# 13th International Joint Conference on Natural Language Processing and the 3rd Conference of the Asia-Pacific Chapter of the Association for Computational Linguistics (IJCNLP-AACL 2023)

Findings of the Association for Computational Linguistics: IJCNLP-AACL 2023



Nusa Dua, Indonesia
1-4 November 2023

ISBN: 978-1-7138-9002-7

**Printed from e-media with permission by:**

Curran Associates, Inc.
57 Morehouse Lane
Red Hook, NY 12571



Printed with permission by Curran Associates, Inc. (2024)



Association for Computational Linguistics
209 N. Eighth Street
Stroudsburg, Pennsylvania 18360

Phone: 1-570-476-8006
Fax: 1-570-476-0860

acl@aclweb.org

**Additional copies of this publication are available from:**

Curran Associates, Inc.
57 Morehouse Lane
Red Hook, NY 12571 USA
Phone: 845-758-0400
Fax: 845-758-2633
Email: curran@proceedings.com
Web: www.proceedings.com

IJCNLP-AACL 2023

# The 13th International Joint Conference on Natural Language Processing and the 3rd Conference of the Asia-Pacific Chapter of the Association for Computational Linguistics

## Findings of the Association for Computational Linguistics: IJCNLP-AACL 2023

November 1 – 4, 2023

The IJCNLP-AACL organizers gratefully acknowledge the support from the following sponsors.

**Platinum**

**Gold**

**Silver**

# Message from the General Chair

Welcome to IJCNLP-AACL 2023, the 17th International Joint Conference on Natural Language Processsing (IJCNLP) and the 3rd Conference of the Asia-Pacific Chapter of the Association for Computational Linguistics (AACL). The conference will be held in Nusa Dua, Bali, Indonesia, during November 1-4, 2023.

The joint conferences of IJCNLP and AACL are organized by alternating leadership in the Asia-Pacific region, in odd years by Asian Federation of Natural Language Processing (AFNLP) and in even years by AACL, except when the annual meetings of ACL are offered in the region every three years, in which case the conferences will be offered and organized solely by ACL. This year, the conference is organized by AFNLP.

As President of AFNLP, I have formed the Conference Coordination Committee (CCC) last year with executive members of AFNLP: Sadao Kurohashi (Vice President), Min Zhang (Secretary), Liang-Chih Yu (Honorary Treasurer), and Minghui Dong (Web Master). Xuanjing Huang has participated in the meetings of the committee as AACL Representative. I am truly thankful for their dedication in the initial stages as CCC members, in particular during the selection of the Local Chairs together with the conference venue and the nomination and appointment of General Chair and Program Committee Chairs, and, after it is decided that I also serve as General Chair of the conference, for their service as respective chairs throughout the conference preparation stages. Their continued support has been of tremendous help and is much appreciated.

I would also like to thank deeply the entire organizing committee of the conference for their hardwork and superb handling of difficult situations, most of all due to the much limited time to address their respective tasks.

- Program Committe Chairs: Yuki Arase, Baotian Hu and Wei Lu have managed the most critical task of establishing the main program of the conference, which includes, among many others, forming and coordinating the Program Committee, constructing the call for papers with a timely theme track, overseeing the review process on both Softconf and ARR, making decisions on paper acceptance, selecting keynote speakers and putting together the program schedule, and most of all communicating with the reviewers, authors, and other committee members over numerous times during the entire process. This is a formidable task, and their efforts for leading to its successful completion are so much appreciated.

- Tutorial Chairs: Yun-Nung (Vivian) Chen and Sadao Kurohashi have gone through the tutorial proposals to select six tutorials that are well balanced both topically and geographically, actively fostering diversity and inclusion.

- Workshop Chairs: Kehai Chen and Lun-Wei Ku have gone over the workshop proposals to select eight strong workshops, NLPMC, WIESP, Eval4NLP, SocialNLP, SEA, FinNLP, NLInt, and ArtOfSafety.

- Demo Chairs: Sriparna Saha and Herry Sujaini have overseen the process of selecting papers among those submitted to the system demonstration session independently of the main program.

- Publication Chairs: Minghui Dong and Kotaro Funakoshi have put together all the documents and articles to construct the conference proceedings expertly, cordially and in a timely manner.

- Sponsorship Chairs: Min Zhang, Satoshi Sekine, Haofeng Wang, and Zhongqing Wang have worked hard to solicit funding to support the conference, and successfully, despite the short time to operate. We are all much grateful to the funding organizations for their generous help.

- Finance Chair: Liang-Chih Yu has always been the person to consult whenever any financial issues arise. Things are not yet fully over at the time of preparing for this message, but are believed to come to self-sustainment, with some room for financial aid as well, thanks to the valiant efforts of all the people involved.
- Website & App Chair: Juntao Li has worked single-handedly and dependably to reflect all the requests to post important news at our conference homepage.
- Publicity & Social Media Chairs: Koustava Goswami and JinYeong Bak have worked to disseminate information over social media as widely as possible whenever there are notable events for the conference.
- Handbook Chairs: Yasuhide Miura and Yunita Sari have worked very hard to meet the deadline for the conference handbook when there is really not much time left. The help of Sonoko Miura as Conference Handbook Designer is also gratefully acknowledged.
- Faculty Advisors to Student Research Workshop (SRW): Hyeju Jang, Yugo Murawaki, and Derek Fai Wong have worked to oversee the SRW, in particular communicating with its chairs, Dongfang Li, Rahmad Mahendra and Zilu Peter Tang. The efforts of the faculty advisors and SRW chairs are much appreciated.
- Diversity & Inclusion Chair: Hwanhee Lee has worked to resolve requests for financial aid, mostly in the form of registration waiver, and as amicably as possible, under a strict limit on granting such requests.
- Registration Chair: Dessi Puji Lestari has worked to oversee the process of registration, together with the kind help of Minghui Dong as the manager of the registration site.
- Local Chairs: Derry Wijaya, Ayu Purwarianti and Adila Alfa Krisnadhi have worked to resolve practically numerous issues, many times beyond the duties of local chairs, after successfully bidding to host the conference in Nusa Dua, Bali, Indonesia. It is with much gratitude and respect that I commend their efforts to the fullest.

In summary, I can only say that their sense of duty and responsibility has been critical to meeting and resolving so many difficulties that we faced along the way. Many, many thanks to all of them.

The mode of the conference has been determined early on to be hybrid, considering the fact that we are not fully over the coronavirus pandemic. However, it has not been quite clear until very recently whether we would need, and can afford, the top-notch professional service of an on-demand video platform such as Underline for a hybrid conference. I am very grateful to all the chairs for the remarkable patience and very happy with the concerted decision to go for the service of Underline, albeit in a limited scope. I wish to thank kindly Damira Mrsic and Sol Rosenberg, representatives of Underline, for the patience and expert help. I also thank Richard Gerber for the help with our use of Softconf.

The Local Chairs made a proposal to host the conference in Nusa Dua early on, but it took all of us a long time to finally come to a decision to choose Grand Hyatt Bali, Nusa Dua, Bali, Indonesia for its exceptional location in the region as the conference venue. Its daytime temperatures are expected to reach 31°C, with the nighttime temperatures of around 24°C. I wish a very pleasant time for all the off-line participants of the conference and an equally memorable time for all the on-line participants.

Welcome to the conference and Nusa Dua!

IJCNLP-AACL 2023 General Chair
Jong C. Park
Korea Advanced Institute of Science and Technology (KAIST)

## Message from the Program Committee Co-Chairs

Welcome to IJCNLP-AACL 2023, the 13th International Joint Conference on Natural Language Processing and the 3rd Conference of the Asia-Pacific Chapter of the Association for Computational Linguistics. This year, we have organized the conference in a hybrid format to accommodate both in-person and virtual participation, making it accessible to everyone regardless of travel constraints. The physical conference takes place in Bali; we are looking forward to discussions on present and future research in NLP with all of you.

This conference has been made possible through the dedicated voluntary efforts of hundreds of individuals. We sincerely thank everyone involved, in particular:

- The incredible team of 30 SACs, 72 ACs, and 427 reviewers who carefully handled submissions.
- Our Best Paper Award Committee, Danushka Bollegala, Jing Jiang, Yang Liu (Tsinghua University), Nanyun (Violet) Peng, Xiaojun Wan, Taro Watanabe, and Koichiro Yoshino, who assessed the candidate papers under the tight schedule.
- Computational Linguistics Editor-in-Chief, Hwee Tou Ng, for exploring the presentation possibility of CL papers with us.
- The ARR technical team, Jonathan Kummerfeld, Nils Dycke, Yoshitomo Matsubara, Dhruv Naik, and Amanda Stent, for supporting IJCNLP-AACL 2023 to have submissions through ARR.
- Rich Gerber at Softconf, who always addressed our inquiries and issues quickly.
- The Program Chairs of conferences going on the same period of time, including Houda Bouamor, Juan Pino, Kalika Bali (EMNLP 2023), Maria Keet, Hung-Yi Lee, Sina Zarrieß (INLG 2023), Svetlana Stoyanchev, Shafiq Joty (SIGDIAL 2023), and Jennifer Dy, Sriraam Natarajan, Kristian Kersting, Sameer Singh, Prasad Tadepalli, Angela Yao (AAAI 2024), whom we cooperated with to preclude multiple submissions.
- The ACL Executive Committee, especially Yusuke Miyao (Conference Officer), for supporting IJCNLP-AACL 2023 with various advice on conference organization.
- The ACL Ethics Committee, Min-Yen Kan, for advising us to conduct ethics reviews.
- The past *ACL conference program chairs, in particular Jordan Boyd-Graber, Naoaki Okazaki, Anna Rogers (ACL 2023) for sharing their experiences that were crucial to avoid pitfalls and practically sharing tools to handle a large volume of submissions.
- ACL Anthology director, Matt Post, for supporting us to publish the proceedings.
- Underline team, Jernej Masnec, Luka Simic, Sol Rosenberg, Borna Bevanda, and Damira Mrsic (Underline Science, Inc.), for their professional services and supports to realize the online part of the conference.

The conference owes its existence to the collaborative efforts of multiple chairs of IJCNLP-AACL 2023. We are deeply grateful to:

- General Chair, Jong C. Park, who was responsible for and led the whole process.
- Publication Chairs, Minghui Dong and Kotaro Funakoshi, for compiling the proceedings and ensuring the correct formatting.

- Handbook Chairs, Yunita Sari and Yasuhide Miura, for creating the conference handbooks.
- Web Chair, Juntao Li, and Publicity & Social Media chairs, JinYeong Bak and Koustava Goswami, for distributing the important information on the web, which allowed efficient and timely communication.
- Local Chairs, Derry Wijaya, Ayu Purwarianti, and Adila Alfa Krisnadhi, who did everything for realizing the physical part of the conference.
- Our assistants, Jindi Yu, Senbao Shi, and Jiaxi Li for their help and support throughout the conference preparation period.

Last but not least, we extend our heartfelt gratitude to all the authors for their invaluable scientific contributions, which are at the very heart of IJCNLP-AACL 2023. We hope everyone will enjoy IJCNLP-AACL 2023 either on-site or online.

## Submission and Acceptance

IJCNLP-AACL 2023 used two submission platforms: direct submission through SoftConf and submissions through ACL Rolling Review (ARR). We received 338 direct submissions (229 long and 109 short) and 25 commitments from ARR (19 long and 6 short), in total 363 valid papers went through the review process. The submissions came from 33 countries and regions of all over the world: 49.2% from Asia-Pacific, 26.7% from North America, 18.7% from Europe, 4.1% from Middle East, and 1.3% from Africa.

The direct submissions were thoroughly reviewed by 427 reviewers under 72 ACs and 30 SACs in 19 tracks. The ARR committed papers were handled by the SACs based on review and meta-review comments gained through ARR. Finally, we have accepted 94 submissions (72 long and 22 short) as the main conference papers accompanied by 37 Findings papers (23 long and 14 short), which results in the acceptance rates of 25.9% for the main conference (29.0% long and 19.1% short) and 36.1% when including the Findings papers (38.3% long and 31.3% short).

In adherence to the ACL code of ethics, we have conducted ethics reviews. Given the limited number of papers that raised ethical concerns, the program chairs assumed the responsibilities of ethics reviewers. Authors of papers that received ethics review comments were requested to address these concerns in their final versions.

The papers accepted to the main conference will be presented in the form of either oral and poster presentations. The presentation modes were determined solely based on the nature of the work, irrespective of review scores. There is no distinction in the proceedings regarding the presentation modes. The Findings papers will have optional lightning talks to introduce highlights of their work.

## Design of Tracks

IJCNLP-AACL 2023 has incorporated 18 general areas reflecting the trends of the field. Most of these areas are consistent with the recent *ACL conferences. In addition, recognizing the conference centers on Asia-Pacific regions, which boast a variety of regional languages with limited language resources, we have introduced a special theme track this year: Large Language Models and Regional/Low-Resource Languages. The most popular areas were "NLP Applications," "Resources and Evaluation," and "Large Language Models and Regional/Low-Resource Languages."

- Dialogue and Interactive Systems
- Discourse and Pragmatics

- Generation and Summarization
- Information Extraction
- Information Retrieval and Text Mining
- Interpretability and Analysis of Models for NLP
- Language Modeling and Analysis
- Linguistic Theories, Cognitive Modeling, and Psycholinguistics
- Machine Learning for NLP
- Machine Translation and Multilingualism
- Multimodality: Speech, Vision, Robotics, and Beyond
- NLP Applications
- Question Answering
- Resources and Evaluation
- Semantics: Lexical, Sentence-level Semantics, Textual Inference, etc.
- Sentiment Analysis, Stylistic Analysis, and Argument Mining
- Society and NLP
- Syntax: Tagging, Chunking, Parsing, etc.
- Theme Track: Large Language Models and Regional/Low-Resource Languages

## Limitations Section and Responsible NLP Checklist

Following ACL 2023, EMNLP 2022, and ARR, we made it mandatory to discuss limitations of a study and submit the responsible NLP checklist to foster the open and honest scientific discussions and promote consideration of responsibility in NLP research. We also encouraged authors to include Ethics Statements whenever there might be potential concerns. The Limitations Section and Ethics Statements did not count towards the page limit.

## Best Paper Awards

Following the new ACL conference awards policy, we organized the Best Paper Award Committee to select the Best Paper Awards followed by Outstanding Paper Awards, together with two special awards, namely Social Impact Award and Resource Award. The committee assessed 15 papers nominated by reviewers. In addition, SACs of each track selected at most a paper for Area Chair's Awards. The award winners will be announced in a dedicated plenary session on November 4, 2023.

IJCNLP-AACL 2023 Program Comittee Co-Chairs
Yuki Arase (Osaka University)
Baotian Hu (Harbin Institute of Technology (Shenzhen))
Wei Lu (Singapore University of Technology and Design)

# Message from the Local Co-Chairs

It is with immense excitement and a profound sense of achievement that we, the local co-chairs of IJCNLP-AACL 2023 - Ayu Purwarianti, Adila Krisnadhi, and myself - welcome you to the breathtaking island of Bali, Indonesia. The significance of this moment cannot be understated, as it marks the very first time that the IJCNLP or ACL conference has found its home in the enchanting Indonesian archipelago. This landmark occasion has doubled our excitement as local chairs, and we are thrilled to share this unique experience with all of you.

Since the moment when we were awarded the privilege of organizing IJCNLP-AACL 2023, we have been tirelessly working to ensure this conference exceeds all expectations. We embarked on an extensive quest to discover the perfect venue and event organizer, negotiated hybrid support, searched for sponsorships, all while meticulously managing the budget, and addressing an array of logistical details, all with the goal of enhancing your experience at the conference. While our commitment to delivering an exceptional event has remained steadfast, we did encounter some noteworthy challenges. The close proximity of EMNLP 2023, scheduled in nearby Singapore just one month after IJCNLP-AACL 2023 and whose submission deadline is also just a month after IJCNLP-AACL 2023's, might have created scheduling dilemmas for prospective authors and participants. We sincerely hope that, despite these challenges, our captivating Bali location will draw participants from around the globe, ensuring IJCNLP-AACL 2023 remains a highlight in the NLP conference calendar.

Another notable challenge has been attracting local participants to the conference. The absence of Scopus indexing for IJCNLP or AACL proceedings, a critical factor for researchers in Indonesia, has presented hurdles. We hope that in the future, as more NLP proceedings are indexed by Scopus, we can generate greater local interest and participation in the region.

On behalf of the local organizing team, I extend my heartfelt gratitude and appreciation to our General Chair, Jong Park; Publication Co-Chair, Minghui Dong; Finance Chair, Liang-Chih Yu; Tutorial Co-Chair, Sadao Kurohashi; Sponsorship Chair, Min Zhang; Registration Chair, Dessi Puji Lestari; and the PC co-chairs who have given so much help and support to the local co-chairs. I have learned a lot from you. Hosting the AACL-IJCNLP 2023 has been an invaluable learning experience for me, and it is an experience I will carry with me. I am also grateful for the contributions and hard work of the entire organizing committee and our kind sponsors, without whom none of this would have been possible.

We look forward to the exciting discussions, sharing of knowledge, and camaraderie that will define IJCNLP-AACL 2023. Welcome to Bali, and we sincerely hope you have one of the most wonderful conference experiences.

Warm regards,

IJCNLP-AACL 2023 Local Co-Chairs
Derry Tanti Wijaya (Monash University Indonesia)
Ayu Purwarianti (Institut Teknologi Bandung)
Adila Krisnadhi (Universitas Indonesia)

# Organizing Committee

**General Chair**

Jong C. Park, Korea Advanced Institute of Science and Technology (KAIST)

**Program Committee Chairs**

Yuki Arase, Osaka University
Baotian Hu, Harbin Insitute of Technology (Shenzhen)
Wei Lu, Singapore University of Technology and Design

**Tutorial Chairs**

Yun-Nung (Vivian) Chen, National Taiwan University
Sadao Kurohashi, Kyoto University

**Workshop Chairs**

Kehai Chen, Harbin Institute of Technology (Shenzhen)
Lun-Wei Ku, Academia Sinica

**Demo Chairs**

Sriparna Saha, Indian Institute of Technology (Patna)
Herry Sujaini, University of Tanjunpura

**Publication Chairs**

Minghui Dong, Institute for Infocomm Research, A*Star
Kotaro Funakoshi, Tokyo Institute of Technology

**Sponsorship Chairs**

Min Zhang, Harbin Institute of Technology (Shenzhen)
Satoshi Sekine, RIKEN, AIP
Haofeng Wang, Tongji University (Shanghai)
Zhongqing Wang, Soochow University

**Finance Chair**

Liang-Chih Yu, Yuan Ze University

**Website & App Chair**

Juntao Li, Soochow University

**Publicity & Social Media Chairs**

Koustava Goswami, Adobe Research India
JinYeong Bak, SungKyunKwan University

### Handbook Chairs

Yasuhide Miura, Fujifilm Corporation
Yunita Sari, Universitas Gadjah Mada
(Conference Handbook Designer: Sonoko Miura)

### Faculty Advisors to Student Research Workshop

Hyeju Jang, Indiana University-Purdue University Indianapolis
Yugo Murawaki, Kyoto University
Derek Fai Wong, University of Macau

### Diversity & Inclusion Chair

Hwanhee Lee, Chung Ang University

### Registration Chair

Dessi Puji Lestari, Bandung Institute of Technology

### Local Chairs

Derry Wijaya, Monash University Indonesia
Ayu Purwarianti, Bandung Institute of Technology
Adila Alfa Krisnadhi, University of Indonesia

### AACL Representative

Xuanjing Huang, Fudan University

# Program Comittee

### Dialogue and Interactive Systems

Senior area chair: Michel Galley
Area chairs: Song Feng, Alexandros Papangelis, Lei Sha, Wei-Nan Zhang

### Discourse and Pragmatics

Senior area chair: Bonnie Webber
Area chair: Yufang Hou

### Generation and Summarization

Senior area chairs: Yue Dong, Dimitra Gkatzia
Area chairs: Meng Cao, Khyathi Raghavi Chandu, Bang Liu, Saad Mahamood, Lili Mou, Arabella Sinclair, Wen Xiao, Jiacheng Xu

### Information Extraction

Senior area chairs: Ruihong Huang, Makoto Miwa
Area chairs: Jun Araki, Prafulla Kumar Choubey, Fenia Christopoulou, Wenlin Yao

### Information Retrieval and Text Mining

Senior area chairs: Sophia Ananiadou, Muhao Chen
Area chairs: Yixin Cao, Fangyu Liu, Tulika Saha, Sheng Zhang, Hongming Zhang

### Interpretability and Analysis of Models for NLP

Senior area chair: Kai-Wei Chang
Area chairs: Sunipa Dev, Yangfeng Ji, Xiaoqing Zheng

### Language Modeling and Analysis

Senior area chairs: Naoya Inoue, Yang Liu (Microsoft)
Area chairs: Benjamin Heinzerling, Reid Pryzant, Keisuke Sakaguchi, Rui Zhang

### Linguistic Theories, Cognitive Modeling, and Psycholinguistics

Senior area chairs: Ashutosh Modi, Yohei Oseki
Area chair: Pranava Madhyastha

### Machine Learning for NLP

Senior area chairs: Lingpeng Kong, Sinno Jialin Pan
Area chairs: Jing Ma, Zhiyong Wu, Jingjing Xu, Shi Zong

**Machine Translation and Multilingualism**

Senior area chairs: Longyue Wang, Deyi Xiong
Area chairs: Liangyou Li, Xing Niu, Elena Voita, Baosong Yang, Biao Zhang

**Multimodality: Speech, Vision, Robotics, and Beyond**

Senior area chairs: Li Dong, Sakriani Sakti
Area chairs: Armen Aghajanyan, Zhe Gan, Florian Metze

**NLP Applications**

Senior area chairs: Jey Han Lau, Mingxuan Wang
Area chairs: Shanbo Cheng, Massimo Piccardi, Ehsan Shareghi, Yangqiu Song, Ekaterina Vylomova, Rong Ye, Zhirui Zhang

**Question Answering**

Senior area chair: Wenpeng Yin
Area chairs: Nitish Gupta, Hangfeng He, Zhiguo Wang

**Resources and Evaluation**

Senior area chairs: Eduardo Blanco, Joel Tetreault
Area chairs: Yvette Graham, Anne Lauscher, Junyi Jessy Li, Liling Tan, Alakananda Vempala

**Semantics: Lexical, Sentence-level Semantics, Textual Inference, etc.**

Senior area chair: Preslav Nakov
Area chairs: Atsushi Fujita, James Thorne, Marcos Zampieri

**Sentiment Analysis, Stylistic Analysis, and Argument Mining**

Senior area chair: Vincent Ng
Area chairs: Henning Wachsmuth, Jianfei Yu

**Society and NLP**

Senior area chair: Wei Gao
Area chairs: Firoj Alam, Shi Feng, Kokil Jaidka, Liang-Chih Yu

**Syntax: Tagging, Chunking, Parsing etc.**

Senior area chair: Kewei Tu
Area chair: Zhenghua Li

**Theme Track: Large Language Models and Regional/Low-Resource Languages**

Senior area chairs: Lei Li, Imed Zitouni
Area chairs: Boxing Chen, Zhiyu Chen, Stephan Peitz, Zhaopeng Tu, Lina Yao

**Reviewers**

Asad Abdi, Haithem Afli, Piush Aggarwal, Akiko Aizawa, Md. Shad Akhtar, Hend Al-Khalifa, Bharat Ram Ambati, Jie An, Anietie Andy, Eiji ARAMAKI, Arturo Argueta, Piyush Arora, Lukasz Augustyniak

Xuefeng Bai, Amir Bakarov, Mithun Balakrishna, Timothy Baldwin, Hritik Bansal, Christine Basta, Gábor Berend, Sabine Bergler, Dario Bertero, Arnab Bhattacharya, Pushpak Bhattacharyya, Anahita Bhiwandiwalla, Michael Bloodgood, Victoria Bobicev, Florian Boudin, Thomas Brovelli (Meyer), Wray Buntine, Miriam Butt

John Calvo Martinez, Ziqiang Cao, Spencer Caplan, Rémi Cardon, Dumitru-Clementin Cercel, Tuhin Chakrabarty, Tanmoy Chakraborty, Yllias Chali, Hou Pong Chan, Kehai Chen, Yubo Chen, Mei-Hua Chen, Xiaocong Chen, Yue Chen, Hsin-Hsi Chen, Fuxiang Chen, Hannah Chen, Sihao Chen, Xinchi Chen, Qian Chen, Qiang Chen, Kanzhi Cheng, Colin Cherry, Emmanuele Chersoni, KEY-SUN CHOI, Monojit Choudhury, Chenhui Chu, Abu Nowshed Chy

Aswarth Abhilash Dara, Avisha Das, Sarthak Dash, Gael de Chalendar, Mathieu Dehouck, Vera Demberg, Yue Deng, Yuntian Deng, Shumin Deng, Chris Develder, Maria Pia di Buono, Luigi Di Caro, Gaël Dias, Miguel Domingo, Shichao Dong, Mingwen Dong, Zi-Yi Dou, Aleksandr Drozd, Wanyu Du, Cunxiao Du, Junwen Duan, Kevin Duh, Jonathan Dunn

Hiroshi Echizen'ya, Steffen Eger, Ramy Eskander

Ming Fang, Hao Fei, Elisabetta Fersini, Alejandro Figueroa, Mauajama Firdaus, Margaret Fleck

Matteo Gabburo, Olivier Galibert, Abbas Ghaddar, Pranav Goel, Carlos Gómez-Rodríguez, Jesús González-Rubio, Isao Goto, Yulia Grishina, Yi Guan, Anupam Guha, Tunga Gungor

Udo Hahn, Na-Rae Han, Ting Han, Jie Hao, Maram Hasanain, Sabit Hassan, Yoshihiko Hayashi, Jie He, DELIA IRAZU HERNANDEZ FARIAS, Tsutomu Hirao, Tosho Hirasawa, Yi-Li Hsu, Po Hu, han hu, zhiyuan hu, Hang Hua, Shujian Huang, Zhongqiang Huang, Kaiyu Huang, Hen-Hsen Huang, Tenghao Huang, Jiangping Huang, Patrick Huber, Jena D. Hwang

Dmitry Ilvovsky, Kenji Imamura, Takashi Inui, Hitoshi Isahara, Etsuko Ishii, Hayate Iso

Palak Jain, Shoaib Jameel, Abhik Jana, Inigo Jauregi Unanue, Yangfeng Ji, Yuxiang Jia, Ridong Jiang, Jyun-Yu Jiang, Aditya Joshi, Prathyusha Jwalapuram

Besim Kabashi, Lis Kanashiro Pereira, Diptesh Kanojia, Sarvnaz Karimi, Börje Karlsson, Marzena Karpinska, Anisia Katinskaia, Daisuke Kawahara, Casey Kennington, Salam Khalifa, Joo-Kyung Kim, Hwichan Kim, David King, Tracy Holloway King, Julien Kloetzer, Philipp Koehn, Mamoru Komachi, Kanako Komiya, Myoung-Wan Koo, Yannis Korkontzelos, Fajri Koto, Canasai Kruengkrai, Lun-Wei Ku, Roland Kuhn, Shankar Kumar

Matthieu Labeau, Albert Y.S. Lam, Stefan Larson, Hung Le, Lung-Hao Lee, Gurpreet Lehal, Alessandro Lenci, Yves Lepage, Piji Li, Yun Li, Sheng Li, Junyi Li, Alexander Hanbo Li, Jiaqi Li, Bangzheng Li, Dongfang Li, Dingcheng Li, Yanran Li, Yuan-Fang Li, Tao Li, Zuchao Li, Weikang Li, Fangtao Li, Wei Li, Peifeng Li, Zekun Li, Lu Li, Baoli LI, Junhui Li, Si Li, Haoran LI, Chao-Chun Liang, Mark Liberman, Gilbert Lim, Marina Litvak, Fenglin Liu, Yongbin Liu, Qun Liu, Yiqun Liu, Yang Janet Liu, Yue Liu, Yao Liu, Zhe Liu, Han Liu, Sharid Loáiciga, Robert L Logan IV, Quanyu Long, Yunfei Long, Di Lu, Hanjia Lyu

Jianqiang Ma, Mounica Maddela, Tarek Mahmoud, Peter Makarov, Valentin Malykh, Muhammad Arslan Manzoor, Bruno Martins, Sahisnu Mazumder, John P. McCrae, Bridget McInnes, Fanchao Meng, Rui Meng, Tao Meng, Zaiqiao Meng, Mohsen Mesgar, Margot Mieskes, SeyedAbolghasem Mirroshandel,

Abhijit Mishra, Yusuke Miyao, Aditya Mogadala, Diego Molla, Sneha Mondal, Manuel Montes, Lori Moon, Hajime Morita, Larry Moss, Pramod Kaushik Mudrakarta, Emir Munoz, Dragos Munteanu

Masaaki Nagata, Tetsuji Nakagawa, Preksha Nema, Nam Nguyen, Nhung Nguyen, Truc-Vien T. Nguyen, Thien Nguyen, Eric Nichols, Garrett Nicolai, Massimo Nicosia, Jian-Yun Nie, Takashi Ninomiya, Masaaki Nishino, Sergiu Nisioi, Joakim Nivre, Pierre Nugues

Atul Kr. Ojha, Antoni Oliver

Santanu Pal, Chester Palen-Michel, Yi-Cheng Pan, Zhufeng Pan, Liang Pang, Nikos Papasarantopoulos, Jacob Parnell, Ioannis Partalas, Prasanna Parthasarathi, Marius Pasca, Sapan Patel, Pavel Pecina, Hengzhi Pei, Flammie Pirinen, Andrei Popescu-Belis, Fred Popowich, Animesh Prasad, Daniel Preotiuc-Pietro, Laurent Prévot, Emily Prud'hommeaux

Xinying Qiu

Alexandre Rademaker, Surangika Ranathunga, Yanghui Rao, Farzana Rashid, Hanumant Redkar, German Rigau, Anthony Rios, Bryan Routledge, Alla Rozovskaya

Fatiha Sadat, Saurav Sahay, Elizabeth Salesky, Avneesh Saluja, German Sanchis-Trilles, Bishal Santra, Anoop Sarkar, Ryohei Sasano, Asad Sayeed, Shigehiko Schamoni, Stephanie Schoch, William Schuler, Ethan Selfridge, Nasredine Semmar, Gregory Senay, Cory Shain, Raksha Sharma, Artem Shelmanov, Yangyang Shi, Tomohide Shibata, Kai Shu, Maryam Siahbani, Carina Silberer, Diego Silva, Michel Simard, Patrick Simianer, Sunayana Sitaram, Amy Siu, Hyun-Je Song, Xingyi Song, Marlo Souza, Balaji Vasan Srinivasan, Felix Stahlberg, Mark Steedman, Kristina Striegnitz, Yixuan Su, Katsuhito Sudoh, Yoshi Suhara, Derwin Suhartono, Alane Suhr, Kai Sun, Chengjie Sun, Marek Suppa

Zeerak Talat, George Tambouratzis, Akihiro Tamura, Bowen Tan, Zhiyang Teng, Camilo Thorne, Yufei Tian, Nasim Tohidi, Takenobu Tokunaga, Marc Tomlinson, Marwan Torki, Samia Touileb, Aashka Trivedi, Chen-Tse Tsai

Kiyotaka Uchimoto, Masao Utiyama

Rob van der Goot, David Vandyke, Natalia Vanetik, Clara Vania, Shikhar Vashishth, Rakesh Verma, Martin Villalba

Xintong Wang, Wei Wang, Di Wang, Hecong Wang, Zhaowei Wang, Guangtao Wang, Zijie Wang, Dexin Wang, Hai Wang, Wenya Wang, Jianzong Wang, Weiyue Wang, Zhongqing Wang, Hsin-Min Wang, Qingyun Wang, Derry Tanti Wijaya, Gijs Wijnholds, Kam-Fai Wong, Xianchao Wu, Stephen Wu, Fangzhao Wu, Zhiyong Wu

Tong Xiao, Jun Xie, Canwen Xu, Qiongkai Xu, Fangzhi Xu, Ruifeng Xu, Wenduan Xu, Hongfei Xu

Yadollah Yaghoobzadeh, Zhaohui Yan, Muqiao Yang, Eugene Yang, Haiqin Yang, Yaqin Yang, Wei Yang, Tae Yano, Kaisheng Yao, Seid Muhie Yimam, Qingyu Yin, Seunghyun Yoon, Masaharu Yoshioka, Heng Yu, Jianfei Yu, Xinchen Yu, Dong Yu, Frances Yung

Fadi Zaraket, Zenan Zhai, Yuqi Zhang, Zhuosheng Zhang, Tianyi Zhang, Wen Zhang, Dongyan Zhao, Xinran Zhao, Chao Zhao, Boyuan Zheng, Houquan Zhou, Yichao Zhou, Guangyou Zhou, Yi Zhu, Wanzheng Zhu, Su Zhu, Bowei Zou, Vilém Zouhar, Arkaitz Zubiaga

# Outstanding Services

## Outstanding ACs

We are indebt to these area chairs who offered a distinguished and professional meta-reviewing.

Jun Araki, Prafulla Kumar Choubey, Fenia Christopoulou, Shi Feng, Kokil Jaidka, Zhenghua Li, Massimo Piccardi, Lei Sha, Elena Voita, Henning Wachsmuth, Wenlin Yao, Rui Zhang

## Outstanding Reviewers

The community has greatly benefited from these outstanding reviewers who delivered particularly insightful and constructive review comments.

Dario Bertero, Hsin-Hsi Chen, Colin Cherry, Sarthak Dash, Tunga Gungor, Hwichan Kim, Zuchao Li, Tao Li, Han Liu, Sergiu Nisioi, Zhufeng Pan, Anoop Sarkar, Akihiro Tamura, Stephen Wu, Frances Yung

## Table of Contents

# Localize, Retrieve and Fuse: A Generalized Framework for Free-Form Question Answering over Tables

**Wenting Zhao**[1] **Ye Liu**[2] **Yao Wan**[3] **Yibo Wang**[1] **Zhongfen Deng**[1] **Philip S. Yu**[1]
[1]Department of Computer Science, University of Illinois at Chicago, IL, USA
[2]Salesforce Research, Palo Alto, USA
[3]School of Computer Sci. & Tech., Huazhong University of Science and Technology, China
{wzhao41,ywang633,zdeng21,psyu}@uic.edu
yeliu@salesforce.com, wanyao@hust.edu.cn

## Abstract

Question answering on tabular data (*a.k.a* TableQA), which aims at generating answers to questions grounded on a provided table, has gained significant attention recently. Prior work primarily produces concise factual responses through information extraction from individual or limited table cells, lacking the ability to reason across diverse table cells. Yet, the realm of free-form TableQA, which demands intricate strategies for selecting relevant table cells and the sophisticated integration and inference of discrete data fragments, remains mostly unexplored. To this end, this paper proposes a generalized three-stage approach: *Table-to-Graph conversion and cell localizing, external knowledge retrieval, and the fusion of table and text (called* TAG-QA*)*, to address the challenge of inferring long free-form answers in generative TableQA. In particular, TAG-QA (1) locates relevant table cells using a graph neural network to gather intersecting cells between relevant rows and columns, (2) leverages external knowledge from Wikipedia, and (3) generates answers by integrating both tabular data and natural linguistic information. Experiments showcase the superior capabilities of TAG-QA in generating sentences that are both faithful and coherent, particularly when compared to several state-of-the-art baselines. Notably, TAG-QA surpasses the robust pipeline-based baseline TAPAS by 17% and 14% in terms of BLEU-4 and PARENT F-score, respectively. Furthermore, TAG-QA outperforms the end-to-end model T5 by 16% and 12% on BLEU-4 and PARENT F-score, respectively.[1]

| Rank | Rider | Team | Speed | Time |
|---|---|---|---|---|
| 1 | Northern Ireland Robert D | Yamaha | 102.46 mph | 1:28.22.2 |
| 2 | Scotland Steve Hislop | Yamaha | 101.27 | 1:29.24.8 |
| 3 | Wales Ian Lougher | Yamaha | 100.62 | 1:29.59.2 |

**[Q]**: Who won in the first three places of The Newcomers Manx Grand Prix race?
**[T5]**: Scotland's Steve Hislop finished second with 101.27 mph and Wales' Ian Lougher finished third with 100.62 mph.
**[TAPAS]**: The Newcomers Manx Grand Prix race was won by the **Spaniard** in the first three places with a time of 1:28.22.2 seconds, 1:29.24.8 seconds and a time of 1:29.59.2.
**[MATE]**: Robert Dunlop won in the first three places, followed by Steve Hislop in the second.
**[Ours]**: The Newcomers Manx Grand Prix race was won by Robert Dunlop from Scotland Steve Hislop in 2nd place and Ian Lougher in 3rd place at 100.62 mph.
**[Reference]**: The Newcomers Manx Grand Prix race was won by Robert Dunlop from Steve Hislop in 2nd place and Ian Lougher in 3rd place at an race speed of 100.62.

Figure 1: A motivating example to show the insights of our proposed approach when comparing with several state-of-the-art methods.

## 1 Introduction

Question answering is to generate precise answers by interacting efficiently with unstructured, structured, or heterogeneous contexts, such as paragraphs, knowledge bases, tables, images, and various combinations thereof (Burke et al., 1997; Yao and Van Durme, 2014; Talmor et al., 2021; Hao et al., 2017). Among these, question answering on tabular data (TableQA) is a challenging task that requires the understanding of table semantics, as well as the ability to reason and infer over relevant table cells (Herzig et al., 2021; Chen et al., 2020b, 2021b).

For the task of TableQA, from our investigation, most current studies are focusing on the factoid TableQA, in which the answer is in a few words or a phrase copied directly from relevant table cells. In particular, current works on factoid TableQA are mainly categorized into two groups: (1) pipeline-based methods consisting of two stages, i.e., cell retrieval and answer reader (Zhu et al., 2021; Chen et al., 2020a); and (2) end-to-end neural networks such as a paradigm of sequence-to-sequence model that takes the context of question answering (e.g., question and table cells) as input to generate natural-language answers (Li et al., 2021b; Pan et al., 2022; Herzig et al., 2021; Pan et al., 2021; Chen, 2023).

Despite much progress made on factoid TableQA, a contradiction between the factoid TableQA and TableQA exists in real scenarios. In factoid TableQA, the answers are always in a short

[1]Source code will be released at https://github.com/wentinghome/TAGQA.



*Findings of the Association for Computational Linguistics: IJCNLP-AACL 2023*, pages 1–12
November 1–4, 2023. ©2023 Asian Federation of Natural Language Processing

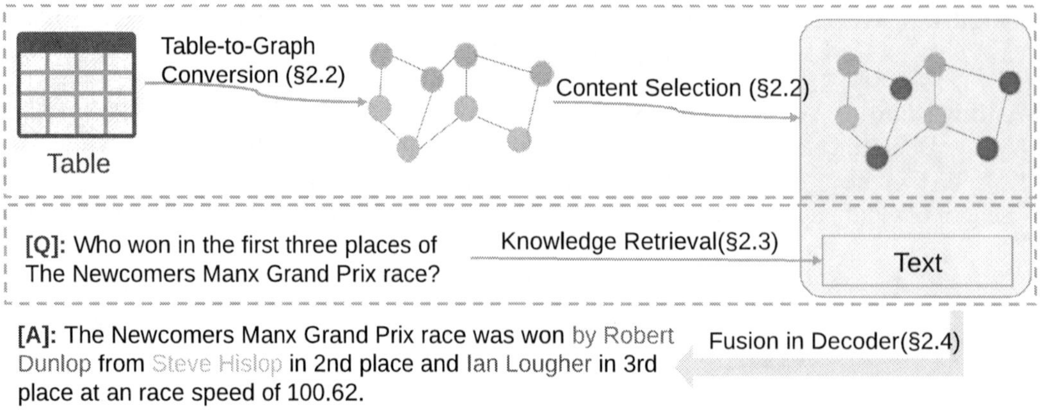


Figure 2: An overview of TAG-QA. The input to TAG-QA is a combination of one table and question, while the output is an answer. The top box shows the content selection process which first converts the table to a graph and selects relevant nodes using GNN. The middle box shows the process of using the spare retrieval technique to retrieve relevant text as complementary information. The rightmost blue box is to integrate the selected cells and retrieved texts to generate the final answer.

form with a few words directly copied from the relevant table cells. However, in real-world scenarios, the answers are expected to be long and informative sentences in a free form, motivating us to target the free-form TableQA in this paper.

It is challenging to generate coherent and faithful free-form answers over tables. (1) *The well-preserved spatial structure of tables is critical for retrieving relevant table cells to the question.* Different from factoid TableQA, free-form TableQA with sophisticated question shares less semantic similarities to the table content, while depending more on the spatial structure of tables to infer multiple related cells such that the related cells may be located in a relatively connected area, e.g., from either a few selected rows or columns. (2) *The selected table cells, containing the key point, are insufficient for composing the entire coherent sentences.* To generate fluent natural-language sentences as answers, external information such as the relevant background knowledge about the question is necessary. (3) *It is expected to aggregate and reason from the question, retrieved table cells, and external knowledge to compose a reasonable answer.* Given the heterogeneous information, a practical model should be capable of aggregating the information efficiently and generating a coherent and fluent free-form answer.

Figure 1 provides a motivating example to illustrate the insights of this paper. Given a table describing "*the 1983 Manx Grand Prix Newcomers Junior Race Results*" and a question "*Who won in the first three places of The Newcomers Manx Grand Prix race?*", the goal is to select relevant cells first and then generate a natural sentence as an answer. From this table, we can observe that the state-of-the-art model TAPAS and MATE only select the "*rider*" while missing the "*rank*" column, providing low cell selection coverage. For the overall generation quality, we can observe that both the end-to-end T5 (Raffel et al., 2020) and the pipeline-based TAPAS (Herzig et al., 2020) and MATE (Eisenschlos et al., 2021) are missing key information from the table by merely mentioning part of the three riders. In addition, the TAPAS introduces a hallucinated rider named "*Spaniard*". These observations motivate us to design a model that can select the relevant cells more accurately and generate faithful answers grounded on the table given a question.

Based on the aforementioned insights, this paper designs a three-stage pipeline framework to tackle the problem of free-form TableQA. Even though the end-to-end TableQA models with high accuracy are prevalently ascribed to the suppression of error accumulated from one-stage training, the long table distracts the model from focusing on relevant table cells, resulting in irrelevant answers. On the other hand, the cell selection module provides a controllable and explainable perspective by extracting a small number of table cells as anchors for the model to generate answers. For the content selection stage, inspired by the recent success of graph models, we convert the table to a graph by designing the node linking and applying a Graph Neural Network (GNN) to aggregate node information and classify whether the table cell is relevant or not. In addition, to generate informative free-form answers, we employ a spare retrieval technique to explore extra knowledge from Wikipedia. Consequently, both the extra knowledge and relevant cells are taken into account to calibrate the pre-trained language model bias. Lastly, we adopt a fusion layer in the decoder to generate the final answer.

To summarize, the primary contributions of this paper are three-fold. (1) To the best of our knowledge, we are the first to convert a semi-structured table into a graph, and then design a graph neural network to retrieve relevant table cells. (2) External knowledge is leveraged to fill in the gap between the selected table cell and the long informative answer by providing background information. (3) Comprehensive experiments on a public dataset named FeTaQA (Nan et al., 2022) are performed to verify the effectiveness of TAG-QA. Experimental results show that TAG-QA outperforms the strong baseline TAPAS by 17% and 14%, and outperforms the end-to-end T5 model by 16% and 12%, in terms of BLEU-4 and PARENT F-score, respectively.

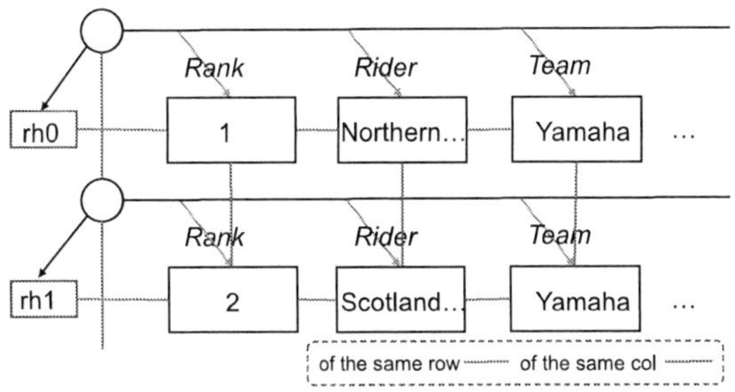


Figure 3: Convert the table shown in Figure 1 into a graphical representation. "*rh0*" is the added row header for the first row. Two relations are considered in the table graph, i.e., "*of the same row*" and "*of the same column*" relations.

## 2 TAG-QA Approach

In this section, we first formulate the problem of TableQA, and introduce the details of our proposed approach TAG-QA.

### 2.1 Problem Formulation

A free-form question-answering task is formulated as generating an answer $a$ to a question $q$ based on a semi-structured table $T$ including table cell content and table meta information such as column, and row header. Different from the factoid table question answering task with a short answer, the free-form QA aims at generating informative and long answers.

### 2.2 Overview

Figure 2 illustrates the overall architecture of our proposed TAG-QA, which is composed of three stages, i.e., relevant table cell localization, relevant external knowledge retrieval, and table-text fusion. *(1) Relevant table cell localization.* We first propose a table-to-graph converter to transform a table into a graph which can preserve the table's spatial information. We think that the graph-based table representation can better assist in selecting relevant table cells. *(2) External knowledge retrieval.* We adopt the sparse retrieval technique to collect external information which can be complementary information for the final answer generation. *(3) Table-text fusion.* We employ the fusion-in-decoder model by taking both the selected table cells and the external sources into account to generate the answer. The above three steps enable our model to generate a faithful free-form answer for a question grounded on the table.

### 2.3 Relevant Table Cell Localization

The initial phase of TAG-QA involves table content selection, a pivotal step that serves as the foundation for subsequent stages. Notably, this stage is of utmost importance as it supplies essential input to the subsequent processes. FeTaQA presents a formidable challenge as a dataset, with a Median/Avg percentage of relevant table cells at 10.7%/16.2%. In order to enhance the precision of the content selection stage, we design a table-to-graph converter to preserve the inherent spatial structure of the tables. We employ GNN to effectively aggregate information at the cell level and subsequently perform a classification task on the table cells.

**Table-to-Graph Converter** State-of-the-art models prefer to adopt the pre-trained Language Models (LMs) to make predictions by transforming the semi-structured table into natural sentences using a pre-defined template . However, they lose the table structure information and deteriorate the performance of downstream tasks.

TAG-QA designs a table-to-graph converter to transform a table into a graph, preserving the table structure by identifying the cell-to-cell relations.

Figure 3 shows an example of transforming a table into a graph. For the $i$-th row, we add an empty row header as $rhi$ which reflects the entire row information. All the table cells from the same row are fully connected, and all the table cells from the same column are also fully connected. Besides, we design two types of relations for the table graph, i.e., "*of the same row*" and "*of the same column*" relations. In particular, "*of the same row*" relation captures the entity information, while "*of the same column*" relation reveals the connection of the same attribute.

In addition, to incorporate the question node into the graph, we create a question node and assign a linking edge between the question and each table cell with the relation "*question to cell*".

**TAG-QA Content Selection** Inspired by QA-GNN (Yasunaga et al., 2021), we propose a content selection module (TAG-CS) that retrieves relevant table cells from the table-based graph. TAG-CS takes the converted table graph from Sec. 2.3 as input, and outputs the question-related table cells. TAG-CS reasons over the table cell level, and each graph node represents a table cell. To fully explore the table semantic and the spatial information, TAG-CS acquires the initial graph node embedding through a pre-trained LM e.g., BERT. Besides, the pre-trained LM and GNN are jointly trained to predict the selected cells.

**GNN Architecture** We use Graph Attention Network (GAT) (Veličković et al., 2017) which leverages masked self-attention layers and employs iterative message passing among neighbors is applied to predict the selected graph node. GAT follows Eq. 1 to update the $i$-th node feature $h_i^l \in \mathbb{R}^D$ at layer $l$ through gathering the weighted attention among its neighbors $\mathcal{N}_i$.

$$h_i^l = f_g\left(\sum_{s \epsilon N_t \cup \{t\}} \alpha_{st} m_{st}\right) + h_t^{l-1} \quad (1)$$

where $\alpha_{st}$ and $m_{st} \in \mathbb{R}^N$ are the self-attention weight and the message passed from source node $s$ to target node $t$ respectively, and $f_g$ is a 2-layer Multi-Layer Perceptron (MLP) with batch normalization. The message $m_{st} \in \mathbb{R}^N$ from node $v_s$ to $v_t$ is computed using Eq. 2.

$$m_{st} = f_m(h_s^{l-1}, u_s, r_{st}) \quad (2)$$

where $u_s \in \mathbb{R}^{T/2}$ is the source node $s$ feature linearly transformed from the one hot vector node type $u_t$. $r_{st} \in \mathbb{R}^T$ is the relation feature from source node $s$ to target node $t$ computed through a 2-layer MLP by taking relation type, source, and target node type into account. $f_m$ is a linear transformation.

The self-attention coefficient $\alpha_{st}$ is updated in Eq. 3. Query and key vectors are linearly transformed by $g_q$ and $g_k$, as node, edge feature, and the previous layer hidden state provided.

$$\alpha_{st} = \frac{exp(\gamma_{st})}{\sum_{t' \epsilon N_s \cup \{s\}} exp(\gamma_{st'}))}, \gamma_{st} = \frac{Q_s^T K_t}{\sqrt{N}} \quad (3)$$

$$Q_s = g_q(h_s^{l-1}, u_s, r_{st}) \quad (4)$$

$$K_t = g_k(h_s^{l-1}, u_t, r_{st}) \quad (5)$$

**GNN Training and Inference** Given a question $q$ and a table $T$, TAG-CS reasons over a graph containing both the table cell nodes and the question node by making predictions on the row and column level. We observe that relevant table cells tend to show up in a relatively connected area, thus we make predictions over row and column headers and choose the intersection area. Compared to predicting over the cell level which results in low recall, our method gains a higher chance to capture relevant table cells. For the training stage, TAG-CS maximizes the cross entropy to predict the row and column for relevant cells.

## 2.4 External Knowledge Retrieval

TAG-QA is the first attempt to leverage the external knowledge to address the table-based free-form QA task. TAG-QA adopts an effective and simple Spare Retrieval based on the TF/IDF approach to select a potentially relevant context from Wikipedia.

**Sparse Retrieval** For TAG-QA, the external knowledge is served as a complimentary background context for the next table and text fusion stage. We choose the spare retrieval method using BM25 (Robertson and Zaragoza, 2009) as a ranking function to retrieve the most relevant text as supplementary information. Given a query $q$ with $m$ keywords $k_1, k_2, \ldots, k_m$, the BM25 ranking score $p_i$ for document $d_i$ is calculated by Eq. 6,

$$p_i = \sum_{j=1}^{m} \frac{idf(q_j) \times tf(q_j, d_i) \times (\alpha + 1)}{tf(k_j, d_i) + \alpha(1 - \beta + \beta \frac{|d_i|}{L_D})} \quad (6)$$

| | Precision | Recall | F-1 |
|---|---|---|---|
| TAPAS (Herzig et al., 2020) | **65.31** | 24.20 | 35.32 |
| MATE (Eisenschlos et al., 2021) | 56.93 | 22.21 | 31.95 |
| TAG-QA (Ours) | 47.60 | **43.06** | **45.22** |

Table 1: Content selection results on FeTaQA dataset.

where $idf$ is the Inverse Document Frequency (IDF), $tf(k_j, d_i)$ is the term frequency of the keyword $k_j$ in document $d_i$, and $L_D$ is the average document length.

### 2.5 Table-Text Fusion

After obtaining the predicted highlighted table cells from the table as well as the support context from Wikipedia, TAG-QA aggregates and combines the two information sources through a sequence-to-sequence model Fusion-in-Decoder (FiD) (Izacard and Grave, 2021). FiD appends the question to each information source, encoding each component independently. It subsequently merges all source features and transmits them to the decoder.

**Fusion in Decoder** Fusion-in-Decoder based on T5 (Raffel et al., 2020) architecture takes question, support context, and the retrieved semi-structured table cells as input. We flatten the highlighted cells as a natural sentence to fit with its pre-trained LM architecture. For the table example shown in Figure 1, the ground-truth selected cells from the first two columns "*Rank*" and "*Rider*" can be linearized as "*Rank is 1* `[SEP]` *Rider is Northern Ireland Robert D* `[SEP]` *Rank is 2* `[SEP]` *Rider is Scotland Steve Hislop* `[SEP]` *Rank is 3* `[SEP]` *Rider is Wales Ian Loug.*", where `[SEP]` is a special token to indicate the end of table slot value.

## 3 Experiments and Analysis

In this section, we explore the following experimental questions: (1) Does proposed TAG-QA generate a more coherent and faithful answer compared with the baseline? (2) Is table cell selection, knowledge retrieval, and fusion necessary for the free-form TableQA? (3) Is it promising to keep enhancing the three modules of TAG-QA?

### 3.1 Dataset

This paper focuses on tackling the challenge of generating long free-form answers, rather than the short factoid responses. Consequently, we have opted for the utilization of the state-of-the-art dataset, *FetaQA* (Nan et al., 2022), as our testbed. The training dataset comprises 7,327 instances, while the development and test sets encompass 1,002 and 2,004 examples, respectively.

### 3.2 Implementation Details

**TAG-CS)** TAG-CS applies BERT checkpoint "`bert-based-uncased`" to learn the table cell representation. For the BERT model, we set the learning rate to $1e$-6 and impose a maximum token length of 35 for each cell. Subsequently, the acquired table cell-level embeddings serve as input node features for our GNN. Within the TAG-CS framework, our GNN module comprises 3 layers, each with node features of 200 dimensions. Additionally, we apply a dropout rate of 0.2 to each layer for regularization.

We train our model on the FeTaQA dataset, configuring it to run for a maximum of 50 epochs. We employ the RAdam optimizer (Liu et al., 2019) with a weight decay of 0.01, utilizing a powerful 24G memory Titan-RTX GPU. To optimize GPU memory usage, we set the maximum number of table cells as 200 and set the batch size as 1. The selection of the best checkpoint is based on the performance of the model on the development set, which is then used for decoding the test set. Additionally, to enhance efficiency, TAG-CS is employed to select intersection cells from the top 3 rows and 3 columns as the relevant cells, drawing upon our accumulated experience in this context.

***Sparse Retrieval)*** Our implementation relies on the PyTorch-based toolkit Pyserini, designed for reproducible information retrieval research using both sparse and dense representations. We utilize the question as the query to retrieve pertinent contextual information from Wikipedia, selecting the first sentence from the top results. We specifically employ the Lucene Indexes, denoted as "enwiki-paragraphs"[2].

***FiD)*** In the context of FiD, TAG-QA employs the Adam optimizer with a learning rate of $1e$-5. We select the best checkpoint for inference purposes. In the inference phase, we utilize beam search with a beam size of 3 and apply a length penalty of 1 when generating answers.

### 3.3 Baselines

To validate the effectiveness of TAG-QA, we choose two different types of methods as baselines, including end-to-end and pipeline-based models.

[2] https://github.com/castorini/pyserini

| | | BLEU-4 | METEOR | ROUGE-L | PARENT (P/R/F) | PARENT-T (P/R/F) |
|---|---|---|---|---|---|---|
| | ***End-to-end*** | | | | | |
| UniLM | Q-fullTab | 17.57 | 28.30 | 39.46 | 38.21/24.18/25.56 | 26.48/53.99/33.70 |
| | Q-Retrieve | 18.46 | 27.21 | 39.36 | 34.12/23.42/23.76 | 20.37/43.41/25.69 |
| | Q-Retrieve-fullTab | 18.89 | 26.86 | 38.86 | 35.29/23.17/23.72 | 22.07/44.83/27.44 |
| BART | Q-fullTab | 7.62 | 25.70 | 25.76 | 39.64/19.68/22.62 | 25.77/39.53/28.78 |
| | Q-Retrieve | 12.20 | 25.15 | 28.27 | 35.55/20.67/22.37 | 18.31/31.07/20.94 |
| | Q-Retrieve-fullTab | 11.97 | 26.41 | 28.24 | 38.45/22.12/23.96 | 20.57/34.36/23.46 |
| T5 | **Q-fullTab*** | 15.66 | 21.80 | 35.48 | 38.88/14.83/18.01 | 25.11/33.62/26.17 |
| | Q-Retrieve | 25.17 | 24.87 | 39.89 | 33.54/20.3/21.68 | 17.35/31.21/20.13 |
| | Q-Retrieve-fullTab | 27.60 | 26.71 | 42.38 | 38.49/23.2/25.06 | 20.98/35.79/24.02 |
| **Oracle-T5** | Q-OracleCell | 21.77 | 28.35 | 42.54 | 53.37/26.39/30.61 | 38.21/54.22/41.49 |
| | Q-Retrieve | 25.17 | 24.87 | 39.89 | 33.54/20.3/21.68 | 17.35/31.21/20.13 |
| | Q-Retrieve-OracleCell | 31.00 | 30.35 | 46.72 | 46.3/28.44/30.93 | 27.07/44.32/30.71 |
| | ***Pipeline*** | | | | | |
| TAPAS-T5 | Q-predCell | 14.50 | 21.18 | 35.51 | 39.14/12.34/15.67 | 25.19/29.47/24.38 |
| | Q-Retrieve-predCell | 26.81 | 26.92 | 42.59 | 39.23/21.96/24.15 | 21.43/34.54/23.61 |
| MATE-T5 | Q-predCell | 14.28 | 21.01 | 35.36 | 39.07/12.2/15.53 | 24.83/29.56/24.25 |
| | Q-Retrieve-predCell | 26.85 | 26.96 | 42.60 | 39.05/21.89/23.99 | 21.1/34.62/23.57 |
| TAGQA-T5 | Q-predCell | 17.08 | 23.22 | 38.38 | 41.84/16.53/20.1 | 27.11/37.03/28.45 |
| | Q-Retrieve-predCell | 28.01(↑ 0.41) | 27.91(↑ 1.20) | 44.16(↑ 1.78) | 41.35/23.87/26.2(↑ 1.14) | 22.89/37.29/25.64(↑ 1.64) |
| TAGQA-FiD | **Q-Retrieve-predCell*** | **31.84**(↑ 16.18) | **30.16**(↑ 8.36) | **49.39**(↑ 13.91) | **47.56/26.20/29.59**(↑ 11.58) | **25.44/39.11/28.26**(↑ 2.09) |

Table 2: Results on FeTaQA dataset. "P/R/F" denotes the precision/recall/F score. We report end-to-end model UniLM, BART and T5, and the pipeline results. The results of various table cell selection strategies TAPAS, MATE and our proposed TAG with T5 as backbone generation model are noted as TAPAS-T5, MATE-T5 and TagQA-T5. To validate the effectiveness of proposed framework components, we test different combinations of source information to models where "Q" is question, "Retrieve" is the retrieved external knowledge, "fullTab" is full table, and "predCell" refers to the selected table cell. And the last row TAGQA-FiD is the proposed method.

| Method | Overall |
|---|---|
| Reference | 4.94 |
| UniLM [end-to-end] (Dong et al., 2019) | 3.88 |
| BART [end-to-end] (Lewis et al., 2020) | 3.67 |
| T5 [end-to-end] (Raffel et al., 2020) | 3.81 |
| Tapas [pipeline] (Herzig et al., 2020) | 3.38 |
| MATE [pipeline] (Eisenschlos et al., 2021) | 3.30 |
| TAG-QA [pipeline] | **3.93** |

Table 3: Results of human evaluation for reference, end-to-end model and pipeline methods. TAG-QA outperforms the pipeline models by a large margin, and achieves performance on par with the strong end-to-end baseline model T5.

Firstly, we compare TAG-QA with strong state-of-the-art end-to-end pre-trained generative LMs. UniLM (Dong et al., 2019), BART (Lewis et al., 2020), and T5 (Radford et al., 2019). For the input format to the end-to-end model, we flatten the table by concatenating special token `[SEP]` in between different table cells, and concatenate with the question as a natural sentence, e.g. "*question [SEP] flattened table*". Furthermore, we compare the performance of our proposed model with pipeline-based methods which include two stages: content selection and answer generation. Content selection makes predictions of relevant cells. We choose two table-based pre-training models: TAPAS (Herzig et al., 2020) and MATE (Eisenschlos et al., 2021). Moreover, T5 is chosen as the baseline model's answer generation backbone due to the integration capacity for the table cell and retrieved knowledge.

### 3.4 Automatic Evaluation Metrics

We use various automatic metrics to evaluate the model performance. Due to the pipeline style of TAG-QA, we report two sets of metrics for content selection and answer generation stages respectively. Firstly, to evaluate the retrieval competency of the table semantic parser, we report Precision, Recall, and F1 scores. Besides, to evaluate the answer generation quality, we choose several automatic evaluation metrics, i.e., BLEU-4 (Papineni et al., 2002), ROUGE-L (Lin, 2004) and METEOR (Banerjee and Lavie, 2005), to evaluate the n-gram match between the generated sentence and the reference answer. Considering the limitation that those metric fails to reflect the faithfulness answer to the fact from the table, we report PARENT (Dhingra et al., 2019) and PARENT-T (Wang et al., 2020) score. PARENT score takes the answer matching with both the reference answer and the table information into account, while PARENT-T focuses on the overlap between the generated answer with the corresponding table.

### 3.5 Results

We first evaluate the TAG-CS content selection stage table semantic parsing results, as shown in Table 1. For the F-1 score, TAG-QA outperforms the strong baseline model TAPAS and MATE by 9.9% and 13.27%. For recall, TAG-QA achieves the best result, demonstrating that TAG-QA retrieves more relevant table cells. For precision, the baseline model outperforms TAG-QA by retrieving fewer cells which includes more relevant cells. However, the low precision and high recall are a trade-off since the relevant cells make a stronger impact on the overall answer generation quality. Thus, we can tolerate a small amount of irrelevant cells and keep the correct cells as many as possible.

In addition, Table 2 shows the measurements of generated answer quality using TAG-QA compared to previous both end-to-end and pipeline-based state-of-the-art models. From overlapping-based metrics BLEU-4, METEOR, and ROUGE-L, TAG-QA outperforms all the end-to-end and pipeline-based models. Specifically, TAG-QA gains 14.27%/1.86%/9.93% more than the best end-to-end model UniLM in "Q-fullTab" while gains 14.76%/8.98%/13.88% in "Q-predCell" setting, more than the best pipeline-based model TAPAS. For faithfulness metric PARENT and PARETN-T, TAG-QA provides the best performance among the pipeline models by outperforming TAPAS on the "Q-predCell" setting by 13.92% and 3.88% on PARENT and PARENT-T. Compared with end-to-end models, TAG-QA gives the best PARENT score while UniLM shows the best result regarding PARENT-T. It's explainable because TAG-QA incorporates information outside of the table to generate answers, achieving a trade-off between being grounded on the table and synthesizing informative answers.

Furthermore, to answer Question 2 "*Are three stages of the framework necessary to generate high-quality answer?*", we conduct an experiment in Table 2 by comparing the T5 model "Q-fullTab" with pipeline methods backend by T5 using "Q-predCell". The result shows proposed TAG for content selection TAGQA-T5 selecting 7% of table cell outperforms T5 with fullTab. This indicates the table cell selection is necessary since relevant cells provide an anchor to generate high answer generation. Moreover, to investigate the effect of retrieval knowledge, we show results in Table 2 by concatenating "Retrieval" to the input. The retrieval

| Model | BLEU | METEOR | PARENT | PARENT-T |
|---|---|---|---|---|
| TAG-QA | **31.84** | **30.16** | **29.59** | **28.26** |
| TAG-QA w/o JT | 31.35 | 29.65 | 28.93 | 27.48 |
| TAG-QA w/o SR | 18.93 | 24.95 | 21.57 | 27.95 |
| TAG-QA w/o FiD | 21.51 | 24.03 | 22.46 | 25.40 |

Table 4: Ablation study of the proposed model. We examine the ablated mode by removing the Joint Training (JT) of TAG-CS, Sparse Retrieval (SR), and FiD.

knowledge enhances model performance by providing background knowledge. The proposed model TAGQA-T5 provides the best result by integrating retrieval and informative selected cells. Lastly, our fusion module further enhanced the overall performance by aggregating tables and text efficiently.

Last but not least, to answer the question "*Is there space to further enhance performance using this framework ?*", we conduct an oracle experiment shown in "Oracle-T5". With the simple Retrieval technique, T5 backend generation, and oracle table cell, the BLEU-4 result is 31%, and PARENT, PARENT-T are over 30%. If a better retrieval and fusion model is used, the model performance can be further boosted.

### 3.6 Analysis

To further evaluate the quality of generated answer by various state-of-the-art models when compared to the ground-truth answer, we perform an additional human evaluation. Besides, we conduct an ablation study for TAG-QA to validate the three building blocks: jointly training of LM and GNN for TAG-CS, external context retrieved from Wikipedia, and FiD model. Furthermore, a case study is presented which shows different answer qualities produced by various models.

**Human Evaluation** Following (Nan et al., 2022), we recruit three human annotators who pass the College English Test (CET-6)[3] to judge the quality of the generated sentence. We randomly draw 100 samples from test examples in FeTaQA dataset and collect answers from TAG-QA and baseline models. Then, we present the generated answers to three human annotators without revealing the name of the model, thus reducing human variance.

We provide instructions for human raters to evaluate the sentence quality from four aspects: faithfulness, fluency, correctness, and adequateness. For each aspect, an annotator is supposed to assign a score ranging from 1 (worst) to 5 (best) based on the answer quality. The "overall" column refers to

[3]A national English as a foreign language test in China.

the average ranking of the model. First, for fluency, the annotator checks if an answer is natural and grammatical. Second, for correctness, we compare the answer with the ground truth by checking if the predicted answer contains the correct information. Third, adequacy reflects if an answer contains all the aspects that are asked. Finally, faithfulness evaluates faithfulness if an answer is faithful and grounded to the contents of the highlighted table region such that it covers all the relevant information from the table while not including other key information outside of the table. From Table 3, we can see TAG-QA ranked the top among all models.

**Ablation Study** To figure out which building blocks are driving the improvements, we examine different ablated models to understand each component of TAG-QA, including joint training of BERT and GNN from TAG-CS, sparse retrieval, and FiD. Table 4 presents the ablation results under different evaluation metrics. We can see that the model performance drops when any component is removed. Especially, ablating the sparse retrieval module results in the most drop in BLEU-4 and PARENT scores, while removing FiD causes the most significant drop in PARENT-T.

**Case Study** To inspect the effect of TAG-QA directly, we present a case study in Figure 4, where a sampled table, question, ground-truth relevant table cells (highlighted in blue), the predicted answers of models, as well as the reference are provided. First, we find that the end-to-end model generally contains more information than pipeline models due to the more abundant table information while they suffer from hallucination. For example, T5 and BART identify the ranking position of "*Leandro de Oliveira*" as "*17th*" while it should be "*73rd*" from the table. Second, for pipeline models, they tend to generate irrelevant information e.g. MATE mentions the duration and points instead of answering the ranking position and the event. Third, both the end-to-end and pipeline models (TAPAS) fail to cover all the relevant information from the table, e.g. UniLM did not capture the event 12km, and TAPAS fails to mention the position 73rd. By contrast, TAG-QA provides the highest table coverage while keeping the fluency of sentences.

## 4 Related Work

In this section, we review the related work to ours from the perspectives of TableQA, GNN for natural language processing, and knowledge-grounded text generation.

| Year | Competition | Venue | Pos | Event |
|---|---|---|---|---|
| RB | Representing Brazil | Representing Brazil | RB | RB |
| 2011 | World Cross Country Championships | Punta Umbría Spain | 73rd | 12 km |
| 2011 | World Cross Country Championships | Punta Umbría Spain | 17th | Team - 12 km |
| 2011 | South American Road Mile Championships | Belém Brazil | 1st | One mile |
| 2011 | South American Championships | Buenos Aires Argentina | 1st | 1500m |
| 2011 | Pan American Games | Guadalajara México | 18th | 200m |

[Q]: What country did Leandro de Oliveira represent at the 2011 World Cross Country Championships and how did he place?
[T5-end-to-end]: Leandro de Oliveira represented Brazil at the 2011 World Cross Country Championships and placed 17th.
[Bart-end-to-end]: Landro de oliveira represented brazil at the 2011 World cross country championships in the 12 km and finished 17th.
[Unilm-end-to-end]: Leandro de Oliveira was representing Brazil at the 2011 World Cross Country Championships in Punta Umbría , Spain , finishing 73rd .
[TAPAS-pipeline]: Leandro de Oliveira represented Brazil at the 2011 World Cross Country Championships.
[MATE-pipeline]: Leandro de Oliveira finished in 37:10 and finished with 326 points.
[Ours-pipeline]: Leandro de Oliveira represented Brazil at the 2011 World Cross Country Championships and placed 73rd in the 12 km race.
[REF]: Leandro de Oliveira represented Brazil at the 2011 World Cross Country Championships and placed 73rd in the 12 km race.

Figure 4: A case study from FeTaQA for qualitative analysis. The highlighted cells are the ground-truth relevant table cells. "*RB*" refers to "*Representing Brazil*". Hallucinated content from the predicted answer is marked in red and the correct content in blue.

**TableQA** FeTaQA is the first TableQA dataset that addresses the significance of free-form answer generation, while most current research work including WikiTableQuestions (Pasupat and Liang, 2015), Spider (Yu et al., 2018), HybridQA (Chen et al., 2020b), OTT-QA (Chen et al., 2020a), and TAT-QA (Zhu et al., 2021) focuses on the short factoid answer generation. The early solution (Zhong et al., 2017; Liang et al., 2017) of addressing the TableQA is to parse the natural question into a machine-executable meaning representations that can be used to query the table. To reduce the labor-intensive logical annotation, a semantic parser trained over weak supervision from denotations has been drawing attention. Plenty of Transformer-based table pre-traininig models demonstrate decent TableQA performance, e.g., TaPas (Herzig et al., 2020), MATE (Eisenschlos et al., 2021), TaBERT (Yin et al., 2020), StruG (Deng et al., 2021), GraPPa (Yu et al., 2021), and TaPEx (Liu et al., 2022a). In addition, rather than explore table structure, RCI (Glass et al., 2021) assumes the row and column are independent, and predicts the probability of containing the answer to a question in each row and column of a table individually.

**GNN for Natural Language Processing** Apart from the extensively renowned causal language models that have showcased impressive results in various task (Vaswani et al., 2017; Parmar et al., 2018; Wang et al., 2023a, 2022, 2023b), a rich variety of language processing tasks gain improvements from exploiting the power of GNN (Li et al., 2015). Tasks such as semantic parsing (Chen et al., 2021a), text classification (Lin et al., 2021), text generation (Fei et al., 2021), question answering (Wang et al., 2021; Yasunaga et al., 2021) can be expressed with a graph structure and handled with graph-based methods. In addition, researchers apply GNN to model the text generation from structured data tasks e.g. graph-to-sequence (Marcheggiani and Perez-Beltrachini, 2018), and AMR-to-text (Ribeiro et al., 2019).

**Knowledge-Grounded Text Generation** Encoder-decoder-based models have been proposed to tackle the generation task by mapping the input to the output sequence. However, the input text is insufficient to provide knowledge to generate decent output due to the lack of commonsense, factual events, and semantic information. Knowledge-grounded text generation incorporating external knowledge such as linguistic features (Liu et al., 2021c), knowledge graph (Liu et al., 2021b; Li et al., 2021a), knowledge base (Eric and Manning, 2017; He et al., 2017; Liu et al., 2022b), and textual knowledge (Liu et al., 2021a; Zhao et al., 2021) help to generate a more logical and informative answer.

## 5 Conclusion

This paper presents a generalized pipeline-based framework TAG-QA for free-form long answer generation for TableQA. The core idea of TAG-QA is to divide the answer generation process into three stages: (1) transform the table into a graph and jointly reason over the question-table graph to select relevant cells; (2) retrieve contextual knowledge from Wikipedia using sparse retrieval, and (3) integrate the selected cells with the content knowledge to predict the final answer. Extensive experiments on a public dataset FeTaQA are conducted to verify the generated answer quality from both the fluency and faithfulness aspects.

## Limitations

One limitation of TAG-CS, which accepts the entire table as input, arises when dealing with large tables, as training both BERT and the graph model simultaneously becomes challenging due to GPU memory constraints. Consequently, one promising avenue for future research involves the efficient modeling of large tables. Furthermore, it's worth noting that the availability of only one public dataset, FeTaQA, for free-form TableQA, has constrained our validation efforts to this single dataset. However, we are committed to expanding the scope of our research in the future by evaluating the performance of our pipeline model, TAG-QA, across multiple free-form TableQA datasets.

## References


Satanjeev Banerjee and Alon Lavie. 2005. Meteor: An automatic metric for mt evaluation with improved correlation with human judgments. In *Proceedings of the acl workshop on intrinsic and extrinsic evaluation measures for machine translation and/or summarization*, pages 65–72.

Robin D Burke, Kristian J Hammond, Vladimir Kulyukin, Steven L Lytinen, Noriko Tomuro, and Scott Schoenberg. 1997. Question answering from frequently asked question files: Experiences with the faq finder system. *AI magazine*, 18(2):57–57.

Wenhu Chen. 2023. Large language models are few(1)-shot table reasoners. In *Findings of the Association for Computational Linguistics: EACL 2023*, pages 1120–1130, Dubrovnik, Croatia. Association for Computational Linguistics.

Wenhu Chen, Ming-Wei Chang, Eva Schlinger, William Wang, and William W Cohen. 2020a. Open question answering over tables and text. *arXiv preprint arXiv:2010.10439*.

Wenhu Chen, Hanwen Zha, Zhiyu Chen, Wenhan Xiong, Hong Wang, and William Wang. 2020b. Hybridqa: A dataset of multi-hop question answering over tabular and textual data. *arXiv preprint arXiv:2004.07347*.

Zhi Chen, Lu Chen, Yanbin Zhao, Ruisheng Cao, Zihan Xu, Su Zhu, and Kai Yu. 2021a. ShadowGNN: Graph projection neural network for text-to-SQL parser. In *Proceedings of the 2021 Conference of the North American Chapter of the Association for Computational Linguistics: Human Language Technologies*, pages 5567–5577, Online. Association for Computational Linguistics.

Zhiyu Chen, Wenhu Chen, Charese Smiley, Sameena Shah, Iana Borova, Dylan Langdon, Reema Moussa, Matt Beane, Ting-Hao Huang, Bryan Routledge, and William Yang Wang. 2021b. FinQA: A dataset of numerical reasoning over financial data. In *Proceedings of the 2021 Conference on Empirical Methods in Natural Language Processing*, pages 3697–3711, Online and Punta Cana, Dominican Republic. Association for Computational Linguistics.

Xiang Deng, Ahmed Hassan Awadallah, Christopher Meek, Oleksandr Polozov, Huan Sun, and Matthew Richardson. 2021. Structure-grounded pretraining for text-to-SQL. In *Proceedings of the 2021 Conference of the North American Chapter of the Association for Computational Linguistics: Human Language Technologies*, pages 1337–1350, Online. Association for Computational Linguistics.

Bhuwan Dhingra, Manaal Faruqui, Ankur Parikh, Ming-Wei Chang, Dipanjan Das, and William Cohen. 2019. Handling divergent reference texts when evaluating table-to-text generation. In *Proceedings of the 57th Annual Meeting of the Association for Computational Linguistics*, pages 4884–4895, Florence, Italy. Association for Computational Linguistics.

Li Dong, Nan Yang, Wenhui Wang, Furu Wei, Xiaodong Liu, Yu Wang, Jianfeng Gao, Ming Zhou, and Hsiao-Wuen Hon. 2019. Unified language model pre-training for natural language understanding and generation. In *Advances in Neural Information Processing Systems*, volume 32. Curran Associates, Inc.

Julian Eisenschlos, Maharshi Gor, Thomas Müller, and William Cohen. 2021. MATE: Multi-view attention for table transformer efficiency. In *Proceedings of the 2021 Conference on Empirical Methods in Natural Language Processing*, pages 7606–7619, Online and Punta Cana, Dominican Republic. Association for Computational Linguistics.

Mihail Eric and Christopher Manning. 2017. A copy-augmented sequence-to-sequence architecture gives good performance on task-oriented dialogue. In *Proceedings of the 15th Conference of the European Chapter of the Association for Computational Linguistics: Volume 2, Short Papers*, pages 468–473, Valencia, Spain. Association for Computational Linguistics.

Zichu Fei, Qi Zhang, and Yaqian Zhou. 2021. Iterative GNN-based decoder for question generation. In *Proceedings of the 2021 Conference on Empirical Methods in Natural Language Processing*, pages 2573–2582, Online and Punta Cana, Dominican Republic. Association for Computational Linguistics.

Michael Glass, Mustafa Canim, Alfio Gliozzo, Saneem Chemmengath, Vishwajeet Kumar, Rishav Chakravarti, Avi Sil, Feifei Pan, Samarth Bharadwaj, and Nicolas Rodolfo Fauceglia. 2021. Capturing row and column semantics in transformer based question answering over tables. In *Proceedings of the 2021 Conference of the North American Chapter of the Association for Computational Linguistics: Human Language Technologies*, pages 1212–1224, Online. Association for Computational Linguistics.

Yanchao Hao, Yuanzhe Zhang, Kang Liu, Shizhu He, Zhanyi Liu, Hua Wu, and Jun Zhao. 2017. An end-to-end model for question answering over knowledge base with cross-attention combining global knowledge. In *Proceedings of the 55th Annual Meeting of the Association for Computational Linguistics (Volume 1: Long Papers)*, pages 221–231, Vancouver, Canada. Association for Computational Linguistics.

Shizhu He, Cao Liu, Kang Liu, and Jun Zhao. 2017. Generating natural answers by incorporating copying and retrieving mechanisms in sequence-to-sequence learning. In *Proceedings of the 55th Annual Meeting of the Association for Computational Linguistics (Volume 1: Long Papers)*, pages 199–208, Vancouver, Canada. Association for Computational Linguistics.

Jonathan Herzig, Thomas Müller, Syrine Krichene, and Julian Eisenschlos. 2021. Open domain question answering over tables via dense retrieval. In *Proceedings of the 2021 Conference of the North American Chapter of the Association for Computational Linguistics: Human Language Technologies*, pages 512–519, Online. Association for Computational Linguistics.

Jonathan Herzig, Pawel Krzysztof Nowak, Thomas Müller, Francesco Piccinno, and Julian Eisenschlos. 2020. TaPas: Weakly supervised table parsing via pre-training. In *Proceedings of the 58th Annual Meeting of the Association for Computational Linguistics*, pages 4320–4333, Online. Association for Computational Linguistics.

Gautier Izacard and Edouard Grave. 2021. Leveraging passage retrieval with generative models for open domain question answering. In *Proceedings of the 16th Conference of the European Chapter of the Association for Computational Linguistics: Main Volume*, pages 874–880, Online. Association for Computational Linguistics.

Mike Lewis, Yinhan Liu, Naman Goyal, Marjan Ghazvininejad, Abdelrahman Mohamed, Omer Levy, Veselin Stoyanov, and Luke Zettlemoyer. 2020. BART: Denoising sequence-to-sequence pre-training for natural language generation, translation, and comprehension. In *Proceedings of the 58th Annual Meeting of the Association for Computational Linguistics*, pages 7871–7880, Online. Association for Computational Linguistics.

Junyi Li, Wayne Xin Zhao, Zhicheng Wei, Nicholas Jing Yuan, and Ji-Rong Wen. 2021a. Knowledge-based review generation by coherence enhanced text planning. In *Proceedings of the 44th International ACM SIGIR Conference on Research and Development in Information Retrieval*, pages 183–192.

Xiao Li, Yawei Sun, and Gong Cheng. 2021b. Tsqa: tabular scenario based question answering. In *Proceedings of the AAAI Conference on Artificial Intelligence*, volume 35, pages 13297–13305.

Yujia Li, Daniel Tarlow, Marc Brockschmidt, and Richard Zemel. 2015. Gated graph sequence neural networks. *arXiv preprint arXiv:1511.05493*.

Chen Liang, Jonathan Berant, Quoc Le, Kenneth D. Forbus, and Ni Lao. 2017. Neural symbolic machines:

Learning semantic parsers on Freebase with weak supervision. In *Proceedings of the 55th Annual Meeting of the Association for Computational Linguistics (Volume 1: Long Papers)*, pages 23–33, Vancouver, Canada. Association for Computational Linguistics.

Chin-Yew Lin. 2004. Rouge: A package for automatic evaluation of summaries. In *Text summarization branches out*, pages 74–81.

Yuxiao Lin, Yuxian Meng, Xiaofei Sun, Qinghong Han, Kun Kuang, Jiwei Li, and Fei Wu. 2021. Bertgcn: Transductive text classification by combining gcn and bert. *arXiv preprint arXiv:2105.05727*.

Liyuan Liu, Haoming Jiang, Pengcheng He, Weizhu Chen, Xiaodong Liu, Jianfeng Gao, and Jiawei Han. 2019. On the variance of the adaptive learning rate and beyond. *arXiv preprint arXiv:1908.03265*.

Qian Liu, Bei Chen, Jiaqi Guo, Morteza Ziyadi, Zeqi Lin, Weizhu Chen, and Jian-Guang Lou. 2022a. TAPEX: Table pre-training via learning a neural SQL executor. In *International Conference on Learning Representations*.

Ye Liu, Kazuma Hashimoto, Yingbo Zhou, Semih Yavuz, Caiming Xiong, and Philip Yu. 2021a. Dense hierarchical retrieval for open-domain question answering. In *Findings of the Association for Computational Linguistics: EMNLP 2021*, Punta Cana, Dominican Republic. Association for Computational Linguistics.

Ye Liu, Yao Wan, Lifang He, Hao Peng, and Philip S Yu. 2021b. Kg-bart: Knowledge graph-augmented bart for generative commonsense reasoning. In *Proceedings of the AAAI Conference on Artificial Intelligence*, volume 35, pages 6418–6425.

Ye Liu, Yao Wan, Jianguo Zhang, Wenting Zhao, and Philip Yu. 2021c. Enriching non-autoregressive transformer with syntactic and semantic structures for neural machine translation. In *Proceedings of the 16th Conference of the European Chapter of the Association for Computational Linguistics: Main Volume*, pages 1235–1244, Online. Association for Computational Linguistics.

Ye Liu, Semih Yavuz, Rui Meng, Dragomir Radev, Caiming Xiong, and Yingbo Zhou. 2022b. Uniparser: Unified semantic parser for question answering on knowledge base and database. In *Proceedings of the 2022 Conference on Empirical Methods in Natural Language Processing*, pages 8858–8869, Abu Dhabi, United Arab Emirates. Association for Computational Linguistics.

Diego Marcheggiani and Laura Perez-Beltrachini. 2018. Deep graph convolutional encoders for structured data to text generation. In *Proceedings of the 11th International Conference on Natural Language Generation*, pages 1–9, Tilburg University, The Netherlands. Association for Computational Linguistics.

Linyong Nan, Chiachun Hsieh, Ziming Mao, Xi Victoria Lin, Neha Verma, Rui Zhang, Wojciech Kryściński, Hailey Schoelkopf, Riley Kong, Xiangru Tang, Mutethia Mutuma, Ben Rosand, Isabel Trindade, Renusree Bandaru, Jacob Cunningham, Caiming Xiong, Dragomir Radev, and Dragomir Radev. 2022. FeTaQA: Free-form Table Question Answering. *Transactions of the Association for Computational Linguistics*, 10:35–49.

Feifei Pan, Mustafa Canim, Michael Glass, Alfio Gliozzo, and Peter Fox. 2021. CLTR: An end-to-end, transformer-based system for cell-level table retrieval and table question answering. In *Proceedings of the 59th Annual Meeting of the Association for Computational Linguistics and the 11th International Joint Conference on Natural Language Processing: System Demonstrations*, pages 202–209, Online. Association for Computational Linguistics.

Feifei Pan, Mustafa Canim, Michael Glass, Alfio Gliozzo, and James Hendler. 2022. End-to-end table question answering via retrieval-augmented generation. *arXiv preprint arXiv:2203.16714*.

Kishore Papineni, Salim Roukos, Todd Ward, and Wei-Jing Zhu. 2002. Bleu: a method for automatic evaluation of machine translation. In *Proceedings of the 40th annual meeting of the Association for Computational Linguistics*, pages 311–318.

Niki Parmar, Ashish Vaswani, Jakob Uszkoreit, Lukasz Kaiser, Noam Shazeer, Alexander Ku, and Dustin Tran. 2018. Image transformer. In *International conference on machine learning*, pages 4055–4064. PMLR.

Panupong Pasupat and Percy Liang. 2015. Compositional semantic parsing on semi-structured tables. In *Proceedings of the 53rd Annual Meeting of the Association for Computational Linguistics and the 7th International Joint Conference on Natural Language Processing (Volume 1: Long Papers)*, pages 1470–1480, Beijing, China. Association for Computational Linguistics.

Alec Radford, Jeff Wu, Rewon Child, David Luan, Dario Amodei, and Ilya Sutskever. 2019. Language models are unsupervised multitask learners.

Colin Raffel, Noam Shazeer, Adam Roberts, Katherine Lee, Sharan Narang, Michael Matena, Yanqi Zhou, Wei Li, and Peter J. Liu. 2020. Exploring the limits of transfer learning with a unified text-to-text transformer. *Journal of Machine Learning Research*, 21(140):1–67.

Leonardo F. R. Ribeiro, Claire Gardent, and Iryna Gurevych. 2019. Enhancing AMR-to-text generation with dual graph representations. In *Proceedings of the 2019 Conference on Empirical Methods in Natural Language Processing and the 9th International Joint Conference on Natural Language Processing (EMNLP-IJCNLP)*, pages 3183–3194, Hong Kong, China. Association for Computational Linguistics.

Stephen Robertson and Hugo Zaragoza. 2009. *The probabilistic relevance framework: BM25 and beyond*. Now Publishers Inc.

Alon Talmor, Ori Yoran, Amnon Catav, Dan Lahav, Yizhong Wang, Akari Asai, Gabriel Ilharco, Hannaneh Hajishirzi, and Jonathan Berant. 2021. Multimodalqa: Complex question answering over text, tables and images. *arXiv preprint arXiv:2104.06039*.

Ashish Vaswani, Noam Shazeer, Niki Parmar, Jakob Uszkoreit, Llion Jones, Aidan N Gomez, Łukasz Kaiser, and Illia Polosukhin. 2017. Attention is all you need. *Advances in neural information processing systems*, 30.

Petar Veličković, Guillem Cucurull, Arantxa Casanova, Adriana Romero, Pietro Lio, and Yoshua Bengio. 2017. Graph attention networks. *International Conference on Learning Representations (ICLR)*.

Kuan Wang, Yuyu Zhang, Diyi Yang, Le Song, and Tao Qin. 2021. Gnn is a counter? revisiting gnn for question answering. *arXiv preprint arXiv:2110.03192*.

Yibo Wang, Congying Xia, Guan Wang, and Philip S. Yu. 2022. Continuous prompt tuning based textual entailment model for e-commerce entity typing. In *2022 IEEE International Conference on Big Data (Big Data)*, pages 1383–1388.

Yibo Wang, Yanbing Xue, Bo Liu, Musen Wen, Wenting Zhao, Stephen Guo, and Philip S Yu. 2023a. Click-conversion multi-task model with position bias mitigation for sponsored search in ecommerce. In *Proceedings of the 46th International ACM SIGIR Conference on Research and Development in Information Retrieval*, pages 1884–1888.

Yibo Wang, Wenting Zhao, Yao Wan, Zhongfen Deng, and Philip S. Yu. 2023b. Named entity recognition via machine reading comprehension: A multi-task learning approach. *arXiv:2309.11027*.

Zhenyi Wang, Xiaoyang Wang, Bang An, Dong Yu, and Changyou Chen. 2020. Towards faithful neural table-to-text generation with content-matching constraints. In *Proceedings of the 58th Annual Meeting of the Association for Computational Linguistics*, pages 1072–1086, Online. Association for Computational Linguistics.

Xuchen Yao and Benjamin Van Durme. 2014. Information extraction over structured data: Question answering with Freebase. In *Proceedings of the 52nd Annual Meeting of the Association for Computational Linguistics (Volume 1: Long Papers)*, pages 956–966, Baltimore, Maryland. Association for Computational Linguistics.

Michihiro Yasunaga, Hongyu Ren, Antoine Bosselut, Percy Liang, and Jure Leskovec. 2021. QA-GNN: Reasoning with language models and knowledge graphs for question answering. In *Proceedings of the 2021 Conference of the North American Chapter of the Association for Computational Linguistics: Human Language Technologies*, pages 535–546, Online. Association for Computational Linguistics.

Pengcheng Yin, Graham Neubig, Wen tau Yih, and Sebastian Riedel. 2020. TaBERT: Pretraining for joint understanding of textual and tabular data. In *Annual Conference of the Association for Computational Linguistics (ACL)*.

Tao Yu, Chien-Sheng Wu, Xi Victoria Lin, bailin wang, Yi Chern Tan, Xinyi Yang, Dragomir Radev, richard socher, and Caiming Xiong. 2021. Gra{pp}a: Grammar-augmented pre-training for table semantic parsing. In *International Conference on Learning Representations*.

Tao Yu, Rui Zhang, Kai Yang, Michihiro Yasunaga, Dongxu Wang, Zifan Li, James Ma, Irene Li, Qingning Yao, Shanelle Roman, Zilin Zhang, and Dragomir Radev. 2018. Spider: A large-scale human-labeled dataset for complex and cross-domain semantic parsing and text-to-SQL task. In *Proceedings of the 2018 Conference on Empirical Methods in Natural Language Processing*, pages 3911–3921, Brussels, Belgium. Association for Computational Linguistics.

Wenting Zhao, Ye Liu, Yao Wan, and Philip Yu. 2021. Attend, memorize and generate: Towards faithful table-to-text generation in few shots. In *Findings of the Association for Computational Linguistics: EMNLP 2021*, pages 4106–4117, Punta Cana, Dominican Republic. Association for Computational Linguistics.

Victor Zhong, Caiming Xiong, and Richard Socher. 2017. Seq2sql: Generating structured queries from natural language using reinforcement learning. *arXiv preprint arXiv:1709.00103*.

Fengbin Zhu, Wenqiang Lei, Youcheng Huang, Chao Wang, Shuo Zhang, Jiancheng Lv, Fuli Feng, and Tat-Seng Chua. 2021. TAT-QA: A question answering benchmark on a hybrid of tabular and textual content in finance. In *Proceedings of the 59th Annual Meeting of the Association for Computational Linguistics and the 11th International Joint Conference on Natural Language Processing (Volume 1: Long Papers)*, pages 3277–3287, Online. Association for Computational Linguistics.

# Named Entity Recognition via Machine Reading Comprehension: A Multi-Task Learning Approach

**Yibo Wang**
Department of Computer Science
University of Illinois Chicago
ywang633@uic.edu

**Wenting Zhao**
Department of Computer Science
University of Illinois Chicago
wzhao41@uic.edu

**Yao Wan**
School of Computer Science and Technology
Huazhong University of Science and Technology
wanyao@hust.edu.cn

**Zhongfen Deng**
Department of Computer Science
University of Illinois Chicago
zdeng21@uic.edu

**Philip S. Yu**
Department of Computer Science
University of Illinois Chicago
psyu@uic.edu

## Abstract

Named Entity Recognition (NER) aims to extract and classify entity mentions in the text into pre-defined types (e.g., organization or person name). Recently, many works have been proposed to shape the NER as a machine reading comprehension problem (also termed MRC-based NER), in which entity recognition is achieved by answering the formulated questions related to pre-defined entity types through MRC, based on the contexts. However, these works ignore the label dependencies among entity types, which are critical for precisely recognizing named entities. In this paper, we propose to incorporate the label dependencies among entity types into a multi-task learning framework for better MRC-based NER. We decompose MRC-based NER into multiple tasks and use a self-attention module to capture label dependencies. Comprehensive experiments on both nested NER and flat NER datasets are conducted to validate the effectiveness of the proposed Multi-NER. Experimental results show that Multi-NER can achieve better performance on all datasets.

## 1 Introduction

Named Entity Recognition (NER), which aims to locate and classify entity mentions in text into pre-defined types, is a fundamental task in information extraction (Chinchor and Robinson, 1997; Nadeau and Sekine, 2007). Typically, NER is formulated as a sequence labeling task, where each token is classified as one of the pre-defined types. However, the sequence labeling models can only assign one label to a token, resulting in the incapability of handling overlapping entities in nested NER (Finkel and Manning, 2009). Figure 1 shows an example of nested NER: *Homeland Security* can be recognized as ORGANIZATION , as well as PERSON.

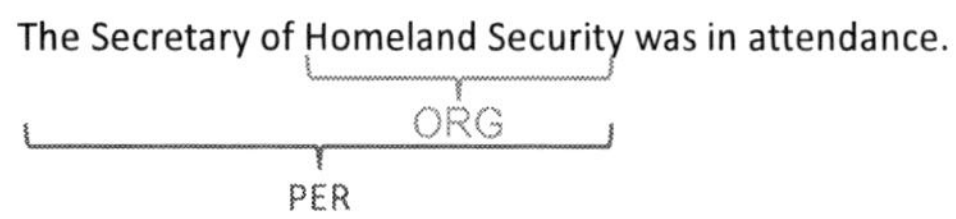


Figure 1: An example of nested NER.

To mitigate this issue, many works resort to formulating NER as a Machine Reading Comprehension (MRC) question answering task (termed MRC-based NER) (Wang et al., 2020; Li et al., 2020; Wang et al., 2022). For example, to recognize the ORGANIZATION, a natural-language question *"Which* ORGANIZATION *is mentioned in the text?"* is formulated. Then the goal of NER is transformed to answer the formulated questions through machine reading comprehension, given the contexts. MRC-based NER provides a unified solution for both flat and nested NER tasks since each entity type has its corresponding entity span positions as the answer, and these output answers are independent of each other.

Despite much progress having been made in MRC-based NER, existing approaches tend to ignore the label dependencies among entity types, which are critical for precise NER. Label dependencies indicate that different entities in the text have some relations with each other. For example, in a sentence *"Ousted WeWork founder Adam Neumann lists his Manhattan penthouse for $37.5 million"*, once *Adam Neumann* is recognized as PERSON, it is expected to help with the recognition



*Findings of the Association for Computational Linguistics: IJCNLP-AACL 2023*, pages 13–19
November 1–4, 2023. 

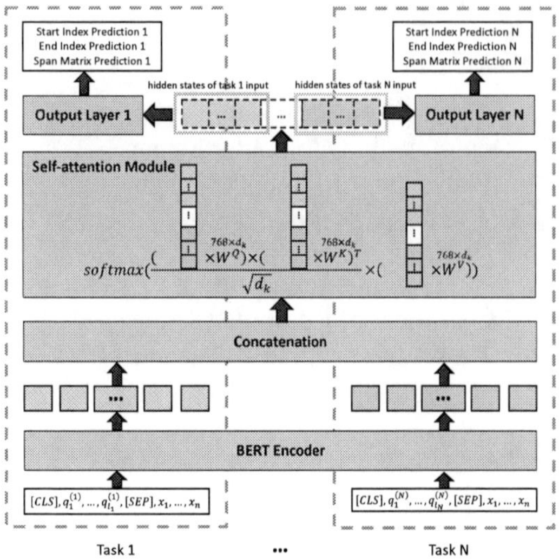

Figure 2: The architecture of our proposed Multi-NER. The input of each task is the concatenation of a question associated with task/entity type and context. The outputs are the corresponding start index prediction, end index prediction, and span matrix prediction.

of *WeWork* as ORGANIZATION because the *founder* preceding a person's name implies an organization.

To leverage the label dependencies among entity types, we propose a novel multi-task learning framework (termed Multi-NER) for MRC-based NER. In Multi-NER, MRC-based NER is decomposed into multiple tasks, each task focusing on one entity type. For each task, the corresponding input is the concatenation of an entity-class-related question and the context, and the output is expected to be the corresponding entity spans (i.e., start and end positions). The input is first encoded via a pre-trained BERT (Devlin et al., 2019). The concatenation of embeddings of all tasks are fed into a self-attention module, which can preserve the label dependencies between different entity types. Finally, task-specific output layers are applied to different tasks.

To validate the effectiveness of our proposed Multi-NER, we conduct experiments on the datasets of both flat NER and nested NER. Experimental results show that Multi-NER can benefit the MRC-based NER in both flat NER and nested NER, with the important label dependencies among entities preserved. Additionally, we also visualize the self-attention maps to examine whether the label dependencies have been successfully captured.

Overall, the contributions of this paper are two-fold: 1) We are the first to propose a multi-task learning framework for MRC-based NER tasks to capture label dependencies between entity types; 2) The introduced self-attention maps are visualized to verify that the self-attention modules can capture label dependencies.

All the source code and datasets are available at https://github.com/YiboWANG214/MultiNER

## 2 Methodology

### 2.1 Problem Formulation

Given a sequence $X = \{x_1, x_2, \ldots, x_n\}$, where $n$ denotes length of $X$, NER aims to find every entity mention in $X$ and assign an entity type $y \in \mathcal{Y}$ to it. BERT-MRC (Li et al., 2020) transforms tagging-style NER to MRC format with a triplet of (QUESTION, ANSWER, CONTEXT). The natural language question $q^{(y)} = \{q_1^{(y)}, \ldots, q_{l_y}^{(y)}\}$, where $l_y$ denotes length of $q^{(y)}$, is related to the entity type $y$ and considered as QUESTION; The positions $P^y_{start,end}$ of entity mentions of $y$ is considered as ANSWER; The input sequence $X$ is considered as CONTEXT. Given $X$ and $q^{(y)}$, the goal of BERT-MRC is to predict $P^y_{start,end}$.

Our Multi-NER applies the same MRC format but further decomposes BERT-MRC into multiple tasks, where each task $i \in \{1, 2, \ldots, |\mathcal{Y}|\}$ only focuses on one entity type. Thus, the task set $\{1, 2, \ldots, |\mathcal{Y}|\}$ and the entity type set $\mathcal{Y}$ are bijection. Instead of processing one QUESTION at a time, Multi-NER processes all QUESTIONs in a multi-task framework. Therefore, in Multi-NER settings, given a CONTEXT $X$ and multiple questions $\{q^{(y)}\}_{y\in\mathcal{Y}}$, the goal is to predict $\{P^y_{start,end}\}_{y\in\mathcal{Y}}$.

### 2.2 Multi-NER

Figure 2 gives an overview of our proposed Multi-NER, which consists of $|\mathcal{Y}|$ tasks, where each task denotes the recognition of one specific entity type. To share information between tasks, one shared encoder is used across tasks, and a self-attention module is employed to capture label dependencies.

**Single Task Learning** For every single task $i \in \{1, 2, \ldots, |\mathcal{Y}|\}$, the input sequence is the concatenation of the natural language question $q^{(i)}$ and the context $X$, as follows:

$$I^{(i)} = \texttt{[CLS]}, q^{(i)}, \texttt{[SEP]}, X\,. \quad (1)$$

The output of task $i$ has three components: start index prediction, end index prediction, and span matrix prediction. The start index prediction is the probability of each token being a start position; the end index prediction is the probability of each token being an end position; the span matrix prediction is the probability of each start-end pair being an entity mention position.

**Task Interactions** Task interactions are two-fold. First, one shared large language model like BERT (Devlin et al., 2019) is used as the encoder for all tasks to make the embedding space consistent. Thus, the embedding of task $i$ is $E^{(i)} = Encoder(I^{(i)})$. Second, a self-attention module (Vaswani et al., 2017) is used across all tasks, accepting the concatenation of the embeddings of every task as input. The self-attention module incorporates information from every task and outputs the concatenation of hidden states

$$E = ATT\left(\left[E^{(1)}, \ldots, E^{(|\mathcal{Y}|)}\right]\right). \quad (2)$$

The self-attention module enables $E$ with the property of capturing the label dependencies between entity types, making $E$ a better representation.

**Model Learning** At training time, all tasks are trained jointly. The loss function for multi-task learning is defined as follows:

$$\mathcal{L} = \sum_{i=1}^{|\mathcal{Y}|}(\alpha\mathcal{L}^{i}_{start} + \beta\mathcal{L}^{i}_{end} + \gamma\mathcal{L}^{i}_{span}), \quad (3)$$

where $\alpha$, $\beta$, and $\gamma$ are tunable weights for start index prediction, end index prediction, and span matrix prediction. $\mathcal{L}^{i}_{start}$, $\mathcal{L}^{i}_{end}$ and $\mathcal{L}^{i}_{span}$ are cross entropy loss of task $i$.

## 3 Experiments

To evaluate the performance of the proposed Multi-NER, we compare it with a state-of-the-art baseline BERT-MRC (Li et al., 2020), on datasets of flat NER and nested NER. We also perform a case study with attention maps visualized to further analyze the ability of Multi-NER to capture label dependencies.

### 3.1 Datasets

We adopt three nested NER datasets (i.e., English ACE-2004 (Mitchell et al., 2005), English ACE-2005 (Walker et al., 2006) and GENIA (Ohta et al., 2002)) and one flat NER dataset (i.e., English CoNLL-2003 (Tjong Kim Sang and De Meulder, 2003)) to evaluate the performance of Multi-NER. ACE-2004 and ACE-2005 are two textual datasets from broadcast, newswire, telephone conversations and weblogs. GENIA is a collection of biomedical literature, containing Medline abstracts. CoNLL-2003 is extracted from Reuters news stories between August 1996 and August 1997. We conducted experiments on both nested NER datasets and flat NER dataset since our model is based on BERT-MRC, which can be applied to both flat and nested NER.

### 3.2 Experimental Settings

For a fair comparison, we select $BERT_{base}$ as the backbone encoder for all models. We adopt a one-layer linear transformation to predict the start index and end index and adopt a two-layer MLP with activation function GELU to predict the span matrix. We set the hidden size as 1,536 and the dropout rate as 0.1. More details of the hyperparameters setting are referred to the Appendix A.1. We follow the same process of question generation in (Li et al., 2020) to use annotation guideline notes, which are the guidelines provided to the annotators when building datasets, as references to construct questions.

### 3.3 Results and Analysis

Table 1 shows the experimental results on both nested NER datasets and flat NER dataset. From this table, we can observe that our Multi-NER achieves 85.34% on ACE 2004, 84.25% on ACE 2005, 81.13% on GENIA, and 92.33% on CoNLL-2003, achieving +1.3%, +0.4%, +1.24% and 1.25% improvement, respectively, when comparing with BERT-MRC. The performance improvements of Multi-NER on all the datasets indicate that formulating MRC-based NER into a multi-task learning framework to obtain label dependencies between different entity types can indeed bring model performance improvement.

Furthermore, the idea behind our proposed multi-task framework is to use different output layers to disambiguate between entity types and use a self-attention module to obtain label dependencies between entity types. To evaluate the contribution of the different output layers and the self-attention module, we also conduct ablation studies on all datasets. The experimental results in Table 2 show that both different output layers and the self-attention module contribute to Multi-NER.

Table 1: Experimental results on nested NER datasets and flat NER dataset.

| Model | Precision | Recall | F1 |
|---|---|---|---|
| | ACE 2004 | | |
| BERT-MRC | 84.63 | 83.46 | 84.04 |
| Multi-NER | 86.01 | 84.68 | 85.34 (+1.3) |
| | ACE 2005 | | |
| BERT-MRC | 83.22 | 84.48 | 83.85 |
| Multi-NER | 84.47 | 84.03 | 84.25 (+0.4) |
| | GENIA | | |
| BERT-MRC | 79.47 | 80.32 | 79.89 |
| Multi-NER | 82.63 | 79.68 | 81.13 (+1.24) |
| | CoNLL-2003 | | |
| BERT-MRC | 90.61 | 91.55 | 91.08 |
| Multi-NER | 91.96 | 92.70 | 92.33 (+1.25) |

Table 2: Ablation studies evaluate the contribution of components of Multi-NER.

| Model | ACE04 | ACE05 | GENIA | CoNLL03 |
|---|---|---|---|---|
| Multi-NER | 85.34 | 84.25 | 81.13 | 92.33 |
| (w/o att) | 84.84 | 84.01 | 80.87 | 91.32 |
| (w/o diff) | 84.72 | 84.05 | 80.58 | 91.55 |

### 3.4 Case Study

To further study the effect of Multi-NER, we examine some randomly selected examples. As an example, for *"Ahbulaity Ahbudurecy , chairman of the Xinjiang Uigur Autonomous Region , presided at the opening ceremony , and leaders such as Tiemuer Dawamaiti , vice - chairman of the Standing Committee of the National People ' s Congress , Shimayi Aimaiti , member of the State Affairs Committee , etc . cut the ribbon for the meeting ."* from

**BERT-MRC:** [ Ahbulaity Ahbudurecy ]PER , [ chairman of [ the Xinjiang Uigur Autonomous Region ]GPE ]PER , presided at the opening ceremony , and [ leaders such as ...... , [ [etc]ORG ]PER ]PER. cut the ribbon for the meeting .

**Multi-NER:** [ Ahbulaity Ahbudurecy ]PER , [ chairman of [ the Xinjiang Uigur Autonomous Region ]GPE ]PER , presided at the opening ceremony , and [ leaders such as ...... , etc ]PER. cut the ribbon for the meeting .

**Ground Truth:** [ Ahbulaity Ahbudurecy ]PER , [ chairman of [ the Xinjiang Uigur Autonomous Region ]GPE ]PER , presided at the opening ceremony , and [ leaders such as ...... , etc . ]PER cut the ribbon for the meeting .

Figure 3: The ground truth, predictions of BERT-MRC and Multi-NER for a randomly selected example. The middle of the sentence is omitted for better presentation. The complete example is referred to Appendix A.2.

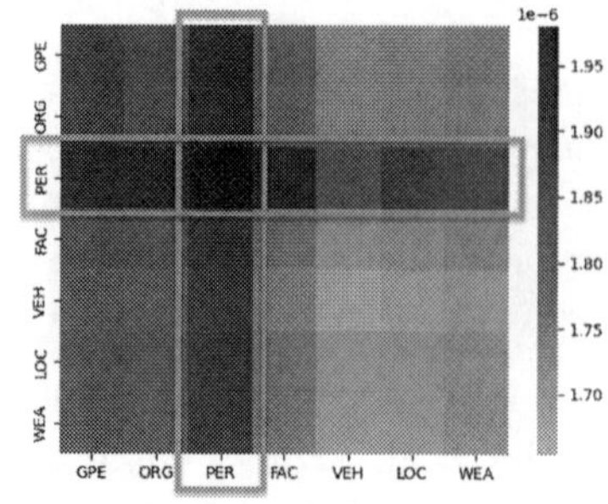


Figure 4: Attention map of the mean scores according to entity types of a randomly selected example from ACE 2004.

ACE 2004, we show the ground-truth entities and predicted results of BERT-MRC and Multi-NER in Figure 3. In BERT-MRC, *etc* is categorized as both ORG and PER, while in Multi-NER and ground truth *etc* is categorized as PER. Ambiguous tokens like *etc* are hard to categorize even with contextual information. However, when applying Multi-NER, different entity types and label dependencies are also considered, which is beneficial to ambiguous tokens.

We also show the attention map of the mean scores according to entity types of this example in Figure 4. We can see that PER has a relatively large impact on other entity types, helping the model improve performance on other entity types with PER information. We attribute it to label dependencies obtained by information sharing between entity types using the self-attention module.

## 4 Related Work

As language models have advanced (Devlin et al., 2019; Raffel et al., 2020; Zhao et al., 2023; Dong et al., 2023; Zhao et al., 2021; Liu et al., 2021), numerous efforts have emerged to enhance the performance of MRC-based NER. Zhang et al. (2022) incorporated different domain knowledge into MRC-based NER task to improve model generalization ability. Liu et al. (2022) proposed to use graph attention networks to capture label dependencies between entity types when applying MRC-based NER to electronic medical records. However, they only use entity type embeddings to build graph attention networks, ignoring the rich information in context. MRC-based NER is applied to different domains. Du et al. (2022) designed an MRC-based method for medical NER through both sequence labeling and span boundary detection. Zhang and Zhang (2022) applied MRC-based NER for financial named entity recognition from literature. Wang et al. (2020) proposed MRC-based NER with the help of a distilled masked language model in e-commerce. Jia et al. (2022) applied MRC-based methods for multimodal named entity recognition.

The span-based methods (Eberts and Ulges, 2020) that formulate nested NER as a span classification task are also mentionable. Wan et al. (2022) improved span representation using retrieval-based span-level graphs based on n-gram similarity. Yuan et al. (2022) integrated heterogeneous factors like inside tokens, boundaries, labels, and related spans to improve the performance of span representation and classification. Shen et al. (2021) improved span-based NER using a two-stage entity identifier to filter out low-quality spans to reduce computational costs.

## 5 Conclusion

In this paper, we propose to incorporate the label dependencies among entity types into a novel multi-task learning framework (termed Multi-NER) for MRC-based NER. A self-attention mechanism is introduced to obtain label dependencies between entity types. Experimental results validate that Multi-NER outperforms BERT-MRC on both nested NER and flat NER. Case study and attention map visualization show that our introduced self-attention module is able to capture label dependencies among entities, contributing to a performance improvement.

## Limitations

One limitation of our proposed Multi-NER lies in that the number of tasks depends on the number of entity types because each entity type is considered as a task. Depending on the model structure we use in Multi-NER, the number of parameters will increase by 4M for each additional entity type with $Max\_Length = 128$. One possible solution to solve this problem is using parameter-efficient fine-tuning methods like Hypernetworks (Ha et al., 2016) to effectively generate task-specific output layers. We leave this problem to our future work.

## References


Nancy Chinchor and Patricia Robinson. 1997. Muc-7 named entity task definition. In *Proceedings of the 7th Conference on Message Understanding*, volume 29, pages 1–21.

Jacob Devlin, Ming-Wei Chang, Kenton Lee, and Kristina Toutanova. 2019. BERT: Pre-training of deep bidirectional transformers for language understanding. In *Proceedings of the 2019 Conference of the North American Chapter of the Association for Computational Linguistics: Human Language Technologies, Volume 1 (Long and Short Papers)*, pages 4171–4186, Minneapolis, Minnesota. Association for Computational Linguistics.

Xiangjue Dong, Jiaying Lu, Jianling Wang, and James Caverlee. 2023. Closed-book question generation via contrastive learning. In *Proceedings of the 17th Conference of the European Chapter of the Association for Computational Linguistics*, pages 3150–3162, Dubrovnik, Croatia. Association for Computational Linguistics.

Xiaojing Du, Jia Yuxiang, and Zan Hongying. 2022. MRC-based medical NER with multi-task learning and multi-strategies. In *Proceedings of the 21st Chinese National Conference on Computational Linguistics*, pages 836–847, Nanchang, China. Chinese Information Processing Society of China.

Markus Eberts and Adrian Ulges. 2020. Span-based joint entity and relation extraction with transformer pre-training. In *ECAI 2020*, pages 2006–2013. IOS Press.

Jenny Rose Finkel and Christopher D Manning. 2009. Nested named entity recognition. In *Proceedings of the 2009 conference on empirical methods in natural language processing*, pages 141–150.

David Ha, Andrew M. Dai, and Quoc V. Le. 2016. Hypernetworks. *CoRR*, abs/1609.09106.

Meihuizi Jia, Xin Shen, Lei Shen, Jinhui Pang, Lejian Liao, Yang Song, Meng Chen, and Xiaodong He. 2022. Query prior matters: A mrc framework for multimodal named entity recognition. In *Proceedings of the 30th ACM International Conference on Multimedia*, pages 3549–3558.

Xiaoya Li, Jingrong Feng, Yuxian Meng, Qinghong Han, Fei Wu, and Jiwei Li. 2020. A unified MRC framework for named entity recognition. In *Proceedings of the 58th Annual Meeting of the Association for Computational Linguistics*, pages 5849–5859, Online. Association for Computational Linguistics.

Shuyue Liu, Junwen Duan, Feng Gong, Hailin Yue, and Jianxin Wang. 2022. Fusing label relations for chinese emr named entity recognition with machine reading comprehension. In *International Symposium on Bioinformatics Research and Applications*, pages 41–51. Springer.

Ye Liu, Yao Wan, Lifang He, Hao Peng, and Philip S. Yu. 2021. Kg-bart: Knowledge graph-augmented bart for generative commonsense reasoning. In *Proceedings of the AAAI Conference on Artificial Intelligence*, volume 35, pages 6418–6425.

Alexis Mitchell, Stephanie Strassel, Shudong Huang, and Ramez Zakhary. 2005. Ace 2004 multilingual training corpus. *Linguistic Data Consortium, Philadelphia*, 1:1–1.

David Nadeau and Satoshi Sekine. 2007. A survey of named entity recognition and classification. *Lingvisticae Investigationes*, 30(1):3–26.

Tomoko Ohta, Yuka Tateisi, Jin-Dong Kim, Hideki Mima, and Junichi Tsujii. 2002. The genia corpus: An annotated research abstract corpus in molecular biology domain. *Proceedings of the human language technology conference*, pages 73–77.

Colin Raffel, Noam Shazeer, Adam Roberts, Katherine Lee, Sharan Narang, Michael Matena, Yanqi Zhou, Wei Li, Peter J Liu, et al. 2020. Exploring the limits of transfer learning with a unified text-to-text transformer. *J. Mach. Learn. Res.*, 21(140):1–67.

Yongliang Shen, Xinyin Ma, Zeqi Tan, Shuai Zhang, Wen Wang, and Weiming Lu. 2021. Locate and label: A two-stage identifier for nested named entity recognition. *arXiv preprint arXiv:2105.06804*.

Erik F. Tjong Kim Sang and Fien De Meulder. 2003. Introduction to the CoNLL-2003 shared task: Language-independent named entity recognition. In *Proceedings of the Seventh Conference on Natural Language Learning at HLT-NAACL 2003*, pages 142–147.

Ashish Vaswani, Noam Shazeer, Niki Parmar, Jakob Uszkoreit, Llion Jones, Aidan N Gomez, Łukasz Kaiser, and Illia Polosukhin. 2017. Attention is all you need. *Advances in neural information processing systems*, 30.

Christopher Walker, Stephanie Strassel, Julie Medero, and Kazuaki Maeda. 2006. Ace 2005 multilingual training corpus. *Linguistic Data Consortium, Philadelphia*, 57:45.

Juncheng Wan, Dongyu Ru, Weinan Zhang, and Yong Yu. 2022. Nested named entity recognition with span-level graphs. In *Proceedings of the 60th Annual Meeting of the Association for Computational Linguistics (Volume 1: Long Papers)*, pages 892–903, Dublin, Ireland. Association for Computational Linguistics.

Qifan Wang, Li Yang, Bhargav Kanagal, Sumit Sanghai, D. Sivakumar, Bin Shu, Zac Yu, and Jon Elsas. 2020. Learning to extract attribute value from product via question answering: A multi-task approach. In *Proceedings of the 26th ACM SIGKDD International Conference on Knowledge Discovery & Data Mining*, KDD '20, page 47–55, New York, NY, USA. Association for Computing Machinery.

Yibo Wang, Congying Xia, Guan Wang, and Philip S. Yu. 2022. Continuous prompt tuning based textual entailment model for e-commerce entity typing. In *2022 IEEE International Conference on Big Data (Big Data)*, pages 1383–1388. IEEE Computer Society.

Zheng Yuan, Chuanqi Tan, Songfang Huang, and Fei Huang. 2022. Fusing heterogeneous factors with triaffine mechanism for nested named entity recognition. In *Findings of the Association for Computational Linguistics: ACL 2022*, pages 3174–3186, Dublin, Ireland. Association for Computational Linguistics.

Yu Zhang, Jian Deng, Ying Ma, and Jianmin Li. 2022. A multi-task approach for machine reading comprehension form named entity recognition tasks. In *2022 3rd International Conference on Artificial Intelligence and Education (IC-ICAIE 2022)*, pages 480–485. Atlantis Press.

Yuzhe Zhang and Hong Zhang. 2022. Finbert-mrc: financial named entity recognition using bert under the machine reading comprehension paradigm. *arXiv preprint arXiv:2205.15485*.

Wenting Zhao, Ye Liu, Yao Wan, Yibo Wang, Zhongfen Deng, and Philip S. Yu. 2023. Localize, retrieve and fuse: A generalized framework for free-form question answering over tables.

Wenting Zhao, Ye Liu, Yao Wan, and Philip Yu. 2021. Attend, memorize and generate: Towards faithful table-to-text generation in few shots. In *Findings of the Association for Computational Linguistics: EMNLP 2021*, pages 4106–4117, Punta Cana, Dominican Republic. Association for Computational Linguistics.

# A Appendix

## A.1 Hyperparameters

The hyperparameter details are shown in Table 3.

## A.2 Examples

The ground truth, predicted results of Multi-NER and BERT-MRC of a randomly selected example are shown in Table 4 and Figure 5. From the table, we can observe that the true positive, false positive, and false negative positions of BERT-MRC and Multi-NER are 8, 4, 3, and 9, 3, 2. Besides, most errors of Multi-NER are due to the ambiguity of the entity mention boundaries like punctuation.

Table 3: Hyperparameters for all models.

| Model | Batch Size | Max Length | Learning Rate | Epoch | # Parameters |
|---|---|---|---|---|---|
| **ACE 2004** | | | | | |
| BERT-MRC | 2 | 128 | 3e-5 | 14 | 112M |
| Multi-NER | 2 | 128 | 2e-5 | 19 | 133M |
| **ACE 2005** | | | | | |
| Model | Batch Size | Max Length | Learning Rate | Epoch | # Parameters |
| BERT-MRC | 2 | 128 | 2e-5 | 11 | 112M |
| Multi-NER | 2 | 128 | 2e-5 | 16 | 133M |
| **GENIA** | | | | | |
| Model | Batch Size | Max Length | Learning Rate | Epoch | # Parameters |
| BERT-MRC | 2 | 180 | 2e-5 | 9 | 112M |
| Multi-NER | 2 | 128 | 2e-5 | 15 | 125M |
| **CoNLL-2003** | | | | | |
| Model | Batch Size | Max Length | Learning Rate | Epoch | # Parameters |
| BERT-MRC | 2 | 200 | 3e-5 | 8 | 112M |
| Multi-NER | 1 | 200 | 2e-5 | 18 | 123M |

Table 4: Results of an example *"Ahbulaity Ahbudurecy , chairman of the Xinjiang Uigur Autonomous Region , presided at the opening ceremony , and leaders such as Tiemuer Dawamaiti , vice - chairman of the Standing Committee of the National People ' s Congress , Shimayi Aimaiti , member of the State Affairs Committee , etc . cut the ribbon for the meeting ."* from ACE 2004.

| entity type | BERT-MRC | Multi-NER | Ground Truth |
|---|---|---|---|
| GPE | (5,9) | (5,9) | (5,9) |
| ORG | (28,37) (32,37) (44,47) (49,49) | (28,37) (32,37) (44,47) | (28,37) (44,47) |
| PER | (0,1) (3,9) (18,49) (21,22) (24,37) (39,40) (49,49) | (0,1) (3,9) (18,49) (21,22) (24,37) (39,40) (39,47) (42,47) | (0,1) (3,9) (18,50) (21,22) (24,37) (39,40) (42,47) (49,50) |
| FAC | - | - | - |
| VEH | - | - | - |
| LOC | - | - | - |
| WEA | - | - | - |

**BERT-MRC:** [ Ahbulaity Ahbudurecy ]PER , [ chairman of [ the Xinjiang Uigur Autonomous Region ]GPE ]PER , presided at the opening ceremony , and [ leaders such as [ Tiemuer Dawamaiti ]PER , [ vice - chairman of [ the Standing Committee of ~~[ the National People ' s Congress ]ORG~~ ]ORG ]PER , [ Shimayi Aimaiti ]PER , **member of** [ **the State Affairs Committee** ]ORG , ~~[ [**etc**]ORG ]PER~~ ]PER. cut the ribbon for the meeting .

**Multi-NER:** [ Ahbulaity Ahbudurecy ]PER , [ chairman of [ the Xinjiang Uigur Autonomous Region ]GPE ]PER , presided at the opening ceremony , and [ leaders such as [ Tiemuer Dawamaiti ]PER , [ vice - chairman of [ the Standing Committee of [ ~~the National People ' s Congress~~ ]ORG ]ORG ]PER , ~~[ [ Shimayi Aimaiti ]PER , [ member of [ the State Affairs Committee ]ORG ]PER ]PER~~ , **etc** ]PER. cut the ribbon for the meeting .

**Ground Truth:** [ Ahbulaity Ahbudurecy ]PER , [ chairman of [ the Xinjiang Uigur Autonomous Region ]GPE ]PER , presided at the opening ceremony , and [ leaders such as [ Tiemuer Dawamaiti ]PER , [ vice - chairman of [ the Standing Committee of the National People ' s Congress ]ORG ]PER , [ Shimayi Aimaiti ]PER , [ [ member of [ the State Affairs Committee ]PER ]ORG ]PER , etc . ]PER cut the ribbon for the meeting .

Figure 5: The ground truth, results of BERT-MRC and Multi-NER of a randomly selected example. Delete lines and underlines represent false positive and bolded tokens represent false negative. Punctuation errors are not indicated in the figure.

# SPEC5G: A Dataset for 5G Cellular Network Protocol Analysis

**Imtiaz Karim, Kazi Samin Mubasshir, Mirza Masfiqur Rahman, Elisa Bertino**
Purdue University
{karim7, kmubassh, rahman75, bertino}@purdue.edu

**Abstract**

5G is the $5^{th}$ generation state-of-the-art cellular network protocol designed to connect virtually everyone and everything with increased speed and reduced latency. Therefore, its development, analysis, and security are critical. However, all approaches to the 5G protocol development and security analysis, e.g., property extraction, protocol summarization, and semantic analysis of the protocol specifications and implementations are completely manual. To reduce such manual efforts, in this paper, we curate SPEC5G–the *first-ever* public 5G dataset for NLP research. The dataset contains 3,547,587 sentences with 134M words, from 13094 cellular network specifications and 13 online websites. By leveraging large-scale pre-trained language models that have achieved state-of-the-art results on NLP tasks, we use this dataset for security-related text classification and summarization. Security-related text classification can be used to extract relevant security-related properties for protocol testing. On the other hand, summarization can help developers and practitioners understand the high-level idea of the protocol, which is itself a daunting task. To ensure the research community can benefit from this work, all the datasets and accompanying codebase are made publicly available[1].

## 1 Introduction

The deployment of the 5G cellular network protocol has generated a lot of enthusiasm in academia and industry, because of its promise of enabling innovative applications, such as autonomous vehicles (Ahmad et al., 2020), remote surgery (sur, 2022), industrial IoT (Satyanarayanan, 2017), augmented reality (Zhang et al., 2017), and multiplayer online gaming (scr, 2022). Therefore the security of 5G protocol is critical. Unfortunately, the 5G protocol development and analysis are all completely manual tasks requiring domain expertise. We observe that for 5G there is an unutilized resource of information available in the form of specifications (Spe, 2022) and numerous tutorials on the Internet. These resources have not yet been utilized.

Recently, a few approaches have been proposed that leverage natural language processing (NLP) and machine learning (ML) to detect risky operations in some of the specifications of 4G LTE (Chen et al., 2021) and to analyze change requests (Chen et al., 2022). These approaches are very limited, not generalizable, and not open-source. Automatic and systematic analysis of 5G networks is still a difficult task. One major problem is the lack of high-quality datasets to train ML models, which would enable the automation of different 5G-related downstream tasks e.g., security-related text classification, protocol summarization, semantic analysis, and automatic programming. In this paper, we address this need by introducing SPEC5G, a high-quality dataset of the 5G protocol specifications. 5G is not a single wireless technology, but an umbrella term used to categorize the fifth generation of wireless communication, including hundreds of different protocols at different layers of the protocol. Some of these protocols are VoWiFi, cellular IoT, IKE, and 5G-AKA. SPEC5G is a complete dataset that covers all these protocols and therefore, has the potential to impact different protocols affecting billions of devices. Such a high-quality dataset would be beneficial to numerous applications in different domains, such as security testing, policy enforcement, automatic code generation, and protocol summarization. It would encourage research and development in novel NLP tasks that are communication protocol-specific and critical for the security analysis of these protocols. Notable examples include formal model extraction from large-scale natural language documents and identifications of conflicting security guidelines.

[1]Datasets and codebase for SPEC5G are publicly available at https://github.com/Imtiazkarimik23/SPEC5G



*Findings of the Association for Computational Linguistics: IJCNLP-AACL 2023*, pages 20–38
November 1–4, 2023. 

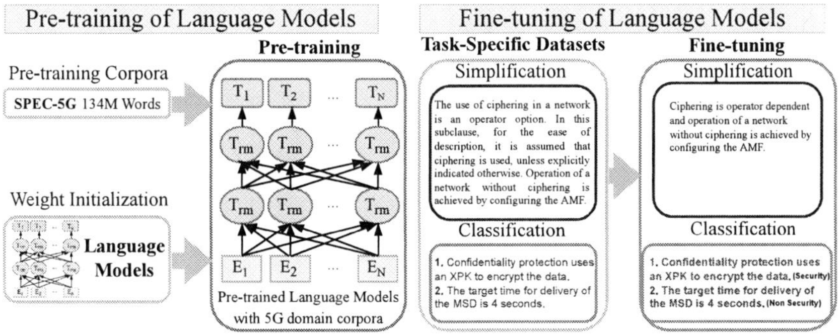


Figure 1: Overview of our pre-training and fine-tuning on downstream tasks using SPEC5G

To show the viability of our SPEC5G dataset, we use it for two downstream tasks (shown in Figure 1). First, we use it for *security-text classification*. In previous 5G security testing (Basin et al., 2018; Cremers and Dehnel-Wild, 2019; Hussain et al., 2019) the properties are manually extracted from the specifications. Using security-text classification, we can automatically identify texts, which specify important security properties to be used for formal verification and other testing approaches. Second, we use SPEC5G for the *paragraph summarization* task. The 5G specification is large and complex with specialized jargon, mostly due to backward compatibility requirements. Therefore, it is really daunting for a software developer to understand the high-level ideas of the protocol specification. With the summarization task, we show that it is possible to summarize and simplify the high-level ideas of the protocol. To achieve those tasks, we created two expert-annotated datasets: one for summarization and one for classification. The summarization dataset contains 713 long articles and their concise summaries. The classification dataset contains 2401 sentences and their class labels (*Non-Security*, *Security*, *Undefined*). Both datasets were annotated by multiple domain experts to ensure quality and fairness. Along with SPEC5G, these two expert annotated datasets have been open-sourced to enhance research.

On the whole, our contributions are three-fold. First, we create the first-ever novel 5G dataset (SPEC5G) of 3,547,587 sentences by pre-processing the 5G specification and scraping data from different 5G tutorials on the Internet. Second, we create two expert-annotated datasets for baseline security-text classification and summarization tasks. We conduct an extensive evaluation of these datasets using several NLP models on the downstream tasks. The results show that the models pre-trained on SPEC5G outperform all baseline models. Third, all these research artifacts have been made available via a public repository. To the best of our knowledge, this is the *first-ever* public 5G dataset created for NLP research.

## 2 Related Work

The introduction of the attention-based transformer architecture by (Vaswani et al., 2017) beaconed the era of transformer-based Language Models (LM) in the field of NLP. A range of high-performing transformer-based language models have since been proposed, each with its own specific use cases. To train such LMs, high-quality large datasets are critical. In the following, we will discuss the research relevant to our work.

**Cellular Networks Research Using NLP.** CREEK (Chen et al., 2022) uses BERT models for detecting security-relevant change requests. For this, they pre-train BERT with a subset of 4G LTE specifications (1546 out of 13094). Moreover, in ATOMIC (Chen et al., 2021) they design a framework to semantically analyze LTE documents using NLP to obtain a set of hazard indicators for generating test cases based on a given threat model. These are the first steps in applying NLP techniques to analyze cellular network specifications. In a technical blog post from Erricson (err, 2022), the authors adopt LMs for the telecom domain and create a telecom question-answering dataset. Though promising, these approaches do not generalize and are ad-hoc and closed-source, thus accentuating the need for a complete and public dataset for 5G.

**Summarization.** Following BookCorpus and Wikidata, researchers have built summarization datasets such as Wikilarge (Zhang and Lapata, 2017), Wikismall (Zhu et al., 2010), and so on (Coster and Kauchak, 2011; Kauchak, 2013). Such datasets are widely used in the field of sentence summarization. Early summarization models mostly relied on statistical machine translation (Wubben et al., 2012; Narayan and Gardent, 2014). Improvements of the machine translation model to obtain a new summarization model are done by (Nisioi et al., 2017) and investigations on how to simplify sentences to different difficulty levels are conducted after this (Scarton and Specia, 2018; Nishihara et al., 2019). Sentence alignment methods to improve sentence summarization are proposed by (Štajner et al., 2017) and (Jiang et al., 2020). There are several corpora related to summarization. A large-scale, human-annotated scientific papers corpus is provided by (Yasunaga et al., 2019). This corpus provides over 1,000 papers in the ACL anthology with their citation networks (e.g., citation sentences, citation counts) and their comprehensive, manual summaries. There is another dataset that has been created for the Computational Linguistics Scientific Document Summarization Shared Task which started in 2014 as a pilot (Jaidka et al., 2014) and which is now a well-developed challenge in its fourth year (Jaidka et al., 2018, 2017). A new dataset for summarisation of computer science publications by exploiting a large resource of the author-provided summaries is introduced by (Collins et al., 2017).

**Sentence Classification.** The Corpus of Linguistic Acceptability (CoLA) (Warstadt et al., 2018) consists of English acceptability judgments drawn from books and journal articles on linguistic theory. Each example is a sequence of words annotated with whether it is an English grammatical sentence. The Stanford Sentiment Treebank (Socher et al., 2013) consists of sentences from movie reviews and human annotations of their sentiment. SciCite (Cohan et al., 2019a) is a large dataset of citation intents for the task of automated analysis of scientific papers by identifying the intent of a citation (e.g., background information, use of methods, comparing results). Researchers have also leveraged other large datasets such as DEFT (Spala et al., 2019) and ACL-ARC (Bird et al., 2008) for the sentence classification tasks. CSABSTRUCT (Cohan et al., 2019b) is another new dataset of manually annotated sentences from computer science abstracts for Sequential Sentence Classification (SSC). Paper Field (Sinha et al., 2015) is built from the Microsoft Academic Graph and maps paper titles to one of 7 fields of study: geography, politics, economics, business, sociology, medicine, and psychology. DBpedia is aimed at extracting structured content from Wikipedia. This is a data extract (after preprocessing, with kernel included) with taxonomic, hierarchical categories, or classes, for 343k Wikipedia articles. A version of this dataset is also a popular baseline for text classification tasks.

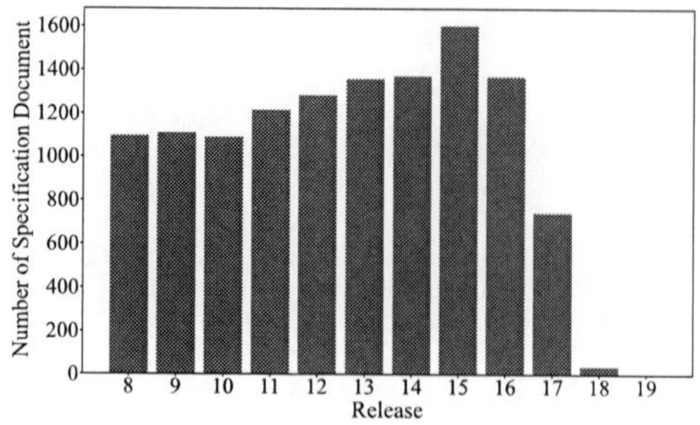


Figure 2: Number of Technical Specifications in subsequent releases from 3GPP. Release 15 has seen the largest number of documents. The current release (Rel-19) has only 1 specification document so far. Mean: 1021.08, median: 1160, min: 1, max: 1601, sd: 491.50, skewness: -1.19, kurtosis: 0.13

## 3 Dataset Curation

In this section, we discuss the collection and preparation of our dataset. A significant amount of data was collected from the 3GPP website (Spe, 2022).

### 3.1 3GPP

The 3rd Generation Partnership Project (3GPP) is an umbrella organization that hosts several organizations from different countries. 3GPP is globally considered the issuer of standards for cellular network protocols. These standards are publicized as releases, e.g., LTE standards were made public from Release 8 and 5G standards from Release 15. The current release is Release 19.

A large number of meeting minutes, Technical Reports (TR) can be found on the 3GPP FTP server (Spe, 2022). 3GPP releases a set of Technical Specifications (TS) as well, which subsequently add features and bug fixes. Figure 2 shows the count of specification documents per release.

### 3.2 Dataset Collection

As stated earlier a significant portion of the dataset has been collected from the 3GPP FTP server. Automated NLP tasks have been hindered in the 5G domain because of noisy data in the standard documentation. Often, the specification documents contain embedded codes, tables, and lists with definitions of varying terminologies, flow diagrams, finite state machines, and so on–which makes it hard to build models that reason and perform well on downstream applications.

Thus, to leverage downstream NLP tasks, we perform extensive preprocessing. Furthermore, we scrape data from 13 blogs, and forums of the internet. The web sources are listed in Table 4 and details about the web sources can be found in Appendix C.5. We extract approximately 17 GB of text data from specification releases and web portals using python web scrapper and Selenium (sel, 2022). Later we apply a set of standard and domain-specific preprocessing to obtain the final dataset.

#### 3.2.1 Preprocessing

5G specifications and web data contain a variety of materials encompassing method and framework documentation, pseudocode, high-level implementations, numerous parameters, field constitution, and so on. At first, the raw data go through standard NLP preprocessing tasks, e.g., removing extra whitespaces, tabs, certain Unicode characters introduced from scrapping, HTML tags, etc. Later, we extend the preprocessing to handle special cases such as code snippets, tables, figures, references to other specification documents, etc. For the list of preprocessing tasks, we refer the reader to Appendix A.1. Finally, this dataset is used to pre-train baseline models for downstream applications.

#### 3.2.2 Dataset Statistics

Our final processed dataset contains 3,547,587 sentences with a total of 134M words. Figure 3 shows the distribution of the number of sentences per document and Figure 4 shows the distribution of tokens per sentence.

### 3.3 Annotation

To demonstrate the effectiveness of SPEC5G, we additionally create and annotate two datasets specific to two NLP tasks - summarization and sentence classification.

#### 3.3.1 Summarization

To prepare the summarization dataset, we randomly select 1500 locations to retrieve articles from the SPEC5G dataset. An article is defined as a sequential collection of sentences. Here we apply another round of manual processing to ensure semantic correctness among the sentences of each of

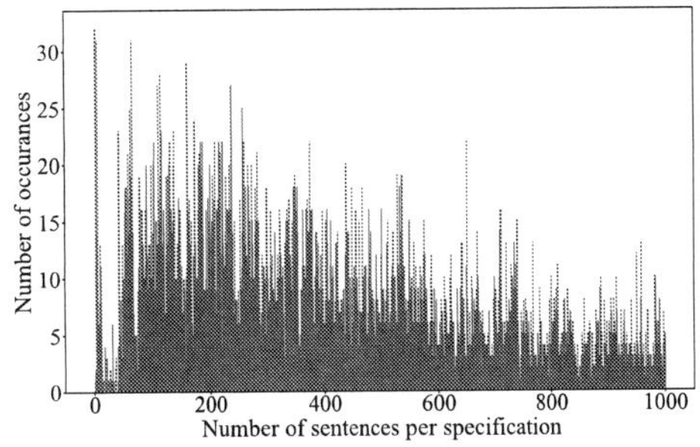


Figure 3: Document distribution based on sentences. Documents with more than 1000 sentences were omitted from the figure for better visualization. Mean: 400.90, median: 356, min: 0, max: 1000, sd: 257.83, skewness: 0.52, kurtosis: -0.73

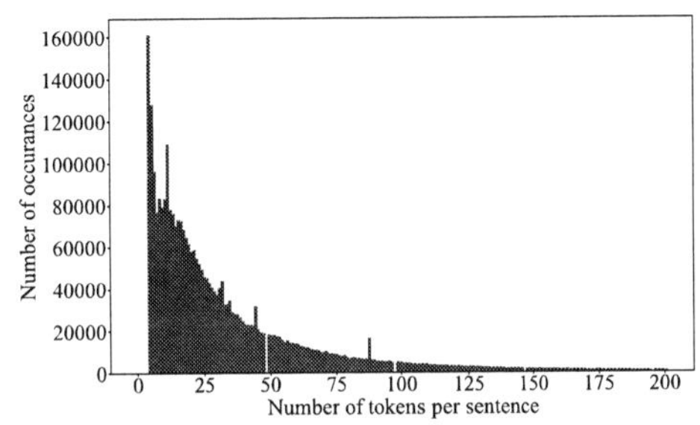


Figure 4: Sentence distribution based on tokens. Sentences with more than 200 tokens were omitted from the figure for better visualization. Mean: 34.89, median: 23, min: 4, max: 200, sd: 34.91, skewness: 1.95, kurtosis: 4.10

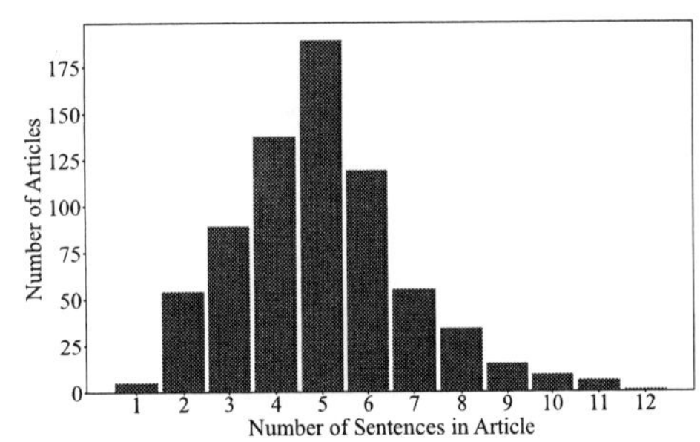


Figure 5: Sentence distribution per article. Mean: 4.97, median: 5, min: 1, max: 12, sd: 1.85, skewness: 0.61, kurtosis: 0.72

the articles. The final curated dataset contains 713 articles, each with 1-12 sentences. The distribution of sentences per article is shown in Figure 5. This dataset is subsequently labeled by 9 domain experts; each label itself is a smaller set of sentences that summarizes the article. The task of annotation (summarizing) varies in difficulty. The annotators have made insightful comments about the articles they have faced challenges with. Another round of manual data cleaning has been done based on the comments which resulted in a very high-quality test set for protocol specification summarization. For the rest of this paper, we refer to this annotated dataset as 5GSum.

### 3.3.2 Security Classification

Similar to the summarization task, we randomly select and annotate 2401 sentences from our SPEC5G dataset to use for multi-class classification. We categorize the data into 3 classes- *Non-Security* (0), *Security* (1), and *Undefined* (2). To discard human bias, the dataset has been labeled by 9 domain experts. We do a 85-5-10 split for train, validation, and test data with 2040, 120, and 241 samples respectively. For the rest of the paper, we refer to this dataset as 5GSC.

Among the 3 classes, the least number of samples are from class 2 (*Undefined*: 484). Yet, the class with the highest number of samples (*Non-Security*: 1303) is about 3 times more than the class with the lowest number of samples. Therefore, the dataset is not highly imbalanced. Overall, this non-uniformity is expected, since most of the specification documents should not be related to *Security* issues and a high amount of *Undefined* statements in 5G specifications would rather mean inconsistencies in implementation.

## 4 Tasks

In this section, we define the downstream tasks: summarization and security sentence classification. Moreover, we discuss the relevance of these downstream tasks with respect to 5G.

### 4.1 Task 1: Summarization

Text summarization is the simplification of the original text to a more understandable text while keeping the main meaning of the original text unchanged (Štajner and Saggion, 2018; Maddela et al., 2020). It can provide convenience for non-native speakers (Petersen and Ostendorf, 2007; Glavaš and Štajner, 2015; Paetzold and Specia, 2016), non-expert readers (Elhadad and Sutaria, 2007; Siddharthan and Katsos, 2010). In the case of 5G standard documents, summarization can help developers and practitioners understand the high-level idea of the protocol, which can be really time-consuming without the summarization.

The document-level text summarization task can be defined as follows. Let $C$ be an original complex article; suppose that $C$ consists of $n$ sentences, denoted as $C = S_1, S_2, \ldots, S_n$. Document-level summarization aims to simplify $C$ into $m$ sentences, which form the simplified article $F$, denoted as $F = T_1, T_2, \ldots, T_m$, where $m$ is not necessarily equal to $n$. $F$ retains the primary meaning of $C$ and is more straightforward than $C$, making it easier for people to understand. The operations for sentence-level summarization include word reservation and deletion, synonym replacement (Xu et al., 2016). In our definition, document-level summarization should allow the loss of information but should not allow the loss of important information. The fact that sentence deletion is a prevalent phenomenon in document summarization is pointed out by (Zhong et al., 2019). We believe that information that has little relevance to the primary meaning should be removed to improve readability.

The objective is to simplify a paragraph without losing important information. Task 1 is more challenging when evaluating a model's ability to reason about unobserved effects.

### 4.2 Task 2: Sentence Classification

Text classification is a classic topic for natural language processing, in which one needs to assign predefined categories to free-text documents. The range of text classification research goes from designing the best features to choosing the best possible machine learning classifiers (Mekala et al., 2021; Liu et al., 2021; Zhang et al., 2022).

The multi-class sentence classification can be defined as follows. Given a sentence $s \in \mathcal{S}$, where $\mathcal{S}$ is some high dimensional sentence space and a finite set of categories or classes $\mathcal{C} = \{c_1, c_2, \ldots, c_n\}$, the objective of multi-class sentence classification is to find a function $\mathcal{F}$ mapping sentences to categories, formally, $\mathcal{F} : \mathcal{S} \rightarrow \mathcal{C}$. Given a dataset $\tilde{\mathcal{D}}$ of $m$ training samples $\{(s_i, c_i)\}_{i=1}^{m}$, we aim to learn the function $\bar{\mathcal{F}}$ that approximates $\mathcal{F}$.

For protocol analysis, an important step is property-guided testing (Hussain et al., 2019). Up to this point, the properties are manually extracted, and the testing is entirely manual. The security classification task aims to label the security-related sentences that in turn can be used as properties and enable semi-automated testing.

## 5 Experiments and Evaluation

In this section we provide a comprehensive assessment of the proposed methodology through rigorous experimentation and evaluation.

### 5.1 Experiment Setup

**Baseline Models:** For baseline models we use base versions of BERT (Devlin et al., 2018), RoBERTa (Liu et al., 2019), XLNet (Yang et al., 2019), BART (Lewis et al., 2019), GPT2 (Radford et al., 2019), T5 (Raffel et al., 2019), ALBERT (Lan et al., 2019), CamemBERT (Martin et al., 2019), LongFormer (Beltagy et al., 2020), Pegasus (Zhang et al., 2019); large versions of GPT2 and mBART (Liu et al., 2020); medium version of GPT2; DistilGPT2 and DistilBERT (Sanh et al., 2019).

**Pre-trained Models:** We pre-train three models- BERT-base, ROBERTa-base, and XLNet-base, on the SPEC5G dataset; we refer to them as BERT5G, ROBERTa5G, and XLNet5G respectively. The reason for training these three models is discussed in Section 7 (Choice of Pre-trained Models). We then fine-tune the pre-trained models for the downstream tasks. The details of the pre-training and fine-tuning are discussed in detail in Section A.2.

**Training Hardware:** We use Google Colab Pro+ to pre-train and fine-tune the models. Around 3000 computing units (CU) of Premium GPU (A100) with high RAM configuration have been consumed to complete all our experiments. For details about CU and training time, we refer to Appendix A.3.

### 5.2 Performance Metric

To measure the performance of the sentence classification task we use standard performance metrics such as accuracy, precision, recall, and F1-score. We discuss the metrics for the summarization task here in detail.

#### 5.2.1 Summarization Metrics

To measure the quality of summarization we use both automatic and human evaluation metrics. For automatic evaluation, we use the commonly used ROUGE score.

**Human Evaluation Metric:** Due to significant dissonance with human evaluation, automatic evaluation metrics are often considered unreliable for summarization quality evaluation. Hence, we resort to human evaluation metrics. The human annotator's rate on a scale from 1 (worst) to 5 (best) on three coarse attributes: (1) *Simplicity:* As the majority of the inferences require speculation, this metric measures how simple and concise the models and the annotators are. (2) *Correctness:* Whether the generated or annotated inferences are grammatically and from a protocol point of view correct. This is very important for the summarization of network protocol specifications. (3) *Contextuality:* Whether the generated or annotated inferences fit the context.

| Model | RG-1 | RG-2 | RG-L |
|---|---|---|---|
| BERT-base | 0.484 | 0.341 | 0.415 |
| BERT5G | **0.543** | **0.382** | **0.472** |
| PEGASUS | 0.239 | 0.120 | 0.199 |
| RoBERTa-base | 0.489 | 0.341 | 0.418 |
| RoBERTa5G | 0.540 | 0.379 | 0.469 |
| BART-base | 0.357 | 0.231 | 0.311 |
| XLNET-base | 0.483 | 0.340 | 0.416 |
| XLNET5G | 0.526 | 0.362 | 0.453 |
| GPT2 | 0.488 | 0.340 | 0.418 |
| GPT2-medium | 0.481 | 0.333 | 0.408 |
| GPT2-large | 0.487 | 0.344 | 0.418 |
| DistilGPT2 | 0.483 | 0.333 | 0.412 |
| T5 | 0.444 | 0.285 | 0.363 |

Table 1: Performance of summarization over the 5GSum dataset based on ROUGE scores.

### 5.3 Performance

We now report the performance of the baseline language models to characterize our dataset.

**Summarization:** We report the models' mid-score fmeasure of ROUGE-1, ROUGE-2, and ROUGE-L in Table 1 and human evaluation scores in Table 3 to show the comparison of the baseline models with the pre-trained models. BERT5G outperforms all the models, though BERT-base was not the best-performing model. This shows the quality of our dataset for technical specification learning.

**Sentence Classification:** We report the performance of the models on the sentence classification task in Table 2. For sentence classification with relatively few classes, BERT, ROBERTa, and XLNet perform the best(Chang et al., 2020). Therefore, we pre-train 3 models- BERT-base, ROBERTa-base, and XLNet-base language models on the SPEC5G dataset. These 3 models along with other baselines are then fine-tuned on the 5GSC dataset to compare their classification performance. We observe that BERT5G, ROBERTa5G, and XLNet5G outperform their corresponding baselines by a significant margin. Additionally, BERT5G outperforms all other models in precision and F1 score. XLNet5G has the highest recall. Interestingly, the baseline GPT2 has the highest accuracy. Despite that, we do not choose GPT2 for pre-training. The reason behind this is discussed in Section 6.

| Model | Precision | Recall | F1 | Acc |
|---|---|---|---|---|
| ALBERT-base | 0.6485 | 0.6587 | 0.6459 | 0.7034 |
| BART-base | 0.6458 | 0.6503 | 0.6432 | 0.7103 |
| BERT-base | 0.6113 | 0.6229 | 0.6157 | 0.6897 |
| BERT5G | **0.6972** | 0.6762 | **0.6856** | 0.7655 |
| CamemBERT | 0.6107 | 0.6272 | 0.6174 | 0.7034 |
| DistilBERT | 0.5819 | 0.5769 | 0.5731 | 0.6621 |
| GPT2 | 0.6133 | 0.5567 | 0.5767 | **0.7973** |
| LongFormer | 06280 | 0.6281 | 0.6274 | 0.7034 |
| mBART-large | 0.6598 | 0.6642 | 0.6606 | 0.7241 |
| ROBERTa-base | 0.5752 | 0.5562 | 0.5631 | 0.6690 |
| ROBERTa5G | 0.5944 | 0.5696 | 0.5785 | 0.6966 |
| XLNet-base | 0.6260 | 0.6339 | 0.6297 | 0.7034 |
| XLNet5G | 0.6480 | **0.6829** | 0.6619 | 0.7103 |

Table 2: Performance of baseline models on classification task over the 5GSC dataset.

## 6 Result Analysis

**Performance Improvements Due to SPEC5G:** The primary objective of our work is to introduce an anchor 5G dataset that might pave the way for future NLP research in 5G and NLP. The models pre-trained on 5G and fine-tuned on respective tasks achieve significant performance improvements, suggesting that such dataset should be considered the gold standard for pre-training models before deploying them for more sophisticated, 5G-oriented NLP applications.

**Best Pre-trained Model:** The scores of both tasks show that BERT5G is the best-performing model. It is not surprising that XLNet5G, the pre-trained version of more recent BERT variant XLNet, is a close competitor. While GPT2 is a good choice for our summarization task, we do not recommend it for security classification. Despite a high accuracy score, GPT2 failed to achieve a contending recall or F1-score. We observe that GPT2 could classify the *Non-Security* samples well (53 out of 70 test samples were correct) which dominates the dataset distribution, while poorly classifying samples from *Security* (11 out of 24 correct) and *Undefined* (4 out of 11 correct). This is the reason for its higher accuracy yet low recall and F1.

**Results of Human Evaluation for Summarization:** We randomly sample 40 inferences generated by each pre-trained model, their non-pre-trained versions, and corresponding gold inference. These inferences are then manually rated by three independent annotators based on the human-evaluation metrics. As shown in Table 3, we observe that the fine-tuned models perform similarly on SPEC5G but fail to reach gold annotation performance. Moreover, as expected, the pre-trained models significantly outperform their non-pre-trained counterparts. We provide some examples of the generated inferences in Figure 6. Inspection of the model-generated inferences reveals that the usage of keywords from the technical specifications is more frequent in inferences generated by models pre-trained on SPEC5G.

| Model | Simplicity | Correctness | Contextuality |
|---|---|---|---|
| Gold | 4.37 | 4.77 | 4.56 |
| BERT-base | 3.2 | 3.87 | 3.3 |
| BERT5G | 3.96 | 4.32 | 3.92 |
| RoBERTa-base | 3.7 | 4.03 | 3.76 |
| RoBERTa5G | 4.02 | 4.2 | 3.94 |
| XLNET-base | 3.57 | 3.84 | 3.53 |
| XLNET5G | 3.97 | 4.31 | 3.91 |

Table 3: Result of the human evaluation for SPEC5G.

## 7 Discussion

**Broader Impact of SPEC5G.** Our dataset can offer valuable insights and applications that extend beyond the immediate scope. It can be very useful also for other specialized communication protocols (like IoT, Bluetooth, Bluetooth Low Energy, Vehicular Protocols, and WiFi). One popular methodology to evaluate the design of communication protocols is to manually extract a formal model, for example in terms of finite state machines, of the protocol and evaluate the model against the desired security and privacy properties (Hussain et al., 2019). One major issue with this approach is that the manual model extraction from the protocol-text is error-prone and not scalable. Therefore, communication protocols are analyzed partially or within a specific scope. The analysis paved by SPEC5G can yield a deeper understanding of network behavior, interference patterns, and potential optimizations that can be applied to a variety of wireless communication scenarios. This can lead to an ecosystem around our initial dataset, which could include models trained on SPEC5G and additional relevant datasets that could be combined with ours.

The versatility can spark innovation in the design and development of future-generation protocols. There is a lot of work to design technologies and protocols for interconnecting cellular networks and non-terrestrial networks (via for example, low earth orbit–LEO satellites); therefore creating datasets for these new protocols would only require addition to a modest amount of new data to SPEC5G.

**Article:** The PDCCH channel is used to send control information to the UEs on a per-slot basis. It is used to schedule downlink transmissions, uplink transmissions, MCS of those transmissions, and HARQ information. The PDCCH can appear on any subcarrier; so the jammer must decode the parameter CORESET freq-domain. The parameter CORESET-time-duration, which can take on values 1, 2, or 3, indicates how many OFDM symbols the PDCCH occupies in each slot. The PDCCH always starts in the first symbol of each slot, is QPSK modulated and uses polar coding.

**Reference:** PDCCH sends per-slot control information to UEs. Schedules downlink, uplink, MCS, and HARQ transmissions. PDCCH can exist on any subcarrier; the jammer must decode CORESET freq-domain. The CORESET-time-duration parameter shows how many OFDM symbols the PDCCH occupies each slot. The PDCCH starts at the first symbol of each slot and uses polar coding.

**BERT-base:** The PDCCH channel is used to send control information to the UEs on a per-slot basis. The PDCCH can appear on any subcarrier; so the jammer must decode the parameter CORESET freq-domain.

**BERT5G:** The PDCCH channel is used to send control information to the UEs on a per-slot basis. The parameter CORESET-time-duration, which can take on values 1, 2, or 3, indicates how many OFDM symbols the PDCCH occupies each slot.

**RoBERTa-base:** The PDCCH channel is used to send control information to the UEs on a per-slot basis. The PDCCH can appear on any subcarrier; so the jammer must decode the parameter CORESET freq-domain.

**RoBERTa5G:** The PDCCH channel is used to send control information to the UEs on a per-slot basis. The parameter CORESET-time-duration, which can take on values 1, 2, or 3, indicates how many OFDM symbols the PDCCH occupies each slot.

**XLNet-base:** The PDCCH channel is used to send control information to the UEs on a per-slot basis. The PDCCH always starts in the first symbol of each slot, is QPSK modulated and uses polar coding.

**XLNet5G:** The PDCCH channel is used to send control information to the UEs on a per-slot basis. The PDCCH always starts in the first symbol of each slot, is QPSK modulated and uses polar coding.

Figure 6: Comparison of summarization task by pre-trained models and their base version. Brown colored lines denotes the base models inability to capture protocol specific sentences in summaries and teal colored lines donotes the sentences introduced by pre-trained models on SPEC5G that are more contextual.

Similarly, models trained on SPEC5G could also be tuned by using a modest amount of new data. By leveraging the insights gained from the interactions within the dataset, researchers and engineers can create protocols that can adapt to evolving communication landscapes. This adaptability will be essential as we move towards more interconnected and heterogeneous networks.

Furthermore, the utility of our dataset reaches beyond those exclusively working on 5G networks. As NLP research and natural language processing techniques continue to evolve, our dataset can serve as a foundation for various research avenues. For instance, the dataset can be employed to develop advanced predictive models, anomaly detection systems, and intelligent network management solutions. These applications are not limited to the realm of 5G but have the potential to influence and enhance NLP research across a broader spectrum.

**Choice of Pre-trained Models.** The motivation behind the choice of the machine learning models is to show the quality of SPEC5G. Hence we only use pre-existing models for the downstream tasks and do not measure the performance of simple baseline models like lead-3 extractive baseline (taking the first 3 sentences of the article as the summary) and the SummaRuNNer extractive model (Nallapati et al., 2016), nor improve the performance of the downstream tasks. We pick the models that perform well in both downstream tasks. Here the chosen models are all encoder-only to maintain consistency between the experiments. Nevertheless, encoder-decoder models or decoder-only models would also benefit from pre-training. It is well known that pre-training on domain-specific data can help to improve the performance of downstream tasks in the domain (Lee et al., 2019; Chalkidis et al., 2020). However, in our case after the first step of preprocessing, BERT only improves 2.73%, XLNet improvement is 1.96% and ROBERTa improves 0.061% in F1 score. Thus, although we commonly know that pre-training improves downstream tasks, evidently the preprocessing of the dataset signifies that process even more. The performance improvement of the base models after pre-training on our dataset indicates that the models could learn and sufficiently generalize their knowledge in technical specifications. We leave exploring the downstream tasks in detail and the criteria for the selection of different models on the technical specification domain as future work.

**Downstream Task Dataset Size.** While the downstream task datasets may seem small, recent high-quality manually annotated datasets had similar sizes–COUGH dataset(1236 labeled sentences)(Zhang et al., 2021) and YASO dataset (2215 labeled sentences)(Orbach et al., 2021). Thus, the current size is comparable to the contemporaries. To address the selection bias of the relatively short test set, the test points are randomly sampled on 3 different runs of each model, and the models are run on 3 different random seeds which show low standard deviation in performance metrics. Therefore, the randomness in the test set removes the selection bias. Moreover, this dataset can easily be used as a seed alongside our trained models for semi-automatic annotation with minimal human effort. Our work enables this direction of using language models in technical specification documents. In the case of the summarization dataset, it is only used as a test set for the models that can already summarize articles. Their performance on summarizing network protocol specification is measured using this test set.

**Project Maintenance.** In the context of the 3GPP, major releases like 3G, 4G, and 5G are published every ten years. However, smaller, incremental functional changes are made each year within these larger frameworks. These updates are designed to be backward compatible and avoid conflicts with the previous releases, ensuring a smooth transition for existing infrastructure and devices. To address the concern with the new releases, we have devised a plan to maintain the quality and relevance of our dataset in the face of these protocol changes. After each major 3GPP release, we will analyze the changes and updates made to the protocol specifications. For each significant protocol update, we will review and re-evaluate the annotations in our dataset. This will involve identifying any modifications, additions, or clarifications in the protocol specifications. The Change Request (CR) procedure used by 3GPP to create revised versions of 3GPP specifications can be used to automatically identify the modifications. Our team will then update the dataset to accurately reflect these changes. Alongside these updates, we will provide summaries of the changes made in each protocol release. This will serve as a "TL;DR" version highlighting the key modifications that have taken place. This way, users can quickly understand what has changed in the context of each new release. Our commitment is to keep our dataset in sync with the evolving protocols and maintain its utility as a valuable resource for researchers, developers, and industry professionals.

## 8 Conclusion

We have created SPEC5G–a new dataset for 5G, 5GSum and 5GSC– expert annotated datasets for 5G protocol summarization and 5G security text classification respectively. To show the usefulness of SPEC5G in protocol specifications learning by the Language Models, we design security sentence classification and summarization tasks for state-of-the-art Language Models to solve.

**Future Work.** Given the specialized nature of 5G terminology in the dataset, it could be utilized for domain adaptation tasks in NLP (for instance, adapting language models to understand and generate content in the context of 5G communications). The dataset could be used to create datasets for named entity recognition tasks, focusing on extracting and categorizing specific entities such as protocols, technologies, companies, and standards relevant to 5G. With the wealth of information present in the dataset, question-answering datasets could also be constructed, where models are trained to answer questions related to 5G concepts, protocols, and technologies. SPEC5G can be used to develop semantic role labeling datasets, assisting in understanding the roles and relationships of various elements in sentences discussing 5G. Datasets for document classification tasks, where the goal is to categorize entire documents or articles based on their content related to 5G concepts can also be created. With content from various sources, the dataset could be used to create parallel corpora for translating technical 5G content between different languages. SPEC5G can be utilized to develop datasets for dependency parsing tasks, improving syntactic analysis and understanding of relationships between words. Generating datasets for topic modeling tasks can help in identifying and categorizing prevalent topics within the 5G domain.

## 9 Limitations

Here we discuss some limitations we faced.

### 9.1 Underspecifications in the standards

In this paper, we introduce SPEC5G, a dataset aimed at the automated analysis of the 5G protocol, and show the usefulness of SPEC5G in two downstream tasks. The performance of the two different downstream tasks on the dataset, in turn, depends on the 5G standards. In some cases, the standards are intentionally kept underspecified and contain ambiguities. The reason for such underspecifications and ambiguities is mainly to give vendors flexibility in the implementation design and performance enhancement. Nonetheless, the SPEC5G dataset can include some of the underspecified behaviors from the standards. These ambiguities existing in the text can be resolved using human expertise. This is precisely how we leverage human expertise for the two downstream tasks in the paper. However, this can be accomplished by using NLP methods that exploit unlabeled data and human knowledge. This is the direction we plan to pursue in the future.

### 9.2 Automation

The aim of SPEC5G is to help automate the manual-intensive tasks of 5G protocol development, analysis, and testing using state-of-the-art NLP techniques. However, it is evident that it is still not possible to completely automate such tasks because of the manual annotation, which requires domain expertise. In spite of the limited annotated data, we show that it is still possible to achieve fairly good results in two downstream tasks. It may not be possible to completely automate the 5G related tasks, but we still hope it can help reduce the large manual efforts which is the current state-of-the-art.

## 10 Ethical Considerations

In regards to the datasets being released, all information is in the public domain and is not subject to any copyrights. To pre-train, we use different language models. It has been reported that the pre-trained masked language models encode unfair social biases such as gender, racial bias, and religious biases (Bommasani et al., 2020). In our case, as we are dealing with a technical domain, we believe these biases do not have any impact on our results. Moreover, we randomly evaluated the model's outputs and found no evidence of these biases. In the case of annotations, the annotators for SPEC5G are all Ph.D. students doing active research in the area of networks. They are provided with specific guidelines (discussed in detail in Appendix C) and are strictly asked not to write any toxic content (hateful or offensive toward any gender, race, sex, or religion) and to consider gender-neutral settings.

## Acknowledgement

We thank the anonymous reviewers for their insightful comments and the annotators: Adrian Li, Charalampos Katsis, Fabrizio Cicala, Mengdie Huang, Sonam Bhardwaj, Yiwei Zhang, and Zilin Shen from cyber2slab of Purdue University for their valuable time and effort in annotating the downstream task datasets. The work reported in this paper has been supported by NSF under grant 2112471 "AI Institute for Future Edge Networks and Distributed Intelligence (AI-EDGE)".

## References

2022. *3GPP, Specifications*. https://www.3gpp.org/ftp/Specs.

2022. *5G-Powered Medical Robot Performs Remote Brain Surgery*. https://www.automate.org/blogs/5g-powered-medical-robot-performs-remote-brain-surgery.

2022. *Adopting neural language models for the telecom domain*. https://www.ericsson.com/en/blog/2022/1/neural-language-models-telecom-domain.

2022. *How to Reduce & Fix Gaming Lag*. https://www.screenbeam.com/wifihelp/wifibooster/how-to-reduce-lag-for-gaming-and-improve-your-internet-speed/.

2022. *Selenium*. https://www.selenium.dev/.

Fawad Ahmad, Hang Qiu, Ray Eells, Fan Bai, and Ramesh Govindan. 2020. CarMap: Fast 3d feature map updates for automobiles. In *17th USENIX Symposium on Networked Systems Design and Implementation (NSDI 20)*, pages 1063–1081, Santa Clara, CA. USENIX Association.

David Basin, Jannik Dreier, Lucca Hirschi, Saša Radomirovic, Ralf Sasse, and Vincent Stettler. 2018. A formal analysis of 5g authentication. In *Proceedings of the 2018 ACM SIGSAC Conference on Computer and Communications Security*, CCS '18, page 1383–1396, New York, NY, USA. Association for Computing Machinery.

Iz Beltagy, Matthew E. Peters, and Arman Cohan. 2020. Longformer: The long-document transformer. *CoRR*, abs/2004.05150.

Steven Bird, Robert Dale, Bonnie Dorr, Bryan Gibson, Mark Joseph, Min-Yen Kan, Dongwon Lee, Brett Powley, Dragomir Radev, and Yee Fan Tan. 2008. The ACL Anthology reference corpus: A reference dataset for bibliographic research in computational linguistics. In *Proceedings of the Sixth International Conference on Language Resources and Evaluation (LREC'08)*, Marrakech, Morocco. European Language Resources Association (ELRA).

Rishi Bommasani, Kelly Davis, and Claire Cardie. 2020. Interpreting pretrained contextualized representations via reductions to static embeddings. In *Proceedings of the 58th Annual Meeting of the Association for Computational Linguistics*, pages 4758–4781.

Ilias Chalkidis, Manos Fergadiotis, Prodromos Malakasiotis, Nikolaos Aletras, and Ion Androutsopoulos. 2020. LEGAL-BERT: the muppets straight out of law school. *CoRR*, abs/2010.02559.

Wei-Cheng Chang, Hsiang-Fu Yu, Kai Zhong, Yiming Yang, and Inderjit S. Dhillon. 2020. Taming pretrained transformers for extreme multi-label text classification. In *KDD 2020*.

Yi Chen, Di Tang, Yepeng Yao, Mingming Zha, XiaoFeng Wang, Xiaozhong Liu, Haixu Tang, and Dongfang Zhao. 2022. Seeing the forest for the trees: Understanding security hazards in the 3GPP ecosystem through intelligent analysis on change requests. In *31st USENIX Security Symposium (USENIX Security 22)*, pages 17–34, Boston, MA. USENIX Association.

Yi Chen, Yepeng Yao, XiaoFeng Wang, Dandan Xu, Chang Yue, Xiaozhong Liu, Kai Chen, Haixu Tang, and Baoxu Liu. 2021. Bookworm game: Automatic discovery of lte vulnerabilities through documentation analysis. In *2021 IEEE Symposium on Security and Privacy (SP)*, pages 1197–1214.

Arman Cohan, Waleed Ammar, Madeleine van Zuylen, and Field Cady. 2019a. Structural scaffolds for citation intent classification in scientific publications. *CoRR*, abs/1904.01608.

Arman Cohan, Iz Beltagy, Daniel King, Bhavana Dalvi, and Dan Weld. 2019b. Pretrained language models for sequential sentence classification. In *Proceedings of the 2019 Conference on Empirical Methods in Natural Language Processing and the 9th International Joint Conference on Natural Language Processing (EMNLP-IJCNLP)*, pages 3693–3699, Hong Kong, China. Association for Computational Linguistics.

Ed Collins, Isabelle Augenstein, and Sebastian Riedel. 2017. A supervised approach to extractive summarisation of scientific papers. In *Proceedings of the 21st Conference on Computational Natural Language Learning (CoNLL 2017)*, pages 195–205, Vancouver, Canada. Association for Computational Linguistics.

Will Coster and David Kauchak. 2011. Learning to simplify sentences using Wikipedia. In *Proceedings of the Workshop on Monolingual Text-To-Text Generation*, pages 1–9, Portland, Oregon. Association for Computational Linguistics.

Cas Cremers and Martin Dehnel-Wild. 2019. Component-based formal analysis of 5g-aka: Channel assumptions and session confusion.

Jacob Devlin, Ming-Wei Chang, Kenton Lee, and Kristina Toutanova. 2018. Bert: Pre-training of deep bidirectional transformers for language understanding. *arXiv preprint arXiv:1810.04805*.

Noemie Elhadad and Komal Sutaria. 2007. Mining a lexicon of technical terms and lay equivalents. In *Biological, translational, and clinical language processing*, pages 49–56, Prague, Czech Republic. Association for Computational Linguistics.

Goran Glavaš and Sanja Štajner. 2015. Simplifying lexical simplification: Do we need simplified corpora? In *Proceedings of the 53rd Annual Meeting of the Association for Computational Linguistics and the 7th International Joint Conference on Natural Language Processing (Volume 2: Short Papers)*, pages 63–68, Beijing, China. Association for Computational Linguistics.

Syed Rafiul Hussain, Mitziu Echeverria, Imtiaz Karim, Omar Chowdhury, and Elisa Bertino. 2019. 5greasoner: A property-directed security and privacy analysis framework for 5g cellular network protocol. In *Proceedings of the 2019 ACM SIGSAC Conference on Computer and Communications Security*, CCS '19, page 669–684, New York, NY, USA. Association for Computing Machinery.

Kokil Jaidka, Muthu Chandrasekaran, Beatriz Fisas, Rahul Jha, Christopher Jones, Min-Yen Kan, Ankur Khanna, Diego Molla Aliod, Dragomir Radev, Francesco Ronzano, and Horacio Saggion. 2014. The computational linguistics summarization pilot task.

Kokil Jaidka, Muthu Chandrasekaran, Devanshu Jain, and Min-Yen Kan. 2017. The cl-scisumm shared task 2017: Results and key insights.

Kokil Jaidka, Muthu Chandrasekaran, Sajal Rustagi, and Min-Yen Kan. 2018. Insights from cl-scisumm 2016: the faceted scientific document summarization shared task. *International Journal on Digital Libraries*, 19:1–9.

Chao Jiang, Mounica Maddela, Wuwei Lan, Yang Zhong, and Wei Xu. 2020. Neural CRF model for sentence alignment in text simplification. *CoRR*, abs/2005.02324.

David Kauchak. 2013. Improving text simplification language modeling using unsimplified text data. In *Proceedings of the 51st Annual Meeting of the Association for Computational Linguistics (Volume 1: Long Papers)*, pages 1537–1546, Sofia, Bulgaria. Association for Computational Linguistics.

Zhenzhong Lan, Mingda Chen, Sebastian Goodman, Kevin Gimpel, Piyush Sharma, and Radu Soricut. 2019. ALBERT: A lite BERT for self-supervised learning of language representations. *CoRR*, abs/1909.11942.

Jinhyuk Lee, Wonjin Yoon, Sungdong Kim, Donghyeon Kim, Sunkyu Kim, Chan Ho So, and Jaewoo Kang. 2019. Biobert: a pre-trained biomedical language representation model for biomedical text mining. *CoRR*, abs/1901.08746.

Mike Lewis, Yinhan Liu, Naman Goyal, Marjan Ghazvininejad, Abdelrahman Mohamed, Omer Levy, Veselin Stoyanov, and Luke Zettlemoyer. 2019. BART: denoising sequence-to-sequence pre-training for natural language generation, translation, and comprehension. *CoRR*, abs/1910.13461.

Yinhan Liu, Jiatao Gu, Naman Goyal, Xian Li, Sergey Edunov, Marjan Ghazvininejad, Mike Lewis, and Luke Zettlemoyer. 2020. Multilingual denoising pre-training for neural machine translation. *CoRR*, abs/2001.08210.

Yinhan Liu, Myle Ott, Naman Goyal, Jingfei Du, Mandar Joshi, Danqi Chen, Omer Levy, Mike Lewis, Luke Zettlemoyer, and Veselin Stoyanov. 2019. Roberta: A robustly optimized BERT pretraining approach. *CoRR*, abs/1907.11692.

Yonghao Liu, Renchu Guan, Fausto Giunchiglia, Yanchun Liang, and Xiaoyue Feng. 2021. Deep attention diffusion graph neural networks for text classification. In *Proceedings of the 2021 Conference on Empirical Methods in Natural Language Processing*, pages 8142–8152, Online and Punta Cana, Dominican Republic. Association for Computational Linguistics.

Mounica Maddela, Fernando Alva-Manchego, and Wei Xu. 2020. Controllable text simplification with explicit paraphrasing. *CoRR*, abs/2010.11004.

Louis Martin, Benjamin Müller, Pedro Javier Ortiz Suárez, Yoann Dupont, Laurent Romary, Éric Villemonte de la Clergerie, Djamé Seddah, and Benoît Sagot. 2019. Camembert: a tasty french language model. *CoRR*, abs/1911.03894.

Dheeraj Mekala, Varun Gangal, and Jingbo Shang. 2021. Coarse2fine: Fine-grained text classification on coarsely-grained annotated data. In *EMNLP*.

Derek Miller. 2019. Leveraging BERT for extractive text summarization on lectures. *CoRR*, abs/1906.04165.

Ramesh Nallapati, Feifei Zhai, and Bowen Zhou. 2016. Summarunner: A recurrent neural network based sequence model for extractive summarization of documents. *CoRR*, abs/1611.04230.

Shashi Narayan and Claire Gardent. 2014. Hybrid simplification using deep semantics and machine translation. volume 1.

Daiki Nishihara, Tomoyuki Kajiwara, and Yuki Arase. 2019. Controllable text simplification with lexical constraint loss. In *Proceedings of the 57th Annual Meeting of the Association for Computational Linguistics: Student Research Workshop*, pages 260–266, Florence, Italy. Association for Computational Linguistics.

Sergiu Nisioi, Sanja Štajner, Simone Paolo Ponzetto, and Liviu P. Dinu. 2017. Exploring neural text simplification models. In *Proceedings of the 55th Annual Meeting of the Association for Computational Linguistics (Volume 2: Short Papers)*, pages 85–91, Vancouver, Canada. Association for Computational Linguistics.

Matan Orbach, Orith Toledo-Ronen, Artem Spector, Ranit Aharonov, Yoav Katz, and Noam Slonim. 2021. YASO: A targeted sentiment analysis evaluation dataset for open-domain reviews. In *Proceedings of the 2021 Conference on Empirical Methods in Natural Language Processing*, pages 9154–9173, Online and Punta Cana, Dominican Republic. Association for Computational Linguistics.

Gustavo Paetzold and Lucia Specia. 2016. Unsupervised lexical simplification for non-native speakers. *Proceedings of the AAAI Conference on Artificial Intelligence*, 30.

Sarah E. Petersen and Mari Ostendorf. 2007. Text simplification for language learners: a corpus analysis. In *SLaTE*.

Alec Radford, Jeff Wu, Rewon Child, David Luan, Dario Amodei, and Ilya Sutskever. 2019. Language models are unsupervised multitask learners.

Colin Raffel, Noam Shazeer, Adam Roberts, Katherine Lee, Sharan Narang, Michael Matena, Yanqi Zhou, Wei Li, and Peter J. Liu. 2019. Exploring the limits of transfer learning with a unified text-to-text transformer. *CoRR*, abs/1910.10683.

Victor Sanh, Lysandre Debut, Julien Chaumond, and Thomas Wolf. 2019. Distilbert, a distilled version of BERT: smaller, faster, cheaper and lighter. *CoRR*, abs/1910.01108.

Mahadev Satyanarayanan. 2017. The emergence of edge computing. *Computer*, 50(1):30–39.

Carolina Scarton and Lucia Specia. 2018. Learning simplifications for specific target audiences. In *Proceedings of the 56th Annual Meeting of the Association for Computational Linguistics (Volume 2: Short Papers)*, pages 712–718, Melbourne, Australia. Association for Computational Linguistics.

Advaith Siddharthan and Napoleon Katsos. 2010. Reformulating discourse connectives for non-expert readers. In *Human Language Technologies: The 2010 Annual Conference of the North American Chapter of the Association for Computational Linguistics*, pages 1002–1010, Los Angeles, California. Association for Computational Linguistics.

Arnab Sinha, Zhihong Shen, Yang Song, Hao Ma, Darrin Eide, Bo-June Hsu, and Kuansan Wang. 2015. An overview of microsoft academic service (mas) and applications. pages 243–246.

Richard Socher, Alex Perelygin, Jean Wu, Jason Chuang, Christopher D. Manning, Andrew Ng, and Christopher Potts. 2013. Recursive deep models for semantic compositionality over a sentiment treebank. In *Proceedings of the 2013 Conference on Empirical Methods in Natural Language Processing*, pages 1631–1642, Seattle, Washington, USA. Association for Computational Linguistics.

Sasha Spala, Nicholas A. Miller, Yiming Yang, Franck Dernoncourt, and Carl Dockhorn. 2019. DEFT: A corpus for definition extraction in free- and semi-structured text. In *Proceedings of the 13th Linguistic Annotation Workshop*, pages 124–131, Florence, Italy. Association for Computational Linguistics.

Sanja Štajner, Marc Franco-Salvador, Simone Paolo Ponzetto, Paolo Rosso, and Heiner Stuckenschmidt. 2017. Sentence alignment methods for improving text simplification systems. In *Proceedings of the 55th Annual Meeting of the Association for Computational Linguistics (Volume 2: Short Papers)*, pages 97–102, Vancouver, Canada. Association for Computational Linguistics.

Sanja Štajner and Horacio Saggion. 2018. Data-driven text simplification. In *Proceedings of the 27th International Conference on Computational Linguistics: Tutorial Abstracts*, pages 19–23, Santa Fe, New Mexico, USA. Association for Computational Linguistics.

Ashish Vaswani, Noam Shazeer, Niki Parmar, Jakob Uszkoreit, Llion Jones, Aidan N. Gomez, Lukasz Kaiser, and Illia Polosukhin. 2017. Attention is all you need. *CoRR*, abs/1706.03762.

Alex Warstadt, Amanpreet Singh, and Samuel R Bowman. 2018. Neural network acceptability judgments. *arXiv preprint arXiv:1805.12471*.

Sander Wubben, Antal van den Bosch, and Emiel Krahmer. 2012. Sentence simplification by monolingual machine translation. In *Proceedings of the 50th Annual Meeting of the Association for Computational Linguistics (Volume 1: Long Papers)*, pages 1015–1024, Jeju Island, Korea. Association for Computational Linguistics.

Wei Xu, Courtney Napoles, Ellie Pavlick, Quanze Chen, and Chris Callison-Burch. 2016. Optimizing statistical machine translation for text simplification. *Transactions of the Association for Computational Linguistics*, 4:401–415.

Zhilin Yang, Zihang Dai, Yiming Yang, Jaime G. Carbonell, Ruslan Salakhutdinov, and Quoc V. Le. 2019. Xlnet: Generalized autoregressive pretraining for language understanding. *CoRR*, abs/1906.08237.

Michihiro Yasunaga, Jungo Kasai, Rui Zhang, Alexander R. Fabbri, Irene Li, Dan Friedman, and Dragomir R. Radev. 2019. Scisummnet: A large annotated corpus and content-impact models for scientific paper summarization with citation networks. *CoRR*, abs/1909.01716.

Jingqing Zhang, Yao Zhao, Mohammad Saleh, and Peter J. Liu. 2019. PEGASUS: pre-training with extracted gap-sentences for abstractive summarization. *CoRR*, abs/1912.08777.

Wuyang Zhang, Jiachen Chen, Yanyong Zhang, and Dipankar Raychaudhuri. 2017. Towards efficient edge cloud augmentation for virtual reality mmogs. In *Proceedings of the Second ACM/IEEE Symposium on Edge Computing*, SEC '17, New York, NY, USA. Association for Computing Machinery.

Xingxing Zhang and Mirella Lapata. 2017. Sentence simplification with deep reinforcement learning. In *Proceedings of the 2017 Conference on Empirical Methods in Natural Language Processing*, pages 584–594, Copenhagen, Denmark. Association for Computational Linguistics.

Xinliang Frederick Zhang, Heming Sun, Xiang Yue, Simon Lin, and Huan Sun. 2021. COUGH: A challenge dataset and models for COVID-19 FAQ retrieval. In *Proceedings of the 2021 Conference on Empirical Methods in Natural Language Processing*, pages 3759–3769, Online and Punta Cana, Dominican Republic. Association for Computational Linguistics.

Yiwen Zhang, Caixia Yuan, Xiaojie Wang, Ziwei Bai, and Yongbin Liu. 2022. Learn to adapt for generalized zero-shot text classification. In *Proceedings of the 60th Annual Meeting of the Association for Computational Linguistics (Volume 1: Long Papers)*, pages 517–527, Dublin, Ireland. Association for Computational Linguistics.

Yang Zhong, Chao Jiang, Wei Xu, and Junyi Jessy Li. 2019. Discourse level factors for sentence deletion in text simplification. *CoRR*, abs/1911.10384.

Zhemin Zhu, Delphine Bernhard, and Iryna Gurevych. 2010. A monolingual tree-based translation model for sentence simplification. volume 2, pages 1353–1361.

## Appendix

## A Preprocessing and Training

In this section, we outline the preprocessing steps undertaken to clean and transform the data, as well as the training methodology employed to optimize the model's performance. By employing rigorous preprocessing and training techniques, we aim to ensure reliable and accurate results in our subsequent analysis.

### A.1 Preprocessing Details

The following preprocessing steps were performed-

- Sentences containing codes (e.g. consecutive '{{', '}}', '((', '))') are removed.
- Some of the remaining html tags present after web scrapping are removed.
- Citations and references are removed.
- Sentences mentioning subsequent figures, and tables are removed.
- Figure/table captions are skipped.
- Sentences containing consequent digits and dots refer to (sub)section headers are removed.
- Some malformed texts appearing from figures and tables after parsing text files from .doc or .pdfs files are filtered out.
- Sentences containing Unicode characters appearing as raw texts are removed.
- Multiple consecutive newlines, tabs, whitespace, and delimiters are processed into one.

- Starting numbers, dots, interpuncts, and hyphens appearing from (un)ordered lists are removed.
- Additional whitespaces after opening parentheses, curly braces, and brackets are removed. Similar to closing ones.
- 3GPP specifications contain numerous mentions of specification documents (i.e. TS 24.301). These do not add any useful features for learning. Those are renamed as "specification document".
- If a sentence contains a high amount of digits, they necessarily are from embedded codes. If more than 20% are seen, we filter out the sentence.
- Few special cases (for example: "e.g.,", "i.e.,") are handled to not be considered as the end of a sentence.
- An additional newline is added after adding all texts from each of the documents/web pages. This is to ensure that certain downstream applications (e.g., summarization) do not get affected by unrelated texts from multiple documents.

### A.2 Training Details

To pre-train BERT Masked Language Model (MLM), we use the Adam optimizer with $\epsilon = 10^{-8}$ and train the model for 10 epochs. The learning rate is $5 \times 10^{-5}$, we set aside 10% of the data as validation to inspect the model performance at every 50k steps. BERTFastTokenizer has been used to tokenize the dataset. We use the same parameters to pre-train ROBERTa MLM for 5 epochs and ROBERTa BPE tokenizer to tokenize the dataset for this setting. For pre-training XLNet Permutation Language Model (PLM), we use the Adam optimizer in the same setting. Since XLNet requires approximately 5 times more than BERT or ROBERTa, we train the model for 1 epoch. We use the SentencePiece tokenizer in this case.

When fine-tuning the classification models, we set the learning rate to be $2 \times 10^{-5}$, weight decay to be 0.01, and batch size to be 16. The Huggingface standard pipeline with the Automodel class has been used for sequence classification. We train each model for 15 epochs.

We use the bert-extractive-summarizer (Miller, 2019) to generate summaries using BERT-base. The Huggingface standard pipeline libraries has been used to generate summaries using sequence-to-sequence models i.e., PEGASUS and T5 that comes with default summarization capability. To generate summary using RoBERTa-base, RoBERTa5G, XLNet5G, and BERT5G, we use the Huggingface Automodel Library. We use another Huggingface library TransformerSummarizer to generate summary using XLNet, GPT2, GPT2-base, GPT2-medium, GPT2-large and DistilGPT2.

### A.3 Compute Unit and Training Duration

A compute unit (CU) is the unit of measurement for the resources consumed. To calculate CUs, one needs to multiply two factors: (1) Memory (GB) - size of the allocated server for task to run and (2) Duration (hours) - how long the server is used. This means, 1 CU = 1 GB memory x 1 hour. We have used around 80-90% of the GPU during training time. By definition of computing units, we have used roughly 100 hours of 30GB GPU time.

Pre-training BERT takes around 36 hours in our experimental setup. Pre-training RoBERTa and XLNET takes around 24 hours each. Fine-tuning each model takes around 5-6 hours.

## B Performance Evaluation of Downstream Tasks

We report the evaluation of performance and metrics used for it in this section.

### B.1 Performance Metrics

For automatic evaluation, we use the commonly used ROUGE score. We use the Python rouge_score library to calculate this. **ROUGE Score:** ROUGE-N measures the number of matching 'n-grams' between the model-generated text and a 'reference'. An n-gram is simply a grouping of tokens/words. A unigram (1-gram) would consist of a single word. A bigram (2-gram) consists of two consecutive words. In ROUGE-N, N denotes the n-gram that is being used. For ROUGE-1 the match rate of unigrams between the model output and reference are measured. ROUGE-2 and ROUGE-3 would use bigrams and trigrams respectively.

**Recall:** The recall counts the number of overlapping n-grams found in both the model output and reference, then divides this number by the total number of n-grams in the reference.

$$recall = \frac{count_n(gram_n)}{count(gram_n)}$$

**Precision:** We use the precision metric — which is calculated in almost the exact same way as recall, but rather than dividing by the reference n-gram count, it is divided by the model n-gram count.

$$precision = \frac{num\ of\ ngrams\ in\ model\ \&\ ref}{num\ of\ ngrams\ in\ model}$$

Now that both the recall and precision values are available, they can be used to calculate the ROUGE F1 score with the following formula:

$$2 * \frac{precision * recall}{precision + recall}$$

**ROUGE-L:** ROUGE-L measures the longest common subsequence (LCS) between the model output and the reference. With this metric, the number of tokens in the longest sequence shared between both are counted. The idea here is that a longer shared sequence would indicate more similarity between the two sequences. The recall and precision calculations can be applied just like before — but this time the match is replaced with LCS.

$$recall = \frac{LCS(gram_n)}{count(gram_n)}$$

## C Annotation Guidelines

Below are the specific guidelines that we have given to the annotators to ensure the standard of annotation.

### C.1 Sentence Classification Guidelines

The annotators are given some general guidelines and are suggested to follow some steps to make the data annotation consistent. They are also provided with some rules and tips.

**General Guidelines:** For this task, an annotator is given a set of sentences. Based on the methods, fields, variables, and/or entities mentioned in the sentence, the annotator's objective is to identify if the sentence implies a potential security concern or sophisticated operation that might involve vulnerable consequences.

**Steps:**

1. Read the sentence carefully.
2. Identify items and the operation that involve a security issue.
3. Decide the label based on the following:
    a) *Non-Security*: The expressed operation cannot be exploited/ The sentence does not describe any security hazard/ does not describe any underspecified criteria/ does not involve complicated, flawed operations.
    b) *Security*: The text discusses situations or operations that might be risky/ The text involves certain properties or variables, exploiting which, one can seriously block the operations, or harm the entity, or breach privacy.
    c) *Undefined*: The discussed operation is not clear/ The sentence does not express all the parties or variables involved/ The sentence entails some previous operation unavailable to the annotator- without which the annotator can not decide about the potential risk.
4. If the sentences do not express any proper context or are semantically incorrect, or have no items with a sentiment expressed towards them, add a comment and proceed to the next data.

**Rules and Tips:**

- Select all items in the sentence that have a security hazard.
- If there are multiple such cases, you may choose any or all of them.
- Optionally, you may provide a comment about your rationalization or feedback about the data (e.g., errors, unclear descriptions.)

### C.2 Summarization Guidelines

Similar to classification guidelines, the annotators are given general guidelines and suggested steps to annotate the summarization dataset. Again, they are also provided with some rules and tips. Below are the guidelines for annotation tasks for summarization.

**General Guidelines:** For this task, an annotator is given a set of articles. Based on the methods, fields, variables, and/or entities mentioned in the sentence, the annotator's objective is to summarize the article without losing important information, correctness and contextuality.

**Steps:**

1. Read the article carefully.
2. Identify the key points.
3. Summarize the article by doing the following:
    a) Deletion: Delete a sentence if it does not convey any important information.

b) Merge and shorten: Merge consecutive sentences if they convey continued information and make the merged sentences concise.

c) Rephrase and shorten: Rephrase a sentence to make it simpler and make it shorter if possible.

4. If the sentences do not express any proper context, or are semantically incorrect, add a comment and proceed to the next sentence.

**Rules and Tips:**

- Select all items in the article that have important information.
- Make the sentences simpler and concise keeping the important information.
- Under each article is a comments box. Optionally, you can provide article-specific feedback in this box. This may include a rationalization of your choice, a description of an error within the article, or the justification of another answer which was also plausible. In general, any relevant feedback would be useful and will help in improving this task.

### C.3 Annotator Agreement

In total nine annotators have annotated the summarization dataset. Each of them is given 70 non-overlapping distinct articles. So there is no disagreement between annotators. Another round of manual cleaning has been done by two meta annotators who have gone through the whole dataset to ensure summarization quality and consistency, by addressing the comments and suggestions made by the annotators in the first round and making necessary changes(update/delete). For example in first round of annotation, annotators put comments like - "The paragraph is vague", "Independent sentences", "The paragraph does not have a logical flow. It cannot be further summarized", "It is not clear what the paragraph is talking about", etc. These comments are addressed by the meta annotators by manually correcting or removing the articles.

For the classification task, 3 annotators (we call them A1, A2, A3 here) separately annotate the dataset- A1 and A2 annotate 800 examples each and A3 annotates 801 examples. In the second step, they are assigned to reevaluate the annotations of each other (A1 reevaluating labels assigned by A3, A2 reevaluating labels assigned by A1, and A3 reevaluating A2). Such reevaluations bring forth disagreements on several labels which are finally resolved by their combined discussion. For example: "The AMF shall not indicate to the SMF to release the emergency PDU session.": A2 labels this as Security, while A3 assigns Undefined. This disagreement is later resolved by discussing their reasoning for the respective labels.

### C.4 Examples

We are listing some example annotated data for both tasks.

#### C.4.1 Sentence Classification:

Here we show a few examples of sentence classification–each containing a sentence and the correct label associated with it.

**Sentence 1:** If the positioning method parameter indicates both E-Cell ID and GNSS positioning, the eNB may use E-Cell ID measurement collection only if the UE does not provide GNSS-based location information.

**Label 1:** *Security*

**Sentence 2:** SIGN_VAR shall be included in the channel quality report.

**Label 2:** *Non-Security*

**Sentence 3:** After performing the attach, the MS should activate PDP context(s) to replace any previously active PDP context(s).

**Label 3:** *Security*

**Sentence 4:** It switches the user from the UTRAN user plane to the GAN user plane

**Label 4:** *Undefined*

**Sentence 5:** If the BSIC cannot be decoded at the next available opportunities re attempts shall be made to decode this BSIC.

**Label 5:** *Non-Security*

**Sentence 6:** This might lead to an empty or even absent structure, if no parameter was modified.

**Label 6:** *Undefined*

### C.4.2 Summarization:

Here are a few examples, each containing an article and its summary.

**Article 1:** As indicated, 5G NR Meas Gap Length is not fixed and 3GPP specifications made it configurable. Having a fixed Meas Gap could cause unnecessary degradation of throughput in the serving cell. The SMTC window and window duration can be set to match SSB transmissions and accordingly, the MGL. For example, if we consider the SMTC window duration as 2 ms and the Meas Gap Length as 6 ms, here 4 ms segment would not be available for transmission, and reception of data in the serving cell will result in low DL/UL throughput.

**Summary 1:** 5G NR Meas Gap Length is adjustable per 3GPP specs. A fixed Meas Gap can degrade serving cell throughput. The SMTC window and duration can match SSB transmissions and the MGL. If the SMTC window duration is 2 ms and Meas Gap Length is 6 ms, a 4 ms segment is not accessible for transmission, resulting in limited DL/UL throughput.

**Article 2:** IMSI-catching attacks have threatened all generations (2G/3G/4G) of mobile telecommunication for decades. As a result of facilitating backward compatibility for legacy reasons, this privacy problem appears to have persisted. However, the 3GPP has now decided to address this issue, albeit at the cost of backward compatibility. In case of identification failure via a 5G-GUTI, unlike earlier generations, 5G security specifications do not allow plain-text transmissions of the SUPI over the radio interface. Instead, an Elliptic Curve Integrated Encryption Scheme (ECIES)-based privacy-preserving identifier containing the concealed SUPI is transmitted. This concealed SUPI is known as SUCI (Subscription Concealed Identifier).

**Summary 2:** Unlike earlier generations, in the case of identification failure via a 5G-GUTI, 5G security specifications do not allow plain-text transmissions of SUPI over the radio interface. Instead, an Elliptic Curve Integrated Encryption Scheme (ECIES)-based privacy-preserving identifier containing the concealed SUPI (also known as SUCI) is transmitted.

**Article 3:** A SUPI is usually a string of 15 decimal digits. The first three digits represent the Mobile Country Code (MCC) while the next two or three form the Mobile Network Code (MNC), identifying the network operator. The remaining (nine or ten) digits are known as Mobile Subscriber Identification Numbers (MSIN) and represent the individual user of that particular operator. SUPI is equivalent to IMSI, which uniquely identifies the ME, and is also a string of 15 digits.

**Summary 3:** SUPI is a string of 15 decimal digits consisting of the Mobile Country Code, Mobile Network Code, and Mobile Subscriber Identification Number. SUPI is equivalent to IMSI which uniquely identifies the ME.

**Article 4:** Next-generation 5G cellular systems will operate in frequencies ranging from around 500 MHz up to 100 GHz. Till now, with LTE and Wi-Fi technologies, we were operating below 6GHz and the channel models were designed and evaluated for operation at frequencies only as high as 6 GHz. The new 5G systems are to operate in bands above 6 GHz and existing channel models will not be valid, hence there is a need for accurate radio propagation models for these higher frequencies, which requires new channel models. The requirements of the new channel model that can support 5G operation across frequency bands up to 100 GHz are based on the existing 3GPP channel models along with extensions to cover additional 5G modeling requirements.

**Summary 4:** 5G will operate in frequencies ranging from around 500 MHz up to 100 GHz. Up to now 4G and WiFi were operating below 6GHz and the channel models were designed and evaluated for operation at frequencies only as high as 6GHz.

**Article 5:** Carrier Aggregation (CA) increases the bandwidth by combining several carriers. Each aggregated carrier is referred to as a Component Carrier (CC). 5G NR CA supports up to 16 contiguous and non-contiguous CCs with different numerologies in the FR1 band and in the FR2 band. A Carrier aggregation configuration includes the type of carrier aggregation (intra-band, contiguous or not, or inter-band), the number of bands, and the bandwidth class. CA Bandwidth Class is a series of alphabets that defines the minimum and maximum bandwidth along with the number of component carriers.

**Summary 5:** Carrier Aggregation (CA) increases the bandwidth by combining several carriers. 5G NR CA supports up to 16 contiguous and non-contiguous CCs with different numerologies.

### C.5 Data Sources

Below we list the websites that were scrapped to create SPEC5G.

| Portal Name | Web Address | Description | # of Sentences | # of Words |
|---|---|---|---|---|
| Artiza Networks | artizanetworks.com | ArtizaNetworks contains tutorials about 3G, 4G, and 5G Radio Access Network (RAN) and Core Network (CN). | 383 | 5182 |
| Event Helix | eventhelix.com | Event Helix is a private corporation based on Maryland. They develop tools for networking and distributed systems and host numerous blogs about 5G Radio, TCP/IP, and so on. | 595 | 6691 |
| 3G LTE Info | 3glteinfo.com | 3G LTE Info offers tutorials and articles for network professionals. These articles encompass GSM, GPRS, 3G, LTE, 5G, Bluetooth, and so on. | 790 | 9651 |
| 4G 5G World | 4g5gworld.com | Powered by NgnGuru Solutions Pvt. Ltd., 4G 5G World delivers news, reports, and tutorials about 4G and 5G advanced technologies. | 80 | 1069 |
| Info NR LTE | info-nrlte.com | Run by telecom experts, Info NR LTE delivers technology overviews about NR LTE and NR 5G. | 508 | 7431 |
| Resurchify | resurchify.com | Resurchify contains research gatherings from conferences, journals, symposiums, meetings from multiple sectors. | 138 | 1815 |
| Share Tech Note | sharetechnote.com | ShareTechNote aims to be a reference guideline on numerous fields, such as, programming languages, engineering, mathematics, advanced technologies. 5G is one of them. | 8325 | 91575 |
| Telecompedia | telecompedia.net | Telecompedia is a tutorial resource written by 4G, 5G, and radio experts from Rakuten Mobile on different 5G related technologies such as D-RAN, Open-RAN, power control etc. | 2173 | 24997 |
| RF Wireless | rfwireless-world.com | Following IEEE and 3GPP standards, RF Wireless hosts articles, tutorials, source code, terminologies about wireless technologies. | 610 | 8032 |
| Tech Play On | techplayon.com | Tech Play On contains technology news and guidelines on 5GNR and LTE. | 5220 | 89035 |
| Telecom Hall | telecomhall.net | A forum to discuss the advances on telecom domain and to guide developers or practitioners. | 7982 | 127712 |
| How LTE Stuff Works | howltestuffworks.blogspot.com | Hosts numerous blogs about 5GNR and LTE. | 4213 | 65520 |
| Pro-Developer Tutorial | prodevelopertutorial.com | Delivers tutorials about C/C++, Git, System design, 4G LTE, 5GNR, shell-scripting, etc. | 3178 | 31708 |

Table 4: List of blogs & forums crawled as part of dataset collection

# PRiSM: Enhancing Low-Resource Document-Level Relation Extraction with Relation-Aware Score Calibration

**Minseok Choi** **Hyesu Lim** **Jaegul Choo**
KAIST AI
{minseok.choi, hyesulim, jchoo}@kaist.ac.kr

## Abstract

Document-level relation extraction (DocRE) aims to extract relations of all entity pairs in a document. A key challenge in DocRE is the cost of annotating such data which requires intensive human effort. Thus, we investigate the case of DocRE in a low-resource setting, and we find that existing models trained on low data overestimate the NA ("no relation") label, causing limited performance. In this work, we approach the problem from a calibration perspective and propose PRiSM, which learns to adapt logits based on relation semantic information. We evaluate our method on three DocRE datasets and demonstrate that integrating existing models with PRiSM improves performance by as much as 26.38 F1 score, while the calibration error drops as much as 36 times when trained with about 3% of data. The code is publicly available at https://github.com/brightjade/PRiSM.

## 1 Introduction

Document-level relation extraction (DocRE) is a fundamental task in natural language understanding, which aims to identify relations between entities that exist in a document. A major challenge in DocRE is the cost of annotating such documents, requiring annotators to consider relations of all possible entity combinations (Yao et al., 2019; Zaporojets et al., 2021; Tan et al., 2022b). However, there is a lack of ongoing studies investigating the low-resource setting in DocRE (Zhou et al., 2023), and we discover that most of the current DocRE models show subpar performance when trained with a small set of data. We argue that the reason is two-fold. First, the long-tailed distribution of DocRE data encourages models to be overly confident in predicting frequent relations and less sure about infrequent ones (Du et al., 2022; Tan et al., 2022a). Out of the 96 relations in DocRED (Yao et al., 2019), a widely-used DocRE dataset, the 7 most frequent relations account for 55% of the total relation triples. Under the low-resource setting, chances to observe infrequent relations become much harder. Second, DocRE models predict the NA ("no relation") label if an entity pair does not express any relation. In DocRED, about 97% of all entity pairs have the NA label. With limited data, there is a much less signal for ground-truth (GT) labels during training, resulting in models overpredicting the NA label instead.

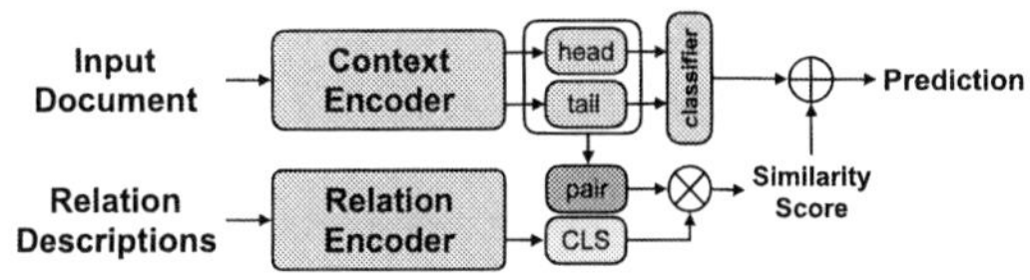


Figure 1: An overview of our proposed method. Top represents the original DocRE framework. PRiSM (bottom) leverages relation descriptions to compute scores for each relation triple. These scores are then used to reweight the prediction logits.

High confidence in common relations and the NA label and low confidence in rare relations suggest that models may be miscalibrated. We hypothesize that lowering the former and raising the latter would improve the overall RE performance. At a high level, we wish to penalize logits of frequent labels (including NA) and supplement logits of infrequent labels such that models are able to predict them without seeing them much during training. To implement such behavior, we leverage relation semantic information, which has proved to be effective in low-resource sentence-level RE (Yang et al., 2020; Dong et al., 2021; Zhang and Lu, 2022).

In this work, we propose the **P**air-**R**elat**i**on **S**imilarity **M**odule (PRiSM) that learns to adapt logits by exploiting semantic information from label descriptions, as depicted in Figure 1. Specifically, we compute a similarity function for each entity pair embedding, constructed from two entities of interest, with relation embeddings, built from corresponding label descriptions. PRiSM then learns re-



*Findings of the Association for Computational Linguistics: IJCNLP-AACL 2023*, pages 39–47
November 1–4, 2023. 

lation representations to output adaptive scores for each relation triple. Note that previous work mostly utilized relation representations for self-supervised learning (Dong et al., 2021; Du et al., 2022; Zhou et al., 2023), whereas PRiSM uses them to directly adjust logits, which brings a calibration effect. To elaborate further, let us say that classification logits are statistical scores and similarities are semantic scores. We have four scenarios: 1) relation is common and GT, 2) relation is common but not GT, 3) relation is uncommon but GT, and 4) relation is uncommon and not GT. In Cases 1 and 4, both statistical and semantic scores are either high or low, and thus, appending PRiSM mostly would not affect the original RE predictions. In Case 2, the statistical score is high, but the semantic score is low, possibly negative to penalize the statistical score. This is the case of PRiSM decreasing the confidence of common relations and NA label. In Case 3, the statistical score is low, but the semantic score is high, which is the case of PRiSM increasing the confidence of uncommon relations. As such, PRiSM incorporates both statistical and semantic scores such that the confidence is adjusted regardless of the relation frequency.

Our technical contributions are three-fold. First, we propose PRiSM, a relation-aware calibration technique that improves model performance and adjusts model confidence on low-resource DocRE. Second, we demonstrate the performance improvement across various state-of-the-art models integrated with PRiSM. Third, we validate the effectiveness of our method on widely-used long-tailed DocRE datasets and calibration metrics.

## 2 Methodology

### 2.1 Problem Formulation

Given a document $d$, a set of $n$ annotated entities $\mathcal{E} = \{e_i\}_{i=1}^{n}$, and a pre-defined set of relations $\mathcal{R} \cup \{\mathsf{NA}\}$, the task of DocRE is to extract the relation triple set $\{(e_h, r, e_t) | e_h \in \mathcal{E}, r \in \mathcal{R}, e_t \in \mathcal{E}\} \subseteq \mathcal{E} \times \mathcal{R} \times \mathcal{E}$ from all possible relation triples, where $(e_h, r, e_t)$ denotes that a relation $r$ holds between head entity $e_h$ and tail entity $e_t$. An entity $e_i$ may appear $k$ times in the document in which we denote corresponding instances as entity mentions $\{m_{ij}\}_{j=1}^{k}$. A relation $r$ exists between an entity pair $(e_h, e_t)$ if any pair of their mentions express the relation, and if they do not express any relation, the entity pair is then labeled as NA.

### 2.2 Document-Level Relation Extraction

Given a document $d$ as an input token sequence $\boldsymbol{x} = [x_t]_{t=1}^{l}$, where $l$ is the length of the token sequence, we explicitly locate the position of entity mentions by inserting a special token "*" before and after each mention. The presence of the entity marker has proved to be effective from previous studies (Zhang et al., 2017; Shi and Lin, 2019; Baldini Soares et al., 2019). The entity-marked document is then fed into a pre-trained language model (PLM) encoder, which outputs the contextual embeddings: $[\boldsymbol{h}_1, \boldsymbol{h}_2, ..., \boldsymbol{h}_l] = \text{Encoder}(\boldsymbol{x})$. We take the embedding of "*" at the start of each mention as its mention-level representation $\boldsymbol{h}_{m_{ij}}$ of the entity $e_i$. For extracting the entity-level representation, we apply the logsumexp pooling over all mentions $\{m_{ij}\}_{j=1}^{k}$ of the entity $e_i$:

$$\boldsymbol{h}_{e_i} = \log \sum_{j=1}^{k} \exp\left(\boldsymbol{h}_{m_{ij}}\right). \tag{1}$$

The logsumexp pooling is a smooth version of max pooling and has been shown to accumulate weak signals from each different mention representation, which results in a better performance (Jia et al., 2019). We pass the embeddings of head and tail entities through a linear layer followed by non-linear activation to obtain the hidden representations: $\boldsymbol{z}_h = \tanh(\boldsymbol{W}_h \boldsymbol{h}_{e_h} + \boldsymbol{b}_h)$ and $\boldsymbol{z}_t = \tanh(\boldsymbol{W}_t \boldsymbol{h}_{e_t} + \boldsymbol{b}_t)$, where $\boldsymbol{W}_h, \boldsymbol{W}_t, \boldsymbol{b}_h, \boldsymbol{b}_t$ are learnable parameters. Then we calculate a score for relation $r$ between entities $h$ and $t$ by taking a bilinear function:

$$s_{(h,r,t)} = \boldsymbol{z}_h^{\top} \boldsymbol{W}_r \boldsymbol{z}_t + \boldsymbol{b}_r, \tag{2}$$

where $\boldsymbol{W}_r, \boldsymbol{b}_r$ are learnable parameters.

### 2.3 PRiSM

Following previous work (Zhang and Lu, 2022), we feed relation descriptions to a PLM encoder to obtain the relation embedding $\boldsymbol{z}_r$ for relation $r$. The details of the relation descriptions used can be found in Appendix A.4. We then construct the entity pair-level representation $\boldsymbol{z}_{(h,t)}$ by mapping the head and tail embeddings to a linear layer followed by non-linear activation: $\boldsymbol{z}_{(h,t)} = \tanh(\boldsymbol{W}_{(h,t)}[\boldsymbol{z}_h; \boldsymbol{z}_t] + \boldsymbol{b}_{(h,t)})$, where $\boldsymbol{z}_h$, $\boldsymbol{z}_t$ are concatenated and $\boldsymbol{W}_{(h,t)}$, $\boldsymbol{b}_{(h,t)}$ are learnable parameters. An adaptive score for relation $r$ between entities $h$ and $t$ is computed by taking a similarity function between the entity pair embedding

| Model | DocRED Dev Ign $F_1$ | DocRED Dev $F_1$ | DocRED Test Ign $F_1$ | DocRED Test $F_1$ | Re-DocRED Dev Ign $F_1$ | Re-DocRED Dev $F_1$ | Re-DocRED Test Ign $F_1$ | Re-DocRED Test $F_1$ |
|---|---|---|---|---|---|---|---|---|
| *3% training examples ($N = 100$)* | | | | | | | | |
| $BERT_{BASE}$ | $10.27 \pm 1.82$ | $10.44 \pm 1.90$ | 11.36 | 11.50 | $28.65 \pm 2.87$ | $29.40 \pm 3.19$ | $28.77 \pm 3.34$ | $29.44 \pm 3.67$ |
| $BERT_{BASE}$ + **PRiSM** | $\mathbf{35.06} \pm 0.94$ | $\mathbf{37.02} \pm 0.88$ | **35.79** | **37.88** | $\mathbf{47.39} \pm 0.79$ | $\mathbf{49.09} \pm 0.90$ | $\mathbf{46.90} \pm 1.59$ | $\mathbf{48.57} \pm 1.73$ |
| $RoBERTa_{BASE}$ | $20.70 \pm 1.91$ | $21.31 \pm 1.87$ | 21.74 | 22.25 | $39.66 \pm 2.25$ | $40.74 \pm 1.89$ | $39.42 \pm 2.80$ | $40.53 \pm 2.43$ |
| $RoBERTa_{BASE}$ + **PRiSM** | $\mathbf{32.40} \pm 0.85$ | $\mathbf{34.49} \pm 0.76$ | **32.20** | **34.32** | $\mathbf{47.71} \pm 1.03$ | $\mathbf{49.40} \pm 1.14$ | $\mathbf{47.31} \pm 0.96$ | $\mathbf{49.04} \pm 1.05$ |
| SSAN-$BERT_{BASE}$ | $10.92 \pm 0.88$ | $11.18 \pm 0.89$ | 11.93 | 12.16 | $28.89 \pm 1.68$ | $29.01 \pm 1.69$ | $28.64 \pm 1.89$ | $29.29 \pm 1.94$ |
| SSAN-$BERT_{BASE}$ + **PRiSM** | $\mathbf{32.86} \pm 2.35$ | $\mathbf{34.76} \pm 2.50$ | **34.00** | **36.03** | $\mathbf{46.49} \pm 1.16$ | $\mathbf{48.11} \pm 1.40$ | $\mathbf{46.51} \pm 1.77$ | $\mathbf{48.11} \pm 2.00$ |
| ATLOP-$BERT_{BASE}$ | $38.99 \pm 2.30$ | $40.50 \pm 2.07$ | 40.88 | 42.37 | $49.45 \pm 2.09$ | $50.60 \pm 1.95$ | $49.24 \pm 2.25$ | $50.32 \pm 2.13$ |
| ATLOP-$BERT_{BASE}$ + **PRiSM** | $\mathbf{40.59} \pm 0.68$ | $\mathbf{42.09} \pm 0.66$ | **40.94** | **42.43** | $\mathbf{50.10} \pm 0.53$ | $\mathbf{51.12} \pm 0.64$ | $\mathbf{50.15} \pm 1.11$ | $\mathbf{51.14} \pm 1.17$ |
| *10% training examples ($N = 305$)* | | | | | | | | |
| $BERT_{BASE}$ | $39.84 \pm 0.92$ | $41.55 \pm 0.99$ | 40.98 | 42.98 | $52.34 \pm 0.66$ | $53.54 \pm 0.80$ | $52.34 \pm 0.68$ | $53.54 \pm 0.84$ |
| $BERT_{BASE}$ + **PRiSM** | $\mathbf{46.01} \pm 0.12$ | $\mathbf{48.02} \pm 0.13$ | **45.52** | **47.83** | $\mathbf{58.10} \pm 0.31$ | $\mathbf{59.86} \pm 0.27$ | $\mathbf{57.75} \pm 0.65$ | $\mathbf{59.53} \pm 0.51$ |
| $RoBERTa_{BASE}$ | $43.42 \pm 1.09$ | $45.20 \pm 1.09$ | 43.78 | 45.63 | $54.82 \pm 1.85$ | $56.10 \pm 1.80$ | $55.36 \pm 2.18$ | $56.67 \pm 2.06$ |
| $RoBERTa_{BASE}$ + **PRiSM** | $\mathbf{46.60} \pm 0.20$ | $\mathbf{48.57} \pm 0.29$ | **47.02** | **49.22** | $\mathbf{59.51} \pm 0.36$ | $\mathbf{61.19} \pm 0.32$ | $\mathbf{59.08} \pm 0.61$ | $\mathbf{60.80} \pm 0.52$ |
| SSAN-$BERT_{BASE}$ | $40.00 \pm 1.62$ | $41.65 \pm 1.63$ | 41.11 | 43.03 | $53.57 \pm 0.83$ | $54.86 \pm 0.81$ | $53.67 \pm 1.55$ | $54.94 \pm 1.52$ |
| SSAN-$BERT_{BASE}$ + **PRiSM** | $\mathbf{46.14} \pm 0.15$ | $\mathbf{48.18} \pm 0.09$ | **45.48** | **47.72** | $\mathbf{58.47} \pm 0.39$ | $\mathbf{60.17} \pm 0.36$ | $\mathbf{58.21} \pm 0.31$ | $\mathbf{59.93} \pm 0.19$ |
| ATLOP-$BERT_{BASE}$ | $49.93 \pm 1.11$ | $51.61 \pm 1.16$ | 50.04 | 51.85 | $60.38 \pm 0.46$ | $61.52 \pm 0.29$ | $60.46 \pm 0.55$ | $61.54 \pm 0.29$ |
| ATLOP-$BERT_{BASE}$ + **PRiSM** | $\mathbf{50.20} \pm 0.68$ | $\mathbf{51.83} \pm 0.64$ | **50.29** | **52.17** | $\mathbf{60.58} \pm 0.18$ | $\mathbf{61.68} \pm 0.17$ | $\mathbf{60.90} \pm 0.37$ | $\mathbf{61.97} \pm 0.40$ |
| *100% training examples ($N = 3053$)* | | | | | | | | |
| $BERT_{BASE}$ | $57.15 \pm 0.17$ | $59.18 \pm 0.05$ | 57.02 | 59.35 | $71.70 \pm 0.61$ | $73.17 \pm 0.55$ | $71.01 \pm 0.88$ | $72.48 \pm 0.78$ |
| $BERT_{BASE}$ + **PRiSM** | $\mathbf{57.82} \pm 0.10$ | $\mathbf{59.93} \pm 0.15$ | **57.17** | **59.52** | $\mathbf{72.92} \pm 0.07$ | $\mathbf{74.25} \pm 0.07$ | $\mathbf{72.35} \pm 0.07$ | $\mathbf{73.69} \pm 0.11$ |
| $RoBERTa_{BASE}$ | $58.24 \pm 0.36$ | $60.19 \pm 0.38$ | 58.00 | 60.10 | $74.00 \pm 0.20$ | $75.20 \pm 0.20$ | $73.56 \pm 0.04$ | $74.75 \pm 0.04$ |
| $RoBERTa_{BASE}$ + **PRiSM** | $\mathbf{58.73} \pm 0.09$ | $\mathbf{60.70} \pm 0.02$ | **58.36** | **60.51** | $\mathbf{74.50} \pm 0.09$ | $\mathbf{75.71} \pm 0.06$ | $\mathbf{74.17} \pm 0.10$ | $\mathbf{75.38} \pm 0.10$ |
| SSAN-$BERT_{BASE}$ | $57.59 \pm 0.35$ | $59.62 \pm 0.24$ | 57.71 | 59.79 | $72.59 \pm 0.15$ | $74.01 \pm 0.15$ | $71.95 \pm 0.11$ | $73.37 \pm 0.11$ |
| SSAN-$BERT_{BASE}$ + **PRiSM** | $\mathbf{58.20} \pm 0.20$ | $\mathbf{60.27} \pm 0.14$ | **58.02** | **60.27** | $\mathbf{73.22} \pm 0.10$ | $\mathbf{74.65} \pm 0.07$ | $\mathbf{72.37} \pm 0.19$ | $\mathbf{73.80} \pm 0.18$ |
| ATLOP-$BERT_{BASE}$ | $59.22 \pm 0.17$ | $61.18 \pm 0.10$ | **58.99** | **61.08** | $72.78 \pm 0.46$ | $73.73 \pm 0.37$ | $72.60 \pm 0.41$ | $73.51 \pm 0.38$ |
| ATLOP-$BERT_{BASE}$ + **PRiSM** | $\mathbf{59.51} \pm 0.09$ | $\mathbf{61.31} \pm 0.05$ | 58.80 | 60.77 | $\mathbf{72.85} \pm 0.29$ | $\mathbf{73.80} \pm 0.35$ | $\mathbf{72.61} \pm 0.59$ | $\mathbf{73.53} \pm 0.53$ |

Table 1: Performance (%) on DocRED and Re-DocRED. Better scores between with and without PRiSM are in bold. The test results for DocRED are obtained by submitting the best dev model predictions to CodaLab[1].

| Model | Macro | Macro@500 | Macro@200 | Macro@100 |
|---|---|---|---|---|
| $N = 100$ | | | | |
| $BERT_{BASE}$ | $0.36 \pm 0.05$ | 0 | 0 | – |
| $BERT_{BASE}$ + **PRiSM** | $\mathbf{7.77} \pm 1.87$ | $\mathbf{4.08} \pm 0.43$ | $\mathbf{0.44} \pm 0.33$ | – |
| $RoBERTa_{BASE}$ | $1.18 \pm 0.28$ | 0 | 0 | – |
| $RoBERTa_{BASE}$ + **PRiSM** | $\mathbf{6.41} \pm 0.77$ | $\mathbf{2.31} \pm 0.82$ | $\mathbf{0.38} \pm 0.28$ | – |
| $N = 305$ | | | | |
| $BERT_{BASE}$ | $9.31 \pm 1.59$ | $3.70 \pm 1.46$ | $0.29 \pm 0.17$ | 0 |
| $BERT_{BASE}$ + **PRiSM** | $\mathbf{20.19} \pm 0.70$ | $\mathbf{14.91} \pm 0.64$ | $\mathbf{7.73} \pm 0.17$ | $\mathbf{2.19} \pm 1.16$ |
| $RoBERTa_{BASE}$ | $14.80 \pm 0.51$ | $9.13 \pm 0.61$ | $3.74 \pm 0.35$ | $0.83 \pm 0.89$ |
| $RoBERTa_{BASE}$ + **PRiSM** | $\mathbf{21.03} \pm 0.27$ | $\mathbf{15.69} \pm 0.48$ | $\mathbf{8.37} \pm 0.16$ | $\mathbf{2.63} \pm 1.25$ |
| $N = 3053$ | | | | |
| $BERT_{BASE}$ | $38.31 \pm 0.39$ | $34.06 \pm 0.45$ | $26.07 \pm 0.72$ | $\mathbf{19.73} \pm 0.96$ |
| $BERT_{BASE}$ + **PRiSM** | $\mathbf{38.89} \pm 0.52$ | $\mathbf{34.57} \pm 0.59$ | $\mathbf{26.51} \pm 0.65$ | $19.57 \pm 0.71$ |
| $RoBERTa_{BASE}$ | $38.67 \pm 1.12$ | $34.28 \pm 1.22$ | $26.14 \pm 1.44$ | $18.69 \pm 1.70$ |
| $RoBERTa_{BASE}$ + **PRiSM** | $\mathbf{39.12} \pm 0.57$ | $\mathbf{34.72} \pm 0.69$ | $\mathbf{26.45} \pm 1.01$ | $\mathbf{19.23} \pm 1.55$ |

Table 2: Dev performance (%) on low-frequency relations in DocRED. Test results cannot be reported because the labels are not accessible.

and relation embedding: $s'_{(h,r,t)} = sim(z_{(h,t)}, z_r)$, where $sim(\cdot)$ is cosine similarity. Formally, the probability of relation $r$ between entities $h$ and $t$ is simply an addition of two scores followed by sigmoid activation:

$$P(r \mid e_h, e_t) = \sigma(s_{(h,r,t)} + \lambda s'_{(h,r,t)}), \quad (3)$$

where $\lambda$ is the scale factor. Finally, we optimize our model with the binary cross-entropy (BCE) loss:

$$\mathcal{L} = -\frac{1}{T} \sum_{<h,t>} \sum_{r} \mathsf{BCE}(P(r|e_h, e_t), \bar{y}_{(h,r,t)}), \quad (4)$$

where $\bar{y}$ is the target label and $T$ is the total number of relation triples.

## 3 Experiments

### 3.1 Dataset

We evaluate our framework on three public DocRE datasets. DocRED (Yao et al., 2019) is a widely-used human-annotated DocRE dataset constructed from Wikipedia and Wikidata. Re-DocRED (Tan et al., 2022b) is a revised dataset from DocRED, addressing the incomplete annotation problem. DWIE (Zaporojets et al., 2021) is a multi-task document-level information extraction dataset consisting of news articles collected from Deutsche Welle. Dataset statistics are shown in Table 5.

### 3.2 Implementation Details

Our framework is built on PyTorch and Huggingface's Transformers library (Wolf et al., 2020). We use the cased BERT (Devlin et al., 2019) and RoBERTa (Liu et al., 2019) for encoding the text and optimize their weights with AdamW (Loshchilov and Hutter, 2019). We tune our hyperparameters to maximize the $F_1$ score on the development set. The additional implementation details are included in Appendix B. During inference, we predict all relation triples that have probabilities higher than the F1-maximizing threshold found in the development set. We conduct our experiments with three different random seeds and report the averaged results. Following Yao et al.

[1] https://codalab.lisn.upsaclay.fr/

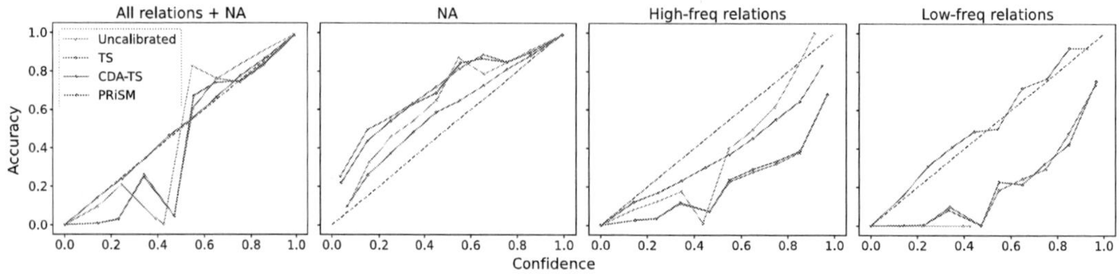


Figure 2: Reliability diagram for $\text{BERT}_{\text{BASE}}$ when trained with 3% of DocRED data.

| Model | Dev $F_1$ | Dev Macro | Test $F_1$ | Test Macro |
|---|---|---|---|---|
| $N = 100$ | | | | |
| $\text{BERT}_{\text{BASE}}$ | $11.97 \pm 1.78$ | $1.79 \pm 0.27$ | $12.41 \pm 2.29$ | $1.87 \pm 0.32$ |
| $\text{BERT}_{\text{BASE}}$ + **PRiSM** | $\mathbf{45.20} \pm 1.60$ | $\mathbf{10.34} \pm 1.91$ | $\mathbf{44.31} \pm 1.47$ | $\mathbf{9.47} \pm 1.46$ |
| $\text{RoBERTa}_{\text{BASE}}$ | $50.27 \pm 1.57$ | $8.55 \pm 0.56$ | $48.29 \pm 1.74$ | $8.95 \pm 0.86$ |
| $\text{RoBERTa}_{\text{BASE}}$ + **PRiSM** | $\mathbf{55.51} \pm 1.11$ | $\mathbf{12.76} \pm 2.03$ | $\mathbf{54.23} \pm 1.24$ | $\mathbf{13.80} \pm 0.64$ |
| $N = 305$ | | | | |
| $\text{BERT}_{\text{BASE}}$ | $52.98 \pm 0.76$ | $15.68 \pm 1.71$ | $52.05 \pm 0.60$ | $14.80 \pm 0.63$ |
| $\text{BERT}_{\text{BASE}}$ + **PRiSM** | $\mathbf{58.23} \pm 0.40$ | $\mathbf{24.62} \pm 0.59$ | $\mathbf{57.05} \pm 0.23$ | $\mathbf{22.43} \pm 0.88$ |
| $\text{RoBERTa}_{\text{BASE}}$ | $65.45 \pm 1.94$ | $21.72 \pm 1.29$ | $62.39 \pm 1.29$ | $20.39 \pm 0.76$ |
| $\text{RoBERTa}_{\text{BASE}}$ + **PRiSM** | $\mathbf{71.18} \pm 1.98$ | $\mathbf{28.36} \pm 1.53$ | $\mathbf{67.12} \pm 2.02$ | $\mathbf{25.82} \pm 0.34$ |
| $N = 587$ | | | | |
| $\text{BERT}_{\text{BASE}}$ | $62.06 \pm 0.33$ | $25.17 \pm 0.37$ | $60.78 \pm 0.25$ | $22.93 \pm 0.40$ |
| $\text{BERT}_{\text{BASE}}$ + **PRiSM** | $\mathbf{66.81} \pm 0.56$ | $\mathbf{28.17} \pm 0.54$ | $\mathbf{66.53} \pm 0.52$ | $\mathbf{29.31} \pm 1.13$ |
| $\text{RoBERTa}_{\text{BASE}}$ | $76.23 \pm 0.72$ | $31.71 \pm 0.13$ | $74.07 \pm 0.77$ | $28.72 \pm 1.54$ |
| $\text{RoBERTa}_{\text{BASE}}$ + **PRiSM** | $\mathbf{78.43} \pm 0.12$ | $\mathbf{32.85} \pm 0.37$ | $\mathbf{78.13} \pm 0.61$ | $\mathbf{33.66} \pm 1.24$ |

Table 3: Performance (%) on the DWIE dataset.

(2019), all models are evaluated on $F_1$ and Ign $F_1$, where Ign $F_1$ excludes the relations shared by the training and development/test sets. Moreover, we measure **Macro**, which computes the average of per-class $F_1$, and **Macro@500**, **Macro@200**, and **Macro@100**, targeting rare relations where the frequency count in the training dataset is less than 500, 200, and 100, respectively.

### 3.3 Experimental Results

To simulate the low-data setting, we reduce the number of training documents $N$ to 100 and 305, which is about 3% and 10% of the original data. To create each of the settings, we repeat random sampling until the label distribution resembles that of the full data. As shown in Table 1, we observe that performance increases consistently across different models when appended with PRiSM. Particularly, PRiSM improves performance by a large margin when trained with just 3% of data, as much as 24.43 Ign $F_1$ and 26.38 $F_1$ on the test set of DocRED for $\text{BERT}_{\text{BASE}}$. We also test PRiSM on $\text{RoBERTa}_{\text{BASE}}$ and two state-of-the-art models SSAN (Xu et al., 2021) and ATLOP (Zhou et al., 2021) and notice a similar trend, indicating that our method is effective on various existing models. We additionally evaluate PRiSM using macro metrics in Table 2 and observe that adding PRiSM improves performance on infrequent relations, especially in the low-data setting. Lastly, we validate our method on

| | $N = 100$ | | | $N = 305$ | | |
|---|---|---|---|---|---|---|
| **Method** | $\boldsymbol{F_1}(\uparrow)$ | **ECE**($\downarrow$) | **ACE**($\downarrow$) | $\boldsymbol{F_1}(\uparrow)$ | **ECE**($\downarrow$) | **ACE**($\downarrow$) |
| Uncalibrated | 10.82 | 0.359% | 0.379% | 42.56 | 0.137% | 0.164% |
| TS | **38.19** | 0.144% | 0.173% | 48.49 | 0.053% | 0.062% |
| CDA-TS | 37.82 | 0.139% | 0.167% | **48.54** | 0.057% | 0.078% |
| PRiSM (ours) | 37.84 | **0.010%** | **0.020%** | 48.10 | **0.023%** | **0.020%** |

Table 4: Comparison of calibration errors (with 10 bins) under a low-resource setting of DocRED.

a different dataset DWIE, as illustrated in Table 3.

### 3.4 Calibration Evaluation

We measure model calibration on two metrics: expected calibration error (ECE) (Naeini et al., 2015) and adaptive calibration error (ACE) (Nixon et al., 2019). ECE partitions predictions into a fixed number of bins and computes a weighted average of the difference between accuracy and confidence over the bins, while ACE puts the same number of predictions in each bin. We compare with general calibration methods such as temperature scaling (TS) (Guo et al., 2017) and class-distribution-aware TS (CDA-TS) (Islam et al., 2021). As reported in Table 4, PRiSM outperforms other methods in both metrics, while also maintaining a comparable RE performance. We also visualize with a reliability diagram (DeGroot and Fienberg, 1983; Niculescu-Mizil and Caruana, 2005) in Figure 2. We observe that PRiSM effectively lowers the confidence of the NA label and raises the confidence of low-frequency relations (bottom 89). For high-frequency relations (top 7), confidence is adjusted in both ways. In any case, PRiSM displays the most stable, closest line to the perfect calibration (blue line).

## 4 Related Work

With the introduction of DocRED (Yao et al., 2019), many approaches were proposed to extract relations from a document (Wang et al., 2019; Ye et al., 2020; Zhang et al., 2021; Xu et al., 2021; Zhou et al., 2021; Xie et al., 2022). The long-tailed data problem of DocRE has been addressed in some studies (Du et al., 2022; Tan et al., 2022a), as well as low-resource DocRE (Zhou et al., 2023); however, most require additional pretraining, which is compute- and cost-intensive, while PRiSM only requires adjusting logits in existing models. Low-resource RE has been extensively studied at the sentence level, and we specifically focus on leveraging label information (Yang et al., 2020; Dong et al., 2021; Zhang and Lu, 2022) in which PRiSM applies it to the document level. In contrast to prior work in calibration (Guo et al., 2017; Islam et al., 2021), our approach is relation-aware, updating logits at a much finer granularity.

## 5 Conclusion and Future Work

In this work, we propose a simple modular framework PRiSM, which exploits relation semantics to update logits. We empirically demonstrate that our method effectively improves and calibrates DocRE models where the data is long-tailed and the NA label is overestimated. For future work, we can apply PRiSM to more tasks such as event extraction and dialogue state tracking, which also enclose long-tailed data and overestimation of "null" labels.

## Limitations

Although our approach is resilient to data scarcity, quite a few annotated documents are still required for the model to learn the pattern. The ultimate goal of DocRE is undoubtedly to build a model that is able to perform well on zero-shot, but we believe our approach takes a step toward that direction. Moreover, we process the long documents (> 512 tokens) in a very naive way, as described in Appendix A.3, and we think that exploration of long-sequence modeling on longer document data could further enrich the field of DocRE.


## Acknowledgements

This work was supported by Institute of Information & communications Technology Planning & Evaluation (IITP) grant funded by the Korea government (MSIT) (No.2019-0-00075, Artificial Intelligence Graduate School Program (KAIST)), the National Supercomputing Center with supercomputing resources including technical support (KSC-2022-CRE-0312), and Samsung Electronics Co., Ltd. We thank the anonymous reviewers for their constructive feedback.


## References


Livio Baldini Soares, Nicholas FitzGerald, Jeffrey Ling, and Tom Kwiatkowski. 2019. Matching the blanks: Distributional similarity for relation learning. In *Proceedings of the 57th Annual Meeting of the Association for Computational Linguistics*, pages 2895–2905, Florence, Italy. Association for Computational Linguistics.

Morris H DeGroot and Stephen E Fienberg. 1983. The comparison and evaluation of forecasters. *Journal of the Royal Statistical Society: Series D (The Statistician)*, 32(1-2):12–22.

Jacob Devlin, Ming-Wei Chang, Kenton Lee, and Kristina Toutanova. 2019. BERT: Pre-training of deep bidirectional transformers for language understanding. In *Proceedings of the 2019 Conference of the North American Chapter of the Association for Computational Linguistics: Human Language Technologies, Volume 1 (Long and Short Papers)*, pages 4171–4186, Minneapolis, Minnesota. Association for Computational Linguistics.

Manqing Dong, Chunguang Pan, and Zhipeng Luo. 2021. MapRE: An effective semantic mapping approach for low-resource relation extraction. In *Proceedings of the 2021 Conference on Empirical Methods in Natural Language Processing*, pages 2694–2704, Online and Punta Cana, Dominican Republic. Association for Computational Linguistics.

Yangkai Du, Tengfei Ma, Lingfei Wu, Yiming Wu, Xuhong Zhang, Bo Long, and Shouling Ji. 2022. Improving long tailed document-level relation extraction via easy relation augmentation and contrastive learning. *arXiv preprint arXiv:2205.10511*.

Chuan Guo, Geoff Pleiss, Yu Sun, and Kilian Q Weinberger. 2017. On calibration of modern neural networks. In *International conference on machine learning*, pages 1321–1330. PMLR.

Mobarakol Islam, Lalithkumar Seenivasan, Hongliang Ren, and Ben Glocker. 2021. Class-distribution-aware calibration for long-tailed visual recognition. *arXiv preprint arXiv:2109.05263*.

Robin Jia, Cliff Wong, and Hoifung Poon. 2019. Document-level n-ary relation extraction with multi-scale representation learning. In *Proceedings of the 2019 Conference of the North American Chapter of the Association for Computational Linguistics: Human Language Technologies, Volume 1 (Long and Short Papers)*, pages 3693–3704, Minneapolis, Minnesota. Association for Computational Linguistics.

Yinhan Liu, Myle Ott, Naman Goyal, Jingfei Du, Mandar Joshi, Danqi Chen, Omer Levy, Mike Lewis, Luke Zettlemoyer, and Veselin Stoyanov. 2019. Roberta: A robustly optimized bert pretraining approach. *arXiv preprint arXiv:1907.11692*.

Ilya Loshchilov and Frank Hutter. 2019. Decoupled weight decay regularization. In *International Conference on Learning Representations*.

Mahdi Pakdaman Naeini, Gregory Cooper, and Milos Hauskrecht. 2015. Obtaining well calibrated probabilities using bayesian binning. In *Proceedings of the AAAI conference on artificial intelligence*, volume 29.

Alexandru Niculescu-Mizil and Rich Caruana. 2005. Predicting good probabilities with supervised learning. In *Proceedings of the 22nd international conference on Machine learning*, pages 625–632.

Jeremy Nixon, Michael W Dusenberry, Linchuan Zhang, Ghassen Jerfel, and Dustin Tran. 2019. Measuring calibration in deep learning. In *CVPR workshops*, volume 2.

OpenAI. 2023. ChatGPT March 23 Version.

Peng Shi and Jimmy Lin. 2019. Simple bert models for relation extraction and semantic role labeling. *arXiv preprint arXiv:1904.05255*.

Qingyu Tan, Ruidan He, Lidong Bing, and Hwee Tou Ng. 2022a. Document-level relation extraction with adaptive focal loss and knowledge distillation. In *Findings of the Association for Computational Linguistics: ACL 2022*, pages 1672–1681, Dublin, Ireland. Association for Computational Linguistics.

Qingyu Tan, Lu Xu, Lidong Bing, Hwee Tou Ng, and Sharifah Mahani Aljunied. 2022b. Revisiting DocRED - addressing the false negative problem in relation extraction. In *Proceedings of the 2022 Conference on Empirical Methods in Natural Language Processing*, pages 8472–8487, Abu Dhabi, United Arab Emirates. Association for Computational Linguistics.

Hong Wang, Christfried Focke, Rob Sylvester, Nilesh Mishra, and William Wang. 2019. Fine-tune bert for docred with two-step process. *arXiv preprint arXiv:1909.11898*.

Thomas Wolf, Lysandre Debut, Victor Sanh, Julien Chaumond, Clement Delangue, Anthony Moi, Pierric Cistac, Tim Rault, Remi Louf, Morgan Funtowicz, Joe Davison, Sam Shleifer, Patrick von Platen, Clara Ma, Yacine Jernite, Julien Plu, Canwen Xu, Teven Le Scao, Sylvain Gugger, Mariama Drame, Quentin Lhoest, and Alexander Rush. 2020. Transformers: State-of-the-art natural language processing. In *Proceedings of the 2020 Conference on Empirical Methods in Natural Language Processing: System Demonstrations*, pages 38–45, Online. Association for Computational Linguistics.

Yiqing Xie, Jiaming Shen, Sha Li, Yuning Mao, and Jiawei Han. 2022. Eider: Empowering document-level relation extraction with efficient evidence extraction and inference-stage fusion. In *Findings of the Association for Computational Linguistics: ACL 2022*, pages 257–268, Dublin, Ireland. Association for Computational Linguistics.

Benfeng Xu, Quan Wang, Yajuan Lyu, Yong Zhu, and Zhendong Mao. 2021. Entity structure within and throughout: Modeling mention dependencies for document-level relation extraction. In *Proceedings of the AAAI conference on artificial intelligence*, volume 35, pages 14149–14157.

Kaijia Yang, Nantao Zheng, Xinyu Dai, Liang He, Shujian Huang, and Jiajun Chen. 2020. Enhance prototypical network with text descriptions for few-shot relation classification. In *Proceedings of the 29th ACM International Conference on Information & Knowledge Management*, pages 2273–2276.

Yuan Yao, Deming Ye, Peng Li, Xu Han, Yankai Lin, Zhenghao Liu, Zhiyuan Liu, Lixin Huang, Jie Zhou, and Maosong Sun. 2019. DocRED: A large-scale document-level relation extraction dataset. In *Proceedings of the 57th Annual Meeting of the Association for Computational Linguistics*, pages 764–777, Florence, Italy. Association for Computational Linguistics.

Deming Ye, Yankai Lin, Jiaju Du, Zhenghao Liu, Peng Li, Maosong Sun, and Zhiyuan Liu. 2020. Coreferential Reasoning Learning for Language Representation. In *Proceedings of the 2020 Conference on Empirical Methods in Natural Language Processing (EMNLP)*, pages 7170–7186, Online. Association for Computational Linguistics.

Klim Zaporojets, Johannes Deleu, Chris Develder, and Thomas Demeester. 2021. Dwie: An entity-centric dataset for multi-task document-level information extraction. *Information Processing & Management*, 58(4):102563.

Ningyu Zhang, Xiang Chen, Xin Xie, Shumin Deng, Chuanqi Tan, Mosha Chen, Fei Huang, Luo Si, and Huajun Chen. 2021. Document-level relation extraction as semantic segmentation. In *Proceedings of the Thirtieth International Joint Conference on Artificial Intelligence, IJCAI-21*, pages 3999–4006. International Joint Conferences on Artificial Intelligence Organization. Main Track.

Peiyuan Zhang and Wei Lu. 2022. Better few-shot relation extraction with label prompt dropout. In *Proceedings of the 2022 Conference on Empirical Methods in Natural Language Processing*, pages 6996–7006, Abu Dhabi, United Arab Emirates. Association for Computational Linguistics.

Yuhao Zhang, Victor Zhong, Danqi Chen, Gabor Angeli, and Christopher D. Manning. 2017. Position-aware attention and supervised data improve slot filling. In *Proceedings of the 2017 Conference on Empirical Methods in Natural Language Processing*, pages 35–45, Copenhagen, Denmark. Association for Computational Linguistics.

Wenxuan Zhou, Kevin Huang, Tengyu Ma, and Jing Huang. 2021. Document-level relation extraction with adaptive thresholding and localized context pooling. In *Proceedings of the AAAI Conference on Artificial Intelligence*, volume 35, pages 14612–14620.

Wenxuan Zhou, Sheng Zhang, Tristan Naumann, Muhao Chen, and Hoifung Poon. 2023. Continual contrastive finetuning improves low-resource relation extraction. In *Proceedings of the 61st Annual Meeting of the Association for Computational Linguistics (Volume 1: Long Papers)*, pages 13249–13263, Toronto, Canada. Association for Computational Linguistics.

# Appendix

## A Additional Dataset Details

### A.1 Data Statistics

We report the statistics for the datasets in Table 5. The test set of DocRED is not included in calculating **% NA** due to its inaccessibility. 14 documents in DWIE are filtered out because of missing labels, and 1 document is removed because the annotated entities did not exist in the input document.

| Statistics | DocRED | Re-DocRED | DWIE |
|---|---|---|---|
| # Train | 3,053 | 3,053 | 587 |
| # Dev | 1,000 | 500 | 100 |
| # Test | 1,000 | 500 | 100 |
| # Relation Types | 97 | 97 | 66 |
| % NA | 97.05% | 94.02% | 97.87% |

Table 5: Dataset statistics. **# Relation Types** includes the NA label. **% NA** indicates a ratio of entity pairs having the NA label over all entity pairs.

### A.2 Class Distribution

We count the number of ground-truth relations in the train sets and visualize their class distribution in Figure 3. We observe that the re-annotation of Re-DocRED further skewed the class distribution, and the DWIE dataset seems to demonstrate a relatively less imbalanced distribution. Nevertheless, a few classes still exhibit high frequency, which PRiSM can handle effectively.

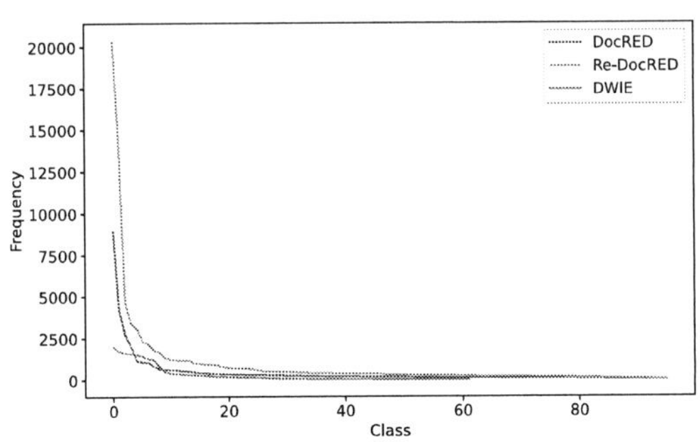


Figure 3: Dataset class distribution.

### A.3 Processing Long Document

For DocRED and Re-DocRED, most of the documents contain less than 512 tokens, and thus we follow the previous work and truncate all of the inputs to 512 tokens, which is the maximum sequence length of BERT. However, we notice that the DWIE dataset mostly contains documents much longer than 512 tokens (as shown in Figure 4) in which the truncation hurts the performance significantly. Therefore, we choose the most naive way of splitting the input document into multiple chunks of length 512 and passing them through the encoder multiple times. The performance improvement over the truncation method is demonstrated in Table 6.

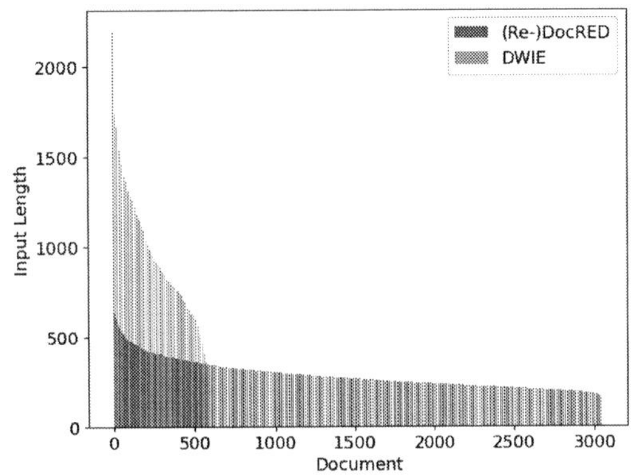


Figure 4: Lengths of input documents in training sets.

| Method | Dev $F_1$ | Test $F_1$ |
|---|---|---|
| $N = 100$ | | |
| Truncation | $36.53 \pm 2.09$ | $35.39 \pm 0.71$ |
| Chunking (ours) | $\mathbf{45.20} \pm 1.60$ | $\mathbf{44.31} \pm 1.47$ |
| $N = 305$ | | |
| Truncation | $53.65 \pm 0.63$ | $51.30 \pm 0.62$ |
| Chunking (ours) | $\mathbf{58.23} \pm 0.40$ | $\mathbf{57.05} \pm 0.23$ |
| $N = 587$ | | |
| Truncation | $61.34 \pm 0.52$ | $59.17 \pm 1.86$ |
| Chunking (ours) | $\mathbf{66.81} \pm 0.56$ | $\mathbf{66.53} \pm 0.52$ |

Table 6: Performance comparison of long document processing methods. The model is fixed with $\text{BERT}_{\text{BASE}}$ + PRiSM evaluating on the DWIE dataset.

### A.4 Relation Descriptions

We provide a small set of relations and their descriptions in DocRED and DWIE in Table 7 and 8. For DocRED, a full list can be found either in their paper (Yao et al., 2019) or link[2]. For DWIE,

[2]https://www.wikidata.org/wiki/Wikidata:Main_Page

a full list is not available publicly; however, we were able to obtain a draft of the annotation documentation from the author. Unannotated relation descriptions were crafted with the help of a large language model (OpenAI, 2023).

| Relation Name | Description |
|---|---|
| head of government | head of the executive power of this town, city, municipality, state, country, or other governmental body |
| country | sovereign state of this item; don't use on humans |
| place of birth | most specific known (e.g. city instead of country, or hospital instead of city) birth location of a person, animal or fictional character |
| country of citizenship | the object is a country that recognizes the subject as its citizen |
| member of sports team | sports teams or clubs that the subject currently represents or formerly represented |

Table 7: DocRED relation descriptions.

| Relation Name | Description |
|---|---|
| based_in0 | Relations between organizations and the countries they are based in |
| in0 | Relations between geographic locations and the countries they are located in |
| citizen_of | Relations between people and the country they are citizens of |
| based_in0-x | Relations between organizations and the nominal variations of the countries they are based in |
| citizen_of-x | Relations between people and the nominal variations of the countries they are citizens of |

Table 8: DWIE relation descriptions.

# B Additional Details for PRiSM

## B.1 Detailed Experimental Setup

**Device.** For all our experiments, we trained the networks on a single NVIDIA TITAN RTX GPU with 24GB of memory.

**Model Size.** PRiSM shares parameters with the PLM used when learning relation representations. The only additional parameter weights come from a linear layer constructing pair representations and an extra embedding space initialized for relation tokens. The number of trainable parameters for each model is illustrated in Table 9.

| Model | # Parameters |
|---|---|
| $\text{BERT}_{\text{BASE}}$ | 108,310,272 |
| $\text{BERT}_{\text{BASE}}$-DocRE | 114,259,297 |
| $\text{BERT}_{\text{BASE}}$-DocRE + **PRiSM** | 115,514,209 |
| $\text{RoBERTa}_{\text{BASE}}$ | 124,645,632 |
| $\text{RoBERTa}_{\text{BASE}}$-DocRE | 130,594,657 |
| $\text{RoBERTa}_{\text{BASE}}$-DocRE + **PRiSM** | 131,849,569 |

Table 9: Comparison of model parameters. **DocRE** includes a bilinear layer and two linear layers for constructing head and tail representations.

**GPU Hours.** Adding PRiSM takes a slightly longer computation time than the existing DocRE models due to having to pass the PLM twice. Note that PRiSM is built for a low-resource setting in which the computation time does not seem to differ as much. The comparison of GPU hours is reported in Table 10.

| Model | Training Hours |
|---|---|
| *3% training examples* | |
| $\text{BERT}_{\text{BASE}}$ | 0.8 |
| $\text{BERT}_{\text{BASE}}$ + **PRiSM** | 0.8 |
| *10% training examples* | |
| $\text{BERT}_{\text{BASE}}$ | 0.8 |
| $\text{BERT}_{\text{BASE}}$ + **PRiSM** | 1.0 |
| *100% training examples* | |
| $\text{BERT}_{\text{BASE}}$ | 2.7 |
| $\text{BERT}_{\text{BASE}}$ + **PRiSM** | 3.5 |

Table 10: GPU hours for DocRED training. Time for evaluating and saving the model every epoch is included.

**Hyperparameters.** We perform a grid search on finding the best hyperparameter configuration and report the tuning range used for our experiments in Table 11. The evaluation on the validation set is performed for every epoch and the tolerance increases by 1 when the validation $F_1$ is worse than the previous evaluation. The training stops early when the count reaches the max tolerance.

| Model | Dataset | Hyperparameter | Range | Best |
|---|---|---|---|---|
| $\text{BERT}_{\text{BASE}}$, $\text{RoBERTa}_{\text{BASE}}$ | (Re-)DocRED | batch size | { 4, 8 } | 4 |
| | | learning rate | { 1e-5, 2e-5, 3e-5, 4e-5, 5e-5, 1e-4 } | 3e-5 |
| | | warmup ratio | { 0, 0.06, 0.1 } | 0.06 |
| | | $\lambda$ | { 1, 5, 10, 100 } | 10 |
| | | max grad norm | { 1.0 } | 1.0 |
| | | max tolerance | { 5 } | 5 |
| | | epoch | { 30 } | 30 |
| $\text{BERT}_{\text{BASE}}$, $\text{RoBERTa}_{\text{BASE}}$ | DWIE | batch size | { 4, 8 } | 4 |
| | | learning rate | { 1e-5, 2e-5, 3e-5, 4e-5, 5e-5, 1e-4 } | 5e-5 |
| | | warmup ratio | { 0, 0.06, 0.1 } | 0.06 |
| | | $\lambda$ | { 1, 5, 10, 100 } | 10 |
| | | max grad norm | { 1.0 } | 1.0 |
| | | max tolerance | { 5 } | 5 |
| | | epoch | { 30 } | 30 |

Table 11: Hyperparameter tuning range and best values used in the experiments.

## B.2 Evaluation Details

We elaborate on the details of calculating calibration errors. We utilize two metrics in our paper. ECE (Naeini et al., 2015) divides the probability interval into a fixed number of bins, calculates the difference between the accuracy of the predictions and the mean of the probabilities (confidence) in each bin, and computes a weighted average over

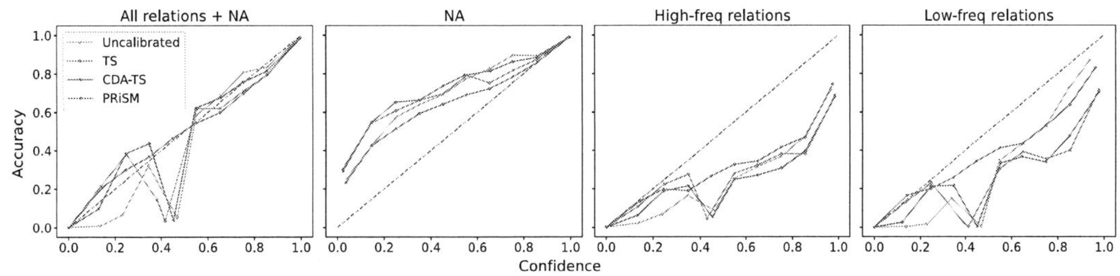


Figure 5: Reliability diagram for $\text{BERT}_{\text{BASE}}$ when trained with 10% of DocRED data.

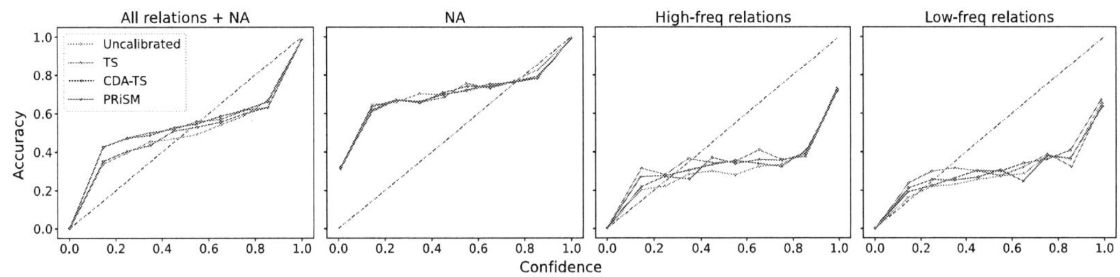


Figure 6: Reliability diagram for $\text{BERT}_{\text{BASE}}$ when trained with 100% of DocRED data.

the bins. Formally, the equation can be written as

$$\text{ECE} = \sum_{b=1}^{B} \frac{n_b}{T} |\text{acc}(b) - \text{conf}(b)|, \tag{5}$$

where $n_b$ is the number of predictions in bin $b$, $B$ is a hyperparameter for the total number of bins, and $T$ is the total number of samples. On the other hand, ACE (Nixon et al., 2019) divides up the probability interval by having the same number of predictions in each bin, thereby mitigating the issue of only calibrating the most confident samples. The equation is written as

$$\text{ACE} = \frac{1}{KR} \sum_{k=1}^{K} \sum_{r=1}^{R} |\text{acc}(r,k) - \text{conf}(r,k)|, \tag{6}$$

where $\text{acc}(r,k)$ and $\text{conf}(r,k)$ are the accuracy and confidence of adaptive calibration range $r$ for class label $k$, respectively.

### B.3 Additional Calibration Results

We visualize the calibration of the rest of the data setting (i.e., 10% and 100% training data) with reliability diagrams in Figure 5 and 6. We notice that PRiSM is still effective with 10% of training data, but with full data, the performance gain is minimal; that is, the line barely moves toward the perfect calibration line.

We understand that calibration results on models other than the $\text{BERT}_{\text{BASE}}$ may be important

| | $N=100$ | | | $N=305$ | | |
|---|---|---|---|---|---|---|
| **Method** | $F_1(\uparrow)$ | **ECE(↓)** | **ACE(↓)** | $F_1(\uparrow)$ | **ECE(↓)** | **ACE(↓)** |
| *DocRED results* | | | | | | |
| BERT | 10.82 | 0.359% | 0.379% | 42.56 | 0.137% | 0.164% |
| BERT + **PRiSM** | **37.84** | **0.010%** | **0.020%** | **48.10** | **0.023%** | **0.020%** |
| RoBERTa | 22.55 | 0.671% | 0.691% | 45.83 | 0.237% | 0.259% |
| RoBERTa + **PRiSM** | **35.10** | **0.015%** | **0.025%** | **48.70** | **0.022%** | **0.020%** |
| SSAN-BERT | 11.93 | 0.368% | 0.390% | 42.82 | 0.128% | 0.152% |
| SSAN-BERT + **PRiSM** | **36.96** | **0.019%** | **0.019%** | **48.28** | **0.023%** | **0.023%** |
| *Re-DocRED results* | | | | | | |
| BERT | 32.75 | 0.367% | 0.407% | 54.44 | 0.185% | 0.190% |
| BERT + **PRiSM** | **49.90** | **0.038%** | **0.048%** | **60.17** | **0.056%** | **0.036%** |
| RoBERTa | 42.40 | 0.722% | 0.718% | 57.61 | 0.191% | 0.208% |
| RoBERTa + **PRiSM** | **50.34** | **0.055%** | **0.051%** | **61.55** | **0.047%** | **0.033%** |
| SSAN-BERT | 30.28 | 0.362% | 0.407% | 55.60 | 0.125% | 0.148% |
| SSAN-BERT + **PRiSM** | **49.04** | **0.050%** | **0.053%** | **60.57** | **0.051%** | **0.036%** |

Table 12: Comparison of calibration errors (with 10 bins) of different models under a low-resource setting of DocRED and Re-DocRED.

in demonstrating the effectiveness of PRiSM. As shown in Table 12, we find that $\text{RoBERTa}_{\text{BASE}}$ and $\text{SSAN-BERT}_{\text{BASE}}$ follow the same trend as $\text{BERT}_{\text{BASE}}$, showing the lowest calibration error when PRiSM is appended. We also observe a similar pattern with the Re-DocRED data. We do not report results for ATLOP because the calibration errors for ATLOP must be computed differently, as it does not use probabilities (confidence) for prediction.

# Improving Query-Focused Meeting Summarization with Query-Relevant Knowledge

**Tiezheng Yu , Ziwei Ji, Pascale Fung**
Center for Artificial Intelligence Research (CAiRE)
Department of Electronic and Computer Engineering
The Hong Kong University of Science and Technology, Clear Water Bay, Hong Kong
{tyuah,zjiad}@connect.ust.hk, pascale@ece.ust.hk

## Abstract

Query-Focused Meeting Summarization (QFMS) aims to generate a summary of a given meeting transcript conditioned upon a query. The main challenges for QFMS are the long input text length and sparse query-relevant information in the meeting transcript. In this paper, we propose a knowledge-enhanced two-stage framework called Knowledge-Aware Summarizer (KAS) to tackle the challenges. In the first stage, we introduce knowledge-aware scores to improve the query-relevant segment extraction. In the second stage, we incorporate query-relevant knowledge in the summary generation. Experimental results on the QMSum dataset show that our approach achieves state-of-the-art performance. Further analysis proves the competency of our methods in generating relevant and faithful summaries.[1]

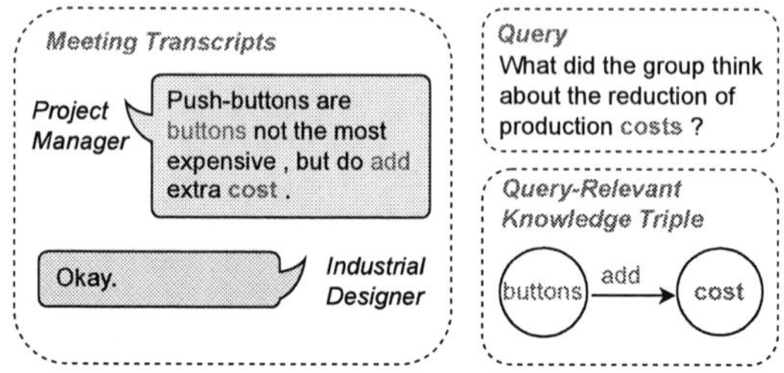


Figure 1: An example of query-relevant knowledge triple extracted from meeting transcripts. The knowledge triple can be used in query-relevant segment extraction as well as summary generation.

## 1 Introduction

Meetings are an essential part of human collaboration and communication. Especially in recent years, the outbreak of Covid-19 has led people to meet online, where most meetings are automatically recorded and transcribed. Query-Focused Meeting Summarization (QFMS) (Zhong et al., 2021) aims to summarize the given meeting transcript conditioned upon a query, which helps people efficiently catch up to the specific part of the meeting they want to know.

There are two main challenges for QFMS: Firstly, meeting transcripts can be so long that current deep learning models cannot encode them at once. Even for models (Beltagy et al., 2020; Xiong et al., 2022) that accept long text input, the cost of computational complexity is enormous. Secondly, query-relevant content is sparsely scattered in the meeting transcripts, meaning a significant part of the transcripts is noisy information when given a particular query. Therefore, the models need to reduce the noisy information's impact effectively.

In this paper, we focus on the two-stage framework, extracting query-relevant segments from the meeting transcripts and then generating the summary based on the selected content. Compared to the end-to-end approaches (Zhu et al., 2020; Pagnoni et al., 2022) that directly encode the entire meeting transcripts, the two-stage framework is better at keeping computational efficiency and easier to scale up to longer inputs. Specifically, we propose Knowledge-Aware Summarizer (KAS) that incorporates query-relevant knowledge in both stages. In the first stage, we extract knowledge triples from the text segments and introduce knowledge-aware scores to improve segment ranking. In the second stage, the extracted query-relevant knowledge triples are utilized as extra input for the summary generation. We conduct experiments on a QFMS dataset named QMSum (Zhong et al., 2021) and achieve state-of-the-art performance. We further investigate how the different numbers of extracted segments affect the final performance. In addition, we manually evaluate the generation quality regarding fluency, relevance and factual correctness.

Our contributions in this work are threefold: (1) Our work demonstrates the effectiveness of leveraging query-relevant knowledge in QFMS. (2) We

[1]The code is released at: https://github.com/TysonYu/KA-QFMS



*Findings of the Association for Computational Linguistics: IJCNLP-AACL 2023*, pages 48–54
November 1–4, 2023. ©2023 Asian Federation of Natural Language Processing

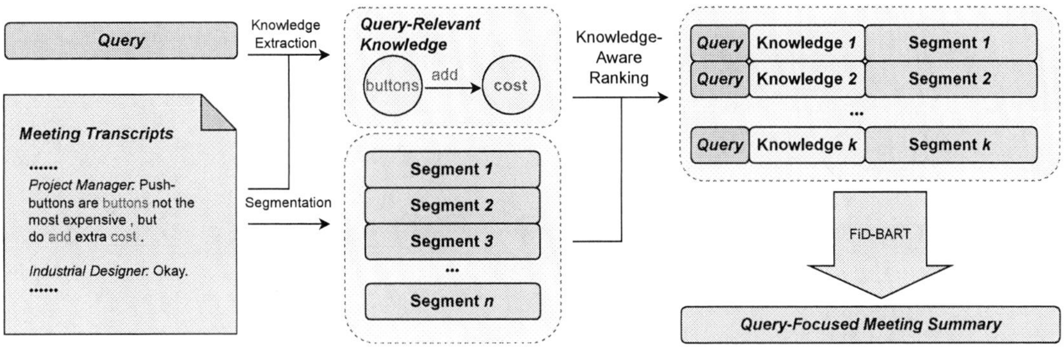


Figure 2: An overview of our proposed framework. We first extract query-relevant knowledge triples based on the query and meeting transcripts and select top-$k$ segments through knowledge-aware ranking. Then we generate the query-focused meeting summary by FiD-BART from query, knowledge and selected meeting transcripts.

propose KAS, a two-stage framework incorporating query-relevant knowledge for QFMS. (3) Experimental results show that our approach achieves state-of-the-art performance on a QFMS dataset (QMSum). Further analysis and human evaluation indicate the advantage of our method.

## 2 Related Works

Existing QFMS methods can be divided into two categories (Vig et al., 2022): two-stage approaches and end-to-end approaches. Two-stage approaches (Zhong et al., 2021; Vig et al., 2022; Zhang et al., 2022) first extract query-relevant snippets and then generate the summary upon the extracted snippets, while end-to-end approaches (Zhu et al., 2020; Zhong et al., 2022; Pagnoni et al., 2022) directly generate summaries from the whole meeting transcripts. However, both types of methods have their disadvantages. For example, most of the two-stage approaches select query-relevant content based on utterance, which ignores the contextual information between multiple utterances. As for the end-to-end approaches, the computational and memory requirements will increase rapidly when the input text becomes longer, making models challenging to adapt to long meeting transcripts. To our knowledge, we are the first to incorporate query-relevant knowledge in QFMS and demonstrate its effectiveness. Besides, we include multiple utterances in each segment to preserve the contextual information, and our approach can easily extend to process long input text.

## 3 Methodology

This section presents our two-stage framework. Firstly, we introduce the extractor, which extracts query-relevant segments and knowledge from the source document. Then, a generative model synthesizes the query, extracted segments, and knowledge into the final summary.

### 3.1 Knowledge-aware Extractor

**Meeting Transcripts Segmentation** To preserve the contextual information between utterances, we split the meeting transcripts into segments, and each segment could contain multiple utterances. To do so, given an input meeting transcripts $T$, we will separate it into $n$ segments $S = \{S_1, S_2, ..., S_n\}$ where each $S_i$ is fewer than $l$ tokens. Specifically, we feed meeting transcripts to the segment utterance by utterance until it reaches $l$.

**Knowledge-aware Ranking** The knowledge-aware ranking approach will select top-$k$ segments according to a combination of semantic search scores and knowledge-aware scores. We apply Multi-QA MPNet (Song et al., 2020) to calculate semantic search scores. Multi-QA MPNet is trained on 215M question-answer pairs from various sources and domains, including Stack Exchange, MS MARCO (Nguyen et al., 2016), WikiAnswers (Fader et al., 2014) and many more. Given the query and the segments, the model outputs 768-dimension vectors to represent them. The semantic search score for each segment is computed according to the cosine similarity:

$$Score_{se} = \frac{MPNet(Q) \cdot MPNet(S_i)}{\|MPNet(Q)\| \, \|MPNet(S_i)\|} \quad (1)$$

To compute the knowledge-aware score for each segment, we first use OpenIE (Angeli et al., 2015) to extractive knowledge triples. Then, to filter out

| Model | ROUGE-1 | ROUGE-2 | ROUGE-L | Average |
|---|---|---|---|---|
| *Two-stage* | | | | |
| MaRGE (Xu and Lapata, 2021) | 31.99 | 8.97 | 27.93 | 22.96 |
| DYLE (Mao et al., 2022) | 34.42 | 9.71 | 30.10 | 24.74 |
| SUMM$^N$ (Zhang et al., 2022) | 34.03 | 9.28 | 29.48 | 24.26 |
| RelReg (Vig et al., 2022) | 34.91 | 11.91 | 30.73 | 25.85 |
| RelReg-W (Vig et al., 2022) | 36.45 | 12.81 | 32.28 | 27.18 |
| *End-to-end* | | | | |
| LED (Beltagy et al., 2020) | 31.60 | 7.80 | 20.50 | 19.97 |
| DialogLM (Zhong et al., 2022) | 34.50 | 9.92 | 30.27 | 24.90 |
| SegEnc-W (Vig et al., 2022) | 37.80 | 13.43 | 33.38 | 28.20 |
| BART-LS (Xiong et al., 2022) | 37.90 | 12.10 | 33.10 | 27.70 |
| SOCRATIC (Pagnoni et al., 2022) | 38.06 | 13.74 | 33.51 | 28.44 |
| KAS (Ours) | **38.80** | **14.01** | **34.26** | **29.02** |

Table 1: Results on QMSum test set. The previous works can be divided into two-stage and end-to-end approaches.

the triples irrelevant to the query, we only keep the triples that contain overlapping words with the query. The knowledge-aware score is obtained by L2 normalizing the number of the remaining triples $m_i$ in each segment:

$$Score_{ka} = \frac{m_i}{\sqrt{\sum_{i=1}^{n} |m_i|^2}} \tag{2}$$

Finally, we calculate the ranking score by summing the semantic search score and the knowledge-aware score:

$$Score_{rank} = Score_{se} + Score_{ka} \tag{3}$$

The segment with the top-$k$ ranking score will be selected for the next stage of summary generation. We denote the remaining segments as $S = \{S_1, S_2, ..., S_k\}$.

### 3.2 Generator

We choose BART-large (Lewis et al., 2020), a transformer-based (Vaswani et al., 2017) generative pre-trained language model, as our backbone model for the generator because of its remarkable performance on text summarization benchmarks. Following the idea of Fusion-in-Decoder (FiD) and its applications in generation tasks (Izacard and Grave, 2021; Su et al., 2022; Vig et al., 2022), we employ FiD-BART for encoding multiple segments independently in the encoder and fuse information from all segments in the decoder jointly through the encoder-decoder attention.

To incorporate the extracted knowledge in the summary generation, we use the knowledge as extra inputs other than the query and segments. In detail, we remove the stop words in the knowledge triples and then merge all the remaining words of knowledge triples in each segment as a set of knowledge phrases. The concatenation of each segment $S_i$, knowledge phrases $K_i$ and the query $Q$ will be processed by FiD-BART encoder:

$$h_{enc}^{i} = Encoder(Q \oplus K_i \oplus S_i) \tag{4}$$

Finally, the decoder performs encoder-decoder attention over the concatenation of all segments' encoder outputs. In this way, the computational complexity grows linearly with the number of segments rather than quadratically, while jointly processing all segments in the decoder enables the model to aggregate information from multiple segments.

## 4 Experiments

### 4.1 Experimental Setup

We choose the top 12 text segments in the segment selection, with each fewer than 512 tokens. For the summary generator, inspired by the effectiveness of pre-finetuning models on relevant datasets to transfer task-related knowledge in the abstractive summarization (Yu et al., 2021; Vig et al., 2022), we initialize our BART-large model using the checkpoint [2] pre-finetuned on WikiSum (Liu et al., 2018).

[2] https://github.com/salesforce/query-focused-sum

| model | ROUGE-1 | ROUGE-2 | ROUGE-L |
|---|---|---|---|
| KAS ($k$=4) | 36.46 | 12.06 | 31.75 |
| KAS ($k$=8) | 37.86 | 13.75 | 33.30 |
| KAS ($k$=12) | **38.80** | **14.01** | **34.26** |

Table 2: Results Our KAS on the QMSum test set with differen number of $k$. $k$ denotes the number of segments that are selected in the first stage.

| model | R-1 | R-2 | R-L | Entity F-1 |
|---|---|---|---|---|
| KAS | **38.80** | **14.01** | **34.26** | **35.59** |
| w/o KA in ranking | 37.71 | 12.96 | 32.94 | 34.03 |
| w/o KA in generator | 37.52 | 13.57 | 33.29 | 35.06 |

Table 3: Ablation results on the QMSum test set without knowledge-Aware (KA). Our KA modules improve the performance of KAS on both stages.

See Appendix A and B for more details of the experimental setup and baselines.

We evaluate the models on the QMSum (Zhong et al., 2021) dataset, which consists of 1,808 query-summary pairs over 232 meetings from product design, academic, and political committee domains. We report ROUGE [3] (Lin, 2004) as the automatic evaluation results.

### 4.2 Main Results

We compare our proposed model with strong baselines and previous state-of-the-art models. As shown in Table 1, our approach outperforms both the two-stage and end-to-end methods by a large margin on all evaluation metrics. We also investigate how the number of selected segments in the first stage affects the final performance. As shown in Table 2, when the number of selected segments grows, the quality of the final summary also improves. Previous end-to-end approaches usually outperform two-stage approaches because they encode the entire meeting transcripts, which conduct lots of computing resources. Our approach performs better by encoding 12 segments of input (6,144 tokens) in the second stage generation than the state-of-the-art end-to-end approach that directly encodes 16384 tokens. Therefore, we strike a balance between performance and efficiency, which is essential in real-world applications. Besides, our approach can easily extend to processing long input text since the ranking method is unsupervised.

[3] https://github.com/pltrdy/files2rouge

| model | Fluency | Relevance | Factual Correctness |
|---|---|---|---|
| SegEnc-W | 4.68 | 4.60 | 3.76 |
| KAS | 4.79 | 4.68 | 4.47 |
| Ground truth | **4.92** | **4.82** | **4.60** |

Table 4: Human evaluation results on QMSum test set.

### 4.3 Ablation Study

We conduct an ablation study to investigate the contribution of the knowledge-aware modules by removing the knowledge-based scoring in the ranking (w/o KA in ranking) and the knowledge input in the summary generation (w/o KA in generator), respectively. Besides, we evaluate the entity-level factual consistency (Nan et al., 2021) of the summary to test the effectiveness of our knowledge-aware modules in keeping the knowledge entities in generated summaries. Specifically, we report the F-1 scores of the entity overlap (Entity F-1) between the source and the generated summary. Table 3 presents that the model's performance decreases in both metrics, especially the Entity F-1, without the knowledge-aware module, which indicates the effectiveness of our method.

### 4.4 Human Evaluation

We further conduct a human evaluation to assess the models on fluency, relevance, and factual correctness. We randomly select 50 samples from the QMSum test set and ask three annotators to score the summary from one to five, with higher scores being better. We compare SegEnc-W because it is the best publicly available model. Table 4 illustrates our approach slightly outperforms SegEnc-W according to fluency and relevance and achieves a significantly better score than SegEnc-W on factual correctness with p-value$<$0.05. Since SegEnc-W and our methods both use BART based generators, it is in line with our expectation that we reach similar fluency and relevance scores. Meanwhile, our proposed query-relevant knowledge can help reduce hallucination and generate more factual correctness summaries. More details of the human evaluation setup are in Appendix C.

## 5 Conclusion

In this paper, we propose a two-stage framework named KAS that incorporates query-relevant knowledge in both stages. Extensive experimental results on the QMSum dataset show the effectiveness of our method. We further conduct detailed analysis and human evaluation to prove our method's capacity to generate fluency, relevant and faithful summaries.

## 6 Limitations

Our method is trained and tested on the only publicly available QFMS dataset named QMSum. QMSum consists of three different domains (Academic, Committee and Product), which makes the evaluation robust. However, QMSum only contains 1,808 samples, which is relatively small. We hope larger QFMS datasets be proposed to accelerate the development of this field.

In the first stage of our approach, we extract a fixed length (6,144 tokens) of the meeting transcripts as the second stage input text. Therefore, the model's performance could be affected since some query-relevant information could be cut off in the first stage.

## 7 Ethics Statement

Although our approach can generate query-focused meeting summaries and achieve a much better factual correctness score than other models, we can not avoid generating hallucinated content from the generative models. We recommend that when our approach is deployed in real-world applications, additional post-processing should be carried out to remove unreliable summaries. In addition, we will indicate that the summary we provide is for reference only, and users need to check the original meeting transcripts to get accurate information.

## References


Gabor Angeli, Melvin Jose Johnson Premkumar, and Christopher D Manning. 2015. Leveraging linguistic structure for open domain information extraction. In *Proceedings of the 53rd Annual Meeting of the Association for Computational Linguistics and the 7th International Joint Conference on Natural Language Processing (Volume 1: Long Papers)*, pages 344–354.

Iz Beltagy, Matthew E Peters, and Arman Cohan. 2020. Longformer: The long-document transformer. *arXiv preprint arXiv:2004.05150*.

Anthony Fader, Luke Zettlemoyer, and Oren Etzioni. 2014. Open question answering over curated and extracted knowledge bases. In *Proceedings of the 20th ACM SIGKDD international conference on Knowledge discovery and data mining*, pages 1156–1165.

Gautier Izacard and Édouard Grave. 2021. Leveraging passage retrieval with generative models for open domain question answering. In *Proceedings of the 16th Conference of the European Chapter of the Association for Computational Linguistics: Main Volume*, pages 874–880.

Diederik P Kingma and Jimmy Ba. 2014. Adam: A method for stochastic optimization. *arXiv preprint arXiv:1412.6980*.

Mike Lewis, Yinhan Liu, Naman Goyal, Marjan Ghazvininejad, Abdelrahman Mohamed, Omer Levy, Veselin Stoyanov, and Luke Zettlemoyer. 2020. Bart: Denoising sequence-to-sequence pre-training for natural language generation, translation, and comprehension. In *Proceedings of the 58th Annual Meeting of the Association for Computational Linguistics*, pages 7871–7880.

Chin-Yew Lin. 2004. Rouge: A package for automatic evaluation of summaries. In *Text summarization branches out*, pages 74–81.

Peter J Liu, Mohammad Saleh, Etienne Pot, Ben Goodrich, Ryan Sepassi, Lukasz Kaiser, and Noam Shazeer. 2018. Generating wikipedia by summarizing long sequences. *arXiv preprint arXiv:1801.10198*.

Ziming Mao, Chen Henry Wu, Ansong Ni, Yusen Zhang, Rui Zhang, Tao Yu, Budhaditya Deb, Chenguang Zhu, Ahmed Awadallah, and Dragomir Radev. 2022. Dyle: Dynamic latent extraction for abstractive long-input summarization. In *Proceedings of the 60th Annual Meeting of the Association for Computational Linguistics (Volume 1: Long Papers)*, pages 1687–1698.

Feng Nan, Ramesh Nallapati, Zhiguo Wang, Cicero dos Santos, Henghui Zhu, Dejiao Zhang, Kathleen Mckeown, and Bing Xiang. 2021. Entity-level factual consistency of abstractive text summarization. In *Proceedings of the 16th Conference of the European Chapter of the Association for Computational Linguistics: Main Volume*, pages 2727–2733.

Tri Nguyen, Mir Rosenberg, Xia Song, Jianfeng Gao, Saurabh Tiwary, Rangan Majumder, and Li Deng. 2016. Ms marco: A human generated machine reading comprehension dataset. *choice*, 2640:660.

Artidoro Pagnoni, Alexander R Fabbri, Wojciech Kryściński, and Chien-Sheng Wu. 2022. Socratic pretraining: Question-driven pretraining for controllable summarization. *arXiv preprint arXiv:2212.10449*.

Kaitao Song, Xu Tan, Tao Qin, Jianfeng Lu, and Tie-Yan Liu. 2020. Mpnet: Masked and permuted pre-training for language understanding. *Advances in Neural Information Processing Systems*, 33:16857–16867.

Dan Su, Xiaoguang Li, Jindi Zhang, Lifeng Shang, Xin Jiang, Qun Liu, and Pascale Fung. 2022. Read before generate! faithful long form question answering with machine reading. In *Findings of the Association for Computational Linguistics: ACL 2022*, pages 744–756.

Ashish Vaswani, Noam Shazeer, Niki Parmar, Jakob Uszkoreit, Llion Jones, Aidan N Gomez, Łukasz Kaiser, and Illia Polosukhin. 2017. Attention is all you need. *Advances in neural information processing systems*, 30.

Jesse Vig, Alexander Richard Fabbri, Wojciech Kryściński, Chien-Sheng Wu, and Wenhao Liu. 2022. Exploring neural models for query-focused summarization. In *Findings of the Association for Computational Linguistics: NAACL 2022*, pages 1455–1468.

Wenhan Xiong, Anchit Gupta, Shubham Toshniwal, Yashar Mehdad, and Wen-tau Yih. 2022. Adapting pretrained text-to-text models for long text sequences. *arXiv preprint arXiv:2209.10052*.

Yumo Xu and Mirella Lapata. 2021. Generating query focused summaries from query-free resources. In *Proceedings of the 59th Annual Meeting of the Association for Computational Linguistics and the 11th International Joint Conference on Natural Language Processing (Volume 1: Long Papers)*, pages 6096–6109.

Tiezheng Yu, Zihan Liu, and Pascale Fung. 2021. Adaptsum: Towards low-resource domain adaptation for abstractive summarization. In *Proceedings of the 2021 Conference of the North American Chapter of the Association for Computational Linguistics: Human Language Technologies*, pages 5892–5904.

Yusen Zhang, Ansong Ni, Ziming Mao, Chen Henry Wu, Chenguang Zhu, Budhaditya Deb, Ahmed Awadallah, Dragomir Radev, and Rui Zhang. 2022. Summn: A multi-stage summarization framework for long input dialogues and documents: A multi-stage summarization framework for long input dialogues and documents. In *Proceedings of the 60th Annual Meeting of the Association for Computational Linguistics (Volume 1: Long Papers)*, pages 1592–1604.

Ming Zhong, Yang Liu, Yichong Xu, Chenguang Zhu, and Michael Zeng. 2022. Dialoglm: Pre-trained model for long dialogue understanding and summarization. In *Proceedings of the AAAI Conference on Artificial Intelligence*, volume 36, pages 11765–11773.

Ming Zhong, Da Yin, Tao Yu, Ahmad Zaidi, Mutethia Mutuma, Rahul Jha, Ahmed Hassan, Asli Celikyilmaz, Yang Liu, Xipeng Qiu, et al. 2021. Qmsum: A new benchmark for query-based multi-domain meeting summarization. In *Proceedings of the 2021 Conference of the North American Chapter of the Association for Computational Linguistics: Human Language Technologies*, pages 5905–5921.

Chenguang Zhu, Ruochen Xu, Michael Zeng, and Xuedong Huang. 2020. A hierarchical network for abstractive meeting summarization with cross-domain pretraining. In *Findings of the Association for Computational Linguistics: EMNLP 2020*, pages 194–203.

## A Experimental Details

We use the off-the-shelf model Multi-QA MPNet [4] for semantic searching. We initialize the generator from the off-the-shelf BART-large model through Hugging Face. We use learning rates $6e^{-5}$ following (Lewis et al., 2020) and Adam optimizer (Kingma and Ba, 2014) to fine-tune KAS. We use a batch size of one and train all models on one RTX 3090 for ten epochs. During decoding, we use beam search with a beam size of five and decode until an end-of-sequence token is emitted. The final results are the average test set performance on the best three checkpoints in the validation set. In addition, the QMSum dataset has MIT License, so we can freely use it.

## B Baselines Details

We conduct both two-stage and end-to-end baselines for comparison. MaRGE (Xu and Lapata, 2021) used **Ma**sked **ROUGE** extractor in the first stage. DYLE (Mao et al., 2022) is a dynamic latent extraction approach for abstractive long-input summarization. SUMM$^N$ (Zhang et al., 2022) is a multi-stage summarization framework for long input dialogues and documents. RelReg (RELevance REGression) (Vig et al., 2022) is similar to MaRGE, which trains a relevance prediction model directly on QFS data using the original, non-masked query. RelReg-W (Vig et al., 2022) uses the same framework as RelReg but initializes the generator from the WikiSum pre-trained checkpoint. LED (Beltagy et al., 2020) is an encoder-decoder transformer-based model that employs efficient attention to process long input text. DialogLM (Zhong et al., 2022) is a pre-trained neural encoder-decoder model for long dialogue understanding and summarization, and it uses a hybrid attention approach by combining sparse local attention with dense global attention. SegEnc-W (Vig et al., 2022) is a fusion-in-decoder method that initialized the model from WikiSum (Liu et al., 2018). BART-LS (Xiong et al., 2022) used pooling-augmented blockwise attention to improve the efficiency and pre-trains the model with a masked-span prediction task with spans of varying lengths. SOCRATIC (Pagnoni et al., 2022) uses a question-driven, unsupervised pretraining objective to improve controllability in summarization tasks, and it

[4]https://huggingface.co/sentence-transformers/multi-qa-mpnet-base-cos-v1

follows the SegEnc framework.

## C Human Evaluation

In Table 4, we conduct a human evaluation of the fluency, relevancy and factual correctness of the generated summaries from the QMSum dataset. In detail, we randomly sample 50 summaries from KAS, SegEnc-W and the ground truth summary from the same meeting transcripts for comparison. Assessments are scored on a scale of one to five, with higher scores being better. Fluency means the summary is grammatically correct and contextually coherent. Relevancy means the summary is relevant to the query. Factual correctness means the summary is faithful according to the information given in the meeting transcripts and does not contain hallucinations. We assign each summary to three annotators and take the average score as the final result. In total, we used three annotators from Hong Kong, and all annotators voluntarily participated in the human evaluation. All annotators agree to have their evaluation results included as part of this paper's results.

# Learning to Diversify Neural Text Generation via *De*generative Model

**Jimin Hong**[*] **ChaeHun Park**[*] **Jaegul Choo**
KAIST AI
{jimmy.h, ddehun, jchoo}@kaist.ac.kr

## Abstract

Neural language models often fail to generate diverse and informative texts, limiting their applicability in real-world problems. While previous approaches have proposed to address these issues by identifying and penalizing undesirable behaviors (e.g., repetition, overuse of frequent words) from language models, we propose an alternative approach based on an observation: models primarily learn attributes within examples that are likely to cause *degeneration* problems. Based on this observation, we propose a new approach to prevent degeneration problems by training two models. Specifically, we first train a model that is designed to amplify undesirable patterns. We then enhance the diversity of the second model by focusing on patterns that the first model fails to learn. Extensive experiments on two tasks, namely language modeling and dialogue generation, demonstrate the effectiveness of our approach.

## 1 Introduction

Neural text generation is a fundamental task including open-ended applications such as language modeling or dialogue generation (Chen et al., 2017). Despite considerable advances in the task, generation models often result in *degeneration* (Li et al., 2016; Dinan et al., 2019; Holtzman et al., 2019) such as repetition or the overproduction of dull and generic texts with lack of diversity.

Previous studies have proposed to overcome these issues as follows: Welleck et al. (2020) suggests to explicitly penalize repetition using unlikelihood objective. Li et al. (2020) applies unlikelihood training (Welleck et al., 2020) to dialogue domain by penalizing overuse of common words in generated responses. Jiang et al. (2019) and Choi et al. (2020) refine the Maximum Likelihood Estimation (MLE) objective by considering the frequency distribution of words. In other words, prior works focus on explicitly defining undesirable behaviors and penalizing them in a training phase. Although these studies have shown promising results, we argue that identifying such negative behaviors of models can be laborious and task-dependent.

Instead, we propose a novel approach that does not require explicitly specifying the negative behaviors of generation models. Our approach is based on a fundamental observation (§3): Models are misguided by attributes within training examples that may be harmful to reflecting human diversity. Based on the observation, we propose LFD: **L**earning **f**rom **D**egeneration, a novel approach to remedy degeneration problems in open-ended applications. Specifically, we first train a model which is designed to *De*generate by amplifying undesirable patterns in examples (§4.2). We then train the second model to enhance its diversity by leveraging the predictions of the first model (§4.3). Experimental results on two representative open-ended generation tasks demonstrate the effectiveness of our approach.

In summary, our contributions include:

- We analyze how the learning dynamics of training examples are affected based on the degree of their diversity on open-ended text generation tasks.
- We propose a novel approach that enhances the overall generation quality, especially diversity.
- LFD can be easily applied regardless of tasks in open-ended applications.

## 2 Related Work

Recent studies have reported that neural generation models often make various forms of degeneration problems (Li et al., 2016; Holtzman et al., 2018; Dinan et al., 2020). Several methods have suggested training objectives to remedy this problem by alleviating token distribution mismatch between hu-

[*] Equal contribution



*Findings of the Association for Computational Linguistics: IJCNLP-AACL 2023*, pages 55–64
November 1–4, 2023. 

man and machine-written texts (Jiang et al., 2019), balancing token distribution (Choi et al., 2020), or directly penalizing negative behaviors on generated texts with auxiliary loss (Welleck et al., 2020; He and Glass, 2020). Wang et al. (2021) address over-confidence issues in text generation by adaptive label smoothing. Li et al. (2022) leverages a task-specific data filtering process Csáky et al. (2020) to build negative teacher for dialogue generation. Such studies are orthogonal to LFD since we mainly focus on training dynamics of examples that are available regardless of tasks.

## 3 Preliminary Study

Previous studies have reported that the generation quality is likely to be degraded due to inherent attributes within the training examples, such as token repetition (Welleck et al., 2020; Fu et al., 2021), a skewed frequency distribution of words (Fagan and Gençay, 2011), and genericness in responses (Csáky et al., 2020). We refer to such attributes as *degenerative attributes* in the paper. In this section, we analyze how such *degenerative attributes* affect the learning dynamics of training examples. We conduct experiments on two open-ended text generation tasks: language modeling and dialogue generation.

### 3.1 Setup

**Dataset** For language modeling, we use WikiText-103 (Merity et al., 2016), a collection of English documents extracted from verified Wikipedia. For dialogue generation, we use DailyDialog (Li et al., 2017) consisting of open-domain dialogues that reflect daily conversations.

**Metrics** We use the following metrics to measure the *degenerative attributes* in each example. For language modeling, we use **Average Frequency** to evaluate the lexical diversity of each example by averaging the frequency of tokens in an example. We also leverage **Repetition** (Welleck et al., 2020) that measures how often each token already appears in the previous part of an example.

For dialogue generation, we regard **Source Entropy** (Csáky et al., 2020) as the measurement of how trivial response is. A response with higher entropy indicates to correspond with more dialogue histories. We also use **Context Overlap** (Li et al., 2020) that calculates the bi-gram overlap between dialogue histories and responses. We describe further details of each metric in Appendix A.1.

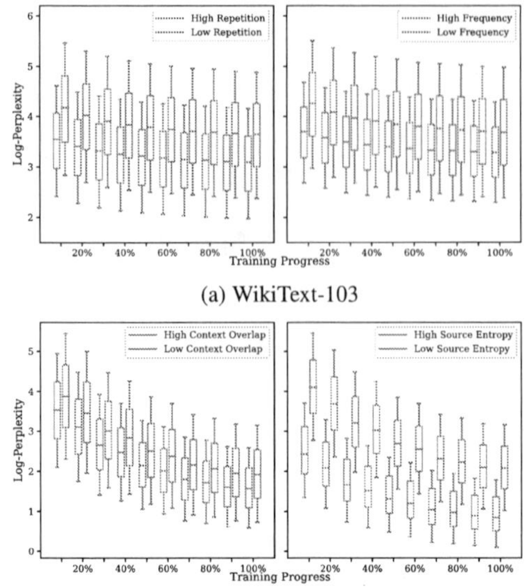


(a) WikiText-103

(b) DailyDialog

Figure 1: Comparisons between two groups with high and low degenerative attributes on language modeling (top) and dialogue generation (bottom) tasks.

**Model** We train 6-layer transformer (Vaswani et al., 2017) decoder and 6-layer transformer encoder-decoder models from scratch for language modeling and dialogue generation tasks, respectively. To analyze the training dynamics of models on each task, we first train models and save their checkpoints at each epoch. We then divide training examples into two groups based on the attribute score[1], and compute log-perplexity at each stage during training.[2]

### 3.2 Analysis

Figure 1 shows log-perplexity of examples with low and high degenerative attributes according to training progress. Specifically, the group with high degenerative attribute usually have lower perplexity than the other group. Even though the perplexity of examples in low degenerative attribute monotonically decreases as training progresses, it does not imply that the model generates diverse sequences in test time since examples with high attributes are still more likely to be produced than others.

## 4 LFD: Learning from *Degeneration*

Based on the analysis (§3), we argue that the model should be prevented from overfitting to degenera-

[1] We choose top and bottom of 5k examples with high and low attribute score, respectively.

[2] For WikiText-103, we compute the average log-perplexity at sentence-level.

tive attributes. Inspired by previous studies (Nam et al., 2020; Sanh et al., 2021), we propose a new training approach consisting of two steps: (a) intentionally train a model $f_{\theta_D}$ to amplify degenerative attributes in examples, and (b) train a diversity-enhanced model $f_{\theta_M}$ by leveraging $f_{\theta_D}$.

### 4.1 Background

Generative language model $f_\theta$ is usually trained to maximize conditional probability distribution of $\mathbf{p}(\mathbf{y}|\mathbf{x},\theta)$, where $\mathbf{x} = (x_1, \ldots, x_{|\mathbf{x}|})$ and $\mathbf{y} = (y_1, \ldots, y_{|\mathbf{y}|})$ are input and target sequences. A typical approach to train the model is optimizing $\theta$ by minimizing the following negative log-likelihood:

$$\mathcal{L}_{\text{MLE}}(\theta, \mathbf{x}, \mathbf{y}) = -\sum_{t=1}^{|\mathbf{y}|} \log p(y_t|y_{<t}, \mathbf{x}, \theta) \quad (1)$$

### 4.2 Training *De*generative Model $f_{\theta_D}$

From the analysis (§3), we observe that the difference between the two groups of examples is significant, especially in the early training phase. We enforce *De*generative model $f_{\theta_D}$ to overfit degeneration attributes captured in a small number of iteration. In particular, we leverage the truncated cross entropy loss (Han et al., 2018) to amplify attributes at token-level. The procedure is following: (a) we train $f_{\theta_D}$ by $K$ step with standard training. (b) After $K$ steps, only $R\%$ of tokens with small loss within a batch are used to update the model $f_{\theta_D}$ by $H$ steps. We expect that tokens are potentially generic when $f_{\theta_D}$ predicts them with high confidence. Conversely, tokens are potentially diverse when $f_{\theta_D}$ predicts them with low confidence.

### 4.3 Enhancing Diversity via *De*generative model $f_{\theta_D}$

Now we explain how to encourage the diversity of the main model $f_{\theta_M}$ by exploiting the predictions of $f_{\theta_D}$. Inspired by Utama et al. (2020), we introduce Product-of-Expert (PoE) to prevent $f_{\theta_M}$ from learning degenerative attributes amplified in $f_{\theta_D}$. Namely, the model $f_{\theta_M}$ is likely to concentrate on attributes that $f_{\theta_D}$ fails to learn. Specifically, the model $f_{\theta_M}$ is trained with the predictions of $f_{\theta_D}$ by combining their outputs as:

$$\begin{aligned}&\sigma_{\text{poe}}(\theta_D, \theta_M, \mathbf{x}, \mathbf{y}, t)\\ &= \log p(y_t|y_{<t}, \mathbf{x}, \theta_D) + \log p(y_t|y_{<t}, \mathbf{x}, \theta_M)\end{aligned} \quad (2)$$

Combined predictions are used to calculate the loss for model optimization. During the training, we only optimize the parameters of $f_{\theta_M}$ while keeping the parameter of $f_{\theta_D}$ as frozen.

$$\begin{aligned}&\mathcal{L}_{\text{PoE}}(\theta_M, \mathbf{x}, \mathbf{y})\\ &= -\sum_{t=1}^{|\mathbf{y}|} \log \text{softmax}(\sigma_{\text{poe}}(\theta_D, \theta_M, \mathbf{x}, \mathbf{y}, t))\end{aligned} \quad (3)$$

The final loss is combined as $\mathcal{L}_{\text{MLE}} + \lambda\mathcal{L}_{\text{PoE}}$. In test time, we generate sequences using $f_{\theta_M}$ only.

| Model | PPL | KLD | ZipC | Rep. | Uniq. |
|---|---|---|---|---|---|
| MLE | **26.3** | 2.3 | 1.16 | 1.3 | 6.0k |
| UL[†] | 26.9 | 2.1 | 1.06 | **0.7** | 7.2k |
| Focal | 26.7 | 2.3 | 1.15 | 1.4 | 5.9k |
| LfD | 26.9 | **1.9** | **0.94** | 0.8 | **8.4k** |
| Human | - | - | 0.93 | 0.2 | 10.9k |
| $f_{\theta_D}$ | 118.15 | 2.9 | 1.20 | 3.6 | 4.1k |
| LfD$_{\text{MLE}}$ | 26.7 | 2.0 | 1.09 | 1.4 | 6.4k |

Table 1: Evaluation results on WikiText-103. Top-$k$ sampling (Fan et al., 2018) is selected as decoding algorithm with $k$=20. We attach † to baselines that explicitly penalize negative behavior (e.g. repetition or frequency). The best and the second best results are highlighted in **bold** and underline, respectively. The results close to human gold standard are regarded as better performance. For **PPL** and **KLD**, the lowest scores are best performances.

## 5 Experiments

### 5.1 Task

We evaluate LFD on language modeling, dialogue generation, and abstractive summarization tasks with datasets described in Section 3.1: WikiText-103 (Merity et al., 2016), DailyDialog (Li et al., 2017), and CNN/DailyMail (Nallapati et al., 2016). Further details of each dataset are in Appendix B.4.

### 5.2 Setup

**Baselines** For language modeling task, we compare LFD with the following baseline models: **MLE**: uses the standard cross entropy in Eq. 1 for training. **Focal** (Lin et al., 2017) downweights the loss of correctly-predicted tokens to deal with imbalance classification. **UL** (Welleck et al., 2020) penalizes the repetitive generation.

For dialogue generation task, in addition to **MLE** and **Focal**, following baselines are compared: **CP** (Pereyra et al., 2017) regularizes the entropy of the model to alleviate over-confident predictions. **FACE** (Jiang et al., 2019) proposes to balance each

| Model | BLEU $n$=2 | BLEU $n$=3 | Distinct $n$=2 | Distinct $n$=3 | self-BLEU $n$=3 | self-BLEU $n$=4 | KLD | Context Overlap | Source Entropy |
|---|---|---|---|---|---|---|---|---|---|
| **MLE** | 15.85 | 8.67 | 5.48 | 15.76 | 96.30 | 92.08 | 2.23 | 12.42 | 0.88 |
| **Dialogue-UL**[†] | 19.19 | 12.22 | 12.21 | 32.78 | 90.47 | 80.62 | 1.38 | 10.49 | 0.66 |
| **FACE**[†] | 7.44 | 3.90 | 14.45 | 42.89 | **85.64** | **71.07** | 1.53 | 3.66 | 0.12 |
| **Focal** | 15.85 | 8.62 | 5.48 | 15.72 | 96.31 | 92.05 | 2.25 | 12.88 | 0.93 |
| **CP** | 19.22 | 12.19 | 11.94 | 31.31 | 90.69 | 81.50 | 1.40 | 10.94 | 0.68 |
| **LfD** | **19.26** | **12.37** | **16.52** | **42.92** | 86.44 | 73.09 | **1.12** | **9.38** | **0.55** |
| **Human** | - | - | 35.97 | 67.00 | 68.72 | 47.34 | - | 9.83 | 0.35 |
| $f_{\theta_D}$ | 13.63 | 6.77 | 1.15 | 2.76 | 99.53 | 99.02 | 4.10 | 16.07 | 1.13 |
| **LfD**$_{\text{MLE}}$ | 19.59 | 12.67 | 15.03 | 39.04 | 88.03 | 76.04 | 1.16 | 9.85 | 0.63 |

Table 2: Evaluation results on DailyDialog. Greedy decoding algorithm is used for all models, following Jiang et al. (2019). The indicators are the same as Table 1. For **BLEU**, we regard the highest scores as the best performances.

token by considering their frequency in a training corpus. **Dialogue-UL** (Li et al., 2020) penalizes the overuse of frequently generated tokens using unlikelihood training. The implementation details of baseline models are described in Appendix B.2.

**Evaluation Metrics** For language modeling, we evaluate with the following metrics: **Perplexity** to quantify the prediction difficulty of sequences by a model. **Zipf Coefficient (ZipC)** (Holtzman et al., 2019) to measure the rank-frequency distribution of words in generated sequence. **Repetition (Rep.)** (Holtzman et al., 2019) to examine whether a sequence is stuck in repetitive loops. **Unique (Uniq.)** (Welleck et al., 2020) to quantify the number of unique tokens in generated sequences. **KL-Divergence (KLD)** (Csáky et al., 2020) to measure the divergence of unigram distributions between the generated texts and reference.

For dialogue generation, we use the following metrics: **BLEU** (Papineni et al., 2002) to measure the n-gram overlap between reference and generated sequences. **Distinct** (Li et al., 2016) to calculate the ratio of unique N-grams among the generated sequences. **self-BLEU** (Zhu et al., 2018) to calculate the BLEU score of each sequence with other generated sequences. Previously mentioned metrics (**KLD**, **Context Overlap**, and **Source Entropy**) are also used. More details of each metric are available in Appendix A.2.

In abstractive summarization, we calculate the ratio of n-grams in a summary that do not appear in a source article **(Novel-n)** (See et al., 2017; Narayan et al., 2018). We also measure the quality of generated summary with **Rouge** (Banerjee and Lavie, 2005).

### 5.3 Main Results

**Language Modeling** As shown in Table 1, our model shows similar token distribution with human-written texts in the corpus (KLD) and competitive performance with other models in PPL. LFD significantly improves both Uniq. and ZipC, having minor gaps with the human texts. Surprisingly, LFD has a competitive result on Rep. with **UL** even in the lack of a penalty on repetition.

**Dialogue Generation** Results in Table 2 show that LFD achieves the best scores in all metrics except for self-BLEU. Interestingly, LFD shows the best BLEU scores, indicating that our approach can also contribute to increasing the similarity of generated responses with answer responses. Although **FACE** shows better self-BLEU scores than LFD, its lower BLEU score may indicate that it fails to generate accurate response.

**Abstractive Summarization** We assume that the diversity of a summary is proportional to its *abstractiveness*. To measure the abstractiveness of summaries, we calculate the ratio of n-grams in a summary that do not appear in a source article (See et al., 2017; Narayan et al., 2018). We also measure the quality of generated summary with ROUGE (Banerjee and Lavie, 2005).

As shown in Table 3, the summaries generated by **MLE** contain fewer novel n-grams (i.e. low abstractivess) than human summaries. LFD enhance the abstractiveness of generated summaries (+10.7%, +64.1%, and +68.5% in Novel-1, Novel-2, and Novel-3 metrics, respectively), although the scores in ROUGE are slightly decreased (e.g., -2.1 points in Rouge-1). Based on these results, we con-

| Model | Rouge-1 | Rouge-2 | Rouge-L | Novel-1(%) | Novel-2(%) | Novel-3(%) |
|---|---|---|---|---|---|---|
| **MLE** | 40.64 | 17.83 | 37.67 | 7.67 | 20.00 | 28.58 |
| **LFD** | 38.54 | 15.48 | 26.56 | 8.59 | 32.81 | 48.16 |
| **Human** | - | - | - | 20.67 | 56.46 | 72.03 |

Table 3: Evaluation results of abstractive summarzation task on CNN/DailyMail dataset. **Novel-N** indicates the ratio of novel N-gram in generated summaries.

firm that the contribution of LFD is still valid in abstractive summarization which is aligned with empirical findings from Goyal et al. (2022)

### 5.4 Amplifying *De*generative Attributes

We also evaluate the following models to confirm the validity of our framework: **1)** $f_{\theta_D}$: We evaluate our *De*generative model in Section 4.2 to check whether it actually captures negative behaviors and degenerate. **2) LfD**$_{\text{MLE}}$: Instead of $f_{\theta_D}$ in Section 4.2, we use **MLE** as a *De*generative model for PoE training. Results are shown in the bottom of Table 1 and Table 2. We first observe that $f_{\theta_D}$ performs significantly worse than other models, especially in diversity metrics, which implies that *De*generative model successfully captures degenerative attributes in the dataset. While **LfD**$_{\text{MLE}}$ also obtains performance gains compared with MLE in the diversity metrics, amplifying degenerative patterns mitigates degeneration and improves diversity more.

## 6 Case Study

We present generation examples for dialogue generation task in Table 4. As we can observe, our method usually increases the diversity of generated responses. For instance, given a dialogue context in the first example (*"Peter, how often do you exercise?"*), both MLE and Dialogue-UL models generate the responses with a generic phrase (*"I'm not sure."*). The FACE generation looks diverse at first glance, but it creates repeated n-gram (e.g., *"after school every day"*, *"day after school class"*). Finally, LFD creates a diverse and natural response by asking a question to the partner (*"How about you?"*).

## 7 Conclusion

In this paper, we discover that examples with low diversity are easy to be learned, leading models to degenerate in open-ended text generation tasks. We propose LFD, a simple training approach that can be widely used to promote diversity without re-

| | |
|---|---|
| **Context** | **A**: Peter, how often do you exercise? |
| **MLE** | I'm not sure. but I often go to the TV. |
| **FACE** | Not bad yet. How about taking photos out every day after work at school every day after school? They are pretty busy at school every day after school every day after school every day after school tomorrow evening every day after school class day after school |
| **UL** | I'm not sure. I often go to a concert. |
| **Ours** | I'm pretty busy. How about you? |
| **Human** | Well, I swim and run every day. |
| **Context** | **A**: Room service. **B**: Good morning . This is room 113 . I'd like some breakfast, please. |
| **MLE** | Ok. How would you like to have your room? |
| **FACE** | Ok sir, here is some money left now and would like some drinks or coffee beans. Would you please fill out this form with us? |
| **UL** | Ok, sir. How would you like to pay? |
| **Ours** | All right, sir. What would you like to order? |
| **Human** | Right. Excuse me. Mrs. Jones? |

Table 4: A generation example on DailyDialog dataset. UL denotes Dialogue-UL.

quiring specified negative behavior. Experimental results on two representative tasks for open-ended generation confirm the validity and effectiveness of our approach.

## Limitations

In this work, we mainly investigate the relationship between the training of the generative model and the *easiness* of undesired behavior that leads to degeneration. For future work, we will extend our analysis of training dynamics into other degeneration problems such as hallucination or inconsistency, which are likely to be undesirable behaviors in other tasks. Another limitation of LfD is that we focus on analyzing the learning dynamics of training examples in terms of the diversity. Since the easily trained examples may consist of complex attributes more than low diversity, diminishing their impact on models may lead to an unintended generation. In future work, we plan to conduct an in-depth analysis for easily trained examples to understand their characteristics.

## Acknowledgements

We thank Radhika Dua for the discussion and feedback on the paper. This work was supported by the Institute of Information & communications Technology Planning & Evaluation (IITP) grant funded by the Korea government (MSIT) (No.2019-0-00075, Artificial Intelligence Graduate School Program (KAIST)), and the Institute of Information & communications Technology Planning & Evaluation (IITP) grant funded by the Korea government(MSIT) (No.2021-0-02068, Artificial Intelligence Innovation Hub).

## References

Satanjeev Banerjee and Alon Lavie. 2005. METEOR: An automatic metric for MT evaluation with improved correlation with human judgments. In *Proceedings of the ACL Workshop on Intrinsic and Extrinsic Evaluation Measures for Machine Translation and/or Summarization*, pages 65–72, Ann Arbor, Michigan. Association for Computational Linguistics.

Daniel Cer, Mona Diab, Eneko Agirre, Iñigo Lopez-Gazpio, and Lucia Specia. 2017. Semeval-2017 task 1: Semantic textual similarity multilingual and crosslingual focused evaluation. In *Proceedings of the 11th International Workshop on Semantic Evaluation (SemEval-2017)*, pages 1–14.

Hongshen Chen, Xiaorui Liu, Dawei Yin, and Jiliang Tang. 2017. A survey on dialogue systems: Recent advances and new frontiers. *Acm Sigkdd Explorations Newsletter*, 19(2):25–35.

Byung-Ju Choi, Jimin Hong, David Keetae Park, and Sang Wan Lee. 2020. F^ 2-softmax: Diversifying neural text generation via frequency factorized softmax. In *Proc. of the Conference on Empirical Methods in Natural Language Processing (EMNLP)*.

Dorin Comaniciu and Peter Meer. 2002. Mean shift: A robust approach toward feature space analysis. *IEEE Transactions on pattern analysis and machine intelligence*, 24(5):603–619.

Richárd Csáky, Patrik Purgai, and Gábor Recski. 2020. Improving neural conversational models with entropy-based data filtering. In *Proc. the Annual Meeting of the Association for Computational Linguistics (ACL)*.

Emily Dinan, Varvara Logacheva, Valentin Malykh, Alexander Miller, Kurt Shuster, Jack Urbanek, Douwe Kiela, Arthur Szlam, Iulian Serban, Ryan Lowe, et al. 2020. The second conversational intelligence challenge (convai2). In *The NeurIPS'18 Competition*, pages 187–208. Springer.

Emily Dinan, Varvara Logacheva, Valentin Malykh, Alexander H Miller, Kurt Shuster, Jack Urbanek, Douwe Kiela, Arthur Szlam, Iulian Serban, Ryan Lowe, et al. 2019. The second conversational intelligence challenge (convai2).

Stephen Fagan and Ramazan Gençay. 2011. An introduction to textual econometrics. *Handbook of empirical economics and finance*, pages 133–154.

Angela Fan, Mike Lewis, and Yann Dauphin. 2018. Hierarchical neural story generation. In *Proceedings of the 56th Annual Meeting of the Association for Computational Linguistics (Volume 1: Long Papers)*, pages 889–898.

Zihao Fu, Wai Lam, Anthony Man-Cho So, and Bei Shi. 2021. A theoretical analysis of the repetition problem in text generation. In *Proceedings of the AAAI Conference on Artificial Intelligence*, volume 35, pages 12848–12856.

Tianyu Gao, Xingcheng Yao, and Danqi Chen. 2021. Simcse: Simple contrastive learning of sentence embeddings. In *Proceedings of the 2021 Conference on Empirical Methods in Natural Language Processing*, pages 6894–6910.

Tanya Goyal, Jiacheng Xu, Junyi Jessy Li, and Greg Durrett. 2022. Training dynamics for text summarization models. In *Findings of the Association for Computational Linguistics: ACL 2022*, pages 2061–2073.

Bo Han, Quanming Yao, Xingrui Yu, Gang Niu, Miao Xu, Weihua Hu, Ivor Tsang, and Masashi Sugiyama. 2018. Co-teaching: Robust training of deep neural networks with extremely noisy labels. In *Proc. the Advances in Neural Information Processing Systems (NeurIPS)*, volume 31.

Tianxing He and James Glass. 2020. Negative training for neural dialogue response generation. In *Proc. the Annual Meeting of the Association for Computational Linguistics (ACL)*.

Ari Holtzman, Jan Buys, Maxwell Forbes, Antoine Bosselut, David Golub, and Yejin Choi. 2018. Learning to write with cooperative discriminators. In *Proc. of Annual Meeting of the Association for Computational Linguistics (ACL)*, pages 1638–1649.

Ari Holtzman, Jan Buys, Maxwell Forbes, and Yejin Choi. 2019. The curious case of neural text degeneration. In *International Conference on Learning Representations (ICLR)*.

Shaojie Jiang, Pengjie Ren, Christof Monz, and Maarten de Rijke. 2019. Improving neural response diversity with frequency-aware cross-entropy loss. In *Proc. of World Wide Web Conference (WWW)*, pages 2879–2885.

Jacob Devlin Ming-Wei Chang Kenton and Lee Kristina Toutanova. 2019. Bert: Pre-training of deep bidirectional transformers for language understanding. In *Proceedings of NAACL-HLT*, pages 4171–4186.

Diederik P Kingma and Jimmy Ba. 2015. Adam: A method for stochastic optimization. In *ICLR (Poster)*.

Jiwei Li, Michel Galley, Chris Brockett, Jianfeng Gao, and William B Dolan. 2016. A diversity-promoting objective function for neural conversation models. In *Proceedings of the 2016 Conference of the North American Chapter of the Association for Computational Linguistics: Human Language Technologies*, pages 110–119.

Margaret Li, Stephen Roller, Ilia Kulikov, Sean Welleck, Y-Lan Boureau, Kyunghyun Cho, and Jason Weston. 2020. Don't say that! making inconsistent dialogue unlikely with unlikelihood training. In *Proc. the Annual Meeting of the Association for Computational Linguistics (ACL)*.

Yanran Li, Hui Su, Xiaoyu Shen, Wenjie Li, Ziqiang Cao, and Shuzi Niu. 2017. Dailydialog: A manually labelled multi-turn dialogue dataset. In *Proceedings of the Eighth International Joint Conference on Natural Language Processing (Volume 1: Long Papers)*, pages 986–995.

Yiwei Li, Shaoxiong Feng, Bin Sun, and Kan Li. 2022. Diversifying neural dialogue generation via negative distillation. In *Proc. of The Annual Conference of the North American Chapter of the Association for Computational Linguistics (NAACL)*.

Tsung-Yi Lin, Priya Goyal, Ross Girshick, Kaiming He, and Piotr Dollár. 2017. Focal loss for dense object detection. In *Proceedings of the IEEE international conference on computer vision*, pages 2980–2988.

Stephen Merity, Caiming Xiong, James Bradbury, and Richard Socher. 2016. Pointer sentinel mixture models. *arXiv preprint arXiv:1609.07843*.

Ramesh Nallapati, Bowen Zhou, Cicero dos Santos, Çağlar Gulçehre, and Bing Xiang. 2016. Abstractive text summarization using sequence-to-sequence rnns and beyond. In *Proceedings of The 20th SIGNLL Conference on Computational Natural Language Learning*, pages 280–290.

Junhyun Nam, Hyuntak Cha, Sungsoo Ahn, Jaeho Lee, and Jinwoo Shin. 2020. Learning from failure: Debiasing classifier from biased classifier. In *Proc. the Advances in Neural Information Processing Systems (NeurIPS)*, volume 33, pages 20673–20684.

Shashi Narayan, Shay B Cohen, and Mirella Lapata. 2018. Don't give me the details, just the summary! topic-aware convolutional neural networks for extreme summarization. In *Proceedings of the 2018 Conference on Empirical Methods in Natural Language Processing*, pages 1797–1807.

Kishore Papineni, Salim Roukos, Todd Ward, and Wei-Jing Zhu. 2002. Bleu: a method for automatic evaluation of machine translation. In *Proceedings of the 40th Annual Meeting of the Association for Computational Linguistics*, pages 311–318, Philadelphia, Pennsylvania, USA. Association for Computational Linguistics.

Gabriel Pereyra, George Tucker, Jan Chorowski, Łukasz Kaiser, and Geoffrey Hinton. 2017. Regularizing neural networks by penalizing confident output distributions. *arXiv preprint arXiv:1701.06548*.

Alec Radford, Jeffrey Wu, Rewon Child, David Luan, Dario Amodei, Ilya Sutskever, et al. 2019. Language models are unsupervised multitask learners. *OpenAI blog*, 1(8):9.

Victor Sanh, Thomas Wolf, Yonatan Belinkov, and Alexander M Rush. 2021. Learning from others' mistakes: Avoiding dataset biases without modeling them. In *Proc. the International Conference on Learning Representations (ICLR)*.

Abigail See, Peter J Liu, and Christopher D Manning. 2017. Get to the point: Summarization with pointer-generator networks. In *Proceedings of the 55th Annual Meeting of the Association for Computational Linguistics (Volume 1: Long Papers)*, pages 1073–1083.

Prasetya Ajie Utama, Nafise Sadat Moosavi, and Iryna Gurevych. 2020. Towards debiasing nlu models from unknown biases. In *Proceedings of the 2020 Conference on Empirical Methods in Natural Language Processing (EMNLP)*, pages 7597–7610.

Ashish Vaswani, Noam Shazeer, Niki Parmar, Jakob Uszkoreit, Llion Jones, Aidan N Gomez, Łukasz Kaiser, and Illia Polosukhin. 2017. Attention is all you need. In *Proc. of Advances in neural information processing systems (NIPS)*, pages 5998–6008.

Yida Wang, Yinhe Zheng, Yong Jiang, and Minlie Huang. 2021. Diversifying dialog generation via adaptive label smoothing. In *Proc. the Annual Meeting of the Association for Computational Linguistics (ACL)*.

Sean Welleck, Ilia Kulikov, Stephen Roller, Emily Dinan, Kyunghyun Cho, and Jason Weston. 2020. Neural text generation with unlikelihood training. In *Proc. the International Conference on Learning Representations (ICLR)*.

Yaoming Zhu, Sidi Lu, Lei Zheng, Jiaxian Guo, Weinan Zhang, Jun Wang, and Yong Yu. 2018. Texygen: A benchmarking platform for text generation models. In *The 41st International ACM SIGIR Conference on Research & Development in Information Retrieval*, pages 1097–1100.

## Appendix

## A Evaluation Metrics

### A.1 Metrics in Preliminary Study

We describe further details in our evaluation metrics 3.1.

**Context Overlap** (Welleck et al., 2020): We measure the ratio of shared bi-gram between contexts and responses as follows:

$$\text{Context Overlap}(x, y) = \frac{|N(x) \cap N(y)|}{|N(y)|} \quad (4)$$

where $N(u)$ denotes the number of n-grams in utterance(s) $u$, while $x$ and $y$ indicate a dialog context and its response, respectively.

**Source Entropy**: We follow clustering-based method with MeanShift (Comaniciu and Meer, 2002) algorithm to obtain entropy value of each response. We employ SimCSE-base (Gao et al., 2021) model finetuned on STS benchmark (Cer et al., 2017) to encode each text to a vector. The source entropy of a response is calculated as

$$\text{H}_{\text{src.}}(c_y, C) = -\sum_{c_i \in C} p(c_i|c_y)\log_2 p(c_i|c_y) \quad (5)$$

where $C$ denotes the set of all clusters and $p(c_i|c_y)$ is the conditional probability of observing a dialog history from cluster $c_i$ given a response $y$ from cluster $c_y$.

**Repetition(Rep.)**: We reinvent **Rep.** metric to compute repetitive patterns in ground-truth tokens inspired by the works (Welleck et al., 2020; Fu et al., 2021). The equation is as follow:

$$\text{Rep}(\mathbf{x}) = \frac{1}{|\mathbf{x}|}\sum_{t=1}^{|\mathbf{x}|} \mathbf{I}[x_t \in x_{0:t-1}] \quad (6)$$

### A.2 Evaluation Metrics in Main Results

**Perplexity**: To measure test perplexity in language modeling using decoder-only model, we regard condition x as 50 prefixes and target y as 100 of ground-truth next tokens.

$$\text{PPL}(\theta, \mathbf{x}, \mathbf{y}) = \frac{1}{|\mathbf{y}|}\sum_{t=1}^{|\mathbf{y}|} e^{-\log p(y_t|y_{<t}, \mathbf{x}, \theta)} \quad (7)$$

## B Implementation Details

### B.1 Training Details

In all experiments, we train language model on a single 3090 RTX GPU with 24GB of memory. We implemented all models with PyTorch using sentence-transformers library from UKPLab[3]. In our experiments, we use 6-layer transformer decoder with GPT2 (Radford et al., 2019) tokenizer and 6-layer transformer encoder-decoder architectures with BERT-base-uncased (Kenton and Toutanova, 2019) tokenizer for language modeling and dialogue generation tasks, respectively. We choose the best checkpoints of models by using their validation loss. We use Adam optimizer (Kingma and Ba, 2015) with linear learning rate scheduler. Learning rate is set to 1e-5 for language modeling task and 1e-4 for dialogue generation task. The value of $\lambda$ that balances $\mathcal{L}_{\text{MLE}}$ and $\mathcal{L}_{\text{PoE}}$ is set to 0.25 and 0.5 for dialogue generation and language modeling task, respectively. We set the $R$ as 0.7 for both tasks, and set $K$ in Section 4.2 as the number of optimization steps for $f_\theta$ during 1 and 3 epochs on WikiText-103 and DailyDialog, respectively. We set the $H$ in Section 4.2 as the number of optimization steps during an epoch on both tasks.

### B.2 Baseline Details

We present more details of our baseline models. We set the weight of repetition penalty in **UL** as 1.0. The penalty weight of **Dialogue-UL** is set to 1000. We set the $\gamma$ in **Focal** as 2.0. **Focal** aim to alleviate the negative effects of degenerative attributes by penalizing over-confident predictions of a model during training. For **CP**, we set the weight of regularization term as 2.5 following the original paper. For **FACE**, we use *Output frequency* with *Pre-weight* configurations for training. The best checkpoint of **FACE** is chosen by using Distinct-1 metrics as suggested by the original paper. In dialogue generation task, we finetune **CP**, **FACE**, **Dialogue-UL**, and LFD starting with **MLE**, and evaluate their performance in every 500 steps to find the best checkpoint.

### B.3 Generation Details

For open-ended text generation, we generate sequences for the evaluation by completing sequences from prefixes. Specifically, we preprocess

[3]https://github.com/UKPLab/sentence-transformers

| Model | BLEU n=2 | BLEU n=3 | Distinct n=2 | Distinct n=3 | self-BLEU n=3 | self-BLEU n=4 | KLD | Context Overlap |
|---|---|---|---|---|---|---|---|---|
| **MLE** | 18.70 | 11.27 | 18.17 | 36.26 | 86.13 | 77.32 | 0.98 | 13.16 |
| **Dialogue-UL**† | 35.18 | 29.54 | 29.24 | 57.55 | 75.37 | 57.94 | 0.41 | **9.45** |
| **LfD** | **35.24** | **29.72** | **33.84** | **63.15** | **71.31** | **51.68** | **0.38** | 9.33 |
| **Human** | - | - | 35.97 | 67.00 | 68.72 | 47.34 | - | 9.83 |

Table 5: Evaluation results on DailyDialog with a pre-trained language model (BERT2BERT). Greedy decoding algorithm is used for all models, following Jiang et al. (2019). The indicators are the same as Table 2.

| Model | PPL | ZipC | Rep. | Uniq. |
|---|---|---|---|---|
| **MLE** | **18.7** | 1.16 | 1.3 | 8.72k |
| **UL**† | 19.1 | 0.95 | **0.7** | 9.22k |
| **Focal** | 21.0 | 1.04 | 1.4 | 8.00k |
| **LfD** | 19.0 | **0.94** | 0.8 | **9.50k** |
| **Human** | - | 0.93 | 0.2 | 10.9k |

Table 6: Evaluation results on WikiText-103 with a pre-trained architecture. Top-$k$ sampling (Fan et al., 2018) is selected as decoding algorithm with $k$=20. For **PPL**, the lowest score is the best performance.

test set of WikiText-103, select the first 50 tokens from each batch as prefixes, and lead models to generate a continuation of 100 tokens from the prefixes. We use top-$k$ sampling with $k$=20 as a decoding algorithm. For dialogue generation, we use a deterministic decoding algorithm (i.e. greedy decoding) following Jiang et al. (2019).

### B.4 Dataset Details

**WikiText-103** WikiText-103 contains 28.4k, 60, and 60 of articles on train, validation, and test split, respectively. We truncate sequence into 512 tokens in each example.

**DailyDialog** DailyDialog dataset contains 13,118, 1000, and 1000 of multi-turn conversations on train, validation, and test split, respectively. Following Jiang et al. (2019), we remove the dialogues with contexts or responses longer than 100 tokens to focus on short conversations. This makes 55,404, 5130, and 4915 pair of dialog history and response in train, validation, and test split, respectively.

## C Experiments with pre-trained language models

We also conduct experiments using pre-trained language models. For dialogue generation task, we use BERT2BERT architecture with BERT-base-uncased. For language modeling task, gpt2-small is used. Experimental results are shown in Table 5 and Table 6 for dialogue generation and language modeling tasks, respectively.

We first find that leveraging pre-trained models generally increase the overall performance of generation models. In dialogue generation task, LFD performs better than Dialogue-UL, a competitive baseline as shown in Table 2, except for Context Overlap scores. In language modeling task, our model usually performs better than other baselines. Based on these results, we confirm the validity of LFD even when they are applied with pre-trained language models.

# A Neighbourhood-Aware Differential Privacy Mechanism for Static Word Embeddings

**Danushka Bollegala**[1,2*] **Shuichi Otake**[3] **Tomoya Machide**[4] **Ken-ichi Kawarabayashi**[3]
University of Liverpool[1], Amazon[2], National Institute of Informatics[3]
International Professional University of Technology in Tokyo[4]

## Abstract

We propose a Neighbourhood-Aware Differential Privacy (NADP) mechanism considering the neighbourhood of a word in a pretrained static word embedding space to determine the minimal amount of noise required to guarantee a specified privacy level. We first construct a nearest neighbour graph over the words using their embeddings, and factorise it into a set of connected components (i.e. neighbourhoods). We then separately apply different levels of Gaussian noise to the words in each neighbourhood, determined by the set of words in that neighbourhood. Experiments show that our proposed NADP mechanism consistently outperforms multiple previously proposed DP mechanisms such as Laplacian, Gaussian, and Mahalanobis in multiple downstream tasks, while guaranteeing higher levels of privacy.

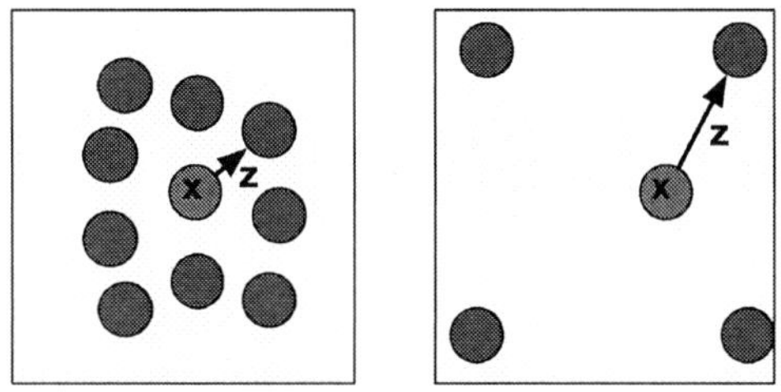


Figure 1: Anonymizing a target word (shown in red) in a dense (left) vs. a sparse (right) neighbourhoods of words (shown in blue). In the sparse neighbourhood, NADP adds a higher level of perturbation noise $z$ to the target word embedding $x$ in order to protect its privacy by disguising it among its neighbours, while in a dense neighbourhood it adds less noise.

## 1 Introduction

Increasingly more NLP models have been trained on private data such as medical conversations, social media posts and personal emails (Abdalla et al., 2020; Lyu et al., 2020b; Song and Shmatikov, 2019). However, we must ensure that sensitive information related to user privacy is not leaked during any stage of the model training process. To protect user privacy, Differential Privacy (DP) mechanisms add random noise to the training data (Feyisetan and Kasiviswanathan, 2021; Krishna et al., 2021; Feyisetan et al., 2020). However, it remains a challenging task to balance the trade-off between user **privacy** vs. **performance** in downstream NLP tasks.

We propose **Neighbourhood-Aware Differential Privacy** (NADP) mechanism, which consists of three steps. First, given a set of words, we compute a nearest neighbour graph considering the similarity between the words (represented by the vertices of the nearest neighbour graph) computed using their word embeddings. Second, we compute the connected components in the nearest neighbour graph to find the *neighbourhoods* of words. Third, we apply Gaussian noise to all words in each neighbourhood, such that the variance of the noise is determined by the words in that neighbourhood.

As illustrated in Figure 1, if all words in a neighbourhood are highly similar to each other (i.e. a *dense* neighbourhood), it would require less perturbation noise to anonymise a word because the addition of small noise can easily *hide* the corresponding word embedding among its neighbours. On the other hand, if the words in a neighbourhood are not very similar to each other (i.e. a *sparse* neighbourhood) we must add higher levels of perturbation noise to a word embedding because its nearest neighbour would be further away in the embedding space. Because words in a language is a discrete set (unlike images for example), there does not exist a word corresponding to all points in the embedding space. Therefore, if we do not add sufficient amount of noise in a sparse

*Contact author: danushka@liverpool.ac.uk



*Findings of the Association for Computational Linguistics: IJCNLP-AACL 2023*, pages 65–79
November 1–4, 2023. 

neighbourhood, we run the risk of easily discovering the target word via a simple nearest neighbour search. Instead of adding the same level of noise to all words in a vocabulary as done in prior DP mechanisms, NADP attempts to minimise the total amount of noise by assigning low noise in dense neighbourhoods and high noise in sparse neighbourhoods. NADP has provable DP guarantees as shown by our theoretical analysis. Moreover, NADP has the following desirable properties that makes it attractive when used for NLP tasks.

**(a)** In NADP, **noise vectors are sampled from the Gaussian distribution**. Many static word embedding algorithms (Pennington et al., 2014; Arora et al., 2016; Mikolov et al., 2013) learn embeddings in the $\ell_2$ space. Moreover, the squared $\ell_2$ norm of a word embedding is known to positively correlate with the frequency of the word in the training corpus (Arora et al., 2016), while the joint co-occurrence probability of a set of words positively correlates with the squared $\ell_2$ norm of the sum of the corresponding word embeddings (Bollegala et al., 2018). Therefore, it is natural to consider Gaussian noise, which corresponds to the $\ell_2$ embedding space used by many static word embedding learning methods rather than the more widely-used Laplacian noise, which relates to the $\ell_1$ norm.

**(b)** Unlike previously proposed DP mechanisms for word embeddings (Feyisetan et al., 2020; Feyisetan and Kasiviswanathan, 2021; Krishna et al., 2021; Xu et al., 2020), NADP **dynamically adjusts the level of noise added to a word embedding considering its neighbourhood**. This enables us to optimally allocate a fixed noise budget over a vocabulary.

**(c)** NADP **adds noise directly to the word embeddings** and does not perform decoding after the noise addition step (Krishna et al., 2021). Decoding is a deterministic process and does not affect DP. Many NLP applications such as text classification, clustering etc. require the input text to be represented in some vector space, and we can use the noise-added input text representations straightaway in such applications without requiring to first decode it back to text. In situations where users train word embeddings on private data on their own and only send/release the embeddings to external machine learning services, we only need to anonymise the word embeddings (Feyisetan and Kasiviswanathan, 2021).

**Results:** *Utility experiments* (§ 5.1) conducted over four downstream NLP tasks show that NADP consistently outperforms previously proposed Laplacian, Gaussian and Mahalanobis mechanisms in downstream tasks. We conduct *privacy experiments* (§ 5.2) to evaluate the level of privacy guaranteed by a DP mechanism for word embeddings. Specifically, we estimate the probability of correctly predicting a word from its perturbed word embedding using the overlap between nearest neighbour sets. To evaluate the level of privacy protected for the entire set of word embeddings, we compute the skewness of the distribution of prediction probabilities. We find that NADP reports near-zero skewness values across a broad range of privacy levels, $\epsilon$, which indicates significantly stronger privacy guarantees compared to other DP mechanisms. Source code implementation of our NADP is publicly available.[1]

## 2 Related Work

Learning models from data with DP guarantees has been studied under *private learning* (Kasiviswanathan et al., 2008). Abadi et al. (2016) proposed a DP stochastic gradient descent by adding Gaussian noise to the gradient of the loss function. Rogers et al. (2016) combined multiple DP algorithms using adaptive parameters. However, compared to continuous input spaces such as in computer vision (Zhu et al., 2020), DP mechanisms for the discrete inputs such as text remain understudied.

Wang et al. (2021) proposed *WordDP* to achieve certified robustness against word substitution attacks in text classification. However, WordDP does *not* seek DP protection for the training data as we consider here, and uses DP randomness for certified robustness during inference time with respect to a testing input. Krishna et al. (2021) proposed AdePT, an autoencoder-based approach to generate differentially private text transformations. However, Habernal (2021) showed that AdePT is *not* differentially private as claimed and proved weaker privacy guarantees. DPText (Alnasser et al., 2021; Beigi et al., 2019) uses an autoencoder to obtain a text representation and adds Laplacian noise to create private representations. However, Habernal (2022) proved that the use of reparametrisation trick for the inverse continuous

[1] https://github.com/shuichiotake/NADP

density function in DPText is inaccurate and that DPText violates the DP guarantees. Such prior attempts show the difficulty in developing theoretically correct DP mechanisms for NLP.

Lyu et al. (2020a) proposed DP Neural Representation (DPNR) to preserve the privacy of text representations by first randomly masking words from the input texts and then adding Laplacian noise. However, unlike NADP DPNR uses a neighbourhood insensitive fixed Laplacian noise distribution. Feyisetan et al. (2020) proposed a DP mechanism where they first add Laplacian noise to word embeddings and then return the nearest neighbour to the noise-added embedding as the output. However, the $\ell_2$ norm of the noise vector scales almost linearly with the dimensionality of the embedding space. To address this issue, in their subsequent work (Feyisetan and Kasiviswanathan, 2021), they projected the word embeddings to a lower-dimensional space before adding Laplacian noise.

Xu et al. (2020) proposed Mahalanobis DP mechanism, which adds elliptical noise considering the covariance structure in the embedding space. Unlike the Gaussian or Laplacian mechanisms, Mahalanobis mechanism adds heterogeneous noise along different directions such that words in sparse regions in the embedding space have sufficient likelihood of replacement without sacrificing the overall utility. They show that Mahalanobis mechanism to be superior to Laplacian mechanism. Mahalanobis mechanism is a special instance of metric (Lipschitz) DP originated in privacy-preserving geolocation studies (Andrés et al., 2013), where Euclidean distance was used as the distance metric. Although metric DP considers the distance between two data points, it does not consider all of the nearest neighbours for each data point when deciding the level of noise that must be applied to a particular data point, unlike our NADP mechanism. Li et al. (2018) used adversarial learning to build NLP models such as part-of-speech (PoS) taggers that cannot predict the writer's age or sex, while can accurately predict the PoS tags. Despite their empirical success, this approach does not have any formal DP guarantees. In contrast, our focus is provably DP mechanisms with formal guarantees.

All of the prior work described thus far, except DPNR and AdePT, focus on static word embeddings as we do in this paper. A natural future extension of this work is DP mechanisms for the contextualised embeddings. However, computational and practical properties of static word embeddings such as, being lightweight to both compute and store, are attractive for resource (e.g. GPU and RAM) limited mobile devices. Considering that such personal mobile devices are used by billions of users and contain highly private data, DP mechanisms for static word embeddings remains an important research topic. Moreover, Gupta and Jaggi (2021) showed that it is possible to distil static word embeddings from pretrained language models that have comparable performance to contextualised word embeddings.

## 3 DP for Word Embeddings

Let us denote the $d$-dimensional embedding of a word $x$ in a vocabulary $\mathcal{X}$ by a vector $\boldsymbol{x} \in \mathbb{R}^d$. We can consider a word embedding algorithm as a function $f : \mathbb{X} \rightarrow \mathbb{R}^d$ that maps the words in a discrete vocabulary space $\mathbb{X}$ to a $d$-dimensional continuous space $\mathbb{R}^d$. We can use a distance metric, $\Gamma$, defined in the embedding space to measure the distance $\Gamma(\boldsymbol{x}_i, \boldsymbol{x}_j)$ between two words $x_i$ and $x_j$ such as the Euclidean distance. We can then find the set of top-$m$ nearest neighbours, $\mathcal{S}_m(x)$, from $\mathcal{X}$ using $\Gamma$ such that for any $y \in \mathcal{S}_m(x)$ and $y' \notin \mathcal{S}_m(x)$, $\Gamma(x, y) \leq \Gamma(x, y')$ holds. The Jaccard similarity, $\mathrm{Jaccard}(x, y)$, between two words $x$ and $y$ is defined using their neighbourhoods as in (1).

$$\mathrm{Jaccard}(x, y) = \frac{|\mathcal{S}_m(x) \cap \mathcal{S}_m(y)|}{|\mathcal{S}_m(x) \cup \mathcal{S}_m(y)|} \quad (1)$$

We define two words $x, y \in \mathcal{X}$ to be in a symmetric *neighbouring* relation, $x \simeq y$, if the following two conditions are jointly satisfied:

**(a)** $x \in \mathcal{S}_m(y)$ or $y \in \mathcal{S}_m(x)$, and

**(b)** $\mathrm{Jaccard}(x, y) \geq \tau$ for a given threshold $\tau \in [0, 1]$.

One could use conjunction instead of disjuction in condition (a) to enforce a mutual nearest neighbour relation. However, doing so results in a large number of small isolated neighbourhoods because two words might not be *mutual* nearest neighbours unless they are synonyms (or highly related). Relaxing the condition (a) to a disjunction would form neighbourhoods where one word might be a neighbour of another but not the inverse such as in hypernym-hyponym pairs. For example, *colour* could be a top nearest neighbour of *crimson*, but *crimson* might not be a top nearest neighbour of *colour*, because there are other prototypical colours such as *red*, *green*, *blue*, etc. than *crimson*.

Let us formally define DP for word embeddings. Because each word is assigned a vector by the word embedding learning algorithm, we can add noise to the embedding vectors to *disguise* a word among its nearest neighbours in the embedding space. However, in doing so we will be perturbing the semantics in the embeddings, thus potentially hurting downstream task performance. Therefore, there exists a *trade-off* between the amount of privacy that can be guaranteed by adding random noise to the embeddings vs. the performance of a downstream NLP task that use those embeddings. A random mechanism operating on word embeddings is said to be DP if Definition 1 holds.

**Definition 1** (Differential Privacy). *A random mechanism $M$ that takes in a vector in the embedding space $\mathbb{X}$ and maps into a space $\mathbb{Y}$ (i.e. $M : \mathbb{X} \rightarrow \mathbb{Y}$) is $(\epsilon, \delta)$-DP with $\epsilon \geq 0$ and $\delta \in [0, 1]$, if for every pair of neighbouring inputs $\boldsymbol{x}, \boldsymbol{x}' \in \mathcal{X}$ and every possible measurable output set $\mathcal{T} \in \mathcal{Y}$ the relationship given by (2) holds:*

$$\Pr[M(\boldsymbol{x}) \in \mathcal{T}] \leq \exp(\epsilon)\Pr[M(\boldsymbol{x}') \in \mathcal{T}] + \delta \tag{2}$$

Here, $\epsilon$ represents the level of privacy ensured by $M$ and smaller $\epsilon$ values result in stronger privacy guarantees. The global $\ell_2$ sensitivity of the embedding space is defined as $\Delta = \sup_{x,x' \in \mathcal{X}, x \simeq x'} ||\boldsymbol{x} - \boldsymbol{x}'||$. Given a set of word embeddings, $\Delta$ can be estimated empirically by computing the maximum Euclidean distance between a word $x$ and its most distant neighbour $x'$ in $\mathcal{S}_m(x)$. As an extreme case, let us consider the smallest possible neighbourhood size corresponding to $m = 2$. Estimating $\Delta$ in this case would amount to finding the maximum Euclidean distance between any pair of neighboring words $x, x' \in \mathcal{V}$. Moreover, the $\Delta$ estimated for $m = 2$ will be larger than the $\Delta$ estimated for any other $m(> 2)$ neighbourhood sizes. Therefore, $\Delta$ is independent of $m$ and can be estimated via a deterministic process (i.e. measuring all pairwise Euclidean distances) from a given set of word embeddings.

**Algorithm 1:** Nearest Neighbour Graph Construction

**Inputs:** Word embeddings $\mathcal{X} = \{\boldsymbol{x}_1, \ldots, \boldsymbol{x}_n\}$, top-$m$ for selecting neighbours, and similarity threshold $\tau \in [0, 1]$.
**Outputs:** Nearest neighbour graph $G(\mathcal{V}, \mathcal{E})$
Initialise $\mathcal{V} = \{x_1, \ldots, x_n\}$, $\mathcal{E} = \{\}$
**for** $i = 1, \ldots, n$ **do**
  **for** $x_j \in \mathcal{S}_m(x_i)$ **do**
    **if** $\text{Jaccard}(x_i, x_j) \geq \tau$ **then**
      $\mathcal{E} = \mathcal{E} + \{(i, j)\}$
Return $G(\mathcal{V}, \mathcal{E})$

### 3.1 Gaussian Mechanism

Gaussian mechanism uses $\ell_2$ norm for estimating the sensitivity due to perturbation and is a more natural fit for word embeddings than, for example, the Laplace mechanism, which is associated with the $\ell_1$ norm. Therefore, we use the Gaussian mechanism as the basis for our proposal.

Let us consider a multivariate zero-mean isotropic Gaussian noise distribution, $\mathcal{N}(\mathbf{0}, \sigma^2\mathbf{I}_d)$, where $\mathbf{I}_d$ is the unit matrix in the $d$-dimensional real space and $\sigma$ is the standard deviation. For each word, $x \in \mathcal{X}$, we sample a random vector $\boldsymbol{z} \sim \mathcal{N}(\mathbf{0}, \sigma\mathbf{I}_d)$ and create a noise-added embedding $M_g(\boldsymbol{x})$ for $x$ as given by (3).

$$M_g(\boldsymbol{x}) = \boldsymbol{x} + \boldsymbol{z} \tag{3}$$

This Gaussian mechanism uses the same $\sigma$ for all words in the vocabulary and is $(\epsilon, \delta)$-DP as claimed in in Theorem 1.[2]

**Theorem 1.** *For any $\epsilon, \delta \in (0, 1)$, the Gaussian mechanism with $\sigma = \Delta\sqrt{2\log(1.25/\delta)}/\epsilon$ is $(\epsilon, \delta)$-DP.*

The proof of Theorem 1 can be found in the Appendix A in (Dwork and Roth, 2014).

## 4 Neighbourhood-Aware Differential Privacy (NADP)

Our proposed DP-mechanism, Neighbourhood-Aware Differential Privacy (NADP), consists of

[2]As a direct extension, we could set a different standard deviations for each dimension of the embedding space. However, doing so did not result in significant performance gains in our preliminary investigations despite the increased parameters.

three main steps. First, we create a nearest neighbour graph where vertices represent the words as described in § 4.1. Next, we factorise this nearest neighbour graph into a set of mutually exclusive neighbourhoods by finding its connected components as described in § 4.2. Finally, for the words that belong to each connected component, we add random noise sampled from Gaussian distributions with zero mean and *different* standard deviations, determined according to the neighbourhood associated with the corresponding connected component. We prove that the proposed NADP mechanism is DP in § 4.3.

### 4.1 Nearest Neighbour Graph Construction

To represent the nearest neighbours of a set $\mathcal{X}$ of words, we construct a nearest neighbour graph, $G = G(\mathcal{X}, \simeq)$ with the symmetric neighbouring relation $\simeq$, vertex set $\mathcal{V}(G) = \mathcal{X}$ and edge set $\mathcal{E}(G) = \{(x, x') \mid x \simeq x'\}$. Given the one-to-one mapping between words and the vertices in the graph, for notational simplicity we denote the $i$-th vertex of the graph by $x_i (\in \mathcal{X})$. Two vertices $x_i$ and $x_j$ are connected by an edge $e_{ij} (\in \mathcal{E})$, if $x_i \simeq x_j$ holds between the corresponding words $x_i$ and $x_j$. As already explained in § 3, we define two words $x_i, x_j \in \mathcal{X}$ to be in a symmetric neighbouring relation, $x_i \simeq x_j$ if the following two conditions are jointly satisfied: (a) $x_i \in \mathcal{S}_m(x_j)$ or $x_j \in \mathcal{S}_m(x_i)$, and (b) $\text{Jaccard}(x_i, x_j) \geq \tau$ for a predefined similarity threshold $\tau \in [0, 1]$.

The pseudo code for constructing the nearest neighbour graph is shown in Algorithm 1. In our experiments, we set $m = 2$, which considers only the top-2 neighbours (i.e. $\mathcal{S}_2$) to ensure only the highly similar neighbours are connected by edges in the nearest neighbour graph. $\tau$ can be used to remove neighbours that have less similarity to a target word across the graph. For example, by setting $\tau = 0.8$, we can ensure that no two words with neighbourhood similarity (measured using the Jaccard coefficient) less than 0.8 will be connected by an edge in $\mathcal{G}$. We empirically study the effect of varying $\tau$ on NADP later in our experiments.

### 4.2 Finding Connected Components

Once a nearest neighbour graph $\mathcal{G}$ is constructed for $\mathcal{X}$, next we identify the regions of neighbours, which we refer to as the *neighbourhoods*. To consider tightly connected neighbourhoods, we propose to factorise $\mathcal{G}$ into a set of mutually exclusive connected components following the procedure described in Algorithm 2. We start by randomly selecting a word $x$ from $\mathcal{X}$ and creating a neighbourhood $\mathcal{X}_1$ consisting all of $x$'s neighbours. We then remove the words in $\mathcal{X}_1$ from $\mathcal{X}$, and repeat this process until all words in $\mathcal{X}$ are included in some neighbourhood. The procedure described in Algorithm 2 for obtaining connected components from $\mathcal{G}$ is simple, efficient and obtains good DP performance in our experiments. Moreover, it does *not* require the number of neighbourhoods, $k$, to be specified in advance as it would be the case for many clustering-based approaches for graph partitioning such as spectral clustering (von Luxburg, 2007). There is a possibility of obtaining long chains when computing connected components using Algorithm 2. However, we did not encounter this issue in our experiments. This is because the nearest neighbour relation that is defined in § 3 requires both mutual nearest neighbourhood and high Jaccard similarity to be satisfied, which reduces the likelihood of forming long chains. Exploring alternative methods for factorising a given graph into a set of mutually exclusive connected components is deferred to future work.

**Algorithm 2:** Finding Connected Components

**Inputs:** Nearest neighbour graph $G(\mathcal{V}, \mathcal{E})$
**Outputs:** Connected components $\{\mathcal{X}_1, \ldots, \mathcal{X}_k\}$
Define $k = 0$
Define $\mathcal{H}_k = \{\}$
**while** $\mathcal{X} \setminus \mathcal{H}_k \neq \emptyset$ **do**
  Choose $x \in \mathcal{X} \setminus \mathcal{H}_k$
  $k = k + 1$
  $\mathcal{X}_k = \{x\}$
  Define $\mathcal{X}' = \{x' | x' \simeq x\} \setminus \mathcal{X}_k$
  $\mathcal{X}_k = \mathcal{X}_k \cup \mathcal{X}'$
  $\mathcal{H}_k = \mathcal{H}_k \cup \mathcal{X}_k$
  **while** $\mathcal{X}' \neq \emptyset$ **do**
    $\mathcal{X}' = \{x' | x' \simeq x \text{ for some } x \in \mathcal{X}_k\} \setminus \mathcal{X}_k$
    $\mathcal{X}_k = \mathcal{X}_k \cup \mathcal{X}'$
    $\mathcal{H}_k = \mathcal{H}_k \cup \mathcal{X}_k$
Return $\{\mathcal{X}_1, \ldots, \mathcal{X}_k\}$

### 4.3 Perturbation of Word Embeddings

In this section, we will first prove that NADP satisfies the DP conditions, and then present an algorithm that can be used to add perturbation noise to the words in each neighbourhood. First note that the trivial relation $x \simeq x$ implies the set $\{||\boldsymbol{x} - \boldsymbol{y}|| \mid x \simeq y\}$ is nonempty and hence we can consider the global $L_2$ sensitivity, $\Delta = \sup_{x \simeq y} ||\boldsymbol{x} - \boldsymbol{y}||$, for any two neighbouring words $x$ and $y$ in the given set of words $\mathcal{X}$. Balle and Wang (2018) proved Theorem 2 that shows a set of word embeddings can be made differentially private by adding Gaussian noise sampled according to $\Delta$, where $\Phi(t)$ the Cumulative Density Function (CDF) of the standard univariate Gaussian distribution, given by (4).

$$\Phi(t) = \frac{1}{\sqrt{2\pi}} \int_{-\infty}^{t} e^{-y^2/2} dy. \tag{4}$$

**Theorem 2** (Balle and Wang (2018))**.** *Let $f : \mathbb{X} \to \mathbb{R}^d$ be a function with global $L_2$ sensitivity $\Delta > 0$. For any $\varepsilon \geq 0$ and $\delta \in [0, 1]$, the Gaussian output perturbation mechanism $M(x) = \boldsymbol{x} + \boldsymbol{z}$ with $\boldsymbol{z} \sim \mathcal{N}(0, \sigma^2 \mathbf{I}_d)$ ($\sigma > 0$) is $(\varepsilon, \delta)$-DP if and only if*

$$\Phi\left(\frac{\Delta}{2\sigma} - \frac{\varepsilon\sigma}{\Delta}\right) - e^{\varepsilon}\Phi\left(-\frac{\Delta}{2\sigma} - \frac{\varepsilon\sigma}{\Delta}\right) \leq \delta. \tag{5}$$

The original proof of Theorem 2 is provided in (Balle and Wang, 2018). However, in § C.1 we provide an alternative proof, which is more concise and can be directly extended to the case of multiple neighbourhoods represented by the connected components in the nearest neighbour graph.

Theorem 3 (see § C.2 for proof) states that NADP satisfies DP conditions.

**Theorem 3** (main)**.** *Let $\{\mathcal{X}_1, \cdots, \mathcal{X}_k\}$ be the connected components of the graph $G(\mathcal{X}, \simeq)$ and let $\sigma_i$ $(1 \leq i \leq k)$ be non-negative real numbers such that $\sigma_i > 0$ whenever $\Delta_i = \sup_{x \simeq y, x, y \in \mathcal{X}_i} ||\boldsymbol{x} - \boldsymbol{y}|| > 0$. For any $\boldsymbol{x} \in \mathcal{X}$, let $i(x)$ $(1 \leq i(x) \leq k)$ be the index such that $x \in \mathcal{X}_{i(x)}$. Then, for any $\varepsilon \geq 0$ and $\delta \in [0, 1]$, the Gaussian output perturbation mechanism $M(x) = \boldsymbol{x} + \boldsymbol{z}$ with $\boldsymbol{z} \sim \mathcal{N}(0, \sigma_{i(x)}^2 \mathbf{I}_d)$ is $(\varepsilon, \delta)$-DP if*

$$\Phi\left(\frac{\Delta_{i(x)}}{2\sigma_{i(x)}} - \frac{\varepsilon\sigma_{i(x)}}{\Delta_{i(x)}}\right) - e^{\varepsilon}\Phi\left(-\frac{\Delta_{i(x)}}{2\sigma_{i(x)}} - \frac{\varepsilon\sigma_{i(x)}}{\Delta_{i(x)}}\right) \leq \delta \tag{6}$$

*for any $x \in \mathcal{X}$ satisfying $\Delta_{i(x)} > 0$.*

**Remark 1.** *We have $\Delta_{i(x)} = 0$ iff the connected component $\mathcal{X}_{i(x)}$ consists of only one word $x$.*

Theorem 3 guarantees that the NADP mechanism described in Algorithm 3 for perturbing a set

**Algorithm 3:** Neighbourhood-Aware Differential Privacy

1 **Inputs:** Connected components $\{\mathcal{X}_1, \ldots, \mathcal{X}_k\}$, $\epsilon \geq 0$, $\delta \in [0, 1]$
2 **Outputs:** Perturbed word embeddings $\hat{\mathcal{X}} = \{\hat{\boldsymbol{x}}_1, \ldots, \hat{\boldsymbol{x}}_n\}$
3 Define $g(u) = \Phi\left(\frac{1}{2u} - \varepsilon u\right) - e^{\varepsilon}\Phi\left(-\frac{1}{2u} - \varepsilon u\right)$
4 Compute $u^* = \min\{u \in \mathbb{R}_{>0} \mid g(u) \leq \delta\}$
5 Define $\hat{\mathcal{X}} = \{\}$
6 **for** $i = 0, \ldots, k$ **do**
7     Compute $\Delta_i = \sup_{x \simeq y, x, y \in \mathcal{X}_i} ||\boldsymbol{x} - \boldsymbol{y}||$
8     Define $\sigma_i = u^* \Delta_i$
9     **for** $x \in \mathcal{X}_i$ **do**
10         Sample $\boldsymbol{z} \sim \mathcal{N}(0, \sigma_i^2 \mathbf{I}_d)$
11         $\hat{\boldsymbol{x}} = \boldsymbol{x} + \boldsymbol{z}$
12         $\hat{\mathcal{X}} = \hat{\mathcal{X}} + \{\hat{\boldsymbol{x}}\}$
13 Return $\hat{\mathcal{X}}$

of word embeddings satisfies DP. Specifically, we can first compute $u^*$ globally for all neighbourhoods (Line 4) as the minimiser of $g(u)$ (given by (7)) such that the DP-condition in (5) is satisfied. We can then determine the standard deviation, $\sigma_i$, corresponding to each neighbourhood, using $u^*$ and the local sensitivity, $\Delta_i$, computed from that neighbourhood. Finally, we sample noise vectors from $\mathcal{N}(0, \sigma_i^2 \mathbf{I}_d)$ and add to all word embeddings in each $\mathcal{X}_i$.

## 5 Experiments

We use the pretrained[3] 300-dimensional GloVe embeddings (Pennington et al., 2014) for 2.8M words, which have also been used in much prior work (Xu et al., 2020; Feyisetan and Kasiviswanathan, 2021) as the static word embeddings.

We build a nearest neighbour graph using the top-1000 frequent words in the English Wikipedia, which resulted in a 73,404 vertex graph. It takes less than 5 minutes to find all connected components of a graph containing 73,404 words used in the paper. Moreover, this is a task independent pre-processing step. Building the neighbourhood graph in a brute force manner requires 3.5

[3]We used 42B token Common Crawl trained embeddings available at https://nlp.stanford.edu/projects/glove/

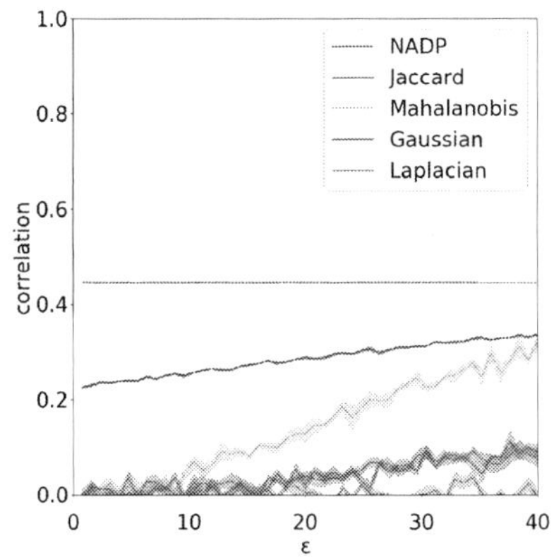


(a) Word-pair similarity prediction.

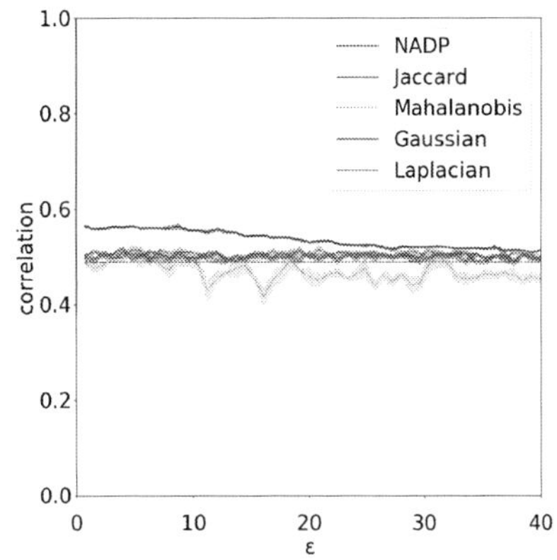


(b) Semantic textual similarity measurement.

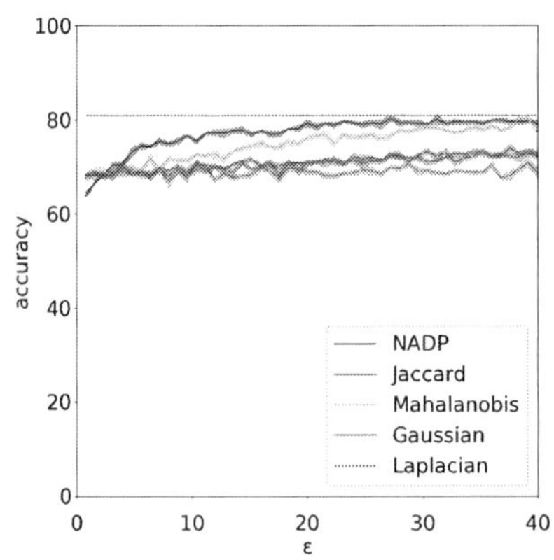


(c) Text classification.

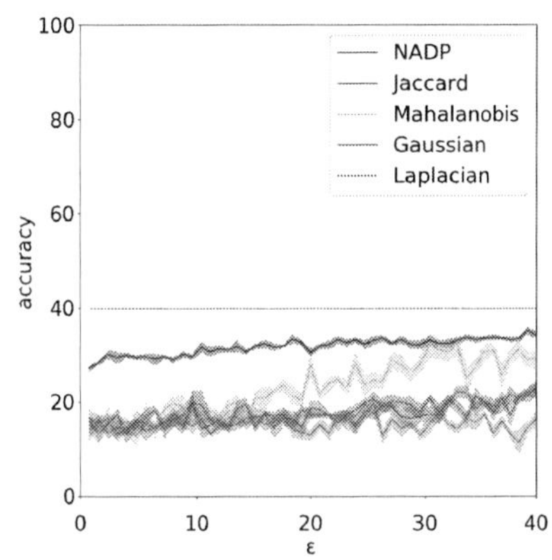


(d) Odd-man-out.

Figure 2: Performance on utility experiments (§ 5.1) shown in sub-figures (a)-(d). Accuracy and correlation (with human ratings) not decreasing with high privacy ($\epsilon$) levels (corresponding to stronger noise levels by DP mechanisms) is desirable. Performance obtained without adding any noise is shown by the horizontal dotted lines.

hours, while approximate nearest neighbour methods such as SCANN (Guo et al., 2020) an be used to do the same in less than 1 minute with over 95% recall.

In our experiments, we compare NADP against the following DP mechanisms: **Gaussian** mechanism described in § 3.1, **Laplacian** mechanism, where noise vectors are sampled from the Laplace distribution with zero location parameter and with different values of the $\epsilon$ scale parameter, **Mahalanobis** mechanism with the recommended parameter values by Xu et al. (2020) (i.e. the Mahalanobis norm $\lambda = 1$ and $\epsilon \in (0, 40]$ are used), which is the current SoTA DP mechanism for static word embeddings.

All of the above mentioned DP-mechanisms apply the same level of random noise to all word embeddings. Therefore, to understand the importance of assigning different levels of noise to different words, we consider a baseline DP mechanism, which we call the **Jaccard** mechanism. We define the density, $\eta(x)$, of the neighbourhood, $\mathcal{S}_k(x)$, of a word $x$ as the average Euclidean distance between $x$ and its nearest neighbours (i.e. $\eta(x) = \frac{1}{k}\sum_{x' \in \mathcal{S}_k(x)} ||\boldsymbol{x} - \boldsymbol{x}'||$). Next, we categorise words into two density categories: dense ($\mathcal{X}_1 = \{x | x \in \mathcal{X}, \eta(x) < \eta_0\}$) vs. sparse ($\mathcal{X}_2 = \{x | x \in \mathcal{X}, \eta(x) \geq \eta_0\}$), based on a density threshold $\eta_0$. Our preliminary experiments showed that splitting into more than two categories did not result in significant performance gains. For a word $x \in \mathcal{X}_i$, we sample a random vector $\boldsymbol{n}(x) \sim \mathcal{N}(\boldsymbol{0}, \sigma_i \mathbf{I}_d)$, for $i \in \{1, 2\}$ and add to $\boldsymbol{x}$. Jaccard is a DP mechanism (see § C.3 for the proof). Note that the density threshold is used only by the Jaccard mechanism and is not required by NADP. It is determined automatically such that we get approximately similar numbers of words in the dense and sparse sets.

## 5.1 Utility Experiments

To evaluate the semantic information preserved in word embeddings, we use the following standard tasks that have been used in much prior work for this purpose (Bollegala, 2022; Bollegala and O'Neill, 2022; Tsvetkov et al., 2015; Faruqui et al., 2015): word similarity measurement, semantic textual similarity (STS), Text Classification, Odd-man-out (Stanovsky and Hopkins, 2018). Due to space limitations, we detail the tasks, datasets and evaluation metrics in Appendix A.

**Results:** Figure 2 shows the performance obtained on utility experiments with noise-added word embeddings for different values of the privacy parameter $\epsilon$, where we use $\tau = 0.5$. The total set of words used in the datasets for all utility experiments is $n = 73404$. Therefore, we set $\delta = 1/73404 \approx 0.000013623$ in all experiments reported in the paper. We repeat each experiment five times and plot the mean and the standard error. Recall that smaller $\epsilon$ values provide stronger DP guarantees. From Figure 2, we see that NADP reports the best performance on all four tasks among the methods compared across all $\epsilon$ values. Among the other methods, Mahalanobis performs second best to NADP in word-pair similarity prediction, text classification and odd-man-out, but performs worst in STS. In word-pair similarity prediction, text classification and odd-man-out tasks, we see the performance of NADP as well as the other methods increase with $\epsilon$ due to less noise being added to the word embeddings.

The performance in STS is comparatively less affected by $\epsilon$ because it is a sentence-level comparison task, which considers all perturbed word embeddings in a sentence, whereas the other three are word-level tasks. We see that Jaccard and Gaussian mechanisms perform similarly in all tasks. This is not surprising given that the Jaccard mechanism is drawing the noise vectors from two independent Gaussian distributions. In particular for high $\epsilon$ values, we see that Gaussian outperforms Laplacian in word-pair similarity prediction, text classification and odd-man-out tasks. This result implies that for making word embeddings differentially private, the $L_2$ sensitivity considered in the Gaussian mechanism is more appropriate than the $L_1$ sensitivity considered in the Laplacian mechanism.

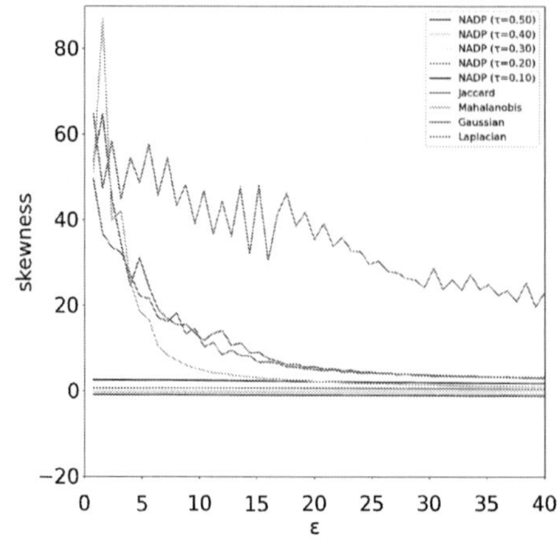


Figure 3: Skewness values for predicting words using their noise-added embeddings. Low skewness values are desirable, and indicate that the prediction probability distribution is similar to the Normal distribution and is not skewed towards a subset of the words.

## 5.2 Privacy Experiments

To empirically measure the level of privacy protected by a DP mechanism, we consider, $p(x|M(x))$, the probability of predicting the word $x$ using its noise-added embedding $M(x)$, as a metric of privacy provided by a DP mechanism. However, it is difficult to accurately estimate probability densities in discrete spaces due to data sparseness. Therefore, we approximate $p(x|M(x))$ by $\frac{|S_m(x) \cap S_m(M(x))|}{|S_m(x) \cup S_m(M(x))|}$, using the nearest neighbour sets. It is noteworthy that this is a conservative estimate of $p(x|M(x))$ because, even if all of the nearest neighbours of $x$ and $M(x)$ fully overlap , there will still be a $1/m$ uncertainty ensuring a nonzero level of privacy.

Due to the differences in neighbourhood densities, some words are likely to be influenced more than the others by a DP mechanism. From a DP point of view we are interested in protecting the privacy of all words in the vocabulary and not just for a subset of it. Therefore, to empirically quantify the global effect on privacy of a DP mechanism, we compute the *skewness* of the distribution of the estimated $p(x|M(x))$ values. If most words

| word | no-noise | Mahalanobis | NADP |
|---|---|---|---|
| misogynist | sexist, chauvinst, bigot | insulting, sexist, racist | scholastic, filicia, shannara |
| police | officers, cops, authorities | police, authorities, officials | posing, smiling, lying |
| hitler | adlof, nazi, stalin | hitler, adolf, nazi | paid, ipo, raided |
| wikileaks | assange, cia, leaked | wikileaks, iran, assange | impetuous, jashari, enraged |
| FBI | cia, investigation, informant | fbi, history, government | asylum, cardoza, sandiego |

Table 1: Top 3 neighbours for words without noise addition to the embeddings (**no-noise**), with SoTA **Mahalanobis** mechanism and the proposed **NADP** mechanism. Mahalanobis mechanism sometimes discloses the original word, whereas NADP mechanism never does.

$x_i$ has lower $p_i = p(x_i|M(x_i))$ values, the probability mass of the $p_i$ distribution will be shifted to the left of the mean, resulting in smaller skewness values (see Appendix B for further explanations). Therefore, smaller skewness values indicate that most words are protected (the probability of being discovered is smaller than the mean) under a DP mechanism.

**Results:** Figure 3 shows the skewness values reported by Jaccard, Mahalanobis, Gaussian, Laplacian mechanisms and the proposed NADP (for different $\tau$) mechanism for different $\epsilon$ values. Overall, we see that NADP reports the lowest skewness values among all DP mechanism compared, indicating that it protects privacy of word embeddings well. We see that the skewness values slightly increase with $\tau$. Recall that when $\tau$ increases the similarity of the neighbours connected to a target word by the symmetric neighbouring relation, $\simeq$, increases in the nearest neighbour graph $\mathcal{G}$. Therefore, when $\tau$ is high, unless when we apply stronger random noise to word embeddings, it becomes easier to discover the original word from its noise-added embedding. However, we note that the performance of NADP is relatively unaffected by different $\tau$ values and skewness values are low for $\tau = 0.1$ setting, which we use in the utility experiments described in § 5.1. Although Gaussian, Jaccard and Mahalanobis mechanisms obtain comparable levels of skewness values when $\epsilon > 15$, for $\epsilon < 5$, where stronger privacy guarantee is required, NADP is the only DP mechanism with near-zero skewness values.

## 6 Investigating the Nearest Neighbours

To obtain qualitative insights into the levels of privacy provided by NADP, for a given word, we compare its top-3 neighbours in the original embedding space (no-noise added), when Mahalanobis and NADP mechanisms are used to add random noise. Table 1 shows the results for some randomly selected set of words. We see that for the words such as *police*, *hitler*, *wikileaks* and *fbi*, even after applying the Mahalanobis mechanism ($\lambda = 1$), we still retrieve the original word as a nearest neighbour. This indicates that Mahalanobis mechanism is unable to anonymise the target words in these cases. Although not reported here due to space limitations, this problem persists even in Jaccard, Gaussian and Laplace mechanisms, which were under performing to the Mahalanobis mechanism in utility and privacy experiments. In the case of *misogynist*, Mahalanobis mechanism retrieves highly similar neighbours such as *sexist*. On the other hand, the neighbours retrieved from the word embeddings anonymised using NADP are semantically less similar to the target word, thus could be considered to be better preserving the privacy of the target word.

## 7 Conclusion

We proposed NADP to make word embeddings indistinguishable from their nearest neighbours with theoretical DP guarantees. We compared NADP against existing DP mechanisms in multiple downstream utility experiments which showed its superior performance. Moreover, we evaluated the level of privacy protection provided by NADP against other DP mechanisms. We found NADP to provide stronger privacy guarantees over a broad range of $\epsilon$ values. In our future work, we plan to extend NADP to sentence/document embeddings and evaluate for languages other than English.

## 8 Ethical Considerations

We do not annotate or release any datasets as part of this research. However, the GloVe word embeddings that we use in our experiments are known to contain various types of unfair social biases such as gender and racial biases (Zhao et al., 2018;

Kaneko and Bollegala, 2019, 2021; Gonen and Goldberg, 2019). It is possible that these biases could get further amplified during the neighbourhood computation and noise-addition processes we perform in this work. Therefore, such social biases must be properly evaluated before the noise-added word embeddings produced by our proposed method are used in real-world NLP applications that are used by users.

## 9 Limitations

Our investigations in this paper was limited to GloVe embeddings, which is one the many avaulable pre-trained static word embeddings. There are other alternative word embeddings such as Skip-Gram with Negative Sampling (SGNS) (Mikolov et al., 2013), PMI-based word embeddings (Arora et al., 2016), fastText embeddings (Bojanowski et al., 2017) etc. that could be used in place of GloVe. However, contextualised word embeddings, obtained using pre-trained Masked Language Models (MLMs) such as BERT (Devlin et al., 2019), RoBERTa (Liu et al., 2019), ALBERT (Lan et al., 2020), etc. have reported superior performance in various downstream tasks, surpassing that by static word embeddings. Therefore, we consider it to be a natural next step to extend our proposed method to anonymise contextualised word embeddings. The theoretical tools that we develop in this paper should be helpful in proving DP conditions for contextualised word embeddings as well.

All the downstream datasets and word embeddings we considered in this work are limited to the English language, which is known to be a morphologically limited language. Therefore, it is important to evaluate our proposed method on other languages using multilingual word embeddings to verify its effectiveness for the languages other than English.

## References


Martin Abadi, Andy Chu, Ian Goodfellow, H. Brendan McMahan, Ilya Mironov, Kunal Talwar, and Li Zhang. 2016. Deep learning with differential privacy. In *CCS*. Association for Computing Machinery, New York, NY, USA, CCS '16, pages 308–318.

Mohamed Abdalla, Moustafa Abdalla, Graeme Hirst, and Frank Rudzicz. 2020. Exploring the privacy-preserving properties of word embeddings: Algorithmic validation study. *JMIR* 22(7):e18055.

Walaa Alnasser, Ghazaleh Beigi, and Huan Liu. 2021. Privacy preserving text representation learning using bert. In *Social, Cultural, and Behavioral Modeling: 14th International Conference, SBP-BRiMS 2021, Virtual Event, July 6–9, 2021, Proceedings*. Springer-Verlag, Berlin, Heidelberg, pages 91–100.

Miguel E. Andrés, Nicolás E. Bordenabe, Konstantinos Chatzikokolakis, and Catuscia Palamidessi. 2013. Geo-indistinguishability: Differential privacy for location-based systems. In *CCS*. Association for Computing Machinery, New York, NY, USA, CCS '13, pages 901–914.

Sanjeev Arora, Yuanzhi Li, Yingyu Liang, Tengyu Ma, and Andrej Risteski. 2016. A latent variable model approach to pmi-based word embeddings. *TACL* 4:385–399.

Sanjeev Arora, Yingyu Liang, and Tengyu Ma. 2017. A simple but tough-to-beat baseline for sentence embeddings. In *Proc. of ICLR*.

Borja Balle and Yu-Xiang Wang. 2018. Improving the Gaussian mechanism for differential privacy: Analytical calibration and optimal denoising. In *ICML*. PMLR, volume 80 of *Proceedings of Machine Learning Research*, pages 394–403.

Ghazaleh Beigi, Kai Shu, Ruocheng Guo, Suhang Wang, and Huan Liu. 2019. Privacy preserving text representation learning. In *Proceedings of the 30th ACM Conference on Hypertext and Social Media*. Association for Computing Machinery, New York, NY, USA, HT '19, pages 275–276.

Piotr Bojanowski, Edouard Grave, Armand Joulin, and Tomas Mikolov. 2017. Enriching word vectors with subword information. *Transactions of the Association for Computational Linguistics* 5:135–146.

Danushka Bollegala. 2022. Learning meta word embeddings by unsupervised weighted concatenation of source embeddings. In *Proc. of the 31st International Joint Conference on Artificial Intelligence (IJCAI-ECAI)*.

Danushka Bollegala and James O'Neill. 2022. A survey on word meta-embedding learning. In *Proc. of the 31st International Joint Conference on Artificial Intelligence (IJCAI-ECAI)*.

Danushka Bollegala, Yuichi Yoshida, and Ken-ichi Kawarabayashi. 2018. Using $k$-way Co-occurrences for Learning Word Embeddings. In *Proc. of AAAI*. pages 5037–5044.

E. Bruni, N. K. Tran, and M. Baroni. 2014. Multimodal distributional semantics. *JAIR* 49:1–47.

Daniel Cer, Mona Diab, Eneko Agirre, Iñigo Lopez-Gazpio, and Lucia Specia. 2017. SemEval-2017 task 1: Semantic textual similarity multilingual and crosslingual focused evaluation. In *SemEval*. Association for Computational Linguistics, Vancouver, Canada, pages 1–14.

Jacob Devlin, Ming-Wei Chang, Kenton Lee, and Kristina Toutanova. 2019. BERT: Pre-training of Deep Bidirectional Transformers for Language Understanding. In *Proc. of NAACL-HLT*.

Cynthia Dwork and Aaron Roth. 2014. *The Algorithmic Foundations of Differential Privacy*, volume 9. Foundations and Trends in TCS.

Manaal Faruqui, Jesse Dodge, Sujay Kumar Jauhar, Chris Dyer, Eduard Hovy, and Noah A. Smith. 2015. Retrofitting word vectors to semantic lexicons. In *Proceedings of the 2015 Conference of the North American Chapter of the Association for Computational Linguistics: Human Language Technologies*. Association for Computational Linguistics, Denver, Colorado, pages 1606–1615.

Oluwaseyi Feyisetan, Borja Balle, Thomas Drake, and Tom Diethe. 2020. Privacy- and utility-preserving textual analysis via calibrated multivariate perturbations. In *WSDM*. Association for Computing Machinery, New York, NY, USA, WSDM '20, pages 178–186.

Oluwaseyi Feyisetan and Shiva Kasiviswanathan. 2021. Private release of text embedding vectors. In *TrustNLP*. Association for Computational Linguistics, Online, pages 15–27.

Daniela Gerz, Ivan Vulić, Felix Hill, Roi Reichart, and Anna Korhonen. 2016. SimVerb-3500: A large-scale evaluation set of verb similarity. In *EMNLP*. Association for Computational Linguistics, Austin, Texas, pages 2173–2182.

Hila Gonen and Yoav Goldberg. 2019. Lipstick on a pig: Debiasing methods cover up systematic gender biases in word embeddings but do not remove them. In *Proceedings of the 2019 Conference of the North American Chapter of the Association for Computational Linguistics: Human Language Technologies, Volume 1 (Long and Short Papers)*. Association for Computational Linguistics, Minneapolis, Minnesota, pages 609–614.

Ruiqi Guo, Philip Sun, Erik Lindgren, Quan Geng, David Simcha, Felix Chern, and Sanjiv Kumar. 2020. Accelerating large-scale inference with anisotropic vector quantization. In Hal Daumé III and Aarti Singh, editors, *Proceedings of the 37th International Conference on Machine Learning*. PMLR, volume 119 of *Proceedings of Machine Learning Research*, pages 3887–3896.

Prakhar Gupta and Martin Jaggi. 2021. Obtaining better static word embeddings using contextual embedding models. In *Proceedings of the 59th Annual Meeting of the Association for Computational Linguistics and the 11th International Joint Conference on Natural Language Processing (Volume 1: Long Papers)*. Association for Computational Linguistics, Online, pages 5241–5253.

Ivan Habernal. 2021. When differential privacy meets NLP: The devil is in the detail. In *EMNLP*. Association for Computational Linguistics, Online and Punta Cana, Dominican Republic, pages 1522–1528.

Ivan Habernal. 2022. How reparametrization trick broke differentially-private text representation learning. In *Proceedings of the 60th Annual Meeting of the Association for Computational Linguistics (Volume 2: Short Papers)*. Association for Computational Linguistics, Dublin, Ireland, pages 771–777.

Felix Hill, Roi Reichart, and Anna Korhonen. 2015. Simlex-999: Evaluating semantic models with (genuine) similarity estimation. *Computational Linguistics* 41(4):665–695.

Minqing Hu and Bing Liu. 2004. Mining and summarizing customer reviews. In *KDD 2004*. pages 168–177.

D. N. Joanes and C. A. Gill. 1998. Comparing measures of sample skewness and kurtosis. *Journal of the Royal Statistical Society: Series D (The Statistician)* 47(1):183–189.

Masahiro Kaneko and Danushka Bollegala. 2019. Gender-preserving debiasing for pre-trained word embeddings. In *Proceedings of the 57th Annual Meeting of the Association for Computational Linguistics*. Association for Computational Linguistics, Florence, Italy, pages 1641–1650.

Masahiro Kaneko and Danushka Bollegala. 2021. Dictionary-based debiasing of pre-trained word embeddings. In *Proceedings of the 16th Conference of the European Chapter of the Association for Computational Linguistics: Main Volume*. Association for Computational Linguistics, Online, pages 212–223.

Shiva Prasad Kasiviswanathan, Homin K. Lee, Kobbi Nissim, Sofya Raskhodnikova, and Adam Smith. 2008. What can we learn privately? In *FOCS*. IEEE.

Satyapriya Krishna, Rahul Gupta, and Christophe Dupuy. 2021. ADePT: Auto-encoder based differentially private text transformation. In *EACL*. Association for Computational Linguistics, Online, pages 2435–2439.

Zhenzhong Lan, Mingda Chen, Sebastian Goodman, Kevin Gimpel, Piyush Sharma, and Radu Soricut. 2020. Albert: A lite bert for self-supervised learning of language representations. In *Proc. of ICLR*.

Yitong Li, Timothy Baldwin, and Trevor Cohn. 2018. Towards robust and privacy-preserving text representations. In *Proceedings of the 56th Annual Meeting of the Association for Computational Linguistics (Volume 2: Short Papers)*. Association for Computational Linguistics, Melbourne, Australia, pages 25–30.

Yinhan Liu, Myle Ott, Naman Goyal, Jingfei Du, Mandar Joshi, Danqi Chen, Omer Levy, Mike Lewis, Luke Zettlemoyer, and Veselin Stoyanov. 2019. RoBERTa: A Robustly Optimized BERT Pretraining Approach.

Lingjuan Lyu, Xuanli He, and Yitong Li. 2020a. Differentially private representation for NLP: Formal guarantee and an empirical study on privacy and fairness. In *EMNLP*. Association for Computational Linguistics, Online, pages 2355–2365.

Lingjuan Lyu, Yitong Li, Xuanli He, and Tong Xiao. 2020b. Towards differentially private text representations. In *SIGIR*. Association for Computing Machinery, New York, NY, USA, pages 1813–1816.

Tomas Mikolov, Kai Chen, and Jeffrey Dean. 2013. Efficient estimation of word representation in vector space. In *ICLR*.

Bo Pang and Lillian Lee. 2005. Seeing stars: Exploiting class relationships for sentiment categorization with respect to rating scales. In *Proc. of ACL*. pages 115–124.

Jeffery Pennington, Richard Socher, and Christopher D. Manning. 2014. Glove: global vectors for word representation. In *Proc. of EMNLP*. pages 1532–1543.

Ryan M Rogers, Aaron Roth, Jonathan Ullman, and Salil Vadhan. 2016. Privacy odometers and filters: Pay-as-you-go composition. In *NeurIPS*. Curran Associates, Inc., volume 29.

Congzheng Song and Vitaly Shmatikov. 2019. Auditing data provenance in text-generation models. In *KDD*. Association for Computing Machinery, New York, NY, USA, KDD '19, pages 196–206.

Gabriel Stanovsky and Mark Hopkins. 2018. Spot the odd man out: Exploring the associative power of lexical resources. In *EMNLP*. Association for Computational Linguistics, Brussels, Belgium, pages 1533–1542.

Yulia Tsvetkov, Manaal Faruqui, Wang Ling, Guillaume Lample, and Chris Dyer. 2015. Evaluation of word vector representations by subspace alignment. In *Proceedings of the 2015 Conference on Empirical Methods in Natural Language Processing*. Association for Computational Linguistics, Lisbon, Portugal, pages 2049–2054.

Ulrike von Luxburg. 2007. A tutorial on spectral clustering. *Statistics and Computing* 17(4):395 – 416.

Wenjie Wang, Pengfei Tang, Jian Lou, and Li Xiong. 2021. Certified robustness to word substitution attack with differential privacy. In *NAACL*. Association for Computational Linguistics, Online, pages 1102–1112.

Janyce Wiebe, Theresa Wilson, and Claire Cardie. 2005. Annotating expressions of opinions and emotions in language. In *LREC*.

Zekun Xu, Abhinav Aggarwal, Oluwaseyi Feyisetan, and Nathanael Teissier. 2020. A differentially private text perturbation method using regularized mahalanobis metric. In *PrivateNLP*. Association for Computational Linguistics, Online, pages 7–17.

Jieyu Zhao, Yichao Zhou, Zeyu Li, Wei Wang, and Kai-Wei Chang. 2018. Learning gender-neutral word embeddings. In *Proceedings of the 2018 Conference on Empirical Methods in Natural Language Processing*. Association for Computational Linguistics, pages 4847–4853.

Yuqing Zhu, Xiang Yu, Manmohan Chandraker, and Yu-Xiang Wang. 2020. Private-knn: Practical differential privacy for computer vision. In *CVPR*. pages 11851–11859.

## Supplementary Materials

## A Downstream Tasks, Datasets and Evaluation Metrics

**Word Similarity:** The cosine similarity between two words, computed using their word embeddings, is compared against the human similarity ratings using the Spearman correlation coefficient. High degree of correlation with human similarity ratings implies that the word embeddings accurately encode the word-level semantics. We aggregate all of the word-pairs and their human similarity ratings in MEN (Bruni et al., 2014), SimLex (Hill et al., 2015) and SimVerb (Gerz et al., 2016) benchmark datasets and report the overall Spearman correlation in Figure 2a.

**Semantic Textual Similarity (STS):** In STS, we are provided with sentence-pairs and the human similarity ratings between the two sentences in each pair. Using the word embeddings, we first create an embedding for each sentence and then compute the cosine similarity between the sentence embeddings. The correlation between the predicted sentence similarities and the human ratings is used as the evaluation metric. We represent each sentence by the centroid of the word embeddings corresponding to the words included in that sentence. Although this is a simple method for creating sentence embeddings from word embeddings, it is known to be a strong unsupervised baseline (Arora et al., 2017), and enables us to directly attribute any differences in performance to the word embeddings – the focus in this work. We use the STS Benchmark dataset (Cer et al., 2017), which contains 1379 test sentence-pairs and show the official score (i.e. class-weighted geometric mean of Spearman and Pearson correlation) in Figure 2b.

**Text Classification:** We train a binary classifier to predict the sentiment (positive vs. negative) of a short review text. Similar to the STS task, we represent a review using the centroid of the word embeddings of the words included in that review. We train a binary logistic regression model to predict sentiment in a review and in Figure 2c report the averaged classification accuracy on the balanced test sets in three standard datasets: Movie reviews dataset (Pang and Lee, 2005), customer reviews dataset (Hu and Liu, 2004) and opinion polarity dataset (Wiebe et al., 2005).

**Odd-man-out:** Stanovsky and Hopkins (Stanovsky and Hopkins, 2018) proposed the *odd-man-out* task, where given a set of five or more words, a system is required to choose the one which does not belong with the others. They annotated a dataset containing 843 sets via crowd sourcing. Pretrained word embeddings can be used to identify the odd-man in a set by repeatedly excluding one word at a time and measuring the average cosine similarity between all remaining pairs of words. Finally, the word when excluded resulting in the highest pairwise similarity is chosen as the odd-man. Unlike previously described tasks, odd-man-out can be carried out in an unsupervised manner, at word-level, and has higher human agreement between the annotators because it does not require numerical ratings. The percentage of correctly solved sets is shown in Figure 2d.

## B Skewness and Privacy

Skewness is a measure of the asymmetry of $p(x|M(x))$ about its mean and can be positive, negative or zero depending on whether $p(x|M(x))$ has respectively a longer left tail, right tail, or perfectly symmetric around the mean (e.g. as in the case of the standard Normal distribution) (Joanes and Gill, 1998). Specifically, if we denote the probability of predicting $i$-th word $x_i$ by $p_i = p(x_i|M(x_i))$, the skewness of the distribution of $p_i$ over $n$ words is given by $\frac{n}{(n-1)(n-2)} \sum_{i=1}^{n} \left(\frac{p_i - \bar{p}_i}{s}\right)^3$, where $\bar{p}_i$ and $s$ are respectively the mean and standard deviation of $\{p_i\}_{i=1}^{n}$.

We study the relationship between the level of privacy protected by the noise added using a particular DP mechanism, $M$ and the skewness of the distribution of $p(x|M(x))$ for the words $w$ in a vocabulary $\mathcal{X}$. For this purpose, we use the Gaussian mechanism described in § 3.1 in the paper where we sample noise vectors $\boldsymbol{z} \in \mathbb{R}^d$ from the $d$-dimensional spherical Gaussian $\mathcal{N}(0, \sigma \mathbf{I}_d)$ with zero-mean and standard deviation $\sigma$, and add this noise to the word embedding, $\boldsymbol{x} \in \mathbb{R}^d$, representing the word $x$. Specifically, $M(x) = \boldsymbol{x} + \boldsymbol{z}$. Next, we gradually increase $\sigma \in [0, 1]$ in step size of $0.05$ and compute the histograms of $p(x|M(x))$ values for the words in $\mathcal{X}$. The histograms and their skewness values are shown in Figure 4.

From Figure 4, we see that when no-noise is being added (i.e. $\sigma = 0$), the histogram peaks at 1, indicating that all words can be trivially discovered from their word embeddings because the closest neighbour of any target word in the embedding space will be itself. Because the distribution is symmetric around this peak, we have a zero skewness. Overall, we see that when we add increasingly high noise, the histograms start shifting towards to the left because less words will be perfectly discovered from the noise added embeddings. Moreover, we see that more probability mass is distributed towards the right side of the mode (peak), resulting in a longer right tail. Consequently, we see skewness values also continuously increase (except at $\sigma = 0.05$, where the distribution has split into two parts) with $\sigma$. This trend stems from the definition of skewness and is independent of the DP mechanism used to generate noise. This result shows that when there are many words with smaller $p(x|M(x))$ values (i.e. distribution has a longer left tail), the skewness values will be smaller, indicating that the privacy is preserved for many words in $\mathcal{X}$.

## C Proofs of Theorems

### C.1 Proof of Theorem 2

*Proof.* For any $\varepsilon \geq 0$ and $\delta \in (0, 1)$, put

$$g(u) = \Phi\left(\frac{1}{2u} - \varepsilon u\right) - e^{\varepsilon}\Phi\left(-\frac{1}{2u} - \varepsilon u\right) \quad (7)$$

and $u^* = \min\{u \in \mathbb{R}_{>0} \mid g(u) \leq \delta\}$.

We will prove the following three statements:

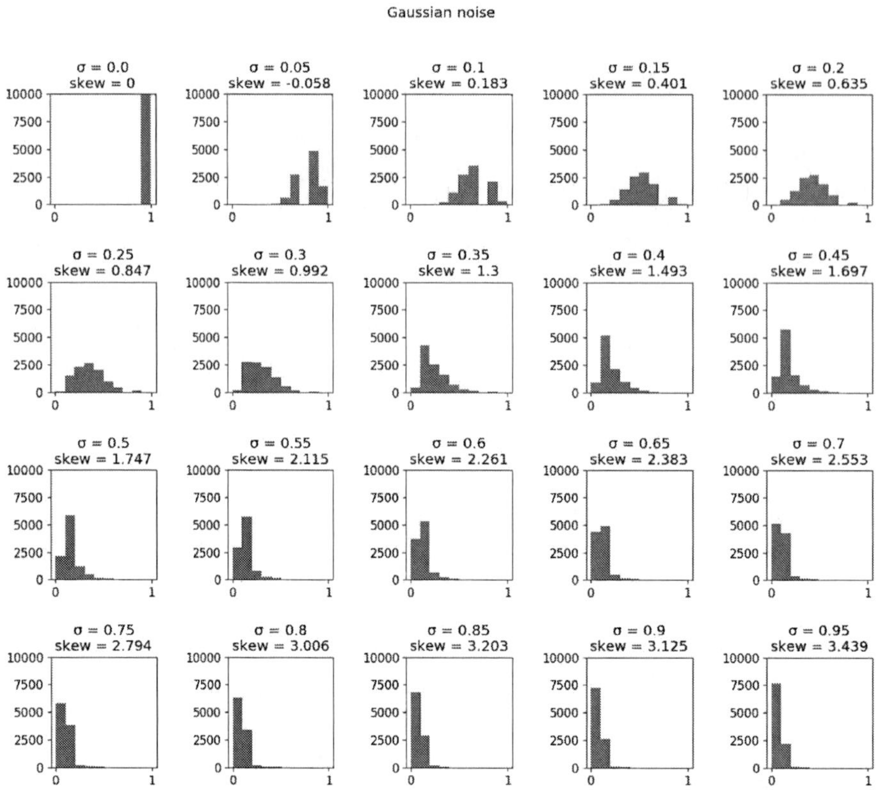


Figure 4: Histogram of $p_i$ values when zero-mean and $\sigma$ standard deviation Gaussian noise is added to the word embeddings. Skewness values (skew) are shown in each histogram alongside with the $\sigma$.

(a) $g(u)$ is strictly decreasing on $(0, \infty)$ with $\lim_{u \to +0} g(u) = 1$, $\lim_{u \to \infty} g(u) = 0$.
(b) The equation $g(u) = \delta$ has the unique solution $u^*$.
(c) Put $\sigma = u^* \Delta$. Then, the Gaussian output perturbation mechanism $M(x) = \boldsymbol{x} + \boldsymbol{z}$ with $\boldsymbol{z} \sim \mathcal{N}(0, \sigma^2 \mathbf{I}_d)$ is $(\varepsilon, \delta)$-DP.
To prove (a) Put

$$\begin{aligned} h(u) &= \sqrt{2\pi} g(u) \\ &= \sqrt{2\pi} \left\{ \Phi\left(\frac{1}{2u} - \varepsilon u\right) - e^{\varepsilon} \Phi\left(-\frac{1}{2u} - \varepsilon u\right) \right\}. \end{aligned}$$

Then,

$$\begin{aligned} h'(u) &= \exp\left(-\frac{1}{2}\left(\frac{1}{2u} - \varepsilon u\right)^2\right) \cdot \left(-\frac{1}{2u^2} - \varepsilon\right) \\ &\quad - \exp(\varepsilon) \cdot \exp\left(-\frac{1}{2}\left(-\frac{1}{2u} - \varepsilon u\right)^2\right) \cdot \left(\frac{1}{2u^2} - \varepsilon\right) \\ &= \exp\left(-\frac{1}{2}\left(\frac{1}{2u} - \varepsilon u\right)^2\right) \cdot \left(-\frac{1}{2u^2} - \varepsilon\right) \\ &\quad - \exp\left(-\frac{1}{2}\left(\frac{1}{2u} - \varepsilon u\right)^2\right) \cdot \left(\frac{1}{2u^2} - \varepsilon\right) \\ &= -\frac{1}{u^2} \cdot \exp\left(-\frac{1}{2}\left(\frac{1}{2u} - \varepsilon u\right)^2\right) < 0 \end{aligned}$$

for any $u > 0$. Therefore, $g(u) = (1/\sqrt{2\pi}) h(u)$ is strictly decreasing on $(0, \infty)$. The latter half of the statement is clear from the definition of $g(u)$.
Next, to prove (b) observe that since $g(u)$ is a continuous function on $(0, \infty)$ satisfying $\lim_{u \to +0} g(u) = 1$ and $\lim_{u \to \infty} g(u) = 0$, $g(u) = \delta$ has a solution $u'$ for any $\delta \in (0, 1)$, which must be unique and satisfy $u' = u^*$ because of the monotonicity of $g(u)$.
Finally, to prove (c) let $\sigma = u^* \Delta$. We then have

$$\begin{aligned} &\Phi\left(\frac{\Delta}{2\sigma} - \frac{\varepsilon\sigma}{\Delta}\right) - e^{\varepsilon} \Phi\left(-\frac{\Delta}{2\sigma} - \frac{\varepsilon\sigma}{\Delta}\right) \\ &= \Phi\left(\frac{1}{2u^*} - \varepsilon u^*\right) - e^{\varepsilon} \Phi\left(-\frac{1}{2u^*} - \varepsilon u^*\right) = g(u^*) \leq \delta, \end{aligned}$$

which implies the mechanism $M(x) = \boldsymbol{x} + \boldsymbol{z}$ with $\boldsymbol{z} \sim \mathcal{N}(0, \sigma^2 \mathbf{I}_d)$ is $(\varepsilon, \delta)$-DP as stated in Theorem 2. □

## C.2 Proof of Theorem 3

*Proof.* For any $i$ $(1 \le i \le k)$, let $\simeq_i$ be the symmetric neighbouring relation obtained by restricting the relation $\simeq$ on $\mathcal{X}_i$. Then, $\Delta_i$ equals to the global $L_2$ sensitivity of $(\mathcal{X}_i, \simeq_i)$ and $\Delta_{i(x)} = \Delta_i$, $\sigma_{i(x)} = \sigma_i$ for any $x \in \mathcal{X}_i$. Hence, if $\Delta_i > 0$, the mechanism $M_i$ obtained by restricting $M$ on $(\mathcal{X}_i, \simeq_i)$ is $(\varepsilon, \delta)$-DP if and only if

$$\Phi\left(\frac{\Delta_{i(x)}}{2\sigma_{i(x)}} - \frac{\varepsilon\sigma_{i(x)}}{\Delta_{i(x)}}\right) - e^{\varepsilon}\Phi\left(-\frac{\Delta_{i(x)}}{2\sigma_{i(x)}} - \frac{\varepsilon\sigma_{i(x)}}{\Delta_{i(x)}}\right) \le \delta$$

for any $x \in \mathcal{X}_i$ by Theorem 2.

Let $x, x' \in \mathcal{X}$ be words such that $x \simeq x'$ and $i$ $(= i(x) = i(x'))$ be the index such that $x, x' \in \mathcal{X}_i$, that is, $x \simeq_i x'$. Now, suppose $\Delta_i > 0$ and (6) holds for any $x \in \mathcal{X}_i$. Then, the mechanism $M_i$ is $(\varepsilon, \delta)$-DP and hence, we have

$$\begin{aligned}\mathbb{P}[M(x) \in E] &= \mathbb{P}[M_i(x) \in E] \\ &\le e^{\varepsilon}\mathbb{P}[M_i(x') \in E] + \delta \\ &= e^{\varepsilon}\mathbb{P}[M(x') \in E] + \delta\end{aligned}$$

for any measurable set $E \subset \mathbb{R}$. Next, suppose $\Delta_{i(x)} = \Delta_{i(x')} = 0$. Then, we have $x = x'$ and hence

$$\mathbb{P}[M(x) \in E] \le e^{\varepsilon}\mathbb{P}[M(x') \in E] + \delta$$

for any measurable set $E \subset \mathbb{R}$, which implies the mechanism $M$ is $(\varepsilon, \delta)$-DP if the condition (6) holds for any $x \in \mathcal{X}$ satisfying $\Delta_{i(x)} > 0$. □

**Corollary 1.** *For any $\varepsilon \ge 0$ and $\delta \in (0, 1)$, put*

$$g(u) = \Phi\left(\frac{1}{2u} - \varepsilon u\right) - e^{\varepsilon}\Phi\left(-\frac{1}{2u} - \varepsilon u\right)$$

*and $u^* = \min\{u \in \mathbb{R}_{>0} \mid g(u) \le \delta\}$. Also, put $\sigma_{i(x)} = u^*\Delta_{i(x)}$ for any $x \in \mathcal{X}$. Then, the Gaussian output perturbation mechanism $M(x) = \boldsymbol{x} + \boldsymbol{z}$ with $\boldsymbol{z} \sim \mathcal{N}(0, \sigma_{i(x)}^2\mathbf{I}_d)$ is $(\varepsilon, \delta)$-DP.*

*Proof.* Suppose $\Delta_{i(x)} > 0$. Then, by definition, we have

$$\begin{aligned}&\Phi\left(\frac{\Delta_{i(x)}}{2\sigma_{i(x)}} - \frac{\varepsilon\sigma_{i(x)}}{\Delta_{i(x)}}\right) - e^{\varepsilon}\Phi\left(-\frac{\Delta_{i(x)}}{2\sigma_{i(x)}} - \frac{\varepsilon\sigma_{i(x)}}{\Delta_{i(x)}}\right) \\ &= \Phi\left(\frac{1}{2u^*} - \varepsilon u^*\right) - e^{\varepsilon}\Phi\left(-\frac{1}{2u^*} - \varepsilon u^*\right) = g(u^*) \le \delta,\end{aligned}$$

which implies the mechanism $M(x) = \boldsymbol{x} + \boldsymbol{z}$ with $\boldsymbol{z} \sim \mathcal{N}(0, \sigma_{i(x)}^2\mathbf{I}_d)$ is $(\varepsilon, \delta)$-DP as claimed in Theorem 3. □

## C.3 Jaccard Mechanism is DP

Theorem 4 claims that the above-mentioned Jaccard mechanism is $(\epsilon, \delta)$-DP.

**Theorem 4** (Jaccard mechanism is DP). *Jaccard mechanism with $\sigma_i = \Delta\alpha_i\sqrt{2\log(1.25/\delta)}/\epsilon$ is $(\epsilon, \delta)$-DP. Here, $\alpha_i$ is a constant that depends only on the density category of a word and $\Delta$ is the global sensitivity over the vocabulary.*

*Proof.* Note that under the Jaccard mechanism, noise vectors, $n(x)$, are sampled from either one of the two Gaussians $\mathcal{N}(\mathbf{0}, \sigma_1\mathbf{I}_d)$ or $\mathcal{N}(\mathbf{0}, \sigma_2\mathbf{I}_d)$ depending on respectively whether $x \in \mathcal{X}_1$ or $x \in \mathcal{X}_2$. Moreover, because $\alpha_i$ depends only on $\mathcal{X}_i$, from $\sigma_i = \Delta\alpha_i\sqrt{2\log(1.25/\delta)}/\epsilon$ and from Theorem 1 we see that each of these underlying Gaussian mechanisms are $(\epsilon, \delta)$-DP. Because $\mathcal{X}_1 \cap \mathcal{X}_2 = \emptyset$ by their definitions, it follows from the compositionality property of DP that the overall Jaccard process is also $(0, \delta)$-DP. This proof can be easily extended to more than two density categories by mathematical induction. □

In our experiments, we use $\eta_0 = 6.0$ such that approximately equal numbers of words in $\mathcal{X}$ belong to each category, corresponding to $\alpha_1 = 1.835$ and $\alpha_2 = 1.276$ for $m = 10$. Global sensitivity $\Delta$ is computed as the average Euclidean distance between a word and its furthermost neighbour.

The ability to guarantee the mean overlap between neighbourhoods before and after the noise addition is important from the point-of-view of NLP tasks that depend on the neighbourhood information such as semantic similarity measurement, bag-of-words representations-based information retrieval and word/text classification tasks, etc. Unlike in the Gaussian mechanism, in the Jaccard mechanism we have a direct relationship between the level of noise and the performance obtained using the anonymised embeddings in the downstream tasks. Moreover, the Jaccard mechanism allows us to set different noise levels to sparse vs. dense regions in the embedding space, which is not possible with other DP mechanisms.

# PhraseSumm: Abstractive Short Phrase Summarization

**Kasturi Bhattacharjee*** **Kathleen McKeown** **Rashmi Gangadharaiah**
AWS AI Labs
{kastb,mckeownk,rgangad}@amazon.com

## Abstract

Prior work in the field of text summarization mostly focuses on generating summaries that are a sentence or two long. In this work, we introduce the task of abstractive short-phrase summarization (**PhraseSumm**), which aims at capturing the central theme of a document through a generated short phrase. We explore BART & T5-based neural summarization models, and measure their effectiveness for the task using both standard summarization metrics as well as human evaluation. Our work showcases the benefits of pre-training the summarization models using tasks such as phrasal paraphrase alignment and NLI before fine-tuning on the task itself, both of which help the model with abstraction and thereby yield improvements over the baselines. Human evaluation reveals that model generated summaries are often judged better than or equal to reference summaries, demonstrating that ROUGE scores underestimate true performance. Finally, we create and release a dataset for this task to enable further research in the area.

## 1 Introduction

Text summarization is a well-studied NLP task of compressing long textual documents to concise, human readable summaries that capture the key semantic information contained in the documents (Nallapati et al., 2017; Dou et al., 2020; Kryscinski et al., 2020; Zhang et al., 2022). In general, there are two main approaches for summarization - *extractive* and *abstractive*. While extractive approaches (Nallapati et al., 2017; Zhong et al., 2019; Wang et al., 2020) focus on copying salient portions of the source document for the summary, abstractive approaches focus on generating novel sentences to create a coherent and succinct summary that remain faithful to the central notions within the input text (Kryscinski et al., 2020; Chen et al., 2021; Ladhak et al., 2021).

| **Utterance** | **Intent Label/Short phrase Summary** |
|---|---|
| **Dataset: CLINC150** | |
| *give me a hand finding my mobile device* | find phone |
| *how to keep my credit score from going down* | improve credit score |
| *i lost my chase bank card and want it labeled as lost* | report lost card |
| **Dataset: SNIPS** | |
| *Give me Steve's address in Manhattan* | Get Place Details |
| *Get me a table at a restaurant near Emily's place for tomorrow 9pm* | Book Restaurant |
| *What is the cheapest restaurant between Balthazar and Lombardi's?* | Compare Places |

Table 1: Examples of utterances & intent labels from CLINC150 & SNIPS datasets. The intent labels are used as short phrase summaries for our task.

Most prior work in both these areas focus on summarizing long documents such as news articles (Eyal et al., 2019; Nenkova et al., 2011; Ahuja et al., 2022), novel chapters (Ladhak et al., 2020; Wu et al., 2021), movie scripts (Chen et al., 2022; Gorinski and Lapata, 2015) etc. to generate summaries that are at least a few sentences in length. However, in this work, we *introduce* ***PhraseSumm***, *a new task* of **abstractive short-phrase summarization** that aims at generating abstractive summaries consisting of a short phrase (2-3 words) from documents that are relatively shorter in length (in our case, mostly consisting of 5-12 words in a single sentence). The short phrase should aim to capture the main theme within the document. To the best of our knowledge, our work is unique in its focus on summarization using short phrases.

Our task involves summarizing an input document using a short phrase which is often not present within the document, and can not, therefore, be obtained using *extractive* techniques alone. Thus, approaches based on topic modeling (Card

*Corresponding author



*Findings of the Association for Computational Linguistics: IJCNLP-AACL 2023*, pages 80–94
November 1–4, 2023. 

et al., 2017; Nguyen and Luu, 2021; Gui et al., 2019) and keyphrase extraction (Papagiannopoulou and Tsoumakas, 2020; Sun et al., 2020; Bennani-Smires et al., 2018) are insufficient for this task. We use intent detection datasets as a proxy for this task, considering utterances as input text and the corresponding intent labels as short-phrase summaries. As shown in Table 1, for most of the cases, the phrase constituting the intent label is not present within the utterance. For instance, **find phone** does not occur in the input utterance *give me a hand finding my mobile device*, but could be inferred from it.

Intent detection is usually framed as a text classification task under the assumption that the entire set of intent labels is known at the time of model training. However, operating within this framework is insufficient if the full label set is not known *apriori*, as can often be the case in real-world scenarios where defining all possible intents can be unrealistic, and we wish to be able to generate intent labels on the fly. This also allows us to *discover* new intents since there can often be more than one suitable intent for each input.

We explore state-of-the-art (SOTA) neural seq2seq text summarization models based on T5-large (Raffel et al., 2020) and BART-large (Lewis et al., 2019) for the task of abstractive short-phrase summarization. Off-the-shelf models are found to be insufficient for this task. Given the need for phrasal paraphrases to be implicitly inferred from the input, we hypothesized that knowledge about paraphrasing and inference would help to improve the model. We demonstrate improvements by pre-training models with phrasal paraphrase alignment (Ouyang et al., 2017) and Natural Language Inference (NLI) (Kumar and Talukdar, 2020; Schick and Schütze, 2021) tasks, before task-specific fine-tuning. Standard summarization metrics such as ROUGE, METEOR, BERTScore & BARTScore are used to evaluate the models, along with human evaluation. Our studies further show that our models are capable of generating short-phrase summaries that may differ from the reference summary, but are still helpful at summarizing the input text, as deemed using human evaluation through Amazon Mechanical Turk. In contrast, we find standard summarization metrics to be unable to capture the usefulness of such summaries.

**Contributions of our paper**:

- In this work, we define a new task of abstractive short-phrase summarization (PhraseSumm), and use intent classification datasets to explore T5-large & BART-large summarization models for the problem.
- We demonstrate the benefits of pre-training models with phrasal paraphrase alignment and NLI tasks, prior to task-specific finetuning, and show improvements over two baselines.
- Further, we show the shortcomings of standard summarization metrics such as ROUGE for this problem, and highlight the importance of human evaluation.
- We release a dataset for this problem, to enable further research in this area [1].

## 2 Related Work

Summarization tasks related to our problem are sentence compression (Kamigaito and Okumura, 2020; Zhao et al., 2019) and news headline generation (Rush et al., 2017; Li et al., 2021; Zhan et al., 2022). However, they differ from our task in terms of the expected length of the generated summary. While we focus on obtaining summaries that constitute 2-3 words in length, both these tasks expect longer generated text. Paraphrase generation is another related task that involves generating paraphrases of input sentences that are semantically similar but may be syntactically different. Notable work in the area includes Gupta et al. (2018) that uses a combination of VAE and LSTM, Egonmwan and Chali (2019) that employ a stacked encoder (Transformer & GRU-RNN)-decoder framework, Fu et al. (2019) that utilize a latent BOW approach for generating paraphrases. Other work includes Prakash et al. (2016); Li et al. (2018); Zhao et al. (2009); Goyal and Durrett (2020). Although related, our task cannot be solved by paraphrase generation since we expect abstractive *short phrase* summaries to be generated for the input.

Other related tasks include topic modeling (Doan and Hoang, 2021) and keyphrase extraction (Papagiannopoulou and Tsoumakas, 2020). Approaches such as TextRank (Kazemi et al., 2020), TopicalPageRank (Sterckx et al., 2015), Bi-LSTM-CRF Sequence Labeling (Alzaidy et al., 2019), FACE (Chau et al., 2020), SIFRank (Sun et al., 2020) have been applied towards keyphrase extraction

[1] `https://github.com/amazon-science/PhraseSumm-short-phrase-summarization`

| Dataset | Number of utterances per split |
|---|---|
| CLINC150 | **train:** 9900, **dev:** 1980, **test_s:** 2970, **test_u:** 1650 |
| SNIPS | **train:** 170, **dev:** 35, **test_s:** 40, **test_u:** 83. |

Table 2: Data statistics for the CLINC150 & SNIPS datasets. **test_s** and **test_u** refer to the test sets with labels seen & unseen during training, respectively. For details, please refer to Section 3.3.

from documents. Further, topic modeling methods such as SCHOLAR (Card et al., 2017), contrastive learning based topic approaches (Nguyen and Luu, 2021), Reinforcement Learning-based methodologies (Gui et al., 2019) have been applied towards neural topic modeling. However, neither keyphrase extraction nor topic modeling suffice for our task since the short phrase summaries required are often not present in the input documents.

We leverage intent detection datasets for this task, namely CLINC150 (Larson et al., 2019) and SNIPS (Coucke et al., 2018), with modifications to fit our problem, details of which we describe in Section 3.3. These datasets have been widely used for intent classification (Casanueva et al., 2020; Zhang et al., 2020; Lee et al., 2021; Chen et al., 2019).

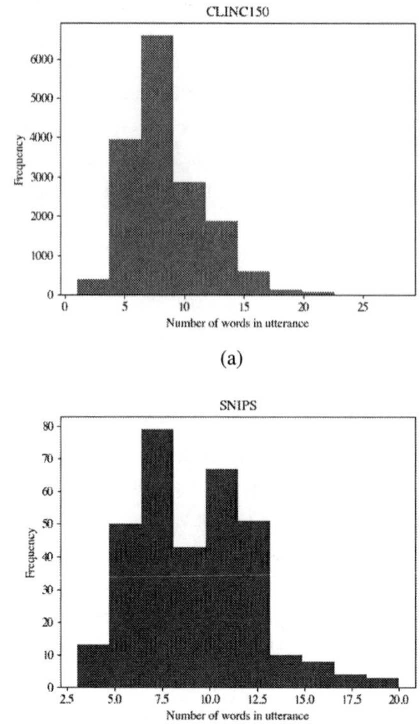


(a)

(b)

Figure 1: Distribution of the number of words in input text for (a) CLINC & (b) SNIPS datasets.

## 3 Datasets

In this section, we introduce the intent classification datasets used for this task. In order to mimic real-world settings where the entire set of intent labels may not be present *apriori*, we describe the creation of test sets with intents unseen during training.

### 3.1 CLINC150

We use an intent classification dataset, CLINC150 (Larson et al., 2019) that contains utterances & intent labels for 10 general domains, e.g. banking, credit cards, kitchen & dining, home, etc. The dataset has 15 intents per domain and comes with pre-defined training, dev, and test splits. Examples are provided in Table 1. The input text length distribution is provided in Figure 1a.

### 3.2 SNIPS

We also leverage another popularly used intent classification dataset SNIPS (Coucke et al., 2018) collected from the Snips personal voice assistant, which also comes with pre-defined train, development & test splits. There are 7 intent labels in all. Examples are provided in Table 1. For the input text length distribution, please refer to Figure 1b.

### 3.3 Modifications for PhraseSumm

We introduce the following modifications for our specific task of PhraseSumm.

**Preprocessing Intent Labels:** For CLINC150, we preprocess the intent labels by replacing underscores with spaces, i.e. *book_hotel* converted to *book hotel* to convert them to phrases. Furthermore, in keeping with our task definition, we retain only *multi-word intent labels* (and their corresponding utterances) from the dataset. For SNIPS, we convert the intent labels to phrases by inserting spaces between each constituent word, e.g. *ComparePlaces* is converted to *Compare Places*. As shown in Table 1 (and discussed in Bhattacharjee et al. (2022)), most intent labels for both datasets are of the form <VERB, NP> (e.g. *find phone*, *Book Restaurant*, etc.)

**Creating test sets with intents/summaries *unseen* during training** In order to simulate real-world scenarios where not all intents may be avail-

| Phrasal Paraphrase Alignment between Extractive & Abstractive Summaries |
|---|
| **EXTRACTIVE:** I see my 10 year old cousins dress. [[*It's almost an exact copy of my wedding dress.*]]<br>**ABSTRACTIVE:** My cousin wore [[*a dress identical to my wedding gown.*]] |
| **EXTRACTIVE:** This guy would break into houses and stand over people as they slept. Deal with it) Eventually this dude turns himself in and not only is he my best friends neighbor [[*I sat with this dude at lunch during this whole fiasco of trying to find this stalker and he played it off a little too well.*]]<br>**ABSTRACTIVE:** My best friend's neighbor would break into houses and stand over people as they slept. [[*I even talked about it with him, and he acted like he had nothing to do with it.*]] |

Table 3: Examples from the Narrative Summarization Corpus (Ouyang et al., 2017). Turker-identified aligned phrases between the extractive & abstractive summaries are indicated with *italicized text* within square brackets ([[]]).

able during training, we randomly pick a subset of the intent labels from the pre-defined train set to create an *unseen label set*. Utterances corresponding to the unseen label set are removed from the train, dev and test sets, and are used to create a separate *unseen labels test set* (details on the unseen labels selected are provided in Appendix Section A.1.1). Thus for each dataset, we have 4 splits : train, dev, test with intents/summaries *seen during training*, test with intents/summaries *unseen during training*, the sizes of which are reported in Table 2.

## 4 Methodology & Experiments

In this section, we elaborate on our proposed approaches and the experiments conducted.

### 4.1 Baselines

We leverage SOTA neural text generation models such as BART-large (Lewis et al., 2019) and T5-large (Raffel et al., 2020) for this short-phrase summarization task. Since our work introduces a new task, there are no existing models to compare to. Thus our **first baseline** (BART-large **OTS**, T5-large **OTS** in Table 5) comprises of the off-the-shelf variants of these models. Specifically, we report the performance of the 406M BART-large[2] and the 770M T5-large models[3]. For our **second baseline**, we fine-tune each of the above models using training data (BART-large **FT**, T5-large **FT** in Table 5) and report performance on both datasets.

### 4.2 Pre-training Tasks

#### 4.2.1 Phrasal Paraphrase Alignment as a Pre-training Task

As demonstrated in Table 1, the given task requires the models to be able to infer the short phrase summary from the input text since the phrases often do not occur within the text itself. For instance, for an utterance of *"Give me Steve's address in Manhattan"*, the desired short phrase summary, that paraphrases the input, is **Get Place Details**. In order to aid the text summarization models towards better paraphrasing and inference, we explore the benefits of pre-training the model on a **phrasal paraphrase alignment task**. For this, we utilize the *Narrative Summarization Corpus* (Ouyang et al., 2017) containing human-annotated extractive and abstractive summaries for 476 personal Reddit narratives. Turkers align phrases between the extractive and abstractive summaries for each annotated narrative, as shown in Table 3. There are 6173 such phrasal paraphrase alignment samples in all. While most other paraphrase generation datasets focus on sentential paraphrases such as PARANMT-50M (Wieting and Gimpel, 2017), or semantically similar question pairs (DataCanary, 2017), the Narrative Summarization Corpus is geared towards paraphrasing *phrases* between extractive & abstractive summaries, which is closer to PhraseSumm. Although PPDB (Ganitkevitch et al., 2013) provides pairs of paraphrased phrases as well, we find the Narrative Summarization Corpus to more often contain paraphrased phrases where there is no overlap in wording between phrases; in contrast, the PPDB consists of paraphrased phrases which could be minor variants of the input phrase. Thus pre-training a model to generate the aligned phrase from the abstractive summary of this dataset is likely to aid the model for the downstream task of PhraseSumm.

We extract these aligned phrases, and *pre-train* BART-large and T5-large models on the phrasal paraphrase alignment task, considering the phrase from the extractive summary as the *input text*, and the *aligned phrase from the abstractive summary* as the desired generated phrase.

#### 4.2.2 NLI as a Pre-training Task

In order to aid summarization models towards inferring intents, many of which are only implicitly expressed in the input, we use NLI as a pre-training

[2]https://huggingface.co/facebook/bart-large
[3]https://huggingface.co/t5-large

| Entailment Pairs | Contradiction Pairs |
|---|---|
| **CLINC150** | |
| **pr:** *how come starbucks declined my card when i tried to use it to pay,* **hyp:** *This text is about card declined*<br>**pr:** *what is the protocol for requesting a vacation,* **hyp:** *This text is about pto request* | **pr:** *i need to order more checks for my us bank account,* **hyp:** *This text is about smart home*<br>**pr:** *tell me if per se in nyc takes reservations,* **hyp:** *This text is about gas type* |
| **SNIPS** | |
| **pr:** *Will it be cloudy at my facebook event?,* **hyp:** *This text is about Get Weather*<br>**pr:** *Any traffic problems to go to my dinner?,* **hyp:** *This text is about Get Traffic Information* | **pr:** *Is there any traffic on US 20?,* **hyp:** *This text is about Book Restaurant*<br>**pr:** *I'd like to know whether Galli is more expensive than Rao's,* **hyp:** *This text is about Get Weather* |

Table 4: Examples of entailment & contradiction pairs created from CLINC150 & SNIPS datasets.

task. Note, however, that framing this as problem an NLI task requires one to know the entire label set *apriori*, and therefore, can not support the generation of novel, unseen intents.

**Creating entailment & contradiction pairs:** The task of NLI requires the creation of positive (**entailment**) and negative (**contradiction**) pairs of premise & hypotheses to train the model. One possible way to obtain such pairs from our respective datasets would be to construct *premises* from the *utterances* & *hypotheses* from *labels*. The premise consists of the utterance itself, while the hypothesis consists of the template *"This text is about {}"* where the corresponding label is inserted in "{}", as proposed in Yin et al. (2019). For instance, an entailment pair would consist of [**premise:** *give me a hand finding my mobile device*, **hypothesis:** *This text is about find phone*], where *find phone* is the intent associated with the utterance. For the contradiction pairs, we first manually identify intents and utterances that are *unrelated* to one another. For instance, for CLINC150, we find the intents (and utterances) corresponding to the following pairs of domains to be vastly different to one another: (***banking, home***), (***auto and commute, kitchen and dining***), (***work, credit cards***). For each domain pair ($D_1$, $D_2$), we select, at random, utterances from intents of $D_1$ to construct premises and intents from $D_2$ to construct hypotheses. The same exercise is performed by constructing premises from $D_2$ and corresponding hypotheses from $D_1$.

When inspecting the SNIPS dataset, we identify pairs of intents whose utterances differ from one another, e.g. (***Share Current Location, Book Restaurant***), (***Compare Places, Get Weather***) (full list in Appendix Section A.1.2). Similar to the method employed for CLINC150, contradiction pairs are created from each such pair of intents. We create 9900 entailment & 902 contradiction pairs from the CLINC150 training set, 170 entailment & 50 contradiction pairs from the SNIPS training set, using which we finetune BART-large & T5-large models on the NLI task.

#### 4.2.3 Cascading NLI & Phrasal Paraphrase Alignment Tasks during Pre-training

In order to combine the benefits of the phrasal paraphrase alignment and NLI tasks, we cascade them during pre-training. As described in Section 4.2.2, we first pre-train the respective BART-large & T5-large checkpoints with the entailment & contradiction pairs created from our intent classification datasets. The finetuned model weights are then used as a starting checkpoint for the phrasal paraphrase alignment task.

### 4.3 Task-specific Fine-tuning

The pretrained models are further finetuned on our specific task. Models pretrained on the phrasal paraphrase alignment task (Section 4.2.1) are further finetuned on the task at hand (BART-large **PA+FT**, T5-large **PA+FT** in Table 5). With models pretrained on NLI (Section 4.2.2), we use the encoder-decoder weights as a starting checkpoint and finetune for PhraseSumm (BART-large **NLI+FT**, T5-large **NLI+FT** checkpoints in Table 5). Finally, the prefix **NLI+PA+FT** in Table 5 refers to models described in Section 4.2.3 that were subsequently finetuned on the PhraseSumm task. We use Adam optimizer with a linear learning rate scheduler for our experiments. For further details on hyperparameter selection, please refer to Appendix Section A.2.

## 5 Evaluation

We measure quantitative performance of models for PhraseSumm using standard summarization metrics while also performing human evaluation on the

| Model | Metrics on Seen Labels /*Unseen Labels* Test Sets | | | | |
|---|---|---|---|---|---|
| | **ROUGE-1** | **ROUGE-2** | **METEOR** | **BERTScore** | **BARTScore** |
| | | CLINC150 | | | |
| BART-large **OTS** | 21.444/*18.704* | 5.281/*2.87* | 27.941/*26.382* | 0.868/*0.859* | -6.128/*-6.078* |
| BART-large **FT** | 96.859/*46.981* | 96.167/*5.273* | 91.581/*27.728* | 0.995/*0.914* | -1.563/*-5.394* |
| BART-large **PA + FT** | 96.552/*43.73* | 95.73/***9.04*** | 91.206/*27.499* | 0.995/*0.915* | -1.59/*-5.477* |
| BART-large **NLI + FT** | 96.964/***47.266*** | 95.889/*7.535* | 91.308/*27.958* | 0.995/*0.913* | -1.589/*-5.357* |
| BART-large **NLI + PA + FT** | **97.792**/*47.239* | **97.391**/*8.889* | **92.531/*30.112*** | **0.997/*0.917*** | **-1.508/*-5.225*** |
| T5-large **OTS** | 54.313/*24.641* | 47.78/*6.586* | 45.303/*14.33* | 0.901/*0.859* | -4.465/*-6.306* |
| T5-large **FT** | 97.785/*29.45* | 97.514/*7.57* | 92.602/*20.545* | 0.997/*0.856* | -1.495/*-6.169* |
| T5-large **PA + FT** | 97.582/*46.678* | 97.144/*10.788* | 92.306/*30.598* | 0.997/*0.912* | -1.508/*-5.265* |
| T5-large **NLI + FT** | 97.678/48.210 | 97.345/12.234 | 92.517/32.456 | **0.998**/0.934 | -1.521/***-5.100*** |
| T5-large **NLI + PA + FT** | **97.891/*48.657*** | **98.112/*13.345*** | **92.671/33.512** | **0.998/*0.945*** | **-1.501/*-5.100*** |
| | | SNIPS | | | |
| BART-large **OTS** | 10.598/*13.913* | 0.0/*0.0* | 11.856/*14.989* | 0.83/*0.858* | -7.533/*-6.386* |
| BART-large **FT** | 93.5/*22.892* | 92.5/*0.0* | 89.064/*13.511* | 0.99/*0.873* | -1.905/*-6.038* |
| BART-large **PA + FT** | 97.0/*25.663* | 95.0/*0.0* | 91.792/***36.288*** | 0.993/*0.876* | -1.703/***-5.794*** |
| BART-large **NLI + FT** | **98.5**/*24.217* | **97.5/*0.0*** | **93.541**/*24.914* | **0.997**/*0.876* | -1.583/*-6.055* |
| BART-large **NLI + PA + FT** | **98.5/*26.145*** | **97.5/*0.0*** | **93.541**/*28.141* | **0.997/*0.878*** | **-1.564**/*-5.987* |
| T5-large **OTS** | 10.747/5.02 | 0.0/0.0 | 13.17/3.356 | 0.807/0.846 | -7.837/-7.01 |
| T5-large **FT** | 92.0/8.10 | 91.34/1.345 | 86.771/8.345 | 0.852/0.823 | -2.34/5.34 |
| T5-large **PA + FT** | 93.5/10.748 | 92.5/2.789 | 88.743/13.196 | 0.989/0.835 | -1.858/-6.212 |
| T5-large **NLI + FT** | 96.5/*10.893* | 95.3/*2.888* | **89.345**/*14.123* | 0.994/*0.800* | -1.823/*-5.901* |
| T5-large **NLI + PA + FT** | **98.23/*26.234*** | **97.67/*3.21*** | **89.345/*14.234*** | **0.999/*0.851*** | **-1.737/*-5.213*** |

Table 5: Performance of T5 & BART based summarization models for the abstractive short phrase summary generation task, across both test sets for CLINC150 & SNIPS (single model runs). Results for the test split with labels unseen during training are *italicized*. The suffixes **OTS** & **FT** stand for off-the-shelf & task-specific fine-tuning, respectively. **NLI+FT** indicates a model pretrained first on the NLI task, and then finetuned for the short phrase summarization task, while **PA+FT** refers to a model pretrained on the phrasal paraphrase alignment task followed by task-specific finetuning. Similarly, **NLI+PA+FT** refers to a model first pretrained on NLI, followed by phrasal paraphrase alignment, and lastly fine-tuned on the task.

| Summaries Compared | Percentage (%) |
|---|---|
| **R:** Reference summary from dataset, **S:** BART-large **NLI + PA + FT** generated summary | **S better than R:** 37.206, **S equivalent to R:** 22.857 |
| **R:** Summary generated by BART-large **FT**, **S:** BART-large **NLI + PA + FT** generated summary | **S better than R:** 37.097, **S equivalent to R:** 29.928 |

Table 6: Quantitative results obtained using human evaluation on the CLINC150 unseen labels test set. We report results for both cases described in Section 5.2.

model predictions, both of which we elaborate on in this Section.

### 5.1 Quantitative Evaluation using Summarization Metrics

Standard summarization metrics such as **ROUGE** (Lin, 2004), **METEOR** (Banerjee and Lavie, 2005), **BERTScore** (Zhang et al., 2019) and **BARTScore** (Yuan et al., 2021) are used to evaluate model performance quantitatively. Table 5 demonstrates the performance of the T5-large and BART-large models across both CLINC150 & SNIPS datasets. Results are reported for *both test sets with labels seen and unseen during training*. Automatic metrics show that the models trained with cascaded NLI & phrasal paraphrase alignment tasks (**NLI+PA+FT**) outperform the first baseline (**OTS**) by a large margin, across all metrics. For instance, for the CLINC150 test set with labels seen during training, BART-large **NLI+PA+FT** demonstrates an improvement over BART-large **OTS** of 76.35 points for ROUGE-1 & 64.59 points for METEOR. Corresponding improvements for the test set with unseen labels during training are 28.54 points for ROUGE-1 & 3.73 points for METEOR. Moreover, improvements are also obtained over the second baseline, i.e models finetuned on the task (without pre-training). BART-large **NLI+PA+FT** improves over BART-large **FT** for the SNIPS test set with seen labels by 5 points for ROUGE-1 & 4.48 points for METEOR. Thus, our proposed approach is able to show performance gains *both for summaries seen and unseen during training.*

### 5.2 Human Evaluation

On inspection of the summaries generated by our models, we often find cases where the model generates a summary that is different from the reference summary, but can be considered an acceptable alternative. Summarization metrics alone, fail to

| Utterance | Reference Summary | Model-generated Summary | ROUGE |
|---|---|---|---|
| *how is my application on new credit card going* | **application status** | **new card** | **R-1**:0.0<br>**R-2**:0.0 |
| *i need you to confirm that there is a reservation under the name david kramer for 7:00 pm at pietro's* | confirm reservation | **restaurant reservation** | **R-1**:50.0<br>**R-2**:0.0 |
| *what's my visa's current rewards balance* | **rewards balance** | **redeem rewards** | **R-1**:50.0<br>**R-2**:0.0 |

Table 7: Examples demonstrating reference short phrase summaries as well as summaries predicted by the best-performing BART-large model (BART-large **NLI + PA + FT**) for the **CLINC150 test set with unseen labels. The summaries selected by Turkers** are indicated in **bold**. If both reference and model-generated summaries are deemed useful, we highlight both. **R-1** and **R-2** refer to ROUGE-1 and ROUGE-2 F1 scores respectively.

capture these differences. Thus, we conduct human evaluation of the test sets using Amazon Mechanical Turk (MTurk), for the following two scenarios.

#### 5.2.1 Comparison between Reference Summary & Model Generated Summary

For test sets with labels unseen during training, we present Turkers with the utterance, the reference summary and the summary generated by the models trained with cascaded NLI & phrasal paraphrase alignment tasks. A Turker is asked to select the summary that best represents the input utterance, or indicate if both summaries are equally applicable. Each example is annotated by 4 Turkers, and a majority vote is considered as the selected summary. We did not encounter ties during the annotation process. IAA is 0.67. The reference and system-generated summaries are shown in random order during annotation, for a fair evaluation. As shown in Table 6, for the CLINC150 test set consisting of labels unseen during training, the BART-large **NLI+PA+FT** model generated summary is found to be equivalent to and better than the reference summary 22.857% and 37.206% of the time, respectively. Furthermore, as illustrated in Table 7, standard summarization metrics such as ROUGE are often unable to capture cases where the model-generated summary is better or at par with the reference summary. For instance, for the utterance *"can you check if my application for a discovery card has been looked over yet"*, the model-generated summary **new card** is considered to be equivalent to the reference summary **application status**, while the corresponding ROUGE-1 & ROUGE-2 scores are 0. For more examples, please refer to Table 11 in the Appendix.

#### 5.2.2 Comparison amongst Models

Similar to the strategy above, we further compare between a baseline model (e.g. BART-large **FT**) and the corresponding *best* model (e.g. BART-large **NLI + PA + FT**) for both the test sets across the datasets. Turkers are asked to select between the two model-generated summaries, or indicate if they find both equally relevant. We find the BART-large **NLI + PA + FT** model generated summaries to outperform those generated by the BART-large **FT** 37.097% of the time, while for 29.928% of cases, both summaries are considered equivalent (Table 6).

#### 5.2.3 Dataset Release

For the CLINC150 dataset, we release the train, dev, and two test sets described in Section 3.3 (under CC-by-4.0 license). For the test set with labels unseen during training, we also provide the model-generated short phrase summaries obtained using BART-large **NLI+PA+FT** model, as alternative to the reference summaries. We also indicate whether the model-generated or the reference summary, or both were selected by Turkers. This is to allow for further research and evaluation for this task[4].

### 5.3 Qualitative Comparison with ChatGPT & GPT3-esque Models

We also qualitatively evaluate the efficacy of OpenAI's ChatGPT [5] & Eleuther AI's GPT-Neo 2.7B (Black et al., 2021) models for this task. The latter is designed using EleutherAI's replication of the GPT-3 architecture. For each utterance, we use a prompt to instruct the model to generate the corresponding short-phrase summary. We experiment with various prompts for the task. As seen

[4]https://github.com/amazon-science/PhraseSumm-short-phrase-summarization

[5]https://openai.com/blog/chatgpt/

| Model | Utterance with *Prompt* | Generated Output | Reference Summary |
|---|---|---|---|
| ChatGPT | can you check if my application for a discovery card has been looked over yet. ***what is the intent here?*** | *I'm sorry, but I am a computer program and do not have the ability to check the status of a credit card application. Your intent here is to check the status of your discovery card application. I recommend contacting the issuer directly for more information.* | application status |
| | ***generate a short-phrase summary for the following:*** "Is Vertigo Sky Lounge more expensive than the bar I usually go to in New York?" | *Comparing Vertigo Sky Lounge's price with a regular bar in New York.* | Compare Places |
| | ***generate a 2 or 3 word summary for the following:*** "Is Vertigo Sky Lounge more expensive than the bar I usually go to in New York?" | **Output1:** *Vertigo Sky Lounge pricing.* **Output2:** *Bar pricing* | |
| GPT-Neo 2.7B | who has seen my cellphone. ***the intent here is*** | *to stop the practice of people like me and others who are trying to get more people to participate. In a video message on the video screen, Obama said that as president, he would make* | find phone |
| | ***Generate a short-phrase summary for:*** "i want to make sure my reservation for 5 at mcdonalds is still set" | *Word Count: 11 words Exact Phrase: 1. make sure* | confirm reservation |

Table 8: Exploring ChatGPT & Eleuther AI's GPT-Neo 2.7B for the task. Prompts used are indicated in ***bold, italicized text***. We find ChatGPT to generate different outputs at different times, for the same utterance & prompt input as illustrated in the 3rd row from the top (**Output1**, **Output2**).

in Table 8, these models tend to either generate long outputs with the intent embedded within them (ChatGPT output for intent ***application status***), or tend to focus on completing the text via generation (e.g. GPT-Neo 2.7B output for intent ***find phone***). Further, ChatGPT, generates different outputs at different points in time, even with the same utterance & prompt as input (see 3rd row of Table 8).

## 5.4 Error Analysis

We inspect a random sample from 20% of the model-generated summaries that yield the lowest ROUGE-1 scores and inspect the errors made by the model w.r.t the reference summary. Three main types of errors are detected: a) **Case 1:** model is unable to capture the intent of the utterance, b) **Case 2:** model generates a summary that could be related to the input but still differs from reference, c) **Case 3:** model generates a clearly acceptable alternative summary to the reference. Examples are provided in Table 9, and in the Appendix (Table 12). Note that we do not find the models to hallucinate when generating the summaries.

| Utterance | Summaries |
|---|---|
| **Case 1:** *do i need to fill up my tires* | **R:**tire pressure, **S:**gas type |
| **Case 2:** *how many rooms are available between 2 and 3* | **R:**schedule meeting, **S:**book hotel |
| **Case 3:** *is there any indication my application for a new credit card has been processed* | **R:**application status, **S:**new card |

Table 9: Examples of errors made by the BART-large NLI+PA+FT model *(best BART model)* on CLINC150 test set with unseen labels during training. **R** stands for reference summary and **S** stands for model-generated summary.

# 6 Conclusion & Future Work

In this work, we introduce a new task of abstractive short-phrase summarization, PhraseSumm, which focuses on generating coherent short-phrase summaries, often inferred or paraphrased from input text. SOTA neural summarization models such as BART-large & T5-large are explored for this task, with model performance measured using standard summarization metrics, along with human evaluation. Our work demonstrates the benefits of pretraining models with phrasal paraphrase alignment and NLI tasks, that aid with paraphrasing and implicitly inferring summaries from input text. Moreover, human evaluation demonstrates that model-generated summaries are often deemed better or equivalent to reference summaries, which summarization metrics fail to capture. We leverage popularly used intent detection datasets - CLINC150 & SNIPS, with desired modifications, and release a dataset to enable further research in this area. As future work, we would be interested in exploring the efficacy of our models in zero & few-shot settings for PhraseSumm.

## 7 Limitations

The datasets we experiment with consist of input text of relatively short length (Figure 1). We would need to experiment with datasets of different input lengths in order to measure the applicability of our proposed methods for longer text. Moreover, our work is limited to English utterances and summaries at this point, thus we cannot conclude on how the models would perform in multilingual settings. Furthermore, there could potentially be other approaches of creating entailment & contradiction pairs for the NLI pre-training task, which remain unexplored.

## References


Ojas Ahuja, Jiacheng Xu, Akshay Gupta, Kevin Horecka, and Greg Durrett. 2022. Aspectnews: Aspect-oriented summarization of news documents. In *Proceedings of the 60th Annual Meeting of the Association for Computational Linguistics (Volume 1: Long Papers)*, pages 6494–6506.

Rabah Alzaidy, Cornelia Caragea, and C. Lee Giles. 2019. Bi-lstm-crf sequence labeling for keyphrase extraction from scholarly documents. In *The World Wide Web Conference*, WWW '19, page 2551–2557, New York, NY, USA. Association for Computing Machinery.

Satanjeev Banerjee and Alon Lavie. 2005. METEOR: An automatic metric for MT evaluation with improved correlation with human judgments. In *Proceedings of the ACL Workshop on Intrinsic and Extrinsic Evaluation Measures for Machine Translation and/or Summarization*, pages 65–72, Ann Arbor, Michigan. Association for Computational Linguistics.

Kamil Bennani-Smires, Claudiu Musat, Andreea Hossmann, Michael Baeriswyl, and Martin Jaggi. 2018. Simple unsupervised keyphrase extraction using sentence embeddings. In *Proceedings of the 22nd Conference on Computational Natural Language Learning*, pages 221–229.

Kasturi Bhattacharjee, Rashmi Gangadharaiah, Kathleen McKeown, and Dan Roth. 2022. What do users care about? detecting actionable insights from user feedback. In *Proceedings of the 2022 Conference of the North American Chapter of the Association for Computational Linguistics: Human Language Technologies: Industry Track*, pages 239–246, Hybrid: Seattle, Washington + Online. Association for Computational Linguistics.

Sid Black, Leo Gao, Phil Wang, Connor Leahy, and Stella Biderman. 2021. GPT-Neo: Large Scale Autoregressive Language Modeling with Mesh-Tensorflow.

Dallas Card, Chenhao Tan, and Noah A. Smith. 2017. Neural models for documents with metadata. In *Annual Meeting of the Association for Computational Linguistics*.

Iñigo Casanueva, Tadas Temčinas, Daniela Gerz, Matthew Henderson, and Ivan Vulić. 2020. Efficient intent detection with dual sentence encoders. In *Proceedings of the 2nd Workshop on Natural Language Processing for Conversational AI*, pages 38–45.

Hung Chau, Igor Labutov, Khushboo Thaker, Daqing He, and Peter Brusilovsky. 2020. Automatic concept extraction for domain and student modeling in adaptive textbooks. *International Journal of Artificial Intelligence in Education*, pages 1 – 27.

Mingda Chen, Zewei Chu, Sam Wiseman, and Kevin Gimpel. 2022. Summscreen: A dataset for abstractive screenplay summarization. In *Proceedings of the 60th Annual Meeting of the Association for Computational Linguistics (Volume 1: Long Papers)*, pages 8602–8615.

Qian Chen, Zhu Zhuo, and Wen Wang. 2019. Bert for joint intent classification and slot filling. *arXiv preprint arXiv:1902.10909*.

Sihao Chen, Fan Zhang, Kazoo Sone, and Dan Roth. 2021. Improving faithfulness in abstractive summarization with contrast candidate generation and selection. In *Proceedings of the 2021 Conference of the North American Chapter of the Association for Computational Linguistics: Human Language Technologies*, pages 5935–5941, Online. Association for Computational Linguistics.

Alice Coucke, Alaa Saade, Adrien Ball, Théodore Bluche, Alexandre Caulier, David Leroy, Clément Doumouro, Thibault Gisselbrecht, Francesco Caltagirone, Thibaut Lavril, Maël Primet, and Joseph Dureau. 2018. Snips voice platform: an embedded spoken language understanding system for private-by-design voice interfaces.

Lili Jiang Meg Risdal Nikhil Dandekar tomtung DataCanary, hilfialkaff. 2017. Quora question pairs.

Thanh-Nam Doan and Tuan-Anh Hoang. 2021. Benchmarking neural topic models: An empirical study. In *Findings of the Association for Computational Linguistics: ACL-IJCNLP 2021*, pages 4363–4368.

Zi-Yi Dou, Pengfei Liu, Hiroaki Hayashi, Zhengbao Jiang, and Graham Neubig. 2020. Gsum: A general framework for guided neural abstractive summarization. *arXiv preprint arXiv:2010.08014*.

Elozino Egonmwan and Yllias Chali. 2019. Transformer and seq2seq model for paraphrase generation. In *Proceedings of the 3rd Workshop on Neural Generation and Translation*, pages 249–255.

Matan Eyal, Tal Baumel, and Michael Elhadad. 2019. Question answering as an automatic evaluation metric for news article summarization. In *Proceedings of the 2019 Conference of the North American Chapter of the Association for Computational Linguistics: Human Language Technologies, Volume 1 (Long and Short Papers)*, pages 3938–3948.

Yao Fu, Yansong Feng, and John P Cunningham. 2019. Paraphrase generation with latent bag of words. *Advances in Neural Information Processing Systems*, 32.

Juri Ganitkevitch, Benjamin Van Durme, and Chris Callison-Burch. 2013. Ppdb: The paraphrase database. In *Proceedings of the 2013 Conference of the North American Chapter of the Association for Computational Linguistics: Human Language Technologies*, pages 758–764.

Philip Gorinski and Mirella Lapata. 2015. Movie script summarization as graph-based scene extraction. In *Proceedings of the 2015 Conference of the North American Chapter of the Association for Computational Linguistics: Human Language Technologies*, pages 1066–1076.

Tanya Goyal and Greg Durrett. 2020. Neural syntactic preordering for controlled paraphrase generation. In *Proceedings of the 58th Annual Meeting of the Association for Computational Linguistics*, pages 238–252.

Lin Gui, Jia Leng, Gabriele Pergola, Yu Zhou, Ruifeng Xu, and Yulan He. 2019. Neural topic model with reinforcement learning. In *Proceedings of the 2019 Conference on Empirical Methods in Natural Language Processing and the 9th International Joint Conference on Natural Language Processing (EMNLP-IJCNLP)*, pages 3478–3483, Hong Kong, China. Association for Computational Linguistics.

Ankush Gupta, Arvind Agarwal, Prawaan Singh, and Piyush Rai. 2018. A deep generative framework for paraphrase generation. In *Proceedings of the aaai conference on artificial intelligence*, volume 32.

Hidetaka Kamigaito and Manabu Okumura. 2020. Syntactically look-ahead attention network for sentence compression. In *Proceedings of the AAAI Conference on Artificial Intelligence*, volume 34, pages 8050–8057.

Ashkan Kazemi, Verónica Pérez-Rosas, and Rada Mihalcea. 2020. Biased textrank: Unsupervised graph-based content extraction.

Wojciech Kryscinski, Bryan McCann, Caiming Xiong, and Richard Socher. 2020. Evaluating the factual consistency of abstractive text summarization. In *Proceedings of the 2020 Conference on Empirical Methods in Natural Language Processing (EMNLP)*, pages 9332–9346, Online. Association for Computational Linguistics.

Sawan Kumar and Partha Talukdar. 2020. Nile: Natural language inference with faithful natural language explanations. In *Proceedings of the 58th Annual Meeting of the Association for Computational Linguistics*, pages 8730–8742.

Faisal Ladhak, Esin Durmus, He He, Claire Cardie, and Kathleen McKeown. 2021. Faithful or extractive? on mitigating the faithfulness-abstractiveness trade-off in abstractive summarization. *arXiv preprint arXiv:2108.13684*.

Faisal Ladhak, Bryan Li, Yaser Al-Onaizan, and Kathleen R McKeown. 2020. Exploring content selection in summarization of novel chapters. In *ACL*.

Stefan Larson, Anish Mahendran, Joseph J. Peper, Christopher Clarke, Andrew Lee, Parker Hill, Jonathan K. Kummerfeld, Kevin Leach, Michael A. Laurenzano, Lingjia Tang, and Jason Mars. 2019. An evaluation dataset for intent classification and out-of-scope prediction. In *Proceedings of the 2019 Conference on Empirical Methods in Natural Language Processing and the 9th International Joint Conference on Natural Language Processing (EMNLP-IJCNLP)*, pages 1311–1316, Hong Kong, China. Association for Computational Linguistics.

Kenton Lee, Kelvin Guu, Luheng He, Tim Dozat, and Hyung Won Chung. 2021. Neural data augmentation via example extrapolation. *arXiv preprint arXiv:2102.01335*.

Mike Lewis, Yinhan Liu, Naman Goyal, Marjan Ghazvininejad, Abdelrahman Mohamed, Omer Levy, Ves Stoyanov, and Luke Zettlemoyer. 2019. Bart: Denoising sequence-to-sequence pre-training for natural language generation, translation, and comprehension. *arXiv preprint arXiv:1910.13461*.

Mingzhe Li, Xiuying Chen, Min Yang, Shen Gao, Dongyan Zhao, and Rui Yan. 2021. The style-content duality of attractiveness: Learning to write eye-catching headlines via disentanglement. In *Proceedings of the AAAI Conference on Artificial Intelligence*, volume 35, pages 13252–13260.

Zichao Li, Xin Jiang, Lifeng Shang, and Hang Li. 2018. Paraphrase generation with deep reinforcement learning. In *Proceedings of the 2018 Conference on Empirical Methods in Natural Language Processing*, pages 3865–3878.

Chin-Yew Lin. 2004. Rouge: A package for automatic evaluation of summaries. In *Text summarization branches out*, pages 74–81.

Ramesh Nallapati, Feifei Zhai, and Bowen Zhou. 2017. Summarunner: A recurrent neural network based sequence model for extractive summarization of documents. In *Thirty-first AAAI conference on artificial intelligence*.

Ani Nenkova, Kathleen McKeown, et al. 2011. Automatic summarization. *Foundations and Trends® in Information Retrieval*, 5(2–3):103–233.

Thong Nguyen and Anh Tuan Luu. 2021. Contrastive learning for neural topic model. *Advances in Neural Information Processing Systems*, 34:11974–11986.

Jessica Ouyang, Serina Chang, and Kathleen McKeown. 2017. Crowd-sourced iterative annotation for narrative summarization corpora. In *Proceedings of the 15th Conference of the European Chapter of the Association for Computational Linguistics: Volume 2, Short Papers*, pages 46–51.

Eirini Papagiannopoulou and Grigorios Tsoumakas. 2020. A review of keyphrase extraction. *Wiley Interdisciplinary Reviews: Data Mining and Knowledge Discovery*, 10(2):e1339.

Aaditya Prakash, Sadid A Hasan, Kathy Lee, Vivek Datla, Ashequl Qadir, Joey Liu, and Oladimeji Farri. 2016. Neural paraphrase generation with stacked residual lstm networks. In *Proceedings of COLING 2016, the 26th International Conference on Computational Linguistics: Technical Papers*, pages 2923–2934.

Colin Raffel, Noam Shazeer, Adam Roberts, Katherine Lee, Sharan Narang, Michael Matena, Yanqi Zhou, Wei Li, Peter J Liu, et al. 2020. Exploring the limits of transfer learning with a unified text-to-text transformer. *J. Mach. Learn. Res.*, 21(140):1–67.

Alexander M Rush, SEAS Harvard, Sumit Chopra, and Jason Weston. 2017. A neural attention model for sentence summarization. In *ACLWeb. Proceedings of the 2015 conference on empirical methods in natural language processing*.

Timo Schick and Hinrich Schütze. 2021. Exploiting cloze-questions for few-shot text classification and natural language inference. In *Proceedings of the 16th Conference of the European Chapter of the Association for Computational Linguistics: Main Volume*, pages 255–269.

Lucas Sterckx, Thomas Demeester, Johannes Deleu, and Chris Develder. 2015. Topical word importance for fast keyphrase extraction. In *Proceedings of the 24th International Conference on World Wide Web*, WWW '15 Companion, page 121–122, New York, NY, USA. Association for Computing Machinery.

Yi Sun, Hangping Qiu, Yu Zheng, Zhongwei Wang, and Chaoran Zhang. 2020. SIFRank: a new baseline for unsupervised keyphrase extraction based on pre-trained language model. *IEEE Access*, 8:10896–10906.

Danqing Wang, Pengfei Liu, Yining Zheng, Xipeng Qiu, and Xuan-Jing Huang. 2020. Heterogeneous graph neural networks for extractive document summarization. In *Proceedings of the 58th Annual Meeting of the Association for Computational Linguistics*, pages 6209–6219.

John Wieting and Kevin Gimpel. 2017. Paranmt-50m: Pushing the limits of paraphrastic sentence embeddings with millions of machine translations. *arXiv preprint arXiv:1711.05732*.

Jeff Wu, Long Ouyang, Daniel M Ziegler, Nisan Stiennon, Ryan Lowe, Jan Leike, and Paul Christiano. 2021. Recursively summarizing books with human feedback. *arXiv preprint arXiv:2109.10862*.

Wenpeng Yin, Jamaal Hay, and Dan Roth. 2019. Benchmarking zero-shot text classification: Datasets, evaluation and entailment approach. *arXiv preprint arXiv:1909.00161*.

Weizhe Yuan, Graham Neubig, and Pengfei Liu. 2021. Bartscore: Evaluating generated text as text generation. *Advances in Neural Information Processing Systems*, 34:27263–27277.

Jiaao Zhan, Yang Gao, Yu Bai, and Qianhui Liu. 2022. Stage-wise stylistic headline generation: Style generation and summarized content insertion. In *Proceedings of the Thirty-First International Joint Conference on Artificial Intelligence, IJCAI-22*, pages 4489–4495. International Joint Conferences on Artificial Intelligence Organization. Main Track.

Jianguo Zhang, Kazuma Hashimoto, Wenhao Liu, Chien-Sheng Wu, Yao Wan, S Yu Philip, Richard Socher, and Caiming Xiong. 2020. Discriminative nearest neighbor few-shot intent detection by transferring natural language inference. In *Proceedings of the 2020 Conference on Empirical Methods in Natural Language Processing (EMNLP)*, pages 5064–5082.

Shengqiang Zhang, Xingxing Zhang, Hangbo Bao, and Furu Wei. 2022. Attention temperature matters in abstractive summarization distillation. In *Proceedings of the 60th Annual Meeting of the Association for Computational Linguistics (Volume 1: Long Papers)*, pages 127–141.

Tianyi Zhang, Varsha Kishore, Felix Wu, Kilian Q Weinberger, and Yoav Artzi. 2019. Bertscore: Evaluating text generation with bert. *arXiv preprint arXiv:1904.09675*.

Shiqi Zhao, Xiang Lan, Ting Liu, and Sheng Li. 2009. Application-driven statistical paraphrase generation. In *Proceedings of the Joint Conference of the 47th Annual Meeting of the ACL and the 4th International Joint Conference on Natural Language Processing of the AFNLP*, pages 834–842.

Yang Zhao, Xiaoyu Shen, Wei Bi, and Akiko Aizawa. 2019. Unsupervised rewriter for multi-sentence compression. In *Proceedings of the 57th Annual Meeting of the Association for Computational Linguistics*, pages 2235–2240, Florence, Italy. Association for Computational Linguistics.

Ming Zhong, Pengfei Liu, Danqing Wang, Xipeng Qiu, and Xuan-Jing Huang. 2019. Searching for effective neural extractive summarization: What works and what's next. In *Proceedings of the 57th Annual Meeting of the Association for Computational Linguistics*, pages 1049–1058.

# A Appendix

## A.1 Datasets

CLINC150 is covered by the CC by 3.0 license, while SNIPS is covered by Apache License 2.0 & the Narrative Summarization Corpus[6] is governed by the MIT license, all of which allow the use of these datasets for research purposes. The 10 domains in the **CLINC150** dataset are *banking, credit cards, kitchen & dining, home, auto & commute, travel, utility, work, small talk and meta*. The predefined train, dev, test splits contain 15K, 3K dev and 4.5K utterances, respectively. The pre-defined training, development and test sets for **SNIPS** contain 13,084, 700 and 700 utterances, respectively.

### A.1.1 Creation of unseen labels test sets

For CLINC150, 10% of the multi-word labels were selected at random for the unseen labels test set, which amounts to 11 labels. In case of the SNIPS dataset, we select 3 out of 7 labels at random for our unseen labels set. Table 10 contains the list of seen & unseen labels for both datasets.

### A.1.2 Creation of contradiction pairs for NLI

For SNIPS, the following is a complete list of intent pairs that were used in the creation of the contradiction pairs: ***(Book Restaurant, Get Weather)***, ***(Share Current Location, Book Restaurant)***, ***(Get Weather, Search Place)***,***(Compare Places, Get Weather)***, ***(Get Traffic Information, Book Restaurant)***.

## A.2 Model training & Hyperparameter Selection

The following are the Hugging Face checkpoints used for model training:

- BART-large
- T5-large

For each of the settings, we conduct a search over a fixed set of hyperparameters, namely the learning rate (lr), number of training epochs, batch size for each task (i.e. both the pretraining tasks described in Sections A.1.1, 4.2.2 & 4.2.3) and the final task specific finetuning. Learning rate is varied between 3e-05 to 5e-05, batch size for BART-large varied between 16 & 32, number of training epochs for PhraseSumm varied between 3, 5, 8, 10. For NLI, the number of training epochs was varied between 1,3, 5; for phrasal paraphrase alignment between 10 & 20. Adam optimizer with betas=(0.9,0.999) and epsilon=1e-08 is used. The max source length in each case is the default value. Model selection was then performed using performance on the dev set. The total number of GPU hours spent across all experiments was 30,840.

The following are the selected hyper-parameters in each case.

- **CLINC150:**
  - BART-large **OTS**: eval batch size 16
  - BART-large **FT**: train batch size 16, eval batch size 16, lr 5e-05, number of epochs 3.
  - BART-large **PA+FT**: train batch size 16, eval batch size 16, lr 5e-05, number of training epochs for PA is 10, for task is 3.
  - BART-large **NLI+FT**: train batch size 16, eval batch size 16, lr 5e-05, number of training epochs for NLI is 1, for task is 10.
  - BART-large **NLI+PA+FT**: train batch size 16, eval batch size 16, lr 5e-05, number of training epochs for NLI is 1, for PA is 10, for task is 3.
  - T5-large **OTS**: eval batch size 8
  - T5-large **FT**: train batch size 8, eval batch size 8, number of training epochs 10.
  - T5-large **PA+FT**: train batch size 8, eval batch size 8, lr 5e-05, number of training epochs for PA is 20, for task is 10.
  - T5-large **NLI+FT**: train batch size 8, eval batch size 8, lr 5e-05, number of training epochs for NLI is 3, for task is 10.
  - T5-large **PA+NLI+FT**: train batch size 8, eval batch size 8, lr 5e-05, number of training epochs for PA is 20, NLI is 5, for task is 10.
- **SNIPS:**
  - BART-large **OTS**: eval batch size 16
  - BART-large **FT**: train batch size 16, eval batch size 16, lr 5e-05, number of epochs 3.
  - BART-large **PA+FT**: train batch size 16, eval batch size 16, lr 5e-05, number of

[6] http://www.cs.columbia.edu/nlp/tools.cgi

| Data Split | Intent Labels |
|---|---|
| CLINC150 Seen Label Set | current location, pto request, where are you from, book flight, measurement conversion, ingredients list, cancel reservation, card declined, whisper mode, flip coin, meal suggestion, nutrition info, report lost card, play music, flight status, credit score, oil change when, change user name, thank you, todo list update, lost luggage, exchange rate, what song, oil change how, restaurant reviews, order checks, restaurant suggestion, restaurant reservation, change language, pto used, shopping list update, new card, reset settings, insurance change, improve credit score, meaning of life, how old are you, shopping list, smart home, who do you work for, find phone, pay bill, are you a bot, tire change, account blocked, freeze account, car rental, cook time, user name, ingredient substitution, tell joke, gas type, meeting schedule, accept reservations, credit limit, update playlist, pin change, travel suggestion, redeem rewards, replacement card duration, how busy, bill due, change speed, jump start, direct deposit, fun fact, plug type, share location, schedule maintenance, interest rate, reminder update, international fees, make call, travel notification, change accent, calendar update, next holiday, sync device, book hotel, last maintenance, expiration date, pto request status, carry on, what are your hobbies, food last, spending history, travel alert, what can i ask you, report fraud, bill balance, what is your name, roll dice, who made you, do you have pets, next song, rollover 401k, min payment, change volume, credit limit change |
| CLINC150 Unseen Label Set | rewards balance, confirm reservation, damaged card, pto balance, change ai name, tire pressure, order status, schedule meeting, application status, todo list, international visa |
| SNIPS Seen Label Set | Get Place Details, Compare Places, Get Weather, Share Current Location, Search Place, Book Restaurant, Get Traffic Information |
| SNIPS Unseen Label Set | Request Ride, Get Directions, Share ETA |

Table 10: Intent label sets for both datasets

training epochs for PA is 10, for task is 3.

- BART-large **NLI+FT**: train batch size 16, eval batch size 16, lr 5e-05, number of training epochs for NLI is 3, for task is 5.
- BART-large **NLI+PA+FT**: train batch size 16, eval batch size 16, lr 5e-05, number of training epochs for NLI is 3, for PA is 10, for task is 5.
- T5-large **OTS**: eval batch size 8
- T5-large **FT**: train batch size 8, eval batch size 8, number of training epochs 5.
- T5-large **PA+FT**: train batch size 8, eval batch size 8, lr 5e-05, number of training epochs for PA is 10, for task is 5.
- T5-large **NLI+FT**: train batch size 8, eval batch size 8, lr 5e-05, number of training epochs for NLI is 3, for task is 10.
- T5-large **PA+NLI+FT**: train batch size 8, eval batch size 8, lr 5e-05, number of training epochs for PA is 10, NLI is 5, for task is 5.

For Eleuther AI's GPT-Neo 2.7B, we use the Hugging Face checkpoint linked here. For the summarization metrics (ROUGE, METEOR, BERTScore), we use the evaluate package from Hugging Face[7]. For BARTScore, we use the author-provided git repo[8].

### A.3 Human Evaluation

We used Amazon Mechanical Turk for our human evaluation. Instructions provided to the annotators were as follows:

**Annotator Instructions:** You have been provided with a text input and three intents, intent_1, intent_2 and intent_3.

Please pick the intent that best describes the given text. If both intent_1 and intent_2 look suitable, please select intent_3 (which says "both intents")

**Example 1:**

**text** *how long is it going to take me to get to bellevue*

**intent_1** greeting

[7]https://huggingface.co/docs/evaluate/index

[8]https://github.com/neulab/BARTScore

**intent_2** distance

**intent_3** both intents

In the above scenario, intent_2 best describes the intent of the text.

**Example 2:**

**text** *could you add that event to my calendar please?*

**intent_1** calendar

**intent_2** calendar update

**intent_3** both intents

In Example 2, intent_3 would be the correct choice since both intent_1 and intent_2 are applicable.

**Annotator Payment** The Turkers were located within the US, and were paid higher than the highest minimum wage of USD 16.50 per hour. We first estimated the amount of time the annotation task would require by conducting an internal annotation over a random sample of size 50. The average time taken per task was $\sim$ 13 secs, with the maximum being 15 secs. Using the maximum time taken as a reference, we estimated 240 tasks to be completed in an hour. In order to set an hourly wage of USD 18.0 (> USD 16.50), we paid the annotators USD 0.075 per task. There were no risks associated with the dataset since it is devoid of any PII or offensive content, as our manual inspection revealed.

### A.4 Results

In Table 11, we present more examples in which the model-generated summary is deemed better or at par with the reference summary by Turkers. Finally, in Table 12, we present more examples of the three cases of errors reported in Section 5.4.

| Utterance | Reference Summary | Model-generated Summary | ROUGE |
|---|---|---|---|
| *can you check if my application for a discovery card has been looked over yet* | **application status** | **new card** | **R-1:**0.0 **R-2:**0.0 |
| *has there been any changes in the status of my credit card application* | application status | **new card** | **R-1:**0.0 **R-2:**0.0 |
| *please confirm my reservation for feburary 21st at 6pm* | **confirm reservation** | **restaurant reservation** | **R-1:**50.0 **R-2:**0.0 |
| *can you please confirm that i have a 6:00 pm table reserved under michelle solomon at devon's* | confirm reservation | **restaurant reservation** | **R-1:**50.0 **R-2:**0.0 |
| *where are rewards from my visa card visible* | rewards balance | **redeem rewards** | **R-1:**50.0 **R-2:**0.0 |
| *i want to track a package i should be getting* | **order status** | **lost luggage** | **R-1:**0.0 **R-2:**0.0 |

Table 11: More examples demonstrating reference short phrase summaries as well as summaries predicted by the best-performing BART-large model (BART-large **NLI + PA + FT**) for the **CLINC150 test set with unseen labels**, which differ from the ground truth. **The summaries selected by Turkers** are indicated in **bold**. Cases for which both reference and model-generated summaries are deemed useful, have both summaries highlighted. **R-1** and **R-2** refer to ROUGE-1 and ROUGE-2 F1 scores respectively.

| Error Type | Utterance | Summaries |
|---|---|---|
| **Case 1:** | *Order a taxi for tomorrow 8am* | **R:** Request Ride, **S:** Book Restaurant |
| | *Tell my friends what time I'll get there* | **R:** Share ETA , **S:** Get Place Details |
| **Case 2:** | *Get me directions to Las Vegas avoiding toll roads* | **S:**Get Traffic Information, **R:**Get Directions |
| | *Share my estimated time of arrival with my mother* | **R:**Share ETA, **S:**Share Current Location |
| **Case 3:** | *Navigate me to Empire State Building using the shortest way* | **S:**Get Traffic Information, **R:**Get Directions |
| | *Directions to La Guardia airport using Waze* | **R:**Get Directions, **S:**Get Traffic Information |

Table 12: Examples of errors made by the BART-large NLI+PA+FT model *(best BART model)* on CLINC150 test set with unseen labels during training. **R** stands for reference summary and **S** stands for model-generated summary.

# Location Aware Modular Biencoder for Tourism Question Answering

**Haonan Li**[♠,♣] **Martin Tomko**[♡] **Timothy Baldwin**[♠,♣]
♠ School of Computing and Information Systems, The University of Melbourne
♡ Department of Infrastructure Engineering, The University of Melbourne
♣ Department of Natural Language Processing, MBZUAI
haonan.li@mbzuai.ac.ae, tomkom@unimelb.edu.au, tb@ldwin.net

## Abstract

Answering real-world tourism questions that seek Point-of-Interest (POI) recommendations is challenging, as it requires both spatial and non-spatial reasoning, over a large candidate pool. The traditional method of encoding each pair of question and POI becomes inefficient when the number of candidates increases, making it infeasible for real-world applications. To overcome this, we propose treating the QA task as a dense vector retrieval problem, where we encode questions and POIs separately and retrieve the most relevant POIs for a question by utilizing embedding space similarity. We use pretrained language models (PLMs) to encode textual information, and train a location encoder to capture spatial information of POIs. Experiments on a real-world tourism QA dataset demonstrate that our approach is effective, efficient, and outperforms previous methods across all metrics. Enabled by the dense retrieval architecture, we further build a global evaluation baseline, expanding the search space by 20 times compared to previous work. We also explore several factors that impact on the model's performance through follow-up experiments. Our code and model are publicly available at https://github.com/haonan-li/LAMB.

**Question:** *Hi! My wife and I are in our late thirties and going to be in Dublin on September 28 and 29th. We are staying in the Grafton Street area. Does anybody have any suggestions for some fairly priced restaurants with great food within walking distance of Grafton Street? Also, What about some good pubs with live local music? (I realize it is a Sun and Mon night and may be slow) Any suggestion would be appreciated! Thanks!*
**Answer ID**: *11_R_4392*
**Answer Name**: The Porterhouse Central, 45-47 Nassau Street, Dublin.

Figure 1: An example of real-world POI recommendation question from the TourismQA dataset (Contractor et al., 2021b). Colored text represents constraints relevant to recommending POIs.

## 1 Introduction

Question answering (QA) models and recommender systems have undergone rapid development in recent years (Seo et al., 2017; Rajpurkar et al., 2016; Kwiatkowski et al., 2019; Lee et al., 2019; Cui et al., 2020; Hamid et al., 2021). However, personalised question answering is still highly challenging and relatively unexplored in the literature. Consider the example question in Figure 1, in the form of a real-world point-of-interest (POI) recommendation question from a travel forum. Answering such questions requires understanding of the question text with possibly explicit (e.g., *in Dublin*) or vague and ambiguous (e.g., *within walking distance of Grafton Street*) spatial constraints, as well as a fast indexing method that supports large-scale reasoning over both spatial and non-spatial (e.g., *fairly priced restaurants*) constraints.

Recently, there has been increased interest in geospatial QA. Most approaches focus on querying structured knowledge bases, based on translating natural language questions into structured queries, e.g., using SPARQL (Punjani et al., 2018; Li et al., 2021; Hamzei et al., 2022). Separately, Contractor et al. (2021b) introduced the task of answering POI-seeking questions using geospatial metadata and reviews that describe POIs. In later work, they proposed a spatial–textual reasoning network that uses distance-aware question embeddings as input and encodes question–POI pairs using attention (Contractor et al., 2021a). However, as their model creates separate question embeddings for each POI, the inference cost increases linearly in the number of POIs, and the model is incompatible with large



*Findings of the Association for Computational Linguistics: IJCNLP-AACL 2023*, pages 95–109
November 1–4, 2023. 

pre-trained models such as BERT (Devlin et al., 2019) or even medium-sized QA models such as BiDAF (Seo et al., 2017).

In this work, we address the question: can we build a more efficient POI recommendation system which supports the use of advanced pre-trained language models as the textual encoder? By presenting the **L**ocation **a**ware **m**odular **b**i-encoder ("LAMB") model. We use a bi-encoder architecture to encode questions and POIs separately, where the question encoder is a textual module and the POI encoder consists of a textual and a location module. By encoding them separately, we cast the task as a retrieval problem based on dense vector similarity between the question and each POI. For training, we combine each question with one positively-labeled POI and multiple negatively-labeled POIs, and use contrastive learning to train the question encoder and POI encoder simultaneously, by maximizing the similarity between the question and positive POI. After training, we generate location-aware dense representations for all POIs using the POI encoder, and index them by city name and entity (POI) type. For inference, we use the question encoder to generate a location-aware representation, and rank the POIs using similarity.

Our contributions are four-fold: (1) we propose a location-aware modular bi-encoder model which fuses spatial and textual information; (2) we demonstrate that the proposed model outperforms the existing SOTA on a real-world tourism QA dataset, with huge improvements in training and inference efficiency; (3) we build new global evaluation baselines by expanding the search space 20× over local evaluation; and finally, (4) we analyse the influence of different training strategies and hyper-parameters through extensive experiments.

## 2 Methodology

In this section, we first formulate the task, and then introduce the POI pre-processing method and the LAMB model. Finally, we describe the efficient training and inference strategies.

### 2.1 Task Formulation

Given a question $q$, the task is to find the most probable POI answer $p$ from a candidate pool $P$, which satisfies spatial and non-spatial constraints in $q$. Each POI in $P$ consists of a *geo-coordinates* $(lat, long)$ of the POI, the multi-granularity location *name* (POI entity name, street, city, postcode), and a list of textual *reviews* $= (r_1, r_2, ...r_n)$. It can be represented as $p = \langle coordinates, name, reviews \rangle$ (see Appendix A for an example).

### 2.2 POI Pre-processing

Reviews of POIs provide useful information to represent POIs, however, each candidate can have hundreds of reviews, the total length greatly exceeding the maximum token length of 512 tokens in general PLMs such as BERT. To choose more representative reviews, previous work (Contractor et al., 2021b) has clustered reviews into $K$ clusters, and then represented the POI using the top-$N$ sentences from each cluster based on distance from the cluster centroid, resulting in $N \times K$ sentences. However, this approach is potentially problematic as clusters can be of varying size and density, and outliers can affect the centroid. To keep representative reviews, $K$ and $N$ should not be too small, e.g., Contractor et al. (2021b,a) set $N = K = 10$.

In this paper, we adopt the SELSUM (Bražinskas et al., 2021) model, which consists of a selector to choose the $M$ most representative reviews and a summarizer to generate a summary of the selected reviews. We use a model pre-trained on the AMASUM dataset, which includes verdicts, pros, and cons, and hundreds of reviews for more than 31,000 summarized Amazon products (see example in Appendix C). We compare the results using clustering, the selection module only, and the full SELSUM model in Appendix C. Our results show that using a 3-sentence summary for each POI achieves comparable results with a clustering approach that represents each POI via 100 sentences, and that using 10 sentences outperforms the clustering method.

### 2.3 Location Aware Modular Bi-encoder

LAMB (see Figure 2) uses a bi-encoder framework to encode questions and POIs. The question encoder is a textual module which takes question text as input, and outputs dense representations. The POI encoder consists of a textual module and a location module, where the textual module encodes a description and/or reviews associated with it, and the location module encodes the multi-granularity location names. The outputs of the textual and location modules are real-valued vectors, which are concatenated to represent a POI. Full details of the model are presented below.

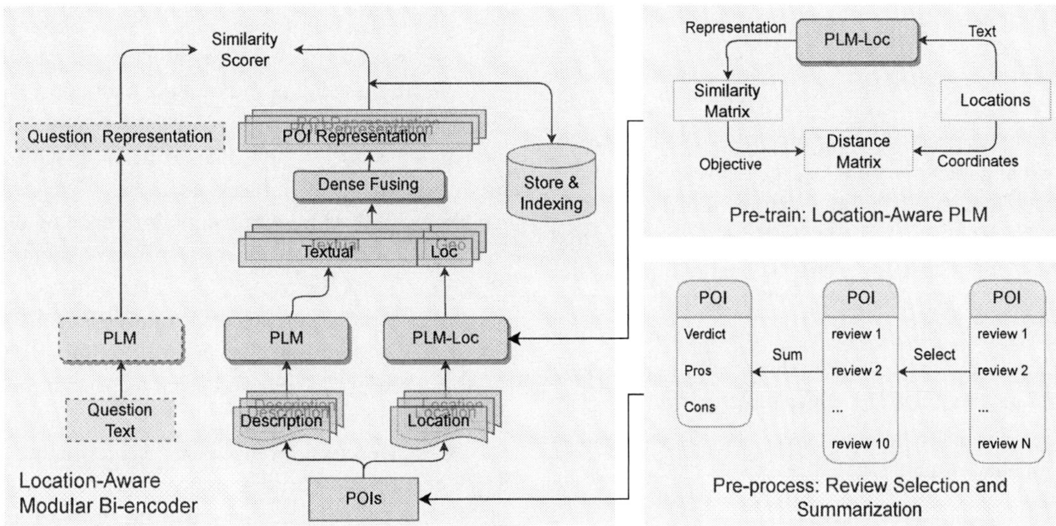


Figure 2: Proposed approach. The reviews of POIs are first selected and summarized by SELSUM (bottom right part). A location module is separately pre-trained under the supervision of geocoordinate-based distances (top right part). The left part is the main LAMB model. The cyan- and salmon-coloured parts are the POI encoder and question encoder, respectively. The orange part is the index of POI embeddings used for inference.

**Textual Module** We use two independent PLMs as the textual encoder for questions and POIs, using the `[CLS]` token representation as the output. For questions, we do not preprocess the question text, while for POIs, we concatenate the preprocessed reviews.

**Location Module** Spatial constraints are crucial in retrieving relevant POIs to a question. However, previous research has shown that PLMs perform poorly in encoding and reasoning over spatial data, especially for geolocation information (Scherrer and Ljubešić, 2021; Hofmann et al., 2022). To enhance the model's ability to capture geospatial information, we employ a location module that explicitly encodes the multi-granularity location name of a POI into a dense vector. We initialize the location module by choosing several transformer blocks from a PLM, and continue pre-training it to learn geo-coordinate-aware location name representations. The training object is designed to pull together pairs of encoded location representations if the locations are physically near each other, and push them apart if they are far from each other.

Formally, for any three POIs $(p_0, p_1, p_2)$, suppose the corresponding locations are $(l_0, l_1, l_2)$, and the encoded representations are $(h_0, h_1, h_2)$. Here $l_i(i = 0, 1, 2)$ is a 1-d vector $[lat_i, long_i]$, representing the latitude and longitude of $p_i$, with $lat_i \in [-90, 90]$ and $long_i \in [-180, 180]$, and $h_i$ is a vector. We choose $p_0$ to be an anchor location, and $d_i(i = 1, 2) \in [0, 1]$ to represent the normalized Haversine distance between $l_0$ and $l_i$, representing the greater-circle distance between two points on a sphere. Similarly, $s_i(i = 1, 2) \in [0, 1]$ represents the cosine similarity between $h_0$ and $h_i$. We use the triplet margin loss, and define the loss function as follows:

$$\mathcal{L} = \begin{cases} \max((s_1 - s_2) + (d_1 - d_2), 0) & \text{if}(d_1 - d_2) > 0 \\ \max((s_2 - s_1) - (d_1 - d_2), 0) & \text{otherwise} \end{cases}$$

In the first case, $d_1 - d_2 > 0$ means that $p_2$ is closer to $p_0$ than $p_1$, and hence we structure the loss to learn a larger $s_2$ (= higher similarity between $p_0$ and $p_2$) and smaller $s_1$ (= lower similarity between $p_0$ and $p_1$). We set the difference between the two distances as a dynamic margin, which controls the rationally-valued similarity difference.

**Question and POI Encoders** As mentioned above, we use a separate textual encoding module $E_P^{text}$ and location encoding module $E_P^{loc}$ to encode each POI. These modules map the review text and location names to fixed-length vectors:

$$r_p^{text} = E_P^{text}(p) \in \mathbb{R}^{1 \times d_1}$$
$$r_p^{loc} = E_P^{loc}(p) \in \mathbb{R}^{1 \times d_2}$$

We concatenate $r_p^{text}$ and $r_p^{loc}$ and then use a dense layer to fuse the representations together, resulting in the POI representation $r_p \in \mathbb{R}^{1\times d}$:

$$r_p = \text{Dense}([r_p^{text}, r_p^{loc}]) \in \mathbb{R}^{1\times d}$$

For questions, we similarly tried using separate text and location modules, and combining their outputs. However, we found that the text may contain distractor locations that should not be considered as spatial constraints, and that context is essential. (e.g., the place name *Italy* in question *Hey I am from Italy, please suggest a restaurant in Berlin that suits my appetite.*) Hence, we use a single textual module $E_Q^{text}$ which directly maps the question text into representation $r_q \in \mathbb{R}^{1\times d}$, of the same dimension as a POI.

### 2.4 Training and Inference

We train the two encoders simultaneously using contrastive learning. We input each question $q_i$ with one positive POI $p_i^+$ and several negative POIs $p_{i,1}^-, ...p_{i,n}^-$ into the model, with the objective to maximize the similarity between the embeddings of $q_i$ and $p_i^+$, while minimizing the similarity between the embeddings of $q_i$ and $p_{i,1}^-, ...p_{i,n}^-$. We use the negative log-likelihood (NLL) loss of the positive POIs as our objective function:

$$\mathcal{L}(q_i, p_i^+, p_{i,1}^-, ...p_{i,n}^-) = -\log \frac{e^{\text{sim}(q_i, p_i^+)}}{e^{\text{sim}(q_i, p_i^+)} + \sum_{j=1}^{n} e^{\text{sim}(q_i, p_{i,j}^-)}}$$

where similarity function $\text{sim}(p, q)$ is the inner product.

**Negative Sampling Strategy** A critical question in contrastive learning is how to construct positive and negative examples. In our case, for each question, there can be more than one answer (= positive) POI. To make use of every positive POI, as well as to adapt to the NLL loss function, we create a training example for each positive POI. For negative samples, all non-answer POIs are candidate negative samples, but previous work (Karpukhin et al., 2020; Xiong et al., 2021a) has shown that high-quality negative samples help to learn a better encoder. In this research, we consider three different types of negative samples: (1) *easy negatives* = random (non-answer) POIs from the entire candidate set; (2) *medium negatives* = random (non-answer) POIs that are in the same city and of the same type (restaurant, attraction, or hotel) as the answer POI; and (3) *hard negatives* = top-$k$ ranked non-answer POIs from the previous epoch.

**Two-phase Training** We conduct two phases of training: first, we use easy and medium negatives to do warm-up training of the model, and provide the model with a relatively easily-optimizable objective; next, we switch over to training with a mixture of medium and hard negatives.[1] We sample hard negatives by performing inference on the training data after each epoch (or a specific number of steps) to find the top-$k$ POIs for each training question. We then create new training instances by randomly sampling $N$ non-answer POIs from the top-$k$ retrieved POIs, and use these to continue training the model.

**Inference** Before inference, we disable the question encoder and generate representations of all POIs using the POI encoder only, and store and index them (as shown in the orange part in Figure 2). During inference, the generated POI representations are loaded into memory. Given a question $q$ at run-time, we encode it using the question encoder, score all candidates using the pre-computed representations, and return the top-$k$ results.

## 3 Experimental Setup

In this section, we introduce the dataset, baselines, and implementation details of our model.

### 3.1 Dataset

We use the TourismQA (Contractor et al., 2021b) dataset, which comprises over 47,000 real-world POI question–answer pairs from 50 cities across the globe. These questions are genuine queries submitted to a trip advisor website,[2] and the answers are real-world responses that have been chosen and authenticated by annotators. The average length of the questions is 87.48 tokens (separated by whitespace). And on average, there are 3.63 POIs as ground truth answers for each question. The dataset contains roughly 114,000 candidate POIs altogether, each with a collection of reviews and metadata such as geo-coordinates and type (restaurant, attraction, or hotel).

We follow Contractor et al. (2021b) in dividing the dataset into a 9:1 train–test split, and constructing a search space by including POIs located in the same city as the ground truth POIs, resulting in an average of approximately 5,300 candidate POIs per question. We believe one reason for earlier work

[1] For convenience, we use "easy" and "hard" negatives to describe the training setting in any single phase.

[2] https://www.tripadvisor.in

to build the candidate pool within a city was that their methods struggled with a large candidate pool. However, in real-world scenarios, the ground truth answer is concealed, and the candidate pool may be extensive, encompassing all POIs in the database. Therefore, we established a new evaluation setting in which the search space comprises all POIs in the world. We refer to this new setting as *global* evaluation (114,000 candidates), and the previous one as *local* evaluation (5,300 candidates).

### 3.2 Evaluation Metrics

Following Contractor et al. (2021b), we evaluate using Accuracy@$N \in \{3, 5, 30\}$ and mean reciprocal rank (MRR) for local evaluation, and use Accuracy@$N \in \{5, 30, 100\}$ for global evaluation. For Accuracy@$N$, if the top-$N$ predictions have a non-empty intersection with the answer POI set, the results are considered to be correct. For MRR, we return the reciprocal rank of the first positive answer POI per question, and average over the questions.

### 3.3 Baselines

We compare ourselves against four baselines, as detailed below.

**Sort by Distance (SD)**: Given all tagged locations with geo-coordinates in the question, we rank POIs by the minimal distance from the tagged locations.

**BM25**: We represent each POI by its combined reviews, and index them using Apache Lucene. Then questions are used as a query to compute BM25 scores for all POIs.

**Cluster-Select-Rerank ("CSR") Model** (Contractor et al., 2021b), which consists of three components: (1) a clustering module that clusters reviews for each POI and selects representative reviews; (2) a Duet (Mitra and Craswell, 2019) retrieval model that selects the best 30 candidate POIs; and (3) a QA-style re-ranker that scores and re-ranks the selected POIs. Note that the cluster module is used to pre-process the POIs, and the selection and re-ranking modules are trained separately and pipelined.

**Spatial-Textual CSR** (Contractor et al., 2021a), which adds a self-attention based geospatial reasoner to the CSR model, and ranks POIs based on the weighted sum of scores from the geo-spatial reasoner and CSR.

### 3.4 LAMB Implementation Details

We implement our model in PyTorch, and use the HuggingFace (Wolf et al., 2020) implementation of DistilBERT (Sanh et al., 2019) as the textual encoder. The location module is comprised of two transformer blocks that are initialized using the first two blocks of a pre-trained DistilBERT model. We continued pre-training for 3 epochs using triplet loss to force the model to learn more spatial information, as described in Section 2.3. During this process, we set the batch size to 8, learning rate to 2e-5, and the max sequence length to 64.

For the main model of LAMB, the maximum length (in subtokens) for both questions and reviews is set to 256. For training, we use a linear learning rate scheduler with an initial learning rate of 2e-5, and the Adam optimizer with default hyperparameters. For each training instance, we use a single positive POI and varying numbers of negatives. We set the batch size to 8 and train for 10 epochs: 5 epochs of phase 1 (easy and medium negatives), and 5 epochs of phase 2 (medium and hard negatives). All experiments were run on a single Nvidia A100 40GB GPU for about 8 hours.

## 4 Results and Analysis

Table 1 shows the overall performance of the baselines and our proposed model. We can see that the sparse-vector retrieval (BM25) and distance-based retrieval (SD) models in the first block of the table perform extremely poorly, demonstrating the difficulty of the task. In contrast, the textual-only pipelined models (CRQA and CSRQA) in the second block improve overall performance substantially, and adding the spatial reasoning subnetwork ("ST+") boosts results again. Note that, since CSRQA is pipelined with a selection model that selects the top-30 results, the spatial-textual module cannot improve Accuracy@30 further.

Compared to the baselines in blocks one and two, our model, LAMB, achieves the state-of-the-art across all metrics. To better understand the impact of different components of our model, we conducted an ablation study by separately removing the training phase 2, review selection and summarization modules, and location module. Overall, the performance dropped when one of these modules or strategies was removed, but still outperformed the previous state-of-the-art. Specifically, removing training phase 2 had a relatively large impact on local evaluation, which we attribute to the process

| Model | Local | | | | Global | | | |
|---|---|---|---|---|---|---|---|---|
| | Acc@3 | Acc@5 | Acc@30 | MRR | Acc@5 | Acc@30 | Acc@100 | MRR |
| SD | 0.83 | 1.11 | 5.62 | 0.011 | 0.83 | 1.11 | 5.62 | 0.011 |
| BM25 | 5.59 | 8.29 | 16.33 | 0.061 | 0.44 | 1.86 | 3.68 | 0.014 |
| CRQA | 16.89 | 23.75 | 52.51 | 0.159 | – | – | – | – |
| ST+CRQA | 19.37 | 26.23 | <u>56.33</u> | 0.175 | – | – | – | – |
| CSRQA | 21.44 | 28.20 | 52.65 | 0.186 | – | – | – | – |
| ST+CSRQA | <u>22.41</u> | <u>28.99</u> | 52.65 | <u>0.193</u> | – | – | – | – |
| LAMB | **24.83** | **32.51** | **60.92** | **0.220** | **14.07** | **32.87** | 49.08 | **0.101** |
| −Phase 2 | 22.49 | 29.35 | 59.20 | 0.201 | 13.22 | 31.89 | **49.68** | 0.094 |
| −SELSUM | 23.90 | 31.20 | 60.52 | 0.216 | 13.28 | 32.12 | 48.63 | 0.096 |
| $-E_{loc}$ | 23.68 | 31.30 | 60.52 | 0.215 | 9.59 | 24.52 | 40.03 | 0.071 |

Table 1: Overall evaluation on the TourismQA dataset. The second block of results are based on the TourismQA paper, wherein the best results are underlined, and "ST" denotes the spatial–textual module. The overall best results are in **bold**. The third block presents the results for the full LAMB model, and also with module ablation.

| Model | Training | Inference | |
|---|---|---|---|
| | Time (h) | #Cand | Time (h) |
| CRQA (±ST) | 360 | 5.3k | 64 |
| CSRQA (±ST) | 360+ | 30 | 2–3 |
| LAMB | 10 | 115k | 0.15 |

Table 2: Runtime comparison, based on a single Nvidia V100 GPU. "#Cand" indicates the number of candidate POIs. For CSRQA, time was estimated by summing the times of the component models.

| Loc Module | Acc@5 | Acc@30 | Acc@100 | MRR |
|---|---|---|---|---|
| w/o Loc | 9.59 | 24.52 | 40.03 | 0.071 |
| 2-$l$ PLM | 9.91 | 25.47 | 41.64 | 0.075 |
| 1-$l$ PLM-Loc | 12.86 | 30.67 | 46.28 | 0.091 |
| 2-$l$ PLM-Loc | **14.07** | **32.87** | **49.08** | **0.101** |
| 4-$l$ PLM-Loc | 10.92 | 27.78 | 43.24 | 0.081 |

Table 3: Results with different location module settings. "PLM" = use PLM directly; "PLM-Loc" = continue to pretrain PLM on location names; and "$N$-$l$" = use $N$ transformer blocks.

of training to distinguish hard negatives. Removing the location module greatly impacted the global evaluation, demonstrating the effectiveness of the location module, particularly when candidates are from around the globe.

Based on our analysis, there are three main reasons why LAMB outperforms previous models: (1) training and inference are end-to-end, avoiding error propagation due to pipelining, as with CSRQA; (2) our use of pre-trained language models as the textual encoder, outperforming static word embeddings or training encoders from scratch; and (3) learning location encodings separately and fusing them with textual representations, providing a soft distance computing method. We provide a comparison between our location module design and other straightforward geo-coordinate-based location/distance modules in Appendix E. From this, we can conclude that compared to strategies that encode geo-coordinates directly, a pretrained location name module better captures spatial information.

### 4.1 Efficiency Comparison

We analyze the computational requirements of the models in Table 2. LAMB is more time efficient than the previously-proposed neural models, requiring around 5% of the training time, and <10% of the inference time. It is also able to handle a much larger candidate pool (in the millions of candidates) compared to C(±S)RQA (in the tens or thousands of candidates). Further analysis of efficiency and usability is provided in Appendix D.

### 4.2 Ablation Study on Model Training

To further understand how different model training options affect the results, we conduct several additional experiments and discuss our findings below.

**Location Module Analysis** In this section, we compare various settings of location modules as shown in Table 3. The table indicates that continuous pretraining of a PLM on location names significantly enhances the module's ability to capture geo-location and distance. Furthermore, using two transformer blocks is sufficient to encode multi-granularity location names, whereas more or fewer layers may lead to overfitting or underfitting.

**Effectiveness of Negative Examples** To investigate the effectiveness of the type and number of negative examples during training, we kept the total

| #HN | Local | | | | Global | | | |
|---|---|---|---|---|---|---|---|---|
| | Acc@3 | Acc@5 | Acc@30 | MRR | Acc@5 | Acc@30 | Acc@100 | MRR |
| 0 | 16.41 | 22.59 | 51.05 | 0.159 | 19.51 | **44.70** | **64.91** | **0.137** |
| 1 | 15.51 | 21.34 | 51.67 | 0.154 | 16.97 | 43.06 | 62.19 | 0.123 |
| 4 | 20.55 | 27.29 | 52.41 | 0.188 | **20.13** | 40.43 | 56.27 | 0.142 |
| 8 | 23.99 | 30.58 | 59.47 | 0.213 | 17.37 | 37.78 | 54.20 | 0.124 |
| 12 | **24.83** | **32.51** | **60.92** | **0.220** | 14.07 | 32.87 | 49.08 | 0.101 |
| 15 | 24.06 | 31.44 | 60.70 | 0.221 | 8.10 | 21.34 | 36.18 | 0.063 |

Table 4: Results with differing numbers of easy/hard negatives, total negatives = 15. #HN: number of hard negatives.

| #Phase 1,2 | Local | | | | Global | | | |
|---|---|---|---|---|---|---|---|---|
| | Acc@3 | Acc@5 | Acc@30 | MRR | Acc@5 | Acc@30 | Acc@100 | MRR |
| 10, 0 | 22.49 | 29.35 | 59.20 | 0.201 | 13.22 | 31.89 | 49.68 | 0.094 |
| 8, 2 | 23.08 | 30.22 | 60.33 | 0.209 | 13.48 | 32.48 | **50.65** | 0.096 |
| 5, 5 | **24.83** | **32.51** | **60.92** | **0.220** | **14.07** | **32.87** | 49.08 | **0.101** |
| 2, 8 | 24.49 | 31.88 | 60.08 | 0.219 | 13.05 | 31.18 | 46.04 | 0.095 |
| 0, 10 | 21.73 | 28.28 | 54.15 | 0.198 | 11.70 | 28.74 | 42.82 | 0.085 |

Table 5: Results with varied epochs in two-phase training, using 10 total training epochs.

number of negatives constant at 15 while varying the mix of easy and hard negatives (as presented in Table 4). As we increase the number of hard negatives, the global evaluation results deteriorate while the local evaluation results improve. This implies that training with easy negatives is more appropriate when the target city or area is unconstrained. The best local evaluation results were achieved when using 12/15 hard negatives, indicating that easy negatives are still necessary for learning general location constraints. We further investigated varying the total number of negatives for contrastive learning, as presented in Table 7 in the Appendix. Our findings indicate that the more negatives we have in each training instance, the better the model performs, but that the relative improvement plateaus beyond around 30.

**Two-Phase Training Strategy** We conducted experiments with different epoch configurations for our two-phase training strategy, as detailed in Table 5. Our results indicate that both phase 1 and phase 2 are essential, aligning with the assumptions stated in Section 2.4. Furthermore, we found that commencing phase 2 training at the midway point was particularly effective.

### 4.3 Human Evaluation

To further investigate the dataset and have a better sense of the overall performance of LAMB, we conducted a small-scale human evaluation. We randomly choose 100 questions from the test set and manually evaluate the top-3 predictions for relevance based on LAMB as presented in Table 1. For this small question set, our estimate of the true Accuracy@3 is around 75%, as compared to the automatic evaluation result of 24%. This is consistent with the human evaluation results reported in (Contractor et al., 2021a), and points to the issue of low label-recall in the dataset: while a given POI may not have been selected by the user who issued the original question, it may well have satisfied the constraints described in the question.

### 4.4 How ChatGPT Performs on TourismQA

During the writing of this paper, ChatGPT (i.e. GPT3.5) was released. We manually tested 100 questions from Section 4.3 by inputting them directly into ChatGPT (GPT-3.5-turbo on 20-March-2023) and getting a single response.[3] The results show that out of the 100 questions, 91 received recommendations for points of interest or areas. However, only 14 of those replies match the ground truth answers, which is lower than our model's performance of 24. We believe that the main reason for this discrepancy is due to differences in the POI databases. The replies from ChatGPT were well-organized and logical, and could even answer many details in the questions beyond the capabilities of our model.

However, we observed that ChatGPT failed to provide an output in many cases: among the 100 replies, sentences such as *As an AI language model,*

[3]Questions and responses are released together with the source code.

*I don't have personal experience in ...* appeared 36 times, while other outputs like *I can recommend that you check out the reviews on websites like TripAdvisor or Booking.com* appeared 13 times. Additionally, ChatGPT tended to recommend popular places, with the word *popular* appearing 44 times in replies, despite not being mentioned in any of the questions. We observed further bias in ChatGPT's recommendations. For example, it recommended *Shake Shack* nine times in response to fast food requests, but never mentioned other international fast-food chains or local chains, even when questions specifically asked for fast food with regional characteristics.

Lastly, ChatGPT's database is not up-to-date, as also mentioned in its replies. Since OpenAI did not provide full training details, the cost of updating the database, including fine-tuning the model, is unclear. In summary, there is still a real need for a comprehensive recommendation system that can be combined with up-to-date website information.

## 5 Related Work

**Geo-Spatial Question Anwering** There has been a strong focus in the literature on component geospatial tasks such as geo-parsing (toponym recognition and disambiguation) (Karimzadeh et al., 2019; Wang et al., 2020a), geo-tagging (tagging toponyms with geographic metadata) (Compton et al., 2014; Middleton et al., 2018), geospatial information retrieval (Purves et al., 2018), and geospatial question analysis (Hamzei et al., 2019).

Based on the type of question, existing work on geospatial QA ("GeoQA") can be classified into four types (Mai et al., 2021): (1) factoid GQA (Li et al., 2021; Hamzei et al., 2022), focusing on answering questions with geographic factoids; (2) geo-analytical QA (Scheider et al., 2020; Xu et al., 2020), focusing on questions with complex spatial analytical intent; (3) visual GQA (Lobry et al., 2020; Janowicz et al., 2020), linking questions to an image or video; and (4) scenario-based GQA (Huang et al., 2019; Contractor et al., 2021b), which associates questions with a scenario described with a map or paragraph of text. Our work corresponds to the last type, and unlike most other work, we do not rely on task-specific query languages or annotations, and focus more on NLP and IR modeling.

**Point-of-Interest (POI) Recommendation** POI recommendation systems have a wide range of applications such as online navigation applications (Zhao et al., 2019a; Yuan et al., 2021), personalized recommendation systems in location-based social networks (Feng et al., 2015; Zhao et al., 2019b), and trip or accommodation advisory systems (Li et al., 2016; Contractor et al., 2021b). In this research, we focus on POI recommendation incorporating both structured information (such as geo-coordinates) and unstructured information (such as textual descriptions). Previous work has explored efficient spatial indexing based on specialized data structures, with textual information as sparse vectors or filters (de Almeida and Rocha-Junior, 2015; Li et al., 2016). Recent work (Contractor et al., 2021b,a) has focused on latent textual representations, which is highly relevant here.

**Textual Encoding and Document Retrieval** Pretrained language models (PLMs) have led to great successes across many NLP tasks (Devlin et al., 2019; Liu et al., 2019; Yang et al., 2019; Lewis et al., 2020; He et al., 2021; Clark et al., 2020). In the field of QA, PLMs have been used to generate representations of questions and documents (Nogueira et al., 2019; Zhang et al., 2020). In this work, we use DistilBERT (Sanh et al., 2019) as our textual encoder, as it is more efficient than BERT and retains much of its expressivity.

Document retrieval has become a mainstay of research in IR and QA. Recently, IR has increasingly moved towards dense vector retrieval methods (Das et al., 2019; Seo et al., 2019; Xiong et al., 2021b). In particular, Karpukhin et al. (2020) proposed DPR based on a dual-encoder approach, and attained impressive results on multiple open-domain question answering benchmarks. Inspired by this, we adopt a bi-encoder framework.

## 6 Conclusion

We have proposed the LAMB model, a location-aware bi-encoder model for answering POI recommendation questions. Experiments on a recently-released tourism question-answering dataset show that our model surpasses existing spatial-textual reasoning models across all metrics. Experiments over LAMB's components and based on changing up the training strategy show the effectiveness of the different design choices used in LAMB. Finally, we analyzed the training and inference efficiency, and demonstrated that our model is resource-efficient at training and inference time, suggesting it can be deployed in real-world tourism applications.

## Limitations

Although we have achieved results that significantly outperform the current state-of-the-art, our work still has some limitations. First, as demonstrated in Section 4.3 and in the earlier work of Contractor et al. (2021a), the TourismQA dataset was collected semi-automatically, and the gold labels have high precision but low recall. Hence any results on this dataset are likely an underestimate of the true model performance. While we currently use the Haversine formula to compute the distance between two locations and supervise the pre-training of the location module, we recognize that this calculation may not reflect the actual distance between two places, taking into account the route direction and vertical height difference. In light of the city's urban design, the Manhattan distance might better represent the true distance between two locations within a city. Additionally, POI density could be a factor that influences user choice in real life, in that people may be more inclined to go to locations with a higher density of restaurants to eat (in order to have more options if a given restaurant doesn't live up to their expectations), rather than travel far to a remote place without other options in the local vicinity. For hotels, on the other hand, some users may prefer privacy and a lower density. Such extra-linguistic features are not explicitly captured in our model.

## References


Arthur Bražinskas, Mirella Lapata, and Ivan Titov. 2021. Learning opinion summarizers by selecting informative reviews. In *Proceedings of the Conference on Empirical Methods in Natural Language Processing (EMNLP)*.

Kevin Clark, Minh-Thang Luong, Quoc V. Le, and Christopher D. Manning. 2020. ELECTRA: pre-training text encoders as discriminators rather than generators. In *Proceedings of the 8th International Conference on Learning Representations*. OpenReview.net.

Ryan Compton, David Jurgens, and David Allen. 2014. Geotagging one hundred million twitter accounts with total variation minimization. In *Proceedings of the 2014 IEEE International Conference on Big Data*, pages 393–401. IEEE Computer Society.

Danish Contractor, Shashank Goel, and Parag Singla. 2021a. Joint spatio-textual reasoning for answering tourism questions. In *Proceedings of the Web Conference 2021*, pages 1978–1989.

Danish Contractor, Krunal Shah, Aditi Partap, Parag Singla, and Mausam. 2021b. Answering poi-recommendation questions using tourism reviews. In *the 30th ACM International Conference on Information and Knowledge Management, Virtual Event, Queensland, Australia, November 1 - 5, 2021*, pages 281–291. ACM.

Zhihua Cui, Xianghua Xu, Xue Fei, Xingjuan Cai, Yang Cao, Wensheng Zhang, and Jinjun Chen. 2020. Personalized recommendation system based on collaborative filtering for IoT scenarios. *IEEE Transactions on Services Computing*, 13(4):685–695.

Rajarshi Das, Shehzaad Dhuliawala, Manzil Zaheer, and Andrew McCallum. 2019. Multi-step retriever-reader interaction for scalable open-domain question answering. In *Proceedings of the 7th International Conference on Learning Representations*. OpenReview.net.

João Paulo Dias de Almeida and João B. Rocha-Junior. 2015. Top-k spatial keyword preference query. *Journal of Information and Data Management*, 6(3):162–177.

Jacob Devlin, Ming-Wei Chang, Kenton Lee, and Kristina Toutanova. 2019. BERT: Pre-training of deep bidirectional transformers for language understanding. In *Proceedings of the 2019 Conference of the North American Chapter of the Association for Computational Linguistics: Human Language Technologies, Volume 1 (Long and Short Papers)*, pages 4171–4186, Minneapolis, Minnesota. Association for Computational Linguistics.

Shanshan Feng, Xutao Li, Yifeng Zeng, Gao Cong, Yeow Meng Chee, and Quan Yuan. 2015. Personalized ranking metric embedding for next new POI recommendation. In *Proceedings of the Twenty-Fourth International Joint Conference on Artificial Intelligence*, pages 2069–2075. AAAI Press.

Rula A Hamid, Ahmed Shihab Albahri, Jwan K Alwan, ZT Al-Qaysi, Osamah Shihab Albahri, AA Zaidan, Alhamzah Alnoor, AH Alamoodi, and BB Zaidan. 2021. How smart is e-tourism? a systematic review of smart tourism recommendation system applying data management. *Computer Science Review*, 39:100337.

Ehsan Hamzei, Haonan Li, Maria Vasardani, Timothy Baldwin, Stephan Winter, and Martin Tomko. 2019. Place questions and human-generated answers: A data analysis approach. In *Proceedings of the 22nd AGILE Conference on Geographic Information Science*, pages 3–19. Springer.

Ehsan Hamzei, Martin Tomko, and Stephan Winter. 2022. Translating place-related questions to geosparql queries. In *Proceedings of the ACM Web Conference 2022*, pages 902–911. ACM.

Pengcheng He, Xiaodong Liu, Jianfeng Gao, and Weizhu Chen. 2021. DeBERTa: decoding-enhanced Bert with disentangled attention. In *Proceedings of the 9th International Conference on Learning Representations*. OpenReview.net.

Valentin Hofmann, Goran Glavaš, Nikola Ljubešić, Janet B Pierrehumbert, and Hinrich Schütze. 2022. Geographic adaptation of pretrained language models. *arXiv preprint arXiv:2203.08565*.

Zixian Huang, Yulin Shen, Xiao Li, Yu'ang Wei, Gong Cheng, Lin Zhou, Xinyu Dai, and Yuzhong Qu. 2019. GeoSQA: A benchmark for scenario-based question answering in the geography domain at high school level. In *Proceedings of the 2019 Conference on Empirical Methods in Natural Language Processing and the 9th International Joint Conference on Natural Language Processing (EMNLP-IJCNLP)*, pages 5866–5871, Hong Kong, China. Association for Computational Linguistics.

Krzysztof Janowicz, Song Gao, Grant McKenzie, Yingjie Hu, and Budhendra Bhaduri. 2020. GeoAI: Spatially explicit artificial intelligence techniques for geographic knowledge discovery and beyond. *International Journal of Geographic Information Science*, pages 625–636.

Xiaoqi Jiao, Yichun Yin, Lifeng Shang, Xin Jiang, Xiao Chen, Linlin Li, Fang Wang, and Qun Liu. 2019. Tinybert: Distilling bert for natural language understanding. *arXiv preprint arXiv:1909.10351*.

Jeff Johnson, Matthijs Douze, and Hervé Jégou. 2021. Billion-scale similarity search with GPUs. *IEEE Trans. Big Data*, 7(3):535–547.

Morteza Karimzadeh, Scott Pezanowski, Alan M MacEachren, and Jan O Wallgrün. 2019. Geotxt: A scalable geoparsing system for unstructured text geolocation. *Transactions in GIS*, 23(1):118–136.

Vladimir Karpukhin, Barlas Oguz, Sewon Min, Patrick Lewis, Ledell Wu, Sergey Edunov, Danqi Chen, and Wen-tau Yih. 2020. Dense passage retrieval for open-domain question answering. In *Proceedings of the 2020 Conference on Empirical Methods in Natural Language Processing (EMNLP)*, pages 6769–6781, Online. Association for Computational Linguistics.

Tom Kwiatkowski, Jennimaria Palomaki, Olivia Redfield, Michael Collins, Ankur Parikh, Chris Alberti, Danielle Epstein, Illia Polosukhin, Jacob Devlin, Kenton Lee, Kristina Toutanova, Llion Jones, Matthew Kelcey, Ming-Wei Chang, Andrew M. Dai, Jakob Uszkoreit, Quoc Le, and Slav Petrov. 2019. Natural questions: A benchmark for question answering research. *Transactions of the Association for Computational Linguistics*, 7:452–466.

Kenton Lee, Ming-Wei Chang, and Kristina Toutanova. 2019. Latent retrieval for weakly supervised open domain question answering. In *Proceedings of the 57th Annual Meeting of the Association for Computational Linguistics*, pages 6086–6096, Florence, Italy. Association for Computational Linguistics.

Mike Lewis, Yinhan Liu, Naman Goyal, Marjan Ghazvininejad, Abdelrahman Mohamed, Omer Levy, Veselin Stoyanov, and Luke Zettlemoyer. 2020. BART: Denoising sequence-to-sequence pre-training for natural language generation, translation, and comprehension. In *Proceedings of the 58th Annual Meeting of the Association for Computational Linguistics*, pages 7871–7880, Online. Association for Computational Linguistics.

Haonan Li, Ehsan Hamzei, Ivan Majic, Hua Hua, Jochen Renz, Martin Tomko, Maria Vasardani, Stephan Winter, and Timothy Baldwin. 2021. Neural factoid geospatial question answering. *Journal of Spatial Information Science*, 23:65–90.

Miao Li, Lisi Chen, Gao Cong, Yu Gu, and Ge Yu. 2016. Efficient processing of location-aware group preference queries. In *Proceedings of the 25th ACM International Conference on Information and Knowledge Management*, pages 559–568. ACM.

Yinhan Liu, Myle Ott, Naman Goyal, Jingfei Du, Mandar Joshi, Danqi Chen, Omer Levy, Mike Lewis, Luke Zettlemoyer, and Veselin Stoyanov. 2019. RoBERTa: A robustly optimized BERT pretraining approach. *ArXiv preprint*, abs/1907.11692.

Sylvain Lobry, Diego Marcos, Jesse Murray, and Devis Tuia. 2020. RSVQA: Visual question answering for remote sensing data. *IEEE Transactions on Geoscience and Remote Sensing*, 58(12):8555–8566.

Gengchen Mai, Krzysztof Janowicz, Rui Zhu, Ling Cai, and Ni Lao. 2021. Geographic question answering: Challenges, uniqueness, classification, and future directions. *AGILE: GIScience Series*, 2:1–21.

Stuart E Middleton, Giorgos Kordopatis-Zilos, Symeon Papadopoulos, and Yiannis Kompatsiaris. 2018. Location extraction from social media: Geoparsing, location disambiguation, and geotagging. *ACM Transactions on Information Systems (TOIS)*, 36(4):1–27.

Bhaskar Mitra and Nick Craswell. 2019. An updated duet model for passage re-ranking. *ArXiv preprint*, abs/1903.07666.

Rodrigo Nogueira, Wei Yang, Jimmy Lin, and Kyunghyun Cho. 2019. Document expansion by query prediction. *ArXiv preprint*, abs/1904.08375.

Dharmen Punjani, K Singh, Andreas Both, Manolis Koubarakis, Ioannis Angelidis, Konstantina Bereta, Themis Beris, Dimitris Bilidas, T Ioannidis, Nikolaos Karalis, and C. Lange. 2018. Template-based question answering over linked geospatial data. In *Proceedings of the 12th Workshop on Geographic Information Retrieval*, page 7.

Ross S Purves, Paul Clough, Christopher B Jones, Mark H Hall, and Vanessa Murdock. 2018. Geographic information retrieval: Progress and challenges in spatial search of text. *Foundations and Trends in Information Retrieval*, 12(2-3):164–318.

Pranav Rajpurkar, Jian Zhang, Konstantin Lopyrev, and Percy Liang. 2016. SQuAD: 100,000+ questions for machine comprehension of text. In *Proceedings of the 2016 Conference on Empirical Methods in Natural Language Processing*, pages 2383–2392, Austin, Texas. Association for Computational Linguistics.

Victor Sanh, Lysandre Debut, Julien Chaumond, and Thomas Wolf. 2019. Distilbert, a distilled version of BERT: smaller, faster, cheaper and lighter. *ArXiv preprint*, abs/1910.01108.

Simon Scheider, Enkhbold Nyamsuren, Han Kruiger, and Haiqi Xu. 2020. Geo-analytical question-answering with GIS. *International Journal of Digital Earth*, pages 1–14.

Yves Scherrer and Nikola Ljubešić. 2021. Social media variety geolocation with GeoBERT. In *Proceedings of the Eighth Workshop on NLP for Similar Languages, Varieties and Dialects*. The Association for Computational Linguistics.

Min Joon Seo, Aniruddha Kembhavi, Ali Farhadi, and Hannaneh Hajishirzi. 2017. Bidirectional attention flow for machine comprehension. In *Proceedings of the 5th International Conference on Learning Representations*. OpenReview.net.

Minjoon Seo, Jinhyuk Lee, Tom Kwiatkowski, Ankur Parikh, Ali Farhadi, and Hannaneh Hajishirzi. 2019. Real-time open-domain question answering with dense-sparse phrase index. In *Proceedings of the 57th Annual Meeting of the Association for Computational Linguistics*, pages 4430–4441, Florence, Italy. Association for Computational Linguistics.

Zhiqing Sun, Hongkun Yu, Xiaodan Song, Renjie Liu, Yiming Yang, and Denny Zhou. 2020. MobileBERT: a compact task-agnostic bert for resource-limited devices. *arXiv preprint arXiv:2004.02984*.

Jimin Wang, Yingjie Hu, and Kenneth Joseph. 2020a. NeuroTPR: A neuro-net toponym recognition model for extracting locations from social media messages. *Transactions in GIS*, 24(3):719–735.

Wenhui Wang, Furu Wei, Li Dong, Hangbo Bao, Nan Yang, and Ming Zhou. 2020b. MiniLM: Deep self-attention distillation for task-agnostic compression of pre-trained transformers. *Advances in Neural Information Processing Systems*, 33:5776–5788.

Thomas Wolf, Lysandre Debut, Victor Sanh, Julien Chaumond, Clement Delangue, Anthony Moi, Pierric Cistac, Tim Rault, Remi Louf, Morgan Funtowicz, Joe Davison, Sam Shleifer, Patrick von Platen, Clara Ma, Yacine Jernite, Julien Plu, Canwen Xu, Teven Le Scao, Sylvain Gugger, Mariama Drame, Quentin Lhoest, and Alexander Rush. 2020. Transformers: State-of-the-art natural language processing. In *Proceedings of the 2020 Conference on Empirical Methods in Natural Language Processing: System Demonstrations*, pages 38–45, Online. Association for Computational Linguistics.

Lee Xiong, Chenyan Xiong, Ye Li, Kwok-Fung Tang, Jialin Liu, Paul N. Bennett, Junaid Ahmed, and Arnold Overwijk. 2021a. Approximate nearest neighbor negative contrastive learning for dense text retrieval. In *Proceedings of the 9th International Conference on Learning Representations*. OpenReview.net.

Wenhan Xiong, Hong Wang, and William Yang Wang. 2021b. Progressively pretrained dense corpus index for open-domain question answering. In *Proceedings of the 16th Conference of the European Chapter of the Association for Computational Linguistics: Main Volume*, pages 2803–2815, Online. Association for Computational Linguistics.

H. Xu, E. Hamzei, E. Nyamsuren, H. Kruiger, S. Winter, M. Tomko, and S. Scheider. 2020. Extracting interrogative intents and concepts from geo-analytic questions. *AGILE: GIScience Series*, 1:23.

Zhilin Yang, Zihang Dai, Yiming Yang, Jaime G. Carbonell, Ruslan Salakhutdinov, and Quoc V. Le. 2019. XLNet: Generalized autoregressive pretraining for language understanding. In *Advances in Neural Information Processing Systems 32: Annual Conference on Neural Information Processing Systems 2019*, pages 5754–5764.

Zixuan Yuan, Hao Liu, Junming Liu, Yanchi Liu, Yang Yang, Renjun Hu, and Hui Xiong. 2021. Incremental spatio-temporal graph learning for online query-poi matching. In *Proceedings of the Web Conference 2021*, pages 1586–1597. ACM / IW3C2.

Zhuosheng Zhang, Yuwei Wu, Junru Zhou, Sufeng Duan, Hai Zhao, and Rui Wang. 2020. SG-Net: Syntax-guided machine reading comprehension. In *Proceedings of the Thirty-Fourth AAAI Conference on Artificial Intelligence*, pages 9636–9643. AAAI Press.

Ji Zhao, Dan Peng, Chuhan Wu, Huan Chen, Meiyu Yu, Wanji Zheng, Li Ma, Hua Chai, Jieping Ye, and Xiaohu Qie. 2019a. Incorporating semantic similarity with geographic correlation for query-poi relevance learning. In *Proceedings of the Thirty-Third AAAI Conference on Artificial Intelligence*, pages 1270–1277. AAAI Press.

Pengpeng Zhao, Haifeng Zhu, Yanchi Liu, Jiajie Xu, Zhixu Li, Fuzhen Zhuang, Victor S. Sheng, and Xiaofang Zhou. 2019b. Where to go next: A spatiotemporal gated network for next POI recommendation. In *Proceedings of the Thirty-Third AAAI Conference on Artificial Intelligence*, pages 5877–5884. AAAI Press.

## A POI Example

Table 6 shows a POI example, from which we can see that many reviews have similar semantics, making it important to choose representative reviews. In this work, we cluster sentences from reviews, and choose reviews evenly from each cluster to make up the textual input.

## B Impact of Total Number of Negative Examples

Table 7 presents experimental results with differing numbers of total negative examples. As the training process is based on contrastive learning, increasing the number of negative examples within a batch leads to an improvement in the model's performance.

## C SELSUM Example and Effectiveness

Figure 3 shows an example of SELSUM model output. Table 8 presents the comparison of using clustered reivews, selected reviews (of SELSUM), and summarized reviews.

## D Efficiency and Usability Analysis

The most important component of LAMB is the textual encoder, which can be replaced by any pretrained language model. With the increased development of model distillation and compression methods (Jiao et al., 2019; Wang et al., 2020b; Sun et al., 2020), LAMB can be made more space and time efficient with advanced encoders. Here, we analyse the model's efficiency and usability by considering: (1) adding a new POI into the database; (2) answering a new question; and (3) maintaining the high accuracy of the model.

**New POI**: To add a new POI to the candidate set, the first step is to do inference using SELSUM model. It is then fed into the POI encoder, and stored for inference purposes. The primary costs of GPU training time and GPU memory consumption can be ignored.

**New Question**: Given a new question, we input it into the question encoder without any preprocessing such as geo-parsing or tagging. After encoding, LAMB ranks the candidate POIs according to vector similarity, based on simple vector dot product. In this paper, we didn't use any special techniques to speed this up, but in practical applications, techniques such as FAISS (Johnson et al., 2021) can be used to achieve sub-linear times.[4]

**Training and Update**: The training of LAMB takes no more than 12 hours on a single GPU. Figure 4 shows the top-$k$ retrieval accuracy with respect to the number of training epochs, based on which we can see that the model already achieves good results after 5 epochs. Once this has happened, there is no need to retrain the model from scratch: as more and more new questions and POIs appear, to maintain high performance of the model, it should be enough to fine-tune it on the new questions and POIs for one or two additional epochs.

## E Comparison to Geo-coordinate-based Location/Distance Module

We compare our location module with straightforward geo-coordinate-based location and distance modules. Specifically, during question preprocessing, we detect location mentions and tag them with geo-coordinates using a geo-tagger. Similar to LAMB, the question location module $E_Q^{loc}$ maps the geo-coordinates of the mentioned locations into fixed-length vectors:

$$r_q^{loc} = E_Q^{loc}([l_1, l_2, ..., l_m]) \in \mathbb{R}^{1 \times d_2}$$

where $m$ is a hyper-parameter determined based on the average number of location mentions in questions ($m = 5$ here). Each $l_i$ is a 2-d vector $[lat_i, long_i]$. If a question contains $n > m$ unique locations, we randomly select $m$ locations as the input to $E_Q^{loc}$, otherwise we pad the input to $m$ with $[0, 0]$. Note that the output dimension $d_2$ is fixed and independent of the number of locations $n$. For POI, we simply set $m = 1$.

**Location Module** The location modules for both questions and POIs are implemented with a multilayer perceptron. Since multiple location mentions (geo-coordinates) may exist in a given question while each POI has a unique geolocation, the sizes of the two location modules are slightly different: POIs are represented as $[lat, long]$ (with size = 2), while questions are represented as $[lat_1, long_1, lat_2, long_2, ..., lat_m, long_m]$ (size = $2m$). We use a 3-layer MLP with dropout of 0.2 and ReLU activation function to map locations into a $2m$-d vector (i.e., $d_2 = 2m$).

**Distance Module** Since the location module indiscriminately encodes location mentions from the

[4] FAISS is an efficient open-source library for approximate nearest-neighbor search.

| Key | Value |
|---|---|
| Name | Donnybrook, 35 Clinton St, New York City, NY 10002-2426 |
| Lat Long | [40.7201861, -73.9846227] |
| Reviews | The place was far from packed, but those who were there were very loud.<br>It was the only place that we didnt have on a list of places to go and I have to say it was one of the high lights of the night.<br>We stumbled across this place whilst enjoying the night life around the lower east side late on a Saturday night.<br>I went in for drinks while I waited for a reservation nearby.<br>On the whole , the atmosphere was not one in which I'd like to stay very long.<br>The loud music wasn't the problem.<br>Turns out that the place is very noisy.<br>They were not serving food when we arrived, but the bar tender ordered a pizza for us which we ate at the bar :-)<br>Definitely include it in an East Village pub crawl<br>Nice bar to grab a beer and a warm pretzel.<br>I wanted a nice pub to sit down and have a beer in peace and quiet.<br>You always find a seat in this place .<br>A great prerequisite to the delancey for the final blow out.<br>A disappointment, but it depends what you're after.<br>We were early for our res at Ivan Ramen down the street.<br>Good beer and good service .<br>They have Magners (just what you need on a hot NYC summer day) The pace is easy going, the staff are friendly and the drinks are reasonably priced (similar to Dublin).<br>Staff is kindle and guinness is a real guinness .<br>Good draft selection and very friendly service<br>The bartender was very friendly.<br>I can't speak to the food, but it was exactly what we needed when we needed it.<br>I had read the reviews, and had high expectations.<br>For a very young audience, I guess it might be fun<br>The music was R&B / HIPHOP / Pop and the whole place had a really good vibe.<br>Everyone up dancing, lots of new yorkers.<br>We stumbled across this "Irish" bar while waiting to check into our hotel. |

Table 6: A POI example, where reviews have been segmented into sentences.

| Negatives | | Local | | | | Global | | | |
|---|---|---|---|---|---|---|---|---|---|
| #N | #HN | Acc@3 | Acc@5 | Acc@30 | MRR | Acc@5 | Acc@30 | Acc@100 | MRR |
| 1* | 0 | 14.98 | 20.75 | 48.30 | 0.140 | 3.57 | 10.64 | 21.80 | 0.020 |
| 3* | 2 | 17.22 | 23.92 | 52.95 | 0.164 | 9.71 | 28.22 | 45.03 | 0.067 |
| 7 | 5 | 19.76 | 25.66 | 56.58 | 0.182 | 11.81 | 29.40 | 48.81 | 0.090 |
| 31 | 16 | 24.24 | 31.56 | **61.33** | 0.218 | 14.51 | 34.06 | 50.72 | 0.105 |
| 47 | 24 | **24.57** | **32.05** | 60.75 | **0.221** | **16.16** | **37.76** | **54.78** | **0.117** |

Table 7: Results with differing numbers of total negatives, with around 3/4 hard negatives. Lines with * signify results with early stopping, because using only hard negatives collapsed the model.

| Review Module | Local | | | | Global | | | |
|---|---|---|---|---|---|---|---|---|
| | Acc@3 | Acc@5 | Acc@30 | MRR | Acc@5 | Acc@30 | Acc@100 | MRR |
| Cluster | 23.90 | 31.20 | 60.52 | 0.216 | 13.28 | 32.12 | 48.63 | 0.096 |
| SEL | 24.87 | 32.08 | 61.17 | 0.221 | 13.28 | 32.05 | 47.96 | 0.095 |
| SELSUM | 24.83 | 32.51 | 60.92 | 0.220 | 14.07 | 32.87 | 49.08 | 0.101 |

Table 8: Comparison of using clustered reviews, selected reviews with SELSUM, and summarized reviews with SELSUM.

question into a fixed-length vector, some of which may be irrelevant or even harmful for POI matching, we add a distance module to explicitly compute a distance score from the location mentions in the question to a POI, followed by min-pooling to choose the minimal distance from the question to a given POI. We use the Haversine formula to compute distances.

To use the distance module, we define similarity between a question $q$ and a POI $p$ using the

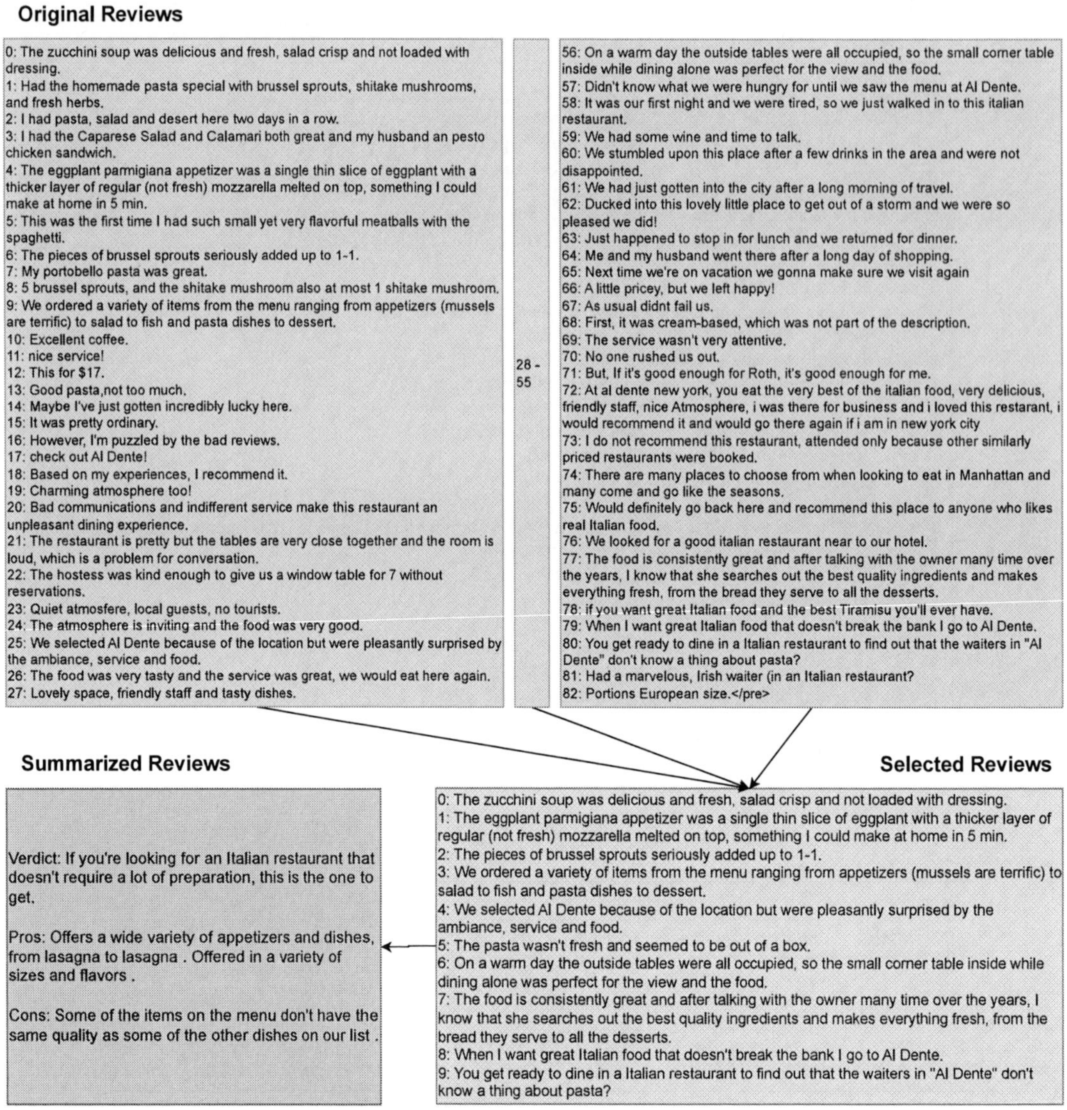


Figure 3: Example of SELSUM output.

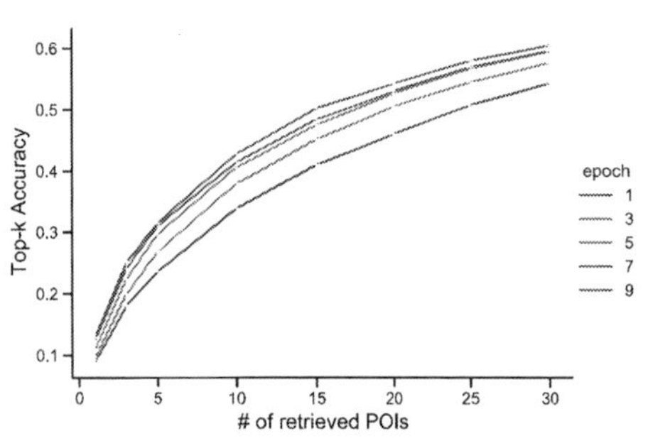


Figure 4: Top-$k$ accuracy with varying numbers of training epochs.

| Module | Acc@3 | Acc@5 | Acc@30 | MRR |
|---|---|---|---|---|
| LAMB Loc | **24.83** | **32.51** | **60.92** | **0.220** |
| Geo-loc | 22.01 | 29.54 | 58.24 | 0.204 |
| Geo-dist | 20.25 | 28.00 | 58.43 | 0.189 |

Table 9: Comparison between LAMB location module and other geo-coordinate-based location/distance modules on local evaluation.

weighted sum of the bi-encoder similarity score and distance score:

$$\text{sim}(p, q) = (1 - \lambda)\text{sim}(r_p, r_q) - \lambda(\text{dist}(p, q))$$

We negate the distance score to ensure the closer

the two locations, the higher the similarity. $\lambda \in [0, 1]$ is a distance score weight, where $\lambda = 0$ means the model does not consider distance at all and $\lambda = 1$ means the model computes scores by distance only.

We compare our location module with these straightforward geo-coordinate-based location/distance modules in Table 9. From the table we can clearly see that our module is much better than the alternatives.

# Joint Representations of Text and Knowledge Graphs for Retrieval and Evaluation

**Teven Le Scao***
Université de Lorraine, Hugging Face
teven.le-scao@loria.fr

**Claire Gardent**
CNRS/LORIA, Université de Lorraine
claire.gardent@loria.fr

## Abstract

A key feature of neural models is that they can produce semantic vector representations of objects (texts, images, speech, etc.) ensuring that similar objects are close to each other in the vector space. While much work has focused on learning representations for other modalities, there are no aligned cross-modal representations for text and knowledge base (KB) elements. One challenge for learning such representations is the lack of parallel data, which we use contrastive training on heuristics-based datasets and data augmentation to overcome, training embedding models on (KB graph, text) pairs. On WEBNLG, a cleaner manually crafted dataset, we show that they learn aligned representations suitable for retrieval. We then fine-tune on annotated data to create EREDAT (Ensembled Representations for Evaluation of DAta-to-Text), a similarity metric between English text and KB graphs. EREDAT outperforms or matches state-of-the-art metrics in terms of correlation with human judgments on WEBNLG even though, unlike them, it does not require a reference text to compare against.

## 1 Introduction

Neural approaches have progressed in capturing semantic relatedness between larger and larger text units, from Word2Vec (Mikolov et al., 2013) to SBERT (Reimers and Gurevych, 2019). Such models have shown to perform well on a wide array of semantic similarity tasks, helped in part by retrieval systems like DPR (Karpukhin et al., 2020a).

Other work has shown that deep representations of knowledge bases (KBs) help improve such tasks as few shot link prediction, analogical reasoning (Pezeshkpour et al., 2018; Pahuja et al., 2021), entity linking (Yu et al., 2020) or cross-lingual entity alignment (Chen et al., 2018; Xu et al., 2019).

In this work, we focus on learning cross-modal representations for English text and KB graphs. Our input graphs are in RDF (Resource Description Framework, (Miller, 1998)) format, a standard where graphs are sets of *(subject, predicate, object)* triples. We linearize those graphs and consider them as text data so that the same model can take text and graphs as input. Given some aligned RDF-text data, our model learns fixed-length latent representations for texts and RDF graphs such that texts and RDF graphs that are semantically similar are close in vector space. This enables retrieval across modalities and allows us to create a cross-modality similarity score which can be used to evaluate the output of RDF-to-text generation models.

One challenge for learning cross-modal RDF-text representations is the lack of parallel data. We train on various RDF-text datasets created using distant supervision techniques, either combining these datasets or using them in isolation. We then compare the performance of the resulting retrieval models (i) on the WEBNLG dataset, a parallel RDF-text dataset where texts are crowdsourced to match the graph (texts and graphs are semantically equivalent), and (ii) on WIKICHUNKS, a more challenging, less well aligned dataset which imitates the conditions in which retrieval on Wikipedia is usually executed. We use the difference in performance between models to analyze the alignment quality of training datasets.

Distance within embedding space can be used to evaluate the output of RDF-to-text generation models (Is the generated text similar to the input graph?). In order to evaluate this metric, we compute correlations between our model's similarity score for graph-text pairs and human judgments of semantic adequacy (input/output semantic similarity) using ratings from the 2020 WEBNLG Challenge. After fine-tuning on data from the 2017 WEBNLG challenge, as well as introducing new classes of data augmentation at pre-training time,

*Corresponding author. teven.lescao@gmail.com



*Findings of the Association for Computational Linguistics: IJCNLP-AACL 2023*, pages 110–122
November 1–4, 2023. 

our best system, EREDAT, is better or on par than existing metrics at correlating with human evaluation, even though it does not require a reference for comparison as do most NLG evaluation metrics such as BLEU (Papineni et al., 2002), TER (Snover et al., 2006), BLEURT (Sellam et al., 2020b), METEOR (Banerjee and Lavie, 2005) or BERT-Score (Zhang* et al., 2020).

Our contributions can be summarised as follows.

- We train a cross-modal RDF-text model to learn aligned (RDF graph, text) representations, making it suitable for cross-modal retrieval. We show that this retrieval model outperforms a state-of-the-art text-only retrieval model by a large margin, demonstrating the effectiveness of our adaptation procedure. We train on several datasets of RDF-text pairs, using the quality of the ensuing retrieval models to analyze the quality of training datasets.

- We provide a novel evaluation metric for RDF-to-text generation models by combining bi- and cross-encoder training procedures and adding adversarial data to address the models' weaknesses. We show that this new metric outperforms other existing RDF-to-text evaluation metrics in terms of correlation with human judgments of semantic adequacy, even though it does not require a costly human reference to compare against. We release our models on `huggingface.co` under the Apache 2.0 license.

## 2 Related Work

We briefly review recent approaches to uni- and cross-modal retrieval, representation learning models, and evaluation metrics for Natural Language Generation (NLG) models.

**Natural Language Retrieval Models.** For natural language, a first class of retrieval models focuses on retrieving sentences that are similar to some input sentence. BERT (Devlin et al., 2019) has been used as a cross-encoder. Two sentences are given with a separator token, cross-attention applies to all input tokens and the resulting representation is fed into a linear layer to score the match. However, this is computationally inefficient as it is not possible to pre-compute and index such representations. A pre-computable model was proposed by (Reimers and Gurevych, 2019) who used twin encoders pre-trained on Natural Language Inference data (Bowman et al., 2015) to set new state-of-the-art performance on a large set of sentence scoring tasks. Further work (Chen et al., 2020; Humeau et al., 2019) combined cross- and bi-encoders to reach a tradeoff between accuracy and efficiency. We differ from those works in that we focus on cross-modal representation learning.

**Representation Learning for Knowledge-Bases.** Various KB embedding models have been proposed to support downstream applications such as KB completion or alignment of different bases. Compositional approaches (Nickel et al., 2011, 2016) use tensor products to model relations as functions of their argument entities. Translational approaches model relations as translation operations from the subject (head) to object (tail) entity (Bordes et al., 2013; Yang et al., 2014; Trouillon et al., 2016). Neural models have also leveraged 2-D convolutions over entity embeddings to predict relations (Dettmers et al., 2018) as well as graph convolutional networks (Schlichtkrull et al., 2018). All these approaches focus on representation learning for Knowledge-Bases entities and relations. In contrast, we focus on cross-modal similarity between a text and a KB graph.

**Cross-Modal Representation Learning and Retrieval.** Some work has focused on incorporating natural language information to improve KB representations. (Han et al., 2016; Toutanova et al., 2015; Wu et al., 2016) encode words and KB entities into a single vector space, and (Wang and Li, 2016; Yamada et al., 2016) learn word and entity embeddings separately then map them into a shared space. Both approaches use text as additional training signal to improve KB representations, and limit themselves to word-level information. Instead, we focus on scoring the similarity between arbitrary-length natural language text and a KB graph. We are not aware of any extant such text-KB models. The best-known cross-modal contrastive model is Radford et al. (2021), which pre-trained an image-text match scoring model.

**Evaluation metrics for Natural Language Generation Models.** Surface-based metrics such as BLEU (Papineni et al., 2002), which measure token overlap between generated and reference text, are commonly used. Methods such as BERT-Score (Zhang* et al., 2020) or BLEURT (Sellam et al., 2020a) which leverage neural representations are currently state-of-the-art. All these methods compute a score by comparing the generated text with human-produced references, rarely available and costly to produce. Some metrics evaluate the generated output with respect to the input rather than to a reference. Wiseman et al. (2017) use the precision of input relations found in the output texts. (Dušek and Kasner, 2020) use a natural language inference pre-trained model to score input-output two-way entailment. For data-to-text generation specifically, (Rebuffel et al., 2021) introduce Data-QuestEval, which uses question answering to compare input graph and output text.

## 3 Learning Cross-Modal RDF-text Representations

### 3.1 Model

Similar to (Schroff et al., 2015; Reimers and Gurevych, 2019), we use twin Transformer encoders to create RDF and text representations such that the embeddings of an RDF graph and of a piece of text with similar content are close in the vector space. A mean-pooling operation creates fixed-sized embeddings $embed(x)$ for $x$ either an RDF graph or a text. RDF graphs are linearized as:

[S] <subject$_1$> [P] <property$_1$> [O] <object$_1$> ... [S] <subject$_n$> [P] <property$_n$> [O] <object$_n$>

where "[S]", "[P]", "[O]" serve as special tokens and are added to the tokenizer vocabulary. This allows us to treat any knowledge base format.

We train this system using a contrastive loss with *in-batch negatives* (Henderson et al., 2017). This variant of contrastive loss computes the pairwise similarities between every text and every RDF in the batch. A softmax is then applied on the RDF axis, which creates a multi-class classification problem: every text data point must be matched to the parallel RDF. The loss can be written as :

$$l = -\sum_{i \in I} \log \left( \frac{\exp(sim(text_i, rdf_i))}{\sum_{j \in J} \exp(sim(text_i, rdf_j))} \right)$$

$$sim(text_i, rdf_j) = \cos(embed(text_i), embed(rdf_j))$$

with $I$ the set of training instances in the batch. Intuitively, this trains the encoder to learn representations that map text items closer to their RDF anchor than to other RDF graphs in the dataset.

In all our experiments, we start from `all-mpnet-base-v2`, a pre-trained sentence-MPNet (Song et al., 2020) model, in order to leverage its strong pre-trained text representations.

### 3.2 Training Datasets

For training, we need $(g, t)$ pairs where $g$ is a Wikidata RDF graph and $t$ is a text in English whose content is similar to $g$. We compare three datasets, all created using distant supervision.

**TeKGen.** (Agarwal et al., 2021) use heuristics to align triples from Wikidata to Wikipedia sentences. The TEKGEN dataset covers 1,041 Wikidata properties and consists of about 6M (graph, text) pairs where each text is a sentence.

**KELM.** The KELM corpus has 15M (graph, text) pairs where graphs are created based on relation co-occurrence counts i.e. frequency of alignment of two properties to the same sentence in the training data (Agarwal et al., 2021). Texts are then generated from these graphs using a T5 model fine-tuned on TEKGEN.

**TREx.** (Elsahar et al., 2018) use word- and sentence-tokenization, coreference resolution, a date-time and a predicate linker, plus various RDF-text alignment methods to create TREX, a dataset aligning 11 million Wikidata triples with 6 million Wikipedia sentences.

### 3.3 Test Datasets

We use two datasets for evaluation: WEBNLG (Gardent et al., 2017) and WIKICHUNKS, which we create in this work. Appendix A shows some statistics for all datasets.

**WebNLG** is a dataset of pairs where the texts were crowdsourced to match the input graph. In WEBNLG the RDF graph is from the DBpedia KB, whereas our models were trained on the Wikidata KB format. To assess the ability of our retrieval model to generalize to different KBs, we evaluate our model both on WEBNLG-DB, the original DBpedia-based dataset, and WEBNLG-WD where the DBpedia graphs have been mapped to Wikidata (Han et al., 2022).

**WikiChunks** consists of 7.3M graph-text pairs where the text is a 100-word *passage* from a Wikipedia dump and the graphs are matching Wikidata graphs. We create matching graphs by aligning all Wikidata *(s, p, o)* triples with a Wikipedia passage such that the subject $s$ of that triple matches

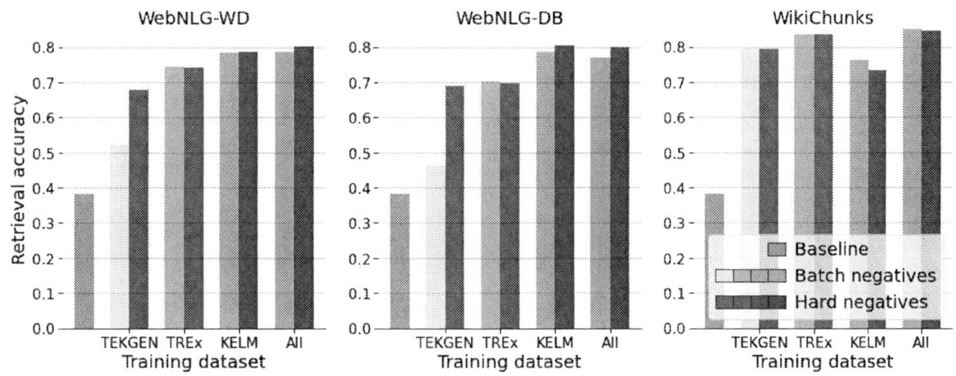


Figure 1: **Retrieval Accuracy** for a variety of training datasets and objectives. Our models outperform the base model (leftmost grey bar) by a large margin. Hard negatives help across the board. Training on an equal mix of datasets yields consistently high performance on aligned (WEBNLG) and noisy (WIKICHUNKS) data.

the entity described by the Wikipedia page from which the passage was extracted and the object $o$, or one of its aliases, is mentioned in that passage. Retrieving on this dataset imitates the conditions in which retrieval on Wikipedia is usually executed (Karpukhin et al., 2020b; Lewis et al., 2020). This is a challenging task as, contrary to WEBNLG, WIKICHUNKS matches are not aligned: the Wikidata graph information is strictly included in the passage, which may contain much more. Several passages may also contain very similar information. We use a subset of 30000 pairs, the same size as WEBNLG, to make results comparable.

We evaluate our representations using a retrieval reformulation of the data-to-text NLG task: Given the embedding of a graph, how well can we identify the most similar text in the corpus? As our evaluation sets have 1-to-1 mappings between sources (the graphs) and targets (the texts), the retrieval performance in the opposite direction does not vary by more than 2%. We consider top-result accuracy.

## 4 Results

### 4.1 General Results

We use `all-mpnet-base-v2`, the state-of-the-art dense sentence embedding model that our models are training from, as a baseline. `all-mpnet-base-v2` can estimate semantic similarity, as our models do, but was only trained on text. It can still process the linearized RDF data, however, as it is in the form of natural text. **The baseline is reasonable, but training yields strong improvements** with a top accuracy of 80% for all settings against 38% for the base model (Figure 1) and 0.003% for random-chance performance.

### 4.2 Generalization to other KB formats

Encoding the RDF data as natural language allows for flexibility in the RDF format, as opposed to earlier graph approaches that encode relations and entities as integers. After fine-tuning on Wikidata graphs, which include relations like `place served by transport hub`, we might be able to generalize to DBPedia, which would use `cityServed` instead, as the base pre-trained model knows all these words. Indeed, we find that **retrieval performance is similar on** WEBNLG-WD **and** WEBNLG-DB.

### 4.3 Batch Size and Negatives

We experiment with adding artificial hard negatives to the batch, and with different batch sizes. Confounders are constructed from the correct graph by corrupting a triple inside that graph, replacing a subject, object or predicate at random with another subject, object or predicate in the dataset. This form of data augmentation is made possible by the formalized nature of RDF graphs: it would be much harder to create confounders on the text side.

**Hard vs. In-batch negatives** Figure 1 shows retrieval accuracy when using only in-batch vs. using in-batch and hard negatives. We see that hard negatives mostly help when retrieving parallel data (WEBNLG) i.e. when small graph-text mismatches strongly impact accuracy. We also see that hard negatives have the strongest impact on the model trained on TEKGEN, which is also the one with the lowest retrieval accuracy. This suggests that hard negatives are most helpful when the training data is noisier than the evaluation data.

**Batch size.** As previous work has found that larger batch sizes improve contrastive training (Qu et al., 2021), we experiment with two batch size set-ups: 192[1] and 2560[2]. We do not find that larger batch sizes consistently improve retrieval accuracy, and keep the smaller ones for practical reasons. Figure 8 in appendix B shows detailed results.

### 4.4 Training Data Quality

The quality of training data has a strong impact on retrieval accuracy. We see that performance varies with the training data used: on WEBNLG retrieval, KELM yields by far the best results followed successively by TREX and TEKGEN. On WIKICHUNKS, which is more loosely aligned, TREX is the best dataset and KELM is slightly behind. We create an equal-mixture dataset by concatenating subsets of equal sizes of each dataset[3]. As the rightmost column in Figure 1 shows, this allows us to capture the best of both worlds. We dub the model trained on this data with hard negatives `all_datasets_hard_negatives`.

The similarity distributions according to `all_datasets_hard_negatives` is shown in Figure 2, which matches those results: KELM is much better aligned. This is in line with intuition as KELM text is generated from the input graphs while TREX and TEKGEN are created using distant supervision. We attempted to bootstrap dataset quality by re-training models on the 50% of the data identified as highest-similarity. We find that this does not increase performance and can even decrease it, probably due to loss of diversity.

### 4.5 Training Data Quantity

As shown in Figure 3, performance plateaus early in training. The advantage of KELM or the concatenated dataset is not due to their larger size.

## 5 Building a Referenceless Metric for Data-to-text Generation

Commonly-used metrics for Natural Language Generation require references to compare the output against, which must be produced by human annotators. Can we leverage our joint embeddings to compare the output text to the input RDF directly, reducing the necessary resources?

[1]The maximum we could fit on an 8-A100 cloud instance.

[2]The maximum we could fit on a larger cluster.

[3]In total, thrice the size of the smallest dataset, TREX.

### 5.1 Fine-tuning on Human Judgments of Semantic Adequacy

Our retrieval models can be used to provide a similarity metric between text and formal data in the form of the scalar product or cosine distance in embedding space. We can further improve this metric by fine-tuning on human judgments of RDF-text adequacy. In order to show the generalization strength of this approach, we fine-tune our `all_datasets_hard_negatives` model on human-rated WEBNLG-2017 items, and evaluate on human-rated WEBNLG-2020 items, which uses different test data and different criteria for the assessment of semantic adequacy by human judges.

(Shimorina et al., 2018) provides human judgments for the output of 10 NLG systems from WEBNLG challenge 2017. Each model was evaluated on a sample of 223 texts yielding a total of 2230 generated texts annotated with human judgments for the following three criteria.

- **Semantic adequacy**: Does the text correctly represent the meaning in the data?
- **Grammaticality**: Is the text grammatical (no spelling or grammatical errors)?
- **Fluency**: Does the text sound natural?

(Castro Ferreira et al., 2020) provides human judgments for the output of 16 NLG systems from WEBNLG Challenge 2020. Each model was evaluated on a sample of 178 texts yielding a total of 2,848 generated texts annotated with human judgments for the following five criteria.

- **Data Coverage**: Does the text include descriptions of *all* predicates in the input?
- **Relevance**: Does the text describe *only* triples present in the graph?
- **Correctness**: For graph predicates, does the text correctly describe their arguments?
- **Text Structure**: Is the text grammatical, well-structured, written in acceptable English?
- **Fluency**: Does the text progress naturally and form a coherent, easy-to-understand whole?

We train on the 2017 *semantic adequacy* metric. To assess how well our similarity metric reflects human judgments of similarity between an RDF graph

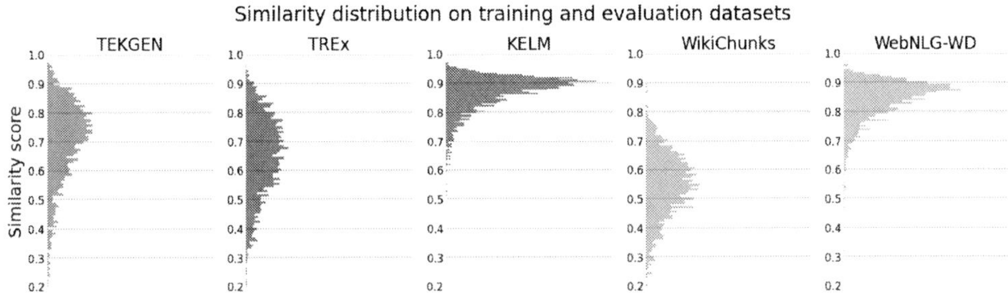


Figure 2: **Pair similarity distributions** according to `all_datasets_hard_negatives` for all datasets.

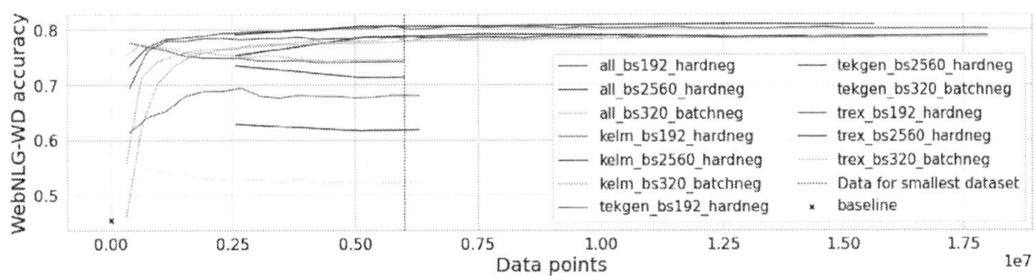


Figure 3: **Performance throughout training** evaluated by WEBNLG-WD accuracy. Training for longer than the size of the smallest datasets does not change performance meaningfully.

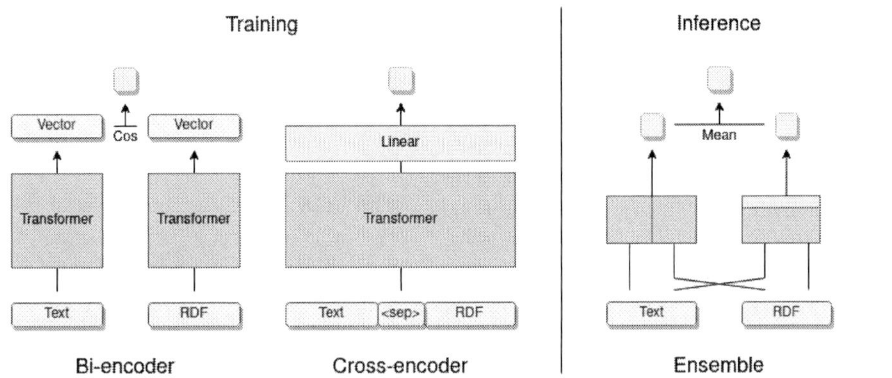


Figure 4: **Fine-tuning setup.** We fine-tune both bi-encoders and cross-encoders on human-rated data. At inference time, we use the mean of a bi-encoder and a cross-encoder as the final metric.

and a Natural Language Text, we compute correlations between our system's scores and the 2020 human judgments of semantic adequacy, namely *data coverage*, *relevance*, and *correctness*[4].

## 5.2 Fine-tuning Procedure

**Bi- and Cross-encoder ensembling** We can fine-tune our pre-trained model as a *cross-encoder*, where there is only one instance of the model, which can attend to both items simultaneously and feed into a linear layer, rather than a *bi-encoder* as previously, where two instances of the model embed the two items separately and the dot product or cosine distance serves as the output. The cross-attention feature allows for higher performance at the cost of making retrieval expensive as all $n^2$ distances must be computed separately (Humeau et al., 2019). However, bi- and cross-encoders perform well on different data points. The scores they give WEBNLG-2020 candidates have surprisingly low Pearson correlation, 0.66. This makes them good candidates for ensembling, and indeed, taking the mean of the bi- and cross-encoder scores yields

[4]We train on WEBNLG-2017 and evaluate on WEBNLG-2020 as semantic adequacy is a more global criterion encompassing coverage, relevance and correctness while the reverse is not true.

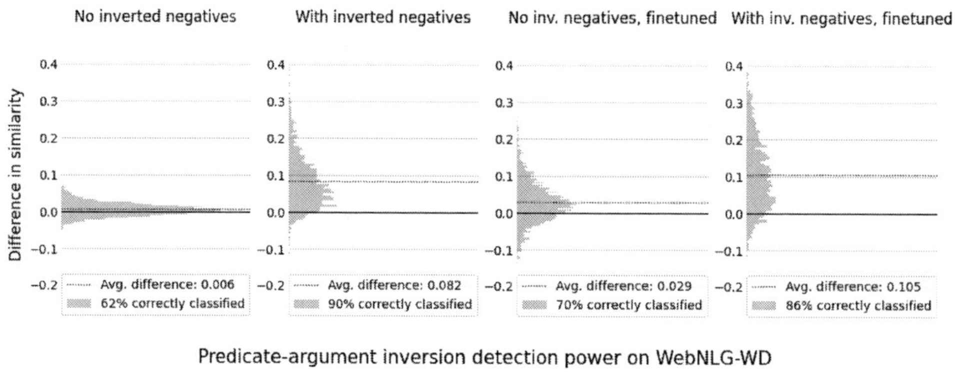


Figure 5: **Difference in similarity between correct and corrupted graph-text pairs.** On the left, `all_datasets_hard_negatives` and `all_datasets_hardinv_negatives` just after pre-training, and on the right, both models after fine-tuning and ensembling on WEBNLG-2017. The system we used as a final metric is the last plot on the right. Models that have seen inverted negatives at pre-training identify correct and corrupted pairs better.

higher correlations with all human judgments. Both architectures and the ensembling method are represented in diagram 4.

**Robustness to inversion** Transformer-based models can sometimes behave as advanced bag-of-word models (Sinha et al., 2021), which would not see a difference if the subject and object are reversed in a triple. In order to examine the robustness, we create an adversarial dataset from all the 1-triple graphs in WEBNLG 2020 with non-symmetrical[5] relationships. In this dataset, for each text, there is a pair with the correct triple and a pair in which the triple's predicate arguments (subject and object) have been inverted e.g., *(André the Giant, larger than, Samuel Beckett)* vs. *(Samuel Beckett, larger than, André the Giant)*. This dataset (WEBNLG-INV) consists of 2793 $(g, t)$, and $(g\_inv, t)$ pairs where $(g, t)$ is a graph of size one with a non-symmetrical relationship in WEBNLG-WD, $t$ is the corresponding text and $g\_inv$ is the corrupted triple.

We report the difference $sim(g, t) - sim(g_{inv}, t)$ in the similarity between text and correct graph on the one hand and text and corrupted graph on the other in Figure 5. The higher, the better the model is at recognizing predicate inversion. `all_datasets_hard_negatives`, the retrieval model presented in Section 3.1, does not do well at this task, with 38% of the inverted triplets estimated more similar to the text than the original ones. (After fine-tuning on WEBNLG-2017 judgments, 30%)

[5]Manually defined. The list is in appendix D.

In order to make our models robust to inversion, at pre-training time, we add inverted negatives to the mix of artificial negatives in the batches: confounding graphs where a random triplet has been inverted. The resulting model, `all_datasets_hardinv_negatives` has the same retrieval accuracy but gains inversion detection abilities. This ability is conserved through fine-tuning, as Figure 5 shows: only 14% of triplets are misclassified.

**The final system we choose as a metric** is the ensemble of a bi- and cross-encoder pre-trained on the concatenation of KELM, TEKGEN and TREX with our two types of data augmentation, then fine-tuned on WEBNLG-2017 human judgments. We call it EREDAT, for Ensembled Representations for Evaluation of DAta-to-Text.

### 5.3 Comparison with other Evaluation Metrics

Correlations with human judgments are shown in Figure 6 for a variety of automated evaluation metrics: three metrics that require a reference (BLEU, BERTscore-F1, and BLEURT, the previous state of the art) and two referenceless metrics (Data-QuestEval and EREDAT). Our metric is the best correlated with all human judgment categories, even including metrics with references. As shown in 7, this advantage is mostly explainable by EREDAT's improved robustness to longer, more complex graphs, which tend to degrade correlation with human judgment. Scatter plots of the underlying distributions are given in appendix C.

As human references are rarely available and

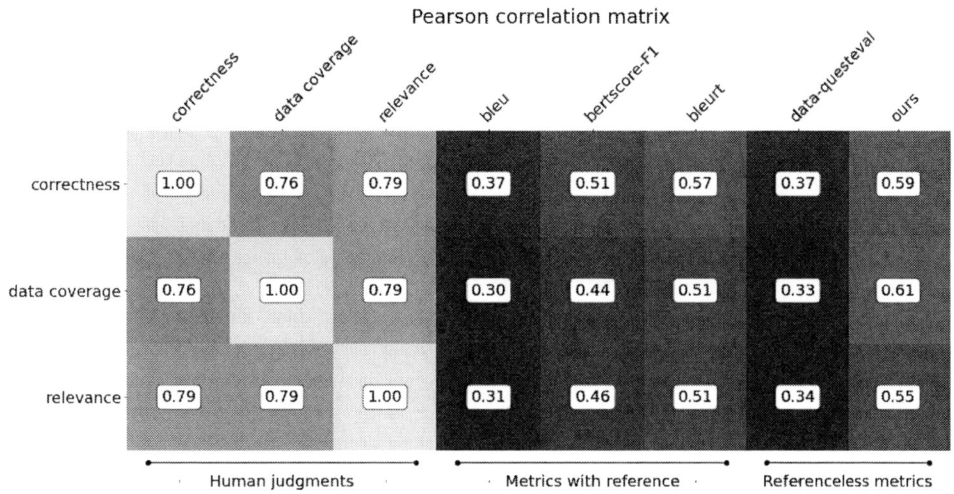


Figure 6: **Pearson correlation between automatic metrics and human judgments.** Lighter and higher is better. EREDAT outperforms the other referenceless metric and matches BLEURT, which requires a reference.

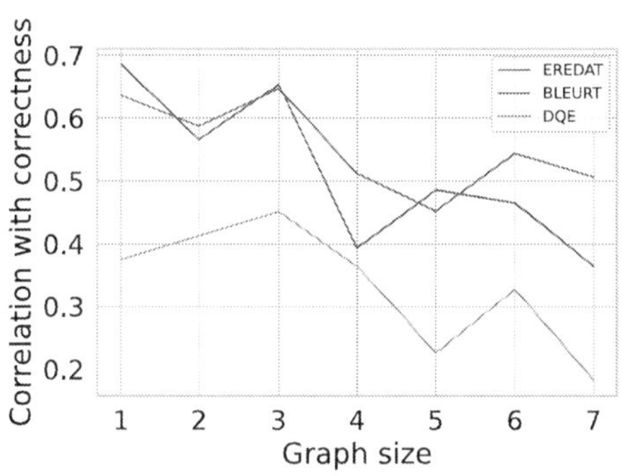


Figure 7: **Correlation with human judgment by graph size** for EREDAT, DQE and BLEURT. Our metric is more robust than BLEURT to longer graphs, and generally much more correlated than DQE, the existing referenceless metric.

costly to produce, and EREDAT attains higher correlation with human judgments without relying on them, it is the most practical choice to evaluate data-to-text generation. In this case, it was not fine-tuned to the same kind of data it was applied to, showing it generalizes to new datasets. If one has a specific dataset or task in mind, even better performance could be attained by training on a set of problem-specific human judgments.

## 6 Conclusion

We presented an architecture and pre-training strategy to measure the similarity between RDF graphs and English texts, introducing novel data augmentation strategies made possible by the RDF structure. Specifically, we introduced a bi-encoder retrieval model trained on unlabeled RDF-text data which achieves high retrieval accuracy on both parallel and real-life, less well aligned datasets. Building from this pre-trained model, we further provided a novel evaluation metric for RDF-to-text generation models which matches state-of-the art metrics in terms of correlation with human judgments of semantic adequacy without needing costly human-written references. This metric can also be used to filter existing text/RDF datasets.

## 7 Limitations and compute statement

This study focuses on English text. Reproducing the proposed approach for use on other languages would require dedicated datasets of similar scale, along with graph/text alignments. Further, the other languages differ quite a lot from English-centric RDF graphs, potentially reducing the suitability of the proposed framework and requiring more advanced multilingual methods. We release our models with the intended use of representation learning and automated RDF-to-text evaluation. Other uses may not be appropriate.

We trained over 2000 models for a total of approximately 2400 GPU-hours (NVIDIA V100s and A100s) of compute on public infrastructure and Google Compute Engine. Most of them were based on `all-mpnet-base-v2`, with 109M parameters.

## 8 Acknowledgments

We thank the anonymous reviewers for their feedback. We gratefully acknowledge the support of the French National Research Agency (Gardent; award ANR-20-CHIA-0003, XNLG "Multilingual, Multi-Source Text Generation").

## References

Oshin Agarwal, Heming Ge, Siamak Shakeri, and Rami Al-Rfou. 2021. Knowledge graph based synthetic corpus generation for knowledge-enhanced language model pre-training. In *Proceedings of the 2021 Conference of the North American Chapter of the Association for Computational Linguistics: Human Language Technologies*, pages 3554–3565, Online. Association for Computational Linguistics.

Satanjeev Banerjee and Alon Lavie. 2005. METEOR: An automatic metric for MT evaluation with improved correlation with human judgments. In *Proceedings of the ACL Workshop on Intrinsic and Extrinsic Evaluation Measures for Machine Translation and/or Summarization*, pages 65–72, Ann Arbor, Michigan. Association for Computational Linguistics.

Antoine Bordes, Nicolas Usunier, Alberto Garcia-Durán, Jason Weston, and Oksana Yakhnenko. 2013. Translating embeddings for modeling multi-relational data. In *Proceedings of the 26th International Conference on Neural Information Processing Systems - Volume 2*, NIPS'13, page 2787–2795, Red Hook, NY, USA. Curran Associates Inc.

Samuel R. Bowman, Gabor Angeli, Christopher Potts, and Christopher D. Manning. 2015. A large annotated corpus for learning natural language inference. In *Proceedings of the 2015 Conference on Empirical Methods in Natural Language Processing*, pages 632–642, Lisbon, Portugal. Association for Computational Linguistics.

Thiago Castro Ferreira, Claire Gardent, Nikolai Ilinykh, Chris van der Lee, Simon Mille, Diego Moussallem, and Anastasia Shimorina. 2020. The 2020 bilingual, bi-directional WebNLG+ shared task: Overview and evaluation results (WebNLG+ 2020). In *Proceedings of the 3rd International Workshop on Natural Language Generation from the Semantic Web (WebNLG+)*, pages 55–76, Dublin, Ireland (Virtual). Association for Computational Linguistics.

Jiecao Chen, Liu Yang, Karthik Raman, Michael Bendersky, Jung-Jung Yeh, Yun Zhou, Marc Najork, Danyang Cai, and Ehsan Emadzadeh. 2020. DiPair: Fast and accurate distillation for trillion-scale text matching and pair modeling. In *Findings of the Association for Computational Linguistics: EMNLP 2020*, pages 2925–2937, Online. Association for Computational Linguistics.

Muhao Chen, Yingtao Tian, Kai-Wei Chang, Steven Skiena, and Carlo Zaniolo. 2018. Co-training embeddings of knowledge graphs and entity descriptions for cross-lingual entity alignment. In *Proceedings of the Twenty-Seventh International Joint Conference on Artificial Intelligence, IJCAI-18*, pages 3998–4004. International Joint Conferences on Artificial Intelligence Organization.

Tim Dettmers, Pasquale Minervini, Pontus Stenetorp, and Sebastian Riedel. 2018. Convolutional 2d knowledge graph embeddings. In *Thirty-second AAAI conference on artificial intelligence*.

Jacob Devlin, Ming-Wei Chang, Kenton Lee, and Kristina Toutanova. 2019. BERT: Pre-training of deep bidirectional transformers for language understanding. In *Proceedings of the 2019 Conference of the North American Chapter of the Association for Computational Linguistics: Human Language Technologies, Volume 1 (Long and Short Papers)*, pages 4171–4186, Minneapolis, Minnesota. Association for Computational Linguistics.

Ondřej Dušek and Zdeněk Kasner. 2020. Evaluating semantic accuracy of data-to-text generation with natural language inference. In *Proceedings of the 13th International Conference on Natural Language Generation*, pages 131–137, Dublin, Ireland. Association for Computational Linguistics.

Hady Elsahar, Pavlos Vougiouklis, Arslen Remaci, Christophe Gravier, Jonathon Hare, Frederique Laforest, and Elena Simperl. 2018. T-REx: A large scale alignment of natural language with knowledge base triples. In *Proceedings of the Eleventh International Conference on Language Resources and Evaluation (LREC 2018)*, Miyazaki, Japan. European Language Resources Association (ELRA).

Claire Gardent, Anastasia Shimorina, Shashi Narayan, and Laura Perez-Beltrachini. 2017. Creating training corpora for NLG micro-planners. In *Proceedings of the 55th Annual Meeting of the Association for Computational Linguistics (Volume 1: Long Papers)*, pages 179–188, Vancouver, Canada. Association for Computational Linguistics.

Kelvin Han, Thiago Castro Ferreira, and Claire Gardent. 2022. Generating questions from Wikidata triples. In *Proceedings of the Thirteenth Language Resources and Evaluation Conference*, pages 277–290, Marseille, France. European Language Resources Association.

Xu Han, Zhiyuan Liu, and Maosong Sun. 2016. Joint representation learning of text and knowledge for knowledge graph completion. *ArXiv*, abs/1611.04125.

Matthew L. Henderson, Rami Al-Rfou, Brian Strope, Yun-Hsuan Sung, László Lukács, Ruiqi Guo, Sanjiv Kumar, Balint Miklos, and Ray Kurzweil. 2017. Efficient natural language response suggestion for smart reply. *CoRR*, abs/1705.00652.

Samuel Humeau, Kurt Shuster, Marie-Anne Lachaux, and Jason Weston. 2019. Real-time inference in multi-sentence tasks with deep pretrained transformers. *CoRR*, abs/1905.01969.

Vladimir Karpukhin, Barlas Oguz, Sewon Min, Patrick Lewis, Ledell Wu, Sergey Edunov, Danqi Chen, and Wen-tau Yih. 2020a. Dense passage retrieval for open-domain question answering. In *Proceedings of the 2020 Conference on Empirical Methods in Natural Language Processing (EMNLP)*, pages 6769–6781, Online. Association for Computational Linguistics.

Vladimir Karpukhin, Barlas Oguz, Sewon Min, Ledell Wu, Sergey Edunov, Danqi Chen, and Wen-tau Yih. 2020b. Dense passage retrieval for open-domain question answering. *CoRR*, abs/2004.04906.

Patrick S. H. Lewis, Ethan Perez, Aleksandra Piktus, Fabio Petroni, Vladimir Karpukhin, Naman Goyal, Heinrich Küttler, Mike Lewis, Wen-tau Yih, Tim Rocktäschel, Sebastian Riedel, and Douwe Kiela. 2020. Retrieval-augmented generation for knowledge-intensive NLP tasks. *CoRR*, abs/2005.11401.

Tomaš Mikolov, Kai Chen, Greg Corrado, and Jeffrey Dean. 2013. Efficient estimation of word representations in vector space.

Eric Miller. 1998. An introduction to the resource description framework. *D-lib Magazine*.

Maximilian Nickel, Lorenzo Rosasco, and Tomaso Poggio. 2016. Holographic embeddings of knowledge graphs. In *Proceedings of the Thirtieth AAAI Conference on Artificial Intelligence*, AAAI'16, page 1955–1961. AAAI Press.

Maximilian Nickel, Volker Tresp, and Hans-Peter Kriegel. 2011. A three-way model for collective learning on multi-relational data. In *Proceedings of the 28th International Conference on International Conference on Machine Learning*, ICML'11, page 809–816, Madison, WI, USA. Omnipress.

Vardaan Pahuja, Yu Gu, Wenhu Chen, Mehdi Bahrami, Lei Liu, Wei-Peng Chen, and Yu Su. 2021. A systematic investigation of KB-text embedding alignment at scale. In *Proceedings of the 59th Annual Meeting of the Association for Computational Linguistics and the 11th International Joint Conference on Natural Language Processing (Volume 1: Long Papers)*, pages 1764–1774, Online. Association for Computational Linguistics.

Kishore Papineni, Salim Roukos, Todd Ward, and Wei-Jing Zhu. 2002. Bleu: a method for automatic evaluation of machine translation. In *Proceedings of the 40th Annual Meeting of the Association for Computational Linguistics*, pages 311–318, Philadelphia, Pennsylvania, USA. Association for Computational Linguistics.

Pouya Pezeshkpour, Liyan Chen, and Sameer Singh. 2018. Embedding multimodal relational data for knowledge base completion. In *Proceedings of the 2018 Conference on Empirical Methods in Natural Language Processing*, pages 3208–3218, Brussels, Belgium. Association for Computational Linguistics.

Yingqi Qu, Yuchen Ding, Jing Liu, Kai Liu, Ruiyang Ren, Wayne Xin Zhao, Daxiang Dong, Hua Wu, and Haifeng Wang. 2021. RocketQA: An optimized training approach to dense passage retrieval for open-domain question answering. In *Proceedings of the 2021 Conference of the North American Chapter of the Association for Computational Linguistics: Human Language Technologies*, pages 5835–5847, Online. Association for Computational Linguistics.

Alec Radford, Jong Wook Kim, Chris Hallacy, Aditya Ramesh, Gabriel Goh, Sandhini Agarwal, Girish Sastry, Amanda Askell, Pamela Mishkin, Jack Clark, Gretchen Krueger, and Ilya Sutskever. 2021. Learning transferable visual models from natural language supervision. In *ICML*.

Clement Rebuffel, Thomas Scialom, Laure Soulier, Benjamin Piwowarski, Sylvain Lamprier, Jacopo Staiano, Geoffrey Scoutheeten, and Patrick Gallinari. 2021. Data-QuestEval: A referenceless metric for data-to-text semantic evaluation. In *Proceedings of the 2021 Conference on Empirical Methods in Natural Language Processing*, pages 8029–8036, Online and Punta Cana, Dominican Republic. Association for Computational Linguistics.

Nils Reimers and Iryna Gurevych. 2019. Sentence-BERT: Sentence embeddings using Siamese BERT-networks. In *Proceedings of the 2019 Conference on Empirical Methods in Natural Language Processing and the 9th International Joint Conference on Natural Language Processing (EMNLP-IJCNLP)*, pages 3982–3992, Hong Kong, China. Association for Computational Linguistics.

Michael Schlichtkrull, Thomas Kipf, Peter Bloem, Rianne Berg, Ivan Titov, and Max Welling. 2018. *Modeling Relational Data with Graph Convolutional Networks*, pages 593–607.

Florian Schroff, Dmitry Kalenichenko, and James Philbin. 2015. Facenet: A unified embedding for face recognition and clustering. *2015 IEEE Conference on Computer Vision and Pattern Recognition (CVPR)*.

Thibault Sellam, Dipanjan Das, and Ankur Parikh. 2020a. BLEURT: Learning robust metrics for text generation. In *Proceedings of the 58th Annual Meeting of the Association for Computational Linguistics*, pages 7881–7892, Online. Association for Computational Linguistics.

Thibault Sellam, Amy Pu, Hyung Won Chung, Sebastian Gehrmann, Qijun Tan, Markus Freitag, Dipanjan Das, and Ankur Parikh. 2020b. Learning to evaluate translation beyond English: BLEURT submissions to the WMT metrics 2020 shared task. In *Proceedings of the Fifth Conference on Machine Translation*, pages 921–927, Online. Association for Computational Linguistics.

Anastasia Shimorina, Claire Gardent, Shashi Narayan, and Laura Perez-Beltrachini. 2018. WebNLG Challenge: Human Evaluation Results. Technical report, Loria & Inria Grand Est.

Koustuv Sinha, Robin Jia, Dieuwke Hupkes, Joelle Pineau, Adina Williams, and Douwe Kiela. 2021. Masked language modeling and the distributional hypothesis: Order word matters pre-training for little. *CoRR*, abs/2104.06644.

Matthew Snover, Bonnie Dorr, Rich Schwartz, Linnea Micciulla, and John Makhoul. 2006. A study of translation edit rate with targeted human annotation. In *Proceedings of the 7th Conference of the Association for Machine Translation in the Americas: Technical Papers*, pages 223–231, Cambridge, Massachusetts, USA. Association for Machine Translation in the Americas.

Kaitao Song, Xu Tan, Tao Qin, Jianfeng Lu, and Tie-Yan Liu. 2020. Mpnet: Masked and permuted pre-training for language understanding. *CoRR*, abs/2004.09297.

Kristina Toutanova, Danqi Chen, Patrick Pantel, Hoifung Poon, Pallavi Choudhury, and Michael Gamon. 2015. Representing text for joint embedding of text and knowledge bases. In *Proceedings of the 2015 Conference on Empirical Methods in Natural Language Processing*, pages 1499–1509, Lisbon, Portugal. Association for Computational Linguistics.

Théo Trouillon, Johannes Welbl, Sebastian Riedel, Éric Gaussier, and Guillaume Bouchard. 2016. Complex embeddings for simple link prediction. In *Proceedings of the 33rd International Conference on International Conference on Machine Learning - Volume 48*, ICML'16, page 2071–2080. JMLR.org.

Zhigang Wang and Juanzi Li. 2016. Text-enhanced representation learning for knowledge graph. In *Proceedings of the Twenty-Fifth International Joint Conference on Artificial Intelligence*, IJCAI'16, page 1293–1299. AAAI Press.

Sam Wiseman, Stuart Shieber, and Alexander Rush. 2017. Challenges in data-to-document generation. In *Proceedings of the 2017 Conference on Empirical Methods in Natural Language Processing*, pages 2253–2263, Copenhagen, Denmark. Association for Computational Linguistics.

Jiawei Wu, Ruobing Xie, Zhiyuan Liu, and Maosong Sun. 2016. Knowledge representation via joint learning of sequential text and knowledge graphs. *arXiv preprint arXiv:1609.07075*.

Kun Xu, Liwei Wang, Mo Yu, Yansong Feng, Yan Song, Zhiguo Wang, and Dong Yu. 2019. Cross-lingual knowledge graph alignment via graph matching neural network. In *Proceedings of the 57th Annual Meeting of the Association for Computational Linguistics*, pages 3156–3161, Florence, Italy. Association for Computational Linguistics.

Ikuya Yamada, Hiroyuki Shindo, Hideaki Takeda, and Yoshiyasu Takefuji. 2016. Joint learning of the embedding of words and entities for named entity disambiguation. In *Proceedings of The 20th SIGNLL Conference on Computational Natural Language Learning*, pages 250–259, Berlin, Germany. Association for Computational Linguistics.

Bishan Yang, Wen-tau Yih, Xiaodong He, Jianfeng Gao, and li Deng. 2014. Embedding entities and relations for learning and inference in knowledge bases.

Haiyang Yu, Ningyu Zhang, Shumin Deng, Hongbin Ye, Wei Zhang, and Huajun Chen. 2020. Bridging text and knowledge with multi-prototype embedding for few-shot relational triple extraction. In *Proceedings of the 28th International Conference on Computational Linguistics*, pages 6399–6410, Barcelona, Spain (Online). International Committee on Computational Linguistics.

Tianyi Zhang*, Varsha Kishore*, Felix Wu*, Kilian Q. Weinberger, and Yoav Artzi. 2020. Bertscore: Evaluating text generation with bert. In *International Conference on Learning Representations*.

## A Dataset statistics

| | # (t,g) | # P | # E |
|---|---|---|---|
| TEKGEN | 6,310,061 | 1041 | 3,939,696 |
| TREX | 6,000,336 | 675 | 3,188,309 |
| KELM | 15,616,551 | 261405 | 5,073,603 |
| WEBNLG-DB | 13,212 | 372 | 3210 |
| WEBNLG-WD | 10,384 | 188 | 2783 |
| WIKICHUNKS | 30,000 | 468 | 20,318 |

Table 1: **Training and test data for retrieval.** # (t,g): Number of graph-text pairs, # T: Number of texts, # G: Number of graphs, # P: Number of distinct properties, # E: Number of distinct entities.

## B Impact of Batch Size

## C Scatter Plot Comparison of BLEURT and EREDAT

## D Symmetrical Relationships in WebNLG

We manually inspected all relationships in WEBNLG and deemed the following to be symmetrical in nature:

"taxon synonym", "partner in business or sport", "opposite of", "partially coincident with", "physically interacts with", "partner", "relative", "related category", "connects with", "twinned administrative body", "different from", "said to be the same as", "sibling", "adjacent station", "shares border with"

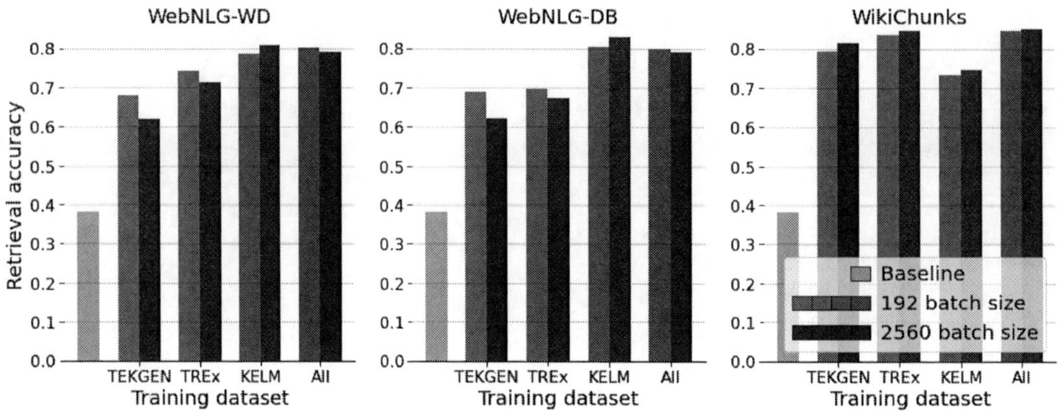


Figure 8: **Small vs. Large Batch Size.** Large batch sizes help a little on data with lower alignement quality (WIKICHUNKS). Overall, the improvement is inconsistent.

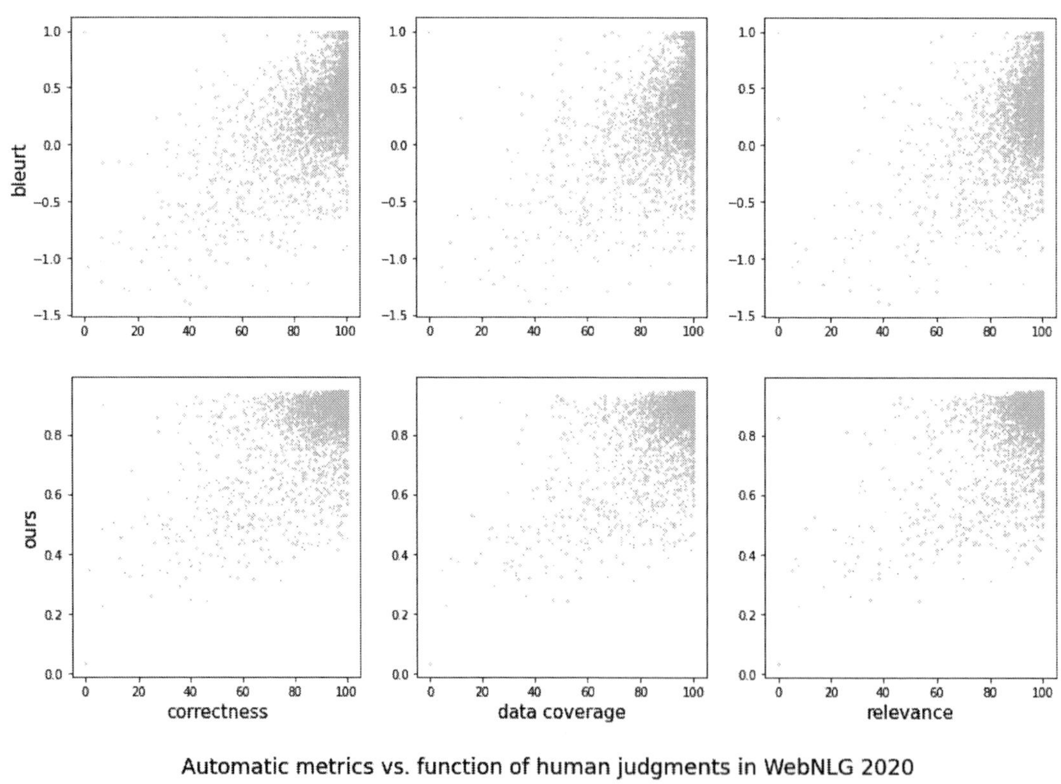


Figure 9: **Human judgment and automated evaluation values for every point in WEBNLG 2020.**

# Unsupervised Multi-document Summarization with Holistic Inference

Haopeng Zhang[1] Sangwoo Cho[2] Kaiqiang Song[2]
Xiaoyang Wang[2] Hongwei Wang[2] Jiawei Zhang[1] Dong Yu[2]
{haopeng,jiawei}@ifmlab.org
{riversong,swcho,shawnxywang,hongweiw,dyu}@global.tencent.com
[1]IFM lab, University of California, Davis [2] Tencent AI Lab, Bellevue, WA

## Abstract

Multi-document summarization aims to obtain core information from a collection of documents written on the same topic. This paper proposes a new holistic framework for unsupervised multi-document extractive summarization. Our method incorporates the holistic beam search inference method associated with the holistic measurements, named Subset Representative Index (SRI). SRI balances the importance and diversity of a subset of sentences from the source documents and can be calculated in unsupervised and adaptive manners. To demonstrate the effectiveness of our method, we conduct extensive experiments on both small and large-scale multi-document summarization datasets under both unsupervised and adaptive settings. The proposed method outperforms strong baselines by a significant margin, as indicated by the resulting ROUGE scores and diversity measures. Our findings also suggest that diversity is essential for improving multi-document summary performance.

## 1 Introduction

The multi-document summarization (**MDS**) is one of the essential tools to obtain core information from a collection of documents written for the same topic. It seeks to find the main ideas from multiple sources with diversified messages. In spite of recent advances in MDS system designs (Mihalcea and Tarau, 2004; Liu and Lapata, 2019a; Xiao et al., 2022), three major challenges hinder its development:

First, existing extractive multi-document summarization systems rely on optimization with *individual* scoring. It becomes sub-optimal when we need to extract multiple summary sentences (Zhong et al., 2020). A typical individual system scores each candidate summary with only measurements of the newly added sentences during inference.

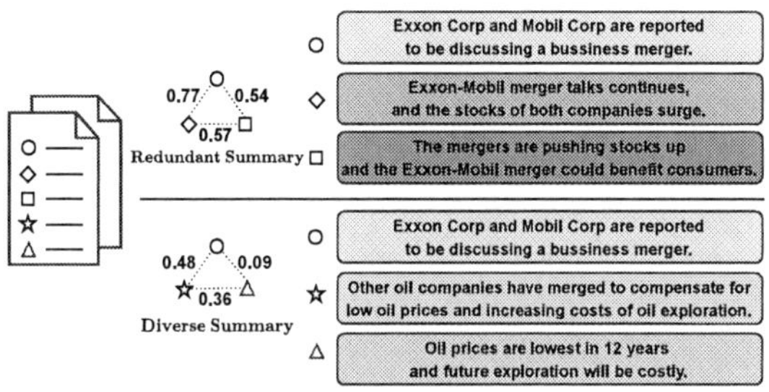


Figure 1: An example of a diverse summary vs. a redundant summary. Sentences in the redundant summary have higher semantic similarity than a diverse summary.

In contrast, the holistic system simultaneously measures all summary sentences and the relations among them. Despite recent efforts in holistic methods on a single document (An et al., 2022; Zhong et al., 2020), how to extract sentences holistically for multi-document summarization remains open. In this work, we propose an inference method that holistically optimizes the extractive summary under multi-document setting.

Second, multi-document summarization naturally contains excessively redundant information (Lebanoff et al., 2018). An ideal summary should provide important information with diversified perspectives (Nenkova and McKeown, 2011). In Figure 1, we show a salient and diversified summary versus a salient but redundant summary. A salient and diversified summary often covers the information thoroughly, while the salient but redundant summary is usually incomplete. Different from existing approaches (Suzuki and Nagata, 2017; Cho et al., 2019b; Xiao and Carenini, 2020) for limiting the repetitions, we introduce **S**ubset **R**epresentative **I**ndex (**SRI**), a holistically balanced measurement between importance and diversity for extractive multi-document summarization.

Finally, recent deep learning-based supervised summarization methods are data-driven and require a massive number of high-quality summaries in the

*Work done during Haopeng Zhang's internship at Tencent AI Lab Seattle.



*Findings of the Association for Computational Linguistics: IJCNLP-AACL 2023*, pages 123–133
November 1–4, 2023. 

training data. Nevertheless, hiring humans to write summaries is always expensive, time-consuming, and thus hard to scale up. This problem becomes more severe for multi-document summarization, since it requires more effort to read more documents. Therefore, existing multi-document summarization datasets are either small-scale (Over and Yen, 2004; Dang and Owczarzak, 2008) or created by acquiring data from the Internet with automatic alignments (Fabbri et al., 2019; Antognini and Faltings, 2020) that could be erroneous. Here we propose an unsupervised multi-document summarization method to tackle the low-resource issue. It can further benefit the unsupervised multi-document summarization, with the adaptive setting using large-scale high-quality single-document summarization data (e.g., CNN/DailyMail (Hermann et al., 2015)).

In this work, we present a novel framework for unsupervised extractive multi-document summarization, aiming to holistically select the extractive summary sentences. The framework contains the holistic beam search inference method associated with the holistic measurements named **SRI** ( **S**ubset **R**epresentative **I**ndex). The SRI is designed as a holistic measurement for balancing the importance of individual sentences and the diversity among sentences within a set. To address data sparsity, we propose to calculate SRI in both unsupervised and adaptive manners. Unsupervised SRI relies on the centrality from graph-based methods (Erkan and Radev, 2004; Mihalcea and Tarau, 2004) for subset importance measurement, while adaptive SRI uses BERT (Devlin et al., 2018) fine-tuned on single document summarization (SDS) corpus for sentence importance measurement. Our method shows performance improvements in both the summary informativeness and diversity scores, indicating our approach can achieve better coverage of documents while maintaining the gist information of multi-documents. We highlight the contributions of our work as follows:

- We propose a novel holistic framework for multi-document extractive summarization. Our framework incorporates a holistic inference method for summary sentence extraction and holistic measurement called Subset Representative Index (SRI) for balancing the importance and diversity of a subset of sentences.
- We propose two unsupervised ways to measure SRI by using graph-based centrality or adapting from a single document corpus.
- We conduct extensive experiments on several benchmark datasets, and the results demonstrate the effectiveness of our paradigm under both unsupervised and adaptive settings. Our findings suggest that effectively modeling sentence importance and pairwise sentence similarity is crucial for extracting diverse summaries and improving summarization performance.

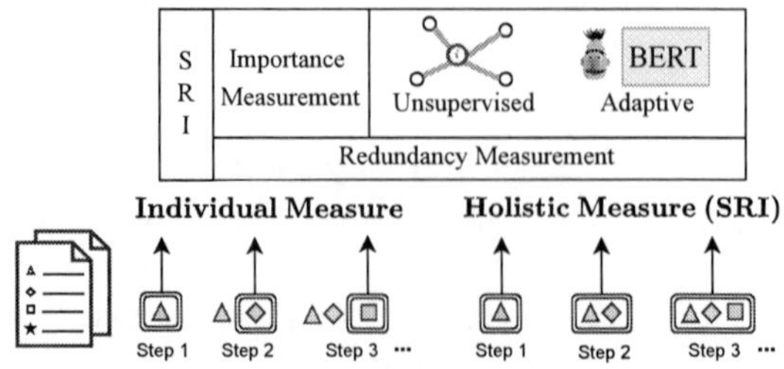


Figure 2: Illustration of the proposed holistic framework for multi-document summarization. The individual inference only resorts to each candidate while the holistic inference is based on all candidates. Orange and Green indicate newly added sentences and already added ones to the summary respectively.

## 2 Related Works

**Multi-document Summarization** Traditional non-neural approaches to multi-document summarization have been both extractive (Carbonell and Goldstein, 1998; Erkan and Radev, 2004; Mihalcea and Tarau, 2004) and abstractive (Ganesan et al., 2010). Recent neural MDS systems rely on Transformer-based encoder-decoder model to process the integrated long documents with hierarchical inter-paragraph attention (Liu and Lapata, 2019a; Fabbri et al., 2019), or attention across representations of different granularity (Jin et al., 2020). This work focuses on unsupervised MDS scenarios where gold reference summaries are unavailable. Prior unsupervised MDS systems are mostly graph-based (Erkan and Radev, 2004; Liu et al., 2021). Similar to our adaptive setting, Lebanoff et al. (2018) proposed to adapt the encoder-decoder framework from a single document corpus, but our work focuses on extractive summarization setting with holistic inference.

**Sentence Importance Measurements** Most works formulate extractive summarization as a sequence classification problem and use sequential neural models with different encoders like recurrent neural networks (Cheng and Lapata, 2016; Nallapati et al., 2016) and pre-trained language models (Liu and Lapata, 2019b; Zhang et al., 2023b). The prediction probabilities are treated as the importance measurement of sentences. On the other hand, unsupervised graph-based methods calculate the importance of sentences with node centrality and rank them for the summaries, including TextRank (Mihalcea and Tarau, 2004), LexRank (Erkan and Radev, 2004), PACSUM (Zheng and Lapata, 2019), and its variants (Liang et al., 2021; Liu et al., 2021). Recent researches (Xu et al., 2019; Wang et al., 2020; Zhang et al., 2022, 2023a) have explored Graph Neural Networks to obtain better representations for each sentence. Graph methods have merits in considering implicit document structure and to adapt with regardless of the input length.

graph neural network message passing or simply

**Redundancy** Considering only the importance of sentences for the summary leads to repeated information, and resolving the redundant contents is an essential problem in the extractive summarization system. Traditional methods to tackle redundancy relies on discrete optimization problem like Maximal Marginal Relevance (MMR) (Carbonell and Goldstein, 1998), Determinantal Point Process (DPP) (Kulesza and Taskar, 2012), and submodular selection (Lin et al., 2009). Trigram blocking is introduced to explicitly reduce redundancy by avoiding sentences that share a 3-gram with the previously added one (Liu and Lapata, 2019b). Paulus et al. (2017) first adopt trigram blocking in decoding for abstractive summarization. Ma et al. (2016) proposed the sentence filtering and beam search methods to for extractive summarization sentence selection. Xiao and Carenini (2020) conducted a systematic study of redundancy in long documents.

## 3 Method

This section provides a detailed description of our proposed holistic MDS summarization framework. We first explain how we formulate the MDS problem holistically in Section 3.1. The overall architecture of our holistic framework is shown in Figure 2, which includes holistic inference methods for summary sentence extraction in Section 3.2, and a new holistic measurement, the Subset Representative Index (SRI) in Section 3.3.

### 3.1 Problem Formulation

Multi-document summarization typically takes a collection of $n$ documents $\mathcal{D} = \{D^{(1)}, \ldots, D^{(n)}\}$ as inputs. Each document contains a varying number of sentences $D^{(i)} = \{s_0^{(i)}, \ldots, s_{l_i}^{(i)}\}$, where $l_i$ is the number of sentences in the $i$-th document. Let $\mathcal{S}$ be the collection of all sentences, i.e. $\mathcal{S} = D^{(1)} \cup \cdots \cup D^{(n)}$. Additionally, let $e_{i,j}$ denote the similarity score between sentence $s_i$ and sentence $s_j$. Our goal is to select a representative subset of sentences $\mathcal{S}' \subset \mathcal{S}$ that maximizes the total importance of the subset while minimizing the redundancy within sentences in the subset at the same time.

### 3.2 Holistic Inference

Most existing approaches for unsupervised extractive summarization formulate it as an individual sentence ranking problem. They first calculate a measurement $\mathcal{M}(s_i)$ (e.g. sentence importance) for each sentence $s_i \in \mathcal{S}$ and rank all sentences in $\mathcal{S}$ accordingly. For summary inference, they directly use an *individual greedy* method that adds one sentence with the highest ranking at a time until the desired total number of summary sentences is reached. In contrast, a holistic summarization method should evaluate a subset of sentences $\mathcal{M}(\mathcal{S}')$ as a whole, then select the best subset $\mathcal{S}'$. The setting formulates the holistic summary inference into a best subset selection problem, which has exponential time complexity.

To address the exponential time complexity issue, we propose several holistic inference methods for summary sentence extraction. These methods optimize subsets of sentences using subset measurements, as opposed to the individual greedy inference method. We describe the different variants of the proposed method as below.

**Holistic Greedy Method.** The most straightforward way to address the exponential time complexity issue is to adopt a greedy approach. Similar to the individual greedy method, the holistic greedy method also adds one sentence at a time. However, it picks the sentence using a subset measurement that takes into account the previously selected sentences. Formally, at each step, the method selects the sentence that maximizes the following objective:

$$\text{argmax}_{s_i \in \mathcal{S} \setminus \mathcal{S}'} \mathcal{M}(\mathcal{S}' \cup \{s_i\}), \qquad (1)$$

where $\mathcal{S}'$ represents the previously selected sentences.

**Holistic Exhaustive Search.** It is a brute-force method that considers every possible subset with the desired number of sentences. However, due to the exponential computation time, it is necessary to first filter out low-importance candidates using $\mathcal{M}(\{s_i\})$ to reduce the search space.

**Holistic Beam Inference** . We also propose Holistic Beam Inference which balances the trade-off between search space size and efficiency. It is a more advanced holistic inference method that adapts the beam-search decoding algorithm. We illustrate the algorithm in Algorithm 1. At each step, it considers the top-k candidate subsets, which enlarges the search space and therefore has a higher chance of finding a better subset solution compared to the holistic greedy method. Meanwhile, the algorithm has linear time complexity, making it more efficient than the holistic exhaustive search method.

**Algorithm 1** Holistic Beam Inference

**Input**: set of sentences $\mathcal{S}$, Measurement $\mathcal{M}(\cdot)$
**Parameter**: # summary sentences $N < |\mathcal{S}|$, beam size $k$
**Output**: the selected subset $\mathcal{S}'$

The candidate set $\mathcal{C} \leftarrow \{\varnothing\}$
**for** $N$ times **do**
  The beam set $\mathcal{C}' \leftarrow \{\varnothing\}$
  **for** $\mathcal{X} \in \mathcal{C}$ **do**
    $\mathcal{X}' \leftarrow$ arg-top-$k$-max$_{s \in \mathcal{S} \setminus \mathcal{X}} \mathcal{M}(\mathcal{X} \cup \{s\})$
    **for** $x \in \mathcal{X}'$ **do**
      Add $\mathcal{X} \cup \{x\}$ to $\mathcal{C}'$
    **end for**
  **end for**
  $\mathcal{C} \leftarrow$ arg-top-$k$-max$_{\mathcal{X} \in \mathcal{C}'} \mathcal{M}(\mathcal{X})$
**end for**
**return** argmax$_{\mathcal{X} \in \mathcal{C}} \mathcal{M}(\mathcal{X})$

### 3.3 Subset Representative Index

To complement the holistic inference methods, we propose a new subset measurement, Subset Representative Index (SRI), denoted as $\mathcal{M}(\mathcal{S}')$. It balances the importance measurement $\mathcal{I}(\mathcal{S}')$ and redundancy measurement $\mathcal{R}(\mathcal{S}')$.

An ideal extractive summary should select the most representative subset from a collection of the input sentences, maximizing the total non-redundant salient information passed to the user. SRI is a holistic subset measurement that balances the importance and redundancy of a subset of sentences from the source documents. Formally, we define SRI as below:

$$\mathcal{M}(\mathcal{S}') = \mathcal{I}(\mathcal{S}') - \lambda \cdot \mathcal{R}(\mathcal{S}'), \tag{2}$$

where $\mathcal{I}(\mathcal{S}')$ measures the informativeness of a set of sentences, and $\mathcal{R}(\mathcal{S}')$ measures the redundancy within the set. The parameter $\lambda$ is used to control the weight of the redundancy in the overall SRI score. We detail the methods for measuring the set importance and redundancy in an unsupervised manner as follows.

**Graph-Based Importance Measurement.** To measure the importance of sentences, we use a graph-based approach. We construct a graph $\mathcal{G} = (\mathcal{V}, \mathcal{E})$, where node $v_i \in \mathcal{V}$ represents sentence $s_i \in \mathcal{S}$, and edge $e_{i,j} \in \mathcal{E}$ represents the similarity between sentence $s_i$ and $s_j$. Our proposed approach for sentence similarity score employs a combination of two methods: TF-IDF and Sentence-BERT (Reimers and Gurevych, 2019). TF-IDF is used to encode sentences with surface-form similarity, while Sentence-BERT is used to encode sentences with semantic similarity:

$$e_{i,j} = \alpha \cdot \mathbf{c}_i^\top \mathbf{c}_j + (1 - \alpha) \cdot \mathbf{r}_i^\top \mathbf{r}_j, \tag{3}$$

where $\mathbf{c}_i$, $\mathbf{c}_j$, $\mathbf{r}_i$ and $\mathbf{r}_j$ are the corresponding TF-IDF features and sentence embeddings for the $i$-th and $j$-th sentences, respectively. The weight term $\alpha \in [0, 1]$ is a configurable hyperparameter to balance between statistical similarity and contextualized similarity.

Inspired from (Mihalcea and Tarau, 2004; Erkan and Radev, 2004), we define the importance of a sentence as its node centrality in the graph, which is calculated as the sum of the weights of edges connected to the node representing this sentence:

$$\mathcal{I}(s_i) = \sum_{s_j \in \mathcal{S} \setminus s_i} e_{i,j}. \tag{4}$$

Similarly, the importance of a subset of sentences is defined as the total weights between the subgraph and the remaining graph:

$$\begin{aligned} \mathcal{I}(\mathcal{S}') &= \frac{1}{|\mathcal{S}| - |\mathcal{S}'|} \sum_{s_i \in \mathcal{S}', s_j \in \mathcal{S} \setminus \mathcal{S}'} e_{i,j} \\ &\approx \frac{1}{|\mathcal{S}|} \sum_{s_i \in \mathcal{S}', s_j \in \mathcal{S} \setminus \mathcal{S}'} e_{i,j}. \end{aligned} \tag{5}$$

Since $|\mathcal{S}'|$ is usually far smaller than $|\mathcal{S}|$ in summarization tasks, we can approximate the denominator by using $|\mathcal{S}|$ directly. This way, the subset importance only takes into account the relationship of the subset with the remaining sentences, rather than considering dependencies within the subset.

**Adaptive Importance Measurement.** In spite of the data sparsity issue in MDS, the Single Document Summarization (SDS) task has abundant high-quality labeled data (Hermann et al., 2015; Narayan et al., 2018; Cohan et al., 2018). We propose a method called adaptive importance measurement, which adapts SDS data for MDS importance measurement. This method utilizes the labeled data from SDS to train a model for predicting the importance of sentences in MDS.

In the adaptive setting, we fine-tune the BERT (Devlin et al., 2018) to a sentence importance scorer on SDS datasets, and then adapt the fine-tuned model to the target MDS datasets. Specifically, we first calculate the normalized salience of a sentence as:

$$f(s_i) = \mathbf{v}^\top \tanh(\mathbf{W}_1 \mathbf{r}_i), \\ \text{salience}(s_i) = \frac{f(s_i)}{\sum_{s_j \in D} f(s_j)}, \tag{6}$$

where $\mathbf{W}$ is a trainable weight, and $\mathbf{r}_i$ is the contextualized representation of sentence $s_i$. Then, we fine-tune BERT to minimize the following loss:

$$R(s_i) = \text{softmax}(\text{ROUGE}(s_i)), \\ \mathcal{L} = -\sum_D \sum_{s_i \in D} R(s_i) \log \text{salience}(s_i). \tag{7}$$

The fine-tuned BERT can be directly adapted to the MDS datasets and calculate the adaptive importance measurement for sentences.

**Redundancy Measurement.** The redundancy measurement for a subset of sentences $\mathcal{S}'$ is defined as the total similarity score of each sentence with its most similar counterpart. This measurement captures the degree of overlap between the sentences in the subset, indicating the level of redundancy present in the selected sentences:

$$\mathcal{R}(\mathcal{S}') = \sum_{s_i \in \mathcal{S}'} \max_{s_j \in \mathcal{S}' \setminus \{s_i\}} e_{i,j}. \tag{8}$$

Overall, we can calculate SRI in both unsupervised and adaptive manners. Our holistic framework extracts summaries as a whole with the holistic inference method, which is guided by SRI to measure the importance and redundancy of a subset of sentences. This approach allows us to balance the importance and redundancy of a summary, making it more informative and coherent.

## 4 Experiments

In this section, we provide details on our experimental setup, including the datasets, evaluation metrics, baselines, and implementation details (Section 4.1). We then present the results of our model on benchmark MDS datasets in both unsupervised (Section 4.2) and adaptive (Section 4.3) settings.

### 4.1 Experimental Setting

**Dataset.** We evaluate our unsupervised method on benchmark multi-document summarization datasets. Particularly, we use MultiNews (Fabbri et al., 2019), WikiSum (Liu et al., 2018), DUC-04 (Over and Yen, 2004), and TAC-11 (Dang and Owczarzak, 2008) datasets. MultiNews is collected from a diverse set of news articles on newser.com. It is a large-scale dataset containing reference summaries written by professional editors. WikiSum is another large-scale dataset that provides documents and summaries from Wikipedia webpages where the documents come from the reference webpages of Wikipedia articles and top-10 Google searches, and the summaries are the lead section of the Wikipedia articles. We use the top-40 high-ranked paragraphs for the document inputs following (Liu and Lapata, 2019a).

For summary extraction, we use the average number of reference sentences: 10 and 5, respectively on MultiNews and WikiSum. For the DUC and TAC datasets, the task is to generate a succinct summary of up to 100 words from a set of 10 news articles. We report results on DUC-04 and TAC-11, which are standard test sets used in previous studies (Hong et al., 2014; Cho et al., 2019a). DUC-03 and TAC-08/09/10 are used for the validation set to tune hyper-parameters. For adaptive setting, we fine-tune BERT on single document summarization dataset CNN/DailyMail (Hermann et al., 2015) and directly adapt to MDS test sets. Table 1 shows the statistics of the datasets in detail.

**Evaluation Metrics.** The extracted summaries are evaluated against human reference summaries using ROUGE (Lin, 2004)[1] for the summarization quality. We report ROUGE-1, ROUGE-2, ROUGE-SU4, and ROUGE-L[2] that respectively measure the overlap of unigrams, bigrams, skip bigrams with a maximum distance of 4 words, and the longest

[1]w/ options -n 2 -m -w 1.2 -c 95 -r 1000 -l 100 for DUC/TAC

[2]Due to some legacy issues, some baselines report the original ROUGE-L, others report ROUGE-Lsum.

| Dataset | # test | # ref. | avg.w/doc | avg.w/sum |
|---|---|---|---|---|
| DUC-04 | 50 | 4 | 4,636 | 109.6 |
| TAC-11 | 44 | 4 | 4,696 | 99.7 |
| Multi-News | 5,622 | 1 | 2,104 | 264.7 |
| Wikisum | 38,205 | 1 | 2,800 | 139.4 |
| CNNDM(SDS) | 11,489 | 1 | 766.1 | 58.2 |

Table 1: Detailed statistics of four multi-document datasets. #test denotes the number of document clusters in the test set, #ref denotes the number of reference summaries, avg.word(doc) denotes the average number of words in the source document cluster, avg.word(sum) denotes the average number of words in the ground truth summary.

common sequence between extracted summary and reference summary. To align with previous works, we report R-1, R-2, R-L for Multinews and Wikisum datasets, and R-1, R-2, R-SU4 for DUC and TAC datasets. For all baseline methods, we report ROUGE results from their original papers if available or use results reported in (Cho et al., 2019a; Liu et al., 2021). We also report the measure of diversity for the generated summaries by calculating a unique n-gram ratio (Xiao and Carenini, 2020; Peyrard et al., 2017) defined as:

$$\text{uniq } n\text{-gram ratio} = \frac{\#\text{ uniq-}n\text{-gram}}{\#n\text{-gram}} \quad (9)$$

**Baselines.** We compare our methods with strong unsupervised summarization baselines. In particular, *MMR* (Carbonell and Goldstein, 1998) combines query relevance with information novelty in the context of summarization. *LexRank* (Erkan and Radev, 2004) computes sentence importance based on eigenvector centrality in a graph representation of sentences. *TextRank* (Mihalcea and Tarau, 2004) adopts PageRank (Page et al., 1999) to compute node centrality recursively based on a Markov chain model. *SumBasic* (Vanderwende et al., 2007) is an extractive approach assuming words frequently occurring in a document cluster are more likely to be included in the summary. *KL-Sum* (Haghighi and Vanderwende, 2009) uses a greedy approach to add a sentence to the summary to minimize the KL divergence. *PRIMERA* (Xiao et al., 2022) is a pyramid-based pre-trained model for MDS that achieves state-of-the-art performance. We compare it under its zero-shot setting.

**Implementation Details.** We run all experiments with 88 Intel(R) Xeon(R) CPUs. We combine the surface indicator based on TF-IDF and contextualized embeddings. We treat each document cluster as a corpus and each sentence as a document when calculating the TF-IDF scores. We employ the pre-trained sentence-transformer (Reimers and Gurevych, 2019) and extract sentence representations using a checkpoint of 'all-mpnet-base-v2'.

The graph edges with low similarity are treated as disconnected to emphasize the connectivity of the graph and avoid noisy edge connections. We keep a threshold $\tilde{e}$ for edge weights such that edges with similarity scores smaller than $\tilde{e}$ will be set to 0. Here $\tilde{e}$ is controlled by a hyper-parameter to be tuned according to datasets. The final representation of edge weight between two sentences $(s_i, s_j)$ is

$$e_{i,j} = \max(\text{sim}(s_i, s_j) - \tilde{e}, 0), \quad (10)$$

where $\tilde{e} = \min(e) + \theta\,(\max(e) - \min(e))$ is the threshold controlled by hyper-parameter $\theta$. For exhaustive search, we filter out the sentences with low centrality and only keep the top 15 sentences at inference.

All hyper-parameters are tuned on validation sets on MultiNews and WikiSum and training sets on DUC and TAC. The best parameters are selected based on the highest R-1 score. More specific, for the balancing factor $\lambda$ in SRI, we use $\{2^{-13}, 2^{-7}, 2^{-4}, 2^{-6}\}$ on DUC, TAC, MultiNews and WikiSum dataset. For $\alpha$ that weighted the contributions of TF-IDF and contextualized sentence similarity, we use 0.9 on News domain datasets and 0.8 on the WikiSum dataset. The edge weight threshold $\theta$ is $\{0, 0, 0.1, 0.1\}$ for DUC, TAC, MultiNews and WikiSum. As for beam search, we use beam size $\{4, 4, 4, 3\}$ on the corresponding datasets.

## 4.2 Unsupervised Summarization Results

The unsupervised summarization results on four benchmark MDS datasets are shown in Table 2.

The summarization performance of our method outperforms strong unsupervised baselines. Note that MultiNews and WikiSum datasets provide abundant training samples and contain shorter input than the DUC or TAC datasets. Our method performs better than the pre-trained model, *PRIMERA* with a zero-shot setting. Compared to the baseline (Sent. greedy) that extracts sentences solely based on importance, balancing diversity with SRI boosts performance by a large margin.

For the DUC-04 and TAC-11 datasets, our proposed methods outperform unsupervised baselines by a large margin. It demonstrates that balancing the summary informativeness and diversity during

| System | *DUC-04* R-1 | R-2 | R-SU | *TAC-11* R-1 | R-2 | R-SU | *MultiNews* R-1 | R-2 | R-L | *WikiSum* R-1 | R-2 | R-L* |
|---|---|---|---|---|---|---|---|---|---|---|---|---|
| ***Unsupervised Systems*** | | | | | | | | | | | | |
| LEAD | 30.77 | 8.27 | 7.35 | 32.88 | 7.84 | 11.46 | 39.41 | 11.77 | 14.51 | 37.63 | 14.75 | 33.76 |
| MMR (1998) | 30.14 | 4.55 | 8.16 | 31.43 | 6.14 | 11.16 | 38.77 | 11.98 | 12.91 | 31.22 | 10.24 | 22.48 |
| LexRank (2004) | 34.44 | 7.11 | 11.19 | 33.10 | 7.50 | 11.13 | 38.27 | 12.70 | 13.20 | 36.12 | 11.67 | 22.52 |
| TextRank (2004) | 33.16 | 6.13 | 10.16 | 33.24 | 7.62 | 11.27 | 38.44 | 13.10 | 13.50 | 23.66 | 7.79 | 21.23 |
| SumBasic (2007) | 29.48 | 4.25 | 8.64 | 31.58 | 6.06 | 10.06 | - | - | - | - | - | - |
| KLSumm (2009) | 31.04 | 6.03 | 10.23 | 31.23 | 7.07 | 10.56 | - | - | - | - | - | - |
| PRIMERA (2022) | 35.10 | 7.20 | 17.90 | - | - | - | 42.00 | 13.60 | 20.80 | 28.00 | 8.00 | 18.00 |
| Individual. Greedy | 34.81 | 7.85 | 11.37 | 34.42 | 8.10 | 11.25 | 40.48 | 13.49 | 16.14 | 37.24 | 10.29 | 32.77 |
| ***Our Methods*** | | | | | | | | | | | | |
| SRI+beam | **36.84** | **8.37** | 12.28 | **35.37** | **8.49** | **11.73** | **44.22** | **14.63** | 18.61 | 38.94 | 15.23 | 34.12 |
| SRI+exh | 36.70 | **8.37** | **12.31** | 35.19 | 8.31 | 11.34 | 43.16 | 14.58 | 18.00 | **39.26** | **16.15** | **34.19** |

Table 2: ROUGE-F1 scores on four datasets under the unsupervised setting. Best unsupervised results are bold. For a fair comparison, we report R-L on Multinews and R-Lsum (See et al., 2017) for WikiSum and limit summaries to 100 words on DUC-04 and TAC-11. R-L are marked with * if reporting ROUGE- Lsum numbers.

| Method | Fluent | Informative | Faithful | Overall |
|---|---|---|---|---|
| MMR | 3.2 | 3.5 | **4.7** | 3.2 |
| PRIMERA | **4.3** | 2.5 | 3.3 | 3.3 |
| SRI | 3.8 | **4.3** | **4.7** | **4.0** |

Table 3: Human evaluation results on a scale of 1-5.

the sentence extraction process is crucial for better summary quality. Note that the input length of DUC/TAC datasets is extremely long spanning an average of 180 sentences. These long input easily exceeds the input capacity of transformer-based models possibly resulting in information loss from documents. The proposed methods on the other hand process documents regardless of the input length or formats (SDS or MDS). Also, our unsupervised methods have the advantage of processing datasets with small training data. The supreme performances on datasets with different input lengths and low-resource data illustrate the effectiveness of our methods. To further verify the model performance, we also conduct a human evaluation by experts on a scale of 5. The results shown in Table 3 also prove our method outputs better summaries in unsupervised setting.

### 4.3 Adptive Summarization Results

The experimental results under the adaptive setting are shown in Table 4. Compared to large pre-trained generation model (BART) and other task-specific pre-trained summarization models (PEGASUS, PRIMERA), our framework shows strong performance when adapting from a single document summarization dataset. We also notice fine-tuning on single document summarization corpus improves the performance of all pre-trained models, but still, our framework achieves the best results under the adaptive setting.

| System | *DUC-04* R-1 | R-2 | R-L | *MultiNews* R-1 | R-2 | R-L |
|---|---|---|---|---|---|---|
| ***Adaptive Systems*** | | | | | | |
| BART(2019) | 24.1 | 4.0 | 15.3 | 27.3 | 6.2 | 15.1 |
| BART (CNNDM) | 29.4 | 6.1 | 16.2 | 36.7 | 8.3 | 17.2 |
| PEGASUS (2020) | 32.7 | 7.4 | 17.6 | 32.0 | 10.1 | 16.7 |
| PEGASUS(CNNDM) | 34.2 | 7.5 | 17.4 | 35.1 | 11.9 | 18.2 |
| LED(2020) | 16.6 | 3.0 | 12.0 | 17.3 | 3.7 | 10.4 |
| PRIMERA (2022) | 35.1 | 7.2 | 17.9 | 42.0 | 13.6 | 20.8 |
| ***Our Systems*** | | | | | | |
| SRI+beam (graph) | 36.8 | 8.4 | 16.4 | 44.2 | **14.6** | 18.6 |
| SRI+beam (CNNDM) | **36.9** | **8.6** | **18.5** | **44.6** | 14.3 | **21.1** |

Table 4: ROUGE-F1 results on DUC-04 and Multinews datasets under the adaptive setting. Models adapted from CNN/DailyMail dataset are marked in the bracket.

## 5 Analysis

### 5.1 Summary Diversity

Other than summary quality, we also test the effectiveness of our SRI in terms of the diversity of the output summaries. We present the unique $n$-gram ratios of output summaries under unsupervised and adaptive settings and the reference summary on the TAC-11 dataset in Figure 3. According to the results, our framework is extremely effective in reducing summary redundancy and increasing summary diversity under both unsupervised and adaptive settings.

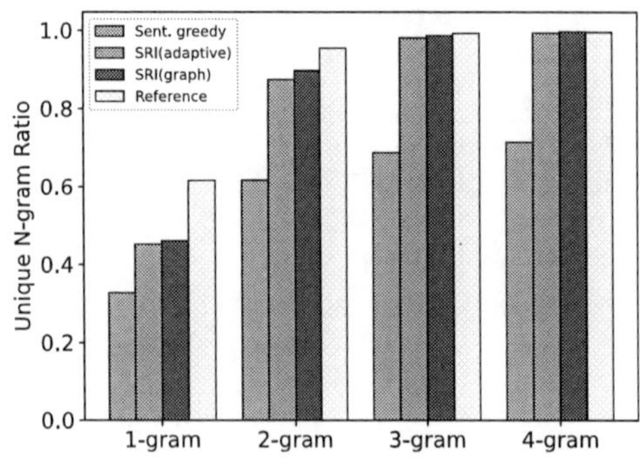


Figure 3: Unique $n$-gram ratios ($n = 1, 2, 3, 4$) of the output summary by different methods on TAC-11.

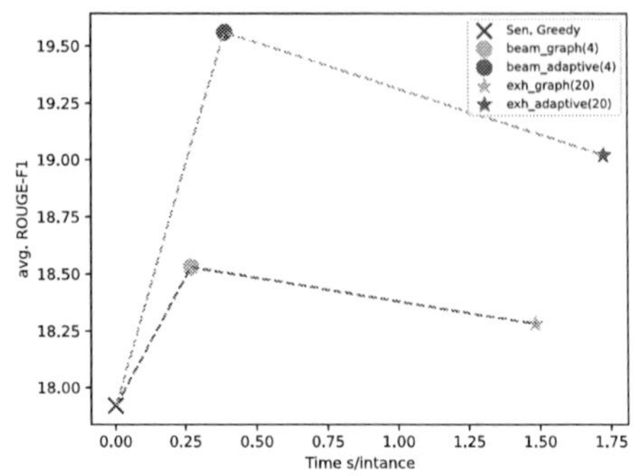


Figure 5: Efficiency vs. average ROUGE (w/o word limit) scores of different inference methods on TAC-11.

| Beam Size | 2 | 3 | 4 | 5 | 6 | 7 | 8 |
|---|---|---|---|---|---|---|---|
| ROUGE-1 | 33.43 | 33.65 | 33.62 | **33.76** | 34.72 | 33.64 | 33.67 |
| ROUGE-2 | 7.71 | **8.00** | 7.87 | 7.93 | 7.84 | 7.86 | 7.85 |
| ROUGE-L* | 28.74 | 29.03 | 28.99 | **29.10** | 29.01 | 28.94 | 29.01 |

Table 5: ROUGE-F1 (w/o word limit) results of SRI-beam with different beam sizes on TAC with $\lambda = 0.125$.

Compared to the ROUGE-F1 results, holistic inference with importance-diversity balancing measurement SRI increases both summary quality and diversity at the same time. The results suggest that considering summary diversity is beneficial in extractive summarization, especially in redundant cases like MDS and long document summarization. Our finding also verifies the crucial rule of effective modeling of sentence importance and similarity.

### 5.2 Hyperparameter Sensitivity

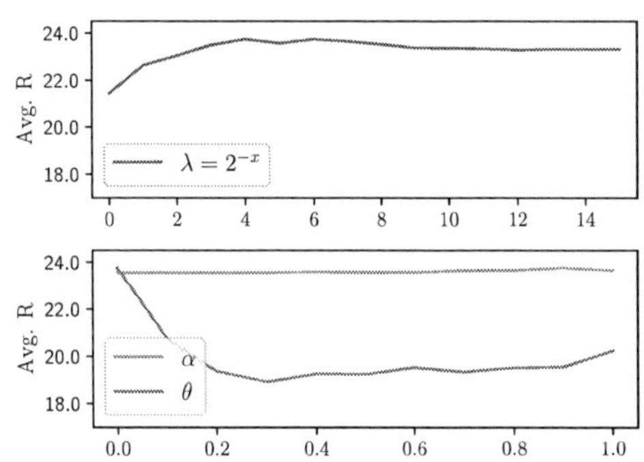


Figure 4: Average ROUGE-F1 (w/o word limit) results with different hyperparameter values on TAC-11.

To test the robustness of our proposed approaches, we study the hyperparameter sensitivity of our proposed methods. The results are shown in Figure 4. The first plot shows the impact of balancing factor $\lambda$ in SRI. The second plot shows the impact of $\alpha$, which balances the contextualized and TF-IDF sentence embedding and the edge weight threshold. The results show that our methods are relatively stable towards the hyperparameter values and could be easily adapted to unseen datasets.

### 5.3 Inference Approaches Analysis

We also compare the efficiency and effectiveness of different inference methods. As in Figure. 5, we compare sentence-level greedy search, set-level greedy search, set-level beam search (beam size = 4), and set-level exhaustive search with pre-filtering as inference methods for both unsupervised and adaptive settings. We pick the filter size of 20 here since the search space without filtering $C(N, K)$ is extremely large. According to the results, all set-level inference methods outperform the sentence-level methods. This suggests that extracting summaries at a set level (holistic) is optimal over the common sentence-level setting that extracts sentences individually. The finding is also consistent with the inherent performance gap between sentence-level and holistic extractors in (Zhong et al., 2020).

Moreover, we realize the set-level beam search and set-level exhaustive search achieve the comparable best performance. However, set-level beam search speed-wise is much more efficient than set-level exhaustive search. We also show the effect of different beam sizes in Table 5. The results indicate that a reasonably small beam size achieves the best ROUGE results, which are both effective and efficient. To conclude, set-level beam search with SRI shows the best overall performance.

## 6 Conclusion

This paper proposes a holistic framework for unsupervised multi-document extractive summarization. Our framework incorporates the holistic beam search inference methods and SRI, a holistically balanced measurement between importance and diversity. We conduct extensive experiments on both small and large-scale MDS datasets under both unsupervised and adaptive settings and the proposed method outperforms strong baselines by a large margin. We also find that balancing summary set importance and diversity benefits both the quality and diversity of output summaries for MDS.

## Limitations

The proposed framework in this paper is mainly designed for low-resource scenarios without gold summaries for multi-document summarization. Adapting the framework for a supervised setting requires further investigation. Recently, large language models (LLM) like ChatGPT have shown strong zero-shot summarization ability, which may raise doubt about the necessity of unsupervised summarization methods.

However, LLM suffers from the hallucination problem and MDS may exceed its input limit (e.g. 4,696 words for TAC) than the input limit of ChatGPT (500-word/4,000-character). In contrast, unsupervised summarization methods can tackle input of arbitrary length and have a faster inference speed than ChatGPT when processing long input documents. In addition, a recent study (Zhang et al., 2023c) shows that ChatGPT's extractive summarization performance is still inferior to existing supervised systems in terms of ROUGE scores.

## Ethical Consideration

Our proposed framework forms summary by directly extracting sentences from source documents. Therefore, the extracted summary may be incoherent or contain unfactual co-references. In addition, the extracted summary will keep biased contents from the source sentences, if any.

## References


Chenxin An, Ming Zhong, Zhiyong Wu, Qin Zhu, Xuanjing Huang, and Xipeng Qiu. 2022. Colo: A contrastive learning based re-ranking framework for one-stage summarization. *arXiv preprint arXiv:2209.14569*.

Diego Antognini and Boi Faltings. 2020. Gamewikisum: a novel large multi-document summarization dataset. In *Proceedings of The 12th Language Resources and Evaluation Conference*, pages 6645–6650, Marseille, France. European Language Resources Association.

Iz Beltagy, Matthew E. Peters, and Arman Cohan. 2020. Longformer: The long-document transformer. *arXiv:2004.05150*.

Jaime Carbonell and Jade Goldstein. 1998. The use of mmr, diversity-based reranking for reordering documents and producing summaries. In *Proceedings of the 21st annual international ACM SIGIR conference on Research and development in information retrieval*, pages 335–336.

Jianpeng Cheng and Mirella Lapata. 2016. Neural summarization by extracting sentences and words. *arXiv preprint arXiv:1603.07252*.

Sangwoo Cho, Logan Lebanoff, Hassan Foroosh, and Fei Liu. 2019a. Improving the similarity measure of determinantal point processes for extractive multi-document summarization. In *Proceedings of the 57th Annual Meeting of the Association for Computational Linguistics*, pages 1027–1038, Florence, Italy. Association for Computational Linguistics.

Sangwoo Cho, Chen Li, Dong Yu, Hassan Foroosh, and Fei Liu. 2019b. Multi-document summarization with determinantal point processes and contextualized representations. In *Proceedings of the 2nd Workshop on New Frontiers in Summarization*, pages 98–103, Hong Kong, China. Association for Computational Linguistics.

Arman Cohan, Franck Dernoncourt, Doo Soon Kim, Trung Bui, Seokhwan Kim, Walter Chang, and Nazli Goharian. 2018. A discourse-aware attention model for abstractive summarization of long documents. *arXiv preprint arXiv:1804.05685*.

Hoa Trang Dang and Karolina Owczarzak. 2008. Overview of the TAC 2008 update summarization task. In *Proceedings of Text Analysis Conference (TAC)*.

Jacob Devlin, Ming-Wei Chang, Kenton Lee, and Kristina Toutanova. 2018. Bert: Pre-training of deep bidirectional transformers for language understanding. *arXiv preprint arXiv:1810.04805*.

Günes Erkan and Dragomir R. Radev. 2004. LexRank: Graph-based lexical centrality as salience in text summarization. *Journal of Artificial Intelligence Research*.

Alexander Fabbri, Irene Li, Tianwei She, Suyi Li, and Dragomir Radev. 2019. Multi-news: A large-scale multi-document summarization dataset and abstractive hierarchical model. In *Proceedings of the 57th Annual Meeting of the Association for Computational Linguistics*, pages 1074–1084, Florence, Italy. Association for Computational Linguistics.

Kavita Ganesan, ChengXiang Zhai, and Jiawei Han. 2010. Opinosis: A graph-based approach to abstractive summarization of highly redundant opinions. In *Proceedings of the International Conference on Computational Linguistics (COLING)*.

Aria Haghighi and Lucy Vanderwende. 2009. Exploring content models for multi-document summarization. In *Proceedings of human language technologies: The 2009 annual conference of the North American Chapter of the Association for Computational Linguistics*, pages 362–370.

Karl Moritz Hermann, Tomas Kocisky, Edward Grefenstette, Lasse Espeholt, Will Kay, Mustafa Suleyman, and Phil Blunsom. 2015. Teaching machines to read and comprehend. *Advances in neural information processing systems*, 28.

Kai Hong, John Conroy, Benoit Favre, Alex Kulesza, Hui Lin, and Ani Nenkova. 2014. A repository of state of the art and competitive baseline summaries for generic news summarization. In *Proceedings of the Ninth International Conference on Language Resources and Evaluation (LREC'14)*, pages 1608–1616, Reykjavik, Iceland. European Language Resources Association (ELRA).

Hanqi Jin, Tianming Wang, and Xiaojun Wan. 2020. Multi-granularity interaction network for extractive and abstractive multi-document summarization. In *Proceedings of the 58th annual meeting of the association for computational linguistics*, pages 6244–6254.

Alex Kulesza and Ben Taskar. 2012. *Determinantal Point Processes for Machine Learning*. Now Publishers Inc.

Logan Lebanoff, Kaiqiang Song, and Fei Liu. 2018. Adapting the neural encoder-decoder framework from single to multi-document summarization. *arXiv preprint arXiv:1808.06218*.

Mike Lewis, Yinhan Liu, Naman Goyal, Marjan Ghazvininejad, Abdelrahman Mohamed, Omer Levy, Ves Stoyanov, and Luke Zettlemoyer. 2019. Bart: Denoising sequence-to-sequence pre-training for natural language generation, translation, and comprehension. *arXiv preprint arXiv:1910.13461*.

Xinnian Liang, Shuangzhi Wu, Mu Li, and Zhoujun Li. 2021. Improving unsupervised extractive summarization with facet-aware modeling. In *Findings of the Association for Computational Linguistics: ACL-IJCNLP 2021*, pages 1685–1697.

Chin-Yew Lin. 2004. Rouge: A package for automatic evaluation of summaries. In *Text summarization branches out*, pages 74–81.

Hui Lin, Jeff Bilmes, and Shasha Xie. 2009. Graph-based submodular selection for extractive summarization. In *2009 IEEE Workshop on Automatic Speech Recognition & Understanding*, pages 381–386. IEEE.

Jingzhou Liu, Dominic JD Hughes, and Yiming Yang. 2021. Unsupervised extractive text summarization with distance-augmented sentence graphs. In *Proceedings of the 44th International ACM SIGIR Conference on Research and Development in Information Retrieval*, pages 2313–2317.

Peter J. Liu, Mohammad Saleh, Etienne Pot, Ben Goodrich, Ryan Sepassi, Lukasz Kaiser, and Noam M. Shazeer. 2018. Generating wikipedia by summarizing long sequences. *ArXiv*, abs/1801.10198.

Yang Liu and Mirella Lapata. 2019a. Hierarchical transformers for multi-document summarization. In *Proceedings of the 57th Annual Meeting of the Association for Computational Linguistics*, pages 5070–5081, Florence, Italy. Association for Computational Linguistics.

Yang Liu and Mirella Lapata. 2019b. Text summarization with pretrained encoders. *arXiv preprint arXiv:1908.08345*.

Shulei Ma, Zhi-Hong Deng, and Yunlun Yang. 2016. An unsupervised multi-document summarization framework based on neural document model. In *Proceedings of COLING 2016, the 26th International Conference on Computational Linguistics: Technical Papers*, pages 1514–1523.

Rada Mihalcea and Paul Tarau. 2004. Textrank: Bringing order into text. In *Proceedings of the 2004 conference on empirical methods in natural language processing*, pages 404–411.

Ramesh Nallapati, Bowen Zhou, Caglar Gulcehre, Bing Xiang, et al. 2016. Abstractive text summarization using sequence-to-sequence rnns and beyond. *arXiv preprint arXiv:1602.06023*.

Shashi Narayan, Shay B Cohen, and Mirella Lapata. 2018. Don't give me the details, just the summary! topic-aware convolutional neural networks for extreme summarization. *arXiv preprint arXiv:1808.08745*.

Ani Nenkova and Kathleen McKeown. 2011. Automatic summarization. *Foundations and Trends in Information Retrieval*.

Paul Over and James Yen. 2004. An introduction to DUC-2004. *National Institute of Standards and Technology*.

Lawrence Page, Sergey Brin, Rajeev Motwani, and Terry Winograd. 1999. The pagerank citation ranking: Bringing order to the web. Technical report, Stanford InfoLab.

Romain Paulus, Caiming Xiong, and Richard Socher. 2017. A deep reinforced model for abstractive summarization. *arXiv preprint arXiv:1705.04304*.

Maxime Peyrard, Teresa Botschen, and Iryna Gurevych. 2017. Learning to score system summaries for better content selection evaluation. In *Proceedings of the Workshop on New Frontiers in Summarization*, pages 74–84.

Nils Reimers and Iryna Gurevych. 2019. Sentence-bert: Sentence embeddings using siamese bert-networks. In *Proceedings of the 2019 Conference on Empirical Methods in Natural Language Processing*. Association for Computational Linguistics.

Abigail See, Peter J Liu, and Christopher D Manning. 2017. Get to the point: Summarization with pointer-generator networks. *arXiv preprint arXiv:1704.04368*.

Jun Suzuki and Masaaki Nagata. 2017. Cutting-off redundant repeating generations for neural abstractive summarization. In *Proceedings of the 15th Conference of the European Chapter of the Association for Computational Linguistics: Volume 2, Short Papers*, pages 291–297, Valencia, Spain. Association for Computational Linguistics.

Lucy Vanderwende, Hisami Suzuki, Chris Brockett, and Ani Nenkova. 2007. Beyond sumbasic: Task-focused summarization with sentence simplification and lexical expansion. *Information Processing & Management*, 43(6):1606–1618.

Danqing Wang, Pengfei Liu, Yining Zheng, Xipeng Qiu, and Xuanjing Huang. 2020. Heterogeneous graph neural networks for extractive document summarization. In *Proceedings of the 58th Annual Meeting of the Association for Computational Linguistics*, pages 6209–6219, Online. Association for Computational Linguistics.

Wen Xiao, Iz Beltagy, Giuseppe Carenini, and Arman Cohan. 2022. PRIMERA: Pyramid-based masked sentence pre-training for multi-document summarization. In *Proceedings of the 60th Annual Meeting of the Association for Computational Linguistics (Volume 1: Long Papers)*, pages 5245–5263, Dublin, Ireland. Association for Computational Linguistics.

Wen Xiao and Giuseppe Carenini. 2020. Systematically exploring redundancy reduction in summarizing long documents. *arXiv preprint arXiv:2012.00052*.

Jiacheng Xu, Zhe Gan, Yu Cheng, and Jingjing Liu. 2019. Discourse-aware neural extractive text summarization. *arXiv preprint arXiv:1910.14142*.

Haopeng Zhang, Xiao Liu, and Jiawei Zhang. 2022. HEGEL: Hypergraph transformer for long document summarization. In *Proceedings of the 2022 Conference on Empirical Methods in Natural Language Processing*, pages 10167–10176, Abu Dhabi, United Arab Emirates. Association for Computational Linguistics.

Haopeng Zhang, Xiao Liu, and Jiawei Zhang. 2023a. Contrastive hierarchical discourse graph for scientific document summarization. In *Proceedings of the 4th Workshop on Computational Approaches to Discourse (CODI 2023)*, pages 37–47, Toronto, Canada. Association for Computational Linguistics.

Haopeng Zhang, Xiao Liu, and Jiawei Zhang. 2023b. Diffusum: Generation enhanced extractive summarization with diffusion. *arXiv preprint arXiv:2305.01735*.

Haopeng Zhang, Xiao Liu, and Jiawei Zhang. 2023c. Extractive summarization via chatgpt for faithful summary generation. *arXiv preprint arXiv:2304.04193*.

Jingqing Zhang, Yao Zhao, Mohammad Saleh, and Peter Liu. 2020. Pegasus: Pre-training with extracted gap-sentences for abstractive summarization. In *International Conference on Machine Learning*, pages 11328–11339. PMLR.

Hao Zheng and Mirella Lapata. 2019. Sentence centrality revisited for unsupervised summarization. *arXiv preprint arXiv:1906.03508*.

Ming Zhong, Pengfei Liu, Yiran Chen, Danqing Wang, Xipeng Qiu, and Xuanjing Huang. 2020. Extractive summarization as text matching. *arXiv preprint arXiv:2004.08795*.

# Predicting Terms in IS-A Relations with Pre-trained Transformers

**Irina Nikishina**[1], **Polina Chernomorchenko**[2], **Anastasiia Demidova**[3], **Alexander Panchenko**[3,4], **and Chris Biemann**[1]
[1]Universität Hamburg, [2]HSE University,
[3]Skolkovo Institute of Science and Technology, [4]AIRI
irina.nikishina@uni-hamburg.de, pvchernomorchenko@edu.hse.ru,
{anastasiia.demidova,a.panchenko}@skol.tech, chris.biemann@uni-hamburg.de

## Abstract

In this paper, we explore the ability of the generative transformers to predict objects in IS-A (hypo-hypernym) relations. We solve the task for both directions of the relations: we learn to predict hypernyms given the input word and hyponyms, given the input concept and its neighbourhood from the taxonomy. To the best of our knowledge, this is the first paper which provides a comprehensive analysis of transformer-based models for the task of hypernymy extraction. Apart from the standard finetuning of various generative models, we experiment with different input formats and prefixes, zero- and few-shot learning strategies, and generation parameters. Results show that higher performance on both subtasks can be achieved by generative transformers with no additional data (like definitions or lemma names). Such models have phenomenally high abilities at the task given a little training and proper prompts in comparison to specialized rule-based and statistical methods as well as encoder-based transformer models.

## 1 Introduction

Nowadays, pre-trained transofmers including ChatGPT[1] and other transformer-based models with instructions (Ouyang et al., 2022) demonstrate high performance on most NLP tasks (Chowdhery et al., 2022; OpenAI, 2023). However, it is not clear, how well they understand the inner structure of a language and could be applied to purely linguistic tasks, e.g. identification of semantic relations. Those tasks have always been important benchmarks for measuring linguistic capabilities of natural language processing approaches, including neural networks (Jawahar et al., 2019; Rogers et al., 2020). They demonstrate whether the models can comprehend language structure and semantic relations between words: synonymy (Wijesiriwardene et al., 2022), hypernymy (Ravichander et al., 2020), negation (Ettinger, 2020), etc.

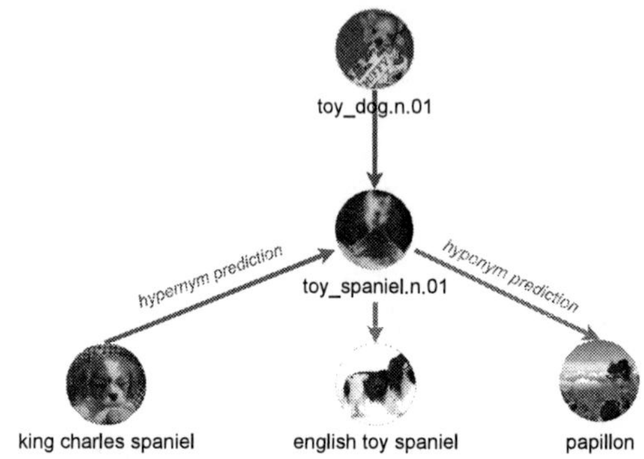


Figure 1: Two formulations of taxonomy enrichment task: attaching new candidates to the existing nodes (red) and generating new candidates at the specified place in the taxonomy (blue).

Applying modern transformers for identifying IS-A relations would allow not only to check the capacities of large language models (LLMs) in linguistics, but also to perform automatic extension of the lexical taxonomic structures with such kinds of relations to alleviate the manual annotation process. Taxonomies play a central role in evaluation tasks, e.g. word-in-context (Armendariz et al., 2020), and are also used for downstream tasks, e.g. (dynamic) entity typing (Del Corro et al., 2015), or for Knowledge Graph Questing Answering (Huang et al., 2019).

There exist several probing experiments for IS-A relation prediction with transformer-based encoder BERT (Devlin et al., 2019; Ettinger, 2020; Hanna and Mareček, 2021). However, to the best of our knowledge, there is no such work on generative transformer models: decoders, e.g. GPT-2 (Radford et al., 2019), or encoder-decoders, e.g. T5 (Raffel et al., 2020).

In this paper, we evaluate generative transformer architectures for two existing Taxonomy Enrichment task formulations (see Figure 1). First, we

[1]`https://openai.com/blog/chatgpt`



*Findings of the Association for Computational Linguistics: IJCNLP-AACL 2023*, pages 134–148
November 1–4, 2023. ©2023 Asian Federation of Natural Language Processing

test zero- and few-shot setups as well as finetuning on the SemEval-2018 Task 9 (Camacho-Collados et al., 2018) dataset on hypernym prediction for English language. We experiment with different prompt formats and the amount of information provided on each hypernym node. Then we evaluate the same models on the hyponym prediction dataset (Nikishina et al., 2022b). Finally, we perform error analysis on the manually selected nodes for hyponym prediction. Thus, we understand the capacities of models for predicting taxonomic relations in both directions.

The main contribution of our work is the first study on using generative transformers for IS-A relationship prediction. We test them in various setups, as it might not be clear, what is the best way to do that: via natural or artificial patterns, few-shot learning or proper fine-tuning, with decoder or encoder-decoder models. We show that prior work based on Hearst (1992) patterns with machine learning classifiers, and encoder-based transformers, are largely outperformed by generative transformers.

Moreover, our approach presents the way for linearization of the context subgraph for using them in LLMs, which can be applied to any task with lexical elements (e.g. synonyms, antonyms, part-of). The methodology may be also generalized to various types of relations available in Knowledge Graphs, such as "capital-of", allowing us to "mine" large pre-trained LMs for new relations.

We also make the code[2] and the models[3] available.

## 2 Related Work

In this section, we overview the task of Taxonomy Enrichment and previous approaches for predicting IS-A relations. We start with a short description of WordNet[4], which is the main data source for most taxonomy-related tasks.

WordNet (Miller, 1995) is a large lexical database of English. Nouns, verbs, adjectives and adverbs are grouped into sets of cognitive synonyms (synsets), each expressing a distinct concept. In this paper, we limit our experiments to nouns represented in 82,115 synsets and 117,798 lemmas. We do not consider other part-of-speech subsets as their hierarchical structure is mostly flat.

Taxonomy Enrichment (Jurgens and Pilehvar, 2016) and Hypernym Discovery (Camacho-Collados et al., 2018) are two main tasks for identifying hypernyms given the input words. The goal of the first task is to attach new words to the correct place in the taxonomy. The second task aims at discovering suitable hypernyms for the input term using a large corpus. Most approaches use static word vector representations like word2vec or fastText (Schlichtkrull and Martínez Alonso, 2016; Bernier-Colborne and Barrière, 2018).

There exist several recent papers on Taxonomy Enrichment that make use of word vector representations and/or large pre-trained language models. For instance, (Nikishina et al., 2022a) present an approach applying numerous of text and graph embeddings as well as their combinations; (Takeoka et al., 2021) solves the same problem, but for the low-resource scenario using BERT-based classifier, while Roller et al. (2018) revise Hearst Patterns for the task. Cho et al. (2020), view taxonomy enrichment as a sequence-to-sequence problem and the authors train an LSTM model on the WordNet data.

## 3 Hypernymy and Hyponymy Prediction

In this section, we introduce two tasks for predicting terms in IS-A relations. We provide formal descriptions for each task and describe the datasets we use for evaluation.

### 3.1 Hypernym Prediction Task

SemEval-2018 Task 9 is the acknowledged benchmark for Hypernym Discovery covering several languages and knowledge domains. Camacho-Collados et al. (2018) define the task as finding the appropriate hypernyms $\{h_1, ..., h_n\}$ for a target input term $t$. At the time of the competition phase, most of the participants of the shared task used Hearst patterns and static word embeddings (Bernier-Colborne and Barrière, 2018; Maldonado and Klubička, 2018; Qiu et al., 2018). A follow-up study (Hanna and Mareček, 2021) analyzes the performance of the BERT model and shows that the encoder-based transformers cannot outperform the state-of-the-art results. To the best of our knowledge, there are no recent studies on large generative transformers like T5 or GPT for this setup.

We use the SemEval-2018 Task 9 (Camacho-Collados et al., 2018) dataset for the hypernym prediction subtask. It consists of a source corpus and input terms with gold hypernyms extracted

[2]https://github.com/orgs/uhh-lt/hypernym-generation

[3]https://huggingface.co/okamifawkes

[4]https://wordnet.princeton.edu

from WordNet (Miller, 1995), Wikidata[5], MultiWiBi (Flati et al., 2016), and Yago (Rebele et al., 2016). In this paper, we focus on the English general domain dataset (subtask 1A), with 3,000 labelled terms (1,500 in both train and test).

### 3.2 Hyponym Prediction Setup

Hyponym prediction (generation) is a less studied lexical semantic task. To the best of our knowledge, there exists only one paper where the authors predict hyponyms at the specific place of the taxonomy (Nikishina et al., 2022b). To solve the task, they combine graph representations with the pretrained BERT model. In this paper, we compare their approach to generative transformers in Section 4.2.

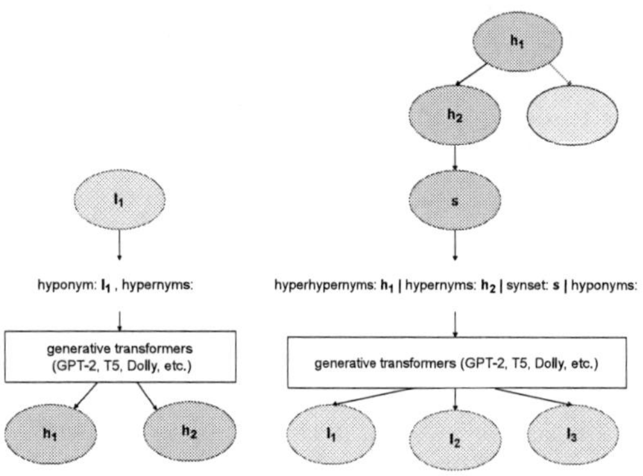


(a) Hypernym prediction (b) Hyponym prediction

Figure 2: Pipelines for predicting IS-A relations for both directions. For hypernym prediction we use the input word in the specific prompt structure, while for the hyponym prediction we linearize the graph structure to feed it to the model as textual input.

The task of Hyponym Prediction is formulated as following. Given subgraph $S = (V, E)$ from a taxonomy $T$, and a leaf node $v_{leaf} \in V$, the goal is to predict new leaves $l_1, ..., l_n$, which relate to $v_{leaf}$ as hyponyms. Edges $E$ denote the closest (hop= 2) IS-A relations between $v_{leaf}$: its hypernyms and hyperhypernyms. In this task formulation, we provide local context, as this information can be used for disambiguation of the synset that can have different meanings, e.g. *"table"* or *"rock"*. Each synset represents only one meaning: if we anticipated children of all meanings at the same time, we would not be able to differentiate, which hyponyms belong to which meanings.

We experiment with following setups: zero-shot, few-shot and model finetuning. We describe the input patterns for zero- and few-shot learning as well as parameters used at the generation step. In this paper, we limit the experiments to the leaf nodes only, as masking and deleting nodes in the middle of the graph needs additional careful study of the graph in order to avoid data leakage. That is why we leave other cases for further experiments.

For this task, we use dataset from Nikishina et al. (2022b). The authors randomly select 1,000 nodes out of 15,646 nodes which children are leaves, i.e., the children do not have hyponyms of their own. They also take into consideration the distance length from the root to the leaf, which should be more than 5 hops. This allows them to exclude the case of predicting very abstract or broad concepts. For each "parental" hypernym all its hyponyms (leaves) were replaced by a single "masked" node and all of the hyponyms are considered as the true answer. All in all, there are 4,376 masked leaves to predict for 1000 synsets.

However, the automatic way of the construction of the CHSP dataset results in occurrence of narrow-field words in the dataset (e.g. "expurgation", "butcherbird", "dot matrix printer"), which hyponyms are too specific for the model to predict. On the other hand, the structure of the WordNet might differ from the pragmatic usage of words in the discourse, so the model would have a different encoded linguistic structure. For instance, according to WordNet, "rottweiler.n.01" is a "shepherd_dog.n.01", which is a "working_dog.n.01" which is a "dog.n.01". At the same time, it is common knowledge that "rottweiler is a dog", therefore, we might expect that models predict "dog" which would not be considered as the correct answer.

To analyse the models performance on common knowledge data, we manually select 22 nodes with hyponyms from the general domain in the English WordNet. Our main guidelines are: (i) to avoid too abstract or general concepts; (ii) to selects ones with numerous instances, subtypes or subclasses, (iii) all the descendants from any level of the chosen node are considered as correct. We are also aware that this dataset is more subjective, however, it is created for additional analysis and not to replace the original dataset. As a result, the selected synsets on average are 7 hops away from the root node and the longest path to a leaf is on average 3. The full list of concepts can be found in Appendix A in Table 7. In this paper, we limit the experiments to the leaf nodes only, as masking and deleting nodes

[5] https://www.wikidata.org

| Model | Hypernym Prediction Average | Hypernym Prediction Best | Hyponym Prediction Average | Hyponym Prediction Best |
|---|---|---|---|---|
| | Zero-shot | | | |
| GPT-2-large | 0.0351±0.0345 | 0.0708 | 0.2677±0.016 | 0.5280 |
| OPT-1.3b | 0.0568±0.0563 | 0.1140 | **0.3081±0.013** | **0.5310** |
| T5-large | **0.0602±0.0591** | **0.1215** | 0.1168±0.001 | 0.1690 |
| | Few-shot | | | |
| GPT-2-large | **0.0610±0.0595** | **0.1234** | 0.4557±0.005 | 0.5940 |
| OPT-1.3b | 0.0585±0.0577 | 0.1177 | **0.4623±0.005** | **0.6030** |
| T5-large | 0.0058±0.0013 | 0.0161 | 0.1144±0.001 | 0.1920 |

Table 1: MRR scores for pre-trained models on zero-shot and few-shot setups for predicting hypernyms and hyponyms. *Average* is average MRR on all 26 Hearst patterns, *Best* denotes the best MRR score.

in the middle of the graph needs additional careful study of the graph in order to avoid data leakage.

## 4 Methodology

The current section presents methodology for zero- and few-shot experiments and the fine-tuning process. It also discusses possible input formats as well as models used in each setup. Figure 2 depicts the strategy for both tasks. The main idea for the hyponym prediction is to transform the input subgraph to the linear form so it can be processed by large language models. For the hypernym prediction task, we do not have a subgraph as input, that is why we provide the input word only. We use the transformers library (Wolf et al., 2020) for all experiments as well as pre-trained models from the same source.

Considering potential data leakage, one may raise a concern about the WordNet being exposed in the LLMs during their pre-training phase. To the best of our knowledge, pre-trained transformers were not trained on the IS-A relationship tasks and WordNet, however, it is quite clear that the model has already seen most of the words from WordNet, which we assume might help to understand the meaning of the input word while predicting hypernyms or retain relevant words from the memory when predicting hyponyms.

### 4.1 Zero- and Few-shot Learning

To conduct zero-shot experiments with pre-trained generative transformers, we utilize numerous Hearst patterns (14 for hypernym prediction and 26 patterns for hyponym prediction) that naturally precede the generation of hyponyms from (Hanna and Mareček, 2021; Hearst, 1992). We evaluate both decoder (*GPT* (Radford et al., 2019), *OPT* (Zhang et al., 2022)), and encoder-decoder (*T5* (Raffel et al., 2020)) architectures. We use top-k sampling ($k = 20$), and restrict the generation length to up to 10 new tokens in addition to the input pattern. The list of the patterns used can be seen in Tables 8 and 9 (as well as the results for each pattern). Additionally, we sample the results multiple times and sort the answers according to their frequency. As a postprocessing step, we lemmatize the output and keep only nouns.

The next step of our experiments is few-shot learning: we design longer prompts to provide the models with more examples. Each of the extended input contains three patterns completed with the correct answers; examples are separated by a line break. Then the prompt is concatenated with a pattern for a test hypernym node.

### 4.2 Fine-tuning Model

Since our main goal is to evaluate the ability of generative models to acquire semantic relationships, we utilize commonly known models such as GPT2 and T5. We finetune them on different versions of the input data: default and processed, described below. We also present the results for bigger recent architectures like Flan-T5 (Chung et al., 2022), GPT-J (Wang and Komatsuzaki, 2021) and Dolly (Conover et al., 2023) to define further result boundaries for LLMs.

To conduct several experiments with model fine-tuning, we do not use patterns from the previous step. From the linguistic perspective, by forcing model to predict hyponyms or hypernyms embodied in a certain context (e.g. *"My favourite [PARENT] is [CHILD]."*), we do not teach it to solve a new task. Instead, we make it guess which specific words should be used. From the taxonomy perspective, such patterns do not allow to insert additional information from the taxonomy for the hyponymy

| Method | MAP | MRR | Pr@1 | Pr@2 | Pr@5 | Pr@10 |
|---|---|---|---|---|---|---|
| word2vec $k$-NN, $k = 20$ | 0.0050 | 0.0210 | 0.0010 | 0.0070 | 0.0109 | 0.0109 |
| fastText $k$-NN, $k = 20$ | 0.0600 | 0.0190 | 0.0000 | 0.0030 | 0.0090 | 0.0090 |
| GloVe $k$-NN, $k = 20$ | 0.0100 | 0.0370 | 0.0000 | 0.0085 | 0.0212 | 0.0208 |
| WebIsaDB (top-20) (Seitner et al., 2016) | 0.0222 | 0.0609 | 0.0639 | 0.0460 | 0.0435 | 0.0354 |
| TAXIDB (top-20) (Panchenko et al., 2016) | 0.0129 | 0.0398 | 0.0425 | 0.0300 | 0.0275 | 0.0198 |
| CHSP (Nikishina et al., 2022b) | - | 0.0215 | 0.0228 | 0.0160 | - | 0.0074 |
| GPT-2 | 0.0390 | 0.1720 | 0.1100 | 0.1040 | 0.0910 | 0.0740 |
| GPT-2 (input & output proc.) | 0.0620 | 0.2320 | 0.1950 | 0.1650 | 0.1190 | 0.0910 |
| T5 | 0.0480 | 0.1889 | 0.1230 | 0.1150 | 0.0962 | 0.0764 |
| T5 (input & output proc.) | 0.0500 | 0.1710 | 0.1130 | 0.1070 | 0.0890 | 0.0690 |
| Flan-T5 | 0.0330 | 0.1330 | 0.0870 | 0.0750 | 0.0630 | 0.0510 |
| Flan-T5 (input & output proc.) | 0.0390 | 0.1410 | 0.0940 | 0.0860 | 0.0710 | 0.0570 |
| GPT-J 8-bit LoRa | 0.1080 | 0.3230 | 0.2250 | 0.1970 | 0.1620 | **0.1230** |
| Dolly 8-bit LoRa | **0.1110** | **0.3240** | **0.2260** | **0.2020** | **0.1640** | 0.1220 |

Table 2: Results for Hyponym Prediction after fine-tuning on CHSP dataset (Nikishina et al., 2022b).

prediction task.

We design the input formats as (1) for hypernym prediction and (2) for hyponym prediction.

(1) hyponym: $l_i$, hypernyms: $h_{1-k}$.

Here we have only an input word $l_i$, with no additional context or definition and expect the model to predict a list of possible hypernyms $h_{1-k}$.

(2) hyperhypernyms: $h_{1-n}$ | hypernyms: $h_{1-m}$ | synset: $s$ | hyponyms: $l_{1-k}$.

In this example, $h_{1-n}$ and $h_{1-m}$ refer to the synset name lists of a certain level, $s$ denotes the target "parental" synset name, and $l_{1-k}$ refers to the output list of lemmas collected from all the descendants of the "parental" synset.

The input & output processed version of the dataset is created with respect to the fact that the output list of correct predictions (both hypernyms and hyponyms) does not have a specific order. Therefore, we can add permutations to the output of the dataset. For each hypernym node, we select 10 random hyponyms and repeat this $n$ times, where $n$ is the total number of hyponyms. Thus, we build a larger dataset of 170,000 examples. As for the input extension, we add three additional examples before the input data. As can be later seen from Tables 2, 3, and 4, such data augmentation improves the results significantly for some models.

All models are trained for three epochs with a batch size of 16. The results are collected as follows: we generate 50 sequences, setting the maximum number of new tokens to 15 and the top-k sampling value to 20. Then we split the output n-grams with a comma (as all models correctly learn the expected output format) and sort the results by frequency. Examples of input and output data are presented in Table 10 in Appendix A.

### 4.3 Baselines

To compare with other approaches, we implement several baselines: Hearst (1992) patterns, Contextualized Hidden State Projection Method (Nikishina et al., 2022b), which is based on BERT, and $k$-Nearest Neighbours ($k = 20$) on three different embeddings: word2vec (Mikolov et al., 2013), fastText (Bojanowski et al., 2017), and GloVe (Pennington et al., 2014). We also fine-tune recent large architectures like GPT-J (Wang and Komatsuzaki, 2021) and Dolly (Conover et al., 2023) to understand further capacities of large language models. However, because of the limitation of computational resources, we finetune Dolly and GPT-J using low-rank adaptation for language models and restrict the model to the 8-bit format. We also ask ChatGPT to list possible hyponyms, using its web interface[6] on the common knowledge dataset for hyponym prediction.

## 5 Experiments

In this section we describe the evaluations metrics, present the result for zero-shot, few-shot and finetuning experiments, and compare performance with different data inputs. We also perform the error analysis for both tasks and explain why certain words or phrases are easier or harder to predict.

[6] Version from 13.04.2023

| Method | MAP | MRR | Pr@1 | Pr@2 | P@5 | Pr@10 |
|---|---|---|---|---|---|---|
| word2vec $k$-NN, $k = 20$ | 0.0400 | 0.1900 | 0.0454 | 0.0681 | 0.1090 | 0.1227 |
| fastText $k$-NN, $k = 20$ | 0.0200 | 0.0700 | 0.0000 | 0.0227 | 0.0363 | 0.0500 |
| GloVe $k$-NN, $k = 20$ | 0.0500 | 0.1900 | 0.0000 | 0.0681 | 0.1363 | 0.1727 |
| WebIsaDB (top-20) (Seitner et al., 2016) | 0.2837 | 0.5834 | 0.4500 | 0.5000 | 0.4300 | 0.3600 |
| TAXIDB (top-20) (Panchenko et al., 2016) | 0.2240 | 0.4917 | 0.4000 | 0.4250 | 0.3600 | 0.2800 |
| CHSP (Nikishina et al., 2022b) | 0.0818 | 0.3377 | 0.3182 | 0.2045 | 0.0818 | 0.0500 |
| GPT-2-large | 0.1270 | 0.6460 | 0.5000 | 0.5000 | 0.4730 | 0.4500 |
| GPT-2-large (input & output proc.) | 0.3030 | 0.7320 | 0.6360 | 0.6820 | 0.6450 | 0.5820 |
| T5-large | 0.1460 | 0.8480 | 0.7730 | 0.6590 | 0.6360 | 0.5360 |
| T5-large (input & output proc.) | 0.1970 | 0.8200 | 0.6820 | 0.7050 | 0.6180 | 0.5230 |
| Flan-T5-large | 0.1170 | 0.7220 | 0.5910 | 0.6360 | 0.4910 | 0.4000 |
| Flan-T5-large (i&o) | 0.1990 | 0.7720 | 0.6820 | 0.6590 | 0.5820 | 0.5450 |
| GPT-J 8-bit LoRa | 0.1780 | 0.9120 | **0.8640** | 0.7500 | 0.6360 | 0.5500 |
| Dolly 8-bit LoRa | 0.1830 | **0.9320** | **0.8640** | **0.8410** | **0.7000** | **0.5680** |
| ChatGPT | **0.3424** | 0.7150 | 0.6363 | 0.6363 | 0.6000 | 0.5091 |

Table 3: Fine-tuning results for the small common knowledge dataset for Hyponym Prediction.

| Method | MAP | MRR | Pr@5 |
|---|---|---|---|
| Bernier-Colborne and Barrière (2018) | 19.78 | 36.10 | 19.03 |
| MSCG-SANITY | 11.83 | 24.79 | 11.60 |
| Hanna and Mareček (2021) | 20.17 | 12.65 | 10.49 |
| GPT-2-large | 13.89 | 37.56 | 11.95 |
| GPT-2-large (input & output proc.) | 19.70 | 35.14 | 19.18 |
| T5-large | **25.68** | 42.40 | **23.03** |
| T5-large (input & output proc.) | 18.67 | 31.19 | 17.66 |
| Flan-T5 | 22.97 | **45.22** | 21.74 |
| Flan-T5 (input & output proc.) | 23.07 | 42.03 | 22.19 |
| GPT-J-6B 8-bit | 19.93 | 38.75 | 18.45 |
| Dolly LoRa 8-bit | 18.54 | 37.89 | 17.21 |

Table 4: Results for Hypernym Prediction on SemEval-2018 Task 9 subtask 1A: English (Camacho-Collados et al., 2018). Transformer-based models are compared against the top-2 participant results. Standard deviation for both *GPT-2-large* and *T5* models is not more than $\pm 0.001$ on 5 runs.

### 5.1 Evaluation Metrics

Generated candidates are compared against the true hypernyms or hyponyms from the taxonomy. We utilize several metrics for both tasks. First, we apply Precision@$k$ (Pr@$k$) metric. Pr@$k$ is the ratio of the correct answers measured at the fixed rank $k$. It allows to understand how many correct answers present in the top-$k$ results. Another metric used for retrieval tasks is Mean Reciprocal Rank (MRR). This metric is more relaxed as it is takes into account the multiplicative inverse of the rank of the first correct answer, but does not reflect coverage. Therefore, we also use the Mean Average Precision (MAP) score which takes into account the total number of gold answers and their rank in the candidate list.

### 5.2 Discussion of the Results

Precision scores for all tested models in zero-shot setup are presented in Table 1. The second and the fourth columns demonstrate the average scores for all 26 patterns for hyponym prediction and 15 options for hypernym one, whereas the third and the fifth show the best results on both datasets. As one can see, no pattern in the zero-shot setting yields acceptable results for hypernymy prediction, while for the hyponym prediction, the best results are shown by *"other [PARENT] such as [CHILD]"*, which is has the highest average MRR score of 0.3.

As it can be seen from Table 1, the few-shot hyponym prediction scores are improved over the zero-shot results. For this task, the best score is reached with the prompt *"I know such types of [PARENT] as"*. It is quite unexpected, since it is not in the top-5 of the best prompts according to average precision scores for the zero-shot setup.

Considering the hypernym prediction few-shot setup, we achieve the best results with the pattern *"[CHILD] is a type of [PARENT]"*. However, the results are increased only with GPT-2. Other models, in their turn, do not produce significantly improved scores. From the T5 model, we obtain lower results over the zero-shot setup. Also, for OPT-1.3b model, almost identical results were received. Thus, as we show later, zero- and few-shot setups lag far behind the finetuning experiments. We explain the low scores for the results by task complexity and unawareness of the WordNet structure by the model.

The fine-tuning results for the Hypernym Prediction task are displayed in Table 4. Tables 2 and

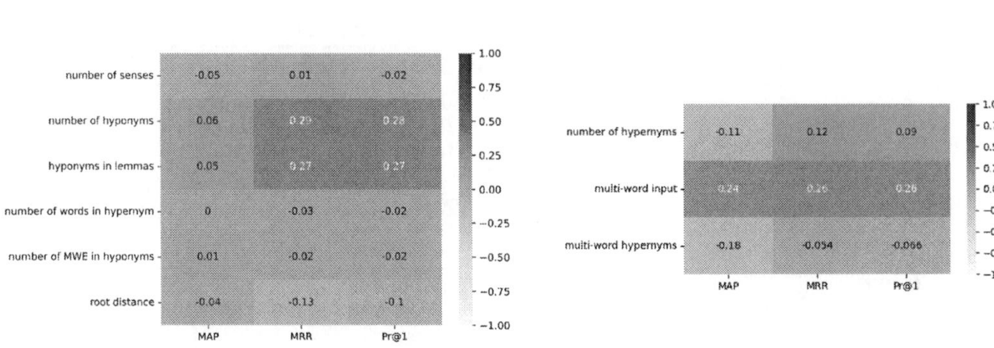


(a) For hyponym prediction (number of senses, number of children, number of children in lemmas, number of words in synset, root distance)

(b) For hypernym prediction (number of hypernyms, multi-word input, multi-word hypernyms)

Figure 3: Pearson correlation scores for the data characteristics of the input and output against MAP, MRR and Pr@1 scores. The colour denotes the correlation strength: the darker the colour is, the stronger the correlation.

3 denote the results on CHSP and small common knowledge datasets, respectively. As we can see, the best performing models are different for two tasks. Interestingly, the results for GPT-J and Dolly on the Hypernym Prediction dataset are not much higher (or even lower) than smaller and older models like GPT-2 and T5. Moreover, they perform on par with the best approaches from SemEval-2018 Task 9. At the same time, both GPT-J and Dolly demonstrate the best performance on the Hyponym Prediction datasets. In comparison to the baselines and previous approaches with transformer encoders, we can see that generative transformers outperform them by a large margin on both datasets. As for ChatGPT, it demonstrates very high results on the small hyponym prediction dataset, however, we cannot compare it with other models directly, as it is used in the zero-shot setup and not finetuned for the task.

When comparing decoders and encoder-decoder architectures, we also see controversial results. On the CHSP dataset, decoders perform better, while the second-best results for the common knowledge dataset are achieved by T5 and Flan-T5. Moreover, those models also perform better for hypernym prediction, outperforming GPT-J and Dolly. By looking at the predictions generated by decoder and encoder-decoder models, we discover that *GPT*-based approaches predict fewer candidates, whereas the answers of *T5*-like models are longer. This explains the higher results for $Pr@1$ and $Pr@2$ of both *GPT*-based approaches and the lower score of *T5-large* on $Pr@10$. Examples are presented in Table 11 in Appendix A.

Another observation is that very high scores are achieved by the same models on the common knowledge dataset in comparison to the automatically constructed CSHP dataset. Even though we cannot draw any conclusion from their comparison, as the datasets are of different size, we still can see that common domain words are easy to predict, as they come numerous descendants and relaxed evaluation setup (all descendants are considered to be the correct answer).

### 5.3 Error Analysis

In order to understand the main difficulties of the models while solving both tasks, we perform both quantitative and manual error analysis.

As for hypernym prediction, we first calculate the scores for entities and concepts separately, as it was done in (Camacho-Collados et al., 2018). The results are displayed in Table 5. We can see that entities are easier to predict than concepts across all models. Camacho-Collados et al. (2018) argue that entities are specific instances of concepts, which are easier to comprehend compared to abstract ideas or categories. As we can see from the data, entities that contain frequently occurring hypernyms like "person" and "city" are easier to guess and to memorize for the models.

We also analyse which words are easier / more difficult to find hyponyms for, even though there is not such word types split in the dataset for the hyponym prediction task. In order to do that, we select top-10 input words according to the MAP and Pr@5 metrics for different models to check, whether there are any common linguistic features. Table 8 demonstrates the top-10 words for the best-performing models. From the obtained lists we can conclude that high MAP scores are achieved for synsets with a small number of hyponyms (often

| Method | MAP | MRR | Pr@5 |
|---|---|---|---|
| | Entities | | |
| Bernier-Colborne and Barrière (2018) | 29.21 | 51.82 | 27.74 |
| MSCG-SANITY | 17.72 | 38.85 | 16.91 |
| GPT-2-large | 25.26 | 46.75 | 23.82 |
| T5-large | **33.76** | <u>62.35</u> | **32.29** |
| Flan-T5 | 29.82 | **62.75** | 27.71 |
| GPT-J-6B 8-bit | <u>32.09</u> | 60.19 | <u>29.66</u> |
| Dolly LoRa 8-bit | 28.04 | 57.00 | 25.79 |
| | Concepts | | |
| Bernier-Colborne and Barrière (2018) | 16.08 | 30.04 | 15.41 |
| MSCG-SANITY | 09.36 | 18.90 | 09.38 |
| GPT-2-large | 15.61 | 28.65 | 15.12 |
| T5-large | **20.71** | **38.77** | **20.07** |
| Flan-T5 | <u>19.68</u> | <u>37.10</u> | <u>18.73</u> |
| GPT-J-6B 8-bit | 14.83 | 29.76 | 13.74 |
| Dolly LoRa 8-bit | 14.55 | 29.87 | 13.61 |

Table 5: Results for Hypernym Prediction on SemEval-2018 Task 9 with Entity and Concept splits.

including words from the synset, for example, the only hyponym of the synset "mousse" is "chocolate mousse"), whereas high Pr@5 scores are achieved for more frequent and general concepts. Then we also calculate the average distance from the top-100 and bottom-100 words to the root word. According to our hypothesis, more general (common) words achieve larger scores than very specific ones. The results confirm that the distance to the root for the top-100 words is on average smaller than for bottom-100 (6.65 hops against 7.82 hops).

We also compute some statistical tests in order to understand the main features of input words or the predicted ones that influence the score. We consider the following features for hyponym prediction: input word ambiguity (in how many other senses this word appears in taxonomy), number of words in the input (is input multi-word expression or not), amount of multi-word expressions in hyponyms, number of hyponyms in nodes, number of hyponym in lemmas (one hyponym node can have different lemma names), distance from the root in hops. For hypernym prediction, we consider only the number of hypernyms to predict, multi-word input and multi-word hypernyms output. We cannot use the same features as for hyponym prediction, as the hypernym prediction data is not related to WordNet. Then we calculate the correlation between the listed features with the average Pr@1, MAP and MRR for all fine-tuned models. We display the result correlation matrices in Figure 3. It is calculated with *pandas* (McKinney et al., 2010); figures are generated using *matplotlib* (Hunter, 2007).

The obtained results indicate that most of our hypotheses have not been confirmed for hyponym prediction, see 3b. A weak positive correlation (0.29) is observed only for number of hyponyms and Pr@1 and number of hyponyms and MRR (0.29). We also see a very weak negative correlation of MRR score and root distance, which is -0.13. Other correlation scores do not exceed 0.1. As for hypernym prediction task, we received a weak positive correlation for multi-word input factor among all scores (0.24 and 0.26). Moreover, we observed a very weak negative effect of the number of hypernyms (-0.11) and multi-word hypernyms (-0.18) on the MAP score. Also, attribute the number of hypernyms has a very weak positive influence on the MRR and Pr@1, which are around 0.1. No other correlation scores surpass 0.1.

As for hypernym prediction correlation scores, we can see a weak correlation between the number of input words and MAP, MRR and Pr@1 metrics, see 3b. We assume that having more words in the predicted hypernym can provide additional examples for the training process, potentially leading to more accurate predictions. Additionally, multi-word input can provide more contextual information and connections between different parts of a phrase, which can help to predict hypernyms.

## 6 Conclusion

In this paper, we explore the practical utility of generative transformer-based models for hyponym and hypernym prediction. We show that promising results can be obtained in both tasks without any additional data, like word definitions or corpora with input term occurrences. Medium-size decoders, and encoder-decoder models yield amazing results after a few epochs of fine-tuning, outperforming other previous baselines by a large margin.

We notice that the fine-tuned sequence-to-sequence outputs contain more plausible candidates, whereas decoders generate fewer candidates with higher quality. Moreover, we cannot conclude which model is the best for both tasks, as the result differ across different datasets. Error analysis of the results shows that there are no specific features like number of senses of the input word in WordNet or number of words to predict that are difficult for the model. Therefore, we assume that generative transformer models demonstrate decent knowledge of IS-A relationships and could be further used for the taxonomy enrichment applications.

| Top-10 words | True hyponyms | Predicted hyponyms |
|---|---|---|
| mousse | chocolate mousse | chocolate mousse, lemon mousse, coffee mousse |
| bull | bullock | bulldog, stud, bullock |
| eclipse | partial eclipse, lunar eclipse, solar eclipse | solar eclipse, lunar eclipse, transit |
| trace | footprint | footprint, trail, track |
| wick | candlewick | candlewick, taper, wax wick |
| learning disorder | dyscalculia, dyslexia, dysgraphia | dyslexia, dysgraphia, dyscalculia |
| nitrite | sodium nitrite | sodium nitrite, nitroglycerin, nitrocellulose |
| reproductive system | male reproductive system, female reproductive system | male reproductive system, sexual system, female reproductive system |
| retinopathy | diabetic retinopathy | diabetic retinopathy, macular degeneration, age-related macular degeneration |
| eclair | chocolate eclair | mille-feuille, chocolate eclair, vanilla eclair |

Table 6: Top-10 synsets with the true hyponyms (at most 3) and predictions (at most 3) according to MAP score.

As the outcome of our research, we also notice that large generative models can not only predict next words (do language modelling), conditioned to some input, but also capture relations between words. Our research further confirms the utility of methodology where information extraction is not directly done on text corpora but on an LLM as a proxy. This new paradigm is useful for several reasons: there is no need to access the original corpus which may be huge and inaccessible, it also allows for certain generalisations required for mining of relations of rare lexical items, and it does not require an explicitly encoded lexical database like WordNet/BabelNet. Our work shows that the very same information may be more compactly stored in the weight of a neural network and explicitly retrieved if needed. This may provide additional computational gain as storage and accessing of large resources like BabelNet featuring millions of nodes and hundreds of millions of relations (hypernyms) between them may be not practical.

As future work, we plan to work with other subtasks for adding new words into taxonomies: insertion of additional nodes in the middle of the graph, crossing two nodes, moving nodes, etc. We also want to solve the tasks for multiple languages using multilingual models and adapters.

## Limitations

We find the main limitation of our work as follows:

- We expect that it is possible to further push quality reported in our work if larger versions of large pre-trained transformers are used, such as T5-3b and T5-11b, as it was the case for multiple other tasks. However, the general trend shall be clear from our experiments.
- We did not test multilingual setting of our approach, which is possible if multilingual version of sequence-to-sequence models are used, such as mT5 or mBERT. This is an important additional experiment to further validation of the method explored in our work.
- Nowadays, dozens of large pre-trained generative models exist and we report results only on a few of them. It may be that, some other base models used could further push the results. Our goal however was to show an example how similar models and not perform and exhaustive search of all models.

## Ethics Statement

We use in our work large neural models, such as T5, pre-trained on real texts including user-generated content. While authors of the models made an effort to filter obviously toxic or biased content, the model itself still can contain certain biases and as a consequence outputs of our methods may render such biases. Methodologically it is however straighforward to apply our techniques on other pre-trained models which were debiased in a required way. Otherwise, we do not see any other ethical concern in our work to the best of our knowledge.


## Acknowledgements

This work was supported by the DFG through the project "ACQuA: Answering Comparative Questions with Arguments" (grants BI 1544/7- 1 and HA 5851/2- 1) as part of the priority program "RATIO: Robust Argumentation Machines" (SPP 1999).

## References

Carlos Santos Armendariz, Matthew Purver, Senja Pollak, Nikola Ljubešić, Matej Ulčar, Ivan Vulić, and Mohammad Taher Pilehvar. 2020. SemEval-2020 task 3: Graded word similarity in context. In *Proceedings of the Fourteenth Workshop on Semantic Evaluation*, pages 36–49, Barcelona (online). International Committee for Computational Linguistics.

Gabriel Bernier-Colborne and Caroline Barrière. 2018. CRIM at SemEval-2018 task 9: A hybrid approach to hypernym discovery. In *Proceedings of the 12th International Workshop on Semantic Evaluation*, pages 725–731, New Orleans, Louisiana. Association for Computational Linguistics.

Piotr Bojanowski, Edouard Grave, Armand Joulin, and Tomas Mikolov. 2017. Enriching word vectors with subword information. *Transactions of the Association for Computational Linguistics*, 5:135–146.

Jose Camacho-Collados, Claudio Delli Bovi, Luis Espinosa-Anke, Sergio Oramas, Tommaso Pasini, Enrico Santus, Vered Shwartz, Roberto Navigli, and Horacio Saggion. 2018. SemEval-2018 task 9: Hypernym discovery. In *Proceedings of the 12th International Workshop on Semantic Evaluation*, pages 712–724, New Orleans, Louisiana. Association for Computational Linguistics.

Yejin Cho, Juan Diego Rodriguez, Yifan Gao, and Katrin Erk. 2020. Leveraging WordNet paths for neural hypernym prediction. In *Proceedings of the 28th International Conference on Computational Linguistics*, pages 3007–3018, Barcelona, Spain (Online). International Committee on Computational Linguistics.

Aakanksha Chowdhery, Sharan Narang, Jacob Devlin, et al. 2022. PaLM: Scaling language modeling with pathways. *CoRR*, abs/2204.02311.

Hyung Won Chung, Le Hou, Shayne Longpre, Barret Zoph, Yi Tay, William Fedus, Eric Li, Xuezhi Wang, Mostafa Dehghani, Siddhartha Brahma, Albert Webson, Shixiang Shane Gu, Zhuyun Dai, Mirac Suzgun, Xinyun Chen, Aakanksha Chowdhery, Sharan Narang, Gaurav Mishra, Adams Yu, Vincent Y. Zhao, Yanping Huang, Andrew M. Dai, Hongkun Yu, Slav Petrov, Ed H. Chi, Jeff Dean, Jacob Devlin, Adam Roberts, Denny Zhou, Quoc V. Le, and Jason Wei. 2022. Scaling instruction-finetuned language models. *CoRR*, abs/2210.11416.

Mike Conover, Matt Hayes, Ankit Mathur, Xiangrui Meng, Jianwei Xie, Jun Wan, Sam Shah, Ali Ghodsi, Patrick Wendell, Zaharia Matei, and Reynold Xin. 2023. Free Dolly: Introducing the World's First Truly Open Instruction-Tuned LLM. `https://www.databricks.com/blog/2023/04/12/dolly-first-open-commercially-viable-instruction-tuned-llm`.

Luciano Del Corro, Abdalghani Abujabal, Rainer Gemulla, and Gerhard Weikum. 2015. FINET: Context-aware fine-grained named entity typing. In *Proceedings of the 2015 Conference on Empirical Methods in Natural Language Processing*, pages 868–878, Lisbon, Portugal. Association for Computational Linguistics.

Jacob Devlin, Ming-Wei Chang, Kenton Lee, and Kristina Toutanova. 2019. BERT: Pre-training of deep bidirectional transformers for language understanding. In *Proceedings of the 2019 Conference of the North American Chapter of the Association for Computational Linguistics: Human Language Technologies, Volume 1 (Long and Short Papers)*, pages 4171–4186, Minneapolis, Minnesota. Association for Computational Linguistics.

Allyson Ettinger. 2020. What BERT is not: Lessons from a new suite of psycholinguistic diagnostics for language models. *Transactions of the Association for Computational Linguistics*, 8:34–48.

Tiziano Flati, Daniele Vannella, Tommaso Pasini, and Roberto Navigli. 2016. MultiWiBi: The multilingual Wikipedia bitaxonomy project. *Artificial Intelligence*, 241:66–102.

Michael Hanna and David Mareček. 2021. Analyzing BERT's knowledge of hypernymy via prompting. In *Proceedings of the Fourth BlackboxNLP Workshop on Analyzing and Interpreting Neural Networks for NLP*, pages 275–282, Punta Cana, Dominican Republic. Association for Computational Linguistics.

Marti A. Hearst. 1992. Automatic acquisition of hyponyms from large text corpora. In *14th International Conference on Computational Linguistics, COLING*, pages 539–545, Nantes, France.

Xiao Huang, Jingyuan Zhang, Dingcheng Li, and Ping Li. 2019. Knowledge graph embedding based question answering. In *Proceedings of the Twelfth ACM International Conference on Web Search and Data Mining*, WSDM '19, page 105–113, New York, NY, USA. Association for Computing Machinery.

J. D. Hunter. 2007. Matplotlib: A 2d graphics environment. *Computing in Science & Engineering*, 9(3):90–95.

Ganesh Jawahar, Benoît Sagot, and Djamé Seddah. 2019. What does BERT learn about the structure of language? In *Proceedings of the 57th Annual Meeting of the Association for Computational Linguistics*, pages 3651–3657, Florence, Italy. Association for Computational Linguistics.

David Jurgens and Mohammad Taher Pilehvar. 2016. SemEval-2016 task 14: Semantic taxonomy enrichment. In *Proceedings of the 10th International Workshop on Semantic Evaluation (SemEval-2016)*, pages 1092–1102, San Diego, California. Association for Computational Linguistics.

Alfredo Maldonado and Filip Klubička. 2018. ADAPT at SemEval-2018 task 9: Skip-gram word embeddings for unsupervised hypernym discovery in specialised corpora. In *Proceedings of the 12th International Workshop on Semantic Evaluation*, pages 924–927, New Orleans, Louisiana. Association for Computational Linguistics.

Wes McKinney et al. 2010. Data structures for statistical computing in python. In *Proceedings of the 9th Python in Science Conference*, volume 445, pages 51–56. Austin, TX.

Tomás Mikolov, Ilya Sutskever, Kai Chen, Gregory S. Corrado, and Jeffrey Dean. 2013. Distributed representations of words and phrases and their compositionality. In *Advances in Neural Information Processing Systems 26: 27th Annual Conference on Neural Information Processing Systems 2013. Proceedings of a meeting held, 2013, Lake Tahoe, Nevada, United States*, pages 3111–3119.

George A. Miller. 1995. WordNet: A lexical database for English. *Commun. ACM*, 38(11):39–41.

Irina Nikishina, Mikhail Tikhomirov, Varvara Logacheva, Yuriy Nazarov, Alexander Panchenko, and Natalia V. Loukachevitch. 2022a. Taxonomy enrichment with text and graph vector representations. *Semantic Web*, 13(3):441–475.

Irina Nikishina, Alsu Vakhitova, Elena Tutubalina, and Alexander Panchenko. 2022b. Cross-modal contextualized hidden state projection method for expanding of taxonomic graphs. In *Proceedings of TextGraphs-16: Graph-based Methods for Natural Language Processing*, pages 11–24, Gyeongju, Republic of Korea. Association for Computational Linguistics.

OpenAI. 2023. GPT-4 technical report. *CoRR*, abs/2303.08774.

Long Ouyang, Jeff Wu, Xu Jiang, Diogo Almeida, Carroll L. Wainwright, Pamela Mishkin, Chong Zhang, Sandhini Agarwal, Katarina Slama, Alex Ray, John Schulman, Jacob Hilton, Fraser Kelton, Luke Miller, Maddie Simens, Amanda Askell, Peter Welinder, Paul F. Christiano, Jan Leike, and Ryan Lowe. 2022. Training language models to follow instructions with human feedback. *CoRR*, abs/2203.02155.

Alexander Panchenko, Stefano Faralli, Eugen Ruppert, Steffen Remus, Hubert Naets, Cédrick Fairon, Simone Paolo Ponzetto, and Chris Biemann. 2016. TAXI at SemEval-2016 task 13: a taxonomy induction method based on lexico-syntactic patterns, substrings and focused crawling. In *Proceedings of the 10th International Workshop on Semantic Evaluation (SemEval-2016)*, pages 1320–1327, San Diego, California. Association for Computational Linguistics.

Jeffrey Pennington, Richard Socher, and Christopher D. Manning. 2014. GloVe: Global vectors for word representation. In *Proceedings of the 2014 Conference on Empirical Methods in Natural Language Processing, EMNLP 2014, October 25-29, 2014, Doha, Qatar, A meeting of SIGDAT, a Special Interest Group of the ACL*, pages 1532–1543. ACL.

Wei Qiu, Mosha Chen, Linlin Li, and Luo Si. 2018. NLP_HZ at SemEval-2018 task 9: a nearest neighbor approach. In *Proceedings of the 12th International Workshop on Semantic Evaluation*, pages 909–913, New Orleans, Louisiana. Association for Computational Linguistics.

Alec Radford, Jeffrey Wu, Rewon Child, David Luan, Dario Amodei, Ilya Sutskever, et al. 2019. Language models are unsupervised multitask learners. *OpenAI blog*, 1(8):9.

Colin Raffel, Noam Shazeer, Adam Roberts, Katherine Lee, Sharan Narang, Michael Matena, Yanqi Zhou, Wei Li, and Peter J. Liu. 2020. Exploring the limits of transfer learning with a unified text-to-text transformer. *Journal of Machine Learning Research*, 21(140):1–67.

Abhilasha Ravichander, Eduard Hovy, Kaheer Suleman, Adam Trischler, and Jackie Chi Kit Cheung. 2020. On the systematicity of probing contextualized word representations: The case of hypernymy in BERT. In *Proceedings of the Ninth Joint Conference on Lexical and Computational Semantics*, pages 88–102, Barcelona, Spain (Online). Association for Computational Linguistics.

Thomas Rebele, Fabian M. Suchanek, Johannes Hoffart, Joanna Biega, Erdal Kuzey, and Gerhard Weikum. 2016. YAGO: A multilingual knowledge base from Wikipedia, WordNet, and Geonames. In *15th International Semantic Web Conference ISWC Proceedings, Part II*, volume 9982 of *Lecture Notes in Computer Science*, pages 177–185, Kobe, Japan. The Semantic Web.

Anna Rogers, Olga Kovaleva, and Anna Rumshisky. 2020. A primer in BERTology: What we know about how BERT works. *Transactions of the Association for Computational Linguistics*, 8:842–866.

Stephen Roller, Douwe Kiela, and Maximilian Nickel. 2018. Hearst patterns revisited: Automatic hypernym detection from large text corpora. In *Proceedings of the 56th Annual Meeting of the Association for Computational Linguistics (Volume 2: Short Papers)*, pages 358–363, Melbourne, Australia. Association for Computational Linguistics.

Michael Schlichtkrull and Héctor Martínez Alonso. 2016. MSejrKu at SemEval-2016 task 14: Taxonomy enrichment by evidence ranking. In *Proceedings of the 10th International Workshop on Semantic Evaluation (SemEval-2016)*, pages 1337–1341, San Diego, California. Association for Computational Linguistics.

Julian Seitner, Christian Bizer, Kai Eckert, Stefano Faralli, Robert Meusel, Heiko Paulheim, and Simone Paolo Ponzetto. 2016. A large DataBase of hypernymy relations extracted from the web. In

*Proceedings of the Tenth International Conference on Language Resources and Evaluation (LREC'16)*, pages 360–367, Portorož, Slovenia. European Language Resources Association (ELRA).

Kunihiro Takeoka, Kosuke Akimoto, and Masafumi Oyamada. 2021. Low-resource taxonomy enrichment with pretrained language models. In *Proceedings of the 2021 Conference on Empirical Methods in Natural Language Processing*, pages 2747–2758, Online and Punta Cana, Dominican Republic. Association for Computational Linguistics.

Ben Wang and Aran Komatsuzaki. 2021. GPT-J-6B: A 6 Billion Parameter Autoregressive Language Model. https://github.com/kingoflolz/mesh-transformer-jax.

Thilini Wijesiriwardene, Vinh Nguyen, Goonmeet Bajaj, Hong Yung Yip, Vishesh Javangula, Yuqing Mao, Kin Wah Fung, Srinivasan Parthasarathy, Amit P. Sheth, and Olivier Bodenreider. 2022. UBERT: A novel language model for synonymy prediction at scale in the UMLS metathesaurus. *CoRR*, abs/2204.12716.

Thomas Wolf, Lysandre Debut, Victor Sanh, Julien Chaumond, Clement Delangue, Anthony Moi, Pierric Cistac, Tim Rault, Remi Louf, Morgan Funtowicz, Joe Davison, Sam Shleifer, Patrick von Platen, Clara Ma, Yacine Jernite, Julien Plu, Canwen Xu, Teven Le Scao, Sylvain Gugger, Mariama Drame, Quentin Lhoest, and Alexander Rush. 2020. Transformers: State-of-the-art natural language processing. In *Proceedings of the 2020 Conference on Empirical Methods in Natural Language Processing: System Demonstrations*, pages 38–45, Online. Association for Computational Linguistics.

Susan Zhang, Stephen Roller, Naman Goyal, Mikel Artetxe, Moya Chen, Shuohui Chen, Christopher Dewan, Mona T. Diab, Xian Li, Xi Victoria Lin, Todor Mihaylov, Myle Ott, Sam Shleifer, Kurt Shuster, Daniel Simig, Punit Singh Koura, Anjali Sridhar, Tianlu Wang, and Luke Zettlemoyer. 2022. OPT: Open pre-trained transformer language models. *CoRR*, abs/2205.01068.

# A Appendix

| Synset | Lemmas |
|---|---|
| coin.n.01 | coin |
| chromatic color.n.01 | chromatic color, chromatic colour, spectral color, spectral colour |
| coat.n.01 | coat |
| jewelry.n.01 | jewelry, jewellery |
| furniture.n.01 | furniture, piece of furniture, article of furniture |
| pasta.n.02 | pasta, alimentary paste |
| cheese.n.01 | cheese |
| room.n.01 | room |
| meat.n.01 | meat |
| wine.n.01 | wine, vino |
| dinosaur.n.01 | dinosaur |
| candy.n.01 | candy, confect |
| beverage.n.01 | beverage, drink, drinkable, potable |
| cloak.n.02 | cloak |
| doll.n.01 | doll, dolly |
| pie.n.01 | pie |
| drum.n.01 | drum, membranophone, tympan |
| makeup.n.01 | makeup, make-up, war paint |
| movie.n.01 | movie, film, picture, moving_picture, moving-picture_show, motion_picture, motion-picture_show, picture_show, pic, flick |
| child's game.n.01 | child's game |
| trouser.n.01 | trouser, pant |
| guitar.n.01 | guitar |

Table 7: Manually selected test synsets for Hyponym Prediction.

| Pattern | GPT-2-large | OPT-1.3b | T5-large | Average |
|---|---|---|---|---|
| Other [PARENT] such as | 0.528 | 0.531 | 0.114 | 0.391 |
| There are a lot of [PARENT] such as | 0.454 | 0.457 | 0.208 | 0.373 |
| There are a lot of [PARENT] here such as | 0.455 | 0.459 | 0.163 | 0.359 |
| There were a lot of [PARENT] such as | 0.469 | 0.434 | 0.155 | 0.353 |
| There were a lot of [PARENT] here such as | 0.452 | 0.438 | 0.166 | 0.352 |
| I know such types of [PARENT] as | 0.416 | 0.451 | 0.118 | 0.328 |
| [PARENT] such as | 0.411 | 0.396 | 0.115 | 0.307 |
| which includes various [PARENT] such as | 0.323 | 0.430 | 0.146 | 0.300 |
| I know such kinds of [PARENT] as | 0.283 | 0.456 | 0.104 | 0.281 |
| My favorite [PARENT] is | 0.326 | 0.415 | 0.100 | 0.280 |
| which includes various [PARENT] like | 0.282 | 0.329 | 0.169 | 0.260 |
| [PARENT] e.g. | 0.296 | 0.346 | 0.118 | 0.253 |
| Other [PARENT] especially | 0.325 | 0.309 | 0.077 | 0.237 |
| My favorite [PARENT] is either | 0.246 | 0.320 | 0.118 | 0.228 |
| I know many types of [PARENT] for example | 0.228 | 0.266 | 0.170 | 0.221 |
| [PARENT] including | 0.202 | 0.318 | 0.059 | 0.193 |
| [PARENT] namely | 0.208 | 0.311 | 0.051 | 0.190 |
| I know many kinds of [PARENT] for example | 0.181 | 0.227 | 0.153 | 0.187 |
| which includes various [PARENT] for example | 0.141 | 0.28 | 0.139 | 0.187 |
| Other [PARENT] for example | 0.181 | 0.193 | 0.103 | 0.159 |
| [PARENT] like | 0.140 | 0.192 | 0.095 | 0.142 |
| There are a lot of [PARENT] here for example | 0.157 | 0.140 | 0.126 | 0.141 |
| There are a lot of [PARENT] for example | 0.091 | 0.130 | 0.083 | 0.101 |
| [PARENT] especially | 0.103 | 0.068 | 0.047 | 0.073 |
| [PARENT] for example | 0.034 | 0.060 | 0.065 | 0.053 |
| [PARENT] for instance | 0.027 | 0.054 | 0.075 | 0.052 |

Table 8: MRR scores for zero-shot hyponyms generation on small common knowledge dataset.

| Pattern | GPT-2-large | OPT-1.3b | T5-large | Average |
|---|---|---|---|---|
| [CHILD] is a type of [PARENT] | 0.0615 | 0.1093 | 0.1215 | 0.0974 |
| [CHILD] which is a kind of [PARENT] | 0.0379 | 0.0785 | 0.0720 | 0.0628 |
| [CHILD] refers to [PARENT] | 0.0653 | 0.1140 | 0.0040 | 0.0611 |
| [CHILD] is child word for [PARENT] | 0.0708 | 0.0735 | 0.0125 | 0.0523 |
| [CHILD] is my favorite [PARENT] | 0.0407 | 0.0458 | 0.0257 | 0.0374 |
| [CHILD] is a [PARENT] | 0.0208 | 0.0198 | 0.0555 | 0.0320 |
| [CHILD] a special case of [PARENT] | 0.0385 | 0.0249 | 0.0088 | 0.0241 |
| [CHILD] which is labeled as [PARENT] | 0.0209 | 0.0293 | 0.0087 | 0.0196 |
| [CHILD] as [PARENT] | 0.0157 | 0.0259 | 0.0079 | 0.0165 |
| [CHILD] belongs to class of [PARENT] | 0.0057 | 0.0040 | 0.0281 | 0.0126 |
| [CHILD] belongs to [PARENT] | 0.0135 | 0.0183 | 0.0039 | 0.0119 |
| [CHILD] is a member of [PARENT] | 0.0139 | 0.0196 | 0.0011 | 0.0115 |
| [CHILD] and other [PARENT] | 0.0061 | 0.0082 | 0.0138 | 0.0094 |
| [CHILD] among other [PARENT] | 0.0027 | 0.0009 | 0.0069 | 0.0035 |
| [CHILD] is one of [PARENT] | 0.0006 | 0.0005 | 0.0031 | 0.0014 |

Table 9: MRR scores for zero-shot hypernyms generation on SemEval 2018 Task-9 dataset.

| Model | | Example |
|---|---|---|
| FLAN-T5 | input | hyponym: buckler, hypernyms: |
| | output | hat, headgear, earmuff, protective covering, clothing, body armor, protection, clothes |
| GPT-2 (Radford et al., 2019) (input&output extended) | input | hyponym: inquisitor , hypernyms: judge, jurisconsult, worker, person<br>hyponym: maliciousness , hypernyms: malevolence, distaste, hatred, hate, malignity<br>hyponym: buckler , hypernyms: body armor<br>hyponym: spelunker , hypernyms: |
| | output | person, explorer, adventurer, traveler, spacer |
| T5-large (Raffel et al., 2020) | input | hyponym: maliciousness, hypernyms: |
| | output | malice, evil, malicious intention, wrongful conduct, wrongdoing |

Table 10: Examples of models outputs after fine-tuning for the Hypernym Prediction task.

| Model | | Example |
|---|---|---|
| GPT-2 (Radford et al., 2019) | input | hyperhypernyms: toiletry.n.01 \| hypernyms: cosmetic.n.01 \| synset: makeup.n.01 \| hyponyms: |
| | output | eyeliner, lip, lip balm |
| GPT-2 (Radford et al., 2019) (input&output extended) | input | hyperhypernyms: garment.n.01 \| hypernyms: overgarment.n.01 \| synset: cloak.n.02 \| hyponyms: burnous, burnoose, burnouse, caftan, kaftan, cape<br>hyperhypernyms: garment.n.01 \| hypernyms: overgarment.n.01 \| synset: coat.n.01 \| hyponyms: box coat, coatee, cutaway, duffel coat, duffle coat, frock coat<br>hyperhypernyms: clothing.n.01 \| hypernyms: garment.n.01 \| synset: trouser.n.01 \| hyponyms: |
| | output | slacks, chino, straitjacket, jean, trews, short trousers, breeches, flannel, churidars, pantaloon, |
| T5-large (Raffel et al., 2020) | input | hyperhypernyms: baked goods.n.01 \| hypernyms: pastry.n.02 \| synset: pie.n.01 \| hyponyms: |
| | output | shepherd's pie, potpie, spud, apple pie, apple pies, baklava, compote, cobbler, strudel, crab cake, pies-a-la-carte, meatloaf, fish pie, trifle, meatpox, pork pie, fruit pie, cheesecake, sausage pie, meatball, applesauce pie, tartlet, steak pie, walnut pie, crabcake, cherry pie, steamer, Victoria pie, crab pie, clam pie, cow pie, hearth pie, sour pie, roulade Pie, scone, roulade pie, Scottish pie, roulade, pies-a-la-mousse, pork-and-veal pie, pork-in-a-brick oven, pork-and-vegetable pie, pie fillet, pork-pie, macaroni pie, bacon-wrapped pie |

Table 11: Examples of models outputs after fine-tuning for the Hyponym Prediction task.

| Top-10 words | True hyponyms | Predicted hyponyms |
|---|---|---|
| vegetable | pinto bean, artichoke, globe artichoke | beet, broccoli, cabbage |
| whale | vaquita, Phocoena sinus, right whale | beaked whale, baleen whale, blue whale |
| military unit | division, naval division, Praetorian Guard | company, airborne unit, artillery unit |
| court game | tennis, lawn tennis, jai alai | volleyball, basketball, tennis |
| dwelling | bed and breakfast, bed-and-breakfast, shooting lodge | cabin, farmhouse, chalet |
| beverage | Burton, Saint Emilion, red wine | ale, beer, alcohol |
| wheeled vehicle | minicar, lorry, camion | carriage, cart, car |
| bread | limpa, baking-powder biscuit, simnel | bun, bap, brioche |
| natural science | statics, cytology, urology | chemistry, biology, botany |
| citrus | grapefruit, citrange, key lime | orange, grapefruit, lemon |

Table 12: Top-10 synsets with the true hyponyms (at most 3) and predictions (at most 3) according to the Pr@5 metric.

# Context Helps Determine Spatial Knowledge from Tweets

**Zhaomin Xiao**
University of North Texas
zhaominxiao@my.unt.edu

**Yan Huang**
University of North Texas
yan.huang@unt.edu

**Eduardo Blanco**
University of Arizona
eduardoblanco@arizona.edu

## Abstract

This paper introduces the problem of determining whether people are located in the locations they mention in their Twitter streams. In particular, we investigate the role of context—tweets published before and after a tweet mentioning a location—in this challenging problem. We present a new corpus of Twitter streams with spatial information. Our analyses show that context is key to define the ground truth, as human judgments depend on whether annotators have access to context. Experimental results show that a neural architecture that takes into account context in addition to the tweet mentioning a location yields better results. We also conduct an error analysis to provide insights into the errors made by our best model.

## 1 Introduction

Information extraction has been popular since decades ago (Cardie, 1997). One of its subareas is geotagging (Cheng et al., 2010; Mahmud et al., 2021; Jurgens et al., 2021), which aims at adding geographical information to an entity. A common example of geotagging is to predict the home location of Twitter users (Elmongui et al., 2015). Geotagging users with their home location is challenging because people change their location often thus they may not tweet from their home location.

Twitter is a social network in which users post short messages known as tweets. Business reports state that the number of daily active users went from 166 million in April 2021 to 229 million in April 2022 (Kemp, 2022). According to a recent report (Dean, 2021), (a) the Twitter app was downloaded over 6 million times in the fourth quarter of 2020, and (b) Twitter users in the US spend on average 158.2 minutes per month on the app. In addition, Beveridge (2021) reports that more than 500 million tweets are published per day.

Users rarely geotag their tweets with their GPS coordinates. Previous studies estimate that only

$t_{before}$ Just sat at the beach and homeboy in front of us rockin our to will smith! Of course.

$t_0$ Miami BEST BEACH!!!

$t_{after}$ I have to go back to work, guys. Don't worry, I'm back to my ol dirtbag routine now

Figure 1: Tweet mentioning *Miami* ($t_0$) and the tweets published before and after ($t_{before}$ and $t_{after}$). $t_0$ by itself is insufficient to determine whether the author was in *Miami*: (a) based on the text, the author could be tweeting about *Miami* from anywhere, and (b) the picture of the sky could be from almost anywhere. Considering context—the tweets published before and after—provides enough evidence to conclude that the author was in *Miami* when he published $t_0$ as he was there on vacation and eventually had to go back to work.

0.85% of tweets are geotagged (Sloan et al., 2013). Alternatively, tweets mentioning a city can still be rich in spatial information. Mentioning a city, however, does not guarantee that the author was in the city when he tweeted—people often tweet about a city from elsewhere (Han et al., 2016).

In this paper, we explore the problem of determining whether people are located in the cities they mention in their tweets. More specifically, we explore the role of context—tweets published before and after the tweet that mentions a city—in this challenging problem. Consider the three tweets in Figure 1, which were published in chronological order from top to bottom. Taking into account only the tweet mentioning *Miami* ($t_0$), it is unsound to conclude that the author was there when he published this tweet. Indeed, the text only states that *Miami* has the *best beach*, and the picture of the sky could be from almost anywhere. The tweets pub-



*Findings of the Association for Computational Linguistics: IJCNLP-AACL 2023*, pages 149–160
November 1–4, 2023. ©2023 Asian Federation of Natural Language Processing

lished before and after, however, provide enough context to conclude that the author was on vacation in *Miami* (*sat in the beach*, *have to go back to work*, etc.) thus he was in *Miami* when he tweeted $t_0$. Note that $t_0$ is the only tweet mentioning *Miami* yet taking into account context is necessary to correctly determine whether the author was there.

While the work presented here could be considered fundamental research, it opens the door to several applications. For example, emergency management systems could issue customized alerts to individuals who were, are, or are about to be located near a natural disaster. Similarly, location information can be utilized to facilitate transportation planning to provide positive long-term and sustainable economic impacts on many regions.

The main contributions of this paper are:[1] (a) a corpus of 3,494 tweets mentioning a city ($t_0$), their context (3 tweets before and 3 tweets after), and annotations indicating whether the author was in the city when he published $t_0$; (b) analysis showing that the problem requires taking into account context—annotations change depending on whether crowdworkers have access to the context; (c) experimental results showing that taking into account tweets published both before and after the tweet mentioning the city is beneficial; and (d) qualitative analysis providing insights into the errors made by our best model, including characteristics of both $t_0$ and the tweets in the context.

## 2 Related Work

Previous works within information extraction have targeted either spatial or temporal information. Works targeting spatial information extraction include event localization (Pustejovsky, 2013), and geolocation prediction (Mousset et al., 2020; Chong and Lim, 2017). Works targeting temporal information extraction include event ordering (Naik et al., 2019; Cassidy et al., 2014; Ning et al., 2020) and event understanding (Ma et al., 2021). In some tasks, such as human interaction prediction (Ke et al., 2016) and facial expression recognition (Zhang et al., 2017), spatial and temporal information are complementary to each other. In these works, spatial/temporal information is used as contextual information.

Various kinds of context have been proved useful in many tasks. Yu et al. (2022) investigate the role of conversational context in annotation and detections of hate speech and counter-hate speech. Wang et al. (2015) use topic, history, and conversation information as context to detect sarcasm in Twitter. Ren et al. (2016) and Vanzo et al. (2014) use similar context to approach the task of sentiment classification. Similar to their works, we also use history tweets as the context. Therefore, the temporal information contained in history tweets is used as the context to extract spatial information.

Most previous works targeting spatial information extraction are centered around events (Mousset et al., 2020; Chong and Lim, 2017; Frisoni et al., 2021). Unlike us, these efforts do not aim at determining spatial information about people. As we shall see, people often mention places despite they are not located there. In addition, knowing the location where an event occurs does not necessarily indicate the location of the participants in the event or people talking about the event. For example, one can state that there is a housing market bubble somewhere without ever stepping foot there. Finally, we note that people change their location often and most events are much shorter than a human lifespan.

More related to our work, Fuchs et al. (2013) analyze personal behavioral patterns using geotagged tweets from the Seattle, Washington area (i.e., tweets published with geographical coordinates within Seattle). Since only 0.85% of tweets are geotagged (Sloan et al., 2013), their work may suffer from lack of generality. We work with tweets mentioning cities across the United States without requiring a geotag. Doudagiri et al. (2018) annotate whether people are located at the locations they tweet about. Their corpus is not publicly available at the time of writing, and experimental results are not presented. The paper presented here is complementary. Xiao and Blanco (2022) work on a task similar to ours, though they investigate the role of modality in the annotation and learning method of spatial information extraction. Differently, we show that context—tweets published before and after—must be taken into account.

## 3 A Corpus of Tweets and Spatial Knowledge

Our main goal is to investigate whether contextual information is beneficial to infer spatial information between authors of tweets and the locations they mention in their tweets. To our knowledge, we

[1]Corpus and code available at `https://github.com/zhaomin1995/aacl2023_repo`

are the first to tackle this problem, so we create a new corpus. Doing so allows us to analyze whether human judgments depend on whether they have access to the context (i.e., tweets published before and after the tweet mentioning a location).

**Collecting Tweets** While one could start with a new collection of tweets, we choose to build upon an existing corpus with spatial annotations disregarding context (Xiao and Blanco, 2022). This corpus contains 6,540 English tweets mentioning a city and crowdsourced annotations indicating whether the author was in the city when he tweeted *based on the content of the tweet and nothing else*. Building upon this corpus allows us to (a) leverage their context-unaware annotations and (b) focus on our main goal: to investigate the role of context.

We refer to the tweets in the existing corpus as *target tweets*. We complement target tweets with the three tweets published immediately before and after within a window of 90 days[2]. We refer to these tweets as *earlier tweets* and *later tweets* respectively. We also refer to both *earlier tweets* and *later tweets* as *context tweets*. An instance thus contains seven tweets: one target tweet mentioning a city, three earlier tweets, and three later tweets (we discarded target tweets without enough context).

**Annotation Guidelines** We aim at capturing spatial information intuitively understood by humans. To this end, we crowdsource annotations from non-experts asking two questions. The first question is "Was the author of the tweet located in *city* when the target tweet was published?". Crowdworkers choose between two options:

- `yes`: the author of the tweets was located in *city* when the target tweet was published; or
- `no`: I cannot tell whether the author of the tweets was located in *city* when the target tweet was published.

Note that `no` does not guarantee that the author was not in *city*. It rather indicates that the crowdworkers cannot establish that the author was in *city*. The results of our pilot annotation show that annotators cannot determine whether the author of the tweet was in *city* in more than 95% of the instances that are not labeled as `yes`.

The second question is "How confident are you about your answer to the first question?" Crowdworkers choose options from a modified Likert scale with five options: *Extremely confident*, *Very confident*, *Moderately confident*, *Slightly confident*, and *Not confident at all*. The second question complements the first question and allows annotators to bridge the semantic gap between `yes` and `no` answers to the first question. During pilot annotations designed to refine the annotation guidelines, we discovered that asking these two questions results in more reliable annotations than, for example, including *probably yes* and *probably no* as options for the first question and skipping the second question.

**Annotation Interface and Process** We crowdsource annotations on Amazon Mechanical Turk. Crowdworkers answer the questions above for one instance (the target tweet mentioning a city, three earlier tweets, and three later tweets) before moving to the next instance. In order to ensure crowdworkers read the tweets in the order they were published, the interface displays the earlier tweets, the target tweet, and the later tweets with short delays in between after workers click on the appropriate button. We display screenshots of tweets from the Twitter's website to ensure that all characters, symbols, emojis, and images are correctly displayed.

A total of 329 annotators participated in our annotation task. The hourly pay for crowd workers ranged from \$9 to \$13 (the federal minimum wage is \$7.25). After collecting multiple annotations for each instance (Section 3.1), we replace `yes` labels with `no` if the confidence level is lower than or equal to *Moderately confident*. Our rationale is that `yes` with low confidence level indicates that there is not enough evidence about the author being located in *city* when the target tweet was published, which is actually the definition of `no`.

### 3.1 Annotation Quality

Ensuring annotation quality is critical in any crowdsourcing effort. Our first defense is to recruit crowdworkers located in the United States with an approval rate above 95%. Second, we do not allow workers to continue to work on our task if the average completing time per Human Intelligence Task in the past (i.e., the average time spent before submitting answers to both questions per instance) is under 8 seconds. We decided on 8 seconds based on observations during pilot annotations—one just cannot read seven tweets and answer two questions in eight seconds. In addition, we split all instances into batches of 500 instances and publish one batch every 8 hours to avoid annotator fatigue.

Our last defense is to collect five annotations per

[2]The 90 days is the maximal time window. If there are more than three tweets within 90 days, we choose the closest three. These seven tweets are published by the same user.

instance and filter out unreliable annotations until we obtain substantial inter-annotator agreement for each batch. We do so using Multi-Annotator Competence Estimation (Hovy et al., 2013, MACE) and Krippendorff's $\alpha$ (Krippendorff, 2011). MACE ranks annotators by their competence scores and adjudicates labels according to these scores. Krippendorff's $\alpha$ is used to measure inter-annotator agreement. $\alpha = 0$ indicates only the agreement expected by chance, while $\alpha = 1$ indicates annotators always agree. Krippendorff's $\alpha$ coefficients at or above 0.6 are considered substantial and above 0.8 (almost) perfect (Artstein and Poesio, 2008). We repeat these steps for each batch until $\alpha \geq 0.6$:

1. Use MACE to calculate competence scores for workers and sort them in descending order.
2. Discard all the annotations by the crowdworker with the lowest score.
3. Calculate the Krippendorff's $\alpha$ coefficient on the remaining annotations.

We discard instances left without annotations after the above steps. The final corpus consists of 3,494 annotated instances with Krippendorff's $\alpha = 0.76$. In the rest of this paper, we work with these instances. We reserve for future work a thorough analysis of the instances with the most disagreements between annotators.

### 3.2 Ethical considerations

Determining where people are located has the potential to open the door to malicious (or unwanted) tracking and surveillance. For example, applications that track location data may turn around and sell that data, revealing someone's every movement—whether it is to a retail store or potential malicious users such as stalkers. Equally important, Twitter users may not be aware that their tweets can be used for research purposes (Fiesler and Proferes, 2018). We are not interested in tracking people or surveillance. Instead, we are interested in investigating the very definition of the problem and analyzing whether and how context complements target tweets. In order to alleviate the issues above, we implemented the following safeguards:

- Our corpus only contains seven tweets per user published within 90 days thus tracking and surveillance are not enabled by this work. Neither user information nor any metadata is included in the public corpus.
- Our analyses and experiments only take into account the text and image in a tweet. We do not consider user information or any metadata.
- We have designed a takedown request process following Mirowski et al. (2019). People can request us to delete tweets via an online form. We will propagate takedown requests to researchers who download the corpus and the license will require them to delete them.

| | | after adding context (our annotations) | |
|---|---|---|---|
| | | `yes` | `no` |
| before adding context (original annotations) | `yes` | 74.5 | 25.5 |
| | `no` | 60.7 | 39.3 |

Table 1: Label percentages depend on whether annotators have access to context (i.e., tweets published before and after). Many labels change if annotators have access to context, especially if the label is `no` (60.7%) before adding context. The *correct* ground truth labels are the ones collected with context.

## 4 Corpus Analysis

The 3,494 instances in our corpus mention 94 unique cities. The most common cities are *Miami* (17% of target tweets) and *Chicago* (6%); other cities account for at most 5% each. The annotation process results in the following label distribution: Most instances are annotated `yes` (67.7%), and around one-third are annotated `no` (32.3%).

**Do labels depend on whether context is available to crowdworkers?** Yes, crowdworkers understand substantially different spatial information depending on whether they have access to context. Table 1 compares our annotations and the original annotations that do not consider context. Note that the *correct* ground truth labels are the ones obtained taking into account context.

Most target tweets annotated `no` without considering context are annotated `yes` considering context (60.7%). The percentage of annotation changes for target tweets annotated `yes` without context is smaller but substantial (25.5%). In other words, figuring out whether the author of a tweet is in the city he tweets about requires looking at context.

We show examples of annotation changes in Figure 2. In the first example, annotators understood that the *target tweet* is a news report about *Philadelphia*. As a result, annotators could not determine whether the author was located in *Philadelphia* when the *target tweet* was published. The later tweet, however, implicitly mentions that the author

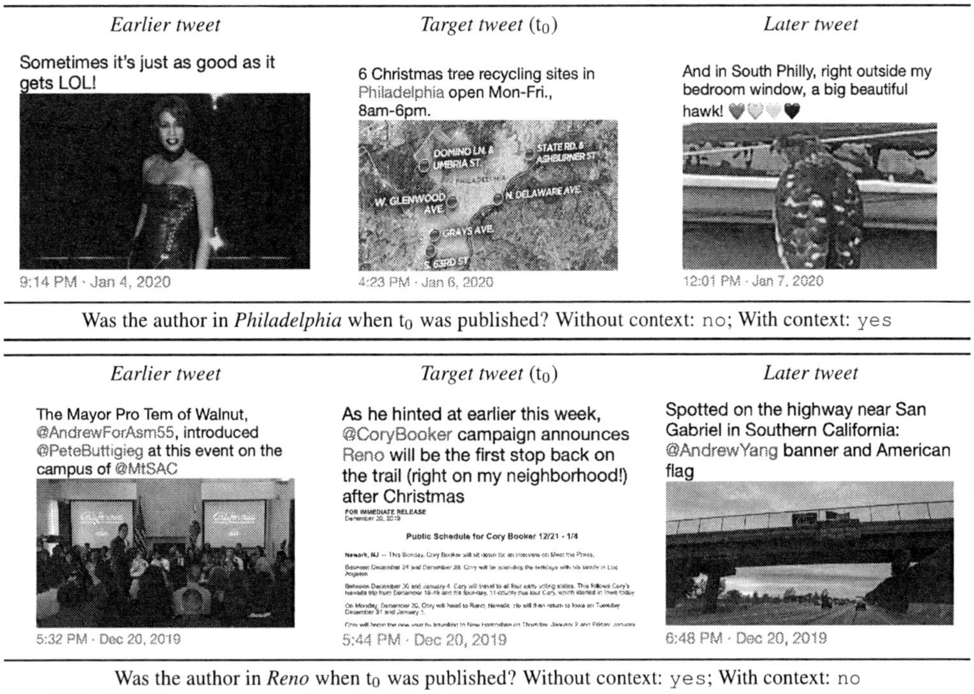


Figure 2: Examples of tweets with different human judgments depending on whether we show context to annotators. Note that the *correct* ground truth is the label obtained when annotators have access to context. We only show selected tweets in the context because of space constraints (recall that we show annotators the three tweets published before and after a target tweet). Annotators understood that the target tweet in the first example was probably a news update and did not conclude that the author was in *Philadelphia* when they did not have access to context. The tweet published after, however, implicitly states that the author lives in that city (his bedroom is in Philly) thus the correct label is yes. The target tweet in the second example is about a local election campaign and annotators understood that the author was in *Reno* looking only at the target tweet. Tweets published before and after within an hour, however, mention distant locations and annotators rightfully concluded that the author was not in Reno.

lives in South Philly—his bedroom is there. Since the target and later tweets were published in consecutive days, annotators concluded that the author was in Philadelphia. In this example, context provides evidence that the target tweet is not just a news report about Philadelphia, but a report from someone who lives there.

In the second example, the *target tweet* shares information about a campaign event to take place in Reno, where the author lives (*right on my neighborhood*). Without context, annotators understood that the author was there when he published the target tweet despite the only information available was that he lives there. Looking at earlier and later tweets, however, annotators concluded that he was not in Reno as he tweeted from *San Gabriel* near Los Angeles shortly after.

## 5 Experiments and Results

We use the 3,494 instances in our corpus to conduct experiments to automatically determine whether authors of tweets are located in the cities they mention in their tweets. Each instance consists of seven tweets published in chronological order. We reduce the problem to a classification task. The inputs to the model are seven tweets. The output is a label indicating whether the author of the tweets was located in the city when the *target tweet* was published (yes or no). We create stratified training and test splits (80% / 20%) and reserve 20% of the training split for validation. Our models do not take into account user information. They make predictions solely based on the tweets' text. [3] We use Pytorch (Paszke et al., 2019) and the pretrained models (i.e., BERT) released by HuggingFace (Wolf et al.,

[3] Since only part of context tweets contain images, we only take into account tweets' text.

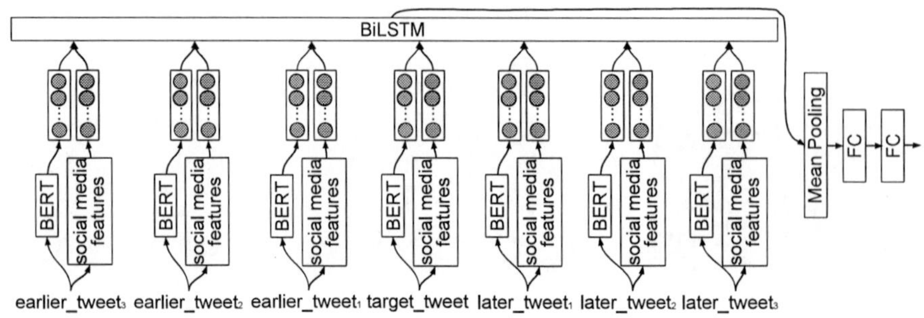


Figure 3: Neural network architecture for determining whether the author of a tweet (target_tweet) is located in the places mentioned in the tweet. We represent the target tweet and context tweets by concatenating their BERT representations and social media features. The BiLSTM processes the sequence of tweets and two fully connected layers after mean pooling make the final prediction.

| | no | | | yes | | | Weighted Average | | |
|---|---|---|---|---|---|---|---|---|---|
| | P | R | F1 | P | R | F1 | P | R | F1 |
| Majority baseline | 0.00 | 0.00 | 0.00 | 0.68 | 1.00 | 0.81 | 0.46 | 0.68 | 0.55 |
| Context-Unaware Network (target tweet) | 0.00 | 0.00 | 0.00 | 0.68 | 1.00 | 0.81 | 0.46 | 0.68 | 0.55 |
| Context-Aware Networks | | | | | | | | | |
| *earlier + target tweets* | 0.00 | 0.00 | 0.00 | 0.68 | 1.00 | 0.81 | 0.46 | 0.68 | 0.55 |
| *target + later tweets* | 0.00 | 0.00 | 0.00 | 0.68 | 1.00 | 0.81 | 0.46 | 0.68 | 0.55 |
| *earlier + target + later tweets* | 0.44 | 0.28 | 0.35 | 0.71 | 0.83 | 0.76 | 0.62 | 0.65 | **0.63** |
| without social media features | 0.39 | 0.30 | 0.34 | 0.70 | 0.78 | 0.74 | 0.60 | 0.62 | 0.61 |

Table 2: Results obtained with the majority baseline, context-unaware network (i.e., only taking into account the *target tweet*), and context-aware networks (three tweets published before and after). The context-unaware network does not outperform the majority baseline, indicating the need of contextual information. The results obtained with context-aware networks demonstrate that it is beneficial to consider (a) both *earlier_tweets* and *later_tweets* (only considering either one does not outperform the baseline), and (b) the social media features.

2020). We train all the neural networks for up to 100 epochs using the Adam optimizer (Kingma and Ba, 2014), categorical cross entropy as the loss function, and batch size 8. We stop the training process before 100 epochs if there is no improvement in the validation set for 10 epochs.

**Context-Unaware Neural Baseline** First, we experiment with a neural network that only takes into account the target tweet ($t_0$) to establish a neural baseline. The inputs of the context-unaware neural network include the tweet text and social media features we extract from the tweet text. The social media features characterize the text in a tweet and include the number of hashtags and features targeting emojis and subjective language. The supplementary materials detail all the features we work with. We use the vector associated with the CLS token returned by BERT [4] (Devlin et al., 2019) as the text representations. We concatenate the text representations and social media features and apply two trainable fully connected layers (sizes: 512 and 2) to make the final prediction (`yes` or `no`). We use dropout (Srivastava et al., 2014) in the second-to-last fully connected layer (rate: 0.2).

**Context-Aware Neural Network** Figure 3 shows the architecture of our context-aware network. The inputs of context-aware networks are the same as the context-unaware network, except that the context-unaware network only uses one tweet (*target tweet*), while the context-aware networks use seven tweets (three *earlier tweets*, one *target tweet*, and three *later tweets*). Since BERT [5] is pretrained using masked language modeling and next sentence prediction—two general tasks not related to extracting spatiotemporal knowledge from social media posts—we extract social media features to enhance the BERT representations. We provide the details

[4]We use bert-base-uncased version of BERT. Note that during the model training process, BERT is held fixed; its parameters are not updated during the training procedure.

[5]Similar to the experiments with the context-unaware neural baseline, BERT is held fixed during the training process.

about social media features in the supplementary materials. The social media features are concatenated with the BERT representations. Note that BERT tokenizer can preprocess the inputs, thus we do not have a data preprocessing step. We use a BiLSTM (size: 1024) (Hochreiter and Schmidhuber, 1997) to encode the sequence of tweets (earlier, target and later tweets). We use a mean pooling layer (Lin et al., 2014) to downsample the feature map and keep the most informative features. We use two fully-connected layers to reduce the dimensionality. The numbers of units in the two fully connected layers are set to 512 and 2, respectively. We use dropout (Srivastava et al., 2014) [6] and ReLU (Nair and Hinton, 2010) in the second-to-last fully connected layer to avoid overfitting and vanishing gradient problems. We experimented with alternative pretrained text encoders and various configurations, including different sizes for the BiLSTM and fully connected layers. Specifically, we have explored BERTweet (Nguyen et al., 2020) and max pooling. However, we do not observe any improvements from these alternative choices.

### 5.1 Results

Table 2 shows the experimental results with the test split using the majority baseline (always `yes`), the context-unaware neural network, and the context-aware networks. The context-unaware network does not outperform the majority baseline. This indicates that the context tweets are essential for the neural network to extract spatial information.

We present results with the context-aware network using four inputs to represent an instance: (a) *earlier tweets* and *target tweet*, (b) *target tweet* and *later tweets*, (c) *earlier tweets*, *target tweet* and *later tweets* (full input), and (d) same as (c) but excluding the social media features. We note several interesting observations:

- Neither *earlier* nor *later tweets* are beneficial by themselves. Only considering either yields the same results than the majority baseline and the context-unaware network.
- The social media features characterizing the text in the tweet are beneficial (F1: 0.61 vs. 0.63). In other words, these features provide information that is not captured in the distributed representation generated by BERT. Note that social media features are beneficial only when combining *earlier* and *later tweets*. Packing any of the *earlier*, *target*, and *later tweets* with social media features does not yield better results (F1: 0.55 vs. 0.63).

[6]Dropout rate is 0.2.

### 5.2 Qualitative Analysis

To better understand what kind of mistakes our best-performing model makes, we perform a qualitative analysis. We randomly picked 100 errors made by the best-performing model. In order to analyze the source of the errors, we divide the errors into two parts. The first part (46% of all errors) contains the errors that occur when the *context tweets* mislead the model. We refer to these errors as *context errors*. The second part (54% of all errors) contains the errors that occur when the target tweets mislead the model. We refer to these errors as *target errors*.

**When and why did context tweets mislead the model?** Figure 4 shows the two most common errors in the *context errors*. We only show one earlier and one later tweet due to space constraints. Note that the percentages are relative to the number of *context errors*. The most common error (63%) occurs when there are multiple references to people and named entities in the context and target tweets. The first example (top) exemplifies this error. The tweets refer to, among others, *Tom Hanks*, *his family*, *Black college student*, and *Peter Liang*. We hypothesize that the model struggles to identify which reference to people, if any, is semantically close to the author. The second most common error (21%) occurs when the publication timestamps is key to make the right prediction. The tweets in the second example (bottom) were published within 5 hours and mention *Denver*, *San Diego*, and *Bahamas*. Taking as a whole, it is not possible to tell whether the author was in any of those locations. The model, however, struggles to figure this out as it does not have access to publication timestamps.

**When and why did target tweets mislead the model?** Figure 5 shows the most common errors in the *target errors*. Note that the percentages are relative to the number of *target errors*. We only show the most common errors and the *target tweets* due to space constraints. The most frequent error (48%) occurs when the target tweet is a news report. In the example (left), the author is reporting on a news event taking place in *Arlington* and the model wrongly predicts `yes` despite there is no evidence that the author was there. The second most common errors (42%) occurs when the target tweet is

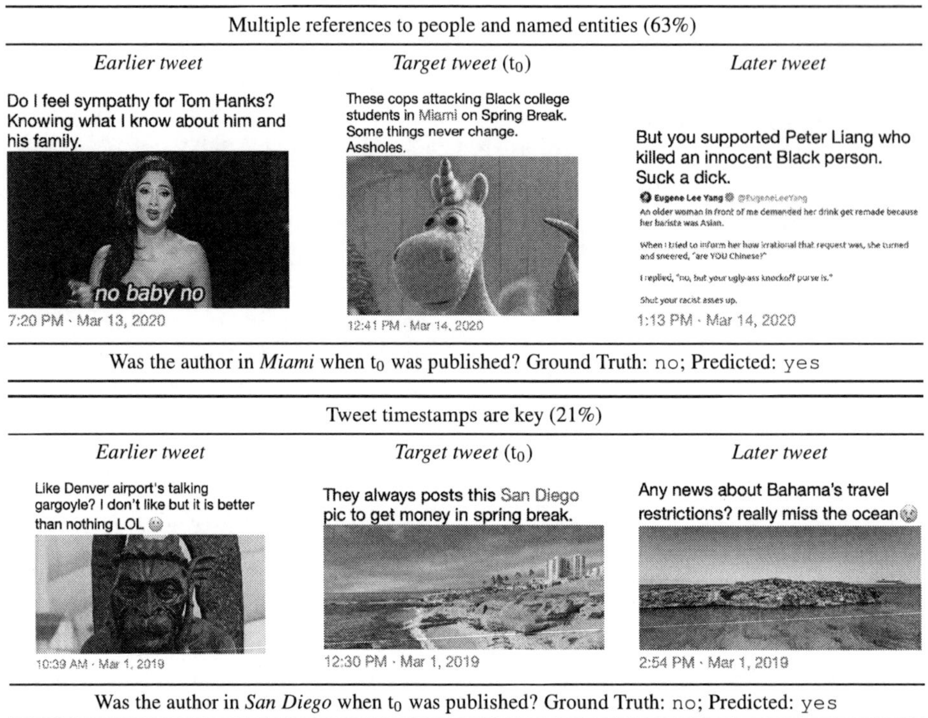


Figure 4: Examples of the most common context-related errors made by the best-performing model (bottom row in Table 2). The most common error (63%) occurs when there are many named entities in the tweets, especially *persons*. The first example (top) illustrates this error type. The many mentions of people (Tom Hanks, his family, Black college students, and Peter Liang) mislead the model. The second most common error (21%) occurs because the model does not have access to tweet timestamps. The second example (bottom) exemplifies this scenario. It is unlikely that somebody is in *Denver*, *San Diego* and *Bahamas* within 5 hours, and the model wrongly predicted that the author was in *San Diego* when he published the target tweet despite earlier and later tweets indicate otherwise.

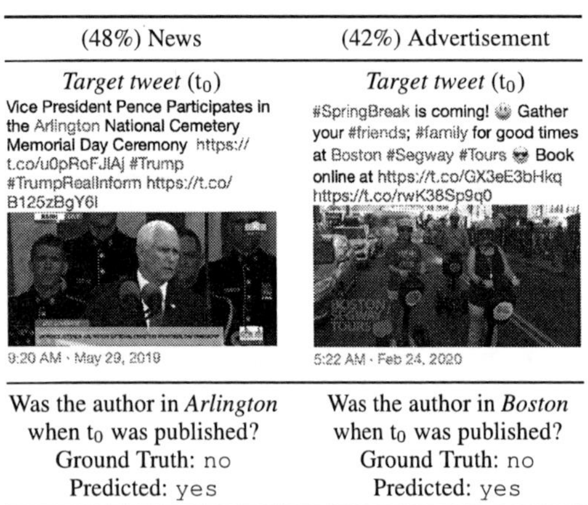


Figure 5: Most common errors made by the best-performing model when it is mislead by the *target tweet*.

an advertisement and the model predicts `yes` despite there is no evidence that the author was in the city at hand, as the example on the right shows. A less common source of errors (10%) occurs when the city mentioned in the target tweet is not a location. For example, *Houston* is sometimes used to refer to the singer rather than the city.

## 6 Conclusions and Future Work

Context does matter in determining the relationship between the authors of tweets and the places they mention in their tweets. We have demonstrated so by (a) analyzing whether human judgments change depending on whether we show them *context tweets* and (b) investigating whether neural networks benefit from incorporating *context tweets*. We found that 36.9% of human judgments change depending on whether we show *context tweets*. Experimental results demonstrate that networks that incorporate *context tweets* yield better results.

We have created a corpus of 3,494 instances

which consists of seven tweets (three *eariler tweets*, one *target tweet*, and three *later tweets*) published in chronological order. The annotations include whether the authors of tweets are in the locations they mention in a *target tweet*. As part of our future work, we plan to experiment with longer contexts and include tweet timestamps. Also, we plan to address the most common cause of errors: multiple mentions to people and named entities. Our research agenda includes investigating how to differentiate between entities mentioned in a tweet and those who participate in the events described in a tweet (including the author), or more generally, described in social media data.

## 7 Limitations

The work presented here has several limitations:

**Corpus and annotations.** First, our corpus only contains tweets written in English and containing a city in the US. While accounting for any location worldwide is outside the scope of the paper, it is possible that the corpus does not generalize to other locales. Second, in order to ensure high agreements, we disregarded annotations of the worse-performing crowdworkers (final corpus size: 3,494 instances). This strategy has the potential to also disregard the most challenging instances (i.e., most ambiguous in the eyes of the annotators) and may simplify the problem of extracting saptial knowledge in general.

**Experiments and results.** Our models rely on large pre-trained transformer that are not available in all languages and require substantial computation. We note, however, that the social media features we define manually do not have this issue and bring substantial improvements. Additional limitations of the current models are described in the Qualitative Analysis (Section 5.2).

## References


Ron Artstein and Massimo Poesio. 2008. Inter-coder agreement for computational linguistics. *Comput. Linguist.*, 34(4):555–596.

Claire Beveridge. 2021. 33 Twitter Stats All Marketers Need to Know in 2022. https://blog.hootsuite.com/twitter-statistics/. Accessed: February, 2021.

Claire Cardie. 1997. Empirical methods in information extraction. *AI Magazine*, 18(4):65.

Taylor Cassidy, Bill McDowell, Nathanael Chambers, and Steven Bethard. 2014. An annotation framework for dense event ordering. In *Proceedings of the 52nd Annual Meeting of the Association for Computational Linguistics (Volume 2: Short Papers)*, pages 501–506, Baltimore, Maryland. Association for Computational Linguistics.

Zhiyuan Cheng, James Caverlee, and Kyumin Lee. 2010. You are where you tweet: A content-based approach to geo-locating twitter users. In *Proceedings of the 19th ACM International Conference on Information and Knowledge Management*, CIKM '10, page 759–768, New York, NY, USA. Association for Computing Machinery.

Wen-Haw Chong and Ee-Peng Lim. 2017. Tweet geolocation: Leveraging location, user and peer signals. In *Proceedings of the 2017 ACM on Conference on Information and Knowledge Management*, CIKM '17, page 1279–1288, New York, NY, USA. Association for Computing Machinery.

Brian Dean. 2021. How Many People Use Twitter in 2021? [New Twitter Stats]. https://backlinko.com/twitter-users. Accessed: October, 2021.

Lingjia Deng and Janyce Wiebe. 2015. MPQA 3.0: An entity/event-level sentiment corpus. In *Proceedings of the 2015 Conference of the North American Chapter of the Association for Computational Linguistics: Human Language Technologies*, pages 1323–1328, Denver, Colorado. Association for Computational Linguistics.

Jacob Devlin, Ming-Wei Chang, Kenton Lee, and Kristina Toutanova. 2019. BERT: Pre-training of deep bidirectional transformers for language understanding. In *Proceedings of the 2019 Conference of the North American Chapter of the Association for Computational Linguistics: Human Language Technologies, Volume 1 (Long and Short Papers)*, pages 4171–4186, Minneapolis, Minnesota. Association for Computational Linguistics.

Vivek Reddy Doudagiri, Alakananda Vempala, and Eduardo Blanco. 2018. Annotating If the Authors of a Tweet are Located at the Locations They Tweet About. In *Proceedings of the Eleventh International Conference on Language Resources and Evaluation (LREC 2018)*, Miyazaki, Japan. European Language Resources Association (ELRA).

Hicham G. Elmongui, H. Morsy, and Riham Mansour. 2015. Inference models for twitter user's home location prediction. *2015 IEEE/ACS 12th International Conference of Computer Systems and Applications (AICCSA)*, pages 1–8.

Casey Fiesler and Nicholas Proferes. 2018. "participant" perceptions of twitter research ethics. *Social Media + Society*, 4(1):2056305118763366.

Giacomo Frisoni, Gianluca Moro, and Antonella Carbonaro. 2021. A survey on event extraction for natural language understanding: Riding the biomedical literature wave. *IEEE Access*, 9:160721–160757.

Georg Fuchs, Gennady L. Andrienko, Natalia V. Andrienko, and Piotr L. Jankowski. 2013. Extracting personal behavioral patterns from geo-referenced tweets.

Bo Han, Afshin Rahimi, Leon Derczynski, and Timothy Baldwin. 2016. Twitter geolocation prediction shared task of the 2016 workshop on noisy user-generated text. In *Proceedings of the 2nd Workshop on Noisy User-generated Text (WNUT)*, pages 213–217, Osaka, Japan. The COLING 2016 Organizing Committee.

Sepp Hochreiter and Jürgen Schmidhuber. 1997. Long short-term memory. *Neural Comput.*, 9(8):1735–1780.

Dirk Hovy, Taylor Berg-Kirkpatrick, Ashish Vaswani, and Eduard Hovy. 2013. Learning whom to trust with MACE. In *Proceedings of the 2013 Conference of the North American Chapter of the Association for Computational Linguistics: Human Language Technologies*, pages 1120–1130, Atlanta, Georgia. Association for Computational Linguistics.

David Jurgens, Tyler Finethy, James McCorriston, Yi Xu, and Derek Ruths. 2021. Geolocation prediction in twitter using social networks: A critical analysis and review of current practice. *Proceedings of the International AAAI Conference on Web and Social Media*, 9(1):188–197.

Qiuhong Ke, Mohammed Bennamoun, Senjian An, Farid Boussaïd, and Ferdous Ahmed Sohel. 2016. Spatial, structural and temporal feature learning for human interaction prediction. *CoRR*, abs/1608.05267.

Simon Kemp. 2022. Twitter Statistics And Trends. `https://datareportal.com/essential-twitter-stats`.

Diederik P. Kingma and Jimmy Ba. 2014. Adam: A method for stochastic optimization. *CoRR*, abs/1412.6980.

Klaus Krippendorff. 2011. Computing krippendorff's alpha-reliability. *Retrieved from https://repository.upenn.edu/asc_papers/43*.

Min Lin, Qiang Chen, and Shuicheng Yan. 2014. Network in network. *CoRR*, abs/1312.4400.

Mingyu Derek Ma, Jiao Sun, Mu Yang, Kung-Hsiang Huang, Nuan Wen, Shikhar Singh, Rujun Han, and Nanyun Peng. 2021. EventPlus: A temporal event understanding pipeline. In *Proceedings of the 2021 Conference of the North American Chapter of the Association for Computational Linguistics: Human Language Technologies: Demonstrations*, pages 56–65, Online. Association for Computational Linguistics.

Jalal Mahmud, Jeffrey Nichols, and Clemens Drews. 2021. Where is this tweet from? inferring home locations of twitter users. *Proceedings of the International AAAI Conference on Web and Social Media*, 6(1):511–514.

Piotr Mirowski, Andras Banki-Horvath, Keith Anderson, Denis Teplyashin, Karl Moritz Hermann, Mateusz Malinowski, Matthew Koichi Grimes, Karen Simonyan, Koray Kavukcuoglu, Andrew Zisserman, and Raia Hadsell. 2019. The streetlearn environment and dataset.

Paul Mousset, Yoann Pitarch, and Lynda Tamine. 2020. End-to-end neural matching for semantic location prediction of tweets. *ACM Trans. Inf. Syst.*, 39(1).

Aakanksha Naik, Luke Breitfeller, and Carolyn Rose. 2019. TDDiscourse: A dataset for discourse-level temporal ordering of events. In *Proceedings of the 20th Annual SIGdial Meeting on Discourse and Dialogue*, pages 239–249, Stockholm, Sweden. Association for Computational Linguistics.

Vinod Nair and Geoffrey E. Hinton. 2010. Rectified linear units improve restricted boltzmann machines. In *ICML*.

Dat Quoc Nguyen, Thanh Vu, and Anh Tuan Nguyen. 2020. BERTweet: A pre-trained language model for English Tweets. In *Proceedings of the 2020 Conference on Empirical Methods in Natural Language Processing: System Demonstrations*, pages 9–14.

Qiang Ning, Hao Wu, Rujun Han, Nanyun Peng, Matt Gardner, and Dan Roth. 2020. TORQUE: A reading comprehension dataset of temporal ordering questions. In *Proceedings of the 2020 Conference on Empirical Methods in Natural Language Processing (EMNLP)*, pages 1158–1172, Online. Association for Computational Linguistics.

Adam Paszke, Sam Gross, Francisco Massa, Adam Lerer, James Bradbury, Gregory Chanan, Trevor Killeen, Zeming Lin, Natalia Gimelshein, Luca Antiga, Alban Desmaison, Andreas Kopf, Edward Yang, Zachary DeVito, Martin Raison, Alykhan Tejani, Sasank Chilamkurthy, Benoit Steiner, Lu Fang, Junjie Bai, and Soumith Chintala. 2019. Pytorch: An imperative style, high-performance deep learning library. In *Advances in Neural Information Processing Systems 32*, pages 8024–8035. Curran Associates, Inc.

James Pustejovsky. 2013. Where things happen: On the semantics of event localization. In *Proceedings of the IWCS 2013 Workshop on Computational Models of Spatial Language Interpretation and Generation (CoSLI-3)*, pages 29–39, Potsdam, Germany. Association for Computational Linguistics.

Yafeng Ren, Yue Zhang, Meishan Zhang, and Donghong Ji. 2016. Context-sensitive twitter sentiment classification using neural network. In *Proceedings of the Thirtieth AAAI Conference on Artificial Intelligence*, AAAI'16, page 215–221. AAAI Press.

Luke Sloan, Jeffrey Morgan, William Housley, Matthew Williams, Adam Edwards, Pete Burnap, and Omer Rana. 2013. Knowing the tweeters: Deriving sociologically relevant demographics from twitter. *Sociological Research Online*, 18(3):74–84.

Nitish Srivastava, Geoffrey Hinton, Alex Krizhevsky, Ilya Sutskever, and Ruslan Salakhutdinov. 2014. Dropout: A simple way to prevent neural networks from overfitting. *Journal of Machine Learning Research*, 15(56):1929–1958.

Andrea Vanzo, Danilo Croce, and Roberto Basili. 2014. A context-based model for sentiment analysis in Twitter. In *Proceedings of COLING 2014, the 25th International Conference on Computational Linguistics: Technical Papers*, pages 2345–2354, Dublin, Ireland. Dublin City University and Association for Computational Linguistics.

Zelin Wang, Zhijian Wu, Ruimin Wang, and Yafeng Ren. 2015. Twitter sarcasm detection exploiting a context-based model. In *Web Information Systems Engineering – WISE 2015*, pages 77–91, Cham. Springer International Publishing.

Thomas Wolf, Lysandre Debut, Victor Sanh, Julien Chaumond, Clement Delangue, Anthony Moi, Pierric Cistac, Tim Rault, Remi Louf, Morgan Funtowicz, Joe Davison, Sam Shleifer, Patrick von Platen, Clara Ma, Yacine Jernite, Julien Plu, Canwen Xu, Teven Le Scao, Sylvain Gugger, Mariama Drame, Quentin Lhoest, and Alexander Rush. 2020. Transformers: State-of-the-art natural language processing. In *Proceedings of the 2020 Conference on Empirical Methods in Natural Language Processing: System Demonstrations*, pages 38–45, Online. Association for Computational Linguistics.

Zhaomin Xiao and Eduardo Blanco. 2022. Are people located in the places they mention in their tweets? a multimodal approach. In *Proceedings of the 29th International Conference on Computational Linguistics*, pages 2561–2571, Gyeongju, Republic of Korea. International Committee on Computational Linguistics.

Xinchen Yu, Eduardo Blanco, and Lingzi Hong. 2022. Hate speech and counter speech detection: Conversational context does matter. In *Proceedings of the 2022 Conference of the North American Chapter of the Association for Computational Linguistics: Human Language Technologies*, pages 5918–5930, Seattle, United States. Association for Computational Linguistics.

Kaihao Zhang, Yongzhen Huang, Yong Du, and Liang Wang. 2017. Facial expression recognition based on deep evolutional spatial-temporal networks. *IEEE Transactions on Image Processing*, 26(9):4193–4203.

## A Supplementary Materials

Table 3 details the social media features used in our experiments. Experimental results (Table 2) show that these features complement the distributed representation obtained with BERT. In other words, combining the representation from BERT and these social media features is beneficial to extract spatiotemporal knowledge.

| | Name | Description |
|---|---|---|
| Hashtags | num hashtag | The number of hashtags |
| | within hashtag | Whether the location is within a hashtag, e.g., *#houston* |
| Emojis | num emoji | The number of emojis |
| | most common emoji | The three most common emojis |
| Subjectivity | num strong_subj | The number of strongly subjective words (e.g., *excoriate*) |
| | num weak_subj | The number of weakly subjective words (e.g., *say*) |
| Other | within mention | Whether the location is within a mention, e.g., *@dallasnews* |
| | num URL | The number of URLs |
| | num token | The number of tokens |
| | num elongated | The number of elongated words (e.g., *looooove*) |
| | num exclamation | The number of exclamation marks |

Table 3: Social media features used to complement the BERT representation of text in a tweet (Section 5, Figure 3). Note that the strongly subjective words and weakly subjective words are from MPQA (Deng and Wiebe, 2015). Experimental results show that taking these social media features into account is beneficial. In other words, these features complement the BERT representation when context (earlier and later tweets) are fed to the network.

# Multilingual Non-Autoregressive Machine Translation without Knowledge Distillation

**Chenyang Huang**[*1], **Fei Huang**[*4], **Zaixiang Zheng**[3],
**Osmar Zaïane**[1], **Hao Zhou**[†2], **Lili Mou**[1]
[1]Dept. of Computing Science, Alberta Machine Intelligence Institute (Amii), University of Alberta
[2]Institute for AI Industry Research (AIR), Tsinghua University
[3]ByteDance Research [4]Damo Academy, Alibaba
chenyangh@ualberta.ca huangfei382@163.com zhengzaixiang@bytedance.com
zhouhao@air.tsinghua.edu.cn zaiane@ualberta.ca doublepower.mou@gmail.com

## Abstract

Multilingual neural machine translation (MNMT) aims at using one single model for multiple translation directions. Recent work applies non-autoregressive Transformers to improve the efficiency of MNMT, but requires expensive knowledge distillation (KD) processes. To this end, we propose an M-DAT approach to non-autoregressive multilingual machine translation. Our system leverages the recent advance of the directed acyclic Transformer (DAT), which does not require KD. We further propose a pivot back-translation (PivotBT) approach to improve the generalization to unseen translation directions. Experiments show that our M-DAT achieves state-of-the-art performance in non-autoregressive MNMT.[1]

## 1 Introduction

Multilingual neural machine translation (MNMT) aims at using a single model for multiple translation directions (Firat et al., 2016). It has attracted the attention of the research community over the years (Bapna and Firat, 2019; Zhang et al., 2021), and has been widely applied in the industry (Johnson et al., 2017). Most state-of-the-art MNMT models are based on the autoregressive Transformer (AT, Vaswani et al., 2017). However, the inference of AT is slow, which results in significant latency in real-world applications (Gu et al., 2018).

Recent work applies the non-autoegressive Transformer (NAT, Gu et al., 2018), which generates target tokens in parallel for efficient inference. However, NAT often generates inconsistent sentences (e.g., with repetitive words). Qian et al. (2021) propose the Glancing Transformer (GLAT), which is trained in a curriculum learning fashion. It tackles the weakness of NAT by focusing less on the training samples that lead to inconsistent generalization.

To accelerate multilingual non-autoregressive translation, Song et al. (2022) propose a Switch-GLAT method, which is based on the Glancing Transformer, and is equipped with back-translation for data augmentation. To the best of our knowledge, Switch-GLAT is currently the only non-autoregressive system for multilingual translation. However, it suffers from two drawbacks. First, Switch-GLAT requires sequence-level knowledge distillation (KD, Kim and Rush, 2016) in every translation direction, which is inconvenient for multilingual tasks. Second, Switch-GLAT is unable to generalize to unseen translation directions (zero-shot translation), which is an essential aspect of multilingual machine translation systems (Johnson et al., 2017; Chen et al., 2017; Gu et al., 2019).

In this work, we propose a multilingual Directed Acyclic Transformer (M-DAT) approach to non-autoregressive multilingual machine translation. Our system leverages the recent directed acyclic Transformer (DAT, Huang et al., 2022b), which does not rely on KD. In addition, we propose a pivot back-translation (PivotBT) approach for the multilingual translation task. Specifically, we back-translate a target sentence to a randomly selected language to obtain an augmented source sentence. The newly generated source sentence and the original target sentence form a synthetic data sample. We observe that if the back-translation direction (e.g., German $\rightarrow$ Romanian) does not exist in the training set (i.e., zero-shot), the augmented source

[*]Work partially done during an internship at ByteDance.
[†]Work partially done while working at ByteDance.
[1]Our code and training/evaluation scripts are available at https://github.com/MANGA-UOFA/M-DAT



*Findings of the Association for Computational Linguistics: IJCNLP-AACL 2023*, pages 161–170
November 1–4, 2023. ©2023 Asian Federation of Natural Language Processing

sentence will be of low quality. Therefore, our proposed PivotBT uses an intermediate language for the back translation (e.g., German → English → Romanian). Our PivotBT is efficient, as the inference of our non-autoregressive model is fast.

We evaluated M-DAT in both supervised and zero-shot translation directions. In the supervised setting, our M-DAT achieves 0.4 higher BLEU scores than the previous state-of-the-art Switch-GLAT, while maintaining fast inference. Moreover, our M-DAT does not require KD, and is convenient to be trained on multilingual datasets. In the zero-shot translation settings, our M-DAT is the first NAT model to effectively generalize to unseen translation directions, and even outperforms a strong autoregressive baseline, which is largely attributed to our proposed PivotBT.

## 2 Related Work

The non-autoregressive Transformer (NAT, Gu et al., 2018) predicts all target words in parallel to achieve fast inference, and has been applied to various text generation tasks, such as machine translation (Gu and Kong, 2021; Huang et al., 2022a), summarization (Su et al., 2021; Liu et al., 2022a,b), and dialogue generation (Zou et al., 2021; Qi et al., 2021). However, the output quality of NAT models tends to be low (Stern et al., 2019; Ghazvininejad et al., 2019), and as a remedy, the Glancing Transformerthe Glancing Transformer (GLAT, Qian et al., 2021) applies an adaptive training algorithm that allows the model to progressively learn more difficult data samples.

Sequence-level knowledge distillation (KD, Kim and Rush, 2016) is commonly used to improve the translation quality of non-autoregressive models. As shown in Zhou et al. (2020), KD data are less complex compared with the original training set, which is easier for NAT models. However, Ding et al. (2021) find that the KD process tends to miss low-frequency words (e.g., proper nouns), which results in worse translation for NAT models. Therefore, there is a need to remove the KD process for NAT models.

The most related work to ours is Switch-GLAT (Song et al., 2022). It combines the Glancing Transformer and knowledge distillation for multilingual machine translation tasks. In addition, Switch-GLAT is equipped with a back-translation technique to augment training data.

Our system is based on the directed acyclic

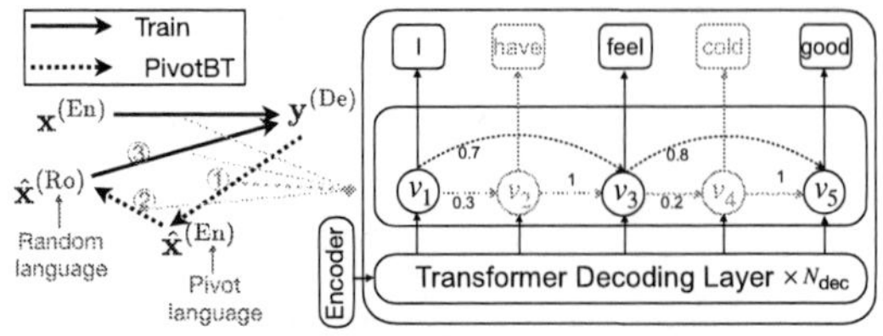


Figure 1: An example of our PivotBT augmenting a German sentence $\mathbf{y}$ to Romanian $\hat{\mathbf{x}}$, where English is used as the pivot language. The training and back-translation steps are accomplished by DAT (Huang et al., 2022b). $N_{\text{dec}}$ is the number of decoding layers.

Transformer (DAT, Huang et al., 2022b), which expands the generation canvas to allow multiple plausible translation fragments. Then, DAT selects the fragments by predicting linkages, which eventually form an output sentence. In this way, M-DAT is more capable of handling complex data samples, and does not rely on KD.

We propose PivotBT to augment the training data to improve the generalization of M-DAT. Our PivotBT is inspired by online back-translation (Zhang et al., 2020), which extends the original back-translation (BT, Sennrich et al., 2016) by randomly picking augmented directions. Different from the previous work, our approach applies pivot machine translation (Cheng et al., 2017) to improve the reliability of the back-translation directions that are unseen in the training set.

## 3 Methodology

Multilingual translation handles multiple translation directions with a single model. Suppose a data sample contains a source sentence $\mathbf{x} = (\mathrm{x}_1, \cdots, \mathrm{x}_{T_\mathrm{x}})$ and a target sentence $\mathbf{y} = (\mathrm{y}_1, \cdots, \mathrm{y}_{T_\mathrm{y}})$, where $T_\mathrm{x}$ and $T_\mathrm{y}$ denote the lengths. In addition, language tags $l_{\text{src}}$ and $l_{\text{tgt}}$ are given to indicate the languages of the source and target sentences, respectively. A multilingual machine translation dataset $\mathcal{D}$ can be represented by $\{(\mathbf{x}^{(i)}, l_{\text{src}}^{(i)}, \mathbf{y}^{(i)}, l_{\text{tgt}}^{(i)})\}_{i=1}^{K}$, where $K$ is the size of the dataset.

Our multilingual Directed Acyclic Transformer (M-DAT) has an encoder–decoder architecture. The encoder of M-DAT takes in an input sentence $\mathbf{x}^{(i)}$ and the target language tag $l_{\text{tgt}}^{(i)}$, whereas the decoder predicts the target-language words independently as the translation.

### 3.1 Directed Acyclic Transformer

To train our system without KD, we adapt the recent directed acyclic Transformer (DAT, Huang et al., 2022b), as it does not use KD but achieves comparable performance to autoregressive models on bilingual machine translation tasks (one direction per model).

In general, DAT expands its output canvas to generate multiple plausible translation fragments. Further, DAT predicts links to select the fragments, which form an output sentence. As seen in Figure 1, DAT predicts extra words and forms the final generation "I feel good", using the predicted links.

Suppose the DAT decoder has $S$ generation steps ($S > T_{\mathrm{y}}$). For each step $s$ within $1 \leq s \leq S$, DAT makes two predictions: word prediction $p_{\text{word}}^{(s)}(\cdot)$ and link prediction $p_{\text{link}}^{(s)}(\cdot)$.

The word prediction $p_{\text{word}}^{(s)}(\cdot)$ gives the distribution over possible words by mapping DAT's $s$th decoder state $\boldsymbol{h}_s$ to the probability distribution over the vocabulary, given by

$$p_{\text{word}}^{(s)}(\cdot) = \operatorname{softmax}(\mathbf{W}_{\text{word}} \boldsymbol{h}_s) \tag{1}$$

where $\mathbf{W}_{\text{word}}$ is a learnable matrix.

The link prediction $p_{\text{link}}^{(s)}(\cdot)$ computes the distribution over the subsequent steps of the $s$th step, determining which follow-up step should be linked to the $s$th step. Specifically, the link prediction leverages the attention mechanism (Bahdanau et al., 2015), which compares the $s$th step's hidden state $\boldsymbol{h}_s$ with the states of subsequent generation steps (from $s+1$ to $S$), given by

$$p_{\text{link}}^{(s)}(\cdot) = \operatorname{softmax}([\boldsymbol{k}_s^\top \boldsymbol{q}_{s+1}; \cdots; \boldsymbol{k}_s^\top \boldsymbol{q}_S]) \tag{2}$$

where $\boldsymbol{k}_s = \mathbf{W}_{\mathrm{k}} \boldsymbol{h}_s$ and $\boldsymbol{q}_s = \mathbf{W}_{\mathrm{q}} \boldsymbol{h}_s$. $\mathbf{W}_{\mathrm{k}}$ and $\mathbf{W}_{\mathrm{q}}$ are learnable matrices. The operation $[;]$ concatenates scalars into a column vector.

Given a reference sequence $\mathbf{y}$ in the training set $\mathcal{D}$, DAT selects $T_{\mathrm{y}}$ of all $S$ generation steps to generate the words in $\mathbf{y}$, where the selected steps are connected by predicted links. We denote the indices of the selected steps by $\boldsymbol{a} = (a_1, \cdots, a_{T_{\mathrm{y}}})$, where $1 = a_1 < \cdots < a_{T_{\mathrm{y}}} = S$. We refer to each selection of the steps $\boldsymbol{a}$ as a *path*.

Consider a groundtruth sequence $\mathbf{y}_{1:T_{\mathrm{y}}}$. The joint probability of the sequence, together with some path $\boldsymbol{a}_{1:T_{\mathrm{y}}}$, is

$$p(\mathbf{y}_{1:T_{\mathrm{y}}}, \boldsymbol{a}_{1:T_{\mathrm{y}}}) = \prod_{t=2}^{T_{\mathrm{y}}} p_{\text{link}}^{(a_{t-1})}(a_t) \prod_{t=1}^{T_{\mathrm{y}}} p_{\text{word}}^{(a_t)}(\mathrm{y}_t) \tag{3}$$

where $p_{\text{link}}^{(a_{t-1})}(a_t)$ is the probability that the two generation steps $a_{t-1}$ and $a_t$ are linked up. Specially, $a_1$ is set to 1, and is not considered as a random variable. $p_{\text{word}}^{(a_t)}(\mathrm{y}_t)$ is the probability of predicting the word $\mathrm{y}_t$ at the $a_t$th generation step.

Finally, the probability of generating the reference sentence $p(\mathbf{y}_{1:T_{\mathrm{y}}})$ is obtained by the marginalization of all possible paths, given by

$$\begin{aligned} p(\mathbf{y}_{1:T_{\mathrm{y}}}) &= \sum_{\boldsymbol{a} \in \Gamma_{S,T_{\mathrm{y}}}} p(\mathbf{y}_{1:T_{\mathrm{y}}}, \boldsymbol{a}_{1:T_{\mathrm{y}}}) \\ &= \sum_{\boldsymbol{a} \in \Gamma_{S,T_{\mathrm{y}}}} \prod_{t=2}^{T_{\mathrm{y}}} p_{\text{link}}^{(a_{t-1})}(a_t) \prod_{t=1}^{T_{\mathrm{y}}} p_{\text{word}}^{(a_t)}(\mathrm{y}_t) \end{aligned} \tag{4}$$

where $\Gamma_{S,T_{\mathrm{y}}} = \{\boldsymbol{a} = (a_1, \cdots, a_{T_{\mathrm{y}}}) | 1 = a_1 < \cdots < a_{T_{\mathrm{y}}} = S\}$ represents all paths of length $T_{\mathrm{y}}$. The computation of (4) is efficient through dynamic programming.[2]

Note that $p_{\text{word}}^{(s)}(\cdot)$ and $p_{\text{link}}^{(s)}(\cdot)$ are independently predicted for different generation steps; thus, DAT is non-autoregressive and is fast in inference.

### 3.2 Pivot Back-Translation

We propose a pivot back-translation (PivotBT) approach to improve the robustness of M-DAT. Following Zhang et al. (2020) and Song et al. (2022), we augment the training data with back-translation (BT, Sennrich et al., 2016). Specifically, a randomly selected language is chosen for such data augmentation.

We observe that when the back-translation direction is unseen (i.e., zero-shot), the synthesized source sentence will be of low quality, which results in a less meaningful synthetic training sample. To this end, we propose to handle the zero-shot scenario by PivotBT, which uses an intermediate language as a pivot and performs multi-step back-translation.

Given a training sample $(\mathbf{x}, l_{\text{src}}, \mathbf{y}, l_{\text{tgt}})$, we first randomly pick a language $l_{\text{aug}}$ from the set of languages in the multilingual training set $\mathcal{D}$. If the back-translation direction $l_{\text{tgt}} \to l_{\text{aug}}$ is in the training set, we directly back-translate $\mathbf{y}$ to $\hat{\mathbf{x}}$ of language $l_{\text{aug}}$. Otherwise, we choose a pivot language $l_{\text{pivot}}$ (e.g., English) such that $l_{\text{tgt}} \to l_{\text{pivot}}$ and $l_{\text{pivot}} \to l_{\text{aug}}$ are both in the training set.[3] In this

[2] We refer readers to Huang et al. (2022b).

[3] Most multilingual translation datasets are English-centric, where using English as $l_{\text{pivot}}$ guarantees the connection of $l_{\text{tgt}}$ and $l_{\text{aug}}$, which is the case of this work. In general, we can use multiple pivot languages to connect $l_{\text{tgt}}$ and $l_{\text{aug}}$ with multiple back-translation steps.

| # | Model Variant | EFD | EFZ | MANY |
|---|---|---|---|---|
| 1 | M-AT w/ standard layout | **34.57** | **31.15** | **30.36** |
| 2 | M-AT w/ shallow decoder | 34.19 | 30.87 | 29.20 |
| 3 | Switch-GLAT* | 33.34 | 29.76 | 28.47 |
| 4 | M-DAT w/ lookahead | 33.72 | 30.39 | 28.69 |
| 5 | w/ $n$-gram beam search | 33.83 | 30.55 | 29.73 |

Table 1: BLEU scores on three WMT datasets. *Trained with sequence-level knowledge distillation.

| Model Variant | IWSLT | | Europarl | |
|---|---|---|---|---|
| | Supervised | 0-Shot | Supervised | 0-Shot |
| M-AT w/ standard layout | **30.00** | 12.87 | **35.79** | 15.84 |
| M-AT w/ shallow decoder | 29.23 | 4.95 | 34.95 | 8.11 |
| Residual M-AT | 29.72 | 17.67 | 35.18 | 26.13 |
| M-DAT w/ lookahead | 28.58 | 18.53 | 34.83 | 25.86 |
| w/ $n$-gram beam search | 29.42 | **19.35** | 35.48 | **27.44** |

Table 2: BLEU scores on IWSLT and Europarl.

| Model Variant | Latency (ms) | Speedup |
|---|---|---|
| M-AT w/ standard layout | 352.4 | 1.0× |
| M-AT w/ shallow decoder | 84.2 | 4.2× |
| Switch-GLAT | **19.6** | **18.0**× |
| M-DAT w/ lookahead | 21.9 | 16.1× |
| w/ $n$-gram beam search | 67.6 | 5.2× |

Table 3: Latency and speedup on WMT-EFD.

way, we are able to obtain an augmented source sentence $\hat{\mathbf{x}}$ by first translating $\mathbf{y}$ to $\hat{\mathbf{x}}_{\text{pivot}}$ of the intermediate language $l_{\text{pivot}}$, and then translating $\hat{\mathbf{x}}_{\text{pivot}}$ to the augmented source sentence $\hat{\mathbf{x}}$ of language $l_{\text{aug}}$. Finally, the newly synthesized sample $(\hat{\mathbf{x}}, l_{\text{aug}}, \mathbf{y}, l_{\text{tgt}})$ is added to the training.

In our PivotBT, the multi-step back-translation is conducted by M-DAT itself. Since M-DAT is fast in inference, the back-translation is also efficient.

We denote the loss of training the real samples in dataset $\mathcal{D}$ by $\mathcal{L}_{\text{real}}$ and that of the synthetic samples by $\mathcal{L}_{\text{PivotBT}}$. The overall training loss of our proposed system is $\mathcal{L} = \mathcal{L}_{\text{real}} + \lambda\mathcal{L}_{\text{PivotBT}}$, where $\lambda$ is a hyperparameter controlling the strength of the back-translation.

## 4 Experiments

### 4.1 Setup

We evaluated M-DAT on five datasets: WMT-EFD, WMT-EFZ, WMT-MANY, IWSLT, and Europarl. The three WMT corpora (Song et al., 2022) only contain supervised directions in the test set, whereas the test sets of IWSLT and Europarl (Liu et al., 2021) contain both supervised directions and unseen directions (zero-shot). The training hyperparameters and evaluate metrics are strictly following Song et al. (2022) and Liu et al. (2021). We provide more details in Appendices A and B.

### 4.2 Main Results

**Supervised Translation.** Table 1 summarizes the BLEU scores of three WMT datasets. We evaluated M-DAT with two decoding algorithms: *lookahead* and *$n$-gram beam search*. The lookahead method directly decodes the generated words in parallel, and jointly maximizes the probability of the next position and predicted tokens, whereas $n$-gram beam search generates a few candidate sentences and ranks them with an $n$-gram language model. We observe that the generation quality with $n$-gram beam search is higher, which is consistent with Huang et al. (2022b).

We also see that M-DAT outperforms Switch-GLAT on average with both lookahead and beam search decoding methods. This makes our M-DAT the state of the art in non-autoregressive multilingual translation. In addition, our system does not rely on KD, which makes it convenient to be trained on multilingual datasets.

To compare M-DAT with the autoregressive multilingual Transformer (M-AT, Johnson et al., 2017), we include two autoregressive Transformer-based variants: 1) the standard layout (Vaswani et al., 2017), which has the same number of encoder layers; and 2) the layout with a shallow decoder, which moves all but one decoding layers to the encoder. The layout with a shallow decoder is suggested by Kasai et al. (2021) as it achieves close results to the standard layout but is faster in inference. We observe that M-DAT is only slightly lower in BLEU scores compared with the M-AT models. This shows our M-DAT, in addition to its efficiency, largely closes the gap between AT and NAT in non-autoregressive multilingual translation tasks.

**Zero-Shot Translation.** The ability to generalize to unseen translation directions is important for multilingual models. In this setting, we do not compare our model with Switch-GLAT as it fails to achieve reasonable performance.[4] Instead, we compare M-DAT with the M-AT models (Johnson et al., 2017), and include a recent study, Residual M-AT (Liu et al., 2021), which relaxes the residual connections in the Transformer encoder to force the decoder to learn more generalized representations.[5]

[4]As seen in the Table 7 of Song et al. (2022), Switch-GLAT only obtained a 2.34 BLEU on a zero-shot dataset.

[5]The numbers of Residual M-AT are based on our replication, and are close to those in Liu et al. (2021).

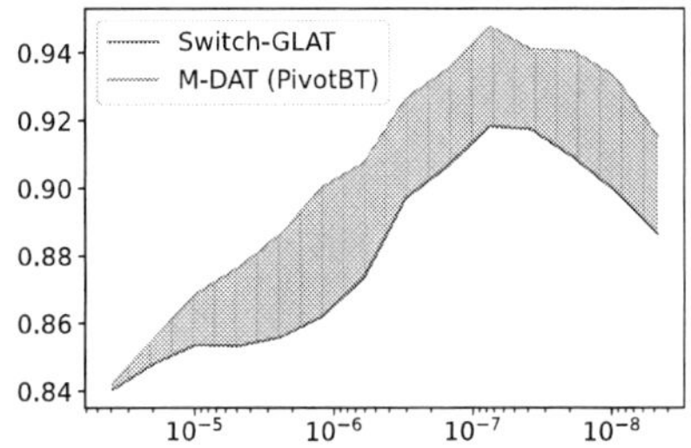


Figure 2: Comparison between M-DAT and Switch-GLAT in the preservation ratio of low-frequency words.

As seen in Table 2, the M-ATs are incapable of zero-shot translation, and are largely outperformed by the Residual M-AT. On the other hand, our M-DAT with the lookahead decoding outperforms Residual M-AT by 0.86 BLEU on the IWSLT dataset, although it is 0.27 lower on the Europarl dataset. With $n$-gram beam search, the improvement is 1.68 BLEU on IWSLT and 1.31 on Europarl. Our M-DAT is the first non-autoregressive model to outperform a strong AT baseline in zero-shot multilingual translation.[6]

**Inference Speed.** We compare the inference speed on the test set of WMT-EFD and present the results in Table 3. The batch size is set to 1 to mimic the real-world scenario, where the user requests come one after another (Gu et al., 2018). As seen, M-DAT with lookahead is about 16 times faster than the standard autoregressive baseline, and is about 4 times faster than M-AT with a shallow decoder. Compared with Switch-GLAT, M-DAT with lookahead is about the same efficiency. Admittedly, M-DAT with beam search is slower, but is still 5.2 times faster than the standard M-AT. In general, M-DAT obtains a good speed–quality trade-off.

### 4.3 Analysis

**Low-Frequency Words.** We analyze the generated text (on the WMT-EFD test set) of our M-DAT and Switch-GLAT. We followed Ding et al. (2021), and computed the percentage of a word being preserved in the translated sentence (in the corresponding language); then we grouped the words by their frequencies in the dataset.[7] As seen in Figure 2, M-DAT keeps more low-frequency words, which verifies our motivation to develop a non-autoregressive multilingual model without the help of knowledge distillation. In addition to the BLEU scores, this result further provides evidence that our M-DAT has better translation quality than Switch-GLAT.

| # | Model Variant | Supervised | Zero-Shot |
|---|---|---|---|
| 1 | M-DAT (PivotBT) | **29.42** | **19.35** |
| 2 | rand-lang & w/o pivot | 29.33 | 18.10 |
| 3 | src-lang & w/o pivot | 29.38 | 13.78 |
| 4 | w/o BT | 28.55 | 13.37 |

Table 4: Ablation study on the IWSLT dataset. The results are generated with $n$-gram beam search.

**Ablation Study.** Table 4 presents an ablation study on the pivot back-translation (PivotBT) of M-DAT using the IWSLT dataset. In addition to PivotBT, we consider 3 variants: 1) *M-DAT rand-lang & w/o pivot*, which randomly selects an augmented source language but does not translate through a pivot language; 2) *M-DAT src-lang & w/o pivot*, which directly back-translates the target sentence to the language of the source sentence; and 3) *M-DAT w/o BT*, which does not augment the training data with back-translation.

In the supervised setting, we observe that back-translation improves the performance (Lines 1–3 vs. Line 4), which is consistent with the findings of previous work (Johnson et al., 2017). Among back-translation methods, *src-lang & w/o pivot* performs the worst in the zero-shot setting (Line 3). We conjuncture that this is because only applying back-translation to the source language makes the model focus too much on the supervised directions, which degenerates the generalization to the zero-shot setting. On the other hand, our PivotBT outperforms the direct random back-translation (*rand-lang & w/o pivot*) and the source-language back-translation (*src-lang & w/o pivot*). This confirms that PivotBT provides the model with better-augmented samples for the zero-shot translation.

## 5 Conclusion

In this work, we propose M-DAT to tackle non-autoregressive multilingual machine translation (MNMT). Our approach leverages the recent directed acyclic Transformer so that we do not need the knowledge distillation process, which is particularly inconvenient in the multilingual translation task. Further, we propose a pivot back-translation method to improve the robustness. Our M-DAT achieves state-of-the-art results on supervised and zero-shot settings for non-autoregressive MNMT.

[6]In our experiments, the autoregressive baseline models are not equipped with PivotBT, as their inefficient inference (as seen in Table 3) makes the training with back-translation impractical. In fact, our PivotBT is another way to take advantage of the fast inference of non-autoregressive models.

[7]We applied the `FastAlign` alignment tool (Dyer et al., 2013) to approximate word preservation.

## 6 Limitation

One possible limitation is that our M-DAT obtains slightly lower BLEU scores compared with autoregressive models in the supervised setting. However, this is not the drawback of this work, as it is understandable that non-autoregressive models trade quality with more efficiency. Nevertheless, our M-DAT outperforms the previous state-of-the-art NAT approach in both supervised and zero-shot settings, and is easier to be deployed since KD is not required. Our PivotBT, in principle, can also be applied to the training of multilingual autoregressive Transformer (M-AT). However, we do not include M-AT with PivotBT for two reasons: 1) the main focus of this research is on the non-autoregressive Transformer; and 2) the decoding of M-AT is much slower than our M-DAT, which makes the training of M-AT with PivotBT impractical.

## Acknowledgments

We would like to thank all reviewers and chairs for their comments. This research was supported in part by the Natural Science Foundation of China under Grant No. 62376133. This research was also supported in part by the Natural Sciences and Engineering Research Council of Canada (NSERC) under Grant Nos. RGPIN-2020-04440 and RGPIN-2020-04465, the Amii Fellow Program, the Canada CIFAR AI Chair Program, the Alberta Innovates Program, and the Digital Research Alliance of Canada (alliancecan.ca).

## References

Naveen Arivazhagan, Ankur Bapna, Orhan Firat, Roee Aharoni, Melvin Johnson, and Wolfgang Macherey. 2019. The missing ingredient in zero-shot neural machine translation. *arXiv preprint arXiv:1903.07091*.

Dzmitry Bahdanau, Kyunghyun Cho, and Yoshua Bengio. 2015. Neural machine translation by jointly learning to align and translate. In *International Conference on Learning Representations*.

Ankur Bapna and Orhan Firat. 2019. Simple, scalable adaptation for neural machine translation. In *Proceedings of the 2019 Conference on Empirical Methods in Natural Language Processing and the 9th International Joint Conference on Natural Language Processing*, pages 1538–1548.

Yun Chen, Yang Liu, Yong Cheng, and Victor O.K. Li. 2017. A teacher-student framework for zero-resource neural machine translation. In *Proceedings of the 55th Annual Meeting of the Association for Computational Linguistics (Volume 1: Long Papers)*, pages 1925–1935.

Yong Cheng, Qian Yang, Yang Liu, Maosong Sun, and Wei Xu. 2017. Joint training for pivot-based neural machine translation. In *Proceedings of the Twenty-Sixth International Joint Conference on Artificial Intelligence*, pages 3974–3980.

Liang Ding, Longyue Wang, Xuebo Liu, Derek F. Wong, Dacheng Tao, and Zhaopeng Tu. 2021. Rejuvenating low-frequency words: Making the most of parallel data in non-autoregressive translation. In *Proceedings of the 59th Annual Meeting of the Association for Computational Linguistics and the 11th International Joint Conference on Natural Language Processing*, pages 3431–3441.

Chris Dyer, Victor Chahuneau, and Noah A. Smith. 2013. A simple, fast, and effective reparameterization of IBM Model 2. In *Proceedings of the 2013 Conference of the North American Chapter of the Association for Computational Linguistics: Human Language Technologies*, pages 644–648.

Orhan Firat, Kyunghyun Cho, and Yoshua Bengio. 2016. Multi-way, multilingual neural machine translation with a shared attention mechanism. In *Proceedings of the 2016 Conference of the North American Chapter of the Association for Computational Linguistics: Human Language Technologies*, pages 866–875.

Marjan Ghazvininejad, Omer Levy, Yinhan Liu, and Luke Zettlemoyer. 2019. Mask-predict: Parallel decoding of conditional masked language models. In *Proceedings of the 2019 Conference on Empirical Methods in Natural Language Processing and the 9th International Joint Conference on Natural Language Processing*, pages 6112–6121.

Jiatao Gu, James Bradbury, Caiming Xiong, Victor O.K. Li, and Richard Socher. 2018. Non-autoregressive neural machine translation. In *International Conference on Learning Representations*.

Jiatao Gu and Xiang Kong. 2021. Fully non-autoregressive neural machine translation: Tricks of the trade. In *Findings of the Association for Computational Linguistics: ACL-IJCNLP*, pages 120–133.

Jiatao Gu, Yong Wang, Kyunghyun Cho, and Victor O.K. Li. 2019. Improved zero-shot neural machine translation via ignoring spurious correlations. In *Proceedings of the 57th Annual Meeting of the Association for Computational Linguistics*, pages 1258–1268.

Chenyang Huang, Hao Zhou, Osmar R Zaïane, Lili Mou, and Lei Li. 2022a. Non-autoregressive translation with layer-wise prediction and deep supervision. In *Proceedings of the AAAI Conference on Artificial Intelligence*, pages 10776–10784.

Fei Huang, Hao Zhou, Yang Liu, Hang Li, and Minlie Huang. 2022b. Directed acyclic Transformer for non-autoregressive machine translation. In *International Conference on Machine Learning*.

Melvin Johnson, Mike Schuster, Quoc V. Le, Maxim Krikun, Yonghui Wu, Zhifeng Chen, Nikhil Thorat, Fernanda Viégas, Martin Wattenberg, Greg Corrado, Macduff Hughes, and Jeffrey Dean. 2017. Google's multilingual neural machine translation system: Enabling zero-shot translation. *Transactions of the Association for Computational Linguistics*, pages 339–351.

Jungo Kasai, Nikolaos Pappas, Hao Peng, James Cross, and Noah A. Smith. 2021. Deep encoder, shallow decoder: Reevaluating non-autoregressive machine translation. In *International Conference on Learning Representations*.

Yoon Kim and Alexander M. Rush. 2016. Sequence-level knowledge distillation. In *Proceedings of the 2016 Conference on Empirical Methods in Natural Language Processing*, pages 1317–1327.

Danni Liu, Jan Niehues, James Cross, Francisco Guzmán, and Xian Li. 2021. Improving zero-shot translation by disentangling positional information. In *Proceedings of the 59th Annual Meeting of the Association for Computational Linguistics and the 11th International Joint Conference on Natural Language Processing (Volume 1: Long Papers)*, pages 1259–1273.

Puyuan Liu, Chenyang Huang, and Lili Mou. 2022a. Learning non-autoregressive models from search for unsupervised sentence summarization. In *Proceedings of the 60th Annual Meeting of the Association for Computational Linguistics (Volume 1: Long Papers)*, pages 7916–7929.

Puyuan Liu, Xiang Zhang, and Lili Mou. 2022b. A character-level length-control algorithm for non-autoregressive sentence summarization. *Advances in Neural Information Processing Systems*, pages 29101–29112.

Kishore Papineni, Salim Roukos, Todd Ward, and Wei-Jing Zhu. 2002. BLEU: A method for automatic evaluation of machine translation. In *Proceedings of the 40th Annual Meeting of the Association for Computational Linguistics*, pages 311–318.

Matt Post. 2018. A call for clarity in reporting BLEU scores. In *Proceedings of the Third Conference on Machine Translation: Research Papers*, pages 186–191.

Weizhen Qi, Yeyun Gong, Jian Jiao, Yu Yan, Weizhu Chen, Dayiheng Liu, Kewen Tang, Houqiang Li, Jiusheng Chen, Ruofei Zhang, et al. 2021. Bang: Bridging autoregressive and non-autoregressive generation with large scale pretraining. In *International Conference on Machine Learning*, pages 8630–8639.

Lihua Qian, Hao Zhou, Yu Bao, Mingxuan Wang, Lin Qiu, Weinan Zhang, Yong Yu, and Lei Li. 2021. Glancing transformer for non-autoregressive neural machine translation. In *Proceedings of the 59th Annual Meeting of the Association for Computational Linguistics and the 11th International Joint Conference on Natural Language Processing (Volume 1: Long Papers)*, pages 1993–2003.

Rico Sennrich, Barry Haddow, and Alexandra Birch. 2016. Improving neural machine translation models with monolingual data. In *Proceedings of the 54th Annual Meeting of the Association for Computational Linguistics (Volume 1: Long Papers)*, pages 86–96.

Zhenqiao Song, Hao Zhou, Lihua Qian, Jingjing Xu, Shanbo Cheng, Mingxuan Wang, and Lei Li. 2022. switch-GLAT: Multilingual parallel machine translation via code-switch decoder. In *International Conference on Learning Representations*.

Mitchell Stern, William Chan, Jamie Kiros, and Jakob Uszkoreit. 2019. Insertion transformer: Flexible sequence generation via insertion operations. In *Proceedings of the International Conference on Machine Learning*, pages 5976–5985.

Yixuan Su, Deng Cai, Yan Wang, David Vandyke, Simon Baker, Piji Li, and Nigel Collier. 2021. Non-autoregressive text generation with pre-trained language models. In *Proceedings of the 16th Conference of the European Chapter of the Association for Computational Linguistics: Main Volume*, pages 234–243.

Ashish Vaswani, Noam Shazeer, Niki Parmar, Jakob Uszkoreit, Llion Jones, Aidan N Gomez, Łukasz Kaiser, and Illia Polosukhin. 2017. Attention is all you need. In *Advances in Neural Information Processing Systems*.

Biao Zhang, Ankur Bapna, Rico Sennrich, and Orhan Firat. 2021. Share or not? Learning to schedule language-specific capacity for multilingual translation. In *International Conference on Learning Representations*.

Biao Zhang, Philip Williams, Ivan Titov, and Rico Sennrich. 2020. Improving massively multilingual neural machine translation and zero-shot translation. In *Proceedings of the 58th Annual Meeting of the Association for Computational Linguistics*, pages 1628–1639.

Chunting Zhou, Jiatao Gu, and Graham Neubig. 2020. Understanding knowledge distillation in non-autoregressive machine translation. In *International Conference on Learning Representations*.

Yicheng Zou, Zhihua Liu, Xingwu Hu, and Qi Zhang. 2021. Thinking clearly, talking fast: Concept-guided non-autoregressive generation for open-domain dialogue systems. In *Proceedings of the 2021 Conference on Empirical Methods in Natural Language Processing*, pages 2215–2226.

| | Directions | Languages | Language pairs |
|---|---|---|---|
| WMT-EFZ | 6 | 3 | en↔fr, en↔zh |
| WMT-EFD | 6 | 3 | en↔fr, en↔de |
| WMT-MANY | 10 | 6 | en↔fr, en↔zh, en↔de, en↔ro, en↔ru |

Table 5: The translation directions of the WMT-EFD, WMT-EFZ, and WMT-MANY datasets.

## A Datasets

**WMT Datasets.** WMT-EFZ, EFD, and MANY are specifically curated for multilingual machine translation; each is a mix of a few general bilingual machine translation corpora.[8] We list the translation directions of the three datasets in Table 5. As seen, both WMT-EFZ and WMT-EFD have 3 languages and 6 translation directions, whereas WMT-MANY has 5 languages and 10 directions.

We strictly followed Song et al. (2022) for data preparation, and we set the vocabulary size as 85K for WMT-EFD and WMT-EFZ, and 95K for WMT-MANY.

**IWSLT Dataset.** We followed Liu et al. (2021) for the IWSLT dataset, and directly obtained the processed data from their published codebase.[9] The vocabulary size of IWSLT is 19K. The IWSLT test set contains 3 supervised language pairs: en↔ro, en↔it, and en↔nl. Additionally, it contains 3 zero-shot language pairs: ro↔it, ro↔nl, and it↔nl. The training set for each supervised direction includes 145K samples.

**Europarl Dataset.** We further include the Europarl dataset to evaluate the multilingual capability of the proposed method. We followed Liu et al. (2021) for data preprocessing. The Europarl test set has 16 supervised directions (containing English) and 56 zero-shot directions (not containing English). The translation directions are detailed in Table 8.

## B Settings

**Evaluation Metrics.** We used BLEU (Papineni et al., 2002) to evaluate the translation quality. To ensure a fair comparison with previous work, we applied two BLEU variants. For the WMT datasets, we followed Song et al. (2022) and applied tokenized BLEU. For the IWSLT and Europarl datasets, we followed Liu et al. (2021) and adopted SacreBLEU (Post, 2018).

We evaluated the latency on a single Tesla V100 GPU with a batch size of 1 to mimic the real-world scenario where the users' requests come one by one. Our evaluation scripts are also available from the released code.

**WMT and Europarl Datasets.** We used the Transformer-base configuration (Vaswani et al., 2017) as the backbone. To train the model, we set the batch size such that it contains 64K tokens, and let the model train for 800K updates. We used the Adam optimizer. The learning rate was warmed up to 5e-4 using 10K updates, and was annealed with the inverse square roots scheduler. The back-translation strength $\lambda$ was set to 0.5. To balance the sizes of different translation directions, we set the upsampling ratio to 1/3. Since the validation set only contains supervised directions for the IWSLT dataset, we further applied the regularization on the encoder representations (Arivazhagan et al., 2019) to prevent overfitting to the supervised directions.

Following the setting in most non-autoregressive machine translation studies (Gu et al., 2018; Gu and Kong, 2021; Song et al., 2022; Huang et al., 2022a), we evaluated both AT and NAT models by averaging the weights of the best 5 checkpoints, which were selected by their BLEU scores on the validation set.

For the neural architecture, both our M-DAT and the M-AT with the standard layout have 6 encoder layers and 6 decoder layers. The shallow-decoder M-AT has 12 encoder layers and 1 decoder layer.

**IWSLT dataset.** Most of the settings for IWSLT are the same as those for the WMT and Europarl datasets, but we made some adaptations. Since the IWSLT dataset is smaller, we set the batch size to 32K tokens. Further, we followed Liu et al. (2021), and set the number of encoders and decoders to 5 for our M-DAT and the M-AT with the standard layout. On the other hand, the M-AT with the shallow-decoder layout M-AT has 10 encoder layers and 1 decoder layer.

## C Detailed Results

We list the per-direction BLEU scores of the three WMT datasets in Table 6, IWSLT in Table 7, and Europarl in Table 8.

As seen, our M-DAT is only slightly outperformed by M-AT (Johnson et al., 2017), and the gap is small. However, our M-DAT outperforms

[8]The corpora are obtained from the WMT workshop: `https://www.statmt.org/wmt17/`

[9]`https://github.com/nlp-dke/NMTGMinor/tree/master/recipes/zero-shot`

| **Supervised Setting** | AVG | en-it | en-nl | en-ro | it-en | nl-en | ro-en |
|---|---|---|---|---|---|---|---|
| M-AT w/ standard layout | **30.0** | **32.7** | 29.0 | **24.4** | **34.6** | 29.8 | **29.5** |
| M-AT w/ shallow decoder | **30.0** | **32.7** | 29.0 | **24.4** | **34.6** | 29.8 | **29.5** |
| Residual M-AT | 29.7 | 32.6 | **29.1** | 23.9 | 33.8 | 29.6 | 29.3 |
| M-DAT w/ lookahead | 28.6 | 30.8 | 27.6 | 22.3 | 33.3 | 29.3 | 28.2 |
| w/ $n$-gram beam search | 29.4 | 32.1 | 28.4 | 23.0 | 34.0 | **30.0** | 29.0 |
| **Zero-Shot Setting** | AVG | it-en | it-ro | nl-it | nl-ro | ro-it | ro-nl |
| M-AT | 12.87 | 13.3 | 12.3 | 13.4 | 11.7 | 14.2 | 12.3 |
| M-AT | 12.87 | 13.3 | 12.3 | 13.4 | 11.7 | 14.2 | 12.3 |
| Residual M-AT | 17.67 | 18.2 | 17.3 | 18.3 | 15.2 | 19.8 | 17.2 |
| M-DAT w/ lookahead | 18.53 | 20.0 | 17.8 | 19.3 | 15.3 | 20.9 | 17.9 |
| w/ $n$-gram beam search | **19.35** | **20.6** | **18.6** | **20.3** | **16.0** | **21.8** | **18.8** |

Table 6: BLEU scores on the IWSLT dataset.

| Model | | AVG | en-fr | fr-en | en-de | de-en | | AVG | en-fr | fr-en | en-zh | zh-en |
|---|---|---|---|---|---|---|---|---|---|---|---|---|
| M-AT w/ standard layout | **WMT-EFD** | **34.57** | **42.30** | **37.88** | 25.85 | **32.23** | **WMT-EFZ** | **31.15** | **42.14** | **37.64** | 21.02 | **23.80** |
| M-AT w/ shallow decoder | | 34.19 | 42.19 | 37.39 | **26.22** | 30.96 | | 30.87 | 42.15 | 37.92 | **21.44** | 21.98 |
| Switch-GLAT | | 33.34 | 40.81 | 36.00 | 25.27 | 31.29 | | 29.76 | 40.54 | 36.48 | 19.47 | 22.55 |
| M-DAT w/ lookahead | | 33.72 | 41.81 | 37.69 | 24.00 | 31.31 | | 30.39 | 41.23 | 36.96 | 20.46 | 22.90 |
| w/ $n$-gram beam search | | 33.83 | 41.54 | 37.84 | 24.23 | 31.70 | | 30.55 | 41.12 | 37.34 | 20.87 | 22.85 |

| **WMT-MANY** | AVG | en-de | de-en | en-fr | fr-en | en-ro | ro-en | en-ru | ru-en | en-zh | zh-en |
|---|---|---|---|---|---|---|---|---|---|---|---|
| M-AT w/ standard layout | **30.36** | 24.67 | **32.16** | 41.67 | **38.00** | **32.86** | **35.65** | **24.22** | **30.47** | 20.66 | 23.27 |
| M-AT w/ shallow decoder | 29.19 | **25.41** | 31.38 | **41.98** | 37.88 | 30.18 | 34.16 | 21.87 | 26.92 | **20.90** | 21.27 |
| Switch-GLAT | 28.47 | 24.18 | 30.49 | 39.47 | 36.30 | 31.93 | 32.40 | 24.16 | 28.33 | 16.25 | 21.23 |
| M-DAT w/ lookahead | 28.69 | 23.48 | 30.30 | 40.78 | 36.76 | 30.77 | 34.83 | 20.14 | 28.30 | 19.61 | 21.94 |
| w/ $n$-gram beam search | 29.73 | 23.91 | 31.52 | 41.12 | 37.63 | 32.11 | 35.44 | 21.45 | 30.09 | 20.60 | **23.42** |

Table 7: BLEU scores on three WMT datasets.

Switch-GLAT in most of the language directions on the WMT datasets.

Moreover, our proposed M-AT outperforms the strong Residual M-AT model (Liu et al., 2021) on all zero-shot translation directions of the IWSLT dataset and of most of the zero-shot directions of the Europarl dataset.

| Direction | M-AT w/ standard layout | M-AT w/ shallow decoder | Residual M-AT | M-DAT w/ lookahead | M-DAT w/ $n$-gram beam search |
|---|---|---|---|---|---|
| da-en | **38.5** | 37.6 | 37.9 | 38.4 | 38.1 |
| de-en | **36.3** | 35.4 | 35.4 | 35.8 | 36 |
| en-da | **36.5** | 35.5 | 36.3 | 34.7 | 35.9 |
| en-de | **28.6** | 27.7 | 27.8 | 26.8 | 28.1 |
| en-es | **43.0** | 42.1 | 42.2 | 41.7 | 42.9 |
| en-fi | 21.9 | 20.5 | 21.5 | 19.8 | **22** |
| en-fr | 38.8 | 38 | 37.8 | 37.2 | **39** |
| en-it | **33.3** | 32.7 | 32.7 | 31.7 | 33.2 |
| en-nl | **30.0** | 28.6 | 29.5 | 28.8 | **30.0** |
| en-pt | **39.3** | 37.9 | 38.3 | 37.7 | 38.8 |
| es-en | **43.2** | 43.0 | 42.6 | 42.7 | 42.1 |
| fi-en | **32.7** | 31.4 | 32.3 | 32.6 | **32.7** |
| fr-en | 38.5 | 38.2 | 38.1 | **38.8** | 38.6 |
| it-en | **36.6** | 36.3 | 36.3 | 36.1 | 36.0 |
| nl-en | **34.5** | 33.3 | 33.6 | 34.1 | 34.3 |
| pt-en | 40.9 | **41.0** | 40.5 | 40.4 | 40 |
| **Average** | **35.79** | 34.95 | 35.18 | 34.83 | 35.48 |
| da-de | 15.2 | 9.8 | 23.85 | 23.5 | **25.1** |
| da-es | 28.1 | 14.8 | 31.08 | 31.7 | **33.3** |
| da-fi | 13.3 | 8.1 | 17.77 | 15.9 | **18.4** |
| da-fr | 22.0 | 13.0 | 28.58 | 28.6 | **30.8** |
| da-it | 18.4 | 10.6 | 26.17 | 25.0 | **26.8** |
| da-nl | 18.3 | 8.8 | 24.24 | 25.1 | **26.6** |
| da-pt | 24.6 | 11.0 | 28.57 | 28.6 | **30.1** |
| de-da | 8.7 | 5.4 | 26.58 | 27.8 | **29.8** |
| de-es | 21.8 | 9.8 | 29.65 | 31.1 | **32.8** |
| de-fi | 8.9 | 5.0 | **19.02** | 15.3 | 17.5 |
| de-fr | 15.7 | 8.6 | 29.2 | 28.5 | **30.4** |
| de-it | 15.2 | 6.8 | **26.27** | 24.3 | 26.0 |
| de-nl | 17.7 | 4.9 | 25.42 | 25.5 | **27.1** |
| de-pt | 15.4 | 6.7 | **28.83** | 28.0 | 29.7 |
| es-da | 11.2 | 5.7 | 29.02 | 29.5 | **30.7** |
| es-de | 12.0 | 5.5 | **24.85** | 23.5 | 24.6 |
| es-fi | 9.0 | 5.7 | **20.28** | 17.0 | 19.0 |
| es-fr | 26.2 | 11.1 | 33.47 | 34.2 | **35.8** |
| es-it | 19.5 | 9.0 | **31.55** | 29.6 | 31.0 |
| es-nl | 13.7 | 4.9 | 25.3 | 25.9 | **27.1** |
| es-pt | 23.9 | 9.8 | 34.24 | 35.5 | **36.9** |
| fi-da | 9.8 | 5.8 | 24.45 | 24.2 | **26.1** |
| fi-de | 9.2 | 5.9 | 20.4 | 19.1 | **20.9** |
| fi-es | 15.2 | 9.8 | 28.74 | 27.6 | **29.2** |
| fi-fr | 12.9 | 7.8 | 25.27 | 25.2 | **27.0** |
| fi-it | 9.3 | 6.5 | **24.37** | 21.5 | 23.1 |
| fi-nl | 11.3 | 5.0 | 20.95 | 21.2 | **22.9** |
| fi-pt | 12.9 | 6.4 | 25.78 | 24.9 | **26.6** |
| fr-da | 9.8 | 7.4 | 25.57 | 26.9 | **28.6** |
| fr-de | 12.9 | 6.9 | 22.08 | 22.2 | **23.7** |
| fr-es | 26.8 | 14.2 | 32.83 | 35.5 | **36.9** |
| fr-fi | 9.9 | 7.1 | 15.56 | 15.4 | **17.5** |
| fr-it | 19.5 | 12.5 | 28.18 | 28.8 | **30.4** |
| fr-nl | 14.6 | 6.2 | 24.33 | 24.6 | **26.5** |
| fr-pt | 20.8 | 10.1 | 30.01 | 32.7 | **34.0** |
| it-da | 9.4 | 4.7 | 24.62 | 25.5 | **26.8** |
| it-de | 10.5 | 5.1 | 21.75 | 20.5 | **21.9** |
| it-es | 22.2 | 10.1 | 31.99 | 33.6 | **34.6** |
| it-fi | 8.6 | 4.7 | **17.45** | 14.6 | 16.7 |
| it-fr | 22.1 | 9.9 | 30.77 | 31.8 | **33.2** |
| it-nl | 12.5 | 4.5 | 22.71 | 23.2 | **24.8** |
| it-pt | 16.7 | 7.9 | 29.8 | 30.4 | **32.1** |
| nl-da | 14.3 | 6.8 | 27.97 | 26.5 | **28.0** |
| nl-de | 13.8 | 6.9 | **25.1** | 22.6 | 24.1 |
| nl-es | 21.9 | 13.6 | 29.78 | 29.7 | **31.4** |
| nl-fi | 9.0 | 5.7 | **17.19** | 14.6 | 16.2 |
| nl-fr | 19.4 | 10.7 | 27.12 | 27.7 | **29.4** |
| nl-it | 16.4 | 8.9 | 24.79 | 23.4 | **25.1** |
| nl-pt | 18.2 | 9.2 | 27.57 | 26.9 | **28.4** |
| pt-da | 11.9 | 6.1 | 26.8 | 28.2 | **29.3** |
| pt-de | 11.5 | 6.3 | **24.42** | 22.4 | 23.7 |
| pt-es | 28.1 | 13.2 | 36.41 | 37.2 | **38.2** |
| pt-fi | 9.8 | 5.9 | 17.26 | 16.4 | **18.3** |
| pt-fr | 25.0 | 12.3 | 33.03 | 34.1 | **35.0** |
| pt-it | 19.2 | 9.7 | 29.96 | 29.5 | **30.3** |
| pt-nl | 12.8 | 5.4 | 24.25 | 25.5 | **26.4** |
| **Average** | 15.84 | 8.11 | 26.13 | 25.86 | **27.44** |

Table 8: BLEU scores on the Europarl dataset.

# Knowledge Injection with Perturbation-based Constrained Attention Network for Word Sense Disambiguation

**Fumiyo Fukumoto**
Interdisciplinary Graduate School
University of Yamanashi
4-3-11, Takeda, Kofu, 400-8511, Japan
fukumoto@yamanashi.ac.jp

**Shou Asakawa**
Graduate School of Engineering
University of Yamanashi
4-3-11, Takeda, Kofu, 400-8511, Japan
G20TK002@yamanashi.ac.jp

## Abstract

Supervised Word Sense Disambiguation (WSD) has been studied intensively for over three decades. However, disentangling diverse contexts is still a challenging problem. This paper addresses the problem and proposes a Perturbation-based constrained attention network (Pconan) for injecting lexical knowledge derived from the WordNet. The Pconan allows modeling beneficial dependencies between the segments/words within the input sequence with the mask-attention technique. We incorporate a perturbation method into our model to mitigate the overfitting problem resulting from intensive learning. The experimental results by using a benchmark dataset show that our method is comparable to the SOTA WSD methods. Our source codes are available online[1].

## 1 Introduction

Computational lexicons such as WordNet (George A. Miller and Miller, 1990) and ACQUILEX (Edward, 1991) have been popular knowledge resources for NLP tasks. There is a large body of WSD work based on neural networks that leverage rich information derived from these resources (Luo et al., 2018b; Vial et al., 2019; Kumar and Talukdar, 2019; Huang et al., 2019; Blevins and Zettlemoyer, 2020; Bevilacqua and Navigli, 2020; Conia and Navigli, 2021). They demonstrated that the external knowledge base is beneficial to disambiguate senses. However, it is often the case that the inputs are long sequences. It hampers WSD attempts with external knowledge. Several authors have attempted to alleviate the issue. (Blevins and Zettlemoyer, 2020) independently embedded the target word with its surrounding contexts and the dictionary definition of each sense. (Bevilacqua and Navigli, 2020) extended (Blevins and Zettlemoyer, 2020) method and integrated relational knowledge into the architecture through a simple additional sparse dot product operation. Their results by using a benchmark dataset were beyond 80%.

The attention mechanism is also one of the major techniques to capture long-term dependencies on their sequence (Vaswani et al., 2017). (Luo et al., 2018a) introduced a co-attention mechanism to generate co-dependent representations to capture both word- and sentence-level information. Their assumption is that lexical knowledge such as gloss sentences and context sentences can help each other to highlight the important words within these sentences, while the sense definition candidates do not all at once take into account during the training process. Several authors focused on the issue (Wang and Wang, 2021). (Barba et al., 2021b) proposed a joint-learning that learns the input context and target word definitions jointly. Subsequently, (Barba et al., 2021a) attempted to process the disambiguation of a target word to be conditioned not only on its context but also on the explicit senses assigned to the surrounding words, while their model has not leveraged external lexical knowledge.

Inspired by the previous work mentioned above, we propose a method to inject lexical knowledge, i.e. example sentences from WordNet to effectively learn a context sentence and lexical knowledge simultaneously. Our model called Perturbation-based constrained attention network (Pconan) allows the modeling of dependencies between the segments/words within the input sequence with the mask-attention technique. The technique makes it possible to concentrate on learning beneficial dependencies only, entirely discarding the others. However, this causes an overfitting problem, especially when the available training data is limited. To alleviate this issue, the Pconan utilizes the perturbation technique (Sato et al., 2019). More specifically, we add noises to the training data and the model learns sense distinctions of the same word by using these noisy data to assign the correct label.

[1] https://github.com/fukumoto-lab/Pconan



*Findings of the Association for Computational Linguistics: IJCNLP-AACL 2023*, pages 171–177
November 1–4, 2023. ©2023 Asian Federation of Natural Language Processing

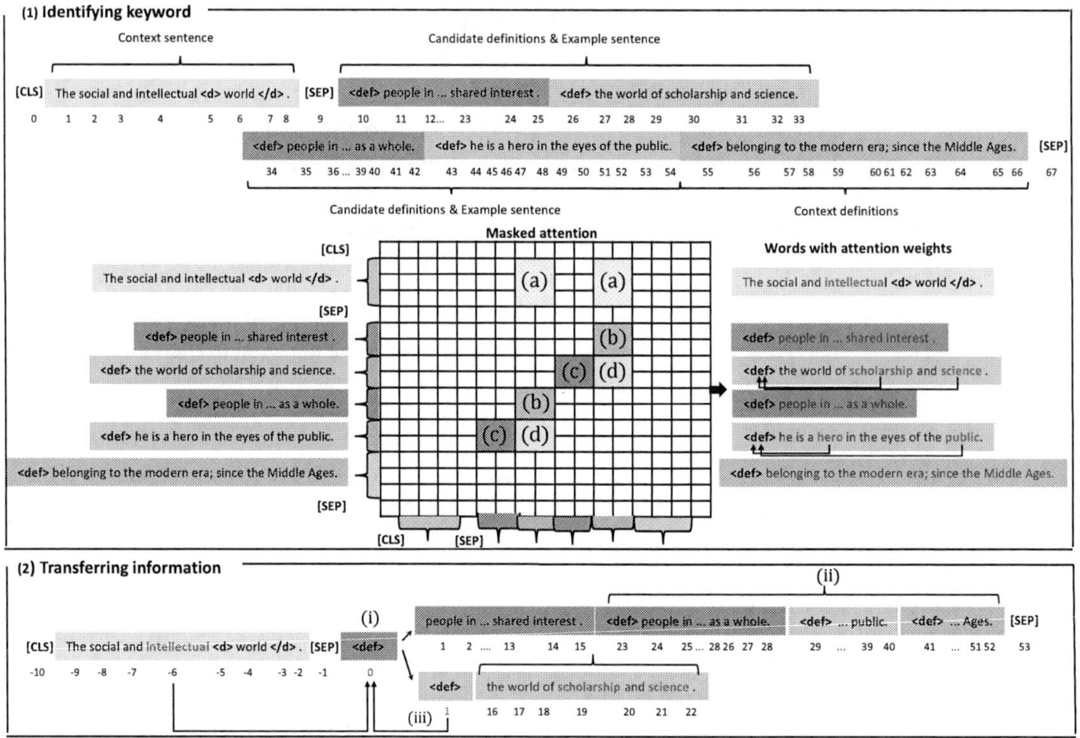


Figure 1: Identifying keyword and transferring information

## 2 Framework

### 2.1 The WSD task definition

For each of the candidate definitions (CDs), our model utilizes an example sentences (ESs) provided by the WordNet.

Let $\mathcal{SI}_{tw(i)}$ be a sense inventory, $tw(i)$ be a current, $i$-th target word appeared in the context sentence $c$. Let also $\mathcal{D}_{tw(i)}$ = <def>$tw(i)_1^{g_1}\cdots tw(i)_{|g_1|}^{g_1}$<def>$es(i)_1^{s_1}\cdots es(i)_{|s_1|}^{s_1}$ <def>$tw(i)_1^{g_N}\cdots tw(i)_{|g_N|}^{g_N}$ <def> $es(i)_1^{s_N}\cdots es(i)_{|s_N|}^{s_N}$ be the CDs for $tw(i)$, along with ESs, where $tw(i)_j^{g_k}$ and $es(i)_j^{s_k}$ be the $j$-th word of the $k$-th CD $g_k$, and ES $s_k$ ($1 \leq k \leq N$), respectively. $N$ is the total number of CDs and <def> stands for the start of each segment. Let also $\widetilde{\mathcal{D}} = \widetilde{s}_1,\cdots,\widetilde{s}_{i-1}$ be a sequence concatenating the context definitions of the senses previously assigned to $\widetilde{w}_1,\cdots,\widetilde{w}_{i-1}$.

For a given $c$ including <d>$tw(i)$</d>, we create an input sequence [CLS] $c$ [SEP] $\mathcal{D}_{tw(i)}$ $\widetilde{\mathcal{D}}$ [SEP]. Here, the inputs to each encoder are padded with DEBERTa-specific start and end symbols: [CLS] and [SEP] (He et al., 2021). The goal of the WSD task is for the input sequence, to find the correct definition $\widetilde{g} \in \mathcal{SI}_{tw(i)}$.

### 2.2 Constrained Attention Network

Our model applies (1) identifying keywords, and (2) transferring information to learn relevant contextual features for WSD. The top of Figure 1 illustrates an example of the input sequence $X$, i.e. [CLS] $c$ [SEP] $\mathcal{D}_{tw(i)}$ $\widetilde{\mathcal{D}}$ [SEP].

For the input sequence $X$ = [CLS] $c$ [SEP] $\mathcal{D}_{tw(i)}$ $\widetilde{\mathcal{D}}$ [SEP], we apply the so-called hard attention technique (Xu et al., 2015; Shen et al., 2018) that a model concentrates solely on learning beneficial dependencies to identify keywords in the sequence, entirely discarding the others. The middle picture of Figure 1 illustrates masked attention for a bi-dimensional matrix. The words aligned on the horizontal axis are heads, and those aligned on the vertical axis are dependents. As illustrated in Figure 1, we discard some segment pairs, each of which consists of a head and dependence on the sequence by masking them as these pairs are not semantically related to each other and do not include keywords that are beneficial to identify the sense of the target word. Table 1 shows pairs that we masked. For example, (b) pairs of candidate definitions and example sentences which do not correspond to each other are masked (purple box

|  | Head | Dependent |
|---|---|---|
| (a) | Context sentence | Example sentence |
| (b) | Candidate definition | Different example sentence |
| (c) | Example sentence | Different candidate definition |
| (d) | Example sentence | Different example sentence |

Table 1: Masked attention between head and dependent.

in Figure 1). The output is a sequence of words with attention weights. In Figure 1, keywords having high weight values are marked in red. From the result of keyword identification, for each candidate definition, we created a sequence for the target candidate definition starting from <def> as follows:

- Context sentence segment perceived as immediately before the CD segment. ((i) in Figure 1)
- <def> of the target CD has two branches. One is that it witnesses other CDs, their ES, and context definitions. ((ii) in Figure 1) Another is that its ES. Relative position of the special token <def> is set to 1. ((iii) in Figure 1)

As shown in "(2) Transferring information" of Figure 1, the structure provides a method to leverage the relative positions of <def> including keywords representation to learn a model more accurately.

### 2.3 Model Architecture

Figure 2 illustrates an overview of our model. Let $\mathbf{E} = [\mathbf{e}_1, \mathbf{e}_2, \cdots, \mathbf{e}_L] \in \mathbb{R}^{d\times L}$ refers to the concatenation of word/token embeddings for the input sequence $X$, and $\mathbf{E}_{rpm} \in \mathbb{R}^{d\times L}$ be relative position matrix of $X$. Here, $\mathbf{e}_k$ and its relative position is obtained by DEBERTa encoding. $d$ refers to the dimension of embedding, and $L$ is the number of words/tokens in $X$. We further utilize a special symbol in $X$ so that the model can capture the difference between the context sentence and others. Let also $\mathbf{r}_k \in \mathbb{R}^d$ be a perturbation vector for the $k$-th word $x_k$ in the input $X$. The perturbed input embedding $\hat{\mathbf{e}}_k$ is computed based on the stochastic gradient descent as follows:

$$\begin{aligned} \hat{\mathbf{e}}_k &= \mathbf{e}_k + \mathbf{r}_k, \\ \mathbf{r}_k &= \epsilon \frac{\mathbf{c}_k}{||\mathbf{c}_k||}, \\ \mathbf{c}_k &= \nabla_{\hat{\mathbf{e}}_k} \mathcal{L}_1(\theta), \end{aligned} \quad (1)$$

where $\epsilon$ refers to a hyperparameter that controls the norm of the perturbation and $\mathcal{L}_1(\theta)$ indicates cross-entropy loss which is given by:

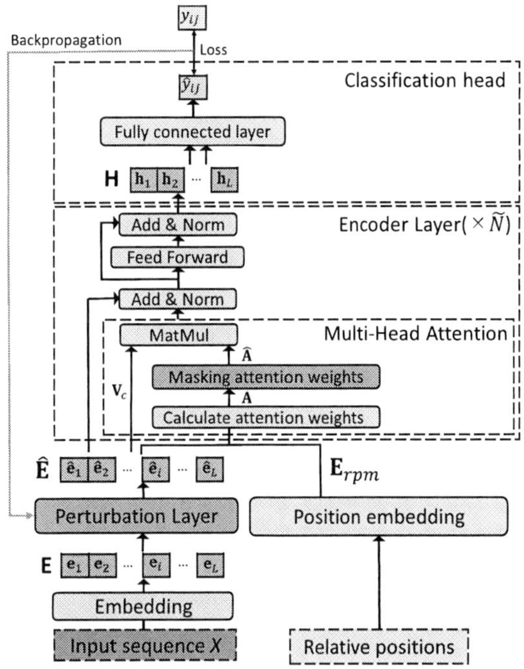


Figure 2: Pconan model architecture.

$$\mathcal{L}_1(\theta) = -\sum_{i=1}^{M}\sum_{j=1}^{N_i} y_{ij}\log \hat{y}_{ij}, \quad (2)$$

where $M$ is the total number of target words in the training data, and $N_i$ is the word sense number of the $i$-th target word, $y_{ij}$ and $\hat{y}_{ij}$ are true and predicted probability of the $i$-th target word that belongs to the $j$-th candidate definition. As shown in Figure 2, for each embedding $\mathbf{e}_k$, we apply Eq.(1) and obtain perturbed sequence. Let $\hat{\mathbf{E}} = [\hat{\mathbf{e}}_1, \hat{\mathbf{e}}_2, \cdots, \hat{\mathbf{e}}_L] \in \mathbb{R}^{d\times L}$ be the concatenation of perturbed sequence. Our constrained attention networks aim to learn relevant contextual keywords for WSD, and finally output attention weights $\mathbf{A}$ for the inputs, $\hat{\mathbf{E}}$ and $\mathbf{E}_{rpm}$. We further obtain $\hat{\mathbf{A}}$ by applying the mask-attention procedure to $\mathbf{A}$. $\hat{\mathbf{E}}$ is linearly projected and we obtain $\mathbf{V}_c$. We multiply $\mathbf{V}_c$ and $\hat{\mathbf{A}}$ by matrix multiplication. Keyword information is transferred by this operation. The result is fed into a feed-forward network, combined with layer normalization and residual connection. Each encoder layer takes the output of the previous layer as input and the number of layers is $\widetilde{N}$. We obtain the matrix $\mathbf{H} = [\mathbf{h}_1, \mathbf{h}_2, \cdots, \mathbf{h}_L] \in \mathbb{R}^{d\times L}$ as an output of the encoder. Each <def> vector that corresponds to the start of the candidate definition is extracted from the matrix $\mathbf{H}$, passed to the fully connected layer and finally, we obtain the probability score $\hat{y}_{ij}$ by the softmax function. The final loss $\mathcal{L}(\theta)$ obtained by our model is given by:

$$\begin{aligned} \mathcal{L}(\theta) &= \mathcal{L}_1(\theta) + \alpha\mathcal{L}_2(\theta), \\ \mathcal{L}_2(\theta) &= \frac{1}{|\mathcal{D}|}\sum_{\mathcal{D}} \mathrm{KL}(p(\cdot|X;\theta)||p(\cdot|X,\mathbf{r};\theta)), \end{aligned} \tag{3}$$

where $\mathcal{D}$ refers to the number of training instances. $\alpha$ indicates a hyperparameter. $\mathrm{KL}(p||q)$ denotes KL-divergence between distributions $p$ and $q$, and $\mathbf{r}$ shows a concatenated vector of $\mathbf{r}_k$ for all $x_k$ ($1 \leq k \leq L$). We train the whole architecture to minimize $\mathcal{L}(\theta)$. Similar to (Barba et al., 2021a) approach, at training time, we use teacher forcing on the context definitions, and at prediction time, we use a greedy decoding strategy and the model deems $\widetilde{g}$ as the most likely definition for a current target word.

## 3 Experiments

### 3.1 Dataset

We performed the experiments on English all-words fine-grained WSD datasets (Alessandro Raganato, 2017b), using SemCor (George A. Miller and Bunker, 1993) as the training corpus. The datasets are Senseval/SemEval data consisting of Senseval-2 (SE2) (Edmonds and Cotton, 2001), Senseval-3 (SE3) (Snyder and Palmer, 2004), SemEval-07 (SE07) (Sameer Pradhan and Palmer, 2007), SemEval-13 (SE13) (Roberto Navigli and Vannella, 2013), and SemEval-15 (SE15) (Moro and Navigli, 2015). Similar to other related work, we chose SE07 as the development set.

### 3.2 Model settings and evaluation metrics

We utilized the hyperparameters with the best performance on SE07 as follows: The dimension of word embedding $d$ was 1,024. The number of maximum words per batch was 1,536. The gradient accumulation and the maximum number of steps were 8.0 and 25,000, respectively. The number of layer $\widetilde{N}$ of DEBERTa was 24 and the learning rate was 3e-6. The initial perturbation was set to 1e-2 and the $\epsilon$ value in Eq.(1) was 3e-6. $\alpha$ in Eq. (3) was set to 1.0. We used Rectified Adam as optimizer (Weijie Liu, 2020). The experiments were conducted by using Pytorch on Nvidia GeForce RTX A6000 (48GB memory). We used the F1-score following (Alessandro Raganato, 2017b).

### 3.3 Comparison Models

We compared our model with the SOTA methods; MSF-SemCor as a frequency based approach, **SVC** (Vial et al., 2019), **GlossBERT** (Huang et al., 2019), **ARES** (Bianca Scarlini, 2020), **EWISER** (Bevilacqua and Navigli, 2020), **BEM** (Blevins and Zettlemoyer, 2020), **WMLC** (Conia and Navigli, 2021), **HCAN** (Luo et al., 2018a), and **KELESC** (Zhang et al., 2022) as a knowledge source integration approach, **SACE** (Wang and Wang, 2021), **ESCHER** (Barba et al., 2021b), and **ConSec** (Barba et al., 2021a) as a joint learning approach.

### 3.4 Results

The results are summarized in Table 2. The performance of joint-learning approaches was better than those of frequency-based and knowledge source integration approaches in all test sets and part-of-speech (POS) patterns. This indicates that the model learned the input context and target word definitions jointly are effective for disambiguation. Our model was statistically significant compared with the second-best method for test sets and POS patterns except for SE3, 15, Adj, and Adv.

### 3.5 Ablation study

We conducted ablation studies to empirically examine our mask-attention technique and perturbation (Prtb). Table 3 shows the results. When we did not utilize the mask-attention and perturbation procedures, the F1-score was 82.1% which is no significant difference compared with ConSec (82.0%) even though ESs are injected. When we applied the mask-attention technique, the improvement was 0.5% at maximum, 82.6%. Among masked attentions, there is also no statistically significant difference between the masked attention (a) context sentence and ES pairs (82.5%) and the combination of (b)$\sim$ (d) (82.3%). However, we gained 0.6% improvement by using (a) $\sim$ (d) and further gained 0.4% improvement by perturbation. From these observations, we can conclude that the perturbation approach helps the mask-attention procedure to boost the WSD task performance.

### 3.6 Qualitative analysis of errors

We performed an error analysis to provide feedback for further improvement of our method. The number of errors for each POS was 590 noun words, 420 for a verb, 120 for an adjective, and 38 for an adverb, 1,168 words in all. The average senses

| | Model | Dev Set | Test Sets | | | | Concatenation of all Datasets | | | | |
|---|---|---|---|---|---|---|---|---|---|---|---|
| | | SE7 | SE2 | SE3 | SE13 | SE15 | Noun | Verb | Adj | Adv | ALL |
| | MFS-SemCor | 54.5 | 65.6 | 66.0 | 63.8 | 67.1 | 67.7 | 49.8 | 73.1 | 80.5 | 65.5 |
| SemCor | SVC (hypernyms) | 69.5 | 77.5 | 77.4 | 76.0 | 78.3 | 79.6 | 65.9 | 79.5 | 85.5 | 76.7 |
| | GlossBERT | 72.5 | 77.7 | 75.2 | 76.1 | 80.4 | 79.8 | 67.1 | 79.6 | 87.4 | 77.0 |
| | ARES | 71.0 | 78.0 | 77.1 | 78.7 | 75.0 | 80.6 | 68.3 | 80.5 | 83.5 | 77.9 |
| | EWISER | 71.0 | 78.9 | 78.4 | 78.9 | 79.3 | 81.7 | 66.3 | 81.2 | 85.8 | 78.3 |
| | BEM | 74.5 | 79.4 | 77.4 | 79.7 | 81.7 | 81.4 | 68.5 | 83.0 | 87.9 | 79.0 |
| | WMLC | 72.2 | 78.4 | 77.8 | 76.7 | 78.2 | 80.1 | 67.0 | 80.5 | 86.2 | 77.6 |
| | HCAN | - | 72.8 | 70.3 | 68.5 | 72.8 | 72.7 | 58.2 | 77.4 | 84.1 | 71.1 |
| | KELESC | 76.7 | 82.2 | 78.1 | 82.2 | 83.0 | 84.3 | 69.4 | 84.0 | 86.7 | 81.2 |
| | SACE | 76.3 | 82.4 | **81.1** | 82.5 | 83.7 | 84.1 | 72.2 | **86.4** | **89.0** | 81.9 |
| | ESCHER | 76.3 | 81.7 | 77.8 | 82.2 | 83.2 | 83.9 | 69.3 | 83.8 | 86.7 | 80.7 |
| | ConSec | 77.4 | 82.3 | 79.9 | 83.2 | **85.2** | 85.4 | 70.8 | 84.0 | 87.3 | 82.0 |
| | **Pconan** | **79.8** | **83.8** | **81.1**$^*$ | **83.9** | 84.7$^*$ | **85.6** | **73.8** | 84.8 | **89.0**$^*$ | **83.0** |

Table 2: Performance comparison: The best score is in boldface and the second best is underlined. $*$ denotes the method (if any) whose score is not statistically significant compared to the best one. We used a t-test, p-value < 0.01.

| Model | ALL |
|---|---|
| ConSec | 82.0 |
| w/o Prtb & w/o (a), (b), (c), and (d) | 82.1$^*$ |
| w/o Prtb & w/o (b), (c), and (d) | 82.5$^*$ |
| w/o Prtb & w/o (a) | 82.3$^*$ |
| w/o Prtb | 82.6 |
| Pconan | 83.0 |

Table 3: Ablation test over the Pconan components: "w/o Prtb" refers to the result without pertubation. $*$ denotes the method whose score is not statistically significant compared to the baseline, ConSec.

[Context sentence]
Skilled ringers use their wrists to <d> advance </d> or retard the next swing so that one bell can swap places with another in the following change.
[Candidate sense & definition & example sentence]
advance#1 <def> **move forward**, also in the metaphorical sense. <def> Times marches on.
advance#5 <def> cause to **move forward** <def> Can you **move** the car seat **forward**?

Figure 3: An example with similar context definitions: The correct sense in <d> advance <d> is advance#5.

for these POS words were 6.7 for nouns, 12.2 for verbs, 5.9 for adjectives, and 5.2 for adverbs. We randomly picked up 100 words from 1,168 and found that there are mainly two types of errors:

**1. Sense distribution:** When the sense distribution of the target word in the training data is unbalanced, most of the target words tend to be assigned to the sense of having much training instances. This was the most frequent error type and 51 words were classified into this type.

**2. The similarity between candidate definitions:** When words that appear one candidate definition are semantically similar or the same as those of other candidate definitions, it is difficult to model beneficial dependencies to identify keywords. For example, in Figure 3, as "move forward" appears in both candidate definitions and example sentence, only a few words such as "car" and "seat" are clues to predict beneficial dependencies which causes an error. 26 words were classified into this type.

We focused on example sentences extracted from WordNet as lexical knowledge. (Vial et al., 2019; Conia and Navigli, 2021) utilized the semantic relationships between senses such as synonymy, hypernymy, and hyponymy derived from the WordNet and reported that the external knowledge contributes to improving WED performance. This is definitely worth trying with Pconan.

## 4 Conclusion

We presented WSD approach for injecting lexical knowledg from the WordNet with perturbation-based constrained attention network. The comparative results with the SOTA WSD methods showed the effectiveness of our method. Future work will include: (i) evaluating our model by using other lexical knowledge such as the semantic relationship between senses, (ii) investigating other perturbation techniques (Gal and Ghahramani, 2016; Wang and Wang, 2021) to improve the performance, and (iii) applying methods (Liu et al., 2020; Xiong et al., 2021) to reduce the overall self-attention complexity for further advantages in efficacy.

## Acknowledgments

We would like to thank anonymous reviewers for their comments and suggestions. This work is supported by SCAT, JKA, Kajima Foundation's Support Program, and JSPS KAKENHI No.23H03402.

## References


Roberto Navigli Alessandro Raganato, Claudio Delli Bovi. 2017b. Neural sequence learning models for word sense disambiguation. In *Proceedings of the 2017 Conference on Empirical Methods in Natural Language Processing*, page 1156–1167.

Edoardo Barba, Luigi Procopio, and Roberto Navigli. 2021a. ConSeC: Word sense disambiguation as continuous sense comprehension. In *Proceedings of the 2021 Conference on Empirical Methods in Natural Language Processing*, pages 1492–1503.

Edonardo Barba, Tommaso Pasini, and Navigli Roberto. 2021b. Esc: Redesigning wsd with extractive sense comprehension. In *Proceedings of the 2021 Conference on the North American Chappter of the Association for Computational Linguistics: Human Language Technologies*, pages 4661–4672.

Michele Bevilacqua and Roberto Navigli. 2020. Breaking through the 80% glass ceiling: Raising the state of the art in word sense disambiguation by incorporating knowledge graph information. In *Proceedings of the 58th Annual Meeting of the Association for Computational Linguistics*, pages 2854–2864.

Roberto Navigli Bianca Scarlini, Tommaso Pasini. 2020. With more contexts comes better performance: Contextualized sense embeddings for all-round word sense disambiguation. In *Proceedings of the 2020 Conference on Empirical Methods in Natural Language Processing (EMNLP)*, page 3528–3539.

Terra Blevins and Luke Zettlemoyer. 2020. Moving down the long tail of word sense disambiguation with gloss- informed bi-encoders. In *Proceedings of the 58th Association for Computational Linguistics*, pages 1006–1017.

Simone Conia and Roberto Navigli. 2021. Framing Word Sense Disambiguation as a multi-label problem for model-agnostic knowledge integration. In *Proceedings of the 16th Conference of the European Chapter of the Association for Computational Linguistics: Main Volume*, pages 3269–3275.

Philip Edmonds and Scott Cotton. 2001. Senseval2: Overview. In *Proceedings of SENSEVAL2 Second International Workshop on Evaluating Word Sense Disambiguation Systems*, page 1–5.

Briscoe Edward. 1991. Lexical issues in natural language processing. In *Proceedings of the Symposium on Natural Language and Speech*, pages 36–68.

Yarin Gal and Zoubin Ghahramani. 2016. A theoretically grounded application of dropout in recurrent neural networks. In *Proceedings of the 30th International Conference on Neural Information Processing Systems*, pages 1027–1035.

Christiane D. Fellbaum D. Gross George A. Miller, R.T. Beckwith and K. Miller. 1990. Introduction to wordnet: An online lexical database. In *International Journal of Lexicography, 3(4)*, pages 235–244.

Randee Tengi George A. Miller, Claudia Leacokc and Ross T Bunker. 1993. A semantic concordance. In *Proceedings of the workshop on Human Language Technology*, pages 303–308.

Pengcheng He, Xiaodong Liu, Jianfeng Gao, and Weizhu Chen. 2021. Deberta: decoding-enhanced bert with disentangled attention. In *9th International Conference on Learning Representations*.

Luyao Huang, Chi Sun, Xipeng Qiu, and Xuanjing Huang. 2019. GlossBERT: BERT for word sense disambiguation with gloss knowledge. In *Proceedings of the 2019 Conference on Empirical Methods in Natural Language Processing and the 9th International Joint Conference on Natural Language Processing (EMNLP-IJCNLP)*, pages 3507–3512.

Sharmistha Jat Karan Saxena Kumar, Sawan and Partha Talukdar. 2019. Zero-shot word sense disambiguation using sense definition embeddings. In *Proceedings of the 57th Annual Meeting of the Association for Computational Linguistics*, pages 5670–5681.

Liyuan Liu, Haoming Jiang, Pengcheng He, Weizhu Chen, Xiaodong Liu, Jianfeng Gao, and Jiawei Han. 2020. On the variance of the adaptive learning rate and beyond. In *Proceedings of the Eighth International Conference on Learning Representations (ICLR 2020)*.

Fuli Luo, Tianyu Liu, Zexue He, Qiaolin Xia, Zhifang Sui, and Baobao Chang. 2018a. Leveraging gloss knowledge in neural word sense disambiguation by hierarchical co-attention. In *Proceedings of the 2018 Conference on Empirical Methods in Natural Language Processing*, pages 1402–1411.

Fuli Luo, Tianyu Liu, Qiaolin Xia, Baobao Chang, and Zhifang Sui. 2018b. Incorporating glosses into neural word sense disambiguation. In *Proceedings of the 56th Annual Meeting of the Association for Computational Linguistics (Volume 1: Long Papers)*, pages 2473–2482.

Andrea Moro and Roberto Navigli. 2015. Semeval2015 task 13: Multilingual all-words sense disambiguation and entity linking. In *Proceedings of the 9th International Workshop on Semantic Evaluation (SemEval 2015)*, page 288–297.

David Jurgens Roberto Navigli and Daniele Vannella. 2013. Semeval-2013 task 12: Multilingual word sense disambiguation. In *Second Joint Conference on Lexical and Computational Semantics (*SEM), Volume 2: Proceedings of the Seventh International Workshop on Semantic Evaluation (SemEval 2013)*, page 222–231.

Dmitriy Dligach Sameer Pradhan, Edward Loper and Martha Palmer. 2007. Semeval-2007 task-17: English lexical sample, srl and all words. In *Proceedings of the Fourth International Workshop on Semantic Evaluations (SemEval-2007)*, page 87–92.

Motoki Sato, Jun Suzuki, and Shun Kiyono. 2019. Effective adversarial regularization for neural machine translation. In *Proceedings of the 57th Annual Meeting of the Association for Computational Linguistics*, pages 204–210.

Tao Shen, Tianyi Zhous, Guodong Long, Jing Jiang, Sen Wang, and chengqi Zhang. 2018. Reinforced self-attention network: a hybrid of hard and soft attention for sequence modeling. In *Proceedings of the Twenty-Seventh International Joint Conference on Artificial Intelligence (IJCAI-18)*, pages 4345–4352.

Benjamin Snyder and Martha Palmer. 2004. The english all-words task. In *Proceedings of SENSEVAL3, the Third International Workshop on the Evaluation of Systems for the Semantic Analysis of Text*, page 41–43.

Ashish Vaswani, Noam Shazeer, Niki Parmar, Jakob Uszkoreit, Llion Jones, Aidan N Gomez, Łukasz Kaiser, and Illia Polosukhin. 2017. Attention is all you need. In *Advances in Neural Information Processing Systems*, page 6000–6010.

Loïc Vial, Benjamin Lecouteux, and Didier Schwab. 2019. Sense Vocabulary Compression through the Semantic Knowledge of WordNet for Neural Word Sense Disambiguation. In *Proceedings of the 10th Global Wordnet Conference*, pages 108–117.

Ming Wang and Yinglin Wang. 2021. Word sense disambiguation: Towards interactive context exploitation from both word and sense perspectives. In *Proceedings of the 59th Annual Meeting of the Association for Computational Linguistics and the 11th International Joint Conference on Natural Language Processing (Volume 1: Long Papers)*, pages 5218–5229.

Zhe Zhao Zhiruo Wang Qi Ju Haotang Deng Ping Wang Weijie Liu, Peng Zhou. 2020. K-BERT: Enabling language representation with knowledge graph. In *Proceedings of the AAAI Conference on Artificial Intelligence*, pages 2901–2908.

Yunyang Xiong, Zhanpeng Zeng, Rudrasis Chakraborty, Mingxing Tan, Glenn Fung, Yin Li, and Vikas Singh. 2021. Nyströmformer: A nystöm-based algorithm for approximating self-attention. In *Proceedings of the Association for the Advancement of Artificial Intelligence*, pages 14138–14148.

Kelvin Xu, Jimmy Ba, Ryan Kiros, Kyunghyun Cho, Aaron Couville, Ruslan Salakhudinov, Rich Zemei, and Yoshua Bengio. 2015. Show, attend and tell: Neural image caption generation with visual attention. In *32nd International Conference on Machine Learning*, pages 2048–2057.

Guobiao Zhang, Wenpeng Lu, Zueping Peng, Shoujin Wang, Baoshuo Kan, and Rui Yu. 2022. Word sense disambiguation with knowledge-enhanced and local self-attention-based extractive sense comprehension. In *Proceedings of the 29th International Conference on Computational Linguistics*, pages 4061–4070.

# The Glass Ceiling of Automatic Evaluation in Natural Language Generation

**Pierre Colombo**[1,2], **Maxime Peyrard**[3], **Nathan Noiry**[4] **Robert West**[3] **Pablo Piantanida**[5]
[1]MICS - CentraleSupélec, [2] Equall,
[3] EPFL, [4] Telecom Paris
[5] ILLS, CNRS - CentraleSupélec
colombo.pierre@centralesupelec.fr

## Abstract

Automatic evaluation metrics capable of replacing human judgments are critical to allowing fast development of new methods. Thus, numerous research efforts have focused on crafting such metrics. In this work, we take a step back and analyze recent progress by comparing the body of existing automatic metrics and human metrics altogether. As metrics are used based on how they rank systems, we compare metrics in the space of system rankings. Our extensive statistical analysis reveals surprising findings: automatic metrics – old and new – are much more similar to each other than to humans. Automatic metrics are not complementary and rank systems similarly. Strikingly, human metrics predict each other much better than the combination of all automatic metrics used to predict a human metric. It is surprising because human metrics are often designed to be independent, to capture different aspects of quality, e.g. *content fidelity* or *readability*. We provide a discussion of these findings and recommendations for future work in the field of evaluation.

## 1 Introduction

Crafting automatic evaluation metrics (AEM) able to replace human judgments is critical to guide progress in natural language generation (NLG), as such automatic metrics allow for cheap, fast, and large-scale development of new ideas. The NLG fields are then heavily influenced by the set of AEM used to decide which systems are valuable. Therefore, a large body of work has focused on improving the ability of AEM to predict human judgments.

Human judgment data is typically employed to decide which metric to select based on correlation analysis with human annotations (Rankel et al., 2013; Owczarzak et al., 2012; Graham, 2015). In this work, we take a step back and investigate the relationship between existing AEM and human judgments globally. We do not make metric recommendation but reflect upon the global progress in the field of automatic evaluation. Our work is motivated by the findings of Fig. 1. It depicts the improvement over time, when new metrics were introduced, in the ability to fit human judgments when using all existing metrics as features. The fit is measured by the correlation with humans of a trained classifier in a 5-fold cross-validation setup. Remarkably, our observations indicate that there have been only minor incremental improvements, and the progress in recent years appears to be reaching a saturation point.

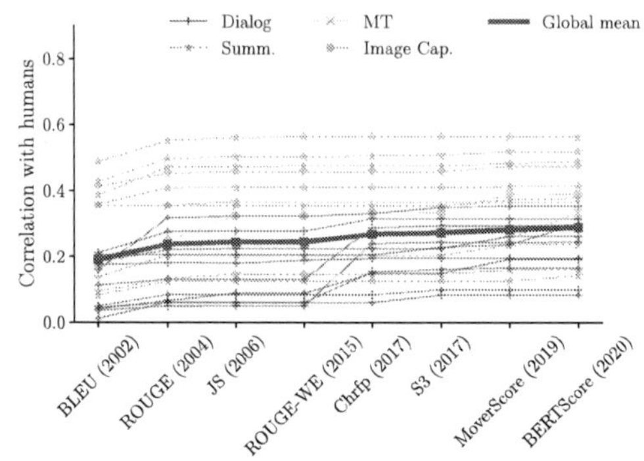


Figure 1: **Correlation with humans over time considering all existing metrics combined.** On the x-axis: evaluation metrics ordered by their release time; y-axis: utterance-level Kendall's $\tau$ with human when training a model to fit human judgments with all metrics available at the time (5-Fold cross-validation with XGBoost regressor). The dotted lines represent different human annotations and datasets. Different variants of the same metrics (like ROUGE-1 and ROUGE-2) are averaged. The datasets and metrics are described in Sec. 2.

Recent works emphasized the importance of viewing metrics in terms of how they rank systems instead of just comparing score values (Novikova et al., 2018; Peyrard et al., 2021; Colombo et al., 2022). Indeed, not only ranking is a more robust framework of comparison, it is also more aligned with the way metrics are used: identifying and extracting the "best system". Thus, we perform



*Findings of the Association for Computational Linguistics: IJCNLP-AACL 2023*, pages 178–183
November 1–4, 2023. ©2023 Asian Federation of Natural Language Processing

our analysis in the space of rankings. i.e., how do metrics rank systems? By analyzing 9 datasets covering 4 tasks and 270k scores, we made the following observations:

**Findings.** (i) Automatic metrics are much more similar to each other, in terms of how they rank systems, than they are to human metrics. It means that AEM, even the more recent transformer-based ones are similar to the older ones when used in practice (ROUGE and BLEU). (ii) This lack of complementarity results in the inability to fit human judgments even when all these metrics are taken together as features for a classifier predicting humans. (iii) Quite surprisingly, different human dimensions – different annotations guidelines such as *readability*, or *content fidelity* – are very predictive of each other, whereas AEM are much less predictive of humans. This finding is striking because human metrics are designed to capture different and independent aspects of quality whereas AEM have been selected precisely for their ability to match humans. We would expect human metrics to be uncorrelated and automatic metric to be highly correlated with humans but we observe the opposite. First, it casts serious doubt about the ability of AEM to replace human judgments. Then, the correlation between independent human annotations of quality hints at some latent inherent *goodness* of systems: good systems are good in different aspect whereas bad systems are bad across all aspects.

Our findings have several consequences that can inform future research. Newly introduced metrics are not complementary to previous ones, resulting in small global improvements. As a way forward, we propose that research, instead of crafting metrics that maximize correlation with humans, focus on making metrics that **also** aim to be explicitly complementary to the set of existing metrics. This would enforce maximal marginal gain and ensure that the field, as a whole, makes progress towards capturing the complexity of human annotations.

For practitioners, it is common practice to report several AEM in the hope to get a better view of system performances. However, reporting several metrics that all produce similar rankings does not bring useful additional information. With our proposal, reporting a set of complementary metrics would better serve the intended purpose.

To help research build upon our work and use our measure of complementarity, we make our code available at `github`.

## 2 Methodology

**Terminology.** Let $\mathscr{X}$ be the space of possible outputs for an NLG task. An NLG metric is a function $m: \mathscr{X} \times \mathscr{X} \rightarrow \mathbb{R}_+$ which, from a given textual candidate $C \in \mathscr{X}$ and corresponding reference $R \in \mathscr{X}$, computes a score $m(C,R)$ reflecting the properties that $C$ should satisfy (*e.g.* fluency, fidelity...). Of course, it is illusory to summarize subtle semantic properties by a single scalar and one is rather seeking for metrics that are able to discriminate between different systems. In fact, crafted AEM are evaluated by comparison to human judgments: one usually computes ranking correlations such as the Kendall's $\tau$. Higher correlations indicate that the AEM is a better replacement for the human metrics.

**Encoding metrics with rankings.** Since the usage of NLG metrics is to rank systems, we choose to represent an NLG metric, automatic or human, by the ranking it induces on a set of systems or utterances. More formally, for $S \geq 1$ NLG systems evaluated on a dataset made of $U \geq 1$ utterances, there exists a natural ranking representations of $m$:

Each utterance $u \in \{1, \ldots, U\}$ induces a ranking $\sigma_u^m \in \mathbb{R}^S$ of the $S$ systems seen as a vector $\sigma_u^m$, where $\sigma_u^m[s]$ is the rank of system $s \in \{1, \ldots, S\}$. For a system $s$, the representation of a metric $m$, noted $\sigma^m[s]$, is sum of *rankings over the utterances*:

$$\sigma^m[s] := \sum_{u=1}^{U} \sigma_u^m(s) \in \mathbb{R}^N. \tag{1}$$

We call this **System level representation.** Symmetrically, each system $s \in \{1, \ldots, S\}$ induces a ranking $\rho_s^m \in \mathbb{R}^U$ of the $U$ utterances, where $\rho_s^m[u]$ is the rank of utterance $u$. The **Utterance level representation** of $m$ is sum of *rankings over the systems*:

$$\rho^m[u] := \sum_{s=1}^{S} \rho_s^n \in \mathbb{R}^K. \tag{2}$$

Using the space of rankings has been shown to be more robust than the raw scores as it is less sensitive to outliers and statistical variations (Novikova et al., 2017; Peyrard et al., 2021; Colombo et al., 2022). Furthermore, this representation is closely tied to Borda counts, which enjoys theoretical properties: the ranking induced by $\sigma^{m,S}$ is a 5-approximation of the Kemeny-consensus which is a good notion of average in the symmetric group

(Kemeny, 1959; Young and Levenglick, 1978; Coppersmith et al., 2006). It is moreover the fastest approximation of the Kemeny-consensus whose computation is NP-hard (Ali and Meilă, 2012).

**Complementarity.** We measure the *complementarity* between two metrics – humans or automatic – by the average over utterances of the distance between their rankings of systems. Formally, for two metrics $m_0$ and $m_1$, complementarity is given by:

$$C(m_0, m_1) := \frac{1}{U} \sum_{u=1}^{U} d_\tau(\sigma_u^{m_0}, \sigma_u^{m_1}), \qquad (3)$$

where $d_\tau$ is the normalized Kendall's distance between the vectors of rank. It is related to the Kendall's rank correlation $\tau$ by: $\tau = 1 - 2d_\tau$.

Similarly, we define the complementarity between a metric $m_0$ and a set of other metrics $\boldsymbol{m} := \{m_i\}_{i=1,\ldots,l}$, as the average pairwise complementarity:

$$C(m_0, \boldsymbol{m}) = \frac{1}{l} \sum_{i=1,\ldots,l} C(m_0, m_i). \qquad (4)$$

Complementarity measures the extent to which a metric ranks systems differently than another metrics or a set of other metrics. Whether comparing two metrics or a metric with set, it is a number between 0 and 1 where 0 indicates that the metrics rank systems in the exact same order and 1 indicates the exact opposite order. In between, it counts the number of inversions between the two rank lists normalized by the number of possible pairs of systems.

## 2.1 Dataset description

To ensure a wide coverage of NLG we focus on four different problems *i.e.*, dialogue generation (using PersonaChat (PC) and TopicalChat (TC) (Mehri and Eskenazi, 2020)), image description (relying on FLICKR (Young et al., 2014)), summary evaluation (via TAC08 (Dang and Owczarzak, 2008), TAC10, TAC11 (Owczarzak and Dang, 2011), RSUM (Bhandari et al., 2020) and SEVAL (Fabbri et al., 2021)), and translation (focusing on multilingual quality estimation (MLQE) Ranasinghe et al. (2021)).
For each task, we gather datasets and rely on AEM such as JS [1-2] (Lin et al., 2006), BLEU (Papineni et al., 2002; Post, 2018), Chrfpp (Popović, 2017), S3 (both variant pyr/resp) (Peyrard et al., 2017), ROUGE (Lin, 2004) (including 5 of its variants

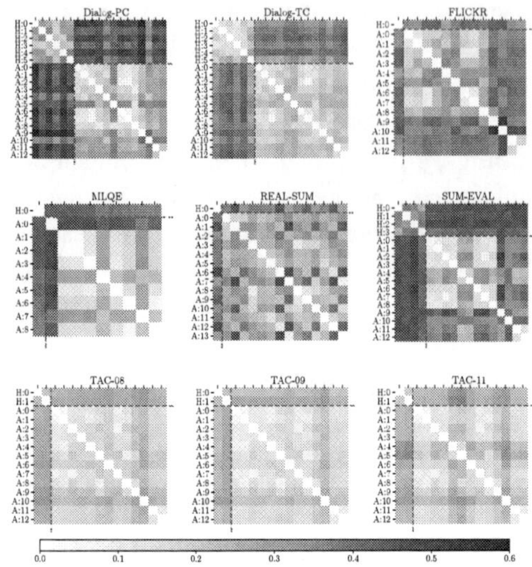


Figure 2: **Complementarity**: For each dataset, the pairwise complementarity between each pair of metrics as computed by Eq. 3 both human and automatic. In these matrix plot, symmetric by design, we ordered metrics to have the human one first and the automatic ones after, the red lines trace the limit between humans and AEM.

(Ng and Abrecht, 2015)), BERTScore (Zhang et al., 2019), MoverScore (Zhao et al., 2019). For MLQE we solely consider several version of BERTScore, MoverScore and ContrastScore. The human evalutions criterion are specific to each dataset and will be identified by starting with an H:. Overall, our final datasets gather over 270k scores.[1]

# 3 Experiments

**Finding 1: Automatic metrics are similar to each other much more than they are to human metric.** In Fig. 2, we report the pairwise complementarity between each pair of metrics as computed by Eq. 3 for both human and AEM. When aggregated over pairs and over datasets, we obtain an average complementarity between: (i) two human metrics of $.16 \pm .01$, (ii) two AEM of $.20 \pm .01$ and (iii) a human and an automatic metric of $.35 \pm .02$.

Importantly, we observe across datasets low complementarity, i.e., strong similarity, between AEM, low complementarity between human metrics but

[1]The selection of these metrics was driven by their widespread usage and recognition, as reported in numerous research papers. In order to streamline our analysis and address practical considerations, we opted to exclude recent metrics, such as those based on GPT-3/4, due to their expensive evaluation requirements on large benchmarks and reliance on proprietary models with undisclosed datasets.

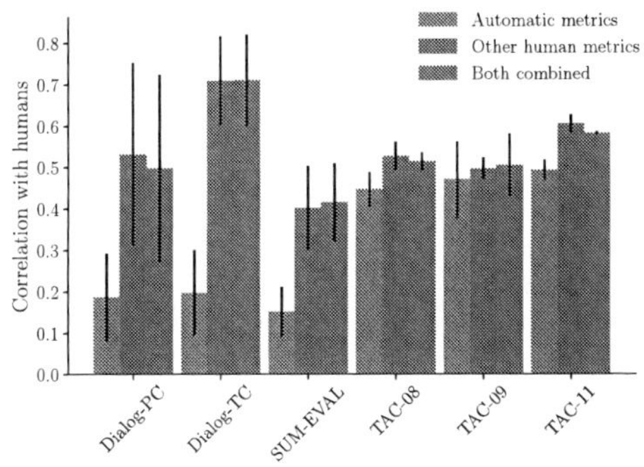


Figure 3: **Human metrics are significantly more predictive of each other than AEM.** On this plot, we report the 5-fold cross-validated result of fitting an XGBoost regressor on various feature sets: (i) all available AEM, (ii) other human metrics when available, and (iii) both automatic and human metrics. The fit is measured as the average instance-level correlation in the test set.

high complementarity, i.e., low similarity, between automatic and human metrics.

We draw two conclusions from this analysis: (i) AEM rank systems similarly but (ii) differently than humans. There is some nuances across datasets. The effect described above is particularly strong in the Dialog, MLQE and SUM-Eval datasets. In particular, we notice that TAC datasets, from the summarization task, have lower complementarity in general, meaning that all metrics, human and automatic, are more similar. Indeed, a lot of works have relied on these datasets to develop new metrics. The more recent REAL-SUM and SUM-Eval reveal much lower metric similarity.

**Finding 2: Automatic metrics even all combined do not explain human metrics.** If AEM are rather different than human metrics, we might wonder whether it is possible to get a good approximation of human judgments by combining existing AEM together. To account for possible correlations, we rely on XGBoost regressors with 5-fold cross-validation to predict human judgments. The training is performed on three different features space: *(i)* AEM only, *(ii)* other human metrics only and *(iii)* both sets of metrics combined. We compute the Kendall's $\tau$ between predictions and ground truths and report the results in Fig. 3.

The plot confirms that AEM struggle to capture human judgment subtlety: correlation rarely exceeds .4 on held-out data. In contrast, human metrics are much more predictive of each others, even if they are often supposed to capture different concepts. Finally, it is worth noting that adding AEM to human ones do not marginally improve the prediction power. These findings cast shadows over recent progress in the field.

## 4 Discussion

Our analysis reveals that studied automatic metrics are not complementary, and recent automatic metrics actually capture the same properties of human judgments as older ones. Furthermore, the studied metrics are not strong predictors of human judgments. Quite surprisingly, other human metrics which are often designed to be independent of each other end-up being more predictive of each other than automatic metrics. This predictability of human metrics from one another can be explained due to the available datasets: when a system is good at extracting content, it is also often good at making the content readable, when a system is bad it is often bad across the board in all human metrics. However, the fact the considered automatic metrics are less predictive than other human dimensions casts some shadow over recent progress in the field. It shows that the current strategy of crafting metrics with slightly better correlation than baselines with one of the human metrics has reached its limit and some qualitative change would be needed.A promising strategy to address the limitations of automatic metrics is to report several of them, hoping that they will together give a more robust overview of system performance. However, this makes sense only if automatic metrics measure different aspects of human judgments, i.e., if they are complementary. In this work, we have seen that metrics are in fact not complementary, as they produce similar rankings of systems.

**Proposition for future work** To foster meaningful progress in the field of automatic evaluation, we propose that future research craft new metrics not only to maximize correlation with human judgments but also to minimize the similarity with the body of existing automatic metrics. This would ensure that the field progresses as whole by focusing on capturing aspects of human judgments that are not already captured by existing metrics. Furthermore, the reporting of several metrics that have been demonstrated to be complementary could become again a valid heuristic to get a robust overview of model performance. In practice, researchers could re-use our code and analysis to enforce complementarity by, for example, enforcing new metrics to have low complementarity as measured by Eq. 3.

## 5 Limitations

Even though we have considered a representative set of automatic evaluation metrics, new ones are constantly introduced and could be added to such an analysis. Similarly, new datasets could be added to the analysis and impact the results. In an effort to make our findings relevant in the long run, we release an easy-to-use code base to replicate our analysis with new metrics and datasets.

Like the majority of analysis on automatic evaluation metrics, ours rely on the assumption that human judgments are valid and meaningful. However, some works have questioned the quality of human judgments in standard datasets.

## References


Alnur Ali and Marina Meilă. 2012. Experiments with kemeny ranking: What works when? *Mathematical Social Sciences*, 64(1):28–40.

John J Bartholdi, Craig A Tovey, and Michael A Trick. 1989. The computational difficulty of manipulating an election. *Social Choice and Welfare*, 6(3):227–241.

Manik Bhandari, Pranav Gour, Atabak Ashfaq, Pengfei Liu, and Graham Neubig. 2020. Re-evaluating evaluation in text summarization.

Vincent D Blondel, Jean-Loup Guillaume, Renaud Lambiotte, and Etienne Lefebvre. 2008. Fast unfolding of communities in large networks. *Journal of statistical mechanics: theory and experiment*, 2008(10):P10008.

Pierre Colombo, Nathan Noiry, Ekhine Irurozki, and Stéphan Clémençon. 2022. What are the best systems? new perspectives on nlp benchmarking. *arXiv preprint arXiv:2202.03799*.

Don Coppersmith, Lisa Fleischer, and Atri Rudra. 2006. Ordering by weighted number of wins gives a good ranking for weighted tournaments. In *Proceedings of the seventeenth annual ACM-SIAM symposium on Discrete algorithm*, pages 776–782.

Hoa Trang Dang and Karolina Owczarzak. 2008. Overview of the tac 2008 update summarization task. In *TAC*.

Cynthia Dwork, Ravi Kumar, Moni Naor, and Dandapani Sivakumar. 2001. Rank aggregation methods for the web. In *Proceedings of the 10th international conference on World Wide Web*, pages 613–622.

Alexander R Fabbri, Wojciech Kryściński, Bryan McCann, Caiming Xiong, Richard Socher, and Dragomir Radev. 2021. Summeval: Re-evaluating summarization evaluation. *Transactions of the Association for Computational Linguistics*, 9:391–409.

Yvette Graham. 2015. Re-evaluating Automatic Summarization with BLEU and 192 Shades of ROUGE. In *Proceedings of the 2015 Conference on Empirical Methods in Natural Language Processing*, pages 128–137. Association for Computational Linguistics.

Ian T Jolliffe and Jorge Cadima. 2016. Principal component analysis: a review and recent developments. *Philosophical Transactions of the Royal Society A: Mathematical, Physical and Engineering Sciences*, 374(2065):20150202.

John G Kemeny. 1959. Mathematics without numbers. *Daedalus*, 88(4):577–591.

Chin-Yew Lin. 2004. Rouge: A package for automatic evaluation of summaries. In *Text summarization branches out*, pages 74–81.

Chin-Yew Lin, Guihong Cao, Jianfeng Gao, and Jian-Yun Nie. 2006. An information-theoretic approach to automatic evaluation of summaries. In *Proceedings of the Human Language Technology Conference of the NAACL, Main Conference*, pages 463–470.

Shikib Mehri and Maxine Eskenazi. 2020. Usr: An unsupervised and reference free evaluation metric for dialog generation. *arXiv preprint arXiv:2005.00456*.

Jun-Ping Ng and Viktoria Abrecht. 2015. Better summarization evaluation with word embeddings for rouge. *arXiv preprint arXiv:1508.06034*.

Jekaterina Novikova, Ondřej Dušek, Amanda Cercas Curry, and Verena Rieser. 2017. Why we need new evaluation metrics for NLG. In *Proceedings of the 2017 Conference on Empirical Methods in Natural Language Processing*, pages 2241–2252, Copenhagen, Denmark. Association for Computational Linguistics.

Jekaterina Novikova, Ondřej Dušek, and Verena Rieser. 2018. RankME: Reliable human ratings for natural language generation. In *Proceedings of the 2018 Conference of the North American Chapter of the Association for Computational Linguistics: Human Language Technologies, Volume 2 (Short Papers)*, pages 72–78, New Orleans, Louisiana. Association for Computational Linguistics.

Karolina Owczarzak, John M. Conroy, Hoa Trang Dang, and Ani Nenkova. 2012. An Assessment of the Accuracy of Automatic Evaluation in Summarization. In *Proceedings of Workshop on Evaluation Metrics and System Comparison for Automatic Summarization*, pages 1–9. Association for Computational Linguistics.

Karolina Owczarzak and Hoa Trang Dang. 2011. Overview of the tac 2011 summarization track: Guided task and aesop task. In *Proceedings of the Text Analysis Conference (TAC 2011), Gaithersburg, Maryland, USA, November*.

Kishore Papineni, Salim Roukos, Todd Ward, and Wei-Jing Zhu. 2002. Bleu: a method for automatic evaluation of machine translation. In *Proceedings of the 40th ACL*, pages 311–318, Philadelphia, Pennsylvania, USA. ACL.

Maxime Peyrard, Teresa Botschen, and Iryna Gurevych. 2017. Learning to score system summaries for better content selection evaluation. In *Proceedings of the Workshop on New Frontiers in Summarization*, pages 74–84.

Maxime Peyrard, Wei Zhao, Steffen Eger, and Robert West. 2021. Better than average: Paired evaluation of nlp systems. *arXiv preprint arXiv:2110.10746*.

Maja Popović. 2017. chrf++: words helping character n-grams. In *Proceedings of the second WMT*, pages 612–618.

Matt Post. 2018. A call for clarity in reporting bleu scores. *arXiv preprint arXiv:1804.08771*.

Tharindu Ranasinghe, Constantin Orasan, and Ruslan Mitkov. 2021. An exploratory analysis of multilingual word-level quality estimation with cross-lingual transformers. *arXiv preprint arXiv:2106.00143*.

Peter A. Rankel, John M. Conroy, Hoa Trang Dang, and Ani Nenkova. 2013. A Decade of Automatic Content Evaluation of News Summaries: Reassessing the State of the Art. In *Proceedings of the 51st Annual Meeting of the Association for Computational Linguistics*, pages 131–136, Sofia, Bulgaria. Association for Computational Linguistics.

H Peyton Young and Arthur Levenglick. 1978. A consistent extension of condorcet's election principle. *SIAM Journal on applied Mathematics*, 35(2):285–300.

Peter Young, Alice Lai, Micah Hodosh, and Julia Hockenmaier. 2014. From image descriptions to visual denotations: New similarity metrics for semantic inference over event descriptions. *Transactions of the Association for Computational Linguistics*, 2:67–78.

Tianyi Zhang, Varsha Kishore, Felix Wu, Kilian Q Weinberger, and Yoav Artzi. 2019. Bertscore: Evaluating text generation with bert.

Wei Zhao, Maxime Peyrard, Fei Liu, Yang Gao, Christian M Meyer, and Steffen Eger. 2019. Moverscore: Text generation evaluating with contextualized embeddings and earth mover distance.

# A Novel Information-Theoretic Objective to Disentangle Representations for Fair Classification

**Pierre Colombo**[1,2], **Nathan Noiry**[3], **Guillaume Staerman**[4], **Pablo Piantanida**[5]
[1]MICS - CentraleSupélec, [2] Equall,
[3] Telecom Paris, [4] Inria Saclay, [5] ILLS, CNRS - CentraleSupélec
colombo.pierre@centralesupelec.fr

## Abstract

One of the pursued objectives of deep learning is to provide tools that learn abstract representations of reality from the observation of multiple contextual situations. More precisely, one wishes to extract *disentangled representations* which are *(i)* low dimensional and *(ii)* whose components are independent and correspond to concepts capturing the essence of the objects under consideration (Locatello et al., 2019b). One step towards this ambitious project consists in learning disentangled representations *with respect to a predefined (sensitive) attribute*, *e.g.*, the gender or age of the writer. Perhaps one of the main application for such disentangled representations is fair classification. Existing methods extract the last layer of a neural network trained with a loss that is composed of a cross-entropy objective and a disentanglement regularizer. In this work, we adopt an information-theoretic view of this problem which motivates a novel family of regularizers that minimizes the mutual information between the latent representation and the sensitive attribute conditional to the target. The resulting set of losses, called `CLINIC`, is *parameter free* and thus, it is easier and faster to train. `CLINIC` losses are studied through extensive numerical experiments by training over 2k neural networks. We demonstrate that our methods offer a better disentanglement/accuracy trade-off than previous techniques, and generalize better than training with cross-entropy loss solely provided that the disentanglement task is not too constraining.

## 1 Introduction

There has been a recent surge towards disentangled representations techniques in deep learning (Mathieu et al., 2019; Locatello et al., 2019a, 2020; Gabbay and Hoshen, 2019). Learning disentangled representations from high dimensional data ultimately aims at separating a few explanatory factors (Bengio et al., 2013) that contain meaningful information on the objects of interest, regardless of specific variations or contexts. A disentangled representation has the major advantage of being less sensitive to accidental variations (*e.g.*, style) and thus generalizes well.

In this work, we focus on a specific disentanglement task which aims at learning a representation independent from a predefined attribute $S$. Such a representation will be called *disentangled with respect to* $S$. This task can be seen as a first step towards the ideal goal of learning a perfectly disentangled representation. Moreover, it is particularly well-suited for fairness applications, such as fair classification, which are nowadays increasingly sought after. When a learned representation $Z$ is disentangled from a sensitive attribute $S$ such as the age or the gender, any decision rule based on $Z$ is independent of $S$, making it fair in some sense.

Learning disentangled representations with respect to a sensitive attribute is challenging and previous works in the Natural Language Processing (NLP) community were based on two types of approach. The first one consists in training an adversary (Elazar and Goldberg, 2018; Coavoux et al., 2018). Despite encouraging results during training, Lample et al. (2018) show that a new adversary trained from scratch on the obtained representation is able to infer the predefined attribute, suggesting that the representation is in fact not disentangled. The second one consists in training a variational surrogate (Cheng et al., 2020; Colombo et al., 2021c; John et al., 2018) of the mutual information (MI) (Cover and Thomas, 2006) between the learned representation and the variable from which one wishes to disentangle it. One of the major weaknesses of both approaches is the presence of an additional optimization loop designed to learn additional parameters during training (the parameters of the adversary for the first method, and the parameters required to approximate the MI for the second one), which is time-consuming and requires



*Findings of the Association for Computational Linguistics: IJCNLP-AACL 2023*, pages 184–198
November 1–4, 2023. ©2023 Asian Federation of Natural Language Processing

careful tuning (see Alg. 1).

**Our contributions.** We introduce a new method to learn disentangled representations, with a particular focus on fair representations in the context of NLP. Our contributions are two-fold:

**(1)** We provide **new perspectives on the disentanglement with respect to a predefined attribute problem** using information-theoretic concepts. Our analysis motivates the introduction of new losses tailored for classification, called CLINIC (**C**onditional mutua**L** **I**nformatio**N** m**I**nimization for fair **C**lassif**I**c**A**tio**N**). It is faster than previous approaches as it does not to require to learn additional parameters. One of the main novelty of CLINIC is to minimize the MI between the latent representation and the sensitive attribute *conditional to the target* which leads to high disentanglement capability while maintaining high-predictive power.

**(2)** We conduct **extensive numerical experiments** which illustrate and validate our methodology. More precisely, we train over 2K neural models on four different datasets and conduct various ablation studies using both Recurrent Neural Networks (RNN) and pre-trained transformers (PT) models. Our results show that the CLINIC's objective is better suited than existing methods, it is faster to train and requires less tuning as it does not have learnable parameters. Interestingly, in some scenarios, it can increase both disentanglement and classification accuracies and thus, overcoming the classical disentanglement-accuracy trade-off.

From a practical perspective, we would like to add that our method is well-suited for fairness applications and is compliant with the *fairness through unawareness principle* that obliges one to fix a single model which is later applied across all groups of interest (Gajane and Pechenizkiy, 2017; Lipton et al., 2018). Indeed, our method only requires access to the sensitive attribute during its learning phase, but the resulting learned prediction function does not take the sensitive variable as an input.

## 2 Related Works

In order to describe existing works, we begin by introducing some useful notations. From an input textual data represented by a random variable (r.v.) $X \in \mathcal{X}$, the goal is to learn a parameter $\theta \in \Theta$ of an encoder $f_\theta : \mathcal{X} \to \mathcal{Z} \subset \mathbb{R}^d$ so as to transform $X$ into a latent vector $Z = f_\theta(X)$ of dimension $d$ that summarizes the useful information of $X$. Additionally, we require the learned embedding $Z$ to be *guarded* (following the terminology of (Elazar and Goldberg, 2018)) from an input sensitive attribute $S \in \mathcal{S}$ associated to $X$, in the sense that no classifier can predict $S$ from $Z$ better than a random guess. The final decision is done through predictor $g_\phi$ that makes a prediction $\hat{Y} = g_\phi(Z) \in \mathcal{Y}$, where $\phi \in \Phi$ refers to the learned parameters. We will consider classification problems where $\mathcal{Y}$ is a discrete finite set.

### 2.1 Disentangled Representations

The main idea behind most of the previous works focusing on the learning of disentangled representations consists in adding a disentanglement regularizer to a learning task objective. The resulting mainstream loss takes the form:

$$\mathcal{L}(\theta, \phi) = \underbrace{\mathcal{L}_{task}}_{\text{target task}} + \lambda \cdot \underbrace{\mathcal{R}\left(f_\theta(X), S; \phi\right)}_{\text{disentanglement}}, \quad (1)$$

where $\phi$ denotes the trainable parameters of the regularizer. Let us describe the two main types of regularizers used in the literature, both having the flaw to require a nested loop, which adds an extra complexity to the training procedure (see Alg. 1).

**Adversarial losses.** They rely on fooling a classifier (the adversary) trained to recover the sensitive attribute $S$ from $Z$. As a result, the corresponding disentanglement regularizer is trained by relying on the cross-entropy (CE) loss between the predicted sensitive attribute and the ground truth label $S$. Despite encouraging results, adversarial methods are known to be unstable both in terms of training dynamics (Sridhar et al., 2021; Zhang et al., 2019) and initial conditions (Wong et al., 2020).

**Losses based on Mutual Information (MI).** These losses, which also rely on learned parameters, aim at minimizing the MI $I(Z; S)$ between $Z$ and $S$, which is defined by

$$I(Z; S) = \mathbb{E}_{ZS}\left[\log \frac{p_{ZS}(Z, S)}{p_Z(Z)p_S(S)}\right], \quad (2)$$

where the joint probability density function (pdf) of the tuple $(Z, S)$ is denoted $p_{ZS}$ and the respective marginal pdfs are denoted $p_Z$ and $p_S$. Recent MI estimators include MINE (Belghazi et al., 2018), NWJ (Nguyen et al., 2010), CLUB (Cheng et al., 2020), DOE (McAllester and Stratos, 2020), $I_\alpha$ (Colombo et al., 2021c), SMILE (Song and Ermon, 2019).

### 2.2 Parameter Free Estimation of MI

The CLINIC's objective can be seen as part of the second type of losses although **it does not involve additional learnable parameters**. MI estimation can be done using contrastive learning surrogates (Chopra et al., 2005) which offer satisfactory approximations with theoretical guarantees (we refer the reader to Oord et al. (2018) for further details). Contrastive learning is connected to triplet loss (Schroff et al., 2015) and has been used to tackle the different problems including self-supervised or unsupervised representation learning (*e.g.* audio (Qian et al., 2021), image (Yamaguchi et al., 2019), text (Reimers and Gurevych, 2019; Logeswaran and Lee, 2018)). It consists in bringing closer pairs of similar inputs, called *positive pairs* and further dissimilar ones, called *negative pairs*. The positive pairs can be obtained by data augmentation techniques (Chen et al., 2020) or using various heuristic (*e.g* similar sentences belong to the same document (Giorgi et al., 2020), backtranslation (Fang et al., 2020) or more complex techniques (Qu et al., 2020; Gillick et al., 2019; Shen et al., 2020)). For a deeper dive in mining techniques used in NLP, we refer the reader to Rethmeier and Augenstein (2021).
One of the novelty of CLINIC is to provide a novel information theoretic objective tailored for fair classification. It incorporates both the sensitive and target labels in the disentanglement regularizer.

### 2.3 Fair Classification and Disentanglement

The increasing use of machine learning systems in everyday applications has raised many concerns about the fairness of the deployed algorithms. Works addressing fair classification can be grouped into three main categories, depending on the step at which the practitioner performs a *fairness intervention* in the learning process: (i) pre-processing (Brunet et al., 2019; Kamiran and Calders, 2012), (ii) in-processing (Colombo et al., 2021c; Barrett et al., 2019) and (iii) post-processing (d'Alessandro et al., 2017) techniques (we refer the reader to Caton and Haas (2020) for exhaustive review). When the attribute for which we want to disentangle the representation is a sensitive attribute (*e.g.* gender, age, race), our method can be considered as an in-process fairness technique.

## 3 Model and Training Objective

In this section, we introduce the new set of losses called CLINIC that is designed to learn disentangled representations. We begin with information theory considerations which allow us to derive a training objective, and then discuss the relation to existing losses relying on MI.

### 3.1 Analysis & Motivations

#### 3.1.1 Problem Analysis.

When learning disentangled representations, the goal is to obtain a representation $Z$ that contains no information about a sensitive attribute $S$ but preserves the maximum amount of information between $Z$ and the target label $Y$. We use Veyne diagrams in Fig. 1 to illustrate the situation. Notice that, for a given task, the MI between $Y$ and $S$ is fixed (*i.e* corresponding to $\mathscr{C}_Y \cap \mathscr{C}_S$). Therefore, any representation $Z$ that maximizes the MI with $Y$ (*i.e* corresponding to $\mathscr{C}_Y \cap \mathscr{C}_Z$) cannot hope to have a mutual information with $S$ lower than $I(Y;S)$. Informally, recalling that $Z = f_\theta(X)$, we would like to solve:

$$\max_{\theta \in \Theta} I(Z;Y) - \lambda \cdot I(Z;S), \tag{3}$$

where $\lambda > 0$ controls the magnitude of the penalization. Existing works (Elazar and Goldberg, 2018; Barrett et al., 2019; Coavoux et al., 2018) rely on the CE loss to maximize the first term, i.e., within the area of $\mathscr{C}_Z \cap \mathscr{C}_Y$ in Fig. 1, and either on adversarial or contrastive methods for minimizing the second term, i.e., the area of $\mathscr{C}_Z \cap \mathscr{C}_S$ in Fig. 1). The ideal objective is to maximize the area of $(\mathscr{C}_Z \cap \mathscr{C}_Y) \setminus \mathscr{C}_S$. We refer to Colombo et al. (2021c) for connections between adversarial learning and MI and to Oord et al. (2018) for connections between contrastive learning and MI.

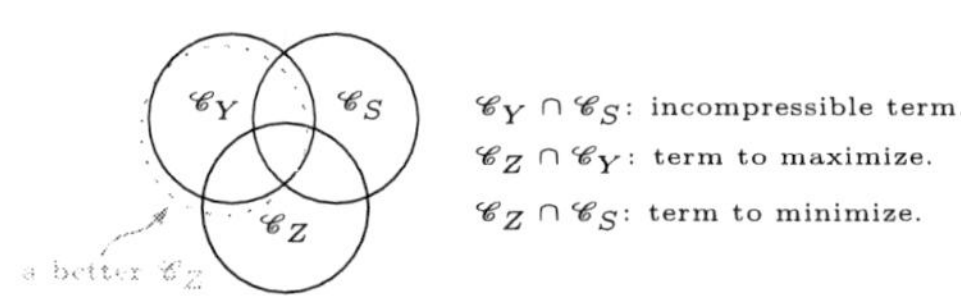


Fig. 1: Veyne diagrams visualization.

#### 3.1.2 Limitations of Previous Methods

Since $I(Z;S) = I(Z;S|Y) + I(Z;S;Y)$, when minimizing $I(Z;S)$, previous work minimize actually the two terms $I(Z;S|Y)$ and $I(Z;S;Y)$. *This could be problematic since $I(Z;S;Y)$ tends to decrease the MI between $Z$ and $Y$, a phenomenon we would like to avoid to keep high performance on our target task.* Our method will bypass this issue by minimizing the conditional mutual information

$I(Z;S|Y)$ solely (this amounts to minimize the area of $(\mathscr{C}_Z \cap \mathscr{C}_S) \setminus (\mathscr{C}_Z \cap \mathscr{C}_S \cap \mathscr{C}_Y)$.

### 3.2 CLINIC

Motivated by the previous analysis CLINIC aims at maximizing the new following ideal objective:

$$\max_{\theta \in \Theta} I(Z;Y) - \lambda \cdot I(Z;S|Y). \quad (4)$$

Minimizing $I(Z;S)$ in Eq. 4 instead of $I(Z;S)$ in Eq. 3 alleviates previously identified flaws.

#### 3.2.1 Estimation of $I(Z;S|Y)$

The estimation of MI related quantities is known to be difficult (Pichler et al., 2020; Paninski, 2003). As a result, to estimate $I(Z;S|Y)$, we develop a tailored made constrastive learning objectives to obtain a parameter free estimator. Let us describe the general form for the loss we adopt on a given input $\{x_i, y_i, s_i\}_{1 \leq i \leq B}$ of size $B$. Recall that $z_i = f_\theta(x_i)$ is the output of the encoder for input $x_i$. For each $1 \leq i \leq B$, in fair classification task we have access to two subsets $\mathscr{P}(i), \mathscr{N}(i) \subset \{1, \ldots, B\} \setminus \{i\}$ corresponding respectively to *positive* and *negative* indices of examples. More precisely, $\mathscr{P}(i)$ (resp. $\mathscr{N}(i)$) corresponds to the set of indices $j \neq i$ such that $z_j$ is similar (resp. dissimilar) to $z_i$. Then, CLINIC consists in minimizing a loss of the form Eq. 1 with $\mathcal{L}_{task}$ given by the CE between the predictions $g_\phi(z_i)$ and the groundtruth labels $y_i$, and with $\mathcal{R}$ given by:

$$\mathcal{R} = \mathcal{R}(Z, \mathscr{P}, \mathscr{N}, B, \tau_p, \tau_n) = -\sum_{i=1}^{B} \mathrm{C}_i, \quad (5)$$

where the contribution $\mathrm{C}_i$ of sample $i$ is

$$\mathrm{C}_i = \frac{1}{|\mathscr{P}(i)|} \sum_{j_p \in \mathscr{P}(i)} \log \frac{e^{z_i \cdot z_{j_p}/\tau_p}}{\sum\limits_{j_n \in \mathscr{N}(i)} e^{z_i \cdot z_{j_n}/\tau_n}}. \quad (6)$$

As emphasized in Eq. 5, the term $\mathcal{R}$ depends on several hyperparameters: the choice of positive and negative examples ($\mathcal{P}(i)$, $\mathcal{N}(i)$), the associated temperatures $\tau_p, \tau_n > 0$ and the batch size $B$. Compared to Eq. 1, the proposed regularizer does not require any additional trainable parameters $\phi$.

#### 3.2.2 Hyperparameters Choice

**Sampling strategy for $\mathscr{P}$ and $\mathscr{N}$.** The choice of positive and negative samples is instrumental for contrastive learning (Wu et al., 2021; Karpukhin et al., 2020; Chen et al., 2020; Zhang and Stratos, 2021; Robinson et al., 2020). In the context of fair classification, the input data take the form $(x_i, s_i, y_i)$ and we consider two natural strategies to define the subsets $\mathcal{P}$ and $\mathcal{N}$. For any given $y$ (resp. $s$), we denote by $\overline{y}$ (resp. $\overline{s}$) a uniformly sampled label in $\mathcal{Y} \setminus \{y\}$ (resp. in $\mathcal{S} \setminus \{s\}$).

**Remark 1.** *It is usual in fairness applications to consider that the sensitive attribute is binary. In that case $\bar{S}$ is deterministic.*

The first strategy ($\mathcal{S}_1$) is to take

$$\mathcal{P}_{\mathcal{S}_1}(i) = \{1 \leq j_p \leq B, \text{ s.t. } y_{j_p} = y_i, s_{j_p} = \bar{s}_i\},$$
$$\mathcal{N}_{\mathcal{S}_1}(i) = \{1 \leq j_n \leq B, \text{ s.t. } y_{j_n} = \bar{y}_i\}.$$

The second strategy ($\mathcal{S}_2$) is to set

$$\mathcal{P}_{\mathcal{S}_2}(i) = \{1 \leq j_p \leq B, \text{ s.t } y_{j_p} = y_i, s_{j_p} = \bar{s}_i\},$$
$$\mathcal{N}_{\mathcal{S}_2}(i) = \{1 \leq j_n \leq B, \text{ s.t } y_{j_n} = \bar{y}_i, s_{j_n} = s_i\}.$$

**Influence of the temperature.** As discussed in Wang and Liu (2021); Wang and Isola (2020) in the case where $\tau_p = \tau_n$, a good choice of temperature parameter is crucial for contrastive learning. Our method offers additional versatility by allowing to fine tune *two* temperature parameters, $\tau_p$ and $\tau_n$, respectively corresponding to the impact one wishes to put on positive and negative examples. For instance, a choice of $\tau_n \ll 1$ tends to focus on hard negative pairs while $\tau_n \gg 1$ makes the penalty uniform among the negatives. We investigate this effect in Ssec. 6.2.

**Influence of the batch size.** Previous works on contrastive losses (Henaff, 2020; Oord et al., 2018; Bachman et al., 2019; Mitrovic et al., 2020) argue for using large batch sizes to achieve good performances. In practice, hardware limits the maximum number of samples that can be stored in memory. Although several works (He et al., 2020; Gao et al., 2021), have been conducted to go beyond the memory usage limitation, every experiment we conducted was performed on a single GPU. Nonetheless, we provide an ablation study with respect to admissible batch sizes in Sssec. A.4.1.

### 3.3 Theoretical Guarantees

There exists a theoretical bound between the contrastive loss of Eq. 5 and the mutual information between two probability laws in the latent space, defined according to the sampling strategy for $\mathscr{P}$ and $\mathscr{N}$. CLINIC's training objective offers theoretical guarantees when approximating $I(Z;S|Y)$ in

Eq. 4. Formally, strategy $\mathcal{S}_1$ and $\mathcal{S}_2$ aim at minimizing the distance between:

$$\underbrace{P_Z(\cdot \mid Y=0, S=0)}_{\mathscr{L}_{0,0}} \text{ and } \underbrace{P_Z(\cdot \mid Y=0, S=1)}_{\mathscr{L}_{0,1}},$$

and between

$$\underbrace{P_Z(\cdot \mid Y=1, S=0)}_{\mathscr{L}_{1,0}} \text{ and } \underbrace{P_Z(\cdot \mid Y=1, S=1)}_{\mathscr{L}_{1,1}}.$$

We prove the following result in **??**.

**Theorem 1.** *For $\epsilon \in \{0,1\}$, denote by $p_\epsilon = |\{1 \leq i \leq B,\ y_i = \epsilon\}|/B$. Then, it holds that*

$$\frac{1}{p_0} I(\mathscr{L}_{0,0}, \mathscr{L}_{0,1}) + \frac{1}{p_1} I(\mathscr{L}_{1,0}, \mathscr{L}_{1,1}) \geq \frac{\log(p_0 B)}{p_0} + \frac{\log(p_1 B)}{p_1} - (\mathcal{R}/B). \quad (7)$$

**Remark 2.** *Th. 1 offers theoretical guarantees that our adaptation of contrastive learning in Eq. 5 is a good approximation of $I(Z; S|Y)$ in Eq. 4.*

**Remark 3.** *To simplify the exposition we restricted to binary $Y$ and $S$. The general case would involved quantities $\mathscr{L}_{y,s}$ with $y \in \mathcal{Y}$ and $S \in \mathcal{S}$.*

## 4 Experimental Setting

In this section, we describe the experimental setting which includes the dataset, the metrics and the different baselines we will consider. Due to space limitations, details on hyperparameters and neural network architectures are gathered in Ap. C. To ensure fair comparisons we re-implement all the models in a unified framework.

### 4.1 Datasets

We use the DIAL dataset (Blodgett et al., 2016) to ensure backward comparison with previous works (Colombo et al., 2021c; Xie et al., 2017; Barrett et al., 2019). We additionally report results on TrustPilot (TRUST) (Hovy et al., 2015) that has also been used in Coavoux et al. (2018). Tweets from the DIAL corpus have been automatically gathered and labels for both polarity (*is the expressed sentiment positive or negative?*) and mention (*is the tweet conversational?*) are available. Sensitive attribute related to the race (*is the author non-Hispanic black or non-Hispanic white?*) has been inferred from both the author geo-location and the used vocabulary. For TRUST the main task consists in predicting a sentiment on a scale of five. The dataset is filtered and examples containing both the author birth date and gender are kept and splits follow Coavoux et al. (2018). These variables are used as sensitive information. To obtain binary sensitive attributes, we follow Hovy and Søgaard (2015) where age is binned into two categories (*i.e.* age under 35 and age over 45).

**A word on the sensitive attribute inference.** Notice that these two datasets are balanced with respect to the chosen sensitive attributes ($S$), which implies that a random guess has 50% accuracy.

### 4.2 Metrics

Previous works on learning disentangled representation rely on two metrics to assess performance.

**Measuring disentanglement** by reporting the accuracy of an adversary trained from scratch to predict the sensitive labels from the latent representation. Since both datasets are balanced, *a perfectly disentangled representation corresponds to an accuracy of the adversary of 50%.*

**Success on the main classification task** which is measured with accuracy (higher is better). As we are interested in controlling the desired degree of disentanglement (Colombo et al., 2021c), we report the trade-off between these two metrics for different models when varying the $\lambda$ parameter, which controls the magnitude of the regularization (see Eq. 1). For our experiments, we choose $\lambda \in [0.001, 0.01, 0.1, 1, 10]$.

**GAP**: To assess fairness we adopt the approach introduced by (Ravfogel et al., 2020), which involves calculating the root mean square of $GAPTPR$ across all main classes. For GAP, lower is better.

### 4.3 Baselines

**Losses.** To compare CLINIC with previous works, we compare against adversarial training (ADV) (Elazar and Goldberg, 2018; Coavoux et al., 2018) and the recently introduced Mutual Information upper bound (Colombo et al., 2021c) ($I_\alpha$) which has been shown to offer more control over the degree of disentanglement than previous estimators. We compare CLINIC with the work of (Chi et al., 2022; Shen et al., 2021; Gupta et al., 2021; Shen et al., 2022) which uses a method that estimates $I(Z; S)$ (see Eq. 4). Beware that this baseline, be denoted as $\mathcal{S}_0$, does not incorporate information on $Y$.

**Encoders.** To provide an exhaustive comparison, we work both with RNN-encoder and PT (*e.g* BERT (Devlin et al., 2018)) based architectures. Contrarily to previous works that use frozen PT (Ravfogel et al., 2020), we fine-tune the encoder during training and evaluate our methods on various types of encoders (*e.g.* DISTILBERT (DIS.) (Sanh et al., 2019), ALBERT (ALB.) (Lan et al., 2019), SQUEEZEBERT (SQU.) (Iandola et al., 2020)). These models are selected based on efficiency.

## 5 Numerical Results

In this section, we gather experimental results on the fair classification task. Because of space constraints, additional results can be found in Ap. A.

### 5.1 Overall Results

We report in Tab. 1 the best model on each dataset for each of the considered methods. In Tab. 1, each row corresponds to a single $\lambda$ which controls the weight of the regularizer (see Eq. 1).

| | | RNN | | | | BERT | | | |
|---|---|---|---|---|---|---|---|---|---|
| Dat. | Loss | $\lambda$ | $Y(\uparrow)$ | $S(\downarrow)$ | GAP | $\lambda$ | $Y(\uparrow)$ | $S(\downarrow)$ | GAP |
| DIAL-S | CE | 0.0 | 62.7 | 73.2 | 44.5 | 0.0 | 76.2 | 76.7 | 44.5 |
| | $\mathcal{S}_0$ | 1.0 | 66.1 | 55.1 | 18.2 | 10 | 74.5 | 66.8 | 39.7 |
| | $\mathcal{S}_1$ | 1.0 | 79.1 | 51.0 | 6.5 | 1.0 | **73.5** | **58.3** | **18.9** |
| | $\mathcal{S}_2$ | 1.0 | **79.9** | **50.0** | **2.9** | 0.1 | 75.1 | 69.4 | 30.2 |
| | ADV | 1.0 | 58.4 | 70.2 | 44.5 | 0.1 | 74.8 | 72.7 | 44.5 |
| | $I_\alpha$ | 0.1 | 55.2 | 72.3 | 44.5 | 0.1 | 74.5 | 70.1 | 44.5 |
| DIAL-M | CE | 0.0 | 77.5 | 62.1 | 12.3 | 0.0 | 82.7 | 79.1 | 41.6 |
| | $\mathcal{S}_0$ | 10 | 76.7 | 54.9 | 6.2 | 10 | 76.6 | 66.6 | 33.9 |
| | $\mathcal{S}_1$ | 10 | 69.3 | 50.0 | 3.9 | 1.0 | 81.6 | 52.0 | 6.1 |
| | $\mathcal{S}_2$ | 10 | **69.3** | **50.0** | **3.5** | 1.0 | **75.0** | **50.0** | **2.7** |
| | ADV | 0.01 | 76.9 | 57.9 | 22.5 | 0.1 | 82.6 | 74.6 | 39.7 |
| | $I_\alpha$ | 0.1 | 75.5 | 55.7 | 21.7 | 10 | 74.9 | 55.0 | 13.9 |
| TRUST-A | CE | 0.0 | 72.9 | 53.0 | 10.2 | 0.0 | 74.9 | 53.8 | 14.9 |
| | $\mathcal{S}_0$ | 10 | 69.3 | 50.0 | 6.3 | 10 | 70.1 | 50.0 | 7.3 |
| | $\mathcal{S}_1$ | 10 | 75.1 | 50.0 | 4.5 | 10 | 75.1 | 50.0 | 5.6 |
| | $\mathcal{S}_2$ | 10 | **71.1** | **50.0** | **53.9** | 10 | **75.1** | **50.0** | **5.0** |
| | ADV | 10 | 65.5 | 50.0 | 5.7 | 10 | 70.1 | 50.0 | 6.9 |
| | $I_\alpha$ | 10 | 75.1 | 55.0 | 6.3 | 10 | 70.1 | 50.0 | 5.9 |
| TRUST-G | CE | 0.0 | 75.4 | 52.0 | 10.2 | 0.0 | 74.9 | 53.8 | 10.2 |
| | $\mathcal{S}_0$ | 10 | 73.1 | 50.0 | 5.3 | 10 | 73.3 | 50.0 | 5.9 |
| | $\mathcal{S}_1$ | 10 | 76.1 | 50.0 | 4.1 | 10 | 76.2 | 50.0 | 4.5 |
| | $\mathcal{S}_2$ | 10 | **75.8** | **50.0** | **3.2** | 10 | **76.2** | **50.0** | **3.2** |
| | ADV | 10 | 56.3 | 50.0 | 5.6 | 10 | 73.2 | 50.0 | 5.9 |
| | $I_\alpha$ | 10 | 76.2 | 50.0 | 4.5 | 10 | 73.2 | 50.3 | 4.7 |

Tab. 1: Overall results on the fair classification task: the columns with $Y$ and $S$ stand for the main and the sensitive task accuracy respectively. $\downarrow$ means lower is better whereas $\uparrow$ means higher is better. The best model is bolded and second best is underlined. CE refers to a model trained based on CE solely (case $\lambda = 0$ in Eq. 1)

**Global performance.** For each dataset, we report the performance of a model trained without disentanglement regularization (CE rows in Tab. 1). Results indicate this model relies on the sensitive attribute $S$ to perform the classification task. In contrast, all disentanglement techniques reduce the predictability of $S$ from the representation $Z$. Among these techniques, we observe that $I_\alpha$ improves upon ADV as already pointed out in Colombo et al. (2021c). Our CLINIC based methods outperform both ADV and $I_\alpha$ baselines, suggesting that contrastive regularization is a promising line of search for future work in disentanglement.

**Comparing the strategies of CLINIC.** Among the three considered sampling strategies for positives and negatives, $\mathcal{S}_1$ and $\mathcal{S}_2$ are the best and always improve performance upon $\mathcal{S}_0$. This is because $\mathcal{S}_1$ and $\mathcal{S}_2$ incorporate knowledge on the target task to construct positive and negative samples, which is crucial to obtain good performance.

**Datasets difficulty.** From Tab. 1, we can observe that some sensitive/main label pairs are more difficult to disentangle than others. In this regard, TRUST is clearly easier to disentangled than DIAL. Indeed, every models except for CE achieve perfect disentanglement. This suggests we are in the case $\mathscr{C}_Y \cap \mathscr{C}_S = \emptyset$ of Fig. 1, meaning that the sensitive attribute $S$ only contains few information on the target $Y$. Within DIAL, sentiment label is the hardest but CLINIC with strategy $\mathcal{S}_1$ achieves a good trade-off between accuracy and disentanglement.

**RNN vs BERT encoder.** Interestingly, the BERT encoder is always harder to disentangle than the RNN encoder. This observation can be seen as an additional evidence that BERT may exhibit gender, age and/or race biases, as already pointed out in Ahn and Oh (2021); Mozafari et al. (2020); de Vassimon Manela et al. (2021).

### 5.2 Controlling the Level of Disentanglement

A major challenge when disentangling representations is *to be able to control the desired level of disentanglement* (Feutry et al., 2018). We report performance on the main task and on the disentanglement task for both BERT (see Fig. 2) and RNN (see Fig. 3) for differing $\lambda$. Notice that we measure the performance of the disentanglement task by reporting the accuracy metric of a classifier trained on the learned representation.

**Results on DIAL.** We report a different behavior when working either with RNN or BERT. From Fig. 3b we observe that CLINIC (especially $\mathcal{S}_1$ and $\mathcal{S}_2$) allows us to both learn perfectly disentangled representation as well as allow a fined grained control over the desirable degree of disentanglement when working with RNN-based encoder. On the other hand, previous methods (*e.g* ADV or $I_\alpha$) either fail to learn disentangled representations (see $I_\alpha$ on Fig. 2a) or do it while losing the ability to predict $Y$ (see ADV on Fig. 2a). As already pointed out in the analysis of Tab. 1, we observe again that it is both easier to learn disentangled representation and to control the desire degree of disentanglement with RNN compared to BERT.

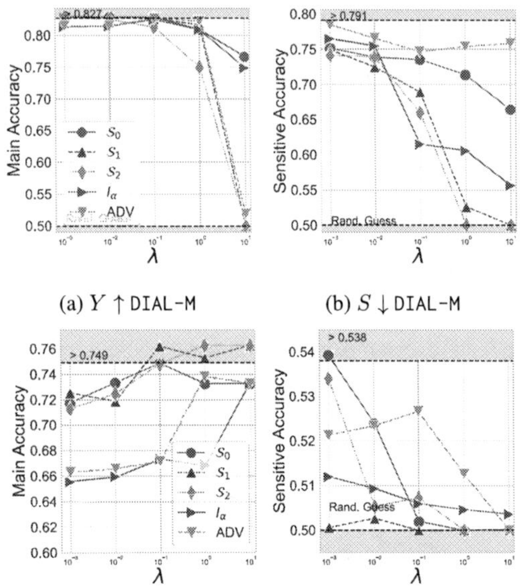


(a) $Y \uparrow$ DIAL-M (b) $S \downarrow$ DIAL-M

(c) $Y \uparrow$ TRUST-G (d) $S \downarrow$ TRUST-G

Fig. 2: Fair Classification results using BERT. Results are given with $B = 256$ and $\tau_p = \tau_n = 0.5$.

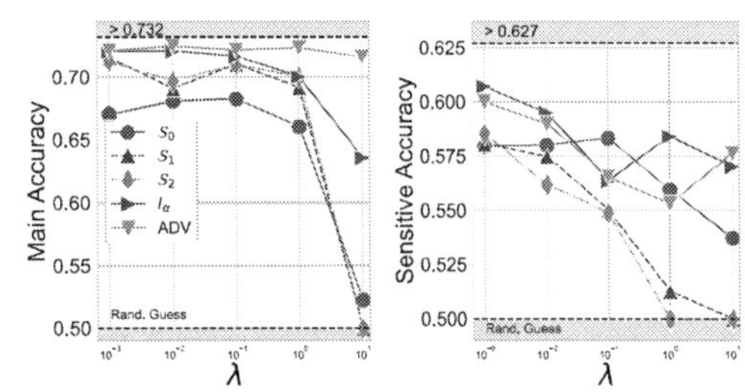


(a) $Y \uparrow$ DIAL-M (b) $S \downarrow$ DIAL-M

Fig. 3: Results on Fair Classification for a RNN.

**Results on TRUST.** This dataset exhibits an interesting behaviour known as spurious correlations (Yule, 1926; Simon, 1954; Pearl et al., 2000). This means that, without any disentanglement penalty, the encoder learns information about the sensitive features that hurts the classification performance on the test set. We also observe that learning disentangled representation with CLINIC (using $S_1$ or $S_2$) outperforms a model trained with CE loss solely. This suggests that CLINIC could *go beyond the standard disentanglement/accuracy trade-off.*

### 5.3 Superiority of the CLINIC's Objective

In this experiment we assess the relevance of using $I(Z;S|Y)$ (Eq. 4) instead of $I(Z;S)$ (Eq. 3). For all the considered $\lambda$, all datasets and all the considered checkpoints, we display in Fig. 6 the disentanglement/accuracy trade-off.

**Analysis.** Each point in Fig. 6 corresponds to a trained model (with a specific $\lambda$). The more a point is at the bottom right, the better it is for our purpose. Notice that the points stemming from our strategies $\mathcal{S}_1$ and $\mathcal{S}_2$ (orange/green) lie further down on the right than the point stemming from $\mathcal{S}_0$ (bleu). For instance, the use of $\mathcal{S}_1$ or $\mathcal{S}_2$ for the RNN provide many models exhibiting perfect sensitive accuracy while maintaining high main accuracy, which is not the case for $\mathcal{S}_0$. For BERT, models trained with $\mathcal{S}_0$ either have high sensitive and main accuracy or low sensitive and main accuracy. On the contrary, there are points stemming from $\mathcal{S}_1$ or $\mathcal{S}_2$ that lies on the bottom right of Fig. 6. *Overall, Fig. 6 validates the use of $I(Z;S|Y)$ instead of $I(Z;S)$.*

### 5.4 Speed up Gain

In contrast with CLINIC, both previous methods ADV and $I_\alpha$ rely on an additional network for the computation of the disentanglement regularizer in Eq. 1. These extra parameters need to be learned with the use of an additional loop during training: at each update of the encoder $f_\theta$, several updates of the network are performed to ensure that the regularizer computes the correct value. This loop is both times consuming and involves extra parameters (*e.g* new learning rates for the additional network) that must be tuned carefully. This makes ADV and $I_\alpha$ more difficult to implement on large-scale datasets. Tab. 2, illustrates both the parameter reduction and the speed up induced by CLINIC.

| | Method | # params. | 1 epoch. |
|---|---|---|---|
| RNN | ADV | 2220 −0.6% | 551 −17% |
| | $I_\alpha$ | 2234 | 663 |
| | CLINIC | 2206 −1.3% | 500 −24% |
| BERT | ADV | 109576 −0.01% | 2424 −10% |
| | $I_\alpha$ | 109591 | 2689 |
| | CLINIC | 109576 −0.03% | 2200 −19% |

Tab. 2: Runtime for 1 epoch (using DIAL-S, $B = 64$ and relying on a single NVIDIA-V100 with 32GB of memory). The model sizes are given in thousand. We compute the relative improvement with respect to the strongest baseline $I_\alpha$ from Colombo et al. (2021c).

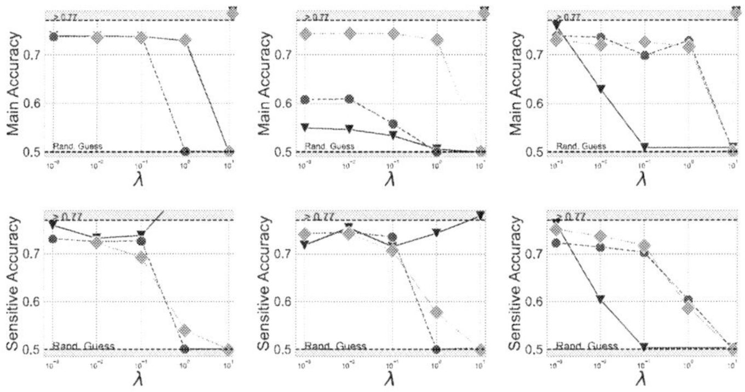


Fig. 4: Ablation study on PT on DIAL-S. Figures from left to right correspond to the performance of ALB., DIS. and SEQU..

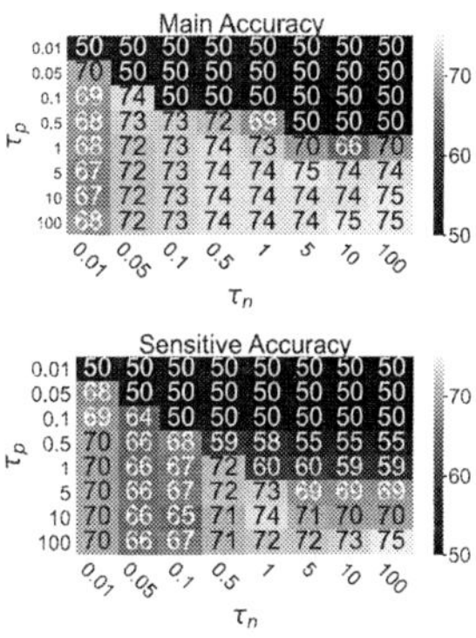


Fig. 5: Ablation study on $(\tau_n, \tau_p)$ for DIAL-S.

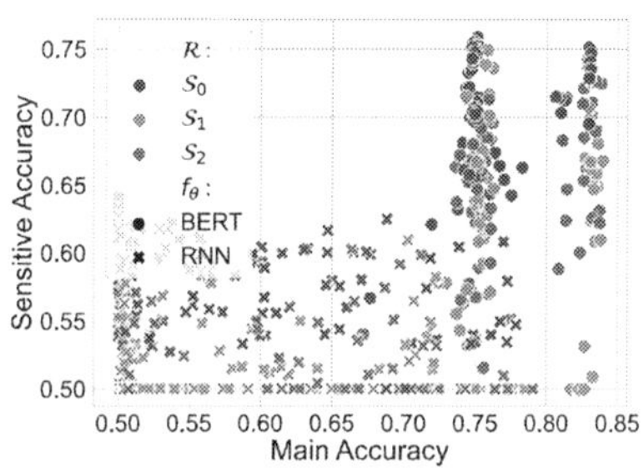


Fig. 6: Disentanglement/accuracy trade-off for various datasets, checkpoints and values of $\lambda$. Point with high sensitive accuracy (*e.g.* in the upper right corner) corresponds to low values of $\lambda$ (*e.g.* $\lambda \in \{10^{-3}, 10^{-2}, 10^{-1}\}$).

## 6 Ablation Study

In this section, we conduct an ablation study on CLINIC with the best sampling strategy ($\mathcal{S}_1$) to better understand the importance of its relative components. We focus on the effect of *(i)* the choice of PT models, *(ii)* the batch size and *(iii)* the temperature. This ablation study is conducted for both DIAL-S and TRUST-A, where we recall that the former is harder to disentangle than the latter. Results on TRUST-A can be found in Ap. A.

### 6.1 Changing the PT Model

**Setting.** As recently pointed out by Bommasani et al. (2021), PT plays a central role in NLP, thus the need to understand their effects is crucial. We test CLINIC with PT that are lighter and require less computation time to finetune than BERT.

**Analysis.** The results of CLINIC trained with SQU., DIS. and ALB. are given in Fig. 4. Overall, we observe that CLINIC consistently achieves better results on all the considered models. Interestingly, for $\lambda > 0.1$, we observe that ADV degenerates: the main task accuracy is around 50% and the sensitive task accuracy either is 50% or reaches a high value. This phenomenon has been reported in Barrett et al. (2019); Colombo et al. (2021c).

### 6.2 Effect of the Temperature

Recall that CLINIC uses two different temperatures (see Eq. 5) denoted by $\tau_p$ and $\tau_n$, corresponding to the magnitude one wishes to put on positive and negatives examples. In this experiment, we study their relative importance on the disentanglement/accuracy trade-off.

**Analysis.** Fig. 5 gathers the performance of CLINIC for different $(\tau_p, \tau_n)$. We observe that low values of $\tau_p$ (*i.e* focusing on easy positive) conduct to uninformative representation (*i.e* low accuracy for $Y$). As $\tau_p$ increases, the choice of $\tau_n$ becomes relevant. Previously introduced supervised contrastive losses (Khosla et al., 2020) only use one temperature thus can only rely on diagonal score from Fig. 5. Since the chosen trade-off depends on the final application, we believe this ablation study validates the use of two temperatures.

## 7 Summary and Concluding Remarks

We introduced CLINIC, a set of novel losses tailored for fair classification. CLINIC both outperform existing disentanglement methods and can go beyond the traditional accuracy/disentanglement trade-off. Future works include (1) improving CLINIC to enable finer control over the disentanglement degree, and (2) developing a way to measure the accuracy/disentanglement trade-off which appears to differ for each dataset.

## 8 Limitations

This paper proposes a novel information-theoretic objective to learn disentangled representations. While the results held for English and studied pre-trained encoders, we observed different behavior depending on the disentanglement difficulty. Overall predicting for which attribute or which data we will be able to see a positive trade-off while disentangling remains an open question.

Additionally, similarly to previous work in the same line of research we also assumed to have access to $S$ which might not be the case for various practical applications. Note that although the main paper focuses on binary attributes for $S$ we report additional results in Ssec. A.1. In general, we believe that our embeddings could be utilized for diverse applications, such as sentence generation and large language models. However, evaluating their performance on these specific tasks falls beyond the scope of this paper. Future research should focus on addressing these aspects.

## References


Anass Aghbalou and Guillaume Staerman. 2023. Hypothesis transfer learning with surrogate classification losses. *arXiv preprint arXiv:2305.19694*.

Jaimeen Ahn and Alice Oh. 2021. Mitigating language-dependent ethnic bias in bert. *arXiv preprint arXiv:2109.05704*.

Philip Bachman, R Devon Hjelm, and William Buchwalter. 2019. Learning representations by maximizing mutual information across views. *arXiv preprint arXiv:1906.00910*.

Maria Barrett, Yova Kementchedjhieva, Yanai Elazar, Desmond Elliott, and Anders Søgaard. 2019. Adversarial removal of demographic attributes revisited. In *Proceedings of the 2019 Conference on Empirical Methods in Natural Language Processing and the 9th International Joint Conference on Natural Language Processing (EMNLP-IJCNLP)*, pages 6331–6336.

Mohamed Ishmael Belghazi, Aristide Baratin, Sai Rajeswar, Sherjil Ozair, Yoshua Bengio, Aaron Courville, and R Devon Hjelm. 2018. Mine: mutual information neural estimation. *arXiv preprint arXiv:1801.04062*.

Y. Bengio, A. Courville, and P. Vincent. 2013. Representation learning: A review and new perspectives. *IEEE Transactions on Pattern Analysis and Machine Intelligence*, 35(8):1798–1828.

Su Lin Blodgett, Lisa Green, and Brendan O'Connor. 2016. Demographic dialectal variation in social media: A case study of African-American English. In *Proceedings of the 2016 Conference on Empirical Methods in Natural Language Processing*, pages 1119–1130, Austin, Texas.

Rishi Bommasani, Drew A Hudson, Ehsan Adeli, Russ Altman, Simran Arora, Sydney von Arx, Michael S Bernstein, Jeannette Bohg, Antoine Bosselut, Emma Brunskill, et al. 2021. On the opportunities and risks of foundation models. *arXiv preprint arXiv:2108.07258*.

Marc-Etienne Brunet, Colleen Alkalay-Houlihan, Ashton Anderson, and Richard Zemel. 2019. Understanding the origins of bias in word embeddings. In *International Conference on Machine Learning*, pages 803–811.

Cristian S Calude and Giuseppe Longo. 2017. The deluge of spurious correlations in big data. *Foundations of science*, 22(3):595–612.

Simon Caton and Christian Haas. 2020. Fairness in machine learning: A survey. *arXiv preprint arXiv:2010.04053*.

Emile Chapuis, Pierre Colombo, Matteo Manica, Matthieu Labeau, and Chloé Clavel. 2020. Hierarchical pre-training for sequence labelling in spoken dialog. In *Findings of the Association for Computational Linguistics: EMNLP 2020*, pages 2636–2648, Online. Association for Computational Linguistics.

Ting Chen, Simon Kornblith, Mohammad Norouzi, and Geoffrey Hinton. 2020. A simple framework for contrastive learning of visual representations. In *International conference on machine learning*, pages 1597–1607.

Pengyu Cheng, Weituo Hao, Shuyang Dai, Jiachang Liu, Zhe Gan, and Lawrence Carin. 2020. Club: A contrastive log-ratio upper bound of mutual information. In *International Conference on Machine Learning*, pages 1779–1788.

Cyril Chhun, Pierre Colombo, Fabian M. Suchanek, and Chloé Clavel. 2022. Of human criteria and automatic metrics: A benchmark of the evaluation of story generation. In *Proceedings of the 29th International Conference on Computational Linguistics*, pages 5794–5836, Gyeongju, Republic of Korea. International Committee on Computational Linguistics.

Jianfeng Chi, William Shand, Yaodong Yu, Kai-Wei Chang, Han Zhao, and Yuan Tian. 2022. Conditional supervised contrastive learning for fair text classification. *arXiv preprint arXiv:2205.11485*.

Sumit Chopra, Raia Hadsell, and Yann LeCun. 2005. Learning a similarity metric discriminatively, with application to face verification. In *2005 IEEE Computer Society Conference on Computer Vision and Pattern Recognition (CVPR'05)*, volume 1, pages 539–546.

Somnath Basu Roy Chowdhury, Sayan Ghosh, Yiyuan Li, Junier B Oliva, Shashank Srivastava, and Snigdha Chaturvedi. 2021. Adversarial scrubbing of demographic information for text classification. *arXiv preprint arXiv:2109.08613*.

Junyoung Chung, Caglar Gulcehre, KyungHyun Cho, and Yoshua Bengio. 2014. Empirical evaluation of gated recurrent neural networks on sequence modeling. *arXiv preprint arXiv:1412.3555*.

Maximin Coavoux, Shashi Narayan, and Shay B Cohen. 2018. Privacy-preserving neural representations of text. *arXiv preprint arXiv:1808.09408*.

Pierre Colombo. 2021. *Learning to represent and generate text using information measures*. Ph.D. thesis, Institut polytechnique de Paris.

Pierre Colombo, Emile Chapuis, Matthieu Labeau, and Chloé Clavel. 2021a. Code-switched inspired losses for spoken dialog representations. In *Proceedings of the 2021 Conference on Empirical Methods in Natural Language Processing*, pages 8320–8337, Online and Punta Cana, Dominican Republic. Association for Computational Linguistics.

Pierre Colombo, Emile Chapuis, Matthieu Labeau, and Chloé Clavel. 2021b. Improving multimodal fusion via mutual dependency maximisation. In *Proceedings of the 2021 Conference on Empirical Methods in Natural Language Processing*, pages 231–245, Online and Punta Cana, Dominican Republic. Association for Computational Linguistics.

Pierre Colombo, Emile Chapuis, Matteo Manica, Emmanuel Vignon, Giovanna Varni, and Chloe Clavel. 2020. Guiding attention in sequence-to-sequence models for dialogue act prediction. In *AAAI*, pages 7594–7601.

Pierre Colombo, Chloe Clavel, and Pablo Piantanida. 2021c. A novel estimator of mutual information for learning to disentangle textual representations. *arXiv preprint arXiv:2105.02685*.

Pierre Colombo, Chloé Clavel, Chouchang Yack, and Giovanna Varni. 2021d. Beam search with bidirectional strategies for neural response generation. In *Proceedings of the 4th International Conference on Natural Language and Speech Processing (ICNLSP 2021)*, pages 139–146, Trento, Italy. Association for Computational Linguistics.

Pierre Colombo, Eduardo Dadalto, Guillaume Staerman, Nathan Noiry, and Pablo Piantanida. 2022a. Beyond mahalanobis distance for textual ood detection. In *Advances in Neural Information Processing Systems*, volume 35, pages 17744–17759. Curran Associates, Inc.

Pierre Colombo, Nathan Noiry, Ekhine Irurozki, and Stéphan Clémençon. 2022b. What are the best systems? new perspectives on nlp benchmarking. *Advances in Neural Information Processing Systems*, 35:26915–26932.

Pierre Colombo, Maxime Peyrard, Nathan Noiry, Robert West, and Pablo Piantanida. 2022c. The glass ceiling of automatic evaluation in natural language generation. *arXiv preprint arXiv:2208.14585*.

Pierre Colombo, Pablo Piantanida, and Chloé Clavel. 2021e. A novel estimator of mutual information for learning to disentangle textual representations. In *Proceedings of the 59th Annual Meeting of the Association for Computational Linguistics and the 11th International Joint Conference on Natural Language Processing (Volume 1: Long Papers)*, pages 6539–6550, Online. Association for Computational Linguistics.

Pierre Colombo, Guillaume Staerman, Chloé Clavel, and Pablo Piantanida. 2021f. Automatic text evaluation through the lens of Wasserstein barycenters. In *Proceedings of the 2021 Conference on Empirical Methods in Natural Language Processing*, pages 10450–10466, Online and Punta Cana, Dominican Republic. Association for Computational Linguistics.

Pierre Colombo, Guillaume Staerman, Nathan Noiry, and Pablo Piantanida. 2022d. Learning disentangled textual representations via statistical measures of similarity. In *Proceedings of the 60th Annual Meeting of the Association for Computational Linguistics (Volume 1: Long Papers)*, pages 2614–2630, Dublin, Ireland. Association for Computational Linguistics.

Pierre Colombo, Wojciech Witon, Ashutosh Modi, James Kennedy, and Mubbasir Kapadia. 2019. Affect-driven dialog generation. In *Proceedings of the 2019 Conference of the North American Chapter of the Association for Computational Linguistics: Human Language Technologies, Volume 1 (Long and Short Papers)*, pages 3734–3743, Minneapolis, Minnesota. Association for Computational Linguistics.

Pierre Jean A. Colombo, Chloé Clavel, and Pablo Piantanida. 2022e. Infolm: A new metric to evaluate summarization & data2text generation. *Proceedings of the AAAI Conference on Artificial Intelligence*, 36(10):10554–10562.

Thomas M. Cover and Joy A. Thomas. 2006. *Elements of Information Theory (Wiley Series in Telecommunications and Signal Processing)*. Wiley-Interscience, USA.

Brian d'Alessandro, Cathy O'Neil, and Tom LaGatta. 2017. Conscientious classification: A data scientist's guide to discrimination-aware classification. *Big data*, 5(2):120–134.

Maxime Darrin, Pablo Piantanida, and Pierre Colombo. 2022. Rainproof: An umbrella to shield text generators from out-of-distribution data. *arXiv preprint arXiv:2212.09171*.

Maxime Darrin, Guillaume Staerman, Eduardo Dadalto Câmara Gomes, Jackie CK Cheung, Pablo Piantanida, and Pierre Colombo. 2023. Unsupervised layer-wise score aggregation for textual ood detection. *arXiv preprint arXiv:2302.09852*.

Maria De-Arteaga, Alexey Romanov, Hanna Wallach, Jennifer Chayes, Christian Borgs, Alexandra Chouldechova, Sahin Geyik, Krishnaram Kenthapadi, and Adam Tauman Kalai. 2019. Bias in bios: A case study of semantic representation bias in a high-stakes setting. In *proceedings of the Conference on Fairness, Accountability, and Transparency*, pages 120–128.

Daniel de Vassimon Manela, David Errington, Thomas Fisher, Boris van Breugel, and Pasquale Minervini. 2021. Stereotype and skew: Quantifying gender bias in pre-trained and fine-tuned language models. In *Proceedings of the 16th Conference of the European Chapter of the Association for Computational Linguistics: Main Volume*, pages 2232–2242.

Jacob Devlin, Ming-Wei Chang, Kenton Lee, and Kristina Toutanova. 2018. Bert: Pre-training of deep bidirectional transformers for language understanding. *arXiv preprint arXiv:1810.04805*.

Emily Dinan, Angela Fan, Ledell Wu, Jason Weston, Douwe Kiela, and Adina Williams. 2020. Multi-dimensional gender bias classification. *arXiv preprint arXiv:2005.00614*.

Tanvi Dinkar, Pierre Colombo, Matthieu Labeau, and Chloé Clavel. 2020. The importance of fillers for text representations of speech transcripts. In *Proceedings of the 2020 Conference on Empirical Methods in Natural Language Processing (EMNLP)*, pages 7985–7993, Online. Association for Computational Linguistics.

Yanai Elazar and Yoav Goldberg. 2018. Adversarial removal of demographic attributes from text data. *arXiv preprint arXiv:1808.06640*.

Hongchao Fang, Sicheng Wang, Meng Zhou, Jiayuan Ding, and Pengtao Xie. 2020. Cert: Contrastive self-supervised learning for language understanding. *arXiv preprint arXiv:2005.12766*.

Clément Feutry, Pablo Piantanida, Yoshua Bengio, and Pierre Duhamel. 2018. Learning anonymized representations with adversarial neural networks. *arXiv preprint arXiv:1802.09386*.

Aviv Gabbay and Yedid Hoshen. 2019. Demystifying inter-class disentanglement. *arXiv preprint arXiv:1906.11796*.

Pratik Gajane and Mykola Pechenizkiy. 2017. On formalizing fairness in prediction with machine learning. *arXiv preprint arXiv:1710.03184*.

Luyu Gao, Yunyi Zhang, Jiawei Han, and Jamie Callan. 2021. Scaling deep contrastive learning batch size under memory limited setup. In *Proceedings of the 6th Workshop on Representation Learning for NLP (RepL4NLP-2021)*, pages 316–321.

Alexandre Garcia, Pierre Colombo, Florence d'Alché Buc, Slim Essid, and Chloé Clavel. 2019. From the token to the review: A hierarchical multimodal approach to opinion mining. In *Proceedings of the 2019 Conference on Empirical Methods in Natural Language Processing and the 9th International Joint Conference on Natural Language Processing (EMNLP-IJCNLP)*, pages 5539–5548, Hong Kong, China. Association for Computational Linguistics.

Daniel Gillick, Sayali Kulkarni, Larry Lansing, Alessandro Presta, Jason Baldridge, Eugene Ie, and Diego Garcia-Olano. 2019. Learning dense representations for entity retrieval. *arXiv preprint arXiv:1909.10506*.

John M Giorgi, Osvald Nitski, Gary D Bader, and Bo Wang. 2020. Declutr: Deep contrastive learning for unsupervised textual representations. *arXiv preprint arXiv:2006.03659*.

Umang Gupta, Aaron M Ferber, Bistra Dilkina, and Greg Ver Steeg. 2021. Controllable guarantees for fair outcomes via contrastive information estimation. In *Proceedings of the AAAI Conference on Artificial Intelligence*, volume 35, pages 7610–7619.

Kaiming He, Haoqi Fan, Yuxin Wu, Saining Xie, and Ross Girshick. 2020. Momentum contrast for unsupervised visual representation learning. In *Proceedings of the IEEE/CVF Conference on Computer Vision and Pattern Recognition*, pages 9729–9738.

Olivier Henaff. 2020. Data-efficient image recognition with contrastive predictive coding. In *International Conference on Machine Learning*, pages 4182–4192. PMLR.

Dirk Hovy, Anders Johannsen, and Anders Søgaard. 2015. User review sites as a resource for large-scale sociolinguistic studies. In *Proceedings of the 24th international conference on World Wide Web*, pages 452–461.

Dirk Hovy and Anders Søgaard. 2015. Tagging performance correlates with author age. In *Proceedings of the 53rd annual meeting of the Association for Computational Linguistics and the 7th international joint conference on natural language processing (volume 2: Short papers)*, pages 483–488.

Forrest N Iandola, Albert E Shaw, Ravi Krishna, and Kurt W Keutzer. 2020. Squeezebert: What can computer vision teach nlp about efficient neural networks? *arXiv preprint arXiv:2006.11316*.

Hamid Jalalzai, Pierre Colombo, Chloé Clavel, Eric Gaussier, Giovanna Varni, Emmanuel Vignon, and Anne Sabourin. 2020. Heavy-tailed representations, text polarity classification & data augmentation. In *Advances in Neural Information Processing Systems*, volume 33, pages 4295–4307. Curran Associates, Inc.

Vineet John, Lili Mou, Hareesh Bahuleyan, and Olga Vechtomova. 2018. Disentangled representation learning for non-parallel text style transfer. *arXiv preprint arXiv:1808.04339*.

Faisal Kamiran and Toon Calders. 2012. Data preprocessing techniques for classification without discrimination. *Knowledge and Information Systems*, 33(1):1–33.

Vladimir Karpukhin, Barlas Oğuz, Sewon Min, Patrick Lewis, Ledell Wu, Sergey Edunov, Danqi Chen, and Wen-tau Yih. 2020. Dense passage retrieval for open-domain question answering. *arXiv preprint arXiv:2004.04906*.

Prannay Khosla, Piotr Teterwak, Chen Wang, Aaron Sarna, Yonglong Tian, Phillip Isola, Aaron Maschinot, Ce Liu, and Dilip Krishnan. 2020. Supervised contrastive learning. *arXiv preprint arXiv:2004.11362*.

Diederik P Kingma and Jimmy Ba. 2014. Adam: A method for stochastic optimization. *arXiv preprint arXiv:1412.6980*.

Pierre Laforgue, Guillaume Staerman, and Stephan Clémençon. 2021. Generalization bounds in the presence of outliers: a median-of-means study. In *International Conference on Machine Learning*, pages 5937–5947. PMLR.

Guillaume Lample, Sandeep Subramanian, Eric Smith, Ludovic Denoyer, Marc'Aurelio Ranzato, and Y-Lan Boureau. 2018. Multiple-attribute text rewriting. In

*International Conference on Learning Representations*.

Zhenzhong Lan, Mingda Chen, Sebastian Goodman, Kevin Gimpel, Piyush Sharma, and Radu Soricut. 2019. Albert: A lite bert for self-supervised learning of language representations. *arXiv preprint arXiv:1909.11942*.

Zachary C Lipton, Alexandra Chouldechova, and Julian McAuley. 2018. Does mitigating ml's impact disparity require treatment disparity? In *Proceedings of the 32nd International Conference on Neural Information Processing Systems*, pages 8136–8146.

Francesco Locatello, Gabriele Abbati, Tom Rainforth, Stefan Bauer, Bernhard Schölkopf, and Olivier Bachem. 2019a. On the fairness of disentangled representations. *arXiv preprint arXiv:1905.13662*.

Francesco Locatello, Stefan Bauer, Mario Lucic, Gunnar Raetsch, Sylvain Gelly, Bernhard Schölkopf, and Olivier Bachem. 2019b. Challenging common assumptions in the unsupervised learning of disentangled representations. In *international conference on machine learning*, pages 4114–4124.

Francesco Locatello, Stefan Bauer, Mario Lucic, Gunnar Rätsch, Sylvain Gelly, Bernhard Schölkopf, and Olivier Bachem. 2020. A sober look at the unsupervised learning of disentangled representations and their evaluation. *arXiv preprint arXiv:2010.14766*.

Lajanugen Logeswaran and Honglak Lee. 2018. An efficient framework for learning sentence representations. *arXiv preprint arXiv:1803.02893*.

Ilya Loshchilov and Frank Hutter. 2017. Decoupled weight decay regularization. *arXiv preprint arXiv:1711.05101*.

Emile Mathieu, Tom Rainforth, Nana Siddharth, and Yee Whye Teh. 2019. Disentangling disentanglement in variational autoencoders. In *International Conference on Machine Learning*, pages 4402–4412.

David McAllester and Karl Stratos. 2020. Formal limitations on the measurement of mutual information. In *Proceedings of the Twenty Third International Conference on Artificial Intelligence and Statistics*, volume 108 of *Proceedings of Machine Learning Research*, pages 875–884.

Jovana Mitrovic, Brian McWilliams, and Melanie Rey. 2020. Less can be more in contrastive learning.

Marzieh Mozafari, Reza Farahbakhsh, and Noël Crespi. 2020. Hate speech detection and racial bias mitigation in social media based on bert model. *PloS one*, 15(8):e0237861.

XuanLong Nguyen, Martin J Wainwright, and Michael I Jordan. 2010. Estimating divergence functionals and the likelihood ratio by convex risk minimization. *IEEE Transactions on Information Theory*.

Aaron van den Oord, Yazhe Li, and Oriol Vinyals. 2018. Representation learning with contrastive predictive coding. *arXiv preprint arXiv:1807.03748*.

Liam Paninski. 2003. Estimation of entropy and mutual information. *Neural computation*, 15(6):1191–1253.

Adam Paszke, Sam Gross, Soumith Chintala, Gregory Chanan, Edward Yang, Zachary DeVito, Zeming Lin, Alban Desmaison, Luca Antiga, and Adam Lerer. 2017. Automatic differentiation in pytorch. In *NIPS 2017 Workshop on Autodiff*.

Judea Pearl et al. 2000. Models, reasoning and inference. *Cambridge, UK: CambridgeUniversityPress*, 19.

Georg Pichler, Pierre Jean A. Colombo, Malik Boudiaf, Günther Koliander, and Pablo Piantanida. 2022. A differential entropy estimator for training neural networks. In *Proceedings of the 39th International Conference on Machine Learning*, volume 162 of *Proceedings of Machine Learning Research*, pages 17691–17715. PMLR.

Georg Pichler, Pablo Piantanida, and Günther Koliander. 2020. On the estimation of information measures of continuous distributions. *arXiv preprint arXiv:2002.02851*.

Marine Picot, Federica Granese, Guillaume Staerman, Marco Romanelli, Francisco Messina, Pablo Piantanida, and Pierre Colombo. 2023. A halfspace-mass depth-based method for adversarial attack detection. *Transactions on Machine Learning Research*.

Marine Picot, Nathan Noiry, Pablo Piantanida, and Pierre Colombo. 2022a. Adversarial attack detection under realistic constraints.

Marine Picot, Guillaume Staerman, Federica Granese, Nathan Noiry, Francisco Messina, Pablo Piantanida, and Pierre Colombo. 2022b. A simple unsupervised data depth-based method to detect adversarial images.

Rui Qian, Tianjian Meng, Boqing Gong, Ming-Hsuan Yang, Huisheng Wang, Serge Belongie, and Yin Cui. 2021. Spatiotemporal contrastive video representation learning. In *Proceedings of the IEEE/CVF Conference on Computer Vision and Pattern Recognition*, pages 6964–6974.

Yanru Qu, Dinghan Shen, Yelong Shen, Sandra Sajeev, Jiawei Han, and Weizhu Chen. 2020. Coda: Contrast-enhanced and diversity-promoting data augmentation for natural language understanding. *arXiv preprint arXiv:2010.08670*.

Shauli Ravfogel, Yanai Elazar, Hila Gonen, Michael Twiton, and Yoav Goldberg. 2020. Null it out: Guarding protected attributes by iterative nullspace projection. *arXiv preprint arXiv:2004.07667*.

Nils Reimers and Iryna Gurevych. 2019. Sentence-bert: Sentence embeddings using siamese bert-networks. *arXiv preprint arXiv:1908.10084*.

Nils Rethmeier and Isabelle Augenstein. 2021. A primer on contrastive pretraining in language processing: Methods, lessons learned and perspectives. *arXiv preprint arXiv:2102.12982*.

Joshua Robinson, Ching-Yao Chuang, Suvrit Sra, and Stefanie Jegelka. 2020. Contrastive learning with hard negative samples. *arXiv preprint arXiv:2010.04592*.

Victor Sanh, Lysandre Debut, Julien Chaumond, and Thomas Wolf. 2019. Distilbert, a distilled version of bert: smaller, faster, cheaper and lighter. *arXiv preprint arXiv:1910.01108*.

Florian Schroff, Dmitry Kalenichenko, and James Philbin. 2015. Facenet: A unified embedding for face recognition and clustering. In *Proceedings of the IEEE conference on computer vision and pattern recognition*, pages 815–823.

Aili Shen, Xudong Han, Trevor Cohn, Timothy Baldwin, and Lea Frermann. 2021. Contrastive learning for fair representations. *arXiv preprint arXiv:2109.10645*.

Aili Shen, Xudong Han, Trevor Cohn, Timothy Baldwin, and Lea Frermann. 2022. Does representational fairness imply empirical fairness? In *Findings of the Association for Computational Linguistics: AACL-IJCNLP 2022*, pages 81–95.

Dinghan Shen, Mingzhi Zheng, Yelong Shen, Yanru Qu, and Weizhu Chen. 2020. A simple but tough-to-beat data augmentation approach for natural language understanding and generation. *arXiv preprint arXiv:2009.13818*.

Herbert A Simon. 1954. Spurious correlation: A causal interpretation. *Journal of the American statistical Association*, 49(267):467–479.

Jiaming Song and Stefano Ermon. 2019. Understanding the limitations of variational mutual information estimators. *arXiv preprint arXiv:1910.06222*.

A Sridhar, Chawin Sitawarin, and David Wagner. 2021. Mitigating adversarial training instability with batch normalization. In *Proceedings of International Conference on Learning Representation Workshop on Security and Safety in Machine Learning Systems*.

Nitish Srivastava, Geoffrey Hinton, Alex Krizhevsky, Ilya Sutskever, and Ruslan Salakhutdinov. 2014. Dropout: a simple way to prevent neural networks from overfitting. *The journal of machine learning research*, 15(1):1929–1958.

Guillaume Staerman. 2022. *Functional anomaly detection and robust estimation*. Ph.D. thesis, Institut polytechnique de Paris.

Guillaume Staerman, Eric Adjakossa, Pavlo Mozharovskyi, Vera Hofer, Jayant Sen Gupta, and Stephan Clémençon. 2023. Functional anomaly detection: a benchmark study. *International Journal of Data Science and Analytics*, 16(16):101–117.

Guillaume Staerman, Pierre Laforgue, Pavlo Mozharovskyi, and Florence d'Alché Buc. 2021a. When ot meets mom: Robust estimation of wasserstein distance. In *Proceedings of The 24th International Conference on Artificial Intelligence and Statistics*, volume 130, pages 136–144.

Guillaume Staerman, Pavlo Mozharovskyi, Stephan Clémençon, and Florence d'Alché Buc. 2019. Functional isolation forest. In *Proceedings of The Eleventh Asian Conference on Machine Learning*, volume 101, pages 332–347.

Guillaume Staerman, Pavlo Mozharovskyi, and Stéphan Clémençon. 2020. The area of the convex hull of sampled curves: a robust functional statistical depth measure. In *Proceedings of the 23nd International Conference on Artificial Intelligence and Statistics*, volume 108, pages 570–579.

Guillaume Staerman, Pavlo Mozharovskyi, and Stéphan Clémençon. 2021b. Affine-invariant integrated rank-weighted depth: Definition, properties and finite sample analysis. *arXiv preprint arXiv:2106.11068*.

Guillaume Staerman, Pavlo Mozharovskyi, Pierre Colombo, Stéphan Clémençon, and Florence d'Alché Buc. 2021c. A pseudo-metric between probability distributions based on depth-trimmed regions. *arXiv preprint arXiv:2103.12711*.

Ashish Vaswani, Noam Shazeer, Niki Parmar, Jakob Uszkoreit, Llion Jones, Aidan N Gomez, Łukasz Kaiser, and Illia Polosukhin. 2017. Attention is all you need. In *Advances in neural information processing systems*, pages 5998–6008.

Feng Wang and Huaping Liu. 2021. Understanding the behaviour of contrastive loss. In *Proceedings of the IEEE/CVF Conference on Computer Vision and Pattern Recognition*, pages 2495–2504.

Tongzhou Wang and Phillip Isola. 2020. Understanding contrastive representation learning through alignment and uniformity on the hypersphere. In *International Conference on Machine Learning*, pages 9929–9939.

Wojciech Witon, Pierre Colombo, Ashutosh Modi, and Mubbasir Kapadia. 2018. Disney at IEST 2018: Predicting emotions using an ensemble. In *Proceedings of the 9th Workshop on Computational Approaches to Subjectivity, Sentiment and Social Media Analysis*, pages 248–253, Brussels, Belgium. Association for Computational Linguistics.

Thomas Wolf, Lysandre Debut, Victor Sanh, Julien Chaumond, Clement Delangue, Anthony Moi, Pierric Cistac, Tim Rault, R'emi Louf, Morgan Funtowicz, and Jamie Brew. Huggingface's transformers: State-of-the-art natural language processing. *arXiv preprint arXiv:1910.03771*.

Eric Wong, Leslie Rice, and J Zico Kolter. 2020. Fast is better than free: Revisiting adversarial training. *arXiv preprint arXiv:2001.03994*.

Chuhan Wu, Fangzhao Wu, and Yongfeng Huang. 2021. Rethinking infonce: How many negative samples do you need? *arXiv preprint arXiv:2105.13003*.

Qizhe Xie, Zihang Dai, Yulun Du, Eduard Hovy, and Graham Neubig. 2017. Controllable invariance through adversarial feature learning. In *Advances in Neural Information Processing Systems*, pages 585–596.

Bing Xu, Naiyan Wang, Tianqi Chen, and Mu Li. 2015. Empirical evaluation of rectified activations in convolutional network. *arXiv preprint arXiv:1505.00853*.

Shin'ya Yamaguchi, Sekitoshi Kanai, Tetsuya Shioda, and Shoichiro Takeda. 2019. Multiple pretext-task for self-supervised learning via mixing multiple image transformations. *arXiv preprint arXiv:1912.11603*.

G Udny Yule. 1926. Why do we sometimes get nonsense-correlations between time-series?–a study in sampling and the nature of time-series. *Journal of the royal statistical society*, 89(1):1–63.

Huan Zhang, Hongge Chen, Chaowei Xiao, Sven Gowal, Robert Stanforth, Bo Li, Duane Boning, and Cho-Jui Hsieh. 2019. Towards stable and efficient training of verifiably robust neural networks. *arXiv preprint arXiv:1906.06316*.

Wenzheng Zhang and Karl Stratos. 2021. Understanding hard negatives in noise contrastive estimation. *arXiv preprint arXiv:2104.06245*.

# Large Language Models and Low-Resource Languages: An Examination of Armenian NLP

**Hayastan Avetisyan** and **David Broneske**
The German Centre for Higher Education Research and Science Studies (DZHW), Germany
avetisyan@dzhw.eu
broneske@dzhw.eu

## Abstract

This paper presents a comprehensive review of Natural Language Processing (NLP) research on Armenian, a language that, despite its rich history and unique linguistic characteristics, is currently low-resource in the field of NLP. We critically synthesize and evaluate various studies in Armenian NLP, highlighting key advancements, challenges, and areas for improvement. A notable aspect of our work is the underlined lack of application of Large Language Models (LLMs) in Armenian NLP, signifying an area of potential exploration and development. Identifying and discussing these challenges and opportunities lays the groundwork for future research directions in Armenian NLP. The emphasis on Armenian also advocates for increased attention to low-resource languages in NLP research, stressing the importance of linguistic diversity and equity. To the best of our knowledge, this is the first paper providing such an extensive review of Armenian NLP, marking a significant contribution to the field.

## 1 Introduction

The evolution of Natural Language Processing (NLP) technologies has revolutionized our interactions with digital systems, paving the way for more human-like dialogues with artificial intelligence. Despite these advancements, a significant number of the world's languages are still considered low-resource in terms of NLP tools and technologies. One such language is Armenian, an Indo-European language with unique complexities and limited digital resources. To address these issues and shed light on the Armenian language in the context of NLP, we present a comprehensive study that contributes to the field in several ways:

1. **Comprehensive Overview of Armenian NLP**: We provide a thorough review of the current state of Armenian Natural Language Processing (NLP), identifying key research, significant advancements, and areas of improvement within the field. We synthesize and critically evaluate the findings from various studies, providing valuable insights for researchers and practitioners alike.

2. **Identifying Challenges and Opportunities**: Our paper highlights the challenges of developing NLP technologies for Armenian, a low-resource language. It elucidates the issues related to the lack of linguistic resources and tools, gaps in machine learning methodologies, and the specific challenges associated with Armenian. This knowledge is essential for future research and resource allocation.

3. **Emphasis on Large Language Models (LLMs)**: Our paper underscores the underutilization of LLMs in Armenian NLP. It examines the potential benefits and challenges of deploying these models in low-resource settings and suggests avenues for future research.

4. **Future Directions**: We present an informed and thorough projection of potential future work in Armenian NLP, covering various aspects such as the development of linguistic resources, the application of machine learning techniques, and the need for multilingual and cross-lingual models. This helps set a clear roadmap for other researchers in the field.

5. **Encouragement of NLP Research for Low-Resource Languages and Promotion of Language Diversity**: By focusing on Armenian, a low-resource language, our paper advocates for more attention to be given to similar languages in NLP research. It stresses the importance of these languages in ensuring linguistic diversity and equity in NLP.

To the best of our knowledge, this is the first comprehensive review focusing specifically on the



*Findings of the Association for Computational Linguistics: IJCNLP-AACL 2023*, pages 199–210
November 1–4, 2023. 

advancements, challenges, and opportunities in Armenian Natural Language Processing. Therefore, our paper fills a crucial gap in the literature, providing a much-needed foundation for further exploration and development in Armenian NLP. This added context further emphasizes the value and novelty of our contributions to the field.

## 2 Exploration of Armenian Natural Language Processing: Key Domains and Literature Review

In the forthcoming chapter, we will present an overview of the current state of Armenian NLP based on the findings of our review. Given the scope limitations, a detailed discussion of the findings cannot be provided. However, for a comprehensive understanding of the literature search process, including the specific databases searched and the keywords employed, and to ensure transparency, please refer to Section A in the appendix.

### 2.1 Linguistic Resources and Tools

The rapid growth of Natural Language Processing (NLP) has primarily been geared toward resource-rich languages such as English, Spanish, and Chinese, overlooking lower-resource languages like Armenian. This oversight results in a scarcity of linguistic resources and tools, which is detrimental to language preservation, linguistic research, and the development of NLP applications for such languages (Silberztein, 2007; Baghdasaryan, 2022; Malajyan et al., 2020; Kindt and Van Elverdinghe, 2022; Megerdoomian, 2009; Vidal-Gorène and Decours-Perez, 2020; Khurshudyan et al., 2022; Saini and Rakholia, 2016).

**NLP Development Platforms**: NooJ, for example, allows users to create grammars and dictionaries while providing parsing capabilities for tokenization, morphology, syntax, and semantics. However, its resources are still insufficient for full-scale Armenian language processing, indicating a need for more comprehensive platforms (Silberztein, 2007).

**Speech Corpora**: The ArmSpeech corpus presents a collection of Armenian speech data, which is essential for speech recognition, synthesis, and spoken language identification systems. Nevertheless, the necessity for similar large-scale resources in other aspects of the Armenian language remains (Baghdasaryan, 2022).

**Semantic and Paraphrase Corpora**: The ARPA corpus, a paraphrase dataset generated using back translation, forms a foundation for paraphrase detection in Armenian. However, the small scale of this corpus (2360 paraphrases) underscores the need for more diverse datasets to enhance NLP tasks (Malajyan et al., 2020).

**Historical Language Resources**: Efforts like the GREgORI Project, which processes historical Armenian manuscripts, are crucial for enhancing Armenian linguistic resources. However, a broader range of Armenian language variations and contexts needs to be included for comprehensive resource development (Kindt and Van Elverdinghe, 2022).

**Language-specific Features and Bootstrapping**: Techniques such as related language bootstrapping can help develop language resources. However, Armenian's unique linguistic features necessitate a language-specific approach rather than a generalized strategy (Megerdoomian, 2009).

**Resource Compilation Platforms**: Calfa compiles and updates existing resources for Classical Armenian, showcasing promising advancements in Armenian NLP. However, the need for larger, interoperable databases persists, indicating the necessity for more systematic efforts (Vidal-Gorène and Decours-Perez, 2020).

**Comprehensive Corpora**: The Eastern Armenian National Corpus (EANC) provides a valuable resource for linguistic studies and various research fields. However, the need for more comprehensive databases covering different time frames, styles, and registers is apparent (Khurshudyan et al., 2022).

**Foundational Resources**: Specific stop-word lists for Armenian are notably lacking, despite being foundational resources in NLP (Saini and Rakholia, 2016).

In conclusion, while progress has been made, further efforts are required to enrich Armenian NLP. This necessitates the creation of more comprehensive resources, the development of tools for diverse NLP tasks, and the promotion of multilingual or cross-lingual learning methods to counterbalance data scarcity. Moreover, it highlights the need for collaboration among researchers, data scientists, and the Armenian community worldwide to create culturally sensitive, community-driven resources.

## 2.2 Evolution of Speech Processing and Recognition

Armenian speech processing and recognition has witnessed transformative advancements across various key sub-domains, primarily automated speech recognition (ASR), speech recognition thresholds (SRT), dialect identification, and evaluation of ASR systems (Davit and Tigran, 2022; Baghdasaryan; Sargsyan and Rahne, 2021; Avetisyan, 2022; Aslanyan et al., 2015; Chakmakjian and Wang, 2022).

**Automated Speech Recognition (ASR) Models**: A dual strategy has marked Progress in this realm. Davit and Tigran (2022) fine-tuned a pre-trained Conformer model yielding notable Armenian ASR outcomes, while Baghdasaryan devised an efficient real-time speech-to-text system using Baidu's Deep Speech and KenLM toolkit. These initiatives signal the feasible extension of ASR applications to languages with limited resources.

**Speech Recognition Thresholds**: Sargsyan and Rahne (2021) innovated a multisyllabic speech audiometry test capable of measuring SRT in Armenian speakers. The results corroborated with equivalent studies in other languages, signifying a universal scope for this approach.

**Dialect Identification**: The work of Avetisyan (2022) illustrated the superiority of neural network models over statistical approaches in Armenian dialect identification. The successful utilization of pre-trained word vectors, even with scarce training data, added to the novelty of their work.

**Evaluation and Future Directions for ASR**: Aslanyan et al. (2015) meticulously assessed current ASR technologies and suggested alternatives to Hidden Markov Models, like Artificial Neural Networks and Sequence Data Mining, to enhance recognition accuracy.

**Challenges of ASR for Bivariant Languages**: The complexities of developing ASR for Armenian, a language with two diverse standard variants, were highlighted by Chakmakjian and Wang (2022). A practical methodology emphasizing the need for a comprehensive understanding of both language variants was proposed for future ASR research.

These studies underscore the advances in Armenian speech processing and recognition, mapping out promising future directions for low-resource languages like Armenian. The collective contribution of these researchers forms a robust foundation for further advancements in the field, highlighting the necessity for continuous exploration and innovation in speech recognition technology.

## 2.3 Progress in Morphology and Syntax

The development of NLP resources for under-documented languages like Armenian has seen noteworthy progress in morphological and syntactic analysis, as highlighted by several key studies (Dolatian et al., 2022; Kindt and Kepeklian, 2022; Vidal-Gorène and Kindt, 2020; Vidal-Gorène et al., 2020; Ghukasyan and Avetisyan, 2021; Arkhangelskiy et al., 2012; Chiarcos et al., 2018).

**Morphological Analysis**: A wide spectrum of tools has been developed, including a morphological transducer by Dolatian et al. (2022) for Western Armenian, and a reusable RNN model by Vidal-Gorène et al. (2020) for various Armenian dialects. The latter indicates the possibility of rapid corpus processing in languages with limited NLP resources.

**Lexical Analysis**: Kindt and Kepeklian (2022) successfully applied a hybrid method combining digital dictionaries and RNN methodologies for analyzing ancient Armenian text, underscoring the utility of traditional and machine learning techniques.

**Lemmatization and POS-Tagging**: There have been advancements in the development of lemmatization and POS-tagging resources for Classical Armenian (Vidal-Gorène and Kindt, 2020), including the creation of a lightweight yet highly accurate lemmatizer (Ghukasyan and Avetisyan, 2021).

**Corpus Creation**: Corpus construction tools, like UniParser and the EANC platform, were utilized by Arkhangelskiy et al. (2012) to construct a morphologically annotated corpus for a minority language, demonstrating the potential for similar initiatives in other low-resource languages.

**Extensions to Universal Morphologies**: Chiarcos et al. (2018) aimed at enhancing the coverage of Universal Morphologies (UniMorph) for the languages of the Caucasus region, pointing towards the potential for further improvement and adaptability of existing tools.

In summary, there is promising progress in the morphological and syntactic analysis of Armenian, with studies indicating the potential of machine learning methodologies and the need for larger, more representative datasets. However, further research is needed to augment the adaptability of these tools across different Armenian dialects and improve their accuracy.

### 2.4 Advancements in Semantics and Named Entity Recognition (NER)

Developments in semantics and Named Entity Recognition (NER) for Armenian have been noteworthy, as exhibited by the research conducted by Mkhitaryan and Madatyan (2022); Podolak and Zeinert (2020); Jain et al. (2019); Tambuscio and Andrews (2021); Vachagan and Tigran (2015); Ghukasyan et al. (2018).

**Semantics**: Exploring temporal expressions in Armenian fairy tales, Mkhitaryan and Madatyan (2022) identified shared schemas with English, thus guiding the future semantic analysis of Armenian texts. Additionally, Vachagan and Tigran (2015) developed algorithms for advanced sentence-level semantic analysis, addressing issues like homonyms.

**Cross-Lingual NER**: Multilingual transformer models were investigated by Podolak and Zeinert (2020) to understand the influence of language-specific features on performance. Meanwhile, Jain et al. (2019) leveraged machine translation to enhance NER in languages with sparsely annotated corpora, exhibiting superior performance for Armenian NER compared to a monolingual model.

**Geolocation NER**: Tambuscio and Andrews (2021) enhanced the detection of geographical entities from historical Armenian text by combining the output of multiple NER tools and utilizing geographical clustering, overcoming the limitations of traditional NER tools for older texts.

**Resources for Armenian NER**: Ghukasyan et al. (2018) made a significant contribution by providing a silver- and gold-standard dataset, setting baseline results for popular models, and sharing Armenian word embeddings, all of which can aid in the development of Armenian NER systems.

In summary, the progress made in Armenian semantics and NER is considerable. However, the potential for improvement is vast, with future directions including refining models, creating more representative datasets, leveraging machine translation for cross-lingual NER, and enhancing semantic analysis techniques. These advancements are essential for fully understanding and preserving the richness of the Armenian language.

### 2.5 Innovations in Document Analysis and Optical Character Recognition

Pioneering developments in document analysis and optical character recognition (OCR) have significantly benefited the preservation and accessibility of low-resource languages, such as Armenian. The works by Vidal-Gorène et al. (2021); Hovakimyan et al.; Islam and Dundua (2015); Tigranyan and Ghukasyan (2020) illustrate this trend:

**Multilevel Annotation Platform**: Vidal-Gorène et al. (2021) created an online, modular interface to annotate handwritten and printed documents. By developing an Armenian manuscript database, they showed the utility of such platforms in automating tasks and managing data. Their tool demonstrates the potential to enrich digital humanities resources, particularly for lesser-documented languages.

**Text Recognition**: Hovakimyan et al. introduced a novel two-layer neural network approach for Armenian text recognition. By outperforming single-layer networks, their work significantly advances the digitization of Armenian texts, expanding the possible applications of complex networks in text recognition.

**Origin Tracing**: Islam and Dundua (2015) employed supervised machine learning to identify the origins of the Georgian Gospel. Their classifier, based on lexical and classical information-theoretic features, distinguishes original from translated documents, underscoring the potential of machine learning in document analysis and multilingual data handling.

**Error Reduction**: The challenge of OCR errors in Armenian texts was addressed by Tigranyan and Ghukasyan (2020). Through a two-step method involving a multilayer perceptron and a convolutional neural network-based sequence transducer, they reduced the word error rate in OCR output, emphasizing the importance of post-processing in OCR tasks.

In summary, these studies signify considerable progress in document analysis and OCR for Armenian, revealing the power of innovative methods and collaborative platforms. However, further research is needed to continue enhancing these resources' quality, accuracy, and breadth, ensuring the preservation and accessibility of Armenian texts.

### 2.6 Emerging Trends in Armenian Text Similarity and Plagiarism Detection

Recent studies in text similarity and plagiarism detection have introduced promising methodologies, particularly for low-resource languages like Armenian. The works by Avetisyan et al. (2023);

Yeshilbashian et al. (2022); Ter-Hovhannisyan and Avetisyan (2022); Margarov et al. (2017) contribute to this growing field:

**Cross-Lingual Plagiarism Detection**: Avetisyan et al. (2023) introduced a cross-lingual plagiarism detection method leveraging multilingual thesauri and pre-trained BERT-based language models. The method's effectiveness across languages and its independence from machine translation or word sense disambiguation make it a fitting solution for less-resourced languages.

**Stylometric Techniques**: Yeshilbashian et al. (2022) used intrinsic stylometric techniques for Armenian text plagiarism detection. They implemented hierarchical clustering models, thereby indicating areas for improvement for longer documents and suggesting refinements for feature sets and parsers.

**Cross-Lingual Sentence Alignment**: The value of pre-trained Transformer-based language models for cross-lingual sentence alignment was underscored by Ter-Hovhannisyan and Avetisyan (2022). They found the XLM-RoBERTa model outperformed others across multiple languages, reinforcing the advantage of a single model trained on various languages in a multilingual context.

**Multi-Layered Analysis**: Margarov et al. (2017) introduced an Armenian text similarity analysis system. By conducting a multi-layered analysis and facilitating user interaction, their approach comprehensively detects plagiarism, including synonym replacement and translation-based plagiarism.

These studies highlight the potential of advanced language models, stylometric techniques, and user-interactive systems for enhancing text similarity and plagiarism detection in Armenian and other low-resource languages. They lay out directions for future research, including refining feature sets, devising efficient model training strategies, and creating more user-interactive systems.

### 2.7 Evolution of Language Modeling for Armenian Language

The field of language modeling has seen significant growth, with research focusing on creating custom models for the Armenian language and enhancing the cross-lingual capabilities of multilingual models.

**Compact Language Modeling**: In Karamyan and Karamyan (2022), a compact and efficient N-gram language model was developed specifically for Armenian. The researchers optimized the model's size and performance using pruning, quantization, and Byte Pair Encoding (BPE) techniques. This research resulted in a compact, high-performing language model for Armenian.

**Cross-lingual Transfer**: In an endeavor to enhance the cross-lingual transfer abilities of Multilingual BERT (mBERT), Kulshreshtha et al. (2020) managed to improve its performance. The researchers achieved this by aligning mBERT with cross-lingual signals, employing parallel corpora supervision, and fine-tuning the alignment. Their study provides valuable insights into strengthening language transfer in multilingual models.

**Word Embedding Models**: On a different track, Avetisyan and Ghukasyan (2019) tested existing Armenian word embedding models and introduced new ones. They employed intrinsic and extrinsic evaluation methods involving a variety of language tasks for comprehensive analysis. The researchers found that different models excelled at different tasks, highlighting the inadequacy of a "one-size-fits-all" approach in choosing an embedding model. They also provided new embeddings that outperformed existing ones in several tasks, contributing to more effective Armenian language processing tools.

In conclusion, efforts in Armenian language modeling are shaping the landscape of language-specific models, enhancing multilingual models' cross-lingual capabilities, and refining word embeddings. These research endeavors contribute to a richer understanding and processing of the Armenian language, driving progress toward more effective natural language processing tools.

## 3 Trends Over Time in Armenian NLP Research

Research on Armenian Natural Language Processing (NLP) has evolved significantly, showcasing notable trends in methods and techniques employed for addressing NLP tasks in the Armenian language.

Initially, Armenian NLP research focused on developing basic tools and methods, such as keyword identification and stemming, to handle specific tasks like plagiarism detection (Margarov et al., 2017). These early studies aimed to overcome the language's unique challenges and lay the foundation for further advancements.

As research progressed, more advanced techniques and algorithms were adopted. Stylometric approaches emerged, enabling the detection of style changes and breaches in Armenian texts (Yeshilbashian et al., 2022). These findings highlighted the potential for more sophisticated language-specific tasks.

Recently, there has been a shift towards utilizing transformer-based models in Armenian NLP. Pretrained multilingual models like BERT and XLM-RoBERTa have shown promising results in tasks requiring a deeper understanding of text semantics and cross-lingual alignment (Avetisyan et al., 2023; Ter-Hovhannisyan and Avetisyan, 2022). However, the application of large language models in Armenian NLP remains relatively unexplored.

In conclusion, Armenian NLP research has transitioned from basic text processing techniques to embracing complex transformer-based models. While significant progress has been made, exploring large language models in Armenian NLP is still in its early stages. This trend emphasizes the need for further research, particularly in applying large language models, to address the unique challenges of the Armenian language and drive the field forward.

## 4 Identification of Gaps, Limitations, and Challenges in Current Research

Based on our review, the main challenges in Armenian Natural Language Processing (NLP) are as follows:

1. **Limited Availability of Large, Labeled Datasets**: Armenian NLP is considerably constrained by the scarcity of large and diverse labeled datasets (Khurshudyan et al., 2022). These datasets are essential for training and evaluating machine learning models, including large language models (LLMs). The lack of such resources limits the capacity to leverage the full potential of LLMs for Armenian NLP tasks.

2. **Shortage of Linguistic Resources and Tools**: The lack of comprehensive linguistic tools, such as parsers, lemmatizers, and tokenizers, poses significant challenges for Armenian NLP. This lack becomes particularly evident in tasks requiring complex linguistic analysis, like stylometry (Yeshilbashian et al., 2022) and plagiarism detection (Avetisyan et al., 2023). Additionally, the absence of resources like a robust Armenian WordNet counterpart constrains the development of applications such as semantic analysis and machine translation.

3. **Less Prevalent Use of Advanced Models**: While studies are leveraging advanced machine learning models such as BERT-based and transformer models for Armenian NLP tasks (Avetisyan et al., 2023; Ter-Hovhannisyan and Avetisyan, 2022), the overall application of such models, especially large language models (LLMs), is still limited. This restricts the understanding and potential benefits of using LLMs in the Armenian NLP.

4. **Handling Dialectal Variations**: Dialectal variations of Armenian (Weitenberg, 2002) can significantly impact the performance of language models if not accounted for during their development and training.

5. **Challenges in Adapting Armenian for NLP Applications**: Armenian, as a unique Indo-European language with a rich history, faces several linguistic challenges integral to its speakers and the broader linguistic landscape. One of the distinctive features of Armenian is its alphabetic script (Sanjian, 1996), which has its own set of characters and symbols, making it distinct from the Roman or Cyrillic scripts. While culturally significant, this uniqueness can pose difficulties regarding digital representation and compatibility with international standards. Adapting Armenian to modern technological applications often requires accurate font development and encoding to ensure proper rendering and functionality. Moreover, the Armenian language has undergone various historical shifts and linguistic influences due to its location at the crossroads of Eastern Europe and Western Asia. These influences, including Persian, Arabic, and Russian, have left their mark on Armenian vocabulary and grammar. Navigating this linguistic history and preserving the purity of the language can be a complex undertaking. Economic factors and government policies are also crucial in shaping the language's trajectory, impacting its promotion, preservation, and accessibility.

Furthermore, handling inflections, word order flexibility, and the rich morphological system of Armenian (Dum-Tragut, 2009) could present unique challenges in developing practical NLP tools and models. These issues require in-depth research to create NLP solutions that accurately capture and process the complexities of the Armenian language. Thus, the intersection of linguistic uniqueness, historical influences, and complex linguistic features necessitates a multidimensional approach to address the challenges of adapting Armenian for modern NLP applications.

6. **Low Commercial Interest**: Due to the limited population of Armenian speakers compared to other languages, there may be less commercial incentive to invest in Armenian NLP research and development. This can slow down progress in this field.

## 5 The utilization of LLMs in Armenian NLP tasks

The recent advancements in natural language processing (NLP) have been significantly driven by the advent and development of large language models (LLMs), such as BERT, GPT-3, and T5. However, despite their evident success, the adoption of LLMs in Armenian NLP tasks has been somewhat limited, as reflected in the current literature (Avetisyan et al., 2023; Yeshilbashian et al., 2022; Ter-Hovhannisyan and Avetisyan, 2022; Margarov et al., 2017).

Only a handful of studies in Armenian NLP have explored the use of Large Language Models (LLMs). For instance, Avetisyan et al. (2023) employed a BERT-based model for cross-lingual plagiarism detection, showcasing its versatility. In a related effort, Ter-Hovhannisyan and Avetisyan (2022) utilized the transformer-based XLM-RoBERTa model for cross-lingual sentence alignment, highlighting its effectiveness in multilingual contexts. Additionally, Kulshreshtha et al. (2020) augmented the cross-lingual transfer abilities of Multilingual BERT (mBERT) to achieve superior performance in language transfer tasks.

Despite the proven efficacy of Large Language Models (LLMs) in various language processing tasks for well-resourced languages, their utilization in Armenian NLP remains limited. The prevailing approaches in Armenian NLP lean towards traditional methods, such as clustering, bag-of-words, and rule-based techniques (Yeshilbashian et al., 2022; Margarov et al., 2017). While these methods have shown relative success, the underutilization of LLMs highlights a research gap and the potential to enhance the performance of Armenian NLP systems.

Given the transformative effect of LLMs on NLP tasks in other languages, the underutilization of LLMs in Armenian NLP calls for future research. Exploring the reasons behind this limited application and identifying potential solutions could greatly benefit Armenian NLP. Therefore, future studies on Armenian NLP should consider the following directions:

1. **Expanding Data Resources**: One of the main challenges in Armenian NLP is the shortage of high-quality and diverse language resources. Future work should prioritize developing and augmenting Armenian language corpora, including web scraping of Armenian text, transcription of spoken language, and translation of existing datasets from other languages. Efforts should be made to ensure these datasets span multiple domains and genres, such as news, academic literature, fiction, and social media posts (Avetisyan et al., 2023).

2. **Fine-tuning of Pre-trained Models**: As demonstrated in studies (Ghukasyan et al., 2018; Avetisyan et al., 2023; Ter-Hovhannisyan and Avetisyan, 2022), fine-tuning pre-trained language models on Armenian-specific tasks can yield impressive results. However, this approach could be extended to other NLP tasks that have not been extensively explored in the Armenian context, such as sentiment analysis, topic modeling, text summarization, and dialogue systems.

3. **Investigating Language-specific Challenges**: Armenian, like any other language, possesses unique linguistic characteristics that can pose challenges for NLP. These characteristics may include complex morphology, dialects, or historical language changes. Understanding these features and how they affect the performance of LLMs is crucial. Future work could explore these challenges and devise strategies to mitigate their effects (Yeshilbashian et al., 2022).

4. **Developing Armenian NLP Applications**: Once sufficient resources and fine-tuned models are in place, efforts should build practical applications for Armenian NLP. These applications could include Armenian sentiment analysis systems, named entity recognizers, chatbots, and machine translation systems (Margarov et al., 2017).

5. **Benchmarking and Evaluation**: Establishing benchmarks for various Armenian NLP tasks is crucial. These benchmarks will provide a clear direction for the research community and enable comparing different models and approaches.

6. **Developing an Armenian-specific Language Model**: While multilingual models have succeeded, creating a large pre-trained language model specifically for Armenian could lead to even better performance. This would require collecting and preprocessing a large Armenian corpus, which could benefit the wider Armenian NLP community.

7. **Cross-lingual Transfer Learning**: While Avetisyan et al. (2023) have successfully used multilingual models, there is a need for more research on techniques for transferring learning from high-resource languages to Armenian. This can help achieve higher accuracy in NLP tasks without requiring extensive Armenian-specific datasets.

8. **Exploration of Smaller Models**: Large language models require significant computational resources due to their size. Exploring the application and performance of smaller models or efficient training methods could enable the broader use of language models in Armenian NLP.

The potential benefits of these efforts are wide-reaching. From a research perspective, they can improve performance across various NLP tasks, deepening our understanding of Armenian language processing. For users, these advancements could lead to more accurate and helpful language technology applications, including better machine translation systems, more effective information retrieval tools, more engaging dialogue systems, and more robust text analysis tools.

In conclusion, by leveraging the potential of LLMs and addressing the unique challenges of Armenian NLP, researchers and practitioners can pave the way for significant advancements in language technology for Armenian. The proposed directions and future work outlined in this paper aim to stimulate further research and collaboration in the field, ultimately contributing to the growth and development of Armenian NLP.

## 6 Conclusion

In conclusion, this paper has taken significant strides in illuminating the state of Natural Language Processing (NLP) research in the Armenian language context, a low-resource language that has been relatively under-explored in the computational linguistics landscape.

Our analysis highlights a substantial gap in deploying Large Language Models (LLMs) in Armenian NLP tasks, despite their proven effectiveness across various NLP tasks for well-resourced languages. This finding underscores the potential of harnessing the power of LLMs to boost Armenian language processing tasks. However, it simultaneously reveals formidable challenges, such as the scarcity of training data, substantial computational resource requirements, and the peculiarities of the Armenian language.

With the rapid advancements in NLP and the growing focus on low-resource languages, our study articulates the imperative and the potential for further exploration of Armenian NLP, armed with the power of LLMs. Our work catalyzes such exploration, setting the stage for what we anticipate will be a future filled with robust development in this area. As part of our contributions, we have also suggested several directions for future work, including training LLMs specifically on Armenian data or fine-tuning existing multilingual models.

Moreover, our paper makes a critical contribution by situating the discourse on Armenian NLP within the broader NLP landscape and emphasizing the need for the NLP community to give equal attention to low-resource languages. This can lead to development of more sophisticated NLP tools for these languages and contribute to a more comprehensive understanding of language diversity—an aspect crucial for the holistic advancement of NLP.

We would like to encourage our fellow researchers and practitioners in NLP to explore low-resource languages, such as Armenian. Investigating such languages holds immense potential for revealing novel approaches and techniques in NLP that can serve a broader range of languages and cultures. This enriches the diversity in the NLP field and presents a unique opportunity to refine and innovate our methodologies.

Engaging with low-resource languages can also significantly reduce the digital divide and promote diversity, ensuring all languages find representation in the digital space. So, let us collectively embrace the challenges of low-resource languages and uncover the vast, untapped potential they offer to advance NLP.

Lastly, it is crucial to acknowledge that the development of Armenian NLP goes beyond technological advancements. It encompasses the preservation of language and cultural heritage. In today's digital world, languages lacking essential NLP resources face the risk of being marginalized. Hence, investing in Armenian NLP ensures the longevity and vitality of the Armenian language in the digital age.

## Limitations

While providing a thorough review of Armenian NLP research, our study has several limitations that should be noted. Primarily, the scope of our review is confined to the set of studies and papers we have access to, which might not encompass the full breadth of relevant work in this area. Further, exploring Armenian as a low-resource language, with its associated challenges, is a broad and multifaceted issue. Although we strive to cover this topic comprehensively, there could be facets that were not fully captured in our discussion.

It is also essential to underscore that our review fundamentally relies on the accuracy and thoroughness of the original papers incorporated into our analysis. Consequently, any inaccuracies or misinterpretations within those works could inadvertently impact the findings of our review.

Moreover, while we endeavored to present a rich snapshot of the current state of Armenian NLP research, the inherently static nature of a review such as this cannot entirely keep pace with the rapid advancements within the field. As such, certain parts of our analysis could potentially become outdated in a relatively short period.

Finally, our paper primarily emphasizes using large language models in Armenian NLP. In focusing on this aspect, there is a chance that other potentially effective approaches, including more traditional linguistic methods, may not have been as extensively explored.

Our suggestions for future work in Armenian NLP represent a projection of potential research directions. Nonetheless, the feasibility and effectiveness of these suggestions would ultimately need to be empirically validated in subsequent research.

## Ethics Statement

We recognize the importance of ethical considerations in research and the broader impact of our work. Throughout the process of conducting this literature review, we have taken into account relevant ethical aspects.

This paper is solely focused on analyzing and synthesizing existing literature without involving human subjects, data collection, or experimentation. As a result, it does not require specific ethical approvals or considerations regarding human subjects, privacy, or data protection.

However, we are dedicated to promoting ethical practices and responsible information use. We have exercised caution to appropriately cite and attribute all the sources used in this review, respecting the intellectual property rights of authors and organizations. We have aimed to accurately and objectively represent the content of the literature, ensuring that no biases or misinterpretations are introduced.

Additionally, we understand the significance of inclusivity and diversity within the field of NLP. In our review, we have deliberately covered a broad range of studies and perspectives to provide a comprehensive and balanced overview of the literature on Armenian NLP. We have consciously tried to accurately represent the Armenian language and its speakers, actively avoiding biases or stereotypes. Our methodologies and models have been developed with fairness and equity in mind, striving to minimize potential biases or discriminatory effects.

Furthermore, we acknowledge the potential societal implications of our work. Our research aims to positively contribute to the Armenian language community by supporting language preservation, linguistic research, and application development for Armenian speakers.

## References

Timofey Arkhangelskiy, Oleg Belyaev, and Arseniy Vydrin. 2012. The creation of large-scale annotated corpora of minority languages using uniparser and the eanc platform. In *Proceedings of COLING 2012: Posters*, pages 83–92.

Levon Aslanyan, Minoosh Heidari, Hasmik Sahakyan, Daryoush Alipour, Jorge Fernández, Angel Castellanos, Juan Castellanos, Leonid Hulianytsky, Anna Pavlenko, Mariam Haroutunian, et al. 2015. On string mining speech recognition.

Karen Avetisyan. 2022. Dialects identification of armenian language. In *Proceedings of the Workshop on Processing Language Variation: Digital Armenian (DigitAm) within the 13th Language Resources and Evaluation Conference*, pages 8–12.

Karen Avetisyan and Tsolak Ghukasyan. 2019. Word embeddings for the armenian language: intrinsic and extrinsic evaluation. *arXiv preprint arXiv:1906.03134*.

Karen Avetisyan, Arthur Malajyan, and Tsolak Ghukasyan. 2023. A simple and effective method of cross-lingual plagiarism detection. *arXiv preprint arXiv:2304.01352*.

Varuzhan H Baghdasaryan. Armenian speech recognition system: Acoustic and language models.

Varuzhan H Baghdasaryan. 2022. Armspeech: Armenian spoken language corpus. *International Journal of Scientific Advances (IJSCIA)*, 3(3):454–459.

Samuel Chakmakjian and Ilaine Wang. 2022. Towards a unified asr system for the armenian standards. In *Proceedings of the Workshop on Processing Language Variation: Digital Armenian (DigitAm) within the 13th Language Resources and Evaluation Conference*, pages 38–42.

Christian Chiarcos, Kathrin Donandt, Maxim Ionov, Monika Rind-Pawlowski, Hasmik Sargsian, Jesse Wichers Schreur, Frank Abromeit, and Christian Fäth. 2018. Universal morphologies for the caucasus region. In *Proceedings of the Eleventh International Conference on Language Resources and Evaluation (LREC 2018)*.

Karamyan Davit and Karamyan Tigran. 2022. A conformer based automated speech recognition for armenian language. *//Scientific Artsakh*, (2 (13)):224–229.

Hossep Dolatian, Daniel Swanson, and Jonathan Washington. 2022. A free/open-source morphological transducer for western armenian. In *Proceedings of the Workshop on Processing Language Variation: Digital Armenian (DigitAm) within the 13th Language Resources and Evaluation Conference*, pages 1–7.

Jasmine Dum-Tragut. 2009. *Armenian: Modern eastern armenian*, volume 14. John Benjamins Publishing.

T Ghukasyan and K Avetisyan. 2021. Research and development of a deep learning-based lemmatizer for the armenian language. - , page 92.

Tsolak Ghukasyan, Garnik Davtyan, Karen Avetisyan, and Ivan Andrianov. 2018. pioner: Datasets and baselines for armenian named entity recognition. In *2018 Ivannikov Ispras Open Conference (ISPRAS)*, pages 56–61. IEEE.

Anna Hovakimyan, Narine Ispiryan, and Gevorg Narimanyan. Armenian texts recognition via neural networks.

Zahurul Islam and Natia Dundua. 2015. Finding the origin of a translated historical document. In *Proceedings of the 29th Pacific Asia Conference on Language, Information and Computation: Posters*, pages 96–105.

Alankar Jain, Bhargavi Paranjape, and Zachary C Lipton. 2019. Entity projection via machine translation for cross-lingual ner. *arXiv preprint arXiv:1909.05356*.

Davit S Karamyan and Tigran S Karamyan. 2022. Compact n-gram language models for armenian. *Mathematical Problems of Computer Science*, 57:30–38.

Victoria Khurshudyan, Timofey Arkhangelskiy, Misha Daniel, Vladimir Plungian, Dmitri Levonian, Alex Polyakov, and Sergei Rubakov. 2022. Eastern armenian national corpus: State of the art and perspectives. In *Proceedings of the Workshop on Processing Language Variation: Digital Armenian (DigitAm) within the 13th Language Resources and Evaluation Conference*, pages 28–37.

Bastien Kindt and Gabriel Kepeklian. 2022. Analyse automatique de l'ancien arménien. évaluation d'une méthode hybride «dictionnaire» et «réseau de neurones» sur un extrait de l'adversus haereses d'irénée de lyon. In *Proceedings of the Workshop on Processing Language Variation: Digital Armenian (DigitAm) within the 13th Language Resources and Evaluation Conference*, pages 13–20.

Bastien Kindt and Emmanuel Van Elverdinghe. 2022. Describing language variation in the colophons of armenian manuscripts. In *Proceedings of the Workshop on Processing Language Variation: Digital Armenian (DigitAm) within the 13th Language Resources and Evaluation Conference*, pages 21–27.

Saurabh Kulshreshtha, José Luis Redondo-García, and Ching-Yun Chang. 2020. Cross-lingual alignment methods for multilingual bert: A comparative study. *arXiv preprint arXiv:2009.14304*.

Arthur Malajyan, Karen Avetisyan, and Tsolak Ghukasyan. 2020. Arpa: Armenian paraphrase detection corpus and models. In *2020 Ivannikov Memorial Workshop (IVMEM)*, pages 35–39. IEEE.

Gevorg Margarov, Gohar Tomeyan, and Maria João Varanda Pereira. 2017. Plagiarism detection system for armenian language. In *2017 Computer Science and Information Technologies (CSIT)*, pages 185–189. IEEE.

Karine Megerdoomian. 2009. Low-density language strategies for persian and armenian. In *Language Engineering for Lesser-Studied Languages*, pages 291–312. IOS Press.

Yelena Mkhitaryan and Lusine Madatyan. 2022. A spatial model of conceptualization of time: With special reference to english and armenian fairy tales. *International Journal of Language and Culture*.

Jowita Podolak and Philine Zeinert. 2020. Master thesis: Developing a cross-lingual named entity recognition model.

Jatinderkumar R Saini and Rajnish M Rakholia. 2016. On continent and script-wise divisions-based statistical measures for stop-words lists of international languages. *Procedia Computer Science*, 89:313–319.

Avedis K Sanjian. 1996. The armenian alphabet. *The world's writing systems*, pages 356–357.

Sona Sargsyan and Torsten Rahne. 2021. Development of speech material for an armenian speech recognition threshold test. *Russian Open Medical Journal*, 10(3):321.

Max Silberztein. 2007. An alternative approach to tagging. In *Natural Language Processing and Information Systems: 12th International Conference on Applications of Natural Language to Information Systems, NLDB 2007, Paris, France, June 27-29, 2007. Proceedings 12*, pages 1–11. Springer.

Marcella Tambuscio and Tara Lee Andrews. 2021. Geolocation and named entity recognition in ancient texts: A case study about ghewond's armenian history. In *CHR*, pages 136–148.

Tatevik Ter-Hovhannisyan and Karen Avetisyan. 2022. Transformer-based multilingual language models in cross-lingual plagiarism detection. In *2022 Ivannikov Memorial Workshop (IVMEM)*, pages 72–80. IEEE.

S Tigranyan and T Ghukasyan. 2020. Post-ocr correction of armenian texts using neural networks. *Vestnik" Scientific Journal of Russian-Armenian University.—2020*.

Vahradyan Vachagan and Apozyan Tigran. 2015. On meanings of words, sentences and texts interpreted for chess and literary eastern armenian.

Chahan Vidal-Gorène and Aliénor Decours-Perez. 2020. Languages resources for poorly endowed languages: The case study of classical armenian. In *Proceedings of The 12th Language Resources and Evaluation Conference*, pages 3145–3152.

Chahan Vidal-Gorène, Boris Dupin, Aliénor Decours-Perez, and Thomas Riccioli. 2021. A modular and automated annotation platform for handwritings: evaluation on under-resourced languages. In *Document Analysis and Recognition–ICDAR 2021: 16th International Conference, Lausanne, Switzerland, September 5–10, 2021, Proceedings, Part III 16*, pages 507–522. Springer.

Chahan Vidal-Gorène, Victoria Khurshudyan, and Anaïd Donabédian-Demopoulos. 2020. Recycling and comparing morphological annotation models for armenian diachronic-variational corpus processing. In *Proceedings of the 7th Workshop on NLP for Similar Languages, Varieties and Dialects*, pages 90–101.

Chahan Vidal-Gorène and Bastien Kindt. 2020. Lemmatization and pos-tagging process by using joint learning approach. experimental results on classical armenian, old georgian, and syriac. In *Proceedings of LT4HALA 2020-1st Workshop on Language Technologies for Historical and Ancient Languages*, pages 22–27.

Jos JS Weitenberg. 2002. Aspects of armenian dialectology. *TRENDS IN LINGUISTICS STUDIES AND MONOGRAPHS*, 137:141–158.

Ye M Yeshilbashian, AA Asatryan, and Ts G Ghukasyan. 2022. Plagiarism detection in armenian texts using intrinsic stylometric analysis. *Programming and Computer Software*, 48(7):435–444.

## A Literature Search and Keywords

The literature search was conducted in prominent academic databases such as the ACL Anthology, IEEE Xplore, Google Scholar, Semantic Scholar, ACM Digital Library, SpringerLink, and ScienceDirect. These databases were chosen due to their extensive coverage of relevant research papers in the field of Natural Language Processing (NLP).

To retrieve relevant literature, we employed a comprehensive set of keywords. These keywords were carefully selected to encompass various aspects of NLP research, including methodologies, techniques, applications, and specific subdomains within NLP. The chosen keywords aimed to capture a broad range of literature pertinent to our research objectives.

By combining general and specific keywords, we sought to cast a wide net to ensure the inclusivity of relevant publications. This approach enabled us to explore diverse perspectives and comprehensively understand the current state of research in NLP.

The selected keywords were rigorously reviewed and refined iteratively to optimize their effectiveness in retrieving relevant literature. The process involved considering synonymous terms, related concepts, and variations in terminology commonly used in the NLP community. This ensured that our search strategy was comprehensive and accounted for different linguistic expressions and terminologies used across the literature.

The selected keywords are as follows: "Armenian language" AND "Natural Language Processing" "Armenian" AND "NLP" "Armenian language" AND "Machine Learning" "Large Language Models" AND "Armenian" "Low-resource" AND "NLP" AND "Armenian" "Armenian language" AND "deep learning" "Transfer learning" AND "Armenian" "Armenian" AND "BERT" "Armenian" AND "Transformer models" "Armenian language" AND "AI" "Neural Networks" AND "Armenian language" "Armenian" AND "Language Models" "Armenian" AND "Text classification" "Armenian" AND "Named Entity Recognition" "Armenian" AND "Sentiment Analysis" "Armenian" AND "Speech Recognition" "Armenian" AND "Language Generation" "Armenian" AND "Text-to-Speech".

# Multi-Target Semantic Parsing with Collaborative Deliberation Network

**Xiang Li**[1,2], **Fangyu Lei**[1,2], **Shizhu He**[1,2]*, **Kang Liu**[1,2], **Jun Zhao**[1,2],
[1]The Laboratory of Cognition and Decision Intelligence for Complex Systems,
Institute of Automation, Chinese Academy of Sciences, Beijing, China
[2] School of Artificial Intelligence, University of Chinese Academy of Sciences,
Beijing, China
`{leifangyu2022, lixiang2022}@ia.ac.cn`
`{shizhu.he, jzhao, kliu}@nlpr.ia.ac.cn`

## Abstract

Semantic parsing aims at mapping natural language utterances into machine-interpretable meaning representations, facilitating user accesses to knowledge bases. However, knowledge in real-world scenarios is often duplicated in multiple storages and different representations. Although researchers have made great success by improving neural semantic parsers, existing works can only handle a specific kind of meaning representation, i.e., the single-target semantic parsing. In this paper, we introduce a multi-target semantic parsing model based on a collaborative deliberation network, which can not only decode multiple meaning representations simultaneously but also allow meaning representations to make use of information from each other while decoding. Experiments show that the proposed model improves the EM accuracy of four MRs averagely by 2.48% to 5.05% on three public datasets [1].

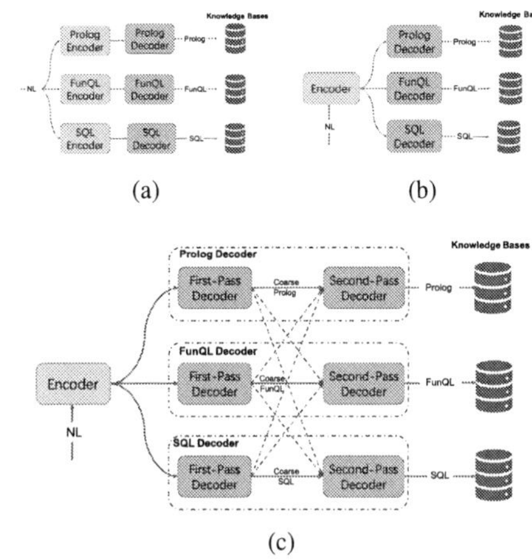


Figure 1: Different implementations for multi-target semantic parsing (MulTSP). (a) Training one parser for each target. (b) A multi-task parser that independently decodes different targets with a shared encoder. (c) The collaborative deliberation network which exploits other coarse decoding outputs to enhance the decoding of any target.

## 1 Introduction

Knowledge bases (KBs) (Bollacker et al., 2008; Lehmann et al., 2015; Weikum et al., 2021) are fundamental facilities for many AI applications. The large amount of structural information they contain is mainly accessed by corresponding formal query language. A variety of query languages are adopted due to the diversity of implementations and domains, such as Prolog for expert systems, and the standardized SQL and SPARQL for relational databases and RDF stores respectively. Semantic parsing (Zelle and Mooney, 1996; Dahl et al., 1994) provides a friendly interface to people unfamiliar with these formal languages by transducing the natural language questions into the underlying query language, which has been widely used in abundant tasks, such as question answering system (Lan et al., 2021; Hu et al., 2018) and robot navigation (Walker et al., 2019). Recently, neural semantic parsing with the notable sequence-to-sequence (Seq2Seq) framework has made impressive progress (Jia and Liang, 2016; Yin and Neubig, 2017; Dong and Lapata, 2018; Peter Shaw and Altun, 2019).

However, recent parsers only focus on single-target semantic parsing designed for only one certain KB and its corresponding query language, whereas in real-world scenarios, the same fact is commonly duplicated and stored in many systems. For example, personnel and financial data are stored in both tabular and graph structures in some businesses, which calls for a multi-target semantic parsing (MulTSP) model with the capability of generating multiple meaning representations (MRs).

There are two approaches to adopt existing technologies for MulTSP. Specifically, the first is to

*Corresponding author

[1]Our implementation can be found on `https://github.com/Xiang-Li-oss/MultiTarget`



*Findings of the Association for Computational Linguistics: IJCNLP-AACL 2023*, pages 211–221
November 1–4, 2023. ©2023 Asian Federation of Natural Language Processing

**train N seq2seq models** (Dong and Lapata, 2016; Jia and Liang, 2016) for N target formal languages independently, which is far from an efficient way for MulTSP. And the second approach is to resort to the **multi-task learning** for all the target formal languages with different decoders, which only exchange information at the encoder. Figure 1(a) and Figure 1(b) illustrate their differences. As recent work has shown (Guo et al., 2020), there's a significant performance gap between different MRs, for example, the FunQL is more competitive than Lambda Calculus and Prolog. This experimental finding suggests the performance of decoding one MR might get improved with the help of other MRs by introducing collaborations among their decoders.

To implement collaborations among decoders of different MRs, a straightforward way is to augment attention mechanism within tokens from all MRs at each decoding timestep. However, this is less likely to succeed due to two concerns: 1) The erroneous alignment problem, in which the tokens of different MRs could be hardly aligned by position and the attention mechanism could be even harmful to the current decoding step, for example, considering parsing *"How large is Texas ?"* to Lambda Calculus and FunQL in Table 1. At 2nd timestep, current token *'('* in FunQL is most likely to be useless for predicting *'size<lo,i>'* in Lambda Calculus. 2) Holistic information ignorance, in which future tokens from one MR are invisible for other MRs. For example, at the 2nd decoding step, *'size'* in FunQL is valuable yet invisible for *'size<lo,i>'* in Lambda Calculus.

To address the aforementioned problems, we present a multi-target semantic parsing model based on a collaborative deliberation network(CDNParser). As shown in Figure 1(c), each decoder in CDNParser performs two-stage decoding through its two child decoders. During the first decoding stage, each first-pass decoder generates a coarse target formal language sequence for its MR without teach forcing. After that, each second-pass decoder will predict final target sequences as well as collaborate with each other by sharing sequences of coarse target logical forms, which are almost complete target sequences for each MR. Through this design, our method meets the requirements of MulTSP and avoids the problem of erroneous alignments and holistic information ignorance.

To evaluate the proposed model in this paper, we have conducted extensive experiments on three public benchmarks. Compared with strong baselines, the experimental results demonstrate that the proposed CDNParser can 1) successfully meet the need for MulTSP, 2) for the EM (exact-match) accuracy of four MRs, CDNParser provides 2.52% average improvement on Geo dataset, 5.05% on Job dataset, and 2.48% on ATIS dataset.

To sum up, our contributions are as follows:

1. We propose to perform multi-target semantic parsing, which supports simultaneous decoding of multiple meaning representations. To our best knowledge, this is the first work for MulTSP task.

2. We propose a MulTSP model by designing a collaborative deliberation network (CDNParser) which allows the decoding process of each MR to utilize the assistance of other MRs.

3. We have conducted detailed experiments on several open datasets. And the experimental results demonstrate that CDNParser can not only decode multiple MRs simultaneously but also achieves better performance.

## 2 Related Work

### 2.1 Semantic Parsing Methods

Various semantic parsing models have been proposed over the past decades, which devotes to converting natural language utterances into logical forms that can be easily executed on a knowledge graph (Kwiatkowski et al., 2011; Andreas et al., 2013; Zhao and Huang, 2015). These systems typically learn lexicalized mapping rules and scoring models to construct a meaning representation for a given input.

Table 1: Examples of MRs for utterance "How large is Texas?" in the Geo domain.

| MR | Logical Form |
|---|---|
| **Prolog** | answer(A, (size(B, A), const(B, stateid(texas)))) |
| **Lambda Calculus** | (size:<lo,i> texas:s) |
| **FunQL** | answer(size(stateid('texas'))) |
| **SQL** | select STATEalias0.AREA from ... where ... STATE_NAME = "texas" |

With the development of neural networks, sequence-to-sequence models have been employed to semantic parsing with remarkable results. The neural-based parsing models avoid the requirement for feature engineering and explicit semantic composition rules (Dong and Lapata, 2016; Jia and Liang, 2016; Ling et al., 2016) in previous methods. Lots of ideas have been explored to improve the performance of these models, including data augmentation (Wu et al., 2021) and designing structural decoders (Dong and Lapata, 2018; Li et al., 2021). Although there have been some efforts to use share parameters for multiple languages or meaning representations, there hasn't been any attempts to study multi-target semantic parsing, which is the main focus of this paper.

### 2.2 Meaning Representations

We adopt four formal languages (that is Meaning Representations, MRs) in this paper: Prolog, Lambda Calculus, FunQL, and SQL. Since these MRs are explored extensively in semantic parsing task, making it easier to obtain labeled data in these MRs. Table 1 shows a logical form for each of the four MRs in the Geo domain.

**Prolog** is a logic programming language for deductive reasoning. Since its birth, it has been extended to many application areas, such as relational databases, mathematical logic, natural language understanding, etc. Prolog is based on first-order predicates logic, incorporating higher-order predicates to handle problems such as quantification and aggregation.

**Lambda calculus** is a formal system for describing operations, which can represent all first-order predicates, and can support some higher-level predicates. Lambda calculus expresses natural language through constants, quantifiers, logical connectives, Lambda operators, etc. These advantages promote the widespread use of Lambda calculus in semantic parsing tasks.

**FunQL** is a variable-free language that abstracts variables away and uses nested structures to represent compositionality. Unlike languages such as Prolog and Lambda calculus, predicates in FunQL take a set of entities as input and return another set of entities as output.

**SQL** is short for Structured Query Language and is a popular relational database query language. Given that SQL is domain-agnostic and has well-established execution engines, the subtask of semantic parsing, Text-to-SQL has also sparked a lot of attention.

### 2.3 Deliberation Network

Deliberation network (Xia et al., 2017) is inspired by human behavior. For example, to write a good document, we usually first create a complete draft and then polish it based on a global understanding of the whole draft. Deliberation network leverages the global information with both looking back and forward in sequence decoding through a deliberation process. (Li et al., 2019a) and (Xiong et al., 2019) apply deliberation network in dialogue system and machine translation and and adopt a new simplified training algorithm instead of the original Monte Carlo based algorithm. In our work, deliberation network acts as a key technology to implement collaborative multi-target decoding among different MRs.

## 3 Proposed Method

Given a dataset $D = \{(x, y^1, ..., y^N)\}$ where $x = \{x_1, x_2, ...x_{T_x}\}$ is the source natural language sequence, for example *"How large is Texas ?"*, and each $y^i = \{y_1^i, y_2^i, ...y_{T_{y^i}}^i\}$ is a target logical form sequence for one MR, such as FunQL sequence *"answer(size(stateid('texas')))"* or Prolog sequence *"answer(A,(size(B,A),const(B, stateid(texas))))"*. $T_x$. and $T_{y^i}$ represent sequence length. Our model is aimed at learning a parser which transforms $x$ into $(y^1, ..., y^N)$, simultaneously.

### 3.1 Model Overview

Figure 2 visualizes the overall architecture of our multi-target semantic parsing model. Our model is based on a collaborative deliberation network. A collaborative deliberation network consists of an encoder $E$ and $N$ ($N$=2 in this example) deliberation decoders $D^i (i = 1, 2, ..., N)$. In this example, two deliberation decoders are responsible for generating Lambda Calculus and FunQL, respectively. Each deliberation decoder is composed of a first-pass decoder $D_1^i$ and a second-pass decoder $D_2^i$, where collaboration happens. Briefly speaking, $E$ is used to encode the source sequence into a sequence of vector representations. Each $D_1^i$ reads the encoder representations and generates a first-pass target sequence as a draft, which further participates in the collaboration mechanism and is provided as input to the second-pass decoders to

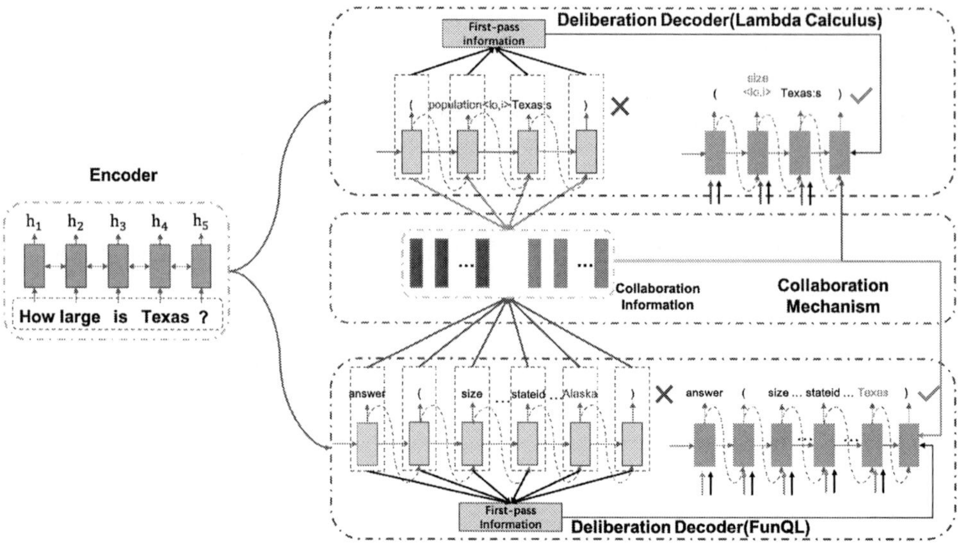


Figure 2: The overview of the collaborative deliberation network for MulTSP. For simplicity, we omit the encoder-decoder attention. The encoder on the left encodes natural language utterances before feeding them to two deliberation decoders. Each decoder performs two-phase decoding to generate Lambda Calculus and FunQL respectively. Moreover, during the second decoding phase, the two decoders are supposed to collaborate.

perform second pass decoding.

### 3.2 Encoder and First-Pass Decoder

When an source sequence $x$ is fed into the encoder $E$, it is encoded into a hidden vector sequence $\{h_1, h_2, ..., h_{T_x}\}$ with the length of $T_x$. To be specific, $h_i = \mathrm{LSTM}(x_i, h_{i-1})$, where $x_i$ is the $i$th word embedding and $h_0$ is intialized to zero vector. For the sake of convenience, in the following part of this section, we will omit the superscript of $y^i$, $D_1^i$, and $D_2^i$ and denote them as $y$, $D_1$, and $D_2$.

Each first-pass decoder $D_1$ will generate a sequence of hidden states $\hat{s}_j(\forall\, j \in [T_{\hat{y}}])$, and the first-pass target logical form sequence $\hat{y}_j(\forall\, j \in [T_{\hat{y}}])$. Next we explain the process in detail.

Identificial to the conventional encoder-decoder model, an additive attention is included in each $D_1$. At timestep $t$, $D_1$ first calculate contextual vector $ctx_e$ as follows:

$$\alpha_i = \frac{\exp(v_e^T \tanh(W_0^e h_i + W_1^e \hat{s}_{t-1}))}{\sum_{k=1}^{T_x} \exp(v_e^T \tanh(W_0^e h_k + W_1^e \hat{s}_{t-1}))}$$

$$ctx_e = \sum_{i=1}^{T_x} \alpha_i h_i$$

where $v_e^T$, $W_0^e$, $W_1^e$ are parameters.

After obtaining $ctx_e$, the hidden state $\hat{s}_i^t$ of first-pass decoder is got by:

$$\hat{s}_t = \mathrm{LSTM}([\hat{y}_{t-1}; ctx_e], \hat{s}_{t-1})$$

After that, the concatenated vector $[\hat{s}_t, ctx_e, \hat{y}_{t-1}]$ will be fed into a feedforward network to predict the probability of $\hat{y}_t$ as:

$$p(\hat{y}_t|x, \hat{y}_{<t}) = \mathrm{softmax}(\mathrm{FFN}([\hat{s}_t, ctx_e, \hat{y}_{t-1}]))$$

Finally, $\hat{y}_t$ is predicted by:

$$\hat{y}_t = \mathrm{argmax}\, p(\hat{y}_t|x, \hat{y}_{<t})$$

### 3.3 Second-Pass Decoder

The second-pass decoder is the key component of our approach since it contains the vital collaboration mechanism. Figure 2 exhibits the behavior of second-pass decoder.

Once first-pass decoder has generated the first-pass target logical form sequences $\hat{y}$ as a draft. It is fed into the second-pass decoder for further collaboration. Besides the sequence $\hat{y}$ and hidden state $\hat{s}$ produced by its corresponding first-pass decoder, the second-pass decoder also collaborates with other second-pass decoders, taking outputs from other first-pass decoders into consideration.

First, the information from source sequence is integrated by calculating contextual vector $ctx'_e$, the computation detail is similar to $ctx_e$ in Section 3.2.

To synthesize information from the first-pass target logical form sequence, we compute the contextual vector $ctx_c$ by:

$$\alpha_i = \frac{\exp(v_c^T \tanh(W_0^c[\hat{s}_i;\hat{y}_i] + W_1^c s_{t-1}))}{\sum_{j=1}^{T_y} \exp(v_c^T \tanh(W_0^c[\hat{s}_j;\hat{y}_j] + W_1^c s_{t-1}))}$$

$$ctx_c = \sum_{i=1}^{T_y} \alpha_i[\hat{s}_i;\hat{y}_i]$$

where $v_c^T$, $W_0^c$, $W_1^c$ are parameters.

Second-pass decoder calculates contextual vector $ctx_o$ to collaborate with other deliberation decoders based on $\hat{y}^o$ and $\hat{s}^o$, where $\hat{y}^o = [y^j \,\forall j = 1, 2, ..., N \wedge j \neq i]$ represents the concatenation of first-pass target logical form sequences predicted by other deliberation decoders. Simmilar for $\hat{s}^o$ and $ctx_o$ is defined as follow:

$$\alpha_i = \frac{\exp(v_o^T \tanh(W_0^o[\hat{s}_i^o;\hat{y}_i^o] + W_1^o s_{t-1}))}{\sum_{j=1}^{T_y} \exp(v_o^T \tanh(W_0^o[\hat{s}_j^o;\hat{y}_j^o] + W_1^o s_{t-1}))}$$

$$ctx_o = \sum_{i=1}^{T_y} \alpha_i[\hat{s}_i^o;\hat{y}_i^o]$$

where $v_o^T$, $W_0^o$, $W_1^o$ are parameters.

After obtaining all of the three contextual vectors, $D_2$ takes the previous hidden state $s_{t-1}$ generated by itself, previously decoded token $y_{t-1}$ to calculate $s_t$ as:

$$s_t = \text{LSTM}([y_{t-1}; ctx_e'; ctx_c], s_{t-1})$$

Finally, the concantenated vector:

$$a_t = [s_t; ctx_e'; ctx_c; ctx_o; y_{t-1}]$$

is fed to a feedforward network followed by a softmax layer to predict the probability of $y_t$. As can be seen from the above computation, the contextual vector $ctx_o$ aggregates the global information extracted from the first-pass logical form sequence of other MRs, making the most use of assistance from other MRs.

### 3.4 Training

Since our model output multiple MRs, we minimize summed training for all MRs:

$$L = \sum_{i=1}^{N} L_i$$

each $L_i$ represents a loss for a certain MR. Next, we explain how $L_i$ is calculated in detail.

In contrast to the original deliberation network (Gu et al., 2019), where they propose a complex training algorithm based on Monte Carlo Method, we follow the works of Xiong et al. (2019) and Li et al. (2019b), maximizing the summed likelihood of the two generated logical form sequences. And $L_i$ is computed as:

$$\begin{aligned} L_i &= L_i^1 + L_i^2 \\ L_i^1 &= -\textstyle\sum_D \sum_{j=1}^{T_{y^i}} \log P(\hat{y}_j^i) \\ L_i^2 &= -\textstyle\sum_D \sum_{j=1}^{T_{y^i}} \log P(y_j^i) \end{aligned}$$

where $P(\hat{y}_j^i)$ is the probability predicted for $j$th token in $i$th MR by first-pass decoder and $P(y_j^i)$ is the probability predicted for $j$th token in $i$th MR by second-pass decoder.

## 4 Experiment

### 4.1 Datasets

We trained our model on the three datasets covering different domains: Geo, ATIS, and Job, each of which has been widely used in previous works and has been labeled with logical forms for four MRs including Prolog, Lambda Calculus, FunQL and SQL.

**Geo** focuses on querying a US geography database, originally containing 880 (utterance, logical form) pairs annotated by (Zelle and Mooney, 1996) through a Prolog-style MR. Latter, (Popescu et al., 2003) and (Rohit J. Kate and Mooney, 2005) proposed to use SQL and FunQL to represent the meanings, respectively. Furthermore, (Zettlemoyer and Collins, 2005) proposed to use Lambda Calculus and manually converted the Prolog logical forms to equivalent expressions in Lambda Calculus. By convention, we adopt the standard 600/280 training/test split.

**ATIS** is a standard semantic parsing dataset about flight booking, consisting of 5410 questions and their corresponding SQL queries. (Zettlemoyer and Collins, 2007) use Lambda Calculus to represent the meanings and automatically map SQL queries to equivalent Lambda Calculus. The standard split has 4480 training instances, 480 development instances and 450 test instances.

**Job** dataset contains 640 utterances and their corresponding Prolog queries to a dataset of job listings. Similar to Geo, (Zettlemoyer and Collins, 2005) proposed to represent the meanings with Lambda Calculus and manually converted Prolog logical forms to equivalent Lambda Calculus logical forms.

Since not all the four MRs introduced above are used in these three domains, following previous works, (Guo et al., 2020) has annotated the above three datasets with all the four MRs by semi-automatically translating logical forms in one MR into others.

### 4.2 Baselines

Our models are compared with two baselines:

1. Seq2Seq model: We formulate semantic parsing task as a neural machine translation task and employ the encoder-decoder architecture to solve it. To predict N MRs, we need N independent Seq2Seq models to generate logical forms for each MR. Each Seq2Seq model contains a one-layer BI-LSTM (Gers et al., 2000) encoder and a one-layer LSTM decoder.

2. Multi-task learning model: Applying multi-task learning to parse multiple MRs. It consists of a one-layer BI-LSTM encoder and multiple one-layer LSTM decoders. Each decoder is responsible for generating logical forms for one MR. The decoders only share the same encoder and have no communication with each other. The crucial distinction between this model and our model is whether to introduce the help of other MRs.

### 4.3 Implementations

We adopt AllenNLP (Gardner et al., 2018) and Pytorch (Paszke et al., 2019) framework to implement each approach. Due to the limited number of test data in each dataset, we run each approach five times and report the mean performance and standard deviation.

Many neural semantic parsing approaches adopt data anonymization to replace entities in utterances with placeholders. However, in this paper, we do not apply data anonymization to avoid bias.

For parameters, we tune the hyper-parameters of each approach on the development set or through cross-validation on the training set. We put the search space of hyper-parameters in Appendix A.

We initialize all parameters uniformly within the interval [-0.1, 0.1]. We use Adam algorithm to update parameters. Gradients are clipped to 5.0 to alleviate the gradient explosion problem. Early stop is used to determine the number of training epochs. We use greedy search to generate logical forms during inference.

### 4.4 Evaluation Metrics

Following previous work (Guo et al., 2020), we use EM (exact-match) accuracy as the evaluation metric, which is defined as the percentage of the samples that are correctly parsed to their gold standard meaning representations.

### 4.5 Experimental Results

At first, we evaluate our model's performance on three standard benchmarks along with baseline models, in performing the MulTSP (multi-target semantic parsing) task. All approaches are required to predict four MRs, namely Prolog, Lambda Calculus, FunQL, and SQL.

Table 2 shows our results. By comparing various methods, we observe that 1) our model consistently outperforms all other candidates. On the one hand, our model achieves the best parsing accuracy among all methods, on the other hand, the performance of our model is more steady, making our method more reliable. For example, on Job dataset, CDNParser achieves 5.05% absolute improvement on average compared to the Seq2Seq model with a lower standard deviation. This justifies the effectiveness of our approach on MulTSP task. 2) Both our model and multi-task learning model can produce all four MRs. However, our model beats the multi-task learning model substantially, indicating that incorporating help from other MRs plays a crucial role in enhancing accuracy.

By comparing the performance of various MRs, we observe that 1) FunQL tends to outperform other MRs and our model's advancement on FunQL is relatively lesser as compared to the other three MRs. One possible reason is that FunQL is more compact than the other MRs due to its elimination of variables and quantifiers, making it easier to predict even without the aid of other MRs. 2) SQL appears to have the poorest performance yet tends to achieve the highest improvement. For example, in Geo dataset, the exact-match accuracy of FunQL

Table 2: Experimental results of our multi-target semantic parsing model and two baseline models. Seq2Seq* reports the results from (Guo et al., 2020). The results are averaged over 5 random seeds (mean±std). We highlight the best performance for every MR and our model's absolute improvement over Seq2Seq*. The poor SQL exact-match accuracy in ATIS is caused by the different distribution of SQL queries in test set.

| Approach | Prolog | Lambda Calculus | FunQL | SQL |
|---|---|---|---|---|
| **GEO** | | | | |
| Seq2Seq* | **70.0**±2.1 | 64.7±2.3 | 76.8±2.4 | 58.0±2.4 |
| Seq2Seq | 66.8±2.9 | 65.7±2.6 | 73.5±2.4 | 57.8±8.0 |
| Multi-Task | 67.9±0.6 | 66.4±1.0 | 74.8±2.0 | 63.8±1.8 |
| CDNParser(ours) | 69.1(-0.9)±0.7 | **68.4**(+3.8)±1.7 | **77.1**(+0.3)±1.3 | **64.9**(+6.9)±0.8 |
| **JOB** | | | | |
| Seq2Seq* | 68.1±2.3 | 65.8±1.3 | 71.4±2.4 | 68.5±3.0 |
| Seq2Seq | 67.8±2.3 | 65.2±1.5 | 71.6±2.6 | 67.9±3.4 |
| Multi-Task | 72.7±1.6 | 70.1±2.2 | 70.7±2.1 | 71.4±1.8 |
| CDNParser(ours) | **73.0**(+4.9)±2.4 | **73.7**(+7.9)±1.1 | **73.0**(+1.6)±1.6 | **74.3**(+5.8)±2.0 |
| **ATIS** | | | | |
| Seq2Seq* | 65.9±1.5 | 68.7±1.8 | 70.8±0.6 | 5.6±0.3 |
| Seq2Seq | 65.1±1.6 | 69.0±1.6 | 70.0±0.8 | 5.6±0.3 |
| Multi-Task | 65.0±2.7 | 72.0±1.7 | 71.4±3.6 | 5.4±0.4 |
| CDNParser(ours) | **68.2**(+2.3)±0.7 | **72.7**(+4.0)±0.5 | **74.3**(+3.5)±1.0 | **5.7**(+0.1)±0.3 |

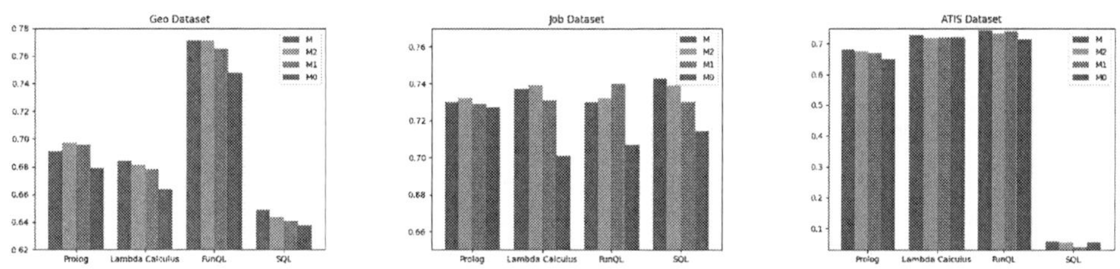


(a) Geo (b) Job (c) ATIS

Figure 3: Experimental results for ablation studies on three datasets. For each MR, four bars in different colors stand for four models with varying degrees of collaboration. As the collaboration weakens from left to right, the EM accuracy of each MR typically displays a declining trend.

is substantially higher than that of SQL in all approaches. However, SQL gets a remarkable 6.9% improvement from our model. This is understandable, SQL is a domain-general language, unlike domain-specific MRs (Prolog, Lambda Calculus, and FunQL), the domain knowledge can not be injected into SQL easily, making it a challenge for neural networks to generate SQL. Therefore, by obtaining assistance from the other three domain-specific MRs, SQL achieves the maximum promotion.

### 4.6 Ablation Study

We conduct ablation study to explore the effects of collaboration mechanism in our model. We assess the performance of several collaboration weakened models. We denote $M$ as our original multi-target semantic parsing model, and $M_2$ as collaborative weakened model, in which each decoder is limited to randomly collaborate with other two out of three decoders. Similarly, each decoder in $M_1$ can only collaborate with one aonther random decoder and decoders in $M_0$ are not allowed to collaborate with each other, Figure 3 summarizes the experimental results.

From the results, we observe that: 1) As the collaboration weakens, the EM accuracy of each MR generally shows a downward trend. 2) When collaboration is completely deactivated, there is often a sudden drop in performance. This implies that the collaboration mechanism is a vital component in our method and the outstanding performance achieved by our model benefits a lot from the mutual assistance among MRs brought by collaboration mechanism.

### 4.7 Analysis

Our main experiment has shown that incorporating information from other MRs can improve semantic parsing performance. We call them auxiliary MRs. This subsection will dive deeper into this subject. We hypothesize that auxiliary MRs contribute differently and fewer MRs could even give better performance according to the results from Figure 3. This brings up an interesting question: *In the case of generating logical forms for a specific MR, how do we choose other auxiliary MRs?*

Table 3: Empirical Transformation Accuracy, row and column respectively represents the source and target MRs.

| | Prolog | Lambda Calculus | FunQL | SQL |
|---|---|---|---|---|
| Prolog | – | 70.4% | 82.3% | 71.2% |
| Lambda Calculus | 59.4% | – | 73.3% | 69.3% |
| FunQL | 71.1% | 72.2% | – | 75.8% |
| SQL | 54.0% | 57.0% | 60.6% | – |

We hypothesize that an MR will be enhanced more by a homogeneous MR than a heterogeneous one. For example, the Prolog is intuitively closer to lambda calculus than SQL. A comprehensive measurement of the similarity is not trivial, and thus we resort to the approximated similarity based on empirical results. Specifically, we employ a Seq2Seq neural network to transform an MR into another one. The 4-by-4 transformation results form a matrix (Table 3). We propose a **Heuristic Selection Strategy** (HSS) based on this matrix: For any MR in demand as the target, the source MRs with higher transformation accuracy are more preferred. For example, taking Prolog as the target, the most similar MR is the FunQL (71.1%), followed by Lambda Calculus (59.4%) and SQL (54.0%). Note the similarity is not symmetric in this setting. When the amount of auxiliary MRs is restricted to 1 (or 2), HSS will choose only FunQL (or Lambda Calculus in addition).

To evaluate HSS, we respectively pick up 2 and 1 auxiliary MRs for each MR, there are 3 choices in both cases as marked by letters in parentheses in Table 4 (or Table 5). P, L, F, and S represent Prolog, Lambda Calculus, FunQL, and SQL is picked respectively. The "↑" indicates the higher EM accuracy than taking all the other 3 MRs as auxiliary MRs, while the "↓" indicates the lower EM accuracy.

Table 4: EM accuracy for each MR when picking up 2 auxiliary MRs.We highlight HSS selection for each MR.

| Target MR | Composition | | |
|---|---|---|---|
| **GEO** | | | |
| Prolog | **69.6(LF)**↑ | 68.8(LS)↓ | 68.0(FS)↓ |
| Lambda | **69.9(PF)**↑ | 67.9(PS)↓ | 67.4(FS)↓ |
| FunQL | **77.0(PL)**↓ | 75.7(PS)↓ | 75.5(LS)↓ |
| SQL | 65.0(PL)↑ | **65.1(PF)**↑ | 64.0(LF)↑ |
| **JOB** | | | |
| Prolog | **74.1(LF)**↑ | 73.3(LS)↑ | 73.6(FS)↑ |
| Lambda | **74.8(PF)**↑ | 74.4(PS)↑ | 73.8(FS)↑ |
| FunQL | **72.9(PL)**↓ | 73.8(PS)↑ | 74.4(LS)↑ |
| SQL | 73.2(PL)↓ | **74.3(PF)**↑ | 73.5(LF)↓ |

Table 5: EM accuracy for each MR when picking up 1 auxiliary MR. We highlight HSS selection for each MR.

| Target MR | Composition | | |
|---|---|---|---|
| **GEO** | | | |
| Prolog | 70.4(L)↑ | **72.0(F)**↑ | 66.3(S)↓ |
| Lambda | 71.6(P)↑ | **70.0(F)**↑ | 69.0(S)↑ |
| FunQL | **78.0(P)**↑ | 77.3(L)↑ | 78.8(S)↑ |
| SQL | 64.9(P)↓ | 65.2(L)↑ | **65.0(F)**↑ |
| **JOB** | | | |
| Prolog | 74.3(L)↑ | **74.1(F)**↑ | 72.7(S)↓ |
| Lambda | 74.7(P)↑ | **75.3(F)**↑ | 75.6(S)↑ |
| FunQL | **71.4(P)**↓ | 73.7(L)↑ | 73.6(S)↑ |
| SQL | 73.5(P)↑ | 73.7(L)↑ | **75.0(F)**↑ |

Table 4 and Table 5 shows that: 1) After choosing one or two auxiliary MRs, the EM accuracy for each MR may either rise or fall, confirming our assumption that auxiliary MRs do not contribute equally. 2) After picking one or two auxiliary MRs following our strategy, the EM accuracy for most MRs increases, proving that our strategy based on heuristic features is empirically reasonable and valuable in practice.

## 5 Conclusion

In this paper, we propose a multi-target semantic parsing model based on a collaborative deliberation network. On the one hand, our model is capable of predicting multiple MRs simultaneously, successfully completing the multi-target semantic parsing task, on the other hand, each MR in our model can leverage assistance information from other MRs thanks to the design of collaboration mechanism in our model. We believe that our method has good application prospects in real-world scenarios due to the diversity of knowledge forms.

## Limitations

Our multi-target semantic parsing model based on collaborative deliberation network focues on specific domain, and is unable to handle multi-domain settings. In the future, we plan to extend our method to adapt multi-domain scenarios.


## Acknowledgement

This work was supported by National Key R&D Program of China (No.2022ZD0118501) and the National Natural Science Foundation of China (No.62376270, No.U1936207, No.61976211). This work was supported by the Youth Innovation Promotion Association CAS, Yunnan Provincial Major Science and Technology Special Plan Projects (No.202202AD080004) and OPPO Research Fund.


## References


Jacob Andreas, Andreas Vlachos, and Stephen Clark. 2013. Semantic parsing as machine translation. In *Proceedings of the 51st Annual Meeting of the Association for Computational Linguistics (Volume 2: Short Papers)*, pages 47–52.

Kurt Bollacker, Colin Evans, Praveen Paritosh, Tim Sturge, and Jamie Taylor. 2008. Freebase: A collaboratively created graph database for structuring human knowledge. In *Proceedings of the 2008 ACM SIGMOD International Conference on Management of Data*, pages 1247–1250.

Deborah A. Dahl, Madeleine Bates, Michael Brown, William Fisher, Kate Hunicke-Smith, David Pallett, Christine Pao, Alexander Rudnicky, and Elizabeth Shriberg. 1994. Expanding the scope of the ATIS task: The ATIS-3 corpus. In *Human Language Technology: Proceedings of a Workshop held at Plainsboro, New Jersey, March 8-11, 1994.*

Li Dong and Mirella Lapata. 2016. Language to logical form with neural attention. In *Proceedings of the 54th Annual Meeting of the Association for Computational Linguistics (Volume 1: Long Papers)*, pages 33–43, Berlin, Germany. Association for Computational Linguistics.

Li Dong and Mirella Lapata. 2018. Coarse-to-fine decoding for neural semantic parsing. In *Proceedings of the 56th Annual Meeting of the Association for Computational Linguistics (Volume 1: Long Papers)*, pages 731–742, Melbourne, Australia. Association for Computational Linguistics.

Matt Gardner, Joel Grus, Mark Neumann, Oyvind Tafjord, Pradeep Dasigi, Nelson F. Liu, Matthew Peters, Michael Schmitz, and Luke Zettlemoyer. 2018. AllenNLP: A deep semantic natural language processing platform. In *Proceedings of Workshop for NLP Open Source Software (NLP-OSS)*, pages 1–6, Melbourne, Australia. Association for Computational Linguistics.

Felix A Gers, Jürgen Schmidhuber, and Fred Cummins. 2000. Learning to forget: Continual prediction with lstm. *Neural computation*, 12(10):2451–2471.

Jiatao Gu, Changhan Wang, and Junbo Zhao. 2019. Levenshtein transformer. *Advances in Neural Information Processing Systems*, 32.

Jiaqi Guo, Qian Liu, Jian-Guang Lou, Zhenwen Li, Xueqing Liu, Tao Xie, and Ting Liu. 2020. Benchmarking meaning representations in neural semantic parsing. In *Proceedings of the 2020 Conference on Empirical Methods in Natural Language Processing (EMNLP)*, pages 1520–1540, Online. Association for Computational Linguistics.

Sen Hu, Lei Zou, and Xinbo Zhang. 2018. A state-transition framework to answer complex questions over knowledge base. In *Proceedings of the 2018 Conference on Empirical Methods in Natural Language Processing*, pages 2098–2108, Brussels, Belgium. Association for Computational Linguistics.

Robin Jia and Percy Liang. 2016. Data recombination for neural semantic parsing. In *Proceedings of the 54th Annual Meeting of the Association for Computational Linguistics*, pages 12–22.

Tom Kwiatkowski, Luke Zettlemoyer, Sharon Goldwater, and Mark Steedman. 2011. Lexical generalization in ccg grammar induction for semantic parsing. In *Proceedings of the 2011 Conference on Empirical Methods in Natural Language Processing*, pages 1512–1523.

Yunshi Lan, Gaole He, Jinhao Jiang, Jing Jiang, Wayne Xin Zhao, and Ji-Rong Wen. 2021. A survey on complex knowledge base question answering: Methods, challenges and solutions. In *Proceedings of the 30th International Joint Conference on Artificial Intelligence.*

Jens Lehmann, Robert Isele, Max Jakob, Anja Jentzsch, Dimitris Kontokostas, Pablo N Mendes, Sebastian Hellmann, Mohamed Morsey, Patrick Van Kleef, Sören Auer, et al. 2015. Dbpedia–a large-scale, multilingual knowledge base extracted from wikipedia. *Semantic web*, 6(2):167–195.

Yuntao Li, Bei Chen, Qian Liu, Yan Gao, Jian-Guang Lou, Yan Zhang, and Dongmei Zhang. 2021. Keep the structure: A latent shift-reduce parser for semantic parsing. In *Proceedings of the Thirtieth International Joint Conference on Artificial Intelligence, IJCAI-21*, pages 3864–3870. International Joint Conferences on Artificial Intelligence Organization. Main Track.

Zekang Li, Cheng Niu, Fandong Meng, Yang Feng, Qian Li, and Jie Zhou. 2019a. Incremental transformer with deliberation decoder for document grounded conversations. In *Proceedings of the 57th Annual Meeting of the Association for Computational Linguistics*, pages 12–21, Florence, Italy. Association for Computational Linguistics.

Zekang Li, Cheng Niu, Fandong Meng, Yang Feng, Qian Li, and Jie Zhou. 2019b. Incremental transformer with deliberation decoder for document grounded conversations. In *Proceedings of the 57th Annual Meeting of the Association for Computational Linguistics*, pages 12–21.

Wang Ling, Phil Blunsom, Edward Grefenstette, Karl Moritz Hermann, Tomáš Kočiský, Fumin Wang, and Andrew Senior. 2016. Latent predictor networks for code generation. In *Proceedings of the 54th Annual Meeting of the Association for Computational Linguistics (Volume 1: Long Papers)*, pages 599–609.

Adam Paszke, Sam Gross, Francisco Massa, Adam Lerer, James Bradbury, Gregory Chanan, Trevor Killeen, Zeming Lin, Natalia Gimelshein, Luca Antiga, et al. 2019. Pytorch: An imperative style, high-performance deep learning library. *Advances in neural information processing systems*, 32.

Angelica Chen Francesco Piccinno Peter Shaw, Philip Massey and Yasemin Altun. 2019. Generating logical forms from graph representations of text and entities. In *Proceedings of the 57th Annual Meeting of the Association for Computational Linguistics*, pages 95–106.

Ana-Maria Popescu, Oren Etzioni, and Henry Kautz. 2003. Towards a theory of natural language interfaces to databases. In *Proceedings of the 8th international conference on Intelligent user interfaces*, pages 149–157.

Yuk Wah Wong Rohit J. Kate and Raymond J. Mooney. 2005. Learning to transform natural to formal languages. pages 1062–1068.

Nick Walker, Yu-Tang Peng, and Maya Cakmak. 2019. Neural semantic parsing with anonymization for command understanding in general-purpose service robots. In *Robot World Cup*, pages 337–350. Springer.

Gerhard Weikum, Luna Dong, Simon Razniewski, and Fabian M. Suchanek. 2021. Machine knowledge: Creation and curation of comprehensive knowledge bases. *Found. Trends Databases*, 10:108–490.

Kun Wu, Lijie Wang, Zhenghua Li, Ao Zhang, Xinyan Xiao, Hua Wu, Min Zhang, and Haifeng Wang. 2021. Data augmentation with hierarchical sql-to-question generation for cross-domain text-to-sql parsing. In *Proceedings of the 2021 Conference on Empirical Methods in Natural Language Processing*, pages 8974–8983.

Yingce Xia, Fei Tian, Lijun Wu, Jianxin Lin, Tao Qin, Nenghai Yu, and Tie-Yan Liu. 2017. Deliberation networks: Sequence generation beyond one-pass decoding. *Advances in neural information processing systems*, 30.

Hao Xiong, Zhongjun He, Hua Wu, and Haifeng Wang. 2019. Modeling coherence for discourse neural machine translation. In *Proceedings of the AAAI conference on artificial intelligence*, volume 33, pages 7338–7345.

Pengcheng Yin and Graham Neubig. 2017. A syntactic neural model for general-purpose code generation. In *Proceedings of the 55th Annual Meeting of the Association for Computational Linguistics*, pages 440–450.

John M. Zelle and Raymond J. Mooney. 1996. Learning to parse database queries using inductive logic programming. In *Proceedings of the 13th National Conference on Artificial Intelligence*, pages 1050–1055.

Luke Zettlemoyer and Michael Collins. 2007. Online learning of relaxed ccg grammars for parsing to logical form. In *Proceedings of the 2007 Joint Conference on Empirical Methods in Natural Language Processing and Computational Natural Language Learning*, pages 678–687.

Luke S. Zettlemoyer and Michael Collins. 2005. Learning to map sentences to logical form: Structured classification with probabilistic categorial grammars. In *Proceedings of the Twenty-First Conference on Uncertainty in Artificial Intelligence*, page 658–666.

Kai Zhao and Liang Huang. 2015. Type-driven incremental semantic parsing with polymorphism. In *Proceedings of the 2015 Conference of the North American Chapter of the Association for Computational Linguistics: Human Language Technologies*, pages 1416–1421.

# A Appedix

## A.1 Preprocess

According to (Jia and Liang, 2016), we preprocess the Prolog logical forms to the De Brujin index notation. We standardize the variable naming of Lambda Calculus based on their occurrence order in logical forms.

## A.2 Hyper-Parameters

For our model, a one-layer bi-directional LSTM is chosen for encoder and a one-layer LSTM is selected as decoder. The embedding dimension of both source and target languages ranges over {100, 200}. The decoder keeps the same hidden dimension as encoder, ranging over {32, 64}. As for the attention model, we apply additive attention. We employ dropout at training time to alleviate over-fitting with rate ranging over {0.1, 0.2, 0.3}. We select batch size from {16, 32, 64}, and select learning rate from {0.005, 0.01}.

# Improving Machine Reading Comprehension through A Simple Masked-Training Scheme

**Xun Yao[†], Junlong Ma[†], Xinrong Hu[†], Jie Yang[◇*], Yuan-Fang Li[‡]**
[†]School of Computer Science and Artificial Intelligence, Wuhan Textile University
[‡]School of Computing and Information Technology, University of Wollongong
[◇]Faculty of Information Technology, Monash University
{yaoxun, hxr}@wtu.edu.cn
jiey@uow.edu.au,
YuanFang.Li@monash.edu

## Abstract

Extractive Question Answering (EQA) is a fundamental problem in Natural Language Understanding, aiming at answering given questions via extracting a contiguous sequence or span of words from a passage. Recent work on EQA has achieved promising performance with the help of pre-trained language models, for which Masked Language Modeling (MLM) is usually adopted as a pre-training task to predict masked tokens. This paper revisits MLM and proposes a simple yet effective method to improve the EQA performance, termed the `[Mask]`-for-Answering method (M4A). Specifically, three masking strategies are first introduced, which produce masked copies of the original passages. Instead of predicting masked tokens as in MLM, both original samples and masked copies are utilized simultaneously for training the EQA model. Importantly, a discrepancy loss is further incorporated to ensure that masked copies remain semantically close to the originals. As such, M4A is able to produce robust embeddings for both original and masked samples and infer correct answers even with masked context. Experimental study on several highly-competitive benchmarks consistently demonstrates the superiority of our proposed method over existing methods. M4A also achieves strong performance in low-resource settings and out-of-domain generalization.

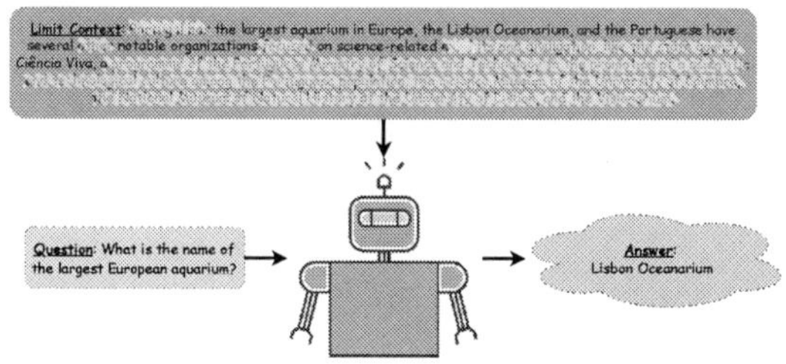


Figure 1: An illustration case from SQuAD (1.1) (Fisch et al., 2019), using the proposed `[Mask]`-for-Answering algorithm (M4A) to infer answer(s) from samples with limit (unmasked) context.

## 1 Introduction

Extractive Question Answering (EQA), a fundamental task for Natural Language Understanding, refers to the process of identifying the answer span (a sequence of continuous words) over the given question and passage. Past years have witnessed a dramatically increasing interest in applications of Pre-trained Language Models (PLMs) for EQA, where PLMs are usually adopted as encoders to form contextual/semantic embeddings for the question-passage pair. Abundant evidences indicate that the strong encoding capability of PLMs has rapidly advanced the EQA performance, compared to traditional word embedding methods, such as GloVe and Word2Vec (Devlin et al., 2019; Joshi et al., 2020; Liu et al., 2019). Recently, how humans approaching reading comprehension becomes a major source of inspiration for enhancing EQA. There is a rich literature to incorporate the human-like reading comprehension strategy with PLMs and achieve remarkable success beyond the vanilla models, as later shown in Section 2.

Notably, when experienced human readers perform question reasoning, they could infer the correct answer using only few sentences (even some parts of one sentence), instead of the entire passage (Paris et al., 1983; Yu et al., 2017). As illustrated in Fig. 1, even with the limit (unmasked) contexts, one could still predict the correct answer of "`Lisbon Oceanarium`" to the given question (of "`the name of the largest European aquarium`"). The observation of humans approaching reading comprehension with limit (unmasked) contexts is the major source of inspiration for this paper.

Accordingly, we propose a simple yet effective mask-training scheme, termed `[Mask]`-for-Answering (M4A). Specifically, M4A introduces

*corresponding author



*Findings of the Association for Computational Linguistics: IJCNLP-AACL 2023*, pages 222–232
November 1–4, 2023. 

three masking strategies to substitute non-answer tokens from the original training passage with `[Mask]` tokens. Additionally, semantic similarity is utilized to maintain the semantic closeness between masked samples and originals. The effectiveness of our training scheme can be intuitively explained from two perspectives: (1) providing strong training signals by strategically masking out potentially-irrelevant contents (non-answer tokens) and (2) data augmentation by simply perturbing the original training samples without additional annotations.

Our method differs from existing methods in the following perspectives. (1) The `[Mask]` token is traditionally utilized to hold out a portion of the input tokens in pre-training PLMs to predict missing tokens (Özkan Tan et al., 2023; Yang et al., 2023). Several studies leverage `[Mask]` to produce pseudo passage-question pairs (Ram et al., 2021; Bian et al., 2021), which is limited by parts of speech (POS) of masked tokens (usually nouns) and the objective is still for predicting masked tokens (the in-domain pre-training). In contrast, M4A directly employs samples with masked tokens in directly optimizing the downstream task objective. Additionally, in M4A non-answer tokens can be masked regardless their POS. (2) Masked samples also play a role of data augmentation, and existing augmentation methods either replace words with synonyms (Ng et al., 2020) or perturb input embeddings (Lee et al., 2021). The former is limited by the set of available synonyms, while our method is independent from synonyms. The latter adds noise on the embedding level (for all tokens) with a prior assumption of a multivariate Gaussian distribution. In contrast, M4A performs masking on the token level, and ensures (ground-truth) answer tokens unmasked.

The main contributions of our proposed work are summarized as follows:

- A novel `[Mask]`-for-Answering method is proposed to produce robust features and incorporate human comprehension skills to infer answers from samples with masked tokens.
- Three masking strategies are introduced to produce masked samples, that are trained simultaneously with original inputs.
- The semantic similarity between original-and-masked pairs is applied to minimize the noise conveyed in masked samples.
- Empirically, our proposed M4A method outperforms recent strong baselines on six standard benchmarks. Intensive ablation studies are also conducted to understand the impact from masking strategies and ratios. Moreover, M4A also demonstrates a strong generalizability in the low-resource training and zero-shot domain adaptation setting.

## 2 Related work

The Extractive Question Answering (EQA) task requires a model to learn informative representation from the context passage, and return a span (continuous words from this passage) that matches the given question. Usually, Pre-trained Language Models (PLMs) are adopted as the encoder to estimate embeddings for the pair of question-passage, which is followed by a decision layer (*i.e.*, two binary classifiers to identify the start and end position of the answer span respectively). Due to the capability of forming semantic representation for input questions and passages, PLMs have significantly advanced the EQA frontier (Devlin et al., 2019; Joshi et al., 2020; Liu et al., 2022).

Inspired by the remarkable success of PLMs, a variety of improvement methods have been proposed to further enhance PLMs with human-reading strategies. A block based attention method is proposed in (Seonwoo et al., 2020), which predicts highly-relevant context about answers. Another similar work is found in (Guan, 2022), that introduces the Block-Skim strategy to identify and skim irrelevant context blocks by utilizing CNN to for EQA. In Sun et al. (2019), different-level attention mechanisms are implemented to simulate the process of back-and-forth reading, highlighting, and self-assessment, while Zhang et al. (2020) considers the reading strategy for multi-round reasoning phrases of reading-attending-excluding, that is, through initial scan *reading*, followed by *attended* intensive reading, and concluding with answer *exclusion*.

In addition to attention-based work, a few studies employed the data-augmentation strategy to fine-tune the EQA task, including synthetic question-answer generation, external knowledge, and input perturbation. As an example, the work from (Ram et al., 2021; Bian et al., 2021) produces synthetic pairs by masking specific words from the passage and training a model to answer questions related to those masked words. Yet, generation-based methods usually suffer from costly computational resource and have limitations on masked words (usually nouns) and question types (mainly cloze-like). KALA (Kang et al., 2022) is proposed to integrate the contextual representation of intermediate PLM layers with related entity and relational representations (from the external Knowledge Graph). With knowledge-augmented representations, KALA improves the performance of the vanilla PLM on various EQA tasks. Additionally, input perturbation is also considered via the word deletion or synonym replacement (Wei and Zou, 2019). SSMBA (Ng et al., 2020) corrupts input sequences via substituting existing tokens with `[Mask]` and then reconstructing them. SWEP (Lee et al., 2021) directly perturbs input embeddings via adjustable Gaussian noises. Using both original and perturbed samples, models are trained to extract token representations to facilitate the subsequent answering task. By comparison, our proposed method neither recovers masked tokens nor perturbs input embeddings. Instead, augmented samples (with `[Mask]` tokens) are directly utilized for the model training while ensuring their semantic similarity with originals.

## 3 Proposed method

The proposed `[Mask]`-for-Answering (M4A) algorithm is detailed in this section. It consists of three main modules: source training, `[Mask]` training, and semantic alignment. Specifically, the second module enables the model to answer questions with incomplete (masked) contents, while the third module ensures semantic correlations between original and masked samples (shown in Fig 2). Notably, the `[Mask]` training module is not utilized during the inference stage, as our ultimate aim is to fine-tune a resilient encoder that can handle masked samples and generate robust features.

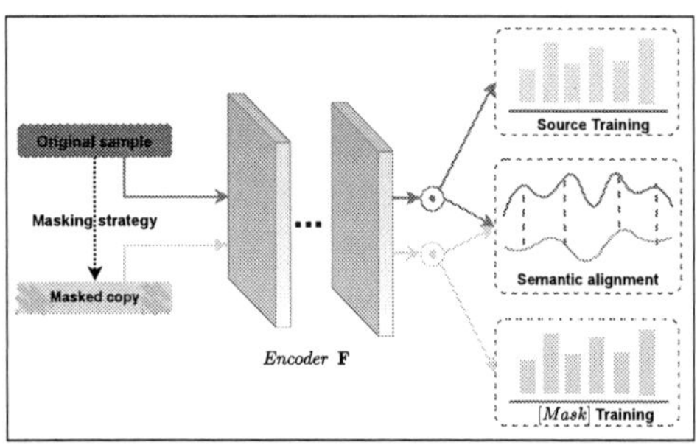


Figure 2: Illustration of the proposed M4A for EQA. Original inputs are masked to produce additional training samples, while their representation similarity is later maximized to remain the semantic alignment.

### 3.1 Source training

Given the input pair of question ($\boldsymbol{q}$) and passage ($\boldsymbol{p}$), the EQA task aims to identify the start and end positions of the correct answer span ($\boldsymbol{a}_{s/e}$) from $\boldsymbol{p}$. Specifically, the input of EQA is a tokenized sequence, $X$ = `[CLS]`$\boldsymbol{q}_1\boldsymbol{q}_2\cdots\ \boldsymbol{q}_{|\boldsymbol{q}|}$`[SEP]`$\boldsymbol{p}_1\boldsymbol{p}_2\cdots\ \boldsymbol{p}_{|\boldsymbol{p}|}$`[SEP]`, where $\boldsymbol{q}_i$ and $\boldsymbol{p}_j$ represents the $i$-th and $j$-th token from $\boldsymbol{q}$ and $\boldsymbol{p}$, respectively. Then the encoder ($\mathbf{F}$, usually a PLM such as BERT (Devlin et al., 2019)) is applied to induce the following probability distribution:

$$\mathrm{p}(\boldsymbol{p}_i = \boldsymbol{a}_{s/e}) \triangleq \frac{\exp(\mathrm{MLP}^{s/e}(\mathbf{F}(\boldsymbol{p}_i)))}{\sum_j^{|\boldsymbol{p}|}\exp(\mathrm{MLP}^{s/e}(\mathbf{F}(\boldsymbol{p}_j)))}, \quad (1)$$

where $\mathbf{F}(\boldsymbol{p}_i)$ represents the extracted feature of $\boldsymbol{p}_i$, and $\mathrm{MLP}^{s/e}$ represents a multilayer perceptron network (usually with one-hidden layer) for predicting the *s*tart and *e*nd of the answer span, respectively. Accordingly, the loss function for EQA is defined as follows:

$$\mathcal{L}_{EQA} \triangleq -\sum_i^{|\boldsymbol{p}|} \mathbb{1}(\boldsymbol{p}_i = \boldsymbol{a}_{s/e}) \log \mathrm{p}(\boldsymbol{p}_i = \boldsymbol{a}_{s/e}), \quad (2)$$

where $\mathbb{1}(\cdot)$ is the indicator function that returns 1 if the condition is true and returns 0 otherwise. Overall, the source training module is to minimize the $\mathcal{L}_{EQA}$ loss using labeled original samples.

### 3.2 `[Mask]` training

The traditional mask-based training (or masked-language modeling (MLM)) aims to predict a set fraction of `[Mask]` tokens given the remaining unmasked text. This fraction is defined as the masking budget ($b_M$), and tokens for masking are chosen by a uniform (or random) sampling until $b_M$ is met. This previous mask-and-predict task is different from ours. In contrast, samples with masked tokens are utilized for training the EQA model directly, while the mask-prediction task is less emphasized.

Given the tokenized input $X$, this module substitutes tokens from the passage $\boldsymbol{p}$ (the second part of $X$) with `[Mask]` to generate the masked copy $X^M$.* Specifically, three masking strategies, *Gaussian*, *U-shaped*, and *Uniform*, are adopted,

*Some masking techniques (such as removing continues words (Joshi et al., 2020) or words with dependency connections (Tian et al., 2022)) may be beneficial to produce more diverse masked copies, and we leave the investigation to future work.

which are differentiated by the distributions of masked tokens. A reference index $r$ is introduced ($r \in [1, |\boldsymbol{p}|]$), where $r$ is explicitly determined by the index of the *start* token from the ground-truth answer span. Then, *Gaussian* favors masking tokens around $r$, while *U-shaped* differs from *Gaussian* by masking more away from $r$ (towards the begin or end of $\boldsymbol{p}$). *Uniform* masks tokens with a uniform probability (similar to the MLM). Note that for all three masking strategies, tokens belonging to the ground-truth answer span are assigned with zero masking probability (never masked), and only non-answer tokens can be masked.

To estimate the masking rate for each token within the passage, probability density functions (PDFs) under different masking strategies are firstly introduced. Assume that PDFs are defined within a range of $[-\Delta, \Delta]$ (where $\Delta > 0$ is a hyper-parameter). Followed by the standard Gaussian distribution $\mathcal{N}(0, 1)$, the PDF for the *Gaussian* masking is accordingly defined as

$$\mathrm{Gau}(x) = \frac{e^{-\frac{x^2}{2}}}{\sqrt{2\pi}}, \quad -\Delta \leq x \leq \Delta.$$

Similarly the PDF for the *U-shaped* distribution is defined as:

$$\mathrm{Ush}(x) = \begin{cases} \mathrm{Gau}(x-\Delta) & \text{if} \quad 0 \leq x \leq \Delta \\ \mathrm{Gau}(x+\Delta) & \text{if} \quad -\Delta \leq x < 0 \end{cases}.$$

To be consistent with *Gaussian* and *U-shaped*, the PDF for *Uniform* is simply given by

$$\mathrm{Uni}(x) = \frac{1}{\Delta-(-\Delta)} = \frac{1}{2\times\Delta}, \quad -\Delta \leq x \leq \Delta.$$

Next, given the reference index $r$, the following mapping function is adopted to project the $t$-th token into this range of $[-\Delta,\Delta]$ by:

$$\mathrm{Map}(t) = \frac{\Delta(t-r)}{\max(r, |X|-r)}. \quad (3)$$

At last, given the masking budget (the fraction of masked tokens) $b_M$, the masking probability for this $t$-th token is further given by:

$$\mathrm{p}(t) = b_m \times |X| \times \frac{f(\mathrm{Map}(t))}{\sum_i^{|X|} f(\mathrm{Map}(i))}, \quad (4)$$

where $f(\cdot)$ represents Gau($\cdot$), Ush($\cdot$), and Uni($\cdot$) for the case of *Gaussian*, *U-shaped*, and *Uniform*, respectively. An illustrating example of the three masking strategies is provided in Fig. 3. At last, masked passages are combined with the given question to form $X^M$, and the resultant loss $\mathcal{L}_{EQA}^{\texttt{[Mask]}}$ is obtained by replacing $X$ with $X^M$ in Eq. (2).

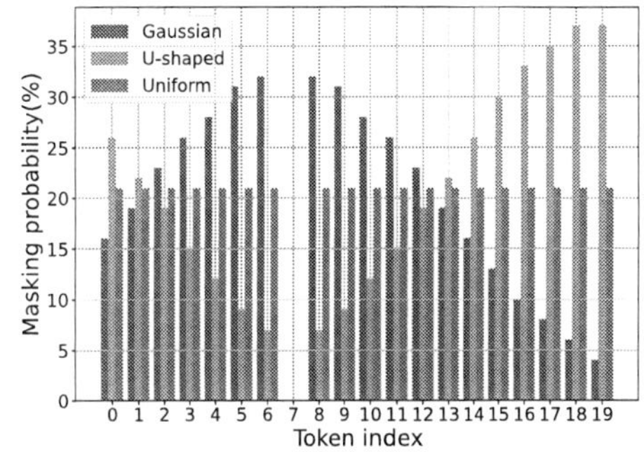


Figure 3: Comparison of proposed masking strategies, where $b_m$ = 20%, the length of the passage is 20 and $\Delta$=2. Presumably, the ground-truth answer token is with the $7^{th}$ index. Specifically, *Gaussian* prefers to mask tokens around the reference index of $r$=7, while more tokens from the begin and end are masked in the *U-shaped* strategy. By contrast, *Uniform* marks tokens with the equally distributed way. Notably, ground-truth answer tokens will never be masked across three cases.

### 3.3 Semantic alignment

The `[Mask]` training module enables the model to answer questions with masked samples $X^M$, which could introduce noise from masked tokens. To reduce the impact of noises, we design the semantic alignment module to suppress noisy signals conveyed in $X^M$, and enforce the semantics of original inputs is preserved even after masking parts of the passage. This is done by minimizing the difference between the distribution of individual-token score (*i.e.*, the probability of being correct-answer tokens) obtained from $X$ and that of the corresponding $X^M$.

To begin with, let $\mathbf{C}$ and $\mathbf{C}^M$ represent feature embedding of original and masked samples, *i.e.*, $\mathbf{C} = \mathbf{F}(X)$ and $\mathbf{C}^M = \mathbf{F}(X^M)$, where $\mathbf{C}/\mathbf{C}^M \in \mathbb{R}^{|X|\times l}$ and $l$ is the hidden dimension. Given two classifiers for identifying the start/end token ($\mathrm{MLP}^{s/e}$) from Eq. (1), the score distribution of individual tokens from $\mathbf{C}$ and $\mathbf{C}^M$ is estimated by:

$$\begin{aligned} d_{\mathbf{C}}^{s/e} &\triangleq \mathrm{softmax}(\mathrm{MLP}^{s/e}(\mathbf{C})) \\ d_{\mathbf{C}^M}^{s/e} &\triangleq \mathrm{softmax}(\mathrm{MLP}^{s/e}(\mathbf{C}^M)), \end{aligned} \quad (5)$$

The Jensen-Shannon divergence ($\mathbb{D}_{\mathrm{JS}}$) is then employed to measure the distribution similarity with the following objective:

$$\mathcal{L}_{ALI} \triangleq \mathbb{D}_{\mathrm{JS}}(d_{\mathbf{C}}^s, d_{\mathbf{C}^M}^s) + \mathbb{D}_{\mathrm{JS}}(d_{\mathbf{C}}^e, d_{\mathbf{C}^M}^e). \quad (6)$$

As such, this loss minimization encourages $\mathbf{F}$ to produce semantically similar representations between the original input $X$ and its masked version

$X^M$. Note that this alignment loss is different from that of `[Mask]` training, as it does not require supervision signals, but only reduces the token-score difference obtained by $X$ and $X^M$.

### 3.4 Overall objective function

In summary, in the proposed M4A, samples with masked tokens are trained simultaneously with originals. Additionally, the semantic alignment loss further ensures masked samples remaining semantically close to original ones. The following joint loss is utilized:

$$\mathcal{L}=\frac{1}{2}\mathcal{L}_{EQA}+\frac{1}{2}\mathcal{L}_{EQA}^{\texttt{[Mask]}}+\lambda\mathcal{L}_{ALI}, \quad (7)$$

where $\lambda$ is a penalty regularizer. During the inference, the `[Mask]` training and semantic alignment modules are discarded, and testing samples follow the traditional steps to extract latent representation via the trained encoder (**F**), before applying the classifiers ($\text{MLP}^{s/e}$) to identify the start and end position of answers.

## 4 Experiments

### 4.1 Setup

Experiments and analysis are carried on a collection of high-competitive EQA tasks. Specifically, six benchmarking datasets from MRQA 2019 (Fisch et al., 2019) are employed, including SQuAD (1.1), HotpotQA, NewsQA, NaturalQ, TriviaQA, and SearchQA. Their statistics are provided in Appendix A.1.

The RoBERTa-base model (Liu et al., 2019) is adopted as the encoder. In addition, with both *Gaussian* and *U-shaped* masking, the reference index $r$ is set as the beginning location of the ground-truth answer token (from training samples), while ground-truth answer tokens are assigned with zero masking probability (never masked). The hyper-parameter is set as $\Delta=2$ for Eq. (3). More training details are provided in Appendix A.2. The F1-evaluation metric, measured by the number of overlapping tokens between the predicted and ground-truth answers, is adopted.

### 4.2 Main results

Our proposed method is compared with the following models. We re-implement them using provided source codes and results are competing with the reported.

- Base (Liu et al., 2019) is implemented using the pre-trained vanilla model (RoBERTa-base) and fine-tuned as described in Section 3.1;
- BLANC (Seonwoo et al., 2020) applies a block-attention strategy to predict answers and supporting contexts (spans surrounding around answers) simultaneously;
- SSMBA (Ng et al., 2020) randomly substitutes tokens with `[Mask]` and recovers them to produce new samples for data augmentation;
- SWEP (Lee et al., 2021) augments the data by perturbing the input embedding with an adjustable Gaussian noise;
- KALA (Kang et al., 2022) augments the original contextual representation using related entity and relational representation from the external Knowledge Graph.

For M4A we set $\lambda = 0.5$ (the ablation study of $\lambda$ is provided later), the masking budget (or the the fraction of masked tokens) as $b_m$ = 20% with the *U-shaped* masking strategy (the impact of different masking strategies are also offered in the ablation study).

Table 1: Comparison among M4A and existing methods. Specifically, M4A achieves $1.66e^{-16}$, $4.47e^{-7}$, $9.91e^{-19}$, $6.92e^{-19}$, $2.58e^{-9}$, and $5.14e^{-13}$ for SQuAD, HotpotQA, NewsQA, NaturalQ, TriviaQA and SearchQA, respectively, in terms of the $p$-values from the T-tests. This statistical significance testing confirms the stability of M4A.

| Model | SQuAD | HotpotQA | NewsQA |
|---|---|---|---|
| Base | 90.3±0.2 | 78.7±0.3 | 69.8±0.4 |
| BLANC | 91.1±0.2 | 77.8±0.1 | 70.7±0.5 |
| SSMBA | 90.1±0.3 | 77.3±0.4 | 69.2±0.2 |
| SWEP | 91.0±0.1 | 78.8±0.1 | 71.7±0.1 |
| KALA | 90.9±0.4 | 77.3±0.5 | 72.7±0.3 |
| M4A | **92.2**±0.1 | **79.2**±0.1 | **72.8**±0.2 |
| **Model** | **NaturalQ** | **TriviaQA** | **SearchQA** |
| Base | 79.6±0.2 | 74.0±0.4 | 81.5±0.3 |
| BLANC | 80.3±0.1 | 75.1±0.1 | 82.6±0.1 |
| SSMBA | 79.8±0.2 | 74.8±0.2 | 82.1±0.1 |
| SWEP | 80.2±0.3 | 75.3±0.2 | 82.5±0.2 |
| KALA | 80.1±0.4 | 75.5±0.3 | 82.4±0.4 |
| M4A | **81.4**±0.1 | **76.3**±0.2 | **83.5**±0.1 |

The comparison results in terms of the mean value and standard deviation over 10 runs are shown in Table 1, in which the best result for each dataset is **bolded**. M4A consistently improves existing models across employed EQA tasks. For instance, the strongest baseline SWEP model achieves an approximately 0.8 absolute-point improvement compared to the vanilla model, while our M4A model enhance a further 1.1 absolute point over SWEP. Thus, it amounts to a comparable improvement and demonstrates the superiority of the proposed masking approach.

Notably, in terms of the computational complexity, the proposed algorithm has a same scale of model-training parameters as the vanilla model (RoBERTa-base). Specifically, M4A reuses two MLPs ($\text{MLP}^{s/e}$ for classifying the start/end answer token from Eq. (1)) in the `[Mask]` training and semantic alignment modules (Eq. (5)). As such, the proposed method does not require extra model parameters. Additionally, during the inference, both the `[Mask]` training and semantic alignment modules are discarded as M4A only requires the trained encoder. As an example, M4A needs only 0.02 seconds per question on the SQuAD testing set.

### 4.3 Ablation study

**On the encoder flexibility.** To start with, we evaluate the impact from the fundamental encoder towards the proposed M4A. Specifically, the BERT-base encoder (Devlin et al., 2019) is implemented as the `Base`, and the strongest baseline `SWEP` from Table 1 is also employed for comparison purposes. Most of the experimental settings, such as the batch size and the sequence length, are in line with the above RoBERTa-base model, except the learning rate is fixed as $3e^{-5}$ and the training epoch is 2 (consistent with `SWEP`). The comparison results over 10 runs are illustrated in Fig. 4, and our M4A method achieves the best F1 score across all datasets, outperforming SWEP. This experiment provides further evidence for M4A's stability on the underlying encoder: it outperforms the current best model SWEP on both RoBERTa and BERT as the encoder. Without explicitly mentioning, the following ablation studies are conducted using the RoBERTa-base encoder.

**On the masking strategy.** The following ablation experiments are performed using SQuAD to evaluate the proposed masking strategies, *i.e.*, *Gaussian*, *U-shaped*, and *Uniform*, whose main difference lies in the distribution of masked tokens. Given $\lambda = 0.5$, $\Delta = 2$, and $b_m = 20\%$, the reference index $r$, again, for *Gaussian* and *U-shaped* is set as the start location of the ground-truth answer token(s), respectively. As for *Uniform*, the token masking probability is set as $b_m$.

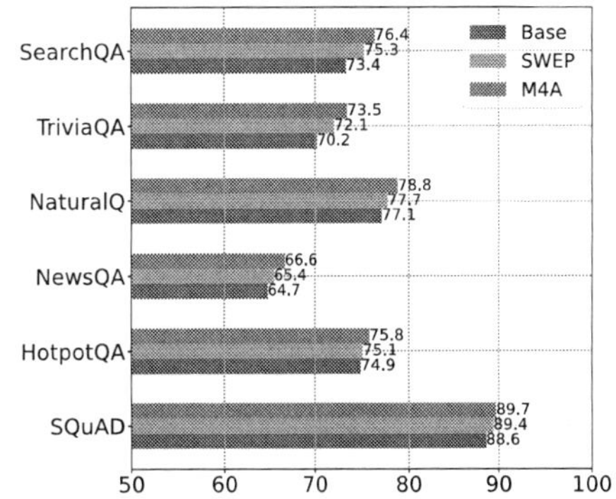


Figure 4: Impact analysis from the underlying encoder.

Table 2: Comparison of the answering performance achieved by different masking strategies.

| Base | Gaussian | U-shaped | Uniform |
|---|---|---|---|
| 90.3±0.2 | 91.7±0.1 | 92.2±0.1 | 92.1±0.1 |

Table 2 compares the three proposed masking strategies, all of which obtain the similar, and higher accuracy than the `Base` model. The result clearly demonstrates the effectiveness of M4A to utilize masked samples for solving EQA. In addition, the U-shaped masking strategy, which masks less tokens around the ground-truth answer(s) but more towards the begin/end of the entire passage, performs the best on the SQuAD dataset. This finding is consistent with BLANC (Seonwoo et al., 2020), from which supporting contexts (spans surrounding around answers) are highlighted via a predetermined soft label. In contrast, our method encourages to remove (via masking) tokens that are far away from answer tokens. Accordingly, the U-shaped masking strategy is adopted for all following experiments. However, we need to point out that the differences among these three masking distributions are relatively moderate (*e.g.*, ±0.25 F1). The contributor to this effectiveness is explored later on the module breakdown part.

**On the masking budget.** The impact from the masking budget (or the the fraction of masked tokens) $b_m$ is validated hereafter. Obviously, more tokens are masked out with a higher value of $b_m$, which also leads to more noisy samples (due to the increase of masked or missing tokens). Specifically, experiments are conduced by varying $b_m$ from 10%

to 100% on the SQuAD dataset. Notably, with $b_M$=100%, all tokens except ground-truth ones are removed.

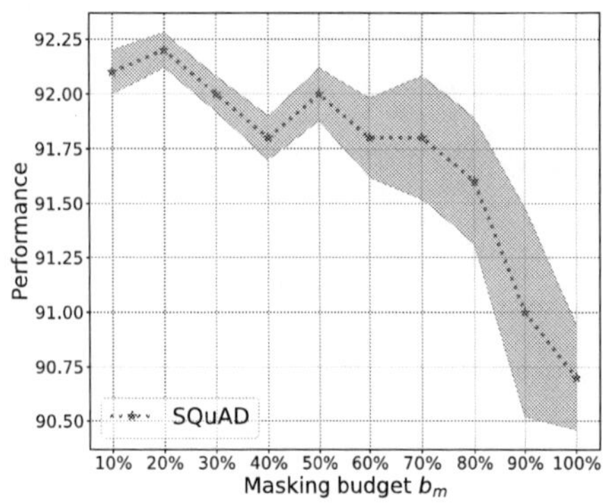


Figure 5: Performance comparison as a function of the masking budgets $b_m$.

The comparison is shown in Fig 5, and results show that the proposed method is relatively insensitive to $b_m$. For instance, with SQuAD the highest performance is observed as 92.2±0.1 ($b_m$ = 20%), which decreases to 90.7±0.2 ($b_m$ = 100%). Surprisingly, even with $b_M$=100%, M4A still obtains a slightly better performance than the `Base` model (90.3 from RoBERTa-base), which shows the lower bound of M4A is the vanilla model. That is, given the very incomplete (masked) passages, M4A is still capable of identifying correct answers, which empirically confirms the robustness and stability of our proposed masking strategy. Furthermore, we argue that such a stable performance (with high masking rate) is a result of the semantic alignment. In the extreme case of $b_M$=100%, for instance, only ground-truth tokens are maintained in the masked sample, and presumably the contribution from the `[Mask]` training loss becomes limited; yet, the semantic alignment loss enforces the encoder to produce robust features for sample with/out masking masking. We further investigate this hypothesis in the model breakdown study below.

**On the module breakdown.** The following experiment examines the effectiveness of M4A from aspects of masked training and semantic alignment. Specifically, the comparison is considered with the following variants: `Base` represents the model trained using only original samples (*w.r.t.* the first term of Eq. (7)); `Mask` only employs U-shaped masking samples for the model training (*w.r.t.* the second term of Eq. (7)); and `Alignment` maximizes the semantic similarity between the original-masked pairs (*w.r.t.* the last term of Eq. (7)).

Table 3: Examination on individual modules of training with masked copies and aligning original-and-masked semantics.

| Base | Mask | Base+Mask |
|---|---|---|
| 90.3 | 90.0 | 90.7 |
| Base+Alignment | Mask+Alignment | Full |
| 91.5 | 91.0 | 92.2 |

Table 3 shows contributions from individual modules using SQuAD with $\lambda$ = 0.5 and $b_m$ = 0.2. To begin with, both the proposed masked training and alignment modules stably improve the performance of the `Base` model. Training with only masked samples, as observed, the `Mask` variant achieves the worst result; the reason is mainly due to the noise brought by the incomplete (or masked) passage(s). Yet, `Base+Mask` achieves the accuracy of 90.7 for SQuAD, which shows the benefit of employing masked copies as the data augmentation. Furthermore, `Alignment` brings a bigger performance boost in comparison with `Mask`. The former achieves the averaged improvement of 1.2 points on top of `Base`, while the latter only obtains a boost of 0.4 points. More importantly, that is also evidenced by the second-place score from `Base+Alignment`, which trains the model without masked samples but only enforces the semantic similarity between the original and masked samples. In other words, with the presence of masked samples, the key contributor to M4A is to restrict their semantic alignment with the original ones (not the way of producing those masked samples, such as the masking budget and the masking strategy). The alignment loss regulates the encoder to generate robust features so to improve the model robustness and performance.

It is worth noting that, the utilization of the masking model proves essential not only for generating supplementary samples that complement the originals, but also for facilitating the Semantic Alignment module to align these masked samples with the original ones. In other words, masked samples form the foundational element on which the alignment depends, although the key contributor to M4A is the semantic alignment. Yet, the proposed masking strategy is also cost-effective, which stands in stark contrast to existing data augmentation techniques that often demand prior domain knowledge and/or resources.

**On the penalty regularizer $\lambda$.** The model

accuracy is also evaluated by varying values of $\lambda$ from 0.1 to 1.0. The comparison is shown in Fig 6 with SQuAD. The result illustrates that the proposed method is robust to $\lambda$, as M4A achieves a stable performance for different scenarios (with an average F1 difference of $\pm 0.35$ approximately).

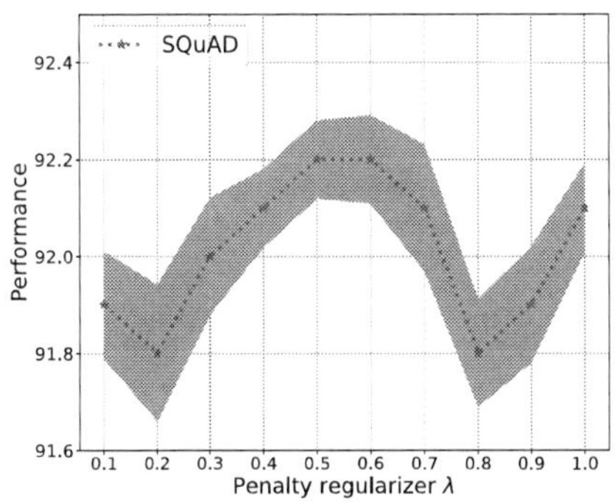


Figure 6: Performance comparison as a function of different $\lambda$.

**On the data augmentation.** This section validates the proposed model from the aspect of the low-resource training, as samples with masked tokens could play a role of the data augmentation. Accordingly, only a small amount (say $m$) of samples (randomly selected from the training set) are utilized for masking and further fine-tuning the model, where $m = [20\%, 40\%, 60\%, 80\%, 100\%]$ ($m = 100\%$ represents the full dataset).

Table 4: Averaged performance (measured by F1) obtained by SWEP/M4A under different percentages of training samples.

| SQuAD | 20% | 40% | 60% | 80% | 100% |
|---|---|---|---|---|---|
| SWEP | 88.4 | 89.6 | 90.1 | 90.7 | 91.0 |
| M4A | 88.6 | 90.4 | 91.5 | 91.9 | 92.2 |

Table 4 shows the accuracy as a function of the sample size using the SQuAD dataset. Compared to the strongest baseline (`SWEP` from Table 1), M4A consistently improves the model performance under all percentages of the training samples. With 40% of labeled data, M4A has achieved even higher accuracy than `SWEP` with 60% samples. Empirically, the result clearly demonstrates the superiority of produced samples with `[Mask]` tokens as an effective data augmentation.

**On out-of-domain generalizability.** In this experiment, we measure M4A's ability via adapting to unseen domains (*i.e.*, datasets) in a zero-shot manner. Following `SSMBA` and `SWEP`, the model is first trained on a single source dataset (SQuAD in this case), and further evaluated on the other two target dataset (*i.e.*, HotpotQA and NaturalQ) without any fine-tuning[†].

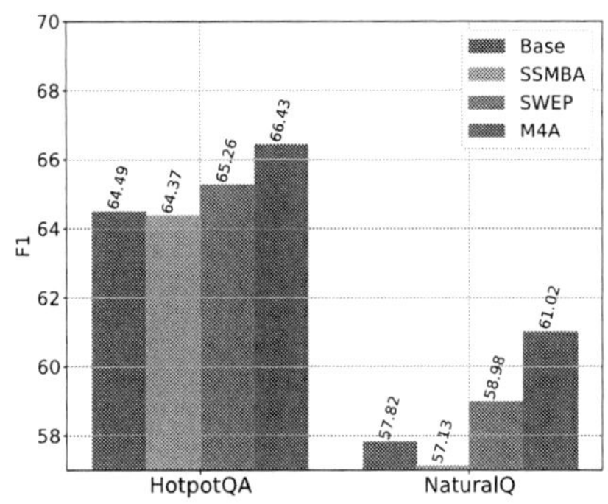


Figure 7: Transferring the EQA model trained by SQuAD to unseen datasets.

Averaged performance from our proposed and other methods is presented in Fig. 7. The `Base` method (directly applying the RoBERTa-base model trained from SQuAD) achieves the worst F1 (60.1 on average) on three subsequent target datasets, which reveals the different data distribution among diverse datasets. Therefore, a direct application of the `Base` model to downstream dataset(s) is ineffective as shown by its low generalizability. Surprisingly, `SSMBA` achieves even worse results than `Base` on HotpotQA and NaturalQ. Notably, `SSMBA` reconstructs masked tokens to produced augmented samples. Yet, new substituted tokens may still cause the semantic drift and lead to poor performance on test sets. In contrast, the average performance of M4A (62.58) is highest across three target datasets. Due to masked samples, M4A is encouraged to produce more robust features, which contributes to the model generalizability to unseen datasets. The comparison indicates that M4A can be regarded as a supplementary pre-training method, along with the traditional Masked Language Modeling (MLM), to offer a robust starting point for fine-tuning unseen datasets.

## 5 Conclusion

This paper proposes a `[Mask]`-for-Answering algorithm (M4A) to tackle the Extractive Question Answering (EQA) task, via simulating human-comprehension skills to infer answers with limit

[†]Notably these three datasets share the same Wikipedia domain background, as shown in Table 5 from Appendix A.1.

context. Specifically, three different masking strategies are introduced to produce masked copies of original samples. Those masked samples are directly utilized for the model training, and regularized by an alignment loss to ensure their semantic similarity with originals. Empirically, M4A achieves statistically better performance than current methods on several benchmark EQA datasets. In addition, M4A also demonstrates the strong capability in the settings of the low-resource training and zero-shot domain adaptation. At last, this masking-then-training strategy, explored by M4A, is also agnostic to downstream tasks, and we will incorporate it with other downstream applications.

## Limitations

`[Mask]` tokens play a critical role, for our proposed M4A, in improving the model inference capability even with masked contents. Yet, the proposed masking strategies mainly focus on the distribution of masked tokens; intuitively, it still cannot be guaranteed that all question-irrelevant contents are masked (or removed). Therefore, masking strategies can be further refined, such as by incorporating external/prior knowledge about passages/questions, masking (stop) words with specific POS, or introducing dependency parsing for identifying trivial words.

Additionally, regarding the Jensen-Shannon divergence employed in this paper, we acknowledge its crucial role in semantic alignment. However, other methods exist for calculating semantic similarity. We defer exploring these alternatives to future work, as they hold potential to enhance the performance further

At last, while current Large Language Models (LLMs), such as GPT-3.5 and Vicuna, achieve impressive achievements across different tasks, including EQA, the proposed method is much more lightweight, based on models that are orders of magnitude smaller (*e.g.*, 110M parameters for BERT-base compared to 7B for Vicuna). Nevertheless, our ablation study highlights the adaptability of our approach as it can be applied to other encoder-decoder language models in a plug-and-play manner. We anticipate enhanced performance by adopting our proposed method using LLMs like Vicuna for EQA.

## Ethical Statement

In terms of reproducibility, we have made the experimental source code available anonymously. Additionally, the benchmark datasets used in our study are publicly accessible. However, it is important to acknowledge the potential presence of hidden biases from Pre-trained Language Models, stemming from biased data they were trained on. Despite utilizing these pre-trained language models for encoding, we did not encounter any biased outcomes. Nevertheless, we carefully considered the low-risk nature of our specific domain during the study.

## Acknowledgments

We express our sincere gratitude to the anonymous reviewers for their invaluable feedback, which has significantly enhanced the depth and presentation of our research. This work was partially supported by the Australian Research Council Discovery Project (DP210101426), the Australian Research Council Linkage Project (LP200201035), and AEGiS Advance Grant(888/008/268), University of Wollongong.

## References

Ning Bian, Xianpei Han, Bo Chen, Hongyu Lin, Ben He, and Le Sun. 2021. Bridging the Gap between Language Model and Reading Comprehension: Unsupervised MRC via Self-Supervision. volume abs/2107.08582. ArXiv preprint.

Jacob Devlin, Ming-Wei Chang, Kenton Lee, and Kristina Toutanova. 2019. BERT: Pre-training of deep bidirectional transformers for language understanding. In *Proceedings of the 2019 Conference of the North American Chapter of the Association for Computational Linguistics: Human Language Technologies, Volume 1 (Long and Short Papers)*, pages 4171–4186, Minneapolis, Minnesota. Association for Computational Linguistics.

Adam Fisch, Alon Talmor, Robin Jia, Minjoon Seo, Eunsol Choi, and Danqi Chen. 2019. MRQA 2019 Shared Task: Evaluating generalization in reading comprehension. In *Proceedings of the 2nd Workshop on Machine Reading for Question Answering*, pages 1–13, Hong Kong, China. Association for Computational Linguistics.

Li Z. Lin Z. Zhu Y. Leng J. Guo M. Guan, Y. 2022. Block-skim: Efficient question answering for transformer. *Proceedings of the AAAI Conference on Artificial Intelligence*, 36(10):10710–10719.

Mandar Joshi, Danqi Chen, Yinhan Liu, Daniel S. Weld, Luke Zettlemoyer, and Omer Levy. 2020. SpanBERT: Improving pre-training by representing and predicting spans. *Transactions of the Association for Computational Linguistics*, 8:64–77.

Minki Kang, Jinheon Baek, and Sung Ju Hwang. 2022. KALA: knowledge-augmented language model adaptation. In *Proceedings of the 2022 Conference of the North American Chapter of the Association for Computational Linguistics: Human Language Technologies*, pages 5144–5167, Seattle, United States. Association for Computational Linguistics.

Seanie Lee, Minki Kang, Juho Lee, and Sung Ju Hwang. 2021. Learning to perturb word embeddings for out-of-distribution QA. In *Proceedings of the 59th Annual Meeting of the Association for Computational Linguistics and the 11th International Joint Conference on Natural Language Processing (Volume 1: Long Papers)*, pages 5583–5595, Online. Association for Computational Linguistics.

Junping Liu, Shijie Mei, Xinrong Hu, Xun Yao, Jack Yang, and Yi Guo. 2022. Seeing the wood for the trees: a contrastive regularization method for the low-resource knowledge base question answering. In *Findings of the Association for Computational Linguistics: NAACL 2022*, pages 1085–1094, Seattle, United States. Association for Computational Linguistics.

Yinhan Liu, Myle Ott, Naman Goyal, Jingfei Du, Mandar Joshi, Danqi Chen, Omer Levy, Mike Lewis, Luke Zettlemoyer, and Veselin Stoyanov. 2019. RoBERTa: A robustly optimized BERT pretraining approach. volume abs/1907.11692. ArXiv preprint.

Nathan Ng, Kyunghyun Cho, and Marzyeh Ghassemi. 2020. SSMBA: Self-supervised manifold based data augmentation for improving out-of-domain robustness. In *Proceedings of the 2020 Conference on Empirical Methods in Natural Language Processing (EMNLP)*, pages 1268–1283, Online. Association for Computational Linguistics.

Scott G. Paris, Marjorie Y. Lipson, and Karen K. Wixson. 1983. Becoming a strategic reader. *Contemporary Educational Psychology*, 8(3):293–316.

Ori Ram, Yuval Kirstain, Jonathan Berant, Amir Globerson, and Omer Levy. 2021. Few-shot question answering by pretraining span selection. In *Proceedings of the 59th Annual Meeting of the Association for Computational Linguistics and the 11th International Joint Conference on Natural Language Processing (Volume 1: Long Papers)*, pages 3066–3079, Online. Association for Computational Linguistics.

Yeon Seonwoo, Ji-Hoon Kim, Jung-Woo Ha, and Alice Oh. 2020. Context-aware answer extraction in question answering. In *Proceedings of the 2020 Conference on Empirical Methods in Natural Language Processing (EMNLP)*, pages 2418–2428, Online. Association for Computational Linguistics.

Kai Sun, Dian Yu, Dong Yu, and Claire Cardie. 2019. Improving machine reading comprehension with general reading strategies. In *Proceedings of the 2019 Conference of the North American Chapter of the Association for Computational Linguistics: Human Language Technologies, Volume 1 (Long and Short Papers)*, pages 2633–2643, Minneapolis, Minnesota. Association for Computational Linguistics.

Yuanhe Tian, Yan Song, and Fei Xia. 2022. Improving relation extraction through syntax-induced pre-training with dependency masking. In *Findings of the Association for Computational Linguistics: ACL 2022*, pages 1875–1886, Dublin, Ireland. Association for Computational Linguistics.

Jason Wei and Kai Zou. 2019. EDA: Easy data augmentation techniques for boosting performance on text classification tasks. In *Proceedings of the 2019 Conference on Empirical Methods in Natural Language Processing and the 9th International Joint Conference on Natural Language Processing (EMNLP-IJCNLP)*, pages 6382–6388, Hong Kong, China. Association for Computational Linguistics.

Dongjie Yang, Zhuosheng Zhang, and Hai Zhao. 2023. Learning better masking for better language model pre-training. In *Proceedings of the 61st Annual Meeting of the Association for Computational Linguistics (Volume 1: Long Papers)*, pages 7255–7267. Association for Computational Linguistics.

Adams Wei Yu, Hongrae Lee, and Quoc Le. 2017. Learning to skim text. In *Proceedings of the 55th Annual Meeting of the Association for Computational Linguistics (Volume 1: Long Papers)*, pages 1880–1890, Vancouver, Canada. Association for Computational Linguistics.

Chenbin Zhang, Congjian Luo, Junyu Lu, Ao Liu, Bing Bai, Kun Bai, and Zenglin Xu. 2020. Read, attend, and exclude: Multi-choice reading comprehension by mimicking human reasoning process. In *Proceedings of the 43rd International ACM SIGIR Conference on Research and Development in Information Retrieval*, SIGIR '20, page 1945–1948, New York, NY, USA. Association for Computing Machinery.

Neşet Özkan Tan, Alex Yuxuan Peng, Joshua Bensemann, Qiming Bao, Tim Hartill, Mark Gahegan, and Michael Witbrock. 2023. Input-length-shortening and text generation via attention values. *arXiv, 2303.07585*.

# A Appendix

## A.1 Employed benchmarks

The statistics for employed datasets are provided in Table 5.

## A.2 Training Details

The RoBERTa-base model (Liu et al., 2019) is adopted as the encoder. The dropout rate across all layers is set as 0.1. The Adam optimizer with a dynamic learning rate is adopted, for which the learning rate is warmed up for 10 thousand steps to a maximum value of $1e^{-4}$ before decaying linearly

Table 5: Employed datasets for the EQA task, where **Domain** represents the passage resource, and **#Train** and **#Test** is the number of training and test samples, respectively.

| **Dataset** | **Domain** | **#Train** | **#Test** |
|---|---|---|---|
| SQuAD(1.1) | Wikipedia | 86,588 | 10,507 |
| HotpotQA | Wikipedia | 72,928 | 5,904 |
| NewsQA | News articles | 74,160 | 4,212 |
| NaturalQ | Wikipedia | 104,071 | 12,836 |
| TriviaQA | Web snippets | 61,688 | 7,785 |
| SearchQA | Web snippets | 117,384 | 16,980 |

to a minimum value of $2e^{-5}$. The training is performed with batches of 8 sequences of length 512. The maximal number of training epoch is 10. For each dataset, 1,000 samples are randomly selected from the training set to form the validation set, and training stops when the validation accuracy fails to improve for one epoch. At last, the proposed model is trained on a machine with four Tesla K80 GPUs.

# A Comprehensive Neural and Behavioral Task Taxonomy Method for Transfer Learning in NLP

**Yunhao Zhang**[1,2]†, **Chong Li**[1,2]†, **Xiaohan Zhang**[1,2], **Xinyi Dong**[3], **Shaonan Wang**[1,2]

[1]State Key Laboratory of Multimodal Artificial Intelligence Systems, Institute of Automation, CAS, Beijing, China

[2]School of Artificial Intelligence, University of Chinese Academy of Sciences, Beijing, China

[3]State Key Laboratory of Cognitive Neuroscience and Learning, Beijing Normal University

{zhangyunhao2021, lichong2021}@ia.ac.cn; 202121061097@mail.bnu.edu.cn;

{shaonan.wang, xiaohan.zhang}@nlpr.ia.ac.cn

## Abstract

Transfer learning is frequently utilized in scenarios with limited labeled examples, where a crucial step is to identify a related task to the target task. CogTaskonomy (Luo et al., 2022) was proposed to acquire a taxonomy of NLP tasks, specifically focusing on assessing the similarities between tasks. This method, inspired by cognitive processes, exhibits notable time efficiency. Nevertheless, it does not fully exploit the task-related information present in cognitive data and lacks a comprehensive evaluation of various types of cognitive data. To address these limitations, this paper proposes a comprehensive neural and behavioral method to investigate the relationship among NLP tasks. Our approach utilizes cognitive data, encompassing both neural data such as fMRI and EEG, as well as behavioral data including eye-tracking and semantic feature ratings. Each data modality is employed to establish a common representation space with Representation Similarity Analysis for projecting task-related representations. To fully leverage the cognitive information, we effectively extract the task-relevant information extracted from neural data through feature ranking. Experimental results on 12 NLP tasks demonstrate that our proposed method outperforms state-of-the-art methods on evaluating task similarity.

## 1 Introduction

Pre-trained Language Models (PLMs) achieve remarkable performance on downstream tasks through fine-tuning on abundant labeled data (Devlin et al., 2019; Radford et al., 2019; Peters et al., 2018). However, their performance tends to degrade when facing with limited labeled data (Chen et al., 2023; Hedderich et al., 2021). To overcome this challenge, researchers employ transfer learning by initially fine-tuning a PLM on a related task with ample labeled data, followed by fine-tuning on the target task (Dwivedi and Roig, 2019; Song et al., 2019). Nevertheless, devising an effective method to identify a suitable similar task remains a challenging endeavor (Ramirez et al., 2023).

To evaluate the relatedness between tasks, different methods have been employed. The first category of method is task embedding, which learns a dedicated high-dimensional representation for each task using a task encoder (James et al., 2018; Lan et al., 2019; Achille et al., 2019; Vu et al., 2020). Despite the low time complexity, modulating the model to adapt for a new task using this method is challenging. Another approach is Taskonomy method (Zamir et al., 2018), which fine-tunes a model on each task, and transfers each fine-tuned model to other tasks in a fully supervised manner. This process can effectively capture task similarity, while it is demanding and time-consuming. The third category encompasses the cognitively inspired CogTaskonomy proposed by Luo et al. (2022). This method projects task-related representations into a shared space based on fMRI and subsequently evaluates the similarity between tasks. It only needs to fine-tune a model for each task separately, which exhibits notable time efficiency. However, shared spaces in CogTaskonomy are not strict shared spaces, and this method does not effectively leverage task-related information from neural data. Our study falls under the third category and improves upon the existing approach by fully utilizing cognitive information to generate an enhanced shared space.

This paper proposes a method, called NBT (A Comprehensive **N**eural and **B**ehavioral **T**ask **T**axonomy Method), integrating both neural data (i.e., fMRI, EEG) and behavioral data (i.e., Eye-tracking, Semantic feature ratings) to investigate the relationship among NLP tasks. We employ each data modality to establish a common representation space with Representation Similarity Analysis (RSA) (Kriegeskorte et al., 2008) for projecting

†Equal Contribution.



*Findings of the Association for Computational Linguistics: IJCNLP-AACL 2023*, pages 233–241
November 1–4, 2023. 

task-related representations. Moreover, to fully exploit cognitive information, we employ feature ranking to effectively extract the task-relevant information extracted from neural data. Results on 12 NLP tasks show that NBT outperforms the previous cognitive-inspired method, and achieves comparable performance to state-of-the-art methods with lower computational time complexity on evaluating task similarity.

## 2 Methods

To evaluate task similarity, we propose NBT as demonstrated in Figure 1, which involves three steps: 1) calculating task-specific representations, 2) generating a shared space from cognitive data, and 3) mapping task-specific representations to cognitive data in a shared space to calculate the task similarity. Each step in Figure 1 is described as follows.

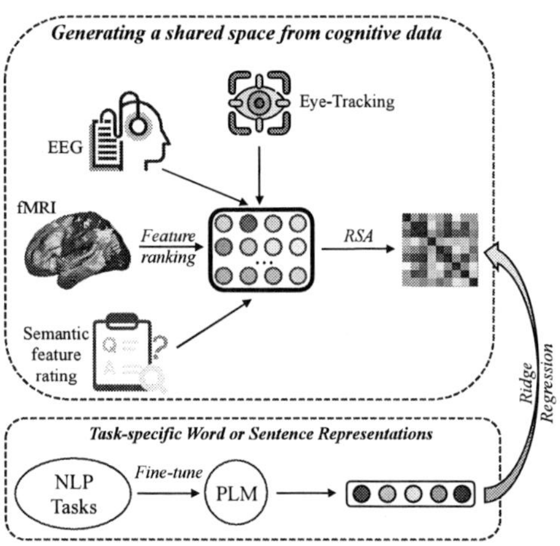


Figure 1: Architecture of NBT.

### 2.1 Extracting Task-Specific Representations

We take task-specific representations through the last layer of PLMs fine-tuned on various NLP tasks. For word-level stimuli, following the method in previous studies (Wang et al., 2022, 2023), we randomly sample a maximum of 1,000 sentences for each target word from Xinhua News corpus[1], and feed sentences into fine-tuned PLMs, with vectors extracted from the last layer. Subsequently, we average vectors of each target word to obtain a task-related representation. For sentence-level stimuli, the sentence representation is obtained by extracting the hidden state of [CLS] token from each sequence in the last layer.

[1]http://www.xinhuanet.com/whxw.htm

### 2.2 Generating a Shared Space from Cognitive Data

To fully extract task-relevant information from high-dimensional fMRI, we select a certain number of voxels by scoring them with their relevance to PLMs. Specifically, regression models are trained for each voxel to predict each dimension of representations of PLMs with this voxel and its adjacent three-dimensional neighbors. The correlation between the true and the predicted representations is regarded as the informative score of each voxel.

Subsequently, we utilize RSA, a widely employed technique for discerning correlations between neuronal responses derived from brain data and models. This facilitates the mapping of cognitive data originating from distinct subject-specific spaces into a unified representational space. It can also help to mitigate the inherent noise in cognitive data. To be more precise, we extract a group of word or sentence cognitive representations $E = \{e_1, e_2, ..., e_n\}$ from cognitive data. For each pair of representations $(e_i, e_j)$, its similarity is measured by the Pearson correlation ($\rho$). Thus, we obtain cognitive data in the representational similarity space $M \in \mathbb{R}^{n \times n}$, where $M_{ij} = \rho(e_i, e_j)$.

### 2.3 Mapping Task-specific Representations to the Shared Space

Finally, we use ridge regression[2] to learn a mapping function between cognitive data $M$ and task-specific representations $P_u \in \mathbb{R}^{n \times w}$ obtained by the PLM $f(\theta_u)$ fine-tuned on the $u$-th task, where $n$ is the number of words or sentences as well as the dimensionality of $M$, and $w$ is the dimensionality of representations of $f(\theta_u)$. The regression coefficients $l$, which is a $n$-dimension vector, and $l_0$ are learned by minimizing

$$\text{loss}(l, l_0) = \|P_u l + l_0 - m\|_2^2 + \lambda \|l\|_2^2 \quad (1)$$

for each column $m \in \mathbb{R}^{n \times 1}$ which is a single dimension of the $M$ matrix. The regularization parameter $\lambda$ for each dimension is set by the nested cross-validation. Each dimension of $M$ and $P_u$ is standardized across training stimuli.

After mapping, we obtain the final predict matrix $\hat{M}_u$ by averaging predict matrices over all participants for the $u$-th task, and calculate the correlation coefficients between $\hat{M}_u$ and $M$ across each dimension to obtain task-specific representation $\text{CogP}_u$ in the shared space, defined as follows:

[2]Compared to Multi-layer Perception, ridge regression has fewer parameters and lower time complexity.

$$\mathrm{CogP}_u = [c(\hat{\boldsymbol{m}}_{u0}, \boldsymbol{m}_0), \ldots, c(\hat{\boldsymbol{m}}_{uh}, \boldsymbol{m}_h) \\ \ldots, c(\hat{\boldsymbol{m}}_{uv}, \boldsymbol{m}_v)], 0 \leq h \leq v \tag{2}$$

where $\hat{m}_{hu}$ and $m_h$ are respectively the predicted and ground-truth vectors of the $h$-th dimension, $n$ is the number of dimensions, and $c(\cdot)$ is the correlation function for vector pairs, e.g., $\rho$ and the coefficient of determination ($R^2$).

We then utilize $s(\cdot)$ involving three different similarity functions (Cosine similarity (cos), $R^2$ and $\rho$) to calculate pairwise task similarity as follows:

$$\mathrm{Sim}_{uu'} = s(\mathrm{Cog\,P}_u, \mathrm{Cog\,P}_{u'}) \tag{3}$$

## 3 Experimental settings

### 3.1 Neural datasets

**fMRI** We utilize the fMRI dataset from Pereira et al. (2018), collecting functional activation data of 627 natural language sentences from 5 participants.

**EEG** We adopt the EEG dataset comprising 1100 sentences and 4384 words obtained from 12 participants, as published by Hollenstein et al. (2018).

### 3.2 Behavioral datasets

**Semantic feature ratings** We use the semantic dataset published by Binder et al. (2016), which includes 535 concepts with 65 semantic features. Each semantic feature of a word has a rating that is the average of annotations from 30 participants.

**Eye-Tracking** The Eye-Tracking dataset in our experiments comes from Hollenstein et al. (2018), which is collected with EEG simultaneously.

### 3.3 Transfer Learning Tasks

Twelve NLP tasks are involved in our experiments, covering sentence/token-level classification, information extraction, and passage ranking tasks (Tjong Kim Sang and De Meulder, 2003; Hendrickx et al., 2010; Nguyen et al., 2016; Rajpurkar et al., 2018; Wang et al., 2019). Task details are shown in Table 1.

| Task | Dataset | #Train |
|---|---|---|
| Acceptability | CoLA | 8,551 |
| Natural Language Inference | MNLI | 392,702 |
| Paraphrase | QQP | 363,846 |
| Paraphrase | MRPC | 3,668 |
| Question Answering | QNLI | 104,743 |
| Sentiment Analysis | SST-2 | 67,349 |
| Entailment | RTE | 2,490 |
| Textual Similarity | STS-B | 5,749 |
| Extractive Question Answering | SQuAD-2.0 | 129,941 |
| Relation Extraction | Semeval-2010 | 8,000 |
| Named Entity Recognition | CoNLL-2003 | 14,042 |
| Passage Reranking | MS MARCO | 3,213,835 |

Table 1: Statistic of tasks used.

### 3.4 Baseline Methods

**Direct Similarity Estimation (DSE)** DSE approximates the similarity of task pairs using the average similarity of sentence representations from PLMs fine-tuned on the corresponding task.

**Analytic Hierarchy Process (AHP)** On the other hand, the similarity of task pairs can be estimated from the pair-wise transfer learning results (Zamir et al., 2018). Given a target task, PLMs transferred from different source tasks are compared on a hold-out dataset to determine the transferability of the target task, which is further used to approximate the similarity between tasks.

**Cognitive Representation Analytics (CRA)** CRA first calculates the Representation Dissimilarity Matrix (RDM) by the dissimilarity of sentence representations, then approximates the similarity between tasks by the similarity between the corresponding RDMs (Luo et al., 2022).

**Cognitive-Neural Mapping (CNM)** CNM calculates the task similarity by mapping sentence representations from multiple fine-tuned PLMs to the same fMRI data (Luo et al., 2022).

### 3.5 Hyperparameters

Most of the hyperparameters used in our transfer-learning and baseline experiments are in line with the ones in Luo et al. (2022). The only exception is that the source model of TinyBERT is distilled from our fine-tuned BERT, rather than initialized from the public models of Jiao et al. (2020) whose download links are missing now.

The hyperparameter $\lambda$ in ridge regression for each dimension is set utilizing nested cross-validation within the training set, respectively. Each voxel is normalized across training stimuli, as is the dimension of representations of PLMs. More formally, the nested cross-validation framework is applied to make sure that the data utilized for the regularization parameter tuning and the data employed to test the model is firmly independent. The interior 10-fold cross-validation is utilized to choose the optimal regularization parameter, and the extrinsic 10-fold nested cross-validation is applied to predict the values using the model with the optimal regularization parameter.

### 3.6 Evaluation Metric

To empirically evaluate the similarity between NLP tasks, we conducted pair-wise transfer learning experiments for each task in Table 1, and quantify it with the actual transfer learning performance (Results are reported in Appendix B). In other words, the more similar the source task is, the better performance on the target task the model gets.

Task Ranking Score (TRS) is used to assess the distance between the task similarity estimated from different methods mentioned before, e.g., DSE, and the empirical task similarity in the transfer learning experiments. Specifically, the task ranking score is obtained from the average ranking of the best source task estimated by the method in the real transfer learning experiment for all target tasks. Then, the random guess leads to $\frac{N}{2}$ in the task ranking score, while the best one always gets 1 under the $N$ tasks setting.

## 4 Results and Analysis

| Method | Complexity | TRS ↓ | |
|---|---|---|---|
| | | TinyBERT | BERT |
| *Baselines* | | | |
| Random | $O(1)$ | 6.0 | 6.0 |
| DSE | $O(n)$ | 4.9 | 4.8 |
| CRA | $O(n)$ | 5.0 | 4.4 |
| CNM | $O(n)$ | 4.1 | 4.6 |
| AHP* | $O(n^2)$ | **1.4** | **2.5** |
| *Ours* | | | |
| $\text{NBT}_{eeg}$ | $O(n)$ | 4.0 | 4.2 |
| $\text{NBT}_{eye}$ | $O(n)$ | 3.6 | 3.8 |
| $\text{NBT}_{sem}$ | $O(n)$ | 3.3 | 3.9 |
| $\text{NBT}_{fmri}$ | $O(n)$ | **2.4** | **2.9** |

Table 2: Task ranking scores (TRS) for different task similarity estimation methods. Results denoted by * come from Luo et al. (2022).

**Main result** Table 2 displays the task ranking scores obtained from various methods. It is evident that NBT outperforms CogTaskonmoy (CNM and CRA), with $\text{NBT}_{fmri}$ exhibiting an average improvement of 41.13% over them. Additionally, $\text{NBT}_{eeg}$, $\text{NBT}_{eye}$ and $\text{NBT}_{sem}$ separately exceed them by 8.93%, 24.40%, and 20.02%. These results suggest that NBT is superior to CogTaskonomy in capturing the relation among NLP tasks by utilizing distinct neural and behavioral data. Although NBT has the same time complexity with CNM, NBT is more efficient than CNM in practice[3]. Moreover, NBT has comparable performance to AHP with lower computational time and less memory.

| Corr. Coef. | Task Sim. | Method | TRS ↓ | |
|---|---|---|---|---|
| | | | TinyBERT | BERT |
| cos | $R^2$ | CNM | 4.3 | 4.8 |
| | | $\text{NBT}_{fmri}$ | 2.7 | 3.3 |
| | $\rho$ | CNM | 4.1 | 4.6 |
| | | $\text{NBT}_{fmri}$ | 2.9 | 3.0 |
| | cos | CNM | 4.2 | 4.4 |
| | | $\text{NBT}_{fmri}$ | 2.9 | 3.2 |
| $\rho$ | $R^2$ | CNM | 4.4 | 4.4 |
| | | $\text{NBT}_{fmri}$ | 2.6 | **2.7** |
| | $\rho$ | CNM | 4.2 | 4.6 |
| | | $\text{NBT}_{fmri}$ | **2.4** | 2.9 |
| | cos | CNM | 4.2 | 4.8 |
| | | $\text{NBT}_{fmri}$ | 3.0 | 3.0 |

Table 3: TRS of $\text{NBT}_{fmri}$ and CNM for BERT and TinyBERT with different measures of task similarity and correlation coefficients.

**Evaluating NBT with different similarity measure combinations** There are multiple options to calculate correlation coefficients of mapping performance (e.g., $\rho$, $R^2$) and task similarity (e.g., cos, $R^2$, $\rho$). To demonstrate the robustness of the proposed method, we evaluate the performance of NBT across various measure combinations. As the CNM utilizes fMRI to measure task relations, we compare it with NBT using identical cognitive data. It can be seen from Table 3 that $\text{NBT}_{fmri}$ has better performance than CNM in all cases. Specifically, $\text{NBT}_{fmri}$ outperforms CNM by 35.39% on average. In addition, TinyBERT and BERT show minimal performance difference using $\text{NBT}_{fmri}$, while TinyBERT is more resilient to different cases compared to BERT with CNM, which indicates that the proposed method has greater generalization for different models.

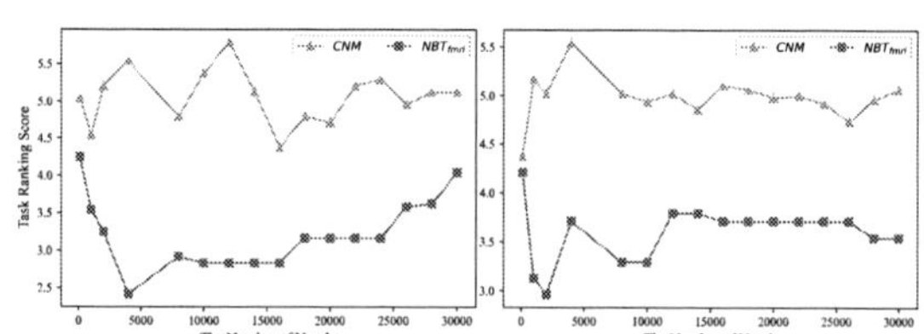


Figure 2: TRS of $\text{NBT}_{fmri}$ and CNM with TinyBERT (left) and BERT (right) predicting different numbers of voxels.

[3]To map a fine-tuned model to fMRI data, NBT only costs 23.3s (for BERT), which is 2.7% of time spent with CNM (879.3s) when the voxel number is 30K

**Evaluating NBT with numbers of voxels** The number of voxels is a critical parameter in the proposed method. In this part, we further evaluate the stability of our proposed method by comparing it with CNM across voxel numbers. Figure 2 shows that $\text{NBT}_{fmri}$ exhibits superior performance to CNM across various numbers of voxels. Moreover, it's hard to predict the number of voxels when achieving the best ranking score using CNM, while $\text{NBT}_{fmri}$ can achieve relatively optimal results in the 2000-10000 voxel range.

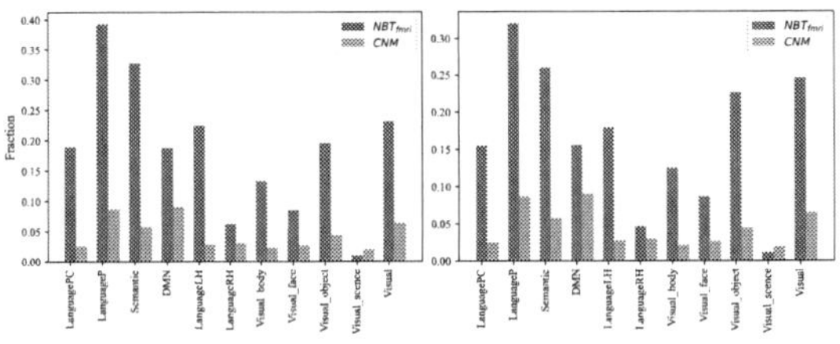

Figure 3: Distribution of informative voxels of $\text{NBT}_{fmri}$ and CNM with TinyBERT (left) and BERT (right) across the brain (averaged over 5 participants).

**Analysis on the spatial distribution of informative voxels** In this section, we explore the distribution of voxels selected by $\text{NBT}_{fmri}$ and CNM across brain networks associated with semantic processing. As can be obtained from Figure 3, $\text{NBT}_{fmri}$ selects a obviously larger proportion of voxels within areas relating to semantic processing compared to CNM, including languagePC, languageP, semantic and languageLH, which suggests the proposed method can effectively extract the task-relevant information from neural signal. Moreover, voxels selected using $\text{NBT}_{fmri}$ also distribute in areas relating to visual semantics, indicating that the method can effectively utilize semantic information from each brain functional area to accurately separate task presentations from neural data.

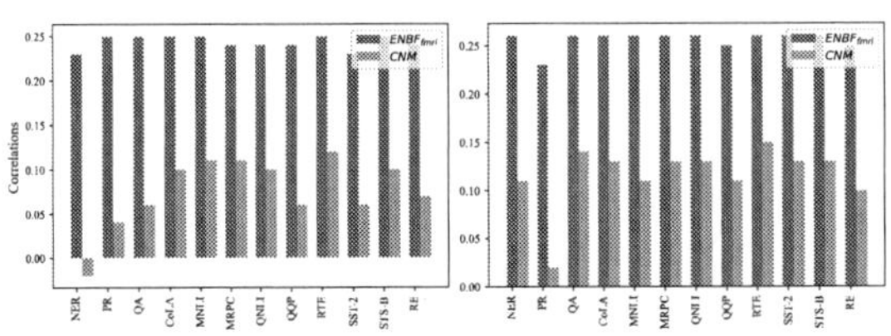

Figure 4: Voxel prediction results of $\text{NBT}_{fmri}$ and CNM with TinyBERT (left) and BERT (right) (averaged over 5 participants and 30K voxels).

**Analysis on the voxel prediction evaluation** In this part, we compare results of the proposed method and CNM on voxel prediction. It can be noticed from Figure 4 that $\text{NBT}_{fmri}$ obtains higher correlation than CNM, suggesting that the proposed method can better establish the connection between neural signals and task-representations of fine-tuned PLMs, and can better isolate task presentations from neural signals.

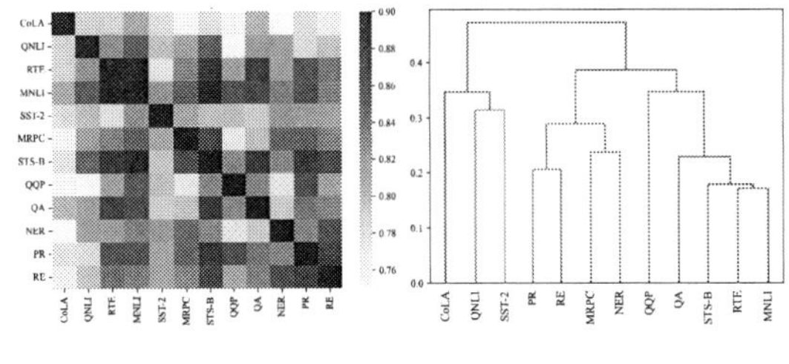

Figure 5: Task similarity matrix from the results of $\text{NBT}_{fmri}$ (left) and taxonomy tree (right).

**Analysis on taxonomy tree of 12 NLP tasks** In this section, we explore the task similarity matrix and the taxonomy tree of 12 NLP tasks from $\text{NBT}_{fmri}$. Compared with the taxonomy tree from CogTaskonomy, "QA, STS-B" and "QNLI, SST-2" are both found to be put in one cluster in two taxonomies. Furthermore, the proposed method clusters three tasks that need to infer semantic relationships (MNLI, STS-B and RTE) in one cluster, while CogTaskonomy divides STS-B into other clusters.

## 5 Conclusion

We propose a comprehensive neural and behavioral method to investigate the similarity between various NLP tasks. This method can fully extract task-relevant information from neural data thus capture task taxonomy and effectively guide transfer learning across diverse NLP tasks, which also can be beneficial for other cross-task learning paradigms, including multi-task learning (Zhang et al., 2021; Chen et al., 2021), meta learning (Yin, 2020) and lifelong learning (Biesialska et al., 2020). Results on 12 tasks show that the proposed method outperforms the previous cognitive-inspired method, and reaches comparable performance to the state-of-the-art method with $O(n)$ computational time complexity on evaluating task similarity.

## Limitations

The proposed method utilizes cognitive data, including neural data such as fMRI and EEG, along with behavioral data such as eye-tracking and semantic feature ratings, to efficiently capture the inter-task relationships in NLP with reduced computational time complexity. Although existing work has proven that human brain contains information about NLP tasks (Oota et al., 2022), it is unclear what kind of task-relevant information human brain contains (i.e., sentence/token-level classification, information extraction, and passage ranking tasks). Moreover, pre-trained models are fine-tuned on downstream tasks in a fully supervised manner, which is different from how human learn and understand new knowledge (Kühl et al., 2022). Therefore, the task similarity based on cognitive data may show different pattern from the real task similarity. Finally, since the proposed method currently exhibits effective performance on NLP, it will be extended to vision and multi-modal domains in our future work.

## References


Alessandro Achille, Michael Lam, Rahul Tewari, Avinash Ravichandran, Subhransu Maji, Charless C Fowlkes, Stefano Soatto, and Pietro Perona. 2019. Task2vec: Task embedding for meta-learning. In *Proceedings of the IEEE/CVF international conference on computer vision*, pages 6430–6439.

Magdalena Biesialska, Katarzyna Biesialska, and Marta R Costa-Jussa. 2020. Continual lifelong learning in natural language processing: A survey. *arXiv preprint arXiv:2012.09823*.

Jeffrey R Binder, Lisa L Conant, Colin J Humphries, Leonardo Fernandino, Stephen B Simons, Mario Aguilar, and Rutvik H Desai. 2016. Toward a brain-based componential semantic representation. *Cognitive neuropsychology*, 33(3-4):130–174.

Jiaao Chen, Derek Tam, Colin Raffel, Mohit Bansal, and Diyi Yang. 2023. An empirical survey of data augmentation for limited data learning in nlp. *Transactions of the Association for Computational Linguistics*, 11:191–211.

Shijie Chen, Yu Zhang, and Qiang Yang. 2021. Multi-task learning in natural language processing: An overview. *arXiv preprint arXiv:2109.09138*.

Jacob Devlin, Ming-Wei Chang, Kenton Lee, and Kristina Toutanova. 2019. BERT: Pre-training of deep bidirectional transformers for language understanding. In *Proceedings of the 2019 Conference of the North American Chapter of the Association for Computational Linguistics: Human Language Technologies, Volume 1 (Long and Short Papers)*, pages 4171–4186, Minneapolis, Minnesota. Association for Computational Linguistics.

Kshitij Dwivedi and Gemma Roig. 2019. Representation similarity analysis for efficient task taxonomy & transfer learning. In *Proceedings of the IEEE/CVF Conference on Computer Vision and Pattern Recognition*, pages 12387–12396.

Michael A. Hedderich, Lukas Lange, Heike Adel, Jannik Strötgen, and Dietrich Klakow. 2021. A survey on recent approaches for natural language processing in low-resource scenarios. In *Proceedings of the 2021 Conference of the North American Chapter of the Association for Computational Linguistics: Human Language Technologies*, pages 2545–2568, Online. Association for Computational Linguistics.

Iris Hendrickx, Su Nam Kim, Zornitsa Kozareva, Preslav Nakov, Diarmuid Ó Séaghdha, Sebastian Padó, Marco Pennacchiotti, Lorenza Romano, and Stan Szpakowicz. 2010. SemEval-2010 task 8: Multi-way classification of semantic relations between pairs of nominals. In *Proceedings of the 5th International Workshop on Semantic Evaluation*, pages 33–38, Uppsala, Sweden. Association for Computational Linguistics.

Nora Hollenstein, Jonathan Rotsztejn, Marius Troendle, Andreas Pedroni, Ce Zhang, and Nicolas Langer. 2018. Zuco, a simultaneous eeg and eye-tracking resource for natural sentence reading. *Scientific data*, 5(1):1–13.

Stephen James, Michael Bloesch, and Andrew J Davison. 2018. Task-embedded control networks for few-shot imitation learning. In *Conference on robot learning*, pages 783–795. PMLR.

Xiaoqi Jiao, Yichun Yin, Lifeng Shang, Xin Jiang, Xiao Chen, Linlin Li, Fang Wang, and Qun Liu. 2020. TinyBERT: Distilling BERT for natural language understanding. In *Findings of the Association for Computational Linguistics: EMNLP 2020*, pages 4163–4174, Online. Association for Computational Linguistics.

Nikolaus Kriegeskorte, Marieke Mur, and Peter A Bandettini. 2008. Representational similarity analysis-connecting the branches of systems neuroscience. *Frontiers in systems neuroscience*, page 4.

Niklas Kühl, Marc Goutier, Lucas Baier, Clemens Wolff, and Dominik Martin. 2022. Human vs. supervised machine learning: Who learns patterns faster? *Cognitive Systems Research*, 76:78–92.

Lin Lan, Zhenguo Li, Xiaohong Guan, and Pinghui Wang. 2019. Meta reinforcement learning with task embedding and shared policy. *arXiv preprint arXiv:1905.06527*.

Yifei Luo, Minghui Xu, and Deyi Xiong. 2022. Cog-Taskonomy: Cognitively inspired task taxonomy is beneficial to transfer learning in NLP. In *Proceedings of the 60th Annual Meeting of the Association for Computational Linguistics (Volume 1: Long Papers)*, pages 904–920, Dublin, Ireland. Association for Computational Linguistics.

Tri Nguyen, Mir Rosenberg, Xia Song, Jianfeng Gao, Saurabh Tiwary, Rangan Majumder, and Li Deng. 2016. Ms marco: A human generated machine reading comprehension dataset. In *the Workshop on Cognitive Computation: Integrating neural and symbolic approaches 2016 co-located with the 30th Annual Conference on Neural Information Processing Systems (NIPS 2016), Barcelona, Spain, December 9, 2016*, volume 1773 of CEUR Workshop Proceedings. CEUR-WS.org.

Subba Reddy Oota, Jashn Arora, Veeral Agarwal, Mounika Marreddy, Manish Gupta, and Bapi Surampudi. 2022. Neural language taskonomy: Which NLP tasks are the most predictive of fMRI brain activity? In *Proceedings of the 2022 Conference of the North American Chapter of the Association for Computational Linguistics: Human Language Technologies*, pages 3220–3237, Seattle, United States. Association for Computational Linguistics.

Francisco Pereira, Bin Lou, Brianna Pritchett, Samuel Ritter, Samuel J Gershman, Nancy Kanwisher, Matthew Botvinick, and Evelina Fedorenko. 2018. Toward a universal decoder of linguistic meaning from brain activation. *Nature communications*, 9(1):963.

Matthew E. Peters, Mark Neumann, Mohit Iyyer, Matt Gardner, Christopher Clark, Kenton Lee, and Luke Zettlemoyer. 2018. Deep contextualized word representations. In *Proceedings of the 2018 Conference of the North American Chapter of the Association for Computational Linguistics: Human Language Technologies, Volume 1 (Long Papers)*, pages 2227–2237, New Orleans, Louisiana. Association for Computational Linguistics.

Alec Radford, Jeffrey Wu, Rewon Child, David Luan, Dario Amodei, Ilya Sutskever, et al. 2019. Language models are unsupervised multitask learners. *OpenAI blog*, 1(8):9.

Pranav Rajpurkar, Robin Jia, and Percy Liang. 2018. Know what you don't know: Unanswerable questions for SQuAD. In *Proceedings of the 56th Annual Meeting of the Association for Computational Linguistics (Volume 2: Short Papers)*, pages 784–789, Melbourne, Australia. Association for Computational Linguistics.

Pierluigi Zama Ramirez, Adriano Cardace, Luca De Luigi, Alessio Tonioni, Samuele Salti, and Luigi Di Stefano. 2023. Learning good features to transfer across tasks and domains. *IEEE Transactions on Pattern Analysis and Machine Intelligence*.

Jie Song, Yixin Chen, Xinchao Wang, Chengchao Shen, and Mingli Song. 2019. Deep model transferability from attribution maps. *Advances in Neural Information Processing Systems*, 32.

Erik F. Tjong Kim Sang and Fien De Meulder. 2003. Introduction to the CoNLL-2003 shared task: Language-independent named entity recognition. In *Proceedings of the Seventh Conference on Natural Language Learning at HLT-NAACL 2003*, pages 142–147.

Tu Vu, Tong Wang, Tsendsuren Munkhdalai, Alessandro Sordoni, Adam Trischler, Andrew Mattarella-Micke, Subhransu Maji, and Mohit Iyyer. 2020. Exploring and predicting transferability across nlp tasks. *arXiv preprint arXiv:2005.00770*.

Alex Wang, Amanpreet Singh, Julian Michael, Felix Hill, Omer Levy, and Samuel R. Bowman. 2019. GLUE: A multi-task benchmark and analysis platform for natural language understanding. In *7th International Conference on Learning Representations, ICLR 2019, New Orleans, LA, USA, May 6-9, 2019*. OpenReview.net.

Shaonan Wang, Yunhao Zhang, Weiting Shi, Guangyao Zhang, Jiajun Zhang, Nan Lin, and Chengqing Zong. 2023. A large dataset of semantic ratings and its computational extension. *Scientific Data*, 10(1):106.

Shaonan Wang, Yunhao Zhang, Xiaohan Zhang, Jingyuan Sun, Nan Lin, Jiajun Zhang, and Chengqing Zong. 2022. An fmri dataset for concept representation with semantic feature annotations. *Scientific Data*, 9(1):721.

Wenpeng Yin. 2020. Meta-learning for few-shot natural language processing: A survey. *arXiv preprint arXiv:2007.09604*.

Amir R Zamir, Alexander Sax, William Shen, Leonidas J Guibas, Jitendra Malik, and Silvio Savarese. 2018. Taskonomy: Disentangling task transfer learning. In *Proceedings of the IEEE conference on computer vision and pattern recognition*, pages 3712–3722.

Yunhao Zhang, Jiajun Yu, Xinyi Dong, and Ping Zhong. 2021. Multi-task support vector machine with pinball loss. *Engineering Applications of Artificial Intelligence*, 106:104458.

## A Correlation selection in NBT$_{fmri}$

There are three options for us to calculate the correlation coefficient ($R^2$, $\rho$, $cos$) on all voxels between predicted values and ground-truth values. We calculate task ranking scores using these options for NBT$_{fmri}$ with TinyBERT and BERT, as shown in Figure 6. Our findings suggest that $\rho$ outperforms $R^2$ in almost all cases.

## B Oracle Task Ranking

After pair-wise transfer learning, we evaluate the performance of models on the validation set of target tasks and report them in Table 4 and Table 5 for BERT and TinyBERT, respectively.

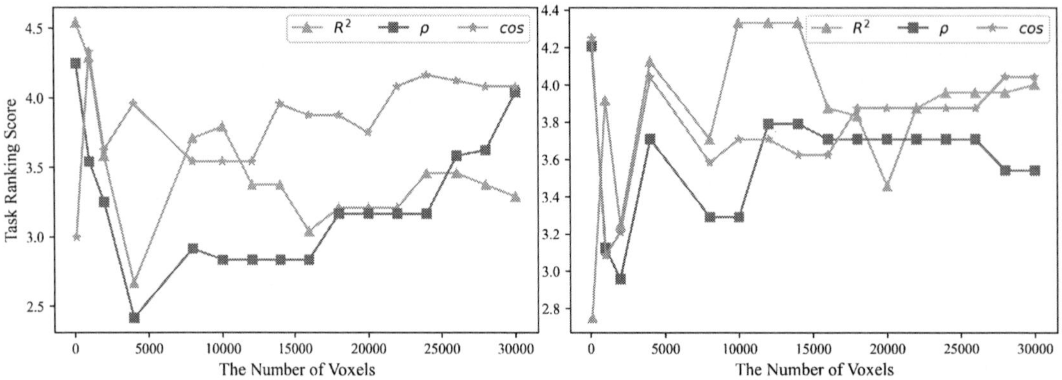


Figure 6: Task ranking scores with different correlation coefficients in NBT$_{fmri}$ based on TinyBERT (left) and BERT (right).

| Source Task | Target Task | | | | | | | | | | | |
|---|---|---|---|---|---|---|---|---|---|---|---|---|
| | **CoLA** | **QNLI** | **RTE** | **MNLI** | **SST-2** | **MRPC** | **STS-B** | **QQP** | **NER** | **RE** | **QA** | **PR** |
| | Mcc | Acc | Acc | Acc | Acc | F1 | $r^s$ | F1 | F1 | F1 | F1 | MRR@10 |
| CoLA | - | 91.40(4) | 64.98(6) | 83.95(8) | 92.55(5) | 90.82(1) | 87.94(7) | 88.04(1) | 93.70(3) | 90.73(4) | 76.02(6) | 65.84(2) |
| QNLI | 55.57(5) | - | 70.40(2) | 84.37(5) | 92.78(3) | 90.16(3) | 88.71(2) | 87.25(10) | 93.53(6) | 89.98(8) | 77.20(1) | 63.21(9) |
| RTE | 55.47(6) | 91.73(1) | - | 84.03(7) | 92.43(6) | 88.04(8) | 88.65(4) | 87.66(7) | 93.48(7) | 90.94(1) | 76.39(3) | 63.47(7) |
| MNLI | 54.84(7) | 91.12(6) | 77.26(1) | - | 93.12(1) | 89.64(6) | 88.65(4) | 87.74(4) | 93.44(8) | 89.20(10) | 75.88(7) | 64.47(4) |
| SST-2 | 56.76(2) | 91.07(7) | 61.73(10) | 84.39(4) | - | 87.78(9) | 87.90(8) | 87.64(8) | 93.60(4) | 90.32(5) | 76.24(5) | 62.75(10) |
| MRPC | 56.77(1) | 91.58(2) | 65.34(4) | 84.51(3) | 92.78(3) | - | 88.18(6) | 87.96(2) | 93.79(2) | 90.84(2) | 75.20(9) | 66.66(1) |
| STS-B | 56.25(4) | 90.39(10) | 65.34(4) | 83.74(10) | 92.89(2) | 90.24(2) | - | 87.59(9) | 93.60(4) | 90.83(3) | 75.04(10) | 61.20(11) |
| QQP | 54.69(8) | 90.55(9) | 63.90(7) | 84.66(1) | 92.43(6) | 89.01(7) | 88.70(3) | - | 93.22(10) | 89.59(9) | 76.93(2) | 64.44(5) |
| NER | 56.50(3) | 91.36(5) | 63.54(8) | 84.32(6) | 92.43(6) | 89.93(4) | 87.73(9) | 87.72(6) | - | 90.02(7) | 74.04(11) | 63.81(6) |
| RE | 53.93(9) | 91.07(7) | 62.09(9) | 83.92(9) | 91.97(9) | 87.46(10) | 87.17(11) | 87.82(3) | 93.85(1) | - | 76.35(4) | 63.31(8) |
| QA | 52.59(10) | 91.47(3) | 67.15(3) | 84.65(2) | 91.86(10) | 89.72(5) | 89.18(1) | 87.74(4) | 93.41(9) | 90.11(6) | - | 65.44(3) |
| PR | 5.20(11) | 89.44(11) | 61.01(11) | 82.49(11) | 91.40(11) | 82.98(11) | 87.44(10) | 87.13(11) | 90.53(11) | 86.75(11) | 75.68(8) | - |

Table 4: Transfer learning results of BERT. Mcc denotes the Matthews correlation coefficient, $r^s$ is the Spearman's rank correlation coefficient, and MRR@10 denotes the Mean Reciprocal Rank for the top 10. The ranking for the source task to the target task is denoted in the right parenthesis.

| Source Task | Target Task | | | | | | | | | | | |
|---|---|---|---|---|---|---|---|---|---|---|---|---|
| | CoLA | QNLI | RTE | MNLI | SST-2 | MRPC | STS-B | QQP | NER | RE | QA | PR |
| | Mcc | Acc | Acc | Acc | Acc | F1 | $r^s$ | F1 | F1 | F1 | F1 | MRR@10 |
| CoLA | - | 78.89(9) | 55.23(9) | 74.65(9) | 86.12(9) | 76.4(11) | 25.15(9) | 82.73(9) | 74.98(10) | 85.46(8) | 47.31(9) | 58.57(9) |
| QNLI | 16.57(8) | - | 61.01(4) | 77.74(8) | 85.67(10) | 87.80(4) | 84.44(7) | 84.94(8) | 85.71(8) | 86.04(6) | 68.44(3) | 62.70(8) |
| RTE | 16.11(9) | 87.55(4) | - | 79.30(5) | 87.84(5) | 87.80(4) | 85.96(3) | 85.40(6) | 87.63(3) | 87.13(2) | 64.25(7) | 63.94(6) |
| MNLI | 28.19(1) | 89.27(2) | 74.01(1) | - | 91.28(1) | 90.36(1) | 87.51(2) | 86.67(1) | 87.18(5) | 88.19(1) | 70.24(1) | 63.99(5) |
| SST-2 | 9.91(10) | 75.93(10) | 55.23(9) | 72.57(10) | - | 80.45(8) | 14.99(11) | 81.78(10) | 70.07(11) | 78.29(10) | 47.03(10) | 55.55(10) |
| MRPC | 19.69(7) | 87.46(5) | 62.82(3) | 79.67(4) | 88.42(4) | - | 85.57(4) | 85.80(3) | 87.20(4) | 85.18(9) | 63.86(8) | 63.31(7) |
| STS-B | 25.86(2) | 85.54(8) | 59.57(6) | 78.93(7) | 86.93(7) | 89.45(2) | - | 85.65(4) | 87.06(6) | 86.78(3) | 64.64(6) | 64.66(2) |
| QQP | 22.29(3) | 86.82(6) | 59.57(6) | 79.92(3) | 87.16(6) | 87.83(3) | 85.42(6) | - | 84.81(9) | 86.08(5) | 67.01(5) | 64.13(4) |
| NER | 5.66(11) | 63.04(11) | 58.12(8) | 68.93(11) | 81.65(11) | 79.60(10) | 19.01(10) | 79.82(11) | - | 76.14(11) | 42.93(11) | 55.34(11) |
| RE | 21.79(4) | 86.45(7) | 55.23(9) | 82.95(1) | 89.56(3) | 80.14(9) | 83.19(8) | 85.49(5) | 88.86(1) | - | 68.14(4) | 65.30(1) |
| QA | 19.81(6) | 88.72(3) | 64.26(2) | 79.01(6) | 86.93(7) | 86.72(7) | 85.53(5) | 85.32(7) | 86.41(7) | 85.79(7) | - | 64.60(3) |
| PR | 20.31(5) | 89.77(1) | 61.01(4) | 82.72(2) | 90.83(2) | 87.69(6) | 87.90(1) | 86.29(2) | 87.89(2) | 86.70(4) | 70.19(2) | - |

Table 5: Transfer learning results of TinyBERT. Mcc denotes the Matthews correlation coefficient, $r^s$ is the Spearman's rank correlation coefficient, and MRR@10 denotes the Mean Reciprocal Rank for the top 10. The ranking for the source task to the target task is denoted in the right parenthesis.

# My Boli: Code-mixed Marathi-English Corpora, Pretrained Language Models and Evaluation Benchmarks

**Tanmay Chavan**[1*], **Omkar Gokhale**[2*], **Aditya Kane**[2*], **Shantanu Patankar**[2*], and **Raviraj Joshi**[3]
Pune Institute of Computer Technology, L3Cube[1]
Georgia Institute of Technology, L3Cube[2]
Indian Institute of Technology Madras, L3Cube[3]
chavantanmay1402@gmail.com, ogokhale3@gatech.edu, adityakane1@gmail.com, spatankar34@gatech.edu, ravirajoshi@gmail.com

## Abstract

The research on code-mixed data is limited due to the unavailability of dedicated code-mixed datasets and pre-trained language models. In this work, we focus on the low-resource Indian language Marathi which lacks any prior work in code-mixing. We present L3Cube-MeCorpus, a large code-mixed Marathi-English (Mr-En) corpus with 10 million social media sentences for pretraining. We also release L3Cube-MeBERT and MeRoBERTa, code-mixed BERT-based transformer models pre-trained on MeCorpus. Furthermore, for benchmarking, we present three supervised datasets MeHate, MeSent, and MeLID for downstream tasks like code-mixed Mr-En hate speech detection, sentiment analysis, and language identification respectively. These evaluation datasets individually consist of manually annotated ~12,000 Marathi-English code-mixed tweets. Ablations show that the models trained on this novel corpus significantly outperform the existing state-of-the-art BERT models. This is the first work that presents artifacts for code-mixed Marathi research. All datasets and models are publicly released at `https://github.com/l3cube-pune/MarathiNLP`.

## 1 Introduction

The modern world has been engulfed by the presence of social media platforms like Twitter and Facebook (Salem and Mourtada, 2011). Moreover, websites like YouTube have witnessed considerable user interaction in the comments section of videos (Siersdorfer et al., 2010). These posts and comments closely reflect the thoughts of the general public. It is common for users from different linguistic backgrounds to discuss social, political, and other topics over such social media. This leads to users using a mixed language for communicating over social media platforms.

Code-mixing is known as the mixing of words from multiple languages while retaining the script of a single language. The Latin script is often used to encapsulate the terms of some languages. For example, a given text can be of the Marathi language written in Latin script, as opposed to the Devanagari script, which is the original script of the Marathi language (Joshi, 2022a). Code-mixed data is inherently difficult to process and analyze due to its linguistic complexity, variance in spelling and grammar, and long-tailed distribution of uncommon terms and phrases, which are often specific to the geography and demographics of the source location. It is observed that a large number of tweets, comments, and posts on social media are code-mixed in nature. Thus, with the advent of social media analytics, effectively analyzing code-mixed data has gained the utmost importance.

Marathi is a language which has its origins in Maharashtra, a state in India. Due to the state's geographic and demographic expanse, Marathi has evolved into a language with multiple varieties and dialects. Recently, there has been some focus on Marathi NLP based on the Devanagari script (Joshi, 2022b,a; Kulkarni et al., 2021; Patil et al., 2022; Litake et al., 2022). However, a large chunk of tweets, posts, and comments in Marathi are in code-mixed form. In spite of this, no efforts have been made to curate models and datasets pertaining to Marathi code-mixed data in the past. This work presents the following.

1. We release three supervised datasets (L3Cube-MeHate, MeLID, and MeSent) and one unsupervised dataset (L3Cube-MeCorpus)[1]. The unsupervised corpus comprises 5 million (70.9M tokens) Roman script code-mixed Marathi-English samples compiled from various sources. We further include 5M Devanagari sentences based on original text making it a 10 million (139.5M tokens) mixed-script MeCorpus.

*First author, equal contribution

[1] MarathiNLP



*Findings of the Association for Computational Linguistics: IJCNLP-AACL 2023*, pages 242–249
November 1–4, 2023. ©2023 Asian Federation of Natural Language Processing

2. The supervised dataset contains labels for code-mixed Marathi-English (Roman script) hate classification, sentiment detection, and language identification. These datasets were manually annotated by native Marathi speakers.

3. Finally, we release a plethora of code-mixed MeBERT-based pre-trained and fine-tuned models for downstream tasks trained on these novel corpora. These models include MeBERT[2], MeBERT-Mixed[3], MeBERT-Mixed-v2[4], MeRoBERTa-Mixed[5], and MeRoBERTa[6]. The models suffixed as 'Mixed' were trained on full 10M MeCorpus while others were trained on 5M Roman MeCorpus. The supervised models include MeSent-RoBERTa[7], MeHate-RoBERTa[8], and MeLID-RoBERTa[9].

This work is a major milestone towards democratizing NLP for the Marathi language. Additionally, we present several ablations with fine-tuned models. This is the first work to present a large unsupervised corpus, multiple pre-trained models, and high-quality supervised datasets. This work is a strong foundation in the domain of Marathi and code-mixed Marathi NLP.

## 2 Related Works

The use of regional scripts, such as Devanagari, Gurmukhi, Bengali, etc., presents a significant challenge in India due to keyboards primarily designed for the Roman script and the population's familiarity with it. The demand for code-mix datasets and models tailored to regional languages has increased exponentially. These resources play a crucial role in enabling enhanced analysis and moderation of social media content that is code-mixed.

In the realm of language models, BERT-based architectures (Vaswani et al., 2017), including variations such as RoBERTa (Liu et al., 2019) and ALBERT (Lan et al., 2019), have gained popularity due to their application in pre-training and fine-tuning on various tasks. Multilingual models like multilingual-BERT, XLM-RoBERTa (Conneau et al., 2019), and MuRIL(Khanuja et al., 2021) have specifically focused on data representations that are multilingual and cross-lingual in nature, offering improvements in accuracy and latency. However, these models are pre-trained on less than a hundred thousand real code-mix texts.

While previous research efforts have addressed code mixing in other Indian languages, the specific domain of code-mix Marathi remains largely unexplored. Notably, there is a scarcity of prior work and an absence of a dedicated code-mix Marathi dataset. However, other Indian languages have seen some notable contributions. For instance, Hande et al. (2020) presents KanCMD a code-mixed Kannada dataset for sentiment analysis and offensive language detection. Chakravarthi et al. (2021) and have released datasets encompassing Tamil-English and Malayalam-English code-mixed texts. Nayak and Joshi (2022) have made available HingCorpus, a Hindi-English code-mix dataset, and also open-sourced pre-trained models trained on code-mix corpora. Srivastava and Singh (2021) provide HinGE, a dataset for the generation and evaluation of code-mixed Hinglish text, and demonstrate techniques for algorithmically creating synthetic Hindi code-mixed texts.

In the realm of transliteration, there have been attempts to pre-train language models using transliterated texts. However, these models often underperform due to the rule-based nature of most transliteration techniques, which struggle to account for the diverse spelling variations present in real-life code-mixed texts (Santy et al., 2021).

## 3 MeCorpus - Pretraining Data Creation

We introduce MeCorpus, a new pre-training corpus of 10 million code-mixed Marathi sentences. This consists of 5M Roman and 5M Devanagari sentences. These sentences are extracted from the social media platforms YouTube and Twitter. We also used synthetic data obtained by transliterating Tweets written in the Devanagari script. The complete data collection process is illustrated in Figure 1.

### 3.1 Twitter data

A part of the pretraining corpus is obtained from the social networking site Twitter. We utilize `snscrape`, a scraper for social networking sites

[2]MeBERT
[3]MeBERT-Mixed
[4]MeBERT-Mixed-v2
[5]MeRoBERT-Mixed
[6]MeRoBERTa
[7]MeSent-RoBERTa
[8]MeHate-RoBERTa
[9]MeLID-RoBERTa

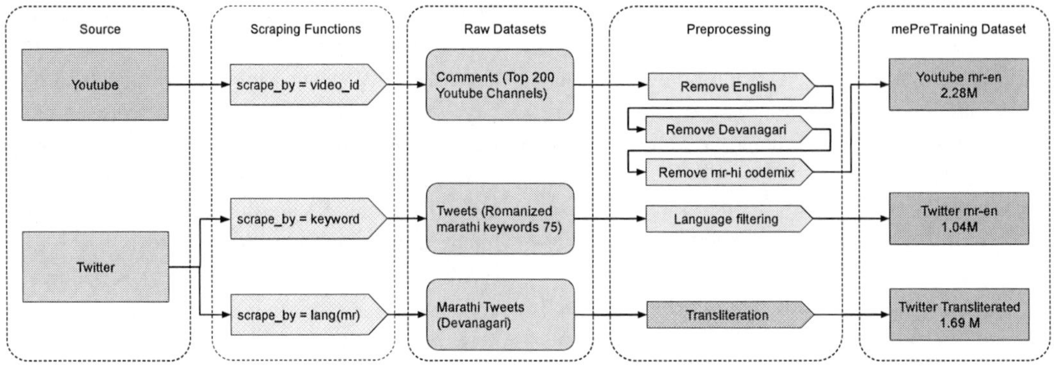


Figure 1: Dataset creation process for our 5 million code-mixed corpora. These 5 million examples are further transliterated to the Devanagari script, which results in a combined corpora of 10 million examples.

to scrape the data from Twitter. We use a keyword-based approach to curate the data. We use frequently used Marathi words as keywords and fetch all the tweets containing the given word. The list of seed keywords is generated by selecting a few common Marathi words and scraping tweets containing these words. Then we identify the most frequently occurring Marathi words in these tweets and add them to our list. The seed words are properly vetted before being added to the list. Proper care is taken to manually check that the word is predominantly exclusive to the Marathi language and doesn't occur in texts from other languages. We fetch a fixed number of tweets belonging to a certain keyword and discard the keyword if the tweets fail to satisfactorily meet the aforementioned conditions after manual verification. Otherwise, we scrape all the tweets containing the keyword and add them to our corpus. This manual verification process ensures that the curated data largely contains Marathi text.

The Twitter data amounts to over a million tweets. All of the tweets at least partly contain code-mixed Marathi. A significant number of the tweets exhibit code-switching between Marathi and English. A small portion of the tweets also contain code-switched Hindi-Marathi text. We anonymize the data before using it for pre-training. The username mentions are replaced with the '@USER' text. We also remove links and hashtags from the tweets. The Twitter corpus contains 50M tokens.

### 3.2 YouTube data

YouTube comments are an excellent source of Code-mixed Marathi data. We scrape all the comments from 200 Marathi YouTube channels using the `youtube-comments-scraper` library. This gave us a mix of English, Devanagari, and code-mixed Marathi sentences. We then removed the Devanagari and English comments to obtain the code-mixed Marathi data. This data was then preprocessed and used in our pre-training dataset. Devanagari words were identified and removed by checking their utf-8 encoding. We remove all comments that have more than 80% Devanagari words. This gives us comments that are either English or Marathi-English code-mixed. We used a fast text classifier to identify sentences that are English. We removed these sentences and were left with code-mixed Marathi sentences. Thus at the end of both filtering steps, we are left with 2,278,097 of the original 7,599,588 comments.

| Source | Number of Sentences |
|---|---|
| Twitter tweets | 1,037,659 |
| Youtube comments | 2,277,108 |
| Transliterated-tweets | 1,685,233 |
| **Total** | **5,000,000** |

Table 1: Source-wise split of the Roman script pretraining corpus (5M).

### 3.3 Transliteration

We scraped around 1.7 million Marathi Devanagari tweets from Twitter using the snscrape library. We then used the indic-trans Python library to transliterate 1,685,233 of these Devanagari tweets to Code-mixed Marathi and added them to our dataset.

## 4 Me Corpus - Transliteration

We created an additional 5 million Devanagari sentences and added them to the corpus. This was done by transliterating the Tweets and YouTube comments mentioned in sections 3.1 and 3.2 respectively to the Devanagari script. We also used the scraped Devanagari tweets mentioned in section 3.3. This gave us a total of 5M Devanagari sentences. These 5M sentences were used to pre-train the multilingual models mentioned in the future sections.

## 5 MeEval - Downstream dataset creation

We aim to create a large dataset of code-mix Marathi-English data, annotated with sentiment and hatefulness. In this study, we selected a set of tweets from a larger corpus of 1,037,659 tweets obtained from the social media platform Twitter. Half of the tweets chosen were posted on Twitter before 2013, and the other half were posted after 2013. This helped to provide a more diachronic distribution of tweets, as the number of tweets posted in the past few years far outnumber the old tweets. The tweets were selected randomly apart from this criteria. This ensures a realistic representation of the sentiment, hate, and profanity distributions present in the real-world data across the past several years. For data annotation, we selected four annotators who are proficient in Marathi, Hindi, and English languages. All four annotators are native Marathi speakers and hold undergraduate-level proficiency in English. Any discrepancies discovered within the dataset were systematically resolved through collaborative consensus among the annotators.

The collected data was labeled according to three distinct categories: sentiment, hate, and language identification. We followed a set of guidelines while labeling the data to ensure the veracity of the annotation. We annotated the data after anonymizing it. This helped remove any bias or knowledge of the entity posting it. We also disregarded any additional information that could be inferred by us based on external context but is not apparent by reading the text by itself. Here, we outline the dataset statistics and annotation procedure. The dataset statistics are described in Table 3. A few annotated examples are presented in Table 2.

### 5.1 MeSent Dataset

The code-mixed Marathi-English sentiment data is termed the MeSent Dataset. Tweets expressing good or heartening emotions such as thankfulness, happiness, applause, and appreciation are labeled positive. Tweets expressing negative or disheartening emotions like strong dissent, disappointment, sorrow, derision, and hate are labeled negative. Plain facts, statements, and simple responses are labeled neutral. If a tweet contains conflicting emotions, the stronger emotion is chosen.

- +1 indicating a *positive* sentiment,
- -1 indicating a *negative* sentiment, and
- 0 indicating a *neutral* sentiment.

While annotating the data, we removed unsuitable and ambiguous tweets. Finally, we selected 4,000 tweets from each sentiment category, leading to the dataset containing a total of 12,000 tweets.

### 5.2 MeHate Dataset

For the hatefulness annotation, we labeled any tweets expressing strongly negative feelings such as insults, mockery, abuse, intimidation, and threats as *hateful*. Any tweet not containing such hateful content is labeled as *non-hateful*. We use 1 for hateful content and 0 for non-hateful content. The MeHate dataset contains 1384 hateful and 1384 non-hateful tweets, totaling 2768 tweets. We also release the full 12k labeled tweets with the majority of non-hate labels.

### 5.3 MeLID dataset

Additionally, a Language Identification (LID) dataset is created. Each word within the selected tweets is labeled based on its language as *Marathi*, *English*, or *Other*. The *Other* category contains invalid words, words from languages other than English or Marathi, and literals such as numbers and proper nouns. The MeLID dataset contains 11,814 tweets. For all three supervised datasets, we provide a pre-defined train, test, and validation split of 80:10:10.

## 6 Models trained on code-mixed MeCorpus

We train several well-known models on our novel pretraining corpora. In this section, we outline these models and their training details.

We used pre-trained BERT, RoBERTa, mBERT, MuRIL, and XLM Roberta as the base models and trained them on the novel MeCorpus using the Masked Language Modelling (MLM) objective. For MLM training, we train the models for two

| Example Text | Hate (MeHate Dataset) | Sentiment (MeSent Dataset) | LID (MeLID Dataset) |
|---|---|---|---|
| Good morning sir mast tumhala bhetayche ahe | 0 (Non-hateful) | 1 (Positive) | ["Good" : ENG, "morning" : ENG, "sir" : ENG, "mast" : MAR, "tumhala" : MAR, "bhetayche" : MAR, "ahe" : MAR ] |
| nalayak jalavu nakos amhala | 1 (Hateful) | -1 (Negative) | ["nalayak" : MAR, "jalavu" : MAR, "nakos" : MAR, "amhala" : MAR ] |
| Ssc cha decision lavkar ghya | 0 (Non-hateful) | 0 (Neutral) | ["Ssc" : OTH, "cha" : MAR, "decision" : ENG, "lavkar" : MAR, "ghya" : MAR ] |

Figure 2: Table containing code-mixed examples with their annotations.

epochs at a learning rate of $2e - 5$, with a weight decay of $0.01$ and a mask probability of $0.15$.

The monolingual models were pre-trained on the Roman 5M codemixed data mentioned in section 3. While the multilingual models were trained on the full 10M corpus (5M Roman + 5M Devanagari sentences) mentioned in section 4. The models pre-trained on mixed-script corpus are suffixed as 'Mixed'.

The resulting models were named similarly to the original models, prefixed with "**me**", which stands for **M**arathi-**E**nglish. Therefore, the models MeBERT, MeBERT-Mixed, MeBERT-Mixed-v2, MeRoBERTa-Mixed, and MeRoBERTa are the BERT, mBERT, MuRIL, XLM-RoBERTa, and RoBERTa models trained on the MeCorpus respectively. Note that these models are further "fine-tuned" on the MeCorpus using the MLM training objective.

## 7 Results

We fine-tune our MeBERT models on the MeSent, MeHate, and MeLID datasets as mentioned in section 5 and test them on the respective test data. The same process is repeated for their base models and a few state-of-the-art Marathi models like Indic-BERT (Kakwani et al., 2020), Marathi-Tweets-BERT (Gokhale et al., 2022), and Marathi Code-mixed Abusive MuRIL (Das et al., 2022). The results obtained from this are showcased in Table 2. It is observed that MeBERT-Mixed-v2 outperforms all other models on the MeHate evaluation set with an F1 score of 78.3%. For the sentiment analysis corpus MeSent, MeRoBERTa outperforms the others by obtaining an F1 score of 67.27%. Testing the models on the MeLID dataset, MeBERT-Mixed-v2 outperforms the other models by obtaining an F1 score of 88.6%. The newly pre-trained code-mixed MeBERT-based models consistently outperform their base models as well as the state-of-the-art Marathi models.

| Model | MeHate | MeSent | MeLID |
|---|---|---|---|
| Indic-BERT | 61.62 | 55.29 | 87.37 |
| MahaTweets-BERT | 63.18 | 57.59 | 87.38 |
| Abusive-MuRIL | 67.69 | - | - |
| BERT | 61.98 | 59.06 | 87.89 |
| MeBERT | 73.78 | 61.92 | 88.01 |
| mBERT | 66.80 | 60.25 | 87.64 |
| MeBERT-Mixed | 77.39 | 65.73 | 88.25 |
| MuRIL | 67.93 | 63.38 | 87.55 |
| MeBERT-Mixed-v2 | **78.3** | 64.23 | **88.6** |
| XLM-RoBERTa | 64.66 | 61.06 | 87.54 |
| MeRoBERTa-Mixed | 78.07 | 67.17 | 87.42 |
| RoBERTa | 66.10 | 58.86 | 86.46 |
| MeRoBERTa | 77.85 | **67.27** | 88.41 |

Table 2: Macro F1 scores (in %) of models on the MeHate, MeSent, and MeLID datasets.

## 8 Conclusion

This work lays the necessary groundwork for future work on code-mixed Marathi. We introduce a novel pretraining corpus of 5 million code-mixed text examples. In addition to that, we present five new models trained on this code-mixed corpus. Furthermore, we present three supervised datasets of 12,000 tweets for hate classification, sentiment analysis, and language identification annotated by native Marathi speakers. We also present thorough ablations and show that our code-mixed MeBERT models outperform the previous state-of-the-art models by a considerable margin.

## Limitations

A major problem while dealing with Romanized Marathi is the lack of a singular correct spelling of words. A Marathi word can be written in several ways in Marathi, all of which are equally valid and correctly convey meaning despite having significantly different spellings. Developing efficient approaches to tackle this issue will lead to a significant increase in performance on NLP tasks dealing with code-mixed languages. Our keyword-based scraping method uses words primarily from the western Maharashtra dialect of Marathi, which might not sufficiently represent samples from other Marathi dialects. Efforts to increase the dataset to include examples from other dialects will make the dataset more diverse and robust.

## Ethics Statement

All of the data used in our experiments has been scraped by legal and valid means, adhering to the provided guidelines. We anonymized the data before usage to protect the privacy of the original authors of the data. This data might contain biases and thus must be used with care. This data also contains strong language which might be unsuitable for some applications. This data should be used only for research purposes and not for training any model for deployment.

## Acknowledgments

This work was done under the L3Cube Pune mentorship program. We would like to express our gratitude towards our mentors at L3Cube for their continuous support and encouragement. This work is a part of the L3Cube-MahaNLP project (Joshi, 2022b).

## References

Bharathi Raja Chakravarthi, Prasanna Kumar Kumaresan, Ratnasingam Sakuntharaj, Anand Kumar Madasamy, Sajeetha Thavareesan, Premjith B, Subalalitha Chinnaudayar Navaneethakrishnan, John P. McCrae, and Thomas Mandl. 2021. Overview of the HASOC-DravidianCodeMix Shared Task on Offensive Language Detection in Tamil and Malayalam. In *Working Notes of FIRE 2021 - Forum for Information Retrieval Evaluation*. CEUR.

Alexis Conneau, Kartikay Khandelwal, Naman Goyal, Vishrav Chaudhary, Guillaume Wenzek, Francisco Guzmán, Edouard Grave, Myle Ott, Luke Zettlemoyer, and Veselin Stoyanov. 2019. Unsupervised cross-lingual representation learning at scale. *arXiv preprint arXiv:1911.02116*.

Mithun Das, Somnath Banerjee, and Animesh Mukherjee. 2022. Data bootstrapping approaches to improve low resource abusive language detection for indic languages. In *Proceedings of the 33rd ACM Conference on Hypertext and Social Media*, pages 32–42.

Omkar Gokhale, Aditya Kane, Tanmay Chavan, Shantanu Patankar, and Raviraj Joshi. 2022. Spread love not hate: Undermining the importance of hateful pre-training for hate speech detection. *arXiv preprint arXiv:2210.04267*.

Adeep Hande, Ruba Priyadharshini, and Bharathi Raja Chakravarthi. 2020. Kancmd: Kannada codemixed dataset for sentiment analysis and offensive language detection. In *Proceedings of the Third Workshop on Computational Modeling of People's Opinions, Personality, and Emotion's in Social Media*, pages 54–63.

Raviraj Joshi. 2022a. L3cube-mahacorpus and mahabert: Marathi monolingual corpus, marathi bert language models, and resources. In *Proceedings of the WILDRE-6 Workshop within the 13th Language Resources and Evaluation Conference*, pages 97–101.

Raviraj Joshi. 2022b. L3cube-mahanlp: Marathi natural language processing datasets, models, and library. *arXiv preprint arXiv:2205.14728*.

Divyanshu Kakwani, Anoop Kunchukuttan, Satish Golla, NC Gokul, Avik Bhattacharyya, Mitesh M Khapra, and Pratyush Kumar. 2020. Indicnlpsuite: Monolingual corpora, evaluation benchmarks and pre-trained multilingual language models for indian languages. In *Findings of the Association for Computational Linguistics: EMNLP 2020*, pages 4948–4961.

Simran Khanuja, Diksha Bansal, Sarvesh Mehtani, Savya Khosla, Atreyee Dey, Balaji Gopalan, Dilip Kumar Margam, Pooja Aggarwal, Rajiv Teja Nagipogu, Shachi Dave, Shruti Gupta, Subhash Chandra Bose Gali, Vish Subramanian, and Partha Talukdar. 2021. Muril: Multilingual representations for indian languages.

Atharva Kulkarni, Meet Mandhane, Manali Likhitkar, Gayatri Kshirsagar, and Raviraj Joshi. 2021. L3cubemahasent: A marathi tweet-based sentiment analysis dataset. In *Proceedings of the Eleventh Workshop on Computational Approaches to Subjectivity, Sentiment and Social Media Analysis*, pages 213–220.

Zhenzhong Lan, Mingda Chen, Sebastian Goodman, Kevin Gimpel, Piyush Sharma, and Radu Soricut. 2019. Albert: A lite bert for self-supervised learning of language representations. *arXiv preprint arXiv:1909.11942*.

Onkar Litake, Maithili Ravindra Sabane, Parth Sachin Patil, Aparna Abhijeet Ranade, and Raviraj Joshi. 2022. L3cube-mahaner: A marathi named entity recognition dataset and bert models. In *Proceedings of the WILDRE-6 Workshop within the 13th Language Resources and Evaluation Conference*, pages 29–34.

Yinhan Liu, Myle Ott, Naman Goyal, Jingfei Du, Mandar Joshi, Danqi Chen, Omer Levy, Mike Lewis, Luke Zettlemoyer, and Veselin Stoyanov. 2019. Roberta: A robustly optimized bert pretraining approach. *arXiv preprint arXiv:1907.11692*.

Ravindra Nayak and Raviraj Joshi. 2022. L3cube-hingcorpus and hingbert: A code mixed hindi-english dataset and bert language models. *arXiv preprint arXiv:2204.08398*.

Hrushikesh Patil, Abhishek Velankar, and Raviraj Joshi. 2022. L3cube-mahahate: A tweet-based marathi hate speech detection dataset and bert models. In *Proceedings of the Third Workshop on Threat, Aggression and Cyberbullying (TRAC 2022)*, pages 1–9.

Fadi Salem and Racha Mourtada. 2011. Civil movements: The impact of facebook and twitter. *Arab Social Media Report*, 1.

Sebastin Santy, Anirudh Srinivasan, and Monojit Choudhury. 2021. BERTologiCoMix: How does code-mixing interact with multilingual BERT? In *Proceedings of the Second Workshop on Domain Adaptation for NLP*, pages 111–121, Kyiv, Ukraine. Association for Computational Linguistics.

Stefan Siersdorfer, Sergiu Chelaru, Wolfgang Nejdl, and Jose San Pedro. 2010. How useful are your comments? analyzing and predicting youtube comments and comment ratings. pages 891–900.

Vivek Srivastava and Mayank Singh. 2021. Hinge: A dataset for generation and evaluation of code-mixed hinglish text. In *Proceedings of the 2nd Workshop on Evaluation and Comparison of NLP Systems*, pages 200–208.

Ashish Vaswani, Noam Shazeer, Niki Parmar, Jakob Uszkoreit, Llion Jones, Aidan N Gomez, Łukasz Kaiser, and Illia Polosukhin. 2017. Attention is all you need. *Advances in neural information processing systems*, 30.

# A Appendix

| Dataset | Sample Count | Average word count | Labels | Count per label |
|---|---|---|---|---|
| **MeLID** | 11,813 | 12 | Marathi | 99,230 |
| | | | English | 26,290 |
| | | | Other | 10,870 |
| **MeSent** | 12,000 | 16 | Positive | 4,000 |
| | | | Neutral | 4,000 |
| | | | Negative | 4,000 |
| **MeHate** | 2,768 | 17 | Non Hate | 1,384 |
| | | | Hate | 1,384 |

Table 3: Statistics for benchmark datasets

# Template Filling for Controllable Commonsense Reasoning

**Dheeraj Rajagopal[♠], Vivek Khetan[♣], Bogdan Sacaleanu[♣],**
**Anatole Gershman[♠] Andrew Fano[♣], Eduard Hovy[♠]**
[♠] Language Technologies Institute, Carnegie Mellon University, Pittsburgh, PA, USA
[♣] Accenture Labs, San Francisco, USA
{dheeraj, anatoleg, hovy}@cs.cmu.edu
{vivek.a.khetan, andrew.e.fano, bogdan.e.sacaleanu}@accenture.com

## Abstract

Large-scale sequence-to-sequence models have shown to be adept at both multiple-choice and open-domain commonsense reasoning tasks. However, the current formulations do not provide the ability to control the various attributes of the reasoning chain. To enable better controllability, we propose to study the *commonsense reasoning as a template filling task* (TemplateCSR) — where the language models fills reasoning templates with the given constraints as control factors. As an approach to TemplateCSR, we (i) propose a dataset of commonsense reasoning template-expansion pairs for *healthcare and well-being* domain and (ii) introduce `ITO`, an instruction fine-tuned sequence-to-sequence model that performs commonsense reasoning across concepts in the template. Our experiments show that our approach outperforms baseline both in generation metrics and factuality metrics. We also present a detailed error analysis on our approach's ability to reliably perform template based commonsense reasoning[1].

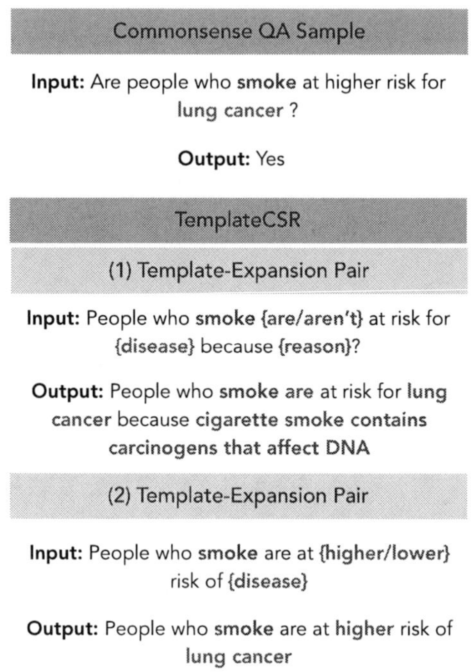


Figure 1: In this example, we show how a commonsense reasoning question can be formulated as two different template-expansion pairs, each focusing on different aspects of reasoning between the concepts *smoking* and *lung cancer*. While formulation (1) focuses on the explanation, (2) aims to understand the qualitative relationship between them.

## 1 Introduction

Commonsense reasoning has been studied across both *multiple choice* (Tandon et al., 2018; Talmor et al., 2019; Lv et al., 2020), and *open-ended knowledge base* settings (Lin et al., 2021a). While multiple choice approaches require a list of answer options, open-ended KB approaches assume that the answer exists in an available knowledge base (KB). Such constraints often limit these systems' ability in practical applications where control is required (e.g. a web search query with specific conditions).

To complement the existing commonsense reasoning efforts, our work aims to enhance the commonsense reasoning capabilities of natural language processing (NLP) systems by studying **template commonsense reasoning** (TemplateCSR) — where reasoning is achieved by filling templates with restricted template slots, rather than selecting answers from a list of candidates or KB. TemplateCSR task is challenging as there are no available annotations and potentially multiple correct expansions for each template. Moreover, the task of designing templates with slots that satisfy arbitrary constrains and their expansion is still an open challenge. For example, for an example reasoning template **People who smoke are at a risk of `{disease}`** , a system needs to first constrain the slot to only *diseases*, and then use the addi-

[1]All code and data will be released publicly



*Findings of the Association for Computational Linguistics: IJCNLP-AACL 2023*, pages 250–260
November 1–4, 2023. ©2023 Asian Federation of Natural Language Processing

tional constraint of *smoking* to arrive at the right answer in the slot. In comparison to Language Model (LM) probing approaches (Ribeiro et al., 2020) that test capabilities of LM that are already trained, we aim to propose a task and train a model for TemplateCSR task.

Figure 1 shows one such example from the *healthcare and well-being* domain, where we show how an existing commonsense reasoning query can be formulated as different template-expansion pairs with control over different aspects of the reasoning. In the first expansion, the reasoning chain focuses on the relationship between *smoking* and *cancer* with the corresponding explanation (`reason`), while the second chain solely focuses on the qualitative relationship between the *smoking* and *cancer*.

To address the above mentioned challenges, our contributions in this paper for TemplateCSR are two-fold. First, we present a dataset of commonsense reasoning templates for the *healthcare and well-being* domain and their corresponding expansions that are valid completions of the template, which we define as template-expansion pairs (Fass and Wilks, 1983). The slots in the templates are open-ended and are not restricted to any particular categories and enable controlling the reasoning chain. Given the recent focus on explainable models for reasoning (Wiegreffe and Marasović, 2021), we also augment templates with an optional free-form explanation slot that explains the reasoning connection between various commonsense concepts. Our TemplateCSR dataset comprises of about 3600 unique template-expansion pairs collected from diverse sources, and we hope to enable SEQ-TO-SEQ systems to effectively learn to fill commonsense reasoning templates.

Next, we present `ITO`, a model that formulates the TemplateCSR challenge as a SEQ-TO-SEQ task where given a template with slots for specific concepts, the goal of the model is to produce meaningful completed sentences for the template. The concept in each slot in the template is provided via an *instruction* (Wei et al., 2022a), which indicates an abstraction of the nature of the slot. The multiple choice *qualifier* slot is used to model the relationship between the concepts and the *explanation* slot generates a free-form text explanation for the reasoning chain. Specifying each slots in free-form text enables control allowing commonsense reasoning questions to specify concepts, the qualitative relationship and the nature of explanation.

In our experiments for the TemplateCSR task, `ITO` outperforms baseline both in terms of generation metrics such as `ROUGE` and `BERTSCORE`, and factual correctness (factuality) metrics such as `FACTCC`. We also evaluate the factuality of the dataset using expert human judges and present a detailed analysis of model failures. While we still observe factual errors, our approach provides deeper understanding of the mistakes, enabling alternate ways to build commonsense reasoning systems via templates using SEQ-TO-SEQ models.

## 2 Dataset

For our use-case, we create dataset samples of commonsense reasoning templates related to *healthcare and well-being*. Incorporating NLP systems for aiding healthy lifestyle has been an active area of research in the past decade (Liberato et al., 2014; Fadhil and Gabrielli, 2017; Doustmohammadian and Bazhan, 2021; Ahne et al., 2022). Inspired by this line of research, we want to collect templates that describe a relation between lifestyle related commonsense concept and a corresponding health related concept. In comparison to existing datasets like *commonsenseqa* (Talmor et al., 2019) which relies on fixed set of relationships from a knowledge-base (Speer and Havasi, 2013), we do not restrict the relationship types or number of concepts or hops, making it close to open-vocabulary text. We believe that our dataset augments well with the existing commonsense reasoning datasets in the community, contributing to the diversity of the data.

Based on the efficacy assessment for NLP systems in health and lifestyle related settings (Laranjo et al., 2018; Abd-alrazaq et al., 2020; Hoermann et al., 2017), we designed our basic template structure. Our basic units for the TemplateCSR task is as follows:

1. *concept slot* : contains an abstract category of a concept. The concept's abstraction is provided in a natural language format in open-vocabulary, without fixed class constraints. In the example shown in figure 2, *people with habit* and *disease* are concept slots.

2. *multiple-choice qualifier slot* : a word or phrase that describes the nature of the relationship between the concepts. This slot

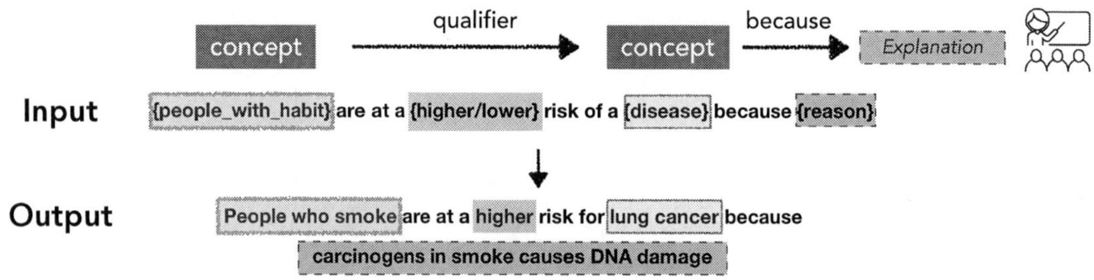


Figure 2: An overview of the overall template structure for our approach. Our goal is to reason across concepts for TemplateCSR. In this example template, concept slots are *people_with_habit* and *disease*, and the multiple choice qualifier slot - *higher/lower* describes their relationship and an explanation *reason* slot aims to get a free-form text explanation for how they are related.

is typically framed as a multiple-choice slot, where the goal is to pick an option from the choices rather than replacing the text in the template slot. Figure 2 shows an example where the slot *higher/lower* is one such multiple-choice qualifier slot.

3. *explanation slot* : this optional field consists of a free-form explanation that explains the reasoning between concepts, typically marked as *reason* slot.

Towards this, we collect a set of template ($x$) and its corresponding expansions ($y$) based on this overall schema for commonsense reasoning. In the example shown in figure 2, the template comprises of two concept slots, (*people with habit* and *disease*). The qualifier slot (*higher/lower*) specifies how one concept is connected to another concept in terms of their qualitative relationship. The template also includes an optional *explanation* slot that specifies in free-form text how smoking is connected to cancer. A valid output for the above-mentioned template is for instance, *people who smoke are at a higher risk for lung cancer because carcinogens in smoke causes DNA damage*, where *people with habit* is replaced by *people who smoke*, and the multiple choice qualifier slot *higher/lower* is replaced by *higher*, and *disease* slot replaced by *lung cancer* and finally the *reason* slot replaced by explanation of the qualitative relationship *carcinogens in smoke causes DNA damage*. In this example, we show how both the template-expansion pairs aim to uncover the relationship between *smoke* and *lung cancer*, while also providing the flexibility to additionally constrain the reasoning chain in any way.

**Task Setup :** To collect our dataset using crowdsourcing, we use amazon mechanical turk platform [2]. Each datapoint took $\sim$120 seconds to annotate, and we paid an average of \$15 per hour. Additionally, we used a filtering step to select master annotators with an approval rate of more than 90%. All the turkers were given specific instructions to input only factual information and not opinionated statements. Specifically, the turkers were instructed to use the following sources: *CDC*[3], *WebMD*[4], *Healthline*[5] and *Mayo Clinic*[6]. The annotators were also instructed to give a template, and at least two corresponding sentences that matches the template. The statistics of the data are as follows: the average sentence length was about *14.57* words, with mean 2.4 slots per template. Some qualitative examples from the dataset are given in the table 1. Overall, our dataset contains about 7000 template-sentence pairs with about 3600 unique templates. Once the templates are collected, the authors post-process the data to verify each template-expansion pair for correctness and validate that we do not have any identifying information like proper names. We then create a standard 70/10/20 train/val/test split.

## 3 Model

Early NLP systems have often relied on rule-based templatic systems (Riloff, 1996; Brin, 1998; Agichtein and Gravano, 1999; Craven et al., 2000) due to their simplistic nature. Compared to machine learning methods, they were often rigid (Yih, 1997). Despite their rigidity, template based

[2] https://www.mturk.com/
[3] https://www.cdc.gov/
[4] https://www.webmd.com/
[5] https://www.healthline.com/
[6] https://www.mayoclinic.org/

| Concepts | Template Expansion Pairs | |
|---|---|---|
| | Sample Template | Valid Expansions for the Template |
| location, disease | {person_at_location} has a {higher/lower} risk of {disease} because {reason_for_risk} | Person who lives in a city has a higher risk<br>- of depression because of stress due to noise<br>Person who lives near a village has a lower risk<br>- of respiratory illness because of lower pollution |
| prescription medication, disease | {person_taking_prescription} has a higher risk of {disease} due to {reason} | Someone on steroids have a higher risk for heart disease<br>- because steroids compromise heart pumping<br>People on insulin have a lower risk of hyperglycemia<br>- because of lower glucose levels. |
| food item, substitute item | {food_item_1} should not be consumed with {food_item_2} because {reason} | Steak should not be consumed with mashed potatoes<br>- because pairing fried foods increases the risk of diabetes.<br>Pizza should not be consumed with French fries because<br>- proteins require a much different stomach<br>- environment than starches for proper digestion |
| behavior change, medical condition | A change in behavior such as {behavior_change} is often associated with {a_medical_condition} because {reason_for_condition} | A change in behavior such as becoming more sedentary is<br>- often associated with obesity<br>- because less activity leads to less calorie burning.<br>A change in behavior such as no longer drinking coffee<br>- is often associated with diminished insomnia<br>- because less caffeine equals improved sleep. |
| symptom, medical condition, everyday action | When severe symptoms like {a_symptom} for a {a_medical_condition} shows up, immediately one should perform {an_action} | When severe symptoms like confusion or disorientation<br>- for heatstroke show up, immediately, one should perform<br>- cooling actions, such as applying cooling towels.<br>When severe symptoms like unconsciousness for a<br>- heart attack show up, immediately one should<br>- call 911 and perform CPR while awaiting help. |
| lifestyle activity, disease | People often do {an_activity} before going to bed in night to prevent risk of {disease}. This is because {reason_for_activity} | People often do reading before going to bed in night<br>- to prevent risk of insomnia. This is because<br>- doing some light reading helps lull you to sleep.<br>People often do teeth brushing before going to bed in night<br>- to prevent risk of tooth decay. This is because<br>- brushing removes cavity-causing plaque from teeth. |

Table 1: Examples from our dataset. Each template has two corresponding sentences. [concept] is a concept, and [text] represents the explanation and [text] represents a qualifier. We show two sentences each for a template. Each template slot is given in free-form text without any restriction in vocabulary.

systems are often easy to comprehend, and lend themselves to easily incorporate domain knowledge (Chiticariu et al., 2013). Our goal is to combine the strengths of both template-based systems and recent advances in pretrained SEQ-TO-SEQ models for the task of commonsense reasoning via template expansion.

In this work, we present ITO (**I**nstruction Fine-tuning for **T**emplate Based C**o**mmonsense Reasoning), an approach that models the TemplateCSR task as a instruction fine-tuning task inspired by the recent advances in instruction based fine-tuning (Wei et al., 2022a).

Table 2 shows an example of our task setup for our ITO approach. In comparison to approaches such as Donahue et al. (2020), our approach does not strictly enforce that sentences only fill missing spans of text. Rather, the expanded sentences are allowed to have additional modifications (token addition, deletion and rewrite). For instance, for the following input template - {person_at_location} has a {higher/lower} risk of {disease} because {reason_for_risk}, a valid expansion is *person who lives in the city has a higher risk of depression due to noise.*

### 3.1 Training

Given a template $x \in \mathcal{X}$ and its corresponding expansion $y \in \mathcal{Y}$, we can train any sequence-to-sequence model that models $p_\theta(y|x)$. Towards this, we use a pretrained sequence-to-sequence model $\mathcal{M}$ to estimate the filled template $y$ for an input $x$. We model the conditional distribution

| Input (Template) | Output (Expansion) |
|---|---|
| The first blank is `person_at_location`.<br>The second blank is `higher/lower`.<br>The third blank is `disease`.<br>The fourth blank is a `reason_for_risk`.<br>`[MASK]` has a `[MASK]` risk of<br>`[MASK]` because `[MASK]` | Person who lives in a city<br>has a higher risk of depression<br>because of higher stress due to noise |

Table 2: Overview of ITO approach for TemplateCSR. Each concept category is given as a instruction to the input and the slots are represented via the [MASK] token. The instruction describes each slot's abstraction and the task is to generate the *output*.

$p_\theta(y \mid x)$ parameterized by $\theta$ as

$$p_\theta(y \mid x) = \prod_{k=1}^{M} p_\theta(y^k \mid x, y^1, .., y^{k-1})$$

where $M$ is the length of $y$.

### 3.2 Inference to Decode Template Expansions

The auto-regressive factorization of SEQ-TO-SEQ $p_\theta$ allows us to effectively cast the constrained decoding of filling the template as generating the sequence given the input $x$. For each expansion, we sample $y_j^1 \sim p_\theta(y \mid \mathbf{x}_j)$. Consequently, we sample $y_j^2 \sim p_\theta(y \mid \mathbf{x}_j, y_j^1)$, and the token generation process is repeated until we reach the end-symbol. For each symbol, the model has to decide between generating a token to replace the template slot or generate part of the template, while also ensuring the overall generated output sequence is consistent with the constraints given in the template.

## 4 Experiments

In this section, we describe the experimental setup, and baselines for our approach. Since our ITO approach is agnostic to the pretrained encoder-decoder architecture type, we perform experiments on two state-of-the-art SEQ-TO-SEQ models - BART and T5.

### 4.1 Experimental Setup

**Metrics** : We use the following evaluation metrics for evaluation for the TemplateCSR task: (i) ROUGE (Lin, 2004) and (ii) BERTSCORE (Zhang et al., 2019). N-gram metrics such as ROUGE are known to be limited, specifically for reasoning tasks. To mitigate this, we use BERTSCORE, which uses the similarity score between the reference and generated output using conceptual embeddings from BERT (Devlin et al., 2019) model, which correlates better towards human judgements.

To perform the evaluation, we compare the generated sentence for the template against the gold annotations in the dataset. We remove the template words from the output and only compare the slot filler concepts to avoid score inflation due to copying. All the experiments were performed on a cluster of 8 NVIDIA V100 GPUs for about 32 GPU hours.

### 4.2 Models

We follow the same experimental settings across the baseline and our approach for all the models. We initialize all the models with their pretrained weights. We use commonly used encoder-decoder architectures for our experiments - BART-BASE, BART-LARGE, T5-BASE and T5-LARGE. The model settings are given in below:

(i) BART-BASE: This pretrained encoder-decoder transformer architecture is based on Lewis et al. (2020). It consists of 12 transformer layers each with 768 hidden size, 16 attention heads and overall with 139M params. (ii) BART-LARGE: Larger version of BART-BASE, with 24 transformer layers, 1024 hidden size, 16 heads and 406M params. (iii) T5-BASE: The T5 model is also a transformer encoder-decoder model based on Raffel et al. (2020) with 220M parameters with 12-layers each with 768 hidden-state, 3072 feed-forward hidden-state and 12 attention heads. (iv) T5-LARGE: T5-Large model version comprises of 770M parameters with 24-layers with 1024 hidden-state, 4096 feed-forward hidden-state and 16 attention heads [7].

| Model | Type | ROUGE-1 | ROUGE-2 | ROUGE-L | BERTSCORE |
|---|---|---|---|---|---|
| T5-BASE | SPL TOKEN | 14.00 | 2.71 | 12.58 | 2.2 |
| T5-BASE | ITO | 14.01 | 2.60 | 12.57 | 6.1 |
| T5-LARGE | SPL TOKEN | 13.74 | 3.11 | 13.74 | 4.8 |
| T5-LARGE | ITO | 16.74 | 4.33 | 15.37 | 6.7 |
| BART-BASE | SPL TOKEN | 17.17 | 5.60 | 16.32 | 3.9 |
| BART-BASE | ITO | 18.89 | 5.87 | 17.96 | 6.3 |
| BART-LARGE | SPL TOKEN | 19.54 | 7.57 | 18.49 | 7.0 |
| BART-LARGE | ITO | 20.58 | 7.32 | 19.58 | 7.6 |

Table 3: Overview of the results compared to baselines. The table shows that BART-BASE performs better than T5-BASE model and BART-LARGE outperforms both. Both in terms of ROUGE and BERTSCORE, we also observe that our INSTRUCTION approach outperforms SPL TOKEN approach. All experiments were done with 5 seeds, and reported are the average.

| Baseline | Template | Output |
|---|---|---|
| SPL TOKEN (Donahue et al., 2020) | [S]person_at_location[/S] has a [S]higher/lower[/S] risk of [S]disease[/S] because [S]reason_for_risk[/S] | Person who lives in a city has a higher risk of depression because of stress due to noise |

Table 4: Baseline Setup: We use Donahue et al. (2020) and use special tokens to indicate the start and end of each slot. The model is trained to predict the output, which is a valid expansion for the template.

### 4.3 Baseline Method

SPL TOKEN: In this approach, we use the special token approach (SPL TOKEN) (Donahue et al., 2020), where we indicate the start and end of each template slot in the input and generate the output sentence. Table 4 shows the baseline setup.

### 4.4 Results

The results across various pretrained encoder-decoder approaches are shown in table 3. In this table, we see that on average, BART models perform better than T5 models on average. We hypothesize this might be an effect of their pretraining task choices and corresponding datasets. We also observe that INSTRUCTION based models outperform the SPL TOKEN based approach. For all of the models and baselines, we used the greedy decoding strategy. Across all the experiments, we found that the ITO approach outperforms SPL TOKEN approach across both ROUGE and BERTSCORE scores for all models.

[7]Implementation adapted from Huggingface (Wolf et al., 2020)

## 5 Factual Correctness Evaluation

**Expert Evaluation of Dataset :** Since our dataset contains health related commonsense knowledge, we additionally verified our data from domain experts. In our case, we selected a subset of 100 data samples from our validation set, and we verified the factual claims by recruiting two annotators with a Doctor of Medicine (M.D.) degree [8]. Each expert annotator labeled either *correct* or *incorrect* for a template-expansion pair. Overall, they found an average of 70% of the samples to be factually correct with an inter-annotator agreement of 80%.

**Model Output Evaluation :** To assess the quality of generated output, we perform additional factuality evaluation towards our best performing models - SPL TOKEN and ITO approach using BART-LARGE. Towards this we use the FACTCC factuality metric (Kryscinski et al., 2020), which uses entailment classification to predict a binary factuality label between the source document and generated output.

Computing factuality using FACTCC metric requires an input source document; (i.e.) the gener-

[8]https://www.upwork.com/

| Model | Type | FACTCC |
|---|---|---|
| BART-LARGE | SPL TOKEN | 65.27 |
| BART-LARGE | ITO | 79.88 |

Table 5: Factual consistency results. In this experiment, we show that our ITO approach outperforms the SPL TOKEN approach in terms of factuality metric FACTCC, showing its relative effectiveness

ated output is compared against the source document for factual correctness. For this evaluation setup, we augmented each generated output $y$ with a source document. Towards this, we use a large scale retrieval corpus based on Nguyen et al. (2016), and retrieve the top similar document $D$ (Lin et al., 2021b) to a generated template expansion. Using the $(D, y)$ pairs, we compute the factual correctness of our best performing models. From the table 5, we observe that our ITO approach outperforms the SPL TOKEN approach for factual correctness by ~14 points in accuracy.

Additionally, we also perform human evaluation of factual correctness. For this experiment, three human judges annotated 100 unique samples for *correctness* - that indicates how many samples were correct from a human perspective. We used our best performing BART-BASE-ITO model for this evaluation. In this experiment, a sentence generated by the model for a given template was given to each human judge and they were asked to evaluate whether the sentence was correct, given the template. The inter-annotator agreement on sentence expansion correctness was substantial with a Fleiss' Kappa score (Fleiss and Cohen, 1973) of 0.73. From our evaluation, we found that human judges rated about 69% of the sentences to be correct given a template, comparable to our FACTCC evaluation metric numbers. Both the automated and human evaluation suggests that our ITO approach has better factual consistency.

## 6 Error Analysis

In this section, we analyze in detail how well language models perform template-expansion task for multihop reasoning. To understand the errors in depth, we complement our automated evaluation with manual error analysis. For this analysis, we randomly select 100 samples from the validation set predictions where the ROUGE scores were low. We observe the following categories of errors that language models exhibit. Table 6 shows the common type of errors and a corresponding example for each type.

**Error Type - Correct but not in gold (17%) :** In several cases, we observe that the output produced by the language models are correct despite not matching the gold answer. This phenomenon is evident when the input template contains multiple possible answers. While the gold answer in the example shown in Table 6 (first row) fills the template using `smoking`, the model generates an answer related to `kidney damage`. While correct, the automated generation metrics such as ROUGE and BERTSCORE score such answers lower.

**Error Type - Wrong commonsense concept (8%) :** In this category of error, the model generates the wrong specification for the given slot. For instance (second row in table 6), the model mistakenly assumes `person taking less medication` as a `socioeconomic condition`. This error type gives a more nuanced understanding on which concept categories the model makes the most mistakes.

**Error Type - Generic Explanation (53%):** In several cases, the model resorts to generic explanation that are *obvious*. A generic explanation repeats the same information as the rest of sentence as an explanation, thereby not providing any new information compared to the rest of the sentence. In the example shown in Table 6 (row 3), the explanation `because of the strain of the heart` is already clear from the concept `chest pain`. A generic explanation is often unreliable in explainable NLP systems since it does not provide any insight into the reasoning capability of the model (Ye and Durrett, 2022).

**Error Type - Factually Incorrect (22%) :** Factual correctness is one of the biggest challenges in NLP applications (Petroni et al., 2020; Pagnoni et al., 2021). The incorrect factual information is also acute for cross-domain reasoning applications as well. As shown in the example (row 4 in table 6), the model incorrectly generates that `people with flu diagnosis` should do `exercise`. Factual correctness in generation models is an active area of research and we believe that template-based approaches can provide additional insight into this phenomenon.

Overall, TemplateCSR remains a challenging

| Error Type | Template | Gold Answer | Generated Answer |
|---|---|---|---|
| Correct but not in gold | Children who are exposed to {environmental_factor} are often at a higher risk for {disease} because {reason} | Children exposed to second hand smoke are at a higher risk for lung disease because of breathing in the cigarette smoke | Children who are exposed to lead paint are often at a higher risk for kidney failure because lead causes kidney damage |
| Wrong commonsense concept | People with {certain_socioeconomic _condition} are at higher risk of {disease} as they are more exposed to {reason} | Person who often inhale a lot of dirt are at a higher risk of hay fever because of allergen content. | Person who often take less medications are at a higher risk of hay fever because of the drug ineffectiveness |
| Generic Explanation | When people with {certain_co-morbidities} show {symptoms}, this is because of {reason_for_patient_state} | When people with diabetes show lethargy, this is because of high glucose levels. | When people with heart disease show chest pain, this is because of the strain on the heart |
| Factually Incorrect | People with a {health_condition} should do {an_activity} because {reason} | People with a cardiovascular disease should do exercise since exercise burns excess fat | People with a flu diagnosis should do exercise because to stay active |

Table 6: Error Analysis based on the BART-BASE-ITO model. We select 100 samples from the validation set and each row shows an example of each class of error.

task for SEQ-TO-SEQ models, specifically on their factual correctness and we believe it opens several avenues for progress in this research direction.

## 7 Related Work

**Knowledge Bases :** Knowledge Bases (KBs) have been the predominant approach to perform commonsense reasoning in the past (Speer and Havasi, 2013). Some of the prominent knowledge bases for commonsense reasoning include DBPedia (Mendes et al., 2012), YAGO (Suchanek et al., 2007) and NELL (Mitchell et al., 2018) or extending KBs with domain knowledge (Khetan et al., 2021, 2022). In this work, we focus on TemplateCSR using LM, which can be viewed as a complementary using KBs for commonsense.

**Language Models for Reasoning:** Using pre-trained language models to generate knowledge has been studied for commonsense reasoning tasks. (Sap et al., 2019; Bosselut et al., 2019; Shwartz et al., 2020; Bosselut et al., 2021). Our work closely aligns with Bosselut et al. (2019, 2021). Compared to Bosselut et al. (2019), where our goal is to extend towards more controllable commonsense reasoning. Our work is also related to recent chain-of-thought prompting approach (Dalvi et al., 2021; Wei et al., 2022b), where a reasoning chain is first generated before the final solution. Compared to chain-of-thought prompting, our approach focuses on controllability of the reasoning process from input, via template slots using instructions, similar to Wei et al. (2022a).

**Language Model Infilling :** Our work also closely relates to the language model infilling work in the literature such as Fedus et al. (2018) and Donahue et al. (2020). Compared to these works which only look at cloze-test infilling, our work aims to expand templates that cannot be directly modeled as cloze-style. Our work is also related to the story generation efforts such as Yao et al. (2019); Fan et al. (2018); Ippolito et al. (2019); Rashkin et al. (2020) but our application differs from them in that we focus on commonsense reasoning instead of content planning for stories.

## 8 Conclusion and Future Work

In this paper, we present the ITO approach that adapts language models to perform the TemplateCSR task via prompting. We collect a dataset for the same, and show that such an approach allows higher control over the reasoning process by enabling practitioners to specify the nature of the template slots. Through both automated and human metrics, we find that our ITO approach outperforms the baselines while also maintaining high factuality. For future work, we hope to extend this line of work towards other controllable generation tasks such as story generation and summarization.

## 9 Limitations and Ethics Considerations

Our work only tests single sentence template-expansion pairs. One of the limitation of our work is that we do not try on longer template sequences, which we want to explore for future work. While we present our dataset and corresponding modeling approaches, we acknowledge the limitations of the system and potential risks if it was used for real-world use-cases due to its factual errors. While we worked diligently with the annotators, and real domain experts to ascertain the quality of the dataset, we believe that there is immense room to be potentially improved and scaled further. We also did not test our dataset efficacy in large-scale models such as GPT-3 due to budget constraints, which we consider another limitation of this work.

As our results show, common sense reasoning and its health related knowledge reasoning is far from solved and we hope this dataset starts a research direction towards addressing this reasoning challenge. In no way, we support using this system for real-world commonsense related advice. The system, dataset and the accompanying publication is intended only for research purposes and ability to test current NLP systems' capabilities.

## References


Alaa A. Abd-alrazaq, Asma Rababeh, Mohannad Alajlani, Bridgette M. Bewick, and Mowafa Said Househ. 2020. Effectiveness and safety of using chatbots to improve mental health: Systematic review and meta-analysis. Journal of Medical Internet Research, 22.

Eugene Agichtein and L. Gravano. 1999. Extracting relations from large plain-text collections.

Adrian Ahne, Vivek Khetan, Xavier Tannier, Md Imbesat Hassan Rizvi, Thomas Czernichow, Francisco Orchard, Charline Bour, Andy E. Fano, and Guy Fagherazzi. 2022. Extraction of explicit and implicit cause-effect relationships in patient-reported diabetes-related tweets from 2017 to 2021: Deep learning approach. JMIR Medical Informatics, 10.

Antoine Bosselut, Ronan Le Bras, and Yejin Choi. 2021. Dynamic neuro-symbolic knowledge graph construction for zero-shot commonsense question answering. In Proceedings of the 35th AAAI Conference on Artificial Intelligence (AAAI).

Antoine Bosselut, Hannah Rashkin, Maarten Sap, Chaitanya Malaviya, Asli Çelikyilmaz, and Yejin Choi. 2019. Comet: Commonsense transformers for automatic knowledge graph construction. In ACL.

S. Brin. 1998. Extracting patterns and relations from the world wide web. In WebDB.

Laura Chiticariu, Yunyao Li, and Frederick R. Reiss. 2013. Rule-based information extraction is dead! long live rule-based information extraction systems! In Proceedings of the 2013 Conference on Empirical Methods in Natural Language Processing, pages 827–832, Seattle, Washington, USA. Association for Computational Linguistics.

M. Craven, Dan DiPasquo, Dayne Freitag, A. McCallum, Tom Michael Mitchell, K. Nigam, and Seán Slattery. 2000. Learning to construct knowledge bases from the world wide web. Artif. Intell., 118:69–113.

Bhavana Dalvi, Peter Jansen, Oyvind Tafjord, Zhengnan Xie, Hannah Smith, Leighanna Pipatanangkura, and Peter Clark. 2021. Explaining answers with entailment trees. In Proceedings of the 2021 Conference on Empirical Methods in Natural Language Processing, pages 7358–7370, Online and Punta Cana, Dominican Republic. Association for Computational Linguistics.

Jacob Devlin, Ming-Wei Chang, Kenton Lee, and Kristina Toutanova. 2019. BERT: Pre-training of deep bidirectional transformers for language understanding. In NAACL 2019, pages 4171–4186, Minneapolis, Minnesota. Association for Computational Linguistics.

Chris Donahue, Mina Lee, and Percy Liang. 2020. Enabling language models to fill in the blanks. In ACL.

Azam Doustmohammadian and Marjan Bazhan. 2021. Social marketing-based interventions to promote healthy nutrition behaviors: a systematic review protocol. Systematic Reviews, 10.

Ahmed Fadhil and Silvia Gabrielli. 2017. Addressing challenges in promoting healthy lifestyles: the al-chatbot approach. Proceedings of the 11th EAI International Conference on Pervasive Computing Technologies for Healthcare.

Angela Fan, Mike Lewis, and Yann Dauphin. 2018. Hierarchical neural story generation. In Proceedings of the 56th Annual Meeting of the Association for Computational Linguistics (Volume 1: Long Papers), pages 889–898, Melbourne, Australia. Association for Computational Linguistics.

Dan Fass and Yorick Wilks. 1983. Preference semantics, iii-formedness, and metaphor. Am. J. Comput. Linguistics, 9:178–187.

William Fedus, Ian Goodfellow, and Andrew M. Dai. 2018. MaskGAN: Better text generation via filling in the ______. In International Conference on Learning Representations.

Joseph L Fleiss and Jacob Cohen. 1973. The equivalence of weighted kappa and the intraclass correlation coefficient as measures of reliability. Educational and psychological measurement, 33(3):613–619.

Simon Hoermann, Kathryn L. McCabe, David N. Milne, and Rafael Alejandro Calvo. 2017. Application of synchronous text-based dialogue systems in mental health interventions: Systematic review. Journal of Medical Internet Research, 19.

Daphne Ippolito, David Grangier, Chris Callison-Burch, and Douglas Eck. 2019. Unsupervised hierarchical story infilling. In Proceedings of the First Workshop on Narrative Understanding, pages 37–43, Minneapolis, Minnesota. Association for Computational Linguistics.

Vivek Khetan, Annervaz K M, Erin Wetherley, Elena Eneva, Shubhashis Sengupta, and Andrew E. Fano. 2021. Knowledge graph anchored information-extraction for domain-specific insights.

Vivek Khetan, Md Imbesat Rizvi, Jessica Huber, Paige Bartusiak, Bogdan Sacaleanu, and Andrew Fano. 2022. MIMICause: Representation and automatic extraction of causal relation types from clinical notes. In Findings of the Association for Computational Linguistics: ACL 2022, Dublin, Ireland. Association for Computational Linguistics.

Wojciech Kryscinski, Bryan McCann, Caiming Xiong, and Richard Socher. 2020. Evaluating the factual consistency of abstractive text summarization. In Proceedings of the 2020 Conference on Empirical Methods in Natural Language Processing (EMNLP), pages 9332–9346, Online. Association for Computational Linguistics.

Liliana Laranjo, Adam G. Dunn, Huong Ly Tong, Ahmet Baki Kocaballi, Jessica A. Chen, Rabia Bashir, Didi Surian, Blanca Gallego, Farah Magrabi, Annie Y. S. Lau, and Enrico W. Coiera. 2018. Conversational agents in healthcare: a systematic review. Journal of the American Medical Informatics Association : JAMIA, 25:1248 – 1258.

Mike Lewis, Yinhan Liu, Naman Goyal, Marjan Ghazvininejad, Abdelrahman Mohamed, Omer Levy, Veselin Stoyanov, and Luke Zettlemoyer. 2020. BART: Denoising sequence-to-sequence pre-training for natural language generation, translation, and comprehension. In Proceedings of the 58th Annual Meeting of the Association for Computational Linguistics, pages 7871–7880, Online. Association for Computational Linguistics.

Selma Coelho Liberato, Ross Stewart Bailie, and Julie K. Brimblecombe. 2014. Nutrition interventions at point-of-sale to encourage healthier food purchasing: a systematic review. BMC Public Health, 14.

Bill Yuchen Lin, Haitian Sun, Bhuwan Dhingra, Manzil Zaheer, Xiang Ren, and William W. Cohen. 2021a. Differentiable open-ended commonsense reasoning. In NAACL.

Chin-Yew Lin. 2004. Rouge: A package for automatic evaluation of summaries. In Text summarization branches out, pages 74–81.

Jimmy Lin, Xueguang Ma, Sheng-Chieh Lin, Jheng-Hong Yang, Ronak Pradeep, and Rodrigo Nogueira. 2021b. Pyserini: A Python toolkit for reproducible information retrieval research with sparse and dense representations. In Proceedings of the 44th Annual International ACM SIGIR Conference on Research and Development in Information Retrieval (SIGIR 2021), pages 2356–2362.

Shangwen Lv, Daya Guo, Jingjing Xu, Duyu Tang, Nan Duan, Ming Gong, Linjun Shou, Daxin Jiang, Guihong Cao, and Songlin Hu. 2020. Graph-based reasoning over heterogeneous external knowledge for commonsense question answering. In AAAI.

Pablo Mendes, Max Jakob, and Christian Bizer. 2012. DBpedia: A multilingual cross-domain knowledge base. In Proceedings of the Eighth International Conference on Language Resources and Evaluation (LREC'12), pages 1813–1817, Istanbul, Turkey. European Language Resources Association (ELRA).

T. Mitchell, W. Cohen, E. Hruschka, P. Talukdar, B. Yang, J. Betteridge, A. Carlson, B. Dalvi, M. Gardner, B. Kisiel, J. Krishnamurthy, N. Lao, K. Mazaitis, T. Mohamed, N. Nakashole, E. Platanios, A. Ritter, M. Samadi, B. Settles, R. Wang, D. Wijaya, A. Gupta, X. Chen, A. Saparov, M. Greaves, and J. Welling. 2018. Never-ending learning. Commun. ACM, 61(5):103–115.

Tri Nguyen, Mir Rosenberg, Xia Song, Jianfeng Gao, Saurabh Tiwary, Rangan Majumder, and Li Deng. 2016. Ms marco: A human generated machine reading comprehension dataset.

Artidoro Pagnoni, Vidhisha Balachandran, and Yulia Tsvetkov. 2021. Understanding factuality in abstractive summarization with FRANK: A benchmark for factuality metrics. In Proceedings of the 2021 Conference of the North American Chapter of the Association for Computational Linguistics: Human Language Technologies, pages 4812–4829, Online. Association for Computational Linguistics.

Fabio Petroni, Patrick Lewis, Aleksandra Piktus, Tim Rocktäschel, Yuxiang Wu, Alexander H. Miller, and Sebastian Riedel. 2020. How context affects language models' factual predictions. In Automated Knowledge Base Construction.

Colin Raffel, Noam Shazeer, Adam Roberts, Katherine Lee, Sharan Narang, Michael Matena, Yanqi Zhou, Wei Li, and Peter J. Liu. 2020. Exploring the limits of transfer learning with a unified text-to-text transformer. Journal of Machine Learning Research, 21(140):1–67.

Hannah Rashkin, Asli Celikyilmaz, Yejin Choi, and Jianfeng Gao. 2020. PlotMachines: Outline-conditioned generation with dynamic plot state tracking. In Proceedings of the 2020 Conference on Empirical Methods in Natural Language Processing (EMNLP), pages 4274–4295, Online. Association for Computational Linguistics.

Marco Tulio Ribeiro, Tongshuang Wu, Carlos Guestrin, and Sameer Singh. 2020. Beyond accuracy: Behavioral testing of NLP models with CheckList. In Proceedings of the 58th Annual Meeting of the Association for Computational Linguistics, pages 4902–4912, Online. Association for Computational Linguistics.

E. Riloff. 1996. Automatically generating extraction patterns from untagged text. In AAAI/IAAI, Vol. 2.

Maarten Sap, Ronan Le Bras, Emily Allaway, Chandra Bhagavatula, Nicholas Lourie, Hannah Rashkin, Brendan Roof, Noah A Smith, and Yejin Choi. 2019. Atomic: An atlas of machine commonsense for if-then reasoning. In Proceedings of the AAAI Conference on Artificial Intelligence, volume 33, pages 3027–3035.

Vered Shwartz, Peter West, Ronan Le Bras, Chandra Bhagavatula, and Yejin Choi. 2020. Unsupervised commonsense question answering with self-talk. arXiv preprint arXiv:2004.05483.

Robyn Speer and Catherine Havasi. 2013. Conceptnet 5: A large semantic network for relational knowledge. In The People's Web Meets NLP.

Fabian M. Suchanek, Gjergji Kasneci, and Gerhard Weikum. 2007. Yago: A core of semantic knowledge. In Proceedings of the 16th International Conference on World Wide Web, WWW '07, page 697–706, New York, NY, USA. Association for Computing Machinery.

Alon Talmor, Jonathan Herzig, Nicholas Lourie, and Jonathan Berant. 2019. Commonsenseqa: A question answering challenge targeting commonsense knowledge. In NAACL.

Niket Tandon, Bhavana Dalvi, Joel Grus, Wen-tau Yih, Antoine Bosselut, and Peter Clark. 2018. Reasoning about actions and state changes by injecting commonsense knowledge. In Proceedings of the 2018 Conference on Empirical Methods in Natural Language Processing, pages 57–66, Brussels, Belgium. Association for Computational Linguistics.

Jason Wei, Maarten Bosma, Vincent Zhao, Kelvin Guu, Adams Wei Yu, Brian Lester, Nan Du, Andrew M. Dai, and Quoc V Le. 2022a. Finetuned language models are zero-shot learners. In International Conference on Learning Representations.

Jason Wei, Xuezhi Wang, Dale Schuurmans, Maarten Bosma, Ed Chi, Quoc Le, and Denny Zhou. 2022b. Chain of thought prompting elicits reasoning in large language models.

Sarah Wiegreffe and Ana Marasović. 2021. Teach me to explain: A review of datasets for explainable natural language processing. In NeurIPS Datasets and Benchmarks.

Thomas Wolf, Lysandre Debut, Victor Sanh, Julien Chaumond, Clement Delangue, Anthony Moi, Pierric Cistac, Tim Rault, Rémi Louf, Morgan Funtowicz, Joe Davison, Sam Shleifer, Patrick von Platen, Clara Ma, Yacine Jernite, Julien Plu, Canwen Xu, Teven Le Scao, Sylvain Gugger, Mariama Drame, Quentin Lhoest, and Alexander M. Rush. 2020. Transformers: State-of-the-art natural language processing. In Proceedings of the 2020 Conference on Empirical Methods in Natural Language Processing: System Demonstrations, pages 38–45, Online. Association for Computational Linguistics.

Lili Yao, Nanyun Peng, Ralph Weischedel, Kevin Knight, Dongyan Zhao, and Rui Yan. 2019. Plan-and-write: Towards better automatic storytelling. Proceedings of the AAAI Conference on Artificial Intelligence, 33(01):7378–7385.

Xi Ye and Greg Durrett. 2022. The unreliability of explanations in few-shot in-context learning.

S. Yih. 1997. Template-based information extraction from tree-structured html documents.

Tianyi Zhang, Varsha Kishore, Felix Wu, Kilian Q. Weinberger, and Yoav Artzi. 2019. Bertscore: Evaluating text generation with bert. ArXiv, abs/1904.09675.

# Temporal Relation Classification in Hebrew


**Guy Yanko**
Efi Arazi School
of Computer Science
Reichman University
guyy1232@gmail.com

**Shahaf Pariente**
Efi Arazi School
of Computer Science
Reichman University
shahafp2@gmail.com

**Kfir Bar**
Efi Arazi School
of Computer Science
Reichman University
kfirbarmail@gmail.com



## Abstract

Temporal Relation Classification (TRC) is a fundamental task in natural language processing (NLP) and is essential for achieving a comprehensive understanding of a natural language. Given a document containing two event mentions, the objective of this task is to discern which of the two events happened first. Existing TRC datasets predominantly consist of texts written in English. To accommodate the growing interest in relevant NLP applications for Hebrew, we introduce a new TRC dataset for Hebrew. Professional annotators labeled Hebrew documents with TRC labels, adhering to guidelines adapted from a similar project on English and with some changes required to address some unique aspects of the Hebrew language. Overall, we annotated a corpus of 28,757 words, corresponding to 7,260 pairs of events. In addition to releasing the new dataset, which can be accessed at `https://github.com/shahafp/TRC-Hebrew`, we train several baseline models for TRC and report their performance.


## 1 Introduction

Events in a story are not necessarily mentioned in a chronological order. Constructing a timeline of events mentioned in a document is crucial for comprehending the primary narrative of the story. The timeline, also known as the chronology of events, can be applied to various use cases. For instance, clinicians may utilize the timeline to conveniently explore their patients' disease progression. Moreover, a model can follow text-based instructions more accurately with a timeline in place. Building a timeline comprises several subtasks, with the two primary subtasks being: 1) Event detection, which involves identifying the most important events in a given text; and 2) Temporal relation classification (TRC), which entails determining the correct order of two given events. Consider the following Hebrew text as an example:

"אכלתי את התפוח אחרי ששטפתי אותו"
"I ate the apple after washing it"

The event detection subtask is about detecting only the relevant events for our domain of interest; in this example: אכלתי "I ate" and שטפתי "I washed". In this case, both words are verbs representing actions which we subsequently mark as events. In the TRC subtask, we classify each pair of events using a closed set of labels to establish their chronological order. In this example, the events אכלתי "I ate" and שטפתי "I washed" should be assigned the label AFTER to indicate that "I ate" occurs after "I washed" in chronological order.

This study focuses on creating a Hebrew dataset for the second subtask, TRC, which is generally defined as a classification problem involving two events accompanied by their contextual information. Utilizing the annotated data, we train multiple TRC baseline models using all available Hebrew language models.

## 2 Related Works

To the best of our knowledge, there is no publicly available Hebrew dataset for TRC. TRC in English, however, has been a subject of considerable focus within the scientific literature.

Ning et al. (2018b) proposed a multi-axis annotation scheme for TRC, improving inter-annotator agreement (IAA), ascending from the conventional 60's to a high of 80's, as measured on the Cohen's Kappa scale. This new annotation scheme enabled the use of crowdsourcing, thereby mitigating the laborious demands on individual annotators. In this work, the authors introduced the most dominant TRC dataset in English, MATRES, which contains news documents manually annotated with TRC labels. Overall, MATRES



*Findings of the Association for Computational Linguistics: IJCNLP-AACL 2023*, pages 261–267
November 1–4, 2023. ©2023 Asian Federation of Natural Language Processing

contains 12,736 training instances and 837 test instances. We derive inspiration from their annotation guidelines and adapt them to Hebrew. According to their guidelines, all verbs mentioned in a document are selected as events. Every pair of events $(n, m)$ is manually labeled with one of four labels reflecting the chronological order between the two. The four labels are: BEFORE ($n$ occurs before $m$), AFTER ($n$ occurs after $m$), EQUAL ($n$ and $m$ occur simultaneously), and VAGUE (it is impossible to determine which event preceded the other). We follow the same guidelines. Previous works on building TRC datasets include TempEval (Verhagen et al., 2007), TimeBankDense (Chambers et al., 2014), RED (OGorman et al., 2016), and TCR (Ning et al., 2018a).

Various computational strategies have been employed to train a TRC model for English. Most of them use language models (Han et al., 2021, 2019a,b), some form of a global inference mechanism (Zhou et al., 2021; Ning et al., 2019; Mathur et al., 2021), and certain linguistic information extracted from the text (Zhang et al., 2021; Wang et al., 2022b,a). The best model for English TRC has been reported recently by (Zhou et al., 2022), who extracted relational syntactic and semantic structures, and encoded them using a graph neural network achieving 84% F1-score on MATRES.

## 3 TRC in Hebrew

We annotated articles from the Universal Dependencies Corpus for Hebrew (Tsarfaty, 2013; McDonald et al., 2013),[1] containing about 500 articles, corresponding to 6,143 sentences. We choose to annotate this dataset since it already contains part-of-speech labels for each word, simplifying the task of identifying all verbs as actions.

### 3.1 Annotation Preparation

To convert the treebank articles into TRC samples, we first identify all events mentioned in each document. Events are defined as any word labeled as a verb, excluding infinitive verbs and gerunds due to their lack of temporal meaning in Hebrew. Next, we create two-sentence sliding windows that run through every article. For instance, an article with three sentences yields two windows, the first spanning the first and second sentences, and the second covering the second and third sentences. For every window, we generate one sample for every pair of events mentioned within the window text. The two events are marked by enclosing them within bracketed special tokens. For example:

[א1] זכיתי [/א1] בלוטו אז [א2] החלטתי [/א2] לקנות רכב חדש

In other words, each sample is a copy of the entire window text, with the two specific events marked with brackets. Overall, we process 78 articles from the treebank, corresponding to 7,260 TRC samples, which we distribute among the annotators.

### 3.2 Annotation Process

We hired two annotators, both possessing academic backgrounds, with one individual having expertise in linguistics. The dataset was curated by two of the authors. We start with a set of annotation pilots to validate and improve our annotation guidelines. We use INCEpTION.[2] The annotators were provided with a set of instructions to assist in determining the appropriate label for each pair of events $(n, m)$. Inspired by the method used in MATRES, we define two guiding questions that can assist the annotators in choosing the correct label:

1. `Q1`: Could it be possible for the start time of $n$ to precede the start time of $m$?
2. `Q2`: Could it be possible for the start time of $m$ to precede the start time of $n$?

From these two binary questions, there are four possible answer combinations, each of which maps to a specific label, according to Table 1.

| Answer to `Q1` | Answer to `Q2` | Label |
|---|---|---|
| Yes | No | BEFORE |
| No | Yes | AFTER |
| No | No | EQUAL |
| Yes | Yes | VAGUE |

Table 1: Label assignment.

Generally, our annotation guidelines derive from those established by MATRES, with some modifications suitable for Hebrew. For more information, please refer to Appendix C. Table 2 summarizes the label distribution of the annotated dataset. We compared the label distribution with that of the original MATRES dataset. The two distributions appear quite similar, except that in our

[1] `https://github.com/UniversalDependencies/UD_Hebrew-HTB`

[2] `https://inception-project.github.io/`

dataset, there are more EQUAL labels and fewer VAGUE labels. Some examples from the dataset can be found in Appendix D.

| Label | Count | Percentage |
|---|---|---|
| BEFORE | 3,092 | 42% (49%) |
| AFTER | 2,374 | 33% (23%) |
| EQUAL | 618 | 9% (2%) |
| VAGUE | 1,176 | 16% (26%) |

Table 2: Label distribution (Total: 7,260). In parentheses: For comparison, the label distribution of the original MATRES dataset is provided.

### 3.3 Multi-Axis Annotations

Events can have temporal relationships only if they share the same axis. Time axes are defined following the method outlined in (Ning et al., 2018b). The guidelines allow for the assignment of each event in a given text to one of three types of axes: main, parallel, and orthogonal. The main axis represents the primary sequence of events in the text, and there exists only one such axis. On the other hand, parallel axis (may be more than one) represents a secondary timeline axis in which events occur on a distinct timeline from the main or another parallel axis. Typically, events that occur in quotation or that form part of a hypothesis are assigned to a parallel axis. Events on a parallel axis can only have temporal relationships with other events on the same axis.

An orthogonal axis, of which there may be more than one in a given story, denotes an alternate timeline originating from an event that belongs to another axis, also known as the "connecting" event. In other words, an orthogonal axis is a branch that stems from the original axis. Generally speaking, a pair of events can have a non-VAGUE temporal relationship only if they belong to the same axis. A connecting event is capable of having a non-VAGUE relationship with events transpiring on the two axes it links together.

The temporal relationship between two events that do not share the same axis is VAGUE. During the annotation pilots, we learned that in most cases, annotators can intuitively understand the concept of using multiple time axes. However, when confronted with complex situations, it was necessary to establish some guidelines for identifying the axes. Our guidelines are released with the dataset.

### 3.4 Inter-Annotator Agreement

After completing two pilot annotation projects, in which we made suitable modifications to the guidelines, we carried out two rounds of annotations. In the first round, all the TRC samples were annotated by at least one annotator, and about 55% were annotated by both annotators to measure consistency and agreement. Following this, we had a detailed discussion with the annotators to clarify any ambiguities in the guidelines. Additionally, we identified the samples that showed disagreement between the two annotators (1,073 windows out of 3,998 windows which were annotated by both annotators) and conducted a second annotation round for these specific samples. After the second round concluded, the authors adjudicated any remaining discrepancies in the annotations.

To measure the inter-annotator agreement (IAA) level, we calculate Cohen's kappa for each round of annotation separately as well as for both rounds combined. In addition to the standard IAA calculations, following common evaluation practices on MATRES (Ning et al., 2018b), we define a relaxed version of IAA. If one annotator labels a sample as VAGUE, and the other as either AFTER or BEFORE, it is not necessarily a complete disagreement, given that VAGUE inherently encompasses both temporal directions. Therefore, in the relaxed IAA we exclude disagreements regarding VAGUE. Table 3 summarizes all IAA values.

| Method | 1st Round | 2st Round | Combined |
|---|---|---|---|
| Standard | 0.62 | 0.53 | 0.81 |
| Relaxed | 0.84 | 0.77 | 0.91 |

Table 3: Cohen's Kappa values for each annotation round and both rounds combined.

## 4 TRC Models

We fine-tune a number of models for Hebrew TRC based on some existing Hebrew foundation language models. The model's input consists of a sentence containing the two events. Inspired by Soares et al. (2019) we mark the events with distinct special tokens, as shown in Section 3.1. We use Hebrew marker; specifically, we employ [1א] to denote the beginning of the first event and [1א/] to denote its ending. The second event is marked similarly, but replacing 1 with 2.[3]

[3]We experimented with alternative marker types, and the results indicate that this approach is optimal. Performance

| Model | Architecture | | | | | |
|---|---|---|---|---|---|---|
| | SEQ-CLS | | ESS | | EMP | |
| | M/ avg | W/ avg | M/ avg | W/ avg | M/ avg | W/ avg |
| AlephBERTGimmel | 0.62 | 0.74 | 0.65 | **0.78** | 0.65 | **0.78** |
| HeBERT | 0.56 | 0.65 | 0.56 | 0.64 | 0.59 | **0.75** |
| mBERT | 0.48 | 0.64 | 0.61 | **0.74** | 0.62 | 0.73 |
| AlephBERT | 0.64 | 0.75 | 0.67 | **0.77** | 0.67 | **0.77** |

Table 4: Relaxed F1 scores. W/ avg = Weighted Average F1; M/ avg = Macro Average F1.

We use four Hebrew language models: AlephBERT (Seker et al., 2022), HeBERT (Chriqui and Yahav, 2022), mBERT cased (bert-base-multilingual) (Devlin et al., 2019), and AlephBERTGimmel (Guetta et al., 2022), all having 110M parameters, obtained directly from Hugging Face's transformer library. Inspired by Soares et al. (2019), we experiment with three sequence classification architectures:

**Sequence Classification (SEQ-CLS).** We use the [CLS] vector as input for the classification layer.

**Event Start State (ESS).** We concatenate the output vector of the start markers of both events, and use it for classification.

**Event Mention Pooling (EMP).** For each event, we apply maxpooling on the output vectors of all its word pieces, excluding markers. The two pooled vectors are concatenated into a single vector, serving as the classification layer's input.

The classification layer is always implemented as a simple linear layer. See Appendix A for training details.

### 4.1 Models Evaluation

We use the macro and weighted average F1 metrics. As previously stated, we adopt the relaxed F1 score metric (ignoring mistakes of non-VAGUE predictions on VAGUE samples). In order to train and evaluate our models, we divide the dataset into training and evaluation sets using an 80/20 split. We ensure that each article is assigned to only one of the sets. The split is released with the dataset. Table 4 summarizes the relaxed F1 scores measured on the evaluation set. The corresponding non-relaxed scores can be found in Appendix B. The best performance is achieved by AlephBERTGimmel using ESS and EMP. To study the relationship between the training-set size and the model performance, we train our AlephBERTGimmel/ESS architecture using a growing size of the training set, and monitor its performance. We train the model using 15%, 25%, 50%, 75%, and 100% of the training set. For each size, we train the model three times using different seeds for training-set sampling. Figure 1 shows the mean of the macro-average F1 scores over the three executions, with a standard deviation of 0.02 for the 15% portion and 0.01 for the rest of the portions. The results show an increasing improvement with the expansion of the training set. However, the improvement becomes less significant after using about 50% of the data, implying that our newly created Hebrew TRC dataset provides an adequate volume of data for constructing robust models.

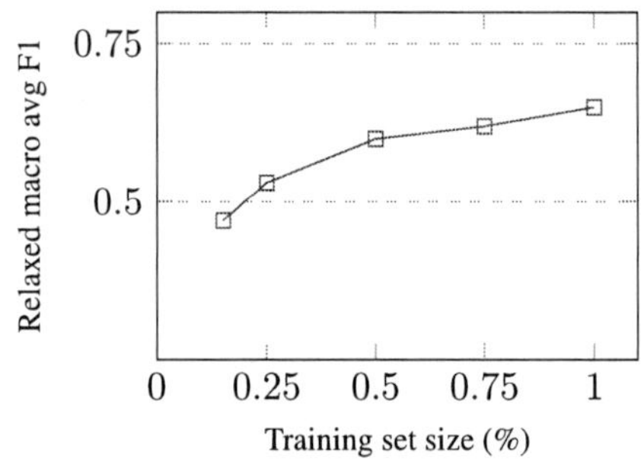


Figure 1: Training on different training set sizes.

## 5 Conclusion

In this study, we present a Hebrew TRC dataset, employing TRC annotation techniques that have been previously validated. The dataset contains 7,260 samples, manually annotated by professional annotators, following guidelines developed as part of this work. While our dataset currently only includes news articles, we plan to add documents from other domains. We fine-tune a range of TRC models under various classification settings

diminished when markers were not used.

and evaluate their performance. We have made the dataset and models accessible for research purposes, under a license (CC BY-NC-SA 4.0).[4]

## 6 Limitations

There are three main limitations to this work, two are related to the dataset itself and the third to the model we provide along with the dataset. First, we use a single, domain-specific source of news articles. While we provide full annotation guidelines, a new domain might require some adjustments. The second limitation is related to VAGUE annotations. Our guidelines label any two events in a window that don't share the same axis as VAGUE. However, a different label could be chosen for such a pair to distinguish it from a pair of events on the same axis, but with both directive questions answered with Yes. The third limitation pertains to the model itself. We have proposed an evaluation methodology termed "relaxed". In this approach, predictions that do not align with the VAGUE label are considered true positives, even when the actual label is VAGUE. This deviation stems from the inherent complexities and variability associated with the VAGUE label.

## References


Nathanael Chambers, Taylor Cassidy, Bill McDowell, and Steven Bethard. 2014. Dense event ordering with a multi-pass architecture. *Transactions of the Association for Computational Linguistics*, 2:273–284.

Avihay Chriqui and Inbal Yahav. 2022. HeBERT & HebEMO: a Hebrew BERT model and a tool for polarity analysis and emotion recognition. *INFORMS Journal on Data Science*.

Jacob Devlin, Ming-Wei Chang, Kenton Lee, and Kristina Toutanova. 2019. Bert: Pre-training of deep bidirectional transformers for language understanding. In *NAACL-HLT (1)*, pages 4171–4186. Association for Computational Linguistics.

Eylon Guetta, Avi Shmidman, Shaltiel Shmidman, Cheyn Shmuel Shmidman, Joshua Guedalia, Moshe Koppel, Dan Bareket, Amit Seker, and Reut Tsarfaty. 2022. Large pre-trained models with extra-large vocabularies: A contrastive analysis of Hebrew BERT models and a new one to outperform them all.

Rujun Han, I Hsu, Mu Yang, Aram Galstyan, Ralph Weischedel, Nanyun Peng, et al. 2019a. Deep structured neural network for event temporal relation extraction. *arXiv preprint arXiv:1909.10094*.


[4]https://github.com/shahafp/TRC-Hebrew


Rujun Han, Qiang Ning, and Nanyun Peng. 2019b. Joint event and temporal relation extraction with shared representations and structured prediction. In *Proceedings of the 2019 Conference on Empirical Methods in Natural Language Processing and the 9th International Joint Conference on Natural Language Processing (EMNLP-IJCNLP)*, pages 434–444, Hong Kong, China. Association for Computational Linguistics.

Rujun Han, Xiang Ren, and Nanyun Peng. 2021. ECONET: Effective continual pretraining of language models for event temporal reasoning. In *Proceedings of the 2021 Conference on Empirical Methods in Natural Language Processing (EMNLP)*, Punta Cana, Dominican Republic.

Puneet Mathur, Rajiv Jain, Franck Dernoncourt, Vlad Morariu, Quan Hung Tran, and Dinesh Manocha. 2021. TIMERS: Document-level temporal relation extraction. In *Proceedings of the 59th Annual Meeting of the Association for Computational Linguistics and the 11th International Joint Conference on Natural Language Processing (Volume 2: Short Papers)*, pages 524–533, Online. Association for Computational Linguistics.

Ryan T McDonald, Joakim Nivre, Yvonne Quirmbach-Brundage, Yoav Goldberg, Dipanjan Das, Kuzman Ganchev, Keith B Hall, Slav Petrov, Hao Zhang, Oscar Täckström, et al. 2013. Universal dependency annotation for multilingual parsing. In *Proc. of ACL*.

Qiang Ning, Zhili Feng, Hao Wu, and Dan Roth. 2018a. Joint reasoning for temporal and causal relations. In *Proceedings of the 56th Annual Meeting of the Association for Computational Linguistics (Volume 1: Long Papers)*, pages 2278–2288, Melbourne, Australia. Association for Computational Linguistics.

Qiang Ning, Sanjay Subramanian, and Dan Roth. 2019. An improved neural baseline for temporal relation extraction. In *Proceedings of the 2019 Conference on Empirical Methods in Natural Language Processing and the 9th International Joint Conference on Natural Language Processing (EMNLP-IJCNLP)*, pages 6203–6209, Hong Kong, China. Association for Computational Linguistics.

Qiang Ning, Hao Wu, and Dan Roth. 2018b. A multi-axis annotation scheme for event temporal relations. In *ACL*.

Tim OGorman, Kristin Wright-Bettner, and Martha Palmer. 2016. Richer event description: Integrating event coreference with temporal, causal and bridging annotation. In *Proceedings of the 2nd Workshop on Computing News Storylines (CNS 2016)*, pages 47–56.

Amit Seker, Elron Bandel, Dan Bareket, Idan Brusilovsky, Refael Greenfeld, and Reut Tsarfaty. 2022. AlephBERT: Language model pre-training and evaluation from sub-word to sentence level. In

*Proceedings of the 60th Annual Meeting of the Association for Computational Linguistics (Volume 1: Long Papers)*, pages 46–56, Dublin, Ireland. Association for Computational Linguistics.

Livio Baldini Soares, Nicholas FitzGerald, Jeffrey Ling, and Tom Kwiatkowski. 2019. Matching the blanks: Distributional similarity for relation learning. *CoRR*, abs/1906.03158.

Reut Tsarfaty. 2013. A unified morpho-syntactic scheme of stanford dependencies. In *Proc. of ACL*.

Marc Verhagen, Robert Gaizauskas, Frank Schilder, Mark Hepple, Graham Katz, and James Pustejovsky. 2007. Semeval-2007 task 15: Tempeval temporal relation identification. In *Proceedings of the fourth international workshop on semantic evaluations (SemEval-2007)*, pages 75–80.

Haoyu Wang, Hongming Zhang, Yuqian Deng, Jacob R Gardner, Muhao Chen, and Dan Roth. 2022a. Extracting or guessing? improving faithfulness of event temporal relation extraction. *arXiv preprint arXiv:2210.04992*.

Liang Wang, Peifeng Li, and Sheng Xu. 2022b. DCT-centered temporal relation extraction. In *Proceedings of the 29th International Conference on Computational Linguistics*, pages 2087–2097.

Shuaicheng Zhang, Lifu Huang, and Qiang Ning. 2021. Extracting temporal event relation with syntactic-guided temporal graph transformer. *arXiv preprint arXiv:2104.09570*.

Jie Zhou, Shenpo Dong, Hongkui Tu, Xiaodong Wang, and Yong Dou. 2022. RSGT: Relational structure guided temporal relation extraction. In *Proceedings of the 29th International Conference on Computational Linguistics*, pages 2001–2010, Gyeongju, Republic of Korea. International Committee on Computational Linguistics.

Yichao Zhou, Yu Yan, Rujun Han, J. Harry Caufield, Kai-Wei Chang, Yizhou Sun, Peipei Ping, and Wei Wang. 2021. Clinical temporal relation extraction with probabilistic soft logic regularization and global inference. In *AAAI*.

## A Training Information

We fine-tune all our models for the duration of 10 epochs, using a learning value of $3 \times 10^{-5}$ and batch-size value of 32. To train our models, we used one Nvidia Tesla T4 with 16GB of memory. It takes about 45 minutes to train each model. The model cards from Hugging Face we use are: AlephBERTGimmel: `imvladikon/alephbertgimmel-base-512`, HeBERT: `avichr/heBERT`, mBERT: `bert-base-multilingual-cased`, and AlephBERT: `onlplab/alephbert-base`.

## B Non-Relaxed F1 Scores

Table 5 summarizes the non-relaxed F1 scores of our experiments with the different models, as reported in the text.

## C Adjustments for Hebrew TRC

We have made some adjustments to the MATRES annotation guidelines of English to accommodate the unique challenges of Hebrew. Two primary additions to the guidelines are:

1. Verbal nouns and infinitive verbs are not counted as events.

2. Auxiliary verbs (in Hebrew פעלי עזר, such as היה, הלך) are not labeled as part of the events. For example, in the text: "היה מתאמן" "he was practicing", only מתאמן is labeled as an event.

For more information, please refer to the annotation guidelines, provided in as supplementary data.

## D Examples

In Table 6 we provide some samples from the dataset, along with their gold labels. We provide one full annotated document (in json format) in the supplementary data.

| Model | Architecture | | | | | |
|---|---|---|---|---|---|---|
| | SEQ_CLS | | ESS | | EMP | |
| | M/ avg | W/ avg | M/ avg | W/ avg | M/ avg | W/ avg |
| AlephBERTGimmel | 0.48 | 0.58 | 0.50 | 0.60 | 0.49 | 0.59 |
| HeBERT | 0.32 | 0.44 | 0.32 | 0.44 | 0.44 | 0.56 |
| mBERT | 0.33 | 0.44 | 0.43 | 0.54 | 0.46 | 0.56 |
| AlephBERT | 0.47 | 0.58 | 0.48 | 0.59 | 0.50 | 0.60 |

Table 5: **Non-relaxed** F1 scores. M/ avg = Macro Average F1; W/ avg = Weighted Average F1.

| Sample | Label |
|---|---|
| במחנה פליטים סמוך לשכם נפגע תושב מקומי מפגיעת רימון גז מדמיע, שנורה בידי חיילים. מקורות פלשתיניים [א1] **מסרו** [/א1] כי חיילים, שירדו ממיניבוס לבן בשכונת ראפידיה בשכם, [א2] **ניפצו** [/א2] בעזרת אבנים זגוגיות של מכוניות חונות של תושבים מקומיים, ביניהן גם את חלונות מכוניתו של דר מוסטפא מקבול. | AFTER |
| האיש שנפל קורבן לכדורי אקדח שנורו על-ידי ערבי, [א1] **הצית** [/א1] במותו את האיבה לערבים. האש הזאת [א2] **תוסיף** [/א2] ללחוש, גם אם הלהבה של יום קבורתו של מאיר כהנא תדעך במקצת. | BEFORE |
| התחרות היתה בהרצליה. קפספקו מתל אביב [א1] **ניצח** [/א1] במירוץ אופניים שהיה סביב כיכר המדינה בתל אביב, לאחר [א2] **שעבר** [/א2] 8 ק"ם ב-41. | AFTER |
| אמנם נוצחנו פעם אחת, אבל לא שיחקנו נגד הגדולות. אם [א1] **ננצח** [/א1] באחד משלושת המשחקים הבאים נגד הפועל תל אביב, מכבי תל אביב והפועל גליל עליון זה יהיה הישג אדיר, [א2] **שיתן** [/א2] לנו דחיפה קדימה". | BEFORE |
| עדיין לא הוגש כתב הגנה. 48 דיירים [א1] **המתגוררים** [/א1] ברחוב החלמונית 3, 5 ו7 בקריית ראשון בראשון-לציון [א2] **הגישו** [/א2] השבוע סדרה של תביעות נגד סולל בונה. | BEFORE |
| משה ויזל, מנכ"ל החברה, זומן לבירורים בהתאחדות חברות הביטוח וכן עם מנהלי חברות ביטוח. [א1] **טענו** [/א1] בפניו שהוא [א2] **כורת** [/א2] את הענף של הביטוח עליו הוא יושב. | AFTER |
| דובר מחלקת המדינה של ארה"ב, אמר אתמול כי ארה"ב "היתה בקשר הדוק עם ישראל במשך כל התקופה" שמאז תחילת המשבר במפרץ. הוא [א1] **חזר** [/א1] [א2] **ושיבח** [/א2] את גישת ה"פרופיל הנמוך" שישראל נוקטת. | EQUAL |
| כך [א1] **עשה** [/א1] גם בליגה להגנה בברוקלין. בארץ [א2] **שיחרר** [/א2] בלמים אצל קבוצות השוליים, והצליח להניח על השולחן רעיונות שגם אנשים מן היישוב הוגים בהם, אך אינם מעיזים לבטא אותם (עד לעת האחרונה). | VAGUE |

Table 6: Examples from the dataset.

# Privacy Adhering Machine *Un-learning* in NLP

**Vinayshekhar Bannihatti Kumar, Rashmi Gangadharaiah, Dan Roth**
AWS AI Labs
{vinayshk,rgangad,drot}@amazon.com

## Abstract

Regulations introduced General Data Protection Regulation (GDPR) in the EU or California Consumer Privacy Act (CCPA) in the US have included provisions on the *right to be forgotten* that mandates industry applications to remove data related to an individual from their systems. In several real world industry applications that use Machine Learning to build models on user data, such mandates require significant effort both in terms of data cleansing as well as model retraining while ensuring the models do not deteriorate in prediction quality due to removal of data. As a result, continuous removal of data and model retraining steps do not scale if these applications receive such requests at a very high frequency. Recently, a few researchers proposed the idea of *Machine Unlearning* to tackle this challenge. Despite the significant importance of this task, the area of Machine Unlearning is under-explored in Natural Language Processing (NLP) tasks. In this paper, we explore the Unlearning framework on various GLUE tasks (Wang et al., 2018), such as, QQP, SST and MNLI. We propose computationally efficient approaches (SISA-FC and SISA-A) to perform *guaranteed* Unlearning that provides significant reduction in terms of both memory (90-95%), time (100x) and space consumption (99%) in comparison to the baselines while having minimal impact on model performance.[1].

## 1 Introduction

The use of user generated content in building ML-based solutions in many industry applications is quite common. As new data is acquired, these ML models undergo constant updates to further improve the performance. Such data can contain sensitive information such as names, account ids, email addresses and so on. Typically, user generated content goes through several redaction systems to remove such sensitive information before being used for retraining purposes. Industry applications also adopt rigorous approval processes with opt-in or opt-out capabilities to ensure that user generated content is used in a safe manner while raising awareness among users on how their generated content will be used.

More recently, the GDPR and CCPA provisioned the right to be forgotten, introducing new regulations that mandates industry applications to support deletion of user generated content when requested by users. Although privacy concerns have gained significant importance now, the scale at which these models are built make it extremely expensive and time-consuming to remove data efficiently while providing *complete removal guarantees*.

Unlearning assures the users that their data has been completely removed when they prefer to have their data erased (Bourtoule et al., 2019). This task is different from Differential Privacy that focuses on models that ensure that the users' information in the training data cannot be inferred and provides guarantees on the effect of an individual examples. Such a task is challenging as removal of data points can have significant deterioration on the performance of the models *aka catastrophic unlearning* (Du et al., 2019; Golatkar et al., 2019; Nguyen et al., 2020, 2022a).

Approaches that guarantee complete removal of users' data points have recently gained momentum (Bourtoule et al., 2019; Nguyen et al., 2022b) but are under explored on NLP tasks. Motivated by SISA (**S**harded, **I**solated, **S**liced and **A**ggregated) training (Bourtoule et al., 2019) applied to CV datasets, we explore an approach that trains multiple ML models in isolation on disjoint shards and its slices. Model checkpoints are saved after training each slice in a shard. When a request for deletion is received, the corresponding datapoint is deleted from its slice and the model checkpoint upto the datapoint is used to further retrain

[1]https://github.com/awslabs/privacy-adhering-machine-unlearning-nlp



*Findings of the Association for Computational Linguistics: IJCNLP-AACL 2023*, pages 268–277
November 1–4, 2023. ©2023 Asian Federation of Natural Language Processing

the model. Although the SISA framework can be applied to any learning algorithm, it is still impractical in NLP settings as storing model checkpoints that include large language models (such as, BERT (Devlin et al., 2018a)) is both space and time consuming. We propose extensions to this SISA framework (1) (**SISA-FC**) requires storing only task-specific layers (2) (**SISA-A**) uses Adapters (Houlsby et al., 2019) that requires storing only the adapter weights. These extensions prevent storing the entire model checkpoints, hence reducing time, memory and space footprints. We further improve upon the approaches by creating shards such that the least number of slices are affected when requests for removal are made, further reducing the time required to retrain the models. To the best of our knowledge this paper makes the first attempt to explore the task of Unlearning on various NLP tasks. The contributions of this paper are summarized as follows:

- We explore the task of Unlearning on various NLP tasks (GLUE tasks such as QQP, SST and MNLI) in both full data as well as few shot settings.
- We explore SISA-FC and SISA-A for NLP-based models that do not require storing large model checkpoints, thereby significantly reducing space, memory and time
- We propose novel ways to partition the data, thereby reducing the number of slices affected and the retraining time while ensuring minimal degradation in the overall model quality.

The paper is organized as follows. Section 2 briefly describes some of the related work in the area of Unlearning. Section 3 describes the NLP datasets used to evaluate the approaches proposed in this paper. Section 4 explains the proposed approaches (SISA-FC and SISA-A) followed by results in Section 5. We finally conclude and provide future extensions to this work in Section 6.

## 2 Related Work

Privacy preserving ML provides guarantees on bounds ensuring the contribution from the data points is as low as possible (Sarwate et al., 2009; Abadi et al., 2016; Jang et al., 2022; Yu et al., 2021; Li et al., 2021). Machine *Unlearning* on the other hand focuses on *complete* removal of training examples, ensuring that there is *zero* contribution of the training sample to the model's learned weights. As a result, Unlearning assures the users that their data has been completely removed when they prefer to have their data erased (Bourtoule et al., 2019). A simple approach to forget training samples would be to re-train the models after removal of the examples. Such an approach is not scalable and computationally expensive when systems receive removal requests at high frequencies. Another challenge this brings is in the deterioration of the performance of the models.

Machine Unlearning has gained significant attention in industry applications as a means to allow users to completely delete their data from ML models (Tahiliani et al., 2021; Nguyen et al., 2022a; Baumhauer et al., 2020). Regulations introduced by regulatory bodies apply to all forms of user generated content. However, most of the recent approaches tackle this problem of Unlearning in Computer Vision (CV) settings (Mehta et al., 2022; Golatkar et al., 2019; Bourtoule et al., 2019). It is imperative to explore unlearning strategies on textual data that can contain user sensitive information or personally identifiable information (PII).

Our work is inspired by SISA training (Bourtoule et al., 2019) which was originally applied to CV datasets. The framework provides a strategic way to limit the influence of a data point in the training procedure. The approach trains models in isolation on disjoint shards created by partitioning the training data. When a request for removal is made, only the affected model is retrained. Shards are further broken down into slices to decrease the time required to unlearn. During inference, they use ensemble strategies to aggregate predictions of individual models. We extend this framework for NLP models. Our paper also proposes approaches to partition the data such that the least number of shards/slices are affected, thereby further reducing the re-training time.

## 3 Datasets

Glue (Wang et al., 2018) tasks are divided into three categories namely , "SINGLE-SENTENCE TASKS", " SIMILARITY AND PARAPHRASE TASKS" , " INFERENCE TASKS". We pick "SST-2" dataset from the first, "QQP" dataset from the second and "MNLI" dataset from the third respectively. In order to test the generalizability of our approach in terms of performance, time taken to retrain models and the memory they

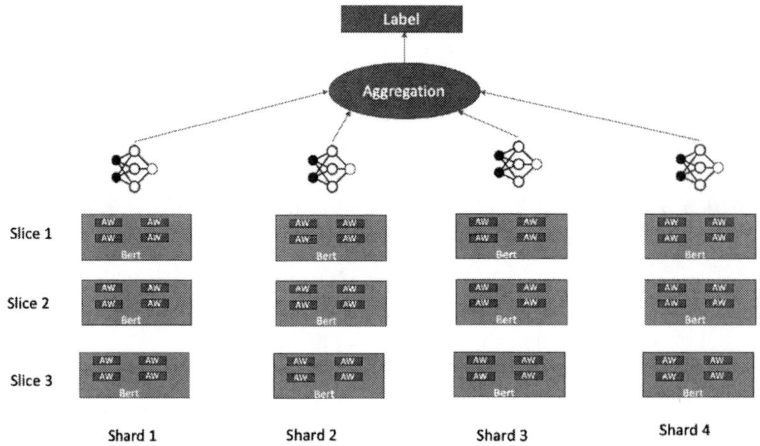


Figure 1: Architecture of SISA-A which uses S slices and R shards. One model is built for each shard and the labels are aggregated using a majority voting strategy.

| Dataset Name | BERT-A | | SISA-A | | Accuracy Reduction (%) | Re-training time gain (%) |
|---|---|---|---|---|---|---|
| | Accuracy | Re-training time (s) | Accuracy | Re-training time (s) | | |
| SST | 0.93 | 1580 | 0.92 | 147 | 1 | 9748 |
| QQP | 0.82 | 1750 | 0.80 | 145 | 2 | 1106 |
| MNLI | 0.75 | 1868 | 0.70 | 145 | 6 | 1188 |

Table 1: We see that our SISA-A (SISA with Adapters) approach is only $1-6\%$ worse when compared to the deletion baseline model (BERT-A BERT model trained using Adapters) but has a 100x improvement in training time over the deletion baseline. This performance is measured upon receiving 16 unlearning requests

occupy on disk, we pick the first $60,000$ samples across each datasets and use 20% of this as our test split. Having the same number of training and evaluation samples helps us to compare training times across different types of NLP tasks. For each of the datasets, we use accuracy to measure model performance. The tasks are explained below:

**SST-2:** This is a movie review corpus from Socher et al. (2013) that consists of a sentence form the review along with the sentiment associated with that sentence.

**QQP:** Quora Question Pair corpus (Wang et al., 2018) consists of two questions and a label indicating if the two questions are duplicates of each other.

**MNLI:** The MNLI (Williams et al., 2017) corpus is built of top of SNLI. This consists of a premise, hypothesis and a label indicating if the premise and hypothesis are in entailment, contradiction or they are neutral.

## 4 Models

The simplest way to make a model forget the datapoint it has seen during training is to remove the datapoint from the training set and re-train the model. However, this is computationally very expensive for large models like BERT (Devlin et al., 2018b) and we need an efficient way to re-training models if we want to forget a datapoint. Bourtoule et al. (2019) presented Sharded, Isolated, Sliced and Aggregated (SISA) training approach in order to "un-learn" a datapoint. While they measured the performance of this approach on computer vision datasets, no work has looked at its performance on NLP datasets. We explain the algorithm and our approach to make it parameter efficient for NLP specific models.

### 4.1 SISA

Figure 1 shows the working of the SISA algorithm. The entire training dataset is split into $S$ shards. Each shard is made up of $R$ slices. There is one model that is trained for every shard. In order to begin training, we can pick any ML model and then use gradient descent to train the model. While training, the model goes through the data, slice by slice saving a checkpoint after training for each slice. Finally once the model finishes training on the final slice, the model is saved and mapped to the shard. This process is continued for all the shards. During inference, each model belonging

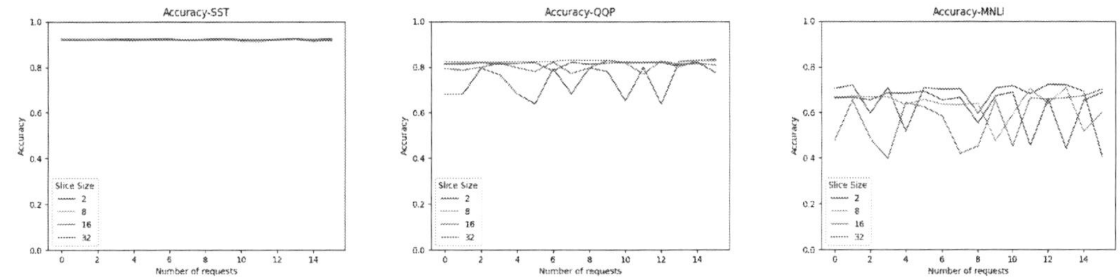


(a) SST (b) QQP (c) MNLI

Figure 2: Performance of SISA-A on the 3 datasets. Number of slices is shown in the legend. We see SISA-A has same or slightly lower performance than the baseline BERT model.

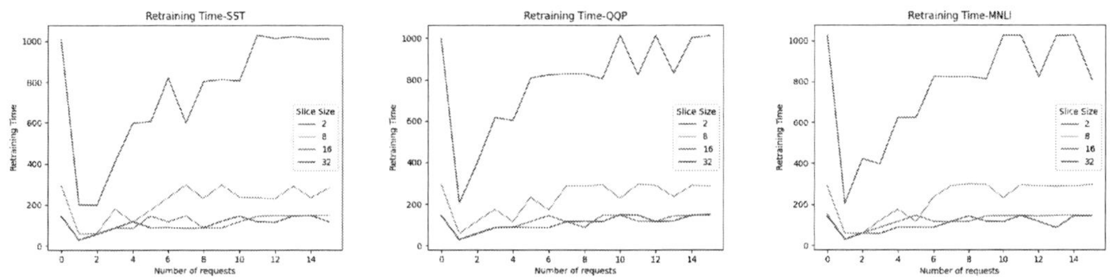


(a) SST (b) QQP (c) MNLI

Figure 3: Re-training time of SISA-A on the 3 datasets. Number of slices is shown in the legend. We see that the re-training time remains fairly constant if the slice size is greater than 8 for a number of un-learning requests.

to a shard predicts the label and the labels are aggregated similar to model ensembling. When an un-learning request comes in, we pick the shard where this data point is present, then go to the slice that contains the un-learning request. We delete the datapoint from this slice, take the checkpoint that was trained up until that checkpoint and continue training the model. This guarantees that the model forgets the un-learning request. During inference we pass the sample through each of the $S$ models, obtain $S$ labels and aggregate using a majority voting strategy.

### 4.2 SISA modified with fully connected Layer (SISA-FC)

While the SISA framework is flexible to be used with any model, in the NLP domain it is not practical to store a checkpoint after each slice. Moreover the pre-training/fine-tuning time of the full model will become a major shortcoming and we need a way to reduce both the training time and the memory footprint of these large models. A simple way to alleviate this short-coming is to use a base model and pre-train it on a generic corpus of text and then add fully connected layers on top of it. Only the parameters from the linear layers are fine tuned in the optimization process. This will reduce the overall training time as the backpropagation of gradients only happens in the final layers and also we will only need to store the weights of these additional parameters.

### 4.3 SISA modified with Adapters (SISA-A)

While adding linear layers to SISA might solves both the training time and the memory footprint issue, the raw performance of the model will take a hit when compared to fine tuning the entire model as is done in a regular NLP setting (Devlin et al., 2018b). One approach to keep the benefits of the linear layer while also optimizing for performance is to use Adapters (Houlsby et al., 2019) in the Encoder blocks of the transformer. While this increases the memory footprint of the model, it only accounts for about $1-5\%$ of the model parameters. Thereby providing us with $95-99\%$ memory benefits.

### 4.4 Baselines:

We compare the performance of SISA-FC and SISA-A with respect to popular NLP settings. We

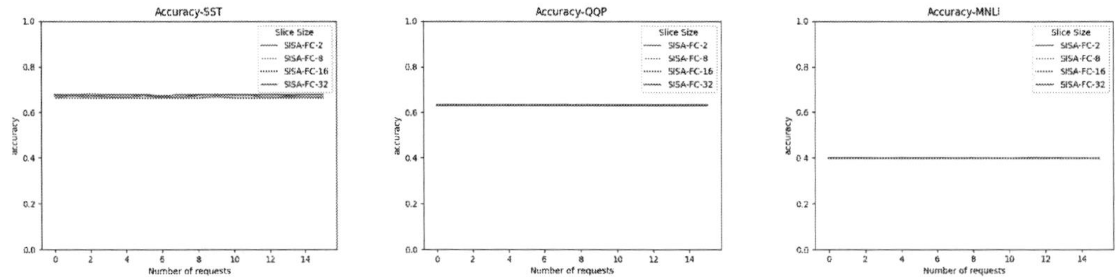


(a) SST (b) QQP (c) MNLI

Figure 4: Performance of SISA-FC on the 3 datasets. Number of slices is shown in the legend. We see the performance of SISA-FC is lower than that of SISA-A.

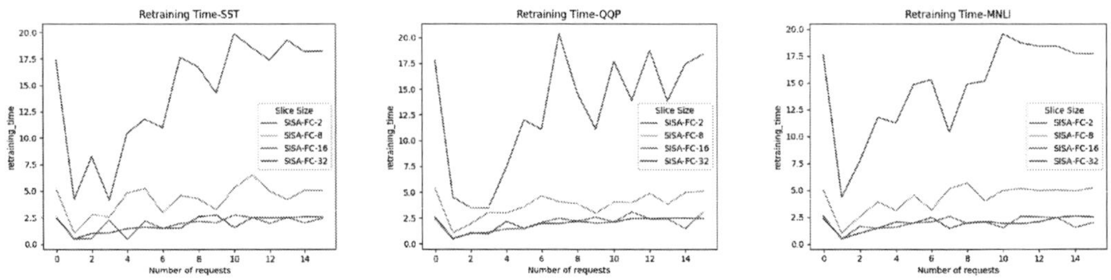


(a) SST (b) QQP (c) Accuracy

Figure 5: Re-training time of SISA-FC on the 3 datasets. Number of slices is shown in the legend. We see that the re-training time remains fairly constant if the slice size is greater than 8 for a number of un-learning requests.

fine-tune Bert on the same samples and show that there is minimal impact on performance. We also show the majority classifier accuracy to show the improvement of SISA-FC and SISA-A against this baseline.

### 4.5 Implementation details:

We use the Bert-base model from Huggingface[2] to train on this task. We used a batch of 16, max length of 256, Adam (Kingma and Ba, 2014) optimizer learning rate of $5e-3$ and train the model for 10 epochs when we are training the SISA-FC model. We also use the same hyper-parameters for SISA-A approach but add adapters using Adapterhub[3] and only update those parameters. We experiment with different slice sizes but keep the number of shards fixed at 5. We ran each experiment 4 times and averaged the results. All the experiments were run on 4 V-100 GPUs with 16GB memory each for a total of 10 days.

[2]https://huggingface.co/

[3]https://docs.adapterhub.ml/training.html

## 5 Experiments and Results

For all the experiments in this paper we use a shard size of 5. We however experiment with different slices sizes (these are shown in the legends of the graphs)

### 5.1 Evaluation Metrics:

In order for an organization to allow customers to opt-out we need mechanisms that will enable re-training of models with low re-training time and memory foot-print while keeping the model performance as close to the original model as possible. Hence we look at the following three metrics :

**Accuracy:** Percentage of samples in the test set that the model predicts accurately.

**Re-training time:** The amount of time taken to delete the un-learning requests from the dataset and then re-train the model.

**Memory:** The amount of memory the final model takes up on disk.

We analyze the model across all the three metrics for upto 16 uniformly randomly sampled un-learning requests unless stated otherwise. An un-learning request is defined as a request to the delete a datapoint from the training set. This is equivalent

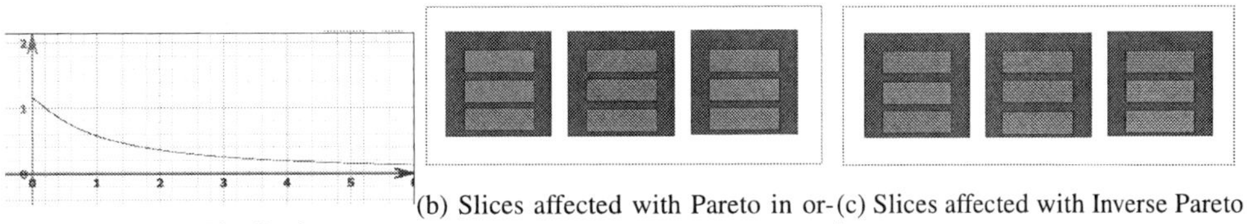

(a) Pareto Distribution (b) Slices affected with Pareto in orange (c) Slices affected with Inverse Pareto in orange

Figure 6: Figure 6a shows the Pareto distribution and the subsequent figures shows how the slices get affected with the Pareto and the inverse Pareto distributions.

to an user opting out of data collection practices.

### 5.2 Analysis of SISA-A

Figure 2 shows the performance of SISA-A for different slice sizes. We see that our approach is able to achieve the same level of performance as the BERT-base model even with the new setup we have with Adapters and SISA 1. While it doesn't drop in accuracy by more than $1-6\%$, we see that the model has a lower training time of 100x. We also see that the memory occupied by the model is much lower than using the original SISA approach which would store the weights of the full model. We also see from Figure 2 that the accuracy of our approach for slice size greater than 2 is almost the same across different slices and remains same for different number of un-learning requests as well. However with larger number of slices we see that the model has a much lower re-training time when compared to a slice size of two from Figure 3. This observation is consistent across all the 3 datasets. It is also to be noted that the re-training time does not increase linearly with more number of un-learning requests. The re-training time does increase with a positive delta. We show in Section 5.5 on how we can make this re-training time flat across multiple un-learning requests. We also see that the model re-training time is constant across all the 3 datasets that were chosen.

### 5.3 Analysis of SISA-FC

Figure 5 shows the performance of SISA-FC for different slice sizes. We observe that the model performance for different un-learning requests is lower than that of SISA-A by $20-30\%$ on all the tasks. This is due to the fact that there are far lesser number of weights that were used to fine-tune the model. However in low memory settings this approach would work better than the SISA-A approach as it occupies lesser memory. We also observe that the re-training time to just train the final layer is much lower than that of SISA-A. But other observations made with respect to SISA-A still holds with SISA-FC.

### 5.4 Comparison Between SISA-FC and SISA-A

From Figures 5, we see that the SISA-A approach significantly outperforms the SISA-FC approach in terms of accuracy. Across different slice sizes we see that we can get an absolute gain of 20-30% in accuracy depending on the task. While the Houlsby et al. (2019) does note this performance difference, the performance difference is only 1%. When we apply adapters to SISA we see that the performance gain is much higher.

### 5.5 Profiling requests based on probability of occurrence

In the above two experiments, we assumed that the un-learning requests are uniformly randomly chosen from all of the training points. However, in a practical setting this might not be the case. Organizations can group customers into high risk and low risk customers based on their probability of opting out. In order to simulate such a scenario, we use the Pareto distribution. Pareto distribution is defined using the equation below:

$$p(x) = a.m^{a}/x^{a+1} \quad (1)$$

When we plot the Pareto distribution we get the curve shown in Figure 6a. 80% of the mass is in the head of the distribution and 20% in the tail. When we sample requests based on this distribution we get data-points belonging to the shards shown in Figure 6b. For the purpose of this experiment we set $m$ to 1 and $a$ to 1.16. However if we take the mirror image of the Pareto distribution and sample from that distribution then the shards that will be affected is shown in Figure 6c. We experiment with both these types of sampling to see its affect on model performance and re-training time.

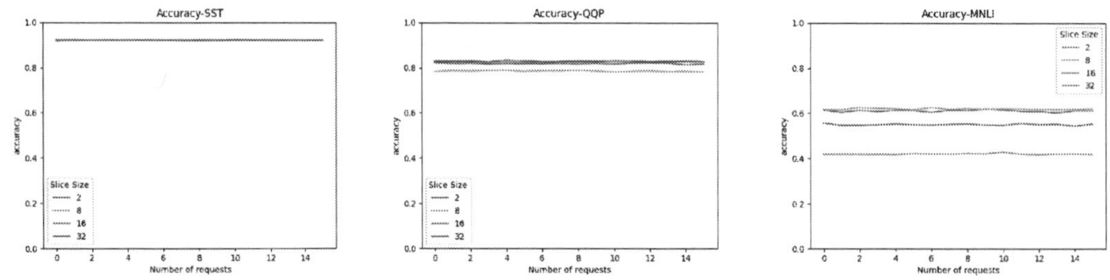


(a) SST (b) QQP (c) MNLI

Figure 7: Accuracy of SISA-A on Inverse Pareto distribution. Number of slices is shown in the legend.

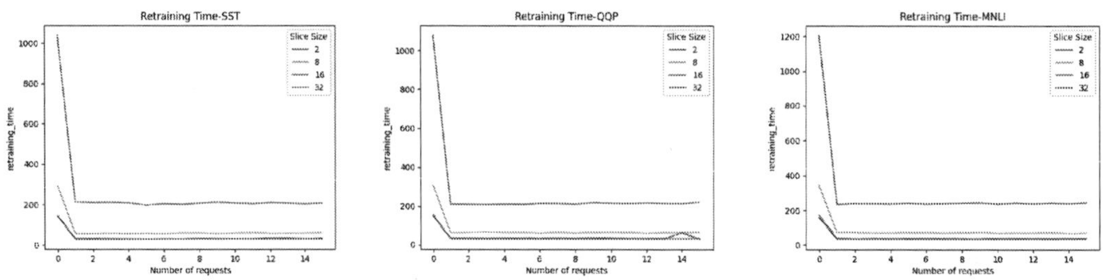


(a) SST (b) QQP (c) Accuracy

Figure 8: Re-training time of SISA-A on Inverse Pareto distribution. Number of slices is shown in the legend.

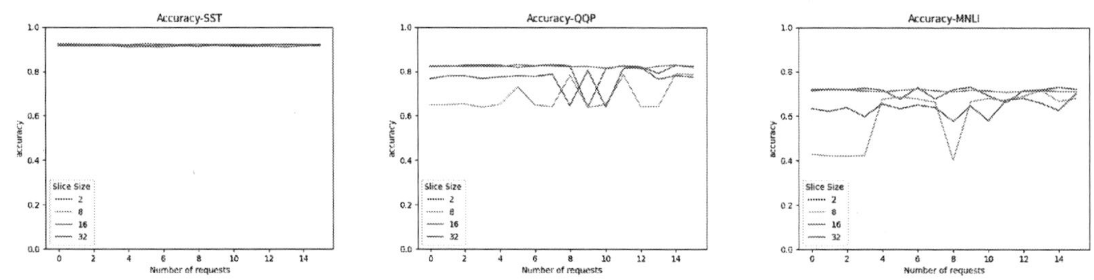


(a) SST (b) QQP (c) MNLI

Figure 9: Accuracy of SISA-A on Pareto distribution. Number of slices is shown in the legend.

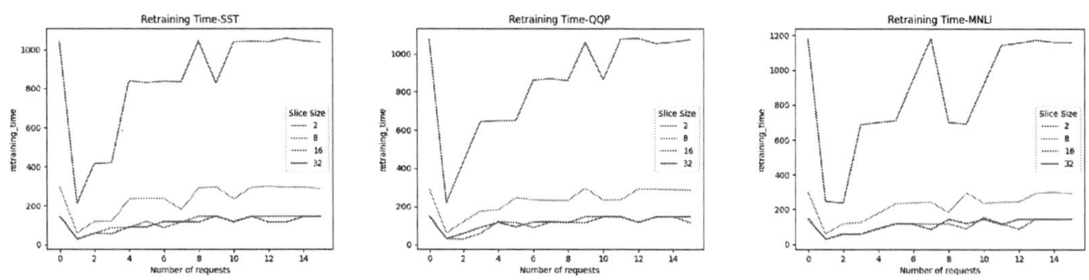


(a) SST (b) QQP (c) MNLI

Figure 10: Re-training time of SISA-A on Pareto distribution. Number of slices is shown in the legend.

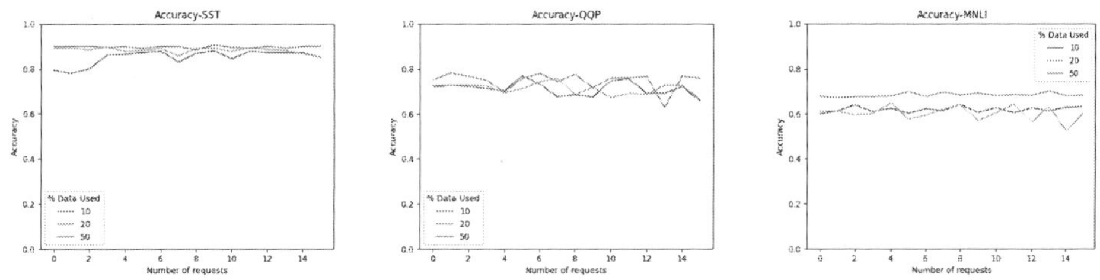


(a) SST (b) QQP (c) Accuracy

Figure 11: Accuracy of SISA-A on partial datasets. Percentage data used is shown in the legend

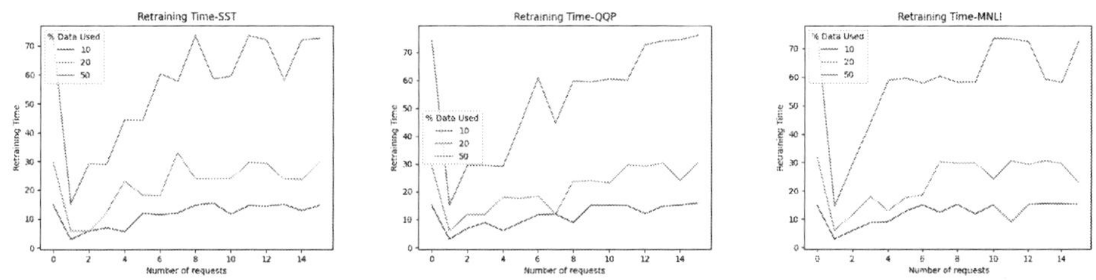


(a) SST (b) QQP (c) Accuracy

Figure 12: Re-training time of SISA-A on partial datasets. Percentage data used is shown in the legend

From Figures 8 and 10, we see that the training time of the inverse Pareto distribution is lesser than that of both the uniform distribution and Pareto distribution by 350% and 360% respectively. We also see that the re-training time of the inverse Pareto distribution is flat across multiple un-learning requests as they only affect the last few slices in the shard, thereby lowering training time. This opens up to possibilities of smarter customer segmentation while training. While we show one simple way to segment customers to gain on re-training time, we leave the possibilities of exploring other such strategies for future work.

## 5.6 Performance on a portion of the data

In the next experiment, we look at the performance of SISA-A on portions of the training set to test the few shot generalizability of this approach. For the purpose of this experiment, we use 5 shards, 16 slices and uniform un-learning requests. Results are shown in Figures 11 and 12. We see that on all the different datasets, the performance in the few-shot setting does not match the performance of the model in the full-data setting. This is one of the major drawbacks of the SISA algorithm in low resource NLP settings. Since the model is forced to look at a portion of the data several times before it is check-pointed, the model tends to overfit on the slice it is training on. We hypothesize this to be the reason for lower model performance.

We also see that the BERT-base model performs much better than the SISA-A approach in the few-shot setting. While we show the short-coming of this approach in the few-shot setting we leave the further exploration to alleviate this issue for future work.

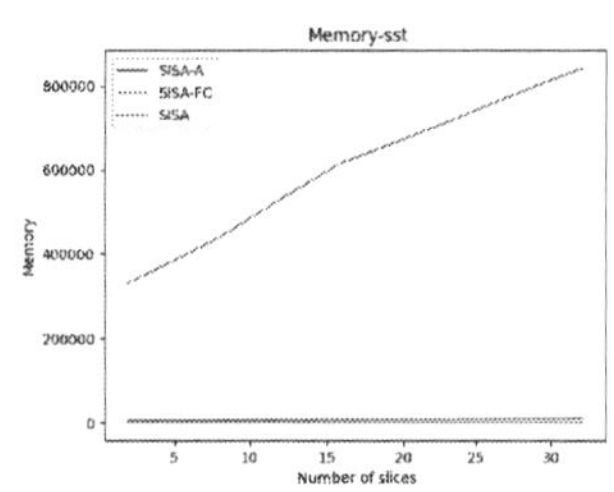


Figure 13: Memory Occupied by the three approaches. We see that the SISA-A and SISA-FC approaches provides a significant memory savings when compared to the base SISA approach

## 5.7 Memory profiling

Figure 13 shows the memory occupied by the three different approaches compared in this work. We see that if we use the BERT model along with the vanilla SISA algorithm, the memory increases linearly as the number of slices increases. But with our approach, the memory increase is far less drastic (SISA-A and SISA-FC).

## 6 Conclusion

The central tenet of privacy regulations in the U.S and EU revolve around the concept of "notice and choice". This allows users to opt-out of data collection if they deem something violates their privacy needs. However, owing to the gap between technology experts and privacy regulators there has not been enough work around opting out of data that has already been used to train ML models. Through the SISA-A and SISA-FC approaches we show the working of the SISA algorithm in the NLP domain on Encoder based models. We show the benefits of our approach in terms of re-training time and disk space usage.

## Limitations

While the experimental results show that it is possible to use SISA in LLMs, it is only limited to Encoder based models because of the requirement of an aggregation layer in SISA. We cannot extend this approach to the decoder based models as is and that is a limitation of our work. Also,as noted in Section 5.6, our results show that SISA-A approches do not work well in the few shot setting because of the tendency of the model to overfit on each slice. In this paper we do point out the lack of generalizability of this approach in the few shot setting. However, we do not discuss steps to mitigate these issues using our technique. Finally, we show how organizations can benefit from segmenting users into different groups based on the probability of opting out. While we show this by using/simulating different distributions we do not perform profiling on actual user data.

## Ethics Statement

In this work we show how we can perform efficient NLP while also adhering to the people's privacy requirements. While we show how organizations can efficiently perform the task of un-learning we cannot prove if the organization indeed performed unlearning on the samples. Also all the associated risks of using pre-trained language models like BERT will remain with this approach as they form the backbone of our framework.

## References


Martin Abadi, Andy Chu, Ian Goodfellow, H. Brendan McMahan, Ilya Mironov, Kunal Talwar, and Li Zhang. 2016. Deep learning with differential privacy. In *Proceedings of the 2016 ACM SIGSAC Conference on Computer and Communications Security*. ACM.

Thomas Baumhauer, Pascal Schöttle, and Matthias Zeppelzauer. 2020. Machine unlearning: Linear filtration for logit-based classifiers.

Lucas Bourtoule, Varun Chandrasekaran, Christopher A. Choquette-Choo, Hengrui Jia, Adelin Travers, Baiwu Zhang, David Lie, and Nicolas Papernot. 2019. Machine unlearning. *CoRR*, abs/1912.03817.

Jacob Devlin, Ming-Wei Chang, Kenton Lee, and Kristina Toutanova. 2018a. BERT: pre-training of deep bidirectional transformers for language understanding. *CoRR*, abs/1810.04805.

Jacob Devlin, Ming-Wei Chang, Kenton Lee, and Kristina Toutanova. 2018b. Bert: Pre-training of deep bidirectional transformers for language understanding. *arXiv preprint arXiv:1810.04805*.

Min Du, Zhi Chen, Chang Liu, Rajvardhan Oak, and Dawn Song. 2019. Lifelong anomaly detection through unlearning. In *Proceedings of the 2019 ACM SIGSAC Conference on Computer and Communications Security*, CCS '19, page 1283–1297, New York, NY, USA. Association for Computing Machinery.

Aditya Golatkar, Alessandro Achille, and Stefano Soatto. 2019. Eternal sunshine of the spotless net: Selective forgetting in deep networks. *CoRR*, abs/1911.04933.

Neil Houlsby, Andrei Giurgiu, Stanislaw Jastrzebski, Bruna Morrone, Quentin de Laroussilhe, Andrea Gesmundo, Mona Attariyan, and Sylvain Gelly. 2019. Parameter-efficient transfer learning for NLP. *CoRR*, abs/1902.00751.

Joel Jang, Dongkeun Yoon, Sohee Yang, Sungmin Cha, Moontae Lee, Lajanugen Logeswaran, and Minjoon Seo. 2022. Knowledge unlearning for mitigating privacy risks in language models.

Diederik P Kingma and Jimmy Ba. 2014. Adam: A method for stochastic optimization. *arXiv preprint arXiv:1412.6980*.

Xuechen Li, Florian Tramèr, Percy Liang, and Tatsunori Hashimoto. 2021. Large language models can be strong differentially private learners. *CoRR*, abs/2110.05679.

Ronak Mehta, Sourav Pal, Vikas Singh, and Sathya N. Ravi. 2022. Deep unlearning via randomized conditionally independent hessians.

Quoc Phong Nguyen, Bryan Kian Hsiang Low, and Patrick Jaillet. 2020. Variational bayesian unlearning. In *Advances in Neural Information Processing Systems*, volume 33, pages 16025–16036. Curran Associates, Inc.

Quoc Phong Nguyen, Ryutaro Oikawa, Dinil Mon Divakaran, Mun Choon Chan, and Bryan Kian Hsiang Low. 2022a. Markov chain monte carlo-based machine unlearning. In *Proceedings of the 2022 ACM on Asia Conference on Computer and Communications Security*. ACM.

Thanh Tam Nguyen, Thanh Trung Huynh, Phi Le Nguyen, Alan Wee-Chung Liew, Hongzhi Yin, and Quoc Viet Hung Nguyen. 2022b. A survey of machine unlearning.

Anand D. Sarwate, Kamalika Chaudhuri, and Claire Monteleoni. 2009. Differentially private support vector machines. *CoRR*, abs/0912.0071.

Richard Socher, Alex Perelygin, Jean Wu, Jason Chuang, Christopher D Manning, Andrew Y Ng, and Christopher Potts. 2013. Recursive deep models for semantic compositionality over a sentiment treebank. In *Proceedings of the 2013 conference on empirical methods in natural language processing*, pages 1631–1642.

Aman Tahiliani, Vikas Hassija, Vinay Chamola, and Mohsen Guizani. 2021. Machine unlearning: Its need and implementation strategies. In *2021 Thirteenth International Conference on Contemporary Computing (IC3-2021)*, IC3 '21, page 241–246, New York, NY, USA. Association for Computing Machinery.

Alex Wang, Amanpreet Singh, Julian Michael, Felix Hill, Omer Levy, and Samuel R. Bowman. 2018. GLUE: A multi-task benchmark and analysis platform for natural language understanding. *CoRR*, abs/1804.07461.

Adina Williams, Nikita Nangia, and Samuel R Bowman. 2017. A broad-coverage challenge corpus for sentence understanding through inference. *arXiv preprint arXiv:1704.05426*.

Da Yu, Saurabh Naik, Arturs Backurs, Sivakanth Gopi, Huseyin A. Inan, Gautam Kamath, Janardhan Kulkarni, Yin Tat Lee, Andre Manoel, Lukas Wutschitz, Sergey Yekhanin, and Huishuai Zhang. 2021. Differentially private fine-tuning of language models. *CoRR*, abs/2110.06500.

# GECTurk: Grammatical Error Correction and Detection Dataset for Turkish

**Atakan Kara, Farrin Marouf Safian, Andrew Bond, Gözde Gül Şahin**
Computer Engineering Department
Koç University, Istanbul, Turkey
`https://gglab-ku.github.io/`

## Abstract

Grammatical Error Detection and Correction (GEC) tools have proven useful for native speakers and second language learners. Developing such tools requires a large amount of parallel, annotated data, which is unavailable for most languages. Synthetic data generation is a common practice to overcome the scarcity of such data. However, it is not straightforward for morphologically rich languages like Turkish due to complex writing rules that require phonological, morphological, and syntactic information. In this work, we present a flexible and extensible synthetic data generation pipeline for Turkish covering more than 20 expert-curated grammar and spelling rules (a.k.a., writing rules) implemented through complex transformation functions. Using this pipeline, we derive 130,000 high-quality parallel sentences from professionally edited articles. Additionally, we create a more realistic test set by manually annotating a set of movie reviews. We implement three baselines formulating the task as i) neural machine translation, ii) sequence tagging, and iii) prefix tuning with a pretrained decoder-only model, achieving strong results. Furthermore, we perform exhaustive experiments on out-of-domain datasets to gain insights on the transferability and robustness of the proposed approaches. Our results suggest that our corpus, GECTurk, is high-quality and allows knowledge transfer for the out-of-domain setting. To encourage further research on Turkish GEC, we release our datasets, baseline models, and the synthetic data generation pipeline at `https://github.com/GGLAB-KU/gecturk`.

## 1 Introduction

Grammatical Error Correction (GEC) is among the well-established NLP tasks with dedicated shared tasks (e.g., BEA (Bryant et al., 2019)), benchmarks, and even specific evaluation measures. With increasing interest from the community, the field is in constant need of novel tools, methods, and more importantly, extensions to other languages.

Recently, there has been an explosion of research about GEC for high-resource languages, especially for English (Rothe et al., 2021; Omelianchuk et al., 2020; Bryant et al., 2019). These recent techniques either formulate the task as neural machine translation, i.e., generation (Rothe et al., 2021), or token classification to detect erroneous tokens (Omelianchuk et al., 2020). The first approach mainly utilizes and engineers vanilla Transformers to generate the corrected text, while the second focuses on engineering a set of errors and transformation rules. Both formulations require a large set of parallel corpora containing grammatically correct and incorrect sentence pairs. Also, the latter approach additionally requires a highly curated dataset with annotations for correcting errors (i.e., location and type of the error). Constructing such a corpus with error annotations is nontrivial—especially for low-resource languages with rich morphology like Turkish. The challenge is due to grammar rules, a.k.a., writing errors being entangled in several layers, such as phonology, morphology, syntax, and semantics. As of today, there are no spelling or grammatical error datasets, as mentioned by Çöltekin et al. (2023), with the exception of the dataset introduced by Arikan et al. (2019).

To address this, we focus on the Turkish Language and utilize the official writing rules established by the Turkish Language Association[1]. We implement corruption, a.k.a. transformation, functions to generate instances that violate a specific rule, which requires challenging analysis of sentences on several linguistic levels, as well as curation of specialized lexicons. Then, we generate a large, synthetic, high-quality annotated corpus by applying transformation functions to professionally edited, modern Turkish articles. In addition to the

[1] `https://tdk.gov.tr/`



*Findings of the Association for Computational Linguistics: IJCNLP-AACL 2023*, pages 278–290
November 1–4, 2023. ©2023 Asian Federation of Natural Language Processing

transformation functions, we implement and share the reverse-transformation functions for validating the generated datasets and developing sequence tagger models, which achieve state-of-the-art in English.

In addition, we compile a corpus of movie reviews and manually annotate 300 sentences with the proposed error types to evaluate the models in a real-life setting. Furthermore, we design and implement several baselines using standard neural machine translation (NMT), sequence tagging and prefix-tuning. The NMT model only generates the correct sentece, but the sequence tagging model is trained to tag the tokens with the error type (if any) and then use our reverse transformation function on this error to generate the correct text. Finally, we perform prefix-tuning (Li and Liang, 2021) on mGPT Shliazhko et al. (2022) for both detection and correction to test more recent techniques.

Our findings indicate that our pipeline approach using smaller models perform better than employing larger pretrained models in an end-to-end fashion when it comes to both synthetic and real-world datasets—particularly for the grammatical error detection task. Conversely, we observe that pretraining benefits the models in more realistic cases, despite the larger models still falling behind their simpler counterparts. Our results from out-of-domain tests imply that training on the synthetic dataset gives a strong prior to both smaller and larger models.

Our contributions can be summarized as follows:

- We propose the first comprehensive, expert-curated grammatical error schema for Turkish that covers 25 error types.
- We present a synthetic data generation pipeline that can be used to create arbitrary sized datasets, and can be easily extended to include new grammatical error types or lexicons, and can easily be modified to include custom tools (e.g., morphological analyzer and disambiguator).
- We present the first large-scale, fine-grained public dataset for Turkish grammatical correction and detection, along with a manually annotated realistic test set and strong baseline models.

We make our datasets, baseline models, and synthetic data generation pipeline publicly available at `https://github.com/GGLAB-KU/gecturk`.

## 2 Related Work

**English GEC** Despite having a long history, with the BEA-2019 Shared Task on Grammatical Error Correction (Bryant et al., 2019), the GEC community started using neural models and formulating GEC as a neural machine translation task (i.e., translate from grammatically incorrect to correct sentences), which has become the dominant approach. Another recent approach, GECToR (Omelianchuk et al., 2020), uses the idea of reverse transformations, which can be applied to a list of source tokens $[x_1, \ldots, x_n]$, in order to produce the desired correct grammar. They use a sequence tagger with a BERT encoder. Each tag corresponds to a transformation where transformations are applied after the sequence tagging finishes. In contrast, the gT5 model released by Xue et al. (2021) is a multilingual mT5 model fine-tuned on artificially corrupted sentences from the mC4 corpus and uses a span prediction and classification task to fix grammatical errors (Rothe et al., 2021). This does require a lot of additional training time, since the original mT5 model is not initially prepared for a similar task. Their model achieves SOTA results in 4 languages while only training once.

**Turkish GEC** Previously, Arikan et al. (2019) proposed a neural sequence tagger model and a synthetically generated dataset to correct "de/da" clitic errors. In Turkish grammar, "de/da" is used both as a locative suffix and a conjuction meaning *also*, *too* that is written separately. For instance, "-de" is a locative suffix in the sentence "Ev**de** (**At** home)"; while used as a conjuction here: "Ben **de** geliyorum (I'm coming **too**)". Mistakes in using these clitics are common among native speakers, often due to some contextual subtleties and oral dialect influencing the written language. Öztürk et al. (2020) combined a contextual word embedding model, namely BERT, with a sequence tagger to correct "de/da" clitic errors. Although these errors are common, they constitute only a small portion of grammatical errors made by native speakers. In addition, while there are various forms of this error, the previous work only considers a few. Our data generation strategy considers multiple versions of the "de/da" clitic errors and many more common grammatical errors.

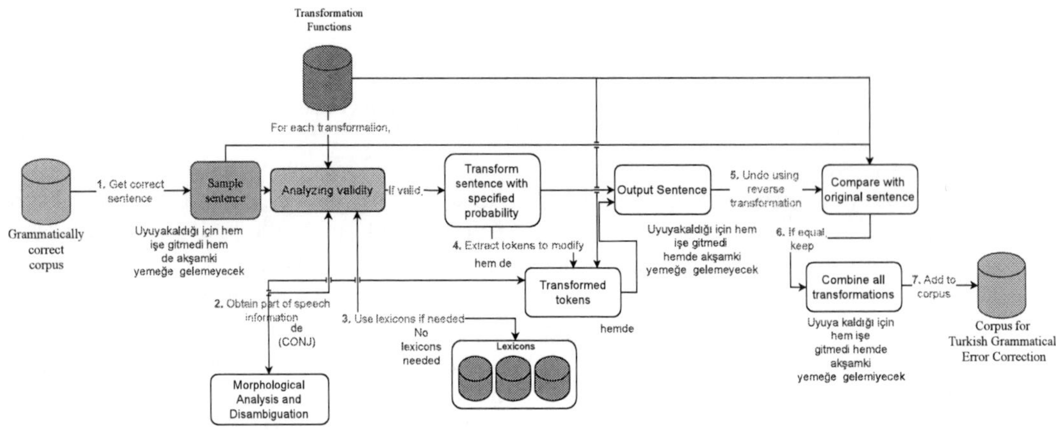


Figure 1: Data generation pipeline. 1) First, a correct sentence is obtained from the grammatically correct corpus. 2) Then, morphological analysis is performed. 3) The validity of the sentence for the transformation function is checked. If the sentence is eligible, the transformation is applied with some probability $p$. 4)First, selecting tokens to modify, 5) then, checking if the reverse transformations can recover the original tokens. 6) If original cannot be recovered, the sentence is removed. If can be recovered 7) the transformed sentence is added to the corpus.

**Parsing-based Approaches** While most of the current approaches focus on reverse transformations and sequence tagging, there are several studies that involve the use of parsing techniques. Flickinger and Yu (2013) create a parsing tree, and identify malformed parts of the tree to detect grammatical errors. da Costa (2021) use symbolic parsers and computational grammars for GEC and GED. On the same research line, Flickinger and Packard use bridged analyses combined with parsing to better allow for connecting two phrases in Head-driven Phrase Structure Grammar (HPSG).

## 3 Synthetic Data Generation

The overall generation process is given in Fig. 1. First, we randomly sample from professionally edited Turkish corpora ( §3.1). Then, sentences are corrupted—if possible—following the expert-curated transformation rules explained in §3.2, as well as the use of a morphological analyzer. Finally, pairs of grammatically correct and corrupted sentences are added to the final Turkish GEC corpus following the $M^2$ scorer (Dahlmeier and Ng, 2012) (MaxMatch) data format.

### 3.1 Corpus

Our proposed data generation pipeline is built upon the assumption that all input sentences are grammatically correct. Hence, we base our study on previously compiled newspaper corpora (Diri and Amasyali, 2003; Amasyalı and Diri, 2006; Can and Amasyalı, 2016; Kemik NLP Group, 2022) that are proofread and went through a professional editing process. The articles are on various topics, including politics, sports, and medicine, and have been written by more than 95 authors for three different newspapers; in total, more than 7000 singly authored documents were collected between 2004-2012. Once we obtained grammatically correct source sentences, we performed several preprocessing steps, such as removing duplicates (2.9% of the combined dataset), ending with 138K unique sentences.

### 3.2 Transformation

The Turkish Language Association (TDK)[2], a government agency founded in 1932, is responsible for providing resources to conduct scientific research on written and oral sources of Turkish. Within this scope, they specify and maintain a comprehensive list of publicly available writing rules[3]. We rely on this expert-curated list to generate forward and backward transformation rules, which we refer to as $f$ and $f^{-1}$ respectively. However, the list is long, and some writing rules are intuitive to native speakers, so that any errors made on these rules sound abnormal to them. We select the grammar rules that are most commonly used incorrectly by native speakers, determined by consulation with Turkish language experts and filtering the list from TDK

[2] https://www.tdk.gov.tr/

[3] https://www.tdk.gov.tr/kategori/icerik/yazim-kurallari/

using their feedback. We do not include any rules that are common for Turkish language learners but rarely made by native speakers. Table 1 provides the full list of the transformation rules produced by this work. The transformations rely on a morphological analyzer, which was essential to get the transformations right for a morphologically rich language like Turkish. For more information on Turkish Morphology, we refer to Oflazer (2014) and Lewis (1985).

**Applying $f$** For each sampled sentence, first, we shuffle the list of $f$s. This ensures that mutually exclusive transformation functions are applied with desired frequencies. Then, we iteratively apply each $f$ on the sentence given with the pseudo-code in Algorithm 1. Here, $f$ gets an input sentence $s$, morphological analysis of the sentence $M_s$, an array of indicators for whether any transformation has been applied to the word— $flags$, and parameter $p \in (0,1)$. The algorithm, then, iterates over tokens (or pairs) and checks whether the token has been transformed. If not, it checks whether the token(s) are eligible for $f$. If eligible, we apply $f$ with the probability $p$, since not all errors are made with the same frequency by native speakers.[4]

**Eligibility Check** Some official writing rules require syntactic analysis at the token and sentence levels. For instance, to apply the transformation function CONJ_DE_SEP, one must perform morphological analysis and disambiguation to analyze the part-of-speech tags at the morpheme level. That is, CONJ_DE_SEP transformation can be applied **only if** a "-de/da" morpheme with a CONJUCTION part-of-speech tag is found. Additionally, a small set of rules requires specialized lexicons, e.g., a list of exceptional foreign words for FOREIGN_R2_EXC. To address the former, we use a state-of-the-art morphological analyzer Dayanik et al. (2018), and the lexicons are taken from the official lists provided by TDK[2].

**Annotation Format** We use the standard GEC annotation format following Ng et al. (2013) and Bryant et al. (2019). An example annotation is given in Fig. 2. Here, S and A refer to the ungrammatical sentence and edit annotations respectively. Each A contains starting and ending indices, the error type, the corrected phrase, and the id of the annotator.

[4]We choose the probabilities intuitively after an initial analysis on web corpus and student essays.

Uyuyakaldığı için hem işe gitmedi hem de akşamki yemeğe gelemeyecek .

(Because they overslept, they didn't go to work and won't be able to come to dinner tonight.)

(a)

Uyuya kaldığı için hem işe gitmedi hemde akşamki yemeğe gelemiyecek .

(b)

S Uyuya kaldığı için hem işe gitmedi hemde akşamki yemeğe gelemiyecek.
A 0 2|||COMP_VERB_ADJ|||Uyuyakaldığı|||REQUIRED|||-NONE-|||0
A 6 7|||CONJ_DE_SEP|||hem de|||REQUIRED|||-NONE-|||0
A 9 10|||PRONOUNC_EXC|||gelemeyecek|||REQUIRED|||-NONE-|||0

(c)

Figure 2: The grammatically correct sentence is given in (a), the transformed version is given in (b), and the annotation format is given in (c).

**Postprocessing** Despite the use of professionally edited source sentences, there are still some grammatically incorrect sentences that slip through. We detect these cases by taking advantage of a key property of our reverse transformations: since each $f$ is reversible, we should see $S = f^{-1}(f(S))$ for each sentence $S$. Therefore, at the end of the transformation process, we perform this check on every generated, grammatically incorrect sentence. If a sentence fails this check, then we know it is problematic, and we remove it from the corpus. The final sentences are thus properly modified in the desired way, with no unintentional side effects.

### 3.3 Annotated Corpus

The annotated corpus includes more than 138K sentences, with 104K error annotations belonging to 25 error types given in Table 1. In this corpus, 50% of sentences are error free, in order for models to learn how to detect/correct sentences that are already grammatically correct. The generative pipeline controls the frequency of those error types, aiming to mimic the human error frequencies (see App. B). As in the dataset of CoNLL-2014 shared task (Ng et al., 2014), some error types appear more frequently than others. These frequencies are by the probability parameters $p$; therefore, the difference between frequencies of error types is an intended result. Our dataset is finally split into a train/val/test set of 70%/15%/15%.

**Algorithm 1** Apply $f$

```
Require: s := sentence, M_s := morphological analysis, flags, p
Ensure: tags
  tags ← []
  n ← Number of tokens in s
  for i = 1 → n do
      if flags[i] and is_eligible(s, M_s) and flipCoin(p) then
          tags.insert("A i {i + 1} ||| ruleID ||| sentence[i] ||| REQUIRED ||| -NONE- ||| 0")
          sentence[i] ← transformed token at index i
          flags[i] ← False
```

### 3.4 Curated Test Corpus

For a more realistic test setting, we used movie reviews from a popular website [5] shared by Altinok (2023). We asked a domain expert to annotate the sentences for the proposed error types, following the standard GEC annotation format. As a results, we curated a test dataset of 300 sentences, wherein half of the sentences were grammatically correct and the other half contained errors.

## 4 Tasks and Models

In this paper, we consider two tasks: Grammatical Error Correction (GEC) and Grammatical Error Detection (GED).

**Grammatical Error Correction (GEC)** takes as input a grammatically incorrect sentence and outputs the corrected version of the sentence. Formally, given an input sentence $\mathbf{x} = (x_1, \cdots, x_T)$ which may contain some grammar mistakes, the aim is to produce an output sentence $\mathbf{y} = (y_1, \cdots, y_{T'})$ which contains no grammatical errors. Conditions are not imposed on how the model produces grammatically correct sentences.

**Grammatical Error Detection (GED)** takes a slightly different approach to this problem, with the goal of producing detailed information about the errors in the source sentence. This includes details about the type of error and the location of the error in the sentence. Formally, given an input sentence $\mathbf{x} = (x_1, \cdots, x_T)$, we can represent the problem as a token-level classification task, where the output is $\mathbf{c} = (c_1, \cdots, c_T)$, and $c_i$ represents the error type of token $i$. Given the knowledge that an error of type $c_k$ occurred at the location from $m$ to $n$, it is then possible to apply the corresponding reverse transformation $f^{-1}$, and fix the error.

[5] www.beyazperde.com

### 4.1 Models

We introduce three models to evaluate the performance of GECTurk: An NMT baseline, a sequence tagger using BERT (Devlin et al., 2019) pretrained on Turkish, and mGPT using prefix-tuning. All models are trained using 1 Nvidia V100 GPU. We only provide the essential information about the models here. More details are available in Appendix A.

**NMT Baseline:** We train a vanilla transformer model (Vaswani et al., 2017) for GEC. This choice is inspired by the most recent shared task on grammatical correction (Bryant et al., 2019), where many of the winning teams used transformer-based models and modeled the problem as a Neural Machine Translation (NMT). The training dataset consists of triples $\{(x_i, y_i, a_i)\}_{i=1}^N$, where $x_i$ is the $i$-th input sentence, $y_i$ is the corresponding ground truth corrected sentence, and $a_i$ are the annotations. During training, the model receives $x_i$ as input and tried to predict $y_i$ as output. Due to the nature of the formulation, NMT is only used for correction.

**Sequence Tagger:** Similar to recent work (Omelianchuk et al., 2020), we train a sequence tagging model using a cased BERT encoder, pretrained on Turkish text (Schweter, 2020) with default configurations and additional linear and softmax layers on the top. The BERT model uses the WordPiece tokenizer (Wu et al., 2016) that segments tokens into subwords. Therefore, each sentence in the dataset is first tokenized into subwords and passed into the BERT encoder. We only hold the first subword's representation for words with multiple subword tokens. Then, the encoder's representations are linearly transformed and passed to the softmax layer to classify into possible error types described in Table 1 or no error. The model is finetuned for token classification objective using cross-entropy loss.

The advantage of this model is the ability to per-

| Category | Rule ID | Description | f | Frequency |
|---|---|---|---|---|
| -DE/-DA | 1. CONJ_DE_SEP | Conjunction "-de/-da" is written separately. | Durumu [oğluna da -> oğlunada] bildirdi. | 12962 |
| | 2. CONJ_DE_VH | Conjunction "-de/-da" must follow the vowel harmony | Çok [da -> de] iyi olmuş. | 101 |
| | 3. CONJ_DE_AR | Conjunction "-de/-da" does not follow phonetic assimilation rules. | Sınıf [da -> ta] temizlendi. | 99 |
| | 4. YADA | "-de/-da" written together with the word "ya" is always written separately. | Sen [ya da -> yada] o buradan gidecek. | 472 |
| | 5. CONJ_DE_APOS | Conjunction "-de/-da" cannot be used with an apostrophe. | [Ayşe de -> Ayşe'de] geldi. | 10859 |
| | 6. CASE_DE | Suffix "-de/-da" is written adjacent. | [Evde -> Ev de] hiç süt kalmamıştı. | 37462 |
| -KI | 7. CONJ_KI_SEP | Conjunction "-ki" is written separately. | Bugün öyle çok [yorulmuş ki -> yorulmuşki] hemen yattı. | 1817 |
| | 8. CONJ_KI_EXC | On some exceptional instances, by convention, the conjunction "-ki" is written adjacent. | [Belki -> Bel ki], [oysaki -> oysa ki], [çünkü -> çünki] | 1395 |
| FOREIGN | 9. FOREIGN_R1 | Words that start with double consonants of foreign origin are written without adding an "-i" between the letters. | [gram -> gıram] | 307 |
| | 15. FOREIGN_R2 | Some foreign origin words undergo consonant assimilation | [sebebi -> sebepi] | 327 |
| | 16. FOREIGN_R2_EXC | Exceptions to the FOREIGN_R2 rule | [evrakı -> evrağı] | 422 |
| BISYL | 13. BISYLL_HAPL_VOW | Some bisyllabic words undergo haplology when they get a suffix starting with a vowel. | [ağzı -> ağızı] | 1567 |
| | 14. BISYLL_HAPL_VOW_EXC | Exception to previous rule | [içeride -> içerde] | 866 |
| LIGHT VERB | 17. LIGHT_VERB_SEP | Light verbs such as "etmek, edilmek, eylemek, olmak, olunmak" are written separately in case of no phonological assimilation | [arz etmek -> arzetmek] | 460 |
| | 18. LIGHT_VERB_ADJ | Light verbs are written adjacent in case of phonological assimilation e.g., liaison | [emretti -> emir etti] | 547 |
| COMPOUND | 20. COMP_VERB_ADJ | Compound words formed by knowing, giving, staying, stopping, coming, and writing are written adjacent if they have a suffix starting with -a, -e, -ı, -i, -u, -ü. | [uyuyakalma -> uyuya kalmak], [gidedurmak -> gide durmak], [çıka gelmek -> çıka gelmek] | 7840 |
| SINGLE | 22. PRONOUN_EXC | Traditionally, some pronouns are written adjacent. | [hiçbir -> hiç bir], [herhangi -> her hangi] | 3867 |
| | 23. SENT_CAP | The first letter of the sentence is capitalized. | [Onlar -> onlar] geldi. | 2613 |
| | 24. CAPPED | Some Arabic and Persian originated words are written with capped letters. | [kâğıt -> kağıt], [karargâh -> karargah] | 834 |
| | 25. ABBREV | Grammatical rules for abbreviations, such as adding suffixes to abbreviations, punctuations with abbreviations etc. | [Alm. -> Alm], [THY'de -> THY'da], [cm'yi -> cm'ye] | 359 |
| | 12. PRONOUNC_EXC | Unlike its pronunciation, verbs ending with "-a/-e" do not mutate when they get a suffix other than "-yor" | [başlayacağım -> başlıyacağım] | 12750 |

Table 1: Selected list of writing rules introduced by Turkish Language Association. $f[arg1- > arg2]$ refers to the transformation function where the correct and corrupted surface forms are given with $arg1$ and $arg2$ respectively.

| Dataset | #s | #a | %e | #e |
|---|---|---|---|---|
| (Ours) GECTurk | 138K | 104K | 49.7% | 25 |
| (Ours) CuratedTest | 300 | 227 | 50% | 25 |
| BOUN | 10K | 6K | 50.0% | 2 |
| BOUN complex | 102 | 105 | 100.0% | 2 |

Table 2: Datasets used for training and evaluation. #s: sentences, #a: annotations, %e: percentage of erroneous sentences, #e: number of errors types

form error detection easily, as opposed to simply error correction. Correction is simply performed with reverse transformations as described previously.

**Prefix Tuning:** Inspired by the recent successes of prefix tuning (Li and Liang, 2021) as an alternative to model fine-tuning, we use OpenPrompt (Ding et al., 2022) to perform prefix tuning on mGPT (Shliazhko et al., 2022). Despite being multilingual and primarily focused on other languages, mGPT achieves encouraging results on morphologically rich languages (Acikgoz et al., 2022). In prefix tuning, we append $N$ trainable (soft) tokens to the front of each input. Therefore, given input $\mathbf{x} = (x_1, \cdots, x_T)$, the new input becomes $\mathbf{x} = (s_1, \cdots, s_N, x_1, \cdots, x_T)$, where the $s_i$'s are the added artificial tokens. We then optimize only these tokens during training, while leaving the original model frozen.

Here, we model both correction and detection tasks in the same sequence generation approach, where the corrected sentence is first generated, and then information about the violated rule, and the location of this error is generated at the end of the sentence. This allows for one trained model to output both results. In order to train this correctly, the target sentence was appended with the details of the error type and location, and used for loss calculations. An example is provided in Fig 6.

## 5 Experimental Setup

### 5.1 Datasets

The list of datasets and their statistics are given in Table 2. GECTurk and MovieReview datasets are already described in §3.3 and §3.4 accordingly. The BOUN dataset (Arikan et al., 2019) is a relatively smaller dataset of 15K training and 2K test sentences, containing only 2 error types. It also includes a complex split, a list of 100 sentences that are mentioned to be extra challenging by the authors.

### 5.2 Evaluation

**Grammatical Error Correction** Following the Omelianchuk et al. (2020) and Bryant et al. (2019), we report Precision ($P$), Recall ($R$), and $F_{0.5}$ scores using the $M^2$ (MaxMatch) scorer (Dahlmeier and Ng, 2012).

**Grammatical Error Detection** To allow for a fair comparison with the BOUN dataset from Arikan et al. (2019), we use the same metrics, namely Precision ($P$), Recall ($R$), and $F_1$. Since the task is modeled as a sequence tagging problem, this aligns with the standard evaluation for sequence tagging, such as in Huang et al. (2015). For all GED results, we report macro metrics, which are computed by taking unweighted average of each classes' result. We use macro metrics over micro ones since distribution of grammatical errors types made by humans are imbalanced. To calculate these scores, we use SeqEval (Nakayama, 2018), a common library for evaluating sequence tagging tasks and use one tag for each error type.

## 6 Experiments and Results

We train the baseline models using the setup explained in Section §5 with three different fixed seeds. The mean and standard deviation of their performances on GEC and GED are given in Table 3. As can be seen, both SeqTag and mGPT provide strong results over 0.94 $F_{0.5}$ score for the GEC task, compared to the NMT baseline model. On the other hand, the detection task is performed more competently by SeqTag—as expected—than mGPT, which again achieves around 0.90 $F_1$ score. Moreover, the experiment on the effect of dataset sizes shows that the proposed dataset is more challenging than existing ones, with a steeper learning curve due to the larger number of error types. More information on the dataset size experiments can be found in Appendix C.

Successful detection does not always translate into successful correction because erroneous edits undermine the grammatical accuracy of the sentence, even when the grammatical error is successfully detected. Here, the $M^2$ scorer does identify this anomaly and explains the decrease in the correction scores. It is also worth noting that GED and GEC are two separate tasks, and models handle them differently. For example, generative models such as mGPT generate both the corrections and detections by predicting the next tokens, so there

| | GECTurk | | | | | |
|---|---|---|---|---|---|---|
| | Detection | | | Correction | | |
| | P | R | $F_1$ | P | R | $F_{0.5}$ |
| NMT | - | - | - | 0.50 ± 0.01 | 0.84 ± 0.01 | 0.55 ± 0.01 |
| SeqTag | 0.90 ± 0.003 | 0.90 ± 0.013 | 0.90 ± 0.006 | 0.98 ± 0.001 | 0.98 ± 0.001 | 0.98 ± 0.001 |
| mGPT | 0.52 ± 0.02 | 0.38 ± 0.004 | 0.41 ± 0.01 | 0.95 ± 0.01 | 0.92 ± 0.03 | 0.94 ± 0.01 |
| | **Curated Test Data** | | | | | |
| NMT | - | - | - | 0.31 | 0.62 | 0.35 |
| SeqTag | 0.94 | 0.87 | 0.89 | 0.85 | 0.80 | 0.84 |
| mGPT | 0.73 | 0.52 | 0.59 | 0.75 | 0.61 | 0.72 |

Table 3: Detection and Correction results of the baselines on GECTurk (in-domain) and curated test dataset (out-of-domain).

isn't necessarily a strong correlation between what is generated for each of them. On the other hand, SeqTag uses a pipeline approach, where it detects the errors first, then applies reverse transformations to fix them. Hence there is a stronger correlation between the detection and correction performances for SeqTag, as expected.

In order to test whether the performance of our models would transfer to different domains, we perform zero-shot experiments on the curated test set from the movie domain. We use our highest performing checkpoints on our synthetic test set, and evaluate without any additional training on the hand-annotated corpus as given in Table 3, second row. For detection, SeqTag performs similarly to synthetic setting, while mGPT's performance *increases dramatically*, proving the importance of being exposed to real-life data during pretraining. However, SeqTag still outperforms mGPT by a large margin due to its classification objective. On the other hand, both models perform significantly worse on the correction task for the currated test data compared to the synthetic setting, suggesting larger room for improvement on this more challenging test set.

### 6.1 Knowledge Transfer

Next, we investigate the transfer capacity of our models on unseen datasets using a different set of errors (i.e., mostly a subset) originally introduced to our models. We first evaluate our pretrained models on the BOUN (Arikan et al., 2019) standard and complex test splits to see their zero-shot ability, seen in Table 4, first row. Surprisingly, our best model, SeqTag, achieves 0,80 $F_1$, on-par with state-of-the-art for the standard split. It also surpasses state-of-the-art accuracy on the complex split by a large margin together with the mGPT model. This suggests that the error type knowledge

| | BOUN Zero-Shot | | | | | | |
|---|---|---|---|---|---|---|---|
| | Detection | | | | Correction | | |
| | P | R | $F_1$ | Acc | P | R | $F_{0.5}$ |
| NMT | - | - | - | - | 0.19 | 0.56 | 0.22 |
| SeqTag | 0.91 | 0.72 | 0.80 | 0.99 | 0.81 | 0.63 | 0.77 |
| mGPT | 0.60 | 0.56 | 0.58 | 0.97 | 0.75 | 0.67 | 0.73 |
| | **BOUN Complex Split Zero-Shot** | | | | | | |
| NMT | - | - | - | - | 0.71 | 0.73 | 0.72 |
| SeqTag | 0.99 | 0.93 | 0.96 | 0.99 | 0.99 | 0.93 | 0.98 |
| mGPT | 0.61 | 0.96 | 0.90 | 0.93 | 0.79 | 0.75 | 0.78 |
| | **BOUN Full Training** | | | | | | |
| NMT | - | - | - | - | 0 | 0 | 0 |
| SeqTag | 0.97 | 0.86 | 0.91 | 0.99 | 0.97 | 0.86 | 0.94 |
| mGPT | 0.61 | 0.48 | 0.53 | 0.97 | 0.85 | 0.73 | 0.82 |
| BOUN Results | 0.92 | 0.82 | 0.87 | 0.71 * | - | - | - |

* This result is for BOUN Complex Split Zero-Shot task.

Table 4: Performance metrics of various models on the BOUN dataset. The table is divided into three sections: models trained on the GECTurk dataset and evaluated zero-shot on two different BOUN splits, and models exclusively trained and evaluated on BOUN.

is mostly transferrable to other domains. Similar to our results on GECTurk, mGPT scores much lower on detection compared to SeqTag. However, the performance of mGPT is higher on BOUN dataset due to the small number of error types that are relatively more balanced. We note that despite the claims made by the authors of the BOUN dataset, our results suggest no additional complexity in the "complex" split as shown in Table 4, second row.

Finally, we investigate the effectiveness of our general approach by training our proposed models from scratch on the BOUN (Arikan et al., 2019) training split, given in Table 4, BOUN Full Training. For this setup, the NMT model was not able to converge, and just produced noise, hence, shown as 0.

Following our previous results, SeqTag achieves $F_1$ score of 0.91, surpassing the state-of-the-art by 0.04 pp, and its zero-shot performance by a large margin (0.11 pp). This suggests that pipeline approach is able to transfer a lot of knowledge. However, there is still a large gap that can be compensated by directly training on the actual domain and error types. On the other hand, the high scores provide cues for the strength of the proposed model. Surprisingly, prefix tuning of mGPT directly on the BOUN training dataset does not increase the performance compared to the zero-shot setting. This suggests two things: i) synthetic dataset such as ours, GECTurk, provides quality prior knowledge on the Turkish grammatical error types and ii) pretrained models have a considerably larger transfer capacity compared to training from scratch, as expected. Furthermore, for languages where the error types are mostly identified and can be fixed by a set of rules, a pipeline approach such as SeqTag proves more effective, efficient and robust.

## 7 Conclusion and Future Work

In this work, we have presented an annotated dataset for Grammatical Error Correction (GEC) and Detection (GED), GECTurk, containing more than 20 Turkish writing error types proposed by Turkish language experts. We have also introduced a flexible and extensible data generation pipeline that can be used to create a synthetic dataset from grammatically correct sentences. We used this pipeline to create a large-scale dataset using multiple opinion columns from Turkish newspapers. In addition, we have manually constructed a more challenging test set by annotating the movie-reviews with the proposed error types.

Finally, we implemented a diverse set of strong baseline models, by training from scratch, fine-tuning, or using prefix tuning. Our results show that smaller models focusing on the simpler problem of detecting the error types outperform large pretrained models on both the synthetic and real-life datasets, especially for the detection task. On the other hand, we observe that pretraining helps the models to handle more realistic cases, even though they still lag behind the simpler models. Our out-of-domain results suggest that training on the synthetic data gives a strong prior to both smaller and larger models.

## Acknowledgements

This work has been supported by the Scientific and Technological Research Council of Türkiye (TÜBİTAK) as part of the project "Automatic Learning of Procedural Language from Natural Language Instructions for Intelligent Assistance" with the number 121C132. We also gratefully acknowledge KUIS AI Lab for providing computational support. We thank our anonymous reviewers and the members of GGLab who helped us improve this paper.

## Limitations

One key issue is that mGPT is very computationally intensive to work with, even when only doing prefix tuning. This meant we could only train for 1 epoch. Another limitation is that the data generation pipeline is very time-consuming due to the use of a morphological analyzer. This means many resources are needed for very large-scale datasets. Additionally, needing hand-crafted rules and reverse transformations makes adding new rules slow.

Another key limitation is the need of dictionaries for exceptions to grammatical rules. Words in Turkish originating from other languages (notably Persian, French, and Arabic) don't always follow normal grammar rules, and thus require special lists of exceptions. While we included as many as possible, our list is not exhaustive, which can lead to rare edge cases where our pipeline fails. While dictionaries allow for adding learned knowledge directly, and is an invaluable part of our pipeline, these edge cases can cause problems during dataset generation.

## Ethical Considerations

One ethical issue is the misuse of grammatical correction models for cheating. Having such models and datasets mean that students can more easily use these to score better than normal on assignments and exams. This is bad for the student's learning, and also affects others who can be negatively impacted by this artificial success.

Despite this, we believe that grammatical error correction models are more beneficial than harmful. Many people, from authors to language learners, can benefit from having grammar corrections. By introducing a dataset and demonstrating models on Turkish, an under-served language in the NLP community, more people will be able to take advantage of this, similar to the many existing tools for English.

## References

Emre Can Acikgoz, Tilek Chubakov, Muge Kural, Gözde Şahin, and Deniz Yuret. 2022. Transformers on multilingual clause-level morphology. In *Proceedings of the The 2nd Workshop on Multi-lingual Representation Learning (MRL)*, pages 100–105, Abu Dhabi, United Arab Emirates (Hybrid). Association for Computational Linguistics.

Duygu Altinok. 2023. A diverse set of freely available linguistic resources for Turkish. In *Proceedings of the 61st Annual Meeting of the Association for Computational Linguistics (Volume 1: Long Papers)*, pages 13739–13750, Toronto, Canada. Association for Computational Linguistics.

M. Fatih Amasyalı and Banu Diri. 2006. Automatic Turkish text categorization in terms of author, genre and gender. In *Natural Language Processing and Information Systems*, pages 221–226, Berlin, Heidelberg. Springer Berlin Heidelberg.

Ugurcan Arikan, Onur Güngör, and Suzan Uskudarli. 2019. Detecting clitics related orthographic errors in Turkish. In *Proceedings of the International Conference on Recent Advances in Natural Language Processing, RANLP 2019, Varna, Bulgaria, September 2-4, 2019*, pages 71–76. INCOMA Ltd.

Christopher Bryant, Mariano Felice, Øistein E. Andersen, and Ted Briscoe. 2019. The BEA-2019 shared task on grammatical error correction. In *Proceedings of the Fourteenth Workshop on Innovative Use of NLP for Building Educational Applications*, pages 52–75, Florence, Italy. Association for Computational Linguistics.

Ender Can and Mehmet Fatih Amasyalı. 2016. Text2arff: A text representation library. In *2016 24th Signal Processing and Communication Application Conference (SIU)*, pages 197–200.

Çagri Çöltekin, A. Seza Doğruöz, and Özlem Çetinoglu. 2023. Correction to: Resources for Turkish natural language processing: A critical survey. *Lang. Resour. Evaluation*, 57(1):489.

Luís Morgado da Costa. 2021. *Using rich models of language in grammatical error detection*. Ph.D. thesis, Nanyang Technological University.

Daniel Dahlmeier and Hwee Tou Ng. 2012. Better evaluation for grammatical error correction. In *Proceedings of the 2012 Conference of the North American Chapter of the Association for Computational Linguistics: Human Language Technologies*, pages 568–572, Montréal, Canada. Association for Computational Linguistics.

Erenay Dayanik, Ekin Akyürek, and Deniz Yuret. 2018. Morphnet: A sequence-to-sequence model that combines morphological analysis and disambiguation. *CoRR*, abs/1805.07946.

Jacob Devlin, Ming-Wei Chang, Kenton Lee, and Kristina Toutanova. 2019. BERT: pre-training of deep bidirectional transformers for language understanding. In *Proceedings of the 2019 Conference of the North American Chapter of the Association for Computational Linguistics: Human Language Technologies, NAACL-HLT 2019, Minneapolis, MN, USA, June 2-7, 2019, Volume 1 (Long and Short Papers)*, pages 4171–4186. Association for Computational Linguistics.

Ning Ding, Shengding Hu, Weilin Zhao, Yulin Chen, Zhiyuan Liu, Haitao Zheng, and Maosong Sun. 2022. Openprompt: An open-source framework for prompt-learning. In *Proceedings of the 60th Annual Meeting of the Association for Computational Linguistics, ACL 2022 - System Demonstrations, Dublin, Ireland, May 22-27, 2022*, pages 105–113. Association for Computational Linguistics.

Banu Diri and Mehmet Fatih Amasyali. 2003. Automatic author detection for Turkish texts.

Dan Flickinger and Woodley Packard. Robust parsing in hpsg: Bridging the coverage chasm. Poster presented at the 22nd International Conference on HPSG. 2015.

Dan Flickinger and Jiye Yu. 2013. Toward more precision in correction of grammatical errors. In *CoNLL Shared Task*.

Zhiheng Huang, Wei Xu, and Kai Yu. 2015. Bidirectional LSTM-CRF models for sequence tagging. *CoRR*, abs/1508.01991.

Kemik NLP Group. 2022. Our datasets. `http://www.kemik.yildiz.edu.tr/data/File/2500koseyazisi.rar`. Online; accessed 26-November-2022]".

Diederik P. Kingma and Jimmy Ba. 2014. Adam: A method for stochastic optimization. *CoRR*, abs/1412.6980.

G. Lewis. 1985. *Turkish Grammar*. Oxford University Press.

Xiang Lisa Li and Percy Liang. 2021. Prefix-tuning: Optimizing continuous prompts for generation. *Proceedings of the 59th Annual Meeting of the Association for Computational Linguistics and the 11th International Joint Conference on Natural Language Processing (Volume 1: Long Papers)*, abs/2101.00190.

Ilya Loshchilov and Frank Hutter. 2019. Decoupled weight decay regularization. In *7th International Conference on Learning Representations, ICLR 2019, New Orleans, LA, USA, May 6-9, 2019*. OpenReview.net.

Hiroki Nakayama. 2018. seqeval: A python framework for sequence labeling evaluation. Software available from https://github.com/chakki-works/seqeval.

Hwee Tou Ng, Siew Mei Wu, Ted Briscoe, Christian Hadiwinoto, Raymond Hendy Susanto, and Christopher Bryant. 2014. The CoNLL-2014 shared task on grammatical error correction. In *Proceedings of the Eighteenth Conference on Computational Natural Language Learning: Shared Task*, pages 1–14, Baltimore, Maryland. Association for Computational Linguistics.

Hwee Tou Ng, Siew Mei Wu, Yuanbin Wu, Christian Hadiwinoto, and Joel Tetreault. 2013. The CoNLL-2013 shared task on grammatical error correction. In *Proceedings of the Seventeenth Conference on Computational Natural Language Learning: Shared Task*, pages 1–12, Sofia, Bulgaria. Association for Computational Linguistics.

Kemal Oflazer. 2014. Turkish and its challenges for language processing. *Lang. Resour. Evaluation*, 48(4):639–653.

Kostiantyn Omelianchuk, Vitaliy Atrasevych, Artem Chernodub, and Oleksandr Skurzhanskyi. 2020. GECToR – grammatical error correction: Tag, not rewrite. In *Proceedings of the Fifteenth Workshop on Innovative Use of NLP for Building Educational Applications*, pages 163–170, Seattle, WA, USA → Online. Association for Computational Linguistics.

Sascha Rothe, Jonathan Mallinson, Eric Malmi, Sebastian Krause, and Aliaksei Severyn. 2021. A simple recipe for multilingual grammatical error correction. In *Proceedings of the 59th Annual Meeting of the Association for Computational Linguistics and the 11th International Joint Conference on Natural Language Processing (Volume 2: Short Papers)*, pages 702–707, Online. Association for Computational Linguistics.

Stefan Schweter. 2020. Berturk - bert models for Turkish.

Oleh Shliazhko, Alena Fenogenova, Maria Tikhonova, Vladislav Mikhailov, Anastasia Kozlova, and Tatiana Shavrina. 2022. mGPT: Few-shot learners go multilingual. *CoRR*, abs/2204.07580.

Ashish Vaswani, Noam Shazeer, Niki Parmar, Jakob Uszkoreit, Llion Jones, Aidan N Gomez, Ł ukasz Kaiser, and Illia Polosukhin. 2017. Attention is all you need. In *Advances in Neural Information Processing Systems*, volume 30. Curran Associates, Inc.

Yonghui Wu, Mike Schuster, Zhifeng Chen, Quoc V. Le, Mohammad Norouzi, Wolfgang Macherey, Maxim Krikun, Yuan Cao, Qin Gao, Klaus Macherey, Jeff Klingner, Apurva Shah, Melvin Johnson, Xiaobing Liu, Lukasz Kaiser, Stephan Gouws, Yoshikiyo Kato, Taku Kudo, Hideto Kazawa, Keith Stevens, George Kurian, Nishant Patil, Wei Wang, Cliff Young, Jason Smith, Jason Riesa, Alex Rudnick, Oriol Vinyals, Greg Corrado, Macduff Hughes, and Jeffrey Dean. 2016. Google's neural machine translation system: Bridging the gap between human and machine translation. *CoRR*, abs/1609.08144.

Linting Xue, Noah Constant, Adam Roberts, Mihir Kale, Rami Al-Rfou, Aditya Siddhant, Aditya Barua, and Colin Raffel. 2021. mT5: A massively multilingual pre-trained text-to-text transformer. In *Proceedings of the 2021 Conference of the North American Chapter of the Association for Computational Linguistics: Human Language Technologies*, pages 483–498, Online. Association for Computational Linguistics.

Hasan Öztürk, Alperen Değirmenci, Onur Güngör, and Suzan Uskudarli. 2020. The role of contextual word embeddings in correcting the 'de/da' clitic errors in Turkish. In *2020 28th Signal Processing and Communications Applications Conference (SIU)*, pages 1–4.

# A Model Details

## A.1 NMT Baseline

For tokenization, we used BerTurk-cased (Schweter, 2020) tokenizer, passed to the NMT model. The transformer model has 6 encoders with embedding size 512, 6 decoder layers, and 8 heads. A dropout of 0.1 is used directly after the positional embeddings. For training, an Adam (Kingma and Ba, 2014) optimizer with $\beta_1 = 0.9$, $\beta_2 = 0.98$, and $\varepsilon = 1e - 9$, and a learning rate of $1e - 4$ is used. We used batch size of 32, and trained the model for 100 epochs on a single V100. We use a standard cross-entropy loss during training, as follows:

$$\mathcal{L}_{GEC}(\hat{y}, y) = -\sum_{n=1}^{N}\sum_{c=1}^{V} log \frac{exp(\hat{y}_{n,c})y_{n,c}}{\sum_{i=1}^{V} exp(\hat{y}_{n,i})} \quad (1)$$

Here, $N$ is the batch size, $V$ is the number of error classes, $x$ is the model output, and $y$ is the target. For the data size experiments, we used the same architecture but with slightly different hyperparameters. For both the 75% and 100% experiments, the model was trained for 100 epochs. For the 50% experiment, we only trained for 50 epochs. When training 10% and 25%, the Adam optimizer is used with the same $\beta$ values, a learning rate of $5e - 4$, and a weight decay of $1e - 4$, for 100 epochs. The zero-shot testing on the BOUN (Arikan et al., 2019) dataset is tokenized with the same tokenizer, and the best pre-trained model from GECTurk is used for evaluation.

## A.2 Sequence Tagger

For training, we used the AdamW (Loshchilov and Hutter, 2019) optimizer for 3 epochs, using batch size 16, learning rate $2e - 5$, weight decay 0.01, $\beta_1 = 0.9$, and $\beta_2 = 0.999$.

## A.3 Prefix Tuning

We used the standard mGPT tokenizer and the OpenPrompt prefix tuning template. All experiments use 5 soft tokens at the beginning. Teacher forcing is used during training, and both the correction and detection tasks are formulated as a sequence generation problem. Following the settings from Acikgoz et al. (2022), we don't use weight decay for the bias and LayerNorm weights. The AdamW optimizer is used, with an initial learning rate of $5e - 5$, linearly decaying to 0 over the entire training. We clip the norm of the gradient at 1.0.

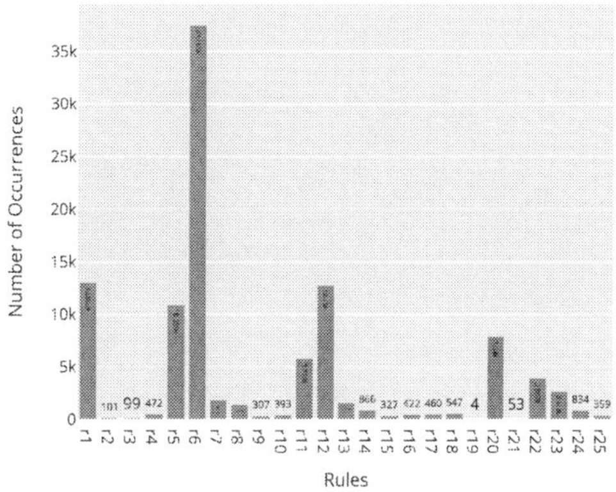


Figure 3: Number of sentences with each writing rule type.

Due to the computational requirements of mGPT, we only train on GECTurk for a single epoch on all experiments. However, on the smaller BOUN dataset, we train for 5 epochs. For inference, we also follow the hyperparameters from Acikgoz et al. (2022), using a temperature of 1.0, top p of 0.9, no repetition penalty, and a beam search of 5 beams. For all experiments, a batch size of 3 was used. The max sequence length, including soft tokens, is set to 512.

# B GECTurk Error Frequencies

Fig. 3 shows the frequencies of each error type in GECTurk dataset.

# C Effect of Dataset Size

In order to obtain a better understanding of how important the dataset size is for this task, we conducted training on $1, 10, 25, 50, 75$, and 100 percent of GECTurk and evaluated each model using the same evaluation measures. Fig. 4 shows how the performance of the models vary with more training data. NMT reaches its top point with around 75% of the training data, while SeqTag and mGPT achieve high $F_{0.5}$ scores with 25% of the training split. However, as discussed before, correction scores can be misleadingly high, since high frequency and easy to correct errors will push the results much higher. Hence we also plot the F1 scores for the detection task both on TurkishGEC and BOUN datasets in Fig. 5. The plot shows that the GECTurk dataset is richer than the BOUN, since SeqTag and mGPT F1 performances are much steeper on the former.

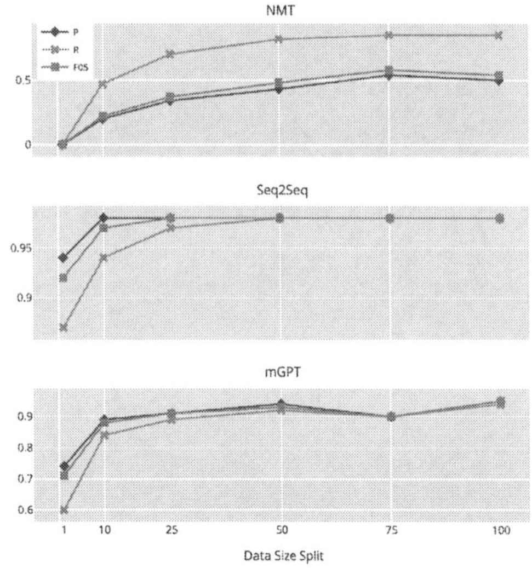


Figure 4: Correction performance of each model trained on varying sizes of GECTurk

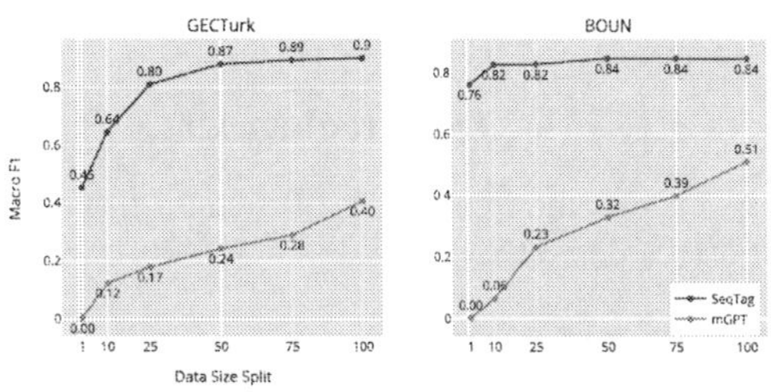


Figure 5: $F_1$ score performance of SeqTag and mGPT on GECTurk and Boun training splits.

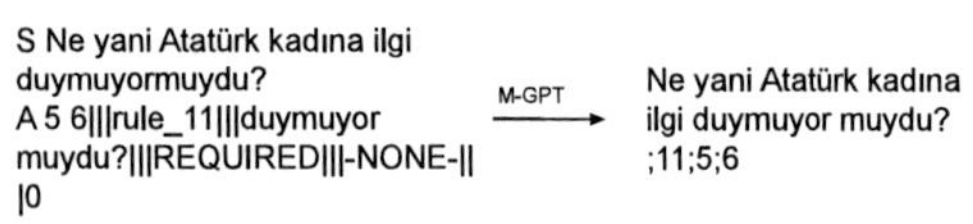


Figure 6: Example output of the mGPT model. The first line performs the grammatical error correction, and subsequent lines allow for detection. The annotations are included for comparison with model outputs, but are not actually provided to the model.

# Interactively Learning Social Media Representations Improves News Source Factuality Detection

**Nikhil Mehta**
Department of Computer Science
Purdue University
West Lafayette, IN 47907
mehta52@purdue.edu

**Dan Goldwasser**
Department of Computer Science
Purdue University
West Lafayette, IN 47907
dgoldwas@purdue.edu

## Abstract

The rise of social media has enabled the widespread propagation of fake news, text that is published with an intent to spread misinformation and sway beliefs. Rapidly detecting fake news, especially as new events arise, is important to prevent misinformation.

While prior works have tackled this problem using supervised learning systems, automatedly modeling the complexities of the social media landscape that enables the spread of fake news is challenging. On the contrary, having humans fact check all news is not scalable. Thus, in this paper, we propose to approach this problem *interactively*, where humans can interact to help an automated system learn a better social media representation quality. On real world events, our experiments show performance improvements in detecting factuality of news sources, even after few human interactions.

## 1 Introduction

Over the last decade, we have witnessed a rise in the proliferation of "fake news" (Lazer et al., 2018), news content which lacks the journalistic standards ensuring its quality while maintaining its appearance. Social media is flooded with inaccurate and incomplete information (Vosoughi et al., 2018), and combating this has attracted significant research interest (Nguyen et al., 2020). However, this is still a hard task, particularly on unseen topics. In this paper, rather than annotating data to learn these topics, we propose to use quick **human interactions** to characterize social media, allowing us to learn a better representation, and detect factuality better.

Instead of fact checking individual articles, some works (Baly et al., 2020) focus on fact-checking sources. While still requiring automated systems due to the number of sources online, source factuality detection can be more scalable, as sources often publish content of similar factuality. Following this, we focus on capturing the factuality levels of sources: *high, mixed, low*.

One concept underlying methods that aim to exploit social information for identifying the factuality of news sources is the *social homophily principle* (McPherson et al., 2001), which captures the tendency of members of the same social group to hold similar views and content preferences. This often leads to the formation of *"echo chambers"* (Jamieson and Cappella, 2008; Quattrociocchi et al., 2016), tightly-knit *"information communities"* that have little interaction with other communities holding different views. Prior work shows how similar news, particularly misinformation, tends to spread more in some of these tightly-knit information communities (Bessi et al., 2016). Thus, identifying them can provide the needed information for capturing the factuality of sources (communities spreading mostly low factuality content in the past are likely to spread low factuality content in the future). In this work, we first capture social information in an information graph, modeling it via a R-GCN (Schlichtkrull et al., 2018).

Many approaches to detect news factuality are often studied in unrealistic settings, as their success hinges on test data being similar to or related to training data. However, a more realistic setup would examine whether a system would be able to generalize to emerging news events: These events introduce different narratives, users, and news sources, that are unseen and do not interact with training content; i.e. test users don't follow train users and test graph nodes aren't connected to train nodes. In this paper, to simulate these settings, we collected new data, consisting of the articles published around specific news events (Black Lives Matter and Climate Change - see Sec 5.1), their sources, and social context. We applied a recent strong baseline system (Mehta et al., 2022), trained over data sampled from past events, and it resulted in significant degradation in performance on the new events (~22% Acc, 19% Macro-F1).

Our main observation in this paper is that even



*Findings of the Association for Computational Linguistics: IJCNLP-AACL 2023*, pages 291–311
November 1–4, 2023. 

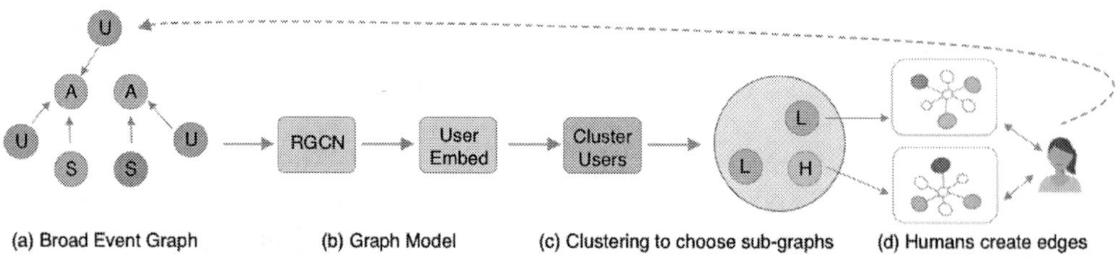


Figure 1: Our framework overview: **Adapting News Source Factuality Detection to Emerging News Events by Interactively Characterizing the Social Media Context of News Articles and Their Sources.** (Key: U = Users, A = Articles, S = Sources, Green/H = High Factuality, Red/L = Low Factuality). From the learned graph model (b), we find pairs of inconsistent users by clustering all user embeddings and looking for conflicting factuality labels (c) (L = low; H = high factuality). Here, the High Factuality user doesn't match the mostly Low Factuality cluster. We then build sub-graphs from these pairs of mismatched users and their community to show human interactors (d), who create new edges based on content similarity. This is far simpler and quicker than identifying factuality, as humans only need to identify which nodes are similar in content. Based on the interactions, we create edges in the broad event graph (a) to do better news source factuality detection (either directly or with more training).

in these challenging settings, the social homophily principle can be exploited to better detect source factuality, **if the system can identify relevant information communities over users engaging with the new content**. This is since users that are part of an information community that propagates fake news, are likely to do so as well. As we later show, automatically detecting the factuality of news sources is difficult, particularly on emerging news events. *Instead*, we suggest an **interactive learning protocol**, in which human judgements dynamically help the model identify these communities. As humans analyzing all emerging news content is clearly infeasible, we propose a novel sampling method for interactions, based on resolving inconsistencies in the model's graph-based social representation. Specifically, we identify pairs of users that are clustered in the same community, but have conflicting factuality predictions, as this indicates inconsistency. We create small sub-graphs corresponding to the social and content preferences of these users and other members of the community, and ask the humans to resolve the conflict: Based on their profile descriptions, social relations and articles endorsed, *is it likely (given the principle of social homophily) that these two users belong to the same community?* The human judgements provide rich feedback for this question, by adding edges to the graph, which connect users, articles, and sources. These edges result in cleaner information communities, which alleviate the difficulty of the source classification task. Fig. 1 describes this.

In summary, we make the following contributions. (1) We are the first to formulate the task of **interactive news source factuality detection** by characterizing social context, and implement an interaction tool for supporting this. (2) We suggest a novel sampling approach for reducing the number of human judgements needed by focusing on social inconsistencies. (3) We focus on one of the most challenging settings of news source factuality detection in emerging news events, collect data, and perform experiments showing how minimal, quick interactions can lead to performance improvements on unseen data. More generally, we propose an interactive framework to learn stronger information communities, and apply it to improve news source factuality detection. In the future, it can also be applied to other social media analysis tasks.

Sec. 3 describes our graph model, Sec. 4 our novel protocol to incorporate interactions, Sec. 5 shows results, and Sec. 6 analyzes them.

## 2 Related Work

Detecting fake news on social media is a popular research topic, studied in supervised learning (Hassan et al., 2017; Pérez-Rosas et al., 2018; Volkova and Jang, 2018; Ma et al., 2018; Shu et al., 2019a,b; Kim et al., 2019), Graphs (Han et al., 2020; Li et al., 2022), zero-shot (Wright et al., 2022), dialogue (Gupta et al., 2022), cross-domain (Huang et al., 2021; Zhu et al., 2022a,b; Mosallanezhad et al., 2022), and low-resource (Lin et al., 2022) settings.

One of the most challenging yet most critical social context fake news detection settings is the early detection of it, where test data has new users, articles, and sources, that do not interact with training data. Recently, researchers have been working on this task, especially at the article/tweet level. Liu and Wu classify news propagation paths, Yuan et al. model user credibility, while Konkobo et al. built a semi-supervised classifier. In our work, we focus on this challenging early detection setting, specifically to identify the factuality of news sources. We show how our *interactive setup* can be useful, even in these settings. If combined with other early detection methods, our framework may lead to further gains, and we leave this for future work.

Using human interactions to improve models has also been popular recently (Brantley et al., 2021), in scenarios such as active learning (Blok et al., 2021), or humans providing general system feedback (Tandon et al., 2022). Other works exploit human feedback for concept discovery (Pacheco et al., 2022, 2023) by communicating human-level symbolic knowledge (Pacheco and Goldwasser, 2021). In contrast, our interactions enable stronger general models, and generalization to new unseen scenarios.

Social homophily has been used to better many NLP tasks, like sentiment analysis, entity linking, and fake news. (West et al., 2014; Yang et al., 2016; Mehta et al., 2022). Particularly, prior work shows how misinformation (and similar news) spreads more in tightly-knit communities, motivating our idea that if we use humans to increase homophily and build better information communities, we can detect facutality better (Bessi et al., 2016; Halberstam and Knight, 2016; Cinelli et al., 2021).

## 3 Graph Model

Similar to Mehta et al., we view fake news source detection as reasoning over relationships between sources, articles, and users in an information graph. We use their graph model[1], briefly explaining it in this sec. Sec. 4 explains our interactive protocol.

The model uses a heterogeneous graph to capture the interaction between social information and news content, and a Relational Graph Convolutional Network (R-GCN) to encode it. The R-GCN allows us to create contextualized node representations for factuality prediction. For example, one way sources are represented is by the articles they publish (which in turn are also represented by their relationships to other nodes).

**Graph Creation**: The graph (see: Fig.1a) consists of 3 types of nodes, each with feature vectors (details: App. A.3.1): (1) $S$, the news *sources*, are our classification targets. (2) $A$, the *articles* published by these sources, (3) $U$, the Twitter *users*. Sources are first connected to articles they publish. Social context is added via Twitter users that interact/connect to sources/ articles/other users. These users provide the means for fake (and real) news spread on social media: **(1) Following Sources/Users:** Users are connected to sources and users they follow. **(2) Propagating Articles:** Articles are connected to users that tweet its title/link.

**Graph Embedding:** As in Mehta et al., we train a R-GCN (Schlichtkrull et al., 2018) to learn graph embeddings, which will be later used to determine where human interaction may be beneficial. We optimize the Classification objective of News Source Factuality Detection (categorical cross-entropy). To predict labels, we pass the source node embeddings from R-GCN through the Softmax activation.

[1] https://github.com/hockeybro12/FakeNews_Inference_Operators

## 4 Interactive Protocol

We hypothesize that understanding content and the context it is provided in is critical to detecting fake news. Specifically, identifying information communities of users, sources, and articles based on their content preferences can be helpful, as a community that mostly shares fake news in the past, is likely to share fake news in the future. Further, users that join this community are likely to share beliefs of the community, and thus also share fake news.

Unfortunately, understanding content on social media and using it to identify information communities is challenging for AI agents. It becomes more difficult as new events with new relationships arise, as the agent does not have enough data to determine what is fake news. This makes the early detection of fake news difficult (see Sec. 5.3). On the other hand, educated humans can more easily understand relationships on social media, even in new events, as they can better analyze social interactions. Thus, humans can clear up model confusion by helping the model identify the information communities or make existing ones bigger. For example, after reading a sample of tweets from users discussing a new event, humans can *quickly* determine if the users are offering the same perspectives, and should be in the same community. This knowledge can help the agent model these users and other content they interact with better. As we later show experimentally, human interactions like these enables us to build strong information communities, which helps the agent, particularly with the early detection of news sources factuality on new news events.

Unlike automated agents, humans cannot analyze all content that pertains to a new event, as it is too massive. Instead, due to the highly connected structure of social media, **small amounts of interactions done in the right places can make significant impact**, as the added information can flow throughout the information graph. Thus, we first discuss in Sec 4.1 how we determine what content humans should interact with and what interactions they should make (i.e. forming/strengthening information communities). Then, in Sec 4.2, we explain how we can incorporate those interactions back into the model to achieve performance improvements.

### 4.1 Soliciting Human Interactions

Now, we discuss 3 different protocols to identify the data on which humans should interact, and then what they should do. In general, we want humans to analyze a sub-graph of the broad information graph characterizing the new event. Given this sub-graph, we ask humans to help form information communities by characterizing the content in the graph based on similarity, i.e. identify if two users are similar, two articles offer the same perspective, etc. This is done by asking humans a series of questions (details : App. B) which enables them to connect nodes in the sub-graph based on content preferences, via a graphical interface we developed. An ex. is shown in App. Fig 2. We then replicate these connections in the broad information graph.

Identifying the sub-graph that will benefit the most from interactions is critical to getting the most value out of each interaction. We build the sub-graphs by first choosing a pair of users, as our end goal is to build stronger user information communities. We explore three different protocols for doing this in 4.1.1 and Sec 4.1.2. After finding these pairs of users, we build the sub-graph to show humans by including these users and their direct connections in the graph. This includes the articles they propagate, other users that propagate those articles, the sources that publish those articles, and up to 3 "influencers" (users with over 1000 followers) that one of these users follows. For each node in the sub-graph, we populate it with relevant information to enable the human interactors to understand content. For ex:, user/source nodes show user bio, tweets, etc. Article nodes show article publish date, headline, and first paragraph. Details: App B.

#### 4.1.1 Baselines

We have two baselines for selecting pairs of users. **(1) Random**, users at random. **(2) Model Confusion** takes an *active learning*-like approach, and chooses users based on a label confusion criterion, calculated by propagating the softmax score of the source prediction downwards to get user confusion. Specifically, to get this score, we look at all the sources the user directly interacts with (articles they propagate and sources they follow), and then take the weighted average of those source's Softmax predicted label to be the user score (thus approximating user confidence). For example, a user interacting with 3 articles predicted with low factuality score of 0.7 and 1 source with high factuality score 0.9 will have confidence 0.75.

#### 4.1.2 Social vs. Factuality Mismatch Criterion

Now, we discuss our novel protocol to determine the pairs of users, seen also in Alg 1. It is designed around one of the key ideas in this paper, homophily, the tendency of users with similar social preferences to have similar content preferences. Our graph model learns to represent both, by creating node embeddings which capture users' similarities, and learning classifiers used for characterizing content by identifying factuality. Intuitively, our protocol is designed to identify users, that based on the current model parameters, break the homophily principle. These users are part of the same social group while at the same time have different factuality predictions, and thus likely different content preferences. When this is true, the model may not have clearly understood the content preferences of these users, which a human can help clear up.

To identify these pairs of users, we first need to compute factuality labels for each user. As the model is trained for source classification, we designed a heuristic to use source labels to compute user labels: We assign users the label of the *most common predicted label* of the sources/articles the user is directly connected to. For ex:, a user following 3 low factuality sources and tweeting 1 mixed factuality article is assigned a low factuality label, as it interacts with more low factuality content.

After computing user labels, we need to find groups of similar users, which we do by k-means clustering all users in the event graph using their model embeddings (Alg 1: 3). Then, we assign each cluster a factuality label based on the most frequently occurring user factuality label in that cluster (Alg 1: 5). Finally, we choose pairs of users that are in the same cluster, but one has a different label than the cluster label, as the model thinks they are similar but predicts their factuality differently, which indicates a sign of confusion (Alg 1: 7-9).

**Algorithm 1** *Social vs. Factuality Mismatch*

**Input:** $U$ (Users), $U_E$ (Graph User Embeddings), $F$ (User Factuality Scores), $P$ (Empty List)
**Output:** $P$ (Pairs of Users To Build Graphs)
$c_{1 \dots k} = \text{k-means}(U_E)$ `K-means Cluster all Users based on Graph User Embeddings`
**for all** $i = 1, \dots, k$ **do** {for each cluster}
  $c_l = \max_{0 \leq u \leq n} F_u$ `Assign Cluster the Label of the most common user`
  **for all** $j = 1, \dots, n$ **do** {for each user}
    **if** $F_j \neq c_l$ **then** {If user label $\neq$ cluster label}
      $U_k = \text{rand}(U)$ where $(F_j \neq F_k) \land (F_k \in c_l)$ `Choose a random user in the cluster with a different label`
      $P$.insert$((U_j, U_k))$ `Add User Pair to List`
    **end if**
  **end for**
**end for**
**return** $P$ (Pairs of Users)

## 4.2 Incorporating Human Interactions

Humans interact by making new connections on the sub-graphs. We then utilize the interactions by connecting the appropriate nodes in the broader event graph. Our goal is to show how human interactions allow us to have a better model that performs well with and without further interactions.

We focus on the challenging **fully inductive setting**: where all test set nodes are not seen at training and are also not connected to training set nodes. Further, we evaluate the important setting of early detection of fake news, where test data comes from unseen emerging events. As we show in Sec 5.3, in these settings, existing models struggle.

We evaluate 3 interaction-based protocols. The three protocols have the same starting point, a graph-based factuality classification system trained over an established dataset (Baly et al., 2020). The protocols are designed to show how interactions can enhance that initial system when making predictions on data from unseen emerging events, and are organized in order of increasing effort required and increasing performance. All involve performing interactions on up to two different data sets (each corresponding to a different emerging event, see Sec 5.1). Since some of the protocols we introduce update the parameters of the model after interaction, we collect data for two events to ensure that all protocols can be evaluated in the fully inductive settings on the second event data (i.e., relying on interactions alone without training).

We hereby refer to the first event as $E1$, and the second as $E2$. Each event is further split into interaction and no interaction halves (ex: $E1\text{-}1/E1\text{-}2$), for comparison and model training (see below).

**(1) Fully Inductive:** In the first protocol, humans interact on the interaction halves of $E1$ and $E2$, and then the interactions are incorporated, without any additional training. This is the most challenging, but no extra effort is necessary for performance improvements.

**(2) Interactions Amplify Model Learning:** Here, our goal is to show how interactions can help us learn a stronger model that performs well without interactions. Thus, we interact on the interaction half of $E1$ (half so we can evaluate how we do on the same event without interactions), use it to train the model, and evaluate it on $E2$ (future event, fully inductive) without any additional interactions.

**(3) Learning to Incorporate Interactions:** In this protocol, we show how training the model after interactions allows the model to learn how to better incorporate them. This enables it to do even better when interactions are provided on future events. To do this, as above, we interact on half of $E1$ and train on it. Then, we evaluate $E2$ on both the interaction and non-interaction half. Both halves of $E2$ are connected, so although interactions are only on half, information can propagate via the graph.

## 4.3 Simulating Human Interactions

Due to constraints involved with human interaction time/cost, to evaluate our models we also designed a heuristic to simulate humans: We hypothesize that two users are similar if they have the same gold factuality label. While our interaction approach prioritizes content preferences for interactions, identifying this automatically is difficult, so this is an approximation. Thus, doing human interactions at the scale of simulated ones could perform better, and we leave it for future work. To get user gold factuality labels, we use the same heuristic as in Sec 4.1 (assinging users the label of the source they are most often connected to). Note that in this simulated interaction setting, we are using the test set to determine user labels, so this setup is not realistic.

# 5 Experiments

## 5.1 Dataset and Collection

To evaluate our model's ability to predict the factuality of news medium, we used the Media Bias/Fact Check dataset (Baly et al., 2018). We expand it by scraping additional sources from Media Bias/Fact Check[2], for better coverage of recent events and increasing the number of sources for evaluation.

[2]https://mediabiasfactcheck.com

| Model | Baly Acc. | Baly F1 | E1-1 Acc | E1-1 F1 |
|---|---|---|---|---|
| Baly | 71.52 | 67.25 | - | - |
| Mehta R-GCN | 68.90 | 63.72 | - | - |
| Mehta BEST | 72.55 | 66.89 | - | - |
| BL: Mehta R-GCN | 66.04 | 54.20 | 43.21 | 34.44 |

Table 1: Baseline results on Baly (Baly et al., 2020) and an inductive future BLM event $E1$-1 (not seen or connected to the training graph). Baseline (BL) is the strong graph classification model from (Mehta et al., 2022) (Mehta R-GCN) that was competitive with the state of the art ((Mehta et al., 2022) - Mehta BEST). Even with this, performance significantly worsens on $E1$, showing that detecting fake news on future events inductively is challenging. BL: Mehta R-GCN was trained on a smaller (Baly et al., 2020) dataset, as some sources were used for evaluation, which is why the performance is slightly lower.

Identically to Baly et al., we labeled the sources on a 3-point factuality scale: *high*, *mixed*, or *low*.

Our goal in this paper is to show how human interactions can help news source factuality detection on new events, where even strong models struggle (Sec 5.3). To do this, we evaluated our model on **two broad events**: *Black Lives Matter (BLM)* and *Climate Change (CLM)*. For each, we scraped data from Twitter over 3 time periods (01/02/2019 - 06/01/19; 06/02/19 - 01/1/21; 02/02/21 - 05/06/22), each of which additionally cover many different sub-events. For each time period, we created a fully inductive graph, consisting of at least 99 sources and their metadata. None of these graphs are connected to each other in any way and no nodes in any of them are common with each other or the training set - making our test settings fully inductive, and very challenging. To ensure this inductive setting, when collecting data for future time periods, we made sure not to include sources/users/articles that we already used in previous time periods, even if they propagated content in those future periods. Combined with Baly et al., we used the first time period for training, to teach the model how to identify fake news in general and as it pertains to an event. We used the 2nd and 3rd time period as $E1$ and $E2$ in the protocols discussed in Sec 4.2. Details (statistics, etc.): A.2. We release our code and data.[3]

## 5.2 Evaluation Method

For both BLM and CLM, we evaluate on the two inductive sub-events ($E1$, $E2$) collected in Sec 5.1. The interaction half is referred to with a -1 and

| Model | E2-1 Acc | E2-1 F1 |
|---|---|---|
| Random Users | 35.21 | 29.99 |
| Confused Users | 36.61 | **32.72** |
| User Clustering | **42.10** | 32.22 |

Table 2: Ablation study on our methods for choosing interactions on $E2$-1. It is clear that finding users based on clustering and then factuality mismatch is best.

the non-interaction with -2, for ex: $E1$-1. For fair comparison, each data split, i.e. $E1$-1, is the same across all evaluations. We report results on Accuracy, Macro F1 (the dataset is unbalanced), and the total number of edges added by all interactions.

We evaluated 3 settings, the first 2 are simulated using gold test set labels (see Sec 4.3), while the last is done by humans: **(1) Interaction Graphs Only:** Edges are added only between users in interaction graphs. **(2) X% of Data:** Edges are added between X% of all possible users that have the same label in the test set that we run interactions on (not only users in interaction sub-graphs). X is 100%, 75%, or 25%. **(3) Human Interactions**: For BLM, we evaluate on two separate versions, each featuring a different source set (and social media data). This section shows results on the first version, when one human interacts on 20 graphs per data split (details in B.1, B.2). The appendix shows the second version of BLM with ***3 different interactors***, showing the same trends. For space, these interaction results/details (including agreement) are in B.2.3. This section also evaluates Climate Change, with 2 interactors interacting on 10 sub-graphs per data split. (for detailed CLM results, see App. C). The human interaction results are also the most realistic evaluation setting, as they don't use any gold test set labels, like the simulated interactions do.

## 5.3 Baselines

We trained our baseline model, from Sec. 3, for Source Factuality Detection on Baly et al. and the first event, where it achieved strong performance, similar to SOTA (Mehta et al., 2022) (we use the same data and methodology) and other baselines (Baly et al., 2020) (SVM). However, when evaluated inductively on a BLM event that was published after dates the training data was collected from - i.e. $E1$-1 - performance significantly worsened (see Table 1). This validated our hypothesis that strong models, even if trained on generic and event specific data, do not translate well to future events. Thus, we propose to use our interactive protocol.

[3]https://github.com/hockeybro12/Fake_News_Interactive_Detection

| Model | E1-1 Acc | E1-1 F1 | E1-2 Acc | E1-2 F1 | E2-1 Acc | E2-1 F1 | # Edges |
|---|---|---|---|---|---|---|---|
| BLM No Interactions | 43.21 | 34.44 | 37.93 | 30.70 | 35.21 | 27.65 | - |
| CLM No Interactions | 40.16 | 32.77 | 39.65 | 31.86 | 34.88 | 30.93 | - |
| BLM Sim. Interactions on Sub-Graphs Only | 44.54 | 36.45 | 37.93 | 30.70 | 42.10 | 32.22 | 2,162 |
| BLM Sim. Interactions on 100% of Data in E1-1 + E2-1 | 49.20 | 40.52 | 37.93 | 30.70 | 44.73 | 36.82 | 133,336 |
| BLM Sim. Interactions on 75% of Data in E1-1 + E2-1 | 46.03 | 38.05 | 37.93 | 30.70 | 50.00 | 40.50 | 74,414 |
| BLM Sim. Interactions on 25% of Data in E1-1 + E1-2 | 46.03 | 37.65 | 37.93 | 30.70 | 42.10 | 32.65 | 8,266 |
| BLM Human Interactions in E1-1 + E2-1 | 44.44 | 35.96 | 37.93 | 30.70 | 44.73 | 30.03 | 84 |
| CLM Human Interactions in E1-1 + E2-1 | 46.72 | 43.94 | 39.65 | 31.86 | 39.53 | 36.95 | 47 |

Table 3: Protocol 1: Interactions results on BLM and Climate Change (CLM) in the difficult, inductive, no training setting. E1 and E2 are the two separate, inductive graphs. E1-1 is the first half that receives interactions, and E1-2 is the second half that doesn't. E2-1 (first half E2) also receives interactions, but it's dev set is not used to select the model. With a minimal number of added edges, human interactions achieve performance improvements in these difficult, inductive settings, with no extra training (compared to No Interactions). Ex: results improve on human BLM E2-1 (~9.5% Acc.) Sim. settings also show improvements.

| Model | E1-2 Acc | E1-2 F1 | E2-1 Acc | E2-1 F1 | # Edges |
|---|---|---|---|---|---|
| BLM No Interactions | 37.93 | 30.70 | 35.21 | 27.65 | - |
| BLM No Interactions Train | 64.86 | 66.91 | 42.10 | 40.10 | - |
| CLM No Interactions Train | 49.29 | 44.84 | 44.77 | 42.35 | - |
| BLM Sim. Interactions on Sub-Graphs Only | 62.16 | 62.95 | 43.66 | 29.47 | 2,162 |
| BLM Sim. Interactions on 100% of Data in E1-1 | 56.75 | 59.27 | 45.07 | 40.18 | 133,336 |
| BLM Sim. Interactions on 75% of Data in E1-1 | 65.51 | 64.01 | 43.66 | 39.11 | 74,414 |
| BLM Sim. Interactions on 25% of Data in E1-1 | 54.05 | 46.48 | 39.43 | 35.09 | 8,266 |
| BLM Human Interactions in E1-1 | 67.56 | 71.56 | 45.07 | 35.18 | 84 |
| CLM Human Interactions in E1-1 | 53.52 | 44.53 | 40.29 | 46.38 | 47 |

Table 4: Protocol 2: Interactions results on BLM + Climate Change (CLM) when we train on interactions, and then apply the model to a new event with no interactions done. E1 and E2 are the two separate, inductive graphs. E1-1 is the interaction half of the $1^{st}$ event and E1-2 is the $2^{nd}$, non-interaction half. E2-1 (non-interaction half) is not connected to E1. Compared to the model that was trained on E1-1 without interactions (No Interactions Train), human interactions lead to a more accurate model for future events, by ~3% better Acc. for BLM and ~4% F1 for CLM (E2-1). Sim. settings also show improvements.

### 5.4 Interactions

We now evaluate our interaction protocols - what portions of the graph to show users and how to incorporate interactions, using the method in Sec 5.2.

#### 5.4.1 Soliciting Interactions

When comparing our methods for choosing what sub-graphs to show on BLM, simulated interactions performance shows a benefit (Table 2) of choosing the users to build interaction graphs for based on confused user clustering. This matches our intuition as if the model predicts a users' factuality differently than other users similar to it, then the model is confused and clearing that could improve performance. Thus, we use this method of choosing sub-graphs throughout the rest of our experiments.

#### 5.4.2 Incorporating Interactions

Now, we evaluate our 3 protocols of incorporating interactions discussed in Sec 4.2, in order of increasing performance and model training required. For space, additional human interaction results are in App. B.2.3 and detailed CLM results in App. C. Note that simulated interactions (4.3) use gold test set labels and thus are only used to test our models.

First, Protocol 1, where we evaluate how the model performs with interactions in the completely inductive setting, so no training is necessary. In Tab. 3, we ran interactions on only the interaction half of each event ($E1$-1 + $E2$-1) and the dev. data (also from $E1$-1), to choose the strongest model. To ensure the dev. set being chosen from $E1$-1 does not bias us into a strong model, we also did interactions on the interaction half of $E2$ and notice stronger performance improvements. Note that $E2$ is a future event and is not connected to $E1$ at all. All settings improve performance. Moreover, on BLM, human interactions improves performance ~9.3% Acc. on E2-1, comparable to simulated interactions with significantly more data, showing the large impact benefit of human interactions.

Next, in Protocol 2, we learn a better model for

| Model | E1-2 Acc | E1-2 F1 | E2-1 Acc | E2-1 F1 | E2-2 Acc | E2-2 F1 | # Edges |
|---|---|---|---|---|---|---|---|
| BLM No Interactions | 37.93 | 30.70 | 35.21 | 27.65 | 30.30 | 24.84 | - |
| BLM No Interactions Train | 64.86 | 66.91 | 42.10 | 40.10 | 45.45 | 42.35 | - |
| CLM No Interactions Train | 49.29 | 44.84 | 44.77 | 42.35 | 44.44 | 33.06 | - |
| BLM Sim. Interactions on Sub-Graphs Only | 62.16 | 62.95 | 57.89 | 48.53 | 45.45 | 43.49 | 2,162 |
| BLM Sim. Interactions on 100% of Data in E1-1 + E1-2 | 56.75 | 59.27 | 57.89 | 61.90 | 36.36 | 35.53 | 133,336 |
| BLM Sim. Interactions on 75% of Data in E1-1 + E1-2 | 65.51 | 64.01 | 63.15 | 61.84 | 45.45 | 43.60 | 74,414 |
| BLM Sim. Interactions on 25% of Data in E1-1 + E1-2 | 54.05 | 46.48 | 44.73 | 31.38 | 51.51 | 45.31 | 8,266 |
| BLM Human Interactions in E1-1 + E2-1 | 67.56 | 71.56 | 50.00 | 43.60 | 51.51 | 40.09 | 84 |
| CLM Human Interactions in E1-1 + E2-1 | 53.52 | 44.53 | 53.48 | 43.07 | 46.80 | 38.73 | 47 |

Table 5: Protocol 3: Results on BLM + Climate Change (CLM) when we train on interactions and then do more in the inductive setting. E1 and E2 are the two separate inductive graphs. E1-1 is the interaction half of E1 that is trained on. E1-2 is the non-interaction half. E2 receives interactions on the interaction half (E2-1), but not the non-interaction half (E2-2). Human interactions improve accuracy on both halves of E2 and F1 on E2-1, compared to no interactions train, and more than only applying interactions without training for them as Tab.3, showing the benefit of training to learn to incorporate interactions.

news source factuality detection after doing interactions, compared to not doing any. In Tab. 4, we ran interactions on the interaction half of $E1$, and then trained on that data. On $E2$ with no interactions done, we can see how this improves accuracy compared to models trained without interactions.

Finally, for Protocol 3, we learn to better incorporate interactions into the model after we train for it. Thus, we train similarly to Protocol 2, but now we also run interactions on the interaction half of $E2$. In Tab. 5, we see accuracy improves on both halves of $E2$ after we learn to incorporate interactions on $E1$, even though $E2$ is inductive. Further, F1 improves on $E1$-1. This shows that training with and then doing interactions helps performance significantly on future events. We hypothesize that this happens as training with interactions enables the model to learn how to incorporate them better, allowing the model to further take advantage of them whenever provided. Further, human interactions based on content preferences provide clearer results compared to simulated ones (without cheating and using test set labels), as the model better learns the social media landscape, shown by it achieving better accuracy on the BLM interacted and non-interacted data (both halves of $E2$).

From these results, we see that our real-world applicable human interactions models result in performance improvements in either Accuracy or Macro F1, often times both. As a whole, all our models improve performance (any non-gain in one of these metrics is offset by significant gains in the other). We additionally hypothesize that performing more interactions (particularly human) will achieve higher and more consistent results.

| Model | Purity | # Edge |
|---|---|---|
| No Inter. | 36.2, 37.8, 33.3 | - |
| P1: Inductive Human | 39.2, 40.2, 35.3 | 84 |
| P2: Train Human | 49.5, 37.4, 41.4 | 84 |
| P3: Train + Inter. Human | 53.4, 41.9, 42.6 | 84 |

Table 6: Purity clustering (sources, articles, users) for the human interaction protocols on E2-1. As training increases with each protocol (P), purity does too, showing that interactions do help to learn better information communities.

## 6 Discussion

Now, we analyze our best BLM interaction model for fake news source detection (for each protocol) on $E2$-1 by answering these research questions:
(1) *Do interactions help learn better communities?*
(2) *What pairs of nodes do humans connect?*
(3) *How can our model be used in the real world?*
(4) *Do interactions change embeddings?* App. D.1

### 6.1 Learned Communities

We analyze how interactions help learn better info. communities. We evaluate cluster-purity by K-means clustering sources, articles, and users before and after interactions are done. To compute purity, each cluster is assigned to the class which is most frequent in it, and then the accuracy of this is measured. Users are assigned gold labels based on the most common label of all the nodes they are directly connected to in the graph. Results in Tab. 6 show purity increases after interactions, showing interactions help learn better communities.

### 6.2 Human Interaction Analysis/Examples

We analyze the interactions to determine what humans connected. We see humans make smart decisions in matching content preferences. Further, we show specific examples, demonstrating the ease, quickness, and lack of subjectivity of the interaction process. These details/ex. are in App. D.2.

### 6.3 Real World Use Case

As shown in Sec. 5, our interactive protocols enable rapidly (humans spent ~3 min/sub-graph) learning better source factuality detection models for new events, even in the most challenging settings when there are no users, articles, or sources in common with prior data. This happens as contrary to providing additional labels, which can be time consuming and hard, interactions clear up content preferences, creating better social homophily and performance.

Specifically, in a real-world use case, interacting at training time learns a better model for the new event setting (Protocol 2 results on E2-1). In addition, this model would become even stronger as more interactions are performed, even without any further training, as seen in Protocol 3. Thus, when new news events happen, humans can interact on a few settings (our interaction sub-graphs) and our setup enables the model to amplify this knowledge to rapidly detect fake news sources on a large scale.

## 7 Summary and Future Work

We proposed an initial protocol to interactively build stronger information communities, applying it on source factuality detection. We focused on the early detection settings, where even strong models can struggle. Our approach of finding sub-graphs and then interacting on them via 3 protocols enables minimal, quick human interactions to achieve significant performance improvements. We hypothesize that our interactive framework can generalize to other social media analysis tasks like bias or topic detection, and testing it is our future work. Additionally, we aim to scale up our interaction process, to include additional human interactions and types of interactions.

## 8 Acknowledgements

We thank the anonymous reviewers of this paper for all of their vital feedback. The project was funded by NSF CAREER award IIS-2048001 and IIS-2135573.

## 9 Ethics Statement

In this section, we first discuss some limitations of our model (9.1), and then expand on that with a discussion on ethics as it relates to our data collection, data usage, human interaction, and the deployment of our models (9.2).

### 9.1 Limitations

This work tackles fake news source detection in English on Twitter (our social media platform of choice). Our methods may or may not apply to other languages with different morphology, and other social networking platforms. We leave the investigation of this to future work, but are optimistic that especially with the benefit of interactivity, our methods may generalize.

The nature of our interactive framework also requires human interactors to interact, which could be a potential limitation. Interactors must have some general understanding of news content and be able to identify if two entities (users, sources, or articles) have similar content relationships. However, as interactors are just looking for content/perspective similarity, they need not be aware of the latest events or be fake news detection specialists. Further, human interactors don't analyze user-specific information or profile users themselves, they just determine if users have similar content relationships.

We used a single GeForce GTX 1080 NVIDIA GPU to train our models, with 12 GB of memory. As our models are largely textual based, they do not require much GPU usage. However, scaling our experiments to larger scale settings in real world settings could require more compute, which may be a potential limitation. Our hyper-parameter search, mentioned in App A.3 was done manually.

### 9.2 Ethics

To the best of our knowledge no code of ethics was violated throughout the experiments done in this paper. We reported all hyper-parameters and other technical details necessary to reproduce our results, and release the code and dataset we collected. We evaluated our model on two datasets that we collected in this paper, and was collected by prior work, but it is possible that results may differ on other datasets. We believe our methodology is solid and applies to any social media fake news setting. Due to lack of space, we placed some of the technical details and discussion to the Appendix section. The results we reported supports our claims in this paper and we believe it is reproducible. Any qualitative result we report is an outcome from a machine learning model that does not represent the authors' personal views. For anything associated with the data we use, we do not include account information and all results are anonymous.

In our dataset release, we include sources, users, and articles, with enough data to produce the results described in the paper and the Appendix. Sources are public information provided in (Baly et al., 2020), and we map each to an ID. We release article graph embeddings, which can be used to train our models. As these embeddings are neural network representations, they can't be mapped back to article text. However, we also release article URLs, so that the articles can be downloaded, if they are still publicly available. Additionally, we release the Twitter data that we used, in complicance with the Twitter API policies [4]. In our dataset release, each user is referenced by their Twitter ID, and their graph ID (the graph ID is meaningless on it's own). We release the mapping of the Twitter ID to the graph ID. By us only releasing Twitter ID's, and not the actual Twitter text or user information, in order to download the exact Twitter data that we used, users must use the Twitter API to gather the latest public information[5]. This ensures that we respect user privacy, in accordance with the policies mentioned by the Twitter API, as only user content that is still public can be downloaded and we are not storing/releasing any data. We also provide the model representations for each user, article, and source we used as our initial embedding in the graph. As these are neural network model embeddings, they can't be mapped back to the individual text. Our data is meant for academic research purposes and should not be used outside of academic research contexts. All our data is in English.

In this paper, we did not use any of the Twitter data for user surveillance purposes, and we encourage the community to do the same, to respect user privacy. We also do not profile users, we only use the user insights as an aggregate to classify news sources. Further, we only use public Twitter profiles, which there are enough of for our framework to work in real-time situations. When doing human interactions, we show humans public Twitter information, so that they can determine user similarity. To do this, we use the Twitter API to determine the Twitter data that is publicly available at the time of interaction, show that to humans, and then discard the Twitter information. Further, in our graph model, we do not store any user-specific information, we only store neural network model embeddings which are used for training and cannot be mapped back to the original text or user. The same is true for articles, so we we are actually discarding all the text (Twitter, article, and source). Users of our framework should also do the same - use public knowledge for interactions and not store any user/article specific data, rather use the appropriate APIs to retrieve the data when needed.

Our framework in general is intended to be used to defend against fake news. While our framework could be used to build better methods of designing fake news, our methodology of interactive fake news detection could guard against that as well. We caution that our models and methods be considered and used carefully. This is because in an area like fake news detection, there are great consequences of wrong model decisions, such as unfair censorship and other social related issues. Further, despite our efforts, it is possible our models are biased, and this should also be taken into consideration. Our protocol of building sub-graphs based on model confusion that we used when showing humans what to interact on, can be used to get insights into the model to help prevent some of these issues as well. However, this is definitely an area of future work.

In the interactive setting we proposed, our approach relies on getting insights from human interactors and using that to improve performance in fake news detection. While that lead to performance improvements in this work and we believe it will hold in different settings, there could be issues, such as biased humans. Running interactions at large scale with multiple human experts per subgraph can help mitigate some of these issues. For example, edges can be weighted in the graph based on how many humans chose to add them. Thus, extremely biased interactors decisions would be given less weight, and maybe even not considered by the model. We leave this for future work. However, despite this, there may still be some human interactor bias that can leak into the final fake news detection model, which is why perhaps important decisions should not be made only by machine learning models, but rather the models be used as a tool.

As mentioned in the Appendix B.2.3, the human interactors we used were Compute Science PhD

[4] https://developer.twitter.com/en/developer-terms/more-on-restricted-use-cases

[5] https://developer.twitter.com/en/docs/twitter-api

students. The interactors were awarded research credits for their work, as the hours they spent working on the task were considered as part of their research credit hours. They were explained the entire process before hand including what the interactions would be used for, and agreed to perform the interaction. The total interaction process took under 3 hours, including the time spent explaining the process.

These and many other issues are things to consider when using fake news detection models such as the one proposed in this work.

## References


Ramy Baly, Georgi Karadzhov, Dimitar Alexandrov, James Glass, and Preslav Nakov. 2018. Predicting factuality of reporting and bias of news media sources. In *Proceedings of the Conference on Empirical Methods in Natural Language Processing*, EMNLP '18, Brussels, Belgium.

Ramy Baly, Georgi Karadzhov, Jisun An, Haewoon Kwak, Yoan Dinkov, Ahmed Ali, James Glass, and Preslav Nakov. 2020. What was written vs. who read it: News media profiling using text analysis and social media context. In *Proceedings of the 58th Annual Meeting of the Association for Computational Linguistics*, ACL '20.

Alessandro Bessi, Fabio Petroni, Michela Del Vicario, Fabiana Zollo, Aris Anagnostopoulos, Antonio Scala, Guido Caldarelli, and Walter Quattrociocchi. 2016. Homophily and polarization in the age of misinformation. *The European Physical Journal Special Topics*, 225:2047–2059.

Pieter M Blok, Gert Kootstra, Hakim Elchaoui Elghor, Boubacar Diallo, Frits K van Evert, and Eldert J van Henten. 2021. Active learning with maskal reduces annotation effort for training mask r-cnn. *arXiv preprint arXiv:2112.06586*.

Kianté Brantley, Soham Dan, Iryna Gurevych, Ji-Ung Lee, Filip Radlinski, Hinrich Schütze, Edwin Simpson, and Lili Yu, editors. 2021. *Proceedings of the First Workshop on Interactive Learning for Natural Language Processing*. Association for Computational Linguistics, Online.

Matteo Cinelli, Gianmarco De Francisci Morales, Alessandro Galeazzi, Walter Quattrociocchi, and Michele Starnini. 2021. The echo chamber effect on social media. *Proceedings of the National Academy of Sciences*, 118(9):e2023301118.

Prakhar Gupta, Chien-Sheng Wu, Wenhao Liu, and Caiming Xiong. 2022. Dialfact: A benchmark for fact-checking in dialogue. In *Proceedings of the 60th Annual Meeting of the Association for Computational Linguistics (Volume 1: Long Papers)*, pages 3785–3801.

Yosh Halberstam and Brian Knight. 2016. Homophily, group size, and the diffusion of political information in social networks: Evidence from twitter. *Journal of public economics*, 143:73–88.

Felix Hamborg, Norman Meuschke, Corinna Breitinger, and Bela Gipp. 2017. news-please: A generic news crawler and extractor. In *Proceedings of the 15th International Symposium of Information Science*, pages 218–223.

Yi Han, Shanika Karunasekera, and Christopher Leckie. 2020. Graph neural networks with continual learning for fake news detection from social media. *arXiv preprint arXiv:2007.03316*.

Naeemul Hassan, Fatma Arslan, Chengkai Li, and Mark Tremayne. 2017. Toward automated fact-checking: Detecting check-worthy factual claims by claimbuster. In *Proceedings of the 23rd ACM SIGKDD International Conference on Knowledge Discovery and Data Mining*, pages 1803–1812.

Yinqiu Huang, Min Gao, Jia Wang, and Kai Shu. 2021. Dafd: Domain adaptation framework for fake news detection. In *International Conference on Neural Information Processing*, pages 305–316. Springer.

Kathleen Hall Jamieson and Joseph N Cappella. 2008. *Echo chamber: Rush Limbaugh and the conservative media establishment.* Oxford University Press.

Jooyeon Kim, Dongkwan Kim, and Alice Oh. 2019. Homogeneity-based transmissive process to model true and false news in social networks. In *Proceedings of the Twelfth ACM International Conference on Web Search and Data Mining*, pages 348–356.

Pakindessama M Konkobo, Rui Zhang, Siyuan Huang, Toussida T Minoungou, Jose A Ouedraogo, and Lin Li. 2020. A deep learning model for early detection of fake news on social media. In *2020 7th International Conference on Behavioural and Social Computing (BESC)*, pages 1–6. IEEE.

David MJ Lazer, Matthew A Baum, Yochai Benkler, Adam J Berinsky, Kelly M Greenhill, Filippo Menczer, Miriam J Metzger, Brendan Nyhan, Gordon Pennycook, David Rothschild, et al. 2018. The science of fake news. *Science*, 359(6380):1094–1096.

Ke Li, Bin Guo, Jiaqi Liu, Jiangtao Wang, Haoyang Ren, Fei Yi, and Zhiwen Yu. 2022. Dynamic probabilistic graphical model for progressive fake news detection on social media platform. *ACM Transactions on Intelligent Systems and Technology (TIST)*.

Hongzhan Lin, Jing Ma, Liangliang Chen, Zhiwei Yang, Mingfei Cheng, and Chen Guang. 2022. Detect rumors in microblog posts for low-resource domains via adversarial contrastive learning. In *Findings of the Association for Computational Linguistics: NAACL 2022*, pages 2543–2556.

Yang Liu and Yi-Fang Wu. 2018. Early detection of fake news on social media through propagation path classification with recurrent and convolutional networks. In *Proceedings of the AAAI conference on artificial intelligence*, volume 32.

Yinhan Liu, Myle Ott, Naman Goyal, Jingfei Du, Mandar Joshi, Danqi Chen, Omer Levy, Mike Lewis, Luke Zettlemoyer, and Veselin Stoyanov. 2019. Roberta: A robustly optimized bert pretraining approach. *arXiv preprint arXiv:1907.11692*.

Jing Ma, Wei Gao, and Kam-Fai Wong. 2018. Rumor detection on twitter with tree-structured recursive neural networks. In *Proceedings of the 56th Annual Meeting of the Association for Computational Linguistics (Volume 1: Long Papers)*, pages 1980–1989.

Miller McPherson, Lynn Smith-Lovin, and James M Cook. 2001. Birds of a feather: Homophily in social networks. *Annual review of sociology*, 27(1):415–444.

Nikhil Mehta, María Leonor Pacheco, and Dan Goldwasser. 2022. Tackling fake news detection by continually improving social context representations using graph neural networks. In *Proceedings of the 60th Annual Meeting of the Association for Computational Linguistics (Volume 1: Long Papers)*, pages 1363–1380.

Ahmadreza Mosallanezhad, Mansooreh Karami, Kai Shu, Michelle V Mancenido, and Huan Liu. 2022. Domain adaptive fake news detection via reinforcement learning. In *Proceedings of the ACM Web Conference 2022*, pages 3632–3640.

Van-Hoang Nguyen, Kazunari Sugiyama, Preslav Nakov, and Min-Yen Kan. 2020. Fang: Leveraging social context for fake news detection using graph representation. In *Proceedings of the 29th ACM International Conference on Information & Knowledge Management*, pages 1165–1174.

Maria Leonor Pacheco and Dan Goldwasser. 2021. Modeling content and context with deep relational learning. *Transactions of the Association for Computational Linguistics*, 9:100–119.

Maria Leonor Pacheco, Tunazzina Islam, Monal Mahajan, Andrey Shor, Ming Yin, Lyle Ungar, and Dan Goldwasser. 2022. A holistic framework for analyzing the COVID-19 vaccine debate. In *Proceedings of the 2022 Conference of the North American Chapter of the Association for Computational Linguistics: Human Language Technologies*, pages 5821–5839, Seattle, United States. Association for Computational Linguistics.

Maria Leonor Pacheco, Tunazzina Islam, Lyle Ungar, Ming Yin, and Dan Goldwasser. 2023. Interactive concept learning for uncovering latent themes in large text collections. In *Findings of the Association for Computational Linguistics: ACL 2023*, pages 5059–5080, Toronto, Canada. Association for Computational Linguistics.

Adam Paszke, Sam Gross, Francisco Massa, Adam Lerer, James Bradbury, Gregory Chanan, Trevor Killeen, Zeming Lin, Natalia Gimelshein, Luca Antiga, Alban Desmaison, Andreas Kopf, Edward Yang, Zachary DeVito, Martin Raison, Alykhan Tejani, Sasank Chilamkurthy, Benoit Steiner, Lu Fang, Junjie Bai, and Soumith Chintala. 2019. Pytorch: An imperative style, high-performance deep learning library. In H. Wallach, H. Larochelle, A. Beygelzimer, F. d'Alché-Buc, E. Fox, and R. Garnett, editors, *Advances in Neural Information Processing Systems 32*, pages 8024–8035. Curran Associates, Inc.

Verónica Pérez-Rosas, Bennett Kleinberg, Alexandra Lefevre, and Rada Mihalcea. 2018. Automatic detection of fake news. In *Proceedings of the 27th International Conference on Computational Linguistics*, pages 3391–3401.

Walter Quattrociocchi, Antonio Scala, and Cass R Sunstein. 2016. Echo chambers on facebook. *Available at SSRN 2795110*.

Nils Reimers and Iryna Gurevych. 2019. Sentence-bert: Sentence embeddings using siamese bert-networks. In *Proceedings of the 2019 Conference on Empirical Methods in Natural Language Processing and the 9th International Joint Conference on Natural Language Processing (EMNLP-IJCNLP)*, pages 3982–3992.

Michael Schlichtkrull, Thomas N Kipf, Peter Bloem, Rianne Van Den Berg, Ivan Titov, and Max Welling. 2018. Modeling relational data with graph convolutional networks. In *European semantic web conference*, pages 593–607. Springer.

Kai Shu, Limeng Cui, Suhang Wang, Dongwon Lee, and Huan Liu. 2019a. defend: Explainable fake news detection. In *Proceedings of the 25th ACM SIGKDD international conference on knowledge discovery & data mining*, pages 395–405.

Kai Shu, Deepak Mahudeswaran, and Huan Liu. 2019b. Fakenewstracker: a tool for fake news collection, detection, and visualization. *Computational and Mathematical Organization Theory*, 25(1):60–71.

Niket Tandon, Aman Madaan, Peter Clark, and Yiming Yang. 2022. Learning to repair: Repairing model output errors after deployment using a dynamic memory of feedback. *NAACL Findings.(to appear)*.

Svitlana Volkova and Jin Yea Jang. 2018. Misleading or falsification: Inferring deceptive strategies and types in online news and social media. In *Companion Proceedings of the The Web Conference 2018*, pages 575–583.

Soroush Vosoughi, Deb Roy, and Sinan Aral. 2018. The spread of true and false news online. *Science*, 359(6380):1146–1151.

Minjie Wang, Da Zheng, Zihao Ye, Quan Gan, Mufei Li, Xiang Song, Jinjing Zhou, Chao Ma, Lingfan Yu, Yu Gai, et al. 2019. Deep graph library: A graph-centric, highly-performant package for graph neural networks. *arXiv preprint arXiv:1909.01315*.

Robert West, Hristo S Paskov, Jure Leskovec, and Christopher Potts. 2014. Exploiting social network structure for person-to-person sentiment analysis. *Transactions of the Association for Computational Linguistics*, 2:297–310.

Dustin Wright, David Wadden, Kyle Lo, Bailey Kuehl, Arman Cohan, Isabelle Augenstein, and Lucy Wang. 2022. Generating scientific claims for zero-shot scientific fact checking. In *Proceedings of the 60th Annual Meeting of the Association for Computational Linguistics (Volume 1: Long Papers)*, pages 2448–2460.

Yi Yang, Ming-Wei Chang, and Jacob Eisenstein. 2016. Toward socially-infused information extraction: Embedding authors, mentions, and entities. In *Proceedings of the 2016 Conference on Empirical Methods in Natural Language Processing*, pages 1452–1461.

Chunyuan Yuan, Qianwen Ma, Wei Zhou, Jizhong Han, and Songlin Hu. 2020. Early detection of fake news by utilizing the credibility of news, publishers, and users based on weakly supervised learning. In *Proceedings of the 28th International Conference on Computational Linguistics*, pages 5444–5454.

Yongchun Zhu, Qiang Sheng, Juan Cao, Shuokai Li, Danding Wang, and Fuzhen Zhuang. 2022a. Generalizing to the future: Mitigating entity bias in fake news detection. In *Proceedings of the 45nd International ACM SIGIR Conference on Research and Development in Information Retrieval*. Association for Computing Machinery.

Yongchun Zhu, Qiang Sheng, Juan Cao, Qiong Nan, Kai Shu, Minghui Wu, Jindong Wang, and Fuzhen Zhuang. 2022b. Memory-guided multi-view multi-domain fake news detection. *IEEE Transactions on Knowledge and Data Engineering*.

# A Supplemental Material: Fake News Source Detection

In this section, we provide implementation details for our models for fake news source detection. The original dataset we used has 859 sources: 452 *high* factuality, 245 *mixed*, and 162 *low*, and was released publicly by (Baly et al., 2020)[6]. We then extended it by scraping sources from the Media Bias/Fact Check website[7], to gain better coverage of more recent events. The dataset does not include any other raw data (articles, sources, etc.), so we must scrape our own.

## A.1 Data Collection

We will release the data and code for this paper upon acceptance. Our data collection process is identical to Mehta et al. as we use their code, but we briefly describe the process here completion. Further details are available in Mehta et al.

Following the process used in Mehta et al., we tried to scrape news articles for each source in the dataset using public libraries (Newspaper3K [8], news-please [9] (Hamborg et al., 2017), and Scrapy [10]). In cases where the webpage of the news source was removed as often happens with fake news websites, we used the Wayback Machine [11] to download the articles, if possible. As explained in Sec 3, we attempted to get up to 300 articles for each source. For the sources we got for the (Baly et al., 2020) dataset, our statistics are the same as Mehta et al. as we use their data, and thus the sources have an average of 109 articles with a STD of 36.

To scrape Twitter data, we used the Twitter API[12]. In order to densely populate the graph, we attempted to scrape up to 5000 followers for each source that had a Twitter account ((72.5% of the sources, the same number as (Baly et al., 2020; Mehta et al., 2022)). Further, to find users that propagate articles, we used the Twitter Search API to search articles. From the returned Twitter results, we use users that mention the article title or the article URL and post their tweet within 3 months of the original article being published. For each user found, we download their profile and add them to our graph, making the appropriate Twitter User to

[6]https://github.com/ramybaly/News-Media-Reliability
[7]https://mediabiasfactcheck.com
[8]https://github.com/codelucas/newspaper
[9]https://github.com/fhamborg/news-please
[10]https://github.com/scrapy/scrapy
[11]https://archive.org/web/
[12]https://developer.twitter.com/en/docs

Article connection as discussed in Sec 3. Finally, we scraped the followers of each Twitter user in the graph, and connected them to any user they followed that was in the graph. This increases the connectivity of the graph and allows us to better capture the social media landscape. To maintain a densely connected graph, we remove users that do not connect to any other node in the graph.

To get the data for the YouTube embeddings for the sources, we used the ones released publicly by (Baly et al., 2020), who were able to scrape YouTube channels for 49% of sources.

### A.2 Event Collection

To collect the data for each event ($E1$ from June 2, 2019 - Jan 1, 2021 and $E2$ from Feb 2, 2021 - May 6, 2022), we filtered by date and downloaded Tweets mentioning certain hashtags and a URL with one of the sources in the dataset. The hashtags/search terms we used to collect data for the *Black Lives Matter* event were: *Black Lives Matter, BLM, blacklivesmatter, Floyd, George Floyd.*

We then filtered the data to find the top *high*, *mixed*, and *low* factuality sources that were mentioned on Twitter for each of these events and time periods. We kept sources that had at least 10 articles with Twitter users propagating them. We ended up with at least 33 sources for each factuality level in each event data split. Other sources that were in the training set of Baly et al. were used to train the initial Graph Embedding. Detailed statistics for the training set and the sources used in one of our Black Lives Matter splits are shown in Table 8.

### A.3 Experimental Settings

#### A.3.1 Initial Embeddings

We used the same initial graph node embedding representations as Mehta et al., which we briefly explain here. The Twitter embedding we used for each source and each Twitter user was a 773 dimensional vector consisting of the SBERT (Reimers and Gurevych, 2019) (RoBERTa (Liu et al., 2019) Base NLI model) representation of their bio (up to the first 512 tokens) concatenated with a variety of numerical features, as follows: (1) a binary number representing whether the source is verified, (2) the number of users a source follows and the number that follow it, (3) the number of tweets the user posts, and (4) the number of favorites/likes the users' tweets have received. The YouTube embedding we used consisted of the following numerical features: the average of the number of views, the number of dislikes, and the number of comments for each video the source posted on YouTube. For articles, we used the same SBERT RoBERTa model to generate an embedding based on the article text, which ends up being a 768 dimensional vector. In all cases where we encoded text for embedding representations, we use SBERT (Reimers and Gurevych, 2019) RoBERTa (Liu et al., 2019) model because it provides semantically meaningful sentence representations for the text.

#### A.3.2 Models and Training

We used the publicly released code of Mehta et al., which was built using PyTorch (Paszke et al., 2019) and DGL (Deep Graph Library) (Wang et al., 2019) in Python. The R-GCN used consists of 5 layers, 128 hidden units, a learning rate of 0.001, and a batch size of 128 for Node Classification. The initial source and article embeddings have hidden dimension 768, while the user one has dimension 773. To do 3-way source classification, the final fully connected layer has size 3.

We trained our models using a 12GB TITAN XP GPU card. To learn the initial model which was used to determine where to perform interactions, it took approximately 2 hours. Training after interactions takes approximately 30 minutes total. Inductive settings do not have any training, and take minutes to run as we only have to compute embeddings for nodes that we are attempting to classify.

We used the development set to evaluate model performance, and choose the best hyperparameters.

## B Supplemental Material: Interaction Graphs

In this section, we provide details about the interaction graphs we showed users in B.1. Then, in B.2, we discuss the interaction process (B.2.1), the details behind the interactions used in the main paper (B.2.2), and finally new interactions on the second Black Lives Matter Split (B.2.3).

### B.1 Interaction Graph Details

The sub-graphs were constructed by first picking pairs of users, and then adding context around them, as discussed in Sec 4.1. The context consists of the article each user propagated, the sources that published it, other users that propagated the same arti-

| Model | T1-1 Acc | T1-1 F1 | T1-2 Acc | T1-2 F1 | T2-1 Acc | T2-1 F1 | # Edges |
|---|---|---|---|---|---|---|---|
| No Interactions | 41.79 | 37.10 | 41.93 | 35.95 | 37.50 | 33.54 | - |
| No Interactions Train | 85.71 | 85.16 | 68.42 | 63.00 | 40.40 | 30.75 | - |
| Protocol 1: Human Interactions in T1-1 | 43.28 | 37.39 | 45.16 | 42.34 | - | - | 65 |
| Protocol 2: Human Interactions in T1-1 | 71.68 | 72.50 | 52.63 | 41.82 | 41.41 | 34.79 | 65 |

Table 7: Additional interaction results across the two of our protocols. With minimal interactions, we still see performance improvements in the fully inductive setting in Protocol 1 using all the interactions done by the three humans. We also see how the interactions allow us to learn a better model in Protocol 2, as seen by the improvements on $T2$-1, despite no interactions performed there (interactions were only on $T1$-1).

| Dataset | Low | Mixed | High |
|---|---|---|---|
| Training Event | 57 | 81 | 153 |
| T1 | 56 | 33 | 33 |
| T2 | 33 | 33 | 33 |

Table 8: Number of sources in our datasets for the training event (added to the training set to train the initial model), T1 (first event) and T2 (second event). The results on these data sets are shown in Table 7.

cles, and finally some additional celebrities (users with more than 1000 followers) that are followed by one of the users in the graph. All articles added to the graph have to be about the same event, and they are found by searching hashtags related to the event (in our case Black Lives Matter or Climate Change, hashtags below) in a four week span on Twitter. An example of an interaction graph that is shown to humans is in Fig. 2

Each node in the interaction graphs also contains metadata to provide more information to the human interactors. As seen in Fig 3, article nodes consist of the headline, article text, article entities, and the date the article was published. As seen in Fig 4 source and user nodes contain Twitter information such as: username, following count, number of followers, whether they are verified, how many tweets they make, what is their model predicted label, their biography, the tweet they made about the article, and other tweets they made about the same event.

Once the graphs are built, we show them to humans and ask a series of questions to guide the interaction process. Each question asks the user to create an edge in the interaction graph based if there is a positive relationship between the two nodes. A Positive relationships mean the nodes have similar content preferences. If a positive relationship doesn't exist, or there is not enough data to clearly determine a positive relationship, humans are asked to not make any edge connections. Thus, humans are asked to ignore potentially subjective cases. Humans identifying positive relationships has multiple benefits for fake news detection: **(1) Simplicity:** It is far simpler than identifying factuality, so it can be used to detect fake news quickly. The simplicity of the interaction process is due to the fact that interactors only have to read a small amount of content (a few user tweets/profile information + up to two article headlines/summaries), compared to reading multiple articles and gaining real world knowledge. On average, human interactors spent 3 minutes per interaction graph, and made an average of 8 connections in this time. **(2) Effectiveness:** Interactions improve social media representation quality and thus social homophily, and that's what leads to performance improvements. Here are the questions we asked human interactors for each sub-graph shown:

1. Are there any users that are similar to each other? Please connect them.
2. Are there any articles that are similar to each other? Please connect them.
3. Are any users likely to propagate any of the articles? Please connect them to the appropriate article.
4. Are any users likely to interact with another user? Please connect those pairs of users.
5. Are any users likely to interact with any sources? Please connect those users of the respective source.

### B.2 Human Interactor Details

In this sub-section, we first discuss the interaction process, including the graphical interface we built for this task (B.2.1). Then, we discuss the two rounds of human interaction protocols we did for

Black Lives Matter. Climate change details follow in Sec C. The first split of Black Lives Matter, Sec B.2.2 was presented in the main paper, and the second split B.2.3 appears in this section.

#### B.2.1 Interaction Process

The human interactors use a graphical interface that displays the interaction graphs. We hosted the interface on a website built for this interaction process. Humans must answer the questions discussed above (Sec B.1) by connecting nodes to create edges, which are then saved on our server and can be incorporated into the broad event graph as new edges, when evaluating the overall performance. The examples of the graphs human interactors see when interacting, and the metadata they are provided with, can be seen in Fig 2, Fig 3, and Fig 4. Examples of connections made are in 6.2.

#### B.2.2 Initial Interactor Details

We now describe the initial interaction session we discussed in the main Paper on Black Lives Matter and used for all the BLM Human results presented there. The interactor used for this session was an Asian-American PhD student in Computer Science and Natural Language Processing. They were explained of the entire process before hand including what the interactions would be used for, and agreed to perform the interaction. They interacted on 20 graphs per data split (E1-1, dev, and E2-1), which took under an hour for each split.

#### B.2.3 Additional Interactor Details

To expand our human interactor sessions, we also ran additional interaction sessions on the Black Lives Matter dataset (and Climate Change in Sec C. For variety, we used a different source split in this setting, that we will also release. For this reason, these additional results are not comparable to the ones in the main paper, and we refer to the new events as $T1$, $T1$-1, $T2$, etc. instead of $E1$, $E1$-1, $E2$, etc. The data collection was the same as before.

For these additional interactions, we used three interactors of Asian descent, all fluent in the English language and all Computer Science PhD students. The interactors were awarded research credits for their work, as the hours that they spent working on the task were considered as part of their research credit hours. They were explained of the entire process before hand including what the interactions would be used for, and agreed to perform the interaction. Each interactor interacted on 10 graphs for $T1$-1, and spent less than one hour. A majority of the time was spent becoming familiar the interaction process, and once complete the interactions went more rapidly. As a test, we had one interactor do interactions on 10 more graphs, and they were able to do 10 graphs in less than 30 minutes, showing how this process can be done rapidly. Moreover, interactors spent an average of 3 mins. per interaction sub-graph, once familiar with the process. Across the three interactors, we had 65 unique edge connections made for $T1$-1. We had 31 edges that were repeated across the interactors, showing a reasonable level of interactor agreement given the the task.

Results for this additional interaction process is in Tab. 7, and they are consistent with the results for the Protocols in the main paper for the single interactor. For Protocol 1, we see improvements in the inductive setting on both the interaction and non-interaction half of $T1$. Thus, interactions help performance even when there is no additional training. Protocol 2 also leads to improvements and shows how interactions (done on $T1$-1) allow us to learn a better model for when no interactions are done (dev. set performance was 43.45% Accuracy). This further shows how interactions can help to build a stronger model, especially on emerging news events. In addition, it is likely that more interactions would lead to more improvements, and we leave this for future work.

## C Supplemental Material: Climate Change

In this section, we expand upon the Climate Change (CLM) dataset results discussed first in Sec 5. We first discuss what search terms we used to collect the data for Climate Change in Sec C.1. Then, in Sec C.2, we explain the interaction process that was used for Climate Change, and the agreement statistics associated with it. Finally, in Sec C.3, we present detailed results for Climate Change, including simulated interactions. All results and conclusions are comparable with the Black Lives Matter results, showing that our approach generalizes across events.

### C.1 Data Collection

We used the same Data Collection process for Climate Change as Black Lives Matter, discussed in Sec 5.1 and Sec A.1. This means we have the same

| Model | E1-1 Acc | E1-1 F1 | E1-2 Acc | E1-2 F1 | E2-1 Acc | E2-1 F1 | E2-2 Acc | E2-2 F1 | # Edges |
|---|---|---|---|---|---|---|---|---|---|
| CLM No Interactions | 40.16 | 32.77 | 39.65 | 31.86 | 34.88 | 30.93 | - | - | - |
| CLM Sim. Interactions on 100% of Data in E1-1 + E2-1 | 46.72 | 41.59 | 39.65 | 31.86 | 44.18 | 41.57 | - | - | 12,602 |
| CLM Human Interactions in E1-1 + E2-1 | 46.72 | 43.94 | 39.65 | 31.86 | 39.53 | 36.95 | - | - | 47 |
| CLM No Interactions Train | - | - | 49.29 | 44.84 | 44.77 | 42.35 | - | - | - |
| CLM Sim. Interactions on 100% of Data in E1-1 | - | - | 56.33 | 50.02 | 44.18 | 43.10 | - | - | 12,602 |
| CLM Human Interactions in E1-1 | - | - | 53.52 | 44.53 | 40.29 | 46.38 | - | - | 47 |
| CLM No Interactions Train | - | - | 49.29 | 44.84 | 44.77 | 42.35 | 44.44 | 33.06 | - |
| CLM Sim. Interactions on 100% of Data in E1-1 + E1-2 | - | - | 56.33 | 50.02 | 41.86 | 36.42 | 34.04 | 24.93 | 12,602 |
| CLM Human Interactions in E1-1 + E1-2 | - | - | 53.52 | 44.53 | 53.48 | 43.07 | 46.80 | 38.73 | 47 |

Table 9: Climate Change Results: Key: E1 and E2 are the two inductive graphs. E1-1/E2-1 is the first half, and E1-2/E2-2 are the second half. # Edges shows the number of edges added by interactions to E1-1. **Protocol 1:** The top third refers to Protocol 1, where interactions result in performance improvements in the difficult, inductive, no training setting. In particular, we see improvements of 6.56% Acc. and 11.17% F1 on $E1$-1. We do not evaluate on $E2$-2, as no interactions are done on that split, so performance does not change. **Protocol 2:** The middle third refers to Protocol 2, where interactions result in performance improvements when we train on the interactions, and then apply the model to a new event with no interactions done. We do not evaluate on $E1$-1, as it is the training set), and $E2$-2, as no interactions are done and performance does not change. **Protocol 3:** The last third refers to Protocol 3, where interactions result in performance improvements when we train on the interactions and then do more interactions in the inductive setting ($E2$-1). We also see improvements in $E2$-2. We don't evaluate on $E1$-1 as it is the training set.

| Dataset | Low | Mixed | High |
|---|---|---|---|
| E1-1 | 30 | 43 | 49 |
| E1-2 | 28 | 41 | 47 |
| E2-1 | 11 | 15 | 17 |
| E2-2 | 13 | 16 | 18 |

Table 10: Number of sources in our dataset for climate change.

3 time periods for Climate Change as Black Lives Matter (BLM). The only difference between BLM and Climate Change are the search terms we used to search Twitter to collect the data. For Climate Change, we used the following search terms: *fracking*, *global warming*, *climate change*, *#savetheplanet*, *#savethetrees*, *#climatechangeisreal*, *#waterpollution*, and *#climatestrike*. Statistics for the number of sources in each data split and their high, mixed, and low factuality distribution are shown in Table 10.

## C.2 Human Interaction Process

For the human interactions done on Climate Change, we used two male human interactors. Both are Computer Science P.h.D. students in Natural Language Processing of Asian descent. The interactions were done on 8 sub-graphs for each time period ($E1$-1, $E2$-1, and the development set), for a total of 24 sub-graphs interacted on. As with Black Lives Matter, interactors spent an average of about 3 minutes on each interaction sub-graph.

## C.3 Climate Change Results

In-depth results for climate change are presented in Table 9. In the main paper, due to lack of space, we presented only baseline and human interaction results, which we expand upon here also showing simulated results. We can see that results improve and are consistent with Black Lives Matter Results for Protocols 1, 2, and 3. Protocol 1 (top third of the table) shows significant Accuracy and F1 improvements in the fully inductive setting, showing the power of minimal human interactions in the right places to improve the model without any training. Protocol 2 (middle third of the table) shows how interactions result in performance improvements when we train on interactions and then apply them in the fully inductive setting with no additional interactions done. Finally, protocol 3 shows improvements when we train on the interactions and then do more interactions in the inductive setting.

The results in this section, combined with the earlier results on Black Lives Matter, show that our approach can generalize across multiple datasets, topics, and events.

| Model | Embedding Change % |
|---|---|
| P1: Inductive Human | 75.39 |
| P2: Train Human | 64.23 |
| P3: Train + Inter. Human | 51.41 |

Table 11: Change of node embeddings after interactions compared to the no interaction model on E2-1. Interactions affect model representations (lower # = more change).

# D Discussion Continued

## D.1 Model Representations

Now, in order to measure the impact of interactions on our graph-based model, we evaluate how much model node embeddings change after they are incorporated. To do this, we compute the difference in the cosine similarity of the embedding of each user node before and after interactions are done, and average the results. The results in Tab. 11 show that even a small amount of interactions can make a significant change in model representations. This shows why minimal amounts of interactions can lead to a strong performance increase.

## D.2 Discussion: Interaction Examples

In this section, we continue our discussion from Sec 6.2 and provide more examples of nodes that humans connected during the interaction process. We first show the connections humans make (Sec. D.2.1), and then discuss what trends we can learn from these connections about our approach (Sec. D.2.2). The connections reveal interesting insights on how humans are connecting nodes based on content preferences. Further, it shows that despite all the content being focused on one event, there are lots of different relevant perspectives identified by the model as realistic points of confusion.

### D.2.1 Interactions Made

We first show examples of pairs of users/articles that were connected by human interactors, describing what they were about. This analysis was done by the authors based on the human interactions.

1. A user with hashtags about taking back the United States by burning and destroying it, and also White Supremacy related hashtags, was connected to an article saying the current President (Biden) was clueless and didn't know what they were doing.

2. Two users with random and unrelated hashtags in their bio and extremely similar tweet language were connected as they were identified to likely both be bots.

3. A user that was a sports fan was connected to a source that reported sports media, but in this case had posted an article about how certain races have been negatively impacted from the coronavirus despite being athletic.

4. An article discussing how the Minnesota Vikings Honored George Floyd's family at their season opener was connected to a source that reported football sports articles that seemed factual.

5. An atheist, socialist, songwriter, and musician student Twitter user was connected to a Bernie Sanders supporter that wanted student loan forgiveness.

6. An influencer who was the mayor of a major city was connected to a seemingly politically aligned news reporter for the same city.

Next, we show snippets (to preserve anonymity) of user bios and articles that were connected, to show how simple the process is. We also provide our explanations of why these users/articles were connected. All of these examples are related to the Climate Change event and the text shown is snippets of the actual text that was shown to humans:

1. **Bio 1:** "what makes you optimistic...sharing optimism of optimistic leaders" **Tweet 1:** "a majority of young people are #optimistic that it's still possible to prevent the worst effects of #climatechange"

   **Bio 2:** "Christian...#Goodnews seeker, ther's plenty of it!"

   **Explanation:** These users were connected by interactors likely because the second user likes good news, and the first user is an optimist specifically sharing good news about climate change!

2. **Article 1:** "...San Diego May Get Climate Update After All.."

   **Article 2:** "Fish prices spike as ...face total depletion"

   **Explanation**: These articles were connected by interactors likely because they both are showing the effects of climate change. It is changing cities, and changing fish prices.

3. **Tweet 1:** "Climate Change...Biggest Hoax in Human History"

**Tweet 2**: "Trump is Hurting Climate Change by letting China take the lead..."

**Explanation:** These users were not connected (and so weren't the corresponding articles), and specifically marked **different**. This is likely because the first user doesn't believe in climate change, while the second is disappointed that President Trump isn't taking more action about it.

4. **Article 1:** "Climate Change...Biggest Hoax in Human History"

   **Article 2:** "California bans sale on new gas-powered cars in 2035"

   **Explanation:** These articles were not connected, and specifically marked **different**. This is likely because the first doesn't believe in climate change, while the second one does, or at least enough to report on the ban of the sale of gas cars to protect the environment.

#### D.2.2 Interactions Task Details and Trends

While humans can be subjective and make mistakes, we specifically designed our interaction task to be simple to try and eliminate as much of this as possible. Humans were asked to determine user similarity based on how users are discussing certain events, not in depth questions like if a text is factual or not. Determining this high level of user similarity is fairly simple, especially for educated humans, whom we envision performing the interactions.

From these examples above, we can see that our goal to reduce the subjectivity and increase simplicity of our interaction task holds true, at least in our experiments. This is why the entire interaction process can be be done rapidly (humans spent 3 mins per interaction graph, leading to the creation of 8 edges) and with high human interactor agreement. From the examples shown, it is clear that users/articles were connected based on content match, which was fairly simple for our educated human interactors to tell. However, this is hard for models, particularly on emerging news events, which is why our interaction setup leads to large performance improvements, even without any training. Also, we note that in most cases, the text defining the user/article similarity was not very subjective, and it is easy to determine the user/article perspective.

It is also possible, but unlikely, that two users/articles making similar statements don't have at least some similarity on an issue, and thus shouldn't be in the same information community. However, on a large scale over a lot of interactions, the text we show humans is likely to capture user/article perspectives and thus content similarity trends. Thus, even if there are a few rare cases in which users are connected but their statements aren't representative of the community they belong to, it isn't likely to make a significant difference in our learned representation and thus source factuality detection performance.

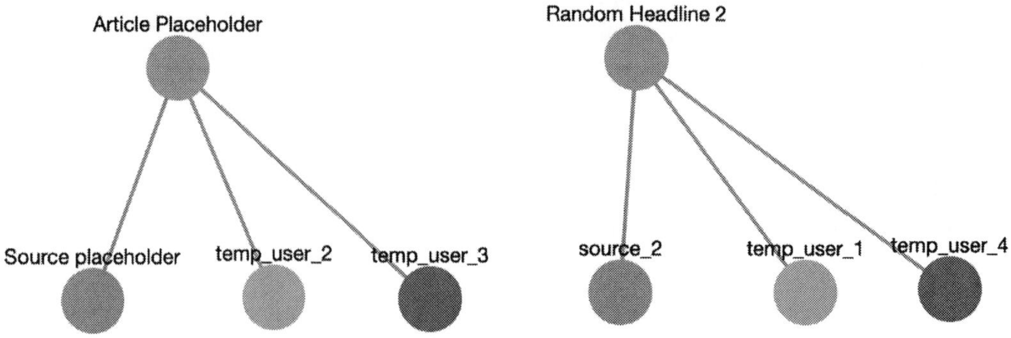


Figure 2: Example of an interaction graph that has been anonymized. The two red nodes are the pairs of users that were identified in Sec 4.1, shown by the Twitter usernames. The two orange nodes are the article nodes, and shown by their headlines without determiners. Blue nodes are other users that propagate the same articles (could be celebrities - users with over 1000 followers, and purple nodes are sources)

.

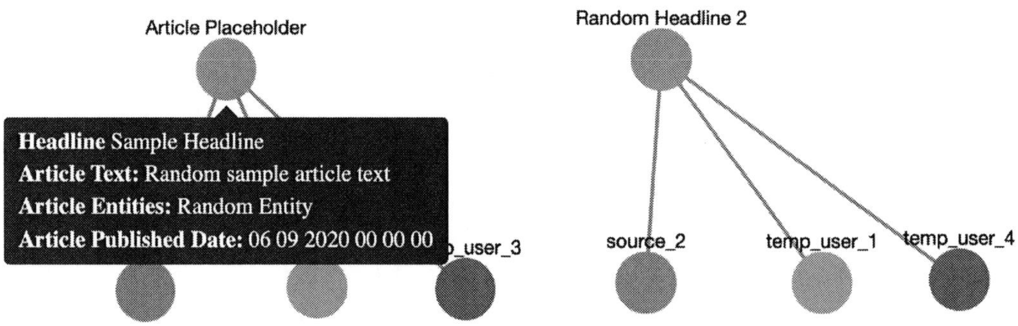


Figure 3: Example of an interaction graph where we can see metadata about an article, by clicking on the article node. This would be filled in during real human interactions, to allow humans to analyze the article and the context around it, but is currently anonymized.

.

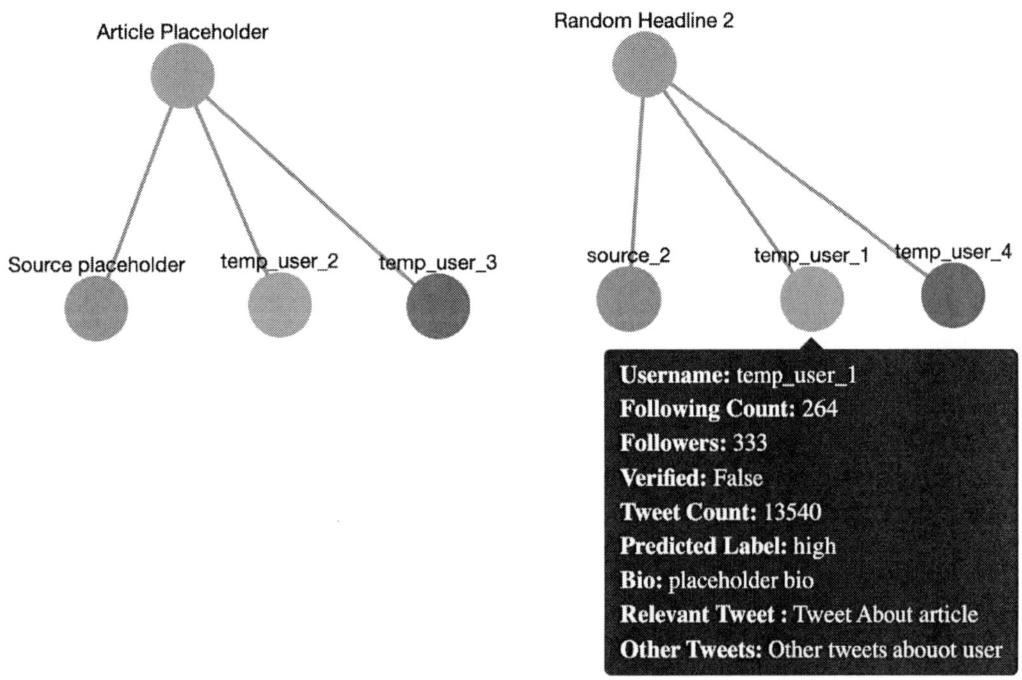


Figure 4: Example of an interaction graph where we can see metadata about a user, by clicking on the user node. This would be filled in (with data from Twitter) during real human interactions, to allow humans to analyze the user and the context around it, but is currently anonymized. Source nodes with Twitter profiles would appear with the same metadata.

# IndIE: A Multilingual Open Information Extraction Tool For Indic Languages

**Ritwik Mishra**[1] , **Simranjeet Singh**[2] , **Rajiv Ratn Shah**[1] , **Ponnurangam Kumaraguru**[3] and **Pushpak Bhattacharyya** [4]

[1] IIIT, Delhi [2] NSUT, Delhi [3] IIIT, Hyderabad [3] IIT Bombay

ritwikm@iiitd.ac.in, simranjeets.ec18@nsut.ac.in
rajivratn@iiitd.ac.in, pk.guru@iiit.ac.in, pb@cse.iitb.ac.in

## Abstract

Open Information Extraction (OIE) is the process of extracting informative facts from open-domain natural language text. A multilingual OIE tool, *IndIE*, has been proposed, which performs chunking, creates a Merged-phrase Dependency Tree (MDT), and generates triples using hand-crafted rules. It is observed that fine-tuned transformer-based chunker outperforms other traditional methods of chunking. A benchmark called *Hindi-BenchIE* has also been developed for automatically evaluating Hindi triples. The developed OIE tool, *IndIE*, has been automatically evaluated on the golden-triples of 112 Hindi sentences. Compared to other multilingual methods, the *IndIE* method generates more meaningful triples with 0.51 F1-score. It is observed that *IndIE* generates more fine-grained triples than other methods. It is conjectured that *IndIE* has the ability to generate meaningful triples for Urdu, Tamil, and Telugu sentences as well because the developed chunker is shown to generalize across various natural languages, and the triple generation rules are based on dependency relations that are common to the aforementioned Indic languages.

## 1 Introduction

India is a linguistically diverse country. Among the top 20 most spoken languages globally, six are native to India (eth, 2021; cen, 2011). Despite being spoken by billions of people, many Indic languages are considered low-resource due to the lack of annotated resources and automated systems available for them (Hirschberg and Manning, 2015). Consequently, there has also been a scarcity of tools for information extraction in Indian languages due to a lack of research work in the field (Gupta et al., 2019; Harish and Rangan, 2020).

Introduced in the mid-1960s, the concept of Information Extraction (IE) deals with extracting structured facts from unstructured text written in a natural language (WILKS, 1964). Extraction of informative facts irrespective of the text domain is called Open Information Extraction (OIE). A standard convention to represent facts is through triples <*head, relation, tail*> where *relation* denotes the link between the two entities, *head* and *tail*. For example, consider the sentence "*PM Modi to visit UAE in Jan marking 50 yrs of diplomatic ties*", one of the possible meaningful triple would be <*PM Modi, to visit, UAE*>.

The biggest strength of OIE tools is their ability to extract triples from large amounts of texts in an unsupervised manner (Gamallo et al., 2012). OIE also serves as an initial step in building or augmenting a knowledge graph out of an unstructured text (Muhammad et al., 2020; Lin et al., 2020).

A triple can be extracted in many different ways depending on the word-order constraints in the given natural language and the expected level of detail in the triples. Consider the sentence, *John sliced an apple with a knife*. Two possible ways to extract facts from this sentence are: (i) <*John, sliced, an apple with a knife*> (ii) <*John, sliced, an apple*>, and <*John, sliced, with a knife*>. Both ways represent the same fact but with different levels of detail. In the case of languages with free word order, like Hindi (Mohanan, 1994), one fact can be represented by many permutations of the elements of a triple. For example, both the following triples <राम ने, खाया, एक सेब> [<*rAm ne, khAya, ek seb*>][1] and <एक सेब, खाया, राम ने> [<*ek seb, khAya, rAm ne*>] represents the same information as the following English triple: <*Ram, ate, an apple*>. However, since the Hindi language uses postpositions (*kaarak*) instead of prepositions (Nagendra, 2019), those word permutations are prohibited that detach the postposition word from

[1] Italicized text written in square brackets represents the ITRANS transliteration, whereas the italicized text in round brackets represents the English translation of the preceding Hindi phrase/sentence



*Findings of the Association for Computational Linguistics: IJCNLP-AACL 2023*, pages 312–326
November 1–4, 2023. ©2023 Asian Federation of Natural Language Processing

its intended subject word because the meaning of the triple changes. For example, the following triple <एक सेब, ने खाया, राम> [<*ek seb*, *ne khAya*, *rAm*>] conveys that <*An apple*, *ate*, *Ram*>.

Our work is primarily focused on automatically extracting triples from Hindi sentences since all the authors of this work are familiar with the language. However, the proposed tool can extract triples from other low-resource Indic languages such as Tamil, Telugu, and Urdu. The main contributions of this paper are as follows:

1. We create and release an OIE benchmark dataset for Hindi sentences, *Hindi-BenchIE*, to facilitate the automatic evaluation of machine-generated triples. To our knowledge, it is the first benchmark that can handle the free-word order nature of Hindi and diverse triple extractions from different OIE systems.

2. We fine-tune a transformer model on manually annotated chunks from six natural languages (*Hindi*, *English*, *Urdu*, *Nepali*, *Gujarati*, and *Bengali*). The resulting model is able to perform chunking on languages it has not seen during the fine-tuning phase.

3. In our research, we also observed that when fine-tuning a pretrained encoder for sequence labeling tasks like chunking, taking an average of subword embeddings or taking the last subword embedding consistently outperformed the traditional way of taking the first subword embedding.

4. We propose a greedy algorithm to extract triples from Hindi text. All the resources and source code will be publicly available on https://github.com/ritwikmishra/IndIE.

## 2 Related Work

Earlier works have used a combination of shallow parsing and hand-crafted rules to extract meaningful entities from English language text (Mohanty et al., 2005; Etzioni et al., 2008; Christensen et al., 2011; Fader et al., 2011). Mausam et al. (2012) used hand-crafted rules and dependency parsing to develop OLLIE, which captured relations mediated by non-verbal phrases like "*is the president of*" extracted triples from English sentences. OLLIE was found to be performing at par with an SRL-based triple extractor. While most of the works dealt with extracting facts in the form of triples, KrakeN was developed to extract facts as N-ary tuples using dependency parsing (Akbik and Löser, 2012). One drawback of earlier rule-based OIE methodologies was their strictly extractive nature, i.e., triples could contain only those explicitly mentioned words in the sentence. Hence, appositive relationships[2] were not extracted by such tools (Zhan and Zhao, 2020). The method we used to extract such appositive relationships is discussed in section 3.3.

Del Corro and Gemulla (2013) developed ClausIE, which identified clauses in an English sentence and then extracted facts by classifying the identified clauses using rules. In order to identify the relations or entities, dependency parsing of sentences was a crucial step in ClausIE and many other works (White et al., 2016; Zhang et al., 2018; Gamallo et al., 2012; Gamallo and Garcia, 2015). Built as an improvement to ClausIE, the MinIE (Gashteovski et al., 2017) tool generated much more fine-grained and concise facts as compared to ClausIE. The triples generated by MinIE had dictionary-like attributes containing information about certainty, polarity, and knowledge source. Due to the availability of manually annotated data for the English, much of the recent OIE research is based on deep neural architectures where the triple extraction problem is divided into the following two sub-problems: (a) Relation extraction and (b) Argument (*head/tail*) extraction using features from the extracted relation (Ro et al., 2020). Span selection (using sequence labeling paradigm) is a common practice to extract relations and their corresponding arguments in such OIE methods (Zhan and Zhao, 2020).

The development of OIE tools for languages other than English is impeded by the need for annotated resources available for them. However, the field of language-independent (multilingual) OIE started in 2015 with two methods. The first method was developed by Manaal and Kumar (*M&K*) (Faruqui and Kumar, 2015), where the authors translated the source language to English using Google translate and then extracted triples using the OLLIE tool. The English triples were projected back to their source language through word alignments. It could handle as many languages as Google can translate, but machine translation has not been regarded as a sustainable solution for OIE

[2] It is a grammatical construction where two noun phrases are written adjacent to each other to convey additional information. For example: *My brother, Bob, likes ice cream*

due to translation errors (Claro et al., 2019). The second method was a rule-based triple extractor called *ArgOE* (Gamallo and Garcia, 2015). In order to generate triples, it expects dependency parse of a sentence in CoNLL format as input. However, the extracted triples contain only verb-mediated relations. *PredPatt* (White et al., 2016) was developed a year later, which also relied on a dependency parse tree and hand-crafted rules to identify predicate-argument structure in a sentence. Another work called *Multi2OIE* modeled the problem of identifying predicate-argument structure through two sequence-labeling tasks using mBERT embeddings and multi-head attention blocks (Ro et al., 2020). The first task identified all the predicates in a sentence, and the second task identified all arguments associated with each predicate. One limitation in identifying predicates with the sequence labeling paradigm is its inability to identify overlapping predicates. For example, consider the following sentence "*Nehru became the prime minister of India in 1947*". Depending on the level of detail (granularity) in triples, two predicates that can be extracted among numerous possible predicates are "*became*" and "*became the prime minister*".

Kolluru et al. (2022) introduced a novel approach to multilingual Open Information Extraction that leverages Natural Language Generation (NLG) techniques and cross-lingual projections. Their method is capable of extracting overlapping relations (predicates) and triple arguments. However, their proposed AACTrans algorithm required parallel corpora for training, and they utilized off-the-shelf translation systems in their experiments. In order to compare the performance of *IndIE*, we have taken the five methods mentioned above (*M&K, ArgOE, PredPatt, Multi2OIE, and Gen2OIE*) as our baselines since they are on similar lines as that of our work.

## 3 Methodology

Our method takes raw text as input and uses the Stanza library (Qi et al., 2020) (version 1.1.1) to perform sentence segmentation and dependency parsing. The primary motivation behind using the Stanza library was its ability to perform shallow parsing on multiple Indic languages. Figure 1 describes the overall procedure of generating triples. It is divided into the following three primary steps: (a) performing chunking and identifying the semantic phrases in the given sentence, (b) creating a Merged-phrases Dependency Tree using the dependency parse tree, and (c) generating triples through our hand-crafted rules. In the following subsections, we discuss the three steps in a more detailed manner.

### 3.1 Chunking

The process of chunking can be defined by capturing non-overlapping multi-word entities in a sentence and classifying them into different syntactic phrases (Tjong Kim Sang and Buchholz, 2000). Chunking is modeled as a sequence labeling task where one chunk tag is predicted for every token of the given sentence. Each chunk tag consists of (i) a boundary label and (ii) a chunk label. The chunk labels can be classified into different syntactic categories, like Noun-Phrases (NP), Verb-Phrases (VP), Adjective-Phrases (JJP), etc. (Bharati et al., 2006). Whereas different notations, like BIO or BIOES, can be used to represent the non-overlapping boundary labels. We use BI notation to mark boundary labels because earlier works have shown its superior precision over other notations (Singh et al., 2005; Sharma et al., 2016).

#### 3.1.1 Dataset

We develop a multilingual chunking tool by fine-tuning a pre-trained transformer on multilingual chunk annotated data. Our chunker is fine-tuned on chunk annotated sentences from Jha (2010)[3] and Bhat et al. (2017)[4]. The former data source comprises 70K chunk-labelled sentences in English, Hindi, Bengali, Nepali, and Gujarati each, whereas the latter data source consists of 16K and 5K chunk-labelled sentences in Hindi and Urdu, respectively. The primary motivation behind using two data sources is to have a large amount of fine-tuning data. The two data sources gave us 0.37 million chunk annotated sentences in total.

#### 3.1.2 Model

Using transformers library (Wolf et al., 2020), we fine-tune different pretrained transformer-based models for the task of chunking because earlier works have shown their superior ability to perform well on shallow parsing tasks (Tran et al., 2020; Doostmohammadi et al., 2020; Li et al., 2021). The word embeddings are obtained by taking an unweighted average of all its subword embeddings. To compare the performance of a transformer-based

[3]from http://tdil-dc.in

[4]from https://universaldependencies.org/

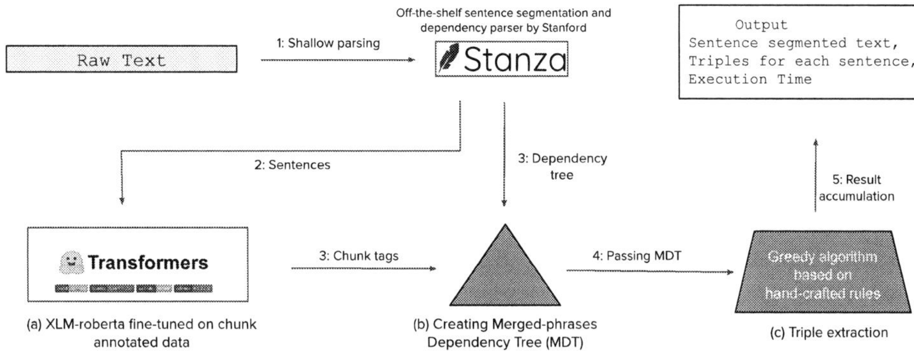


Figure 1: Overall architecture of the *IndIE* tool. The three primary steps are (a) Chunk tag prediction, (b) Creating Merged-phrases Dependency Tree (MDT), and (c) Triple generation. The three steps are run for each sentence segmented by the Stanza library (Qi et al., 2020).

chunker, we train a Conditional Random Field (CRF) model using the scikit-learn (Pedregosa et al., 2011) library. We also implemented a second-order Hidden Markov Model (HMM) with Viterbi decoding to predict the chunk tags. Both the models are the traditional methods used for chunking in Indic languages (Bharati and Mannem, 2007). Appendix B contains the implementation details for the baseline models.

A given text is parsed by the Stanza library (Qi et al., 2020), which performs sentence segmentation, POS tagging, and dependency parsing. Each segmented sentence is passed to our chunker, which predicts the chunk tags for each token. The predicted chunk tags identify the non-overlapping phrases (or multi-word expressions). A syntactically rich phrase is constructed by concatenating all the attributes of its member tokens. Each phrase is stored in a list in order of its appearance in the sentence. The list of phrases is then passed to the next step, which creates the Merged-phrases Dependency Tree.

### 3.2 Merged-phrases Dependency Tree (MDT)

Dependency trees have been used extensively in OIE to aid in the generation of triples from raw text (White et al., 2016; Zhang et al., 2018; Gamallo et al., 2012; Gamallo and Garcia, 2015; Del Corro and Gemulla, 2013). A traditional dependency tree is constructed at a token level, i.e., the leaves of the tree are the tokens present in the sentence, and the edges connecting them represent the dependency relation between the two tokens. A Merged-phrases Dependency Tree (*MDT*) is a coarse tree where each node contains a phrase or a multi-word expression from the sentence. An online tool by explosion.ai[5] illustrates the difference very well. One head is identified in each phrase (similar to Dobrovolskii (2021)), and the dependency relation between two heads is used as the dependency relation between the two corresponding phrases. The token-level dependency tree serves as a guiding tool to identify the dependency relationships between the identified phrases. Figure 2 illustrates the comparison between a traditional dependency tree and a generated *MDT* using an example of a Hindi sentence. It differs from a constituency tree as it does not conserve the syntactic relationships between the head and the rest of the tokens in each phrase. To the best of our knowledge, there is no publicly available tool for either constituency tree parsing or *MDT* parsing of sentences in Indic languages. Therefore, we developed a rule-based method to generate *MDT* from a traditional dependency tree.

The phenomenon of Complex Predicates (CPs) is common in Hindi, where a single action is represented by a noun-verb combination (called *conjunct verbs*) or a verb-verb combination (called *compound verbs*) (Burton-Page, 1957; Fatma, 2018). An *MDT* proves to be more useful in representing a sentence where the traditional dependency tree fails to parse CPs in languages like Hindi. For example, consider the sentence प्रारंभिक खगोलविदों का मानना था कि पृथ्वी ब्रह्मांड के केंद्र में है [*prarambhik khagolvido ka mAn-na tha ki prithvi brahm-And ke kendr me hae*] (*Early astronomers believed that Earth is in the center of the universe*), where the action of *believed* is represented by the Hindi *compound verb* मानना था

[5]https://explosion.ai/demos/displacy/

[*mAn-na tha*]. In the token-level dependency tree of this sentence, the following parent → child structure is generated: था [*tha*] (past-tense-inflection) $\xrightarrow{\text{nsubj}}$ मानना [*mAn-na*] (*to believe*), which is incorrect; the correct structure would be मानना [*mAn-na*] (*to believe*) $\xrightarrow{\text{aux}}$ था [*tha*] (past-tense-inflection). A chunker identifies *compound verbs* as a single Verb Phrase, thus generating a meaningful *MDT*. It has also been observed that, without a Multi-word Entity Recognition tool, identification of triple arguments becomes difficult by using dependency parsing alone (Gamallo et al., 2012). Gulordava and Merlo (2016) also have shown that the performance of a dependency parser degrades for natural languages having free word-order.

### 3.3 Triple generation

We use hand-crafted rules for capturing the *head*, *relation*, and *tail* from the *MDT* of a sentence. Similar to Mesquita et al. (2013), our hand-crafted rules are constructed by studying all the possible dependency relations in Hindi[6]. The rules are developed by carefully analyzing 80 different Hindi sentences, covering 26 out of 27 possible dependency relations in Hindi. One dependency relation that is not covered in our chosen Hindi sentences is *vocative*. Since it occurs only in 6 out of 16K dependency-annotated sentences in the data by Bhat et al. (2017), we observed that the Stanza dependency parsing tool fails to predict *vocative* relation in Hindi. In the dependency annotated data[7] of Tamil, Telugu, and Urdu, the percentage of nodes that are connected to their parents using a Hindi dependency relation are 96%, 98%, and nearly 100%, respectively. Hence, the authors are of the opinion that triple extraction rules based on Hindi dependency relations have wide coverage and could find their applicability in other Indic languages.

In the final set of rules, there are more than 100 decision-making statements (such as if-else). Therefore, we will not be explaining all the triple extraction rules here for the sake of brevity. Appendix E contains an abstracted algorithm illustrating the triple extraction procedure.

One novel property of our hand-crafted rules is their ability to capture *appositive* relationships between two entities. Earlier multilingual methods were unable to capture such *appositive* relationships. For example, in the sentence, शरमीला टैगोर के बेटे सैफ अली खान को मिला पद्म श्री पुरस्कार [*sharmila taegore ke bete saef ali khAn ko mila padm shri puraskAr*] (*Son of Sharmila Tagore, Saif Ali Khan, was awarded Padma Shri*), there exists an appositive *is-a* relationship between *Saif Ali Khan* and *Son of Sharmila Tagore*. Our system captures such appositive relationships that are expressed by *nominal modifier* (*nmod*) and *appositional modifier* (*appos*) dependency relation in the *MDT*. Our method selects the parent of these relations as <*head*>, and the child as <*tail*> of the triple. Mesquita et al. (2013) used the English auxiliary verb '*be*' to represent the <*relation*> for appositive relationships in English. We used the Hindi auxiliary verb है [*hae*] (*is/be*) to denote the <*relation*> of a triple that contains an *appositive* relationship in a Hindi sentence. The overall dataflow of the proposed architecture is illustrated in Appendix A using an example.

## 4 Triple Evaluation

The quality of generated triples is generally evaluated by getting them annotated by native speakers of that language. However, the procedure is time and cost intensive. Moreover, the lack of availability of Indic language annotators creates a hurdle in the manual evaluation process. On the other hand, automatic evaluation methods based on gold annotations (like CaRB (Bhardwaj et al., 2019)) do not consider the fact that there can be multiple ways to extract meaningful triples. Therefore, extending a work titled *BenchIE* (Gashteovski et al., 2021), we developed an automatic evaluation method, *Hindi-BenchIE*, based on multiple gold annotations to evaluate Hindi triples generated by any OIE tool.

#### *Hindi-BenchIE*

A natural language sentence is generally composed of one or more facts. In the original work of *BenchIE* (Gashteovski et al., 2021), multiple triples were written manually (called *golden triples*) to represent a single fact of the sentence. In our proposed benchmark, *Hindi-BenchIE*, we extend the *BenchIE* notations by introducing the following two subcategories of *golden triples*: (a) *essential-triples* and (b) *compensatory-triples*. An *essential-triple* is a triple that contains all the information needed to represent a fact. There might be some phrases in an *essential-triple* without which the

[6] `https://universaldependencies.org/treebanks/hi_hdtb/index.html`

[7] from https://universaldependencies.org/

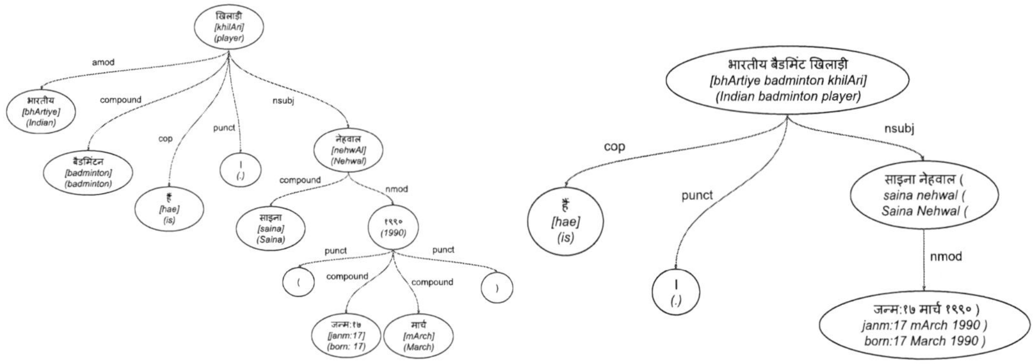


Figure 2: A comparison between a traditional dependency tree (left) and a Merged-phrases Dependency Tree (right) for the given Hindi sentence: साइना नेहवाल ( जन्म:१७ मार्च १९९० ) भारतीय बैडमिंटन खिलाड़ी हैं । [*saina nehwAl ( janm 17 mArch 1990 ) bhArtiye badminton khilAri hae*] which translates to *Saina Nehwal ( born:17 March 1990) is (an) Indian badminton player* . where predicted chunk labels are Noun Phrase (NP) , Verb Phrase (VP) , and Miscellaneous (BLK)

rest of the triple remains meaningful. We term such phrases as *vulnerable-phrases* in this work. However, an ideal OIE benchmark should ensure that no information is lost in the automatically generated triples. Moreover, if any information is lost, then the given OIE methodology should be penalized for it. Therefore, a *compensatory-triple* contains the information that is lost in the absence of a *vulnerable-phrase* in the generated triple. Moreover, *Hindi-BenchIE* supports the interchangeability of *head* and *tail* in a triple since Hindi is a free word-order language. These modifications facilitate annotation, as manually extracting triples for free word-order languages would otherwise require significant human effort.

In order to differentiate apposition relationships, we use an explicit keyword named '*property*' as a *relation*. In this work, a single-annotator manually extracted *golden-triples* for 112 Hindi sentences in different clusters. We release[8] the manually extracted triples for Hindi sentences since such resources are scarce in the field of multilingual OIE (Claro et al., 2019).

The number of True Positives and False Positives is calculated over all the *golden-triples* of the corresponding sentence (much like the *BenchIE*). In our work, False Negatives are calculated as the number of missing *essential-triples*, and the number of missing *compensatory-triples* that corresponds to a missing *vulnerable-phrase* (if any).

[8]https://github.com/ritwikmishra/hindi-benchie

## 5 Results

In order to compare our fine-tuned chunker with other traditional methods, we divided the chunk annotated data into training-set and test-set in a 50:50 ratio. We observed that the overall accuracy of our fine-tuned xlm-roberta-base (Conneau et al., 2020) chunker (91%) was superior to the other baselines of CRF (84%) and HMM (12%). The low performance on HMM is due to the sparsity in the *emission matrix* because of Out Of Vocabulary (OOV) words. Over multiple random splits, we observed that more than 80% of the test-set word bigrams were absent in the HMM training set. Due to the poor performance of HMM, we decided to use only the CRF for further comparisons. To test our chunker's multilingual nature, we curated language-specific test-sets and removed them from the training-set. This approach aligns with the principles of Leave One Language Out (LOLO) strategy, a technique documented in prior research (Ahuja et al., 2022; Srinivasan et al., 2021). Compared to CRF, the transformer-based chunker gave better accuracy on the languages it had never seen during the learning or fine-tuning phase. Table 1 compares our fine-tuned chunker and CRF chunker.

We also observed that a single linear layer and an unweighted average of subword embeddings gave the best chunking accuracy. It is important to note, however, that employing subword embedding averaging introduces a temporal overhead into the chunking process. As an alternative to the unweighted average, we observed that taking the last

| Model | Hindi | English | Urdu | Nepali | Gujarati | Bengali |
|---|---|---|---|---|---|---|
| XLM | **78%** | **60%** | **84%** | **65%** | **56%** | **66%** |
| CRF | 67% | 56% | 71% | 58% | 53% | 53% |

Table 1: A comparison of (fine-tuned) XLM chunker and CRF chunker on the languages which are removed from training-set. The numbers represent the accuracy obtained by each model when sentences from the given language are used only in the test-set. We observe that XLM chunker always perform better on unseen languages.

subword embedding is consistently better than the the conventional approach of taking the first subword embedding, a practice suggested by (Devlin et al., 2018) for Named Entity Recognition (NER) task, which is similar to chunking as both are sequence labeling tasks. For a comprehensive presentation of the results derived from our chunker ablation studies, please refer to Appendix C.

### 5.1 IndIE vs Others

To compare the performance of our triple extractor (*IndIE*), we used the following five baselines: (i) *M&K* (Faruqui and Kumar, 2015), (ii) *ArgOE* (Gamallo and Garcia, 2015), (iii) *PredPatt* (White et al., 2016), (iv) *Multi2OIE* (Ro et al., 2020), and (v) *Gen2OIE* (Kolluru et al., 2022) , because of their multilingual nature. The source code for *M&K* is not publicly available, but the authors have released a dataset of sentences and the corresponding triples generated by their method[9]. We randomly sampled sentences from *M&K* to create the *Hindi-BenchIE* benchmark. We used a fixed seed in order to make the random sampling reproducible.

It is essential to convey here that *PredPatt* is not designed as a triple extractor. The output generated by the method resembles an entity extractor. Appendix D shows the output of *PredPatt* on a Hindi sentence and the rules we developed to convert *PredPatt* output to triples format.

Our method, *IndIE*, performs better than other methods on *Hindi-BenchIE* golden set. Table 2 compares different OIE methods' performance. In this metric, failing to generate any triple on a given sentence penalizes the recall value of that method. In such cases, the smallest number of *essential-triples* are added to the *False Negatives* while calculating the recall. The overall results indicate that our proposed method, *IndIE*, extracted more meaningful triples from Hindi sentences than other multilingual OIE tools.

[9] https://www.kaggle.com/shankkumar/multilingualopenrelations15

## 6 Discussion

Motivated by qualitative observations, Table 3 presents quantitative insights about the generated triples from various methods. We observed that methods such as *ArgOE* and *PredPatt* generated more coarse triples than other methods. Coarse triples have a high sentence coverage percentage. They identify the root action in the sentence, and the remaining text is placed in the argument of triple. For example, for the following sentence 007 के गुप्त नाम से प्रसिद्ध यह एजेंट फ़्लेमिंग की बारह पुस्तकों व दो लघुकथाओं में मौजूद है। [*007 ke nAm se prasidha yeh Ejant phleming ki bArah pustakon va do laghukathaon me maaujUd hae*] (*Renowned by the name of 007, this agent appears in twelve books and two short stories by Fleming.*). The triple extracted by *ArgOE* is as follows: <007 के गुप्त नाम से प्रसिद्ध यह एजेंट, है, फ़्लेमिंग की बारह पुस्तकों व दो लघुकथाओं में मौजूद> [*<007 ke nAm se prasidha yeh Ejant, hae, phleming ki bArah pustakon va do laghukathaon me maaujUd>*] (*<Renowned by the name of 007 this agent, is, present in twelve books and two short stories by Fleming>*). Fine-grained triples are essential for downstream tasks, such as creating a knowledge-base from raw text (Zhang et al., 2021), whereas coarse triples could result in overspecific relations or entities.

The yield of triples by *Gen2OIE* method is better than other methods. However, since the source code of *M&K* is unavailable, we cannot determine the number of sentences for which the method returns no triples. Since *M&K* and *Gen2OIE* method generates triples in English and then uses word alignments to obtain Hindi triples, they often generate non-meaningful Hindi triples because the incorrect word alignments separate the postpositional word (*kaarak*) from its preceding word. As a result, more triples are generated with misplaced *kaarak*. For example, for the given sentence जब कोई मतैक्य नहीं हुआ तो विक्रम ने एक हल सोचा। [*jab koi mataekya nahin hua to vikram ne ek hal sochA*] (*When there was no consensus, Vikram thought of a solution.*), the *Gen2OIE* method generated a triple as <विक्रम, सोचा, ने एक हल> [*<vikram, sochA, ne ek hal>*] (Ungrammatical). Similar to *Gen2OIE*, the *IndIE* can generate overlapped arguments in the extracted triples. For instance, the two triples generated for the following sentence मैं शब्द की आत्मा

|  | *ArgOE* | *M&K* | *Multi2OIE* | *PredPatt* | *Gen2OIE* | *IndIE* |
|---|---|---|---|---|---|---|
| Precision | 0.17 | 0.07 | 0.005 | 0.22 | 0.23 | **0.49** |
| Recall | 0.04 | 0.08 | 0.01 | 0.05 | 0.35 | **0.53** |
| F1-score | 0.07 | 0.08 | 0.008 | 0.09 | 0.28 | **0.51** |

Table 2: Performance of different OIE methods on *Hindi-BenchIE* golden set. It is observed that *IndIE* outperforms other methods on the *Hindi-BenchIE* golden set.

|  | *ArgOE* | *M&K* | *Multi2OIE* | *PredPatt* | *Gen2OIE* | *IndIE* |
|---|---|---|---|---|---|---|
| # Triples | 51 | 199 | 59 | 48 | **278** | 277 |
| # Sentences with no triples | 69 | NA | 68 | 66 | **0** | 2 |
| Avg. Tokens in a Triple | 12 | 10 | **7** | 12 | 10 | **7** |
| Avg. Sentence Coverage of a Triple | 73% | 64% | 49% | 76% | 66% | **46%** |
| Triples with misplaced *kaarak* | 1.9% | 44% | 20% | 39% | 16% | **0.7%** |

Table 3: Triple statistics of different OIE methods on *Hindi-BenchIE* golden set of 112 sentences. Non-unique tokens are considered while counting the number of tokens in a triple. Sentence coverage is calculated by $1 - |unique(sent) - unique(triple)|/|unique(sent)|$ . It can be observed that *IndIE* triples have the least sentence coverage and *kaarak* errors. Hence, *IndIE* generates more fine-grained triples than other methods.

समझकर ही इस श्रेष्ठ तत्त्व की उपासना करता हूं । [*main shabd ki Atma samajhkar hee is shreshth tatv ki upAsna karta hun*] (*I worship this supreme element after understanding the soul of the word.*) are as follows <मैं,उपासना करता हूं,इस श्रेष्ठ तत्त्व की> [<*main, upAsna karta hun, is shrestha tatv ki*>] (<*I, worship, this supreme element*>) and <इस श्रेष्ठ तत्त्व की उपासना करता हूं,समझकर ही,आत्मा> [<*is shreshtha tatv ki upAsna karta hoon, samajhkar hee, Atma*>] (<*worship this supreme element, after understanding, soul*>).

In our experiments, the zero-shot *Multi2OIE* method performs poorly on every metric, which is expected since neural methods are known to generate incorrect facts as compared to rule-based methods (Gashteovski et al., 2021). Therefore, a promising direction is to train a neural OIE method based on the output of a rule-based OIE tool for a given language.

### 6.1 Limitations

The utilization of hand-crafted rules in the triple extraction process imposes constraints on the scalability and versatility of the IndIE pipeline. Furthermore, while we provide a rationale supporting the potential application of the IndIE tool to other Indic languages, we encountered challenges in creating a benchmark akin to Hindi-BenchIE due to a scarcity of annotators for these languages. Consequently, the performance of IndIE on other Indic languages remains a matter of conjecture. The number of sentences in our automatic evaluation benchmark, *Hindi-BenchIE*, is much smaller than the original work of *BenchIE*. Since manually generating triples requires more effort than triple annotation, the single-annotator of *Hindi-BenchIE* was able to generate more than 500 triples for 112 Hindi sentences only. Hence, we believe that the benchmark can be further refined with the efforts of the Indic-nlp community. We also acknowledge the fact that the multilingual nature of *IndIE* is limited to the intersection between the set of languages on which xlm-roberta-base has been pretrained and the set of languages supported by the Stanza library.

## 7 Conclusion

The low resource nature of Indic languages has been an impediment in the development of their NLP tools. In this work, we developed an Open Information Extraction (OIE) tool, *IndIE*, that generates triples from unstructured Hindi sentences. It first predicts the chunk tags for the given sentence and then creates a Merged-Phrase Dependency Tree (MDT) to generate the triples using the hand-crafted rules. We used a multilingual pretrained transformer model and fine-tuned it with chunk annotated sentences from English and five Indic languages. It was observed that, in sequence labeling tasks (such as chunking), taking the average of subword token embeddings is more valuable than other paradigms. We created *Hindi-BenchIE*, a benchmark for automatically evaluating Hindi triples based on a set of 112 Hindi sentences to compare the performance of various multilingual

OIE tools. It was observed that the *IndIE* generates more informative and fine-grained triples than other baselines.

### 7.1 Future Work

We plan to explore different methods to merge the fine-grained triples to make them more informative. Further linguistic efforts are needed to analyze and capture the appositive relationships in Agglutinative Indic languages such as Tamil and Telugu. Expanding the golden triples in *Hindi-BenchIE* and developing similar benchmarks for other Indic languages is also an important direction to keep the field of OIE in Indic languages alive. Co-reference resolution is an important area to explore to generate more meaningful triples with resolved pronominal references. Moreover, the viability of OIE-based approaches needs to be explored where the length of input text sequence exceeds the capability of transformer-based models, like open-domain Question-Answering and document-level textual similarity.

## Acknowledgements

Ritwik Mishra wishes to extend his appreciation to the University Grant Commission (UGC) of India for their partial support through the UGC Junior Research Fellowship (JRF) program. He would also like to express his gratitude to ACM-India for his selection as a recipient of the Anveshan-Setu fellowship and for assigning Prof. Pushpak Bhattacharya as his mentor. Rajiv Ratn Shah is partly supported by the Infosys Center for AI, the Center of Design and New Media, and the Center of Excellence in Healthcare at IIIT Delhi.

## References

2011. Census of india.

2021. What are the top 200 most spoken languages?

Kabir Ahuja, Antonios Anastasopoulos, Barun Patra, Graham Neubig, Monojit Choudhury, Sandipan Dandapat, Sunayana Sitaram, and Vishrav Chaudhary. 2022. The sumeval 2022 shared task on performance prediction of multilingual pre-trained language models. In Proceedings of the First Workshop on Scaling Up Multilingual Evaluation, pages 1–7.

Alan Akbik and Alexander Löser. 2012. Kraken: N-ary facts in open information extraction. In Proceedings of the Joint Workshop on Automatic Knowledge Base Construction and Web-scale Knowledge Extraction (AKBC-WEKEX), pages 52–56.

Akshar Bharati and Prashanth R Mannem. 2007. Introduction to shallow parsing contest on south asian languages. In Proceedings of the IJCAI and the Workshop On Shallow Parsing for South Asian Languages (SPSAL), pages 1–8. Citeseer.

Akshar Bharati, Rajeev Sangal, Dipti Misra Sharma, and Lakshmi Bai. 2006. Anncorra: Annotating corpora guidelines for pos and chunk annotation for indian languages. LTRC-TR31, pages 1–38.

Sangnie Bhardwaj, Samarth Aggarwal, and Mausam Mausam. 2019. CaRB: A crowdsourced benchmark for open IE. In Proceedings of the 2019 Conference on EMNLP-IJCNLP, pages 6262–6267, Hong Kong, China. Association for Computational Linguistics.

Riyaz Ahmad Bhat, Rajesh Bhatt, Annahita Farudi, Prescott Klassen, Bhuvana Narasimhan, Martha Palmer, Owen Rambow, Dipti Misra Sharma, Ashwini Vaidya, Sri Ramagurumurthy Vishnu, et al. 2017. The hindi/urdu treebank project. In Handbook of linguistic annotation, pages 659–697. Springer.

John Burton-Page. 1957. Compound and conjunct verbs in hindi1. Bulletin of the School of Oriental and African Studies, 19(3):469–478.

Janara Christensen, Stephen Soderland, and Oren Etzioni. 2011. An analysis of open information extraction based on semantic role labeling. In Proceedings of the sixth international conference on Knowledge capture, pages 113–120.

Daniela Barreiro Claro, Marlo Souza, Clarissa Castellã Xavier, and Leandro Oliveira. 2019. Multilingual open information extraction: Challenges and opportunities. Information, 10(7):228.

Alexis Conneau, Kartikay Khandelwal, Naman Goyal, Vishrav Chaudhary, Guillaume Wenzek, Francisco Guzmán, Edouard Grave, Myle Ott, Luke Zettlemoyer, and Veselin Stoyanov. 2020. Unsupervised cross-lingual representation learning at scale. In ACL.

Luciano Del Corro and Rainer Gemulla. 2013. Clausie: clause-based open information extraction. In Proceedings of the 22nd international conference on World Wide Web, pages 355–366.

Jacob Devlin, Ming-Wei Chang, Kenton Lee, and Kristina Toutanova. 2018. BERT: pre-training of deep bidirectional transformers for language understanding. CoRR, abs/1810.04805.

Vladimir Dobrovolskii. 2021. Word-level coreference resolution. In Proceedings of the 2021 Conference on Empirical Methods in Natural Language Processing, pages 7670–7675.

Ehsan Doostmohammadi, Minoo Nassajian, and Adel Rahimi. 2020. Persian ezafe recognition using transformers and its role in part-of-speech tagging. In Findings of the Association for Computational Linguistics: EMNLP 2020, pages 961–971.

Oren Etzioni, Michele Banko, Stephen Soderland, and Daniel S Weld. 2008. Open information extraction from the web. Communications of the ACM, 51(12):68–74.

Anthony Fader, Stephen Soderland, and Oren Etzioni. 2011. Identifying relations for open information extraction. In Proceedings of the 2011 conference on empirical methods in natural language processing, pages 1535–1545.

Manaal Faruqui and Shankar Kumar. 2015. Multilingual open relation extraction using cross-lingual projection. In North American Chapter of the ACL: Human Language Technologies, pages 1351–1356.

Shamim Fatma. 2018. Conjunct verbs in hindi. Trends in Hindi Linguistics, pages 217–244.

Pablo Gamallo and Marcos Garcia. 2015. Multilingual open information extraction. In Portuguese Conference on Artificial Intelligence, pages 711–722. Springer.

Pablo Gamallo, Marcos Garcia, and Santiago Fernández-Lanza. 2012. Dependency-based open information extraction. In Proceedings of the joint workshop on unsupervised and semi-supervised learning in NLP, pages 10–18.

Kiril Gashteovski, Rainer Gemulla, and Luciano del Corro. 2017. Minie: minimizing facts in open information extraction. Association for Computational Linguistics.

Kiril Gashteovski, Mingying Yu, Bhushan Kotnis, Carolin Lawrence, Goran Glavas, and Mathias Niepert. 2021. Benchie: Open information extraction evaluation based on facts, not tokens. arXiv preprint arXiv:2109.06850.

Kristina Gulordava and Paola Merlo. 2016. Multi-lingual dependency parsing evaluation: a large-scale analysis of word order properties using artificial data. Transactions of the Association for Computational Linguistics, 4:343–356.

Vaishali Gupta, Nisheeth Joshi, and Iti Mathur. 2019. Advanced machine learning techniques in natural language processing for indian languages. In Smart Techniques for a Smarter Planet, pages 117–144. Springer.

BS Harish and R Kasturi Rangan. 2020. A comprehensive survey on indian regional language processing. SN Applied Sciences, 2(7):1–16.

Julia Hirschberg and Christopher D Manning. 2015. Advances in natural language processing. Science, 349(6245):261–266.

Kushal Jain, Adwait Deshpande, Kumar Shridhar, Felix Laumann, and Ayushman Dash. 2020. Indic-transformers: An analysis of transformer language models for indian languages. arXiv preprint arXiv:2011.02323.

Girish Nath Jha. 2010. The TDIL program and the Indian langauge corpora intitiative (ILCI). In Proceedings of the Seventh International Conference on Language Resources and Evaluation (LREC'10), Valletta, Malta. European Language Resources Association (ELRA).

Keshav Kolluru, Muqeeth Mohammed, Shubham Mittal, Soumen Chakrabarti, et al. 2022. Alignment-augmented consistent translation for multilingual open information extraction. In Proceedings of the 60th Annual Meeting of the Association for Computational Linguistics (Volume 1: Long Papers), pages 2502–2517.

Hongwei Li, Hongyan Mao, and Jingzi Wang. 2021. Part-of-speech tagging with rule-based data preprocessing and transformer. Electronics, 11(1):56.

Xueling Lin, Haoyang Li, Hao Xin, Zijian Li, and Lei Chen. 2020. Kbpearl: a knowledge base population system supported by joint entity and relation linking. Proceedings of the VLDB Endowment, 13(7):1035–1049.

Mausam, Michael Schmitz, Stephen Soderland, Robert Bart, and Oren Etzioni. 2012. Open language learning for information extraction. In Proceedings of the 2012 Joint Conference on Empirical Methods in Natural Language Processing and Computational Natural Language Learning, pages 523–534, Jeju Island, Korea. Association for Computational Linguistics.

Filipe Mesquita, Jordan Schmidek, and Denilson Barbosa. 2013. Effectiveness and efficiency of open relation extraction. In Proceedings of the 2013 Conference on Empirical Methods in Natural Language Processing, pages 447–457.

Tara Mohanan. 1994. Case ocp: A constraint on word order in hindi. Theoretical perspectives on word order in South Asian languages, 185:216.

Rajat Mohanty, Anupama Dutta, and Pushpak Bhattacharyya. 2005. Semantically relatable sets: building blocks for representing semantics. In MT Summit, volume 5. Citeseer.

Iqra Muhammad, Anna Kearney, Carrol Gamble, Frans Coenen, and Paula Williamson. 2020. Open information extraction for knowledge graph construction. In International Conference on Database and Expert Systems Applications, pages 103–113. Springer.

Jaya S Nagendra. 2019. Basic grammar, hindi. In A Brief History of Languages, volume 1, page 190. Atlantic.

F. Pedregosa, G. Varoquaux, A. Gramfort, V. Michel, B. Thirion, O. Grisel, M. Blondel, P. Prettenhofer, R. Weiss, V. Dubourg, J. Vanderplas, A. Passos, D. Cournapeau, M. Brucher, M. Perrot, and E. Duchesnay. 2011. Scikit-learn: Machine learning in Python. Journal of Machine Learning Research, 12:2825–2830.

Slav Petrov, Dipanjan Das, and Ryan McDonald. 2012. A universal part-of-speech tagset. In Proceedings of the Eighth International Conference on Language Resources and Evaluation (LREC'12), pages 2089–2096.

Peng Qi, Yuhao Zhang, Yuhui Zhang, Jason Bolton, and Christopher D. Manning. 2020. Stanza: A Python natural language processing toolkit for many human languages. In Proceedings of the 58th Annual Meeting of the Association for Computational Linguistics: System Demonstrations.

Youngbin Ro, Yukyung Lee, and Pilsung Kang. 2020. Multi$^2$oie: Multilingual open information extraction based on multi-head attention with bert. In Proceedings of the 2020 Conference on Empirical Methods in Natural Language Processing: Findings, pages 1107–1117.

Anna Rogers, Olga Kovaleva, and Anna Rumshisky. 2020. A primer in bertology: What we know about how bert works. Transactions of the Association for Computational Linguistics, 8:842–866.

Arnav Sharma, Sakshi Gupta, Raveesh Motlani, Piyush Bansal, Manish Shrivastava, Radhika Mamidi, and Dipti Misra Sharma. 2016. Shallow parsing pipeline-hindi-english code-mixed social media text. In Proceedings of the 2016 Conference of the North American Chapter of the Association for Computational Linguistics: Human Language Technologies, pages 1340–1345.

Akshay Singh, Sushma Bendre, and Rajeev Sangal. 2005. Hmm based chunker for hindi. In Companion Volume to the Proceedings of Conference including Posters/Demos and tutorial abstracts.

Anirudh Srinivasan, Sunayana Sitaram, Tanuja Ganu, Sandipan Dandapat, Kalika Bali, and Monojit Choudhury. 2021. Predicting the performance of multilingual nlp models. arXiv preprint arXiv:2110.08875.

EF Tjong Kim Sang and S Buchholz. 2000. Introduction to the conll-2000 shared task: Chunking. ACL.

Thi Oanh Tran, Phuong Le Hong, et al. 2020. Improving sequence tagging for vietnamese text using transformer-based neural models. In Proceedings of the 34th Pacific Asia Conference on Language, Information and Computation, pages 13–20.

Aaron Steven White, Drew Reisinger, Keisuke Sakaguchi, Tim Vieira, Sheng Zhang, Rachel Rudinger, Kyle Rawlins, and Benjamin Van Durme. 2016. Universal decompositional semantics on universal dependencies. In Proceedings of the 2016 Conference on Empirical Methods in Natural Language Processing, pages 1713–1723.

YORICK WILKS. 1964. Text searching with templates. Cambridge Language Research Unit Memo, ML, (165).

Thomas Wolf, Lysandre Debut, Victor Sanh, Julien Chaumond, Clement Delangue, Anthony Moi, Pierric Cistac, Tim Rault, Rémi Louf, Morgan Funtowicz, Joe Davison, Sam Shleifer, Patrick von Platen, Clara Ma, Yacine Jernite, Julien Plu, Canwen Xu, Teven Le Scao, Sylvain Gugger, Mariama Drame, Quentin Lhoest, and Alexander M. Rush. 2020. Transformers: State-of-the-art natural language processing. In Proceedings of the 2020 Conference on Empirical Methods in Natural Language Processing: System Demonstrations, pages 38–45, Online. Association for Computational Linguistics.

Junlang Zhan and Hai Zhao. 2020. Span model for open information extraction on accurate corpus. In Proceedings of the AAAI Conference on Artificial Intelligence, volume 34, pages 9523–9530.

Sheng Zhang, Xutai Ma, Rachel Rudinger, Kevin Duh, and Benjamin Van Durme. 2018. Cross-lingual decompositional semantic parsing. In Proceedings of the 2018 Conference on Empirical Methods in Natural Language Processing, pages 1664–1675.

Zixuan Zhang, Nikolaus Parulian, Heng Ji, Ahmed Elsayed, Skatje Myers, and Martha Palmer. 2021. Fine-grained information extraction from biomedical literature based on knowledge-enriched abstract meaning representation. In Proceedings of the 59th Annual Meeting of the Association for Computational Linguistics and the 11th International Joint Conference on Natural Language Processing (Volume 1: Long Papers), pages 6261–6270.

## A Illustration

The overall dataflow of the proposed architecture is illustrated using the following raw (multi-sentence) text in Hindi: शर्मीला टैगोर के बेटे सैफ अली खान को 2010 में पद्म श्री पुरस्कार मिला। वह एक भारीतय अभिनेता है। [*sharmila taegor ke bete saef ali khAn ko 2010 me padm shri puraskAr mila. veh ek bhArtiye abhinetA hae*] *(Son of Sharmila Tagore, Saif Ali Khan, was awarded with Padma Shri award in 2010. He is an Indian actor)*. The raw text is fed to the Stanza library for sentence segmentation and dependency parsing of each sentence. In stage (a) of the architecture, as shown in Figure 1, segmented sentences are passed to the chunking model to predict the chunk tags for each word of the given sentence. Predicted chunked phrases from the stage (a) are as follows:

Sentence 1 - {शर्मीला टैगोर के [*sharmila taegore ke*] *(Sharmila Tagore's)*}_NP , {बेटे [*bete*] *(son)*}_NP , {सैफ अली खान को [*saef ali khAn ko*] *(to Saif Ali Khan)*}_NP , {2010 में [*2010 me*] *(in 2010)*}_NP , {पद्म श्री

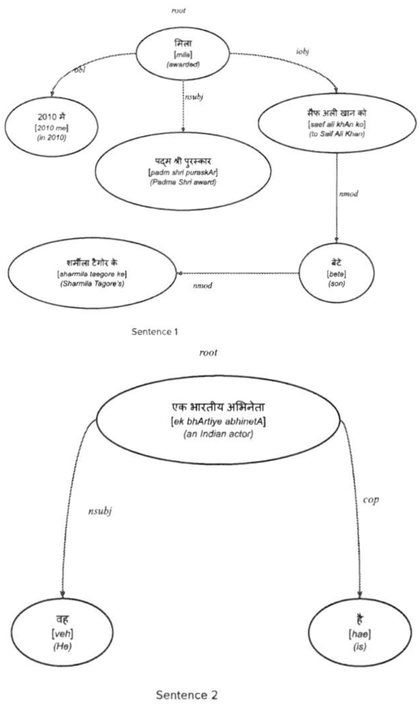


Figure 3: The generated *MDTs* after sentence segmentation, chunking, and dependency parsing of the following raw text: शर्मीला टैगोर के बेटे सैफ अली खान को 2010 में पद्म श्री पुरस्कार मिला। वह एक भारीतय अभिनेता है। *[sharmila taegor ke bete saef ali khAn ko 2010 me padm shri puraskAr mila. veh ek bhArtiye abhinetA hae] (Son of Sharmila Tagore, Saif Ali Khan, was awarded with Padma Shri award in 2010. He is an Indian actor).*

पुरस्कार *[padm shri puraskAr] (Padma Shri award)}*_NP , {मिला *[mila] (awarded)}*_VGF

Sentence 2 - {वह *[veh] (He)}*_NP , {एक भारीतय अभिनेता *[ek bhArtiye abhinetA] (an Indian actor)}*_NP , {है *[hae] (is)}*_VGF

The chunked phrases and dependency tree for each sentence are passed to the stage (b) of the architecture to construct *MDT* for each sentence. Figure 3 illustrates the *MDTs* generated at the output of stage (b). For each sentence, triples are generated using its corresponding *MDT* and our hand-crafted rules. All the triples extracted by the *IndIE* tool for the aforementioned raw text are shown in Table 4. The output of stage (c) consists of the following three types: (i) a list of segmented sentences, (ii) extracted triples, and (iii) execution time for each sentence.

| | <head> | <relation> | <tail> |
|---|---|---|---|
| Sentence 1 | पद्म श्री पुरस्कार *[padm shri puraskAr] (Padma Shri award)* | मिला *[mila] (awarded)* | सैफ अली खान को *[saef ali khAn ko] (to Saif Ali Khan)* |
| | 2010 में *[2010 me] (in 2010)* | मिला *[mila] (awarded)* | पद्म श्री पुरस्कार *[padm shri puraskAr] (Padma Shri award)* |
| | सैफ अली खान को *[saef ali khAn ko] (to Saif Ali Khan)* | है *[hae] (is)* | बेटे *[bete] (son)* |
| | बेटे *[bete] (son)* | है *[hae] (is)* | शर्मीला टैगोर के *[sharmila taegore ke] (Sharmila Tagore's)* |
| Sentence 2 | वह *[veh] (He)* | है *[hae] (is)* | एक भारीतय अभिनेता *[ek bhArtiye abhinetA] (an Indian actor)* |

Table 4: Triples extracted through hand-crafted rules of the proposed IndIE tool for the following raw text in Hindi: शर्मीला टैगोर के बेटे सैफ अली खान को 2010 में पद्म श्री पुरस्कार मिला। वह एक भारीतय अभिनेता है। *[sharmila taegor ke bete saef ali khAn ko 2020 me padm shri puraskAr mila. veh ek bhArtiye abhinetA hae] (Son of Sharmila Tagore, Saif Ali Khan, was awarded with Padma Shri award in 2010. He is an Indian actor).*

## B Chunking Baselines

We used the scikit-learn scikit-learn python library to implement[10] the CRF model. The following features were used for each word of the sentence: (a) bias ← 1.0, (b) word text, (c) POS tag of the word, (d) POS tags of preceding two words, and (e) POS tags of succeeding two words. The values of L1 and L2 regularization were obtained through grid search. We used the word text and its POS tag as features for the HMM model.

Our fine-tuned chunker is an end-to-end model for chunking because it takes input in raw text. However, CRF and HMM model expects already POS tagged sentences. The chunk annotated sentences from the Bhat et al. (2017) are POS tagged in upos format (Petrov et al., 2012), whereas sentences from the Jha (2010) are POS tagged with a scheme called AnnCorra (Bharati et al., 2006). It is an extension to the Penn tagset and tailored for Indian languages. In the absence of a publicly available POS tagger for AnnCorra, we created a mapping from AnnCorra to upos tagset for standardizing the POS tags in the entire dataset. We passed all the Hindi and English sentences from the (**?**) dataset through Stanza library, generating POS tags in upos format. Therefore, we create a mapping from AnnCorra (Penn tagset) to upos tagset which helped us in standardizing the POS

[10]https://sklearn-crfsuite.readthedocs.io/en/latest/tutorial.html

tag format across all sentences.

## C Chunking Ablation

We experimented with three approaches to handle sub-word token embeddings and observed that averaging sub-word token embeddings gave better accuracy as compared to the first sub-word token embedding or last sub-word token embedding, as shown in Table 5. Since averaging the sub-word token embeddings requires additional processing, its fine-tuning time (6 hours/epoch) and inference time (29 milliseconds/sentence) is more than fine-tuning time (45 minutes/epoch) and inference time (17 milliseconds/sentence) for the other two approaches. Hence, if accuracy is preferred over inference time, then we recommend taking an average of sub-word token embeddings for a sequence labeling task; otherwise simply taking the last sub-word token embedding gives better performance with equal inference time than the traditional technique of taking the first sub-word token embedding. In our experiments, we used the embeddings from `last_hidden_state` of the model. However, since some methods in the literature suggest that early layers of a transformer are responsible for learning shallow features of the text (Rogers et al., 2020), we experimented by taking average embeddings of the first two hidden layers of the model as well. It turns out that using embeddings from early layers actually decreased the accuracy (86%) for the chunking task. Confirming the findings of Jain et al. (Jain et al., 2020), we observed that xlm-roberta-base (Conneau et al., 2020) gave the best accuracy (92%) over other pretrained models.

## D PredPatt

Figure 4 shows the output of *PredPatt* on a Hindi sentence. Table 6 contains the rules we developed to convert *PredPatt* output to triples format.

## E Algorithm

```
label: sent_91
sentence: अभ्रक आदि की खानों में मोमबत्तियाँ भी प्रयुक्त होती है .
          [abhrak Adi ki khAno me mombattiya bhi prayukt hoti hae]
          (In the mines of Mica candles are also used)

ppatt:
  अभ्रक की खानों में ?a प्रयुक्त होती है
      ?a: मोमबत्तियाँ
  [abhrak ki khAno me ?a prayukt hoti hae
      ?a: mombattiya]
  (In the mines of Mica ?a are used
      ?a: candles)
```

Figure 4: Output of *PredPatt* on a Hindi sentence अभ्रक आदि की खानों में मोमबत्तियाँ भी प्रयुक्त होती है [*abhrak Adi ki khAno me mombattiya bhi prayukt hoti hae*] (*In the mines of Mica candles are also used*). In the given sentence, *candles* is the *Entity1*, and it is represented with '?a' notation.

Triple generator algorithm from Merged-phrase Dependency Tree (MDT)

```
function EXTRACT(MDT, t, Q)
    if 'cop' ∈ t.children.dep_rel then
        if |t.children| ≤ 2 then
            Head, Tail ← FIND_HEAD(MDT, t) , t
            Rel ← x where (x ∈ t.children ∧ x.dep_rel = 'cop')
        else
            Head, Tail ← FIND_HEAD(MDT, t) , FIND_TAIL(MDT, t)
            Rel ← t + x where (x ∈ t.children ∧ x.dep_rel = 'cop')
        end if
    else if 'advcl' == t.dep_rel then
        Head ← q.Tail + q.Rel where (q ∈ Q ∧ t.parent ∈ q)
        Rel, Tail ← t , FIND_TAIL(MDT, t)
    else if 'acl' == t.dep_rel then
        Head ← t.closest_phrase(q.Tail, q.Head) where (q ∈ Q ∧ t.parent ∈ q)
        Rel, Tail ← t , FIND_TAIL(MDT, t)
    else if 'conj' == t.dep_rel then
        if ∃q ∈ Q such that q.Head == t.parent then
            Head, Rel, Tail ← t , q.Rel , q.Tail
        else if ∃q ∈ Q such that q.Tail == t.parent then
            Head, Rel, Tail ← q.Head , q.Rel , t
        end if
    else
        if t.is_clausal() == True then
            Head, Rel, Tail ← t.pronoun , t.verb , t − (t.pronoun ∩ t.verb)
        else
            if t.is_a_relationship() == True then //appositive relationship
                Head, Rel, Tail ← t , FIND_TAIL(MDT, t) , t.is_a_label
            else
                Head, Rel, Tail ← FIND_HEAD(MDT, t) , t , FIND_TAIL(MDT, t)
            end if
        end if
    end if
    if Head, Rel, Tail then
        Q.add([Head, Rel, Tail])
    end if
    if t.contain_args() == True then
        Q ← EXTRACT(MDT, t)
    else
        for each t_c ∈ t.children do
            Q ← EXTRACT(MDT, t_c)
        end for
    end if
    return Q
end function
triples ← EXTRACT(MDT, t_root, {})
```

| Classification Layers | First sub-word token embedding | Last sub-word token embedding | Average embedding of all sub-word tokens |
|---|---|---|---|
| 1 | 82±10 (50±20) | 89±0.5 (62±1.0) | **91±0.0 (65±0.5)** |
| 2 | 86±1.8 (51±6.2) | 89±0.5 (54±7.4) | **90±0.5 (54±4.5)** |
| 3 | 79±14 (43±13) | 82±11 (41±12) | **90±0.5 (48±2.2)** |

Table 5: A comparison of three approaches for solving the sub-word token embeddings for chunking task. Four different random seeds were used to calculate the mean and standard deviation for the given samples. All the experiments were run on the combined data of Jha et al. (Jha, 2010) and Bhat et al.(Bhat et al., 2017). The numbers written outside round brackets represent the accuracy, whereas numbers inside round brackets represent the macro average.

| **Rule No.** | **Sentence Structure** | **Extracted Triple** |
|---|---|---|
| 1 | ^ phrase1 Entity1 phrase2 $ | <phrase1 , phrase2 , Entity1> |
| 2 | ^ Entity1 phrase1 Entity2 phrase2 $<br>^ Entity1 Entity2 phrase1 $<br>^ phrase1 Entity1 Entity2 $<br>^ Entity1 phrase1 Entity2 $ | <Entity1 , phrase1 , Entity2> |
| 3 | ^ phrase1 Entity1 Entity2 phrase2 $<br>^ phrase1 Entity1 phrase2 Entity2 $<br>^ phrase1 Entity1 phrase2 Entity2 phrase3 $ | <Entity1 , phrase2 , Entity2> |
| 4 | Any other sentence structure | Discard |

Table 6: The rules we used to extract triples from *PredPatt* output. Considering the sentence given in Figure 4, Rule number 1 is applied to the sentence. The symbol ^ indicates the start of the sentence, and the symbol $ indicates the end of the sentence.

# Mitigating Word Bias in Zero-shot Prompt-based Classifiers

**Adian Liusie, Potsawee Manakul, Mark J. F. Gales**
ALTA Institute, Department of Engineering, University of Cambridge
al826@cam.ac.uk, pm574@cam.ac.uk, mjfg@eng.cam.ac.uk

## Abstract

Prompt-based classifiers are an attractive approach for zero-shot classification. However, the precise choice of the prompt template and label words can largely influence performance, with semantically equivalent settings often showing notable performance difference. This discrepancy can be partly attributed to word biases, where the classifier may be biased towards classes. To address this problem, it is possible to optimise classification thresholds on a labelled data set, however, this mitigates some of the advantages of prompt-based classifiers. This paper instead approaches this problem by examining the expected marginal probabilities of the classes. Here, probabilities are reweighted to have a uniform prior over classes, in an unsupervised fashion. Further, we draw a theoretical connection between the class priors and the language models' word prior, and offer the ability to set a threshold in a zero-resource fashion. We show that matching class priors correlates strongly with the oracle upper bound performance and demonstrate large consistent performance gains for prompt settings over a range of NLP tasks.[1]

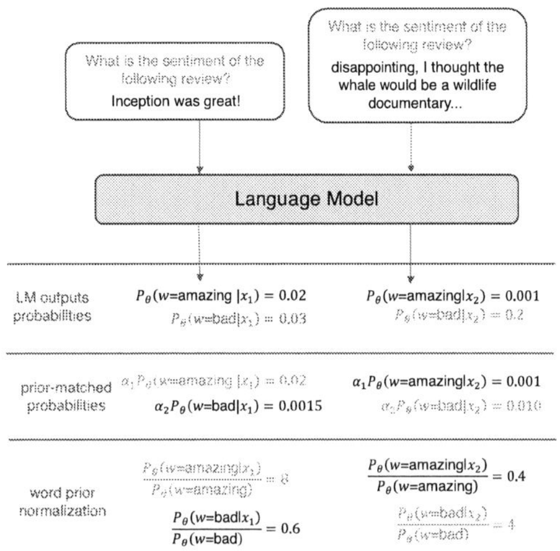


Figure 1: Instead of using the raw LM output probabilities of the label words, we consider mitigating bias by finding weights that make the classifier unbiased over classes. This is connected to normalising by word priors, which we use as a zero-resource de-biasing approach.

## 1 Introduction

Large language models (LLM) have shown impressive general ability for natural language processing (NLP) tasks. LLMs can effectively handle a range of NLP tasks through 'prompting', where a natural language instruction is added to the input, conditioning the model to the task at hand. Prompting can either be an emergent ability learned through scaling up model size (Brown et al., 2020; Wei et al., 2022) or an ability learned through instruction tuning (Wei et al., 2021; Chung et al., 2022; Ouyang et al., 2022). Despite the recent popularity of prompting, there is a known sensitivity of prompt-based LLMs to elements such as prompt template and label words (Gao et al., 2021; Schick and Schütze, 2021). Previous works have demonstrated that prompt templates can significantly impact task performance (Shin et al., 2020; Zhou et al.) and that factors such as chosen label words can influence system performance for classification tasks (Zhao et al., 2021; Holtzman et al., 2021).

This work focuses on the influence of 'word biases' for prompt-based classifiers. i.e. the bias that prompts may have towards certain classes, independent of the input text. To account for this bias, one could use a labelled dataset to find optimal class decision thresholds. This, however, requires labelled task data, which may limit the zero-shot benefits of prompt-based classifiers. We propose a simple unsupervised solution of re-weighting probabilities, where we use unlabelled data to search for weight parameters that ensure a uniform prior over classes. We show that this prior matching leads to greater

[1] code available on github at https://github.com/adianliusie/robust-prompt-classifier



*Findings of the Association for Computational Linguistics: IJCNLP-AACL 2023*, pages 327–335
November 1–4, 2023. ©2023 Asian Federation of Natural Language Processing

robustness for diverse prompt settings and that the unsupervised weights which debias the classifier is highly correlated with the oracle weights that maximise accuracy. Further, we provide theoretical analysis that draws a connection between word priors and inherent class bias, which we use to motivate a zero-resource normalisation approach that is competitive with prior matching. Overall, we demonstrate that our unsupervised approach highly reduces sensitivity to the chosen prompt and label words, and that settings which initially fail can often be made effective through a simple probability re-weighting.

Our contributions are 1) We propose a simple unsupervised probability re-weighting method, and empirically demonstrate greater robustness to prompt and label word choice, with large accuracy gains across prompt settings for a range of standard NLP tasks. 2) We theoretically connect the weight parameters to word priors and use this to motivate a zero-resource re-weighting approach. 3) We show that the weights of prior matching are highly correlated with the optimal oracle weights that maximize accuracy, illustrating that our approach is a near-optimal use of a system's output probabilities.

## 2 Mitigating Bias by Re-weighting

**Prompt-based classifiers** Given an input sequence $\mathbf{x} \in \mathcal{X}$, large language models (LLMs) model $P_\theta(\mathbf{w}|\mathbf{x})$, the output probability distribution over all possible sequences $\mathbf{w} \in \mathcal{X}$. For a classification task $\mathcal{T}$, a prompt-based classifier 1) reformats the input text $\mathbf{x}$ to prompt $\mathbf{p} \in \mathcal{X}$ by including the task instruction, and 2) selects class words $\{w_k\}_{1:K}$ which are associated to each output class $\{y_k\}_{1:K}$. For example in sentiment classification, one can use prompt *'what is the sentiment of the following review? <x>'*, (where <x> is the current input $\mathbf{x}$, e.g. *'Inception was absolutely brilliant'*), and class words $w_0$=*bad* and $w_1$=*good* for the negative and positive classes respectively. For a prompt classifier, $Q = \{\mathbf{p}, \{w_k\}_{1:K}\}$, class probabilities can be set to be proportional to the probability of the associated class word, where the final decision $\hat{y}$ is the class with the highest probability (Zhao et al., 2021; Jiang et al., 2020).

$$\tilde{P}_\theta(y_k|\mathbf{x}, Q) = \frac{P_\theta(w_k|\mathbf{p}(\mathbf{x}))}{\sum_{w_i} P_\theta(w_i|\mathbf{p}(\mathbf{x}))} \quad (1)$$

$$\hat{y} = \underset{k}{\operatorname{argmax}}\ \tilde{P}_\theta(y_k|\mathbf{x}, Q) \quad (2)$$

However, as a large language model, the prompt-based classifier may return probabilities that are influenced by distributional statistics of words (Gardner et al., 2021; Liusie et al., 2022). This may lead to inherent class bias, where label words may have high probability not because they better answer the prompt, but because they have a high LM prior.

**Optimal Weights** To account for this, one can define weight parameters $\boldsymbol{\alpha} = \{\alpha_k\}_{1:K}$, where each $\alpha_k \in \mathbb{R}^+$ scales the probabilities of the classifier,

$$\hat{P}_\theta(y_k|\mathbf{x}, Q, \boldsymbol{\alpha}) = \frac{\alpha_k \tilde{P}_\theta(y_k|\mathbf{x}, Q)}{\sum_i \alpha_i \tilde{P}_\theta(y_i|\mathbf{x}, Q)} \quad (3)$$

Given labelled task dataset $\mathcal{D} = \{(\mathbf{x}^{(j)}, y^{(j)})\}_{j=1}^N$, one can then find the optimal weights $\boldsymbol{\alpha}^*$ that maximises the accuracy of the prompt classifier $\hat{P}_\theta(y_k|\mathbf{x}, Q, \boldsymbol{\alpha})$ over the dataset,

$$\boldsymbol{\alpha}^* = \underset{\boldsymbol{\alpha}}{\operatorname{argmax}}\ \text{Accuracy}(Q, \boldsymbol{\alpha}, \mathcal{D}) \quad (4)$$

**Prior-Matching** The previous approach requires labelled data, which may limit the benefit of using prompt-based classifiers. As an alternative, one can find the values $\bar{\alpha}$ that ensure that the classifier is unbiased, such that the class prior $\hat{P}(y_k|Q, \boldsymbol{\alpha})$ matches the true prior $P(y_k)$

$$\hat{P}_\theta(y_k|Q, \boldsymbol{\alpha}) = \mathbb{E}_{\mathbf{x}}\{\hat{P}_\theta(y_k|\mathbf{x}, Q, \boldsymbol{\alpha})\} \quad (5)$$

$$\approx \frac{1}{N}\sum_{j=1}^{N} \hat{P}_\theta(y_k^{(j)}|\mathbf{x}^{(j)}, Q, \boldsymbol{\alpha}) \quad (6)$$

$$\bar{\alpha} = \underset{\alpha}{\operatorname{argmin}} \sum_{\forall y_k} |\hat{P}_\theta(y_k|Q, \boldsymbol{\alpha}) - P(y_k)| \quad (7)$$

A deterministic solution that exactly matches the distributions exists, which can be found with a search with 1 degree of freedom (that can be accounted for by setting $\alpha_1 = 1$). If there is no expected class bias, one can assume equal probabilities over all classes, $P(y_k) = \mathcal{U}(y_k) = \frac{1}{N}$. This approach is therefore unsupervised and only requires text inputs $\mathcal{D}_x = \{\mathbf{x}^{(j)}\}_{j=1}^M$, which therefore can be applied at inference to any test set.

**Null-Input Approximation** The dependence of prior-matching on unlabelled dataset $\mathcal{D}_x$ is a drawback. In Appendix A, we show that one can make the analytical approximation

$$\bar{\alpha}_k \approx \frac{1}{\mathbb{E}_x\{P_\theta(w_k|\mathbf{x}, Q)\}} = \frac{1}{P_\theta(w_k|Q)} \quad (8)$$

| method | inputs | labels | imdb | rt | amazon | snli | mnli | qqp |
|---|---|---|---|---|---|---|---|---|
| baseline | ✗ | ✗ | 85.4±12.7 | 78.8±14.0 | 86.0±13.8 | 45.2±13.7 | 43.5±11.3 | 65.4±14.0 |
| null-input | ✗ | ✗ | 92.1±3.2 | 89.1±3.8 | 95.0±1.8 | 75.2±10.4 | 66.1±9.7 | 77.4±6.6 |
| prior-match | ✓ | ✗ | 93.1±3.3 | 90.9±1.6 | 96.0±0.8 | 78.5±9.3 | 69.8±9.7 | 79.1±2.4 |
| optimal | ✓ | ✓ | 93.5±2.7 | 91.2±1.5 | 96.1±0.7 | 79.4±8.2 | 70.8±8.6 | 82.3±2.8 |

Table 1: Average dataset accuracy and standard deviations, over all prompts and label words. **baseline** and **null-input** are zero-resource classification methods, **prior matching** uses the text inputs but not labels, while **optimal** is an oracle approach that uses the labels to search for the best thresholds. Results for FlanT5 large

Inspired by Zhao et al. (2021), we consider a resource-free approximation of the word prior (equation 8) by considering the output word probabilities of the null input $\emptyset$ (i.e. an empty string).

$$P_\theta(w_k|Q) \approx P_\theta(w_k|\mathbf{p}(\emptyset)) \tag{9}$$

This enables a zero-resource approximation of weight parameters $\bar{\alpha}$.

## 3 Experiments

### 3.1 Experimental Setup

**Data** Experimental results are run on standard NLP benchmarks, including sentiment classification (*IMDB* (Maas et al., 2011), *Rotten Tomatoes* (Pang and Lee, 2005) and *amazon*), natural language inference (*SNLI* (Bowman et al., 2015) and *MNLI* (Williams et al., 2018)) and paraphrase detection (*QQP* (Wang et al., 2018)). Evaluation is reported on standard test sets, except for amazon polarity where 5000 test examples were randomly sampled.

**Models** We use FlanT5 large[2] (Chung et al., 2022), a T5 with further instruction-tuning stage where the system was trained in a multi-task fashion over 1,836 tasks, each prepended with a natural instruction prompt. This work evaluates FlanT5 for different NLP tasks with arbitrary prompting set ups. For each task, we select 6 prompt templates and for binary classification tasks consider 25 possible class words pairs, while for NLI we have 64 class word triplets (where all permutations of valid class words are considered). All prompts and label words used are given in Appendix B. Further experiments for FlanT5 base and Llama-2-chat can be found in Appendix D.

**Methods** We consider 4 different methods to leverage LLM probabilities for classification. Class word probability via equation 1 (**baseline**). Normalised probabilities calculated using null-inputs priors via equation 9 (**null-input**). Optimising $\alpha_k$ with a search to have unbiased class prior via equation 7 (**prior-match**). The oracle upper-bound performance, found by optimising the optimal accuracy threshold via equation 4 (**optimal**).

[2]https://huggingface.co/google/flan-t5-large

### 3.2 Experimental Results

**Classification Robustness** Table 1 shows the mean and standard deviation of accuracies among all prompt and class word settings for a given task. We observe large consistent gains from both re-weighting approaches, with prior-matching increasing baseline accuracy by between 6.7% to 12.1% for sentiment classification, 13.7% for qqp, and over 25% for natural language inference. Prior-matching also demonstrates performance very similar to the oracle upper-bound, often within 1%, showing that the unsupervised prior-match approach is competitive with the supervised threshold search. Prior-matching also performs better than null-input by a small margin in all tasks, where this small gap confirms that the word-prior normalisation is a very reasonable zero-shot approximation.

**Prompt Robustness** Figure 2 illustrates a box-plot of rotten tomatoes performance over all class-words for each considered method, over all 6 prompts. As observed in Table 1, naively using raw label word probabilities (dark blue) leads to considerable fluctuations in accuracy; some prompt and label word settings lead to reasonable accuracy (92%+ accuracy), however there is observed brittleness to label word choice, with many settings demonstrating poor performance. Prior matching (green) leads to significant robustness, with nearly all sensible settings above 85% accuracy. We further find that, as shown in Table 1, the unsupervised approach has accuracies very comparable to those

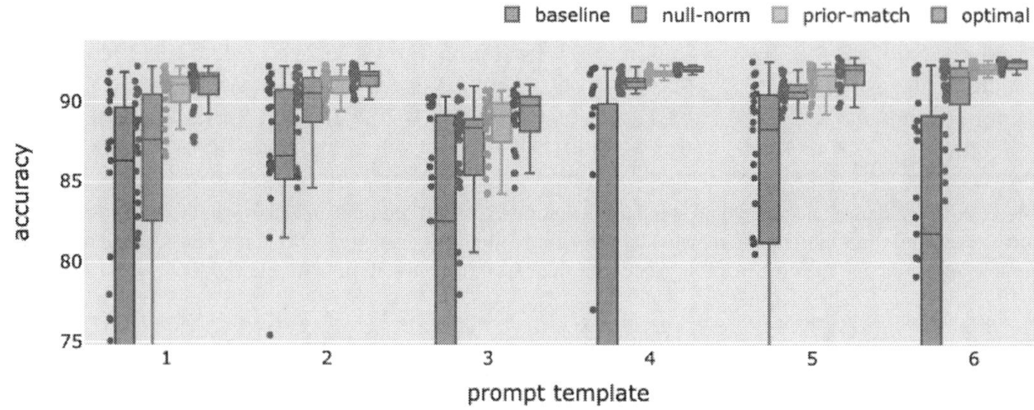


Figure 2: boxplots of the accuracy of all label-word pairs for **rotten tomatoes**, over all the considered prompts

when using optimal thresholds.

In Figure 3, we consider similar boxplots for SNLI and observe larger gains through reweighting. This was as higher probabilities are often assigned to the entailment and contradiction labels words, leading to under-classification of the neutral class. We observe greater sensitivity to prompt choice and label words for snli than as observed in rotten tomatoes, even with reweighting.

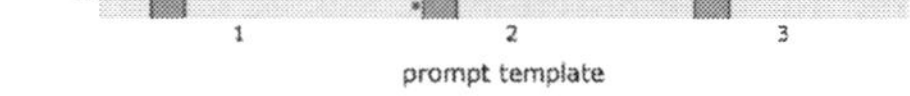


Figure 3: boxplots of the accuracy of all label-word sets for **snli**, for the first 3 prompts

**Weight Alignment** Figure 4 shows a scatter plot of the weights found by the optimal threshold search $\alpha^*$ (equation 4), with those found from the unsupervised prior matching method $\bar{\alpha}$ (equation 7) and the zero-resource word prior approximation (equation 9). We see a clear linear relationship between optimal and prior-match, illustrating that accounting for the marginal bias is almost equivalent with maximising accuracy, however, achieved in an unsupervised fashion. Null-input is also well correlated with the optimal thresholds, but there is a less direct relationship. Similar linear relationships are observed also for other binary-classification tasks and prompts, as shown in Appendix C.

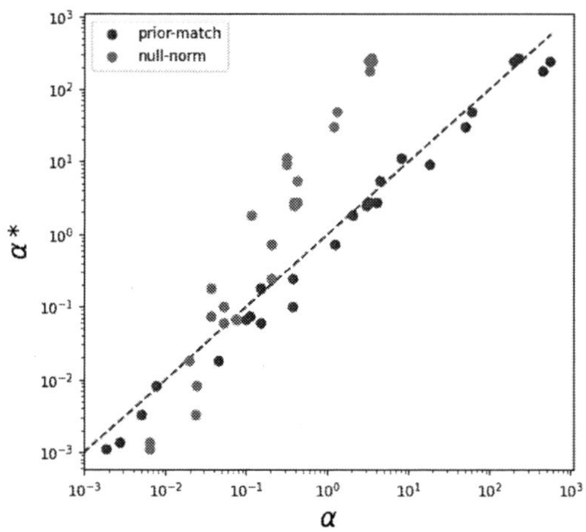


Figure 4: Scatter plot of the optimal weights $\alpha^*$ (equation 4) with the prior match weights $\bar{\alpha}$ (equation 7) and the approximation via null-input (equation 9), for all settings of prompt 1 on **amazon**

## 4 Conclusions

This paper analyzes prompt-based classifiers and demonstrates that inherent class bias is a significant factor that influences the sensitivity of the system to prompt and label words. We propose an unsupervised approach of prior matching, which we demonstrate performs competitively to the supervised alternative of searching for optimal thresholds, while avoiding the need for labelled data. We relate prior matching with word biases, and motivate a zero-resource approach of debiasing model probabilities. We show that our methods lead to practical approaches that reduce the sensitivity to design choices such as prompts and label words.

## Limitations

This work considered sentiment classification, natural language inference, and paraphrase detection, and could have been extended over a greater suite of tasks to guarantee its effectiveness. Further, this paper ran experiments on FlanT5 and Llama2, and this work has not yet explored a larger range of prompted language models. FlanT5 has also been instruction-tuned on similar tasks, so the findings may be limited in scenarios where known capabilities have to be elicited from models robustly.

## Ethical Considerations

Though this work suggests methods to improve the robustness of prompt-based classifiers to prompts and label words, this does not imply that all design choices will work. In some set ups, the system may be ineffective and have poor generalisation over the task. Deploying machine learning classifiers in real-world classification settings has many associated risks, and careful analysis should be made before deploying such systems.

## Acknowledgements

This work is supported by Cambridge University Press & Assessment (CUP&A), a department of The Chancellor, Masters, and Scholars of the University of Cambridge, and the Cambridge Commonwealth, European & International Trust.

## References

Samuel R. Bowman, Gabor Angeli, Christopher Potts, and Christopher D. Manning. 2015. A large annotated corpus for learning natural language inference. In *Proceedings of the 2015 Conference on Empirical Methods in Natural Language Processing*, pages 632–642, Lisbon, Portugal. Association for Computational Linguistics.

Tom Brown, Benjamin Mann, Nick Ryder, Melanie Subbiah, Jared D Kaplan, Prafulla Dhariwal, Arvind Neelakantan, Pranav Shyam, Girish Sastry, Amanda Askell, et al. 2020. Language models are few-shot learners. *Advances in neural information processing systems*, 33:1877–1901.

Hyung Won Chung, Le Hou, Shayne Longpre, Barret Zoph, Yi Tay, William Fedus, Eric Li, Xuezhi Wang, Mostafa Dehghani, Siddhartha Brahma, et al. 2022. Scaling instruction-finetuned language models. *arXiv preprint arXiv:2210.11416*.

Tianyu Gao, Adam Fisch, and Danqi Chen. 2021. Making pre-trained language models better few-shot learners. In *Proceedings of the 59th Annual Meeting of the Association for Computational Linguistics and the 11th International Joint Conference on Natural Language Processing (Volume 1: Long Papers)*, pages 3816–3830.

Matt Gardner, William Merrill, Jesse Dodge, Matthew E Peters, Alexis Ross, Sameer Singh, and Noah A Smith. 2021. Competency problems: On finding and removing artifacts in language data. In *Proceedings of the 2021 Conference on Empirical Methods in Natural Language Processing*, pages 1801–1813.

Ari Holtzman, Peter West, Vered Shwartz, Yejin Choi, and Luke Zettlemoyer. 2021. Surface form competition: Why the highest probability answer isn't always right. In *Proceedings of the 2021 Conference on Empirical Methods in Natural Language Processing*, pages 7038–7051.

Zhengbao Jiang, Frank F Xu, Jun Araki, and Graham Neubig. 2020. How can we know what language models know? *Transactions of the Association for Computational Linguistics*, 8:423–438.

Adian Liusie, Vatsal Raina, Vyas Raina, and Mark Gales. 2022. Analyzing biases to spurious correlations in text classification tasks. In *Proceedings of the 2nd Conference of the Asia-Pacific Chapter of the Association for Computational Linguistics and the 12th International Joint Conference on Natural Language Processing (Volume 2: Short Papers)*, pages 78–84, Online only. Association for Computational Linguistics.

Andrew L. Maas, Raymond E. Daly, Peter T. Pham, Dan Huang, Andrew Y. Ng, and Christopher Potts. 2011. Learning word vectors for sentiment analysis. In *Proceedings of the 49th Annual Meeting of the Association for Computational Linguistics: Human Language Technologies*, pages 142–150, Portland, Oregon, USA. Association for Computational Linguistics.

Long Ouyang, Jeffrey Wu, Xu Jiang, Diogo Almeida, Carroll Wainwright, Pamela Mishkin, Chong Zhang, Sandhini Agarwal, Katarina Slama, Alex Ray, et al. 2022. Training language models to follow instructions with human feedback. *Advances in Neural Information Processing Systems*, 35:27730–27744.

Bo Pang and Lillian Lee. 2005. Seeing stars: Exploiting class relationships for sentiment categorization with respect to rating scales. In *Proceedings of the 43rd Annual Meeting of the Association for Computational Linguistics (ACL'05)*, pages 115–124, Ann Arbor, Michigan. Association for Computational Linguistics.

Timo Schick and Hinrich Schütze. 2021. Exploiting cloze-questions for few-shot text classification and natural language inference. In *Proceedings of the 16th Conference of the European Chapter of the Association for Computational Linguistics: Main Volume*, pages 255–269.

Taylor Shin, Yasaman Razeghi, Robert L Logan IV, Eric Wallace, and Sameer Singh. 2020. Autoprompt: Eliciting knowledge from language models with automatically generated prompts. In *Proceedings of the 2020 Conference on Empirical Methods in Natural Language Processing (EMNLP)*, pages 4222–4235.

Alex Wang, Amanpreet Singh, Julian Michael, Felix Hill, Omer Levy, and Samuel Bowman. 2018. GLUE: A multi-task benchmark and analysis platform for natural language understanding. In *Proceedings of the 2018 EMNLP Workshop BlackboxNLP: Analyzing and Interpreting Neural Networks for NLP*, pages 353–355, Brussels, Belgium. Association for Computational Linguistics.

Jason Wei, Maarten Bosma, Vincent Zhao, Kelvin Guu, Adams Wei Yu, Brian Lester, Nan Du, Andrew M Dai, and Quoc V Le. 2021. Finetuned language models are zero-shot learners. In *International Conference on Learning Representations*.

Jason Wei, Yi Tay, Rishi Bommasani, Colin Raffel, Barret Zoph, Sebastian Borgeaud, Dani Yogatama, Maarten Bosma, Denny Zhou, Donald Metzler, et al. 2022. Emergent abilities of large language models. *arXiv preprint arXiv:2206.07682*.

Adina Williams, Nikita Nangia, and Samuel Bowman. 2018. A broad-coverage challenge corpus for sentence understanding through inference. In *Proceedings of the 2018 Conference of the North American Chapter of the Association for Computational Linguistics: Human Language Technologies, Volume 1 (Long Papers)*, pages 1112–1122, New Orleans, Louisiana. Association for Computational Linguistics.

Zihao Zhao, Eric Wallace, Shi Feng, Dan Klein, and Sameer Singh. 2021. Calibrate before use: Improving few-shot performance of language models. In *International Conference on Machine Learning*, pages 12697–12706. PMLR.

Yongchao Zhou, Andrei Ioan Muresanu, Ziwen Han, Keiran Paster, Silviu Pitis, Harris Chan, and Jimmy Ba. Large language models are human-level prompt engineers. In *NeurIPS 2022 Foundation Models for Decision Making Workshop*.

## A Derivation of Zero-Resource Equation

For a prompt classifier $Q = \{\mathbf{p}, \{w_k\}_{1:K}\}$, class probabilities are assumed to be proportional to the probability of the associated class word,

$$\tilde{P}_\theta(y_k|\mathbf{x}, Q) = \frac{P_\theta(w_k|\mathbf{p}(\mathbf{x}))}{\sum_{w_i} P_\theta(w_i|\mathbf{p}(\mathbf{x}))} \tag{10}$$

Given the task dataset $\mathcal{D} = \{\{\mathbf{x}^{(j)}, y^{(j)}\}\}_{j=1}^N$, one can calculate the assumed prior of the prompt classifier over the output classes,

$$\begin{aligned}\tilde{P}_\theta(y_k|Q) &= \mathbb{E}_\mathbf{x}\{\tilde{P}_\theta(y_k|Q, \mathbf{x})\} && (11)\\ &\approx \frac{1}{N}\sum_{j=1}^{N} \tilde{P}_\theta(y_k|Q, \mathbf{x}^{(j)}) && (12)\\ &= \frac{1}{N}\sum_{j=1}^{N} \frac{P_\theta(w_k|\mathbf{p}(\mathbf{x}^{(j)}))}{\sum_{w_i} P_\theta(w_i|\mathbf{p}(\mathbf{x}^{(j)}))} && (13)\end{aligned}$$

This can be compared to the actual prior of the task/domain,

$$P(y_k) \approx P(y_k|\mathcal{D}) = \frac{1}{N}\sum_{j=1}^{N} \mathbb{1}(y, y^{(j)}) \tag{14}$$

If $\mathcal{D}$ is sufficiently large, then an unbiased classifier should have a class prior similar to that approximated via the labels. However, if they diverge, one may wish to debias the classifier by scaling class probabilities by factors $\alpha_k$,

$$\begin{aligned}\hat{P}_\theta(y_k|\mathbf{x}, Q, \boldsymbol{\alpha}) &= \frac{\alpha_k \tilde{P}_\theta(y_k|\mathbf{x}, Q)}{\sum_i \alpha_i \tilde{P}_\theta(y_i|\mathbf{x}, Q)} && (15)\\ &= \frac{\alpha_k P_\theta(w_k|\mathbf{x}, Q)}{Z(\mathbf{x}, Q, \boldsymbol{\alpha})} && (16)\end{aligned}$$

Where $Z(\mathbf{x}, Q, \boldsymbol{\alpha}) = \sum_i \alpha_i P_\theta(w_i|\mathbf{x}, Q, \boldsymbol{\alpha})$ and $P_\theta(w_k|\mathbf{x}, Q) \equiv P_\theta(w_k|\mathbf{p}(\mathbf{x}))$. The parameters $\bar{\boldsymbol{\alpha}}$ that lead to an unbiased classifier can then be determined in a deterministic fashion.

$$\bar{\boldsymbol{\alpha}} = \underset{\boldsymbol{\alpha}}{\text{argmin}} \sum_{\forall y_k} |\hat{P}_\theta(y_k|Q, \boldsymbol{\alpha}) - P(y_k)| \tag{17}$$

Note that by constraining $\alpha_1 = 1$, there will exist a deterministic solution that ensures that $\hat{P}_\theta(y_k|Q, \boldsymbol{\alpha}) = P(y_k)$. For given weight parameters $\boldsymbol{\alpha}$, Consider the prompt-classifier priors, $\hat{P}_\theta(y_k|Q, \boldsymbol{\alpha})$. One can approximate this using a Taylor series of the expectation of a ratio, yielding

$$\begin{aligned}\hat{P}_\theta(y_k|Q, \boldsymbol{\alpha}) &= \mathbb{E}_\mathbf{x}[\hat{P}_\theta(y_k|\mathbf{x}, Q, \boldsymbol{\alpha})] && (18)\\ &= \mathbb{E}_\mathbf{x}[\frac{\alpha_k P_\theta(w_k|\mathbf{x}, Q)}{Z(\mathbf{x}, Q, \boldsymbol{\alpha})}] && (19)\\ &\approx \frac{\mathbb{E}_\mathbf{x}[\alpha_k P_\theta(w_k|\mathbf{x}, Q)]}{\mathbb{E}_\mathbf{x}[Z(\mathbf{x}, Q, \boldsymbol{\alpha})]} && (20)\\ &= \frac{\alpha_k P_\theta(w_k|Q)}{Z(Q, \boldsymbol{\alpha})} && (21)\end{aligned}$$

By equating the predicted prior with the true prior, we find an approximation for $\bar{\alpha}_k$

$$\hat{P}_\theta(y_k|Q) = P(y_k|\mathcal{D}) \tag{22}$$

$$\frac{\alpha_k P_\theta(w_k|Q)}{Z(Q)} = P(y_k|\mathcal{D}) \tag{23}$$

$$\Rightarrow \alpha_k = \frac{Z(Q) \cdot P(y_k|\mathcal{D})}{P_\theta(w_k|Q)} \tag{24}$$

A final insight is that in many cases it is assumed that there should be no inherent class bias, and so $P(y_k|\mathcal{D})$ can be assumed to be uniform and be included in the normalisation term.

# B Prompts and Label Words

## B.1 Sentiment Classification

| prompt |
|---|
| classify the following review: |
| how was the movie? |
| which word best describes the text? |
| what is the sentiment? |
| what is the reviewer's verdict? |
| is the following movie good or bad? |

Table 2: sentiment classification prompts

| positive | negative |
|---|---|
| good | bad |
| great | terrible |
| amazing | poor |
| fantastic | horrible |
| positive | negative |

Table 3: label words for sentiment classification

## B.2 Natural Language Inference

| prompt |
|---|
| is the second text an entailment of the first text? |
| does the second text directly follow from the first text? |
| are the texts related? |
| are the texts consistent? |
| does text 1 imply text 2? |
| can text 2 be logically derived from text 1? |
| does the hypothesis logically follow the premise? |

Table 4: NLI prompts

| entailment | neutral | contradiction |
|---|---|---|
| yes | maybe | no |
| correct | unclear | incorrect |
| yeah | potentially | nope |
| follows | neutral | contradiction |

Table 5: label words for NLI

## B.3 Paraphrase Identification

| prompt |
|---|
| is the second text a paraphrase of the first text? |
| are the two texts semantically equivalent? |
| are the texts paraphrases of each other? |
| do the texts have the same meaning? |
| is the meaning of text 1 the same as in text 2? |
| would the two texts be classified as paraphrases? |

Table 6: NLI prompts

| paraphrase | not paraphrase |
|---|---|
| yes | no |
| correct | incorrect |
| yeah | not |
| positive | negative |
| true | false |

Table 7: label words for sentiment classification

# C Threshold Alignment Plots

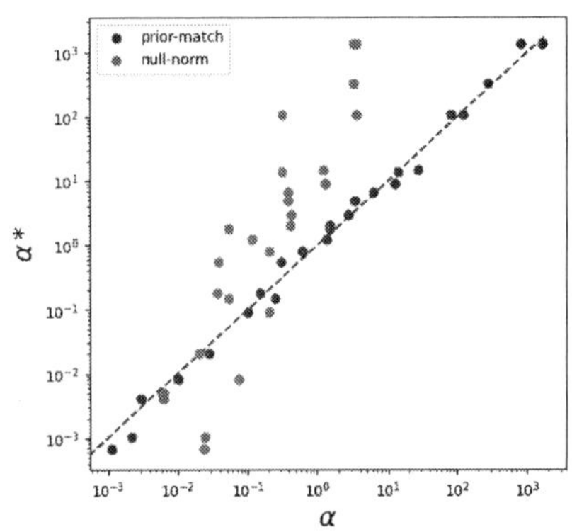


Figure 5: weights alignment plot for **rotten tomatoes**

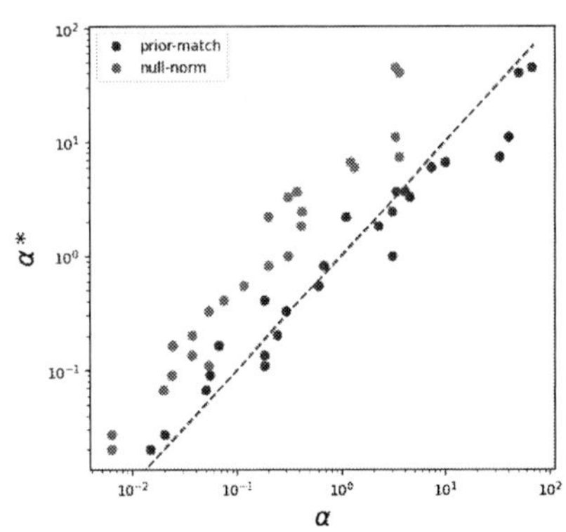


Figure 6: weights alignment plot for **imdb**

## D Impact of LLM Choice

| method | inputs | labels | imdb | rt | amazon | snli | mnli | qqp |
|---|---|---|---|---|---|---|---|---|
| baseline | ✗ | ✗ | 82.1±11.1 | 70.1±11.7 | 83.4±12.8 | 37.4±6.1 | 37.0±4.3 | 52.5±11.4 |
| null-input | ✗ | ✗ | 87.5±3.2 | 78.5±4.8 | 91.1±2.3 | 41.8±3.8 | 40.2±4.1 | 53.9±10.2 |
| prior-match | ✓ | ✗ | 89.1±2.4 | 80.8±2.9 | 92.0±1.3 | 44.7±6.3 | 41.8±3.8 | 58.5±5.5 |
| optimal | ✓ | ✓ | 89.3±2.0 | 81.2±2.9 | 92.1±1.4 | 47.6±5.9 | 43.5±3.7 | 65.3±2.9 |

Table 8: Robustness performance when using FlanT5 base as the base LLM (set-up equivalent to Table 1).

| method | inputs | labels | imdb | rt | amazon | snli | mnli | qqp |
|---|---|---|---|---|---|---|---|---|
| baseline | ✗ | ✗ | 85.8±8.7 | 78.4±10.3 | 86.4±10.3 | 35.1±2.7 | 36.9±3.2 | 51.0±11.6 |
| null-input | ✗ | ✗ | 87.4±6.9 | 83.2±6.6 | 90.7±6.4 | 37.9±5.4 | 39.4±3.7 | 51.8±8.4 |
| prior-match | ✓ | ✗ | 90.5±3.1 | 86.3±3.7 | 93.1±2.4 | 39.5±5.4 | 41.2±3.1 | 52.6±1.9 |
| optimal | ✓ | ✓ | 90.8±2.8 | 86.7±3.6 | 93.2±2.4 | 42.8±4.6 | 42.8±2.3 | 66.8±0.4 |

Table 9: Robustness performance when using Llama-2-chat 7B as the base LLM.

Tables 8 and 9 show the prompt-based classifier performance for the different methods when using different FlanT5-base and LLama-2-chat 7B respectively. For sentiment classification and natural language tasks, we similarly observe that the various re-weighting methods lead to considerable boosts in accuracy. Both null-norm and prior-match again lead to performance near that to the optimal weights, with considerable performance boost over the baseline. However, for paraphrase detection, we only observe moderate performance boosts over the baseline setting with a larger performance discrepancy with the optimal weights.

## E Boxplots

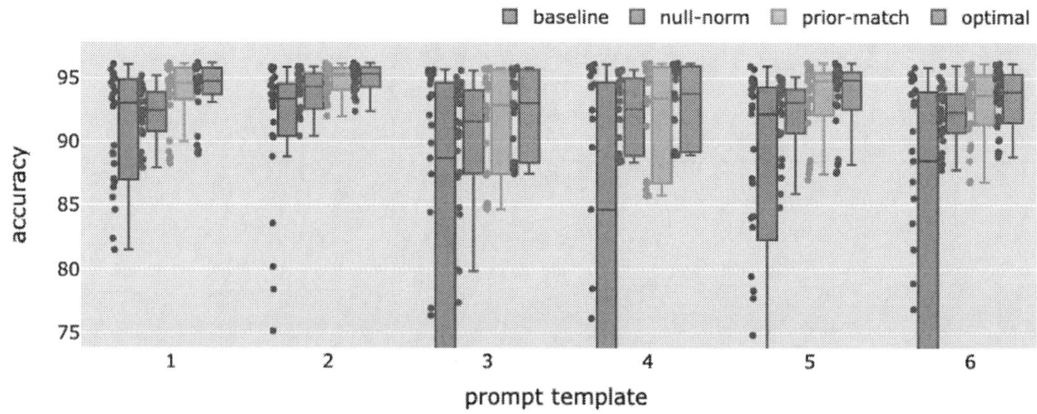


Figure 7: boxplots of the accuracy of all label-word pairs on **IMDB**, over all the considered prompts

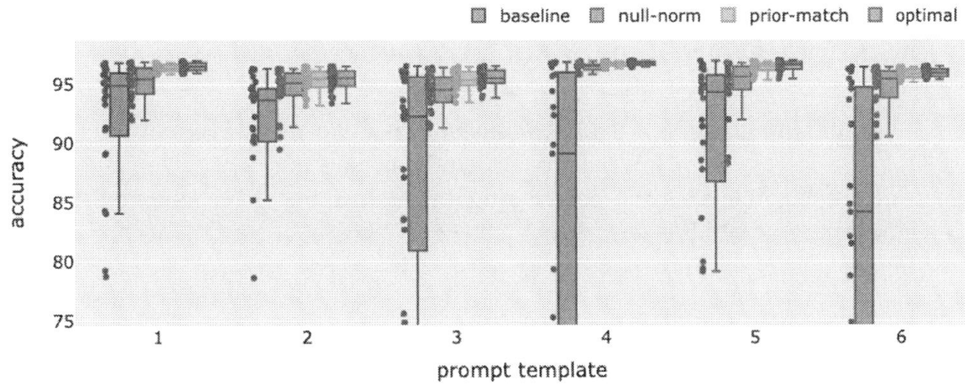


Figure 8: boxplots of the accuracy of all label-word pairs on **amazon**, over all the considered prompts

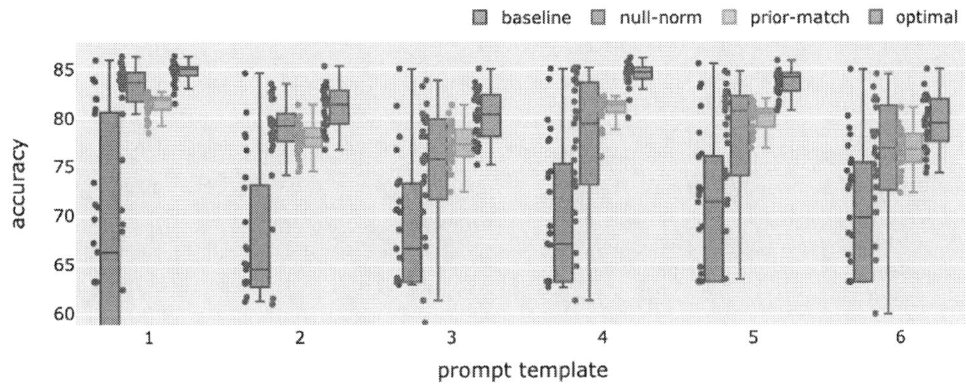


Figure 9: boxplots of the accuracy of all label-word pairs on **qqp**, over all the considered prompts

# Mixing It Up: Inducing Empathy and Politeness using Multiple Behaviour-aware Generators for Conversational Systems

**Mauajama Firdaus**[1*] and **Priyanshu Priya**[2*] and **Asif Ekbal**[2]
[1]University of Alberta, Canada
[2]Department of Computer Science and Engineering, Indian Institute of Technology Patna, India
[1]mauzama.03@gmail.com,{[2]priyanshu_2021cs26,asif}@iitp.ac.in

## Abstract

Politeness is a key component that can assist in building a strong customer-agent relationship. With the ongoing increase in customer-care systems, it is crucial to have healthy relations with the users providing satisfaction and a better customer experience. In this regard, it is significant to model the different polite behaviors in an agent to help the user in reaching the intended objectives. In our current work, we propose the task of polite behavior-aware generation considering the affective state of the user and the conversational context. We design a Transformer based encoder-decoder framework with three major components i.e., Affective tracker, Behaviour-aware generators, and Polite generator. The *affective tracker* is a context encoder that captures the contextual information along with the affective information in the utterances; the *behavior-aware generators* independently attends to the context information to compute behavior-aware polite representations and finally, *polite generator* generates the final polite response considering the representations from different generators. Experimental results on the CYCCD dataset prove that our approach generates contextually correct and relevant responses compared to the state-of-the-art approaches and the baselines.

## 1 Introduction

The technological advancements in Artificial Intelligence (AI) and Natural Language Processing (NLP) have led to the proliferation of conversational systems (chatbots and personal assistants like Amazon's Alexa, Google's Home, and Apple's Siri) in our daily lives. These conversational systems that aim to assist users in numerous ways like making reservations, booking flights, scheduling appointments and many more are prevalent in several areas such as hospitality, education, and health care, to name a few. The success of these systems significantly depends on their ability to effectively communicate with the users. Thus, the research in recent times has been inclined towards modulating biases, styles, and control in text generation to improve these interactions.

Customer care is a typical application area for automated task-oriented conversational systems. These systems provide potentially cost-effective and reliable solutions for customer care. Nowadays, companies rely heavily on customer care service to successfully guide and assist customers and establish long-term and healthy relationships with them. Customers generally interact with conversational agents with diverse expectations and attitudes (Følstad and Skjuve, 2019). In such situation, if the agent fails to satisfy their expectations or fix their issue as desired, they may get frustrated or furious quickly (Jain et al., 2018). To avoid this, it is imperative for customer care agents to mimic human-like (Fink, 2012) behaviour during the conversation.

Politeness and empathy, which encompass social belongingness are a few fundamental sociolinguistic cues of humans (Brown et al., 1987; Maslow, 1943). The use of social language by the agents facilitates building rapport and emotional connection with the customers. Politeness has been investigated recently (Golchha et al., 2019; Firdaus et al., 2022a; Priya et al., 2023a; Mishra et al., 2023a, 2022a; Firdaus et al., 2022b; Mishra et al., 2022b, 2023c,b; Priya et al., 2023b) to ensure user satisfaction and to build strong user relations. Politeness could have different behavioral aspects linguistically such as one could be apologetic, appreciative, empathetic, or could be respectful by always greeting and assuring. Such behavioral patterns could lead to different responses that are contextually plausible and interactive.

Emotion and sentiment of the user are essential for meeting the user's wants appropriately and facilitating the creation of smooth and amicable conver-

*The authors are jointly first authors.



*Findings of the Association for Computational Linguistics: IJCNLP-AACL 2023*, pages 336–347
November 1–4, 2023. ©2023 Asian Federation of Natural Language Processing

| Dialog Context | Customer Sentiment | Customer Emotion | Generic Response | Polite Response | Polite behaviour |
|---|---|---|---|---|---|
| I need a software update urgently, but I am unable to connect to the network. | Negative | Frustrated | What is happening with your internet? | Please don't worry, we can help! Kindly tell what is happening with your internet? | *Assurance* |
| Hey, i got stomach ache from your inflight meal on monday. | Negative | Anger | Send us a dm. | That's really sad to hear. We are sorry, please send us a dm. | *Apology* |
| Hi! I want help. | Neutral | Hopeful | What are you looking for? | Hey good morning! Good to have you with us, please let us know what are you looking for? | *Greet* |
| Dear this new update is awesome, got great new apps! | Positive | Joy | The update has many features. | Thank you very much, please checkout the exciting features in the update. | *Appreciation* |
| I lost my bag. | Negative | Sad | We will look into the matter. | That's really disappointing to hear. Please have patience until we look into the matter. | *Empathy* |

Table 1: Examples of variation in polite behaviour in accordance with user's affective state (emotion and sentiment)

sations (Beale and Creed, 2009; Shi and Yu, 2018; Firdaus et al., 2020a, 2022c, 2023; Singh et al., 2022; Samad et al., 2022; Madasu et al., 2022; Firdaus et al., 2022c,d). The usage of user feedback in the form of emotion and sentiment is essential for generating contextually coherent polite responses reflecting relevant polite behaviour in the responses as depicted in Table 1. For the first example in Table 1, it can be seen that the user's emotion and sentiment are negative. The appropriate response in such a scenario could either exhibit empathy or apologize or provide assurance. For this particular example, the polite behaviour is assurance which could help in smoother conversations with the user.

In our current work, we take a step ahead and address the task of behaviour-aware polite response generation. To the best of our knowledge, this is one of the very first attempts that addresses the linguistically driven different behavioural patterns of the polite generation. We build an end-to-end transformer-based encoder-decoder architecture for the task of behaviour-aware polite response generation. Our proposed architecture captures the complete affective information in the form of emotion and sentiment from the conversational context and uses this knowledge for generating behaviour-aware polite customer care responses.

In summary, the key contributions of our work are three-fold. We first introduce the task of behaviour-guided polite response generation for customer-care systems. Second, we design a transformer-based encoder-decoder network having three crucial components, i.e., an affective tracker, behaviour-aware generators, and a final polite generator to capture the emotional quotient from the context and generate behaviour-wise response representations and finally generate the polite response using the weighted-sum approach. Lastly, experimental analysis on the CY-CCD dataset shows that our approach performs better than all the existing baselines and generates more informative and varying responses.

## 2 Related Work

Natural language generation (NLG) module has been gaining prominence in a variety of applications, including dialogue systems (Shen et al., 2018; Zhang et al., 2018), question answering systems (Indurthi et al., 2017; Duan et al., 2017), and various other natural language interfaces. Users' feelings in the form of sentiments and emotions have been exploited in (Acosta, 2009; Pittermann et al., 2010; Shi and Yu, 2018; Firdaus et al., 2021b; Dias et al., 2022; Firdaus et al., 2021a, 2020b,d) to give humanly essence to the system, thereby facilitating better user experience. Emotion recognition and sentiment analysis in customer support system is essential for understanding and to provide better customer support (Herzig et al., 2016; Wang et al., 2020a).

Politeness in customer support systems is important for attaining customer satisfaction and retention (Bickmore and Picard, 2005; Bickmore et al., 2009; Liao et al., 2016; Wang et al., 2020b). In the past, (Gupta et al., 2007) explored building more affective and socially intelligent dialogue systems by incorporating different politeness strategies in the responses. Lately, (Niu and Bansal, 2018a) proposed a reinforcement learning (RL)-based model to induce politeness in chit-chat conversations without parallel data. Golchha et al. (2019); Firdaus et al. (2020c) presented a method for increasing user satisfaction by instilling courteous nature in the customer-care responses by exploiting reinforced pointer networks. Madaan et al. (2020) devised a tag and generate framework for transforming non-polite sentences into polite ones. Firdaus et al. (2022a) transformed generic customer-care responses into polite ones based on user's sentiment and conversational history using an RL-based approach. Firdaus et al. (2022b) designed a reinforced deliberation network based framework to inculcate politeness in the responses according to the personalized user information (age and gender) and dialog context.

Our present work is different in the sense that we aim to incorporate different polite behaviour in the generated responses according to emotion and sentiment of the user. The inclusion of user feedback in the form of emotion and sentiment provides complete affective information, which in turn, enhances the quality of generation and makes the responses contextually coherent with the dialog.

## 3 Methodology

In this section, we present the problem definition of our current task and provide a detailed description of our proposed approach. Our approach focuses on generating responses based on the speaker's emotional state from the conversational context constrained by the different polite behaviour such as *Appreciation, Empathy, Apology, Greeting, and Assurance*.

### 3.1 Problem Definition

Our current work aims at generating contextually appropriate responses based on different polite behaviour. Precisely, the conversation has an alternating set of utterances from the customer ($U^i$) and the customer care agent ($A^i$). We represent the conversational context as $C = (\mathcal{U}^1, \mathcal{A}^1, \mathcal{U}^2, \mathcal{A}^2, \cdots, \mathcal{U}^i)$ and each utterance is a sequence of words $w_1, w_2, \ldots, w_N$.

Similar to (Golchha et al., 2019), we use the output distribution from DeepMoji (Felbo et al., 2017) (pre-trained on the emoji prediction task) to get the emotional embeddings ($E^{emo}$) associated with both the customer and agent utterances. In addition, we also use the sentiment information ($E^{sen}$) along with the emotional embeddings to get complete affective information. This information is added with every utterance to assist in generating the final behaviour-aware polite response.

### 3.2 Approach

In this section, we describe each component of our proposed model in detail. Overall, our model is composed of three components: a *Affective tracker*, *Behaviour-aware generators* and a final *Polite generator* as shown in Figure 1. The *Affective tracker* is basically the context encoder that provides the representation of the context and computes a distribution over the possible sentiment and emotion categories for the context. The *Behaviour-aware generators* independently attend to this distribution to compute their own representation. Finally, the *Polite generator* takes the weighted sum of representation from the different generators and generates the final polite response. We also incorporate speaker information as embedding in the input with every utterance. This is used to facilitate the encoder to differentiate between the customer and agent utterances.

**Affective Tracker:** The context encoder uses a standard transformer encoder (Vaswani et al., 2017) for the sentiment and emotion (Affective) tracker. To capture the hierarchical nature of the conversation, we use a hierarchical transformer encoder to capture the utterance-level and dialogue-level representations. We use the utterance transformer to get the encoded utterance representation. To learn the representation of each utterance $U^i$, $U^i = w_1^i, w_2^i, \ldots, w_N^i$ is first mapped into continuous space

$$T_u = (t_1^i, t_2^i, \ldots, t_{|U^i|}^i); where[t_j^i = e(w_j^i) + p_j] \tag{1}$$

where, $e(w_j^i)$ and $p_j$ are the word and positional embedding of every word $w_j^i$ in an utterance, respectively. For words, we use Glove embeddings and adopt the sine-cosine positional embedding (Vaswani et al., 2017) as it performs better and does not introduce additional trainable parameters.

The utterance encoder (a Transformer) converts $T_u$ into a list of hidden representations $h_1^i, h_2^i, \ldots, h_{|U^i|}^i$. We use the last hidden representation $h_{|U^i|}^i$ (i.e. the representation at the EOS token) as the textual representation of the utterance $U^i$. Specifically, the final utterance representation $E^U$ is the sum of the final textual representation $h_{|U^i|}^i$, the positional embedding $E^p$ (Vaswani et al., 2017), the speaker embedding $E^s$, the emotion embedding $E^{emo}$ and the sentiment embedding $E^{sen}$ of the corresponding utterance.

$$E^U(C) = h_{|U^i|}^i + E^p(C) + E^s(C) + E^{emo} + E^{sen} \tag{2}$$

In a similar fashion, we encode the agent utterances as well.

The final utterance representation is used as input for the dialogue transformer that encodes the dialog context into a context representation. In order to compute the weighted sum of the output tensor, we add a query token $QRY$ at the start of each input sequence, similar to BERT (Devlin et al., 2018). If a transformer-context encoder is designated as $TRS_{enc}$, then the relevant context

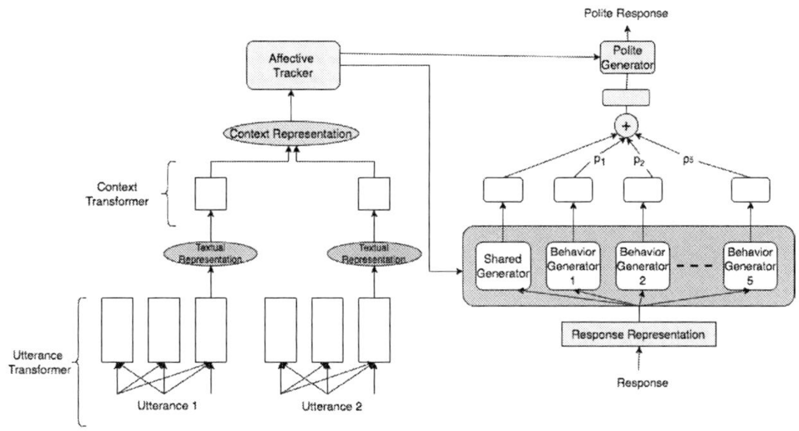


Figure 1: Architectural diagram of our proposed behaviour-aware polite generator

representation is:

$$H^C = TRS_{enc}(E^U([QRY;C])) \quad (3)$$

where [;] denotes concatenation, H $\in R^{L_{model}}$ where $L$ is the dialogue length. Then, we determine the final representation of the token $QRY$ as $q = H_0$ where $q \in R^{d_{model}}$, which is then used as the query for generating the sentiment and emotion distribution.

**Behaviour-aware Generators:** The behaviour-aware generators mainly consist of (1) a shared behaviour generator that learns shared information for all the emotions and their corresponding polite behaviour and (2) $n$ independently parameterized Transformer decoders (Vaswani et al., 2017) that learns how to appropriately react in a polite-manner given a particular affective state.

A standard transformer decoder layer block, abbreviated as $TRS_{dec}$, models all of the generators and is composed of three sub-components: a position-wise fully connected feed-forward network, multi-head attention over the output of the Affective tracker, and a multi-head self-attention over the response input embedding.

As a result, we specify the generator's set as $G = [TRS^0_{dec}, ..., TRS^n_{dec}]$. Each generator constructs its own polite response representation $P_i$ using the target sequence altered by one $r_{0:t-1}$.

$$P_i = TRS^i_{dec}(H^C, E^R(r_{0:t-1})) \quad (4)$$

where $TRS^i_{dec}$ refers to the $i^{th}$ generator, including the shared one. From a conceptual standpoint, we anticipate that the shared generator, $TRS^0_{dec}$, will produce a general representation that will aid the model in capturing the discourse context. On the other hand, we anticipate that each behaviour-aware generator will develop its ability to react in a designated polite behaviour based upon a certain emotion and sentiment. In order to simulate this phenomenon, we give each behaviour-aware generator a varied weight based on the user's emotional distribution, while giving the shared listener a set weight of 1.

To illustrate, we create a Key-Value Memory Network (Miller et al., 2016) and represent each memory slot as a pair of vectors $(k_i, P_i)$, where $k_i \in R^{d_{model}}$ signifies the key vector and $P_i$ is from Equation 4. The key vectors $k$ are then addressed using the encoder-informed query $q$ by performing a dot product and then a Softmax function as follows:

$$v_i = \frac{e^{q^T k_i}}{\sum_{j=1}^{n} e^{q^T k_i}} \quad (5)$$

The weight of each listener is determined by using each $v_i$ as the score given to $P_i$. Given the speaker's affective state $e_t$, we oversee each weight $v_i$ throughout training by using a cross-entropy loss function to maximize the likelihood of the emotion state $e_t$:

$$\mathcal{L}_1 = -logp_{e_t} \quad (6)$$

Finally, the weighted sum of the shared generator output $P_0$ and the memory values $P_i$ is used to calculate the combined output representation.

$$P_M = P_0 + \sum_{i=1}^{n} v_i P_i \quad (7)$$

**Polite Generator:** The polite generator is then implemented using a second transformer decoder layer, which further transforms the behaviour-aware generator's representation and produces the final response. On the basis of emotion and sentiment, each behaviour-aware generator is thought to specialize in a certain polite behaviour, and the polite generator compiles the ideas from different generators to create the final response.

Therefore, we define another $TRS_{dec}^{final}$, and an affine transformation $W \in R^{d_{model} \times |P|}$ to compute:

$$P_{fin} = TRS_{dec}^{final}(H, P_M) \quad (8)$$

$$S_t = p(r_{1:t}|C, r_{0:t-1}) = softmax(P_{fin}^T W) \quad (9)$$

where $P_{fin} \in R^{d_{model} \times t}$ is the output of the polite generator and $p(r_{1:t}|C, r_{0:t-1})$ is the distribution over the vocabulary for the next tokens. The response prediction is then optimized using a standard maximum likelihood estimator (MLE):

$$\mathcal{L}_2 = -logp(S_t|C) \quad (10)$$

Finally, by minimizing the weighted-sum of two losses, all the parameters are jointly trained end-to-end to optimize behaviour selection and response generation:

$$\mathcal{L} = \alpha\mathcal{L}_1 + \beta\mathcal{L}_2 \quad (11)$$

where $\alpha$ and $\beta$ are trainable hyperparameters to balance the two loss functions.

## 4 Dataset and Experiments

In this section, we present the dataset used for our experiments followed by training details, baselines, and evaluation metrics.

### 4.1 Dataset

For our current work, we use the CYCCD dataset (Golchha et al., 2019)[1] having interactions between customers and professional customer care agents of companies on their Twitter handles. The CYCCD Twitter data was taken from the dataset made available on Kaggle by Thought vector. We use the generic and polite annotated version of the CYCCD dataset in a similar manner as (Golchha et al., 2019). The dataset consists of 140k, 20k and 40k conversations in training, validation and test set respectively.

As the CYCCD dataset was not annotated for different polite behaviour, therefore we do the polite-behaviour annotations for the dataset. To annotate the CYCCD dataset with behavioural information, we employ crowd-workers from Amazon Mechanical Turk (AMT) that label every utterance with the provided set of labels (i.e., assurance, empathy, apology, greeting, appreciation). For labelling the utterances, the workers were asked to follow the instructions and guidelines provided for annotation.

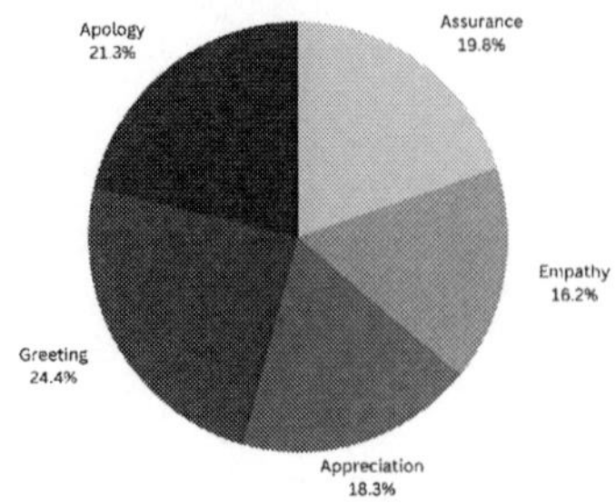


Figure 2: Polite-behaviour distribution in the CYCCD dataset

Some of the significant guidelines for annotation were as follows: (i). Every utterance of a given dialogue was to be marked with the provided labels; (ii) In addition, the workers were asked to provide the overall behaviour label for every sentence in an utterance as well. For cases where we found different annotations in polite behaviour for a particular sentence, we remove them from the dataset, and we also drop the entire conversation to maintain coherence among the utterances. A majority voting scheme was used for selecting the final label for every sentence. We observe a multi-rater Kappa (McHugh, 2012) agreement ratio of approximately 75%, which can be considered as reliable. The polite-behaviour distribution of the CYCCD dataset is provided in Figure 2.

### 4.2 Training Details

We used 300-dimensional word embedding and 300 hidden sizes in each and every experiment. We use word embedding initialized with Glove (Pennington et al., 2014) embedding pre-trained on Twitter and share it across the encoder and decoder. The rest of the parameters are randomly initialized. We employ two self-attention layers, each with two attention heads and a 40-element embedding dimension. We substitute a 1D convolution with 50 filters of width 3 for the Positionwise Feedforward sub-layer. We use batch sizes of 1 while testing while using batches of 16 during training.

In order to train our model, we used the AMSGrad (Reddi et al., 2019) as the optimizer to mitigate the slow convergence issues and changed the learning rate following (Vaswani et al., 2017). For

[1] https://github.com/Mauajama/Courteously-Yours

| | Model Description | PPL | BLEU-4 | Rouge-L | PA |
|---|---|---|---|---|---|
| Existing Approaches | *Seq2Seq* (Sutskever et al., 2014) | 1.112 | 0.145 | 0.278 | 0.38 |
| | *HRED* (Serban et al., 2015) | 1.085 | 0.198 | 0.308 | 0.45 |
| | *Polite-RL* (Niu and Bansal, 2018b) | 1.028 | 0.224 | 0.321 | 0.69 |
| | *PT-TGA* (Madaan et al., 2020) | 1.032 | 0.251 | 0.332 | 0.68 |
| | *PG-RL* (Golchha et al., 2019) | 1.018 | 0.264 | 0.339 | 0.73 |
| | *HT + RL + SE* (Firdaus et al., 2022a) | 1.004 | 0.275 | 0.352 | 0.77 |
| **Proposed Approach** | **AT + BG + PG** | **0.987** | **0.310** | **0.382** | **0.81** |
| Ablation Study | *HT* | 1.015 | 0.269 | 0.343 | 0.70 |
| | *HT + AT + PG* | 1.002 | 0.286 | 0.365 | 0.78 |
| | *HT + BG + PG* | 0.995 | 0.288 | 0.371 | 0.79 |

Table 2: Automatic evaluation results. Here, PPL: Perplexity, PA: Politeness accuracy, HT: Hierarchical transformer, AT: Affective Tracker, BG: Behaviour-aware generator, PG: Polite Generator

simplicity, we set the weight of both losses $\alpha$ and $\beta$ to 1. *Affective Tracker* may assign weights to the *behaviour-generators* at random during the initial training phase and may send noisy gradient flow back to the incorrect *generators*, which can hinder model convergence.

### 4.3 Baselines

To demonstrate the effectiveness of our proposed model, we compare it with the previous state-of-the-art (SoTA) models:

**Seq2Seq:** It is the standard encoder-decoder framework with an attention mechanism that has been widely used in the generation, machine translation, etc. (Sutskever et al., 2014).

**HRED:** It is a hierarchical encoder-decoder model proposed for text-based dialogue systems (Serban et al., 2015).

**Polite-RL:** We implement the Polite-RL framework to induce politeness in responses in a similar manner as (Niu and Bansal, 2018b).

**PT-TGA:** We implement the politeness transfer framework presented in (Madaan et al., 2020) that uses a tag and generate approach to incorporate politeness.

**PG-RL:** We also take the reinforced pointer generator network employed in (Golchha et al., 2019) as one of the baselines to infuse politeness in generic responses.

**HT+RL+SE:** We also compare with the reinforced transformer network having sentiment information (Firdaus et al., 2022a) as one of the baselines to generate polite responses.

### 4.4 Evaluation Metrics

In this section, we describe both the automatic and manual evaluation metrics used to evaluate the performance of our proposed model.

**Automatic Evaluation Metrics:** To evaluate the model at the relevance and grammatical level, we report the results using the standard metrics like Perplexity (Chen et al., 1998), Rouge-L (Lin, 2004) and BLEU-4 (Papineni et al., 2002). We also report the Politeness Accuracy as a metric to measure the degree of politeness in the responses. We compute the politeness score using a pre-trained classifier, BERT (Devlin et al., 2018)[2] for measuring the degree of politeness in the generated responses similar to (Niu and Bansal, 2018b). The classifier takes as input the generated response and generates a probability value giving us the politeness accuracy of the generated response.

**Manual Evaluation Metrics:** We recruit six annotators (in a similar manner as (Firdaus et al., 2022c; Tian et al., 2019)) from a third-party company, having high-level language skills. We sampled 250 responses per model for evaluation with the utterance and the conversational history provided for generation. First, we evaluate the quality of the response on two conventional criteria: *Fluency* and *Relevance*. These are rated on a five-scale, where 1, 3, and 5 indicate unacceptable, moderate, and excellent performance, respectively, while 2 and 4 are used for unsure.

Secondly, we evaluate the politeness quotient of a response in terms of *Politeness Appropriateness* metric that measures whether the politeness induced in the response is in accordance with the user's affective state (both emotion and sentiment) and the dialogue history. Here, 0 indicates irrelevant or contradictory, and 1 indicates consistent with the provided persona and dialogue context.

We compute Fleiss' kappa (Fleiss, 1971) to mea-

[2]The classifier is trained on the Stanford Politeness Corpus (Danescu-Niculescu-Mizil et al., 2013) and achieves an accuracy of 92%.

| | Model Description | F | R | PA |
|---|---|---|---|---|
| Existing Approaches | *Seq2Seq* (Sutskever et al., 2014) | 3.82 | 3.73 | 48% |
| | *HRED* (Serban et al., 2015) | 3.86 | 3.78 | 52% |
| | *Polite-RL* (Niu and Bansal, 2018b) | 3.91 | 3.79 | 61% |
| | *PT-TGA* (Madaan et al., 2020) | 4.03 | 3.85 | 64% |
| | *PG-RL* (Golchha et al., 2019) | 4.11 | 4.06 | 67% |
| | *HT + RL + SE* (Firdaus et al., 2022a) | 4.23 | 4.17 | 75% |
| **Proposed Approach** | **AT + BG + PG** | **4.35** | **4.53** | **80%** |
| Ablation Study | *HT* | 4.09 | 4.03 | 65% |
| | *HT + AT + PG* | 4.25 | 4.19 | 76% |
| | *HT + BG + PG* | 4.28 | 4.22 | 78% |

Table 3: Human evaluation results. Here, F: Fluency, R: Relevance, PA: Politeness Appropriateness, HT: Hierarchical transformer, AT: Affective Tracker, BG: Behaviour-aware generator, PG: Polite Generator

sure inter-rater consistency. The Fleiss' kappa for fluency and relevance are 0.53 and 0.49, indicating moderate agreement. For politeness appropriateness, we obtain 0.65 as the kappa score indicating substantial agreement.

## 5 Results and Analysis

In this section, we present the results of both automatic and manual evaluation. In addition, we also provide a few examples of our generated responses to showcase the effectiveness of our proposed model followed by a brief error analysis of our approach and the baselines.

**Automatic Evaluation Results:** To illustrate the efficacy of our model we provide the automatic evaluation results in Table 2. The table shows the results of different existing approaches that generate polite responses followed by the results of our model and the ablation study for our approach. The perplexity of our approach is the lowest compared to the existing approaches, i.e., *0.987* indicating the responses are fluent and grammatically correct.

The BLEU-4 and Rouge-L metrics provide information regarding content preservation to avoid loss of information or inconsistent generation. From the table, we see that the *Seq2Seq* model has the lowest scores for both the metrics followed by the *HRED* approach. This indicates the inability of LSTM-based models to capture long-term information for a consistent and informative generation. In addition, the reinforced approach *Polite-RL* shows slight improvement compared to the basic models. The *PG-RL* framework gives better scores for both BLEU-4 and Rouge-L using pointer generator network that directly copies the words from the context. Our approach performs better for both the metrics with the ability of transformers to capture better representations from the dialogue context.

We also provide the politeness accuracy of the generated responses in the table. Our approach has an improvement of 4% and 8% compared to the *HT+RL+SE* and *PG-RL* frameworks, respectively. Even though the *HT+RL+SE* approach uses sentiment information for polite response generation, we outperform their approach with the help of affective tracker that captures the overall emotional content from the context for the consistent and relevant polite generation.

We also provide the ablation study of our approach in Table 2. The *HT* approach without the affective tracker and the behaviour-aware generators gives the lowest scores for all the metrics. By adding the affective tracker there is a gain in performance proving the significance of capturing the overall emotional quotient from the context. We also show the performance without the affective tracker, having only the behaviour-aware generators and the final polite generator. The performance is slightly better but still lower than the proposed approach indicating the importance of all the components in the proposed method.

**Manual Evaluation Results:** In Table 3, we provide the results of human evaluation on the CY-CCD dataset. From the table, we see that the fluency scores of our proposed method is the highest compared to all the existing and the ablated models. The responses are fluent and grammatically correct making the responses complete.

In the case of the relevance metric, we gain an improvement of around 0.4% compared to the *HT+RL+SE* framework that uses sentiment information as feedback to generate consistent and relevant polite responses. We perform better as we employ the entire emotional content present in the context using the affective tracker for generating behaviour-aware polite responses that are in accordance with the context.

Finally, the politeness appropriateness scores are highest with an increase of 5% and 13% from the *HT+RL+SE* and *PG-RL* frameworks. This could be contributed to the behaviour-aware generators that assist in generating correct polite responses in accordance with the ongoing dialogue. This also ensures that the different polite behaviours are important to generate the correct and appropriate responses. The performance of the proposed approach is significantly better than all the existing approaches and the ablated models.

**Case Study and Discussion:** In Table 4, we

| Context | *Hey, i got food poisoning from your inflight meal on Sunday* |
|---|---|
| $\mathbf{BG}_{apology}$ | We are sorry for the inconvenience, we would look into this. |
| $\mathbf{BG}_{empathy}$ | That's sad to hear, we would get you a refund for this. |
| $\mathbf{BG}_{assurance}$ | Don't worry, we will get in touch with the staff and help you with this. |
| **Context** | *Order 2 zinger box meals n got free popcorn chicken, yayyyy* |
| $\mathbf{BG}_{greeting}$ | Hello, good morning!!! Have a nice meal. |
| $\mathbf{BG}_{appreciation}$ | That's nice, hope you have a great meal ahead. |
| $\mathbf{BG}_{assurance}$ | We hope to surprise you again in the future, keep ordering. |
| **Context** | *I need the software update urgently, the battery lasts literally half a day* |
| $\mathbf{BG}_{greeting}$ | Good evening!!! Please DM us the information. |
| $\mathbf{BG}_{apology}$ | We apologize, but we will help you with the updates at the earliest. |
| $\mathbf{BG}_{assurance}$ | We are here to help! Tell us what you need. |
| **Context** | *Had a flight delay yesterday due to less ground staff, got credit points for the delay and free lunch.* |
| $\mathbf{BG}_{greeting}$ | Good evening!!! Have a good flight next time you fly with us. |
| $\mathbf{BG}_{apology}$ | We regret the inconvenience, by the flight delay, we will take better care of you in future. |
| $\mathbf{BG}_{empathy}$ | We are happy you got free food. Let us know if you need to book flights next time. |

Table 4: Examples of polite responses in accordance to the polite behaviour

present a few examples of the generated response. From the table, we see that for a given context there are multiple plausible polite responses in accordance with the behaviour and nature of politeness. Also, the responses are consistent and relevant.

For the first example, "Hey, I got food poisoning from your inflight..." could be responded to in one of the three ways such as the agent could be apologetic about the situation, empathize with the customer or assure the user for a better outcome. In either of the above-mentioned behaviours, politeness is a key component and is well represented in the generated response showcasing the effectiveness of our proposed method. For the last example, "I need the software update urgently, the battery lasts.. ", the agent shows variations in polite behaviour and helps the user with the said problem either by just greeting, apologizing, or assuring the user. From the generated responses, it is clear that polite behaviour is significant for generating relevant, interactive, and better responses.

In addition, from the last example in Table 4, we see that the generator is capable of generating responses capturing the information in the context. This concludes the fact that the proposed approach is not only capable of variating politeness in responses but also inculcates informative knowledge from the context. We also perform an error analysis for the proposed approach to properly evaluate the performance of our approach in comparison to the baselines. Some of the errors encountered by the models are:

**Loss of information:** For a few responses, we see that the generated polite response lacks some of the information presents in the context making the response inconsistent with the ongoing dialogue. For example, the ground-truth response is "*The order from KFC has been taken and will be delivered soon*" while the generated response is "*We will look into this and call the service center.*"

**Polite-behaviour inconsistency:** In some cases, we see that the responses fail to capture the correct polite behaviour and generate responses that are inconsistent with the context. For the context "*The fries were soggy and the burger was stale*" the generated response is "*Thank you for ordering, enjoy your meal.*" The generated response is incorrect as the agent should either be apologizing for the order or assuring the customer that the feedback will be taken care of in the future.

## 6 Conclusion and Future Work

In our current work, we focus on the variations in politeness based on the different behavioural pattern linguistically present in polite phrases such as *greeting*, *apology*, *appreciation*, *assurance* and *empathy*. We design a transformer-based encoder-decoder network with three major components an affective tracker, behaviour-aware generators, and a polite generator to incorporate politeness in responses according to the context. Experimental analysis of the CYCCD dataset shows that the proposed approach effectively infuses the behaviour-wise polite phrases in the responses.

In the future, we intend to use unsupervised techniques to incorporate politeness in responses to create robust end-to-end systems. Also, the usage of politeness is important for goal-oriented conversations, therefore we plan to apply politeness to different domains.

## Limitations

Our paper focuses on incorporating behaviour-aware politeness in responses according to the dialogue context for polite response generation. The primary limitation is the availability of labeled data for modeling the variations in politeness for the different user-related queries. Nevertheless, we employed crowd workers for the data annotation which even though is a time-consuming and costly process yet is the most reliable way of getting the data annotated. Due to the unavailability of the polite behaviour-annotated dataset, we conducted experiments using CYCCD dataset only. In future, we will attempt to extend the experiments to more task-oriented datasets. Also, because of limited computational resources in academia, we weren't able to conduct experiments using LLMs such as GPT2, GPT3, PaLM, LLaMa, etc.

## Acknowledgements

Priyanshu Priya acknowledges the financial support provided by the Department of Science and Technology, Ministry of Science and Technology, Government of India, through the Innovation in Science Pursuit for Inspired Research (INSPIRE) Fellowship.

## References

Jaime Cesar Acosta. 2009. Using emotion to gain rapport in a spoken dialog system.

Russell Beale and Chris Creed. 2009. Affective interaction: How emotional agents affect users. *International journal of human-computer studies*, 67(9):755–776.

Timothy W Bickmore, Laura M Pfeifer, and Brian W Jack. 2009. Taking the time to care: empowering low health literacy hospital patients with virtual nurse agents. In *Proceedings of the SIGCHI conference on human factors in computing systems*, pages 1265–1274.

Timothy W Bickmore and Rosalind W Picard. 2005. Establishing and maintaining long-term human-computer relationships. *ACM Transactions on Computer-Human Interaction (TOCHI)*, 12(2):293–327.

Penelope Brown, Stephen C Levinson, and Stephen C Levinson. 1987. *Politeness: Some universals in language usage*, volume 4. Cambridge university press.

Stanley Chen, Douglas H. Beeferman, and Ronald Rosenfeld. 1998. Evaluation metrics for language models.

Cristian Danescu-Niculescu-Mizil, Moritz Sudhof, Dan Jurafsky, Jure Leskovec, and Christopher Potts. 2013. A computational approach to politeness with application to social factors. *arXiv preprint arXiv:1306.6078*.

Jacob Devlin, Ming-Wei Chang, Kenton Lee, and Kristina Toutanova. 2018. BERT: pre-training of deep bidirectional transformers for language understanding. *Proceedings of the 2019 Conference of the North American Chapter of the Association for Computational Linguistics: Human Language Technologies, NAACL-HLT 2019, Minneapolis, MN, USA, June 2-7, 2019, Volume 1 (Long and Short Papers)*, pages 4171–4186.

Isabel Dias, Ricardo Rei, Patrícia Pereira, and Luisa Coheur. 2022. Towards a sentiment-aware conversational agent. In *Proceedings of the 22nd ACM International Conference on Intelligent Virtual Agents*, pages 1–3.

Nan Duan, Duyu Tang, Peng Chen, and Ming Zhou. 2017. Question generation for question answering. In *Proceedings of the 2017 conference on empirical methods in natural language processing*, pages 866–874.

Bjarke Felbo, Alan Mislove, Anders Søgaard, Iyad Rahwan, and Sune Lehmann. 2017. Using millions of emoji occurrences to learn any-domain representations for detecting sentiment, emotion and sarcasm. In *Conference on Empirical Methods in Natural Language Processing (EMNLP)*.

Julia Fink. 2012. Anthropomorphism and human likeness in the design of robots and human-robot interaction. In *International conference on social robotics*, pages 199–208. Springer.

Mauajama Firdaus, Hardik Chauhan, Asif Ekbal, and Pushpak Bhattacharyya. 2020a. Emosen: Generating sentiment and emotion controlled responses in a multimodal dialogue system. *IEEE Transactions on Affective Computing*, 13(3):1555–1566.

Mauajama Firdaus, Hardik Chauhan, Asif Ekbal, and Pushpak Bhattacharyya. 2020b. Meisd: A multimodal multi-label emotion, intensity and sentiment dialogue dataset for emotion recognition and sentiment analysis in conversations. In *Proceedings of the 28th international conference on computational linguistics*, pages 4441–4453.

Mauajama Firdaus, Hardik Chauhan, Asif Ekbal, and Pushpak Bhattacharyya. 2021a. More the merrier: Towards multi-emotion and intensity controllable response generation. In *Proceedings of the AAAI Conference on Artificial Intelligence*, volume 35, pages 12821–12829.

Mauajama Firdaus, Asif Ekbal, and Pushpak Bhattacharyya. 2020c. Incorporating politeness across languages in customer care responses: Towards building a multi-lingual empathetic dialogue agent. In

*Proceedings of the 12th Language Resources and Evaluation Conference*, pages 4172–4182.

Mauajama Firdaus, Asif Ekbal, and Pushpak Bhattacharyya. 2022a. Polise: Reinforcing politeness using user sentiment for customer care response generation. In *Proceedings of the 29th International Conference on Computational Linguistics*, pages 6165–6175.

Mauajama Firdaus, Umang Jain, Asif Ekbal, and Pushpak Bhattacharyya. 2021b. Seprg: sentiment aware emotion controlled personalized response generation. In *Proceedings of the 14th International Conference on Natural Language Generation*, pages 353–363.

Mauajama Firdaus, Arunav Shandilya, Asif Ekbal, and Pushpak Bhattacharyya. 2022b. Being polite: Modeling politeness variation in a personalized dialog agent. *IEEE Transactions on Computational Social Systems*.

Mauajama Firdaus, Gopendra Vikram Singh, Asif Ekbal, and Pushpak Bhattacharyya. 2023. Affect-gcn: a multimodal graph convolutional network for multiemotion with intensity recognition and sentiment analysis in dialogues. *Multimedia Tools and Applications*, pages 1–22.

Mauajama Firdaus, Nidhi Thakur, and Asif Ekbal. 2022c. Sentiment guided aspect conditioned dialogue generation in a multimodal system. In *European Conference on Information Retrieval*, pages 199–214. Springer.

Mauajama Firdaus, Naveen Thangavelu, Asif Ekba, and Pushpak Bhattacharyya. 2020d. Persona aware response generation with emotions. In *2020 International Joint Conference on Neural Networks (IJCNN)*, pages 1–8. IEEE.

Mauajama Firdaus, Naveen Thangavelu, Asif Ekbal, and Pushpak Bhattacharyya. 2022d. I enjoy writing and playing, do you: A personalized and emotion grounded dialogue agent using generative adversarial network. *IEEE Transactions on Affective Computing*.

Joseph L Fleiss. 1971. Measuring nominal scale agreement among many raters. *Psychological bulletin*, 76(5):378.

Asbjørn Følstad and Marita Skjuve. 2019. Chatbots for customer service: user experience and motivation. In *Proceedings of the 1st international conference on conversational user interfaces*, pages 1–9.

Hitesh Golchha, Mauajama Firdaus, Asif Ekbal, and Pushpak Bhattacharyya. 2019. Courteously yours: inducing courteous behavior in customer care responses using reinforced pointer generator network. In *Proceedings of the 2019 Conference of the North American Chapter of the Association for Computational Linguistics: Human Language Technologies, Volume 1 (Long and Short Papers)*, pages 851–860.

Swati Gupta, Marilyn A Walker, and Daniela M Romano. 2007. How rude are you?: Evaluating politeness and affect in interaction. In *International Conference on Affective Computing and Intelligent Interaction*, pages 203–217. Springer.

Jonathan Herzig, Guy Feigenblat, Michal Shmueli-Scheuer, David Konopnicki, Anat Rafaeli, Daniel Altman, and David Spivak. 2016. Classifying emotions in customer support dialogues in social media. In *SIGDIAL Conference*, pages 64–73.

Sathish Reddy Indurthi, Dinesh Raghu, Mitesh M Khapra, and Sachindra Joshi. 2017. Generating natural language question-answer pairs from a knowledge graph using a rnn based question generation model. In *Proceedings of the 15th Conference of the European Chapter of the Association for Computational Linguistics: Volume 1, Long Papers*, pages 376–385.

Mohit Jain, Pratyush Kumar, Ramachandra Kota, and Shwetak N Patel. 2018. Evaluating and informing the design of chatbots. In *Proceedings of the 2018 designing interactive systems conference*, pages 895–906.

Q Vera Liao, Matthew Davis, Werner Geyer, Michael Muller, and N Sadat Shami. 2016. What can you do? studying social-agent orientation and agent proactive interactions with an agent for employees. In *Proceedings of the 2016 acm conference on designing interactive systems*, pages 264–275.

Chin-Yew Lin. 2004. Rouge: a package for automatic evaluation of summaries.

Aman Madaan, Amrith Setlur, Tanmay Parekh, Barnabas Poczos, Graham Neubig, Yiming Yang, Ruslan Salakhutdinov, Alan W Black, and Shrimai Prabhumoye. 2020. Politeness transfer: A tag and generate approach. *arXiv preprint arXiv:2004.14257*.

Avinash Madasu, Mauajama Firdaus, and Asif Eqbal. 2022. A unified framework for emotion identification and generation in dialogues. *arXiv preprint arXiv:2205.15513*.

Abraham Harold Maslow. 1943. A theory of human motivation. *Psychological review*, 50(4):370.

Mary L McHugh. 2012. Interrater reliability: The kappa statistic. *Biochemia medica: Biochemia medica*, 22(3):276–282.

Alexander Miller, Adam Fisch, Jesse Dodge, Amir-Hossein Karimi, Antoine Bordes, and Jason Weston. 2016. Key-value memory networks for directly reading documents. *arXiv preprint arXiv:1606.03126*.

Kshitij Mishra, Mauajama Firdaus, and Asif Ekbal. 2022a. Please be polite: Towards building a politeness adaptive dialogue system for goal-oriented conversations. *Neurocomputing*, 494:242–254.

Kshitij Mishra, Mauajama Firdaus, and Asif Ekbal. 2022b. Predicting politeness variations in goal-oriented conversations. *IEEE Transactions on Computational Social Systems*.

Kshitij Mishra, Mauajama Firdaus, and Asif Ekbal. 2023a. Genpads: Reinforcing politeness in an end-to-end dialogue system. *Plos one*, 18(1):e0278323.

Kshitij Mishra, Priyanshu Priya, and Asif Ekbal. 2023b. Help me heal: A reinforced polite and empathetic mental health and legal counseling dialogue system for crime victims. In *Proceedings of the AAAI Conference on Artificial Intelligence*, volume 37, pages 14408–14416.

Kshitij Mishra, Priyanshu Priya, and Asif Ekbal. 2023c. Pal to lend a helping hand: Towards building an emotion adaptive polite and empathetic counseling conversational agent. In *Proceedings of the 61st Annual Meeting of the Association for Computational Linguistics (Volume 1: Long Papers)*, pages 12254–12271.

Tong Niu and Mohit Bansal. 2018a. Polite dialogue generation without parallel data. *Transactions of the Association for Computational Linguistics*, 6:373–389.

Tong Niu and Mohit Bansal. 2018b. Polite dialogue generation without parallel data. *TACL*, 6:373–389.

Kishore Papineni, Salim Roukos, Todd Ward, and Wei-Jing Zhu. 2002. Bleu: a method for automatic evaluation of machine translation. In *Proceedings of the 40th Annual Meeting of the Association for Computational Linguistics, July 6-12, 2002, Philadelphia, PA, USA*, pages 311–318. Association for Computational Linguistics.

Jeffrey Pennington, Richard Socher, and Christopher Manning. 2014. Glove: Global vectors for word representation. In *Proceedings of the 2014 Conference on Empirical Methods in Natural Language Processing, EMNLP 2014, October 25-29, 2014, Doha, Qatar, A meeting of SIGDAT, a Special Interest Group of the ACL*, pages 1532–1543.

Johannes Pittermann, Angela Pittermann, and Wolfgang Minker. 2010. Emotion recognition and adaptation in spoken dialogue systems. *International Journal of Speech Technology*, 13(1):49–60.

Priyanshu Priya, Mauajama Firdaus, and Asif Ekbal. 2023a. A multi-task learning framework for politeness and emotion detection in dialogues for mental health counselling and legal aid. *Expert Systems with Applications*, 224:120025.

Priyanshu Priya, Kshitij Mishra, Palak Totala, and Asif Ekbal. 2023b. Partner: A persuasive mental health and legal counselling dialogue system for women and children crime victims. In *Proceedings of the Thirty-Second International Joint Conference on Artificial Intelligence, IJCAI-23*, pages 6183–6191. International Joint Conferences on Artificial Intelligence Organization. AI for Good.

Sashank J Reddi, Satyen Kale, and Sanjiv Kumar. 2019. On the convergence of adam and beyond. *6th International Conference on Learning Representations, ICLR 2018, Vancouver, BC, Canada, April 30 - May 3, 2018, Conference Track Proceedings*.

Azlaan Mustafa Samad, Kshitij Mishra, Mauajama Firdaus, and Asif Ekbal. 2022. Empathetic persuasion: reinforcing empathy and persuasiveness in dialogue systems. In *Findings of the Association for Computational Linguistics: NAACL 2022*, pages 844–856.

Iulian V Serban, Alessandro Sordoni, Yoshua Bengio, Aaron Courville, and Joelle Pineau. 2015. Hierarchical neural network generative models for movie dialogues. *arXiv preprint arXiv:1507.04808*, 7(8):434–441.

Xiaoyu Shen, Hui Su, Shuzi Niu, and Vera Demberg. 2018. Improving variational encoder-decoders in dialogue generation. In *Proceedings of the AAAI conference on artificial intelligence*, volume 32.

Weiyan Shi and Zhou Yu. 2018. Sentiment adaptive end-to-end dialog systems. *arXiv preprint arXiv:1804.10731*.

Gopendra Vikram Singh, Mauajama Firdaus, Asif Ekbal, and Pushpak Bhattacharyya. 2022. Emoint-trans: A multimodal transformer for identifying emotions and intents in social conversations. *IEEE/ACM Transactions on Audio, Speech, and Language Processing*, 31:290–300.

Ilya Sutskever, Oriol Vinyals, and Quoc V Le. 2014. Sequence to sequence learning with neural networks. In *Advances in neural information processing systems*, pages 3104–3112.

Zhiliang Tian, Wei Bi, Xiaopeng Li, and Nevin L Zhang. 2019. Learning to abstract for memory-augmented conversational response generation. In *Proceedings of the 57th Conference of the Association for Computational Linguistics, ACL 2019, Florence, Italy, July 28- August 2, 2019, Volume 1: Long Papers*, pages 3816–3825.

Ashish Vaswani, Noam Shazeer, Niki Parmar, Jakob Uszkoreit, Llion Jones, Aidan N Gomez, Łukasz Kaiser, and Illia Polosukhin. 2017. Attention is all you need. In *Advances in neural information processing systems*, pages 5998–6008.

Jiancheng Wang, Jingjing Wang, Changlong Sun, Shoushan Li, Xiaozhong Liu, Luo Si, Min Zhang, and Guodong Zhou. 2020a. Sentiment classification in customer service dialogue with topic-aware multi-task learning. In *Proceedings of the AAAI Conference on Artificial Intelligence*, volume 34, pages 9177–9184.

Yi-Chia Wang, Alexandros Papangelis, Runze Wang, Zhaleh Feizollahi, Gokhan Tur, and Robert Kraut. 2020b. Can you be more social? injecting politeness and positivity into task-oriented conversational agents. *arXiv preprint arXiv:2012.14653*.

Hainan Zhang, Yanyan Lan, Jiafeng Guo, Jun Xu, and Xueqi Cheng. 2018. Reinforcing coherence for sequence to sequence model in dialogue generation. In *IJCAI*, pages 4567–4573.

# Few-Shot Adaptation for Parsing Contextual Utterances with LLMs

**Kevin Lin** [†*] **Patrick Xia** [‡] **Hao Fang** [‡]
[†] UC Berkeley [‡] Microsoft Semantic Machines
k-lin@berkeley.edu {patrickxia, hao.fang}@microsoft.com

## Abstract

We evaluate the ability of semantic parsers based on large language models (LLMs) to handle contextual utterances. In real-world settings, there typically exists only a limited number of annotated contextual utterances due to annotation cost, resulting in an imbalance compared to non-contextual utterances. Therefore, parsers must adapt to contextual utterances with a few training examples. We examine four major paradigms for doing so in conversational semantic parsing *i.e.,* Parse-with-Utterance-History, Parse-with-Reference-Program, Parse-then-Resolve, and Rewrite-then-Parse. To facilitate such cross-paradigm comparisons, we construct *SMCalFlow-EventQueries*, a subset of contextual examples from SMCalFlow with additional annotations. Experiments with in-context learning and fine-tuning suggest that Rewrite-then-Parse is the most promising paradigm when holistically considering parsing accuracy, annotation cost, and error types.

## 1 Introduction

A key challenge in conversational semantic parsing (CSP) is handling *contextual* utterances (*i.e.,* utterances that can only be understood with its context) by mapping them to *non-contextual* programs that can be fulfilled by an executor without relying on the dialogue state. Many approaches have been proposed, *e.g.,* directly mapping the contextual utterance with utterance history to a non-contextual program (Suhr et al., 2018), or mapping to an intermediate contextual program which is then resolved (usually in a deterministic manner) to a non-contextual program (Semantic Machines et al., 2020; Cheng et al., 2020). In these prior works, there is often an assumption of having a substantial corpus of annotated data encompassing both non-contextual utterances and contextual utterances for training a parser. However, in practice, it is more expensive to collect and annotate contextual utterances compared to non-contextual utterances, due to the dependency on the conversation history. Furthermore, annotating non-contextual utterances usually precedes annotating contextual utterances. To reflect such real-world settings, we study few-shot adaptation for parsing contextual utterances, where we first build a parser using a large number of annotated non-contextual utterances, and then adapt it for parsing contextual utterances using a few (or even zero) annotated contextual utterances.

Recent work has shown that large language models (LLMs) are capable of semantic parsing using a few examples (Shin et al., 2021; Shin and Van Durme, 2022). Hence, in this work, we conduct a focused study on few-shot adaptation using LLMs for CSP. Specifically, we consider four major paradigms: Parse-with-Utterance-History, Parse-with-Reference-Program, Parse-then-Resolve, and Rewrite-then-Parse. One challenge of carrying out a comparative study on these paradigms is the lack of annotated data, since existing CSP datasets such as SMCalFlow (Semantic Machines et al., 2020) and CoSQL (Yu et al., 2019) are often annotated based on a single paradigm. Therefore, we construct a new dataset, *SMCalFlow-EQ*, derived from a subset of SMCalFlow dialogues with annotations for all four paradigms.

Our experiments consider both in-context learning (ICL) using GPT-3.5 and fine-tuning (FT) using T5-base 220M (Raffel et al., 2020) for building and adapting parsers. ICL typically has lower accuracy compared to FT, although the two are not strictly comparable as they use different models. The only exception is Parse-with-Reference-Program, suggesting that GPT-3.5 is effective at editing programs using natural language. Overall, we find Rewrite-then-Parse to be the most promising approach, as it achieves similar accuracy to other paradigms in both ICL and FT experiments, while requiring only a few annotated examples for to de-

[*] Work done at Microsoft Semantic Machines.



*Findings of the Association for Computational Linguistics: IJCNLP-AACL 2023*, pages 348–360
November 1–4, 2023. 

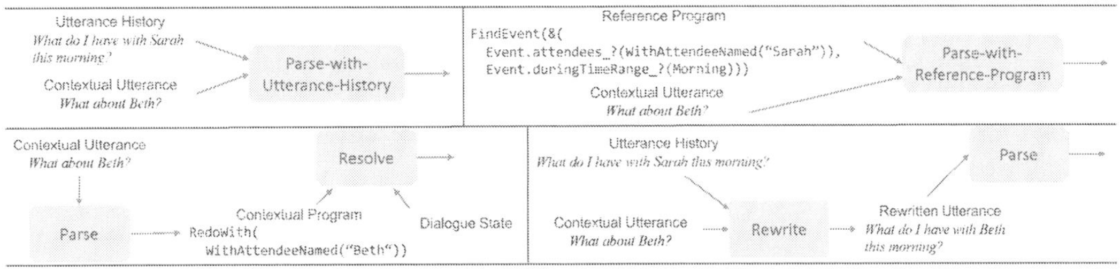


Figure 1: Four canonical paradigms of conversational semantic parsing for contextual utterances.

velop a query rewriter and no additional program annotations. We release code and data to facilitate future work on parsing contextual utterances.[1]

## 2 Background: LLM-Based Parsing

Following Shin et al. (2021) and Roy et al. (2022), we formulate parsing as a constrained decoding problem, where an LLM is used to predict the next token and a context-free grammar (CFG) is used to validate the predicted token. A program is represented as a sequence of S-expression tokens $y_1 y_2 \dots y_L$. The space of all valid S-expressions is governed by a CFG denoted by $\mathcal{G}$, which can be automatically derived from function definitions and types used in the domain (see Appendix A).

To generate the program for a user utterance, we first feed the LLM with the user utterance and necessary context information as a sequence of tokens. Then the S-expression of the program is generated incrementally. At each decoding step $l$, we only keep the partial prefix sequence $y_1 y_2 \dots y_l$ if it is allowed by $\mathcal{G}$. This validation can be efficiently performed via Earley's parsing algorithm (Earley, 1970) using the parsing state of the partial sequence $y_1 y_2 \cdots y_{l-1}$.

In this paper, we consider both ICL and FT for constructing LLM-based parsers. For ICL, we prompt the pre-trained LLM with $K_{\text{ICL}}$ demonstration examples retrieved via BM25 (Robertson and Walker, 1994; Robertson and Zaragoza, 2009), following Rubin et al. (2022) and Roy et al. (2022). For FT, we continue training the LLM on $K_{\text{FT}}$ demonstration examples, producing a new model to be used during constrained decoding.

## 3 Few-Shot Adaptation

In this paper, we assume there are a large number ($M$) of annotated non-contextual utterances, $\mathcal{D} = \{(\boldsymbol{x}^{(1)}, \boldsymbol{y}^{(1)}), \dots, (\boldsymbol{x}^{(M)}, \boldsymbol{y}^{(M)})\}$, where $\boldsymbol{x}^{(i)}$ denotes the $i$-th non-contextual utterance in the dataset, $\boldsymbol{y}^{(i)}$ is the corresponding non-contextual program, and $M$ is the number of annotated examples. These examples are used to derive a grammar $\mathcal{G}_1$ and build the parser $\mathcal{P}_1$ for non-contextual utterances via either ICL or FT.

For a contextual utterance $\boldsymbol{u}_t$ at the $t$-th turn of a dialogue, the goal is to obtain the non-contextual program $\boldsymbol{y}_t$ using the *utterance history* $\boldsymbol{h}_t = [\boldsymbol{u}_{<t}]$, the corresponding programs $\boldsymbol{y}_{<t}$, and/or other information recorded in the dialogue state. Figure 1 illustrates four canonical paradigms for parsing contextual utterances. For each of these paradigms, we would like to obtain a new parser by adapting from the base parser $\mathcal{P}_1$ using $N$ demonstration examples, where $N \ll M$.

### 3.1 Parsing Paradigms

**Parse-with-Utterance-History**: In this paradigm, the parser directly predicts $\boldsymbol{y}_t$ by conditioning on the contextual utterance $\boldsymbol{u}_t$ and its history $\boldsymbol{h}_t$. This paradigm has been used in contextual semantic parsing (Zettlemoyer and Collins, 2009; Suhr et al., 2018) and belief state tracking (Mrkšić et al., 2017).

**Parse-with-Reference-Program**: This paradigm assumes that the salient additional context to parse $\boldsymbol{u}_t$ is captured by a *reference program*, which is a non-contextual program to be revised and typically that from the preceding turn, $\boldsymbol{y}_{t-1}$. The parsing process can be viewed as editing the reference program based on the contextual utterance which directly yields $\boldsymbol{y}_t$. Zhang et al. (2019) employs a similar strategy by using a copy operation during parsing to copy tokens from the reference program for text-to-SQL.

**Parse-then-Resolve**: This paradigm divides the task into two steps, leading to a modularized system with a parser followed by a resolver. $\boldsymbol{u}_t$ is first mapped to an intermediate program $\tilde{\boldsymbol{y}}_t$ which contains specialized contextual symbols. These contex-

[1] https://github.com/microsoft/few_shot_adaptation_for_parsing_contextual_utterances_with_llms

tual symbols (marking ellipsis or coreference) are resolved deterministically using the dialogue state determined from $\boldsymbol{y}_{<t}$, resulting in the final non-contextual prediction $\boldsymbol{y}_t$. Several recent datasets for CSP have adopted this paradigm (Semantic Machines et al., 2020; Cheng et al., 2020).

**Rewrite-then-Parse**: This paradigm modularizes the system using a rewriter followed by a parser. The history $\boldsymbol{h}_t$ and contextual utterance $\boldsymbol{u}_t$ are first rewritten into a single non-contextual utterance $\boldsymbol{u}'_t$ Then, $\boldsymbol{u}'_t$ is parsed to $\boldsymbol{y}_t$ by a single-turn semantic parser. This paradigm is closely related to incomplete utterance rewriting (Liu et al., 2020) and conversational query rewriting (Rastogi et al., 2019; Yu et al., 2020; Chen et al., 2020; Song et al., 2020; Inoue et al., 2022; Mao et al., 2023) though the parsing step is usually unnecessary or overlooked in these related studies. Using this paradigm, the rewriter and the parser can be independently developed and maintained.

### 3.2 Adaptation via ICL

For ICL, we use GPT-3.5 and the following prompt template provided by Shin et al. (2021) and Roy et al. (2022), where placeholders {X1}, {X2}, ... are demonstrations input, {Y1}, {Y2}, ... are demonstrations output, and {X′} is the test input.

```
Let's translate what a human user says into what
a computer might say.

Human: {X1}
Computer: {Y1}

Human: {X2}
Computer: {Y2}

...

Human: {X'}
Computer:
```

For Parse-with-Utterance-History, Parse-with-Reference-Program, and Parse-then-Resolve, the input placeholders are respectively instantiated as $\boldsymbol{h} \mid \boldsymbol{u}$, $\boldsymbol{r} \mid \boldsymbol{u}$, and $\boldsymbol{u}$, where the character | is used as the separator. The output placeholders are all instantiated by non-contextual programs $\boldsymbol{y}$, except for Parse-then-Resolve which uses $\tilde{\boldsymbol{y}}$ instead. The test input placeholder follows the same form as demonstration input placeholders. New CFG rules are derived from the program annotations of contextual utterances, *i.e.*, $\tilde{\boldsymbol{y}}$ and $\boldsymbol{y}$, yielding two new grammars $\mathcal{G}_\alpha$ and $\mathcal{G}_\beta$, respectively. During constrained decoding, the joint grammar $\mathcal{G}_1 \cup \mathcal{G}_\alpha$ is used for Parse-then-Resolve, whereas $\mathcal{G}_1 \cup \mathcal{G}_\beta$ is used for the other three paradigms. In other words, the adaptation only changes the set of demonstration examples used during prompt instantiation and augments the CFG used during constrained decoding.

For Rewrite-then-Parse, we can re-use the same grammar $\mathcal{G}_1$ and parser $\mathcal{P}_1$ used for non-contextual utterances, without any annotated programs for contextual utterances.

### 3.3 Adaptation via FT

For FT, the parser $\mathcal{P}_1$ for non-contextual utterances uses an LLM $\mathcal{M}_1$ fine-tuned from T5-base 220M (Raffel et al., 2020). To adapt this parser for contextual utterances, we continue fine-tuning $\mathcal{M}_1$ on annotated contextual utterances, except for Rewrite-then-Parse which uses $\mathcal{P}_1$ itself. Similar to ICL, different forms of token sequences are used for different paradigms, *i.e.*, $\boldsymbol{h} \mid \boldsymbol{u} \mid \boldsymbol{y}$ for Parse-with-Utterance-History, $\boldsymbol{r} \mid \boldsymbol{u} \mid \boldsymbol{y}$ for Parse-with-Utterance-History, and $\boldsymbol{u} \mid \tilde{\boldsymbol{y}}$ for Parse-then-Resolve. The new grammar is constructed identically to ICL as well.

### 3.4 Data Annotation Effort

An important axis when comparing different parsing paradigms is the data annotation effort. For Parse-with-Utterance-History, annotating the non-contextual program for a contextual utterance can be a cognitively demanding task, as it needs to account for the full utterance history. Data annotation for Parse-with-Reference paradigm is similar to the Parse-with-Utterance-History, though it may be less cognitively intensive because the human annotator only needs to make a a few edits as opposed to performing a full parse. Compared with Parse-with-Utterance-History, annotations of intermediate programs in the Parse-then-Resolve paradigm are much less context-dependent and more concise, which potentially makes the parser more data efficient. However, this comes at a cost of placing a greater burden on the resolver, which uses custom-designed contextual symbols based on the domain; their expressiveness can greatly affect the quality of the annotations and the complexity of the resolver. Finally, collecting annotations for the the utterance rewriting task is relatively easy and domain independent compared to collecting annotations for parsers which often requires learning a domain-specific language.

## 4 Experiments

### 4.1 Data

Existing CSP datasets are often annotated based on only one or two paradigms, making it difficult to compare across different paradigms comprehensively. To address this challenge, we construct a dataset *SMCalFlow-EventQueries* (*SMCalFlow-EQ*) derived from a subset of SMCalFlow (Semantic Machines et al., 2020). It contains 31 training and 100 test instances in total. Each instance consists of a contextual user utterance $\boldsymbol{u}$ during an event-related query (*e.g.*, "*what about Tuesday?*"), the corresponding contextual/intermediate program $\tilde{\boldsymbol{y}}$ and non-contextual program $\boldsymbol{y}$, the utterance history $\boldsymbol{h}$, the reference program $\boldsymbol{r}$, and the rewritten non-contextual utterance $\boldsymbol{u}'$. The programs ($\boldsymbol{y}$, $\tilde{\boldsymbol{y}}$, $\boldsymbol{r}$) are semi-automatically derived from the original SMCalFlow annotations. The rewritten non-contextual utterances $\boldsymbol{u}'$ are manually annotated by domain experts. See Appendix B for details of the dataset construction and examples.

We additionally use 8892 training and 100 test instances of non-contextual utterances (*e.g.*, "*do I have any meetings scheduled after Thursday?*"), each paired with their corresponding non-contextual programs, semi-automatically derived from SMCalFlow as well. These instances are used to construct and evaluate the base parser $\mathcal{P}_1$ for non-contextual utterances.

### 4.2 Experimental Results

For Parse-with-Reference-Program, we use the oracle reference program, which is the non-contextual program of the preceding turn.[2] For Parse-then-Resolve, we assume an oracle resolver is available, which in practice can be implemented as a rule-based system. The rewriter used for Rewrite-then-Parse is implemented via GPT-3.5, and details are provided in Appendix D. We also consider using the oracle rewritten utterances annotated in the contextual subset of *SMCalFlow-EQ*.

We evaluate the program exact match accuracy on the *SMCalFlow-EQ* test set for all paradigms. Table 1 presents the experimental results. Across all paradigms, FT achieves higher exact match than ICL by 7.9% to 29.4% absolute gain. For FT, Rewrite-then-Parse with oracle rewritten utterances performs the best. There is no significant difference

[2]It is possible that the reference program is from an earlier turn or does not appear in the history, though the contextual subset does not contain such examples.

| Paradigm | ICL | FT |
|---|---|---|
| Parse-with-Utterance-History | 51.8 | 81.2 |
| Parse-with-Reference-Program | 86.1* | 78.2 |
| Parse-then-Resolve | 70.5* | 82.4 |
| Rewrite-then-Parse | 65.3* | 75.2 |
| Rewrite-then-Parse (oracle) | 76.2* | 94.0* |

Table 1: Exact match accuracy on *SMCalFlow-EQ* test set. For both ICL and FT, we test each paradigm against the corresponding Parse-with-Utterance-History predictions using McNemar's test and show statistically significant ($p < 0.05$) results with *.

among other approaches, including Rewrite-then-Parse using the GPT-3.5 rewriter which does not require additional fine-tuning. For ICL, Parse-with-Reference-Program performs the best, suggesting it is easier for GPT-3.5 to softly edit a program than parsing directly from natural language. Rewrite-then-Parse using oracle rewritten utterances is still better than the remaining approaches. By comparing the results of Rewrite-then-Parse, it is clear that improving the rewriter can lead to a corresponding improvement in parsing accuracy.

We manually examine incorrect predictions made by parsers for contextual utterances and identify common error categories: incorrect top-level program types, alternative parses for the input, extra constraints, missing constraints, and constraints with incorrect arguments/functions (see Table A5 for examples).

For ICL, the most common error type is incorrect function calls. 30% of the errors made by Parse-with-Reference-Program are due to incorrect function use. In particular, the model struggles with predicting rare functions such as negations, potentially because the only knowledge of the target language is from the contextual subset of *SMCalFlow-EQ*.

For FT, 33% of the errors in Parse-then-Resolve are from incorrect top-level program types. Introducing new symbols increases the program space, especially different intermediate programs that have similar functions, suggesting that the design of these specialized contextual symbols is crucial. For Parse-with-Utterance-History, we find that 40% of the errors come from missing constraints, indicating that jointly learn parsing and consolidating constraints from multiple turns is challenging for the parsing model. For Rewrite-then-Parse, 55% of the errors are due to incorrect arguments, and 45% are due to differences in capitalization (*e.g.*, the

| Paradigm | ICL | FT |
|---|---|---|
| Parse-with-Utterance-History | 63.5 | 84.5 |
| Parse-with-Reference-Program | 79.5* | 83.0 |
| Parse-then-Resolve | 73.5* | 85.5 |
| Rewrite-then-Parse | 69.5* | 82.0 |
| Rewrite-then-Parse (oracle) | 75.0* | 90.5* |

Table 2: Exact match accuracy on *SMCalFlow-EQ* test set combined with non-contextual utterances. For both ICL and FT, we test each paradigm against the corresponding Parse-with-Utterance-History predictions using McNemar's test and show statistically significant ($p < 0.05$) results indicated with $^\star$.

rewriter converts a lowercase name to uppercase) which is arguably less critical.

We also examine the overall parsing accuracy on the joint test set of contextual and non-contextual utterances. We use a binary classifier which takes the user utterance as input and determines whether to use the parser for non-contextual utterances or the parser for contextual utterances. The classifier is obtained by fine-tuning the RoBERTa-base (Liu et al., 2019) to on *SMCalFlow-EQ* utterances. The overall classification accuracy is 95.5%. The results are summarized in Table 2. We use exact match accuracy as the evaluation metric, where the prediction is treated as correct only when classification and parsing are both correct.

## 5 Conclusion

We study a real-world CSP setting, *i.e.,* few-shot adaptation for parsing contextual utterances with LLMs, and compare four different paradigms using both ICL and FT. To facilitate the study, we construct a new dataset, *SMCalFlow-EQ* with annotations for all paradigms. Experiments show that ICL with GPT-3.5 usually underperforms FT with T5-base except for Parse-with-Reference-Program, suggesting GPT-3.5 is good at editing programs via natural language in these data conditions. Overall, Rewrite-then-Parse stands out as a promising approach for future development of LLM-based CSP, as it performs as well as other paradigms but require only a few annotated exampels for the rewriter and no additional program annotation.

## 6 Limitations

Due to the cost of collecting program annotations for all paradigms, the size of the *SMCalFlow-EQ* test set is relatively small and we only study dialogues from SMCalFlow. While the experiments results are informative under significance test, it would be useful for future work to conduct a similar study on larger and diverse datasets.

The LLMs used in this work are pre-trained primarily on English, and the *SMCalFlow-EQ* also only contains English utterances. It would be interesting to study the few-shot adaptation problem on other languages.

## Acknowledgements

We would like to thank Benjamin Van Durme, Matt Gardner, Adam Pauls, and Jason Wolfe for valuable discussions on this paper.

## References

Zheng Chen, Xing Fan, and Yuan Ling. 2020. Pre-training for query rewriting in a spoken language understanding system. In *Proceedings of 2020 IEEE International Conference on Acoustics, Speech and Signal Processing (ICASSP)*, pages 7969–7973.

Jianpeng Cheng, Devang Agrawal, Héctor Martínez Alonso, Shruti Bhargava, Joris Driesen, Federico Flego, Dain Kaplan, Dimitri Kartsaklis, Lin Li, Dhivya Piraviperumal, Jason D. Williams, Hong Yu, Diarmuid Ó Séaghdha, and Anders Johannsen. 2020. Conversational semantic parsing for dialog state tracking. In *Proceedings of the 2020 Conference on Empirical Methods in Natural Language Processing (EMNLP)*, pages 8107–8117, Online. Association for Computational Linguistics.

Jay Earley. 1970. An efficient context-free parsing algorithm. *Communications of the ACM*, 13(2):94–102.

Jeremy Howard and Sebastian Ruder. 2018. Universal language model fine-tuning for text classification. In *Proceedings of the 56th Annual Meeting of the Association for Computational Linguistics (Volume 1: Long Papers)*, pages 328–339, Melbourne, Australia. Association for Computational Linguistics.

Shumpei Inoue, Tsungwei Liu, Son Nguyen, and Minh-Tien Nguyen. 2022. Enhance incomplete utterance restoration by joint learning token extraction and text generation. In *Proceedings of the 2022 Conference of the North American Chapter of the Association for Computational Linguistics: Human Language Technologies*, pages 3149–3158, Seattle, United States. Association for Computational Linguistics.

Qian Liu, Bei Chen, Jian-Guang Lou, Bin Zhou, and Dongmei Zhang. 2020. Incomplete utterance rewriting as semantic segmentation. In *Proceedings of the 2020 Conference on Empirical Methods in Natural Language Processing (EMNLP)*, pages 2846–2857, Online. Association for Computational Linguistics.

Yinhan Liu, Myle Ott, Naman Goyal, Jingfei Du, Mandar Joshi, Danqi Chen, Omer Levy, Mike Lewis, Luke Zettlemoyer, and Veselin Stoyanov. 2019. RoBERTa: A robustly optimized BERT pretraining approach. *arXiv:1907.11692*.

Kelong Mao, Zhicheng Dou, Haonan Chen, Fengran Mo, and Hongjin Qian. 2023. Large language models know your contextual search intent: A prompting framework for conversational search. *arXiv:2303.06573*.

Joram Meron. 2022. Simplifying semantic annotations of SMCalFlow. In *Proceedings of the 18th Joint ACL - ISO Workshop on Interoperable Semantic Annotation within LREC2022*, pages 81–85, Marseille, France. European Language Resources Association.

Nikola Mrkšić, Diarmuid Ó Séaghdha, Tsung-Hsien Wen, Blaise Thomson, and Steve Young. 2017. Neural belief tracker: Data-driven dialogue state tracking. In *Proceedings of the 55th Annual Meeting of the Association for Computational Linguistics (Volume 1: Long Papers)*, pages 1777–1788, Vancouver, Canada. Association for Computational Linguistics.

Colin Raffel, Noam Shazeer, Adam Roberts, Katherine Lee, Sharan Narang, Michael Matena, Yanqi Zhou, Wei Li, and Peter J Liu. 2020. Exploring the limits of transfer learning with a unified text-to-text transformer. *The Journal of Machine Learning Research*, 21(1):5485–5551.

Pushpendre Rastogi, Arpit Gupta, Tongfei Chen, and Mathias Lambert. 2019. Scaling multi-domain dialogue state tracking via query reformulation. In *Proceedings of the 2019 Conference of the North American Chapter of the Association for Computational Linguistics: Human Language Technologies, Volume 2 (Industry Papers)*, pages 97–105, Minneapolis, Minnesota. Association for Computational Linguistics.

Stephen Robertson and Hugo Zaragoza. 2009. The probabilistic relevance framework: BM25 and beyond. *Foundations and Trends in Information Retrieval*, 3(4):333–389.

Stephen E. Robertson and Stephen Walker. 1994. Some simple effective approximations to the 2-Poisson model for probabilistic weighted retrieval. In *Proceedings of the 17th Annual International ACM SIGIR Conference on Research and Development in Information Retrieval*, pages 232–241, Dublin, Ireland.

Subhro Roy, Sam Thomson, Tongfei Chen, Richard Shin, Adam Pauls, Jason Eisner, and Benjamin Van Durme. 2022. BenchCLAMP: A benchmark for evaluating language models on semantic parsing. *arXiv:2206.10668*.

Ohad Rubin, Jonathan Herzig, and Jonathan Berant. 2022. Learning to retrieve prompts for in-context learning. In *Proceedings of the 2022 Conference of the North American Chapter of the Association for Computational Linguistics: Human Language Technologies*, pages 2655–2671, Seattle, United States. Association for Computational Linguistics.

Semantic Machines, Jacob Andreas, John Bufe, David Burkett, Charles Chen, Josh Clausman, Jean Crawford, Kate Crim, Jordan DeLoach, Leah Dorner, Jason Eisner, Hao Fang, Alan Guo, David Hall, Kristin Hayes, Kellie Hill, Diana Ho, Wendy Iwaszuk, Smriti Jha, Dan Klein, Jayant Krishnamurthy, Theo Lanman, Percy Liang, Christopher H. Lin, Ilya Lintsbakh, Andy McGovern, Aleksandr Nisnevich, Adam Pauls, Dmitrij Petters, Brent Read, Dan Roth, Subhro Roy, Jesse Rusak, Beth Short, Div Slomin, Ben Snyder, Stephon Striplin, Yu Su, Zachary Tellman, Sam Thomson, Andrei Vorobev, Izabela Witoszko, Jason Wolfe, Abby Wray, Yuchen Zhang, and Alexander Zotov. 2020. Task-oriented dialogue as dataflow synthesis. *Transactions of the Association for Computational Linguistics*, 8:556–571.

Noam Shazeer and Mitchell Stern. 2018. Adafactor: Adaptive learning rates with sublinear memory cost. In *International Conference on Machine Learning*, pages 4596–4604. PMLR.

Richard Shin, Christopher Lin, Sam Thomson, Charles Chen, Subhro Roy, Emmanouil Antonios Platanios, Adam Pauls, Dan Klein, Jason Eisner, and Benjamin Van Durme. 2021. Constrained language models yield few-shot semantic parsers. In *Proceedings of the 2021 Conference on Empirical Methods in Natural Language Processing*, pages 7699–7715, Online and Punta Cana, Dominican Republic. Association for Computational Linguistics.

Richard Shin and Benjamin Van Durme. 2022. Few-shot semantic parsing with language models trained on code. In *Proceedings of the 2022 Conference of the North American Chapter of the Association for Computational Linguistics: Human Language Technologies*, pages 5417–5425, Seattle, United States. Association for Computational Linguistics.

Shuangyong Song, Chao Wang, Qianqian Xie, Xinxing Zu, Huan Chen, and Haiqing Chen. 2020. A two-stage conversational query rewriting model with multi-task learning. In *Companion Proceedings of the Web Conference 2020*, WWW '20, page 6–7, New York, NY, USA. Association for Computing Machinery.

Alane Suhr, Srinivasan Iyer, and Yoav Artzi. 2018. Learning to map context-dependent sentences to executable formal queries. In *Proceedings of the 2018 Conference of the North American Chapter of the Association for Computational Linguistics: Human Language Technologies, Volume 1 (Long Papers)*, pages 2238–2249, New Orleans, Louisiana. Association for Computational Linguistics.

Shi Yu, Jiahua Liu, Jingqin Yang, Chenyan Xiong, Paul Bennett, Jianfeng Gao, and Zhiyuan Liu. 2020. Few-shot generative conversational query rewriting. In

*Proceedings of the 43rd International ACM SIGIR Conference on Research and Development in Information Retrieval*, SIGIR '20, page 1933–1936, New York, NY, USA.

Tao Yu, Rui Zhang, Heyang Er, Suyi Li, Eric Xue, Bo Pang, Xi Victoria Lin, Yi Chern Tan, Tianze Shi, Zihan Li, Youxuan Jiang, Michihiro Yasunaga, Sungrok Shim, Tao Chen, Alexander Fabbri, Zifan Li, Luyao Chen, Yuwen Zhang, Shreya Dixit, Vincent Zhang, Caiming Xiong, Richard Socher, Walter Lasecki, and Dragomir Radev. 2019. CoSQL: A conversational text-to-SQL challenge towards cross-domain natural language interfaces to databases. In *Proceedings of the 2019 Conference on Empirical Methods in Natural Language Processing and the 9th International Joint Conference on Natural Language Processing (EMNLP-IJCNLP)*, pages 1962–1979, Hong Kong, China. Association for Computational Linguistics.

Luke Zettlemoyer and Michael Collins. 2009. Learning context-dependent mappings from sentences to logical form. In *Proceedings of the Joint Conference of the 47th Annual Meeting of the ACL and the 4th International Joint Conference on Natural Language Processing of the AFNLP*, pages 976–984, Suntec, Singapore. Association for Computational Linguistics.

Rui Zhang, Tao Yu, Heyang Er, Sungrok Shim, Eric Xue, Xi Victoria Lin, Tianze Shi, Caiming Xiong, Richard Socher, and Dragomir Radev. 2019. Editing-based SQL query generation for cross-domain context-dependent questions. In *Proceedings of the 2019 Conference on Empirical Methods in Natural Language Processing and the 9th International Joint Conference on Natural Language Processing (EMNLP-IJCNLP)*, pages 5338–5349, Hong Kong, China. Association for Computational Linguistics.

## A CFG for Constrained Decoding

The CFG used for constrained decoding can be automatically derived from function definitions and types used in the domain. For example, given a function FN($\arg_1, \cdots, \arg_N$) with corresponding argument types $\tau_1, \cdots, \tau_N$ and output type $\tau_O$, we can automatically derive a CFG rule $\mathrm{NT}_{\tau_O} \rightarrow$ ( FN ( $\mathrm{NT}_{\tau_1} \cdots \mathrm{NT}_{\tau_N}$ ) ) where $\mathrm{NT}_{\tau_i}$ denotes the non-terminal symbol for the type $\tau_i$, and the function name FN and the parentheses are terminal symbols in $\mathcal{G}$. For each primitive type (*e.g.*, "string", "number"), we additionally define CFG rules to expand the non-terminal of the primitive type to terminals representing acceptable values of the type (sometimes using regular expressions).

## B Dataset Construction and Examples

The original SMCalFlow data only provide annotations of *contextual programs* for individual utterances. We develop a heuristic-based implementation of `NewClobber` and `ReviseConstraint` to propose candidates of the corresponding non-contextual programs. Specifically, given the non-contextual program

```
(NewClobber (
    (intension)
    (slotConstraint)
    (value)))
```

we modify the non-contextual program of the preceding turn by replacing its fragment satisfying the `slotConstraint` with the new fragment `value`. Similarly, given the non-contextual program

```
(ReviseConstraint (
  (rootLocation)
  (oldLocation)
  (newConstraint)))
```

we modify the non-contextual program of the preceding turn by replacing a fragment `oldConstraint` which satisfies the `oldLocation` and is governed by a bigger fragment satisfying the `rootLocation` with a new fragment

```
(& ((oldConstraint) (newConstraint)))
```

*i.e.,* conjoining the two constraints regardless whether they conflicts with each other. For both cases, when there are multiple possible replacements, all resulting candidates are proposed. These candidates are manually reviewed and edited by the authors to finalize non-contextual program annotations. For example, if `newConstraint` contradicts with a part of `oldConstraint`, we drop the such conflicting parts in the `oldConstraint`.

Furthermore, as noted by Meron (2022), the original annotations of SMCalFlow can be complex and contain many boilerplate segments. Therefore, we use heuristics to simplify the original annotations to obtain programs that are shorter and potentially easier to read and predict. Similar to Meron (2022), the simplification was implemented via a set of tree transformation rules, which convert specific sub-trees of the original program into simplified sub-trees. The list of sub-tree transformations are provided in Table A2–Table A4.

Two data specialists are asked to produce the annotations for the rewritten non-contextual utterances in the contextual subset. They are provided with instructions and training materials, which explains how to rewrite a contextual user utterance with its preceding utterance into a single non-contextual utterance. Each example takes 10 to 30 seconds to annotate. Additionally, annotators were asked to provide a confidence from 0 (least confident) to 3 (most confident) in the rewritten utterance. The average confidence was 2.9. Then they are asked to review the each other's annotations and answer whether they agree with each other. In our pilot data collection, the agreement rate between the two data specialists was 93.3%.

Table A1 provides some examples from in *SMCalFlow-EQ*.

## C Fine-tuning Experiment Hyperparameters

For fine-tuning, we employ the Adafactor optimizer (Shazeer and Stern, 2018) and set the batch size to 32. The slanted triangular learning rate scheduler (Howard and Ruder, 2018) is used with a maximum learning rate of $10^{-5}$ and 1000 warmup steps. We fine-tune $\mathcal{M}_0$ for 10000 steps on the non-contextual subset to obtain $\mathcal{M}_1$, and another 10000 steps on the corresponding data to obtain the models for individual paradigms. For constrained decoding, the maximum output sequence length is 1000.

| Utterance | Last Utterance | Oracle Rewritten Utterance | Non-Contextual Program | Contextual Program |
|---|---|---|---|---|
| What about later next week? | Did I have any meetings early next week? | Did I have any meetings later next week? | `(QueryEventResponseIsNonEmpty (FindEventWrapperWithDefaults (Event.duringDateRangeConstraint_? (LateDateRange (NextWeekList)))))` | `(Execute (ReviseConstraint (DefaultRootLocation) (^(Event) ConstraintTypeIntension) (Event.duringDateRangeConstraint_? (LateDateRange (NextWeekList)))))` |
| Actual I meant the day after tomorrow. | Is there any appointments tomorrow? | Is there any appointments the day after tomorrow? | `(QueryEventResponseIsNonEmpty (FindEventWrapperWithDefaults (Event.onDate_? (adjustByPeriod (Tomorrow) (toDays 1)))))` | `(Execute (ReviseConstraint (DefaultRootLocation) (^(Event) ConstraintTypeIntension) (Event.onDate_? (adjustByPeriod (Tomorrow) (toDays 1)))))` |
| What about training? | Is there a vacation scheduled for me? | Is there a training scheduled for me? | `(QueryEventResponseIsNonEmpty (FindEventWrapperWithDefaults (Event.subject_? (?~= \"training\"))))` | `(Execute (ReviseConstraint (DefaultRootLocation) (^(Event) ConstraintTypeIntension) (Event.subject_? (?~= \"training\"))))` |

Table A1: Dataset examples.

## D Rewriter Implementation

The rewriter used for Rewrite-then-Parse is implemented via GPT-3.5 (`text-davinci-003`). The prompt template is shown below, where placeholders {H1}, {H2}, ... are for the utterance history (*i.e.,* the preceding utterances), {X1}, {X2}, ... are for contextual user utterances, {Z1}, {Z2}, ... are for rewritten non-contextual utterances, and {H'} and {X'} are for test input.

```
Combine the utterances into a single utterance
with the meaning of the last utterance.

Last Utterance: {H1}
Current Utterance: {X1}
Rewritten Utterance: {Z1}

Last Utterance: {H2}
Current Utterance: {X2}
Rewritten Utterance: {Z2}

...

Last Utterance: {H'}
Current Utterance: {X'}
Rewritten Utterance:
```

We sample 8 demonstration examples are sampled uniformly from the contextual subset training instances. Greedy decoding is used with 50 maximum tokens and no frequency or presence penalty. The BLEU score using the oracle rewritten utterances as reference is 93.6.

| Original | Simplified |
|---|---|
| `(& (^($type) EmptyStructConstraint) ($c))` | `($c)` |
| `(& ($c) (^($type) EmptyStructConstraint))` | `($c)` |
| `(> (size (QueryResponse.results ($response))), 0L)` | `(QueryEventResponseIsNonEmpty ($response))` |
| `(AttendeeListHasRecipientConstraint (RecipientWithNameLike (^(Recipient) EmptyStructConstraint) (PersonName.apply $name)))` | `(WithAttendeeNamed ($name))` |
| `(AttendeeListHasRecipient (Execute (refer (extensionConstraint (RecipientWithNameLike (^(Recipient) EmptyStructConstraint) (PersonName.apply $name))))))` | `(WithAttendeeNamed ($name))` |
| `(AttendeeListExcludeRecipient (Execute (refer (extensionConstraint (RecipientWithNameLike (^(Recipient) EmptyStructConstraint) (PersonName.apply $name))))))` | `(WithoutAttendeeNamed ($name))` |

Table A2: List of sub-tree transformations for simplifying SMCalFlow programs (part 1).

| Original | Simplified |
|---|---|
| `(EventAtTime ($event) ($time))` | `(& ($event) (Event.atTime_? ($time)))` |
| `(EventDuringRangeTime ($event) ($timeRange))))` | `(& ($event) (Event.duringTimeRangeConstraint_? ($timeRange)))` |
| `(EventOnDate ($date) ($event))` | `(& ($event) (Event.onDate_? ($date)))` |
| `(EventDuringDateRange ($event) ($dateRange))))` | `(& ($event) (Event.duringDateRangeConstraint_? ($dateRange)))` |
| `(EventOnDateTime (DateAtTimeWithDefaults (($date) ($time)) ($event)))` | `(& ($event) (& (Event.onDate_? ($date)) (Event.atTime_? ($time))))` |
| `(EventOnDateAfterTime (($date) ($event) ($time)))` | `(& ($event) (& (Event.onDate_? ($date)) (Event.afterTime_? ($time))))` |
| `(EventOnDateBeforeTime (($date) ($event) ($time)))` | `(& ($event) (& (Event.onDate_? ($date)) (Event.beforeTime_? ($time))))` |
| `(EventOnDateFromTimeToTime (($date) ($event) ($time1) ($time2)))` | `(& ($event) (& (Event.onDate_? ($date)) (Event.betweenTimeAndTime_? ($time1) ($time2))))` |

Table A3: List of sub-tree transformations for simplifying SMCalFlow programs (part 2).

| Original | Simplified |
|---|---|
| `(EventAfterDateTime (($event) ($dateTime)))` | `(& ($event) (Event.afterDateTime_? ($dateTime)))` |
| `(EventBeforeDateTime (($event) ($dateTime)))` | `(& ($event) (Event.beforeDateTime_? ($dateTime)))` |
| `(EventOnDateWithTimeRange (EventOnDate ($date) ($event)) ($timeRange))` | `(& ($event) (& (Event.onDate_? ($date)) (Event.duringTimeRangeConstraint_? ($timeRange))))` |
| `(EventOnDateWithTimeRange (EventDuringRange ($event) ($dateRange) ($timeRange)))` | `(& ($event) (& (Event.duringDateRangeConstraint_? ($dateRange)) (Event.duringTimeRangeConstraint_? ($timeRange))))` |
| `(EventDuringRangeDateTime ($event) ($dateTimeRange))` | `(& ($event) (Event.duringDateTimeRangeConstraint_? ($dateTimeRange)))` |

Table A4: List of sub-tree transformations for simplifying SMCalFlow programs (part 3).

<table>
<tr><th>Error Type</th><th>Gold</th><th>Predicted</th></tr>
<tr><td>Top-level Incorrect</td><td><pre>(Execute (ReviseConstraint
    (DefaultRootLocation) (^(Event)
    ConstraintTypeIntension) (&
    (Event.attendees_?
    (WithAttendeeNamed "kim")) (&
    (Event.onDate_? (Tomorrow))
    (Event.subject_? (?~= "lunch
    meeting"))))))</pre></td><td><pre>(Execute (NewClobber (DefaultIntension)
    (^(Recipient)
    ConstraintTypeIntension) (intension
    (RecipientWithNameLike (^(Recipient)
    EmptyStructConstraint)
    (PersonName.apply "kim")))))</pre></td></tr>
<tr><td>Alternate parse</td><td><pre>(FindEventWrapperWithDefaults (&
    (Event.attendees_?
    (WithAttendeeNamed "Barry"))
    (Event.start_? (DateTime.date_? (?=
    (Tomorrow))))))</pre></td><td><pre>(FindEventWrapperWithDefaults (&
    (Event.attendees_?
    (WithAttendeeNamed "Barry"))
    (Event.onDate_? (Tomorrow))))</pre></td></tr>
<tr><td>Extra Constraint</td><td><pre>(QueryEventResponseIsNonEmpty
    (FindEventWrapperWithDefaults
    (Event.attendees_? (&
    (WithAttendeeNamed "Marco")
    (WithAttendeeNamed "Peyton")))))</pre></td><td><pre>(QueryEventResponseIsNonEmpty
    (FindEventWrapperWithDefaults (&
    (Event.attendees_?
    (WithAttendeeNamed "Peyton")) (&
    (Event.attendees_?
    (WithAttendeeNamed "Marco"))
    (Event.duringDateRangeConstraint_?
    (FullMonthofMonth (Date.month
    (Today))))))))</pre></td></tr>
<tr><td>Missing Constraint</td><td><pre>(QueryEventResponseIsNonEmpty
    (FindEventWrapperWithDefaults (&
    (Event.attendees_?
    (WithAttendeeNamed "Bob")) (&
    (Event.duringTimeRangeConstraint_?
    (Afternoon)) (Event.onDate_?
    (Tomorrow))))))</pre></td><td><pre>(QueryEventResponseIsNonEmpty
    (FindEventWrapperWithDefaults (&
    (Event.attendees_?
    (WithAttendeeNamed "Bob"))
    (Event.duringTimeRangeConstraint_?
    (Afternoon)))))</pre></td></tr>
<tr><td>Constraint With Incorrect Function</td><td><pre>(Execute (NewClobber (DefaultIntension)
    (extensionConstraint
    (^(LocationKeyphrase)
    AlwaysTrueConstraint)) (intension
    (LocationKeyphrase.apply "EVO"))))</pre></td><td><pre>(Execute (NewClobber (DefaultIntension)
    (^(Recipient)
    ConstraintTypeIntension) (intension
    (RecipientWithNameLike (^(Recipient)
    EmptyStructConstraint)
    (PersonName.apply "EVO")))))</pre></td></tr>
<tr><td>Constraint With Incorrect Argument</td><td><pre>(QueryEventResponseIsNonEmpty
    (FindEventWrapperWithDefaults
    (Event.onDate_? (adjustByPeriod
    (Tomorrow) (toDays 1)))))</pre></td><td><pre>(QueryEventResponseIsNonEmpty
    (FindEventWrapperWithDefaults
    (Event.onDate_? (adjustByPeriod
    (Tomorrow) (toDays 2)))))</pre></td></tr>
</table>

Table A5: Error examples with gold parses.

# Exploring the Use of Large Language Models for Reference-Free Text Quality Evaluation: An Empirical Study

**Yi Chen**[♡♠*], **Rui Wang**[♡♠*], **Haiyun Jiang**[†], **Shuming Shi**, **Ruifeng Xu**[♡♣♠†]
[♡]Harbin Institute of Technology, Shenzhen, China
[♣]Peng Cheng Laboratory, Shenzhen, China
[♠]Guangdong Provincial Key Laboratory of Novel Security Intelligence Technologies
yichennlp@gmail.com,ruiwangnlp@outlook.com,xuruifeng@hit.edu.cn

## Abstract

Evaluating the quality of generated text is a challenging task in NLP, due to the inherent complexity and diversity of text. Recently, large language models (LLMs) have garnered significant attention due to their impressive performance in various tasks. Therefore, we present this paper to investigate the effectiveness of LLMs, especially ChatGPT, and explore ways to optimize their use in assessing text quality. We compared three kinds of reference-free evaluation methods. The experimental results prove that ChatGPT is capable of evaluating text quality effectively from various perspectives without reference and demonstrates superior performance than most existing automatic metrics. In particular, the Explicit Score, which utilizes ChatGPT to generate a numeric score measuring text quality, is the most effective and reliable method among the three exploited approaches. However, directly comparing the quality of two texts may lead to suboptimal results. We believe this paper will provide valuable insights for evaluating text quality with LLMs and have released the used data[1].

## 1 Introduction

Automated evaluation of text generation quality has posed a long-standing challenge in the field of natural language processing (NLP). On the one hand, the diverse forms of textual expression make it impossible for reference-based methods to account for all possible situations(Zhang* et al., 2020; Yuan et al., 2021; Chen et al., 2022b). On the other hand, devising reliable metrics without reference is not a straightforward task and can also be problematic (Sun and Zhou, 2012; Niu et al., 2021; Shen et al., 2022). Furthermore, different types of text necessitate evaluation of distinct aspects, e.g. coherence, fluency, and consistency (Fabbri et al., 2021a; Mehri and Eskenazi, 2020a; Wang et al., 2023b), which makes it hard to design metrics for each type of text and dimension separately.

Nowadays, large language models (LLMs) (Brown et al., 2020; Ouyang et al., 2022; Chung et al., 2022; Chowdhery et al., 2022; Zhang et al., 2022; Touvron et al., 2023; Du et al., 2022) represented by ChatGPT[2] have revolutionized the field of NLP by achieving remarkable results in a wide range of NLP tasks (Song et al., 2023; Chen et al., 2022a). Recent studies (Fu et al., 2023; Wang et al., 2023a; Kocmi and Federmann, 2023; Ji et al., 2023) have also demonstrated the potential of LLMs in evaluating the quality of generated texts. In this paper, we present an empirical study that compares different methods for text quality evaluation using LLMs in a reference-free mode. The key insights from our empirical findings are as follows:

- **How accurately can ChatGPT assess text quality without references?** (§4.1)

It is feasible for ChatGPT to evaluate text quality without reference, and it outperforms commonly used metrics even with a simple prompt design.

- **What is the most effective approach to evaluate text quality using ChatGPT?** (§4)

Generally, using ChatGPT to generate an explicit score for text quality is the best and most stable method among the three we compared. We suggest using greedy decoding for more reliable results.

- **Why may directly comparing two texts using ChatGPT yield suboptimal results?** (§5.1)

Due to its strict standard for "high-quality" text, ChatGPT often considers most generated texts unsatisfactory. Therefore, distinguishing between two subpar texts becomes challenging for ChatGPT.

- **Why is Implicit Score generally less effective than Explicit Score?** (§5.2)

*Equal Contribution.
†Corresponding Authors.
[1]https://github.com/MilkWhite/LLMs_for_Reference_Free_Text_Quality_Evaluation
[2]https://openai.com/blog/chatgpt



*Findings of the Association for Computational Linguistics: IJCNLP-AACL 2023*, pages 361–374
November 1–4, 2023. 

Compared to generating an Explicit Score with ChatGPT, using the confidence of text-davinci models to determine text quality (Implicit Score) is less effective due to different distribution characteristics. Implicit Score has a narrow range and peak structure, while Explicit Score allows better differentiation with its smoother distribution.

- **How can prompt design impact ChatGPT in generating an Explicit Score?** (§5.3)

When prompting ChatGPT for an Explicit Score, it would be better to avoid detailed scoring criteria if such criteria lack clear definitions for each score range. A general description of the evaluation standard is enough. Also, making ChatGPT provide justifications in a "chain-of-thought" manner before scoring can lead it to prioritize its reasoning process over the text. These justifications tend to be templated and similar across different texts, reducing the discriminative power of the final score.

## 2 Method

We explore two different reference-free paradigms, i.e., *Individual Score* and *Pairwise Comparison* for text evaluation using ChatGPT and text-davinci models. Individual Score assesses the quality of a single text by a numerical score, while Pairwise Comparison focuses on the relative quality of two texts and requires a direct comparison to determine which one is superior. Within the Individual Score paradigm, two methods are typically exploited: *Explicit Score*, obtained through direct text generation, and *Implicit Score*, obtained through the token probabilities outputted by the model.

### 2.1 Individual Score

**Explicit Score** Conditioned on a given input text (optional), we prompt ChatGPT to directly generate a score to measure the absolute quality of each text individually in terms of a specific aspect or the overall performance. An example prompt designed for scoring the overall quality of a storyline is shown as follows:

========= PROMPT FOR EXPLICIT SCORE =========

Score the following storyline given the beginning of the story on a continual scale from 0 (worst) to 100 (best), where a score of 0 means "The storyline makes no sense and is totally not understandable" and a score of 100 means "The storyline is perfect-written and highly consistent with the given beginning of the story".

The beginning of the story:
`[Conditioned Text]`

Storyline:
`[Generated Text]`

Score:

**Implicit Score** Given the LLM's potential insensitivity to numerical values and the lack of explicit instructions for aligning score intervals with specific criteria, score fluctuations may occur across different samples. Therefore, we propose an alternative approach by framing the problem as a binary Yes or No question, where the confidence level of answering "yes" serves as the Implicit Score. An illustrative example is presented below:

========= PROMPT FOR IMPLICIT SCORE =========

Consider the following storyline written according to the given beginning of the story:

The beginning of the story:
`[Conditioned Text]`

Storyline:
`[Generated Text]`

Question: Is the storyline well-written and consistent with the beginning of the story?

Answer:

Unfortunately, access to ChatGPT's token probabilities is currently unavailable. Text-davinci-003 is similar to ChatGPT in that they are both trained through supervised instruction tuning and Reinforcement Learning from Human Feedback (RLHF) based on GPT-3.5, and they both exhibit excellent performance in following and fulfilling human instructions. Therefore, we utilize text-davinci-003 to derive the Implicit Score as a baseline metric instead. To facilitate a more comprehensive comparison, we also obtain the Implicit Score from text-davinci-001, an earlier version of the text-davinci series model which is based on GPT-3 and has not been trained using RLHF. Due to a limitation of the OpenAI API, only the top 5 most probable tokens are returned with log probabilities. Therefore, we instead estimate the Implicit Score using the following formula:

$$
\begin{aligned}
p(\text{yes}) &= \sum_{t \in \mathcal{T}_{top5} \cap \mathcal{T}_{yes}} p(t), \\
p(\text{no}) &= \sum_{t \in \mathcal{T}_{top5} \cap \mathcal{T}_{no}} p(t), \qquad (1) \\
\text{Implicit Score} &= \max(p(yes), 1 - p(no)).
\end{aligned}
$$

Here, $p(t)$ represents the probability of predicting token $t$ immediately following the prompt "Answer:". The sets $\mathcal{T}_{yes}$ and $\mathcal{T}_{no}$ consist of the affirmative and negative response tokens, respectively, i.e., $\mathcal{T}_{yes} = \{$" Yes", "Yes", " yes", "yes"$\}$, and $\mathcal{T}_{no} = \{$" No", "No", " no", "no"$\}$.

### 2.2 Pairwise Comparison

Another paradigm to assess text quality is by directly comparing a pair of generated texts based on the same input. This method primarily focuses on the relative quality of the texts. For instance, a prompt for comparing the overall quality of two storylines written according to the same initial story beginning is shown as follows:

====== PROMPT FOR PAIRWISE COMPARISON ======

Consider the following two storylines written according to the given beginning of the story:

The beginning of the story:
`[Conditioned Text]`

Storyline-1:
`[Generated Text-1]`

Storyline-2:
`[Generated Text-2]`

Question: Which storyline is better-written and more consistent with the beginning of the story? Please answer with one of the following options.

Options:
(A) Storyline-1
(B) Storyline-2
(C) Both storylines are equally well-written and consistent with the beginning of the story.

Answer: I will choose Option

## 3 Experimental Setup

### 3.1 Tasks and Datasets

We conduct experiments on four distinct natural language generation tasks: Text Summarization, Dialogue Response Generation, Story Generation, and Paraphrase Generation.

**Text Summarization** aims to summarize the key points of a given long text. SummEval (Fabbri et al., 2021b) is a collection of human annotations for 16 model-generated summaries on 100 CNN/DaliyMail news over 4 dimensions: coherence (COH), fluency (FLU), consistency (CON), and relevance (REL). Due to the budget limit, we randomly sample 20 news and corresponding annotations from SummEval for evaluation.

**Dialogue Response Generation** aims to generate a response based on the preceding dialogue. We conduct experiments on the dialogue-level FED dataset (Mehri and Eskenazi, 2020a), which contains fine-grained human judgments for 124 conversations. The evaluation aspects include coherence (COH), error recovery (ERR), consistency (CON), diversity (DIV), topic depth (DEP), likeability (LIK), understanding (UND), flexibility (FLE), informativeness (INF), inquisitiveness (INQ) and overall performance (Overall). However, we do not include ERR in our evaluation since some annotations are missing.

**Story Generation** aims to automatically write a storyline based on a given beginning of the story. We employ OpenMEVA-ROC (Guan et al., 2021) for evaluation, which contains 200 story beginnings and 5 corresponding machine-generated storylines for each beginning. Each storyline is manually annotated in terms of overall quality.

**Paraphrase Generation** aims to rephrase a sentence in different words or forms while preserving its original meaning. We use Twitter-Para (Xu et al., 2014, 2015) for evaluation, containing 761 input sentences and each input has 9.41 paraphrase candidates on average. We adopt the test set (Shen et al., 2022) extended from Twitter-Para by adding 20% of the input sentences as candidates, denoted as Twitter (Extend).

### 3.2 Chosen Metrics

Following the settings of previous works, we select baseline metrics from the following widely used metrics accordingly: **ROUGE-1**, **ROUGE-2** and **ROUGE-L** (Lin, 2004); **BERTScore** (Zhang* et al., 2020); **MoverScore** (Zhao et al., 2019); **PRISM** (Thompson and Post, 2020); **BARTScore** and its enhanced versions, **BARTScore+CNN** and **BARTScore+CNN+Para** (Yuan et al., 2021); **BERT-R** (Ghazarian et al., 2019); **GPT-2** (Radford et al., 2019); **USR** (Mehri and Eskenazi, 2020b); **S-DiCoh** (Mesgar et al., 2020); **FED** (Mehri and Eskenazi, 2020a); **DynaEval** (Zhang et al., 2021); **SelfEval** (Ma et al., 2022); **PPL** (Guan et al., 2021); **iBLEU** (Sun and Zhou, 2012); **BERT-iBLEU** (Niu et al., 2021); **ParaScore** (Shen et al., 2022). Note that, Shen et al. (2022) also use a reference-free

| Metrics | Spear. | | | |
|---|---|---|---|---|
| | COH | FLU | CON | REL |
| ROUGE-1 | 21.6 | 10.5 | 10.9 | 42.6 |
| ROUGE-2 | 30.7 | 19.1 | 20.7 | 36.9 |
| ROUGE-L | 17.4 | 10.2 | 9.6 | 40.0 |
| BERTScore | 28.5 | 10.6 | 13.4 | 29.5 |
| MoverScore | 22.5 | 11.8 | 14.6 | 39.2 |
| PRISM | 23.7 | 17.5 | 35.2 | 16.9 |
| BARTScore | 33.4 | 20.9 | 34.8 | 24.8 |
| +CNN | 43.3 | 28.7 | 42.7 | 36.1 |
| +CNN+Para | 40.1 | 27.2 | 41.0 | 32.0 |
| IMPLICIT SCORE | | | | |
| text-davinci-001 | -1.7 | -5.6 | 19.7 | 8.4 |
| text-davinci-003 | **57.4** | **32.9** | 35.2 | 28.1 |
| EXPLICIT SCORE | | | | |
| ChatGPT (sampling) | 45.8 | 22.1 | 41.2 | 39.2 |
| ChatGPT (greedy) | 52.2 | 19.3 | **43.3** | **46.0** |

Table 1: Sample-level Spearman (Spear.) correlation of different aspects on SummEval.

version of BERTScore and ParaScore, denoted as **BERTScore.Free** and **ParaScore.Free**.

### 3.3 Meta Evaluation

**Individual Score** In order to assess the reliability of Individual Scores, we utilize the Spearman (Zar, 2005) and Pearson (Mukaka, 2012) correlation coefficients. As SummEval and OpenMEVA provide an equivalent number of model-generated results for each input, we present the sample-level correlations for these datasets. Whereas, for Twitter (Extend) and the dialog-level FED datasets, we report the dataset-level correlations instead.

**Pairwise Comparison** To avoid an excessive volume of requests when testing all permutations of pairwise comparisons in each dataset using ChatGPT, we have opted to randomly sample 200 pairs from each dataset as an approximation. To estimate the reliability of metrics for pairwise comparison, Kendall's Tau-b (Kendall, 1945) is employed to evaluate the correlation between two measured variables. A detailed explanation of Kendall's Tau-b is shown in Appendix C.

## 4 Main Experiments

### 4.1 Individual Score

Notably, as shown in Tables 1 to 4, even without providing reference or calibration details for different score ranges, ChatGPT's Explicit Score has already correlated with human scores better than most commonly used automated metrics. On Twitter (Extend), it is only outperformed by ParaScore and ParaScore.Free, which requires the use of reference or hyper-parameter adjustments on a dev set. Additionally, the performance of the Explicit Score further improves when we use greedy search instead of Top-P sampling for decoding.

It is worth noting that the Implicit Score based on text-davinci-003 also shows promising results. This suggests that LLMs' confidence level in determining whether a text meets a specific standard (yes or no) can reflect the text's quality to some extent. Besides, the Implicit Score based on text-davinci-003 performs better than that based on text-davinci-001 in most cases, perhaps due to RLHF, allowing text-davinci-003 to provide answers that align with human instructions better.

### 4.2 Pairwise Comparison

Scoring individual samples without providing detailed criteria for each score range may lead to inconsistent evaluation standards across different samples. Alternatively, we hypothesize that a direct comparison of quality between a pair of samples is more likely to yield reliable evaluation results from ChatGPT. However, our analysis in Tables 5 to 8 suggests that direct pairwise comparison is not as effective as expected, and eliminating the influence of sampling in decoding is not always advantageous for comparison.

We further categorize the texts for comparison into three levels of difficulty, namely hard, medium, and easy, based on the difference in human scores. The larger the score difference between a pair of texts, the easier it is to discern the better one. The performance of various metrics on distinct difficulty levels is shown in Tables 7 and 8. Overall, the metrics exhibit an increasing trend in performance as the difficulty decreases.

Moreover, our investigation indicates that the Implicit Score derived from text-davinci-003 outperforms or performs comparably to the Explicit Score based on ChatGPT when comparing hard text pairs. This finding may be attributed to the higher precision of the Implicit Score, which is based on the model's output token probability (a floating-point number), as opposed to the model's generated Explicit Score, which is limited to integer values ranging from 0 to 100.

| Metrics | Spear. | | | | | | | | | |
|---|---|---|---|---|---|---|---|---|---|---|
| | COH | CON | DIV | DEP | LIK | UND | FLE | INF | INQ | Overall |
| BERT-R | 22.9 | 16.3 | 19.6 | 19.2 | 28.1 | 19.8 | 25.3 | 21.1 | 33.7 | 24.8 |
| GPT-2 | 12.3 | 9.1 | 14.7 | 9.7 | 17.9 | 7.0 | 13.4 | 11.6 | 7.1 | 12.3 |
| USR | 19.4 | 16.9 | 24.2 | 34.1 | 22.1 | 17.2 | 20.9 | 28.8 | 18.8 | 28.8 |
| S-DiCoh | 3.8 | 1.7 | 5.9 | 4.6 | -7.0 | -10.0 | 4.4 | 2.8 | -5.4 | -7.3 |
| FED | 25.1 | 11.6 | 44.9 | 52.2 | 26.2 | 30.6 | 40.8 | 33.7 | 29.8 | 44.3 |
| DynaEval | 42.3 | 35.2 | 33.2 | 43.9 | 39.8 | 36.1 | 38.9 | 39.6 | 38.8 | 48.2 |
| SelfEval | 43.6 | 34.7 | 26.3 | 32.7 | 39.0 | 40.6 | 31.7 | 31.8 | 42.1 | 43.5 |
| IMPLICIT SCORE | | | | | | | | | | |
| text-davinci-001 | 37.9 | 33.0 | 36.1 | 26.2 | 35.0 | 57.5 | 39.5 | 54.8 | 45.0 | 39.4 |
| text-davinci-003 | 46.8 | 43.8 | 24.9 | 53.4 | **57.3** | 57.6 | 45.0 | 55.1 | **59.0** | **58.0** |
| EXPLICIT SCORE | | | | | | | | | | |
| ChatGPT (sampling) | 57.8 | **47.8** | 44.5 | 51.5 | 47.2 | **61.7** | 49.4 | 61.7 | 42.8 | 55.8 |
| ChatGPT (greedy) | **62.4** | 47.5 | **48.3** | **55.5** | 55.4 | 60.0 | **54.8** | **62.0** | 42.3 | 54.2 |

Table 2: Dataset-level Spearman (Spear.) correlation of different aspects on dialogue-level FED.

| Metrics | Spear. | Pear. |
|---|---|---|
| ROUGE-1 | 1.4 | 2.0 |
| ROUGE-2 | 3.5 | 4.1 |
| ROUGE-L | 1.3 | 2.1 |
| BERTScore | 14.0 | 12.0 |
| Perplexity | 32.4 | 33.0 |
| BARTScore | -6.5 | -8.2 |
| +CNN | 4.9 | 2.6 |
| +CNN+Para | 6.4 | 5.0 |
| IMPLICIT SCORE | | |
| text-davinci-001 | 30.3 | 32.9 |
| text-davinci-003 | 37.9 | 43.4 |
| EXPLICIT SCORE | | |
| ChatGPT (sampling) | 47.6 | 49.0 |
| ChatGPT (greedy) | **49.9** | **51.7** |

Table 3: Sample-level Spearman (Spear.) and Pearson (Pear.) correlation on OpenMEVA.

| Metrics | Spear. | Pear. |
|---|---|---|
| iBLEU | 3.2 | 1.1 |
| BERTScore | 43.2 | 42.7 |
| BERTScore.Free | 41.9 | 31.6 |
| BARTScore+CNN+Para | 27.6 | 28.0 |
| BERT-iBLEU | 41.6 | 32.7 |
| ParaScore | **53.0** | **52.7** |
| ParaScore.Free | 49.5 | 49.6 |
| IMPLICIT SCORE | | |
| text-davinci-001 | 15.8 | 15.9 |
| text-davinci-003 | 44.4 | 40.3 |
| EXPLICIT SCORE | | |
| ChatGPT (sampling) | 45.1 | 44.3 |
| ChatGPT (greedy) | 46.5 | 45.4 |

Table 4: Dataset-level Spearman (Spear.) and Pearson (Pear.) correlation on Twitter (Extend).

| Metrics | Kend. | | | |
|---|---|---|---|---|
| | COH | FLU | CON | REL |
| IMPLICIT SCORE | | | | |
| text-davinci-001 | -3.2 | -4.3 | 9.3 | 12.9 |
| text-davinci-003 | 46.9 | **24.5** | 35.3 | 29.1 |
| EXPLICIT SCORE | | | | |
| ChatGPT (sampling) | **50.3** | 8.6 | 31.7 | 44.3 |
| ChatGPT (greedy) | 43.7 | 16.8 | **32.8** | **52.5** |
| COMPARISON | | | | |
| ChatGPT (sampling) | 22.6 | 7.8 | 24.2 | 30.5 |
| ChatGPT (greedy) | 34.5 | 17.4 | 22.0 | 34.0 |

Table 5: Estimated Kendall's tau-b (Kend.) correlation of different aspects on SummEval.

## 5 Detailed Analysis

### 5.1 Why does the pairwise comparison paradigm perform worse?

In the main experiments, it is noteworthy that direct pairwise comparison using ChatGPT did not yield satisfactory results. To investigate whether this was caused by poorly designed prompts, alternative prompts were also evaluated. These prompts are briefly described in Table 9, with detailed information provided in Appendix B. Surprisingly, changing the prompt did not improve performance, but rather worsened it, as illustrated in Figure 1.

To gain further insights, we examined the confusion matrices of results based on different prompts, as shown in Figure 2. Our analysis revealed that, although we have provided the option of "both storylines equally good" in the default prompt (Prompt V1), ChatGPT still tended to choose one storyline that it deemed "better", as observed from Fig-

| Metrics | Kend. | | | | | | | | | |
|---|---|---|---|---|---|---|---|---|---|---|
| | COH | CON | DIV | DEP | LIK | UND | FLE | INF | INQ | Overall |
| IMPLICIT SCORE | | | | | | | | | | |
| text-davinci-001 | 33.3 | 32.0 | 29.6 | 25.1 | 25.6 | 49.9 | 32.8 | 44.8 | 49.5 | 33.6 |
| text-davinci-003 | 28.8 | 30.5 | 18.8 | 36.9 | 41.9 | 43.2 | 34.0 | 45.8 | 43.0 | 36.7 |
| EXPLICIT SCORE | | | | | | | | | | |
| ChatGPT (sampling) | 48.4 | **44.1** | 32.4 | 47.5 | 46.7 | 48.0 | 36.2 | 45.6 | **45.9** | **44.2** |
| ChatGPT (greedy) | **50.2** | 39.6 | **45.5** | **53.5** | **50.8** | **53.7** | 50.5 | **47.7** | 38.1 | 41.7 |
| COMPARISON | | | | | | | | | | |
| ChatGPT (sampling) | 28.3 | 16.1 | 28.5 | 31.5 | 43.0 | 27.5 | **55.5** | 35.2 | 24.5 | 38.6 |
| ChatGPT (greedy) | 24.3 | 13.7 | 28.5 | 33.8 | 41.9 | 27.5 | 55.5 | 34.1 | 25.6 | 37.5 |

Table 6: Estimated Kendall's tau-b (Kend.) correlation of different aspects on dialogue-level FED.

| Metrics | Kend. | | | |
|---|---|---|---|---|
| | Hard | Medium | Easy | All |
| IMPLICIT SCORE | | | | |
| text-davinci-001 | 6.3 | 29.8 | 44.4 | 16.6 |
| text-davinci-003 | **27.9** | 36.8 | 66.7 | 33.2 |
| EXPLICIT SCORE | | | | |
| ChatGPT (sampling) | 18.5 | 47.3 | 74.3 | 31.2 |
| ChatGPT (greedy) | 16.8 | **62.6** | **82.5** | **36.2** |
| COMPARISON | | | | |
| ChatGPT (sampling) | 8.1 | 22.8 | 33.3 | 14.5 |
| ChatGPT (greedy) | 9.9 | 29.8 | 55.6 | 19.7 |

Table 7: Estimated Kendall's tau-b (Kend.) correlation on OpenMEVA.

| Metrics | Kend. | | | |
|---|---|---|---|---|
| | Hard | Medium | Easy | All |
| IMPLICIT SCORE | | | | |
| text-davinci-001 | 21.6 | 34.6 | 13.6 | 20.4 |
| text-davinci-003 | 25.5 | 19.2 | 59.1 | 28.6 |
| EXPLICIT SCORE | | | | |
| ChatGPT (sampling) | **27.8** | **40.0** | 53.8 | **34.9** |
| ChatGPT (greedy) | 15.3 | 38.5 | 57.0 | 31.2 |
| COMPARISON | | | | |
| ChatGPT (sampling) | 14.6 | 31.0 | **68.3** | 31.3 |
| ChatGPT (greedy) | 10.0 | 22.2 | 65.1 | 26.3 |

Table 8: Estimated Kendall's tau-b (Kend.) correlation on Twitter (Extend).

ure 2(a). This could be attributed to the bias introduced by adding "Answer: I will choose Option" at the end of the prompt, which may have induced the model to make a biased choice at the beginning of the answer. To address this issue, we modified the prompt to require ChatGPT to present its reasoning process before making the final decision

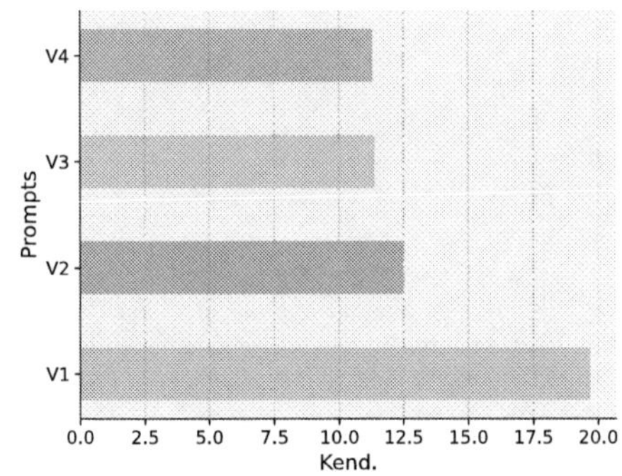


Figure 1: Estimated Kendall's tau-b (Kend.) correlation of Pairwise Comparison using ChatGPT with different prompts on OpenMEVA. We use greedy decoding for Prompt V1~V3. Whereas, for Prompt V4 we use Top-P sampling five times to obtain multiple results and vote for the final decision.

(Prompt V4). With this prompt, the model was more likely to choose the "tie" option, as indicated by the "s1=s2" column in Figure 2(b).

After analyzing ChatGPT's reasoning process, we discovered that ChatGPT frequently concludes that "the quality of the two given storylines is equally poor." As a result, we prompted ChatGPT to choose the "worse" storyline instead of the "better" one (Prompt V3). However, this questioning approach did not yield a better outcome. In addition, Figure 2(c) shows that although Prompt V3 is a mirrored version of Prompt V1, which changes the prompt from selecting the better option to choosing the worse one, ChatGPT's results based on these two prompts are not always consistent. For example, in one case, ChatGPT selected Storyline-1 as better based on Prompt V1, but under the guidance of Prompt V3, it may not necessarily choose Storyline-2 as worse.

Overall, we speculate that the poor quality of the

| | PROMPTS FOR PAIRWISE COMPARISON ON STORY GENERATION |
|---|---|
| PROMPT V1 | The default prompt where we first provide the beginning of the story and the corresponding two storylines for comparison before presenting the question. |
| PROMPT V2 | A revised version of Prompt V1 where we first propose the question, then provide the beginning of the story and present the two storylines to be compared in the form of options. |
| PROMPT V3 | A mirrored version of Prompt V1 where we instruct the model to choose "which one is worse" instead of "which one is better" from the two given storylines. |
| PROMPT V4 | A "chain-of-thought" version of Prompt V1 where we require the model to illustrate the reasoning process before presenting the final answer. |
| | PROMPTS FOR EXPLICIT SCORE ON STORY GENERATION |
| PROMPT V1 | The default prompt where we only specify the rating criteria for zero and full marks. |
| PROMPT V2 | A rephrased version of Prompt V1. |
| PROMPT V3 | A simplified version of Prompt V1 where we only describe the dimensions that need to be evaluated. |
| PROMPT V4 | A detailed prompt where we divide the scores into 5 scales and list the corresponding evaluation criteria for each score scale. |
| PROMPT V5 | A "chain-of-thought" version of Prompt V1 where we require the model to first present the reasons for the evaluation, and then provide the final score. |

Table 9: Prompts designed for Pairwise Comparison and Explicit Score for assessing the quality of storylines in story generation. Note that Prompt V4 of Explicit Score is cited from (Wang et al., 2023a).

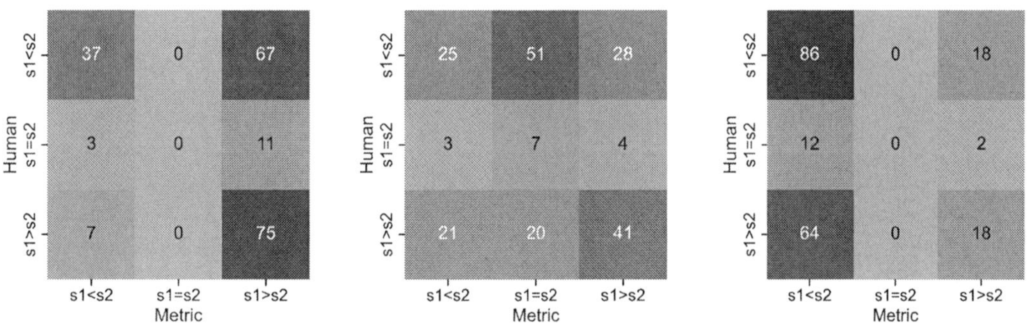


(a) Prompt V1 (Default) (b) Prompt V4 ("Chain-of-Thought" ) (c) Prompt V3 (Mirrored)

Figure 2: Confusion matrices of pairwise comparisons on OpenMEVA based on different prompts using ChatGPT. Prompt V1 is the default prompt used in the main experiments. Prompt V4 and V3 are the "chain-of-thought" and "mirrored" versions of Prompt V1 respectively. Details of these prompts are presented in Table 9 and Appendix B.

candidate texts used in our experiments is the main reason why comparing pairs directly with ChatGPT did not yield good results. ChatGPT perceives the candidate texts as generally low quality, making it to select a "better" or "worse" one from them. This might lead to ChatGPT's unstable decisions.

## 5.2 Why does Explicit Score generally perform better than Implicit Score?

In order to obtain the Explicit Score, we utilize ChatGPT to generate scores in a natural language format. However, as we do not have access to ChatGPT's token probabilities, we instead rely on the confidence of text-davinci series models to determine the Implicit Score, which reflects how well a text meets a particular evaluation criterion. As stated in the Main Experiments (§4), the Explicit

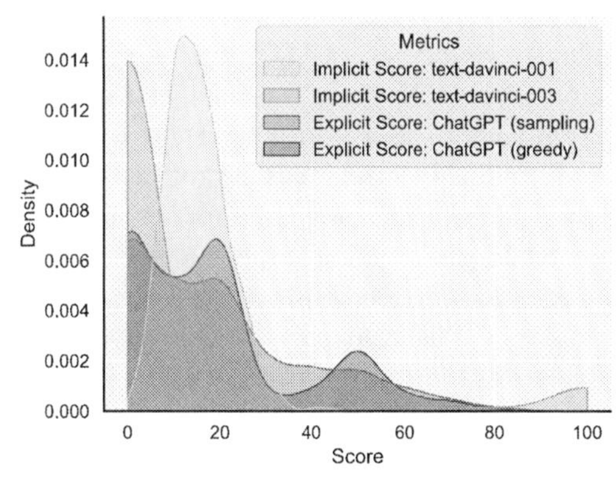


Figure 3: Distribution of different types of Individual Scores on OpenMEVA. The Implicit Score is rescaled into [0,100].

| Explicit Score | Spear. | Pear. |
|---|---|---|
| ChatGPT | | |
| w/ Prompt V1 (greedy) | 49.9 | 51.7 |
| w/ Prompt V2 (greedy) | **50.8** | **53.6** |
| w/ Prompt V3 (greedy) | 49.4 | 52.0 |
| w/ Prompt V4 (greedy) | 46.1 | 48.4 |
| w/ Prompt V5 (sampling) | 47.2 | 50.8 |

Table 10: Sample-level Spearman (Spear.) and Pearson (Pear.) correlation for Explicit Score based on ChatGPT with different prompts on OpenMEVA. We use greedy decoding for Prompt V1∼V4. Whereas, for Prompt V5, we employ Top-P sampling five times to generate multiple reasons and average the resulting scores.

Score is generally more effective than the Implicit Score. This difference in effectiveness could be attributed not only to the variation in the models used but also to the distribution of the two scores. Figure 3 illustrates that the Implicit Score distribution has a peaked structure and is concentrated within a small range. In contrast, the Explicit Score distribution is smoother, allowing for greater discrimination between scores for different texts.

### 5.3 How does the prompt design affect Explicit Score?

We also investigate the impact of prompt design on the performance of rating Explicit Scores generated by ChatGPT. The detailed prompts are provided in Appendix A, and their main features and differences are summarized in Table 9. Our results, presented in Table 10, indicate that paraphrasing (V2) or simplifying (V3) the default prompt (V1) does not significantly affect the performance of Explicit Score based on ChatGPT. In contrast, refining scoring criteria (V4) or providing reasons before scoring (V5) results in a slight decrease in performance. The former may be due to the fact that the refined scoring rules in Prompt V4 do not fully match the standards used for actual manual annotation, and dividing scores into five scales reduces the distinction between scores for different samples. The latter may be due to the overall low quality of the dataset. Our observation indicates that ChatGPT's evaluations for each text are similar and mostly negative. After giving reasons before scoring, ChatGPT's scoring focuses more on the reasons rather than the text itself, resulting in lower scores for each text based on Prompt V5 and reducing the distinction between scores. The detailed distribution of scores derived from different prompts is demonstrated using a violin plot in Figure 4.

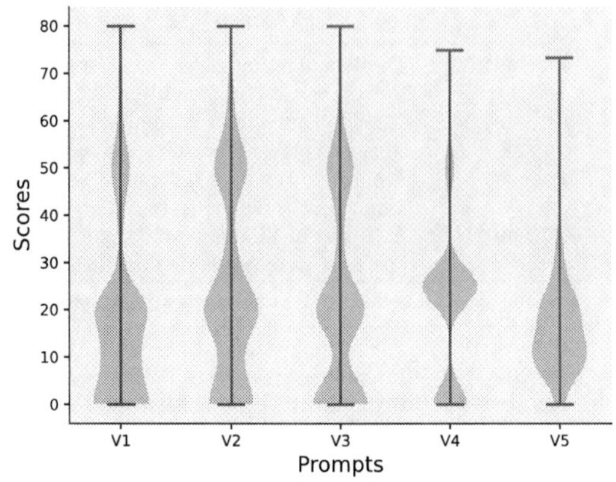


Figure 4: Distribution of Explicit Scores based on ChatGPT with different prompts on OpenMEVA. For Prompt V4, the scores are normalized into [0, 100].

## 6 Related Work

In the field of text quality evaluation, researchers have devised two main lines of approaches: reference-based and reference-free methods. The reference-based text evaluation aims to assess the quality by comparing outputs with ground truth, e.g. ROUGE (Lin, 2004), BERTScore (Zhang* et al., 2020) and BARTScore (Yuan et al., 2021). However, due to the inherent complexity and diversity of text, it is impossible to obtain references covering the entire spectrum of potential outputs. This limitation has prompted researchers to explore reference-free evaluation methods without relying on predefined references e.g. iBLEU (Sun and Zhou, 2012) and ParaScore (Shen et al., 2022). In this line, a reliable sentence representation model is required (Gao et al., 2021; Shen et al., 2023a,b). Recent studies have indicated that LLM-based evaluation methods can exhibit good consistency with human evaluation in assessing text quality (Fu et al., 2023; Wang et al., 2023a; Kocmi and Federmann, 2023; Ji et al., 2023). However, most of these works are preliminary explorations or require gold references. On the contrary, we are the first to conduct extensive experiments to investigate the optimal evaluation approaches using LLMs without references, and moreover propose some clues for customized text evaluation.

## 7 Conclusion

This paper explores the feasibility of LLMs, specifically ChatGPT and text-davinci series models, for evaluating text quality in a reference-free mode. Through an empirical study, we compare different methods for the evaluation of text quality and recommend the use of an Explicit Score generated by ChatGPT as the most effective and stable approach. This paper also highlights the potential problem of directly comparing the quality of two texts using ChatGPT and the limitations of Implicit Scores obtained through the confidence of text-davinci series models. The prompt design is another crucial factor impacting the performance of the Explicit Score generated by ChatGPT. Overall, this paper demonstrates the potential of LLMs in evaluating text quality without reference and we hope it will provide useful insights for future research.

## Limitations

- **Meta Evaluation Strategy**

We primarily assess the reliability of metrics based on their correlation with human scores. However, it should be noted that the consistency between scores annotated by different raters may not always be high in certain datasets. Hence, the correlation with human ratings may not always reflect the performance of metrics appropriately.

- **Coverage of Texts**

We only conducted experiments on four text-generation tasks. Additionally, the quality distribution of the evaluated texts may be non-uniform, potentially lacking in extremely high-quality texts. Even if a metric performs well in evaluating a set of low-quality texts, it does not necessarily imply the same level of discrimination for high-quality texts, and vice versa. Furthermore, our evaluation has been limited to short texts, omitting the consideration of long-text generation.

- **Coverage of Models**

We utilize OpenAI's API to access their language models, including ChatGPT (gpt3.5-turbo-0301), text-davinci-003, and text-davinci-001. However, these models may be updated over time, which can result in inconsistencies in experimental outcomes. Moreover, we have not considered a wider range of LLMs, such as text-babbage-001, text-curie-001, and the FLAN-T5 series. Regrettably, due to API limitations, we were unable to obtain results from the more powerful GPT4 model.

- **Prompt Design**

Our exploration of prompts was limited to a few basic variations. Future research may benefit from more sophisticated prompt designs, such as incorporating few-shot demonstrations, providing more precise annotation guidelines, or guiding the model through multi-turn conversations to facilitate a more accurate assessment of text quality.

## Acknowledgements

This research was supported in part by the National Natural Science Foundation of China(62006062, 62176076), the Guangdong Provincial Key Laboratory of Novel Security Intelligence Technologies(2022B121201000 5), Natural Science Foundation of Guangdong(2023A1515012922), and Key Technologies Research and Development Program of Shenzhen JSGG20210802154400001.

## References


Tom Brown, Benjamin Mann, Nick Ryder, Melanie Subbiah, Jared D Kaplan, Prafulla Dhariwal, Arvind Neelakantan, Pranav Shyam, Girish Sastry, Amanda Askell, et al. 2020. Language models are few-shot learners. *Advances in neural information processing systems*, 33:1877–1901.

Nuo Chen, Yan Wang, Haiyun Jiang, Deng Cai, Ziyang Chen, and Jia Li. 2022a. What would harry say? building dialogue agents for characters in a story. *arXiv preprint arXiv:2211.06869*.

Yi Chen, Haiyun Jiang, Lemao Liu, Rui Wang, Shuming Shi, and Ruifeng Xu. 2022b. Mcpg: A flexible multi-level controllable framework for unsupervised paraphrase generation. In *Findings of the Association for Computational Linguistics: EMNLP 2022*, pages 5948–5958.

Aakanksha Chowdhery, Sharan Narang, Jacob Devlin, Maarten Bosma, Gaurav Mishra, Adam Roberts, Paul Barham, Hyung Won Chung, Charles Sutton, Sebastian Gehrmann, et al. 2022. Palm: Scaling language modeling with pathways. *arXiv preprint arXiv:2204.02311*.

Hyung Won Chung, Le Hou, Shayne Longpre, Barret Zoph, Yi Tay, William Fedus, Eric Li, Xuezhi Wang, Mostafa Dehghani, Siddhartha Brahma, et al. 2022. Scaling instruction-finetuned language models. *arXiv preprint arXiv:2210.11416*.

Zhengxiao Du, Yujie Qian, Xiao Liu, Ming Ding, Jiezhong Qiu, Zhilin Yang, and Jie Tang. 2022. GLM: General language model pretraining with autoregressive blank infilling. In *Proceedings of the 60th Annual Meeting of the Association for Computational Linguistics (Volume 1: Long Papers)*, pages 320–335, Dublin, Ireland. Association for Computational Linguistics.

Alexander R. Fabbri, Wojciech Kryściński, Bryan McCann, Caiming Xiong, Richard Socher, and Dragomir Radev. 2021a. SummEval: Re-evaluating summarization evaluation. *Transactions of the Association for Computational Linguistics*, 9:391–409.

Alexander R Fabbri, Wojciech Kryściński, Bryan McCann, Caiming Xiong, Richard Socher, and Dragomir Radev. 2021b. Summeval: Re-evaluating summarization evaluation. *Transactions of the Association for Computational Linguistics*, 9:391–409.

Jinlan Fu, See-Kiong Ng, Zhengbao Jiang, and Pengfei Liu. 2023. Gptscore: Evaluate as you desire.

Tianyu Gao, Xingcheng Yao, and Danqi Chen. 2021. Simcse: Simple contrastive learning of sentence embeddings. *arXiv preprint arXiv:2104.08821*.

Sarik Ghazarian, Johnny Wei, Aram Galstyan, and Nanyun Peng. 2019. Better automatic evaluation of open-domain dialogue systems with contextualized embeddings. In *Proceedings of the Workshop on Methods for Optimizing and Evaluating Neural Language Generation*, pages 82–89, Minneapolis, Minnesota. Association for Computational Linguistics.

Jian Guan, Zhexin Zhang, Zhuoer Feng, Zitao Liu, Wenbiao Ding, Xiaoxi Mao, Changjie Fan, and Minlie Huang. 2021. OpenMEVA: A benchmark for evaluating open-ended story generation metrics. In *Proceedings of the 59th Annual Meeting of the Association for Computational Linguistics and the 11th International Joint Conference on Natural Language Processing (Volume 1: Long Papers)*, pages 6394–6407, Online. Association for Computational Linguistics.

Yunjie Ji, Yan Gong, Yiping Peng, Chao Ni, Peiyan Sun, Dongyu Pan, Baochang Ma, and Xiangang Li. 2023. Exploring chatgpt's ability to rank content: A preliminary study on consistency with human preferences.

M. G. Kendall. 1945. The treatment of ties in ranking problems. *Biometrika*, 33(3):239–251.

Tom Kocmi and Christian Federmann. 2023. Large language models are state-of-the-art evaluators of translation quality.

Chin-Yew Lin. 2004. ROUGE: A package for automatic evaluation of summaries. In *Text Summarization Branches Out*, pages 74–81, Barcelona, Spain. Association for Computational Linguistics.

Longxuan Ma, Ziyu Zhuang, Weinan Zhang, Mingda Li, and Ting Liu. 2022. SelF-eval: Self-supervised fine-grained dialogue evaluation. In *Proceedings of the 29th International Conference on Computational Linguistics*, pages 485–495, Gyeongju, Republic of Korea. International Committee on Computational Linguistics.

Shikib Mehri and Maxine Eskenazi. 2020a. Unsupervised evaluation of interactive dialog with DialoGPT. In *Proceedings of the 21th Annual Meeting of the Special Interest Group on Discourse and Dialogue*, pages 225–235, 1st virtual meeting. Association for Computational Linguistics.

Shikib Mehri and Maxine Eskenazi. 2020b. USR: An unsupervised and reference free evaluation metric for dialog generation. In *Proceedings of the 58th Annual Meeting of the Association for Computational Linguistics*, pages 681–707, Online. Association for Computational Linguistics.

Mohsen Mesgar, Sebastian Bücker, and Iryna Gurevych. 2020. Dialogue coherence assessment without explicit dialogue act labels. In *Proceedings of the 58th Annual Meeting of the Association for Computational Linguistics*, pages 1439–1450, Online. Association for Computational Linguistics.

Mavuto M Mukaka. 2012. A guide to appropriate use of correlation coefficient in medical research. *Malawi medical journal*, 24(3):69–71.

Tong Niu, Semih Yavuz, Yingbo Zhou, Nitish Shirish Keskar, Huan Wang, and Caiming Xiong. 2021. Unsupervised paraphrasing with pretrained language models. In *Proceedings of the 2021 Conference on Empirical Methods in Natural Language Processing*, pages 5136–5150, Online and Punta Cana, Dominican Republic. Association for Computational Linguistics.

Long Ouyang, Jeffrey Wu, Xu Jiang, Diogo Almeida, Carroll Wainwright, Pamela Mishkin, Chong Zhang, Sandhini Agarwal, Katarina Slama, Alex Ray, et al. 2022. Training language models to follow instructions with human feedback. *Advances in Neural Information Processing Systems*, 35:27730–27744.

Alec Radford, Jeffrey Wu, Rewon Child, David Luan, Dario Amodei, Ilya Sutskever, et al. 2019. Language models are unsupervised multitask learners. *OpenAI blog*, 1(8):9.

Lingfeng Shen, Haiyun Jiang, Lemao Liu, and Shuming Shi. 2023a. Sen2pro: A probabilistic perspective to sentence embedding from pre-trained language model. *arXiv preprint arXiv:2306.02247*.

Lingfeng Shen, Haiyun Jiang, Lemao Liu, and Shuming Shi. 2023b. A simple and plug-and-play method for unsupervised sentence representation enhancement. *arXiv preprint arXiv:2305.07824*.

Lingfeng Shen, Lemao Liu, Haiyun Jiang, and Shuming Shi. 2022. On the evaluation metrics for paraphrase generation. In *Proceedings of the 2022 Conference on Empirical Methods in Natural Language Processing*, pages 3178–3190, Abu Dhabi, United Arab Emirates. Association for Computational Linguistics.

Mingyang Song, Haiyun Jiang, Shuming Shi, Songfang Yao, Shilong Lu, Yi Feng, Huafeng Liu, and Liping Jing. 2023. Is chatgpt a good keyphrase generator? a preliminary study. *arXiv preprint arXiv:2303.13001*.

Hong Sun and Ming Zhou. 2012. Joint learning of a dual SMT system for paraphrase generation. In *Proceedings of the 50th Annual Meeting of the Association for Computational Linguistics (Volume 2: Short Papers)*, pages 38–42, Jeju Island, Korea. Association for Computational Linguistics.

Brian Thompson and Matt Post. 2020. Automatic machine translation evaluation in many languages via zero-shot paraphrasing. In *Proceedings of the 2020 Conference on Empirical Methods in Natural Language Processing (EMNLP)*, pages 90–121, Online. Association for Computational Linguistics.

Hugo Touvron, Thibaut Lavril, Gautier Izacard, Xavier Martinet, Marie-Anne Lachaux, Timothée Lacroix, Baptiste Rozière, Naman Goyal, Eric Hambro, Faisal Azhar, et al. 2023. Llama: Open and efficient foundation language models. *arXiv preprint arXiv:2302.13971*.

Jiaan Wang, Yunlong Liang, Fandong Meng, Haoxiang Shi, Zhixu Li, Jinan Xu, Jianfeng Qu, and Jie Zhou. 2023a. Is chatgpt a good nlg evaluator? a preliminary study.

Rui Wang, Jianzhu Bao, Fei Mi, Yi Chen, Hongru Wang, Yasheng Wang, Yitong Li, Lifeng Shang, Kam-Fai Wong, and Ruifeng Xu. 2023b. Retrieval-free knowledge injection through multi-document traversal for dialogue models. In *Annual Meeting of the Association for Computational Linguistics*.

Wei Xu, Chris Callison-Burch, and Bill Dolan. 2015. SemEval-2015 task 1: Paraphrase and semantic similarity in Twitter (PIT). In *Proceedings of the 9th International Workshop on Semantic Evaluation (SemEval 2015)*, pages 1–11, Denver, Colorado. Association for Computational Linguistics.

Wei Xu, Alan Ritter, Chris Callison-Burch, William B. Dolan, and Yangfeng Ji. 2014. Extracting lexically divergent paraphrases from Twitter. *Transactions of the Association for Computational Linguistics*, 2:435–448.

Weizhe Yuan, Graham Neubig, and Pengfei Liu. 2021. Bartscore: Evaluating generated text as text generation. In *Advances in Neural Information Processing Systems*, volume 34, pages 27263–27277. Curran Associates, Inc.

Jerrold H Zar. 2005. Spearman rank correlation. *Encyclopedia of biostatistics*, 7.

Chen Zhang, Yiming Chen, Luis Fernando D'Haro, Yan Zhang, Thomas Friedrichs, Grandee Lee, and Haizhou Li. 2021. DynaEval: Unifying turn and dialogue level evaluation. In *Proceedings of the 59th Annual Meeting of the Association for Computational Linguistics and the 11th International Joint Conference on Natural Language Processing (Volume 1: Long Papers)*, pages 5676–5689, Online. Association for Computational Linguistics.

Susan Zhang, Stephen Roller, Naman Goyal, Mikel Artetxe, Moya Chen, Shuohui Chen, Christopher Dewan, Mona Diab, Xian Li, Xi Victoria Lin, et al. 2022. Opt: Open pre-trained transformer language models. *arXiv preprint arXiv:2205.01068*.

Tianyi Zhang*, Varsha Kishore*, Felix Wu*, Kilian Q. Weinberger, and Yoav Artzi. 2020. Bertscore: Evaluating text generation with bert. In *International Conference on Learning Representations*.

Wei Zhao, Maxime Peyrard, Fei Liu, Yang Gao, Christian M. Meyer, and Steffen Eger. 2019. MoverScore: Text generation evaluating with contextualized embeddings and earth mover distance. In *Proceedings of the 2019 Conference on Empirical Methods in Natural Language Processing and the 9th International Joint Conference on Natural Language Processing (EMNLP-IJCNLP)*, pages 563–578, Hong Kong, China. Association for Computational Linguistics.

# A Different Prompts for Explicit Score on Story Generation

======= PROMPT FOR EXPLICIT SCORE V1 =======

Score the following storyline given the beginning of the story on a continual scale from 0 (worst) to 100 (best), where a score of 0 means "The storyline makes no sense and is totally not understandable" and a score of 100 means "The storyline is perfect-written and highly consistent with the given beginning of the story".

The beginning of the story:
`[Conditioned Text]`

Storyline:
`[Generated Text]`

Score:

======= PROMPT FOR EXPLICIT SCORE V2 =======

On a scale of 0 to 100, evaluate the storyline based on the given beginning. A score of 0 indicates that the storyline is incomprehensible, while a score of 100 means that the storyline is flawlessly written and logically follows from the beginning of the story.

The beginning of the story:
`[Conditioned Text]`

Storyline:
`[Generated Text]`

Score:

======= PROMPT FOR EXPLICIT SCORE V3 =======

Score the overall quality of the following storyline given the beginning of the story on a continual scale from 0 (worst) to 100 (best). Consider whether the storyline is well-written and consistent with the given beginning of the story.

The beginning of the story:
`[Conditioned Text]`

Storyline:
`[Generated Text]`

Score:

# B Different Prompts for Pairwise Comparison on Story Generation

======= PROMPT FOR EXPLICIT SCORE V4 =======

Score the following storyline given the beginning of the story with one to five stars. Where

- one star means "Nonsense",
- two stars mean "The storyline has some connections with the beginning, but is not understandable",
- three stars mean "The storyline has some connections with the beginning and is understandable",
- four stars mean "The storyline is consistent with the beginning and possibly involves a few grammar mistakes",
- and five stars mean "Perfect storyline and grammar".

The beginning of the story:
`[Conditioned Text]`

Storyline:
`[Generated Text]`

Stars (1-5):

======= PROMPT FOR EXPLICIT SCORE V5 =======

Score the following storyline given the beginning of the story on a continual scale from 0 (worst) to 100 (best), where a score of 0 means "The storyline makes no sense and is totally not understandable" and a score of 100 means "The storyline is perfect-written and highly consistent with the given beginning of the story". Please first give your reason carefully (indicated by "Reason:") and then decide your final score (indicated by "Score: 1-100").

The beginning of the story:
`[Conditioned Text]`

Storyline:
`[Generated Text]`

===== PROMPT FOR PAIRWISE COMPARISON V1 =====

Consider the following two storylines written according to the given beginning of the story:

The beginning of the story:
`[Conditioned Text]`

Storyline-1:
`[Generated Text-1]`

Storyline-2:
`[Generated Text-2]`

Question: Which storyline is better-written and more consistent with the beginning of the story? Please answer with one of the following options.

Options:
(A) Storyline-1
(B) Storyline-2
(C) Both storylines are equally well-written and consistent with the beginning of the story.

Answer: I will choose Option

===== PROMPT FOR PAIRWISE COMPARISON V2 =====

Question: Which storyline is better-written and more consistent with the beginning of the story? Please answer with one of the following options.

The beginning of the story:
`[Conditioned Text]`

Options:
(A) `[Generated Text-1]`
(B) `[Generated Text-2]`
(C) Both storylines are equally well-written and consistent with the beginning of the story.

Answer: I will choose Option

===== PROMPT FOR PAIRWISE COMPARISON V3 =====

Consider the following two storylines written according to the given beginning of the story:
The beginning of the story:
`[Conditioned Text]`

Storyline-1:
`[Generated Text-1]`

Storyline-2:
`[Generated Text-2]`

Question: Which storyline has poorer writing and is less consistent with the beginning of the story? Please answer with one of the following options.

Options:
(A) Storyline-1
(B) Storyline-2
(C) Both storylines are equally poor-written and inconsistent with the beginning of the story.

Answer: I will choose Option

===== PROMPT FOR PAIRWISE COMPARISON V4 =====

Consider the following two storylines written according to the given beginning of the story:
The beginning of the story:
`[Conditioned Text]`

Storyline-1:
`[Generated Text-1]`

Storyline-2:
`[Generated Text-2]`

Question: Which storyline is better-written and more consistent with the beginning of the story? Please first give your reason carefully (indicated by "Reason:") and then choose one of the following options (indicated by "Answer: A/B/C").

Options:
(A) Storyline-1
(B) Storyline-2
(C) Both storylines are equally well-written (poor-written) and consistent (inconsistent) with the beginning of the story.

## C An Explanation of Kendall's Tall-b

Kendall's Tau-b is a measure of the correlation between two variables, specifically designed to handle ties and ranks. The formula to calculate Kendall's Tau-b is as follows:

$$\tau_B = \frac{P - Q}{\sqrt{(P + Q + T)(P + Q + U)}}. \tag{2}$$

where P is the number of concordant pairs, Q is the number of discordant pairs, T is the number of ties only in human judgments, and U is the number of ties only in the given metric. To better understand the calculation of P, Q, T, and U, we can refer to the following table:

| | | Metric | | |
|---|---|---|---|---|
| | | $s_1 < s_2$ | $s_1 = s_2$ | $s_1 > s_2$ |
| Human | $s_1 < s_2$ | P | U | Q |
| | $s_1 = s_2$ | T | - | T |
| | $s_1 > s_2$ | Q | U | P |

# A Text-to-Text Model for Multilingual Offensive Language Identification

**Tharindu Ranasinghe*** 
Aston University
Birmingham, UK
t.ranasinghe@aston.ac.uk

**Marcos Zampieri*** 
George Mason University
Fairfax, VA, USA
mzampier@gmu.edu

## Abstract

The ubiquity of offensive content on social media is a growing cause for concern among companies and government organizations. Recently, transformer-based models such as BERT, XLNET, and XLM-R have achieved state-of-the-art performance in detecting various forms of offensive content (e.g. hate speech, cyberbullying, and cyberaggression). However, the majority of these models are limited in their capabilities due to their encoder-only architecture, which restricts the number and types of labels in downstream tasks. Addressing these limitations, this study presents the first pre-trained model with encoder-decoder architecture for offensive language identification with text-to-text transformers (T5) trained on two large offensive language identification datasets; SOLID and CCTK. We investigate the effectiveness of combining two datasets and selecting an optimal threshold in semi-supervised instances in SOLID in the T5 retraining step. Our pre-trained T5 model outperforms other transformer-based models fine-tuned for offensive language detection, such as fBERT and HateBERT, in multiple English benchmarks. Following a similar approach, we also train the first multilingual pre-trained model for offensive language identification using mT5 and evaluate its performance on a set of six different languages (German, Hindi, Korean, Marathi, Sinhala, and Spanish). The results demonstrate that this multilingual model achieves a new state-of-the-art on all the above datasets, showing its usefulness in multilingual scenarios. Our proposed T5-based models will be made freely available to the community.

## 1 Introduction

The widespread of offensive posts on social media platforms can have detrimental effects on users' mental health among other undesirable consequences. The relation between offensive language and mental health along with potential risks of self harm and depression has been widely addressed by previous studies (Bonanno and Hymel, 2013; Bannink et al., 2014; Bucur et al., 2021). To address this important issue, one of the most commonly employed strategies is to train systems to identify offensive content (Pavlopoulos et al., 2021a) mitigating its spread on social media platforms. By proactively identifying potentially harmful content, social media platforms aim to establish a safer and more inclusive environment for all users.

Early approaches to identifying offensive language ranged from classical machine learning models, such as support vector machines (Malmasi and Zampieri, 2017, 2018), to deep learning models based on word embeddings (Hettiarachchi and Ranasinghe, 2019). With the introduction of BERT (Devlin et al., 2019), transformer models have shown excellent results in offensive language identification (Zia et al., 2022). More recently, domain-specific language models for offensive language identification, such as fBERT (Sarkar et al., 2021), HateBERT (Caselli et al., 2021), and ToxicBERT[1]. have provided state-of-the-art in multiple offensive language identification benchmarks.

The aforementioned models can be grouped into two main categories following their training strategies. Models such as ToxicBERT have been trained using a classification objective by adding a classification layer on top of a BERT model and training on a large offensive language dataset. A clear limitation of this approach is that the trained model can only predict the classes that appear on the dataset. On the other hand, models such as fBERT (Sarkar et al., 2021) and HateBERT (Caselli et al., 2021) have been trained with a masked language modelling (MLM) objective. fBERT (Sarkar et al., 2021) has been trained on the offensive tweets in

**WARNING: This paper contains examples that are offensive in nature.**

*The two authors contributed equally to this work.

[1]ToxicBERT is available at https://huggingface.co/unitary/toxic-bert



*Findings of the Association for Computational Linguistics: IJCNLP-AACL 2023*, pages 375–384
November 1–4, 2023. ©2023 Asian Federation of Natural Language Processing

the SOLID (Rosenthal et al., 2021) dataset, while HateBERT (Caselli et al., 2021) has been trained on banned posts from Reddit Abusive Language dataset. The MLM strategy is not dependent on the number of classes present in the dataset. However, it is not possible to concatenate two datasets annotated with different annotation taxonomies under this strategy without mapping them into a common label (e.g. a general offensive class). This is a critical issue in offensive language identification as different datasets use different annotation schemes and problem formulations (e.g. hate speech, offensive, toxic, profanity). As a result, MLM based models are only trained on one dataset, which can limit their capabilities.

To address this important shortcoming, we introduce FT5, a pre-trained T5 model (Raffel et al., 2020) trained on two large-scale offensive language identification datasets. Since T5 follows a text-to-text approach, it does not rely on a classification layer. Therefore T5 (Raffel et al., 2020) can be used to train an offensive language identification model using different datasets without relying on the number of classes. We show that the proposed FT5 outperforms the plain T5 implementation as well as HateBERT (Caselli et al., 2021) and fBERT (Sarkar et al., 2021) on various offensive and hate speech detection tasks. To the best of our knowledge, this is the first pre-trained offensive language identification model based on T5.

All the previous models, such as ToxicBERT, HateBERT (Caselli et al., 2021) and fBERT (Sarkar et al., 2021) only supports English and training a large language model using similar approaches in low-resource languages can be difficult due to data scarcity. In this paper, we address this limitation by training a multilingual offensive language model, mFT5, which uses mT5 (Xue et al., 2021) as the base model. the results confirm that fine-tuned mFT5 produces state-of-the-art results in six languages, outperforming strong transformer-based models. To the best of our knowledge, mFT5 is the first multilingual model on offensive language opening exciting avenues for a multitude of languages.

The contributions of this paper are as follows:

1. An empirical evaluation of semi-supervised learning techniques that can be applied to train text-to-text models such as T5 (Raffel et al., 2020) and mT5 (Xue et al., 2021) in offensive language identification

2. A comprehensive evaluation of the effect of combining different datasets in pre-training text-to-text models.

3. The first-ever cross-lingual evaluation of mT5 (Xue et al., 2021) model in both high-resource and low-resource language settings.

4. The release of the FT5 and mFT5 made freely available to the research community, which are high-performing, state-of-the-art pre-trained models based on T5 for English and multilingual offensive language identification[2].

## 2 Related Work

### 2.1 Offensive Language Identification

The use of large pre-trained transformer models has become prevalent in NLP. This includes the development of various offensive language identification systems, which are based on transformer architectures, such as BERT (Devlin et al., 2019). These systems have demonstrated top performance in well-known competitions such as HASOC (Mandl et al., 2019), HatEval (Basile et al., 2019), OffensEval (Zampieri et al., 2019b, 2020), TRAC (Kumar et al., 2018), and TSD (Pavlopoulos et al., 2021b). Many of these competitions feature multilingual datasets opening opportunities for the use of cross-lingual models (Ranasinghe and Zampieri, 2020, 2021; Nozza, 2021). The outstanding results achieved by these systems provide concrete evidence that pre-trained transformer models are well-suited for detecting offensive content in both monolingual and multilingual settings.

User-generated content and offensive language online possess unique characteristics that are often not adequately captured by models trained on standard texts. Consequently, research has focused on the task of fine-tuning pre-trained models specifically for this challenging domain. There are several transformer models such as HateBERT (Caselli et al., 2021), fBERT (Sarkar et al., 2021) built for this purpose. In this study, we address the aforementioned limitations of fine-tuned transformer-based models. We propose the first multilingual domain-specific pre-trained offensive language identification model.

[2]https://github.com/TharinduDR/FT5

## 2.2 T5 Models

T5 models introduced by Raffel et al. (2020) have been widely used in many NLP tasks such as text classification (Bird et al., 2023), semantic similarity (Ni et al., 2022) and named entity recognition (Tavan and Najafi, 2022). As the T5 architecture follows a text-to-text approach, multi task learning can be used to improve the results with t5 (Raffel et al., 2020). Following the initial T5 model, multilingual T5 (mT5) models have also been proposed by Xue et al. (2021) which has provided excellent results in multilingual benchmarks. Several studies have used T5 in offensive language identification (Sabry et al., 2022; Adewumi et al., 2022). However, these studies only fine-tune the general T5 models for offensive language identification. To the best of our knowledge, this paper presents the first pre-trained domain specific T5 model for offensive language identification.

# 3 Methodology

**Training Data** In this study, we use two large offensive language identification datasets to retrain the T5 models; SOLID (Rosenthal et al., 2021) with over 9 million English tweets and CCTK with over 1.8 million posts from the civil comments platform. SOLID was the official dataset of SemEval-2020 Task 12 (OffensEval) (Zampieri et al., 2020). SOLID's annotation follows the OLID taxonomy (Zampieri et al., 2019a), which uses its level A (offensive vs non-offensive). Each instance in SOLID has been annotated semi-automatically with the mean and the standard deviation (STD) of the value for offensiveness predicted by four different machine learning models. CCTK was released for the Jigsaw Unintended Bias in Toxicity Classification Kaggle competition[3]. Each instance in CCTK has been annotated with one of the binary labels (toxic vs not toxic). Finally, we used multiple datasets for testing presented in Sections 4 and 5.

**Retraining T5** We select the *t5-large*[4] (Raffel et al., 2020) and train it using the instances from SOLID (Rosenthal et al., 2021) and CCTK. For the instances in SOLID, the input texts to the model were tweets, and the output texts were "OFF" if the mean value in SOLID is above 0.5 and "NOT" otherwise. We used different thresholds (0.05, 0.1, 0.15 and 0.2) for the STD value to filter the most confident examples from SOLID. For each threshold, we consider appending/ not appending the CCTK dataset. For the instances in CCTK, the input texts to the model were the posts, and the output texts were "TOX" if the text is toxic and "NOT" if they are not toxic. As shown in Figure 1 we use "OLID_A" prefix for SOLID instances and "CCTK" prefix for CCTK instances. To create mFT5, we select *mt5-large* (Xue et al., 2021)[5] and repeat the same process. For both models, we use the same configurations; a batch-size of 16, Adam optimiser with learning rate 1e−4, and a linear learning rate warm-up over 10% of the training data and trained the models over ten epochs. We use a cluster of four GeForce RTX 3090 GPUs to train the models.

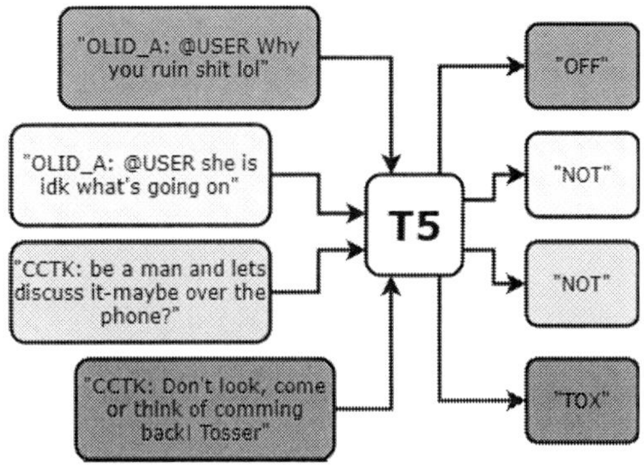


Figure 1: T5/ MT5 pre-training process

# 4 English Experiments and Results

To determine the effectiveness and portability of the trained FT5, we conducted a series of experiments using benchmark datasets in English and compared our model with a general-purpose T5 model. We used the same set of configurations for all the datasets evaluated in order to ensure consistency between all the experiments. This also provides a good starting configuration for researchers who intend to use FT5 on a new dataset. For the sentence-level tasks; the input to the model is the text and the output is the related label. For the token level tasks the input to the model is the text and the output is the text with "[OFF]" placeholders infront of the offensive tokens as shown in Figure 2.

For each dataset, we used different task spe-

[3]https://www.kaggle.com/c/jigsaw-unintended-bias-in-toxicity-classification

[4]t5-large model is available in HuggingFace at https://huggingface.co/t5-large

[5]mt5-large model is available in HuggingFace at https://huggingface.co/google/mt5-large

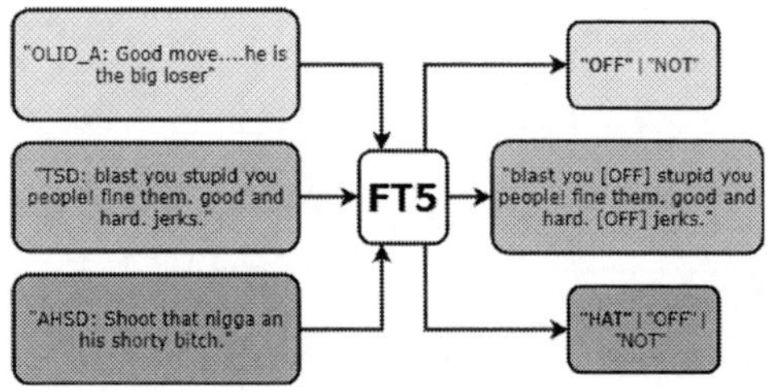


Figure 2: FT5 fine-tuning process for different tasks.

cific prefixes (OLID_A for OLID, TSD for toxic spans detection etc.). We used a batch-size of eight, Adam optimizer with learning rate 1e−4, and a linear learning rate warm-up over 10% of the training data. During the training process, the parameters of the transformer model were updated. The models were trained using only training data. Furthermore, they were evaluated while training using an evaluation set that had one fifth of the rows in training data. We performed early stopping if the evaluation loss did not improve over ten evaluation steps. All the models were trained for three epochs. These experiments were also conducted in a GeForce RTX 3090 GPU. All the experiments were conducted for ten times and we report the mean and standard deviation for each experiment.

**AHSD** In fine-grain aggression detection, classifying offensive language and hate speech is challenging. Hate speech contains explicit instances targeted towards a specific group of people intended to degrade or insult. Davidson et al. (2017) compiled a 24,783 English tweets dataset annotated with one of three labels – "hate speech", "only offensive", and "neither". The dataset contains 1,430 hate speech, 19,190 only offensive, and 4,163 instances that are neither. We further split the dataset into training and test sets in a 4:1 ratio.

**OLID** We use OLID, the official dataset for OffensEval 2019 (Zampieri et al., 2019b), one of the the most popular offensive language identification shared tasks. The dataset has 13,240 training and 860 test instances. There are 4,400 and 240 offensive posts in the training and test dataset, respectively. For the experiment, we chose sub-task A, a binary classification task between offensive and non-offensive posts.

**TRAC** TRAC was released for TRAC shared task 2020 (Kumar et al., 2020). The dataset has 4200 training and 1200 test instances with three classes: overtly aggressive, covertly aggressive and non-aggressive. TRAC is the most heterogeneous dataset we used in terms of data sources containing posts from Facebook, Twitter, and YouTube.

**TSD** For token-level prediction we use TSD, released within the scope of SemEval-2021 Task 5: Toxic Spans Detection for English (Pavlopoulos et al., 2021a). The dataset contains 10,000 posts (comments) from the publicly available Civil Comments dataset (Borkan et al., 2019). If a post is toxic, it has been annotated for its toxic spans.

**HateX** HateXplain dataset (Mathew et al., 2021) was also for offensive language identification at the token level. The dataset contains 11535 training and 3844 testing instances from GAB and twitter. We only used the word level annotations.

### 4.1 Sentence-level Offensive Language Identification

To evaluate the sentence-level tasks, we used the macro F1 score computed on predicted sentence labels and gold sentence labels.

We present the results for the SOLID data selection thresholds and data augmentation with CCTK in Table 1 in terms of $F_1$ Macro. For most of the datasets tested, the 0.1 STD SOLID threshold combined with the CCTK provided the best results. Having a large number of training instances provides better results up to a certain STD threshold in SOLID, and results do not improve with adding further training instances. Furthermore, the results show that the combination of CCTK and SOLID provides better results than having one dataset in the training set. This confirms our previous assumption that T5 can take advantage of multiple datasets via text to text transfer learning.

We select the T5 model retrained on SOLID filtered with 0.1 STD combined with the CCTK dataset as the FT5 model, which provided the best result in most of the datasets. We then compare the performance of FT5 with fBERT and HateBERT.

As can be seen in Table 2, FT5 outperforms fBERT and HateBERT in all of the datasets. Since the datasets contain offensive language identification, fine grained offensive language identification and fine-grained aggression identification, we can validate the effectiveness of the proposed FT5 model for offensive and aggressive language sentence-level classification tasks.

| Train Dataset(s) | STD | Inst. | Sentence-level | | | Token-level | |
|---|---|---|---|---|---|---|---|
| | | | AHSD | OLID | TRAC | TSD | HateX |
| SOLID | 0.05 | 18,169 | 0.832 ±0.009 | 0.807±0.006 | 0.849 ±0.005 | 0.542 ±0.004 | 0.801 ±0.006 |
| | 0.1 | 215,602 | 0.846 ±0.005 | 0.819±0.002 | 0.854 ±0.003 | 0.601 ±0.005 | 0.816 ±0.005 |
| | 0.15 | 1,282,474 | 0.870 ±0.005 | 0.813±0.003 | **0.870 ±0.002** | 0.591 ±0.008 | 0.801 ±0.006 |
| | 0.2 | 6,595,397 | 0.859 ±0.003 | 0.805±0.005 | 0.865 ±0.005 | 0.561 ±0.005 | 0.795 ±0.006 |
| SOLID+CCTK | 0.05 | 1,823,043 | 0.865 ±0.004 | 0.819±0.003 | 0.859 ±0.007 | 0.609 ±0.004 | 0.815 ±0.004 |
| | 0.1 | 2,020,476 | **0.886 ±0.004** | **0.823 ±0.002** | 0.869 ±0.005 | **0.648 ±0.005** | **0.825 ±0.004** |
| | 0.15 | 3,087,348 | 0.872 ±0.005 | 0.816±0.004 | 0.864 ±0.005 | 0.605 ±0.006 | 0.812 ±0.007 |
| | 0.2 | 8,400,271 | 0.868 ±0.005 | 0.809±0.006 | 0.858 ±0.006 | 0.589 ±0.012 | 0.808 ±0.009 |
| CCTK | NA | 1,804,874 | 0.832 ±0.009 | 0.813±0.006 | 0.842 ±0.005 | 0.595±0.004 | 0.809 ±0.006 |

Table 1: FT5 results for different sentence-level and token-level offensive language detection benchmarks.

| Dataset | Model | Macro F1 |
|---|---|---|
| AHSD | **FT5** | **0.886±0.004** |
| | fBERT | 0.878±0.005 |
| | HateBERT | 0.846±0.009 |
| | T5 | 0.821±0.012 |
| OLID | **FT5** | **0.823±0.002** |
| | fBERT | 0.810±0.005 |
| | HateBERT | 0.803±0.009 |
| | T5 | 0.775±0.006 |
| TRAC | **FT5** | **0.869±0.003** |
| | fBERT | 0.859±0.005 |
| | HateBERT | 0.848±0.006 |
| | T5 | 0.846±0.010 |

Table 2: The test set macro $F_1$ scores for sentence-level datasets and models. Results are ordered by performance. Best results are shown in bold font.

| Dataset | Model | Macro F1 |
|---|---|---|
| TSD | **FT5** | **0.648±0.012** |
| | fBERT | 0.530±0.021 |
| | T5 | 0.421±0.019 |
| | HateBERT | 0.410±0.027 |
| HateX | **FT5** | **0.825±0.008** |
| | fBERT | 0.812±0.009 |
| | HateBERT | 0.792±0.016 |
| | T5 | 0.775±0.025 |

Table 3: The test set macro $F_1$ scores for sentence-level datasets and models. Results are ordered by performance. Best results are shown in bold font.

### 4.2 Token-level Offensive Language Identification

Multiple studies on token-level offensive language identification has discussed the need for accurate token-level predictions for improved model explainability (Mathew et al., 2021; Zampieri et al., 2023). Motivated by recent studies, we investigate our model performance on token-level offensive language identification. The token-level tasks were evaluated using the macro F1 score computed on predicted character offsets and gold character offsets (Da San Martino et al., 2019).

FT5 outperforms fBERT and HateBERT in all of the token-level offensive language identification datasets too as can be seen in Table 3. There is a clear improvement with the TSD dataset where the FT5 model outperforms the fBERT model by 0.11 macro F1 score which is over a 20% boost.

## 5 Multilingual Experiments and Results

To determine the effectiveness and portability of our multilingual model; mFT5, we conducted a series of experiments using benchmark datasets covering high-resource, mid-resource and low-resource languages. These datasets are summarised in Table 4. We used the same set of configurations we used for English experiments. The models were trained using the training set and evaluated on the test sets of each dataset.

### 5.1 Sentence-level Offensive Language Identification

For sentence-level offensive language identification, we mapped the labels of each dataset to its closet annotation scheme as we did for English

| Language | Source(s) | Train, dev, test size | Labels | Sentence-level | Token-level |
|---|---|---|---|---|---|
| German (Risch et al., 2021) | Facebook | 2076, 519, 649 | Toxic<br>Not-toxic | TOX, NOT | NA |
| Spanish (Plaza-del Arco et al., 2021) | Twitter<br>Instagram<br>Youtube | 30163, 7540, 9425 | Offensive individual target<br>Offensive group target<br>Offensive other target<br>Expletive language<br>Non-offensive | OFF, NOT | NA |
| Hindi (Mandl et al., 2019) | Twitter | 5120, 1280, 1600 | Offensive<br>Not offensive | OFF, NOT | NA |
| Korean (Jeong et al., 2022) | Naver<br>YouTube | 25876, 6468, 8085 | Offensive<br>Not offensive | OFF, NOT | Available |
| Sinhala (Ranasinghe et al., 2022) | Twitter | 6000, 1500, 2500 | Offensive<br>Not offensive | OFF, NOT | Available |
| Marathi (Gaikwad et al., 2021) | Twitter | 2889, 722, 510 | Offensive<br>Not offensive | OFF, NOT | NA |

Table 4: Datasets that were used to evaluate mFt5 model. **Source** column displays the platform data extracted,**Train, dev, test size** column shows the number of instances of the train, dev and test sets. **Label** column shows the original labels and **Sentence-level** column show the output label in sentence-level experimenst discussed in Section 5. **Token-level** column shows the availability of the token-level data.

| Train Dataset(s) | STD | Inst. | High Resource | | Mid Resource | | Low Resource | |
|---|---|---|---|---|---|---|---|---|
| | | | German | Spanish | Hindi | Korean | Sinhala | Marathi |
| SOLID | 0.05 | 18,169 | 0.567 ±0.010 | 0.832 ±0.009 | 0.799 ±0.005 | 0.735 ±0.004 | 0.748 ±0.008 | 0.789 ±0.016 |
| | 0.1 | 215,602 | 0.601 ±0.002 | 0.846 ±0.005 | 0.807 ±0.003 | 0.776 ±0.005 | 0.756 ±0.008 | 0.825 ±0.009 |
| | 0.15 | 1,282,474 | 0.598 ±0.007 | 0.870 ±0.005 | 0.839 ±0.002 | 0.781 ±0.008 | 0.784 ±0.007 | **0.858 ±0.006** |
| | 0.2 | 6,595,397 | 0.588 ±0.006 | 0.859 ±0.003 | 0.825 ±0.005 | 0.757 ±0.005 | 0.766 ±0.008 | 0.844 ±0.010 |
| SOLID +CCTK | 0.05 | 1,823,043 | 0.611 ±0.004 | 0.852±0.005 | 0.859 ±0.007 | 0.769 ±0.004 | 0.812±0.016 | 0.835 ±0.009 |
| | 0.1 | 2,020,476 | **0.653±0.031** | **0.886 ±0.004** | **0.845 ±0.005** | **0.799±0.004** | **0.856±0.007** | 0.854±0.006 |
| | 0.15 | 3,087,348 | 0.642±0.005 | 0.872 ±0.005 | 0.822 ±0.005 | 0.778 ±0.006 | 0.856 ±0.006 | 0.849±0.008 |
| | 0.2 | 8,400,271 | 0.611 ±0.005 | 0.843±0.012 | 0.818 ±0.006 | 0.765 ±0.012 | 0.836 ±0.006 | 0.811±0.005 |
| CCTK | NA | 1,804,874 | 0.628 ±0.009 | 0.829±0.006 | 0.825 ±0.005 | 0.775±0.004 | 0.796 ±0.005 | 0.801 ±0.003 |

Table 5: mFT5 results for different multilingual offensive language detection benchmarks.

benchmarks; OLID level A (offensive, not offensive) or CCTK (toxic, non toxic). Following this, Spanish, Hindi, Korean, Sinhala and Marathi labels were mapped to OLID level A, and German labels were mapped to CCTK as shown in *sentence-level* column in Table 4. We use "OLID_A" prefix for Spanish, Hindi, Korean, Sinhala and Marathi instances and "CCTK" prefix for German instances. In the training process, we started with different pre-trained models on the configurations described in Section 3. The input to the model is the text preceded by the relevant prefix, and the output is the related label. We performed individual experiments for each language separately.

We present the results for the SOLID data selection thresholds and data augmentation with CCTK in Table 5 in terms of $F_1$ Macro for each test set. For most of the datasets tested, the 0.1 STD SOLID threshold combined with the CCTK provided the best results. Having a large number of training instances provides better results up to a certain STD threshold in SOLID, and results do not improve with adding further training instances. Furthermore, the results show that the combination of CCTK and SOLID provides better results than having one dataset in the training set. This confirms our previous assumption that T5 can take advantage of multiple datasets via text to text transfer learning. We select the T5 model retrained on SOLID filtered with 0.1 STD combined with the CCTK dataset as the FT5 model, which provided the best result in five out of six datasets.

We then compare the performance of mFT5 with mBERT and XLM-R base models. These models are trained on the training set of each dataset by adding a classification layer on top of the transformer model. As shown in Table 6, mFT5 outperforms mBERT and XLM-R in all of the datasets. Since these datasets contain high-resource and low-resource languages as well as data from different social media platforms, we can validate the effectiveness of the proposed mFT5 model for offensive language identification in multiple languages and platforms.

| Dataset | Model | Macro F1 |
|---|---|---|
| German | **mFT5** | **0.653±0.031** |
| | XLM-R | 0.621±0.023 |
| | mBERT | 0.572±0.013 |
| | mFT5* | 0.438±0.015 |
| | mT5 | 0.398±0.016 |
| Spanish | **mFT5** | **0.886±0.004** |
| | XLM-R | 0.853±0.005 |
| | mBERT | 0.821±0.008 |
| | mFT5* | 0.785±0.005 |
| | mT5 | 0.626±0.027 |
| Hindi | **mFT5** | **0.845±0.003** |
| | XLM-R | 0.811±0.007 |
| | mBERT | 0.798±0.006 |
| | mFT5* | 0.745±0.007 |
| | mT5 | 0.612±0.012 |
| Korean | **mFT5** | **0.799±0.004** |
| | XLM-R | 0.765±0.006 |
| | mBERT | 0.755±0.008 |
| | mFT5* | 0.736±0.008 |
| | mT5 | 0.715±0.005 |
| Sinhala | **mFT5** | **0.856±0.007** |
| | XLM-R | 0.834±0.005 |
| | mFT5* | 0.746±0.009 |
| | mT5 | 0.538±0.029 |
| | mBERT | 0.531±0.013 |
| Marathi | **mFT5** | **0.854±0.006** |
| | XLM-R | 0.843±0.003 |
| | mBERT | 0.821±0.006 |
| | mFT5* | 0.708±0.012 |
| | mT5 | 0.421±0.017 |

Table 6: The test set macro $F_1$ scores for coarse-grained offensive language detection. Results are ordered by performance. The best results are shown in bold font.

**Zero-shot Offensive Language Identification** - We also experimented with zero-shot cross-lingual offensive language identification with the mFT5 model. With this setting, we did not train the mFT5 on the language-specific training data. The results are shown in mFT5* rows in Table 6. While zero-shot cross-lingual experiments did not provide the best results, they provided very competitive results compared to the baselines. The results confirm the strong cross-lingual nature of the pre-trained mFT5 model in detecting offensive language. It should also be noted that an MLM approach similar to fBERT and HateBERT needs labelled data to fine-tune and will not be able to provide zero-shot offensive language identification. Therefore, mFT5 is useful for low-resource languages where the training data is scarce.

### 5.2 Token-level Offensive Language Identification

We also experimented with token-level offensive language identification in the datasets where the token-level labels are available; Korean and Sinhala. The input to the model is the text, and the output is the text with "[OFF]" placeholders in front of the offensive tokens. To evaluate the models, we used the macro F1 score computed on predicted offensive tokens and gold offensive tokens. We compared the results with token classification architecture in mBERT and XLM-R large models.

| Dataset | Model | Macro F1 |
|---|---|---|
| Korean | **mFT5** | **0.489±0.004** |
| | XLM-R | 0.466±0.009 |
| | mBERT | 0.453±0.013 |
| | mT5 | 0.311±0.016 |
| Sinhala | **mFT5** | **0.743±0.009** |
| | XLM-R | 0.723±0.013 |
| | mT5 | 0.316±0.023 |
| | mBERT | 0.00 |

Table 7: The test set macro $F_1$ scores for token-level offensive language detection. Results are ordered by performance. The best results are shown in bold font.

As shown in Table 7, mFT5 outperforms mBERT and XLM-R in all of the token-level offensive language identification datasets too. It should be noted that pre-trained models with task-specific heads such as toxic-bert will not be able to perform token-level tasks. However, our text-to-text approach in mFT5 provided state-of-the-art results at token-level too.

## 6 Conclusion and Future Work

Neural transformer models have outperformed previous state-of-the-art deep learning models across different NLP tasks including offensive language identification. Following impressive results in international benchmark competitions, domain-specific pre-trained neural transformers such as ToxicBERT, fBERT and HateBERT have been proposed for offensive language identification. As discussed in this paper, these models have limitations which makes it difficult extend them in to different datasets. We address these limitations by proposing FT5, a *t5-large* model that has been trained using over 2 million instances from the SOLID and CCTK datasets. The FT5 model achieves better results in both sentence-level and token-level tasks across different offensive language identification benchmarks.

This paper also introduced mFT5. To the best of our knowledge, mFT5 is the first pre-trained multilingual offensive language detection model. The model uses the *mt5-large* and is trained using the same data used to train FT5. We show that the proposed FmT5 model achieves better results in both sentence-level and token-level tasks compared to the mBERT, XLM-R, and the vanilla mT5 model across different offensive language identification benchmark datasets. We show that the model performs consistently well across different languages and platforms. Furthermore, the model showed strong zero-shot cross-lingual results opening exciting new avenues for multilingual offensive language detection.

In future work, we would like to extend the proposed FT5 model to the identification of offensive spans along with their targets using the recently released TBO dataset (Zampieri et al., 2023). We believe that modelling targets and offensive expressions jointly is an important step towards improving explainability in offensive language identification systems. Another important direction we have been exploring is the computational efficiency. We have recently experimented with teacher-student architectures using knowledge distillation (KD) and we have shown that the use of KD results in lightweight models that are more computationally efficient and perform on par with larger models (Ranasinghe and Zampieri, 2023). We would like to investigate teacher-student architectures using the proposed FT5 model. Finally, we are interested in the application of multilingual models to low-resource scenarios. Thousands of languages and dialects are spoken in the world, but research on offensive language identification is still (mostly) restricted to English and a few other high-resource languages. We believe that the release of mT5 will encourage research on offensive language identification models for low-resource languages, dialects, and other challenging linguistic scenarios such as code-mixed texts.

## Limitations

Training a T5 model requires a large amount of computing resources. We noted that training a T5 model can take more GPU resources than training a BERT model such as fBERT (Sarkar et al., 2021). Therefore, we did not experiment with large T5 models such as T5-XL and T5-XXL. While these models might perform better than T5-Large models we experimented with, they would consume more resources, limiting their potential use cases.

## Ethics Statement

FT5 and mFT5 are essentially T5 models for offensive language identification, which is trained on multiple publicly available datasets. We used multiple datasets referenced in this paper which were previously collected and annotated to evaluate the models. No new data collection has been carried out as part of this work. We have not collected or processed writers'/users' information, nor have we carried out any form of user profiling to protect users' privacy and identity.

We believe that content moderation should be a trustworthy and transparent process applied to clearly harmful content so it does not hinder individual freedom of expression rights. We encourage research in automatically detecting offensive content on the web trough a trustworthy and transparent process. Using our proposed models for this purpose will alleviate the psychological burden for social media moderators who are exposed to large amounts offensive content while ensuring a more transparent moderation process.

## Acknowledgments

We would like to thank the anonymous AACL-IJCNLP reviewers for their insightful feedback. We further thank the creators of the datasets used in this paper for making the datasets publicly available for our research.

The computational experiments in this paper were conducted on an Aston EPS Machine Learning Server, funded by the EPSRC Core Equipment Fund, Grant EP/V036106/1.

## References

Tosin Adewumi, Sana Sabah Sabry, Nosheen Abid, Foteini Liwicki, and Marcus Liwicki. 2022. T5 for hate speech, augmented data and ensemble. *arXiv preprint arXiv:2210.05480.*

Rienke Bannink, Suzanne Broeren, Petra M van de Looij-Jansen, Frouwkje G de Waart, and Hein Raat. 2014. Cyber and Traditional Bullying Victimization as a Risk Factor for Mental Health Problems and Suicidal Ideation in Adolescents. *PloS one*, 9(4).

Valerio Basile, Cristina Bosco, Elisabetta Fersini, Debora Nozza, Viviana Patti, Francisco Manuel Rangel Pardo, Paolo Rosso, and Manuela Sanguinetti. 2019. Semeval-2019 task 5: Multilingual detection of hate speech against immigrants and women in twitter. In *Proceedings of SemEval.*

Jordan J. Bird, Anikó Ekárt, and Diego R. Faria. 2023. Chatbot interaction with artificial intelligence: human data augmentation with t5 and language transformer ensemble for text classification. *Journal of Ambient Intelligence and Humanized Computing*, 14(4):3129–3144.

Rina A Bonanno and Shelley Hymel. 2013. Cyber bullying and internalizing difficulties: Above and beyond the impact of traditional forms of bullying. *Journal of youth and adolescence*, 42(5):685–697.

Daniel Borkan, Lucas Dixon, Jeffrey Sorensen, Nithum Thain, and Lucy Vasserman. 2019. Nuanced metrics for measuring unintended bias with real data for text classification. In *Proceedings of WWW.*

Ana-Maria Bucur, Marcos Zampieri, and Liviu P. Dinu. 2021. An exploratory analysis of the relation between offensive language and mental health. In *Findings of ACL.*

Tommaso Caselli, Valerio Basile, Jelena Mitrović, and Michael Granitzer. 2021. Hatebert: Retraining bert for abusive language detection in english. In *Proceedings of WOAH.*

Giovanni Da San Martino, Seunghak Yu, Alberto Barrón-Cedeño, Rostislav Petrov, and Preslav Nakov. 2019. Fine-grained analysis of propaganda in news article. In *Proceedings of EMNLP.*

Thomas Davidson, Dana Warmsley, Michael W. Macy, and Ingmar Weber. 2017. Automated hate speech detection and the problem of offensive language. In *Proceedings of ICWSM.*

Jacob Devlin, Ming-Wei Chang, Kenton Lee, and Kristina Toutanova. 2019. BERT: Pre-training of Deep Bidirectional Transformers for Language Understanding. In *Proceedings of NAACL.*

Saurabh Sampatrao Gaikwad, Tharindu Ranasinghe, Marcos Zampieri, and Christopher Homan. 2021. Cross-lingual offensive language identification for low resource languages: The case of Marathi. In *Proceedings of RANLP.*

Hansi Hettiarachchi and Tharindu Ranasinghe. 2019. Emoji powered capsule network to detect type and target of offensive posts in social media. In *Proceedings of RANLP.*

Younghoon Jeong, Juhyun Oh, Jaimeen Ahn, Jongwon Lee, Jihyung Mon, Sungjoon Park, and Alice Oh. 2022. Kold: Korean offensive language dataset. In *Findings of the ACL.*

Ritesh Kumar, Atul Kr Ojha, Shervin Malmasi, and Marcos Zampieri. 2018. Benchmarking Aggression Identification in Social Media. In *Proceedings of TRAC.*

Ritesh Kumar, Atul Kr. Ojha, Shervin Malmasi, and Marcos Zampieri. 2020. Evaluating aggression identification in social media. In *Proceedings of TRAC.*

Shervin Malmasi and Marcos Zampieri. 2017. Detecting hate speech in social media. In *Proceedings of RANLP.*

Shervin Malmasi and Marcos Zampieri. 2018. Challenges in discriminating profanity from hate speech. *Journal of Experimental & Theoretical Artificial Intelligence*, 30(2):187–202.

Thomas Mandl, Sandip Modha, Prasenjit Majumder, Daksh Patel, Mohana Dave, Chintak Mandlia, and Aditya Patel. 2019. Overview of the hasoc track at fire 2019: Hate speech and offensive content identification in indo-european languages. In *Proceedings of FIRE.*

Binny Mathew, Punyajoy Saha, Seid Muhie Yimam, Chris Biemann, Pawan Goyal, and Animesh Mukherjee. 2021. HateXplain: A Benchmark Dataset for Explainable Hate Speech Detection. In *Proceedings of AAAI.*

Jianmo Ni, Gustavo Hernandez Abrego, Noah Constant, Ji Ma, Keith Hall, Daniel Cer, and Yinfei Yang. 2022. Sentence-t5: Scalable sentence encoders from pre-trained text-to-text models. In *Findings of the ACL.*

Debora Nozza. 2021. Exposing the limits of zero-shot cross-lingual hate speech detection. In *Proceedings of ACL.*

John Pavlopoulos, Jeffrey Sorensen, Léo Laugier, and Ion Androutsopoulos. 2021a. SemEval-2021 task 5: Toxic spans detection. In *Proceedings of SemEval.*

John Pavlopoulos, Jeffrey Sorensen, Léo Laugier, and Ion Androutsopoulos. 2021b. SemEval-2021 task 5: Toxic spans detection. In *Proceedings of SemEval*.

Flor Miriam Plaza-del Arco, Arturo Montejo-Ráez, L. Alfonso Ureña-López, and María-Teresa Martín-Valdivia. 2021. OffendES: A new corpus in Spanish for offensive language research. In *Proceedings of RANLP*.

Colin Raffel, Noam Shazeer, Adam Roberts, Katherine Lee, Sharan Narang, Michael Matena, Yanqi Zhou, Wei Li, and Peter J Liu. 2020. Exploring the limits of transfer learning with a unified text-to-text transformer. *Journal of Machine Learning Research*, 21:1–67.

Tharindu Ranasinghe, Isuri Anuradha, Damith Premasiri, Kanishka Silva, Hansi Hettiarachchi, Lasitha Uyangodage, and Marcos Zampieri. 2022. Sold: Sinhala offensive language dataset. *arXiv preprint arXiv:2212.00851*.

Tharindu Ranasinghe and Marcos Zampieri. 2020. Multilingual Offensive Language Identification with Cross-lingual Embeddings. In *Proceedings of EMNLP*.

Tharindu Ranasinghe and Marcos Zampieri. 2021. Multilingual offensive language identification for low-resource languages. *Transactions on Asian and Low-Resource Language Information Processing*, 21(1):1–13.

Tharindu Ranasinghe and Marcos Zampieri. 2023. Teacher and student models of offensive language in social media. In *Findings of the ACL*.

Julian Risch, Anke Stoll, Lena Wilms, and Michael Wiegand. 2021. Overview of the GermEval 2021 shared task on the identification of toxic, engaging, and fact-claiming comments. In *Proceedings of the GermEval*.

Sara Rosenthal, Pepa Atanasova, Georgi Karadzhov, Marcos Zampieri, and Preslav Nakov. 2021. SOLID: A Large-Scale Weakly Supervised Dataset for Offensive Language Identification. In *Findings of the ACL*.

Sana Sabah Sabry, Tosin Adewumi, Nosheen Abid, György Kovács, Foteini Liwicki, and Marcus Liwicki. 2022. Hat5: Hate language identification using text-to-text transfer transformer. *arXiv preprint arXiv:2202.05690*.

Diptanu Sarkar, Marcos Zampieri, Tharindu Ranasinghe, and Alexander Ororbia. 2021. fbert: A neural transformer for identifying offensive content. In *Findings of EMNLP*.

Ehsan Tavan and Maryam Najafi. 2022. MarSan at SemEval-2022 task 11: Multilingual complex named entity recognition using t5 and transformer encoder. In *Proceedings of SemEval*.

Linting Xue, Noah Constant, Adam Roberts, Mihir Kale, Rami Al-Rfou, Aditya Siddhant, Aditya Barua, and Colin Raffel. 2021. mT5: A massively multilingual pre-trained text-to-text transformer. In *Proceedings of NAACL*.

Marcos Zampieri, Shervin Malmasi, Preslav Nakov, Sara Rosenthal, Noura Farra, and Ritesh Kumar. 2019a. Predicting the type and target of offensive posts in social media. In *Proceedings of NAACL*.

Marcos Zampieri, Shervin Malmasi, Preslav Nakov, Sara Rosenthal, Noura Farra, and Ritesh Kumar. 2019b. SemEval-2019 Task 6: Identifying and Categorizing Offensive Language in Social Media (OffensEval). In *Proceedings of SemEval*.

Marcos Zampieri, Skye Morgan, Kai North, Tharindu Ranasinghe, Austin Simmmons, Paridhi Khandelwal, Sara Rosenthal, and Preslav Nakov. 2023. Target-based offensive language identification. In *Proceedings of ACL*.

Marcos Zampieri, Preslav Nakov, Sara Rosenthal, Pepa Atanasova, Georgi Karadzhov, Hamdy Mubarak, Leon Derczynski, Zeses Pitenis, and Çağrı Çöltekin. 2020. SemEval-2020 Task 12: Multilingual Offensive Language Identification in Social Media (OffensEval 2020). In *Proceedings of SemEval*.

Haris Bin Zia, Ignacio Castro, Arkaitz Zubiaga, and Gareth Tyson. 2022. Improving zero-shot cross-lingual hate speech detection with pseudo-label fine-tuning of transformer language models. In *Proceedings of ICWSM*.

# Few-shot Named Entity Recognition with Supported and Dependent Label Representations

**Yasuhide Miura**
Fujifilm Corporation
yasuhide.a.miura@fujifilm.com

**Takumi Takahashi**
Fujifilm Corporation
takumi.c.takahashi@fujifilm.com

## Abstract

We explore the problem of few-shot named entity recognition (NER) by introducing two ideas to improve label representations. Recently, the use of token representations with a distance metric has been shown to be effective in few-shot NER, and we take an approach to use label representations along with token representations. Firstly, we add *support examples* to a label name (e.g., "person; example: Federic Krupp, Gao, Honecker, Bush, Deverow") when obtaining a label representation. Secondly, we estimate a transition score among labels with a bilinear function among label representations. The proposed approach is evaluated on 4 open few-shot NER datasets and we found that the approach can improve the performance of one-stage few-shot NER.

## 1 Introduction

The advance of large language models (e.g., BERT, GPT) has brought some of natural language understanding tasks to be tackled with few training samples. One such task that has especially gathered an attention from researchers is named entity recognition (NER) where a simple nearest neighbor classification using an NER model and a distance metric has shown to achieve a moderate performance in a few-shot setting (Yang and Katiyar, 2020). Ma et al. (2022a) proposed a related but slightly different approach where they prepare an additional BERT to encode labels into representations.

We extend an idea to use label representations to improve few-shot NER. A simple approach to obtain label representations is to encode just label names (Ma et al., 2022a), and we add randomly sampled label examples to label names and encode the combined label names and examples to improve label representations. Figure 1 illustrates our approach to use label examples as the supports of label names. In this approach, an input text and all labels are encoded with a dual encoder architecture. For each token, similarities against all labels are calculated to decide a label. The extension to add label examples may seem like a naive approach to improve label representations but this approach follows previous findings to obtain fine-grained label representations. Firstly, in the context of zero-shot NER, Aly et al. (2021) explored the effectiveness of using label descriptions to encode labels. They have found that the use of label name is a strong baseline to represent a label and a label description can further improve the performance of zero-shot NER depending on its quality. One downside of using label descriptions is that fine-grained descriptions are not always available in an NER dataset. Secondly, an approach to use multiple examples to estimate a label is a well-known approach of Prototypical Networks (Snell et al., 2017). In a typical Prototypical Networks setting, a label prototype can be represented as an average of multiple examples.

We further extend the approach to use label representations in few-shot NER by estimating a label dependency between two labels. A straightforward approach to model label dependencies in NER is to add a Conditional Random Field (CRF, Lafferty et al., 2001) layer after a token encoder (Lample et al., 2016). However, this CRF layer is known to be difficult to transfer since it directly learns a $K \times K$ transition matrix over $K$ labels (Yang and Katiyar, 2020; Hou et al., 2020). We estimate a transition score between two labels with a trainable function which maps two label representations into a single scalar score. We show that this estimation works quite effectively in the dual encoder architecture.

In summary, the contributions of this paper are the followings:

1. We propose an approach to sample *support examples* to improve label representations for few-shot NER and confirm its effectiveness on 4 few-shot NER datasets.



*Findings of the Association for Computational Linguistics: IJCNLP-AACL 2023*, pages 385–391
November 1–4, 2023. 

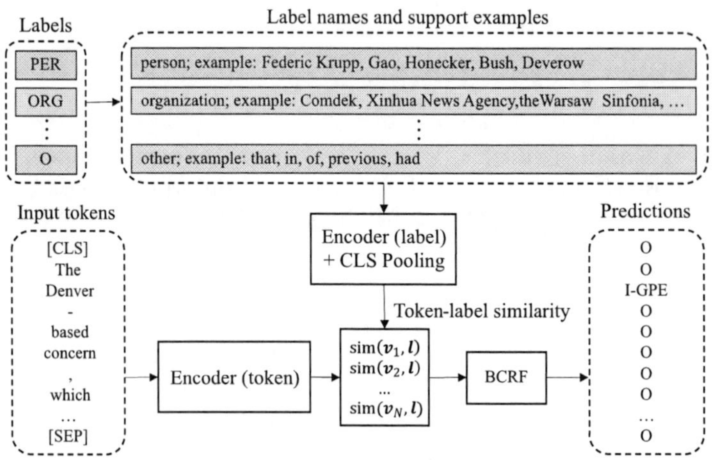


Figure 1: The overview of our approach to encode label representations by adding randomly sampled *support examples*. *Encoder* is a large language model such as BERT, *sim* is a similarity function among representations, $v_n$ is the token representation of $n$-th token, $l$ is label representations and *BCRF* is Bilinear-trainsition CRF (§3.3).

2. We define a trainable function between two label representation to estimate a transition score of the two labels and show its transfer capability in a few-shot setting.

## 2 Related Work

### 2.1 One-stage Few-shot NER

The use of distance metric has shown to be effective in a few-shot setting, where Wiseman and Stratos (2019) and Yang and Katiyar (2020) found that a nearest neighbor search among token representations can be a promising approach for few-shot NER. Fritzler et al. (2019) and Hou et al. (2020) have explored Prototypical Networks to model token-level entity prototypes in few-shot NER. These ideas are further investigated to train a model with a contrastive learning objective (Das et al., 2022). Like these approaches, our approach is in the paradigm of one-stage few-shot NER where named entities are recognized simply as the labels of input tokens.

### 2.2 Two-stage Few-shot NER

Recently, the paradigm of two-stage few-shot NER (Wang et al., 2022a) where entity spans are extracted in the first stage and their types are recognized in the second stage are investigated to extend the one-stage few-shot NER. In this paradigm, span or entity prototypes are defined (Wang et al., 2022b; Ji et al., 2022; Ma et al., 2022b; Wang et al., 2022a) to achieve stronger performances with the complexity of an additional stage.

### 2.3 Label Representation in NER

The use of label description has been also explored in a low-resource NER. Aly et al. (2021) explored the effect of label description in a zero-shot NER and Wang et al. (2021) has utilized label descriptions along with entity representations in a few-shot and a zero-shot NER. Ma et al. (2022a) has shown that simply using label names is quite effective in few-shot NER. Our approach extends these ideas to use support samples to improve label representation in few-shot NER.

## 3 Method

### 3.1 Dual Encoder Model

We followed the approach of dual encoders that was taken by Aly et al. (2021) and Ma et al. (2022a) as the base architecture of our model. As shown in Figure 1, we prepare an encoder for an input tokens and an encoder for labels. Given input tokens $\boldsymbol{u}_I$, the tokens are encoded with a language model $\boldsymbol{v} = \mathrm{LM}_{\mathrm{token}}(\boldsymbol{u}_I)$. The tokens of given labels $\boldsymbol{u}_L$ are similarly encoded with another language model $\boldsymbol{m} = \mathrm{LM}_{\mathrm{label}}(\boldsymbol{u}_L)$, and the representations of CLS[1] are pooled as label representations $\boldsymbol{l}$. For each token representation $\boldsymbol{v}_n$, similarities against all label representations are calculated with a similarity function as $\boldsymbol{o}_n = \mathrm{sim}(\boldsymbol{v}_n, \boldsymbol{l})$. These token-label similarities are used to calculate a loss against true labels. As done in previous studies, we first pre-finetune this model on a large scale NER

[1]A special token of a language model that is prepended to an input text.

**Algorithm 1** Support example sampling

**Require:** input_text $x$, label $y$, training_texts $\boldsymbol{X}$, # of example $n$

$S \leftarrow \phi$
**while** $|S| < n$ **do**
  // Sample a text including $y$ from $\boldsymbol{X}$
  $x_y \leftarrow \text{sample\_text}(\boldsymbol{X}, y)$
  **if** $x_y \neq x$ **then**
    **if** $y \neq \text{O}$ **then**
      $s_y \leftarrow \text{sample\_entity}(x_y)$
    **else**
      $s_y \leftarrow \text{sample\_word}(x_y)$
    **end if**
    $S \leftarrow S \uplus \{s_y\}$
  **end if**
**end while**
**return** $S$

dataset (e.g., OntoNotes 5.0) and then fine-tune it on a few-shot NER dataset.

### 3.2 Support Example Sampling

The dual encoder model encodes label tokens to obtain label representations. Our idea improves label representations by extending label tokens with support examples. Algorithm 1 shows processes to sample support examples $S$ for input text $x$ and label $y$. In the case of *PER* label in Figure 1, $n = 5$ examples of *Federic Krupp*, *Gao*, *Honecker*, *Bush* and *Deverow* are sampled from entire training data $\boldsymbol{X}$[2]. These examples are then combined with the label name *person* with the fixed text snippet of "; example:"[3]. One exceptional label that needs to be considered in this sampling is *O* label. Since *O* is not a label for named entity and does not have an entity boundary, we decided to samples a non-entity word from text $x_y$.

### 3.3 Estimation of Transition Score

Lample et al. (2016) have shown that a CRF layer can be added to a token encoder to improve NER. However, the few-shot transfer of this CRF layer is known to be difficult since the prediction score is defined as $s(\boldsymbol{x}, \boldsymbol{y}) = \sum_i A_{y_i,y_{i+1}} + \sum_i P_{i,y_i}$ where $i$ is a token index, $\boldsymbol{A}$ is a transition matrix and $\boldsymbol{P}$ is an emission matrix. A typical approach to realize $\boldsymbol{A}$ is to prepare a trainable $K \times K$ matrix when there are $K$ labels. We estimate a transition score among two labels $A_{y_i,y_{i+1}}$ simply with a bilinear function as

$$A_{y_i,y_{i+1}} = \boldsymbol{l}_i^T W \boldsymbol{l}_{i+1} + b \tag{1}$$

where $W$ is a trainable weight matrix of size $D \times D$, $b$ is a bias and $D$ is the embedding size of the label encoder. We call a score estimated with this approach **B**ilinear-transition **CRF** (BCRF) score. The estimation of a transition score has been investigated in a more resource rich setting in Hu et al. (2020). Our BCRF score takes a simple estimation approach since we focus on a resource poor few-shot setting.

## 4 Experiment

### 4.1 Datasets and Baselines

We evaluate the effectiveness of our approach using 4 datasets: Few-NERD (Ding et al., 2021), CoNLL-2003 (Tjong Kim Sang and De Meulder, 2003), WNUT-2017 (Derczynski et al., 2017) and i2b2-2014 (Stubbs and Özlem Uzuner, 2015). Few-NERD is a large-scale dataset specialized for the evaluation of few-shot NER. CoNLL-2003, WNUT-2017 and i2b2-2014 are datasets that were used in a few-shot domain transfer setting in previous studies (Yang and Katiyar, 2020; Ma et al., 2022a; Das et al., 2022; Ji et al., 2022).

We compare our approach against various state-of-the-art one-stage baselines (§2.1) and two-stage baselines (§2.2). For the one-stage baselines, we compare against ProtoBERT (Snell et al., 2017), StructShot (Yang and Katiyar, 2020), LabelSem (Ma et al., 2022a) and CONTaiNER (Das et al., 2022). For the two-stage baselines, we compare against ESD (Wang et al., 2022b), MAML-ProtoNet (Ma et al., 2022b), EPNet (Ji et al., 2022) and SpanProto (Wang et al., 2022a). For the scores of ProtoBERT, StructShot and CONTaiNER, we refer to the values reported in Das et al. (2022). For the scores of LabelSem, ESD, MAML-ProtoNet, EPNet and SpanProto, we refer to the values reported in the original papers.

### 4.2 Model Configuration

We first pre-finetuned the dual encoder model (§3.1) on a large-scale NER dataset. The training section is used for Few-NERD and OntoNotes 5.0 (Weischedel et al., 2013) is used for CoNLL-2003, WNUT-2017 and i2b2-2014. BERT base (cased) is used as language models and dot product is used as the similarity function of the model. IO scheme is

[2]This sampling is done for every training batch. This random process is important for the dual encoder model to avoid overfitting to certain examples.

[3]In 1-shot NER, this algorithm can fail to sample examples. In such case, we used the text snippet of "; example: none".

| | | INTRA | | | | INTER | | | |
|---|---|---|---|---|---|---|---|---|---|
| | | 5-way | | 10-way | | 5-way | | 10-way | |
| Stage | Model | 1~2-S | 5~10-S | 1~2-S | 5~10-S | 1~2-S | 5~10-S | 1~2-S | 5~10-S |
| one | ProtoBERT | 23.45 | 41.93 | 19.76 | 34.61 | 44.44 | 58.80 | 39.09 | 53.97 |
| | StructShot | 35.92 | 38.83 | 25.38 | 26.39 | 57.33 | 57.16 | 49.46 | 49.39 |
| | CONTaiNER | 40.40 | 53.71 | 33.82 | 47.51 | 56.10 | 61.90 | 48.36 | 57.13 |
| | DualEnc++$_{proposed}$ | 50.81 | $\underline{64.20}$ | **46.89** | $\underline{58.64}$ | 63.98 | $\underline{72.04}$ | 62.31 | $\underline{69.95}$ |
| | -BCRF | 49.51 | 61.09 | 43.90 | 54.86 | 61.56 | 69.88 | 58.90 | 67.10 |
| | -SupEx | 49.71 | 63.95 | 46.26 | 58.41 | 62.76 | 72.06 | 61.62 | 69.95 |
| | -SupEx, +BCRF[R] | 17.14 | 39.55 | 12.51 | 29.39 | 23.07 | 51.83 | 17.06 | 42.27 |
| two | ESD | 36.08 | 52.14 | 30.00 | 42.15 | 59.29 | 69.06 | 52.16 | 64.00 |
| | MAML-ProtoNet | $\underline{52.04}$ | 63.23 | 43.50 | 56.84 | $\underline{68.77}$ | 71.62 | $\underline{63.26}$ | 68.32 |
| | EPNET | 43.36 | 58.85 | 36.41 | 46.40 | 62.49 | 65.24 | 54.39 | 62.37 |
| | SpanProto | **54.49** | **73.10** | $\underline{45.39}$ | **64.63** | **73.36** | **82.68** | **66.26** | **78.69** |

Table 1: The episode evaluation $F_1$ scores on Few-NERD over 5000 episodes. The shaded models are the proposed model with alternative configurations (§5): -SupEx is without support examples, -BCRF is trained on cross-entropy loss, +BCRF[R] is trained on BCRF with randomly initialized label embeddings. The bold values are the best scores and the underlined values are the second-best scores for each $N$-way $K$-shot setting.

| | | 1-shot | | | 5-shot | | |
|---|---|---|---|---|---|---|---|
| Stage | Model | CoNLL | WNUT | i2b2 | CoNLL | WNUT | i2b2 |
| one | ProtoBERT | $49.9_{\pm 8.6}$ | $17.4_{\pm 4.9}$ | $13.4_{\pm 3.0}$ | $61.3_{\pm 9.1}$ | $22.8_{\pm 4.5}$ | $17.9_{\pm 1.8}$ |
| | StructShot | $62.4_{\pm 10.5}$ | $24.2_{\pm 8.0}$ | $21.4_{\pm 3.5}$ | $74.8_{\pm 2.4}$ | $30.4_{\pm 6.5}$ | $30.3_{\pm 2.1}$ |
| | CONTaiNER | $61.2_{\pm 10.7}$ | $27.5_{\pm 1.9}$ | $21.5_{\pm 1.7}$ | $\underline{75.8}_{\pm 2.7}$ | $32.5_{\pm 3.8}$ | $36.7_{\pm 2.1}$ |
| | LabelSem | $(68.4_{\pm 6.7})$ | $(38.3_{\pm 1.7})$ | $(61.9_{\pm 4.3})$ | $(76.6_{\pm 2.1})$ | $(40.8_{\pm 2.1})$ | $(76.8_{\pm 2.0})$ |
| | DualEnc++$_{proposed}$ | $\mathbf{71.0}_{\pm 3.8}$ | $\mathbf{36.1}_{\pm 4.9}$ | $\mathbf{44.4}_{\pm 5.1}$ | $74.8_{\pm 5.1}$ | $\mathbf{40.3}_{\pm 2.3}$ | $\mathbf{46.5}_{\pm 4.9}$ |
| two | EPNet | $\underline{64.8}_{\pm 10.4}$ | $\underline{32.3}_{\pm 4.8}$ | $\underline{27.5}_{\pm 4.6}$ | $\mathbf{78.8}_{\pm 2.7}$ | $\underline{38.4}_{\pm 5.2}$ | $\underline{44.9}_{\pm 2.7}$ |

Table 2: The $F_1$ scores on CoNLL-2003, WNUT-2017 and i2b2-2014. The scores of the proposed models are average with standard deviation on 10 different $K$-shot samples. The bold values are the best scores and the underlined values are the second-best scores for each $K$-shot setting with the greedy sampling algorithm (Yang and Katiyar, 2020). The values with parenthesis are the scores with the downsampling algorithm (Hou et al., 2020).

used as the tagging scheme of NER. The Viterbi algorithm is used to decide the best label sequence as in the decoding process of CRF. The further detail of the training configuration, label configuration and dataset statistics are shown in §A.1, §A.2 and §A.3, respectively.

### 4.3 Evaluation

Table 1 shows the result on Few-NERD over INTRA and INTER configurations. In Few-NERD, coarse-grained entity types are shared (INTER) or not shared (INTRA) among the training data and the test data. DualEnc++ has shown best scores on all 8 settings against one-stage previous models. For the comparison against two-stages models, DualEnc++ has shown best or second-best scores on 5 settings. Table 2 shows the results on CoNLL-2003, WNUT-2017 and i2b2-2014.

## 5 Discussions

### 5.1 The Effects of Support Examples and BCRF

We examined the effects of two ideas with an ablation study on Few-NERD. The -SupEx and -BCRF scores in Table 1 shows the result of ablation study. BCRF and support examples have shown effective on all 8 settings. We further confirmed the performance of BCRF without the label encoder by using randomly initialized label embeddings as in Hu et al. (2020) (-SupEx, +BCRF[R]). The low performance of this setting indicates the strength of BCRF combined with the label encoder.

### 5.2 The Effects of $n$ Support Examples

The labels encoder encodes $n$ support examples to obtain label representations. In the experiment (§4.3), we chose $n = 5$ so that our approach can consider enough examples in the 5~10 shot settings of Few-NERD. We have additionally tried $n = 1, 3$ on Few-NERD and found the result to be quite stable regardless of the value of $n$. The standard deviation of $F_1$ score was largest on INTRA 10-way 1~2 shot with the value of $47.27 \pm 0.33$. The more detailed effect of the number of support examples can be confirmed in §A.4.

## 6 Conclusion

We proposed two ideas to improve label representations that can be effective for few-shot NER. These ideas have shown effectiveness to achieve strong performances compared against previous one-stage approaches and comparable performances to some of two-stage approaches. As future work, we would like to explore whether these ideas can be applied to span representations which have shown superiority compared to simpler token representations that we have explored in this study.

## Limitations

Our approach has shown strong performances on 4 widely used few-shot NER datasets. Additional datasets and transfer settings have been tested in previous studies (Fritzler et al., 2019; Yang and Katiyar, 2020; Wang et al., 2021; Ma et al., 2022a; Das et al., 2022; Ma et al., 2022b; Ji et al., 2022) and our approach can be suboptimal on them. The result of few-shot domain transfer settings in CoNLL-2003, WNUT-2017 and i2b2-2014 depends on randomly sampled few-shot samples. Since these random samples differ among our approach and previous studies, the comparison is not a fair comparison in an exact manner. This variance in random samples is alleviated in Few-NERD since the episode evaluation use pre-sampled 5000 episodes. The evaluation of our approach requires certain amount of computational resources to run, especially in Few-NERD. Even though a single episode evaluation can be done quite quickly (e.g., 3 minutes), the full evaluation on Few-NERD will take $3 \times 5000 \times 8$ minutes $\approx 2000$ hours on single gpu.

## Ethics Statement

The language resources used in our paper are all publicly available from the corresponding websites. The licenses of the resources are: CC BY-SA 4.0 for Few-NERD, LDC User Agreement for Non-Members[4] for OntoNotes 5.0, CoNLL-2003 license[5] for CoNLL-2003, CC-BY 4.0 for WNUT-2017 and i2b2 Data Use Agreement[6] for i2b2-2014. The resources consist of online encyclopedia (Few-NERD), newswire (CoNLL-2003, OntoNotes 5.0), broadcast news (OntoNotes 5.0), broadcast conversation (OntoNotes 5.0), telephone conversation (OntoNotes 5.0), web data (OntoNotes 5.0), social media (WNUT-2017) and clinical narratives (i2b2-2014). Protected health information in the clinical narratives are de-identified and we have made the agreement with the data provider on a research and development use of them.

[4] https://catalog.ldc.upenn.edu/LDC2013T19

[5] https://www.clips.uantwerpen.be/conll2003/ner/

[6] https://n2c2.dbmi.hms.harvard.edu/data-sets

## References


Rami Aly, Andreas Vlachos, and Ryan McDonald. 2021. Leveraging type descriptions for zero-shot named entity recognition and classification. In *Proceedings of the 59th Annual Meeting of the Association for Computational Linguistics and the 11th International Joint Conference on Natural Language Processing (Volume 1: Long Papers)*, pages 1516–1528, Online. Association for Computational Linguistics.

Sarkar Snigdha Sarathi Das, Arzoo Katiyar, Rebecca Passonneau, and Rui Zhang. 2022. CONTaiNER: Few-shot named entity recognition via contrastive learning. In *Proceedings of the 60th Annual Meeting of the Association for Computational Linguistics (Volume 1: Long Papers)*, pages 6338–6353, Dublin, Ireland. Association for Computational Linguistics.

Leon Derczynski, Eric Nichols, Marieke van Erp, and Nut Limsopatham. 2017. Results of the WNUT2017 shared task on novel and emerging entity recognition. In *Proceedings of the 3rd Workshop on Noisy User-generated Text*, pages 140–147, Copenhagen, Denmark. Association for Computational Linguistics.

Ning Ding, Guangwei Xu, Yulin Chen, Xiaobin Wang, Xu Han, Pengjun Xie, Haitao Zheng, and Zhiyuan Liu. 2021. Few-NERD: A few-shot named entity recognition dataset. In *Proceedings of the 59th Annual Meeting of the Association for Computational Linguistics and the 11th International Joint Conference on Natural Language Processing (Volume 1: Long Papers)*, pages 3198–3213, Online. Association for Computational Linguistics.

Alexander Fritzler, Varvara Logacheva, and Maksim Kretov. 2019. Few-shot classification in named entity recognition task. In *Proceedings of the 34th ACM/SIGAPP Symposium on Applied Computing*, SAC '19, page 993–1000, New York, NY, USA. Association for Computing Machinery.

Yutai Hou, Wanxiang Che, Yongkui Lai, Zhihan Zhou, Yijia Liu, Han Liu, and Ting Liu. 2020. Few-shot slot tagging with collapsed dependency transfer and label-enhanced task-adaptive projection network. In *Proceedings of the 58th Annual Meeting of the Association for Computational Linguistics*, pages 1381–1393, Online. Association for Computational Linguistics.

Zechuan Hu, Yong Jiang, Nguyen Bach, Tao Wang, Zhongqiang Huang, Fei Huang, and Kewei Tu. 2020. An investigation of potential function designs for neural CRF. In *Findings of the Association for Computational Linguistics: EMNLP 2020*, pages 2600–2609, Online. Association for Computational Linguistics.

Bin Ji, Shasha Li, Shaoduo Gan, Jie Yu, Jun Ma, Huijun Liu, and Jing Yang. 2022. Few-shot named entity recognition with entity-level prototypical network enhanced by dispersedly distributed prototypes. In *Proceedings of the 29th International Conference on Computational Linguistics*, pages 1842–1854, Gyeongju, Republic of Korea. International Committee on Computational Linguistics.

John D. Lafferty, Andrew McCallum, and Fernando C. N. Pereira. 2001. Conditional random fields: Probabilistic models for segmenting and labeling sequence data. In *Proceedings of the Eighteenth International Conference on Machine Learning*, ICML '01, page 282–289, San Francisco, CA, USA. Morgan Kaufmann Publishers Inc.

Guillaume Lample, Miguel Ballesteros, Sandeep Subramanian, Kazuya Kawakami, and Chris Dyer. 2016. Neural architectures for named entity recognition. In *Proceedings of the 2016 Conference of the North American Chapter of the Association for Computational Linguistics: Human Language Technologies*, pages 260–270, San Diego, California. Association for Computational Linguistics.

Ilya Loshchilov and Frank Hutter. 2019. Decoupled weight decay regularization. In *International Conference on Learning Representations*.

Jie Ma, Miguel Ballesteros, Srikanth Doss, Rishita Anubhai, Sunil Mallya, Yaser Al-Onaizan, and Dan Roth. 2022a. Label semantics for few shot named entity recognition. In *Findings of the Association for Computational Linguistics: ACL 2022*, pages 1956–1971, Dublin, Ireland. Association for Computational Linguistics.

Tingting Ma, Huiqiang Jiang, Qianhui Wu, Tiejun Zhao, and Chin-Yew Lin. 2022b. Decomposed meta-learning for few-shot named entity recognition. In *Findings of the Association for Computational Linguistics: ACL 2022*, pages 1584–1596, Dublin, Ireland. Association for Computational Linguistics.

Jake Snell, Kevin Swersky, and Richard Zemel. 2017. Prototypical networks for few-shot learning. In *Advances in Neural Information Processing Systems*, volume 30. Curran Associates, Inc.

Amber Stubbs and Özlem Uzuner. 2015. Annotating longitudinal clinical narratives for de-identification: The 2014 i2b2/UTHealth corpus. *Journal of Biomedical Informatics*, 58:S20–S29.

Erik F. Tjong Kim Sang and Fien De Meulder. 2003. Introduction to the CoNLL-2003 shared task: Language-independent named entity recognition. In *Proceedings of the Seventh Conference on Natural Language Learning at HLT-NAACL 2003*, pages 142–147.

Jianing Wang, Chengyu Wang, Chuanqi Tan, Minghui Qiu, Songfang Huang, Jun Huang, and Ming Gao. 2022a. SpanProto: A two-stage span-based prototypical network for few-shot named entity recognition. In *Proceedings of the 2022 Conference on Empirical Methods in Natural Language Processing*, pages 3466–3476, Abu Dhabi, United Arab Emirates. Association for Computational Linguistics.

Peiyi Wang, Runxin Xu, Tianyu Liu, Qingyu Zhou, Yunbo Cao, Baobao Chang, and Zhifang Sui. 2022b. An enhanced span-based decomposition method for few-shot sequence labeling. In *Proceedings of the 2022 Conference of the North American Chapter of the Association for Computational Linguistics: Human Language Technologies*, pages 5012–5024, Seattle, United States. Association for Computational Linguistics.

Yaqing Wang, Haoda Chu, Chao Zhang, and Jing Gao. 2021. Learning from language description: Low-shot named entity recognition via decomposed framework. In *Findings of the Association for Computational Linguistics: EMNLP 2021*, pages 1618–1630, Punta Cana, Dominican Republic. Association for Computational Linguistics.

Ralph Weischedel, Martha Palmer, Mitchell Marcus, Hovy Eduard, Sameer Pradhan, Lance Ramshaw, Nianwen Xue, Ann Taylor, Jeff Kaufman, Michelle Franchini, Mohammed El-Bachouti, Robert Belvin, and Ann Houston. 2013. OntoNotes Release 5.0.

Sam Wiseman and Karl Stratos. 2019. Label-agnostic sequence labeling by copying nearest neighbors. In *Proceedings of the 57th Annual Meeting of the Association for Computational Linguistics*, pages 5363–5369, Florence, Italy. Association for Computational Linguistics.

Yi Yang and Arzoo Katiyar. 2020. Simple and effective few-shot named entity recognition with structured nearest neighbor learning. In *Proceedings of the 2020 Conference on Empirical Methods in Natural Language Processing (EMNLP)*, pages 6365–6375, Online. Association for Computational Linguistics.

# A Appendix

## A.1 Training Configuration

The model is pre-finetuned for 3 epochs and is further fine-tuned on a few-shot dataset for 100 epochs. We optimized the model with support examples (§3.2) and BCRF scores (§3.3) using AdamW (Loshchilov and Hutter, 2019). The learning rate of the optimization is set to $1e^{-5}$ following Ma et al. (2022a) with linear warmup throughout pre-finetuning and fine-tuning for BERT-base

| Dataset | #train | #dev | #test |
|---|---|---|---|
| OntoNotes 5.0 | 59.9K | 8.5K | 8.3K |
| Few-NERD | 131.8K | 18.8K | 37.6K |
| CoNLL-2003 | 14.0K | 3.3K | 3.5K |
| WNUT-2017 | 3.4K | 0.8K | 1.1K |
| i2b2-2014 | 51.5K | 23.2K | 48.5K |

Table 3: The number of sentences included in the datasets of the experiment (§4).

(cased). Transformers library[7] and PyTorch[8] are used to implement the proposed model. The number of support examples is set to $n = 5$. NVIDIA Tesla V100 with 32GB memory is used to train and evaluate the proposed model. The training time of the proposed model is short: 1–8 minutes for a 100 epochs fine-tuning on a target dataset.

## A.2 Label Configuration

The model uses label names along with support examples to obtain label representations (§3.2). We used the label names defined in Ma et al. (2022a) for CoNLL-2003, WNUT-2017 and i2b2-2014. For example, "person" is used as the label name of "PER" in CoNLL-2003. We combined the coarse type and the fine type of a named entity with hyphen in Few-NERD which is available in Table 8 of Ding et al. (2021). For example, "Location-GPE" is used for the named entity with the coarse type of "Location" and the fine type of "GPE". We additionally prepared "start of sentence" and "end of sentence" label names for BCRF which are used in the first token of a sentence and the last token of a sentence, respectively.

## A.3 Dataset Statistics

Table 3 shows the number of sentences included in OntoNotes 5.0, Few-NERD, CoNLL-2003, WNUT-2017 and i2b2-3014. For OntoNotes 5.0, we used the splits of CoNLL-2012[9] following the setting of Yang and Katiyar (2020). The language of the datasets is English for all datasets. All datasets are designed to evaluate NER, and Few-NERD is specifically designed for few-shot settings. Note that the actual training splits of the experiment (§4) are samples of the training split in Table 3.

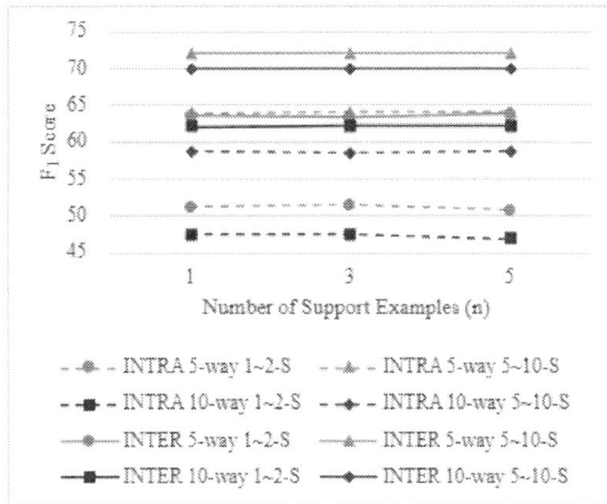


Figure 2: The $F_1$ scores on Few-NERD with varying number of support examples.

## A.4 The Number of Support Examples and Its Effects

Figure 2 shows the changes in $F_1$ score when the number of support examples are in $n = 1, 3, 5$. The performance is quite stable regardless of the value of $n$ in our approach, and the standard deviation of $F_1$ score was largest on INTRA 10-way 1~2 with the value of $47.27 \pm 0.33$ and was smallest on INTRA 10-way 5~10 shot with the value of $58.62 \pm 0.03$.

[7]https://huggingface.co/transformers
[8]https://pytorch.org/
[9]http://conll.cemantix.org/2012/data.html

# What Learned Representations and Influence Functions Can Tell Us About Adversarial Examples

**Shakila Mahjabin Tonni** and **Mark Dras**
School of Computing, Macquarie University
shakila.tonni@mq.edu.au, mark.dras@mq.edu.au

## Abstract

Adversarial examples, deliberately crafted using small perturbations to fool deep neural networks, were first studied in image processing and more recently in NLP. While approaches to detecting adversarial examples in NLP have largely relied on search over input perturbations, image processing has seen a range of techniques that aim to characterise adversarial subspaces over the learned representations.

In this paper, we adapt two such approaches to NLP, one based on nearest neighbors and influence functions and one on Mahalanobis distances. The former in particular produces a state-of-the-art detector when compared against several strong baselines; moreover, the novel use of influence functions provides insight into how the nature of adversarial example subspaces in NLP relate to those in image processing, and also how they differ depending on the kind of NLP task.

## 1 Introduction

The high sensitivity of deep neural networks (DNNs) to slight modifications of inputs is widely recognised and makes DNNs a convenient target for adversarial attacks (Szegedy et al., 2014). Creating malicious inputs or adversarial examples by adding small perturbations to the model's inputs can cause the model to misclassify the inputs that would be predicted correctly otherwise. Such adversarial attacks are highly successful in both image and Natural Language Processing (NLP) domains.

In the image domain, due to the straightforwardness of creating adversarial images by calibrating noise to the original records, researchers have explored many high-performing adversarial attacks (Papernot et al., 2016b; Moosavi-Dezfooli et al., 2016; Carlini and Wagner, 2017, for example). The perturbations of the input images degrade the model's performance with a high success rate and are generally imperceptible to a human.

Work in the NLP space has followed that in image processing. Here, in addition to the goal of impacting the model's prediction, adversarial text examples need to be syntactically and semantically sound to the reader. Consequently, adversarial attack techniques on text use semantics-preserving textual changes at the character level, word level and phrase level or sentence level (Pruthi et al., 2019; Alzantot et al., 2018; Li et al., 2020, for example). Table 1 illustrates two examples, showing different types of attack formulation in NLP.

In the image domain, defence against adversarial attack can be 'proactive' or 'reactive' (Cohen et al., 2020), where proactive defence refers to improving the model's robustness (Madry et al., 2018; Gopinath et al., 2018; Cohen et al., 2019) and reactive defence focuses on detecting real adversarial examples before they are passed to neural networks (Feinman et al., 2017; Ma et al., 2018; Lee et al., 2018; Papernot and McDaniel, 2018). Broadly speaking, for reactive methods, the detection of adversarial examples involves taking a conceptualisation of the space of learned representations and the adversarial subspaces within them (Tanay and Griffin, 2016; Tramèr et al., 2017), and then characterising the differences in some function of the learned representations between the actual and the adversarial inputs produced by the DNN; for example, Ma et al. (2018) applied a local intrinsic dimensionality (LID) measure to the learned representations and used that to successfully distinguish normal and adversarial images.

In the NLP space, relatively fewer adversarial defence techniques have been proposed. Among them, many focus on enhancing the models' robustness proactively through adversarial training (Jia et al., 2019; Pruthi et al., 2019; Jin et al., 2020); generating textual samples for proactive adversarial training is computationally expensive because of necessary search and constraints based on sentence encoding (Yoo and Qi, 2021). Reactive adversarial



*Findings of the Association for Computational Linguistics: IJCNLP-AACL 2023*, pages 392–411
November 1–4, 2023. ©2023 Asian Federation of Natural Language Processing

text detection techniques have mostly been different from their image counterparts, in that they typically modify the input by e.g. repeatedly checking word substitutions (Mozes et al., 2021; Wang et al., 2022; Zhou et al., 2019) rather than trying to characterise the learned representations; consequently, they focus on detecting synonym-substitution adversarial examples. An exception is the work of Liu et al. (2022), which both adapts LID to the text space and proposes the new MultiDistance Representation Ensemble (MDRE) method; their state-of-the-art results suggest that the detection methods based on learned representations drawn from the image processing domain are a promising source of ideas for NLP.

The particular focus of the present paper is the use of influence functions in adversarial detection methods, proposed for image processing by Cohen et al. (2020). They propose that distances to nearest neighbors (used by previous methods) and influence functions, which measure the impact of every training sample on validation or test set data, can be used complementarily to detect adversarial examples: they argue, with support from the strong results from their method, that adversarial examples locate in different regions of the learned representation space of their neighbors with respect to influence functions, compared to original datapoints (Fig 1). Specifically, in the image space, for original datapoints, nearest neighbors and influence function training points overlap, but for adversarial examples, they do not. Influence functions have only relatively recently begun to be explored in NLP, with Han et al. (2020) finding that, with the variety of classification tasks in NLP, the information provided by influence functions differs from image processing and is task-dependent. In this paper, noting significant differences between inputs in NLP and image processing (continuous versus discrete) and attack types, we explore whether and how they can help in NLP in detecting adversarial examples using learned representations, and what this can tell us about the nature of adversarial subspaces.

We also adapt a second method from the image processing literature, by Lee et al. (2018), which uses a Mahalanobis-based confidence score; this was a strong baseline for Cohen et al. (2020), giving an additional perspective on the nature of adversarial subspaces in NLP.

The contributions of this paper are as follows:

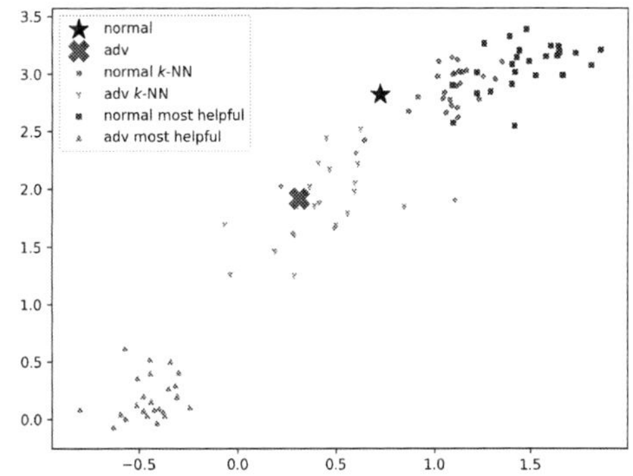


Figure 1: Adversarial examples characterised by divergence in learned representations between nearest neighbors and training points selected by influence functions, unlike original examples (from (Cohen et al., 2020)).

- An adaptation of two adversarial detection techniques from the image processing literature, MAHAL confidence (Lee et al., 2018) and Nearest Neighbor Influence Functions (NNIF) (Cohen et al., 2020), into the text domain; we show that we can achieve SOTA results relative to several strong, recent baselines.
- An analysis of how influence functions work in this context, contributes to understanding both the nature of adversarial subspaces in the text space and what information influence functions can provide.

## 2 Related Work

**Adversarial Defences for Image** An intuitive adversarial defence is to train a deep neural network to be robust against adversarial input samples by e.g. mixing adversarial samples with the training data (Goodfellow et al., 2015; Madry et al., 2018; Xie et al., 2019); popular platforms like Cleverhans (Papernot et al., 2016a) are available to support robust training. However, such defences, termed as 'proactive', are expensive and vulnerable to optimisation attacks (Cohen et al., 2020).

In contrast, others have proposed 'reactive' defences that identify the variations in the representations learned by the DNN on the original input images to separate the adversarial samples; typically, these posit that adversarial examples can be characterised as belonging to particular subspaces (Tramèr et al., 2017), and the different approaches aim to capture the nature of these subspaces in different ways, with detectors such as logistic regression classifiers built over the learned representations. Feinman et al. (2017) built detectors us-

| Original Text | at last, a movie that handles the probability of alien visits with the appropriate depth and loving warmth. | Positive |
|---|---|---|
| Char-level (Pruthi et al., 2019) | at last, a movie that handles the probability of alien visits with the appr0priate depth and loving warDmth | Negative |
| Word-level (Alzantot et al., 2018) | at last, a movie that handles the probability of alien trips with the adequate depth and loving warmth | Negative |

Table 1: Examples of textual adversarial instances on IMDB and the prediction of $\text{BERT}_{\text{BASE}}$ on them

ing kernel density estimation on the last hidden layer of a DNN. Ma et al. (2018) characterised the dimensional properties of adversarial subspaces using Local Intrinsic Dimensionality (LID), applied to the distribution of distances to neighbors in the region around a sample. Papernot and McDaniel (2018), noting that DNNs are poorly calibrated (Guo et al., 2017), proposed Deep k-Nearest Neighbors (DKNN), a KNN classifier constructed over the hidden layers of a DNN classifier; such a DKNN classifier could match the performance of the DNN while also providing better confidence estimates of prediction, and these confidence estimates are used in identifying adversarial examples. Lee et al. (2018) constructed Mahalanobis distance-based confidence scores from DNNs, using these scores to construct a detection classifier. Cohen et al. (2020) investigated the use of influence functions in adversarial image detection that explain the decisions of a model by identifying influential training examples, and comparing these points to those found in a DKNN approach, using the differences in distributions between real examples and adversarial ones to construct classifiers that outperformed the approaches above. In this paper, we focus on the last two and adapt them to NLP.

**Adversarial Defences for Text** Improving adversarial robustness remains a widely used mechanism in defending textual adversaries (Li et al., 2016, 2017; Ribeiro et al., 2018; Jones et al., 2020). In NLP, however, there have been fewer reactive methods. To prevent character-level and word-level adversarial perturbations Zhou et al. (2019) proposed the learning to discriminate perturbations (DISP) framework that detects and replaces suspicious words. Mozes et al. (2021) emphasised word frequencies in the texts in determining adversarial perturbations, arguing that adversarially infused words are less likely to occur, and constructed a rule-based, model-agnostic frequency-guided word substitutions (FGWS) algorithm. The approach of Wang et al. (2022) voted the prediction label for a set of samples generated by random word substitutions from a sentence and matched the voted prediction label with the original sentence's prediction label to detect word-level adversaries. Anomaly Detection with Frequency-Aware Randomization (ADFAR) as proposed by Bao et al. (2021) adds anomaly detection as an additional optimization training objective and augments the training set with random rare-frequency word substitutions of the original sentences. Rather than focus on word substitution as the above methods, Mosca et al. (2022) trained an adversarial detector on Shapley additive explanations (Fidel et al., 2020).

In NLP, only Liu et al. (2022) has used the idea of constructing detectors over learned representations as in the image domain, which explored the idea of adapting the LID (Ma et al., 2018) method above. In addition, they proposed the MultiDistance Representation Ensemble Method (MDRE) algorithm that puts together learned representations from multiple DNN models to detect adversarial texts. Unlike other approaches, the same detector could apply to different types of attacks (character-based, word-based, syntax-based) and MDRE in particular improved over baseline methods across the range of attacks. This motivates our adaptation of more recent techniques from the image domain.

**Influence Functions** The influence function (IF) is a statistical method that captures the dependence of an estimator on any one of the sample (training) points. Koh and Liang (2017) were the first to adapt IFs to image DNNs as a method for interpreting the model's decision: the IF finds the most influential training samples, both helpful and harmful, contributing to each prediction. The essence of the approach is to consider a point $z$ from the training set and compute the change to parameters $\theta$ if $z$ were upweighted by a small $\epsilon$; they then defined closed-form expressions $\mathcal{I}(z, z_{\text{test}})$ to identify the most influential points $z$ on a test point $z_{\text{test}}$.

IFs were first applied to NLP deep architectures by Han et al. (2020), and compared with established gradient-based saliency maps as a way of interpreting input feature importance, using sentiment classification and natural language inference (NLI) as testbeds. Their first finding was that IFs are reliable for deep NLP architectures. Their second interesting finding was that while IFs and saliency measures were consistent for sentiment classification, they differed for NLI: they concluded that for more complex understanding tasks like NLI, IFs captured more useful interpretive information. They also found IFs to be useful for identifying and quantifying the effect of data artifacts on model prediction. A few other works have continued investigating the usefulness of IFs in NLP, such as Guo et al. (2021), who proposed a faster method for IF computation by restricting candidates to top-$k$ nearest neighbors.

## 3 Methods

### 3.1 NNIF Detector

We follow Cohen et al. (2020)'s Nearest Neighbor Influence Function (NNIF) method and apply it to NLP architectures. The essence of it is, for some point $z$ that may be regular or adversarial, to identify the training points that are most influential and those that are nearest neighbors to $z$, and to build a classifier based on those that will predict whether $z$ is regular or adversarial based on differences in relative distributions (Fig 1).

We take a DNN classifier and dataset for some particular task (e.g. sentiment classification); we refer to this DNN as the TARGET MODEL. For each test sample $z_{\text{test}}$, we compute the influence scores $\mathcal{I}(z, z_{\text{test}})$ for all training points $z$, given the target model, and select the top $M$ most helpful and $M$ most harmful (details App B). We then construct a DKNN classifier in the style of Papernot and McDaniel (2018), using the hidden layers of the target model and the training points. For each $z_{\text{test}}$ we find the ranks $\mathcal{R}$ and distances $\mathcal{D}$ using this DKNN for the training examples identified by the IFs; we denote by $\mathcal{R}^{M\uparrow}, \mathcal{D}^{M\uparrow}, \mathcal{R}^{M\downarrow}, \mathcal{D}^{M\downarrow}$ the ranks and distances of the $2M$ most helpful and harmful training examples, respectively. We finally construct a logistic regression classifier with features $(\mathcal{R}^{M\uparrow}, \mathcal{D}^{M\uparrow}, \mathcal{R}^{M\downarrow}, \mathcal{D}^{M\downarrow})$ to detect whether an input is adversarial or not.

Where the target model of Cohen et al. (2020) is a ResNet model, ours is a large language model (LLM) base with additional layers that are fine-tuned for the chosen tasks (§4.3). The hidden layers we use for NNIF are then the pre-final additional layers on top of the DNN (§4.5).

### 3.2 MAHAL Detector

Here we follow Lee et al. (2018), who build a detector that captures the variation in the probability density of the class-conditional Gaussian distribution of the learned representation by the model. Motivated, like Papernot and McDaniel (2018), by the problem that DNNs are poorly calibrated (Guo et al., 2017), they replace the final softmax layer with a Gaussian Discriminant Analysis (GDA) softmax classifier.

For a set of training points $\{(x_1, y_1), ..., (x_n, y_n)\}$ with the label $y \in \{1, 2, \dots, C\}$, the class mean $\hat{\mu}_c$ and covariance $\hat{\sum}$ are computed for each class $c$ to approximate the generative classifier's parameters from the pre-trained target DNN $f(x)$. Next, from the obtained class-conditional Gaussian distribution, the Mahalanobis distance between a test sample $x$ and its closest distribution is measured to find the confidence score $M(x) = \max_c -(f(x) - \hat{\mu}_c)^T \widehat{\Sigma}^{-1}(f(x) - \hat{\mu}_c)$. Finally, we label the Mahalanobis scores for the test samples as positive and adversarial samples as negative and input this feature set to an LR detector.

Lee et al. (2018) propose two calibration techniques to improve the detection accuracy and make regular and out-of-distribution samples more separable: (1) *input pre-processing*, where they add a small noise in a controllable manner to the test samples; and (2) *feature ensemble*, which combines the confidence scores from all the hidden layers of the DNN including the final features. Both together substantially improve the performance of the base approach; each individually reaches almost the combination of the two. As for our NNIF detector in §3.1, our target DNN will have several hidden layers, and we explore models both with final layer-only representations and feature ensembles over all hidden layers. The input preprocessing of (1) is appropriate to the continuous space of images, but not in an obvious way to text, so we do not use that.

## 4 Experimental Setup

We broadly follow the setup of Liu et al. (2022), as the prior NLP work that has used learned representations to detect adversarial examples.

### 4.1 Tasks and Datasets

We work on the sentiment analysis and the natural language inference tasks, two widely tasks used in the adversarial example generation (Pruthi et al., 2019; Alzantot et al., 2018; Ribeiro et al., 2018; Ren et al., 2019; Iyyer et al., 2018; Yoo and Qi, 2021; Li et al., 2020, 2021; Jin et al., 2020). In addition, these are the two tasks that were used for the investigation of the use of influence functions in NLP (Han et al., 2020).

**Sentiment Analysis** For the sentiment analysis, we use the IMDB dataset (Maas et al., 2011) that has 50,000 movie reviews, split into 25,000 training and 25,000 test examples with binary labels indicating positive or negative sentiment. IMDB dataset has 262 words per review on average. In all experiments, we use 512 maximum sequence lengths for the language models on IMDB.

**Natural Language Inference** The Multi-Genre NLI (MULTINLI) dataset (Williams et al., 2018), used for the natural language inference (NLI) task, contains pairs of sentences annotated with textual entailment information. The test examples are mismatched with train examples and are collected from different sources. The dataset has 392,702 training and 9,832 testing examples labelled as three classes: entailment, neutral, and contradiction. Each text of the dataset has 34 words on average. On this dataset, we set the maximum sequence length to 256.

### 4.2 Attack Methods

We use the implementations from Liu et al. (2022) of two widely used attack methods that apply character-level and word-level perturbations to construct adversarial examples. We take a $\text{BERT}_{\text{BASE}}$ model (§4.3) as the target model. An adversarial attack is successful when the adversaries have different predictions than the target mode's original predictions. Our two methods are (more details in §A.1):

- CHARATT (Pruthi et al., 2019). This is a character-level attack that tweaks the original texts by randomly swapping, dropping and adding characters or adding a keyboard mistake.
- WORDATT (Alzantot et al., 2018). This is a word-level attack that allows the attacker to alter practically every word from the sentence if required with the context-preserving synonymous words. This implementation follows Jia et al. (2019) in speeding up the synonym search.

### 4.3 Target Model

Following (Liu et al., 2022), we use a pre-trained BERT-base-cased model, adding a fully connected dense layer of 768 nodes, a layer of 50% dropout, and another dense layer of 768 nodes. The dataset split is 80-20 train-test. We train the model for 3 epochs with $5e^{-5}$ learning rate and AdamW optimization without freezing any layer of the backbone model. This $\text{BERT}_{\text{BASE}}$ model achieves 92.90% and 82.01% test accuracies on the IMDB and MULTINLI datasets respectively. The accuracies of the clean model and the model under attack are given in Table 6; we note that in all the cases, CHARATT degrades the classifier's performance comparatively more than WORDATT. Sizes for IMDB and MULTINLI datasets and number of generated adversarial texts from them are in Table 5.

### 4.4 Detectors

For data to train the adversarial example detectors on, we follow standard practice in image processing (Ma et al., 2018; Cohen et al., 2020) and Liu et al. (2022) and use only those examples that are correctly classified by the target model (§4.3) from the overall test set. Adversarial attacks are then applied to these examples; the originals (labelled positive) and their adversarial alternatives (negative) then form the DETECTION DATASET. Due to the computational intensity of estimating the influential training records for the NNIF method, we limit our detectors to having 10k records (5k tests and 5k adversarial texts) and follow a similar data size for all the other detection methods for comparability. We split the detection dataset 80-20 train-test, and construct and evaluate logistic regression classifiers as detectors over this detection dataset split for our proposed methods (§4.5) and baselines (§4.6).

### 4.5 NNIF and Mahalanobis Methods

**NNIF** We adapt the standard NNIF implementation of Cohen et al. (2020). For influence score calculation, Cohen et al. (2020) uses the Darkon module for the image; we instead incorporate the influence function calculation from Han et al. (2020)[1] which uses Linear time Stochastic Second-Order Algorithm (Agarwal et al., 2017) for faster convergence, and makes several adaptations to NLP. We build the DkNN containing one layer with $l_2$ distance and brute-force search.

Because IF calculations are expensive, like Cohen et al. (2020) and Han et al. (2020) we only

[1] `https://github.com/xhan77/influence-function-analysis`

sample from among all neighbors: we compute the IF on 6K training datapoints uniformly randomly sampled (Cohen et al. (2020) sample 10K neighbors from 49K training points). We choose $M = 500$ for our main results, which is at the top end of the range of values of $M$ selected by Cohen et al. (2020); we show in §5.2 that, unlike the image processing domain, results in our experiments are broadly monotonically increasing as $M$ increases.

Note that we don't use the faster variant of IF computation of Guo et al. (2021), as NNIF requires *separate* perspectives from IFs and kNNs, and FASTIF restricts IF search to subsets of kNNs.

**MAHAL** As per §3.2, we compute the mean and covariance for each class and calculate the Mahalanobis distance score for each normal instance and its adversarial counterpart. Like Ma et al. (2018), we consider both using only the final layer of the model and stacking scores from each layer of the model (feature ensembling). Feature ensembling is always better, so we only include those in the main results, but do separately analyse the contribution of the feature ensembling.

**Code** For both of these, our code uses the implementation of Cohen et al. (2020) as a starting point and adapts as above.[2]

### 4.6 Baseline Detection Methods

We evaluate six adversarial text detection methods as our baseline detectors. The first four are from Liu et al. (2022) (we omit the language model, as it operates essentially at the chance), while the other two are also recent high-performing systems.[3] We give more details on the methods in §A.2.

**DISP** (Zhou et al., 2019). This is a system that aims to correct any adversarial perturbations before an example is passed to a classifier. Liu et al. (2022) adapt this to detecting the adversarial examples.

**FGWS** (Mozes et al., 2021). This algorithm uses a word frequency threshold and calibrated replacement approach to detect adversarial examples. It is only designed to work against word-level attacks.

**LID** (Liu et al., 2022). From among image processing detection methods, Liu et al. (2022) adapted the Local Intrinsic Dimensionality (LID) approach of Ma et al. (2018). This technique creates a distribution over local distances for a test record concerning its neighbors from the training set; it then applies these to the outputs of each layer from the target model to create a detection classifier.

[2]Code: https://github.com/SJabin/NNIF.

[3]We do not include ADFAR (Bao et al., 2021), as it works and performs similarly to (and was proposed concurrently with) RSV, but has a more complex code implementation.

| Dataset | Detector | CHAR ATTACK | WORD ATTACK |
|---|---|---|---|
| IMDB | DISP * | 0.8936 | 0.7714 |
| | FGWS | — | 0.7546 |
| | LID | 0.814 | 0.675 |
| | MDRE | 0.846 | 0.7025 |
| | RSV | — | <u>0.8876</u> |
| | SHAP | 0.812 | 0.764 |
| | NNIF | **1.0** | **0.899** |
| | MAHAL | <u>0.9167</u> | 0.8147 |
| MULTINLI | DISP * | **0.7496** | 0.6137 |
| | FGWS | — | 0.6112 |
| | LID | 0.7035 | 0.5838 |
| | MDRE | 0.687 | 0.6231 |
| | RSV | — | 0.6054 |
| | SHAP | 0.614 | <u>0.697</u> |
| | NNIF | <u>0.745</u> | **0.7351** |
| | MAHAL | 0.6972 | 0.6211 |

Table 2: Accuracy of detection classifiers (**best**, <u>second</u>). DISP results reported from Liu et al. (2022).

**MDRE** (Liu et al., 2022). This has similarities to LID above but uses Euclidean distance rather than the LID measure, and creates an ensemble using different Transformer models (like Liu et al. (2022), we use $\text{BERT}_{\text{BASE}}$, $\text{RoBERTa}_{\text{BASE}}$, $\text{XLNet}_{\text{BASE}}$, $\text{BART}_{\text{BASE}}$).

**RSV** (Wang et al., 2022). In this Randomized Substitution and Vote approach, the assumption is that a word-level attacker aims to find an optimal synonym substitution that mutually influences other words in the sentence. Hence, Wang et al. (2022) randomly replaces words from the text with synonyms in order to destroy the mutual interaction between words and eliminate adversarial perturbation. Like FGWS, this is only designed to work against word-level attacks.

**SHAP** (Mosca et al., 2022). In this approach, an adversarial detector is trained using the SHapley Additive exPlanations (SHAP) values of the training data for each test data item using the SHAP explainer (Fidel et al., 2020). They experiment on multiple classifiers as the detectors: logistic regression, random forest, support vector and neural network. In our main results, we report the best classifier for each dataset and attack.

## 5 Evaluation

### 5.1 Main Results

Results on the detector baselines are in Table 2. (All SHAP detector classifiers in Table 8.) Overall, NNIF is the best, performing with 100% accuracy on CHARATT for sentiment analysis (more than

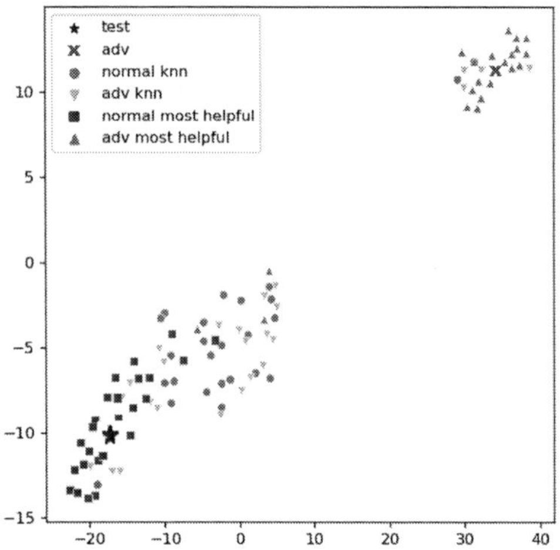


Figure 2: The correspondence between the helpful training records based on IFs in the embedding space of a DNN trained on the IMDB dataset. We present (using t-SNE) the embedding space of a DNN for an actual example (black star) with its adversarial version (purple cross) along with their 25 nearest neighbors (blue) and most helpful samples based on the IF (red).

8% better than the second) and 90% on WORDATT (more than 1% better than the second, RSV, which is tailored to word-level attacks). For MULTINLI WORDATT, it is around 4% better than the second best. The only one where it is not best, CHARATT, is only very slightly below the best performer DISP. (We note that for DISP we report the accuracy values from Liu et al. (2022). This means that the DISP detector used more data in its training set, and so has an advantage in this respect.) MAHAL also performs quite strongly, either better or similar to the baseline detectors, although not as strongly as NNIF; this mirrors the findings in image processing. MDRE results are lower than in Liu et al. (2022) as a consequence of using less data for training all detection classifiers, as discussed in §4.4.

In terms of aggregate task performance, in all our experiments, the detection accuracy on the natural language inference task is lower than the sentiment analysis task in general. As the MULTINLI dataset is a three-class problem and additionally uses mismatched test sentences, the detection is innately harder.

## 5.2 Analyses

**Regions around adversarial examples** The assumption underpinning the Cohen et al. (2020) method is that influential training samples and nearest neighbors should overlap for normal examples, but less so for adversarial examples: having two views on 'nearby' points is key, illustrated in Fig 1.

| Dataset | Attack | Penultimate layer | Feature Ensemble |
|---|---|---|---|
| IMDB | CHARATT | 0.5967 | 0.9167 |
| | WORDATT | 0.536 | 0.8147 |
| MULTINLI | CHARATT | 0.5172 | 0.6972 |
| | WORDATT | 0.4983 | 0.6212 |

Table 3: Detection accuracy of Mahalanobis detector in two settings: penultimate layer (no calibration) and feature ensemble.

We produce an analogous figure in Fig 2 for a randomly selected IMDB test point and its adversarial counterpart generated by WORDATT. We plot 25 nearest neighbors and 25 most helpful IF points using t-SNE (van der Maaten and Hinton, 2008). Ideally, normal neighbors and influence points (blue) should be more tightly grouped and closer to the test point (star); Cohen et al. (2020) expect that for the adversarial point (cross), the neighbors (orange down triangle) should often be separated from the influence points (red up triangle). We see this to some extent in Fig 2 with many adversarial neighbors near the normal point but adversarial influence points near the adversarial point.

This is more difficult to see than in the idealised schematic of Fig 1, so for one view of differences in this pair of points we separate IFs and NNs in Fig 3 with recalculated t-SNE for each. It is apparent that the IFs by themselves do a good job of separating normal from adversarial examples here, while the NNs are more mixed. We give representative examples for the other datasets and attacks in App C. The same pattern is true for the IMDB example on WORDATT. For both MULTINLI, however, the IFs are less clearly separating the points, so the NNIF method relies on combining the two (NN, IF) views in the detector.

To verify whether this is more generally true than just visually for Fig 3, we aim to measure how separable the samples of these plots are. As a measure of separability, we train 2000 SVC binary classifiers, one for each of our 1000 sampled test and adversarial point pairs, for both IFs and NNs. Each classifier is trained using GridsearchCV on the top 100 points in t-SNE space (either IFs or NNs), so each classifier corresponds to a plot like those in Fig 3 (App D). Accuracies averaged across the 1000 classifiers are in Table 4, with $p$-values for a one-tailed test of proportions (positing alternative hypothesis $H_1$ that the IF classifier is more accurate). Table 4 indicates that the IF points are

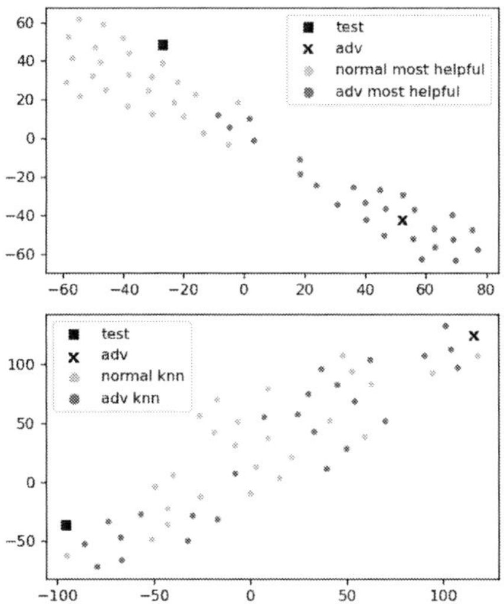


Figure 3: Normal and adversarial train subspace observed on the IMDB record used in Fig 2 under WORDATT by influence function (top) and DKNN (bottom)

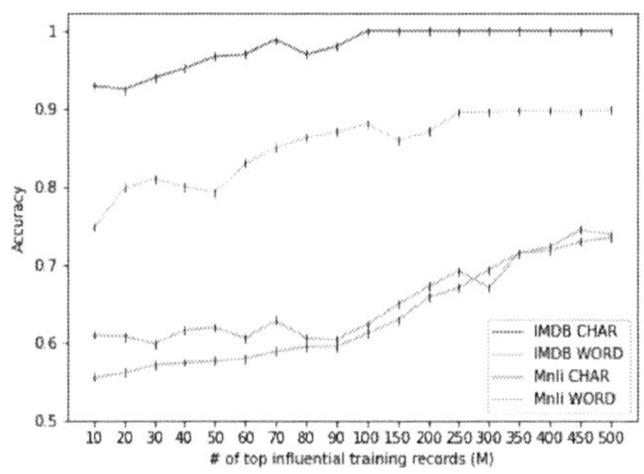


Figure 4: Accuracy of NNIF for different values of M.

generally much more clearly separable and so IF points contribute especially strongly to the method, except for MULTINLI against WORDATT, where they are essentially the same and the method relies on the two-view aspect of NNIF. This observation about the relative importance of the IF contribution was not made by Cohen et al. (2020), and so may be specific to NLP tasks, although this would require more investigation to verify. We also note that our results align with observations of Han et al. (2020), that in the harder task of MULTINLI (§5.1, Table 4), IFs provide a different perspective to characterising the datapoint of interest. We give some text examples in App E.

To look further into the more challenging combination of MULTINLI and CHARATT (as the one case in Table 2 where NNIF was not the highest scoring, albeit by a small margin), we consider a successful and an unsuccessful detection case by NNIF, with the actual examples given in the appendices in Tables 11 and 12, and the corresponding t-SNE plots of IF and NNs in Figs 5 and 6, respectively. The IFs in Fig 5 (the correct example) are somewhat more clustered, with the red (adversarial) points mostly in the top right, than the IFs in Fig 6 (the incorrect example); this lines up with the results of Table 4 in that separability of IF does seem to matter for MULTINLI +CHARATT.

| Attack | Avg Acc NNIF | Avg Acc KNN | $p$-value |
|---|---|---|---|
| IMDB CHARATT | 0.6875 | 0.5626 | $< .00001$ |
| IMDB WORDATT | 0.7812 | 0.5644 | $< .00001$ |
| MULTINLI CHARATT | 0.6399 | 0.5625 | $< .00001$ |
| MULTINLI WORDATT | 0.5603 | 0.5632 | 0.448 |

Table 4: SVC accuracy of linearly separating the 2D-t-SNE embedding subspace of neighboring train samples of 1000 test records and their adversarial versions

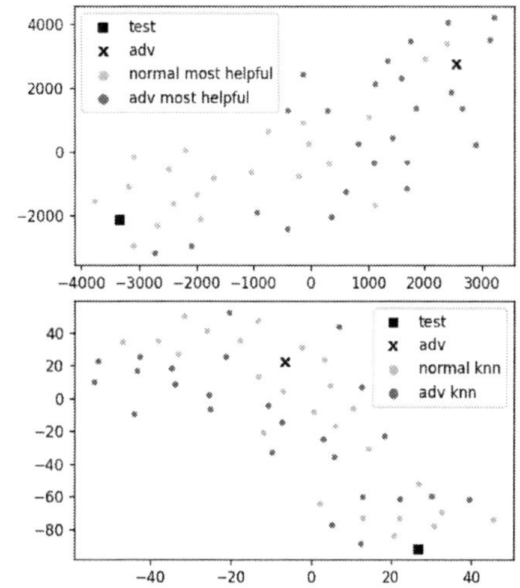


Figure 5: Normal and adversarial subspace of the MULTINLI CHARATT text in Table 10 by IF (top) and DKNN (bottom)

**Varying $M$ in NNIF** Fig 4 plots the accuracies of the NNIF method for both tasks and attacks, for a range of values of $M$. The accuracy broadly monotonically increases until plateaus for the IMDB results, although the MULTINLI results look to be still increasing. This is a contrast with the image processing results of Cohen et al. (2020), where much smaller values of $M$ (e.g. 30) produced better results. It is unclear what characteristics of our tasks (fewer classes, more long-distance dependencies, ...) lead to this difference.

**Ablation for MAHAL** Table 3 shows the accuracies of MAHAL using only the final layer or the feature ensemble. As with Lee et al. (2018), the feature ensemble produces much better results. The im-

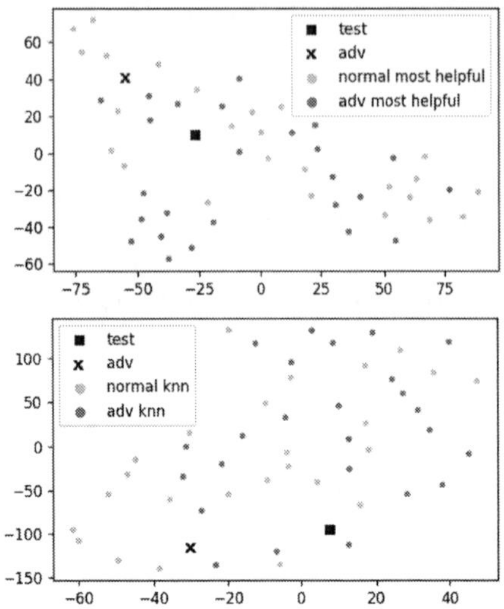


Figure 6: Normal and adversarial subspace by IF (top) and DkNN (bottom) on the unsuccessful detection by NNIF of the MultiNLI CharAtt text in Table 12

provement is larger for IMDB, but still important for MultiNLI, as without the ensemble, detection is essentially at the chance. Noting that the target model of Lee et al. (2018) had many more hidden layers in the ensemble, it is an open question as to whether introducing additional dense layers into our LLM-based model might improve detection while still preserving target model performance.

## 6 Conclusion and Future Work

We have adapted from image processing two methods, NNIF (Cohen et al., 2020) and Mahal (Lee et al., 2018), that detect adversarial examples using learned representations. Both perform strongly, with NNIF the best on three of four task/attack combinations, and a close second on the fourth, against several strong baselines.

Our analysis shows that influence function points make a particularly important contribution to the NNIF method. The MultiNLI task is more challenging for all methods; here it is the complementary nature of information from influence functions and nearest neighbors, supporting observations by Han et al. (2020) about the different perspective of influence functions in this more complex NLP task.

The NNIF method is computationally expensive, so future work will look at ways to make it more efficient. Additionally, to gain a fuller understanding of what information influence functions can provide in NLP tasks, future work will look at a wider range of tasks and attacks.

## 7 Limitations

The major limitation is the computationally expensive calculation of influence functions in our NNIF method. For this, following Cohen et al. (2020) we restrict the data size to 10k (5k test, 5k adversarial) for NNIF and follow a similar approach for other methods for comparability. This helps faster explanation generation in SHAP as well. We use a small architecture as recommended in Han et al. (2020) for the $\text{BERT}_{\text{BASE}}$ model for NNIF and other detectors. As noted in the paper, we recognise that there is the FastIF method of Guo et al. (2021) for speeding up influence function calculation, but because of the restriction of influence function points to nearest neighbors, it is not suitable for our application.

We use only two datasets/tasks and two attack methods, partly because of the computational expense of NNIF. While they are commonly used in the adversarial example literature as well as the analysis of influence functions in NLP by Han et al. (2020) and represent different levels of task complexity and attack type, a wider range of datasets/tasks and attack methods is needed for a full characterisation of influence functions and the nature of adversarial subspaces.

For all experiments, we restrict the maximum sequence length following Liu et al. (2022), which may influence the detectors' performance, especially for the NLI task, that requires the model to learn from a hypothesis and premise text pairs.

For the detector baselines, we used the most available methods. There are two recent contemporaneous methods by Wang et al. (2022) and (Bao et al., 2021) that explore the idea that adversarial perturbations are typically rare-frequency words, and create augmented training sets by replacing those words in each sentence with synonyms. For the detection, Wang et al. (2022) matches the voted prediction with the obtained prediction and (Bao et al., 2021) trains the model on a separate auxiliary learning objective. Between these two works, we choose the RSV from Wang et al. (2022) in our work. For RSV, we follow the similar setting from Wang et al. (2022) in choosing the vote number, word substitution rate and stop word selection for both IMDB and MultiNLI. A different setting for MultiNLI may improve the result.

## References


Naman Agarwal, Brian Bullins, and Elad Hazan. 2017. Second-order stochastic optimization for machine learning in linear time. *J. Mach. Learn. Res.*, 18:116:1–116:40.

Moustafa Alzantot, Yash Sharma, Ahmed Elgohary, Bo-Jhang Ho, Mani Srivastava, and Kai-Wei Chang. 2018. Generating natural language adversarial examples. In *Proceedings of the 2018 Conference on Empirical Methods in Natural Language Processing*, pages 2890–2896, Brussels, Belgium. Association for Computational Linguistics.

Rongzhou Bao, Jiayi Wang, and Hai Zhao. 2021. Defending pre-trained language models from adversarial word substitutions without performance sacrifice. *CoRR*, abs/2105.14553.

Nicholas Carlini and David A. Wagner. 2017. Towards evaluating the robustness of neural networks. In *2017 IEEE Symposium on Security and Privacy, SP 2017, San Jose, CA, USA, May 22-26, 2017*, pages 39–57. IEEE Computer Society.

Ciprian Chelba, Tomás Mikolov, Mike Schuster, Qi Ge, Thorsten Brants, Phillipp Koehn, and Tony Robinson. 2014. One billion word benchmark for measuring progress in statistical language modeling. In *INTERSPEECH 2014, 15th Annual Conference of the International Speech Communication Association, Singapore, September 14-18, 2014*, pages 2635–2639. ISCA.

Gilad Cohen, Guillermo Sapiro, and Raja Giryes. 2020. Detecting adversarial samples using influence functions and nearest neighbors. In *2020 IEEE/CVF Conference on Computer Vision and Pattern Recognition, CVPR 2020, Seattle, WA, USA, June 13-19, 2020*, pages 14441–14450. Computer Vision Foundation / IEEE.

Jeremy M. Cohen, Elan Rosenfeld, and J. Zico Kolter. 2019. Certified adversarial robustness via randomized smoothing. In *Proceedings of the 36th International Conference on Machine Learning, ICML 2019, 9-15 June 2019, Long Beach, California, USA*, volume 97 of *Proceedings of Machine Learning Research*, pages 1310–1320. PMLR.

Zihang Dai, Zhilin Yang, Yiming Yang, Jaime Carbonell, Quoc Le, and Ruslan Salakhutdinov. 2019. Transformer-XL: Attentive language models beyond a fixed-length context. In *Proceedings of the 57th Annual Meeting of the Association for Computational Linguistics*, pages 2978–2988, Florence, Italy. Association for Computational Linguistics.

Reuben Feinman, Ryan R. Curtin, Saurabh Shintre, and Andrew B. Gardner. 2017. Detecting adversarial samples from artifacts. *CoRR*, abs/1703.00410.

Christiane Fellbaum. 2005. Wordnet and wordnets. In Alex Barber, editor, *ELL*, pages 2–665. Elsevier.

Gil Fidel, Ron Bitton, and Asaf Shabtai. 2020. When explainability meets adversarial learning: Detecting adversarial examples using SHAP signatures. In *2020 International Joint Conference on Neural Networks, IJCNN 2020, Glasgow, United Kingdom, July 19-24, 2020*, pages 1–8. IEEE.

Ian J. Goodfellow, Jonathon Shlens, and Christian Szegedy. 2015. Explaining and harnessing adversarial examples. In *3rd International Conference on Learning Representations, ICLR 2015, San Diego, CA, USA, May 7-9, 2015, Conference Track Proceedings*.

Divya Gopinath, Guy Katz, Corina S. Pasareanu, and Clark W. Barrett. 2018. Deepsafe: A data-driven approach for assessing robustness of neural networks. In *Automated Technology for Verification and Analysis - 16th International Symposium, ATVA 2018, Los Angeles, CA, USA, October 7-10, 2018, Proceedings*, volume 11138 of *Lecture Notes in Computer Science*, pages 3–19. Springer.

Chuan Guo, Geoff Pleiss, Yu Sun, and Kilian Q. Weinberger. 2017. On calibration of modern neural networks. In *Proceedings of the 34th International Conference on Machine Learning, ICML 2017, Sydney, NSW, Australia, 6-11 August 2017*, volume 70 of *Proceedings of Machine Learning Research*, pages 1321–1330. PMLR.

Han Guo, Nazneen Rajani, Peter Hase, Mohit Bansal, and Caiming Xiong. 2021. FastIF: Scalable influence functions for efficient model interpretation and debugging. In *Proceedings of the 2021 Conference on Empirical Methods in Natural Language Processing*, pages 10333–10350, Online and Punta Cana, Dominican Republic. Association for Computational Linguistics.

Xiaochuang Han, Byron C. Wallace, and Yulia Tsvetkov. 2020. Explaining black box predictions and unveiling data artifacts through influence functions. In *Proceedings of the 58th Annual Meeting of the Association for Computational Linguistics*, pages 5553–5563, Online. Association for Computational Linguistics.

Mohit Iyyer, John Wieting, Kevin Gimpel, and Luke Zettlemoyer. 2018. Adversarial example generation with syntactically controlled paraphrase networks. In *Proceedings of the 2018 Conference of the North American Chapter of the Association for Computational Linguistics: Human Language Technologies, Volume 1 (Long Papers)*, pages 1875–1885, New Orleans, Louisiana. Association for Computational Linguistics.

Robin Jia, Aditi Raghunathan, Kerem Göksel, and Percy Liang. 2019. Certified robustness to adversarial word substitutions. In *Proceedings of the 2019 Conference on Empirical Methods in Natural Language Processing and the 9th International Joint Conference on Natural Language Processing (EMNLP-IJCNLP)*, pages 4129–4142, Hong Kong, China. Association for Computational Linguistics.

Di Jin, Zhijing Jin, Joey Tianyi Zhou, and Peter Szolovits. 2020. Is BERT really robust? A strong baseline for natural language attack on text classification and entailment.

Erik Jones, Robin Jia, Aditi Raghunathan, and Percy Liang. 2020. Robust encodings: A framework for combating adversarial typos. In *Proceedings of the 58th Annual Meeting of the Association for Compu-*

*tational Linguistics*, pages 2752–2765, Online. Association for Computational Linguistics.

Pang Wei Koh and Percy Liang. 2017. Understanding black-box predictions via influence functions. In *Proceedings of the 34th International Conference on Machine Learning, ICML 2017, Sydney, NSW, Australia, 6-11 August 2017*, volume 70 of *Proceedings of Machine Learning Research*, pages 1885–1894. PMLR.

Kimin Lee, Kibok Lee, Honglak Lee, and Jinwoo Shin. 2018. A simple unified framework for detecting out-of-distribution samples and adversarial attacks. In *Advances in Neural Information Processing Systems 31: Annual Conference on Neural Information Processing Systems 2018, NeurIPS 2018, December 3-8, 2018, Montréal, Canada*, pages 7167–7177.

Dianqi Li, Yizhe Zhang, Hao Peng, Liqun Chen, Chris Brockett, Ming-Ting Sun, and Bill Dolan. 2021. Contextualized perturbation for textual adversarial attack. In *Proceedings of the 2021 Conference of the North American Chapter of the Association for Computational Linguistics: Human Language Technologies*, pages 5053–5069, Online. Association for Computational Linguistics.

Linyang Li, Ruotian Ma, Qipeng Guo, Xiangyang Xue, and Xipeng Qiu. 2020. BERT-ATTACK: Adversarial attack against BERT using BERT. In *Proceedings of the 2020 Conference on Empirical Methods in Natural Language Processing (EMNLP)*, pages 6193–6202, Online. Association for Computational Linguistics.

Yitong Li, Trevor Cohn, and Timothy Baldwin. 2016. Learning robust representations of text. In *Proceedings of the 2016 Conference on Empirical Methods in Natural Language Processing*, pages 1979–1985, Austin, Texas. Association for Computational Linguistics.

Yitong Li, Trevor Cohn, and Timothy Baldwin. 2017. Robust training under linguistic adversity. In *Proceedings of the 15th Conference of the European Chapter of the Association for Computational Linguistics: Volume 2, Short Papers*, pages 21–27, Valencia, Spain. Association for Computational Linguistics.

Na Liu, Mark Dras, and Wei Emma Zhang. 2022. Detecting textual adversarial examples based on distributional characteristics of data representations. In *Proceedings of the 7th Workshop on Representation Learning for NLP*, pages 78–90, Dublin, Ireland. Association for Computational Linguistics.

Xingjun Ma, Bo Li, Yisen Wang, Sarah M. Erfani, Sudanthi N. R. Wijewickrema, Grant Schoenebeck, Dawn Song, Michael E. Houle, and James Bailey. 2018. Characterizing adversarial subspaces using local intrinsic dimensionality. In *6th International Conference on Learning Representations, ICLR 2018, Vancouver, BC, Canada, April 30 - May 3, 2018, Conference Track Proceedings*. OpenReview.net.

Andrew L. Maas, Raymond E. Daly, Peter T. Pham, Dan Huang, Andrew Y. Ng, and Christopher Potts. 2011. Learning word vectors for sentiment analysis. In *Proceedings of the 49th Annual Meeting of the Association for Computational Linguistics: Human Language Technologies*, pages 142–150, Portland, Oregon, USA. Association for Computational Linguistics.

Aleksander Madry, Aleksandar Makelov, Ludwig Schmidt, Dimitris Tsipras, and Adrian Vladu. 2018. Towards deep learning models resistant to adversarial attacks. In *6th International Conference on Learning Representations, ICLR 2018, Vancouver, BC, Canada, April 30 - May 3, 2018, Conference Track Proceedings*. OpenReview.net.

Stephen Merity, Caiming Xiong, James Bradbury, and Richard Socher. 2017. Pointer sentinel mixture models.

Seyed-Mohsen Moosavi-Dezfooli, Alhussein Fawzi, and Pascal Frossard. 2016. Deepfool: A simple and accurate method to fool deep neural networks. In *2016 IEEE Conference on Computer Vision and Pattern Recognition, CVPR 2016, Las Vegas, NV, USA, June 27-30, 2016*, pages 2574–2582. IEEE Computer Society.

Edoardo Mosca, Lukas Huber, Marc Alexander Kühn, and Georg Groh. 2022. Detecting word-level adversarial text attacks via shapley additive explanations. In *Proceedings of the 7th Workshop on Representation Learning for NLP, RepL4NLP@ACL 2022, Dublin, Ireland, May 26, 2022*, pages 156–166. Association for Computational Linguistics.

Maximilian Mozes, Pontus Stenetorp, Bennett Kleinberg, and Lewis Griffin. 2021. Frequency-guided word substitutions for detecting textual adversarial examples. In *Proceedings of the 16th Conference of the European Chapter of the Association for Computational Linguistics: Main Volume*, pages 171–186, Online. Association for Computational Linguistics.

Nikola Mrkšić, Diarmuid Ó Séaghdha, Blaise Thomson, Milica Gašić, Lina M. Rojas-Barahona, Pei-Hao Su, David Vandyke, Tsung-Hsien Wen, and Steve Young. 2016. Counter-fitting word vectors to linguistic constraints. In *Proceedings of the 2016 Conference of the North American Chapter of the Association for Computational Linguistics: Human Language Technologies*, pages 142–148, San Diego, California. Association for Computational Linguistics.

Nicolas Papernot, Fartash Faghri, Nicholas Carlini, Ian Goodfellow, Reuben Feinman, Alexey Kurakin, Cihang Xie, Yash Sharma, Tom Brown, Aurko Roy, et al. 2016a. Technical report on the cleverhans v2. 1.0 adversarial examples library. *arXiv preprint arXiv:1610.00768*.

Nicolas Papernot and Patrick D. McDaniel. 2018. Deep k-nearest neighbors: Towards confident, interpretable and robust deep learning. *CoRR*, abs/1803.04765.

Nicolas Papernot, Patrick D. McDaniel, Somesh Jha, Matt Fredrikson, Z. Berkay Celik, and Ananthram Swami. 2016b. The limitations of deep learning in adversarial settings. In *IEEE European Symposium on Security and Privacy, EuroS&P 2016, Saarbrücken, Germany, March 21-24, 2016*, pages 372–387. IEEE.

Jeffrey Pennington, Richard Socher, and Christopher Manning. 2014. GloVe: Global vectors for word representation. In *Proceedings of the 2014 Conference on Empirical Methods in Natural Language Processing (EMNLP)*, pages 1532–1543, Doha, Qatar. Association for Computational Linguistics.

Danish Pruthi, Bhuwan Dhingra, and Zachary C. Lipton. 2019. Combating adversarial misspellings with robust word recognition. In *Proceedings of the 57th Annual Meeting of the Association for Computational Linguistics*, pages 5582–5591, Florence, Italy. Association for Computational Linguistics.

Shuhuai Ren, Yihe Deng, Kun He, and Wanxiang Che. 2019. Generating natural language adversarial examples through probability weighted word saliency. In *Proceedings of the 57th Annual Meeting of the Association for Computational Linguistics*, pages 1085–1097, Florence, Italy. Association for Computational Linguistics.

Marco Tulio Ribeiro, Sameer Singh, and Carlos Guestrin. 2018. Semantically equivalent adversarial rules for debugging NLP models. In *Proceedings of the 56th Annual Meeting of the Association for Computational Linguistics (Volume 1: Long Papers)*, pages 856–865, Melbourne, Australia. Association for Computational Linguistics.

Christian Szegedy, Wojciech Zaremba, Ilya Sutskever, Joan Bruna, Dumitru Erhan, Ian J. Goodfellow, and Rob Fergus. 2014. Intriguing properties of neural networks. In *2nd International Conference on Learning Representations, ICLR 2014, Banff, AB, Canada, April 14-16, 2014, Conference Track Proceedings*.

Thomas Tanay and Lewis D. Griffin. 2016. A boundary tilting persepective on the phenomenon of adversarial examples. *CoRR*, abs/1608.07690.

Florian Tramèr, Nicolas Papernot, Ian J. Goodfellow, Dan Boneh, and Patrick D. McDaniel. 2017. The space of transferable adversarial examples. *CoRR*, abs/1704.03453.

Laurens van der Maaten and Geoffrey Hinton. 2008. Visualizing data using t-sne. *Journal of Machine Learning Research*, 9(86):2579–2605.

Xiaosen Wang, Yifeng Xiong, and Kun He. 2022. Detecting textual adversarial examples through randomized substitution and vote. In *Uncertainty in Artificial Intelligence, Proceedings of the Thirty-Eighth Conference on Uncertainty in Artificial Intelligence, UAI 2022, 1-5 August 2022, Eindhoven, The Netherlands*, volume 180 of *Proceedings of Machine Learning Research*, pages 2056–2065. PMLR.

Adina Williams, Nikita Nangia, and Samuel Bowman. 2018. A broad-coverage challenge corpus for sentence understanding through inference. In *Proceedings of the 2018 Conference of the North American Chapter of the Association for Computational Linguistics: Human Language Technologies, Volume 1 (Long Papers)*, pages 1112–1122, New Orleans, Louisiana. Association for Computational Linguistics.

Cihang Xie, Yuxin Wu, Laurens van der Maaten, Alan L. Yuille, and Kaiming He. 2019. Feature denoising for improving adversarial robustness. In *IEEE Conference on Computer Vision and Pattern Recognition, CVPR 2019, Long Beach, CA, USA, June 16-20, 2019*, pages 501–509. Computer Vision Foundation / IEEE.

Jin Yong Yoo and Yanjun Qi. 2021. Towards improving adversarial training of NLP models. In *Findings of the Association for Computational Linguistics: EMNLP 2021*, pages 945–956, Punta Cana, Dominican Republic. Association for Computational Linguistics.

Yichao Zhou, Jyun-Yu Jiang, Kai-Wei Chang, and Wei Wang. 2019. Learning to discriminate perturbations for blocking adversarial attacks in text classification. In *Proceedings of the 2019 Conference on Empirical Methods in Natural Language Processing and the 9th International Joint Conference on Natural Language Processing (EMNLP-IJCNLP)*, pages 4904–4913, Hong Kong, China. Association for Computational Linguistics.

## A Experimental Setup Details

The size of the datasets and the number of adversarial samples generated by each of the attack methods are given in Tab. 5. Obtained accuracies of the $\text{BERT}_{\text{BASE}}$ model are in Tab. 6 and the other models used in MDRE are in Tab. 7

### A.1 Attack Methods

**CHARATT.** We implement CHARATT as proposed by Pruthi et al. (2019). It tweaks the original texts by randomly swapping, dropping and adding characters or adding a keyboard mistake. *Swapping* refers to exchanging places of two adjacent internal characters. *Dropping* removes a character and *Adding* inserts a new character at a randomly selected position. *Keyboard mistakes* is for substituting a character with one of its adjacent characters in keyboards.

In our experiments, we allow a maximum of half the words from the original text to be perturbed, so the maximum number of possible attacks on the IMDB and MULTINLI datasets is 256 and 128 per sentence, respectively.

**WORDATT.** Alzantot et al. (2018) proposed an effective and widely used adversarial attack that we incorporate in our work as WORDATT.

This method allows the attacker to alter practically every word from the sentence if required with the context-preserving synonymous words. The synonym search is done over a large search space that includes the GloVe word vectors (Pennington et al., 2014), counter-fitting word vectors (Mrkšić et al., 2016), and the Google 1 billion words language model (Chelba et al., 2014). Then, following the natural selection methods, crossover and mutation techniques from the population-based genetic algorithm are applied to generate the next set of adversarial sentences. On each iteration, several adversarial texts that are unsuccessful in changing the model's prediction are removed from the pool.

However, Jia et al. (2019) found that the algorithm is computationally expensive and recommended using a faster language model and stopping the semantic drift of the algorithm that refers to applying the language model on the synonyms picked from previous iterations as well to choose words from their neighboring word-space.

We incorporate the above recommendations by utilising a faster Transformer-XL architecture (Dai et al., 2019) that is pretrained on the WikiText-103 dataset (Merity et al., 2017) and prohibiting the semantic drift by finding all test examples words' neighbors only before attacks. We also restrict the minimum number of perturbations to one-fifth of the maximum sequence length which is 102 and 51 for the IMDB and MULTINLI, respectively.

### A.2 Baseline Detection Methods

The first four are from Liu et al. (2022) (we omit the language model, as it operates essentially at the chance), and we use the implementations from there.[4]

**Learning to Discriminate Perturbations (DISP) (Zhou et al., 2019).** DISP is one of the commonly used baselines for adversarial text detection that identifies a set of character-level of word-level perturbed tokens and then applies an embedding estimator that predicts embeddings for each perturbed token and maps them to the actual word to repair the perturbations.

If the model's prediction on an adversarial text restored by DISP remains the same class as the prediction on its original version, we consider it a successful detection of an adversarial example.

**Frequency-guided word substitutions (FGWS) (Mozes et al., 2021).** Mozes et al. (2021) verifies that in the case of word-level attacks, the synonym replacements normally occur in low frequency. They use this concept in a model-agnostic rule-based adversarial text detection algorithm Frequency-Guided Word Substitutions (FGWS).

Firstly, the algorithm sets a word frequency threshold to identify infrequent words that have frequencies lower than this value. Then the algorithm replaces those words with their high-frequency synonyms and selects the replaced sentences as adversarial samples if the model's prediction confidence scores for the replacements change over a threshold. They use WordNet (Fellbaum, 2005) and GloVe vectors (Pennington et al., 2014) to find the synonyms. They experiment by taking $\{0\text{-th}, 10\text{-th}, \cdots, 100\text{-th}\}$ percentile of word frequencies in the training set as the word-frequency threshold. Finally, on these selected alternative sentences, if the prediction confidence differs from their corresponding original sentence's prediction confidence by more than a certain amount, the original sentences are determined as adversarial examples.

**Local Intrinsic Dimensionality (LID) (Liu et al., 2022).** From the image processing detection methods, Liu et al. (2022) adapt the Local Intrinsic

[4] https://github.com/NaLiuAnna/MDRE

| Dataset | Training. | Validation. | Testing. | Correctly Predicted Test Examples | Adversarial/Original Examples | |
|---|---|---|---|---|---|---|
| | | | | | character-level | word-level |
| IMDB | 20,000 | 5,000 | 25,000 | 23,226 | 12,299 | 9,627 |
| MULTINLI | 314,162 | 78,540 | 9,832 | 8,062 | 7,028 | 3,240 |

Table 5: The number of examples used in experiments

| Dataset | Clean Accuracy | CHAR ATTACK | WORD ATTACK |
|---|---|---|---|
| IMDB | 0.9290 | 0.3656 | 0.6999 |
| MULTINLI | 0.8201 | 0.4848 | 0.6864 |

Table 6: $\text{BERT}_{\text{BASE}}$ classifier accuracy on the clean and adversarial examples

Dimensionality (LID) approach of Ma et al. (2018). This technique creates a local distance distribution for a test record to its neighbors from the training set. They apply this to transformer models by taking the outputs of each layer from the target model to represent the training records.

Following Liu et al. (2022), we use the $\text{BERT}_{\text{BASE}}$ model and implement a logistic regression classifier as the detector, and tune the size of the neighbors $k$ through a grid search over 100, 1000, and the range [10, 42) with a step size 2.

**MultiDistance Representation Ensemble Method (MDRE) (Liu et al., 2022).** Motivated by the notion that adversarial examples are out-of-distribution samples as recognized in Lee et al. (2018) and Feinman et al. (2017), Liu et al. (2022) assume that texts with the same prediction label lie on similar data submanifold and adversarial perturbation on these texts put them to another data submanifold, thus altering the model's prediction on them.

They measure the Euclidean distance between each reference datapoint and the nearest neighbors from the training datapoints with similar predicted labels and establish that this distance will be greater for the adversarial reference point than the normal one. They further use ensemble learning to combine distances between representations learned from multiple DNNs and build a binary logistic regression model to detect adversarial examples.

Following (Liu et al., 2022), we also use four learning models: [$\text{BERT}_{\text{BASE}}$, $\text{RoBERTa}_{\text{BASE}}$, $\text{XLNet}_{\text{BASE}}$, $\text{BART}_{\text{BASE}}$] in our experiments. Table 7 reports the clean accuracies of the other target classifiers used in feature ensembling in MDRE.

**Randomized Substitution and Vote (RSV) (Wang et al., 2022).** A word-level attacker's target is to find an optimal synonym substitution that mutually influences other words in the sentence. Taking this optimization target of the adversary, Wang et al. (2022) resort to randomly substituting words from the text with their synonyms and argue that this random word substitution destroys the mutual interaction between words and eliminates adversarial perturbation.

At first, they generate a set of perturbed samples by randomly replacing some words from a text with their arbitrary synonyms. Then the model's output logits for the processed samples are accumulated and voted to determine a prediction label for the text samples. If the original text's prediction doesn't match the voted prediction label it is considered as an adversarial example.

We use their code.[5]

**SHapley Additive exPlanations (SHAP) (Mosca et al., 2022).** In this work, Mosca et al. (2022) adopt an adversarial image detection method for word-level attacks on text. They train an adversarial detector with the SHapley Additive exPlanations (SHAP) values of the training data for each of the test data using the SHAP explainer proposed and implemented by Fidel et al. (2020).

They experiment on multiple classifiers as the detectors such as logistic regression, random-forest classifier, support vector classifier and a neural network. They also show that the detector doesn't require a large number of training samples for it to be successful. In our work, we follow the same and report the best accuracy obtained among the four detectors.

We use their code.[6] Accuracies of all the detectors are in Table 8.

## B Computing Influence Function

For a datapoint $z_i = (x_i, y_i)$ from the training set $\{(x_1, y_1), \ldots, (x_i, y_i) \in (X, Y)\}$ and model parameters $\theta \in \Theta$, the loss of the model be $L(z, \theta)$

[5] https://github.com/JHL-HUST/RSV

[6] https://github.com/huberl/adversarial_shap_detect_Repl4NLP

| Dataset | Attack Method | $\text{BERT}_{\text{BASE}}$ | $\text{RoBERTa}_{\text{BASE}}$ | $\text{XLNet}_{\text{BASE}}$ | $\text{BART}_{\text{BASE}}$ |
|---|---|---|---|---|---|
| IMDB | Clean | 0.9290 | 0.9532 | 0.9336 | 0.9429 |
| | CHARATT | 0.3656 | 0.8613 | 0.5770 | 0.8286 |
| | WORDATT | 0.6999 | 0.8714 | 0.7918 | 0.8425 |
| MULTINLI | Clean | 0.8201 | 0.8671 | 0.8630 | 0.8455 |
| | CHARATT | 0.4848 | 0.7104 | 0.6670 | 0.6457 |
| | WORDATT | 0.6864 | 0.7068 | 0.6870 | 0.6296 |

Table 7: Different classifier accuracies on both clean and adversarial dataset for MDRE.

| Dataset | Attack | Logistic Regression | Random Forest | SVC | DNN |
|---|---|---|---|---|---|
| IMDB | CHARATT | 0.740 | 0.804 | 0.803 | 0.812 |
| | WORDATT | 0.605 | 0.764 | 0.684 | 0.75 |
| MULTINLI | CHARATT | 0.588 | 0.614 | 0.613 | 0.61 |
| | WORDATT | 0.528 | 0.697 | 0.633 | 0.621 |

Table 8: Detection accuracy obtained from four detector classifiers used in SHAP.

and the optimized parameters are:

$$\theta' = \arg\min_{\theta \in \Theta} \frac{1}{n} \sum_{i=1}^{n} L(z_i, \theta)$$

The influence score is then calculated by observing the impact of a modification in the weight of a train datapoint on the decision of the prediction for the test datapoint. Assume we upweigh the training datapoint $z$ by a small $\epsilon$ amount, which produces below $\theta'$:

$$\theta'_{\epsilon,z} = \arg\min_{\theta \in \Theta} \frac{1}{n} \sum_{i=1}^{n} L(z_i, \theta) + \epsilon L(z, \theta)$$

Then, according to Koh and Liang (2017), the influence of the boosted $z$ on the parameters $\theta'$ can be defined by:

$$\frac{d\theta'_{\epsilon,z}}{d\epsilon}\Big|_{\epsilon=0} = -H_{\theta'}^{-1} \nabla_\theta L(z, \theta') \quad (1)$$

where $H'_\theta = \frac{1}{n} \sum_{i=1}^{n} \nabla_\theta^2 L(z_i, \theta')$ is the Hessian of the model.

Applying the chain rule to the Eq. 1 can be derived to the below form that measures the influence $I_{up,loss}$ of $z$ on the loss of a test point $z_{test}$:

$$I_{up,loss}(z, z_{test}) = - \nabla_\theta L(z_{test}, \theta') H_\theta^{-1} \nabla_\theta L(z, \theta') \quad (2)$$

The NNIF method uses the $I_{up,loss}$ score.

| Parameters | Values |
|---|---|
| C | [ 1, 10, 1000, 10000] |
| gamma | [1, .1, .01, 0.001, 'auto'] |
| kernel | ['linear', 'rbf', 'poly', 'sigmoid'] |

Table 9: Gridsearch parameters for building SVC.

## C Illustrations of Regions Around Test and Adversarial Points

Looking at the training samples that influence the prediction of a test datapoint, gives us an illustration of the decision subspace of the DNN on it. To illustrate the subspace, we measure the top 25 influential (IF) and nearest neighbor (NN) training embeddings for a test record and its adversarial counterpart for each attack and plot them along with the test and adversarial points. All embeddings are reduced to two dimensions by using t-SNE. Figures 7 and 8 show an example each for the IMDB and MULTINLI datasets, respectively. On each figure, the top row depicts the IF-based training points and the bottom row shows the NN-based training points.

## D Separability of Points: IF vs NN

We build SVC classifiers on the neighboring train embeddings to evaluate how well the influence function is describing the learned subspace of the DNN than the DKNN. The best SVC classifiers over NNs and IF points for each of the 1000 test and adversarial example pairs are estimated through GridSearch over the parameters as depicted in Table 9.

## E Experimental Results Examples

NNIF combines the DKNN ranking on top of the influence scores to select the best training instances for a test datapoint. In Tables 10, 11 and 12 we illustrate examples for WORDATT and CHARATT respectively, showing the top three helpful and harm-

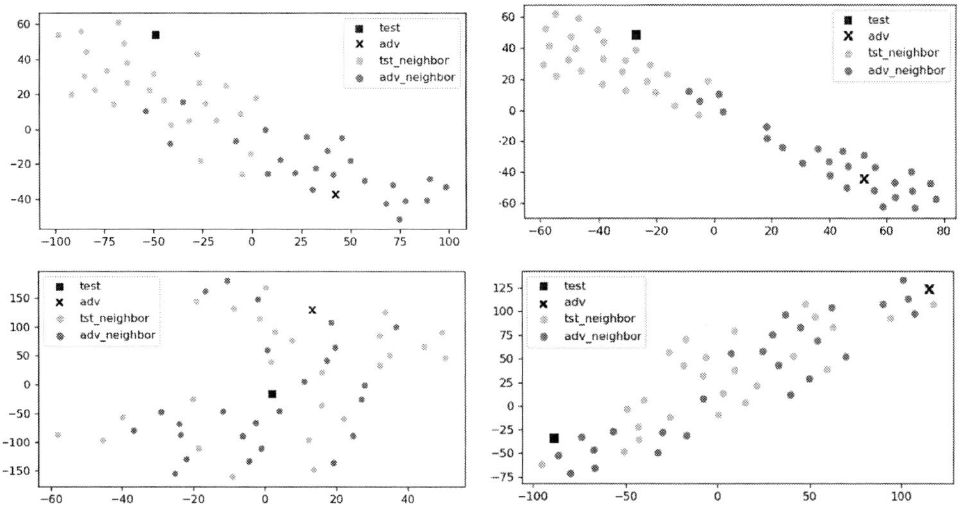


(a) CHARATT (b) WORDATT

Figure 7: Embedding subspace (applied t-SNE) of a test sample from the IMDB dataset (black-square) and its adversarial version (purple-cross) generated by three types of attacks. The top set of images shows the 25 most influential training samples and the bottom set shows the top 25 nearest neighbors (KNN).

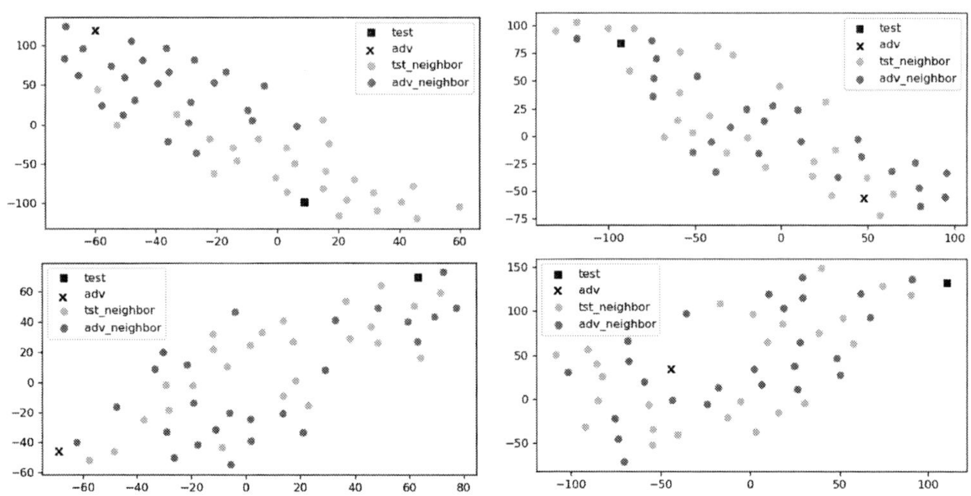


(a) CHARATT (b) WORDATT

Figure 8: Embedding subspace (applied t-SNE) of a test sample from the MULTINLI dataset (black-square) and its adversarial version (purple-cross) generated by three types of attacks. The top set of images shows the 25 most influential training samples and the bottom set shows the top 25 nearest neighbors (KNN).

ful training instances for the detection of the adversarial attack. We also show the DKNN rankings of the top training instances filtered by the IF scores in the table.

As DISP performs better in one of the experimental settings in Liu et al. (2022), we further pick one example sentence from the paper that DISP detects correctly and observe NNIF's performance on it. NNIF is also able to detect the sentence correctly. In Table 13 we show the influential instances for this prediction as well.

| | Original text - label Entailment - prediction Entailment | |
|---|---|---|
| | **Premise:** Address your remarks to the chair illustrates metonymy a figure of speech in which something is called by the name of something else associated with it.<br>**Hypothesis:** Using one word to refer to something that is associated with it is a figure of speech. | |
| | **WordAtt- prediction Contradiction** | |
| | **Premise:** Address your remarks to the chair draws metonymy a digit of speech in which something is called by the name of something else associated with it .<br>**Hypothesis:** Using one word to refer to something that is associated with it is a digit of speech | |
| | **Top Helpful** | **NNIF Rank** |
| 1 | **Premise:** my adult women friends are anguishing over over some of these choices.<br>**Hypothesis:** I don't have any woman friends. | 2185 |
| 2 | **Premise:** Vrenna, now! Jon kicked the barrel and it broke open.<br>**Hypothesis:** Jon told Vrenna what to do. | 4956 |
| 3 | **Premise:** I brought my Gauntlet to bear; electricity leaping out.<br>**Hypothesis:** My gauntlet was magical and electricity jumped out of it. | 5473 |
| | **Top Harmful** | **NNIF Rank** |
| 1 | **Premise:** Examining the elements of the definition also may help make this distinction clear.<br>**Hypothesis:** Ignoring the elements of the definition also may help make this distinction clear. | 4308 |
| 2 | **Premise:** the uniformed services, recognize that promotional material received by a uniformed service member traveling on official business at government expense belongs to the government and must be relinquished in accordance with service regulations.<br>**Hypothesis:** The material belongs to the government even after the hand out. | 5819 |
| 3 | **Premise:** The emergency department at Harborview probably sees 50 times as many patients with alcohol problems as the psychiatry or family medicine departments.<br>**Hypothesis:** The family medicine departments do not treat alcohol problems. | 2221 |

Table 10: Top three helpful and harmful train instances based on IF score and further ranking of them by DkNN for a correctly predicted adversarial text by NNIF for MultiNLI WordAtt

| | Original text - label Entailment - prediction Entailment | |
|---|---|---|
| | **Premise:** Although a seemingly mundane, tactical aspect of business, a firm's inventory strategy reflects its approach to managing risk.<br>**Hypothesis:** It is possible to determine a firm's risk management philosophy by examining their inventory strategy. | |
| | **CharAtt- prediction Neutral** | |
| | **Premise:** Although a seemingly mundane , tactcial aspect of business , a firm 's itnventory strategxy reflects its approach to managing risk.<br>**Hypothesis:** It is possible to determine a firm 's risk management philkosophy by examining their inventory strategxy. | |
| | **Top Helpful** | **NNIF Rank** |
| 1 | **Premise:** Online investment guru Tokyo Joe was sued by the SEC in a civil fraud case.<br>**Hypothesis:** Tokyo Joe has been sued before. | 5091 |
| 2 | **Premise:** Wesray's purchase of Avis was trendy in three ways.<br>**Hypothesis:** There are three reasons why Wesray's purchase of Avis is trendy. | 266 |
| 3 | **Premise:** yeah i don't mind that um my husband never cared for fast food so we didn't go that often but you know i have no problem with uh going to a McDonald's or a Wendy's.<br>**Hypothesis:**My husband and I did not eat that much fast food. | 5630 |
| | **Top Harmful** | **NNIF Rank** |
| 1 | **Premise:** In accordance with the prescribed statutory process, on August 17, 2001, we reported to the Congress, the President, the Vice President, and other officials that the NEPDG had not provided the requested records.<br>**Hypothesis:** We told Congress that the NEPDG had failed to give us the records. | 1346 |
| 2 | **Premise:** The case for not acting until you have to was put most vividly by Senate Assistant Majority Leader Don Nickles of Oklahoma, in a remark that also captures the hard-nosed attitude regarding humanitarian concerns.<br>**Hypothesis:** The statement summarized their sentiment. | 1044 |
| 3 | **Premise:** Predicting that he would get a lot of heat for treating the minister with respect, Novak said that Farrakhan was more measured and a lot less confrontational and provocative than a lot of the politicians we talk to regularly on this program.<br>**Hypothesis:** Predicting he would get a lot of hear for respecting the minister, Novak said Farrakhan was measured and less confrontational. | 5623 |

Table 11: Top three helpful and harmful train instances based on IF score and further ranking of them by DkNN for a correctly predicted adversarial text by NNIF for MultiNLI CharAtt

| | Original text - label Neutral - prediction Neutral | |
|---|---|---|
| | **Premise:** And, instead of providing an open-ended guarantee on prices to its distributors, the company would guarantee the price for only two weeks after purchase by the distributor, refusing to take back computers unless they malfunctioned.<br>**Hypothesis:** The distributor could potentially lose out due to this method. | |
| | **CHARATT- prediction Contradiction** | |
| | **Premise:** And , instead of providing an openedned guaantee on pices to its disrtibutors , the comapny wuld guaantee the price for only two weeks after purchase by the distributor, refusing to take badk computers ulness they malfunctioned .<br>**Hypothesis:** Tehe distributor could potelntially lose out de to this mehgod . | |
| | **Top Helpful** | **NNIF Rank** |
| 1 | **Premise:** No it was gas because you washed your legs all over because you did it in shorts.<br>**Hypothesis:** Your legs were washed all over due to having done it in shorts. | 2373 |
| 2 | **Premise:** Leaving the British official who twice searched his luggage none the wiser, he managed by meticulous observation to memorize the principal features of the power loom well enough to produce his own version of it on his return to Boston.<br>**Hypothesis:** He failed at retaining the information in his head but managed to build a rough prototype of the power loom anyway. | 4706 |
| 3 | **Premise:** Bin Ladin shares Qutb's stark view, permitting him and his followers to rationalize even unprovoked mass murder as righteous defense of an embattled faith.<br>**Hypothesis:** Bin Ladin views his actions as a defense of his faith. | 925 |
| | **Top Harmful** | **NNIF Rank** |
| 1 | **Premise:** As graduates of the class of 1990, we would like to leave behind something tangible, in appreciation for the support and encouragement we have received from other students in the School of Engineering and Technology.<br>**Hypothesis:** We want leave a concrete symbol of our appreciation to the school. | 1336 |
| 2 | **Premise:** Fortunately, not all reports are as disturbing as Hochschild's.<br>**Hypothesis:** Thankfully, not all reports are as terrifying as Hochschild's. | 4817 |
| 3 | **Premise:** Of the two, the W geographical listings seem more W lists Aylesbury, which, through some grievous, egregious fault, is not in the geographical section of the L but does appear in the A-Z section (because of the ducks).<br>**Hypothesis:** For some reason, the ducks put the topic in the A-Z section. | 268 |

Table 12: MULTINLI CHARATT adversarial text that the NNIF fails to detect; showing top three helpful and harmful train instances based on IF score and further ranking of them by DKNN

| Original text - label Entailment prediction Entailment | |
|---|---|
| **Premise**: Finally, it might be worth mentioning that the program has the capacity to store in a temporary memory buffer about 100 words (proper names, for instance) that it has identified as not stored in its dictionary.<br>**Hypothesis**: It's possible to store words in a temporary dictionary, if they don't appear in a regular dictionary. | |
| **WORDATT- prediction Neutral** | |
| **Premise**: Finally, it might be worth mentioning that the program has the capacity to store in a temporary memory buffer about 100 words (proper names, for instance) that it has identified as not stored in its dictionary.<br>**Hypothesis**: It's possible to shopping words in a temporary dictionary, if they don't appear in a regular dictionary. | |
| **Repaired text by DISP** | |
| **Premise**: Finally, it might be worth that that the program has the capacity to store in a temporary memory buffer about 100 words (proper names, for instance) that it has identified as not stored in its dictionary.<br>**Hypothesis**: It's possible to **do** words in a temporary dictionary, if they don't appear in a regular dictionary. | |
| **Repaired text by FGWS** | |
| **Premise**: Finally, it might be worth **name** that the program has the capacity to store in a temporary memory pilot about 100 words (proper names, for instance) that it has identified as not stored in its dictionary.<br>**Hypothesis**: It's possible to shopping words in a temporary dictionary, if they don't appear in a regular dictionary. | |
| **Top Helpful** | **NNIF Rank** |
| 1 **Premise:** yeah i mean they're they're throwing more money at it now than ever before and things are getting worse.<br>**Hypothesis:** The money is going to the wrong things, so it's not fixing the problem. | 1295 |
| 2 **Premise:**I put $75 on the New England Patriots as a 2.5-point underdog and $50 on a Boston Red Sox playoff game against the Cleveland Indians.<br>**Hypothesis:** I bet a total of $125 dollars on the New England Patriots and the Boston Red Sox. | 3870 |
| 3 **Premise:** Graffiti written by Russian soldiers can be seen in the caves of Antiparos.<br>**Hypothesis:** Russian soldiers drew graffiti on the walls of The Louvre. | 4122 |
| **Top Harmful** | **NNIF Rank** |
| 1 **Premise:** But I am most serious.<br>**Hypothesis:** I'm not joking at all. | 808 |
| 2 **Premise:** the uniformed services, recognize that promotional material received by a uniformed service member traveling on official business at government expense belongs to the government and must be relinquished in accordance with service regulations<br>**Hypothesis:** TThe material belongs to the government even after the hand out. | 2835 |
| 3 **Premise:** According to NIST, accreditation is the formal authorization by the management official for system operation and an explicit acceptance of risk.<br>**Hypothesis:** Accreditation is the formal authorization by the management official for system operation and an explicit acceptance of risk, according to NIST. | 2908 |

Table 13: Example sentence from Liu et al. (2022) that is predicted correctly by NNIF, DISP, LID, MDRE and incorrectly by FGWS

# Supervised Clustering Loss for Clustering-Friendly Sentence Embeddings: an Application to Intent Clustering

**Giorgio Barnabò**
Amazon Alexa AI
Sapienza University of Rome
giorgio.barnabo@uniroma1.it

**Antonio Uva**
Amazon Alexa AI
antonuva@amazon.it

**Sandro Pollastrini**
Amazon Alexa AI
kvantumo@amazon.it

**Chiara Rubagotti**
Amazon Alexa AI
crubagot@amazon.it

**Davide Bernardi**
Amazon Alexa AI
dvdbe@amazon.it

## Abstract

Modern virtual assistants are trained to classify customer requests into a taxonomy of predesigned intents. Requests that fall outside of this taxonomy, however, are often unhandled and need to be clustered to define new experiences. Recently, state-of-the-art results in intent clustering were achieved by training a neural network with a latent structured prediction loss. Unfortunately, though, this new approach suffers from a quadratic bottleneck as it requires to compute a joint embedding representation for all pairs of utterances to cluster. To overcome this limitation, we instead cast the problem into a representation learning task, and we adapt the latent structured prediction loss to fine-tune sentence encoders, thus making it possible to obtain clustering-friendly single-sentence embeddings. Our experiments show that the supervised clustering loss returns state-of-the-art results in terms of clustering accuracy and adjusted mutual information.

## 1 Introduction

Many virtual assistants like Alexa, Cortana, Google Home, and Siri have a Natural Language Understanding (NLU) component that categorizes customers' requests into supported experiences, organized by domains and intents. However, when user requests don't fit into these categories, NLU models can fail, causing friction in human-machine interaction. Analyzing these out-of-scope utterances can help expand the assistant's capabilities, but manually inspecting all failing utterances is unfeasible. Therefore, automation is needed, such as clustering frictional utterances into new required experiences. This approach is valuable for expanding the assistants' capabilities in a user-driven way. One way is to use pre-trained sentence embeddings with unsupervised clustering algorithms. Another option is to train a clustering model in a supervised manner using utterances with known intents. This supervised approach has been successful in co-reference resolution (Finley and Joachims, 2005) and has been recently applied to intent clustering. A seminal work by Haponchyk et al. (2018) uses measures of utterance similarity as input to either Latent Structural Support Vector Machines (LSSVM) or to a Latent Structured Perceptron (LSP) (Yu and Joachims, 2009; Fernandes et al., 2014). The same two algorithms - LSSVM and LSP - were later used by Haponchyk and Moschitti (2021) to train a fully Neural Supervised Clustering architecture (NSC) with utterances encoded through pre-trained large language models - e.g. BERT (Devlin et al., 2019). Supervised clustering techniques use graph structures to represent clusters and are highly effective, but have a quadratic complexity due to the need for edge weights between all possible sample pairs. In the NSC case, for example, all pairs of utterances must pass through a convolutional neural network at both training- and inference-time.

To avoid this, we propose using the supervised clustering loss to fine-tune sentence encoders, producing clustering-friendly single-sentence embeddings. This turns supervised clustering into a metric or representation learning problem where we force embeddings to be globally more suitable for intent clustering. Our approach has the advantage of scaling linearly with the number of samples, as embeddings only need to be computed for all utterances, not all pairs. To validate our approach, we perform experiments on CLINC150 (Larson et al., 2019), BANKING77 (Casanueva et al., 2020), DSTC11 (Galley et al., 2022), HUW64 (Liu et al., 2021) and Massive (FitzGerald et al., 2022): these are 5 public benchmark datasets for intent clustering, both monolingual and multilingual. For each dataset we fine-tune mBERT (Devlin et al., 2019), XLM roBERTa (Conneau et al., 2020) and two state-of-the-art sentence encoders (All Mpnet Base and Paraphrase Multilingual Mpnet) with either our supervised clustering loss or one among cross entropy loss, cosine similarity loss, contrastive loss or triplet margin loss. Results show that, regardless of base sentence encoder or algorithm chosen to perform clustering, our proposed fine-tuning strategy induces state-of-the-art embeddings that perform equally or better than those obtained with all other tested metric learning losses, when evaluated on the intent clustering task. Our code has been attached to this submission and will be publicly released upon acceptance.

## 2 Related Works

This work lies at the intersection of three research areas: intent clustering, sentence embeddings, and structured



*Findings of the Association for Computational Linguistics: IJCNLP-AACL 2023*, pages 412–430
November 1–4, 2023. 

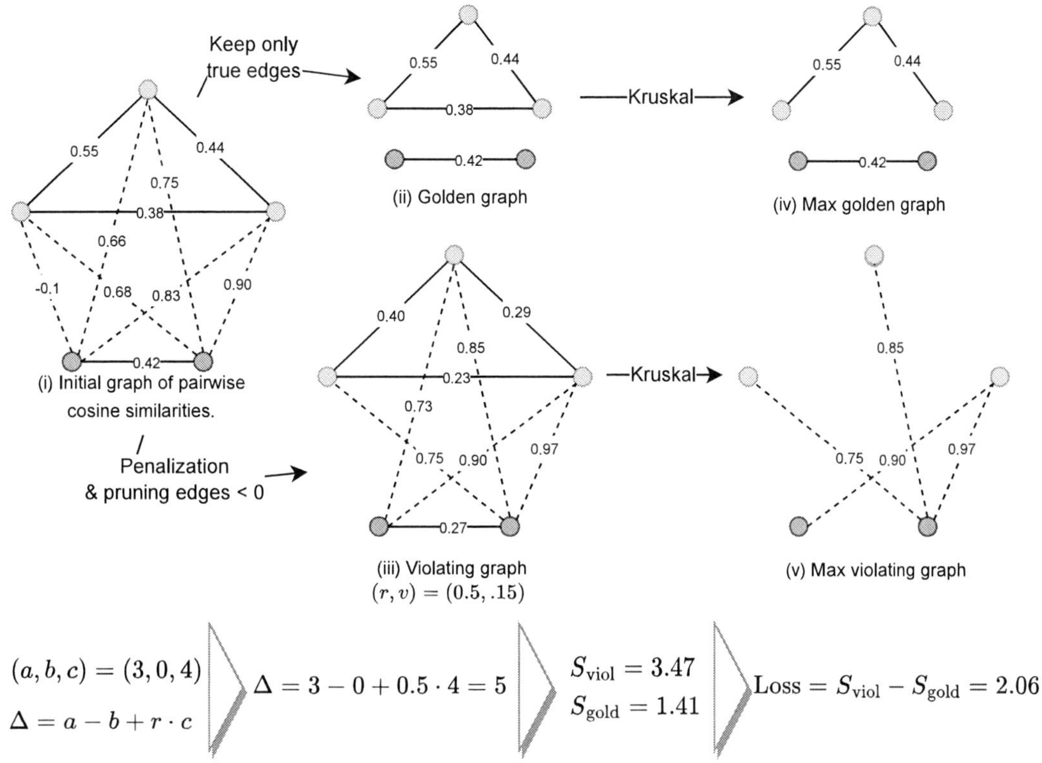


Figure 1: A sample calculation of the supervised clustering loss on two clusters (yellow points vs green points)

prediction - which we will briefly review below.

### 2.1 Intent Clustering

During the past few years, intent clustering has been a very active research topic. While it has been shown that pre-trained transformers perform poorly on out-of-scope detection (Zhang et al., 2022a), fine-tuning in a contrastive or semi-supervised fashion has proven beneficial (Casanueva et al., 2020; Zhang et al., 2021c; Mehri and Eric, 2021; Zhang et al., 2021d; Mou et al., 2022). Early works mostly focus on unsupervised clustering methods (Shi et al., 2018; Perkins and Yang, 2019; Chatterjee and Sengupta, 2020), but semi-supervision has now gained popularity (Forman et al., 2015; Zhang et al., 2022b). Lin et al. (2020), for example, propose to first perform supervised training on known intents and then use pseudo-labeling on unlabeled utterances to learn a better embedding space. Quite similarly, and in line with Deep Clustering (Caron et al., 2018), Zhang et al. (2021b) propose to first pre-train on known intents and then perform k-means clustering to assign pseudo-labels on unlabeled data. Finally, a structured prediction loss was used to directly teach both support vector machines (Finley and Joachims, 2005; Haponchyk et al., 2018) and neural networks (Haponchyk and Moschitti, 2021) to directly output intent clusters for some input utterances. This latter thread of research is the starting point of our work.

### 2.2 Sentence Embeddings

Current state-of-the-art sentence embeddings (Reimers and Gurevych, 2019, 2021; Liao, 2021; Kim et al., 2021; Giorgi et al., 2021) are obtained by fine-tuning pre-trained BERT-based architectures on SNLI (Bowman et al., 2015) and Multi-NLI (Williams et al., 2018) data with either a cross entropy loss, a contrastive loss, or a triplet margin loss. Gao et al. (2021) and Yan et al. (2021) precisely show that contrastive loss can avoid an anisotropic embedding space. As for intent-friendly word and sentence embeddings, some works propose to pre-train BERT on open domain dialogs in a self-supervised manner (Mehri et al., 2020; Wu et al., 2020; Henderson et al., 2020; Hosseini-Asl et al., 2020). On the other hand, Zhang et al. (2020) formulated intent recognition as a sentence similarity task. Another common option consists in pre-training with a contrastive loss on intent detection tasks (Vulić et al., 2021; Zhang et al., 2021d). Finally, and more generally, Zhang et al. (2021a) show that combining a contrastive loss with a clustering objective can improve short text clustering.

### 2.3 Structured Prediction

While in optimization problems local solutions often produce optimal results, structured prediction represents a valid alternative to solve NLP tasks requiring complex output, such as syntactic parsing (Roth and Yih, 2004), co-reference resolution (Yu and Joachims, 2009; Fernandes et al., 2014), and clustering (Finley and Joachims, 2005; Haponchyk et al., 2018). Nonetheless, relatively few works extend structured prediction theory to deep learning (LeCun et al., 2006; Durrett and Klein, 2015; Weiss et al., 2015; Kiperwasser and Goldberg, 2016; Peng et al., 2018; Milidiú and Rocha, 2018; Xu et al., 2018; Wang et al., 2019). In particular, when it comes to clustering, designing a differentiable loss function that captures the global characteristics of good clustering is particularly hard; for this reason, when dealing with coreference resolution - a closely related task - Lee et al. (2017) use simple losses, which already perform well but do not strictly take into account the cluster structure. Haponchyk and Moschitti (2021), on the other hand, represent clusters using graph structures and use LSSVM (Yu and Joachims, 2009) and LSP (Fernandes et al., 2014) - two structured prediction algorithms - to compute an augmented loss for training a deep clustering architecture.

## 3 Supervised Clustering Loss for Clustering-Friendly Representation Learning

In this section, we demonstrate how a structured learning approach - which utilizes *latent representations of graph structures* for predicting clusters from a set of utterances - can be instead used to fine-tune sentence encoders to be more clustering-friendly. Our approach is unique in that it leverages supervised clustering principles for the fine-tuning of sentence-transformers using examples of clusters, known as *gold clusters*. This allows for the creation of "cluster-friendly" embeddings, whose cosine similarities can be used to directly cluster the embedded utterances using various clustering algorithms such as threshold-based, K-Means, or Hierarchical Clustering.

Our fine-tuning loss represents utterances as nodes of a *fully-connected weighted graph*. The edge weights correspond to the cosine similarities between connected pairs of utterances (as defined by Eq. 2). By pruning the edges whose weight is below a certain threshold (i.e., the cosine similarity is less than 0), we can obtain a clustering. This clustering, however, is only used at training time to compute a clustering-sensitive loss, whose back-propagation contributes to the creation of more clustering-friendly sentence embeddings.

We begin by briefly explaining how we can leverage a supervised clustering loss to fine-tune sentence encoders, followed by a detailed description of the mathematical computation behind the loss.

### 3.1 Intuitive explanation of the Supervised Clustering Loss

Our loss function is inspired by the *Neural Supervised Clustering* (NSC) (Haponchyk and Moschitti, 2021). Specifically, the computation of the loss accounts for the differences between the gold clustering and the embedding-based clustering. The loss is made up of two components: a difference between two *scores* based on edge weights (Eqs. 9, 10), and a *structural-loss* based edge comparison (Eq. 8). Following the example in Figure 1:

1. at each learning step, we use the actual embeddings to compute a similarity matrix for the current clustering scenario, represented as a fully-connected graph (i);
2. using the gold clustering, we construct a first graph, called *gold graph* (ii), keeping only edges that connect nodes in the same clusters and pruning the others; its connected components now represent the gold clusters;
3. we construct a second graph, called *violating graph* (iii), perturbing the similarity matrix (i) by penalizing the edges connecting nodes in the same clusters; in this context, $v$ is a real number between 0 and 1, representing the penalization factor on gold edges, while $r$ represent what percentage of this penalization is transferred onto wrong edges;
4. we prune all the edges with weight below 0, resulting in a disconnected graph (iii), whose connected components are the predicted clusters;
5. to perform the comparison between the two resulting clusterings, we keep the minimum possible connectivity which preserves the connected components and select the strongest edges by applying Kruskal's Maximum Spanning Tree to each connected components, resulting in graphs (iv) and (v);
6. we compute a score for each graph - as the weight sum of the remaining edges, and the structural loss - as the difference between the number of edges of the gold graph and the numbers of correct and incorrect edges of the max-violating graph.
7. finally, we perform back propagation only in case the structural loss is greater than zero (which happens in the case of imperfect matching between the two graphs).

### 3.2 Algorithm details

Let $\{(x_i, y_i)\}_{i=1}^n$ be a set of samples to be clustered, where $x_i$ represents the $i$-th object and $y_i$ its cluster assignment. Let's further assume that $\text{Net}_\theta(.)$ is a generic neural network that encodes the objects $\{x_i\}_{i=1}^n$ into $k-$dimensional real-valued vectors, such that:

$$A = [\hat{x}_1, ..., \hat{x}_n] = \text{Net}_\theta([x_1, ..., x_n]), \quad (1)$$

where $A \in \mathbb{R}^{n \times k}$ contains all the $n$ objects encoded with $\text{Net}_\theta(.)$.

The first step to compute the supervised clustering loss is to represent the clustering scenario $\{(x_i, y_i)\}_{i=1}^n$ through an undirected weighted graph, where the $i$-th node corresponds to $x_i$ and the edge $e_{ij} = cosine\_similarity(\hat{x}_i, \hat{x}_j)$. In practice, the weighted adjacency matrix $S$ with the pairwise cosine similarities fully defines the aforementioned graph. $S$ can be efficiently computed through matrix multiplication in the following way:

$$S = 1 - \frac{\bar{A}\bar{A}^T}{2}, \tag{2}$$

where $\bar{A}$ is just the $l_2$-normalized version of $A$. Now, let $D$ and $\bar{D}$ be two $(n, n)$-dimensional matrices such that:

$$D_{ij} = \begin{cases} 1 & \text{if } y_i = y_j \\ 0 & \text{otherwise} \end{cases} \quad \bar{D}_{ij} = \begin{cases} 1 & \text{if } y_i \neq y_j \\ 0 & \text{otherwise} \end{cases} \tag{3}$$

In other words, $D$ is a mask for all the edges connecting any two samples sharing the same cluster (positive edges from now on), while $\bar{D}$ does the same for all the edges connecting any two samples in different clusters (negative edges from now on).

We will now define two graphs through their respective weighted adjacency matrices: i. a gold one where only positive edges are kept, and ii. a violating one, where weights on positive edges are decreased while weights on negative edges are increased.

$$S^{gold} = S \circ D \tag{4}$$

$$S^{viol} = max(0, S + v \cdot (r \cdot \bar{D} - D)) \tag{5}$$

In both equations, all operations are element-wise - for instance $S_{ij}^{viol} = \max(0, S_{ij} + v \cdot (r \cdot \bar{D}_{ij} - D_{ij}))$. The parameters $v, r \in \mathbb{R}^+$ are tunable. They are meant to perturb the similarity matrix to make the edge selection for the correct clusters more challenging and more robust to fluctuation; $v$ controls the impact of this perturbation, while $r$ is used to unbalance the importance between positive and negative edges. On the possibly fully connected graph $S^{viol}$, we define clusters as the connected components obtained after neglecting all the edges, whose weights are less than a threshold $\tau$. The next step is to exploit Kruskal's algorithm to compute the maximum spanning forest for both graphs.

$$H^{gold} = MaxSpanningForest(S^{gold}) \tag{6}$$

$$H^{viol} = MaxSpanningForest(S^{viol}) \tag{7}$$

In other words, $H^{gold}$ and $H^{viol}$ are two $(n, n)$-dimensional matrices whose elements are equal to 1 if the edge $e_{ij}$ is included in the maximum spanning forest for $S^{gold}$ and $S^{viol}$ respectively. Intuitively, the nodes appearing in the same connected component in $H$ are considered part of the same cluster.

$H^{\text{gold}}$ results having the same clusters as $D$ (i.e., the gold clusters), but $D$'s connected components are fully-connected, whereas $H^{\text{gold}}$'s are minimally connected by virtue of Kruskal's algorithm (for a subgraph of $n$ nodes, it has just $n - 1$ edges, instead of the fully-connected $n^2$).

We are now ready to compute the loss. Let's first define some additional quantities: $a = sum(H^{gold})$, $b = sum(D \circ H^{viol})$ and $c = sum(\bar{D} \circ H^{viol})$ - where $a$ is equal to the number of edges included in the maximum spanning forest on $S^{gold}$, while $b$ is equal to the number of positive edges included in $H^{viol}$, and $c$ to the number of negative edges included in $H^{viol}$. These three values are combined into a delta whose value decreases as more positive edges are included into the violating forest and increases when more negative ones are added:

$$\Delta = a - b + r \cdot c \tag{8}$$

Finally, let's compute two intermediate scores:

$$s_{gold} = sum(S \circ H^{gold}) \tag{9}$$

$$s_{viol} = sum(S \circ H^{viol}), \tag{10}$$

where $s_{gold}$ and $s_{viol}$ represent the sum of all edge weights/cosine similarities of the maximum spanning forest on the gold and violating graphs respectively. The supervised clustering loss will then be equal to:

$$\mathcal{L} = \begin{cases} s_{viol} - s_{gold} & \text{if } \Delta > 0 \\ 0 & \text{otherwise} \end{cases} \tag{11}$$

A graphical sample calculation of the supervised clustering loss can be found in figure 1.

Remark that the gradient cannot flow though the $\Delta$ component, nonetheless it is influenced by it by virtue of the condition for which $\mathcal{L} = 0$ if $\Delta \leq 0$.

### 3.3 Time Complexity of the Algorithm

The time complexity for the computation of the supervised clustering loss is $O(n^2 \log n)$, where $n$ is the number of utterances (see Sec. C.1 in the Appendix). This is still more efficient than other losses commonly used for fine-tuning sentence embeddings. For example, the naive implementation of the triplet loss has $O(n^3)$ complexity (Murphy, 2022). However, our experiments have shown that training time is not a significant issue for either loss, as the stopping criterion is typically triggered after just a few epochs.

## 4 Baseline Metric Losses

Using the same notation as in section 3, we will now define four other very well-known losses that proved effective in fine-tuning sentence encoders (Liao, 2021; Reimers and Gurevych, 2019; Nicosia and Moschitti, 2017). We used these losses as strong baselines for comparing the performance of our supervised clustering loss. Unlike the supervised clustering loss, these losses work on pairs or triplets of items and try to reorganize the embedding space simply by pushing away samples not sharing the same label while pulling closer those that do.

Let then $(x_i, x_j)$ be any two samples encoded with $Net_\theta(.)$ into $k-$dimensional real-valued vectors, and $(y_i, y_j)$ their respective cluster assignments. We will define the Binary Classification Loss as:

$$\begin{cases} ln(\sigma(W(x_i, x_y, |x_i - x_y|))) & \text{if } y_i = y_j \\ 1 - ln(\sigma(W(x_i, x_y, |x_i - x_y|))) & \text{otherwise} \end{cases} \tag{12}$$

where $W(x_i, x_y, |x_i - x_y|))$ is just a linear projection applied to the concatenation of the two embeddings and their distance. Using instead the cosine similarity between $x_i$ and $x_j$ we can define the Cosine Similarity Loss as:

$$\begin{cases} [1 - cos\_sim(x_i, x_j)]^2 & \text{if } y_i = y_j \\ cos\_sim(x_i, x_j)^2 & \text{otherwise} \end{cases} \quad (13)$$

where the embeddings of samples sharing the same cluster are forced to have cosine similarity close to 1, while keeping the embeddings of non-related samples further apart. On the same line, the Contrastive Loss (Hadsell et al., 2006) can be defined as:

$$\begin{cases} cos\_dist(x_i, x_j)^2 & \text{if } y_i = y_j \\ max[0, m - cos\_dist(x_i, x_j)]^2 & \text{otherwise} \end{cases} \quad (14)$$

in this case, we force the embeddings of samples inside the same cluster to have cosine distance equal to zero, while keeping the cosine distance of non-related utterances above the margin $m$.

To conclude, we will present the Triplet Margin Loss which takes as input triples of samples $(x_i, x_j, x_k)$ such that $y_i = y_j \neq y_k$ - where the first element is called the anchor, while the second and the third are commonly referred to as the positive and negative examples. The core idea behind this loss is to adjust the relative distances among the samples in each training triplet by minimizing the following quantity:

$$max[0, cos\_dist(x_i, x_j) - cos\_dist(x_i, x_k) - m] \quad (15)$$

in short, for all triplets, we want to cosine distance between the anchor and the negative to be higher than the distance between the anchor and the positive by at least the margin $m$.

## 5 Batch Sampling and Training Procedure

To fine-tune sentence embeddings, the training set plays a crucial role. The losses used for fine-tuning require specific samples to be manually engineered. The supervised clustering loss needs a 'clustering scenario' as input, while the other losses require pairs or triplets of samples with labels equal to 1 if they share the same cluster and 0 otherwise. To train, a common procedure involves randomly selecting $k$ clusters from the training set and then randomly sampling $m$ representatives from each cluster to form a training batch. A training epoch consists of n training batches.

For check-pointing and the stopping criterion, the Precision Recall Area Under the Curve (PRAUC) is monitored on pairs of utterances from the development set. At each training step, $m * k$ utterances are randomly sampled from the development set to calculate the cosine similarity among the sentence embeddings. At the end of each epoch, the PRAUC is computed using the true labels of pairs sharing the same cluster as 1 and pairs with different clusters as 0. This criterion ensures that the average cosine similarity between utterances with the same intent is higher than the average cosine similarity between utterances with different intents during training.

## 6 Experiments

In this section, we present experimental results on intent clustering using five losses applied to four sentence encoders, with resulting utterance embeddings clustered using Agglomerative Hierarchical Clustering. Appendix includes results from DBSCAN and a connected components-based procedure.

### 6.1 Benchmark Datasets

We experimented on five datasets commonly used for benchmarking intent classification and clustering: CLINC150 (Larson et al., 2019), BANKING77 (Casanueva et al., 2020), DSTC11 (Galley et al., 2022), HUW64 (Liu et al., 2021), and Massive (FitzGerald et al., 2022). The first four are in English, while Massive is multilingual and larger in size with almost 1 million manually translated utterances in 51 languages. To reduce its size, we randomly included 20% of the utterances. DSTC11 and BANKING77 are single-domain, while the rest are multi-domain. In essence, our study focuses on in-domain intent clustering. See Table 1 and Section A of the Appendix for dataset statistics and information on data acquisition and usage terms.

### 6.2 Base Models for Utterance Encoding

In our experiments, we rely on four different transformer-based sentence encoders and see whether our fine-tuning strategies improve their representation power when it comes to intent clustering:

1. Average pooling of the word-level **BERT** embeddings (Devlin et al., 2019). BERT was trained on the top 104 languages with the largest Wikipedia, using both a Masked Language Modeling (MLM) and a Next Sentence Prediction objectives,
2. Average pooling of the word-level **XLM roBERTa** embeddings (Conneau et al., 2020). XLM roBERTa is build on top of BERT but modifies key hyper-parameters, removing the next-sentence pretraining objective and training with much larger mini-batches and learning rates,
3. **All Mpnet Base** (Reimers and Gurevych, 2019) maps English-only sentences and paragraphs to a 768-dimensional-dense vector space and was shown to be the best performing sentence encoder in English (HuggingFaceTeam, 2022). The model was trained on multiple corpora of sentence pairs using a Binary Classification Loss on top of a linear classifier that takes as input a concatenation of the two sentence embeddings,
4. **Paraphrase Multilingual Mpnet** (Reimers and Gurevych, 2020) maps sentences and paragraphs to a 768 dimensional dense vector space and was

| DATASET | # domains | # intents | # languages | # total utterances | Avg utt. per intent | # train intent | # dev intent | # test intent |
|---|---|---|---|---|---|---|---|---|
| CLINC150 | 10 | 150 | 1 (en) | 22500 | 150 | 90 | 30 | 30 |
| DSTC11 | 1 | 22 | 1 (en) | 2093 | 95 | 13 | 4 | 5 |
| HWU64 | 21 | 64 | 1 (en) | 11106 | 174 | 38 | 12 | 14 |
| BANKING77 | 1 | 77 | 1 (en) | 13242 | 172 | 46 | 15 | 16 |
| Massive | 18 | 60 | 51 | 759966 | 12666 | 30 | 22 | 16 |

Table 1: Intent Clustering Benchmark Dataset Statistics

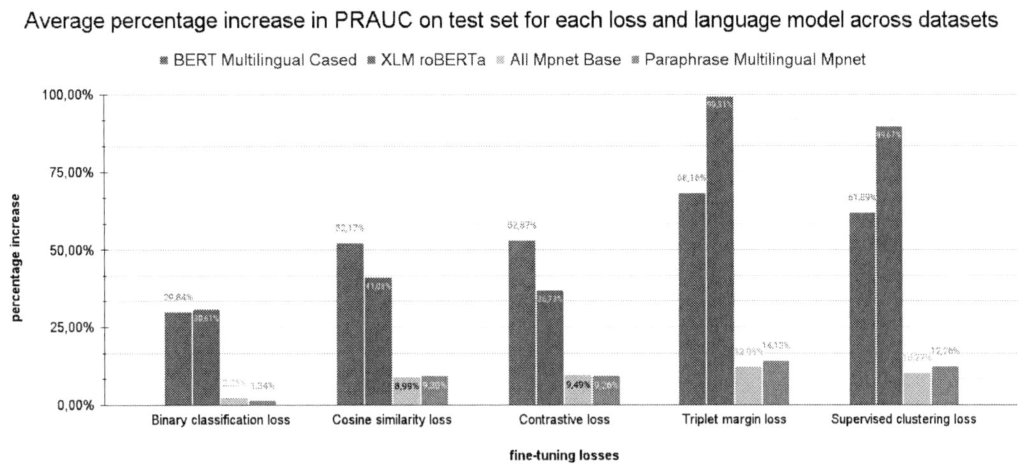


Figure 2: Fine-tuning always leads from moderate to large improvements in PRAUC on test utterances. The supervised clustering loss and the triplet margin loss clearly outperform all other losses. Increases on All Mpnet Base and Paraphrase Multilingual Mpnet are less pronounced because they were already on semantic similarity.

shown to be the best performing multilingual sentence encoder (HuggingFaceTeam, 2022). The model was trained on 1B sentence pairs using a Binary Classification Loss on top of the cosine similarity scores.

All Mpnet Base and Paraphrase Multilingual Mpnet nonetheless were trained quite similarly to Sentence-BERT, but with more data.

### 6.3 Experimental setting

We randomly assign 60% of intents to the training set, 20% to the development set, and 20% to the test set for each of the 5 benchmark datasets. As detailed in section 5, the 4 base sentence encoders are separately fine-tuned using all training intent utterances and each of the five losses. Hyper-parameters are dataset-specific - see table 5 in the Appendix, and a max training epoch of 20 with 5 epochs of patience before early-stopping is set. The best parameters for the supervised clustering loss, triplet margin loss, and contrastive loss are selected via a grid search over specified intervals to obtain the highest PRAUC on the validation set. This procedure is repeated 5 times with different splits. The best parameters for the losses are stable across datasets and experiments: table 6 also shows the best values we used to obtain the final models. The final models consist of 20 fine-tuned models for each dataset (one per encoder-loss pair) except Massive, for which there are 15 fine-tuned models due to its multilingual nature. Information on hardware and computational cost can be found in section B of the Appendix.

Base and fine-tuned models are then used to extract embeddings for all the utterances in the development and test sets. After computing the matrix of pairwise cosine distances, we cluster utterances into tentative intents using agglomerative hierarchical clustering - an algorithm that recursively merges pairs of clusters based on a linkage criterion and a distance threshold. In the Appendix, we also report results using DBSCAN, and a procedure based on connected components. DBSCAN finds core samples of high density and expands clusters from them; in this case, the user needs to choose the minimum distance for two samples to be considered neighbors ($\epsilon$) and the minimum number of samples around a candidate core sample. The third algorithm simply takes as clusters the connected components, after cutting all the edges below a certain threshold. The hyper-parameters of these three algorithms are optimized on the development set with respect to either the clustering accuracy or the adjusted mutual information score (AMIS). Table 7 in the Appendix contains the hyper-

| DATASET | LOSS | BASE SENTENCE ENCODERS | | | | | | | |
|---|---|---|---|---|---|---|---|---|---|
| | | BERT Multilingual Cased | | XLM roBERTa | | Paraphrase Multilingual Mpnet | | All Mpnet Base | |
| | | Average inter-intent pairwise cosine similarity | Average within-intent pairwise cosine similarity | Average inter-intent pairwise cosine similarity | Average within-intent pairwise cosine similarity | Average inter-intent pairwise cosine similarity | Average within-intent pairwise cosine similarity | Average inter-intent pairwise cosine similarity | Average within-intent pairwise cosine similarity |
| BANKING77 | No fine-tuning | 58.90% | 67.10% | 99.60% | 99.70% | 30.90% | 58.30% | 23.60% | 56.00% |
| | Binary classification loss | 21.20% | 66.50% | 99.60% | 99.70% | 31.50% | 59.90% | 27.80% | 61.80% |
| | Cosine similarity loss | 39.80% | 69.90% | 41.00% | 68.40% | 29.70% | 72.10% | 31.60% | 72.80% |
| | Contrastive loss | 32.70% | 65.80% | 32.80% | 65.30% | 22.50% | 68.80% | 23.20% | 69.90% |
| | Triplet margin loss | 25.80% | 61.20% | 48.70% | 74.60% | 16.40% | 61.60% | 13.80% | 61.10% |
| | Supervised clustering loss | 11.70% | 39.70% | 20.60% | 54.10% | 3.50% | 45.10% | 2.60% | 44.90% |
| CLINC150 | No fine-tuning | 54.10% | 67.50% | 99.60% | 99.70% | 16.90% | 61.70% | 9.90% | 53.10% |
| | Binary classification loss | 50.00% | 70.20% | 99.50% | 99.70% | 17.40% | 61.40% | 10.90% | 53.70% |
| | Cosine similarity loss | 28.10% | 78.20% | 41.60% | 71.10% | 14.90% | 79.60% | 20.20% | 77.40% |
| | Contrastive loss | 20.80% | 74.70% | 22.80% | 74.70% | 8.70% | 77.30% | 15.80% | 73.00% |
| | Triplet margin loss | 21.00% | 65.90% | 37.30% | 80.10% | 5.40% | 65.50% | 6.30% | 63.70% |
| | Supervised clustering loss | 6.70% | 44.10% | 24.50% | 63.40% | 3.20% | 50.50% | 1.60% | 49.50% |
| DSTC11 | No fine-tuning | 64.90% | 69.90% | 99.70% | 99.70% | 35.60% | 62.20% | 30.10% | 57.80% |
| | Binary classification loss | 34.90% | 68.90% | - | - | - | - | 24.50% | 70.10% |
| | Cosine similarity loss | 61.25% | 79.35% | 48.05% | 78.10% | 38.80% | 77.95% | 35.90% | 75.50% |
| | Contrastive loss | 27.60% | 63.90% | 45.20% | 68.90% | 24.50% | 67.30% | 28.10% | 72.60% |
| | Triplet margin loss | 34.90% | 61.30% | 47.05% | 78.35% | 12.80% | 66.50% | 12.80% | 68.95% |
| | Supervised clustering loss | 19.45% | 49.30% | 19.45% | 63.15% | 5.70% | 55.80% | 7.05% | 58.30% |
| HWU64 | No fine-tuning | 47.90% | 62.60% | 99.40% | 99.60% | 16.00% | 53.80% | 11.10% | 42.80% |
| | Binary classification loss | 44.70% | 65.90% | 95.40% | 97.90% | 15.80% | 54.10% | 11.80% | 42.90% |
| | Cosine similarity loss | 38.30% | 68.30% | 98.30% | 99.20% | 22.40% | 78.10% | 16.40% | 48.40% |
| | Contrastive loss | 32.80% | 65.80% | 98.40% | 99.20% | 16.30% | 75.60% | 15.40% | 76.70% |
| | Triplet margin loss | 18.70% | 69.90% | 39.90% | 79.80% | 9.50% | 59.20% | 6.00% | 57.10% |
| | Supervised clustering loss | 6.20% | 43.00% | 97.40% | 98.40% | 1.70% | 46.00% | 1.50% | 41.20% |
| Massive | No fine-tuning | 41.60% | 46.60% | 99.30% | 99.40% | 22.80% | 55.90% | - | - |
| | Binary classification loss | 34.90% | 63.50% | 99.20% | 99.30% | 19.10% | 53.40% | - | - |
| | Cosine similarity loss | 40.60% | 64.40% | 98.70% | 98.80% | 31.00% | 66.70% | - | - |
| | Contrastive loss | 30.60% | 62.90% | 98.70% | 98.20% | 22.30% | 62.90% | - | - |
| | Triplet margin loss | 34.50% | 61.50% | 56.00% | 77.30% | 14.40% | 54.70% | - | - |
| | Supervised clustering loss | 8.70% | 30.00% | 20.30% | 49.30% | 2.50% | 46.40% | - | - |

Table 2: Pre-fine-tuning and post-fine-tuning average inter-intent and within-intent pairwise similarity on test utterances. The gap between the average inter-intent and within-intent pairwise similarities increases for all datasets, losses and base sentence encoders. In other words, whatever loss we use, utterances that share the same intent get closer while drifting apart from utterances with different intents. Interestingly enough, the supervised clustering loss behaves in a markedly different manner, yes reducing the within-intent pair-wise similarity, but also leading the inter-intent pair-wise similarity very close to zero. This is equal to say that the supervised clustering loss induces a topological space which is different from the one created by the other losses.

parameter search spaces. Test utterances are eventually clustered using the best hyper-parameters and the same metrics are computed. For each dataset, the whole experimental procedure - from fine-tuning to clustering - is repeated 5 times with different seeds and splits and average results are reported with their variance.

### 6.4 Performance of Fine-Tuning Strategies

Figure 2 shows that fine-tuning always leads to moderate or large improvements in PRAUC on test utterances, regardless of the loss or base sentence encoder chosen. The supervised clustering loss and the triplet margin loss are especially effective fine-tuning strategies. All Mpnet Base and Paraphrase Multilingual Mpnet show less pronounced increases since they were already fine-tuned on sentence similarity tasks. Table 8 in the Appendix confirms these results when broken down by dataset. Table 2 shows that improvements in PRAUC are reflected in average inter-intent and within-intent pairwise similarities- which should be interpreted jointly. In an ideal scenario, a loss should push the within-intent average cosine similarity close to 1 and the inter-intent average cosine similarity to 0. Nonetheless, in our analysis, we show that things go differently.

The gap between the average inter-intent and within-intent pairwise similarities increases for all datasets, losses and base sentence encoders. In other words, whatever loss we use, utterances that share the same intent get closer while drifting apart from utterances with different intents. Interestingly enough, however, while most losses increase the average within-intent pairwise similarity, the supervised clustering loss behaves in a markedly different manner, yes reducing the within-intent pair-wise similarity, but also leading the inter-intent pair-wise similarity very close to zero. This is equal to say that the supervised clustering loss induces a topological space which is different from the one created by the other losses. This is further confirmed when looking at figures 3, 4, 5, 6, 7, 8 in the Appendix - which show the tSNE plots of the BANKING77 test utterances when XLM-RoBERTa is used as base sentence encoder.

### 6.5 New Intent Clustering Results

The results of experiments with agglomerative hierarchical clustering using different datasets, sentence encoders, and losses are shown in tables 3 and 4. Although we performed comparable experiments with DBSCAN and a procedure based on connected components (see the Appendix), for every dataset the highest clustering accuracy and adjusted mutual information score were achieved with agglomerative hierarchical clustering on embeddings obtained from one of the four sentence encoders, fine-tuned with either the supervised clustering loss or the triplet margin loss. Moreover, since the supervised clustering loss re-arranges the embedding space by retaining edges only among utterances sharing the same intent, embeddings obtained from any sentence encoder fine-tuned with such loss are expected to be particularly suitable for agglomerative hierarchical clustering.

As shown in table 3, when we optimize the clustering algorithm hyper-parameters with respect to the adjusted mutual information score, in 13 cases out of 19 the supervised clustering loss proved to induce more clustering friendly embeddings, resulting in higher clustering performance. As further shown in table 4, the clustering behavior slightly changes when we optimize

| Average adjusted mutual information score on test set for all combinations of datasets, base sentence encoders and clustering algorithms when optimizing wrt the adjusted mutual information score | | | | | | | | | |
|---|---|---|---|---|---|---|---|---|---|
| Clustering algorithm | Base sentence encoder | Dataset | No Fine-Tuning | Binary classification loss | Cosine similarity loss | Contrastive loss | Triplet margin loss | Supervised clustering loss | BEST LOSS |
| Agglomerative Hierarchical Clustering | BERT Multilingual Cased | BANKING77 | 0.53±0.02 | 0.55±0.05 | 0.67±0.03 | 0.66±0.04 | 0.76±0.03 | **0.77±0.05** | **Supervised clustering loss** |
| | | CLINC150 | 0.73±0.02 | 0.76±0.03 | 0.77±0.04 | 0.77±0.04 | 0.84±0.03 | **0.85±0.02** | **Supervised clustering loss** |
| | | DSTC11 | 0.29±0.05 | 0.52±0.10 | 0.47±0.14 | 0.50±0.10 | 0.60±0.06 | **0.63±0.10** | **Supervised clustering loss** |
| | | HWU64 | 0.61±0.02 | 0.63±0.02 | 0.67±0.04 | 0.67±0.04 | **0.72±0.05** | **0.72±0.04** | Triplet & Supervised |
| | | Massive | 0.27±0.01 | 0.36±0.05 | 0.45±0.04 | 0.46±0.04 | **0.51±0.04** | **0.51±0.06** | Triplet & **Supervised** |
| | Paraphrase Multilingual Mpnet | BANKING77 | 0.74±0.02 | 0.72±0.07 | 0.76±0.06 | 0.75±0.05 | **0.83±0.02** | 0.81±0.03 | Triplet margin loss |
| | | CLINC150 | 0.86±0.03 | 0.87±0.02 | 0.88±0.03 | 0.87±0.03 | 0.92±0.02 | **0.93±0.01** | **Supervised clustering loss** |
| | | DSTC11 | 0.52±0.15 | 0.36±0.34 | 0.65±0.08 | 0.72±0.06 | 0.73±0.11 | **0.75±0.11** | **Supervised clustering loss** |
| | | HWU64 | 0.79±0.05 | 0.76±0.01 | 0.79±0.03 | 0.79±0.01 | 0.79±0.04 | **0.81±0.04** | **Supervised clustering loss** |
| | | Massive | 0.60±0.09 | 0.60±0.06 | 0.65±0.06 | 0.64±0.06 | **0.71±0.06** | 0.70±0.05 | Triplet margin loss |
| | All Mpnet Base | BANKING77 | 0.84±0.01 | 0.83±0.01 | 0.83±0.02 | 0.83±0.03 | **0.88±0.02** | 0.86±0.02 | Triplet margin loss |
| | | CLINC150 | 0.91±0.02 | 0.90±0.02 | 0.92±0.02 | 0.92±0.02 | **0.94±0.01** | **0.94±0.01** | Triplet & **Supervised** |
| | | DSTC11 | 0.49±0.17 | 0.63±0.16 | 0.75±0.14 | 0.71±0.12 | **0.78±0.11** | 0.70±0.10 | Triplet margin loss |
| | | HWU64 | 0.81±0.05 | 0.81±0.05 | 0.79±0.03 | 0.80±0.01 | 0.79±0.05 | **0.85±0.03** | **Supervised clustering loss** |
| | XLM roBERTa | BANKING77 | 0.48±0.01 | 0.60±0.04 | 0.66±0.06 | 0.66±0.04 | 0.73±0.06 | **0.75±0.03** | **Supervised clustering loss** |
| | | CLINC150 | 0.66±0.02 | 0.72±0.07 | 0.74±0.05 | 0.71±0.07 | 0.86±0.03 | **0.86±0.01** | **Supervised clustering loss** |
| | | DSTC11 | 0.28±0.02 | 0.42±0.00 | 0.53±0.04 | 0.53±0.04 | **0.68±0.05** | 0.65±0.10 | Triplet margin loss |
| | | HWU64 | 0.52±0.04 | 0.61±0.09 | 0.56±0.05 | 0.55±0.07 | 0.73±0.05 | **0.77±0.04** | **Supervised clustering loss** |
| | | Massive | 0.20±0.01 | 0.28±0.12 | 0.23±0.11 | 0.19±0.02 | 0.51±0.06 | **0.58±0.04** | **Supervised clustering loss** |

Table 3: Average adjusted mutual information score on test set using agglomerative hierarchical clustering, for all combinations of datasets and base sentence encoders - when optimizing wrt the adjusted mutual information score

| Average clustering accuracy on test set for all combinations of datasets, base sentence encoders and clustering algorithms when optimizing wrt the clustering accuracy | | | | | | | | | |
|---|---|---|---|---|---|---|---|---|---|
| Clustering algorithm | Base sentence encoder | Dataset | No Fine-Tuning | Binary classification loss | Cosine similarity loss | Contrastive loss | Triplet margin loss | Supervised clustering loss | BEST LOSS |
| Agglomerative Hierarchical Clustering | BERT Multilingual Cased | BANKING77 | 0.32±0.05 | 0.37±0.06 | 0.52±0.04 | 0.50±0.08 | **0.62±0.05** | **0.62±0.08** | Triplet & **Supervised** |
| | | CLINC150 | 0.56±0.06 | 0.53±0.05 | 0.56±0.04 | 0.57±0.06 | 0.68±0.03 | **0.71±0.06** | **Supervised clustering loss** |
| | | DSTC11 | 0.33±0.05 | 0.65±0.10 | 0.56±0.08 | 0.60±0.11 | 0.65±0.14 | **0.73±0.10** | **Supervised clustering loss** |
| | | HWU64 | 0.52±0.04 | 0.51±0.03 | 0.56±0.06 | 0.55±0.04 | **0.59±0.06** | 0.56±0.04 | Triplet margin loss |
| | | Massive | 0.22±0.03 | 0.41±0.07 | 0.46±0.04 | 0.51±0.04 | **0.55±0.07** | 0.53±0.08 | Triplet margin loss |
| | Paraphrase Multilingual Mpnet | BANKING77 | 0.62±0.06 | 0.56±0.08 | 0.64±0.06 | 0.62±0.03 | **0.72±0.03** | 0.69±0.06 | Triplet margin loss |
| | | CLINC150 | 0.65±0.07 | 0.65±0.04 | 0.70±0.08 | 0.69±0.08 | 0.79±0.05 | **0.83±0.05** | **Supervised clustering loss** |
| | | DSTC11 | 0.57±0.09 | 0.48±0.17 | 0.75±0.10 | 0.73±0.06 | 0.75±0.15 | **0.77±0.09** | **Supervised clustering loss** |
| | | HWU64 | 0.73±0.09 | 0.74±0.10 | 0.69±0.05 | 0.67±0.03 | **0.75±0.07** | 0.68±0.05 | Triplet margin loss |
| | | Massive | 0.62±0.09 | 0.61±0.07 | 0.68±0.05 | 0.60±0.08 | 0.67±0.11 | **0.73±0.08** | **Supervised clustering loss** |
| | All Mpnet Base | BANKING77 | 0.70±0.04 | 0.67±0.05 | 0.68±0.04 | 0.71±0.07 | **0.78±0.04** | 0.73±0.04 | Triplet margin loss |
| | | CLINC150 | 0.75±0.06 | 0.75±0.06 | 0.77±0.05 | 0.78±0.08 | 0.81±0.03 | **0.82±0.04** | **Supervised clustering loss** |
| | | DSTC11 | 0.56±0.12 | 0.67±0.09 | 0.78±0.16 | **0.83±0.12** | 0.78±0.14 | 0.77±0.14 | Cosine similarity loss |
| | | HWU64 | 0.70±0.11 | 0.69±0.09 | 0.67±0.05 | 0.67±0.08 | 0.74±0.05 | **0.78±0.08** | **Supervised clustering loss** |
| | XLM roBERTa | BANKING77 | 0.32±0.02 | 0.41±0.03 | 0.52±0.04 | 0.50±0.05 | 0.59±0.08 | **0.62±0.04** | **Supervised clustering loss** |
| | | CLINC150 | 0.54±0.03 | 0.60±0.10 | 0.55±0.03 | 0.55±0.04 | **0.71±0.06** | 0.70±0.04 | Triplet margin loss |
| | | DSTC11 | 0.36±0.08 | 0.68±0.00 | 0.57±0.19 | 0.61±0.18 | **0.74±0.08** | 0.71±0.09 | Triplet margin loss |
| | | HWU64 | 0.42±0.02 | 0.52±0.12 | 0.37±0.02 | 0.44±0.11 | 0.65±0.08 | **0.73±0.07** | **Supervised clustering loss** |
| | | Massive | 0.23±0.02 | 0.30±0.09 | 0.26±0.09 | 0.22±0.02 | 0.52±0.04 | **0.61±0.04** | **Supervised clustering loss** |

Table 4: Average clustering accuracy on test set using agglomerative hierarchical clustering, for all combinations of datasets and base sentence encoders - when optimizing wrt the clustering accuracy

with respect to the clustering accuracy, with the supervised clustering loss outperforming other losses in 11 out of 19 cases. Overall, the supervised clustering loss and the triplet margin loss tended to perform similarly and significantly better than other tested losses. However, in some cases, one loss outperformed the other by up to 8 percentage points in clustering accuracy or adjusted mutual information score, indicating that the best loss depends on both the dataset and the base language model chosen. Further investigation is warranted. Notably, even pre-trained sentence encoders benefited significantly from fine-tuning with either the supervised clustering loss or the triplet margin loss, underscoring the difference between intent similarity and semantic similarity.

## 7 Conclusions and Future Work

We proposed a supervised clustering loss to fine-tune sentence encoders, enabling the production of clustering-friendly sentence embeddings. These embeddings can be used with any unsupervised clustering algorithm to discover new intents, overcoming the quadratic bottleneck of current supervised clustering architectures. Extensive experiments on 5 benchmark datasets, including both monolingual and multilingual data, and 4 different base sentence encoders showed that our fine-tuning strategy induced embeddings that perform equally or better than those obtained with all other tested metric learning losses when comparing their performance on intent clustering. In the future, we plan to analyze the characteristics of the embedding spaces induced by different losses to understand why the supervised clustering loss works well with agglomerative hierarchical clustering but not with DBSCAN. Notably, regardless of the loss or sentence encoder chosen, fine-tuned embeddings always improve the performance of unsupervised intent clustering.

## 8 Limitations and Ethical Considerations

Our work suggests further research on supervised clustering algorithms, investigating the performance of sentence embeddings generated using different clustering algorithms and losses. Additionally, more exploration is needed on the structural and topological differences in embedding space between supervised clustering loss and other losses. Although our experiments demonstrate the effectiveness of supervised clustering loss, we acknowledge the need for further investigation into the circumstances in which triplet margin loss may be preferable. Finally, while we strive to consider less conventional requests, biases in clustering systems may lead to oversimplification of people's requests, and we welcome further research on addressing this issue.

## References


Samuel R. Bowman, Gabor Angeli, Christopher Potts, and Christopher D. Manning. 2015. A large annotated corpus for learning natural language inference. In *Proceedings of the 2015 Conference on Empirical Methods in Natural Language Processing*, pages 632–642, Lisbon, Portugal. Association for Computational Linguistics.

Mathilde Caron, Piotr Bojanowski, Armand Joulin, and Matthijs Douze. 2018. Deep clustering for unsupervised learning of visual features. In *Proceedings of the European conference on computer vision (ECCV)*, pages 132–149.

Iñigo Casanueva, Tadas Temčinas, Daniela Gerz, Matthew Henderson, and Ivan Vulić. 2020. Efficient intent detection with dual sentence encoders. In *Proceedings of the 2nd Workshop on Natural Language Processing for Conversational AI*, pages 38–45, Online. Association for Computational Linguistics.

Ajay Chatterjee and Shubhashis Sengupta. 2020. Intent mining from past conversations for conversational agent. In *Proceedings of the 28th International Conference on Computational Linguistics*, pages 4140–4152, Barcelona, Spain (Online). International Committee on Computational Linguistics.

Alexis Conneau, Kartikay Khandelwal, Naman Goyal, Vishrav Chaudhary, Guillaume Wenzek, Francisco Guzmán, Edouard Grave, Myle Ott, Luke Zettlemoyer, and Veselin Stoyanov. 2020. Unsupervised cross-lingual representation learning at scale. In *Proceedings of the 58th Annual Meeting of the Association for Computational Linguistics*, pages 8440–8451, Online. Association for Computational Linguistics.

Jacob Devlin, Ming-Wei Chang, Kenton Lee, and Kristina Toutanova. 2019. BERT: Pre-training of deep bidirectional transformers for language understanding. In *Proceedings of the 2019 Conference of the North American Chapter of the Association for Computational Linguistics: Human Language Technologies, Volume 1 (Long and Short Papers)*, pages 4171–4186, Minneapolis, Minnesota. Association for Computational Linguistics.

Greg Durrett and Dan Klein. 2015. Neural CRF parsing. In *Proceedings of the 53rd Annual Meeting of the Association for Computational Linguistics and the 7th International Joint Conference on Natural Language Processing (Volume 1: Long Papers)*, pages 302–312, Beijing, China. Association for Computational Linguistics.

Eraldo Rezende Fernandes, Cícero Nogueira dos Santos, and Ruy Luiz Milidiú. 2014. Latent trees for coreference resolution. *Computational Linguistics*, 40(4):801–835.

Thomas Finley and Thorsten Joachims. 2005. Supervised clustering with support vector machines. In *Proceedings of the 22nd international conference on Machine learning*, pages 217–224.

Jack FitzGerald, Christopher Hench, Charith Peris, Scott Mackie, Kay Rottmann, Ana Sanchez, Aaron Nash, Liam Urbach, Vishesh Kakarala, Richa Singh, et al. 2022. Massive: A 1m-example multilingual natural language understanding dataset with 51 typologically-diverse languages. *arXiv preprint arXiv:2204.08582*.

George Forman, Hila Nachlieli, and Renato Keshet. 2015. Clustering by intent: a semi-supervised method to discover relevant clusters incrementally. In *Joint European Conference on Machine Learning and Knowledge Discovery in Databases*, pages 20–36. Springer.

Michel Galley, Yun-Nung Chen, Raghav Gupta, Zhang Chen, Paul Crook, Seungwhan Moon, Chulaka Gunasekara, Satwik Kottur, Sarik Ghazarian, and Behnam Hedayatnia. 2022. Dstc11: The eleventh dialog system technology challenge. `https://dstc11.dstc.community/`. Accessed: 2010-09-30.

Tianyu Gao, Xingcheng Yao, and Danqi Chen. 2021. SimCSE: Simple contrastive learning of sentence embeddings. In *Proceedings of the 2021 Conference on Empirical Methods in Natural Language Processing*, pages 6894–6910, Online and Punta Cana, Dominican Republic. Association for Computational Linguistics.

John Giorgi, Osvald Nitski, Bo Wang, and Gary Bader. 2021. DeCLUTR: Deep contrastive learning for unsupervised textual representations. In *Proceedings of the 59th Annual Meeting of the Association for Computational Linguistics and the 11th International Joint Conference on Natural Language Processing (Volume 1: Long Papers)*, pages 879–895, Online. Association for Computational Linguistics.

Raia Hadsell, Sumit Chopra, and Yann LeCun. 2006. Dimensionality reduction by learning an invariant mapping. In *2006 IEEE Computer Society Conference on Computer Vision and Pattern Recognition (CVPR'06)*, volume 2, pages 1735–1742. IEEE.

Iryna Haponchyk and Alessandro Moschitti. 2021. Supervised neural clustering via latent structured output learning: Application to question intents. In *Proceedings of the 2021 Conference of the North American Chapter of the Association for Computational Linguistics: Human Language Technologies*, pages 3364–3374, Online. Association for Computational Linguistics.

Iryna Haponchyk, Antonio Uva, Seunghak Yu, Olga Uryupina, and Alessandro Moschitti. 2018. Supervised clustering of questions into intents for dialog system applications. In *Proceedings of the 2018 Conference on Empirical Methods in Natural Language Processing*, pages 2310–2321, Brussels, Belgium. Association for Computational Linguistics.

Matthew Henderson, Iñigo Casanueva, Nikola Mrkšić, Pei-Hao Su, Tsung-Hsien Wen, and Ivan Vulić. 2020. ConveRT: Efficient and accurate conversational representations from transformers. In *Findings of the Association for Computational Linguistics: EMNLP 2020*, pages 2161–2174, Online. Association for Computational Linguistics.

Ehsan Hosseini-Asl, Bryan McCann, Chien-Sheng Wu, Semih Yavuz, and Richard Socher. 2020. A simple language model for task-oriented dialogue. *Advances in Neural Information Processing Systems*, 33:20179–20191.

HuggingFaceTeam. 2022. Comparison of sentence encoder performances. `https://www.sbert.net/docs/pretrained_models.html`. Accessed: 2022-10-18.

Taeuk Kim, Kang Min Yoo, and Sang-goo Lee. 2021. Self-guided contrastive learning for BERT sentence representations. In *Proceedings of the 59th Annual Meeting of the Association for Computational Linguistics and the 11th International Joint Conference on Natural Language Processing (Volume 1: Long Papers)*, pages 2528–2540, Online. Association for Computational Linguistics.

Eliyahu Kiperwasser and Yoav Goldberg. 2016. Simple and accurate dependency parsing using bidirectional LSTM feature representations. *Transactions of the Association for Computational Linguistics*, 4:313–327.

Stefan Larson, Anish Mahendran, Joseph J. Peper, Christopher Clarke, Andrew Lee, Parker Hill, Jonathan K. Kummerfeld, Kevin Leach, Michael A. Laurenzano, Lingjia Tang, and Jason Mars. 2019. An evaluation dataset for intent classification and out-of-scope prediction. In *Proceedings of the 2019 Conference on Empirical Methods in Natural Language Processing and the 9th International Joint Conference on Natural Language Processing (EMNLP-IJCNLP)*, pages 1311–1316, Hong Kong, China. Association for Computational Linguistics.

Yann LeCun, Sumit Chopra, Raia Hadsell, M Ranzato, and Fujie Huang. 2006. A tutorial on energy-based learning. *Predicting structured data*, 1(0).

Kenton Lee, Luheng He, Mike Lewis, and Luke Zettlemoyer. 2017. End-to-end neural coreference resolution. In *Proceedings of the 2017 Conference on Empirical Methods in Natural Language Processing*, pages 188–197, Copenhagen, Denmark. Association for Computational Linguistics.

Danqi Liao. 2021. Sentence embeddings using supervised contrastive learning. *arXiv preprint arXiv:2106.04791*.

Ting-En Lin, Hua Xu, and Hanlei Zhang. 2020. Discovering new intents via constrained deep adaptive clustering with cluster refinement. In *Proceedings of the AAAI Conference on Artificial Intelligence*, volume 34, pages 8360–8367.

Xingkun Liu, Arash Eshghi, Pawel Swietojanski, and Verena Rieser. 2021. Benchmarking natural language understanding services for building conversational agents. In *Increasing Naturalness and Flexibility in Spoken Dialogue Interaction*, pages 165–183. Springer.

Shikib Mehri and Mihail Eric. 2021. Example-driven intent prediction with observers. In *Proceedings of the 2021 Conference of the North American Chapter of the Association for Computational Linguistics: Human Language Technologies*, pages 2979–2992, Online. Association for Computational Linguistics.

Shikib Mehri, Mihail Eric, and Dilek Z. Hakkani-Tür. 2020. Dialoglue: A natural language understanding benchmark for task-oriented dialogue. *ArXiv*, abs/2009.13570.

Ruy Luiz Milidiú and Rafael Rocha. 2018. Structured prediction networks through latent cost learning. In *2018 IEEE Symposium Series on Computational Intelligence (SSCI)*, pages 645–649.

Yutao Mou, Keqing He, Pei Wang, Yanan Wu, Jingang Wang, Wei Wu, and Weiran Xu. 2022. Watch the neighbors: A unified k-nearest neighbor contrastive learning framework for ood intent discovery. *arXiv preprint arXiv:2210.08909*.

Kevin P Murphy. 2022. *Probabilistic machine learning: an introduction*. MIT press.

Massimo Nicosia and Alessandro Moschitti. 2017. Accurate sentence matching with hybrid siamese networks. In *Proceedings of the 2017 ACM on Conference on Information and Knowledge Management*, CIKM '17, page 2235–2238, New York, NY, USA. Association for Computing Machinery.

Hao Peng, Sam Thomson, and Noah A. Smith. 2018. Backpropagating through structured argmax using a SPIGOT. In *Proceedings of the 56th Annual Meeting of the Association for Computational Linguistics (Volume 1: Long Papers)*, pages 1863–1873, Melbourne, Australia. Association for Computational Linguistics.

Hugh Perkins and Yi Yang. 2019. Dialog intent induction with deep multi-view clustering. In *Proceedings of the 2019 Conference on Empirical Methods in Natural Language Processing and the 9th International Joint Conference on Natural Language Processing (EMNLP-IJCNLP)*, pages 4016–4025, Hong Kong, China. Association for Computational Linguistics.

Nils Reimers and Iryna Gurevych. 2019. Sentence-BERT: Sentence embeddings using Siamese BERT-networks. In *Proceedings of the 2019 Conference on Empirical Methods in Natural Language Processing and the 9th International Joint Conference on Natural Language Processing (EMNLP-IJCNLP)*, pages 3982–3992, Hong Kong, China. Association for Computational Linguistics.

Nils Reimers and Iryna Gurevych. 2020. Making monolingual sentence embeddings multilingual using knowledge distillation. In *Proceedings of the 2020 Conference on Empirical Methods in Natural Language Processing (EMNLP)*, pages 4512–4525, Online. Association for Computational Linguistics.

Nils Reimers and Iryna Gurevych. 2021. The curse of dense low-dimensional information retrieval for large index sizes. In *Proceedings of the 59th Annual Meeting of the Association for Computational Linguistics and the 11th International Joint Conference on Natural Language Processing (Volume 2: Short Papers)*, pages 605–611, Online. Association for Computational Linguistics.

Dan Roth and Wen-tau Yih. 2004. A linear programming formulation for global inference in natural language tasks. In *Proceedings of the Eighth Conference on Computational Natural Language Learning (CoNLL-2004) at HLT-NAACL 2004*, pages 1–8, Boston, Massachusetts, USA. Association for Computational Linguistics.

Chen Shi, Qi Chen, Lei Sha, Sujian Li, Xu Sun, Houfeng Wang, and Lintao Zhang. 2018. Auto-dialabel: Labeling dialogue data with unsupervised learning. In *Proceedings of the 2018 Conference on Empirical Methods in Natural Language Processing*, pages 684–689, Brussels, Belgium. Association for Computational Linguistics.

Ivan Vulić, Pei-Hao Su, Samuel Coope, Daniela Gerz, Paweł Budzianowski, Iñigo Casanueva, Nikola Mrkšić, and Tsung-Hsien Wen. 2021. ConvFiT: Conversational fine-tuning of pretrained language models. In *Proceedings of the 2021 Conference on Empirical Methods in Natural Language Processing*, pages 1151–1168, Online and Punta Cana, Dominican Republic. Association for Computational Linguistics.

Po-Wei Wang, Priya Donti, Bryan Wilder, and Zico Kolter. 2019. Satnet: Bridging deep learning and logical reasoning using a differentiable satisfiability solver. In *International Conference on Machine Learning*, pages 6545–6554. PMLR.

David Weiss, Chris Alberti, Michael Collins, and Slav Petrov. 2015. Structured training for neural network transition-based parsing. In *Proceedings of the 53rd Annual Meeting of the Association for Computational Linguistics and the 7th International Joint Conference on Natural Language Processing (Volume 1: Long Papers)*, pages 323–333, Beijing, China. Association for Computational Linguistics.

Adina Williams, Nikita Nangia, and Samuel Bowman. 2018. A broad-coverage challenge corpus for sentence understanding through inference. In *Proceedings of the 2018 Conference of the North American Chapter of the Association for Computational Linguistics: Human Language Technologies, Volume 1 (Long Papers)*, pages 1112–1122, New Orleans, Louisiana. Association for Computational Linguistics.

Chien-Sheng Wu, Steven C.H. Hoi, Richard Socher, and Caiming Xiong. 2020. TOD-BERT: Pre-trained natural language understanding for task-oriented dialogue. In *Proceedings of the 2020 Conference on Empirical Methods in Natural Language Processing (EMNLP)*, pages 917–929, Online. Association for Computational Linguistics.

Jingyi Xu, Zilu Zhang, Tal Friedman, Yitao Liang, and Guy Broeck. 2018. A semantic loss function for deep learning with symbolic knowledge. In *International conference on machine learning*, pages 5502–5511. PMLR.

Yuanmeng Yan, Rumei Li, Sirui Wang, Fuzheng Zhang, Wei Wu, and Weiran Xu. 2021. ConSERT: A contrastive framework for self-supervised sentence representation transfer. In *Proceedings of the 59th Annual Meeting of the Association for Computational Linguistics and the 11th International Joint Conference on Natural Language Processing (Volume 1: Long Papers)*, pages 5065–5075, Online. Association for Computational Linguistics.

Chun-Nam John Yu and Thorsten Joachims. 2009. Learning structural svms with latent variables. In *Proceedings of the 26th Annual International Conference on Machine Learning*, ICML '09, page 1169–1176, New York, NY, USA. Association for Computing Machinery.

Dejiao Zhang, Feng Nan, Xiaokai Wei, Shang-Wen Li, Henghui Zhu, Kathleen McKeown, Ramesh Nallapati, Andrew O. Arnold, and Bing Xiang. 2021a. Supporting clustering with contrastive learning. In *Proceedings of the 2021 Conference of the North American Chapter of the Association for Computational Linguistics: Human Language Technologies*, pages 5419–5430, Online. Association for Computational Linguistics.

Hanlei Zhang, Hua Xu, Ting-En Lin, and Rui Lyu. 2021b. Discovering new intents with deep aligned clustering. In *Proceedings of the AAAI Conference on Artificial Intelligence*, volume 35, pages 14365–14373.

Haode Zhang, Yuwei Zhang, Li-Ming Zhan, Jiaxin Chen, Guangyuan Shi, Xiao-Ming Wu, and Albert Y.S. Lam. 2021c. Effectiveness of pre-training for few-shot intent classification. In *Findings of the*

*Association for Computational Linguistics: EMNLP 2021*, pages 1114–1120, Punta Cana, Dominican Republic. Association for Computational Linguistics.

Jianguo Zhang, Trung Bui, Seunghyun Yoon, Xiang Chen, Zhiwei Liu, Congying Xia, Quan Hung Tran, Walter Chang, and Philip Yu. 2021d. Few-shot intent detection via contrastive pre-training and fine-tuning. In *Proceedings of the 2021 Conference on Empirical Methods in Natural Language Processing*, pages 1906–1912, Online and Punta Cana, Dominican Republic. Association for Computational Linguistics.

Jianguo Zhang, Kazuma Hashimoto, Wenhao Liu, Chien-Sheng Wu, Yao Wan, Philip Yu, Richard Socher, and Caiming Xiong. 2020. Discriminative nearest neighbor few-shot intent detection by transferring natural language inference. In *Proceedings of the 2020 Conference on Empirical Methods in Natural Language Processing (EMNLP)*, pages 5064–5082, Online. Association for Computational Linguistics.

Jianguo Zhang, Kazuma Hashimoto, Yao Wan, Zhiwei Liu, Ye Liu, Caiming Xiong, and Philip Yu. 2022a. Are pre-trained transformers robust in intent classification? a missing ingredient in evaluation of out-of-scope intent detection. In *Proceedings of the 4th Workshop on NLP for Conversational AI*, pages 12–20, Dublin, Ireland. Association for Computational Linguistics.

Yuwei Zhang, Haode Zhang, Li-Ming Zhan, Xiao-Ming Wu, and Albert Lam. 2022b. New intent discovery with pre-training and contrastive learning. In *Proceedings of the 60th Annual Meeting of the Association for Computational Linguistics (Volume 1: Long Papers)*, pages 256–269, Dublin, Ireland. Association for Computational Linguistics.

# A Dataset licenses and release

DSTC11, Massive and HUW64 datasets are licensed under the Apache-2.0 License, while CLINC150 and BANKING77 are released under the cc-by-4.0 Creative Commons Public Licence. Massive can be downloaded from `https://github.com/jianguoz/Few-Shot-Intent-Detection`, DSTC11 from `https://github.com/amazon-science/dstc11-track2-intent-induction` and all the other datasets from `https://github.com/jianguoz/Few-Shot-Intent-Detection`. None of the dataset contains any offensive content or information that names or uniquely identifies individual people. Finally, our code includes a pre-processing script for every dataset that allows to turn the downloaded files into the format required in our pipeline.

# B Hardware Infrastructure and Computational Budget

We perform our experiments on one Amazon EC2 P3.16 instance, a 64-bit architecture with 488 GB of RAM, Intel Xeon E5-2686 v4 (64-core CPU running at 2.30GHz) and 8x Nvidia Tesla V100 Tensor Core GPUs with 128 GB of VRAM.

# C Time Complexity

## C.1 Supervised Clustering Loss

Assumomg $V$ is the number of nodes (utterances), and $E$ is the number of edges (all utterances pairs) in figure 1, the time complexity is $O(V^2 \log V)$.

This result is the sum of the complexities for the following steps:

1. Computation of the S similarity matrix (Eq. 2) has quadratic complexity $O(V^2)$.

2. Element-wise product (Eq. 4) and pairwise addition/subtraction (Eq. 5) have quadratic complexity $O(V^2)$.

3. Computing the maximum spanning forests (MSF) by Kruskal's algorithm (Eq. 6) and (Eq. 7) is $(E \log V)$. In our case, the gold MSF will be computed only on correct positive edges $E^+$, while the most-violating MSF will be computed on all the predicted positive edges E (both correct and incorrect). In the worst case, $E$ is equal to all pairs of utterances $V^2$ (all nodes connected = all pairs of utterances classified as being similar). So, the resulting complexity is $O(V^2 \log V)$.

4. Computing the structural loss (Eq. 8) has $O(V)$ complexity. This is due to the fact that in the worst case scenario (i.e., a fully connected graph), Kruskal's algorithm would return $V - 1$ edges, resulting in a $O(V)$ complexity for both element-wise products and summations.

5. For the scores $s_{gold}$ (Eq. 9) and $s_{viol}$ (Eq. 10) the previous argument applies as well.

6. Computing the loss (Eq. 11) has $O(1)$ complexity.

Therefore, the overall complexity of the supervised clustering loss is $O(V^2 \log V)$.

## C.2 Supervised Clustering predictions

After the system has been trained, the time complexity for prediction is $O(V'^2)$, where $V'$ is the number of utterances to be clustered. This is due to the following steps:

1. Computation of the S similarity matrix (Eq. 2) has quadratic complexity $O(V'^2)$.

2. Computation of the connected components is linear in terms of the edges, hence has complexity $O(V'^2)$.

# D Experiment Hyper-parameters

You can find here details of the experimented hyper-parameters of training datasets (Table 5), losses (Table 6), and clustering algorithms (Table 7).

# E Fine-tuning complete experimental results

Please find below average PRAUC (Table 8) for pre-training and post-training on train, dev, and test sets for each dataset, loss, and base sentence encoder.

# F Clustering complete experimental results

You can find here average clustering accuracy (Table 9) and adjusted mutual information score (Table 10) on test set for all combinations of datasets, base sentence encoders, and clustering algorithms.

# G tSNE plots of test utterance embeddings

Figures 3, 4, 5, 6, 7, 8 show the tSNE plots of the BANKING77 test utterances when XLM-RoBERTa is used as base sentence encoder. All plots where obtained with the following hyper-parameters:

- Perplexity = 20
- Learning rate: 200
- Iterations: 2000

As shown in figure 3, when no fine-tuning is performed - the point cloud is scattered all around. Same thing happens when the binary classification loss is used to fine-tune the model. In contrast, after fine-tuning with the cosine similarity loss or with contrastive learning - figures 5 and 6, respectively - intents are much better separated. Such visual clustering further improves when the triplet margin loss or the supervised clustering loss are used as fine-tuning strategies - see figures 7 and 8.

| DATASET | # intents per batch | # utterances per intent | # batches train epoch | # batches val epoch |
|---|---|---|---|---|
| CLINC150 | 30 | 5 | 5 | 5 |
| DSTC11 | 4 | 30 | 4 | 2 |
| HWU64 | 12 | 15 | 4 | 4 |
| BANKING77 | 15 | 8 | 5 | 5 |
| Massive | 12 | 10 | 5 | 5 |

Table 5: Dataset-specific training hyper-parameters

| LOSS | Hyper-parameters | Search space | Optimal values |
|---|---|---|---|
| Supervised Clustering Loss | c | ([0,1]; step: 0.05) | 0.15 |
| | r | ([0,1]; step: 0.05) | 0.5 |
| Triplet Margin Loss | m | ([0,1]; step: 0.05) | 0.15 |
| Contrastive Loss | m | ([0,2]; step: 0.10) | 1.75 |
| Binary Classification Loss | - | - | - |
| Cosine Similarity Loss | - | - | - |

Table 6: Losses: hyper-parameter search spaces and optimal values

| ALGORITHM | Hyper-parameters | Search space |
|---|---|---|
| Agglomerative Hierarchical Clustering | Linkage | ward, complete, average |
| | Distance Threshold | ([0,1]; step: 0.05) |
| DBSCAN | Eps | ([0,1]; step: 0.05) |
| | Min Samples | [2, 5, 10, 15, 20, 25, 30] |
| Connected components | Cut Threshold | ([0,1]; step: 0.05) |

Table 7: Clustering algorithms: hyper-parameters search spaces

| DATASET | LOSS | BASE SENTENCE ENCODER | | | | | | | | | | | | | | | | | | | | | | | |
|---|---|---|---|---|---|---|---|---|---|---|---|---|---|---|---|---|---|---|---|---|---|---|---|---|---|
| | | BERT Multilingual Cased | | | | | | XLM roBERTa | | | | | | Paraphrase Multilingual Mpnet | | | | | | All Mpnet Base | | | | | |
| | | Pre Fine-Tuning PRAUC on Train Set | Post Fine-Tuning PRAUC on Train Set | Pre Fine-Tuning PRAUC on Dev Set | Post Fine-Tuning PRAUC on Dev Set | Pre Fine-Tuning PRAUC on Test Set | Post Fine-Tuning PRAUC on Test Set | Pre Fine-Tuning PRAUC on Train Set | Post Fine-Tuning PRAUC on Train Set | Pre Fine-Tuning PRAUC on Dev Set | Post Fine-Tuning PRAUC on Dev Set | Pre Fine-Tuning PRAUC on Test Set | Post Fine-Tuning PRAUC on Test Set | Pre Fine-Tuning PRAUC on Train Set | Post Fine-Tuning PRAUC on Train Set | Pre Fine-Tuning PRAUC on Dev Set | Post Fine-Tuning PRAUC on Dev Set | Pre Fine-Tuning PRAUC on Test Set | Post Fine-Tuning PRAUC on Test Set | Pre Fine-Tuning PRAUC on Train Set | Post Fine-Tuning PRAUC on Train Set | Pre Fine-Tuning PRAUC on Dev Set | Post Fine-Tuning PRAUC on Dev Set | Pre Fine-Tuning PRAUC on Test Set | Post Fine-Tuning PRAUC on Test Set |
| | Binary classification loss | | 55,40% | | 47,85% | | 46,32% | | 56,80% | | 54,07% | | 49,32% | | 71,13% | | 68,32% | | 66,42% | | 78,02% | | 80,45% | | 76,25% |
| | Cosine similarity loss | | 71,93% | | 67,97% | | 61,50% | | 68,78% | | 63,58% | | 60,43% | | 82,97% | | 79,82% | | 73,95% | | 85,93% | | 85,37% | | 80,55% |
| BANKING77 | Contrastive loss | 39,02% | 70,33% | 39,30% | 67,03% | 38,55% | 60,28% | 35,70% | 69,00% | 36,03% | 64,40% | 34,35% | 61,28% | 67,87% | 81,82% | 68,40% | 80,00% | 64,83% | 73,62% | 76,00% | 86,27% | 78,23% | 85,68% | 75,13% | 80,67% |
| | Triplet margin loss | | 76,72% | | 70,53% | | 67,08% | | 79,10% | | 73,17% | | 70,53% | | 81,32% | | 78,08% | | 74,90% | | 85,72% | | 84,42% | | 80,33% |
| | Supervised clustering loss | | 81,68% | | 72,82% | | 68,93% | | 79,25% | | 73,12% | | 70,07% | | 85,88% | | 81,72% | | 78,10% | | 90,73% | | 85,85% | | 83,10% |
| | Binary classification loss | | 58,68% | | 55,20% | | 57,23% | | 51,60% | | 48,80% | | 51,32% | | 82,43% | | 80,78% | | 80,27% | | 85,45% | | 85,08% | | 84,32% |
| | Cosine similarity loss | | 70,02% | | 66,00% | | 66,67% | | 63,25% | | 60,35% | | 58,32% | | 89,80% | | 84,00% | | 82,52% | | 94,27% | | 90,05% | | 89,60% |
| CLINC150 | Contrastive loss | 53,48% | 71,00% | 52,38% | 65,82% | 52,72% | 66,62% | 46,67% | 60,93% | 46,83% | 58,07% | 47,33% | 56,73% | 82,53% | 90,48% | 81,60% | 84,30% | 80,95% | 83,13% | 85,95% | 94,18% | 85,57% | 90,80% | 84,78% | 89,13% |
| | Triplet margin loss | | 82,85% | | 77,22% | | 76,60% | | 82,65% | | 76,65% | | 75,53% | | 93,00% | | 87,90% | | 87,63% | | 94,35% | | 90,90% | | 90,47% |
| | Supervised clustering loss | | 85,85% | | 76,38% | | 76,48% | | 83,57% | | 77,08% | | 75,52% | | 94,53% | | 88,02% | | 87,78% | | 96,42% | | 92,13% | | 91,47% |
| | Binary classification loss | | 83,40% | | 77,20% | | 76,78% | | 69,30% | | 55,80% | | 70,60% | | 92,25% | | 78,40% | | 81,25% | | 88,63% | | 90,15% | | 88,63% |
| | Cosine similarity loss | | 90,77% | | 81,85% | | 82,90% | | 88,02% | | 82,67% | | 76,18% | | 95,18% | | 90,63% | | 90,72% | | 96,33% | | 93,25% | | 95,72% |
| DSTC11 | Contrastive loss | 48,35% | 91,38% | 47,38% | 82,22% | 47,08% | 82,17% | 44,50% | 85,83% | 43,30% | 80,82% | 43,20% | 76,23% | 85,80% | 95,22% | 80,00% | 90,78% | 80,95% | 90,78% | 84,32% | 96,58% | 83,35% | 93,20% | 81,05% | 94,88% |
| | Triplet margin loss | | 87,32% | | 82,20% | | 83,15% | | 87,68% | | 84,50% | | 83,57% | | 92,73% | | 88,98% | | 92,23% | | 94,20% | | 91,42% | | 93,23% |
| | Supervised clustering loss | | 95,53% | | 84,52% | | 86,52% | | 94,00% | | 87,30% | | 86,37% | | 95,78% | | 90,17% | | 92,12% | | 95,98% | | 93,50% | | 93,87% |
| | Binary classification loss | | 53,02% | | 55,07% | | 53,45% | | 49,22% | | 48,33% | | 49,03% | | 76,95% | | 73,48% | | 75,25% | | 71,98% | | 71,83% | | 72,75% |
| | Cosine similarity loss | | 69,77% | | 63,87% | | 62,28% | | 38,43% | | 36,17% | | 40,15% | | 86,52% | | 77,27% | | 78,87% | | 83,57% | | 77,58% | | 77,45% |
| HWU64 | Contrastive loss | 47,22% | 67,42% | 49,87% | 64,12% | 50,17% | 62,58% | 33,55% | 38,82% | 35,17% | 38,62% | 37,33% | 40,53% | 74,50% | 84,35% | 72,77% | 76,63% | 76,50% | 77,78% | 73,00% | 85,70% | 71,47% | 80,22% | 73,95% | 79,82% |
| | Triplet margin loss | | 74,07% | | 67,30% | | 65,82% | | 59,52% | | 55,55% | | 58,70% | | 84,93% | | 78,50% | | 79,73% | | 87,82% | | 81,22% | | 82,65% |
| | Supervised clustering loss | | 82,55% | | 69,73% | | 69,53% | | 74,35% | | 67,73% | | 70,78% | | 89,83% | | 80,28% | | 81,60% | | 92,08% | | 82,63% | | 83,77% |
| | Binary classification loss | | 56,71% | | 49,09% | | 43,13% | | 34,97% | | 38,05% | | 32,90% | | 68,08% | | 71,07% | | 66,17% | - | - | - | - | - | - |
| | Cosine similarity loss | | 64,48% | | 53,60% | | 50,85% | | 31,87% | | 31,40% | | 29,63% | | 79,02% | | 74,05% | | 70,92% | - | - | - | - | - | - |
| Massive | Contrastive loss | 30,97% | 65,98% | 30,57% | 54,57% | 29,06% | 53,03% | 26,52% | 25,37% | 26,17% | 25,43% | 24,78% | 24,73% | 63,93% | 78,82% | 65,73% | 74,55% | 62,48% | 71,45% | - | - | - | - | - | - |
| | Triplet margin loss | | 63,75% | | 56,23% | | 53,00% | | 65,88% | | 60,32% | | 57,60% | | 79,28% | | 76,25% | | 73,33% | - | - | - | - | - | - |
| | Supervised clustering loss | | 70,57% | | 56,97% | | 56,38% | | 70,62% | | 63,57% | | 60,50% | | 80,07% | | 76,25% | | 74,15% | - | - | - | - | - | - |

Table 8: Average pre-training and post-training PRAUC on train, dev and test sets for each dataset, loss and base sentence encoder. Regardless of the loss or base sentence encoder chosen, fine-tuning always leads from moderate to large improvements in PRAUC on test utterances. This is especially true when the supervised clustering loss or the triplet margin loss are used as fine-tuning strategies. In general, increases are much less pronounced on All Mpnet Base and Paraphrase Multilingual Mpnet since these two models were already fine-tuned on sentence similarity tasks and datasets.

| Clustering algorithm | Base sentence encoder | Dataset | No Fine-Tuning | Binary classification loss | Cosine similarity loss | Contrastive loss | Triplet margin loss | Supervised clustering loss | BEST LOSS |
|---|---|---|---|---|---|---|---|---|---|
| **Average clustering accuracy on test set for all combinations of datasets, base sentence encoders and clustering algorithms when optimizing wrt the clustering accuracy** | | | | | | | | | |
| Agglomerative Hierarchical Clustering | BERT Multilingual Cased | BANKING77 | 0.32±0.05 | 0.37±0.06 | 0.52±0.04 | 0.5±0.08 | 0.62±0.05 | 0.62±0.08 | **Supervised clustering loss** |
| | | CLINC150 | 0.56±0.06 | 0.53±0.05 | 0.56±0.04 | 0.57±0.06 | 0.68±0.03 | 0.71±0.06 | **Supervised clustering loss** |
| | | DSTC11 | 0.33±0.05 | 0.65±0.1 | 0.56±0.08 | 0.6±0.11 | 0.65±0.14 | 0.73±0.1 | **Supervised clustering loss** |
| | | HWU64 | 0.52±0.04 | 0.51±0.03 | 0.56±0.06 | 0.55±0.04 | 0.59±0.06 | 0.56±0.04 | Triplet margin loss |
| | | Massive | 0.22±0.03 | 0.41±0.07 | 0.46±0.04 | 0.51±0.04 | 0.55±0.07 | 0.53±0.08 | Triplet margin loss |
| | Paraphrase Multilingual Mpnet | BANKING77 | 0.62±0.06 | 0.56±0.08 | 0.64±0.06 | 0.62±0.03 | 0.72±0.03 | 0.69±0.06 | Triplet margin loss |
| | | CLINC150 | 0.65±0.07 | 0.65±0.04 | 0.7±0.08 | 0.69±0.08 | 0.79±0.05 | 0.83±0.05 | **Supervised clustering loss** |
| | | DSTC11 | 0.57±0.09 | 0.48±0.17 | 0.75±0.1 | 0.73±0.06 | 0.75±0.15 | 0.77±0.09 | **Supervised clustering loss** |
| | | HWU64 | 0.73±0.09 | 0.74±0.1 | 0.69±0.05 | 0.67±0.03 | 0.75±0.07 | 0.68±0.05 | Triplet margin loss |
| | | Massive | 0.62±0.09 | 0.61±0.07 | 0.68±0.05 | 0.6±0.08 | 0.67±0.11 | 0.73±0.08 | **Supervised clustering loss** |
| | All Mpnet Base | BANKING77 | 0.7±0.04 | 0.67±0.05 | 0.68±0.04 | 0.71±0.07 | 0.78±0.04 | 0.73±0.04 | Triplet margin loss |
| | | CLINC150 | 0.75±0.06 | 0.75±0.06 | 0.77±0.05 | 0.78±0.08 | 0.81±0.03 | 0.82±0.04 | **Supervised clustering loss** |
| | | DSTC11 | 0.56±0.12 | 0.67±0.09 | 0.78±0.16 | 0.83±0.12 | 0.78±0.14 | 0.77±0.14 | Cosine similarity loss |
| | | HWU64 | 0.7±0.11 | 0.69±0.09 | 0.67±0.05 | 0.67±0.08 | 0.74±0.05 | 0.78±0.08 | **Supervised clustering loss** |
| | XLM roBERTa | BANKING77 | 0.32±0.02 | 0.41±0.03 | 0.52±0.04 | 0.5±0.05 | 0.59±0.08 | 0.62±0.04 | **Supervised clustering loss** |
| | | CLINC150 | 0.54±0.03 | 0.6±0.1 | 0.55±0.03 | 0.55±0.04 | 0.71±0.06 | 0.7±0.04 | Triplet margin loss |
| | | DSTC11 | 0.36±0.08 | 0.68±0.0 | 0.57±0.19 | 0.61±0.18 | 0.74±0.08 | 0.71±0.09 | Triplet margin loss |
| | | HWU64 | 0.42±0.02 | 0.52±0.12 | 0.37±0.02 | 0.44±0.11 | 0.65±0.08 | 0.73±0.07 | **Supervised clustering loss** |
| | | Massive | 0.23±0.02 | 0.3±0.09 | 0.26±0.09 | 0.22±0.02 | 0.52±0.04 | 0.61±0.04 | **Supervised clustering loss** |
| Connected Components | BERT Multilingual Cased | BANKING77 | 0.13±0.02 | 0.17±0.04 | 0.39±0.09 | 0.36±0.08 | 0.43±0.09 | 0.46±0.1 | **Supervised clustering loss** |
| | | CLINC150 | 0.23±0.05 | 0.25±0.04 | 0.37±0.04 | 0.34±0.06 | 0.49±0.07 | 0.51±0.02 | **Supervised clustering loss** |
| | | DSTC11 | 0.4±0.11 | 0.38±0.11 | 0.52±0.08 | 0.49±0.1 | 0.54±0.12 | 0.46±0.11 | Triplet margin loss |
| | | HWU64 | 0.23±0.02 | 0.23±0.03 | 0.38±0.08 | 0.34±0.05 | 0.45±0.07 | 0.44±0.11 | Triplet margin loss |
| | | Massive | 0.24±0.02 | 0.23±0.07 | 0.27±0.07 | 0.29±0.06 | 0.3±0.08 | 0.32±0.1 | **Supervised clustering loss** |
| | Paraphrase Multilingual Mpnet | BANKING77 | 0.36±0.03 | 0.43±0.06 | 0.51±0.07 | 0.51±0.05 | 0.46±0.09 | 0.45±0.11 | Cosine similarity loss |
| | | CLINC150 | 0.51±0.06 | 0.49±0.08 | 0.58±0.12 | 0.57±0.1 | 0.66±0.08 | 0.63±0.02 | Triplet margin loss |
| | | DSTC11 | 0.44±0.12 | 0.66±0.09 | 0.69±0.12 | 0.7±0.08 | 0.71±0.13 | 0.72±0.08 | **Supervised clustering loss** |
| | | HWU64 | 0.48±0.09 | 0.5±0.09 | 0.48±0.18 | 0.52±0.16 | 0.57±0.11 | 0.53±0.08 | Triplet margin loss |
| | | Massive | 0.35±0.06 | 0.39±0.1 | 0.44±0.05 | 0.41±0.05 | 0.41±0.05 | 0.39±0.08 | Contrastive loss |
| | All Mpnet Base | BANKING77 | 0.48±0.04 | 0.5±0.06 | 0.49±0.08 | 0.55±0.09 | 0.55±0.05 | 0.54±0.06 | Cosine similarity loss |
| | | CLINC150 | 0.53±0.08 | 0.52±0.07 | 0.71±0.06 | 0.63±0.06 | 0.67±0.02 | 0.62±0.06 | Contrastive loss |
| | | DSTC11 | 0.39±0.14 | 0.67±0.13 | 0.67±0.12 | 0.67±0.1 | 0.77±0.1 | 0.73±0.1 | Triplet margin loss |
| | | HWU64 | 0.47±0.04 | 0.44±0.09 | 0.41±0.18 | 0.43±0.09 | 0.57±0.09 | 0.46±0.13 | Triplet margin loss |
| | XLM roBERTa | BANKING77 | 0.08±0.0 | 0.11±0.04 | 0.35±0.07 | 0.33±0.05 | 0.39±0.08 | 0.51±0.07 | **Supervised clustering loss** |
| | | CLINC150 | 0.04±0.0 | 0.04±0.0 | 0.26±0.18 | 0.22±0.22 | 0.49±0.23 | 0.48±0.22 | Triplet margin loss |
| | | DSTC11 | 0.4±0.11 | 0.57±0.0 | 0.55±0.11 | 0.5±0.12 | 0.52±0.09 | 0.46±0.14 | binary_classification |
| | | HWU64 | 0.08±0.0 | 0.13±0.1 | 0.11±0.06 | 0.09±0.03 | 0.36±0.15 | 0.12±0.09 | Triplet margin loss |
| | | Massive | 0.24±0.02 | 0.24±0.03 | 0.23±0.03 | 0.23±0.03 | 0.41±0.1 | 0.39±0.04 | Triplet margin loss |
| DBSCAN | BERT Multilingual Cased | BANKING77 | 0.19±0.02 | 0.26±0.08 | 0.45±0.07 | 0.41±0.09 | 0.48±0.08 | 0.49±0.1 | **Supervised clustering loss** |
| | | CLINC150 | 0.25±0.05 | 0.28±0.04 | 0.38±0.07 | 0.4±0.07 | 0.54±0.05 | 0.53±0.02 | Triplet margin loss |
| | | DSTC11 | 0.39±0.1 | 0.52±0.06 | 0.59±0.12 | 0.5±0.11 | 0.54±0.17 | 0.57±0.1 | Contrastive loss |
| | | HWU64 | 0.29±0.05 | 0.37±0.06 | 0.42±0.09 | 0.46±0.06 | 0.51±0.05 | 0.44±0.09 | Triplet margin loss |
| | | Massive | 0.25±0.03 | 0.39±0.08 | 0.43±0.07 | 0.47±0.08 | 0.5±0.07 | 0.45±0.05 | Triplet margin loss |
| | Paraphrase Multilingual Mpnet | BANKING77 | 0.42±0.06 | 0.42±0.07 | 0.55±0.06 | 0.48±0.06 | 0.53±0.03 | 0.49±0.13 | Contrastive loss |
| | | CLINC150 | 0.5±0.09 | 0.5±0.07 | 0.57±0.13 | 0.61±0.1 | 0.65±0.1 | 0.64±0.03 | Triplet margin loss |
| | | DSTC11 | 0.56±0.07 | 0.69±0.06 | 0.7±0.13 | 0.78±0.07 | 0.64±0.06 | 0.71±0.07 | Cosine similarity loss |
| | | HWU64 | 0.52±0.12 | 0.5±0.15 | 0.61±0.12 | 0.59±0.14 | 0.66±0.1 | 0.53±0.04 | Triplet margin loss |
| | | Massive | 0.5±0.05 | 0.45±0.09 | 0.52±0.05 | 0.55±0.08 | 0.47±0.09 | 0.54±0.07 | Cosine similarity loss |
| | All Mpnet Base | BANKING77 | 0.47±0.05 | 0.49±0.07 | 0.58±0.08 | 0.57±0.09 | 0.61±0.06 | 0.55±0.08 | Triplet margin loss |
| | | CLINC150 | 0.5±0.05 | 0.54±0.08 | 0.71±0.07 | 0.67±0.04 | 0.67±0.02 | 0.64±0.05 | Contrastive loss |
| | | DSTC11 | 0.61±0.04 | 0.62±0.09 | 0.71±0.1 | 0.69±0.1 | 0.75±0.07 | 0.68±0.12 | Triplet margin loss |
| | | HWU64 | 0.41±0.07 | 0.47±0.11 | 0.53±0.14 | 0.58±0.11 | 0.62±0.09 | 0.52±0.11 | Triplet margin loss |
| | XLM roBERTa | BANKING77 | 0.11±0.01 | 0.3±0.04 | 0.39±0.07 | 0.44±0.05 | 0.53±0.04 | 0.49±0.05 | Triplet margin loss |
| | | CLINC150 | 0.14±0.03 | 0.28±0.05 | 0.32±0.14 | 0.26±0.18 | 0.5±0.15 | 0.5±0.21 | **Supervised clustering loss** |
| | | DSTC11 | 0.39±0.1 | 0.41±0.0 | 0.58±0.1 | 0.56±0.13 | 0.52±0.07 | 0.59±0.09 | **Supervised clustering loss** |
| | | HWU64 | 0.24±0.02 | 0.28±0.05 | 0.19±0.05 | 0.24±0.16 | 0.58±0.1 | 0.39±0.06 | Triplet margin loss |
| | | Massive | 0.23±0.02 | 0.27±0.05 | 0.27±0.04 | 0.24±0.03 | 0.52±0.05 | 0.47±0.06 | Triplet margin loss |

Table 9: Average clustering accuracy on test set for all combinations of datasets, base sentence encoders and clustering algorithms when optimizing wrt the clustering accuracy. It is worth mentioning that gaps in performance between the Supervised Clustering Loss and the Triplet Margin Loss are quite narrow, with confidence intervals often overlapping. On the contrary, all other losses clearly lag behind in terms of performance. Nevertheless, in all cases, fine-tuning any of the base sentence encoders with any of the losses proved beneficial - regardless of the dataset or clustering algorithm adopted.

| **Average adjusted mutual information score on test set for all combinations of datasets, base sentence encoders and clustering algorithms when optimizing wrt the adjusted mutual information score** | | | | | | | | | |
|---|---|---|---|---|---|---|---|---|---|
| Clustering algorithm | Base sentence encoder | Dataset | No Fine-Tuning | Binary classification loss | Cosine similarity loss | Contrastive loss | Triplet margin loss | Supervised clustering loss | BEST LOSS |
| Agglomerative Hierarchical Clustering | BERT Multilingual Cased | BANKING77 | 0.53±0.02 | 0.55±0.05 | 0.67±0.03 | 0.66±0.04 | 0.76±0.03 | 0.77±0.05 | **Supervised clustering loss** |
| | | CLINC150 | 0.73±0.02 | 0.76±0.03 | 0.77±0.04 | 0.77±0.04 | 0.84±0.03 | 0.85±0.02 | **Supervised clustering loss** |
| | | DSTC11 | 0.29±0.05 | 0.52±0.1 | 0.47±0.14 | 0.5±0.1 | 0.6±0.06 | 0.63±0.1 | **Supervised clustering loss** |
| | | HWU64 | 0.61±0.02 | 0.63±0.02 | 0.67±0.04 | 0.67±0.04 | 0.72±0.05 | 0.72±0.04 | Triplet margin loss |
| | | Massive | 0.27±0.01 | 0.36±0.05 | 0.45±0.04 | 0.46±0.04 | 0.51±0.04 | 0.51±0.06 | **Supervised clustering loss** |
| | Paraphrase Multilingual Mpnet | BANKING77 | 0.74±0.02 | 0.72±0.07 | 0.76±0.06 | 0.75±0.05 | 0.83±0.02 | 0.81±0.03 | Triplet margin loss |
| | | CLINC150 | 0.86±0.03 | 0.87±0.02 | 0.88±0.03 | 0.87±0.03 | 0.92±0.02 | 0.93±0.01 | **Supervised clustering loss** |
| | | DSTC11 | 0.52±0.15 | 0.36±0.34 | 0.65±0.08 | 0.72±0.06 | 0.73±0.11 | 0.75±0.11 | **Supervised clustering loss** |
| | | HWU64 | 0.79±0.05 | 0.76±0.01 | 0.79±0.03 | 0.79±0.01 | 0.79±0.04 | 0.81±0.04 | **Supervised clustering loss** |
| | | Massive | 0.6±0.09 | 0.6±0.06 | 0.65±0.06 | 0.64±0.06 | 0.71±0.06 | 0.7±0.05 | Triplet margin loss |
| | All Mpnet Base | BANKING77 | 0.84±0.01 | 0.83±0.01 | 0.83±0.02 | 0.83±0.03 | 0.88±0.02 | 0.86±0.02 | Triplet margin loss |
| | | CLINC150 | 0.91±0.02 | 0.9±0.02 | 0.92±0.02 | 0.92±0.02 | 0.94±0.01 | 0.94±0.01 | **Supervised clustering loss** |
| | | DSTC11 | 0.49±0.17 | 0.63±0.16 | 0.75±0.14 | 0.71±0.12 | 0.78±0.11 | 0.7±0.1 | Triplet margin loss |
| | | HWU64 | 0.81±0.05 | 0.81±0.05 | 0.79±0.03 | 0.8±0.01 | 0.79±0.05 | 0.85±0.03 | **Supervised clustering loss** |
| | XLM roBERTa | BANKING77 | 0.48±0.01 | 0.6±0.04 | 0.66±0.06 | 0.66±0.04 | 0.73±0.06 | 0.75±0.03 | **Supervised clustering loss** |
| | | CLINC150 | 0.66±0.02 | 0.72±0.07 | 0.74±0.05 | 0.71±0.07 | 0.86±0.03 | 0.86±0.01 | **Supervised clustering loss** |
| | | DSTC11 | 0.28±0.02 | 0.42±0.0 | 0.53±0.04 | 0.53±0.04 | 0.68±0.05 | 0.65±0.1 | Triplet margin loss |
| | | HWU64 | 0.52±0.04 | 0.61±0.09 | 0.56±0.05 | 0.55±0.07 | 0.73±0.05 | 0.77±0.04 | **Supervised clustering loss** |
| | | Massive | 0.2±0.01 | 0.28±0.12 | 0.23±0.11 | 0.19±0.02 | 0.51±0.06 | 0.58±0.04 | **Supervised clustering loss** |
| Connected Components | BERT Multilingual Cased | BANKING77 | 0.23±0.02 | 0.26±0.09 | 0.52±0.07 | 0.52±0.05 | 0.58±0.08 | 0.6±0.09 | **Supervised clustering loss** |
| | | CLINC150 | 0.38±0.04 | 0.43±0.05 | 0.51±0.15 | 0.58±0.06 | 0.72±0.04 | 0.72±0.03 | Triplet margin loss |
| | | DSTC11 | 0.13±0.03 | 0.37±0.13 | 0.43±0.12 | 0.44±0.15 | 0.5±0.11 | 0.33±0.15 | Triplet margin loss |
| | | HWU64 | 0.31±0.04 | 0.32±0.07 | 0.45±0.1 | 0.41±0.11 | 0.57±0.07 | 0.54±0.13 | Triplet margin loss |
| | | Massive | 0.14±0.03 | 0.18±0.07 | 0.22±0.08 | 0.22±0.11 | 0.25±0.14 | 0.32±0.1 | **Supervised clustering loss** |
| | Paraphrase Multilingual Mpnet | BANKING77 | 0.54±0.05 | 0.45±0.16 | 0.66±0.06 | 0.65±0.04 | 0.59±0.12 | 0.49±0.2 | contrastive_learning |
| | | CLINC150 | 0.69±0.05 | 0.7±0.06 | 0.72±0.18 | 0.76±0.08 | 0.83±0.04 | 0.78±0.08 | Triplet margin loss |
| | | DSTC11 | 0.37±0.12 | 0.58±0.02 | 0.6±0.15 | 0.61±0.11 | 0.65±0.12 | 0.65±0.11 | **Supervised clustering loss** |
| | | HWU64 | 0.55±0.1 | 0.52±0.1 | 0.58±0.18 | 0.57±0.13 | 0.64±0.12 | 0.62±0.08 | Triplet margin loss |
| | | Massive | 0.32±0.08 | 0.33±0.15 | 0.45±0.08 | 0.39±0.13 | 0.41±0.06 | 0.4±0.08 | contrastive_learning |
| | All Mpnet Base | BANKING77 | 0.59±0.07 | 0.67±0.04 | 0.69±0.07 | 0.71±0.06 | 0.69±0.02 | 0.63±0.13 | Cosine similarity loss |
| | | CLINC150 | 0.72±0.07 | 0.69±0.07 | 0.82±0.06 | 0.8±0.07 | 0.82±0.05 | 0.82±0.01 | **Supervised clustering loss** |
| | | DSTC11 | 0.19±0.17 | 0.5±0.11 | 0.47±0.29 | 0.55±0.22 | 0.65±0.17 | 0.67±0.13 | **Supervised clustering loss** |
| | | HWU64 | 0.49±0.14 | 0.46±0.15 | 0.5±0.15 | 0.62±0.11 | 0.68±0.08 | 0.62±0.07 | Triplet margin loss |
| | XLM roBERTa | BANKING77 | 0.01±0.0 | 0.15±0.13 | 0.46±0.08 | 0.49±0.08 | 0.53±0.09 | 0.63±0.06 | **Supervised clustering loss** |
| | | CLINC150 | 0.0±0.0 | 0.0±0.0 | 0.37±0.31 | 0.28±0.34 | 0.62±0.31 | 0.63±0.32 | **Supervised clustering loss** |
| | | DSTC11 | 0.04±0.01 | 0.03±0.0 | 0.45±0.11 | 0.39±0.09 | 0.46±0.09 | 0.33±0.19 | Triplet margin loss |
| | | HWU64 | 0.0±0.0 | 0.08±0.16 | 0.09±0.18 | 0.03±0.06 | 0.51±0.26 | 0.08±0.16 | Triplet margin loss |
| | | Massive | 0.0±0.0 | 0.08±0.1 | 0.04±0.08 | 0.0±0.0 | 0.34±0.09 | 0.36±0.08 | **Supervised clustering loss** |
| DBSCAN | BERT Multilingual Cased | BANKING77 | 0.27±0.06 | 0.32±0.08 | 0.58±0.05 | 0.55±0.06 | 0.57±0.11 | 0.64±0.07 | **Supervised clustering loss** |
| | | CLINC150 | 0.4±0.04 | 0.45±0.05 | 0.58±0.08 | 0.57±0.08 | 0.71±0.05 | 0.71±0.04 | **Supervised clustering loss** |
| | | DSTC11 | 0.2±0.05 | 0.38±0.13 | 0.49±0.13 | 0.5±0.14 | 0.59±0.11 | 0.39±0.11 | Triplet margin loss |
| | | HWU64 | 0.41±0.04 | 0.49±0.06 | 0.55±0.1 | 0.61±0.04 | 0.58±0.13 | 0.57±0.11 | Cosine similarity loss |
| | | Massive | 0.12±0.03 | 0.29±0.11 | 0.34±0.07 | 0.36±0.07 | 0.4±0.08 | 0.42±0.09 | **Supervised clustering loss** |
| | Paraphrase Multilingual Mpnet | BANKING77 | 0.56±0.06 | 0.55±0.09 | 0.66±0.04 | 0.61±0.07 | 0.53±0.23 | 0.58±0.15 | contrastive_learning |
| | | CLINC150 | 0.64±0.1 | 0.71±0.05 | 0.77±0.08 | 0.69±0.24 | 0.82±0.04 | 0.8±0.03 | Triplet margin loss |
| | | DSTC11 | 0.39±0.18 | 0.63±0.04 | 0.71±0.09 | 0.75±0.06 | 0.71±0.07 | 0.72±0.09 | Cosine similarity loss |
| | | HWU64 | 0.52±0.14 | 0.59±0.09 | 0.66±0.2 | 0.71±0.09 | 0.75±0.07 | 0.66±0.05 | Triplet margin loss |
| | | Massive | 0.44±0.08 | 0.52±0.13 | 0.51±0.06 | 0.5±0.05 | 0.46±0.13 | 0.57±0.06 | **Supervised clustering loss** |
| | All Mpnet Base | BANKING77 | 0.63±0.03 | 0.66±0.03 | 0.66±0.08 | 0.65±0.09 | 0.64±0.14 | 0.63±0.16 | contrastive_learning |
| | | CLINC150 | 0.73±0.04 | 0.71±0.06 | 0.81±0.06 | 0.78±0.1 | 0.79±0.06 | 0.77±0.04 | contrastive_learning |
| | | DSTC11 | 0.5±0.13 | 0.56±0.2 | 0.71±0.09 | 0.73±0.07 | 0.76±0.1 | 0.73±0.11 | Triplet margin loss |
| | | HWU64 | 0.51±0.09 | 0.52±0.13 | 0.62±0.08 | 0.62±0.12 | 0.65±0.09 | 0.6±0.07 | Triplet margin loss |
| | XLM roBERTa | BANKING77 | 0.03±0.02 | 0.42±0.08 | 0.5±0.13 | 0.52±0.1 | 0.66±0.03 | 0.65±0.06 | Triplet margin loss |
| | | CLINC150 | 0.21±0.04 | 0.45±0.06 | 0.46±0.2 | 0.39±0.24 | 0.7±0.13 | 0.67±0.25 | Triplet margin loss |
| | | DSTC11 | 0.06±0.04 | 0.24±0.0 | 0.49±0.14 | 0.47±0.11 | 0.56±0.13 | 0.46±0.16 | Triplet margin loss |
| | | HWU64 | 0.31±0.05 | 0.38±0.07 | 0.28±0.14 | 0.19±0.07 | 0.62±0.13 | 0.51±0.07 | Triplet margin loss |
| | | Massive | 0.08±0.03 | 0.13±0.1 | 0.08±0.1 | 0.02±0.01 | 0.43±0.06 | 0.32±0.1 | Triplet margin loss |

Table 10: Average adjusted mutual information score on test set for all combinations of datasets, base sentence encoders and clustering algorithms when optimizing wrt the adjusted mutual information score. It is worth mentioning that gaps in performance between the Supervised Clustering Loss and the Triplet Margin Loss are quite narrow, with confidence intervals often overlapping. On the contrary, all other losses clearly lag behind in terms of performance. Nevertheless, in all cases, fine-tuning any of the base sentence encoders with any of the losses proved beneficial - regardless of the dataset or clustering algorithm adopted.

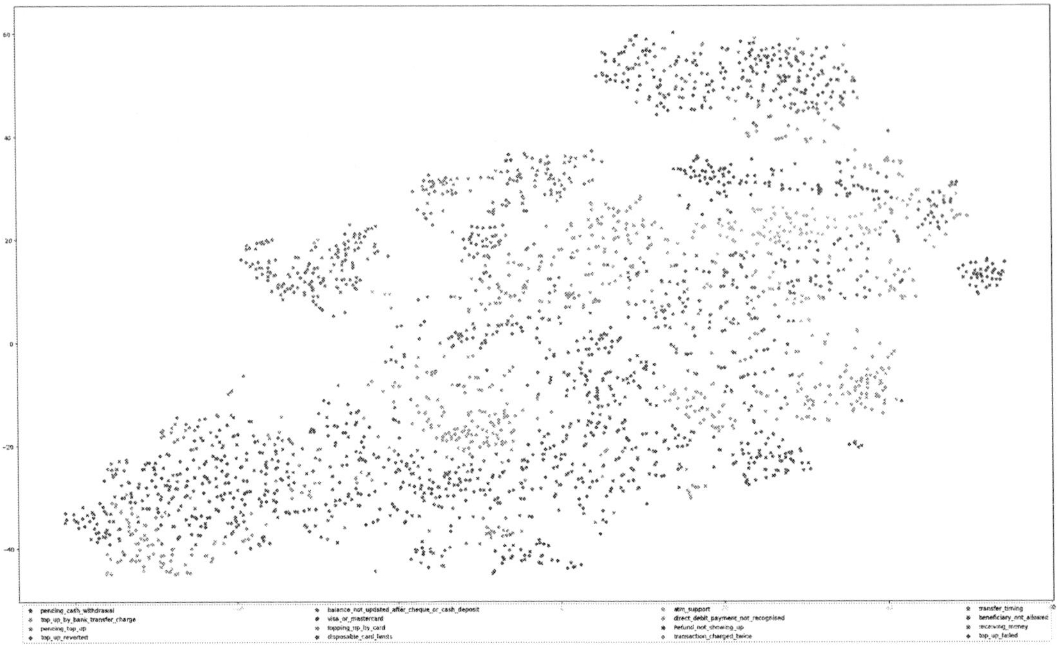


Figure 3: tSNE plots of BANKING77 test utterances when xml-RoBERTa is used to extract the embeddings.

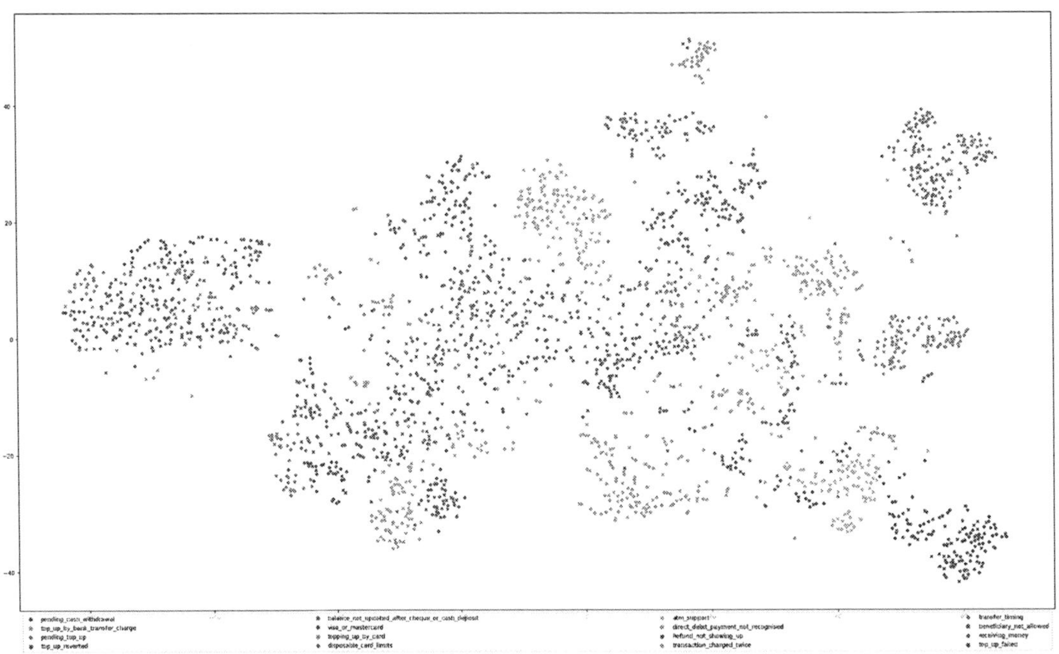


Figure 4: tSNE plots of BANKING77 test utterances when xml-RoBERTa - fine-tuned with the binary classification loss - is used to extract the embeddings.

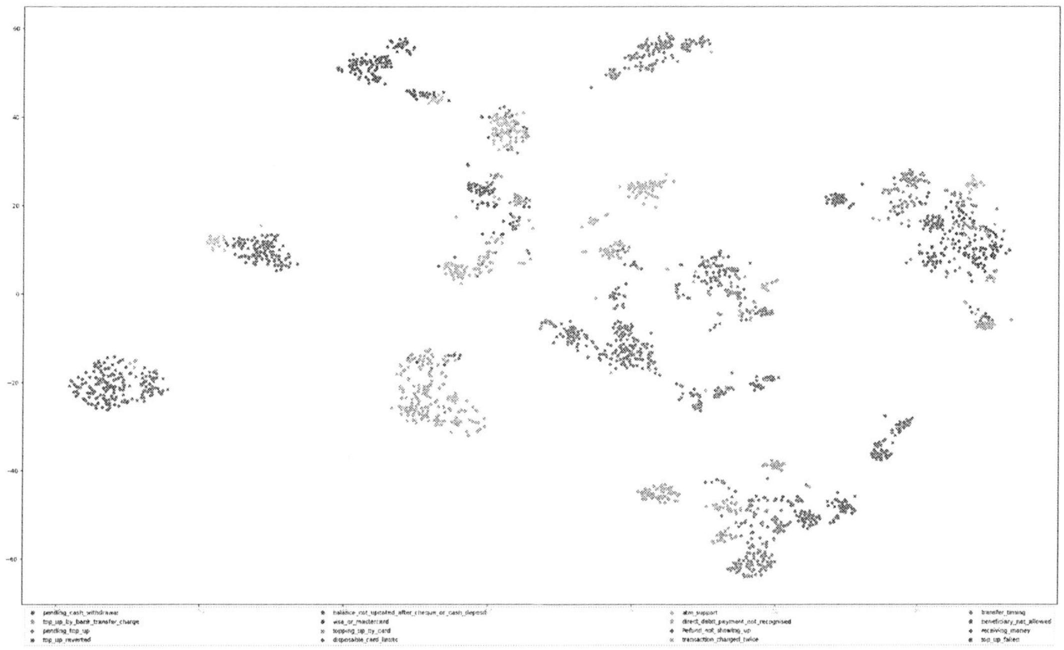

Figure 5: tSNE plots of BANKING77 test utterances when xml-RoBERTa - fine-tuned with the cosine similarity loss - is used to extract the embeddings.

Figure 6: tSNE plots of BANKING77 test utterances when xml-RoBERTa - fine-tuned with the contrastive learning loss - is used to extract the embeddings.

Figure 7: tSNE plots of BANKING77 test utterances when xml-RoBERTa - fine-tuned with the triplet margin loss - is used to extract the embeddings.

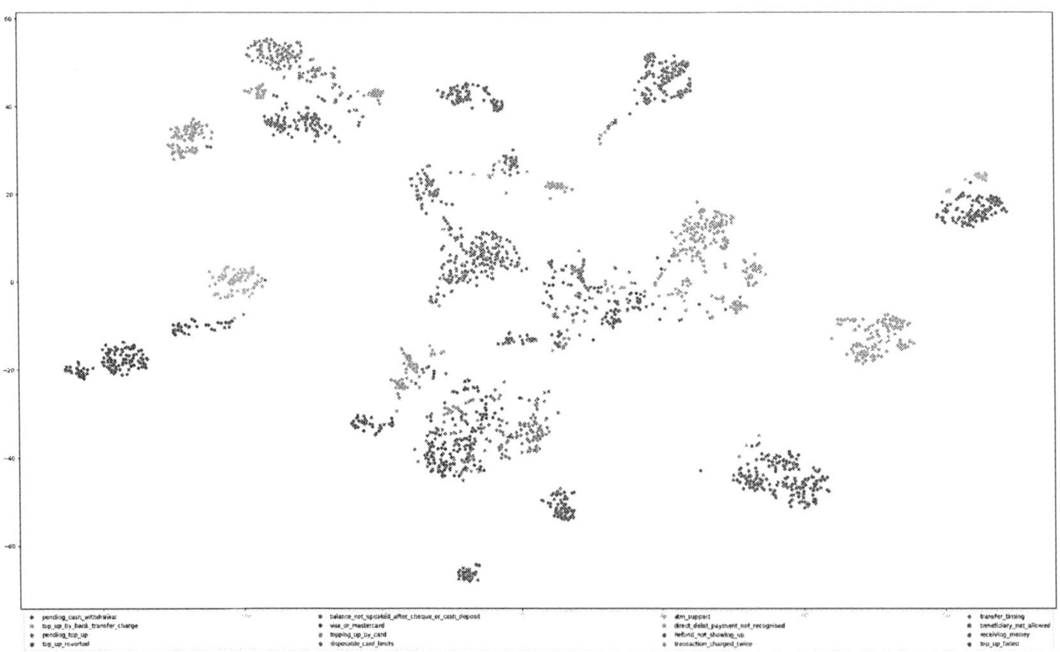


Figure 8: tSNE plots of BANKING77 test utterances when xml-RoBERTa - fine-tuned with the supervised clustering loss - is used to extract the embeddings.

# STRONG – Structure Controllable Legal Opinion Summary Generation


**Yang Zhong**
University of Pittsburgh
Pittsburgh, PA
yaz118@pitt.edu

**Diane Litman**
University of Pittsburgh
Pittsburgh, PA
dlitman@pitt.edu



## Abstract

We propose an approach for the structure controllable summarization of long legal opinions that considers the argument structure of the document. Our approach involves using predicted argument role information to guide the model in generating coherent summaries that follow a provided structure pattern. We demonstrate the effectiveness of our approach on a dataset of legal opinions and show that it outperforms several strong baselines with respect to ROUGE, BERTScore, and structure similarity.


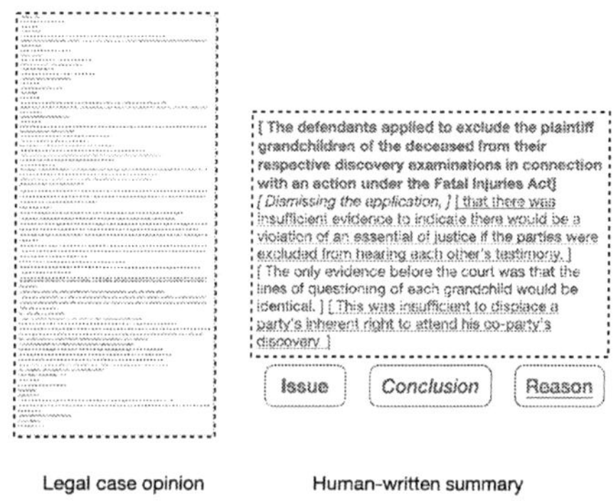


Figure 1: Example of a legal case opinion with its summary. The summary is annotated with oracle argument structure labels (one **Issue**, one *Conclusion*, and two Reasons). Presenting an issue followed by a conclusion and reasons is the dataset's most common normalized structure pattern (54%). Complete descriptions of patterns are in Appendix A.

## 1 Introduction

Discourse structure plays an essential role in text generation in domains ranging from news (Van Dijk, 2013) to peer-reviewed articles (Shen et al., 2022b). In the legal domain, it's equally important to draft a summary that can follow a blueprint (Xu et al., 2021). For instance, in Figure 1, given a long legal opinion with thousands of words as input, a legal expert organized the summary by making the argument clear in terms of the issues the decision addressed, the decision's conclusion, and the reasoning behind the decision.

While progress has been made in controllable generation, limited research has controlled discourse structure. Recently, Spangher et al. (2022) and Shen et al. (2022a) proposed approaches to generate sentences with discourse structure labels. However, no existing controllable generation work addresses the legal domain, where the argumentative structure is pivotal. While prior work in the legal field highlighted the significance of argumentative structure from the input (Elaraby and Litman, 2022), the potential for utilizing argument structure to guide text generation remains unexplored.

Based on a corpus analysis showing that experts use common patterns to summarize legal opinions (the most frequent one is shown in Figure 1), we develop a novel structure-prompting approach called STRONG (**S**tructure con**TR**ollable legal **OpiN**ion summary **G**eneration). STRONG is implemented using Longformer Encoder Decoder (Beltagy et al., 2020) coupled with automatically created structure prompts. Results demonstrate that STRONG outperforms summarization models without structure control and improves inference time over models with structure control from other domains. We make our models available at `https://github.com/cs329yangzhong/STRONG`.

## 2 Related Work

Prior work on controllable generation (Hu et al., 2017; Goyal and Durrett, 2020b; Dou et al., 2021; He et al., 2022) has focused on inner-sentence token-level attributes (e.g., syntactic structure) or full-text stylistic features (e.g., sentiment/topic). Recent research started looking at generating long texts adhering to discourse structures derived from news or article reviews (Ghazvininejad et al., 2022; Ji and Huang, 2021; Spangher et al., 2022; Shen et al., 2022b). Shen et al. (2022a) framed the task




*Findings of the Association for Computational Linguistics: IJCNLP-AACL 2023*, pages 431–448

| Split | Case/Summ pairs | Case len | Summ len | sents |
|---|---|---|---|---|
| *No Manual Annotations* | | | | |
| Train | 21794 | 3979.4 | 276.2 | 10.9 |
| Valid | 2724 | 4067.4 | 279.8 | 11.0 |
| Test | 2723 | 3899.9 | 278.8 | 10.9 |
| *Manual IRC Annotations* | | | | |
| 1049-test | 1049 | 3741.1 | 245.4 | 11.0 |

Table 1: Dataset statistics of CanLII. Case/Summary len is the text length in terms of the number of words, while sents is the sentence count per summary.

as a sentence-by-sentence generation, which led to a longer inference time compared to token generation baselines. *We explore structure control in legal opinions, which is challenging due to long input texts and argumentative discourse structures.*

In the legal domain, besides directly adopting the raw document-summary pairs into supervised training using abstractive summarization models such as BART (Lewis et al., 2020) and Longformer Encoder Decoder (LED) (Beltagy et al., 2020), Elaraby and Litman (2022) proposed highlighting the salient argumentative sentences in the inputs and training a model that is argument-aware. *We instead focus on improving argument structure adherence by exploiting the summaries' annotated discourse structures to create structure prompts rather than by manipulating the original articles.*

## 3 Dataset

We leverage the CanLII dataset of legal case opinions and human-written abstractive summaries.[1][2] It consists of 28,290 legal opinions and human-written summary pairs. For testing, we first leverage the annotated subset produced by Xu et al. (2021), including 1,049 pairs with manually annotated **IRC argument labels**: *Issues* (the legal questions addressed in the case), *Conclusions* (the court's decisions for the related issue), *Reasons* (text snippets illustrating the reasons for the court's decision) and *Non_IRC* (none of the above). We further split the remaining 27,241 unannotated pairs into 80/10/10 percent for model training, validation, and extra testing. Corpus statistics are in Table 1.

As introduced in §1 and Figure 1, legal experts devised different strategies to construct the summaries. We thus analyze the patterns of the IRC labels in the 1,049 annotated summaries. To comprehend the high-level structures better, we remove the Non_IRC tags and collapse adjacent text segments with the same tag into one. The most common "normalized" patterns are "Issue – Conclusion – Reason" (54%) and "Issue – Conclusion – Reason – Conclusion" (9%). Pie charts of the top normalized and original patterns are in Appendix A.

## 4 Method

Figure 2 illustrates our proposed STRONG approach. We start by extending the small-scale annotations to the larger dataset. Since we only have the 1,049 test set manually annotated with oracle summary argument labels, different from Elaraby and Litman (2022) who used a classifier on input sentences, we propose to train a sentence classifier on summary sentences (Stage 1) and then utilize it to predict silver labels for all unannotated summaries in Stage 2.[3] Our approach distinguishes itself from Shen et al. (2022b), which relied solely on manually annotated structure sequences, resulting in a smaller training set than our larger dataset with silver labels. In the next step of Stage 2, we introduce special marker tokens to guide the model in generating summaries following specified structure patterns. Specifically, we extract the argumentative "IRC" labels from summary sentences, concatenate them with split " | " tokens and prepend before the original input text, and connect them with a special marker "==>". This operationalizes the argument mining of salient information blueprint, providing better guidance for the model in generating legal summaries. That is, Stage 2 utilizes the predicted structure labels to fine-tune the LED model. Once the model has been trained, we generate summaries using different sets of structure labels for the two test sets during Stage 3 of the inference process.

## 5 Experimental Setup

We compare STRONG to two baselines. **NoStructure** uses the Longformer-Encoder-Decoder (LED) base model for generating summaries. The second baseline re-implements **SentBS** (Shen et al., 2022a)

[1]The data was obtained through an agreement with the Canadian Legal Information Institute (CanLII): `https://www.canlii.org/en/`

[2]The corpus is moderately abstractive: The overlap ratios for the 1/2/3-gram between the source document and the human-authored summaries stand at 89.7%, 62.0%, and 42.1%, respectively, which suggests a moderate level of abstractiveness of the dataset compared to others such as TL;DR (Völske et al., 2017). It can thus serves as a useful testbed for abstractive summarization.

[3]We include the model details in Appendix B.2.

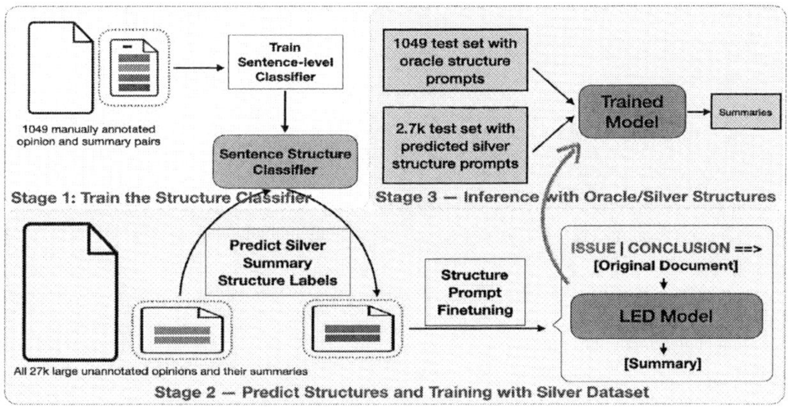


Figure 2: Illustration of our structure prompting approach (STRONG).

and is structure-aware. It uses a prompt-based backbone model to generate sentences, optimizing candidate selections based on the model likelihood and structure label probability. All implementation details are in Appendix B.

All experiments are evaluated using ROUGE-1 (R-1), ROUGE-2 (R-2), ROUGE-L (R-L) F1 (Lin, 2004), BERTScore (BS) (Zhang et al., 2020), and structure similarity (*SS*) (Shen et al., 2022b). More details on the structure metric are in Appendix C.

## 6 Results and Analysis

### 6.1 Automatic Result

This section addresses two research questions: **RQ1**. Does STRONG improve summarization quality compared to baselines? **RQ2**. How do models compare in preserving structure? We then conduct analyses based on the observations and perform a small-scale human evaluation.

**RQ1.** Using the left results section of Table 2, we first compare STRONG with the NoStructure baseline on traditional ROUGE and BERTScore summarization metrics. For the 1049 test set, when the maximum generation output length is limited to 256 tokens, we observe that STRONG obtains an average of 2.1, 0.7, 2.1, and 0.2 improvements across ROUGE-1, 2, L, and BERTScore (rows 3 vs. 2), which are **significant** based on 95% confidence intervals. STRONG also outperformed the re-implemented SentBS baseline (rows 3 vs. 1). We also explored the impact of increasing the maximum output length to 512 tokens, based on the observation that oracle summaries tended to be longer (Table 1). Similar trends were seen when the maximum output length is increased to 512 tokens (rows 5 vs. 4), as well as when all analyses are repeated using the 2,723 silver set (rows 6-8, 9-10). This illustrates that the target structure information helps STRONG generate higher-quality summaries. Appendices D and E present examples and analysis to demonstrate model output differences in content coverage.

**RQ2.** In the 1049 test set, compared to the NoStructure model (row 2), the STRONG model (row 3) significantly improves the structure similarity scores by 0.03. While SentBS (row 1) outperforms both methods (rows 2/3), the tradeoff is increasing inference time (last column). In contrast, with the extended 512 generation length where we could not even run SentBS, STRONG obtained the best oracle test set performance in the table, with a margin of 0.1 compared to SentBS (rows 5 vs. 1). Albeit imperfect, on the silver test set where our IRC sentence classifier predicts the structure labels, STRONG also gains 0.1 improvements to NoStructure (rows 7 vs. 8, and 9 vs. 10), and now even surpasses SentBS (row 6 vs. 8) on structure similarity while again reducing inference time.

### 6.2 Length Control

The second to last column of Table 2 shows that STRONG generates the longest summaries, which may have impacted the above assessments. We thus force NoStructure and STRONG to continue generating tokens until reaching the same specified limit of {64, 128, 256, and 512} tokens.[4] Table 3

[4]The generation length of SentBS cannot be rigidly regulated, considering that it adheres to a sentence-by-sentence generation paradigm, and the inconsistencies in the length of structural prompts result in diverse outputs.

| ID | Model | R-1 | R-2 | R-L | BS | SS | Avg Length | Infer. Time |
|---|---|---|---|---|---|---|---|---|
| | | | | 1049 Oracles | | | | |
| *Max output of 256 tokens* | | | | | | | | |
| 1 | SentBS | 48.31 | 23.86 | 44.73 | 86.87 | 0.436 | 129.6 | 8.5 hours♦ |
| 2 | NoStructure* | 50.33 | 25.84 | 46.47 | 87.39 | 0.344 | 159.2 | 2.2 hours |
| 3 | STRONG* | 52.47 | 26.54 | 48.57 | 87.63 | 0.372 | 186.3 | 2.5 hours |
| *Max output of 512 tokens* | | | | | | | | |
| 4 | NoStructure | 51.61 | 26.72 | 47.76 | 87.49 | 0.383 | 198.1 | 4.2 hours |
| 5 | STRONG* | **55.90** | **28.61** | **51.97** | **87.78** | **0.535** | 263.0 | 4.3 hours |
| | | | | 2723 Silver Test Set | | | | |
| *Max output of 256 tokens* | | | | | | | | |
| 6 | SentBS | 49.24 | 25.43 | 45.58 | 85.47 | 0.470 | 118.0 | 21.5 hours♦ |
| 7 | NoStructure* | 50.76 | 26.84 | 46.78 | 87.75 | 0.330 | 160.6 | 6.2 hours |
| 8 | STRONG* | 52.84 | 27.90 | 48.73 | 87.97 | 0.493 | 179.3 | 6.3 hours |
| *Max output of 512 tokens* | | | | | | | | |
| 9 | NoStructure | 52.22 | 27.57 | 48.18 | 87.69 | 0.440 | 196.9 | 13.0 hours |
| 10 | STRONG* | **57.17** | **29.87** | **52.93** | **88.10** | **0.543** | 255.9 | 13.1 hours |

Table 2: Results of different models on the CanLII oracle and silver test sets. BS refers to BERTScore, SS means structure similarity, respectively. Models with * mean all results are statistically different from the previous row, based on 95% confidence intervals. All results are reported as an average of 3 runs initialized with random seeds. Best results are highlighted with **bold**, and best results under the 256 token settings are underlined. Rows 1 and 6 (with ♦) experiment with an RTX3090Ti card with larger memory, which will make the inference time faster than on the default cards, which are RTX5000s and used for all other experiments.

| Model | Control Len. | R-1 | R-2 | R-L | BS |
|---|---|---|---|---|---|
| NoStructure | No | 50.33 | 25.84 | 46.47 | 87.39 |
| STRONG | No | 52.47 | 26.54 | 48.57 | 87.63 |
| NoStructure | Yes | 50.74 | 25.91 | 47.07 | 87.17 |
| STRONG | Yes | 50.96 | 26.26 | 47.33 | 87.39 |

Table 3: Results of models when summary has a maximum (top) versus controlled (bottom) length of 256 tokens. Although STRONG still outperforms the baseline, the delta is reduced when the length is controlled.

shows the results for the 256 token limit,[5] and indicates that the Table 2 performance gap (repeated in the first two rows of Table 3) diminishes when the length is controlled (the last two rows). This suggests that the structural benefits of STRONG become less important when output length is fixed. However, controlled length can lead to incomplete generations (see an example in Appendix D.1), and STRONG can dynamically adjust and generate similar length summaries compared to the oracle when they can stop generation if needed. Additionally, for both NoStructure and STRONG, we observe a drop in ROUGE performance for extremely long summaries (512 tokens) compared to smaller output lengths (see Appendix D.1), likely because 512 tokens deviate from the distribution of human summarization lengths. We additionally experimented with another setup to adjust the minimum generation length of each model and with higher length penalties. These results are detailed in Table 9, located in Appendix D.2. We observed that our STRONG model outperformed the baseline and reinforced the notion that structural information plays a crucial role in guiding the model to produce summaries with the appropriate length and level of detail.

| Model | SUMMAC$_{\text{CONV}}$ |
|---|---|
| *Max output of 256 tokens* | |
| SentBS | 0.660 |
| NoStructure | 0.663 |
| STRONG | 0.704* |
| *Max output of 512 tokens* | |
| NoStructure | 0.658 |
| STRONG | 0.697* |

Table 4: Results of the average factuality scores for models in Table 2 over the CanLII oracle test set. * means the result is significantly different from the previous row using paired t-test.

[5] An analysis of additional lengths is in Appendix D.1.

### 6.3 Factuality

To evaluate the factuality of generated text, we picked the $\text{SUMMAC}_{\text{CONV}}$ score from Laban et al. (2022), which utilizes the NLI model to detect summary inconsistencies and performs well on multiple factuality benchmarks (details in the original paper) compared to other metrics such as FactCC (Kryscinski et al., 2020) and DAE (Goyal and Durrett, 2020a). As shown in Table 4, our STRONG model obtains the highest scores, which means the highest consistency between document and generated summaries.

### 6.4 Human Evaluation

Human evaluation is under-explored for legal tasks, as it is labor-intensive due to long documents / summaries and requires evaluators with legal expertise (Jain et al., 2021). As a first step, we conducted a small-scale human evaluation using five legal decisions to assess the quality of summaries generated by all models in Table 2. Three legal experts were asked to evaluate the coherence of the generated texts and assess the coverage of argumentative components when compared to the oracle summaries crafted by the human CanLII experts.[6] The evaluator feedback indicated that longer summaries could potentially introduce more factual errors, and there was inconsistency in terms of fluency and readability, with mixed performance observed (one annotator reported issues in two cases). On the other hand, the advantage of controllable structure generation was more evident when generating longer summaries. In two out of five cases, the summaries generated by STRONG were preferred in the 512-length setting, while under the 256-length setting, only one STRONG-generated summary was favored.

## 7 Conclusion

We proposed the STRONG approach for improving the summarization of long legal opinions by providing target-side structure information. STRONG accepts different types of prompts and generates summaries accordingly. Experiments demonstrated that the content coverage, summary length, structure adherence, and inference time are all improved with STRONG compared to prior structure-control and no-structure baselines.

[6] We provide the evaluation details in Appendix F.

## Limitations

Our research results are constrained by our dependence on a single dataset for experimentation as well as by computing resource limitations. While prior work demonstrated that the SentBS approach could obtain negligible performance drop with regard to automatic metrics such as ROUGE and BERTScore compared to a finetuning structure prompted baseline, our current experiment is hindered by extreme demand of GPU memories given the much longer legal input and large parameter searching space. We also demonstrate that the slowness of compared work is more severe when transferring the model to our tasks. Further experiments on more extensive setups of the prior baselines can be important for future work to verify the past work's conclusions. We recognize that our methodology relies on annotated data for structure labels, particularly when adapting to novel domains. In future research, we aim to investigate zero-shot learning techniques to enable structure classification without the necessity for annotations.

While our paper uses standard summarization metrics and a similarity measure particularly related to our focus on structure controllability, we do not yet extensively investigate how STRONG impacts factuality besides the $\text{SUMMAC}_{\text{CONV}}$ score (Laban et al., 2022). A recent study (Wan et al., 2023) demonstrates that improvements in factuality-related metrics come with the sacrifice of dropping automatic metrics such as ROUGE and BERTScore, while Min et al. (2023) harness the power of LLMs to evaluate the factuality of long-form text generation. Deviating from prior work (Zhong and Litman, 2022) that studies the extractive summarization task, we focused on the abstractive summarization, which has shown to surpass the performance of extractive methods by a noticeable margin, while both strategies introduce unfaithfulness (Zhang et al., 2023). Another limitation is that we only exploited the IRC structure representations due to the availability of oracle summary annotations. Exploring the use of structures based on other methods such as Lu et al. (2018) is a promising area for future work. Also, the automatic evaluation metrics may be deficient compared to human evaluations, thus unfaithfully representing the final quality of generated summaries compared to real legal experts. Moreover, in a real application, end users may propose and inquire about different outputs with self-designed structure prompts[7], which remains an open-ended challenge and may need human validation for future works.

## Ethical Considerations

Using generated abstractive summary results from legal opinions remains a problem, as abstractive summarization models have been found to contain hallucinated artifacts that do not faithfully present the source texts (Kryscinski et al., 2019; Zhao et al., 2020). The generation results of our models may carry certain levels of non-factual information and need to be used with extra care. Similarly, CanLII has taken measures (i.e., blocking search indexing) to limit the disclosure of defendants' identities, while abstractive approaches may cause potential user information leakage.

## Acknowledgements

This work is supported by the National Science Foundation under Grant No. 2040490 and by Amazon. We want to thank the members of the Pitt AI Fairness and Law Project members, the Pitt PETAL group, and anonymous reviewers for their valuable comments in improving this work.

## References

Iz Beltagy, Matthew E Peters, and Arman Cohan. 2020. Longformer: The long-document transformer. *arXiv preprint arXiv:2004.05150*.

Jacob Devlin, Ming-Wei Chang, Kenton Lee, and Kristina Toutanova. 2019. BERT: Pre-training of deep bidirectional transformers for language understanding. In *Proceedings of the 2019 Conference of the North American Chapter of the Association for Computational Linguistics: Human Language Technologies, Volume 1 (Long and Short Papers)*, pages 4171–4186, Minneapolis, Minnesota. Association for Computational Linguistics.

Zi-Yi Dou, Pengfei Liu, Hiroaki Hayashi, Zhengbao Jiang, and Graham Neubig. 2021. GSum: A general framework for guided neural abstractive summarization. In *Proceedings of the 2021 Conference of the North American Chapter of the Association for Computational Linguistics: Human Language Technologies*, pages 4830–4842, Online. Association for Computational Linguistics.

Mohamed Elaraby and Diane Litman. 2022. ArgLegalSumm: Improving abstractive summarization of legal documents with argument mining. In *Proceedings of the 29th International Conference on Computational Linguistics*, pages 6187–6194, Gyeongju, Republic of Korea. International Committee on Computational Linguistics.

Marjan Ghazvininejad, Vladimir Karpukhin, Vera Gor, and Asli Celikyilmaz. 2022. Discourse-aware soft prompting for text generation. In *Proceedings of the 2022 Conference on Empirical Methods in Natural Language Processing*, pages 4570–4589, Abu Dhabi, United Arab Emirates. Association for Computational Linguistics.

Tanya Goyal and Greg Durrett. 2020a. Evaluating factuality in generation with dependency-level entailment. In *Findings of the Association for Computational Linguistics: EMNLP 2020*, pages 3592–3603, Online. Association for Computational Linguistics.

Tanya Goyal and Greg Durrett. 2020b. Neural syntactic preordering for controlled paraphrase generation. In *Proceedings of the 58th Annual Meeting of the Association for Computational Linguistics*, pages 238–252, Online. Association for Computational Linguistics.

Junxian He, Wojciech Kryscinski, Bryan McCann, Nazneen Rajani, and Caiming Xiong. 2022. CTRLsum: Towards generic controllable text summarization. pages 5879–5915.

Zhiting Hu, Zichao Yang, Xiaodan Liang, Ruslan Salakhutdinov, and Eric P. Xing. 2017. Toward controlled generation of text. In *ICML'17*, page 1587–1596. JMLR.org.

Deepali Jain, Malaya Dutta Borah, and Anupam Biswas. 2021. Summarization of legal documents: Where are we now and the way forward. *Computer Science Review*, 40:100388.

Haozhe Ji and Minlie Huang. 2021. DiscoDVT: Generating long text with discourse-aware discrete variational transformer. In *Proceedings of the 2021 Conference on Empirical Methods in Natural Language Processing*, pages 4208–4224, Online and Punta Cana, Dominican Republic. Association for Computational Linguistics.

Wojciech Kryscinski, Nitish Shirish Keskar, Bryan McCann, Caiming Xiong, and Richard Socher. 2019. Neural text summarization: A critical evaluation. In *Proceedings of the 2019 Conference on Empirical Methods in Natural Language Processing and the 9th International Joint Conference on Natural Language Processing (EMNLP-IJCNLP)*, pages 540–551, Hong Kong, China. Association for Computational Linguistics.

Wojciech Kryscinski, Bryan McCann, Caiming Xiong, and Richard Socher. 2020. Evaluating the factual consistency of abstractive text summarization. In *Proceedings of the 2020 Conference on Empirical Methods in Natural Language Processing (EMNLP)*, pages 9332–9346, Online. Association for Computational Linguistics.

[7]We provide an example of feeding different prompts to generate diverse summaries in Appendix E.1.

Philippe Laban, Tobias Schnabel, Paul N. Bennett, and Marti A. Hearst. 2022. SummaC: Re-visiting NLI-based models for inconsistency detection in summarization. *Transactions of the Association for Computational Linguistics*, 10:163–177.

Mike Lewis, Yinhan Liu, Naman Goyal, Marjan Ghazvininejad, Abdelrahman Mohamed, Omer Levy, Veselin Stoyanov, and Luke Zettlemoyer. 2020. Bart: Denoising sequence-to-sequence pre-training for natural language generation, translation, and comprehension. In *Proceedings of the 58th Annual Meeting of the Association for Computational Linguistics*, pages 7871–7880.

Chin-Yew Lin. 2004. ROUGE: A package for automatic evaluation of summaries. In *Text Summarization Branches Out*, pages 74–81, Barcelona, Spain. Association for Computational Linguistics.

Yinhan Liu, Myle Ott, Naman Goyal, Jingfei Du, Mandar Joshi, Danqi Chen, Omer Levy, Mike Lewis, Luke Zettlemoyer, and Veselin Stoyanov. 2019. Roberta: A robustly optimized bert pretraining approach. *arXiv preprint arXiv:1907.11692*.

Zhengdong Lu, Xianggen Liu, Haotian Cui, Yukun Yan, and Daqi Zheng. 2018. Object-oriented neural programming (OONP) for document understanding. In *Proceedings of the 56th Annual Meeting of the Association for Computational Linguistics (Volume 1: Long Papers)*, pages 2717–2726, Melbourne, Australia. Association for Computational Linguistics.

Sewon Min, Kalpesh Krishna, Xinxi Lyu, Mike Lewis, Wen tau Yih, Pang Wei Koh, Mohit Iyyer, Luke Zettlemoyer, and Hannaneh Hajishirzi. 2023. Factscore: Fine-grained atomic evaluation of factual precision in long form text generation.

Chenhui Shen, Liying Cheng, Lidong Bing, Yang You, and Luo Si. 2022a. SentBS: Sentence-level beam search for controllable summarization. In *Proceedings of the 2022 Conference on Empirical Methods in Natural Language Processing*, pages 10256–10265, Abu Dhabi, United Arab Emirates. Association for Computational Linguistics.

Chenhui Shen, Liying Cheng, Ran Zhou, Lidong Bing, Yang You, and Luo Si. 2022b. MReD: A meta-review dataset for structure-controllable text generation. In *Findings of the Association for Computational Linguistics: ACL 2022*, pages 2521–2535, Dublin, Ireland. Association for Computational Linguistics.

Alexander Spangher, Yao Ming, Xinyu Hua, and Nanyun Peng. 2022. Sequentially controlled text generation. In *Findings of the Association for Computational Linguistics: EMNLP 2022*, pages 6848–6866, Abu Dhabi, United Arab Emirates. Association for Computational Linguistics.

Teun A Van Dijk. 2013. *News as discourse*. Routledge.

Michael Völske, Martin Potthast, Shahbaz Syed, and Benno Stein. 2017. TL;DR: Mining Reddit to learn automatic summarization. In *Proceedings of the Workshop on New Frontiers in Summarization*, pages 59–63, Copenhagen, Denmark. Association for Computational Linguistics.

David Wan, Mengwen Liu, Kathleen McKeown, Markus Dreyer, and Mohit Bansal. 2023. Faithfulness-aware decoding strategies for abstractive summarization. In *Proceedings of the 17th Conference of the European Chapter of the Association for Computational Linguistics*, pages 2864–2880, Dubrovnik, Croatia. Association for Computational Linguistics.

Thomas Wolf, Lysandre Debut, Victor Sanh, Julien Chaumond, Clement Delangue, Anthony Moi, Pierric Cistac, Tim Rault, Remi Louf, Morgan Funtowicz, Joe Davison, Sam Shleifer, Patrick von Platen, Clara Ma, Yacine Jernite, Julien Plu, Canwen Xu, Teven Le Scao, Sylvain Gugger, Mariama Drame, Quentin Lhoest, and Alexander Rush. 2020. Transformers: State-of-the-art natural language processing. In *Proceedings of the 2020 Conference on Empirical Methods in Natural Language Processing: System Demonstrations*, pages 38–45, Online. Association for Computational Linguistics.

Huihui Xu, Jaromir Savelka, and Kevin Ashley. 2021. Accounting for sentence position and legal domain sentence embedding in learning to classify case sentences. In *Legal Knowledge and Information System*.

Shiyue Zhang, David Wan, and Mohit Bansal. 2023. Extractive is not faithful: An investigation of broad unfaithfulness problems in extractive summarization. *ACL*.

Tianyi Zhang, Varsha Kishore, Felix Wu, Kilian Q Weinberger, and Yoav Artzi. 2020. Bertscore: Evaluating text generation with bert. In *International Conference on Learning Representations*.

Zheng Zhao, Shay B. Cohen, and Bonnie Webber. 2020. Reducing quantity hallucinations in abstractive summarization. In *Findings of the Association for Computational Linguistics: EMNLP 2020*, pages 2237–2249, Online. Association for Computational Linguistics.

Lucia Zheng, Neel Guha, Brandon R. Anderson, Peter Henderson, and Daniel E. Ho. 2021. When does pretraining help? assessing self-supervised learning for law and the casehold dataset. In *Proceedings of the 18th International Conference on Artificial Intelligence and Law*. Association for Computing Machinery.

Yang Zhong and Diane Litman. 2022. Computing and exploiting document structure to improve unsupervised extractive summarization of legal case decisions. In *Proceedings of the Natural Legal Language Processing Workshop 2022*, pages 322–337, Abu Dhabi, United Arab Emirates (Hybrid). Association for Computational Linguistics.

## A IRC Structure Patterns

We report the distribution of different structure patterns with the normalized version (we remove the neighboring duplicated labels and ignore the Non_IRCs for better structure presentation) in Figure 3. We observe that most 1049 test summaries are annotated in an Issue – Conclusion – Reasoning pattern, while the remaining have different reordering of latter patterns. Legal experts sometimes employ the "Conclusion then Reasoning" pattern (3.6%) to strengthen the validity of the case summary. We found 54 distinct normalized structure patterns without considering the Non_IRCs and varying numbers of neighboring sentences. This suggests that legal experts employed diverse strategies to construct the summaries and confirms the importance of structure modeling in text generation tasks. Regarding the original patterns (excluding Non_IRCs), as shown in Figure 4, the numbers of Issue and Reasoning sentences varied.

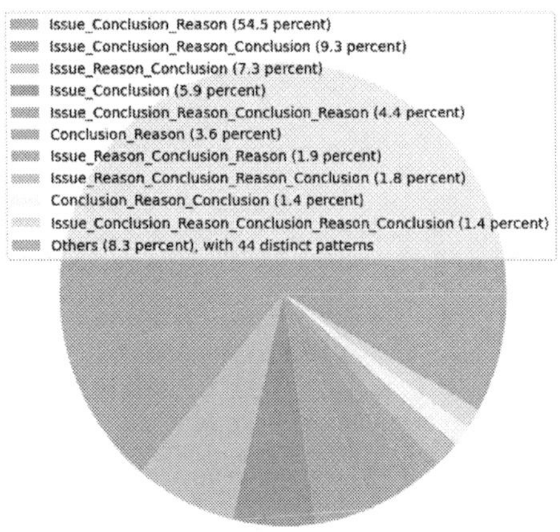


Figure 3: Pattern distribution of normalized summary structures, here we exclude the Non-IRC labels.

## B Implementation Details

All of our BART-based experiments and the sentence classification model are conducted on Quadro RTX 5000 GPUs, each with 16 GB RAM. For SentBS models, we adopted the authors' original codebase workflow[8] and reimplemented it on an RTX 3090Ti GPU to satisfy the minimum RAM requirements.

[8] `https://github.com/Shen-Chenhui/SentBS`

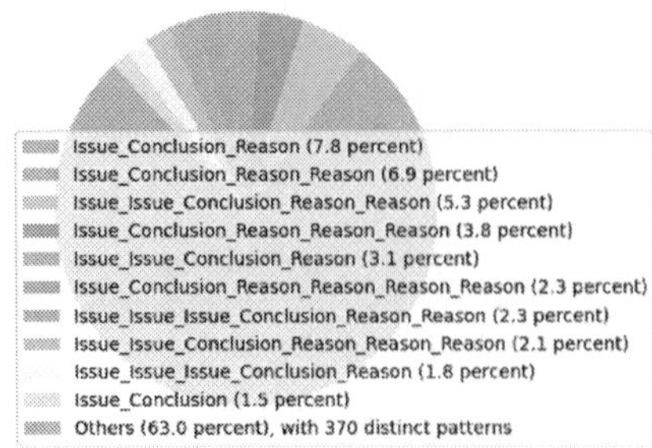


Figure 4: Pattern distribution of summary structures, here we exclude the Non-IRC labels.

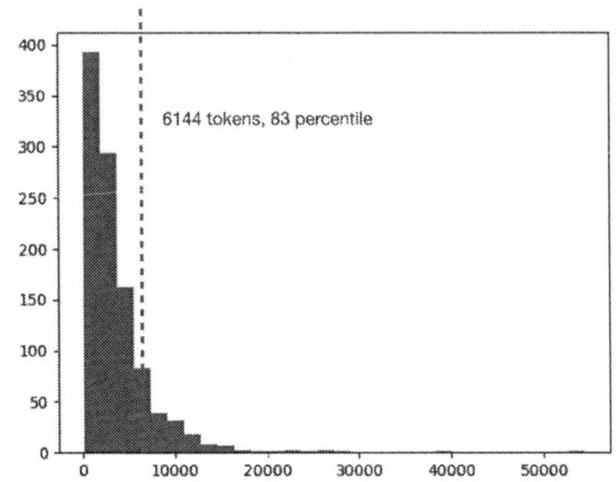


Figure 5: Input case length distribution of the 1049 test set, for models truncated at 6144 tokens, we retain 83 percent complete inputs.

### B.1 NoStructure and STRONG model

All models are implemented with the Huggingface library (Wolf et al., 2020) using PyTorch, initialized with the *"allenai/led-base-16384"* checkpoint[9]. We train all our models with the same learning rate of 2e−5. We train the models for 16k steps, using the gradient step of 4, batch size of 1, and save the best checkpoints at every 1,000 steps, based on the ROUGE-2 F1 score of the validation set evaluations. Each model is trained with three randomized seeds, and we report the final averaged results. For training summarization models, we set the min/maximum inference summary length to 64/256 tokens. We employed beam-search with a beam size of 4 for all experiments. We additionally experimented with 512 output lengths in the main results. We truncate the input length to 6,144 tokens for the LED-base model due to our GPU

[9] `https://huggingface.co/allenai/led-base-16384/tree/main`

| Data Split | I-$F_1$ | R-$F_1$ | C-$F_1$ | Non-$F_1$ | Macro $F_1$ |
|---|---|---|---|---|---|
| Valid | 76.7 | 66.3 | 76.7 | 76.0 | 73.8 |
| Test | 75.3 | 71.8 | 81.0 | 76.7 | 75.9 |

Table 5: IRC label classifier performance on the 1049 subset's validation and test split.

| | R-1 | R-2 | R-L | Infer. time | Avg length |
|---|---|---|---|---|---|
| sentence-ctrl | 48.31 | 23.86 | 44.73 | 8.5 hours | 129.6 |
| segment-ctrl | 42.79 | 21.56 | 39.59 | 6 hours | 77.7 |

Table 6: SentBS results with different structure sequences.

limitation, and analyze the effects of contents truncations.[10] For inference, we do a batch decoding with a batch size of 5 and report the total inference time accordingly.

### B.2 IRC Classifier Training

Our argument role (IRC) classifier leverages a finetuned *legalBERT* (Zheng et al., 2021) model due to its performance gain compared to other contextualized models such as BERT (Devlin et al., 2019) and ROBERTa (Liu et al., 2019) as shown in Elaraby and Litman (2022) to predict sentence IRC labels as a four-way classification task. We implemented the model with the PyTorch Lightning framework[11]. We split sentences from the 1049 annotated summaries into a 80/10/10 randomized setting for train, validation, and testing. For model training, we set the learning rate of 2e−5, training for 15 epochs, and leveraged the validation loss for early stopping criteria with a patience of 5. The final prediction macro-F1 is 0.7586. The detailed sentence classifier result is shown in Table 5.

### B.3 SentBS Re-Implementation

The original SentBS (Shen et al., 2022a) approach is implemented with a backbone of the BART-large (Lewis et al., 2020) model and using a V100 Graphic Card with 32GB memory. We first replaced the BART-large backbone with our trained LED models. Due to the limitation of GPU memory, the model failed to load on our prior RTX 5000 GPUs with the basic setting of beam size of 2. We instead ran the model on a GTX 3090Ti card with 24 GB memory, inference with the SentBS's "beam search + nucleus sampling" option, generation size of 4, beam size of 2, a top-p ratio at 0.9, and the maximum decoding length of 256 tokens. All other parameters are consistent with the original article experiment. Besides the sentence label searching, we additionally experiment with the segment-ctrl setup, where the target summary labels are deduplicated to spans with non-repeated IRC labels. The results are shown in Table 6. We tested the model's performance on the original MReD dataset, which gives 34.77/9.69/30.99 regarding ROUGE scores, which is comparable to the original paper's result 34.61/9.96/30.87 with our evaluation script.

## C Structure Similarity Evaluations

As mentioned in §5, we adopted a metric from the human evaluation introduced in Shen et al. (2022b) to measure the structure-similarity between a system output summary and a given oracle summary with the oracle structure prompt. In our actual implementation, the similarity score is computed by

$$1 - (\frac{minimum\_edit\_distance(S_i, O_i)}{max(len(S_i), len(O_i))}$$

where the edit distance is computed as the Levenshtein Distance, with equal penalties for replace, insert, and delete operations. We report the average similarity score of the test sets in the table results. Given that the sentence classification model can make wrong predictions, we estimate an upper bound by making predictions of the human-written summary sentences, which resulted in 0.781 for the original similarity score. Albeit not perfect, we can still assume that a generation model performs better on the structure-controlled generation task if the computed similarity becomes higher.

[10]We plot the length distribution of input documents in Figure 5.

[11]https://github.com/Lightning-AI/lightning

## D More Analysis on the Generation

### D.1 Controlled Length

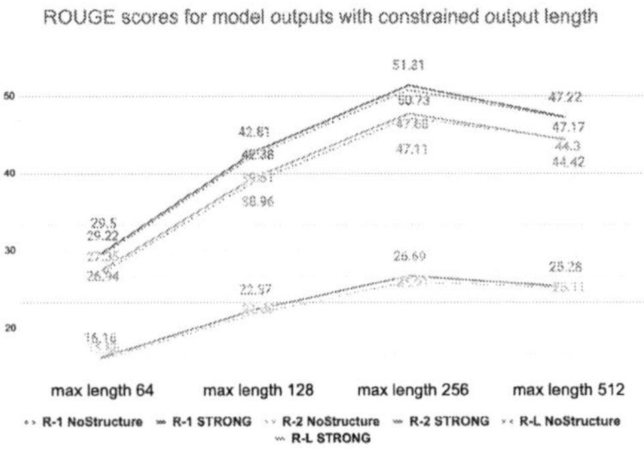


Figure 6: ROUGE scores for NoStructure and STRONG models with 64, 128, 256, and 512 output token limits.

We compare the ROUGE scores between the NoStructure and STRONG models and visualize the results in Figure 6. The findings suggest that the performance gap between the models diminishes, indicating that the structural benefits of the STRONG model for summary organization become less significant when the output length is fixed. Additionally, we observed a drop in performance for extremely long summaries (512 tokens) as they deviated from the distribution of human summarization lengths. The BERTScore performance is shown in Table 7, where we observe a similar trend.

However, controlled length can lead to the incomplete generation problem, as the model can not stop generation until it hits the desired token limit. As shown in Table 8, models obtain incomplete last sentences under the controlled length setting.

### D.2 Controlled Min Length

We set the minimum length parameter of the generation to (64, 128, 256, and 512) and fixed the maximum length at 512. We modified the length penalty to 2.0, aiming to prompt the model to generate longer sequences. Table 9 indicates that our approach yields summaries with higher ROUGE scores when a larger length penalty is applied. This positive impact remains consistent even when we set the minimum length to less than 256 tokens. These findings reinforce the notion that structural information plays a crucial role in guiding the model to produce summaries with the appropriate length and level of detail. Interestingly, in the extreme scenario where we set the minimum tokens to 512, both models perform similarly.

### D.3 Complete ROUGE scores

To evaluate the advantages brought by the proposed methods, alongside diagnosing the effects of augmenting the maximum generation length, we report the complete ROUGE scores of the models on the 1049 test set in Table 10. Initial observations highlight that the incorporation of structural information fosters enhancements in ROUGE recall scores, despite inducing a slight decrement in precision (as evidenced in row 2/3 and row 4/5). Additionally, the expansion of maximum output length significantly boosts the ROUGE recall, which can be attributed to the coverage of more n-grams. However, a corresponding decline in the precision score has been observed. This observation echoed with the preliminary human evaluation, which suggested that the longer outputs occasionally encompassed with higher error rate of contents, thus having lower quality.

| Length | noStructure | | | STRONG | | |
|---|---|---|---|---|---|---|
| | **BS - P** | **BS - R** | **BS - F1** | **BS - P** | **BS - R** | **BS - F1** |
| 64 | 89.08 | 83.36 | 86.09 | 89.22 | 83.38 | 86.17 |
| 128 | 88.27 | 85.64 | 86.91 | 88.47 | 85.67 | 87.02 |
| 256 | 86.79 | 87.50 | 87.17 | 87.04 | 87.80 | 87.39 |
| 512 | 84.56 | 88.49 | 86.46 | 84.62 | 88.86 | 86.66 |

Table 7: Evaluation of models under Controlled Length, BS - P, BS - R, and BS - F1 denote BERTScore for Precision, Recall, and F1-Score, respectively. The table presents the evaluation results of models under different controlled lengths. There still exists difference between the two models, while overall the 512 length generation becomes worse.

| Model | Generated Summary |
|---|---|
| Reference | The appellant was convicted of indecent assault against two young girls. He appealed on five grounds related to a substantial conflict in the evidence. Dismissing the appeal, that there was no error on the part of the trial judge in weighing the evidence. |
| NoStructure **max** | The appellant was convicted of two counts of indecent assault against two girls, aged 13 and 16. He was sentenced to nine months imprisonment, to be followed by two years probation. The appellant appealed.Dismissing the appeal, that there was no error on the part of the trial judge in conducting the trial or in weighing the evidence. After carefully reviewing the evidence, the verdict was not unreasonable or not supported by the evidence and the appeal was dismissed. |
| NoStructure **controlled** | The appellant was convicted of two counts of indecent assault against two girls, aged 13 and 17, respectively. He was sentenced to nine months imprisonment with respect to the first assault, followed by two years probation. The appellant appealed.Dismissing the appeal, that there was no error on the part of the trial judge in conducting the trial or in weighing the evidence. ...... There was a substantial conflict in the evidence as to the appellant's guilt, **and he had been sentenced to 9 months imprisonment for the assault on the complainant, to** |
| STRONG **max** | The appellant was convicted of two counts of indecent assault against two young girls. He was sentenced to nine months imprisonment with respect to the first assault, to be followed by two years probation, and one month consecutive for the second assault. The appellant appealed.Dismissing the appeal, that there was no error on the part of the trial judge in conducting the trial or in weighing the evidence. After carefully reviewing the evidence, the court could not say that the verdict was unreasonable or not supported by the evidence and the appeal was dismissed. |
| STRONG **controlled** | The appellant was convicted of two counts of indecent assault against two girls. He was sentenced to nine months imprisonment with respect to the first count and two years probation on the second count. The appellant appealed both convictions.Dismissing the appeal, that there was no error on the part of the trial judge in conducting the trial or in weighing the evidence. ...... **as the evidence did not support the appellant's contention that the assault was committed in bad faith and that the appellant had committed the second offence in good faith and in** |

Table 8: A sample of 256 token generation for NoStructure and STRONG models under the max and control length settings. **Bold** sentences are incomplete under the controlled length setting.

| Length | noStructure | | | STRONG | | |
|---|---|---|---|---|---|---|
| | **R-1** | **R-2** | **R-L** | **R-1** | **R-2** | **R-L** |
| 64 | 52.00 | 26.82 | 48.19 | 55.68 | 28.30 | 51.74 |
| 128 | 52.42 | 26.97 | 48.61 | 55.51 | 28.22 | 51.62 |
| 256 | 52.30 | 26.92 | 48.73 | 53.88 | 27.65 | 50.22 |
| 512 | 47.09 | 24.98 | 44.32 | 46.96 | 24.95 | 44.04 |

Table 9: Evaluation of models under Controlled Minimum Length. The table presents the evaluation results of models under different controlled minimum lengths. A difference still exists between the two models, while overall, the 512 length generation becomes worse.

| ID | Model | R-1 Precision | R-1 Recall | R-1 F1 | R-2 Precision | R-2 Recall | R-2 F1 | R-L Precision | R-L Recall | R-L F1 |
|---|---|---|---|---|---|---|---|---|---|---|
| 1049 Oracles | | | | | | | | | | |
| *Max output of 256 token* | | | | | | | | | | |
| 1 | SentBS | 59.93 | 44.93 | 48.27 | 29.75 | 22.10 | 23.80 | 55.65 | 41.45 | 44.67 |
| 2 | NoStructure* | 60.45 | 47.99 | 50.15 | 31.31 | 24.31 | 25.65 | 56.04 | 44.17 | 46.33 |
| 3 | STRONG* | 58.84 | 52.47 | 52.62 | 30.38 | 26.93 | 27.04 | 54.67 | 48.40 | 48.70 |
| *Max output of 512 token* | | | | | | | | | | |
| 4 | NoStructure | 57.88 | 53.67 | 51.99 | 30.14 | 27.53 | 26.85 | 53.76 | 49.62 | 48.19 |
| 5 | STRONG* | 53.33 | 61.99 | 55.74 | 27.13 | 31.52 | 28.33 | 49.61 | 57.53 | 51.80 |

Table 10: The Complete ROUGE results for various models on the CanLII 1049 oracle dataset.

## E Examples of Different System Outputs

### E.1 Different Prompts' Effects

In Table 11, we generate multiple summaries according to different prompts using the best-performing STRONG method and set the maximum length of generation at 512 tokens. We find that the outputs follow the structure prompts to a certain degree. For instance, Variant 1 quickly jumped to the reasoning parts after the first two sentences, while Variant 2 started with multiple clear conclusion sentences on the court's decision and the main issues.

### E.2 Sample Outputs

In Table 12, we show the examples for different methods under the 256 token max generation limit. We further ask three legal experts to rate the different outputs and analyze on the coverage of argumentative roles. We find that SentBS does a good job of stating an issue, but never reaches the conclusion. The NoStructure – 256 model fails to give a good statement of the issues, and our STRONG – 256 produces a more coherent and clear presentation. We additionally include the 512-token version of NoStructure and STRONG outputs in Table 13. Compared to the shorter NoStructure output that does not clearly state the issue, and it also doesn't reveal how the issue came out, the legal expert reported that the STRONG - 512 version is very clear and comprehensive. He also raised some concerns about the privacy problem of leaking the decedent's full name.

## F Human Evaluation Details

We conducted evaluations with a total of three legal experts, all of whom hold a J.D. degree and possess a minimum of four years of experience in providing professional legal services. The experts were assigned five randomly sampled legal cases, each accompanied by the oracle reference summary, as well as the generated outputs from the following five models: (1) SentBS with a length of 256 tokens, (2) NoStructure with a length of 256 tokens, (3) STRONG with a length of 256 tokens, (4) NoStructure with a length of 512 tokens, and (5) STRONG with a length of 512 tokens. The experts were presented with the reference summary and all five system outputs in the same row of an Excel file. They were then asked to provide reflections on the faithfulness and coherence of each system output while considering the inclusion of essential argument roles components such as Issue, Reason, and Conclusion compared to the reference summary. Given that the instruction does not specifically inquire about the ranking nor ask evaluators to provide numerical scores, the primary author instead offers an interpretation of the free-text reflections by conducting comparative analyses across various outputs and allocating a relative ranking. We release all reflections for further studies in `https://github.com/cs329yangzhong/STRONG`. Table 14 shows one example of evaluators' reflections on a case, and Table 15 shows the author's ranking interpretation.

| Prompt | Summary |
|---|---|
| *Human Written Summary* | |
| Issue I Conclusion I Conclusion I Reason | At issue was the interim custody of the child and child support. HELD: Interim custody was given to the petitioner with access to the respondent. The respondent was ordered to pay interim child support in the amount of $193 per month. On an interim custody application, the Court must take into account the status quo. |
| *Generations* | |
| Issue I Conclusion I Conclusion I Reason | At issue was the interim custody of the child and child support. The parties began cohabitating in May 1998 and separated in April 2000.HELD: The petitioner was awarded interim custody with reasonable access including every second weekend, reasonable telephone access and reasonable access during holiday periods. Both parents were ordered to complete the Parenting After Separation course. There was an unhealthy degree of constant bickering. |
| *Variant 1:* Issue I Conclusion I Reason I Reason I Reason | The petitioner was awarded interim custody with reasonable access including every second weekend, reasonable telephone access and reasonable access during holiday periods. Both parents were ordered to complete the Parenting After Separation course. The parties raised in their material the issue of each other's lack of cooperation and communication. While the Court was not in position to decide whether the accusations of each party were substantiated, it could say with relative certainty that there was an unhealthy degree of constant bickering. It was evident that as long as the parties work on establishing better communication, the child would benefit from contact with both parents with minimal disruption. |
| *Variant 2:* Conclusion I Issue I Issue I Reason I Reason | Interim custody of the child was awarded to the mother. The father was ordered to pay interim child support of $193 per month. Both parents were ordered to complete the Parenting After Separation course.HELD: The mother was awarded interim custody with reasonable access including every second weekend, reasonable telephone access and reasonable access during holiday periods. Interim child support was ordered in the amount of $125 per month and the father was to pay his proportionate share of childcare costs. There was an unhealthy degree of constant bickering. It was evident that as long as the parties worked on establishing better communication, the child would benefit from contact with both parents with minimal disruption. |

Table 11: An example of the difference between generated summaries based on different prompts using our best structure prompt model STRONG. The original legal decision id is 2003skqb487.

**ORACLE**
Statutes – Interpretation – Limitation of Civil Rights Act, Section 2 The plaintiff bank applied by notice of application for a deficiency judgment against the defendant pertaining to the non-purchase money portion of the outstanding indebtedness to the plaintiff pursuant to her mortgage and to some other costs related to the mortgage. The original mortgage executed by the plaintiff was for $191,000 of which $176,000 was advanced to purchase her condominium and $15,000, eight per cent of the total, was advanced for other purchases. The property sold for $156,000 pursuant to a judicial sale. The sale proceeds were distributed to pay outstanding property taxes, commission, and the principal and interest due under the mortgage in the amount of $141,945 and the net sale proceeds were to be distributed pro rata. As at November 1, 2017, the principal and interest owing on the non-purchase money portion of the mortgage was $21,250. The plaintiff requested judgment for the deficiency in the amount of $9,900 with interest to the date of judgment. It claimed it was entitled to solicitor-client costs and other costs accrued by it under the mortgage. The issue was whether such costs should be subject to the pro rata calculation for the nonpurchase portion of the mortgage, that is, 8 percent of the total costs incurred. HELD: The application was granted. The court found that the plaintiff was entitled to a deficiency judgment for principal and interest owed under the mortgage in the amount requested. It was also entitled to judgment against the mortgagee for eight percent of the solicitor-client costs, condominium fees and property management charges.

**SentBS**
Statutes – Interpretation – Condominium Property Act, 1993, Section 63 The plaintiff bank applied by notice of application for a deficiency judgment against the defendant, Partridge, pertaining to the non-purchase money portion of the outstanding indebtedness to the plaintiff pursuant to her mortgage. Partridge had originally executed a mortgage for $191,000, of which $176,000 was advanced to purchase her condominium unit and $15,000 for other purchases. The non-Purchase money amount of the loan advanced and secured by the mortgage was 8RBC applied for solicitor-client costs and other costs accrued by RBC under the mortgage. The issue was whether the pro rata distribution applied solely to the indebtedness of principal and accrued interest, or applied to all costs of outstanding mortgage, including solicitor and client costs permitted under the mortgages. In its application, RBC had calculated the proceeds from the judicial sale that must be distributed pro ratus between the purchase money and non-paid balances owing, resulting in the deficiency of principal. For the deficiency amount to be set at the rate of 2.

**NoStructure – 256**
The petitioner was awarded interim custody with reasonable access including every second weekend, reasonable telephone access and reasonable access during holiday periods. Both parents were ordered to complete the Parenting After Separation course. The parties raised in their material the issue of each other's lack of cooperation and communication. While the Court was not in position to decide whether the accusations of each party were substantiated, it could say with relative certainty that there was an unhealthy degree of constant bickering. It was evident that as long as the parties work on establishing better communication, the child would benefit from contact with both parents with minimal disruption.

**STRONG – 256**
Mortgage – Foreclosure – Determination of InterestThe plaintiff bank applied by notice of application for a deficiency judgment against the defendant, Partridge, pertaining to the non-purchase money portion of the outstanding indebtedness to it pursuant to her mortgage. The plaintiff also applied to have its lawyers' costs assessed on solicitor-client basis. Partridge had originally executed a mortgage for $191,000, of which $176,000 was advanced to purchase her condominium unit and $15,000 for other purchases. Thus, the mortgage was 8 percent of the total mortgage.HELD: The plaintiff's application was granted and the plaintiff was granted judgment against Partridge in the amount of $9,901.23 with interest from November 1, 2017, to the date of judgment at the rate of 2.79 per cent per annum. It was entitled to solicitor and other costs accrued by the plaintiff under its mortgage.

Table 12: Different models' outputs for the legal decision (id: 5_2018skqb216). The structure prompt is "Non_IRC | Non_IRC | Non_IRC | Non_IRC | Non_IRC | Issue | Issue | Issue | Conclusion | Conclusion | Conclusion ".

| **NoStructure – 512** |
|---|
| Mortgages – Foreclosure – DischargeThe plaintiff applied by notice of application for a deficiency judgment against the defendant pertaining to the non-purchase money portion of the outstanding indebtedness to the plaintiff pursuant to her mortgage. The plaintiff also applied to have its lawyers' costs assessed on solicitor-client basis.HELD: The plaintiff was granted judgment in the amount of $9,901.23 with interest from November 1, 2017 to the date of judgment at the rate of 2.79 per cent per annum for the deficiency of principal and interest owed under the mortgage. |
| **STRONG – 512** |
| Mortgage – Foreclosure – Pro RataDebtor and Creditor – Mortgage – Non-purchase MoneyThe plaintiff, Royal Bank of Canada, applied by notice of application for a deficiency judgment against the defendant, Doreen Pearl Partridge, pertaining to the non-payment of outstanding indebtedness to the plaintiff pursuant to her mortgage. The property sold pursuant to an Order Nisi for Sale by Real Estate Listing for $156,000 was distributed to pay outstanding property taxes, real estate commission and the principal and interest due under the mortgage in the sum of $141,945.36. At issue was whether the pro rata distribution applied solely to the indebtedness of principal and accrued interest, or applied to all costs of the outstanding mortgage, including solicitor-client costs permitted under it. Partridge had originally executed a mortgage for $191,000 of which $176,000 advanced to purchase her condominium unit and $15,000 for other purchases. Thus, the mortgage was 8 percent of the total mortgage.HELD: The plaintiff was granted judgment against Partridge in the amount of $9,901.23 with interest from November 1, 2017 to the date of judgment at the rate of 2.79 per cent per annum. It was entitled to solicitor and client costs and other costs accrued by the plaintiff under its mortgage, that is, 8 per cent of its total outstanding mortgage costs incurred. Section 63 of The Condominium Property Act, 1993 allows the condominium corporation to register a lien against the title of the unit for unpaid contributions to the common expense fund or the reserve fund. Secondly, the plaintiff claimed $1,461.92 for its payment of property management charges for securing and caring for the property, appraisal fee and utilities. These charges were permitted by s. 8(1) of the Limitation of Civil Rights Act (LCRA) and any inspections and administration fees had not been claimed by RBC. Further, the property management charge was recoverable under the terms of the mortgage. |

Table 13: NoStructure and Strong models' outputs for the legal decision (id: 5_2018skqb216) under 512 max length generations. The structure prompt is "Non_IRC | Non_IRC | Non_IRC | Non_IRC | Non_IRC | Issue | Issue | Issue | Conclusion | Conclusion | Conclusion ".

| Model Output | Annotator Reflection |
|---|---|
| SentBS | Does a good job stating an issue, but never reaches the conclusion. |
| NoStructure – 256 | No good statement of the issue, but maybe readers could infer the issue based on the conclusion "It was entitled to solicitor and other costs accrued by the plaintiff under its mortgage." The interest payment isn't important enough to be in the summary |
| STRONG – 256 | Fairly coherent, but it's not totally clear the dispute is about "solicitor and client costs permitted under the mortgages. |
| NoStructure – 512 | It's not very clear about the issue, and it also doesn't reveal how the issue came out. |
| STRONG – 512 | This is very clear. Using the defendant's full name might be a privacy problem. I also wonder if there's a copyright problem with using the subject classification system at the start of the summary. It looks like it's from the Law Society of Saskatchewan. |

Table 14: A sample of the human evaluation on different model outputs. It corresponds to Annotator 3's reflection for the second legal decision summary group in Table 15.

<table>
<tr><th>Annotator</th><th>SentBS</th><th>NoStructure-256</th><th>STRONG-256</th><th>NoStructure-512</th><th>STRONG-512</th></tr>
<tr><td>Anno. 1</td><td>5</td><td>1</td><td>3</td><td>1</td><td>4 (too detailed)</td></tr>
<tr><td>Anno. 2</td><td colspan="5">N/A</td></tr>
<tr><td>Anno. 3</td><td>3 (fluency problem)</td><td>1</td><td>3 (same as sentbs)</td><td>2</td><td>5</td></tr>
<tr><td>Anno. 1</td><td>5 (no conclusion)</td><td>4 (no issue)</td><td>3</td><td>2</td><td>1 (fairly clear)</td></tr>
<tr><td>Anno. 2</td><td>5 (lack conclusion)</td><td>2</td><td>4 (factual errors)</td><td>2 (lack conclusion)</td><td>1 (very good)</td></tr>
<tr><td>Anno. 3</td><td>5 (never concludes)</td><td>3 (good)</td><td>3</td><td>2 (was nice, but ...)</td><td>1 (great)</td></tr>
<tr><td>Anno. 1</td><td colspan="5">N/A</td></tr>
<tr><td>Anno. 2</td><td>5 (wrong issue)</td><td>1</td><td>3 (too many details)</td><td>4 (erratic contents)</td><td>2 (too detailed)</td></tr>
<tr><td>Anno. 3</td><td>5 (very confusing)</td><td>1</td><td>3 (bad grammar)</td><td>4 (not reliable)</td><td>2</td></tr>
<tr><td>Anno. 1</td><td>3</td><td>3</td><td>5</td><td>1</td><td>2</td></tr>
<tr><td>Anno. 2</td><td>4 (no I, C)</td><td>4 (same to SentBS)</td><td>3 (no issue)</td><td>1</td><td>2 (fairly good)</td></tr>
<tr><td>Anno. 3</td><td colspan="5">N/A</td></tr>
<tr><td>Anno. 1</td><td colspan="5">N/A</td></tr>
<tr><td>Anno. 2</td><td>2 (not good)</td><td>2 (same to SentBS)</td><td>2 (same to SentBS)</td><td>1</td><td>5 (bad summary)</td></tr>
<tr><td>Anno. 3</td><td>3 (generally good)</td><td>3</td><td>2</td><td>1</td><td>5 (bad summary)</td></tr>
</table>

Table 15: The inferred rankings of different system outputs, determined based on human reflections over five legal decision summaries. Some annotators did not annotate a specific summary, and the row is represented by "N/A".